Collins

Collins
German
Dictionary

editors/Redaktion
Veronika Schnorr • Ute Nicol • Peter Terrell
Bob Grossmith • Helga Holtkamp • Horst Kopleck
Beate Wengel • John Whitlam

editorial staff/Manuskriptbearbeitung
Joyce Littlejohn • Elspeth Anderson
Christine Bahr • John Podbielski

series editor/Gesamtleitung
Lorna Sinclair Knight

INTRODUCTION

We are delighted you have decided to buy the Collins German Dictionary and hope you will enjoy and benefit from using it at home, at school, on holiday or at work.

The innovative use of colour guides you quickly and efficiently to the word you want, and the comprehensive wordlist provides a wealth of modern and idiomatic phrases not normally found in a dictionary this size.

In addition, the supplement provides you with guidance on using the dictionary, along with entertaining ways of improving your dictionary skills.

We hope that you will enjoy using it and that it will significantly enhance your language studies.

ZUM GEBRAUCH IHRES COLLINS WÖRTERBUCHS

Das Wörterbuch enthält eine Fülle von Informationen, die mithilfe von unterschiedlichen Schriften und Schriftgrößen, Symbolen, Abkürzungen und Klammern vermittelt werden. Die dabei verwendeten Regeln und Symbole werden in den folgenden Abschnitten erklärt.

Stichwörter

Die Wörter, die Sie im Wörterbuch nachschlagen — „Stichwörter" — sind alphabetisch geordnet. Sie sind in Farbe gedruckt, damit man sie schnell erkennt. Die beiden Stichwörter oben links und rechts auf jeder Doppelseite geben das erste bzw. letzte Wort an, das auf den betreffenden Seiten behandelt wird.

Informationen zur Verwendung oder zur Form bestimmter Stichwörter stehen in Klammern hinter der Lautschrift. Sie erscheinen meist in abgekürzter Form und sind kursiv gedruckt (z. B. (*fam*), (*COMM*)).

Wo es angebracht ist, werden mit dem Stichwort verwandte Wörter im selben Artikel behandelt (z. B. accept, acceptance). Sie sind wie das Stichwort fett, aber etwas kleiner gedruckt.

Häufig verwendete Ausdrücke, in denen das Stichwort vorkommt (z. B. **to be cold**), sind in einer anderen Schrift halbfett gedruckt.

Lautschrift

Die Lautschrift für jedes Stichwort (zur Angabe seiner Aussprache) steht in eckigen Klammern direkt hinter dem Stichwort (z. B. Quark [kvark]; knead [niːd]). Die Symbole der Lautschrift sind auf Seite xii erklärt.

Übersetzungen

Die Übersetzungen des Stichworts sind normal gedruckt. Wenn es mehr als eine Bedeutung oder Verwendung des Stichworts gibt, sind diese durch ein Semikolon voneinander getrennt. Vor den Übersetzungen stehen oft andere, kursiv gedruckte Wörter in Klammern. Sie geben an, in welchem Zusammenhang das Stichwort erscheinen könnte (z. B. rough (*voice*) oder (*weather*)), oder sie sind Synonyme (z. B. rough (*violent*)).

Schlüsselwörter

Besonders behandelt werden bestimmte deutsche und englische Wörter, die man als „Schlüsselwörter" der jeweiligen Sprache betrachten kann. Diese Wörter kommen beispielsweise sehr häufig vor oder werden unterschiedlich verwendet (z. B. sein, auch; get, that). Mithilfe von Rauten und Ziffern können Sie die verschiedenen Wortarten und Verwendungen unterscheiden. Weitere nützliche Hinweise finden Sie kursiv und in Klammern in der jeweiligen Sprache des Benutzers.

Grammatische Informationen

Wortarten stehen in abgekürzter Form kursiv gedruckt hinter der Aussprache des

Stichworts (z. B. *vt, adv, conj*).

Die unregelmäßigen Formen englischer Substantive und Verben stehen in Klammern vor der Wortart (z. B. **man** (*pl* **men**) *n*, **give** (*pt* **gave**, *pp* **given**) *vt*).

Die deutsche Rechtschreibreform

Dieses Wörterbuch folgt durchweg der reformierten deutschen Rechtschreibung. Alle Stichwörter auf der deutsch-englischen Seite, die von der Rechtschreibreform betroffen sind, sind mit ▲ gekennzeichnet. Alte Schreibungen, die sich wesentlich von der neuen Schreibung unterscheiden und an einem anderen alphabetischen Ort erscheinen, sind jedoch weiterhin aufgeführt und werden zur neuen Schreibung verwiesen. Diese alten Schreibungen sind mit △ gekennzeichnet.

USING YOUR COLLINS GERMAN DICTIONARY

A wealth of information is presented in the dictionary, using various typefaces, sizes of type, symbols, abbreviations and brackets. The conventions and symbols used are explained in the following sections.

Headwords

The words you look up in a dictionary — "headwords" — are listed alphabetically. They are printed in colour for rapid identification. The two headwords appearing at the top left and top right of each double page indicate the first and last word dealt with on the pages in question.

Information about the usage or form of certain headwords is given in brackets after the phonetic spelling. This usually appears in abbreviated form and in italics (e.g. (*umg*), (*COMM*)).

Where appropriate, words related to headwords are grouped in the same entry (Gluck, glucken) in a slightly smaller bold type than the headword.

Common expressions in which the headword appears are shown in a different bold roman type (e.g. **Glück haben**).

Phonetic spellings

The phonetic spelling of each headword (indicating its pronunciation) is given in square brackets immediately after the headword (e.g. Quark [kvark]). A list of these symbols is given on page xii.

Meanings

Headword translations are given in ordinary type and, where more than one meaning or usage exists, these are separated by a semi-colon. You will often find other words in italics in brackets before the translations. These offer suggested contexts in which the headword might appear (e.g. eng (*Kleidung*) or (*Freundschaft*)) or provide synonyms (e.g. eng (*fig: Horizont*)).

"Key" words

Special status is given to certain German and English words which are considered as "key" words in each language. They may, for example, occur very frequently or have several types of usage (e.g. sein, auch; get, that). A combination of lozenges and numbers helps you to distinguish different parts of speech and different meanings. Further helpful information is provided in brackets and in italics in the relevant language for the user.

Grammatical information

Parts of speech are given in abbreviated form in italics after the phonetic spellings of headwords (e.g. *vt, adv, konj*).

Genders of German nouns are indicated as follows: *m* for a masculine and *f* for a feminine and *nt* for a neuter noun. The genitive and plural forms of regular nouns are shown on the table on page xi. Nouns which do not follow these rules have the genitive and plural in brackets immediately preceding the gender (e.g. **Spaß**, (-es, ⸚e), *m*).

Adjectives are normally shown in their basic form (e.g. **groß** *adj*), but where they are only used attributively (i.e. before a noun) feminine and neuter endings follow in brackets (**hohe (r, s)** *adj attrib*).

German spelling reform
The German spelling reform has been fully implemented in this dictionary. All headwords on the German-English side which are affected by the spelling changes are marked with ▲, but old spellings which are markedly different from the new ones and have a different alphabetical position are still listed and are cross-referenced to the new spellings. The old spellings are marked with △.

ABKÜRZUNGEN

ABBREVIATIONS

Abkürzung	abk, abbr	abbreviation
Akkusativ	acc	accusative
Adjektiv	adj	adjective
Adverb	adv	adverb
Landwirtschaft	AGR	agriculture
Akkusativ	akk	accusative
Anatomie	ANAT	anatomy
Architektur	ARCHIT	architecture
Astrologie	ASTROL	astrology
Astronomie	ASTRON	astronomy
attributiv	attrib	attributive
Kraftfahrzeuge	AUT	automobiles
Hilfsverb	aux	auxiliary
Luftfahrt	AVIAT	aviation
besonders	bes	especially
Biologie	BIOL	biology
Botanik	BOT	botany
britisch	BRIT	British
Chemie	CHEM	chemistry
Film	CINE	cinema
Handel	COMM	commerce
Komparativ	compar	comparative
Computer	COMPUT	computing
Konjunktion	conj	conjunction
Kochen und Backen	COOK	cooking
zusammengesetztes Wort	cpd	compound
Dativ	dat	dative
bestimmter Artikel	def art	definite article
Diminutiv	dimin	diminutive
kirchlich	ECCL	ecclesiastical
Eisenbahn	EISENB	railways
Elektrizität	ELEK, ELEC	electricity
besonders	esp	especially
und so weiter	etc	et cetera
etwas	etw	something
Euphemismus, Hüllwort	euph	euphemism
Interjektion, Ausruf	excl	exclamation
Femininum	f	feminine
übertragen	fig	figurative
Finanzwesen	FIN	finance
nicht getrennt gebraucht	fus	(phrasal verb) inseparable
Genitiv	gen	genitive
Geografie	GEOG	geography
Geologie	GEOL	geology
Grammatik	GRAM	grammar

German	Abbreviation	English
Geschichte	HIST	history
unpersönlich	impers	impersonal
unbestimmter Artikel	indef art	indefinite article
umgangssprachlich (! vulgär)	inf(!)	informal (! particularly offensive)
Infinitiv, Grundform	infin	infinitive
nicht getrennt gebraucht	insep	inseparable
unveränderlich	inv	invariable
unregelmäßig	irreg	irregular
jemand	jd	somebody
jemandem	jdm	(to) somebody
jemanden	jdn	somebody
jemandes	jds	somebody's
Rechtswesen	JUR	law
Kochen und Backen	KOCH	cooking
Komparativ	kompar	comparative
Konjunktion	konj	conjunction
Sprachwissenschaft	LING	linguistics
Literatur	LITER	of literature
Maskulinum	m	masculine
Mathematik	MATH	mathematics
Medizin	MED	medicine
Meteorologie	MET	meteorology
Militär	MIL	military
Bergbau	MIN	mining
Musik	MUS	music
Substantiv, Hauptwort	n	noun
nautisch, Seefahrt	NAUT	nautical, naval
Nominativ	nom	nominative
Neutrum	nt	neuter
Zahlwort	num	numeral
Objekt	obj	object
oder	od	or
sich	o.s.	oneself
Parlament	PARL	parliament
abschätzig	pej	pejorative
Fotografie	PHOT	photography
Physik	PHYS	physics
Plural	pl	plural
Politik	POL	politics
Präfix, Vorsilbe	pp	prefix
Präposition	präp, prep	preposition
Typografie	PRINT	printing
Pronomen, Fürwort	pron	pronoun
Psychologie	PSYCH	psychology
1. Vergangenheit, Imperfekt	pt	past tense
Radio	RAD	radio
Eisenbahn	RAIL	railways
Religion	REL	religion

PHONETIC SYMBOLS / LAUTSCHRIFT

[ː] *length mark/Längezeichen* ['] *stress mark/Betonung*
[|] *glottal stop/Knacklaut*

all vowel sounds are approximate only
alle Vokallaute sind nur ungefähre Entsprechungen

bet	[b]	Ball		[e]	Metall
dim	[d]	dann		[eː]	geben
face	[f]	Fass	set	[ɛ]	hässlich
go	[g]	Gast		[ɛ̃ː]	Cousin
hit	[h]	Herr	pity	[ɪ]	Bischof
you	[j]	ja		[i]	vital
cat	[k]	kalt	green	[iː]	viel
lick	[l]	Last	rot	[ɔ]	Post
must	[m]	Mast	board	[ɔː]	
nut	[n]	Nuss		[o]	Moral
bang	[ŋ]	lang		[oː]	oben
pepper	[p]	Pakt		[õ]	Champignon
red	[r]	Regen		[ø]	ökonomisch
sit	[s]	Rasse		[œ]	gönnen
shame	[ʃ]	Schal	full	[u]	kulant
tell	[t]	Tal	root	[uː]	Hut
chat	[tʃ]	tschüs	come	[ʌ]	
vine	[v]	was		[ʊ]	Pult
wine	[w]			[y]	physisch
loch	[x]	Bach		[yː]	für
	[ç]	ich		[ʏ]	Müll
zero	[z]	Hase	above	[ə]	bitte
leisure	[ʒ]	Genie	girl	[əː]	
join	[dʒ]				
thin	[θ]		lie	[aɪ]	weit
this	[ð]		now	[au]	
	[a]	Hast		[aʊ]	Haut
hat	[æ]		day	[eɪ]	
	[ɑː]	Bahn	fair	[ɛə]	
farm	[ɑː]		beer	[ɪə]	
	[ã]	Ensemble	toy	[ɔɪ]	
fiancé	[ɑ̃ː]			[ɔʏ]	Heu
			pure	[uə]	

['] r can be pronounced before a vowel; Bindungs-R

REGULAR GERMAN NOUN ENDINGS

nom		gen	pl
-ant	*m*	-anten	-anten
-anz	*f*	-anz	-anzen
-ar	*m*	-ar(e)s	-are
-chen	*nt*	-chens	-chen
-e	*f*	-	-n
-ei	*f*	-ei	-eien
-elle	*f*	-elle	-ellen
-ent	*m*	-enten	-enten
-enz	*f*	-enz	-enzen
-ette	*f*	-ette	-etten
-eur	*m*	-eurs	-eure
-euse	*f*	-euse	-eusen
-heit	*f*	-heit	-heiten
-ie	*f*	-ie	-ien
-ik	*f*	-ik	-iken
-in	*f*	-in	-innen
-ine	*f*	-ine	-inen
-ion	*f*	-ion	-ionen
-ist	*m*	-isten	-isten
-ium	*nt*	-iums	-ien
-ius	*m*	-ius	-iusse
-ive	*f*	-ive	-iven
-keit	*f*	-keit	-keiten
-lein	*nt*	-leins	-lein
-ling	*m*	-lings	-linge
-ment	*nt*	-ments	-mente
-mus	*m*	-mus	-men
-schaft	*f*	-schaft	-schaften
-tät	*f*	-tät	-täten
-tor	*m*	-tors	-toren
-ung	*f*	-ung	-ungen
-ur	*f*	-ur	-ṳren

PHONETIC SYMBOLS / LAUTSCHRIFT

[ː] *length mark/Längezeichen* ['] *stress mark/Betonung*
[|] *glottal stop/Knacklaut*

all vowel sounds are approximate only
alle Vokallaute sind nur ungefähre Entsprechungen

bet	[b]	**B**all		[e]	Metall
dim	[d]	**d**ann		[eː]	geben
face	[f]	**F**ass	set	[ɛ]	hässlich
go	[g]	**G**ast		[ɛ̃ː]	Cous**in**
hit	[h]	**H**err	pity	[ɪ]	Bischof
you	[j]	**j**a		[i]	vital
cat	[k]	**k**alt	green	[iː]	viel
lick	[l]	**L**ast	rot	[ɔ]	Post
must	[m]	**M**ast	board	[ɔː]	
nut	[n]	**N**uss		[o]	Moral
bang	[ŋ]	la**ng**		[oː]	oben
pepper	[p]	**P**akt		[õ]	Champig**non**
red	[r]	**R**egen		[ø]	**ö**konomisch
sit	[s]	**R**asse		[œ]	g**ö**nnen
shame	[ʃ]	**Sch**al	full	[u]	kulant
tell	[t]	**T**al	root	[uː]	Hut
chat	[tʃ]	**tsch**üs	come	[ʌ]	
vine	[v]	**w**as		[ʊ]	Pult
wine	[w]			[y]	ph**y**sisch
loch	[x]	Ba**ch**		[yː]	für
	[ç]	**ich**		[ʏ]	Müll
zero	[z]	**H**ase	above	[ə]	bitte
leisure	[ʒ]	**G**enie	girl	[əː]	
join	[dʒ]				
thin	[θ]		lie	[aɪ]	weit
this	[ð]		now	[au]	
	[a]	H**a**st		[aʊ]	Haut
hat	[æ]		day	[eɪ]	
	[ɑː]	**B**ahn	fair	[ɛə]	
farm	[ɑː]		beer	[ɪə]	
	[ã]	**En**semble	toy	[ɔɪ]	
fiancé	[ɑ̃ː]			[ɔʏ]	Heu
			pure	[uə]	

[ʳ] r can be pronounced before a vowel; Bindungs-R

xiv

ZAHLEN

NUMBERS

ein(s)	1	one
zwei	2	two
drei	3	three
vier	4	four
fünf	5	five
sechs	6	six
sieben	7	seven
acht	8	eight
neun	9	nine
zehn	10	ten
elf	11	eleven
zwölf	12	twelve
dreizehn	13	thirteen
vierzehn	14	fourteen
fünfzehn	15	fifteen
sechzehn	16	sixteen
siebzehn	17	seventeen
achtzehn	18	eighteen
neunzehn	19	nineteen
zwanzig	20	twenty
einundzwanzig	21	twenty-one
zweiundzwanzig	22	twenty-two
dreißig	30	thirty
vierzig	40	forty
fünfzig	50	fifty
sechzig	60	sixty
siebzig	70	seventy
achtzig	80	eighty
neunzig	90	ninety
hundert	100	a hundred
hunderteins	101	a hundred and one
zweihundert	200	two hundred
zweihunderteins	201	two hundred and one
dreihundert	300	three hundred
dreihunderteins	301	three hundred and one
tausend	1000	a thousand
tausend(und)eins	1001	a thousand and one
fünftausend	5000	five thousand
eine Million	1000000	a million

erste(r, s)	1.	first	1st
zweite(r, s)	2.	second	2nd
dritte(r, s)	3.	third	3rd
vierte(r, s)	4.	fourth	4th
fünfte(r, s)	5.	fifth	5th
sechste(r, s)	6.	sixth	6th

siebte(r, s)	7.	seventh	7th
achte(r, s)	8.	eighth	8th
neunte(r, s)	9.	ninth	9th
zehnte(r, s)	10.	tenth	10th
elfte(r, s)	11.	eleventh	11th
zwölfte(r, s)	12.	twelfth	12th
dreizehnte(r, s)	13.	thirteenth	13th
vierzehnte(r, s)	14.	fourteenth	14th
fünfzehnte(r, s)	15.	fifteenth	15th
sechzehnte(r, s)	16.	sixteenth	16th
siebzehnte(r, s)	17.	seventeenth	17th
achtzehnte(r, s)	18.	eighteenth	18th
neunzehnte(r, s)	19.	nineteenth	19th
zwanzigste(r, s)	20.	twentieth	20th
einundzwanzigste(r, s)	21.	twenty-first	21st
dreißigste(r, s)	30.	thirtieth	30th
hundertste(r, s)	100.	hundredth	100th
hunderterste(r, s)	101.	hundred-and-first	101st
tausendste(r, s)	1000.	thousandth	1000th

Brüche usw.

Fractions etc.

ein Halb	$\frac{1}{2}$	a half	
ein Drittel	$\frac{1}{3}$	a third	
ein Viertel	$\frac{1}{4}$	a quarter	
ein Fünftel	$\frac{1}{5}$	a fifth	
null Komma fünf	0,5	(nought) point five	0.5
drei Komma vier	3,4	three point four	3.4
sechs Komma acht neun	6,89	six point eight nine	6.89
zehn Prozent	10%	ten per cent	
hundert Prozent	100%	a hundred per cent	

Beispiele

Examples

er wohnt in Nummer 10	he lives at number 10
es steht in Kapitel 7	it's in chapter 7
auf Seite 7	on page 7
er wohnt im 7. Stock	he lives on the 7th floor
er wurde 7.	he came in 7th
Maßstab eins zu zwanzigtausend	scale one to twenty thousand

UHRZEIT

THE TIME

wie viel Uhr ist es?, wie spät ist es?

what time is it?

es ist ...

it's ...

Mitternacht, zwölf Uhr nachts
ein Uhr (morgens *or* früh)
fünf nach eins, ein Uhr fünf
zehn nach eins, ein Uhr zehn
Viertel nach eins, ein Uhr fünfzehn
fünf vor halb zwei, ein Uhr
  fünfundzwanzig
halb zwei, ein Uhr dreißig
fünf nach halb zwei, ein Uhr
  fünfunddreißig
zwanzig vor zwei, ein Uhr vierzig
Viertel vor zwei, ein Uhr
  fünfundvierzig
zehn vor zwei, ein Uhr fünfzig
zwölf Uhr (mittags), Mittag
halb eins (mittags *or* nachmittags),
  zwölf Uhr dreißig
zwei Uhr (nachmittags)

halb acht (abends)

midnight, twelve p.m.
one o'clock (in the morning), one (a.m.)
five past one
ten past one
a quarter past one, one fifteen
twenty-five past one, one twenty-five

half past one, one thirty
twenty-five to two, one thirty-five

twenty to two, one forty
a quarter to two, one forty-five

ten to two, one fifty
twelve o'clock, midday, noon
half past twelve, twelve thirty (p.m.)

two o'clock (in the afternoon), two
  (p.m.)
half past seven (in the evening), seven
  thirty (p.m.)

um wie viel Uhr?

at what time?

um Mitternacht
um sieben Uhr

at midnight
at seven o'clock

in zwanzig Minuten
vor fünfzehn Minuten

in twenty minutes
fifteen minutes ago

DEUTSCH – ENGLISCH
GERMAN – ENGLISH

A, a

Aal [aːl] **(-(e)s, -e)** *m* eel

Aas [aːs] **(-es, -e** *od* **Äser)** *nt* carrion

SCHLÜSSELWORT
---

ab [ap] *präp +dat* from; **Kinder ab 12 Jahren**
children from the age of 12; **ab morgen**
from tomorrow; **ab sofort** as of now
♦ *adv* 1 off; **links ab** to the left; **der Knopf
ist ab** the button has come off; **ab nach
Hause!** off you go home

2 (*zeitlich*): **von da ab** from then on; **von
heute ab** from today, as of today

3 (*auf Fahrplänen*): **München ab 12.20**
leaving Munich 12.20

4: **ab und zu** *od* **an** now and then *od* again

Abänderung [ˈapˌɛndərʊŋ] *f* alteration

Abbau [ˈapbaʊ] **(-(e)s)** *m* (*+gen*) dismantling;
(*Verminderung*) reduction (in); (*Verfall*)
decline (in); (*MIN*) mining; quarrying;
(*CHEM*) decomposition; **a~en** *vt* to
dismantle; (*Bergbau*) to mine; to quarry;
(*verringern*) to reduce; (*CHEM*) to break
down

abbeißen [ˈapbaɪsən] (*unreg*) *vt* to bite off

abbekommen [ˈapbəkɔmən] (*unreg*) *vt* to
(*Deckel, Schraube, Band*) to loosen; **etwas ~**
(*beschädigt werden*) to get damaged;
(: *Person*) to get injured

abbestellen [ˈapbəʃtɛlən] *vt* to cancel

abbezahlen [ˈapbətsaːlən] *vt* to pay off

abbiegen [ˈapbiːgən] (*unreg*) *vi* to turn off;
(*Straße*) to bend ♦ *vt* to bend; (*verhindern*)
to ward off

abbilden [ˈapbɪldən] *vt* to portray;
Abbildung *f* illustration

abblenden [ˈapblɛndən] *vt, vi* (*AUT*) to dip
(*BRIT*), to dim (*US*)

Abblendlicht [ˈapblɛntlɪçt] *nt* dipped (*BRIT*)
od dimmed (*US*) headlights *pl*

abbrechen [ˈapbrɛçən] (*unreg*) *vt, vi* to
break off; (*Gebäude*) to pull down; (*Zelt*) to
take down; (*aufhören*) to stop; (*COMPUT*) to
abort

abbrennen [ˈapbrɛnən] (*unreg*) *vt* to burn
off; (*Feuerwerk*) to let off ♦ *vi* (*aux sein*) to
burn down

abbringen [ˈapbrɪŋən] (*unreg*) *vt*: **jdn von
etw ~** to dissuade sb from sth; **jdn vom
Weg ~** to divert sb

abbröckeln [ˈapbrœkəln] *vt, vi* to crumble
off *od* away

Abbruch [ˈapbrʊx] *m* (*von Verhandlungen etc*)
breaking off; (*von Haus*) demolition; **jdm/
etw ~ tun** to harm sb/sth; **a~reif** *adj* only
fit for demolition

abbrühen [ˈapbryːən] *vt* to scald;
abgebrüht (*umg*) hard-boiled

abbuchen [ˈapbuːxən] *vt* to debit

abdanken [ˈapdaŋkən] *vi* to resign; (*König*)
to abdicate; **Abdankung** *f* resignation;
abdication

abdecken [ˈapdɛkən] *vt* (*Loch*) to cover;
(*Tisch*) to clear; (*Plane*) to uncover

abdichten [ˈapdɪçtən] *vt* to seal; (*NAUT*) to
caulk

abdrehen [ˈapdreːən] *vt* (*Gas*) to turn off;
(*Licht*) to switch off; (*Film*) to shoot ♦ *vi*
(*Schiff*) to change course

Abdruck [ˈapdrʊk] *m* (*Nachdrucken*)
reprinting; (*Gedrucktes*) reprint;
(*Gipsabdruck, Wachsabdruck*) impression;
(*Fingerabdruck*) print; **a~en** *vt* to print, to
publish

abdrücken [ˈapdrʏkən] *vt* (*Waffe*) to fire;
(*Person*) to hug, to squeeze

Abend [ˈaːbənt] **(-s, -e)** *m* evening; **guten ~**
good evening; **zu ~ essen** to have dinner
od supper; **heute ~** this evening; **~brot** *nt*
supper; **~essen** *nt* supper; **~garderobe** *f*

Spelling Reform: ▲ *new spelling* △ *old spelling (to be phased out)*

evening dress; **~kasse** *f* box office; **~kleid** *nt* evening dress; **~kurs** *m* evening classes *pl*; **~land** *nt* (*Europa*) West; **a~lich** *adj* evening; **~mahl** *nt* Holy Communion; **~rot** *nt* sunset; **a~s** *adv* in the evening

Abenteuer ['a:bəntɔʏər] (**-s, -**) *nt* adventure; **~film** *m* adventure film; **a~lich** *adj* adventurous; **~urlaub** *m* adventure holiday

Abenteurer (**-s, -**) *m* adventurer; **~in** *f* adventuress

aber ['a:bər] *konj* but; (*jedoch*) however
♦ *adv*: **das ist ~ schön** that's really nice; **nun ist ~ Schluss!** now that's enough!; **vielen Dank – ~ bitte!** thanks a lot – you're welcome; **A~glaube** *m* superstition; **~gläubisch** *adj* superstitious

aberkennen ['ap|ɛrkɛnən] (*unreg*) *vt* (*JUR*): **jdm etw ~** to deprive sb of sth, to take sth (away) from sb

abermals ['a:bəma:ls] *adv* once again

Abertausend, abertausend ['a:bətauzənt] *indef pron* **tausend** *od* **Tausend und ~** thousands upon thousands

Abf. *abk* (= *Abfahrt*) dep.

abfahren ['apfa:rən] (*unreg*) *vi* to leave, to depart ♦ *vt* to take *od* cart away; (*Strecke*) to drive; (*Reifen*) to wear; (*Fahrkarte*) to use

Abfahrt ['apfa:rt] *f* departure; (*SKI*) descent; (*Piste*) run; **~szeit** *f* departure time

Abfall ['apfal] *m* waste; (*von Speisen etc*) rubbish (*BRIT*), garbage (*US*); (*Neigung*) slope; (*Verschlechterung*) decline; **~eimer** *m* rubbish bin (*BRIT*), garbage can (*US*); **a~en** (*unreg*) *vi* (*auch fig*) to fall *od* drop off; (*sich neigen*) to fall *od* drop away

abfällig ['apfɛlɪç] *adj* disparaging, deprecatory

abfangen ['apfaŋən] (*unreg*) *vt* to intercept; (*Person*) to catch; (*unter Kontrolle bringen*) to check

abfärben ['apfɛrbən] *vi* to lose its colour; (*Wäsche*) to run; (*fig*) to rub off

abfassen ['apfasən] *vt* to write, to draft

abfertigen ['apfɛrtɪgən] *vt* to prepare for dispatch, to process; (*an der Grenze*) to clear; (*Kundschaft*) to attend to

Abfertigungsschalter *m* (*Flughafen*)

check-in desk

abfeuern ['apfɔʏərn] *vt* to fire

abfinden ['apfɪndən] (*unreg*) *vt* to pay off
♦ *vr* to come to terms; **sich mit jdm ~/ nicht ~** to put up with/not get on with sb

Abfindung *f* (*von Gläubigern*) payment; (*Geld*) sum in settlement

abflauen ['apflauən] *vi* (*Wind, Erregung*) to die away, to subside; (*Nachfrage, Geschäft*) to fall *od* drop off

abfliegen ['apfli:gən] (*unreg*) *vi* (*Flugzeug*) to take off; (*Passagier auch*) to fly ♦ *vt* (*Gebiet*) to fly over

abfließen ['apfli:sən] (*unreg*) *vi* to drain away

Abflug ['apflu:k] *m* departure; (*Start*) take-off; **~halle** *f* departure lounge; **~zeit** *f* departure time

Abfluss ▲ ['apflʊs] *m* draining away; (*Öffnung*) outlet; **~rohr** *nt* drain pipe; (*von sanitären Anlagen auch*) waste pipe

abfragen ['apfra:gən] *vt* (*bes SCH*) to test orally (on)

Abfuhr ['apfu:r] (**-, -en**) *f* removal; (*fig*) snub, rebuff

abführen ['apfy:rən] *vt* to lead away; (*Gelder, Steuern*) to pay ♦ *vi* (*MED*) to have a laxative effect

Abführmittel ['apfy:rmɪtəl] *nt* laxative

abfüllen ['apfʏlən] *vt* to draw off; (*in Flaschen*) to bottle

Abgabe ['apga:bə] *f* handing in; (*von Ball*) pass; (*Steuer*) tax; (*eines Amtes*) giving up; (*einer Erklärung*) giving

Abgang ['apgaŋ] *m* (*von Schule*) leaving; (*THEAT*) exit; (*Abfahrt*) departure; (*der Post, von Waren*) dispatch

Abgas ['apga:s] *nt* waste gas; (*AUT*) exhaust

abgeben ['apge:bən] (*unreg*) *vt* (*Gegenstand*) to hand *od* give in; (*Ball*) to pass; (*Wärme*) to give off; (*Amt*) to hand over; (*Schuss*) to fire; (*Erklärung, Urteil*) to give; (*darstellen, sein*) to make ♦ *vr*: **sich mit jdm/etw ~** to associate with sb/bother with sth; **jdm etw ~** (*überlassen*) to let sb have sth

abgebrüht ['apgəbry:t] (*umg*) *adj* (*skrupellos*)

hard-boiled

abgehen ['apge:ən] (*unreg*) *vi* to go away, to leave; (*THEAT*) to exit; (*Knopf etc*) to come off; (*Straße*) to branch off ♦ *vt* (*Strecke*) to go *od* walk along; **etw geht jdm ab** (*fehlt*) sb lacks sth

abgelegen ['apgəle:gən] *adj* remote

abgemacht ['apgəmaxt] *adj* fixed; **~!** done!

abgeneigt ['apgənaikt] *adj* disinclined

abgenutzt ['apgənʊtst] *adj* worn

Abgeordnete(r) ['apgəʔɔrdnətə(r)] *f(m)* member of parliament; elected representative

abgeschlossen ['apgəʃlɔsən] *adj attrib* (*Wohnung*) self-contained

abgeschmackt ['apgəʃmakt] *adj* tasteless

abgesehen ['apgəze:ən] *adj*: **es auf jdn/ etw ~ haben** to be after sb/sth; **~ von ...** apart from ...

abgespannt ['apgəʃpant] *adj* tired out

abgestanden ['apgəʃtandən] *adj* stale; (*Bier auch*) flat

abgestorben ['apgəʃtɔrbən] *adj* numb; (*BIOL, MED*) dead

abgetragen ['apgətra:gən] *adj* shabby, worn out

abgewinnen ['apgəvinən] (*unreg*) *vt*: **einer Sache etw/Geschmack ~** to get sth/ pleasure from sth

abgewöhnen ['apgəvø:nən] *vt*: **jdm/sich etw ~** to cure sb of sth/give sth up

abgrenzen ['apgrɛntsən] *vt* (*auch fig*) to mark off; to fence off

Abgrund ['apgrʊnt] *m* (*auch fig*) abyss

abhacken ['aphakən] *vt* to chop off

abhaken ['apha:kən] *vt* (*auf Papier*) to tick off

abhalten ['aphaltən] (*unreg*) *vt* (*Versammlung*) to hold; **jdn von etw ~** (*fern halten*) to keep sb away from sth; (*hindern*) to keep sb from sth

abhanden [ap'handən] *adj*: **~ kommen** to get lost

Abhandlung ['aphandlʊŋ] *f* treatise, discourse

Abhang ['aphaŋ] *m* slope

abhängen ['aphɛŋən] *vt* (*Bild*) to take down; (*Anhänger*) to uncouple; (*Verfolger*) to shake off ♦ *vi* (*unreg: Fleisch*) to hang; **von jdm/ etw ~** to depend on sb/sth

abhängig ['aphɛŋiç] *adj*: **~ (von)** dependent (on); **A~keit** *f*: **A~keit (von)** dependence (on)

abhärten ['aphɛrtən] *vt, vr* to toughen (o.s.) up; **sich gegen etw ~** to inure o.s. to sth

abhauen ['aphauən] (*unreg*) *vt* to cut off; (*Baum*) to cut down ♦ *vi* (*umg*) to clear off *od* out

abheben ['aphe:bən] (*unreg*) *vt* to lift (up); (*Karten*) to cut; (*Geld*) to withdraw, to take out ♦ *vi* (*Flugzeug*) to take off; (*Rakete*) to lift off ♦ *vr* to stand out

abheften ['aphɛftən] *vt* (*Rechnungen etc*) to file away

abhetzen ['aphɛtsən] *vr* to wear *od* tire o.s. out

Abhilfe ['aphilfə] *f* remedy; **~ schaffen** to put things right

abholen ['apho:lən] *vt* (*Gegenstand*) to fetch, to collect; (*Person*) to call for; (*am Bahnhof etc*) to pick up, to meet

abholzen ['aphɔltsən] *vt* (*Wald*) to clear

abhorchen ['aphɔrçən] *vt* (*MED*) to listen to a patient's chest

abhören ['aphø:rən] *vt* (*Vokabeln*) to test; (*Telefongespräch*) to tap; (*Tonband etc*) to listen to

Abhörgerät *nt* bug

Abitur [abi'tu:r] (**-s, -e**) *nt* German school-leaving examination; **~i'ent(in)** *m(f)* candidate for school-leaving certificate

---

Abitur

*The **Abitur** is the German school-leaving examination taken in four subjects by pupils at a **Gymnasium** at the age of 18 or 19. It is necessary for entry to university.*

Abk. *abk* (= *Abkürzung*) abbr.

abkapseln ['apkapsəln] *vr* to shut *od* cut o.s. off

abkaufen ['apkaufən] *vt*: **jdm etw ~** (*auch fig*) to buy sth from sb

abkehren ['apkeːrən] *vt (Blick)* to avert, to turn away ♦ *vr* to turn away

abklingen ['apklɪŋən] *(unreg) vi* to die away; *(Radio)* to fade out

abknöpfen ['apknœpfən] *vt* to unbutton; **jdm etw ~** *(umg)* to get sth off sb

abkochen ['apkɔxən] *vt* to boil

abkommen ['apkɔmən] *(unreg) vi* to get away; **von der Straße/von einem Plan ~** to leave the road/give up a plan; **A~ (-s, -)** *nt* agreement

abkömmlich ['apkœmlɪç] *adj* available, free

abkratzen ['apkratsən] *vt* to scrape off ♦ *vi (umg)* to kick the bucket

abkühlen ['apkyːlən] *vt* to cool down ♦ *vr (Mensch)* to cool down *od* off; *(Wetter)* to get cool; *(Zuneigung)* to cool

abkürzen ['apkʏrtsən] *vt* to shorten; *(Wort auch)* to abbreviate; **den Weg ~** to take a short cut

Abkürzung *f (Wort)* abbreviation; *(Weg)* short cut

abladen ['aplaːdən] *(unreg) vt* to unload

Ablage ['aplaːgə] *f (für Akten)* tray; *(für Kleider)* cloakroom

ablassen ['aplasən] *(unreg) vt (Wasser, Dampf)* to let off; *(vom Preis)* to knock off ♦ *vi:* **von etw ~** to give sth up, to abandon sth

Ablauf ['aplaʊf] *m (Abfluss)* drain; *(von Ereignissen)* course; *(einer Frist, Zeit)* expiry *(BRIT)*, expiration *(US)*; **a~en** *(unreg) vi (abfließen)* to drain away; *(Ereignisse)* to happen; *(Frist, Zeit, Pass)* to expire ♦ *vt (Sohlen)* to wear (down *od* out)

ablegen ['apleːgən] *vt* to put *od* lay down; *(Kleider)* to take off; *(Gewohnheit)* to get rid of; *(Prüfung)* to take, to sit; *(Zeugnis)* to give

Ableger **(-s, -)** *m* layer; *(fig)* branch, offshoot

ablehnen ['apleːnən] *vt* to reject; *(Einladung)* to decline, to refuse ♦ *vi* to decline, to refuse

ablehnend *adj (Haltung, Antwort)* negative; *(Geste)* disapproving; **ein ~er Bescheid** a rejection

Ablehnung *f* rejection; refusal

ableiten ['aplaɪtən] *vt (Wasser)* to divert; *(deduzieren)* to deduce; *(Wort)* to derive; **Ableitung** *f* diversion; deduction; derivation; *(Wort)* derivative

ablenken ['aplɛŋkən] *vt* to turn away, to deflect; *(zerstreuen)* to distract ♦ *vi* to change the subject; **Ablenkung** *f* distraction

ablesen ['apleːzən] *(unreg) vt* to read out; *(Messgeräte)* to read

ablichten ['aplɪçtən] *vt* to photocopy

abliefern ['apliːfarn] *vt* to deliver; **etw bei jdm ~** to hand sth over to sb

Ablieferung *f* delivery

ablösen ['apløːzən] *vt (abtrennen)* to take off, to remove; *(in Amt)* to take over from; *(Wache)* to relieve

Ablösung *f* removal; relieving

abmachen ['apmaxən] *vt* to take off; *(vereinbaren)* to agree; **Abmachung** *f* agreement

abmagern ['apmaːgərn] *vi* to get thinner

Abmagerungskur *f* diet; **eine ~ machen** to go on a diet

abmarschieren ['apmarʃiːrən] *vi* to march off

abmelden ['apmɛldən] *vt (Zeitungen)* to cancel; *(Auto)* to take off the road ♦ *vr* to give notice of one's departure; *(im Hotel)* to check out; **jdn bei der Polizei ~** to register sb's departure with the police

abmessen ['apmɛsən] *(unreg) vt* to measure; **Abmessung** *f* measurement

abmontieren ['apmɔntiːrən] *vt* to take off

abmühen ['apmyːən] *vr* to wear o.s. out

Abnahme ['apnaːmə] *f (+gen)* removal; *(COMM)* buying; *(Verringerung)* decrease (in)

abnehmen ['apneːmən] *(unreg) vt* to take off, to remove; *(Führerschein)* to take away; *(Prüfung)* to hold; *(Maschen)* to decrease ♦ *vi* to decrease; *(schlanker werden)* to lose weight; **(jdm) etw ~** *(Geld)* to get sth (out of sb); *(kaufen, umg: glauben)* to buy sth (from sb); **jdm Arbeit ~** to take work off sb's shoulders

Abnehmer **(-s, -)** *m* purchaser, customer

Abneigung ['apnaɪgʊŋ] *f* aversion, dislike

abnorm [ap'nɔrm] *adj* abnormal

abnutzen ['apnʊtsən] *vt* to wear out; **Abnutzung** *f* wear (and tear)

Abo ['abo] (*umg*) *nt abk* = **Abonnement**

Abonnement [abɔn(ə)'mãː] (**-s, -s**) *nt* subscription; **Abonnent(in)** [abɔ'nɛnt(ɪn)] *m(f)* subscriber; **abonnieren** *vt* to subscribe to

Abordnung ['apɔrdnʊŋ] *f* delegation

abpacken ['appakən] *vt* to pack

abpassen ['appasən] *vt* (*Person, Gelegenheit*) to wait for

Abpfiff ['appfɪf] *m* final whistle

abplagen ['appla:gən] *vr* to wear o.s. out

abprallen ['appralən] *vi* to bounce off; to ricochet

abraten ['apra:tən] (*unreg*) *vi*: **jdm von etw ~** to advise *or* warn sb against sth

abräumen ['aprɔymən] *vt* to clear up *od* away

abreagieren ['apreagi:rən] *vt*: **seinen Zorn (an jdm/etw) ~** to work one's anger off (on sb/sth) ♦ *vr* to calm down

abrechnen ['aprɛçnən] *vt* to deduct, to take off ♦ *vi* to settle up; (*fig*) to get even

Abrechnung *f* settlement; (*Rechnung*) bill

Abrede ['apre:də] *f*: **etw in ~ stellen** to deny *od* dispute sth

Abreise ['apraɪzə] *f* departure; **a~n** *vi* to leave, to set off

abreißen ['apraɪsən] (*unreg*) *vt* (*Haus*) to tear down; (*Blatt*) to tear off

abrichten ['aprɪçtən] *vt* to train

abriegeln ['apri:gəln] *vt* (*Straße, Gebiet*) to seal off

Abruf ['apru:f] *m*: **auf ~** on call; **a~en** (*unreg*) *vt* (*Mensch*) to call away; (*COMM: Ware*) to request delivery of

abrunden ['aprʊndən] *vt* to round off

abrupt [a'brʊpt] *adj* abrupt

abrüsten ['aprʏstən] *vi* to disarm; **Abrüstung** *f* disarmament

abrutschen ['aprʊtʃən] *vi* to slip; (*AVIAT*) to sideslip

Abs. *abk* (= *Absender*) sender, from

Absage ['apza:gə] *f* refusal; **a~n** *vt* to cancel, to call off; (*Einladung*) to turn down

♦ *vi* to cry off; (*ablehnen*) to decline

absahnen ['apza:nən] *vt* to skim ♦ *vi* (*fig*) to rake in

Absatz ['apzats] *m* (*COMM*) sales *pl*; (*Bodensatz*) deposit; (*neuer Abschnitt*) paragraph; (*Treppenabsatz*) landing; (*Schuhabsatz*) heel; **~gebiet** *nt* (*COMM*) market

abschaffen ['apʃafən] *vt* to abolish, to do away with; **Abschaffung** *f* abolition

abschalten ['apʃaltən] *vt, vi* (*auch umg*) to switch off

abschätzen ['apʃɛtsən] *vt* to estimate; (*Lage*) to assess; (*Person*) to size up

abschätzig ['apʃɛtsɪç] *adj* disparaging, derogatory

Abschaum ['apʃaʊm] (**-(e)s**) *m* scum

Abscheu ['apʃɔy] (**-(e)s**) *m* loathing, repugnance; **~ erregend** repulsive, loathsome; **a~lich** [ap'ʃɔylɪç] *adj* abominable

abschicken ['apʃɪkən] *vt* to send off

abschieben ['apʃi:bən] (*unreg*) *vt* to push away; (*Person*) to pack off; (: *POL*) to deport

Abschied ['apʃi:t] (**-(e)s, -e**) *m* parting; (*von Armee*) discharge; (**von jdm**) **~ nehmen** to say goodbye (to sb), to take one's leave (of sb); **seinen ~ nehmen** (*MIL*) to apply for discharge; **~sbrief** *m* farewell letter; **~sfeier** *f* farewell party

abschießen ['apʃi:sən] (*unreg*) *vt* (*Flugzeug*) to shoot down; (*Geschoss*) to fire

abschirmen ['apʃɪrmən] *vt* to screen

abschlagen ['apʃla:gən] (*unreg*) *vt* (*abhacken, COMM*) to knock off; (*ablehnen*) to refuse; (*MIL*) to repel

abschlägig ['apʃlɛ:gɪç] *adj* negative

Abschlagszahlung *f* interim payment

Abschlepp- ['apʃlɛp] *zW*: **~dienst** *m* (*AUT*) breakdown service (*BRIT*), towing company (*US*); **a~en** *vt* to (take in) tow; **~seil** *nt* towrope

abschließen ['apʃli:sən] (*unreg*) *vt* (*Tür*) to lock; (*beenden*) to conclude, to finish; (*Vertrag, Handel*) to conclude ♦ *vr* (*sich isolieren*) to cut o.s. off; **~d** *adj* concluding

Abschluss ▲ ['apʃlʊs] *m* (*Beendigung*) close,

conclusion; (*COMM: Bilanz*) balancing; (*von Vertrag, Handel*) conclusion; **zum ~** in conclusion; **~feier** f (*SCH*) end of term party; **~prüfung** f final exam

abschneiden [ˈapʃnaɪdən] (*unreg*) vt to cut off ♦ vi to do, to come off

Abschnitt [ˈapʃnɪt] m section; (*MIL*) sector; (*Kontrollabschnitt*) counterfoil; (*MATH*) segment; (*Zeitabschnitt*) period

abschrauben [ˈapʃraubən] vt to unscrew

abschrecken [ˈapʃrɛkən] vt to deter, to put off; (*mit kaltem Wasser*) to plunge in cold water; **~d** adj deterrent; **~des Beispiel** warning

abschreiben [ˈapʃraɪbən] (*unreg*) vt to copy; (*verloren geben*) to write off; (*COMM*) to deduct

Abschrift [ˈapʃrɪft] f copy

Abschuss ▲ [ˈapʃʊs] m (*eines Geschützes*) firing; (*Herunterschießen*) shooting down; (*Tötung*) shooting

abschüssig [ˈapʃʏsɪç] adj steep

abschwächen [ˈapʃvɛçən] vt to lessen; (*Behauptung, Kritik*) to tone down ♦ vr to lessen

abschweifen [ˈapʃvaɪfən] vi to digress

abschwellen [ˈapʃvɛlən] (*unreg*) vi (*Geschwulst*) to go down; (*Lärm*) to die down

abschwören [ˈapʃvøːrən] vi (+*dat*) to renounce

absehbar [ˈapzeːbaːr] adj foreseeable; **in ~er Zeit** in the foreseeable future; **das Ende ist ~** the end is in sight

absehen [ˈapzeːən] (*unreg*) vt (*Ende, Folgen*) to foresee ♦ vi: **von etw ~** to refrain from sth; (*nicht berücksichtigen*) to leave sth out of consideration

abseilen [ˈapzaɪlən] vr (*Bergsteiger*) to abseil (down)

abseits [ˈapzaɪts] adv out of the way ♦ präp +*gen* away from; **A~** nt (*SPORT*) offside

absenden [ˈapzɛndən] (*unreg*) vt to send off, to dispatch

Absender (-s, -) m sender

absetzen [ˈapzɛtsən] vt (*niederstellen, aussteigen lassen*) to put down; (*abnehmen*) to take off; (*COMM: verkaufen*) to sell; (*FIN: abziehen*) to deduct; (*entlassen*) to dismiss; (*König*) to depose; (*streichen*) to drop; (*hervorheben*) to pick out ♦ vr (*sich entfernen*) to clear off; (*sich ablagern*) to be deposited

Absetzung f (*FIN: Abzug*) deduction; (*Entlassung*) dismissal; (*von König*) deposing

absichern [ˈapzɪçərn] vt to make safe; (*schützen*) to safeguard ♦ vr to protect o.s.

Absicht [ˈapzɪçt] f intention; **mit ~** on purpose; **a~lich** adj intentional, deliberate

absinken [ˈapzɪŋkən] (*unreg*) vi to sink; (*Temperatur, Geschwindigkeit*) to decrease

absitzen [ˈapzɪtsən] (*unreg*) vi to dismount ♦ vt (*Strafe*) to serve

absolut [apzoˈluːt] adj absolute; **A~ismus** m absolutism

absolvieren [apzɔlˈviːrən] vt (*SCH*) to complete

absonder- [ˈapzɔndər] zW: **~lich** adj odd, strange; **~n** vt to separate; (*ausscheiden*) to give off, to secrete ♦ vr to cut o.s. off; **A~ung** f separation; (*MED*) secretion

abspalten [ˈapʃpaltən] vt to split off

abspannen [ˈapʃpanən] vt (*Pferde*) to unhitch; (*Wagen*) to uncouple

abspeisen [ˈapʃpaɪzən] vt (*fig*) to fob off

abspenstig [ˈapʃpɛnstɪç] adj: **(jdm) ~ machen** to lure away (from sb)

absperren [ˈapʃpɛrən] vt to block od close off; (*Tür*) to lock; **Absperrung** f (*Vorgang*) blocking od closing off; (*Sperre*) barricade

abspielen [ˈapʃpiːlən] vt (*Platte, Tonband*) to play; (*SPORT: Ball*) to pass ♦ vr to happen

Absprache [ˈapʃpraːxə] f arrangement

absprechen [ˈapʃprɛçən] (*unreg*) vt (*vereinbaren*) to arrange; **jdm etw ~** to deny sb sth

abspringen [ˈapʃprɪŋən] (*unreg*) vi to jump down/off; (*Farbe, Lack*) to flake off; (*AVIAT*) to bale out; (*sich distanzieren*) to back out

Absprung [ˈapʃprʊŋ] m jump

abspülen [ˈapʃpyːlən] vt to rinse; (*Geschirr*) to wash up

abstammen [ˈapʃtamən] vi to be descended; (*Wort*) to be derived; **Abstammung** f descent; derivation

Abstand ['apʃtant] *m* distance; (*zeitlich*) interval; **davon ~ nehmen, etw zu tun** to refrain from doing sth; **mit ~ der Beste** by far the best

abstatten ['apʃtatən] *vt* (*Dank*) to give; (*Besuch*) to pay

abstauben ['apʃtaubən] *vt, vi* to dust; (*umg: stehlen*) to pinch; (: *schnorren*) to scrounge

Abstecher ['apʃtɛçər] (**-s, -**) *m* detour

abstehen ['apʃteːən] (*unreg*) *vi* (*Ohren, Haare*) to stick out; (*entfernt sein*) to stand away

absteigen ['apʃtaɪgən] (*unreg*) *vi* (*vom Rad etc*) to get off, to dismount; **(in die zweite Liga) ~** to be relegated (to the second division)

abstellen ['apʃtɛlən] *vt* (*niederstellen*) to put down; (*entfernt stellen*) to pull out; (*hinstellen: Auto*) to park; (*ausschalten*) to turn *od* switch off; (*Missstand, Unsitte*) to stop

Abstellraum *m* storage room

abstempeln ['apʃtɛmpəln] *vt* to stamp

absterben ['apʃtɛrbən] (*unreg*) *vi* to die; (*Körperteil*) to go numb

Abstieg ['apʃtiːk] (**-(e)s, -e**) *m* descent; (*SPORT*) relegation; (*fig*) decline

abstimmen ['apʃtɪmən] *vi* to vote ♦ *vt*: **~ (auf +***akk***)** (*Instrument*) to tune (to); (*Interessen*) to match (with); (*Termine, Ziele*) to fit in (with) ♦ *vr* to agree

Abstimmung *f* vote

Abstinenz [apsti'nɛnts] *f* abstinence; teetotalism; **~ler(in)** (**-s, -**) *m(f)* teetotaller

abstoßen ['apʃtoːsən] (*unreg*) *vt* to push off *od* away; (*verkaufen*) to unload; (*anekeln*) to repel, to repulse; **~d** *adj* repulsive

abstrakt [ap'strakt] *adj* abstract ♦ *adv* abstractly, in the abstract

abstreiten ['apʃtraɪtən] (*unreg*) *vt* to deny

Abstrich ['apʃtrɪç] *m* (*Abzug*) cut; (*MED*) smear; **~e machen** to lower one's sights

abstufen ['apʃtuːfən] *vt* (*Hang*) to terrace; (*Farben*) to shade; (*Gehälter*) to grade

Absturz ['apʃtʊrts] *m* fall; (*AVIAT*) crash

abstürzen ['apʃtʏrtsən] *vi* to fall; (*AVIAT*) to crash

absuchen ['apzuːxən] *vt* to scour, to search

absurd [ap'zʊrt] *adj* absurd

Abszess ▲ [aps'tsɛs] (**-es, -e**) *m* abscess

Abt [apt] (**-(e)s, ⁻e**) *m* abbot

Abt. *abk* (= *Abteilung*). dept.

abtasten ['aptastən] *vt* to feel, to probe

abtauen ['aptauən] *vt, vi* to thaw

Abtei [ap'taɪ] (**-, -en**) *f* abbey

Abteil [ap'taɪl] (**-(e)s, -e**) *nt* compartment; **'a~n** *vt* to divide up; (*abtrennen*) to divide off; **~ung** *f* (*in Firma, Kaufhaus*) department; (*in Krankenhaus*) section; (*MIL*) unit

abtippen ['aptɪpən] *vt* (*Text*) to type up

abtransportieren ['aptranspɔrti:rən] *vt* to take away, to remove

abtreiben ['aptraɪbən] (*unreg*) *vt* (*Boot, Flugzeug*) to drive off course; (*Kind*) to abort ♦ *vi* to be driven off course; to abort

Abtreibung *f* abortion

abtrennen ['aptrɛnən] *vt* (*lostrennen*) to detach; (*entfernen*) to take off; (*abteilen*) to separate off

abtreten ['aptreːtən] (*unreg*) *vt* to wear out; (*überlassen*) to hand over, to cede ♦ *vi* to go off; (*zurücktreten*) to step down

Abtritt ['aptrɪt] *m* resignation

abtrocknen ['aptrɔknən] *vt, vi* to dry

abtun ['aptuːn] (*unreg*) *vt* (*fig*) to dismiss

abwägen ['apvɛːgən] (*unreg*) *vt* to weigh up

abwälzen ['apvɛltsən] *vt* (*Schuld, Verantwortung*): **~ (auf +***akk***)** to shift (onto)

abwandeln ['apvandəln] *vt* to adapt

abwandern ['apvandərn] *vi* to move away; (*FIN*) to be transferred

abwarten ['apvartən] *vt* to wait for ♦ *vi* to wait

abwärts ['apvɛrts] *adv* down

Abwasch ['apvaʃ] (**-(e)s**) *m* washing-up; **a~en** (*unreg*) *vt* (*Schmutz*) to wash off; (*Geschirr*) to wash (up)

Abwasser ['apvasər] (**-s, -wässer**) *nt* sewage

abwechseln ['apvɛksəln] *vi, vr* to alternate; (*Personen*) to take turns; **~d** *adj* alternate; **Abwechslung** *f* change; **abwechslungsreich** *adj* varied

abwegig ['apveːgɪç] *adj* wrong

Abwehr ['apveːr] (-) f defence; (Schutz) protection; (~dienst) counterintelligence (service); **a~en** vt to ward off; (Ball) to stop

abweichen ['apvaiçən] (unreg) vi to deviate; (Meinung) to differ

abweisen ['apvaizən] (unreg) vt to turn away; (Antrag) to turn down; **~d** adj (Haltung) cold

abwenden ['apvɛndən] (unreg) vt to avert ♦ vr to turn away

abwerfen ['apvɛrfən] (unreg) vt to throw off; (Profit) to yield; (aus Flugzeug) to drop; (Spielkarte) to discard

abwerten ['apvɛrtən] vt (FIN) to devalue

abwertend adj (Worte, Sinn) pejorative

Abwertung f (von Währung) devaluation

abwesend ['apveːzənt] adj absent

Abwesenheit ['apveːzənhait] f absence

abwickeln ['apvɪkəln] vt to unwind; (Geschäft) to wind up

abwimmeln ['apvɪməln] (umg) vt (Menschen) to get shot of

abwischen ['apvɪʃən] vt to wipe off od away; (putzen) to wipe

Abwurf ['apvʊrf] m throwing off; (von Bomben etc) dropping; (von Reiter, SPORT) throw

abwürgen ['apvʏrgən] (umg) vt to scotch; (Motor) to stall

abzahlen ['aptsaːlən] vt to pay off

abzählen ['aptseːlən] vt, vi to count (up)

Abzahlung f repayment; **auf ~ kaufen** to buy on hire purchase

abzapfen ['aptsapfən] vt to draw off; **jdm Blut ~** to take blood from sb

abzäunen ['aptsɔʏnən] vt to fence off

Abzeichen ['aptsaiçən] nt badge; (Orden) decoration

abzeichnen ['aptsaiçnən] vt to draw, to copy; (Dokument) to initial ♦ vr to stand out; (fig: bevorstehen) to loom

abziehen ['aptsiːən] (unreg) vt to take off; (Tier) to skin; (Bett) to strip; (Truppen) to withdraw; (subtrahieren) to take away, to subtract; (kopieren) to run off ♦ vi to go away; (Truppen) to withdraw

abzielen ['aptsiːlən] vi: **~ auf** +akk to be aimed at

Abzug ['aptsuːk] m departure; (von Truppen) withdrawal; (Kopie) copy; (Subtraktion) subtraction; (Betrag) deduction; (Rauchabzug) flue; (von Waffen) trigger

abzüglich ['aptsyːkliç] präp +gen less

abzweigen ['aptsvaigən] vi to branch off ♦ vt to set aside

Abzweigung f junction

ach [ax] excl oh; **~ ja!** (oh) yes; **~ so!** I see; **mit A~ und Krach** by the skin of one's teeth

Achse ['aksə] f axis; (AUT) axle

Achsel ['aksəl] (-, -n) f shoulder; **~höhle** f armpit

acht [axt] num eight; **~ Tage** a week; **A~1** (-, -en) f eight; (beim Eislaufen etc) figure eight

Acht2 (-, -en) f: **~ geben (auf** +akk) to pay attention (to); **sich in ~ nehmen (vor** +dat) to be careful (of), to watch out (for); **etw außer ~ lassen** to disregard sth; **a~bar** adj worthy

acht- zW: **~e(r, s)** adj eighth; **A~el** num eighth; **~en** vt to respect ♦ vi: **~en (auf** +akk) to pay attention (to); **~en, daß ...** to be careful that ...

ächten ['ɛçtən] vt to outlaw, to ban

Achterbahn ['axtər-] f roller coaster

acht- zW: **~fach** adj eightfold; **~geben** △ (unreg) vi siehe **Acht2**; **~hundert** num eight hundred; **~los** adj careless; **~mal** adv eight times; **~sam** adj attentive

Achtung ['axtʊŋ] f attention; (Ehrfurcht) respect ♦ excl look out!; (MIL) attention!; **alle ~!** good for you/him etc

achtzehn num eighteen

achtzig num eighty

ächzen ['ɛçtsən] vi to groan

Acker ['akər] (-s, ") m field; **a~n** vt, vi to plough; (umg) to slog away

ADAC [aːdeːʔaˈtseː] abk (= Allgemeiner Deutscher Automobil-Club) ≈ AA, RAC

Adapter [aˈdaptər] (-s, -) m adapter

addieren [aˈdiːrən] vt to add (up); **Addition** [aditsiˈoːn] f addition

Adel ['aːdəl] (-s) m nobility; **a~ig** adj noble;

a~n *vt* to raise to the peerage
Ader ['a:dər] (-, -n) *f* vein
Adjektiv ['atjɛktiːf] (-s, -e) *nt* adjective
Adler ['a:dlər] (-s, -) *m* eagle
adlig *adj* noble
Adopt- *zW:* **a~ieren** [adɔp'tiːrən] *vt* to adopt; **~ion** [adɔptsi'oːn] *f* adoption; **~iveltern** *pl* adoptive parents; **~ivkind** *nt* adopted child
Adressbuch ▲ *nt* directory; (*privat*) address book
Adress- *zW:* **~e** [a'drɛsə] *f* address; **a~ieren** [adrɛ'siːrən] *vt:* **a~ieren (an** +*akk*) to address (to)
Adria ['a:dria] (-) *f* Adriatic
Advent [at'vɛnt] (-(e)s, -e) *m* Advent; **~skalender** *m* Advent calendar; **~skranz** *m* Advent wreath
Adverb [at'vɛrp] *nt* adverb
Aerobic [ae'roːbik] *nt* aerobics *sg*
Affäre [a'fɛːrə] *f* affair
Affe ['afə] (-n, -n) *m* monkey
Affekt [a'fɛkt] (-(e)s, -e) *m:* **im ~ handeln** to act in the heat of the moment; **a~iert** [afɛk'tiːrt] *adj* affected
Affen- *zW:* **a~artig** *adj* like a monkey; **mit a~artiger Geschwindigkeit** like a flash; **~hitze** (*umg*) *f* incredible heat
affig ['afɪç] *adj* affected
Afrika ['a:frika] (-s) *nt* Africa; **~ner(in)** [-'ka:nər(ɪn)] (-s, -) *m(f)* African; **a~nisch** *adj* African
AG [a:'ge:] *abk* (= *Aktiengesellschaft*) ≈ plc (*BRIT*), ≈ Inc. (*US*)
Agent [a'gɛnt] *m* agent; **~ur** *f* agency
Aggregat [agre'ga:t] (-(e)s, -e) *nt* aggregate; (*TECH*) unit
Aggress- *zW:* **~ion** [agrɛsi'oːn] *f* aggression; **a~iv** [agrɛ'siːf] *adj* aggressive; **~ivität** [agrɛsivi'tɛːt] *f* aggressiveness
Agrarpolitik [a'graːr-] *f* agricultural policy
Ägypten [ɛ'gʏptən] (-s) *nt* Egypt; **ägyptisch** *adj* Egyptian
aha [a'ha:] *excl* aha
ähneln ['ɛːnəln] *vi* +*dat* to be like, to resemble ♦ *vr* to be alike *od* similar
ahnen ['a:nən] *vt* to suspect; (*Tod, Gefahr*) to

have a presentiment of
ähnlich ['ɛːnlɪç] *adj* (+*dat*) similar (to); **Ä~keit** *f* similarity
Ahnung ['a:nʊŋ] *f* idea, suspicion; presentiment; **a~slos** *adj* unsuspecting
Ahorn ['a:hɔrn] (-s, -e) *m* maple
Ähre ['ɛːrə] *f* ear
Aids [eːdz] *nt* AIDS *sg*
Airbag ['ɛːəbæk] (-s, -s) *m* airbag
Akademie [akade'mi:] *f* academy; **Aka'demiker(in)** (-s, -) *m(f)* university graduate; **akademisch** *adj* academic
akklimatisieren [aklimati'zi:rən] *vr* to become acclimatized
Akkord [a'kɔrt] (-(e)s, -e) *m* (*MUS*) chord; **im ~ arbeiten** to do piecework
Akkordeon [a'kɔrdeɔn] (-s, -s) *nt* accordion
Akku ['aku] (-s, -s) *m* rechargeable battery
Akkusativ ['akuzati:f] (-s, -e) *m* accusative
Akne ['aknə] *f* acne
Akrobat(in) [akro'ba:t(ɪn)] (-en, -en) *m(f)* acrobat
Akt [akt] (-(e)s, -e) *m* act; (*KUNST*) nude
Akte ['aktə] *f* file
Akten- *zW:* **~koffer** *m* attaché case; **a~kundig** *adj* on the files; **~schrank** *m* filing cabinet; **~tasche** *f* briefcase
Aktie ['aktsiə] *f* share
Aktien- *zW:* **~gesellschaft** *f* public limited company; **~index** (-(es), -e *od* -**indices**) *m* share index; **~kurs** *m* share price
Aktion [aktsi'oːn] *f* campaign; (*Polizeiaktion, Suchaktion*) action
Aktionär [aktsio'nɛːr] (-s, -e) *m* shareholder
aktiv [ak'tiːf] *adj* active; (*MIL*) regular; **~ieren** [-'viːrən] *vt* to activate; **A~i'tät** *f* activity
Aktualität [aktuali'tɛːt] *f* topicality; (*einer Mode*) up-to-dateness
aktuell [aktu'ɛl] *adj* topical; up-to-date
Akupunktur [akupʊŋk'tuːər] *f* acupuncture
Akustik [a'kʊstɪk] *f* acoustics *pl*
akut [a'kuːt] *adj* acute
Akzent [ak'tsɛnt] *m* accent; (*Betonung*) stress
akzeptabel [aktsɛp'ta:bl̩] *adj* acceptable
akzeptieren [aktsɛp'tiːrən] *vt* to accept
Alarm [a'larm] (-(e)s, -e) *m* alarm; **a~bereit** *adj* standing by; **~bereitschaft** *f* stand-by;

a~ieren [-'mi:rən] *vt* to alarm
Albanien [al'ba:niən] **(-s)** *nt* Albania
albanisch *adj* Albanian
albern ['albərn] *adj* silly
Albtraum ▲ ['alptraum] *m* nightmare
Album ['album] **(-s, Alben)** *nt* album
Alge ['algə] *f* algae
Algebra ['algebra] **(-)** *f* algebra
Algerier(in) [al'ge:ri:r] **(-s, -)** *m(f)* Algerian
algerisch *adj* Algerian
alias ['a:lias] *adv* alias
Alibi ['a:libi] **(-s, -s)** *nt* alibi
Alimente [ali'mentə] *pl* alimony *sg*
Alkohol ['alkohol] **(-s, -e)** *m* alcohol; **a~frei** *adj* non-alcoholic; **~iker(in)** [alko'ho:likər(m)] **(-s, -)** *m(f)* alcoholic; **a~isch** *adj* alcoholic; **~verbot** *nt* ban on alcohol
All [al] **(-s)** *nt* universe
all'abendlich *adj* every evening
allbekannt *adj* universally known

alle(r, s) ['alə(r,s)] *adj* 1 *(sämtliche)* all; **wir alle** all of us; **alle Kinder waren da** all the children were there; **alle Kinder mögen ...** all children like ...; **alle beide** both of us/them; **sie kamen alle** they all came; **alles Gute** all the best; **alles in allem** all in all 2 *(mit Zeit- oder Maßangaben)* every; **alle vier Jahre** every four years; **alle fünf Meter** every five metres
♦ *pron* everything; **alles was er sagt** everything he says, all that he says
♦ *adv (zu Ende, aufgebraucht)* finished; **die Milch ist alle** the milk's all gone, there's no milk left; **etw alle machen** to finish sth up

Allee [a'le:] *f* avenue
allein [a'lain] *adv* alone; *(ohne Hilfe)* on one's own, by oneself ♦ *konj* but, only; **nicht ~** *(nicht nur)* not only; **~ stehend** single; **A~erziehende(r)** *f(m)* single parent; **A~gang** *m*: **im A~gang** on one's own
allemal ['alə'ma:l] *adv (jedes Mal)* always; *(ohne weiteres)* with no bother; *siehe* **Mal**

allenfalls ['alən'fals] *adv* at all events; *(höchstens)* at most
aller- ['alər] *zW*: **~beste(r, s)** *adj* very best; **~dings** *adv (zwar)* admittedly; *(gewiss)* certainly
Allergie [aler'gi:] *f* allergy; **al'lergisch** *adj* allergic
aller- *zW*: **~hand** *(umg)* *adj inv* all sorts of; **das ist doch ~hand!** that's a bit much; **~hand!** *(lobend)* good show!; **A~'heiligen** *nt* All Saints' Day; **~höchstens** *adv* at the very most; **~lei** *adj inv* all sorts of; **~letzte(r, s)** *adj* very last; **A~seelen** **(-s)** *nt* All Souls' Day; **~seits** *adv* on all sides; **prost ~seits!** cheers everyone!

i **Allerheiligen** *(All Saints' Day)* is celebrated on November 1st and is a public holiday in some parts of Germany and in Austria. **Allerseelen** *(All Souls' Day)* is celebrated on November 2nd in the Roman Catholic Church. It is customary to visit cemeteries and place lighted candles on the graves of relatives and friends.

Allerwelts- *in zW (Durchschnitts-)* common; *(nichts sagend)* commonplace
alles *pron* everything; **~ in allem** all in all; **~ Gute!** all the best!
Alleskleber **(-s, -)** *m* multi-purpose glue
allgemein ['algəmain] *adj* general; **im A~en** in general; **~ gültig** generally accepted; **A~wissen** *nt* general knowledge
Alliierte(r) [ali'i:rtə(r)] *m* ally
all- *zW*: **~jährlich** *adj* annual; **~mächtig** *adj* almighty; **~mählich** *adj* gradual; **A~tag** *m* everyday life; **~täglich** *adj, adv* daily; *(gewöhnlich)* commonplace; **~tags** *adv* on weekdays; **~'wissend** *adj* omniscient; **~zu** *adv* all too; **~ oft** all too often; **~ viel** too much
Allzweck- ['altsvek-] *in zW* multi-purpose
Alm [alm] **(-, -en)** *f* alpine pasture
Almosen ['almo:zən] **(-s, -)** *nt* alms *pl*
Alpen ['alpən] *pl* Alps; **~vorland** *nt* foothills *pl* of the Alps

Alphabet [alfa'be:t] **(-(e)s, -e)** *nt* alphabet;
a~isch *adj* alphabetical

Alptraum ['alptraum] = **Albtraum**

SCHLÜSSELWORT

als [als] *konj* **1** (*zeitlich*) when; (*gleichzeitig*)
as; **damals, als ...** (in the days) when ...;
gerade, als ... just as ...
2 (*in der Eigenschaft*) than; **als Antwort** as
an answer; **als Kind** as a child
3 (*bei Vergleichen*) than; **ich kam später als
er** I came later than he (did) *od* later than
him; **lieber ... als ...** rather ... than ...;
nichts als Ärger nothing but trouble
4: als ob/wenn as if

also ['alzo:] *konj* so; (*folglich*) therefore; **~ gut**
od **schön!** okay then; **~, so was!** well
really!; **na ~!** there you are then!

Alsterwasser ['alstər-] *nt* shandy (*BRIT*),
beer and lemonade

Alt [alt] **(-s, -e)** *m* (*MUS*) alto

alt *adj* old; **alles beim A~en lassen** to leave
everything as it was

Altar [al'ta:r] **(-(e)s, -äre)** *m* altar

Alt- *zW*: **~bau** *m* old building; **a~bekannt**
adj long-known; **~bier** *nt* top-fermented
German dark beer; **~eisen** *nt* scrap iron

Alten(wohn)heim *nt* old people's home

Alter ['altər] **(-s, -)** *nt* age; (*hohes*) old age;
im ~ von at the age of; **a~n** *vi* to grow
old, to age

Alternativ- [alternati:f] *in zW* alternative;
~e *f* alternative

Alters- *zW*: **~grenze** *f* age limit; **~heim** *nt*
old people's home; **~rente** *f* old age
pension; **a~schwach** *adj* (*Mensch*) frail;
~versorgung *f* old age pension

Altertum ['altərtu:m] *nt* antiquity

alt- *zW*: **A~glas** *nt* glass for recycling;
A~glascontainer *m* bottle bank; **~klug**
adj precocious; **~modisch** *adj* old-
fashioned; **A~papier** *nt* waste paper;
A~stadt *f* old town

Alufolie ['a:lufo:liə] *f* aluminium foil

Aluminium [alu'mi:niʊm] **(-s)** *nt* aluminium,
aluminum (*US*)

Alzheimerkrankheit ['altshaimər'kraŋkhait]
f Alzheimer's (disease)

am [am] = **an dem**; **~ Schlafen**; (*umg*)
sleeping; **~ 15. März** on March 15th; **~
besten/schönsten** best/most beautiful

Amateur [ama'tø:r] *m* amateur

Amboss ▲ ['ambɔs] **(-es, -e)** *m* anvil

ambulant [ambu'lant] *adj* outpatient;
Ambulanz *f* outpatients *sg*

Ameise ['a:maizə] *f* ant

Ameisenhaufen *m* ant hill

Amerika [a'me:rika] **(-s)** *nt* America;
~ner(in) [-'ka:nər] **(-s, -)** *m(f)* American;
a~nisch [-'ka:nɪʃ] *adj* American

Amnestie [amnes'ti:] *f* amnesty

Ampel ['ampəl] **(-, -n)** *f* traffic lights *pl*

amputieren [ampu'ti:rən] *vt* to amputate

Amsel ['amzəl] **(-, -n)** *f* blackbird

Amt [amt] **(-(e)s, -er)** *nt* office; (*Pflicht*) duty;
(*TEL*) exchange; **a~ieren** [am'ti:rən] *vi* to
hold office; **a~lich** *adj* official

Amts- *zW*: **~richter** *m* district judge;
~stunden *pl* office hours; **~zeichen** *nt*
dialling tone; **~zeit** *f* period of office

amüsant [amy'zant] *adj* amusing

amüsieren [amy'zi:rən] *vt* to amuse ♦ *vr* to
enjoy o.s.

Amüsierviertel *nt* nightclub district

SCHLÜSSELWORT

an [an] *präp +dat* **1** (*räumlich: wo?*) at; (*auf,
bei*) on; (*nahe bei*) near; **an diesem Ort** at
this place; **an der Wand** on the wall; **zu
nahe an etw** too near to sth; **unten am
Fluss** down by the river; **Köln liegt am
Rhein** Cologne is on the Rhine
2 (*zeitlich: wann?*) on; **an diesem Tag** on
this day; **an Ostern** at Easter
3: arm an Fett low in fat; **an etw sterben**
to die of sth; **an (und für) sich** actually
♦ *präp +akk* **1** (*räumlich: wohin?*) to; **er ging
ans Fenster** he went (over) to the
window; **etw an die Wand hängen/
schreiben** to hang/write sth on the wall
2 (*zeitlich: woran?*): **an etw denken** to think
of sth
3 (*gerichtet an*) to; **ein Gruß/eine Frage**

Spelling Reform: ▲ *new spelling* △ *old spelling (to be phased out)*

an dich greetings/a question to you ♦ *adv* **1** (*ungefähr*) about; **an die hundert** about a hundred
2 (*auf Fahrplänen*): **Frankfurt an 18.30** arriving Frankfurt 18.30
3 (*ab*): **von dort/heute an** from there/today onwards
4 (*angeschaltet, angezogen*) on; **das Licht ist an** the light is on; **ohne etwas an** with nothing on; *siehe auch* **am**

analog [ana'lo:k] *adj* analogous; **A~ie** [-'gi:] *f* analogy
Analphabet(in) [an|alfa'be:t(ın)] **(-en, -en)** *m(f)* illiterate (person)
Analyse [ana'ly:zə] *f* analysis
analysieren [analy'zi:rən] *vt* to analyse
Ananas ['ananas] **(-, -** *od* **-se)** *f* pineapple
Anarchie [anar'çi:] *f* anarchy
Anatomie [anato'mi:] *f* anatomy
anbahnen ['anba:nən] *vt, vr* to open up
Anbau ['anbau] *m* (*AGR*) cultivation; (*Gebäude*) extension; **a~en** *vt* (*AGR*) to cultivate; (*Gebäudeteil*) to build on
anbehalten ['anbəhaltən] (*unreg*) *vt* to keep on
anbei [an'bai] *adv* enclosed
anbeißen ['anbaisən] (*unreg*) *vt* to bite into ♦ *vi* to bite; (*fig*) to swallow the bait; **zum A~** (*umg*) good enough to eat
anbelangen ['anbəlaŋən] *vt* to concern; **was mich anbelangt** as far as I am concerned
anbeten ['anbe:tən] *vt* to worship
Anbetracht ['anbətraxt] *m*: **in ~** +*gen* in view of
anbieten ['anbi:tən] (*unreg*) *vt* to offer ♦ *vr* to volunteer
anbinden ['anbındən] (*unreg*) *vt* to tie up; **kurz angebunden** (*fig*) curt
Anblick ['anblık] *m* sight; **a~en** *vt* to look at
anbraten ['anbra:tən] *vt* to brown
anbrechen ['anbrɛçən] (*unreg*) *vt* to start; (*Vorräte*) to break into ♦ *vi* to start; (*Tag*) to break; (*Nacht*) to fall
anbrennen ['anbrɛnən] (*unreg*) *vi* to catch fire; (*KOCH*) to burn

anbringen ['anbrɪŋən] (*unreg*) *vt* to bring; (*Ware*) to sell; (*festmachen*) to fasten
Anbruch ['anbrox] *m* beginning; **~ des Tages/der Nacht** dawn/nightfall
anbrüllen ['anbrylən] *vt* to roar at
Andacht ['andaxt] **(-, -en)** *f* devotion; (*Gottesdienst*) prayers *pl*; **andächtig** *adj* ['andɛçtıç] devout
andauern ['andauərn] *vi* to last, to go on; **~d** *adj* continual
Anden ['andən] *pl* Andes
Andenken ['andɛŋkən] **(-s, -)** *nt* memory; souvenir
andere(r, s) ['andərə(r, z)] *adj* other; (*verschieden*) different; **ein ~s Mal** another time; **kein ~r** nobody else; **von etw ~m sprechen** to talk about something else; **~rseits** *adv* on the other hand
andermal *adv*: **ein ~** some other time
ändern ['ɛndərn] *vt* to alter, to change ♦ *vr* to change
andernfalls ['andərnfals] *adv* otherwise
anders ['andərs] *adv*: **~ (als)** differently (from); **wer ~?** who else?; **jd/irgendwo ~** sb/somewhere else; **~ aussehen/klingen** to look/sound different; **~artig** *adj* different; **~herum** *adv* the other way round; **~wo** *adv* somewhere else; **~woher** *adv* from somewhere else
anderthalb ['andərt'halp] *adj* one and a half
Änderung ['ɛndəruŋ] *f* alteration, change
Änderungsschneiderei *f* tailor (*who does alterations*)
anderweitig ['andər'vaıtıç] *adj* other ♦ *adv* otherwise; (*anderswo*) elsewhere
andeuten ['andɔytən] *vt* to indicate; (*Wink geben*) to hint at; **Andeutung** *f* indication; hint
Andrang ['andraŋ] *m* crush
andrehen ['andre:ən] *vt* to turn *od* switch on; **jdm etw ~** (*umg*) to unload sth onto sb
androhen ['andro:ən] *vt*: **jdm etw ~** to threaten sb with sth
aneignen ['an|aignən] *vt*: **sich** *dat* **etw ~** to acquire sth; (*widerrechtlich*) to appropriate sth

---

Rechtschreibreform: ▲ *neue Schreibung* △ *alte Schreibung (auslaufend)*

aneinander [an|aɪ'nandər] *adv* at/on/to *etc* one another *od* each other; **~ geraten** to clash

Anekdote [anɛk'do:tə] *f* anecdote

anekeln ['an|e:kəln] *vt* to disgust

anerkannt ['an|ɛrkant] *adj* recognized, acknowledged

anerkennen ['an|ɛrkɛnən] (*unreg*) *vt* to recognize, to acknowledge; (*würdigen*) to appreciate; **~d** *adj* appreciative

Anerkennung *f* recognition, acknowledgement; appreciation

anfachen ['anfaxən] *vt* to fan into flame; (*fig*) to kindle

anfahren ['anfa:rən] (*unreg*) *vt* to deliver; (*fahren gegen*) to hit; (*Hafen*) to put into; (*fig*) to bawl out ♦ *vi* to drive up; (*losfahren*) to drive off

Anfahrt ['anfa:rt] *f* (*~sweg, ~szeit*) journey

Anfall ['anfal] *m* (*MED*) attack; **a~en** (*unreg*) *vt* to attack; (*fig*) to overcome ♦ *vi* (*Arbeit*) to come up; (*Produkt*) to be obtained

anfällig ['anfɛlɪç] *adj* delicate; **~ für etw** prone to sth

Anfang ['anfaŋ] (*-(e)s, -fänge*) *m* beginning, start; **von ~ an** right from the beginning; **zu ~** at the beginning; **~ Mai** at the beginning of May; **a~en** (*unreg*) *vt, vi* to begin, to start; (*machen*) to do

Anfänger(in) ['anfɛŋər(ɪn)] (*-s, -*) *m(f)* beginner

anfänglich ['anfɛŋlɪç] *adj* initial

anfangs *adv* at first; **A~buchstabe** *m* initial *od* first letter; **A~gehalt** *nt* starting salary

anfassen ['anfasən] *vt* to handle; (*berühren*) to touch ♦ *vi* to lend a hand ♦ *vr* to feel

anfechten ['anfɛçtən] (*unreg*) *vt* to dispute

anfertigen ['anfɛrtɪgən] *vt* to make

anfeuern ['anfɔyərn] *vt* (*fig*) to spur on

anflehen ['anfle:ən] *vt* to implore

anfliegen ['anfli:gən] (*unreg*) *vt* to fly to

Anflug ['anflu:k] *m* (*AVIAT*) approach; (*Spur*) trace

anfordern ['anfɔrdərn] *vt* to demand; (*COMM*) to requisition

Anforderung *f* (*+gen*) demand (for)

Anfrage ['anfra:gə] *f* inquiry; **a~n** *vi* to inquire

anfreunden ['anfrɔyndən] *vr* to make friends

anfügen ['anfy:gən] *vt* to add; (*beifügen*) to enclose

anfühlen ['anfy:lən] *vt, vr* to feel

anführen ['anfy:rən] *vt* to lead; (*zitieren*) to quote; (*umg: betrügen*) to lead up the garden path

Anführer *m* leader

Anführungszeichen *pl* quotation marks, inverted commas

Angabe ['anga:bə] *f* statement; (*TECH*) specification; (*umg: Prahlerei*) boasting; (*SPORT*) service

angeben ['ange:bən] (*unreg*) *vt* to give; (*anzeigen*) to inform on; (*bestimmen*) to set ♦ *vi* (*umg*) to boast; (*SPORT*) to serve

Angeber (*-s, -*) (*umg*) *m* show-off; **Angebe'rei** (*umg*) *f* showing off

angeblich ['ange:plɪç] *adj* alleged

angeboren ['angəbo:rən] *adj* inborn, innate

Angebot ['angəbo:t] *nt* offer; **~ (an** +*dat*) (*COMM*) supply (of)

angebracht ['angəbraxt] *adj* appropriate, in order

angegriffen ['angəgrɪfən] *adj* exhausted

angeheitert ['angəhaɪtərt] *adj* tipsy

angehen ['ange:ən] (*unreg*) *vt* to concern; (*angreifen*) to attack; (*bitten*) **jdn ~ (um)** to approach sb (for) ♦ *vi* (*Feuer*) to light; (*umg: beginnen*) to begin; **~d** *adj* prospective

angehören ['angəhø:rən] *vi* (+ *dat*) to belong to; (*Partei*) to be a member of

Angehörige(r) ['angəhø:rɪgə(r)] *f(m)* relative

Angeklagte(r) ['angəkla:ktə(r)] *f(m)* accused

Angel ['aŋəl] (*-, -n*) *f* fishing rod; (*Türangel*) hinge

Angelegenheit ['angəle:gənhaɪt] *f* affair, matter

Angel- *zW*: **~haken** *m* fish hook; **a~n** *vt* to catch ♦ *vi* to fish; **~n** (*-s*) *nt* angling, fishing; **~rute** *f* fishing rod; **~schein** *m* fishing permit

angemessen ['angəmɛsən] *adj* appropriate, suitable

Spelling Reform: ▲ *new spelling* △ *old spelling (to be phased out)*

angenehm [ˈangəneːm] *adj* pleasant; **~!** (*bei Vorstellung*) pleased to meet you

angeregt [angəreːkt] *adj* animated, lively

angesehen [ˈangəzeːən] *adj* respected

angesichts [ˈangəzɪçts] *präp +gen* in view of, considering

angespannt [ˈangəʃpant] *adj* (*Aufmerksamkeit*) close; (*Arbeit*) hard

Angestellte(r) [ˈangəʃtɛltə(r)] *f(m)* employee

angestrengt [ˈangəʃtrɛŋt] *adv* as hard as one can

angetan [ˈangətaːn] *adj*: **von jdm/etw ~ sein** to be impressed by sb/sth; **es jdm ~ haben** to appeal to sb

angetrunken [ˈangətrʊŋkən] *adj* tipsy

angewiesen [ˈangəviːzən] *adj*: **auf jdn/etw ~ sein** to be dependent on sb/sth

angewöhnen [ˈangəvøːnən] *vt*: **jdm/sich etw ~** to get sb/become accustomed to sth

Angewohnheit [ˈangəvoːnhait] *f* habit

angleichen [ˈanglaiçən] (*unreg*) *vt, vr* to adjust

Angler [ˈaŋlər] **(-s, -)** *m* angler

angreifen [ˈangraifən] (*unreg*) *vt* to attack; (*beschädigen*) to damage

Angreifer (-s, -) *m* attacker

Angriff [ˈangrɪf] *m* attack; **etw in ~ nehmen** to make a start on sth

Angst (-, ̈e) *f* fear; **jdm ist a~** sb is afraid *od* scared; **~ haben (vor +dat)** to be afraid *od* scared (of); **~ haben um jdn/etw** to be worried about sb/sth; **jdm ~ machen** to scare sb; **~hase** (*umg*) *m* chicken, scaredy-cat

ängst- [ˈɛŋst] *zW*: **~igen** *vt* to frighten ♦ *vr*: **sich ~igen (vor +dat od um)** to worry (o.s.) (about); **~lich** *adj* nervous; (*besorgt*) worried; **Ä~lichkeit** *f* nervousness

anhaben [ˈanhaːbən] (*unreg*) *vt* to have on; **er kann mir nichts ~** he can't hurt me

anhalt- [ˈanhalt] *zW*: **~en** (*unreg*) *vt* to stop ♦ *vi* to stop; (*andauern*) to persist; **(jdm) etw ~en** to hold sth up (against sb); **jdn zur Arbeit/Höflichkeit ~en** to make sb work/be polite; **~end** *adj* persistent;

A~er(in) (-s, -) *m(f)* hitch-hiker; **per A~er fahren** to hitch-hike; **A~spunkt** *m* clue

anhand [anˈhant] *präp +gen* with

Anhang [ˈanhaŋ] *m* appendix; (*Leute*) family; supporters *pl*

anhäng- [ˈanhɛŋ] *zW*: **~en** (*unreg*) *vt* to hang up; (*Wagen*) to couple up; (*Zusatz*) to add (on); **A~er (-s, -)** *m* supporter; (*AUT*) trailer; (*am Koffer*) tag; (*Schmuck*) pendant; **A~erschaft** *f* supporters *pl*; **~lich** *adj* devoted; **A~lichkeit** *f* devotion; **A~sel (-s, -)** *nt* appendage

Anhäufung [ˈanhɔyfʊŋ] *f* accumulation

anheben [ˈanheːbən] (*unreg*) *vt* to lift up; (*Preise*) to raise

anheizen [ˈanhaitsən] *vt* (*Stimmung*) to lift; (*Moral*) to boost

Anhieb [ˈanhiːb] *m*: **auf ~** at the very first go; (*kurz entschlossen*) on the spur of the moment

Anhöhe [ˈanhøːə] *f* hill

anhören [ˈanhøːrən] *vt* to listen to; (*anmerken*) to hear ♦ *vr* to sound

animieren [aniˈmiːrən] *vt* to encourage, to urge on

Anis [aˈniːs] **(-es, -e)** *m* aniseed

Ank. *abk* (= *Ankunft*) arr.

Ankauf [ˈankauf] *m* (*von Wertpapieren, Devisen, Waren*) purchase; **a~en** *vt* to purchase, to buy

Anker [ˈaŋkər] **(-s, -)** *m* anchor; **vor ~ gehen** to drop anchor

Anklage [ˈanklaːgə] *f* accusation; (*JUR*) charge; **~bank** *f* dock; **a~n** *vt* to accuse; **jdn (eines Verbrechens) a~n** (*JUR*) to charge sb (with a crime)

Ankläger [ˈanklɛːgər] *m* accuser

Anklang [ˈanklaŋ] *m*: **bei jdm ~ finden** to meet with sb's approval

Ankleidekabine *f* changing cubicle

ankleiden [ˈanklaidən] *vt, vr* to dress

anklopfen [ˈanklɔpfən] *vi* to knock

anknüpfen [ˈanknʏpfən] *vt* to fasten *od* tie on; (*fig*) to start ♦ *vi* (*anschließen*): **~ an** *+akk* to refer to

ankommen [ˈankɔmən] (*unreg*) *vi* to arrive; (*näher kommen*) to approach; (*Anklang* *finden*): **bei jdm (gut) ~** to go down well with sb; **es kommt darauf an** it depends; (*wichtig sein*) that (is what) matters; **es darauf ~ lassen** to let things take their course; **gegen jdn/etw ~** to cope with sb/sth; **bei jdm schlecht ~** to go down badly with sb

ankreuzen ['ankrɔʏtsən] *vt* to mark with a cross; (*hervorheben*) to highlight

ankündigen ['ankʏndɪgən] *vt* to announce; **Ankündigung** *f* announcement

Ankunft ['ankʊnft] (**-, -künfte**) *f* arrival; **~szeit** *f* time of arrival

ankurbeln ['ankʊrbəln] *vt* (*fig*) to boost

Anlage ['anla:gə] *f* disposition; (*Begabung*) talent; (*Park*) gardens *pl*; (*Beilage*) enclosure; (*TECH*) plant; (*FIN*) investment; (*Entwurf*) layout

Anlass ▲ ['anlas] (**-es, -lässe**) *m*: **~ (zu)** cause (for); (*Ereignis*) occasion; **aus ~** +*gen* on the occasion of; **~ zu etw geben** to give rise to sth; **etw zum ~ nehmen** to take the opportunity of sth

anlassen (*unreg*) *vt* to leave on; (*Motor*) to start ♦ *vr* (*umg*) to start off

Anlasser (**-s, -**) *m* (*AUT*) starter

anlässlich ▲ ['anlɛslɪç] *präp* +*gen* on the occasion of

Anlauf ['anlaʊf] *m* run-up; **a~en** (*unreg*) *vi* to begin; (*neuer Film*) to show; (*SPORT*) to run up; (*Fenster*) to mist up; (*Metall*) to tarnish ♦ *vt* to call at; **rot a~en** to blush; **angelaufen kommen** to come running up

anlegen ['anle:gən] *vt* to put; (*anziehen*) to put on; (*gestalten*) to lay out; (*Geld*) to invest ♦ *vi* to dock; **etw an etw** *akk* **~** to put sth against *od* on sth; **ein Gewehr ~ (auf** +*akk*) to aim a weapon (at); **es auf etw** *akk* **~** to be out for sth/to do sth; **sich mit jdm ~** (*umg*) to quarrel with sb

Anlegestelle *f* landing place

anlehnen ['anle:nən] *vt* to lean; (*Tür*) to leave ajar; **(sich) an etw** *akk* **~** to lean on/against sth

Anleihe ['anlaɪə] *f* (*FIN*) loan

anleiten ['anlaɪtən] *vt* to instruct; **Anleitung** *f* instructions *pl*

anliegen ['anli:gən] (*unreg*) *vi* (*Kleidung*) to cling; **A~** (**-s, -**) *nt* matter; (*Wunsch*) wish; **~d** *adj* adjacent; (*beigefügt*) enclosed

Anlieger (**-s, -**) *m* resident; **„~ frei"** "residents only"

anmachen ['anmaxən] *vt* to attach; (*Elektrisches*) to put on; (*Zigarette*) to light; (*Salat*) to dress

anmaßen ['anma:sən] *vt*: **sich** *dat* **etw ~** (*Recht*) to lay claim to sth; **~d** *adj* arrogant

Anmaßung *f* presumption

anmelden ['anmɛldən] *vt* to announce ♦ *vr* (*sich ankündigen*) to make an appointment; (*polizeilich, für Kurs etc*) to register

Anmeldung *f* announcement; appointment; registration

anmerken ['anmɛrkən] *vt* to observe; (*anstreichen*) to mark; **sich** *dat* **nichts ~ lassen** to not give anything away

Anmerkung *f* note

anmieten ['anmi:tən] *vt* to rent; (*auch Auto*) to hire

Anmut ['anmu:t] (**-**) *f* grace; **a~en** *vt* to give a feeling; **a~ig** *adj* charming

annähen ['annɛ:ən] *vt* to sew on

annähern ['annɛ:ərn] *vr* to get closer; **~d** *adj* approximate

Annäherung *f* approach

Annäherungsversuch *m* advances *pl*

Annahme ['anna:mə] *f* acceptance; (*Vermutung*) assumption

annehm- ['anne:m] *zW*: **~bar** *adj* acceptable; **~en** (*unreg*) *vt* to accept; (*Namen*) to take; (*Kind*) to adopt; (*vermuten*) to suppose, to assume ♦ *vr* (+*gen*) to take care (of); **A~lichkeit** *f* comfort

Annonce [a'nõ:sə] *f* advertisement

annoncieren [anõ'si:rən] *vt, vi* to advertise

annullieren [anʊ'li:rən] *vt* to annul

anonym [ano'ny:m] *adj* anonymous

Anorak ['anorak] (**-s, -s**) *m* anorak

anordnen ['anɔrdnən] *vt* to arrange; (*befehlen*) to order

Anordnung *f* arrangement; order

anorganisch ['anɔrga:nɪʃ] *adj* inorganic

anpacken ['anpakən] *vt* to grasp; (*fig*) to tackle; **mit ~** to lend a hand

anpassen ['anpasən] vt: (jdm) ~ to fit (on sb); to adapt ♦ vr to adapt
anpassungsfähig adj adaptable
Anpfiff ['anpfɪf] m (SPORT) (starting) whistle; kick-off; (umg) rocket
anprallen ['anpralən] vi: ~ (gegen od an +akk) to collide (with)
anprangern ['anpranərn] vt to denounce
anpreisen ['anpraɪzən] (unreg) vt to extol
Anprobe ['anproːbə] f trying on
anprobieren ['anprobiːrən] vt to try on
anrechnen ['anrɛçnən] vt to charge; (fig) to count; jdm etw hoch ~ to think highly of sb for sth
Anrecht ['anrɛçt] nt: ~ (auf +akk) right (to)
Anrede ['anreːdə] f form of address; a~n vt to address; (belästigen) to accost
anregen ['anreːgən] vt to stimulate; angeregte Unterhaltung lively discussion; ~d adj stimulating
Anregung f stimulation; (Vorschlag) suggestion
anreichern ['anraɪçərn] vt to enrich
Anreise ['anraɪzə] f journey; a~n vi to arrive
Anreiz ['anraɪts] m incentive
Anrichte ['anrɪçtə] f sideboard; a~n vt to serve up; Unheil a~n to make mischief
anrüchig ['anrʏçɪç] adj dubious
anrücken ['anrʏkən] vi to approach; (MIL) to advance
Anruf ['anruːf] m call; ~beantworter [-bə-'antvɔrtər] (-s, -) m answering machine; a~en (unreg) vt to call out to; (bitten) to call on; (TEL) to ring up, to phone, to call
ans [ans] = an das
Ansage ['anzaːgə] f announcement; a~n vt to announce ♦ vr to say one will come; ~r(in) (-s, -) m(f) announcer
ansammeln ['anzaməln] vt (Reichtümer) to amass ♦ vr (Menschen) to gather, to assemble; (Wasser) to collect; Ansammlung f collection; (Leute) crowd
ansässig ['anzɛsɪç] adj resident
Ansatz ['anzats] m start; (Haaransatz) hairline; (Halsansatz) base; (Verlängerungsstück) extension; (Veranschlagung) estimate; ~punkt m starting point

anschaffen ['anʃafən] vt to buy, to purchase; Anschaffung f purchase
anschalten ['anʃaltən] vt to switch on
anschau- ['anʃaʊ] zW: ~en vt to look at; ~lich adj illustrative; A~ung f (Meinung) view; aus eigener A~ung from one's own experience
Anschein ['anʃaɪn] m appearance; allem ~ nach to all appearances; den ~ haben to seem, to appear; a~end adj apparent
anschieben ['anʃiːbən] vt to push
Anschlag ['anʃlaːk] m notice; (Attentat) attack; (COMM) estimate; (auf Klavier) touch; (Schreibmaschine) character; a~en ['anʃlaːgən] (unreg) vt to put up; (beschädigen) to chip; (Akkord) to strike; (Kosten) to estimate ♦ vi to hit; (wirken) to have an effect; (Glocke) to ring; an etw akk a~en to hit against sth
anschließen ['anʃliːsən] (unreg) vt to connect up; (Sender) to link up ♦ vi: an etw akk ~ to adjoin sth; (zeitlich) to follow sth ♦ vr: sich jdm/etw ~ to join sb/sth; (beipflichten) to agree with sb/sth; sich an etw akk ~ to adjoin sth; ~d adj adjacent; (zeitlich) subsequent ♦ adv afterwards
Anschluss ▲ ['anʃlʊs] m (ELEK, EISENB) connection; (von Wasser etc) supply; im ~ an +akk following; ~ finden to make friends; ~flug m connecting flight
anschmiegsam ['anʃmiːkzaːm] adj affectionate
anschnallen ['anʃnalən] vt to buckle on ♦ vr to fasten one's seat belt
anschneiden ['anʃnaɪdən] (unreg) vt to cut into; (Thema) to introduce
anschreiben ['anʃraɪbən] (unreg) vt to write (up); (COMM) to charge up; (benachrichtigen) to write to
anschreien ['anʃraɪən] (unreg) vt to shout at
Anschrift ['anʃrɪft] f address
Anschuldigung ['anʃʊldɪgʊŋ] f accusation
anschwellen ['anʃvɛlən] (unreg) vi to swell (up)
anschwindeln ['anʃvɪndəln] vt to lie to
ansehen ['anzeːən] (unreg) vt to look at;

jdm etw ~ to see sth (from sb's face); **jdn/etw als etw ~** to look on sb/sth as sth; **~ für** to consider; **A~ (-s)** *nt* respect; *(Ruf)* reputation

ansehnlich ['anze:nlɪç] *adj* fine-looking; *(beträchtlich)* considerable

ansetzen ['anzɛtsən] *vt (festlegen)* to fix; *(entwickeln)* to develop; *(Fett)* to put on; *(Blätter)* to grow; *(zubereiten)* to prepare ♦ *vi (anfangen)* to start, to begin; *(Entwicklung)* to set in; *(dick werden)* to put on weight ♦ *vr (Rost etc)* to start to develop; **~ an** +*akk (anfügen)* to fix on to; *(anlegen, an Mund etc)* to put to

Ansicht ['anzɪçt] *f (Anblick)* sight; *(Meinung)* view, opinion; **zur ~** on approval; **meiner ~ nach** in my opinion; **~skarte** *f* picture postcard; **~ssache** *f* matter of opinion

ansonsten [an'zɔnstən] *adv* otherwise

anspannen ['anʃpanən] *vt* to harness; *(Muskel)* to strain; **Anspannung** *f* strain

anspielen ['anʃpi:lən] *vi (SPORT)* to start play; **auf etw** *akk* **~** to refer *od* allude to sth

Anspielung *f:* **~ (auf** +*akk)* reference (to), allusion (to)

Anspitzer ['anʃpɪtsər] **(-s, -)** *m* pencil sharpener

Ansporn ['anʃpɔrn] **(-(e)s)** *m* incentive

Ansprache ['anʃpra:xə] *f* address

ansprechen ['anʃprɛçən] *(unreg) vt* to speak to; *(bitten, gefallen)* to appeal to ♦ *vi:* **(auf etw** *akk)* **~** to react (to sth); **jdn auf etw** *akk* **(hin) ~** to ask sb about sth; **~d** *adj* attractive

anspringen ['anʃprɪŋən] *(unreg) vi (AUT)* to start ♦ *vt* to jump at

Anspruch ['anʃprʊx] *m (Recht):* **~ (auf** +*akk)* claim (to); **hohe Ansprüche stellen/ haben** to demand/expect a lot; **jdn/etw in ~ nehmen** to occupy sb/take up sth; **a~slos** *adj* undemanding; **a~svoll** *adj* demanding

anstacheln ['anʃtaxəln] *vt* to spur on

Anstalt ['anʃtalt] **(-, -en)** *f* institution; **~en machen, etw zu tun** to prepare to do sth

Anstand ['anʃtant] *m* decency

anständig ['anʃtendɪç] *adj* decent; *(umg)* proper; *(groß)* considerable

anstandslos *adv* without any ado

anstarren ['anʃtarən] *vt* to stare at

anstatt [an'ʃtat] *präp* +*gen* instead of ♦ *konj:* **~ etw zu tun** instead of doing sth

Ansteck- ['anʃtek] *zW:* **a~en** *vt* to pin on; *(MED)* to infect; *(Pfeife)* to light; *(Haus)* to set fire to ♦ *vr:* **ich habe mich bei ihm angesteckt** I caught it from him ♦ *vi (fig)* to be infectious; **a~end** *adj* infectious; **~ung** *f* infection

anstehen ['anʃte:ən] *(unreg) vi* to queue (up) *(BRIT)*, to line up *(US)*

ansteigen ['anʃtaigən] *vi (Straße)* to climb; *(Gelände, Temperatur, Preise)* to rise

anstelle, an Stelle [an'ʃtɛlə] *präp* +*gen* in place of; **~n** [an-] *vt (einschalten)* to turn on; *(Arbeit geben)* to employ; *(machen)* to do ♦ *vr* to queue (up) *(BRIT)*, to line up *(US)*; *(umg)* to act

Anstellung *f* employment; *(Posten)* post, position

Anstieg ['anʃti:k] **(-(e)s, -e)** *m (+gen)* climb; *(fig: von Preisen etc)* increase (in)

anstiften ['anʃtɪftən] *vt (Unglück)* to cause; **jdn zu etw ~** to put sb up to sth

anstimmen ['anʃtɪmən] *vt (Lied)* to strike up with; *(Geschrei)* to set up

Anstoß ['anʃto:s] *m* impetus; *(Ärgernis)* offence; *(SPORT)* kick-off; **der erste ~** the initiative; **~ nehmen an** +*dat* to take offence at; **a~en** *(unreg) vt* to push; *(mit Fuß)* to kick ♦ *vi* to knock, to bump; *(mit der Zunge)* to lisp; *(mit Gläsern):* **a~en (auf** +*akk)* to drink (to), to drink a toast (to)

anstößig ['anʃtø:sɪç] *adj* offensive, indecent

anstreichen ['anʃtraiçən] *(unreg) vt* to paint

anstrengen ['anʃtrɛŋən] *vt* to strain; *(JUR)* to bring ♦ *vr* to make an effort; **~d** *adj* tiring

Anstrengung *f* effort

Anstrich ['anʃtrɪç] *m* coat of paint

Ansturm ['anʃtʊrm] *m* rush; *(MIL)* attack

Antarktis [ant'|arktɪs] **(-)** *f* Antarctic

antasten ['antastən] *vt* to touch; *(Recht)* to infringe upon; *(Ehre)* to question

Anteil ['antail] **(-s, -e)** *m* share; *(Mitgefühl)*

sympathy; ~ **nehmen (an** +*dat)* to share (in); (*sich interessieren*) to take an interest (in); ~**nahme (-)** *f* sympathy

Antenne [an'tɛnə] *f* aerial

Anti- ['anti] *in zW* anti; ~**alko'holiker** *m* teetotaller; **a~autori'tär** *adj* anti-authoritarian; ~**babypille** *f* contraceptive pill; ~**biotikum** [antibi'o:tikʊm] **(-s, -ka)** *nt* antibiotic

antik [an'ti:k] *adj* antique; **A~e** *f* (*Zeitalter*) ancient world

Antiquariat [antikvari'a:t] **(-(e)s, -e)** *nt* secondhand bookshop

Antiquitäten [antikvi'tɛːtən] *pl* antiques; ~**händler** *m* antique dealer

Antrag ['antra:k] **(-(e)s, -träge)** *m* proposal; (*PARL*) motion; (*Gesuch*) application; ~**steller(in) (-s, -)** *m(f)* claimant; (*für Kredit*) applicant

antreffen ['antrɛfən] (*unreg*) *vt* to meet

antreiben ['antraɪbən] (*unreg*) *vt* to drive on; (*Motor*) to drive

antreten ['antre:tən] (*unreg*) *vt* (*Amt*) to take up; (*Erbschaft*) to come into; (*Beweis*) to offer; (*Reise*) to start, to begin ♦ *vi* (*MIL*) to fall in; (*SPORT*) to line up; **gegen jdn ~** to play/fight (against) sb

Antrieb ['antri:p] *m* (*auch fig*) drive; **aus eigenem ~** of one's own accord

antrinken ['antrɪŋkən] (*unreg*) *vt* (*Flasche, Glas*) to start to drink from; **sich** *dat* **Mut/einen Rausch ~** to give o.s. Dutch courage/get drunk; **angetrunken sein** to be tipsy

Antritt ['antrɪt] *m* beginning, commencement; (*eines Amts*) taking up

antun ['antu:n] (*unreg*) *vt*: **jdm etw ~** to do sth to sb; **sich** *dat* **Zwang ~** to force o.s.; **sich** *dat* **etwas ~** to (try to) take one's own life

Antwort ['antvɔrt] **(-, -en)** *f* answer, reply; **a~en** *vi* to answer, to reply

anvertrauen ['anfɛrtraʊən] *vt*: **jdm etw ~** to entrust sb with sth; **sich jdm ~** to confide in sb

anwachsen ['anvaksən] (*unreg*) *vi* to grow; (*Pflanze*) to take root

Anwalt ['anvalt] **(-(e)s, -wälte)** *m* solicitor; lawyer; (*fig*) champion

Anwältin ['anvɛltɪn] *f siehe* **Anwalt**

Anwärter ['anvɛrtər] *m* candidate

anweisen ['anvaɪzən] (*unreg*) *vt* to instruct; (*zuteilen*) to assign

Anweisung *f* instruction; (*COMM*) remittance; (*Postanweisung, Zahlungsanweisung*) money order

anwend- ['anvɛnd] *zW*: ~**bar** [anvɛnt-] *adj* practicable, applicable; ~**en** (*unreg*) *vt* to use, to employ; (*Gesetz, Regel*) to apply; **A~ung** *f* use; application

anwesend ['anve:zənt] *adj* present; **die A~en** those present

Anwesenheit *f* presence

anwidern ['anvi:dərn] *vt* to disgust

Anwohner(in) ['anvo:nər(ɪn)] **(-s, -)** *m(f)* neighbour

Anzahl ['antsa:l] *f*: ~ **(an** +*dat)* number (of); **a~en** *vt* to pay on account; ~**ung** *f* deposit, payment on account

Anzeichen ['antsaɪçən] *nt* sign, indication

Anzeige ['antsaɪgə] *f* (*Zeitungsanzeige*) announcement; (*Werbung*) advertisement; (*bei Polizei*) report; ~ **erstatten gegen jdn** to report sb (to the police); **a~n** *vt* (*zu erkennen geben*) to show; (*bekannt geben*) to announce; (*bei Polizei*) to report

anziehen ['antsi:ən] (*unreg*) *vt* to attract; (*Kleidung*) to put on; (*Mensch*) to dress; (*Seil*) to pull tight; (*Schraube*) to tighten; (*Knie*) to draw up ♦ *vr* to get dressed; ~**d** *adj* attractive

Anziehung *f* (*Reiz*) attraction; ~**skraft** *f* power of attraction; (*PHYS*) force of gravitation

Anzug ['antsu:k] *m* suit; (*Herankommen*): **im ~ sein** to be approaching

anzüglich ['antsy:klɪç] *adj* personal; (*anstößig*) offensive; **A~keit** *f* offensiveness; (*Bemerkung*) personal remark

anzünden ['antsʏndən] *vt* to light

anzweifeln ['antsvaɪfəln] *vt* to doubt

apathisch [a'pa:tɪʃ] *adj* apathetic

Apfel ['apfəl] **(-s, ⸚)** *m* apple; ~**saft** *m* apple juice; ~**sine** [-'zi:nə] *f* orange; ~**wein** *m* cider

Apostel [a'pɔstəl] **(-s, -)** *m* apostle

Apotheke [apo'te:kə] *f* chemist's (shop), drugstore (*US*); **a~npflichtig** [-pflɪçtɪç] *adj* available only at a chemist's shop (*BRIT*) or pharmacy; **~r(in)** **(-s, -)** *m(f)* chemist, druggist (*US*)

Apotheke

ⓘ The **Apotheke** is a pharmacy selling medicines available only on prescription and toiletries. The pharmacist is qualified to give advice on medicines and treatments.

Apparat [apa'ra:t] **(-(e)s, -e)** *m* piece of apparatus; camera; telephone; (*RADIO, TV*) set; **am ~!** speaking!; **~ur** [-'tu:r] *f* apparatus

Appartement [apart(ə)'mã:] **(-s, -s)** *nt* flat

appellieren [ape'li:rən] *vi*: **~ (an** +*akk*) to appeal (to)

Appetit [ape'ti:t] **(-(e)s, -e)** *m* appetite; **guten ~!** enjoy your meal; **a~lich** *adj* appetizing; **~losigkeit** *f* lack of appetite

Applaus [ap'laʊs] **(-es, -e)** *m* applause

Aprikose [apri'ko:zə] *f* apricot

April [a'prɪl] **(-(s), -e)** *m* April

Aquarell [akva'rɛl] **(-s, -e)** *nt* watercolour

Äquator [ɛ'kva:tɔr] **(-s, -e)** *m* equator

Arab- ['arap] *zW*: **~er(in)** **(-s, -)** *m(f)* Arab; **~ien** [a'ra:biən] **(-s)** *nt* Arabia; **a~isch** [a'ra:bɪʃ] *adj* Arabian

Arbeit ['arbaɪt] **(-, -en)** *f* work *no art*; (*Stelle*) job; (*Erzeugnis*) piece of work; (*wissenschaftliche*) dissertation; (*Klassenarbeit*) test; **das war eine ~** that was a hard job; **a~en** *vi* to work ♦ *vt* to work, to make; **~er(in)** **(-s, -)** *m(f)* worker; (*ungelernt*) labourer; **~erschaft** *f* workers *pl*, labour force; **~geber** **(-s, -)** *m* employer; **~nehmer** **(-s, -)** *m* employee

Arbeits- *in zW* labour; **a~am** *adj* industrious; **~amt** *nt* employment exchange; **~erlaubnis** *f* work permit; **a~fähig** *adj* fit for work, able-bodied; **~gang** *m* operation; **a~kräfte** *pl* (*Mitarbeiter*) workforce; **a~los** *adj*

unemployed, out-of-work; **~lose(r)** *f(m)* unemployed person; **~losigkeit** *f* unemployment; **~markt** *m* job market; **~platz** *m* job; place of work; **a~scheu** *adj* workshy; **~tag** *m* work(ing) day; **a~unfähig** *adj* unfit for work; **~zeit** *f* working hours *pl*; **~zimmer** *nt* study

Archäologe [arçeo'lo:gə] **(-n, -n)** *m* archaeologist

Architekt(in) [arçi'tɛkt(ɪn)] **(-en, -en)** *m(f)* architect; **~ur** [-'tu:r] *f* architecture

Archiv [ar'çi:f] **(-s, -e)** *nt* archive

arg [ark] *adj* bad, awful ♦ *adv* awfully, very

Argentinien [argen'ti:niən] **(-s)** *nt* Argentina, the Argentine

argentinisch *adj* Argentinian

Ärger ['ɛrgər] **(-s)** *m* (*Wut*) anger; (*Unannehmlichkeit*) trouble; **ä~lich** *adj* (*zornig*) angry; (*lästig*) annoying, aggravating; **ä~n** *vt* to annoy ♦ *vr* to get annoyed

arg- *zW*: **~listig** *adj* cunning, insidious; **~los** *adj* guileless, innocent

Argument [argu'mɛnt] *nt* argument

argwöhnisch *adj* suspicious

Arie ['a:riə] *f* aria

Aristokrat [arɪsto'kra:t] **(-en, -en)** *m* aristocrat; **~ie** [-'ti:] *f* aristocracy

Arktis ['arktɪs] **(-)** *f* Arctic

Arm [arm] **(-(e)s, -e)** *m* arm; (*Flussarm*) branch

arm *adj* poor

Armatur [arma'tu:r] *f* (*ELEK*) armature; **~enbrett** *nt* instrument panel; (*AUT*) dashboard

Armband *nt* bracelet; **~uhr** *f* (wrist) watch

Arme(r) *f(m)* poor man (woman); **die ~n** the poor

Armee [ar'me:] *f* army

Ärmel ['ɛrməl] **(-s, -)** *m* sleeve; **etw aus dem ~ schütteln** (*fig*) to produce sth just like that; **~kanal** *m* English Channel

ärmlich ['ɛrmlɪç] *adj* poor

armselig *adj* wretched, miserable

Armut ['armu:t] **(-)** *f* poverty

Aroma [a'ro:ma] **(-s, Aromen)** *nt* aroma; **~therapie** *f* aromatherapy; **a~tisch**

[aro'ma:tɪʃ] adj aromatic

arrangieren [arã'ʒi:rən] vt to arrange ♦ vr to come to an arrangement

Arrest [a'rɛst] (-(e)s, -e) m detention

arrogant [aro'gant] adj arrogant

Arsch [arʃ] (-es, ⁼e) (umg!) m arse (BRIT!), ass (US!)

Art [a:rt] (-, -en) f (Weise) way; (Sorte) kind, sort; (BIOL) species; **eine ~ (von) Frucht** a kind of fruit; **Häuser aller ~** houses of all kinds; **es ist nicht seine ~, das zu tun** it's not like him to do that; **ich mache das auf meine ~** I do that my (own) way

Arterie [ar'te:riə] f artery; **~nverkalkung** f arteriosclerosis

artig ['a:rtɪç] adj good, well-behaved

Artikel [ar'ti:kəl] (-s, -) m article

Artillerie [artɪlə'ri:] f artillery

Artischocke [artɪ'ʃɔkə] f artichoke

Artist(in) [ar'tɪst(ɪn)] (-en, -en) m(f) (circus/variety) artiste od performer

Arznei [a:rts'naɪ] f medicine; **~mittel** nt medicine, medicament

Arzt [a:rtst] (-es, ⁼e) m doctor; **~helferin** f (doctor's) receptionist

Ärztin ['ɛ:rtstɪn] f doctor

ärztlich ['ɛ:rtstlɪç] adj medical

As △ [as] (-ses, -se) nt = **Ass**

Asche ['aʃə] f (-, -n) ash, cinder

Aschen- zW: **~bahn** f cinder track; **~becher** m ashtray

Aschermittwoch m Ash Wednesday

Äser ['ɛ:zər] pl von **Aas**

Asiat(in) [azi'a:t(ɪn)] (-en, -en) m(f) Asian; **asiatisch** [-'a:tɪʃ] adj Asian

Asien ['a:ziən] (-s) nt Asia

asozial ['azotsia:l] adj antisocial; (Familien) asocial

Aspekt [as'pɛkt] (-(e)s, -e) m aspect

Asphalt [as'falt] (-(e)s, -e) m asphalt; **a~ieren** vt to asphalt

Ass ▲ [as] (-es, -e) nt ace

aß etc [a:s] vb siehe **essen**

Assistent(in) [asɪs'tɛnt(ɪn)] m(f) assistant

Assoziation [asotsiatsi'o:n] f association

Ast [ast] (-(e)s, ⁼e) m bough, branch

ästhetisch [ɛs'te:tɪʃ] adj aesthetic

Asthma ['astma] (-s) nt asthma; **~tiker(in)** (-s, -) m(f) asthmatic

Astro- [astro] zW: **~loge** (-n, -n) m astrologer; **~lo'gie** f astrology; **~'naut** (-en, -en) m astronaut; **~'nom** (-en, -en) m astronomer; **~no'mie** f astronomy

Asyl [a'zy:l] (-s, -e) nt asylum; (Heim) home; (Obdachlosenasyl) shelter; **~ant(in)** [azy'lant(ɪn)] (-en, -en) m(f) asylum-seeker

Atelier [atəli'e:] (-s, -s) nt studio

Atem ['a:təm] (-s) m breath; **den ~ anhalten** to hold one's breath; **außer ~** out of breath; **a~beraubend** adj breathtaking; **a~los** adj breathless; **~not** f difficulty in breathing; **~pause** f breather; **~zug** m breath

Atheismus [ate'ɪsmʊs] m atheism

Atheist m atheist; **a~isch** adj atheistic

Athen [a'te:n] (-s) nt Athens

Äthiopien [eti'o:piən] (-s) nt Ethiopia

Athlet [at'le:t] (-en, -en) m athlete

Atlantik [at'lantɪk] (-s) m Atlantic (Ocean)

Atlas ['atlas] (- od -ses, -se od **Atlanten**) m atlas

atmen ['a:tmən] vt, vi to breathe

Atmosphäre [atmo'sfɛ:rə] f atmosphere; **atmosphärisch** adj atmospheric

Atmung ['a:tmʊŋ] f respiration

Atom [a'to:m] (-s, -e) nt atom; **a~ar** adj atomic; **~bombe** f atom bomb; **~energie** f atomic od nuclear energy; **~kern** m atomic nucleus; **~kraftwerk** nt nuclear power station; **~krieg** m nuclear od atomic war; **~müll** m atomic waste; **~strom** m (electricity generated by) nuclear power; **~versuch** m atomic test; **~waffen** pl atomic weapons; **a~waffenfrei** adj nuclear-free; **~zeitalter** nt atomic age

Attentat [atɛn'ta:t] (-(e)s, -e) nt: **~ (auf +akk)** (attempted) assassination (of)

Attentäter [atɛn'tɛ:tər] m (would-be) assassin

Attest [a'tɛst] (-(e)s, -e) nt certificate

Attraktion [atraktsi'o:n] f (Tourismus, Zirkus) attraction

attraktiv [atrak'ti:f] adj attractive

Attrappe [a'trapə] f dummy

Attribut [atri'buːt] **(-(e)s, -e)** *nt* (*GRAM*) attribute

ätzen ['ɛtsən] *vi* to be caustic; **~d** *adj* (*Säure*) corrosive; (*fig: Spott*) cutting

au [au] *excl* ouch!; **~ ja!** oh yes!

Aubergine [ober'ʒiːnə] *f* aubergine, eggplant

auch [aux] *adv* **1** (*ebenfalls*) also, too, as well; **das ist auch schön** that's nice too *od* as well; **er kommt - ich auch** he's coming - so am I, me too; **auch nicht** not ... either; **ich auch nicht** nor I, me neither; **oder auch** or; **auch das noch!** not that as well! **2** (*selbst, sogar*) even; **auch wenn das Wetter schlecht ist** even if the weather is bad; **ohne auch nur zu fragen** without even asking **3** (*wirklich*) really; **du siehst müde aus - bin ich auch** you look tired - (so) I am; **so sieht es auch aus** it looks like it too **4** (*auch immer*): **wer auch** whoever; **was auch** whatever; **wie dem auch sei** be that as it may; **wie sehr er sich auch bemühte** however much he tried

auf [auf] *präp +dat* (*wo?*) on; **auf dem Tisch** on the table; **auf der Reise** on the way; **auf der Post/dem Fest** at the post office/ party; **auf der Straße** on the road; **auf dem Land/der ganzen Welt** in the country/the whole world

♦ *präp +akk* **1** (*wohin?*) on(to); **auf den Tisch** on(to) the table; **auf die Post gehen** go to the post office; **auf das Land** into the country; **etw auf einen Zettel schreiben** to write sth on a piece of paper **2**: **auf Deutsch** in German; **auf Lebenszeit** for my/his lifetime; **bis auf ihn** except for him; **auf einmal** at once; **auf seinen Vorschlag (hin)** at his suggestion

♦ *adv* **1** (*offen*) open; **auf sein** (*umg*) (*Tür, Geschäft*) to be open; **das Fenster ist auf** the window is open

2 (*hinauf*) up; **auf und ab** up and down; **auf und davon** up and away; **auf!** (*los!*) come on! **3** (*aufgestanden*) up; **auf sein** to be up; **ist er schon auf?** is he up yet?

♦ *konj*: **auf dass** (so) that

aufatmen ['aufʔaːtmən] *vi* to heave a sigh of relief

aufbahren ['aufbaːrən] *vt* to lay out

Aufbau ['aufbau] *m* (*Bauen*) building, construction; (*Struktur*) structure; (*aufgebautes Teil*) superstructure; **a~en** *vt* to erect, to build (up); (*Existenz*) to make; (*gestalten*) to construct; **a~en (auf +***dat***)** (*gründen*) to found *od* base (on)

aufbauschen ['aufbauʃən] *vt* to puff out; (*fig*) to exaggerate

aufbekommen ['aufbəkɔmən] (*unreg*) *vt* (*öffnen*) to get open; (*Hausaufgaben*) to be given

aufbessern ['aufbɛsərn] *vt* (*Gehalt*) to increase

aufbewahren ['aufbəvaːrən] *vt* to keep; (*Gepäck*) to put in the left-luggage office (*BRIT*) *od* baggage check (*US*)

Aufbewahrung *f* (safe)keeping; (*Gepäckaufbewahrung*) left-luggage office (*BRIT*), baggage check (*US*)

aufbieten ['aufbiːtən] (*unreg*) *vt* (*Kraft*) to summon (up); (*Armee, Polizei*) to mobilize

aufblasen ['aufblaːzən] (*unreg*) *vt* to blow up, to inflate ♦ *vr* (*umg*) to become bigheaded

aufbleiben ['aufblaɪbən] (*unreg*) *vi* (*Laden*) to remain open; (*Person*) to stay up

aufblenden ['aufblɛndən] *vt* (*Scheinwerfer*) to switch on full beam ♦ *vi* (*Fahrer*) to have the lights on full beam; (*AUT: Scheinwerfer*) to be on full beam

aufblicken ['aufblɪkən] *vi* to look up; **~ zu** to look up at; (*fig*) to look up to

aufblühen ['aufblyːən] *vi* to blossom, to flourish

aufbrauchen ['aufbrauxən] *vt* to use up

aufbrausen ['aufbrauzən] *vi* (*fig*) to flare up; **~d** *adj* hot-tempered

Spelling Reform: ▲ *new spelling* △ *old spelling (to be phased out)*

aufbrechen ['aʊfbrɛçən] (*unreg*) *vt* to break *od* prise (*BRIT*) open ♦ *vi* to burst open; (*gehen*) to start, to set off

aufbringen ['aʊfbrɪŋən] (*unreg*) *vt* (*öffnen*) to open; (*in Mode*) to bring into fashion; (*beschaffen*) to procure; (*FIN*) to raise; (*ärgern*) to irritate; **Verständnis für etw ~** to be able to understand sth

Aufbruch ['aʊfbrʊx] *m* departure

aufbrühen ['aʊfbryːən] *vt* (*Tee*) to make

aufbürden ['aʊfbʏrdən] *vt*: **jdm etw ~** to burden sb with sth

aufdecken ['aʊfdɛkən] *vt* to uncover

aufdrängen ['aʊfdrɛŋən] *vt*: **jdm etw ~** to force sth on sb ♦ *vr* (*Mensch*): **sich jdm ~** to intrude on sb

aufdrehen ['aʊfdreːən] *vt* (*Wasserhahn etc*) to turn on; (*Ventil*) to open up

aufdringlich ['aʊfdrɪŋlɪç] *adj* pushy

aufeinander [aʊf|aɪ'nandər] *adv* on top of each other; (*schießen*) at each other; (*vertrauen*) each other; **~ folgen** to follow one another; **~ folgend** consecutive; **~ prallen** to hit one another

Aufenthalt ['aʊf|ɛnthalt] *m* stay; (*Verzögerung*) delay; (*EISENB: Halten*) stop; (*Ort*) haunt

Aufenthaltserlaubnis *f* residence permit

auferlegen ['aʊf|ɛrleːgən] *vt*: **(jdm) ~** to impose (upon sb)

Auferstehung ['aʊf|ɛrsteːʊŋ] *f* resurrection

aufessen ['aʊf|ɛsən] (*unreg*) *vt* to eat up

auffahr- ['aʊffaːr] *zW*: **~en** (*unreg*) *vi* (*herankommen*) to draw up; (*hochfahren*) to jump up; (*wütend werden*) to flare up; (*in den Himmel*) to ascend ♦ *vt* (*Kanonen, Geschütz*) to bring up; **~en auf** +*akk* (*Auto*) to run *od* crash into; **~end** *adj* hot-tempered; **A~t** *f* (*Hausauffahrt*) drive; (*Autobahnauffahrt*) slip road (*BRIT*), (*freeway*) entrance (*US*); **A~unfall** *m* pile-up

auffallen ['aʊffalən] (*unreg*) *vi* to be noticeable; **jdm ~** to strike sb

auffällig ['aʊffɛlɪç] *adj* conspicuous, striking

auffangen ['aʊffaŋən] (*unreg*) *vt* to catch; (*Funkspruch*) to intercept; (*Preise*) to peg

auffassen ['aʊffasən] *vt* to understand, to comprehend; (*auslegen*) to see, to view

Auffassung *f* (*Meinung*) opinion; (*Auslegung*) view, concept; (*auch:* **~sgabe**) grasp

auffindbar ['aʊffɪntbaːr] *adj* to be found

auffordern ['aʊffɔrdərn] *vt* (*befehlen*) to call upon, to order; (*bitten*) to ask

Aufforderung *f* (*Befehl*) order; (*Einladung*) invitation

auffrischen ['aʊffrɪʃən] *vt* to freshen up; (*Kenntnisse*) to brush up; (*Erinnerungen*) to reawaken ♦ *vi* (*Wind*) to freshen

aufführen ['aʊffyːrən] *vt* (*THEAT*) to perform; (*in einem Verzeichnis*) to list, to specify ♦ *vr* (*sich benehmen*) to behave

Aufführung *f* (*THEAT*) performance; (*Liste*) specification

Aufgabe ['aʊfgaːbə] *f* task; (*SCH*) exercise; (*Hausaufgabe*) homework; (*Verzicht*) giving up; (*von Gepäck*) registration; (*von Post*) posting; (*von Inserat*) insertion

Aufgang ['aʊfgaŋ] *m* ascent; (*Sonnenaufgang*) rise; (*Treppe*) staircase

aufgeben ['aʊfgeːbən] (*unreg*) *vt* (*verzichten*) to give up; (*Paket*) to send, to post; (*Gepäck*) to register; (*Bestellung*) to give; (*Inserat*) to insert; (*Rätsel, Problem*) to set ♦ *vi* to give up

Aufgebot ['aʊfgəboːt] *nt* supply; (*Eheaufgebot*) banns *pl*

aufgedunsen ['aʊfgədʊnzən] *adj* swollen, puffed up

aufgehen ['aʊfgeːən] (*unreg*) *vi* (*Sonne, Teig*) to rise; (*sich öffnen*) to open; (*klar werden*) to become clear; (*MATH*) to come out exactly; **~ (in** +*dat*) (*sich widmen*) to be absorbed (in); **in Rauch/Flammen ~** to go up in smoke/flames

aufgelegt ['aʊfgəleːkt] *adj*: **gut/schlecht ~ sein** to be in a good/bad mood; **zu etw ~ sein** to be in the mood for sth

aufgeregt ['aʊfgəreːkt] *adj* excited

aufgeschlossen ['aʊfgəʃlɔsən] *adj* open, open-minded

aufgeweckt ['aʊfgəvɛkt] *adj* bright, intelligent

aufgießen ['aʊfgiːsən] (*unreg*) *vt* (*Wasser*) to

pour over; (*Tee*) to infuse

aufgreifen ['aufgraifən] (*unreg*) *vt* (*Thema*) to take up; (*Verdächtige*) to pick up, to seize

aufgrund, auf Grund [auf'grunt] *präp* +*gen* on the basis of; (*wegen*) because of

aufhaben ['aufha:bən] (*unreg*) *vt* to have on; (*Arbeit*) to have to do

aufhalsen ['aufhalzən] (*umg*) *vt*: **jdm etw ~** to saddle *od* lumber sb with sth

aufhalten ['aufhaltən] (*unreg*) *vt* (*Person*) to detain; (*Entwicklung*) to check; (*Tür, Hand*) to hold open; (*Augen*) to keep open ♦ *vr* (*wohnen*) to live; (*bleiben*) to stay; **sich mit etw ~** to waste time over sth

aufhängen ['aufhɛŋən] (*unreg*) *vt* (*Wäsche*) to hang up; (*Menschen*) to hang ♦ *vr* to hang o.s.

Aufhänger (**-s, -**) *m* (*am Mantel*) loop; (*fig*) peg

aufheben ['aufhe:bən] (*unreg*) *vt* (*hochheben*) to raise, to lift; (*Sitzung*) to wind up; (*Urteil*) to annul; (*Gesetz*) to repeal, to abolish; (*aufbewahren*) to keep ♦ *vr* to cancel itself out; **bei jdm gut aufgehoben sein** to be well looked after at sb's; **viel A~(s) machen (von)** to make a fuss (about)

aufheitern ['aufhaitərn] *vt, vr* (*Himmel, Miene*) to brighten; (*Mensch*) to cheer up

aufhellen ['aufhɛlən] *vt, vr* to clear up; (*Farbe, Haare*) to lighten

aufhetzen ['aufhɛtsən] *vt* to stir up

aufholen ['aufho:lən] *vt* to make up ♦ *vi* to catch up

aufhorchen ['aufhɔrçən] *vi* to prick up one's ears

aufhören ['aufhø:rən] *vi* to stop; **~, etw zu tun** to stop doing sth

aufklappen ['aufklapən] *vt* to open

aufklären ['aufklɛ:rən] *vt* (*Geheimnis etc*) to clear up; (*Person*) to enlighten; (*sexuell*) to tell the facts of life to; (*MIL*) to reconnoitre ♦ *vr* to clear up

Aufklärung *f* (*von Geheimnis*) clearing up; (*Unterrichtung, Zeitalter*) enlightenment; (*sexuell*) sex education; (*MIL, AVIAT*) reconnaissance

aufkleben ['aufkle:bən] *vt* to stick on;

Aufkleber (**-s, -**) *m* sticker

aufknöpfen ['aufknœpfən] *vt* to unbutton

aufkommen ['aufkɔmən] (*unreg*) *vi* (*Wind*) to come up; (*Zweifel, Gefühl*) to arise; (*Mode*) to start; **für jdn/etw ~** to be liable *od* responsible for sb/sth

aufladen ['aufla:dən] (*unreg*) *vt* to load

Auflage ['aufla:gə] *f* edition; (*Zeitung*) circulation; (*Bedingung*) condition

auflassen ['auflasən] (*unreg*) *vt* (*offen*) to leave open; (*aufgesetzt*) to leave on

auflauern ['auflauərn] *vi*: **jdm ~** to lie in wait for sb

Auflauf ['auflauf] *m* (*KOCH*) pudding; (*Menschenauflauf*) crowd

aufleben ['aufle:bən] *vi* (*Mensch, Gespräch*) to liven up; (*Interesse*) to revive

auflegen ['aufle:gən] *vt* to put on; (*Telefon*) to hang up; (*TYP*) to print

auflehnen ['aufle:nən] *vt* to lean on ♦ *vr* to rebel

Auflehnung *f* rebellion

auflesen ['aufle:zən] (*unreg*) *vt* to pick up

aufleuchten ['aufloyçtən] *vi* to light up

auflisten ['auflistən] *vt* to list

auflockern ['auflɔkərn] *vt* to loosen; (*fig: Eintönigkeit etc*) to liven up

auflösen ['auflø:zən] *vt* to dissolve; (*Haare etc*) to loosen; (*Missverständnis*) to sort out ♦ *vr* to dissolve; to come undone; to be resolved; **(in Tränen) aufgelöst sein** to be in tears

Auflösung *f* dissolving; (*fig*) solution

aufmachen ['aufmaxən] *vt* to open; (*Kleidung*) to undo; (*zurechtmachen*) to do up ♦ *vr* to set out

Aufmachung *f* (*Kleidung*) outfit, get-up; (*Gestaltung*) format

aufmerksam ['aufmɛrkza:m] *adj* attentive; **jdn auf etw** *akk* **~ machen** to point sth out to sb; **A~keit** *f* attention, attentiveness

aufmuntern ['aufmuntərn] *vt* (*ermutigen*) to encourage; (*erheitern*) to cheer up

Aufnahme ['aufna:mə] *f* reception; (*Beginn*) beginning; (*in Verein etc*) admission; (*in Liste etc*) inclusion; (*Notieren*) taking down; (*PHOT*) shot; (*auf Tonband etc*) recording;

a~fähig adj receptive; **~prüfung** f entrance test

aufnehmen ['aufne:mən] (unreg) vt to receive; (hochheben) to pick up; (beginnen) to take up; (in Verein etc) to admit; (in Liste etc) to include; (fassen) to hold; (notieren) to take down; (fotografieren) to photograph; (auf Tonband, Platte) to record; (FIN: leihen) to take out; **es mit jdm ~ können** to be able to compete with sb

aufopfern ['aufʔɔpfərn] vt, vr to sacrifice; **~d** adj selfless

aufpassen ['aufpasən] vi (aufmerksam sein) to pay attention; **auf jdn/etw ~** to look after od watch sb/sth; **aufgepasst!** look out!

Aufprall ['aufpral] (**-s, -e**) m impact; **a~en** vi to hit, to strike

Aufpreis ['aufprais] m extra charge

aufpumpen ['aufpumpən] vt to pump up

aufräumen ['aufrɔymən] vt, vi (Dinge) to clear away; (Zimmer) to tidy up

aufrecht ['aufrɛçt] adj (auch fig) upright; **~erhalten** (unreg) vt to maintain

aufreg- ['aufre:g] zW: **~en** vt to excite ♦ vr to get excited; **~end** adj exciting; **A~ung** f excitement

aufreibend ['aufraibənt] adj strenuous

aufreißen ['aufraisən] (unreg) vt (Umschlag) to tear open; (Augen) to open wide; (Tür) to throw open; (Straße) to take up

aufreizen ['aufraitsən] vt to incite, to stir up; **~d** adj exciting, stimulating

aufrichten ['aufrɪçtən] vt to put up, to erect; (moralisch) to console ♦ vr to rise; (moralisch): **sich ~ (an** +dat) to take heart (from)

aufrichtig ['aufrɪçtɪç] adj sincere, honest; **A~keit** f sincerity

aufrücken ['aufrʏkən] vi to move up; (beruflich) to be promoted

Aufruf ['aufru:f] m summons; (zur Hilfe) call; (des Namens) calling out; **a~en** (unreg) vt (Namen) to call out; (auffordern): **jdn a~en (zu)** to call upon sb (for)

Aufruhr ['aufru:r] (**-(e)s, -e**) m uprising, revolt

aufrührerisch ['aufryːrərɪʃ] adj rebellious

aufrunden ['aufrundən] vt (Summe) to round up

Aufrüstung ['aufrʏstʊŋ] f rearmament

aufrütteln ['aufrʏtəln] vt (auch fig) to shake up

aufs [aufs] = **auf das**

aufsagen ['aufzaːgən] vt (Gedicht) to recite

aufsässig ['aufzɛsɪç] adj rebellious

Aufsatz ['aufzats] m (Geschriebenes) essay; (auf Schrank etc) top

aufsaugen ['aufzaugən] (unreg) vt to soak up

aufschauen ['aufʃauən] vi to look up

aufscheuchen ['aufʃɔyçən] vt to scare od frighten away

aufschieben ['aufʃiːbən] (unreg) vt to push open; (verzögern) to put off, to postpone

Aufschlag ['aufʃlaːk] m (Ärmelaufschlag) cuff; (Jackenaufschlag) lapel; (Hosenaufschlag) turn-up; (Aufprall) impact; (Preisaufschlag) surcharge; (Tennis) service; **a~en** [-gən] (unreg) vt (öffnen) to open; (verwunden) to cut; (hochschlagen) to turn up; (aufbauen: Zelt, Lager) to pitch, to erect; (Wohnsitz) to take up ♦ vi (aufprallen) to hit; (teurer werden) to go up; (Tennis) to serve

aufschließen ['aufʃliːsən] (unreg) vt to open up, to unlock ♦ vi (aufrücken) to close up

aufschlussreich ▲ adj informative, illuminating

aufschnappen ['aufʃnapən] vt (umg) to pick up ♦ vi to fly open

aufschneiden ['aufʃnaidən] (unreg) vt (Brot) to cut up; (MED) to lance ♦ vi to brag

Aufschneider (**-s, -**) m boaster, braggart

Aufschnitt ['aufʃnɪt] m (slices of) cold meat

aufschrauben ['aufʃraubən] vt (festschrauben) to screw on; (lösen) to unscrew

aufschrecken ['aufʃrɛkən] vt to startle ♦ vi (unreg) to start up

aufschreiben ['aufʃraibən] (unreg) vt to write down

aufschreien ['aufʃraiən] (unreg) vi to cry out

Aufschrift ['aufʃrɪft] f (Inschrift) inscription; (auf Etikett) label

Rechtschreibreform: ▲ *neue Schreibung* △ *alte Schreibung (auslaufend)*

Aufschub ['aʊfʃuːp] (**-(e)s, -schübe**) *m* delay, postponement

Aufschwung ['aʊfʃvʊŋ] *m* (*Elan*) boost; (*wirtschaftlich*) upturn, boom; (*SPORT*) circle

aufsehen ['aʊfzeːən] (*unreg*) *vi* to look up; ~ **zu** to look up at; (*fig*) to look up to; **A~ (-s)** *nt* sensation, stir; ~ **erregend** sensational

Aufseher(in) (**-s, -**) *m(f)* guard; (*im Betrieb*) supervisor; (*Museumsaufseher*) attendant; (*Parkaufseher*) keeper

auf sein ▲ *siehe* **auf**

aufsetzen ['aʊfzɛtsən] *vt* to put on; (*Dokument*) to draw up ♦ *vr* to sit up(right) ♦ *vi* (*Flugzeug*) to touch down

Aufsicht ['aʊfzɪçt] *f* supervision; **die ~ haben** to be in charge

Aufsichtsrat *m* (supervisory) board

aufsitzen ['aʊfzɪtsən] (*unreg*) *vi* (*aufrecht hinsitzen*) to sit up; (*aufs Pferd, Motorrad*) to mount, to get on; (*Schiff*) to run aground; **jdm ~** (*umg*) to be taken in by sb

aufsparen ['aʊfʃpaːrən] *vt* to save (up)

aufsperren ['aʊfʃpɛrən] *vt* to unlock; (*Mund*) to open wide

aufspielen ['aʊfʃpiːlən] *vr* to show off

aufspießen ['aʊfʃpiːsən] *vt* to spear

aufspringen ['aʊfʃprɪŋən] (*unreg*) *vi* (*hochspringen*) to jump up; (*sich öffnen*) to spring open; (*Hände, Lippen*) to become chapped; **auf etw** *akk* ~ to jump onto sth

aufspüren ['aʊfʃpyːrən] *vt* to track down, to trace

aufstacheln ['aʊfʃtaxəln] *vt* to incite

Aufstand ['aʊfʃtant] *m* insurrection, rebellion; **aufständisch** ['aʊfʃtɛndɪʃ] *adj* rebellious, mutinous

aufstehen ['aʊfʃteːən] (*unreg*) *vi* to get up; (*Tür*) to be open

aufsteigen ['aʊfʃtaɪgən] (*unreg*) *vi* (*hochsteigen*) to climb; (*Rauch*) to rise; **auf etw** *akk* ~ to get onto sth

aufstellen ['aʊfʃtɛlən] *vt* (*aufrecht stellen*) to put up; (*aufreihen*) to line up; (*nominieren*) to nominate; (*formulieren: Programm etc*) to draw up; (*leisten: Rekord*) to set up

Aufstellung *f* (*SPORT*) line-up; (*Liste*) list

Aufstieg ['aʊfʃtiːk] (**-(e)s, -e**) *m* (*auf Berg*) ascent; (*Fortschritt*) rise; (*beruflich, SPORT*) promotion

aufstocken ['aʊfʃtɔkən] *vt* (*Kapital*) to increase

aufstoßen ['aʊfʃtoːsən] (*unreg*) *vt* to push open ♦ *vi* to belch

aufstützen ['aʊfʃtʏtsən] *vt* (*Körperteil*) to prop, to lean; (*Person*) to prop up ♦ *vr*: **sich auf etw** *akk* ~ to lean on sth

aufsuchen ['aʊfzuːxən] *vt* (*besuchen*) to visit; (*konsultieren*) to consult

Auftakt ['aʊftakt] *m* (*MUS*) upbeat; (*fig*) prelude

auftanken ['aʊftaŋkən] *vi* to get petrol (*BRIT*) *od* gas (*US*) ♦ *vt* to refuel

auftauchen ['aʊftaʊxən] *vi* to appear; (*aus Wasser etc*) to emerge; (*U-Boot*) to surface; (*Zweifel*) to arise

auftauen ['aʊftaʊən] *vt* to thaw ♦ *vi* to thaw; (*fig*) to relax

aufteilen ['aʊftaɪlən] *vt* to divide up; (*Raum*) to partition; **Aufteilung** *f* division; partition

Auftrag ['aʊftraːk] (**-(e)s, -träge**) *m* order; (*Anweisung*) commission; (*Aufgabe*) mission; **im ~ von** on behalf of; **a~en** [-gən] (*unreg*) *vt* (*Essen*) to serve; (*Farbe*) to put on; (*Kleidung*) to wear out; **jdm etw a~en** to tell sb sth; **dick a~en** (*fig*) to exaggerate; **~geber (-s, -)** *m* (*COMM*) purchaser, customer

auftreiben ['aʊftraɪbən] (*unreg*) *vt* (*umg: beschaffen*) to raise

auftreten ['aʊftreːtən] (*unreg*) *vt* to kick open ♦ *vi* to appear; (*mit Füßen*) to tread; (*sich verhalten*) to behave; **A~ (-s)** *nt* (*Vorkommen*) appearance; (*Benehmen*) behaviour

Auftrieb ['aʊftriːp] *m* (*PHYS*) buoyancy, lift; (*fig*) impetus

Auftritt ['aʊftrɪt] *m* (*des Schauspielers*) entrance; (*Szene: auch fig*) scene

aufwachen ['aʊfvaxən] *vi* to wake up

aufwachsen ['aʊfvaksən] (*unreg*) *vi* to grow up

Aufwand ['aʊfvant] (**-(e)s**) *m* expenditure; (*Kosten auch*) expense; (*Luxus*) show

Spelling Reform: ▲ *new spelling* △ *old spelling (to be phased out)*

aufwändig ▲ ['aʊfvɛndɪç] *adj* costly

aufwärmen ['aʊfvɛrmən] *vt* to warm up; *(alte Geschichten)* to rake up

aufwärts ['aʊfvɛrts] *adv* upwards; **A~entwicklung** *f* upward trend

Aufwasch ['aʊfvaʃ] *m* washing-up

aufwecken ['aʊfvɛkən] *vt* to wake up, to waken up

aufweisen ['aʊfvaɪzən] *(unreg) vt* to show

aufwenden ['aʊfvɛndən] *(unreg) vt* to expend; *(Geld)* to spend; *(Sorgfalt)* to devote

aufwendig *adj siehe* **aufwändig**

aufwerfen ['aʊfvɛrfən] *(unreg) vt (Fenster etc)* to throw open; *(Probleme)* to throw up, to raise

aufwerten ['aʊfvɛrtən] *vt (FIN)* to revalue; *(fig)* to raise in value

aufwickeln ['aʊfvɪkəln] *vt (aufrollen)* to roll up; *(umg: Haar)* to put in curlers

aufwiegen ['aʊfviːgən] *(unreg) vt* to make up for

Aufwind ['aʊfvɪnt] *m* up-current

aufwirbeln ['aʊfvɪrbəln] *vt* to whirl up; **Staub ~** *(fig)* to create a stir

aufwischen ['aʊfvɪʃən] *vt* to wipe up

aufzählen ['aʊftsɛːlən] *vt* to list

aufzeichnen ['aʊftsaɪçnən] *vt* to sketch; *(schriftlich)* to jot down; *(auf Band)* to record

Aufzeichnung *f (schriftlich)* note; *(Tonbandaufzeichnung)* recording; *(Filmaufzeichnung)* record

aufzeigen ['aʊftsaɪgən] *vt* to show, to demonstrate

aufziehen ['aʊftsiːən] *(unreg) vt (hochziehen)* to raise, to draw up; *(öffnen)* to pull open; *(Uhr)* to wind; *(umg: necken)* to tease; *(großziehen: Kinder)* to raise, to bring up; *(Tiere)* to rear

Aufzug ['aʊftsuːk] *m (Fahrstuhl)* lift, elevator; *(Aufmarsch)* procession, parade; *(Kleidung)* get-up; *(THEAT)* act

aufzwingen ['aʊftsvɪŋən] *(unreg) vt:* **jdm etw ~** to force sth upon sb

Augapfel ['aʊkʔapfəl] *m* eyeball; *(fig)* apple of one's eye

Auge ['aʊgə] *(-s, -n) nt* eye; *(Fettauge)* globule of fat; **unter vier ~n** in private

Augen- *zW:* **~blick** *m* moment; **im ~blick** at the moment; **a~blicklich** *adj (sofort)* instantaneous; *(gegenwärtig)* present; **~braue** *f* eyebrow; **~optiker(in)** *m(f)* optician; **~weide** *f* sight for sore eyes; **~zeuge** *m* eye witness

August [aʊˈgʊst] **(-(e)s** *od* **-, -e)** *m* August

Auktion [aʊktsiˈoːn] *f* auction

Aula ['aʊla] **(-, Aulen** *od* **-s)** *f* assembly hall

SCHLÜSSELWORT

aus [aʊs] *präp +dat* **1** *(räumlich)* out of; *(von ... her)* from; **er ist aus Berlin** he's from Berlin; **aus dem Fenster** out of the window

2 *(gemacht/hergestellt aus)* made of; **ein Herz aus Stein** a heart of stone

3 *(auf Ursache deutend)* out of; **aus Mitleid** out of sympathy; **aus Erfahrung** from experience; **aus Spaß** for fun

4: aus ihr wird nie etwas she'll never get anywhere

♦ *adv* **1** *(zu Ende)* finished, over; **aus sein** to be over; **aus und vorbei** over and done with

2 *(ausgeschaltet, ausgezogen)* out; *(Aufschrift an Geräten)* off; **aus sein** *(nicht brennen)* to be out; *(abgeschaltet sein: Radio, Herd)* to be off; **Licht aus!** lights out!

3 *(nicht zu Hause):* **aus sein** to be out

4 *(in Verbindung mit von):* **von Rom aus** from Rome; **vom Fenster aus** out of the window; **von sich aus** *(selbstständig)* of one's own accord; **von ihm aus** as far as he's concerned

---

ausarbeiten ['aʊsʔarbaɪtən] *vt* to work out

ausarten ['aʊsʔartən] *vi* to degenerate

ausatmen ['aʊsʔaːtmən] *vi* to breathe out

ausbaden ['aʊsbaːdən] *(umg) vt:* **etw ~ müssen** to carry the can for sth

Ausbau ['aʊsbaʊ] *m* extension, expansion; removal; **a~en** *vt* to extend, to expand; *(herausnehmen)* to take out, to remove; **a~fähig** *adj (fig)* worth developing

ausbessern ['aʊsbɛsərn] *vt* to mend, to

repair

ausbeulen ['ausbɔylən] *vt* to beat out

Ausbeute ['ausbɔytə] *f* yield; (*Fische*) catch; **a~n** *vt* to exploit; (*MIN*) to work

ausbild- ['ausbɪld] *zW:* **~en** *vt* to educate; (*Lehrling, Soldat*) to instruct, to train; (*Fähigkeiten*) to develop; (*Geschmack*) to cultivate; **A~er (-s, -)** *m* instructor; **A~ung** *f* education; training, instruction; development; cultivation

ausbleiben ['ausblaɪbən] (*unreg*) *vi* (*Personen*) to stay away, not to come; (*Ereignisse*) to fail to happen, not to happen

Ausblick ['ausblɪk] *m* (*auch fig*) prospect, outlook, view

ausbrechen ['ausbreçən] (*unreg*) *vi* to break out ♦ *vt* to break off; **in Tränen/Gelächter ~** to burst into tears/out laughing

ausbreiten ['ausbraɪtən] *vt* to spread (out); (*Arme*) to stretch out ♦ *vr* to spread; **sich über ein Thema ~** to expand *od* enlarge on a topic

ausbrennen ['ausbrenən] (*unreg*) *vt* to scorch; (*Wunde*) to cauterize ♦ *vi* to burn out

Ausbruch ['ausbrux] *m* outbreak; (*von Vulkan*) eruption; (*Gefühlsausbruch*) outburst; (*von Gefangenen*) escape

ausbrüten ['ausbry:tən] *vt* (*auch fig*) to hatch

Ausdauer ['ausdauər] *f* perseverance, stamina; **a~nd** *adj* persevering

ausdehnen ['ausde:nən] *vt, vr* (*räumlich*) to expand; (*zeitlich, auch Gummi*) to stretch; (*Nebel, fig: Macht*) to extend

ausdenken ['ausdɛŋkən] (*unreg*) *vt:* **sich** *dat* **etw ~** to think sth up

Ausdruck ['ausdrʊk] *m* expression, phrase; (*Kundgabe, Gesichtsausdruck*) expression; (*COMPUT*) print-out, hard copy; **a~en** *vt* (*COMPUT*) to print out

ausdrücken ['ausdrykən] *vt* (*auch vr:* *formulieren, zeigen*) to express; (*Zigarette*) to put out; (*Zitrone*) to squeeze

ausdrücklich *adj* express, explicit

ausdrucks- *zW:* **~los** *adj* expressionless, blank; **~voll** *adj* expressive; **A~weise** *f*

mode of expression

auseinander [ausaɪˈnandər] *adv* (*getrennt*) apart; **~ schreiben** to write as separate words; **~ bringen** to separate; **~ fallen** to fall apart; **~ gehen** (*Menschen*) to separate; (*Meinungen*) to differ; (*Gegenstand*) to fall apart; **~ halten** to tell apart; **~ nehmen** to take to pieces, to dismantle; **~ setzen** (*erklären*) to set forth, to explain; **sich ~ setzen** (*sich verständigen*) to come to terms, to settle; (*sich befassen*) to concern o.s.; **A~setzung** *f* argument

ausfahren ['ausfa:rən] (*unreg*) *vt* (*spazieren fahren: im Auto*) to take for a drive; (: *im Kinderwagen*) to take for a walk; (*liefern*) to deliver

Ausfahrt *f* (*des Zuges etc*) leaving, departure; (*Autobahnausfahrt*) exit; (*Garagenausfahrt etc*) exit, way out; (*Spazierfahrt*) drive, excursion

Ausfall ['ausfal] *m* loss; (*Nichtstattfinden*) cancellation; (*MIL*) sortie; (*radioaktiv*) fall-out; **a~en** (*unreg*) *vi* (*Zähne, Haare*) to fall *od* come out; (*nicht stattfinden*) to be cancelled; (*wegbleiben*) to be omitted; (*Person*) to drop out; (*Lohn*) to be stopped; (*nicht funktionieren*) to break down; (*Resultat haben*) to turn out; **~straße** *f* arterial road

ausfertigen ['ausfɛrtɪgən] *vt* (*förmlich: Urkunde, Pass*) to draw up; (*Rechnung*) to make out

Ausfertigung ['ausfɛrtɪgʊŋ] *f* drawing up; making out; (*Exemplar*) copy

ausfindig ['ausfɪndɪç] *adj:* **~ machen** to discover

ausfließen ['ausfli:sən] (*unreg*) *vt* (*her~*): **~ (aus)** to flow out (of); (*auslaufen: Öl etc*): **~ (aus)** to leak (out of)

Ausflucht ['ausfluxt] (**-, -flüchte**) *f* excuse

Ausflug ['ausflu:k] *m* excursion, outing; **Ausflügler** ['ausfly:klɐr] (**-s, -**) *m* tripper

Ausflugslokal *nt* tourist café

Ausfluss ▲ ['ausflʊs] *m* outlet; (*MED*) discharge

ausfragen ['ausfra:gən] *vt* to interrogate, to question

ausfressen ['ausfresən] (*unreg*) *vt* to eat up;

Spelling Reform: ▲ *new spelling* △ *old spelling (to be phased out)*

(aushöhlen) to corrode; *(umg: anstellen)* to be up to

Ausfuhr ['ausfuːr] *(-, -en) f* export, exportation ♦ *in zW* export

ausführ- ['ausfyːr] *zW:* **~en** *vt (verwirklichen)* to carry out; *(Person)* to take out; *(Hund)* to take for a walk; *(COMM)* to export; *(erklären)* to give details of; **~lich** *adj* detailed ♦ *adv* in detail; **A~lichkeit** *f* detail; **A~ung** *f* execution, performance; *(Durchführung)* completion; *(Herstellungsart)* version; *(Erklärung)* explanation

ausfüllen ['ausfʏlən] *vt* to fill up; *(Fragebogen etc)* to fill in; *(Beruf)* to be fulfilling for

Ausgabe ['ausgaːbə] *f (Geld)* expenditure, outlay; *(Aushändigung)* giving out; *(Gepäckausgabe)* left-luggage office; *(Buch)* edition; *(Nummer)* issue; *(COMPUT)* output

Ausgang ['ausgaŋ] *m* way out, exit; *(Ende)* end; *(~spunkt)* starting point; *(Ergebnis)* result; *(Ausgehtag)* free time, time off; **kein ~** no exit

Ausgangs- *zW:* **~punkt** *m* starting point; **~sperre** *f* curfew

ausgeben ['ausgeːbən] *(unreg) vt (Geld)* to spend; *(austeilen)* to issue, to distribute ♦ *vr:* **sich für etw/jdn ~** to pass o.s. off as sth/sb

ausgebucht ['ausgəbuːxt] *adj (Vorstellung, Flug, Maschine)* fully booked

ausgedient ['ausgədiːnt] *adj (Soldat)* discharged; *(verbraucht)* no longer in use; **~ haben** to have done good service

ausgefallen ['ausgəfalən] *adj (ungewöhnlich)* exceptional

ausgeglichen ['ausgəglɪçən] *adj* (well-) balanced; **A~heit** *f* balance; *(von Mensch)* even-temperedness

ausgehen ['ausgeːən] *(unreg) vi* to go out; *(zu Ende gehen)* to come to an end; *(Benzin)* to run out; *(Haare, Zähne)* to fall *od* come out; *(Feuer, Ofen, Licht)* to go out; *(Strom)* to go off; *(Resultat haben)* to turn out; **mir ging das Benzin aus** I ran out of petrol *(BRIT) od* gas *(US)*; **von etw ~** *(wegführen)* to lead away from sth; *(herrühren)* to come

from sth; *(zugrunde legen)* to proceed from sth; **wir können davon ~, dass ...** we can take as our starting point that ...; **leer ~** to get nothing

ausgelassen ['ausgəlasən] *adj* boisterous, high-spirited

ausgelastet ['ausgəlastət] *adj* fully occupied

ausgelernt ['ausgəlɛrnt] *adj* trained, qualified

ausgemacht ['ausgəmaxt] *adj* settled; *(umg: Dummkopf etc)* out-and-out, downright; **es war eine ~e Sache, dass ...** it was a foregone conclusion that ...

ausgenommen ['ausgənɔmən] *präp +gen* except ♦ *konj* except; **Anwesende sind ~** present company excepted

ausgeprägt ['ausgəprɛːkt] *adj* distinct

ausgerechnet ['ausgərɛçnət] *adv* just, precisely; **~ du/heute** you of all people/ today of all days

ausgeschlossen ['ausgəflɔsən] *adj (unmöglich)* impossible, out of the question

ausgeschnitten ['ausgəfnɪtən] *adj (Kleid)* low-necked

ausgesprochen ['ausgəfprɔxən] *adj (Faulheit, Lüge etc)* out-and-out; *(unverkennbar)* marked ♦ *adv* decidedly

ausgezeichnet ['ausgətsaɪçnət] *adj* excellent

ausgiebig ['ausgiːbɪç] *adj (Gebrauch)* thorough, good; *(Essen)* generous, lavish; **~ schlafen** to have a good sleep

ausgießen ['ausgiːsən] *vt* to pour out; *(Behälter)* to empty

Ausgleich ['ausglaɪç] *(-(e)s, -e) m* balance; *(Vermittlung)* reconciliation; *(SPORT)* equalization; **zum ~ einer Sache** *gen* in order to offset sth; **a~en** *(unreg) vt* to balance (out); to reconcile; *(Höhe)* to even up ♦ *vi (SPORT)* to equalize

ausgraben ['ausgraːbən] *(unreg) vt* to dig up; *(Leichen)* to exhume; *(fig)* to unearth

Ausgrabung *f* excavation; *(Ausgraben auch)* digging up

Ausguss ▲ ['ausgus] *m (Spüle)* sink; *(Abfluss)* outlet; *(Tülle)* spout

aushalten ['aushaltən] *(unreg) vt* to bear, to

stand; (Geliebte) to keep ♦ vi to hold out;
das ist nicht zum A~ that is unbearable

aushandeln ['aʊshandəln] vt to negotiate

aushändigen ['aʊshɛndɪgən] vt: **jdm etw ~**
to hand sth over to sb

Aushang ['aʊshaŋ] m notice

aushängen ['aʊshɛŋən] (unreg) vt (Meldung)
to put up; (Fenster) to take off its hinges
♦ vi to be displayed

ausharren ['aʊsharən] vi to hold out

ausheben ['aʊshe:bən] (unreg) vt (Erde) to
lift out; (Grube) to hollow out; (Tür) to take
off its hinges; (Diebesnest) to clear out; (MIL)
to enlist

aushecken ['aʊshɛkən] (umg) vt to cook up

aushelfen ['aʊshɛlfən] (unreg) vi: **jdm ~** to
help sb out

Aushilfe ['aʊshɪlfə] f help, assistance;
(Person) (temporary) worker

Aushilfs- zW: ~**kraft** f temporary worker;
a~**weise** adv temporarily, as a stopgap

ausholen ['aʊsho:lən] vi to swing one's arm
back; (zur Ohrfeige) to raise one's hand;
(beim Gehen) to take long strides

aushorchen ['aʊshɔrçən] vt to sound out,
to pump

auskennen ['aʊskɛnən] (unreg) vr to know a
lot; (an einem Ort) to know one's way
about; (in Fragen etc) to be knowledgeable

Ausklang ['aʊsklaŋ] m end

auskleiden ['aʊsklaɪdən] vr to undress ♦ vt
(Wand) to line

ausklingen ['aʊsklɪŋən] (unreg) vi (Ton, Lied)
to die away; (Fest) to peter out

ausklopfen ['aʊsklɔpfən] vt (Teppich) to
beat; (Pfeife) to knock out

auskochen ['aʊskɔxən] vt to boil; (MED) to
sterilize; **ausgekocht** (fig) out-and-out

Auskommen (-s) nt: **sein A~ haben** to
have a regular income; a~ (unreg) vi: **mit
jdm a~** to get on with sb; **mit etw a~** to
get by with sth

auskosten ['aʊskɔstən] vt to enjoy to the
full

auskundschaften ['aʊskʊntʃaftən] vt to
spy out; (Gebiet) to reconnoitre

Auskunft ['aʊskʊnft] (-, **-künfte**) f

information; (nähere) details pl, particulars
pl; (Stelle) information office; (TEL) directory
inquiries sg

auslachen ['aʊslaxən] vt to laugh at, to
mock

ausladen ['aʊsla:dən] (unreg) vt to unload;
(umg: Gäste) to cancel an invitation to

Auslage ['aʊsla:gə] f shop window (display);
~**n** pl (Ausgabe) outlay sg

Ausland ['aʊslant] nt foreign countries pl;
im ~ abroad; **ins ~** abroad

Ausländer(in) ['aʊslɛndər(ɪn)] (-s, -) m(f)
foreigner

ausländisch adj foreign

Auslands- zW: ~**gespräch** nt
international call; ~**reise** f trip abroad;
~**schutzbrief** m international travel cover

auslassen ['aʊslasən] (unreg) vt to leave
out; (Wort etc auch) to omit; (Fett) to melt;
(Kleidungsstück) to let out ♦ vr: **sich über
etw** akk ~ to speak one's mind about sth;
seine Wut etc **an jdm ~** to vent one's rage
etc on sb

Auslassung f omission

Auslauf ['aʊslaʊf] m (für Tiere) run; (Ausfluss)
outflow, outlet; a~**en** (unreg) vi to run out;
(Behälter) to leak; (NAUT) to put out (to
sea); (langsam aufhören) to run down

Ausläufer ['aʊslɔʏfər] m (von Gebirge) spur;
(Pflanze) runner; (MET: von Hoch) ridge;
(: von Tief) trough

ausleeren ['aʊsle:rən] vt to empty

auslegen ['aʊsle:gən] vt (Waren) to lay out;
(Köder) to put down; (Geld) to lend;
(bedecken) to cover; (Text etc) to interpret

Auslegung f interpretation

ausleiern ['aʊslaɪərn] vi (Gummi) to wear
out

Ausleihe ['aʊslaɪə] f issuing; (Stelle) issue
desk; a~**n** (unreg) vt (verleihen) to lend; **sich
dat etw a~n** to borrow sth

Auslese ['aʊsle:zə] f selection; (Elite) elite;
(Wein) choice wine; a~**n** (unreg) vt to
select; (umg: zu Ende lesen) to finish

ausliefern ['aʊsli:fərn] vt to deliver (up), to
hand over; (COMM) to deliver; **jdm / etw
ausgeliefert sein** to be at the mercy of

Spelling Reform: ▲ new spelling △ old spelling (to be phased out)

sb/sth

auslöschen ['aʊslœʃən] *vt* to extinguish; *(fig)* to wipe out, to obliterate

auslosen ['aʊslo:zən] *vt* to draw lots for

auslösen ['aʊslø:zən] *vt (Explosion, Schuss)* to set off; *(hervorrufen)* to cause, to produce; *(Gefangene)* to ransom; *(Pfand)* to redeem

ausmachen ['aʊsmaxən] *vt (Licht, Radio)* to turn off; *(Feuer)* to put out; *(entdecken)* to make out; *(vereinbaren)* to agree; *(beilegen)* to settle; *(Anteil darstellen, betragen)* to represent; *(bedeuten)* to matter; **macht es Ihnen was aus, wenn ...?** would you mind if ...?

ausmalen ['aʊsma:lən] *vt* to paint; *(fig)* to describe; **sich** *dat* **etw ~** to imagine sth

Ausmaß ['aʊsma:s] *nt* dimension; *(fig auch)* scale

ausmessen ['aʊsmɛsən] *(unreg) vt* to measure

Ausnahme ['aʊsna:mə] *f* exception; **~fall** *m* exceptional case; **~zustand** *m* state of emergency

ausnahms- *zW*: **~los** *adv* without exception; **~weise** *adv* by way of exception, for once

ausnehmen ['aʊsne:mən] *(unreg) vt* to take out, to remove; *(Tier)* to gut; *(Nest)* to rob; *(umg: Geld abnehmen)* to clean out; *(ausschließen)* to make an exception of ♦ *vr* to look, to appear; **~d** *adj* exceptional

ausnützen ['aʊsnʏtsən] *vt (Zeit, Gelegenheit)* to use, to turn to good account; *(Einfluss)* to use; *(Mensch, Gutmütigkeit)* to exploit

auspacken ['aʊspakən] *vt* to unpack

auspfeifen ['aʊspfaɪfən] *(unreg) vt* to hiss/ boo at

ausplaudern ['aʊsplaʊdərn] *vt (Geheimnis)* to blab

ausprobieren ['aʊsprobi:rən] *vt* to try (out)

Auspuff ['aʊspʊf] **(-(e)s, -e)** *m (TECH)* exhaust; **~rohr** *nt* exhaust (pipe)

ausradieren ['aʊsradi:rən] *vt* to erase, to rub out; *(fig)* to annihilate

ausrangieren ['aʊsrãʒi:rən] *(umg) vt* to chuck out

ausrauben ['aʊsraʊbən] *vt* to rob

ausräumen ['aʊsrɔymən] *vt (Dinge)* to clear away; *(Schrank, Zimmer)* to empty; *(Bedenken)* to dispel

ausrechnen ['aʊsrɛçnən] *vt* to calculate, to reckon

Ausrede ['aʊsre:də] *f* excuse; **a~n** *vi* to have one's say ♦ *vt*: **jdm etw a~n** to talk sb out of sth

ausreichen ['aʊsraɪçən] *vi* to suffice, to be enough; **~d** *adj* sufficient, adequate; *(SCH)* adequate

Ausreise ['aʊsraɪzə] *f* departure; **bei der ~** when leaving the country; **~erlaubnis** *f* exit visa; **a~n** *vi* to leave the country

ausreißen ['aʊsraɪsən] *(unreg) vt* to tear *od* pull out ♦ *vi (Riss bekommen)* to tear; *(umg)* to make off, to scram

ausrenken ['aʊsrɛŋkən] *vt* to dislocate

ausrichten ['aʊsrɪçtən] *vt (Botschaft)* to deliver; *(Gruß)* to pass on; *(Hochzeit etc)* to arrange; *(in gerade Linie bringen)* to get in a straight line; *(angleichen)* to bring into line; *(TYP)* to justify; **ich werde es ihm ~** I'll tell him; **etwas/nichts bei jdm ~** to get somewhere/nowhere with sb

ausrotten ['aʊsrɔtən] *vt* to stamp out, to exterminate

Ausruf ['aʊsru:f] *m (Schrei)* cry, exclamation; *(Bekanntmachung)* proclamation; **a~en** *(unreg) vt* to cry out, to exclaim; to call out; **~ezeichen** *nt* exclamation mark

ausruhen ['aʊsru:ən] *vt, vr* to rest

ausrüsten ['aʊsrʏstən] *vt* to equip, to fit out

Ausrüstung *f* equipment

ausrutschen ['aʊsrʊtʃən] *vi* to slip

Aussage ['aʊsza:gə] *f (JUR)* statement; **a~n** *vt* to say, to state ♦ *vi (JUR)* to give evidence

ausschalten ['aʊsʃaltən] *vt* to switch off; *(fig)* to eliminate

Ausschank ['aʊsʃaŋk] **(-(e)s, -schänke)** *m* dispensing, giving out; *(COMM)* selling; *(Theke)* bar

Ausschau ['aʊsʃaʊ] *f*: **~ halten (nach)** to look out (for), to watch (for); **a~en** *vi*: **a~en (nach)** to look out (for), to be on the look-out (for)

ausscheiden ['aʊsʃaɪdən] *(unreg) vt* to take

out; (MED) to secrete ♦ vi: ~ **(aus)** to leave;
(SPORT) to be eliminated (from) od knocked
out (of)
Ausscheidung f separation; secretion;
elimination; (aus Amt) retirement
ausschenken ['aʊsʃɛŋkən] vt (Alkohol,
Kaffee) to pour out; (COMM) to sell
ausschildern ['aʊsʃɪldərn] vt to signpost
ausschimpfen ['aʊsʃɪmpfən] vt to scold, to
tell off
ausschlafen ['aʊsʃlaːfən] (unreg) vi, vr to
have a good sleep ♦ vt to sleep off; **ich bin
nicht ausgeschlafen** I didn't have od get
enough sleep
Ausschlag ['aʊsʃlaːk] m (MED) rash;
(Pendelausschlag) swing; (Nadelausschlag)
deflection; **den ~ geben** (fig) to tip the
balance; a~en [-gən] (unreg) vt to knock
out; (auskleiden) to deck out; (verweigern) to
decline ♦ vi (Pferd) to kick out; (BOT) to
sprout; a~gebend adj decisive
ausschließen ['aʊsʃliːsən] (unreg) vt to shut
od lock out; (fig) to exclude
ausschließlich adj exclusive ♦ adv
exclusively ♦ präp +gen exclusive of,
excluding
Ausschluss ▲ ['aʊsʃlʊs] m exclusion
ausschmücken ['aʊsʃmʏkən] vt to
decorate; (fig) to embellish
ausschneiden ['aʊsʃnaɪdən] (unreg) vt to
cut out; (Büsche) to trim
Ausschnitt ['aʊsʃnɪt] m (Teil) section; (von
Kleid) neckline; (Zeitungsausschnitt) cutting;
(aus Film etc) excerpt
ausschreiben ['aʊsʃraɪbən] (unreg) vt (ganz
schreiben) to write out (in full); (ausstellen)
to write (out); (Stelle, Wettbewerb etc) to
announce, to advertise
Ausschreitung ['aʊsʃraɪtʊŋ] f (usu pl) riot
Ausschuss ▲ ['aʊsʃʊs] m committee,
board; (Abfall) waste, scraps pl; (COMM:
auch: ~ware) reject
ausschütten ['aʊsʃʏtən] vt to pour out;
(Eimer) to empty; (Geld) to pay ♦ vr to
shake (with laughter)
ausschweifend ['aʊsʃvaɪfənt] adj (Leben)
dissipated, debauched; (Fantasie)

extravagant
aussehen ['aʊszeːən] (unreg) vi to look; **es
sieht nach Regen aus** it looks like rain; **es
sieht schlecht aus** things look bad; A~ (-
s) nt appearance
aus sein ▲ siehe aus
außen ['aʊsən] adv outside; (nach ~)
outwards; ~ **ist es rot** it's red (on the)
outside
Außen- zW: ~**dienst** m: **im ~dienst sein**
to work outside the office; ~**handel** m
foreign trade; ~**minister** m foreign
minister; ~**ministerium** nt foreign office;
~**politik** f foreign policy; a~**politisch** adj
(Entwicklung, Lage) foreign; ~**seite** f
outside; ~**seiter** (-s, -) m outsider;
~**stände** pl outstanding debts;
~**stehende(r)** f(m) outsider; ~**welt** f
outside world
außer ['aʊsər] präp +dat (räumlich) out of;
(abgesehen von) except ♦ konj
(ausgenommen) except; ~ **Gefahr** out of
danger; ~ **Zweifel** beyond any doubt; ~
Betrieb out of order; ~ **Dienst** retired; ~
Landes abroad; ~ **sich** dat sein to be
beside o.s.; ~ **sich** akk **geraten** to go wild;
~ **wenn** unless; ~ **dass** except; ~**dem** konj
besides, in addition
äußere(r, s) ['ɔʏsərə(r,s)] adj outer, external
außergewöhnlich adj unusual
außerhalb präp +gen outside ♦ adv outside
äußerlich adj external
äußern vt to utter, to express; (zeigen) to
show ♦ vr to give one's opinion; (Krankheit
etc) to show itself
außerordentlich adj extraordinary
außerplanmäßig adj unscheduled
äußerst ['ɔʏsərst] adv extremely, most; ~**e(r,
s)** adj utmost; (räumlich) farthest; (Termin)
last possible; (Preis) highest
Äußerung f remark, comment
aussetzen ['aʊszɛtsən] vt (Kind, Tier) to
abandon; (Boote) to lower; (Belohnung) to
offer; (Urteil, Verfahren) to postpone ♦ vi
(aufhören) to stop; (Pause machen) to have a
break; **jdm/etw ausgesetzt sein** to be
exposed to sb/sth; **an jdm/etw etwas ~** to

find fault with sb/sth

Aussicht ['auszɪçt] *f* view; (*in Zukunft*) prospect; **etw in ~ haben** to have sth in view

Aussichts- *zW*: **a~los** *adj* hopeless; **~punkt** *m* viewpoint; **a~reich** *adj* promising; **~turm** *m* observation tower

aussöhnen ['auszø:nən] *vt* to reconcile ♦ *vr* to reconcile o.s., to become reconciled

aussondern ['auszɔndərn] *vt* to separate, to select

aussortieren ['auszɔrti:rən] *vt* to sort out

ausspannen ['ausʃpanən] *vt* to spread *od* stretch out; (*Pferd*) to unharness; (*umg: Mädchen*): **(jdm) jdn ~** to steal sb (from sb) ♦ *vi* to relax

aussperren ['ausʃpɛrən] *vt* to lock out

ausspielen ['ausʃpi:lən] *vt* (*Karte*) to lead; (*Geldprämie*) to offer as a prize ♦ *vi* (*KARTEN*) to lead; **jdn gegen jdn ~** to play sb off against sb; **ausgespielt haben** to be finished

Aussprache ['ausʃpra:xə] *f* pronunciation; (*Unterredung*) (frank) discussion

aussprechen ['ausʃprɛçən] (*unreg*) *vt* to pronounce; (*äußern*) to say, to express ♦ *vr* (*sich äußern*): **sich ~ (über** +*akk*) to speak (about); (*sich anvertrauen*) to unburden o.s. (about *od* on); (*diskutieren*) to discuss ♦ *vi* (*zu Ende sprechen*) to finish speaking

Ausspruch ['ausʃprʊx] *m* saying, remark

ausspülen ['ausʃpy:lən] *vt* to wash out; (*Mund*) to rinse

Ausstand ['ausʃtant] *m* strike; **in den ~ treten** to go on strike

ausstatten ['ausʃtatən] *vt* (*Zimmer etc*) to furnish; (*Person*) to equip, to kit out

Ausstattung *f* (*Ausstatten*) provision; (*Kleidung*) outfit; (*Aufmachung*) make-up; (*Einrichtung*) furnishing

ausstechen ['ausʃtɛçən] (*unreg*) *vt* (*Augen, Rasen, Graben*) to dig out; (*Kekse*) to cut out; (*übertreffen*) to outshine

ausstehen ['ausʃte:ən] (*unreg*) *vt* to stand, to endure ♦ *vi* (*noch nicht da sein*) to be outstanding

aussteigen ['ausʃtaɪgən] (*unreg*) *vi* to get

out, to alight

ausstellen ['ausʃtɛlən] *vt* to exhibit, to display; (*umg: ausschalten*) to switch off; (*Rechnung etc*) to make out; (*Pass, Zeugnis*) to issue

Ausstellung *f* exhibition; (*FIN*) drawing up; (*einer Rechnung*) making out; (*eines Passes etc*) issuing

aussterben ['ausʃtɛrbən] (*unreg*) *vi* to die out

Aussteuer ['ausʃtɔyər] *f* dowry

Ausstieg ['ausʃti:k] (**-(e)s, -e**) *m* exit

ausstopfen ['ausʃtɔpfən] *vt* to stuff

ausstoßen ['ausʃto:sən] (*unreg*) *vt* (*Luft, Rauch*) to give off, to emit; (*aus Verein etc*) to expel, to exclude; (*Auge*) to poke out

ausstrahlen ['ausʃtra:lən] *vt, vi* to radiate; (*RADIO*) to broadcast

Ausstrahlung *f* radiation; (*fig*) charisma

ausstrecken ['ausʃtrɛkən] *vt, vr* to stretch out

ausstreichen ['ausʃtraɪçən] (*unreg*) *vt* to cross out; (*glätten*) to smooth (out)

ausströmen ['ausʃtrø:mən] *vi* (*Gas*) to pour out, to escape ♦ *vt* to give off; (*fig*) to radiate

aussuchen ['auszu:xən] *vt* to select, to pick out

Austausch ['austauʃ] *m* exchange; **a~bar** *adj* exchangeable; **a~en** *vt* to exchange, to swap

austeilen ['austaɪlən] *vt* to distribute, to give out

Auster ['austər] (**-, -n**) *f* oyster

austoben ['austo:bən] *vr* (*Kind*) to run wild; (*Erwachsene*) to sow one's wild oats

austragen ['austra:gən] (*unreg*) *vt* (*Post*) to deliver; (*Streit etc*) to decide; (*Wettkämpfe*) to hold

Australien [aus'tra:liən] (**-s**) *nt* Australia; **Australier(in)** (**-s, -**) *m(f)* Australian; **australisch** *adj* Australian

austreiben ['austraɪbən] (*unreg*) *vt* to drive out, to expel; (*Geister*) to exorcize

austreten ['austre:tən] (*unreg*) *vi* (*zur Toilette*) to be excused ♦ *vt* (*Feuer*) to tread out, to trample; (*Schuhe*) to wear out; (*Treppe*) to wear down; **aus etw ~** to leave sth

austrinken ['austrɪŋkən] (*unreg*) *vt* (*Glas*) to drain; (*Getränk*) to drink up ♦ *vi* to finish one's drink, to drink up

Austritt ['austrɪt] *m* emission; (*aus Verein, Partei etc*) retirement, withdrawal

austrocknen ['austrɔknən] *vt, vi* to dry up

ausüben ['aus|y:bən] *vt* (*Beruf*) to practise, to carry out; (*Funktion*) to perform; (*Einfluss*) to exert; **einen Reiz auf jdn ~** to hold an attraction for sb; **eine Wirkung auf jdn ~** to have an effect on sb

Ausverkauf ['ausfɛrkauf] *m* sale; **a~en** *vt* to sell out; (*Geschäft*) to sell up; **a~t** *adj* (*Karten, Artikel*) sold out; (*THEAT: Haus*) full

Auswahl ['ausva:l] *f*: **eine ~ (an** +*dat*) a selection (of), a choice (of)

auswählen ['ausvɛ:lən] *vt* to select, to choose

Auswander- ['ausvandər] *zW*: **~er** *m* emigrant; **a~n** *vi* to emigrate; **~ung** *f* emigration

auswärtig ['ausvɛrtɪç] *adj* (*nicht am/vom Ort*) out-of-town; (*ausländisch*) foreign

auswärts ['ausvɛrts] *adv* outside; (*nach außen*) outwards; **~ essen** to eat out; **A~spiel** ['ausvɛrtsʃsi:l] *nt* away game

auswechseln ['ausvɛksəln] *vt* to change, to substitute

Ausweg ['ausve:k] *m* way out; **a~los** *adj* hopeless

ausweichen ['ausvaiçən] (*unreg*) *vi*: **jdm/ etw ~** to move aside *od* make way for sb/ sth; (*fig*) to side-step sb/sth; **~d** *adj* evasive

ausweinen ['ausvainən] *vr* to have a (good) cry

Ausweis ['ausvais] *m* (**-es, -e**) identity card; passport; (*Mitgliedsausweis, Bibliotheksausweis etc*) card; **a~en** [-zən] (*unreg*) *vt* to expel, to banish ♦ *vr* to prove one's identity; **~kontrolle** *f* identity check; **~papiere** *pl* identity papers; **~ung** *f* expulsion

ausweiten ['ausvaitən] *vt* to stretch

auswendig ['ausvɛndɪç] *adv* by heart

auswerten ['ausvɛrtən] *vt* to evaluate; **Auswertung** *f* evaluation, analysis; (*Nutzung*) utilization

auswirken ['ausvɪrkən] *vr* to have an effect; **Auswirkung** *f* effect

auswischen ['ausvɪʃən] *vt* to wipe out; **jdm eins ~** (*umg*) to put one over on sb

Auswuchs ['ausvu:ks] *m* (out)growth; (*fig*) product

auszahlen ['austsa:lən] *vt* (*Lohn, Summe*) to pay out; (*Arbeiter*) to pay off; (*Miterbe*) to buy out ♦ *vr* (*sich lohnen*) to pay

auszählen ['austsɛ:lən] *vt* (*Stimmen*) to count

auszeichnen ['austsaiçnən] *vt* to honour; (*MIL*) to decorate; (*COMM*) to price ♦ *vr* to distinguish o.s.

Auszeichnung *f* distinction; (*COMM*) pricing; (*Ehrung*) awarding of decoration; (*Ehre*) honour; (*Orden*) decoration; **mit ~** with distinction

ausziehen ['austsi:ən] (*unreg*) *vt* (*Kleidung*) to take off; (*Haare, Zähne, Tisch etc*) to pull out; (*nachmalen*) to trace ♦ *vr* to undress ♦ *vi* (*aufbrechen*) to leave; (*aus Wohnung*) to move out

Auszubildende(r) ['austsubɪldəndə(r)] *f(m)* trainee

Auszug ['austsu:k] *m* (*aus Wohnung*) removal; (*aus Buch etc*) extract; (*Konto~*) statement; (*Ausmarsch*) departure

Auto ['auto] (**-s, -s**) *nt* (motor)car; **~ fahren** to drive; **~atlas** *m* road atlas; **~bahn** *f* motorway; **~bahndreieck** *nt* motorway junction; **~bahngebühr** *f* toll; **~bahnkreuz** *nt* motorway intersection; **~bus** *m* bus; **~fähre** *f* car ferry; **~fahrer(in)** *m(f)* motorist, driver; **~fahrt** *f* drive; **a~gen** [-'ge:n] *adj* autogenous; **~'gramm** *nt* autograph

Autobahn

*An **Autobahn** is a motorway. In former West Germany there is a widespread motorway network but in the former **DDR** the motorways are somewhat less extensive. There is no overall speed limit but a limit of 130 km/hour is recommended and there are lower mandatory limits on certain stretches of road. As yet there are no tolls payable on*

German Autobahnen. However, a yearly toll is payable in Switzerland and tolls have been introduced in Austria.

Auto- *zW:* **~'mat** (**-en, -en**) *m* machine; **~matik** [aʊtoˈmaːtɪk] *f* (*AUT*) automatic; **a~'matisch** *adj* automatic; **a~nom** [-ˈnoːm] *adj* autonomous

Autor(in) [ˈaʊtɔr(ɪn)] (**-s, -en**) *m(f)* author

Auto- *zW:* **~radio** *nt* car radio; **~reifen** *m* car tyre; **~reisezug** *m* motorail train; **~rennen** *nt* motor racing

autoritär [aʊtoriˈtɛːr] *adj* authoritarian

Autorität *f* authority

Auto- *zW:* **~telefon** *nt* car phone; **~unfall** *m* car *od* motor accident; **~vermietung** *m* car hire (*BRIT*) *od* rental (*US*); **~waschanlage** *f* car wash

Axt [akst] (**-, ⁻e**) *f* axe

B, b

Baby [ˈbeːbi] (**-s, -s**) *nt* baby; **~nahrung** *f* baby food; **~sitter** (**-s, -**) *m* baby-sitter

Bach [bax] (**-(e)s, ⁻e**) *m* stream, brook

Backbord (**-(e)s, -e**) *nt* (*NAUT*) port

Backe [ˈbakə] *f* cheek

backen [ˈbakən] (*unreg*) *vt, vi* to bake

Backenzahn *m* molar

Bäcker [ˈbɛkər(ɪn)] (**-s, -**) *m* baker; **~ei** *f* bakery; (*~eiladen*) baker's (shop)

Back- *zW:* **~form** *f* baking tin; **~obst** *nt* dried fruit; **~ofen** *m* oven; **~pflaume** *f* prune; **~pulver** *nt* baking powder; **~stein** *m* brick

Bad [baːt] (**-(e)s, ⁻er**) *nt* bath; (*Schwimmen*) bathe; (*Ort*) spa

Bade- [ˈbaːdə] *zW:* **~anstalt** *f* (swimming) baths *pl*; **~anzug** *m* bathing suit; **~hose** *f* bathing *od* swimming trunks *pl*; **~kappe** *f* bathing cap; **~mantel** *m* bath(ing) robe; **~meister** *m* baths attendant; **b~n** *vi* to bathe, to have a bath ♦ *vt* to bath; **~ort** *m* spa; **~tuch** *nt* bath towel; **~wanne** *f* bath (tub); **~zimmer** *nt* bathroom

Bagatelle [bagaˈtɛlə] *f* trifle

Bagger [ˈbagər] (**-s, -**) *m* excavator; (*NAUT*) dredger; **b~n** *vt, vi* to excavate; to dredge

Bahn [baːn] (**-, -en**) *f* railway, railroad (*US*); (*Weg*) road, way; (*Spur*) lane; (*Rennbahn*) track; (*ASTRON*) orbit; (*Stoffbahn*) length; **b~brechend** *adj* pioneering; **~Card** [ˈbaːnkaːrd] (**-, -s**) ® *f* ≈ railcard; **~damm** *m* railway embankment; **b~en** *vt:* **sich/ jdm einen Weg b~en** to clear a way/a way for sb; **~fahrt** *f* railway journey; **~fracht** *f* rail freight; **~hof** (**-, -s**) *m* station; **auf dem ~hof** at the station; **~hofshalle** *f* station concourse; **~linie** *f* (railway) line; **~steig** *m* platform; **~übergang** *m* level crossing, grade crossing (*US*)

Bahre [ˈbaːrə] *f* stretcher

Bakterien [bakˈteːriən] *pl* bacteria *pl*

Balance [baˈlãːsə] *f* balance, equilibrium

balan'cieren *vt, vi* to balance

bald [balt] *adv* (*zeitlich*) soon; (*beinahe*) almost; **~ig** [ˈbaldɪç] *adj* early, speedy

Baldrian [ˈbaldriaːn] (**-s, -e**) *m* valerian

Balkan [ˈbalkaːn] (**-s**) *m:* **der ~** the Balkans *pl*

Balken [ˈbalkən] (**-s, -**) *m* beam; (*Tragbalken*) girder; (*Stützbalken*) prop

Balkon [balˈkõː] (**-s, -s** *od* **-e**) *m* balcony; (*THEAT*) (dress) circle

Ball [bal] (**-(e)s, ⁻e**) *m* ball; (*Tanz*) dance, ball

Ballast [ˈbalast] (**-(e)s, -e**) *m* ballast; (*fig*) weight, burden

Ballen [ˈbalən] (**-s, -**) *m* bale; (*ANAT*) ball; **b~** *vt* (*formen*) to make into a ball; (*Faust*) to clench ♦ *vr* (*Wolken etc*) to build up; (*Menschen*) to gather

Ballett [baˈlɛt] (**-(e)s, -e**) *nt* ballet

Ballkleid *nt* evening dress

Ballon [baˈlõː] (**-s, -s** *od* **-e**) *m* balloon

Ballspiel *nt* ball game

Ballungsgebiet [ˈbalʊŋsgəbiːt] *nt* conurbation

Baltikum [ˈbaltikʊm] (**-s**) *nt:* **das ~** the Baltic States

Banane [baˈnaːnə] *f* banana

Band¹ [bant] (**-(e)s, ⁻e**) *m* (*Buchband*) volume

Band² (-(e)s, ⁻er) nt (Stoffband) ribbon, tape; (Fließband) production line; (Tonband) tape; (ANAT) ligament; **etw auf ~ aufnehmen** to tape sth; **am laufenden ~** (umg) non-stop

Band³ (-(e)s, -e) nt (Freundschaftsband etc) bond

Band⁴ [bɛnt] (-, -s) f band, group

band etc vb siehe **binden**

Bandage [ban'daːʒə] f bandage

banda'gieren vt to bandage

Bande ['bandə] f band; (Straßenbande) gang

bändigen ['bɛndɪɡən] vt (Tier) to tame; (Trieb, Leidenschaft) to control, to restrain

Bandit [ban'diːt] (-en, -en) m bandit

Band- zW: **~nudel** f (KOCH: gew pl) ribbon noodles pl; **~scheibe** f (ANAT) disc; **~wurm** m tapeworm

bange ['baŋə] adj scared; (besorgt) anxious; **jdm wird es ~** sb is becoming scared; **jdm B~ machen** to scare sb; **~n** vi: **um jdn/ etw ~n** to be anxious od worried about sb/sth

Bank¹ [baŋk] (-, ⁻e) f (Sitz~) bench; (Sand~ etc) (sand)bank, (sand)bar

Bank² [baŋk] (-, -en) f (Geldbank) bank; **~anweisung** f banker's order; **~einzug** m direct debit

Bankett [baŋ'kɛt] (-(e)s, -e) nt (Essen) banquet; (Straßenrand) verge (BRIT), shoulder (US)

Bankier [baŋki'eː] (-s, -s) m banker

Bank- zW: **~konto** m bank account; **~leitzahl** f bank sort code number; **~note** f banknote; **~raub** m bank robbery

Bankrott [baŋ'krɔt] (-(e)s, -e) m bankruptcy; **~ machen** to go bankrupt; **b~** adj bankrupt

Bankverbindung f banking arrangements pl; **geben Sie bitte Ihre ~ an** please give your account details

Bann [ban] (-(e)s, -e) m (HIST) ban; (Kirchenbann) excommunication; (fig: Zauber) spell; **b~en** vt (Geister) to exorcize; (Gefahr) to avert; (bezaubern) to enchant; (HIST) to banish

Banner (-s, -) nt banner, flag

Bar (-, -s) f bar

bar [baːr] adj (+gen) (unbedeckt) bare; (frei von) lacking (in); (offenkundig) utter, sheer; **~e(s) Geld** cash; **etw (in) ~ bezahlen** to pay sth (in) cash; **etw für ~e Münze nehmen** (fig) to take sth at its face value

Bär [bɛːr] (-en, -en) m bear

Baracke [ba'rakə] f hut

barbarisch [bar'baːrɪʃ] adj barbaric, barbarous

Bar- zW: **b~fuß** adj barefoot; **~geld** nt cash, ready money; **b~geldlos** adj non-cash

Barkauf m cash purchase

Barkeeper ['baːrkiːpər] (-s, -) m barman, bartender

barmherzig [barm'hɛrtsɪç] adj merciful, compassionate

Baron [ba'roːn] (-s, -e) m baron; **~in** f baroness

Barren ['barən] (-s, -) m parallel bars pl; (Goldbarren) ingot

Barriere [bari'eːrə] f barrier

Barrikade [bari'kaːdə] f barricade

Barsch [barʃ] (-(e)s, -e) m perch

barsch [barʃ] adj brusque, gruff

Bar- zW: **~schaft** f ready money; **~scheck** m open od uncrossed cheque (BRIT), open check (US)

Bart [baːrt] (-(e)s, ⁻e) m beard; (Schlüsselbart) bit; **bärtig** ['bɛːrtɪç] adj bearded

Barzahlung f cash payment

Base ['baːzə] f (CHEM) base; (Kusine) cousin

Basel ['baːzəl] nt Basle

Basen pl von **Base**; **Basis**

basieren [ba'ziːrən] vt to base ♦ vi to be based

Basis ['baːzɪs] (-, **Basen**) f basis

Bass ▲ [bas] (-es, ⁻e) m bass

Bassin [ba'sɛ̃ː] (-s, -s) nt pool

basteln ['bastəln] vt to make ♦ vi to do handicrafts

bat etc [baːt] vb siehe **bitten**

Bataillon [batal'joːn] (-s, -e) nt battalion

Batik ['baːtɪk] f (Verfahren) batik

Batterie [batə'riː] f battery

Bau [bau] (-(e)s) m (~en) building,

construction; (*Aufbau*) structure; (*Körperbau*) frame; (*~stelle*) building site; (*pl ~e: Tierbau*) hole, burrow; (: *MIN*) working(s); (*pl ~ten: Gebäude*) building; **sich im ~ befinden** to be under construction; **~arbeiten** *pl* building *od* construction work *sg*; **~arbeiter** *m* building worker

Bauch [baʊx] **(-(e)s, Bäuche)** *m* belly; (*ANAT auch*) stomach, abdomen; **~fell** *nt* peritoneum; **b~ig** *adj* bulbous; **~nabel** *m* navel; **~redner** *m* ventriloquist; **~schmerzen** *pl* stomachache; **~weh** *nt* stomachache

Baudenkmal *nt* historical monument

bauen ['baʊən] *vt, vi* to build; (*TECH*) to construct; **auf jdn/etw ~** to depend *od* count upon sb/sth

Bauer¹ ['baʊər] **(-n** *od* **-s, -n)** *m* farmer; (*Schach*) pawn

Bauer² ['baʊər] **(-s, -)** *nt od m* (bird)cage

Bäuerin ['bɔʏərɪn] *f* farmer; (*Frau des Bauers*) farmer's wife

bäuerlich *adj* rustic

Bauern- *zW*: **~haus** *nt* farmhouse; **~hof** *m* farm(yard)

Bau- *zW*: **b~fällig** *adj* dilapidated; **~gelände** *f* building site; **~genehmigung** *f* building permit; **~gerüst** *nt* scaffolding; **~herr** *m* purchaser; **~kasten** *m* box of bricks; **~land** *nt* building land; **b~lich** *adj* structural

Baum [baʊm] **(-(e)s, Bäume)** *m* tree

baumeln ['baʊməln] *vi* to dangle

bäumen ['bɔʏmən] *vr* to rear (up)

Baum- *zW*: **~schule** *f* nursery; **~stamm** *m* tree trunk; **~stumpf** *m* tree stump; **~wolle** *f* cotton

Bau- *zW*: **~plan** *m* architect's plan; **~platz** *m* building site

bauspar- *zW*: **~en** *vi* to save with a building society; **B~kasse** *f* building society; **B~vertrag** *m* building society savings agreement

Bau- *zW*: **~stein** *m* building stone, freestone; **~stelle** *f* building site; **~teil** *nt* prefabricated part (of building); **~ten** *pl von* **Bau**; **~unternehmer** *m* building

contractor; **~weise** *f* (method of) construction; **~werk** *nt* building; **~zaun** *m* hoarding

Bayern ['baɪərn] *nt* Bavaria

bayrisch ['baɪrɪʃ] *adj* Bavarian

Bazillus [ba'tsɪlʊs] **(-, Bazillen)** *m* bacillus

beabsichtigen [bə'apzɪçtɪgən] *vt* to intend

beacht- [bə'|axt] *zW*: **~en** *vt* to take note of; (*Vorschrift*) to obey; (*Vorfahrt*) to observe; **~lich** *adj* considerable; **B~ung** *f* notice, attention, observation

Beamte(r) [bə'|amtə(r)] **(-n, -n)** *m* official; (*Staatsbeamte*) civil servant; (*Bankbeamte etc*) employee

Beamtin *f siehe* **Beamte(r)**

beängstigend [bə'|ɛŋstɪgənt] *adj* alarming

beanspruchen [bə'|anʃprʊxən] *vt* to claim; (*Zeit, Platz*) to take up, to occupy; **jdn ~** to take up sb's time

beanstanden [bə'|anʃtandən] *vt* to complain about, to object to

beantragen [bə'|antra:gən] *vt* to apply for, to ask for

beantworten [bə'|antvɔrtən] *vt* to answer; **Beantwortung** *f* (*+gen*) reply (to)

bearbeiten [bə'|arbaɪtən] *vt* to work; (*Material*) to process; (*Thema*) to deal with; (*Land*) to cultivate; (*CHEM*) to treat; (*Buch*) to revise; (*umg: beeinflussen wollen*) to work on

Bearbeitung *f* processing; cultivation; treatment; revision

Bearbeitungsgebühr *f* handling charge

Beatmung [bə'|a:tmʊŋ] *f* respiration

beaufsichtigen [bə'|aʊfzɪçtɪgən] *vt* to supervise; **Beaufsichtigung** *f* supervision

beauftragen [bə'|aʊftra:gən] *vt* to instruct; **jdn mit etw ~** to entrust sb with sth

Beauftragte(r) *f(m)* representative

bebauen [bə'baʊən] *vt* to build on; (*AGR*) to cultivate

beben ['be:bən] *vi* to tremble, to shake; **B~ (-s, -)** *nt* earthquake

Becher ['bɛçər] **(-s, -)** *m* mug; (*ohne Henkel*) tumbler

Becken ['bɛkən] **(-s, -)** *nt* basin; (*MUS*) cymbal; (*ANAT*) pelvis

bedacht [bə'daxt] *adj* thoughtful, careful;
auf etw *akk* ~ **sein** to be concerned about
sth

bedächtig [bə'dɛçtıç] *adj* (*umsichtig*)
thoughtful, reflective; (*langsam*) slow,
deliberate

bedanken [bə'daŋkən] *vr*: **sich (bei jdm)** ~
to say thank you (to sb)

Bedarf [bə'darf] **(-(e)s)** *m* need,
requirement; (*COMM*) demand; **je nach** ~
according to demand; **bei** ~ if necessary; ~
an etw *dat* **haben** to be in need of sth

Bedarfs- *zW*: **~fall** *m* case of need;
~haltestelle *f* request stop

bedauerlich [bə'dauərlıç] *adj* regrettable

bedauern [bə'dauərn] *vt* to be sorry for;
(*bemitleiden*) to pity; **B~ (-s)** *nt* regret;
~swert *adj* (*Zustände*) regrettable; (*Mensch*)
pitiable, unfortunate

bedecken [bə'dɛkən] *vt* to cover

bedeckt *adj* covered; (*Himmel*) overcast

bedenken [bə'dɛŋkən] (*unreg*) *vt* to think
over, to consider

Bedenken (-s, -) *nt* (*Überlegen*)
consideration; (*Zweifel*) doubt; (*Skrupel*)
scruple

bedenklich *adj* doubtful; (*bedrohlich*)
dangerous, risky

Bedenkzeit *f* time to think

bedeuten [bə'dɔytən] *vt* to mean; to signify;
(*wichtig sein*) to be of importance; **~d** *adj*
important; (*beträchtlich*) considerable

bedeutsam *adj* (*wichtig*) significant

Bedeutung *f* meaning; significance;
(*Wichtigkeit*) importance; **b~slos** *adj*
insignificant, unimportant; **b~svoll** *adj*
momentous, significant

bedienen [bə'di:nən] *vt* to serve; (*Maschine*)
to work, to operate ♦ *vr* (*beim Essen*) to
help o.s.; **sich jds / einer Sache** ~ to make
use of sb/sth

Bedienung *f* service; (*Kellnerin*) waitress;
(*Verkäuferin*) shop assistant; (*Zuschlag*)
service (charge)

Bedienungsanleitung *f* operating
instructions *pl*

bedingen [bə'dıŋən] *vt* (*verursachen*) to

cause

bedingt *adj* (*Richtigkeit, Tauglichkeit*) limited;
(*Zusage, Annahme*) conditional

Bedingung *f* condition; (*Voraussetzung*)
stipulation; **b~slos** *adj* unconditional

bedrängen [bə'drɛŋən] *vt* to pester, to
harass

bedrohen [bə'dro:ən] *vt* to threaten;
Bedrohung *f* threat, menace

bedrücken [bə'drykən] *vt* to oppress, to
trouble

bedürf- [bə'dyrf] *zW*: **~en** (*unreg*) *vi* +*gen* to
need, to require; **B~nis (-ses, -se)** *nt*
need; **~tig** *adj* in need, poor, needy

beeilen [bə'ailən] *vr* to hurry

beeindrucken [bə'aindrʊkən] *vt* to
impress, to make an impression on

beeinflussen [bə'ainflʊsən] *vt* to influence

beeinträchtigen [bə'aintrɛçtıgən] *vt* to
affect adversely; (*Freiheit*) to infringe upon

beend(ig)en [bə'ɛnd(ıg)ən] *vt* to end, to
finish, to terminate

beengen [bə'ɛŋən] *vt* to cramp; (*fig*) to
hamper, to oppress

beerben [bə'ɛrbən] *vt*: **jdn** ~ to inherit from
sb

beerdigen [bə'e:rdıgən] *vt* to bury;
Beerdigung *f* funeral, burial

Beere ['be:rə] *f* berry; (*Traubenbeere*) grape

Beet [be:t] **(-(e)s, -e)** *nt* bed

befähigen [bə'fɛ:ıgən] *vt* to enable

befähigt *adj* (*begabt*) talented; ~ (**für**)
(*fähig*) capable (of)

Befähigung *f* capability; (*Begabung*) talent,
aptitude

befahrbar [bə'fa:rba:r] *adj* passable; (*NAUT*)
navigable

befahren [bə'fa:rən] (*unreg*) *vt* to use, to
drive over; (*NAUT*) to navigate ♦ *adj* used

befallen [bə'falən] (*unreg*) *vt* to come over

befangen [bə'faŋən] *adj* (*schüchtern*) shy,
self-conscious; (*voreingenommen*) biased

befassen [bə'fasən] *vr* to concern o.s.

Befehl [bə'fe:l] **(-(e)s, -e)** *m* command,
order; **b~en** (*unreg*) *vt* to order ♦ *vi* to give
orders; **jdm etw b~en** to order sb to do
sth; **~sverweigerung** *f* insubordination

befestigen [bə'fɛstɪgən] *vt* to fasten; (*stärken*) to strengthen; (*MIL*) to fortify; **~ an** +*dat* to fasten to

Befestigung *f* fastening; strengthening; (*MIL*) fortification

befeuchten [bə'fɔyçtən] *vt* to damp(en), to moisten

befinden [bə'fɪndən] (*unreg*) *vr* to be; (*sich fühlen*) to feel ♦ *vt*: **jdn/etw für** *od* **als etw ~** to deem sb/sth to be sth ♦ *vi*: **~ (über** +*akk*) to decide (on), to adjudicate (on); **B~ (-s)** *nt* health, condition; (*Meinung*) view, opinion

befolgen [bə'fɔlgən] *vt* to comply with, to follow

befördern [bə'fœrdərn] *vt* (*senden*) to transport, to send; (*beruflich*) to promote; **Beförderung** *f* transport; promotion

befragen [bə'fra:gən] *vt* to question

befreien [bə'fraɪən] *vt* to set free; (*erlassen*) to exempt; **Befreiung** *f* liberation, release; (*Erlassen*) exemption

befreunden [bə'frɔyndən] *vr* to make friends; (*mit Idee etc*) to acquaint o.s.

befreundet *adj* friendly

befriedigen [bə'fri:dɪgən] *vt* to satisfy; **~d** *adj* satisfactory

Befriedigung *f* satisfaction, gratification

befristet [bə'frɪstət] *adj* limited

befruchten [bə'fruxtən] *vt* to fertilize; (*fig*) to stimulate

Befruchtung *f*: **künstliche ~** artificial insemination

Befugnis [bə'fu:knɪs] **(-, -se)** *f* authorization, powers *pl*

befugt *adj* authorized, entitled

Befund [bə'fʊnt] **(-(e)s, -e)** *m* findings *pl*; (*MED*) diagnosis

befürchten [bə'fʏrçtən] *vt* to fear; **Befürchtung** *f* fear, apprehension

befürworten [bə'fy:rvɔrtən] *vt* to support, to speak in favour of; **Befürworter (-s, -)** *m* supporter, advocate

begabt [bə'ga:pt] *adj* gifted

Begabung [bə'ga:bʊŋ] *f* talent, gift

begann *etc* [bə'gan] *vb siehe* **beginnen**

begeben [bə'ge:bən] (*unreg*) *vr* (*gehen*) to betake o.s.; (*geschehen*) to occur; **sich ~ nach** *od* **zu** to proceed to(wards); **B~heit** *f* occurrence

begegnen [bə'ge:gnən] *vi*: **jdm ~** to meet sb; (*behandeln*) to treat sb; **einer Sache** *dat* **~** to meet with sth

Begegnung *f* meeting

begehen [bə'ge:ən] (*unreg*) *vt* (*Straftat*) to commit; (*abschreiten*) to cover; (*Straße etc*) to use, to negotiate; (*Feier*) to celebrate

begehren [bə'ge:rən] *vt* to desire

begehrt *adj* in demand; (*Junggeselle*) eligible

begeistern [bə'gaɪstərn] *vt* to fill with enthusiasm, to inspire ♦ *vr*: **sich für etw ~** to get enthusiastic about sth

begeistert *adj* enthusiastic

Begierde [bə'gi:rdə] *f* desire, passion

begierig [bə'gi:rɪç] *adj* eager, keen

begießen [bə'gi:sən] (*unreg*) *vt* to water; (*mit Alkohol*) to drink to

Beginn [bə'gɪn] **(-(e)s)** *m* beginning; **zu ~** at the beginning; **b~en** (*unreg*) *vt, vi* to start, to begin

beglaubigen [bə'glaʊbɪgən] *vt* to countersign; **Beglaubigung** *f* countersignature

begleichen [bə'glaɪçən] (*unreg*) *vt* to settle, to pay

Begleit- [bə'glaɪt] *zW*: **b~en** *vt* to accompany; (*MIL*) to escort; **~er (-s, -)** *m* companion; (*Freund*) escort; (*MUS*) accompanist; **~schreiben** *nt* covering letter; **~umstände** *pl* concomitant circumstances; **~ung** *f* company; (*MIL*) escort; (*MUS*) accompaniment

beglücken [bə'glʏkən] *vt* to make happy, to delight

beglückwünschen [bə'glʏkvʏnʃən] *vt*: **~ (zu)** to congratulate (on)

begnadigen [bə'gna:dɪgən] *vt* to pardon; **Begnadigung** *f* pardon, amnesty

begnügen [bə'gny:gən] *vr* to be satisfied, to content o.s.

begonnen *etc* [bə'gɔnən] *vb siehe* **beginnen**

begraben [bə'gra:bən] (*unreg*) *vt* to bury; **Begräbnis (-ses, -se)** [bə'grɛ:pnɪs] *nt* burial, funeral

begreifen [bə'graɪfən] (*unreg*) *vt* to understand, to comprehend

begreiflich [bə'graɪflɪç] *adj* understandable

begrenzen [bə'grɛntsən] *vt* (*beschränken*) to limit

Begrenztheit [bə'grɛntsthaɪt] *f* limitation, restriction; (*fig*) narrowness

Begriff [bə'grɪf] (**-(e)s, -e**) *m* concept, idea; **im ~ sein, etw zu tun** to be about to do sth; **schwer von ~** (*umg*) slow, dense

begriffsstutzig *adj* slow, dense

begründ- [bə'grʏnd] *zW:* **~en** *vt* (*Gründe geben*) to justify; **~et** *adj* well-founded, justified; **B~ung** *f* justification, reason

begrüßen [bə'gryːsən] *vt* to greet, to welcome; **Begrüßung** *f* greeting, welcome

begünstigen [bə'gʏnstɪgən] *vt* (*Person*) to favour; (*Sache*) to further, to promote

begutachten [bə'guːtʔaxtən] *vt* to assess

begütert [bə'gyːtərt] *adj* wealthy, well-to-do

behaart [bə'haːrt] *adj* hairy

behagen [bə'haːgən] *vi:* **das behagt ihm nicht** he does not like it

behaglich [bə'haːklɪç] *adj* comfortable, cosy; **B~keit** *f* comfort, cosiness

behalten [bə'haltən] (*unreg*) *vt* to keep, to retain; (*im Gedächtnis*) to remember

Behälter [bə'hɛltər] (**-s, -**) *m* container, receptacle

behandeln [bə'handəln] *vt* to treat; (*Thema*) to deal with; (*Maschine*) to handle

Behandlung *f* treatment; (*von Maschine*) handling

beharren [bə'harən] *vi:* **auf etw** *dat* **~** to stick od keep to sth

beharrlich [bə'harlɪç] *adj* (*ausdauernd*) steadfast, unwavering; (*hartnäckig*) tenacious, dogged; **B~keit** *f* steadfastness; tenacity

behaupten [bə'haʊptən] *vt* to claim, to assert, to maintain; (*sein Recht*) to defend ♦ *vr* to assert o.s.

Behauptung *f* claim, assertion

beheben [bə'heːbən] (*unreg*) *vt* to remove

behelfen [bə'hɛlfən] (*unreg*) *vr:* **sich mit etw ~** to make do with sth

behelfsmäßig *adj* improvised, makeshift;

(*vorübergehend*) temporary

behelligen [bə'hɛlɪgən] *vt* to trouble, to bother

beherbergen [bə'hɛrbərgən] *vt* to put up, to house

beherrsch- [bə'hɛrʃ] *zW:* **~en** *vt* (*Volk*) to rule, to govern; (*Situation*) to control; (*Sprache, Gefühle*) to master ♦ *vr* to control o.s.; **~t** *adj* controlled; **B~ung** *f* rule; control; mastery

beherzigen [bə'hɛrtsɪgən] *vt* to take to heart

beherzt *adj* courageous, brave

behilflich [bə'hɪlflɪç] *adj* helpful; **jdm ~ sein (bei)** to help sb (with)

behindern [bə'hɪndərn] *vt* to hinder, to impede

Behinderte(r) *f(m)* disabled person

Behinderung *f* hindrance; (*Körperbehinderung*) handicap

Behörde [bə'høːrdə] *f* (*auch pl*) authorities *pl*

behördlich [bə'høːrtlɪç] *adj* official

behüten [bə'hyːtən] *vt* to guard; **jdn vor etw** *dat* **~** to preserve sb from sth

behutsam [bə'huːtzaːm] *adj* cautious, careful; **B~keit** *f* caution, carefulness

---

SCHLÜSSELWORT

---

bei [baɪ] *präp +dat* **1** (*nahe bei*) near; (*zum Aufenthalt*) at, with; (*unter, zwischen*) among; **bei München** near Munich; **bei uns** at our place; **beim Friseur** at the hairdresser's; **bei seinen Eltern wohnen** to live with one's parents; **bei einer Firma arbeiten** to work for a firm; **etw bei sich haben** to have sth on one; **jdn bei sich haben** to have sb with one; **bei Goethe** in Goethe; **beim Militär** in the army

2 (*zeitlich*) at, on; (*während*) during; (*Zustand, Umstand*) in; **bei Nacht** at night; **bei Nebel** in fog; **bei Regen** if it rains; **bei solcher Hitze** in such heat; **bei meiner Ankuft** on my arrival; **bei der Arbeit** when I'm *etc* working; **beim Fahren** while driving

---

beibehalten ['baɪbəhaltən] (*unreg*) *vt* to keep, to retain

beibringen ['baɪbrɪŋən] (*unreg*) *vt* (*Beweis, Zeugen*) to bring forward; (*Gründe*) to adduce; **jdm etw ~** (*lehren*) to teach sb sth; (*zu verstehen geben*) to make sb understand sth; (*zufügen*) to inflict sth on sb

Beichte ['baɪçtə] *f* confession; **b~n** *vt* to confess ♦ *vi* to go to confession

beide(s) ['baɪdə(s)] *pron, adj* both; **meine ~n Brüder** my two brothers, both my brothers; **die ersten ~n** the first two; **wir ~** we two; **einer von ~n** one of the two; **alles ~s** both (of them)

beider- ['baɪdər] *zW*: **~lei** *adj inv* of both; **~seitig** *adj* mutual, reciprocal; **~seits** *adv* mutually ♦ *präp +gen* on both sides of

beieinander [baɪaɪˈnandər] *adv* together

Beifahrer ['baɪfaːrər] *m* passenger

Beifall ['baɪfal] (**-(e)s**) *m* applause; (*Zustimmung*) approval

beifügen ['baɪfyːgən] *vt* to enclose

beige ['beːʒ] *adj* beige, fawn

beigeben ['baɪgeːbən] (*unreg*) *vt* (*zufügen*) to add; (*mitgeben*) to give ♦ *vi* (*nachgeben*) to give in

Beihilfe ['baɪhɪlfə] *f* aid, assistance; (*Studienbeihilfe*) grant; (*JUR*) aiding and abetting

beikommen ['baɪkɔmən] (*unreg*) *vi* +*dat* to get at; (*einem Problem*) to deal with

Beil [baɪl] (**-(e)s**, **-e**) *nt* axe, hatchet

Beilage ['baɪlaːgə] *f* (*Buchbeilage etc*) supplement; (*KOCH*) vegetables and potatoes *pl*

beiläufig ['baɪlɔyfɪç] *adj* casual, incidental ♦ *adv* casually, by the way

beilegen ['baɪleːgən] *vt* (*hinzufügen*) to enclose, to add; (*beimessen*) to attribute, to ascribe; (*Streit*) to settle

Beileid ['baɪlaɪt] *nt* condolence, sympathy; **herzliches ~** deepest sympathy

beiliegend ['baɪliːgənt] *adj* (*COMM*) enclosed

beim [baɪm] = **bei dem**

beimessen ['baɪmɛsən] (*unreg*) *vt* (+*dat*) to attribute (to), to ascribe (to)

Bein [baɪn] (**-(e)s**, **-e**) *nt* leg

beinah(e) ['baɪnaː(ə)] *adv* almost, nearly

Beinbruch *m* fracture of the leg

beinhalten [bəˈɪnhaltən] *vt* to contain

Beipackzettel ['baɪpaktsɛtəl] *m* instruction leaflet

beipflichten ['baɪpflɪçtən] *vi*: **jdm/etw ~** to agree with sb/sth

beisammen [baɪˈzamən] *adv* together; **B~sein** (**-s**) *nt* get-together

Beischlaf ['baɪʃlaːf] *m* sexual intercourse

Beisein ['baɪzaɪn] (**-s**) *nt* presence

beiseite [baɪˈzaɪtə] *adv* to one side, aside; (*stehen*) on one side, aside; **etw ~ legen** (*sparen*) to put sth by

beisetzen ['baɪzɛtsən] *vt* to bury; **Beisetzung** *f* funeral

Beisitzer ['baɪzɪtsər] (**-s**, **-**) *m* (*bei Prüfung*) assessor

Beispiel ['baɪʃpiːl] (**-(e)s**, **-e**) *nt* example; **sich** +*dat* **an jdm ein ~ nehmen** to take sb as an example; **zum ~** for example; **b~haft** *adj* exemplary; **b~los** *adj* unprecedented; **b~sweise** *adv* for instance *od* example

beißen ['baɪsən] (*unreg*) *vt, vi* to bite; (*stechen: Rauch, Säure*) to burn ♦ *vr* (*Farben*) to clash; **~d** *adj* biting, caustic; (*fig auch*) sarcastic

Beistand ['baɪʃtant] (**-(e)s**, **-̈e**) *m* support, help; (*JUR*) adviser

beistehen ['baɪʃteːən] (*unreg*) *vi*: **jdm ~** to stand by sb

beisteuern ['baɪʃtɔyərn] *vt* to contribute

Beitrag ['baɪtraːk] (**-(e)s**, **-̈e**) *m* contribution; (*Zahlung*) fee, subscription; (*Versicherungsbeitrag*) premium; **b~en** ['baɪtraːgən] (*unreg*) *vt, vi*: **b~en (zu)** to contribute (to); (*mithelfen*) to help (with)

beitreten ['baɪtreːtən] (*unreg*) *vi* +*dat* to join

Beitritt ['baɪtrɪt] *m* joining, membership

Beiwagen ['baɪvaːgən] *m* (*Motorradbeiwagen*) sidecar

beizeiten [baɪˈtsaɪtən] *adv* in time

bejahen [bəˈjaːən] *vt* (*Frage*) to say yes to, to answer in the affirmative; (*gutheißen*) to agree with

bekämpfen [bəˈkɛmpfən] *vt* (*Gegner*) to fight; (*Seuche*) to combat ♦ *vr* to fight;

Bekämpfung f fight, struggle

bekannt [bə'kant] adj (well-)known; (nicht fremd) familiar; **~ geben** to announce publicly; **mit jdm ~ sein** to know sb; **~ machen** to announce; **jdn mit jdm ~ machen** to introduce sb to sb; **das ist mir ~** I know that; **es/sie kommt mir ~ vor** it/she seems familiar; **B~e(r)** f(m) acquaintance; friend; **B~enkreis** m circle of friends; **~lich** adv as is well known, as you know; **B~machung** f publication; announcement; **B~schaft** f acquaintance

bekehren [bə'ke:rən] vt to convert ♦ vr to be od become converted

bekennen [bə'kɛnən] (unreg) vt to confess; (Glauben) to profess; **Farbe ~** (umg) to show where one stands

Bekenntnis [bə'kɛntnɪs] (-ses, -se) nt admission, confession; (Religion) confession, denomination

beklagen [bə'kla:gən] vt to deplore, to lament ♦ vr to complain

bekleiden [bə'klaɪdən] vt to clothe; (Amt) to occupy, to fill

Bekleidung f clothing

beklemmen [bə'klɛmən] vt to oppress

beklommen [bə'klɔmən] adj anxious, uneasy

bekommen [bə'kɔmən] (unreg) vt to get, to receive; (Kind) to have; (Zug) to catch, to get ♦ vi: **jdm ~** to agree with sb

bekömmlich [bə'kœmlɪç] adj easily digestible

bekräftigen [bə'krɛftɪgən] vt to confirm, to corroborate

bekreuzigen [bə'krɔʏtsɪgən] vr to cross o.s.

bekunden [bə'kʊndən] vt (sagen) to state; (zeigen) to show

belächeln [bə'lɛçəln] vt to laugh at

beladen [bə'la:dən] (unreg) vt to load

Belag [bə'la:k] (-(e)s, ⁻e) m covering, coating; (Brotbelag) spread; (Zahnbelag) tartar; (auf Zunge) fur; (Bremsbelag) lining

belagern [bə'la:gərn] vt to besiege; **Belagerung** f siege

Belang [bə'laŋ] (-(e)s) m importance; **~e** pl (Interessen) interests, concerns; **b~los** adj trivial, unimportant

belassen [bə'lasən] (unreg) vt (in Zustand, Glauben) to leave; (in Stellung) to retain

belasten [bə'lastən] vt to burden; (fig: bedrücken) to trouble, to worry; (COMM: Konto) to debit; (JUR) to incriminate ♦ vr to weigh o.s. down; (JUR) to incriminate o.s.; **~d** adj (JUR) incriminating

belästigen [bə'lɛstɪgən] vt to annoy, to pester; **Belästigung** f annoyance, pestering

Belastung [bə'lastʊŋ] f load; (fig: Sorge etc) weight; (COMM) charge, debit(ing); (JUR) incriminatory evidence

belaufen [bə'laʊfən] (unreg) vr: **sich ~ auf** +akk to amount to

beleben [bə'le:bən] vt (anregen) to liven up; (Konjunktur, jds Hoffnungen) to stimulate ♦ vr (Augen) to light up; (Stadt) to come to life

belebt [bə'le:pt] adj (Straße) busy

Beleg [bə'le:k] (-(e)s, -e) m (COMM) receipt; (Beweis) documentary evidence, proof; (Beispiel) example; **b~en** vt to cover; (Kuchen, Brot) to spread; (Platz) to reserve, to book; (Kurs, Vorlesung) to register for; (beweisen) to verify, to prove; (MIL: mit Bomben) to bomb; **~schaft** f personnel, staff; **b~tes Brot** open sandwich

belehren [bə'le:rən] vt to instruct, to teach; **Belehrung** f instruction

beleibt [bə'laɪpt] adj stout, corpulent

beleidigen [bə'laɪdɪgən] vt to insult, to offend; **Beleidigung** f insult; (JUR) slander, libel

beleuchten [bə'lɔʏçtən] vt to light, to illuminate; (fig) to throw light on

Beleuchtung f lighting, illumination

Belgien ['bɛlgiən] nt Belgium; **Belgier(in)** m(f) Belgian; **belgisch** adj Belgian

belichten [bə'lɪçtən] vt to expose

Belichtung f exposure; **~smesser** m exposure meter

Belieben [bə'li:bən] nt: **(ganz) nach ~** (just) as you wish

beliebig [bə'li:bɪç] adj any you like ♦ adv as you like; **ein ~es Thema** any subject you like od want; **~ viel/viele** as much/many as you like

beliebt [bəˈliːpt] *adj* popular; **sich bei jdm ~ machen** to make o.s. popular with sb; **B~heit** *f* popularity

beliefern [bəˈliːfərn] *vt* to supply

bellen [ˈbɛlən] *vi* to bark

belohnen [bəˈloːnən] *vt* to reward; **Belohnung** *f* reward

Belüftung [bəˈlʏftʊŋ] *f* ventilation

belügen [bəˈlyːgən] (*unreg*) *vt* to lie to, to deceive

belustigen [bəˈlʊstɪgən] *vt* to amuse; **Belustigung** *f* amusement

bemalen [bəˈmaːlən] *vt* to paint

bemängeln [bəˈmɛŋəln] *vt* to criticize

bemerk- [bəˈmɛrk] *zW:* **~bar** *adj* perceptible, noticeable; **sich ~bar machen** (*Person*) to make *od* get o.s. noticed; (*Unruhe*) to become noticeable; **~en** *vt* (*wahrnehmen*) to notice, to observe; (*sagen*) to say, to mention; **~enswert** *adj* remarkable, noteworthy; **B~ung** *f* remark; (*schriftlich auch*) note

bemitleiden [bəˈmɪtlaɪdən] *vt* to pity

bemühen [bəˈmyːən] *vr* to take trouble *od* pains; **Bemühung** *f* trouble, pains *pl*, effort

benachbart [bəˈnaxbaːrt] *adj* neighbouring

benachrichtigen [bəˈnaːxrɪçtɪgən] *vt* to inform; **Benachrichtigung** *f* notification, information

benachteiligen [bəˈnaːxtaɪlɪgən] *vt* to put at a disadvantage; to victimize

benehmen [bəˈneːmən] (*unreg*) *vr* to behave; **B~ (-s)** *nt* behaviour

beneiden [bəˈnaɪdən] *vt* to envy; **~swert** *adj* enviable

benennen [bəˈnɛnən] (*unreg*) *vt* to name

Bengel [ˈbɛŋəl] **(-s, -)** *m* (little) rascal *od* rogue

benommen [bəˈnɔmən] *adj* dazed

benoten [bəˈnoːtən] *vt* to mark

benötigen [bəˈnøːtɪgən] *vt* to need

benutzen [bəˈnʊtsən] *vt* to use

Benutzer **(-s, -)** *m* user

Benutzung *f* utilization, use

Benzin [bɛntˈsiːn] **(-s, -e)** *nt* (*AUT*) petrol

(*BRIT*), gas(oline) (*US*); **~kanister** *m* petrol (*BRIT*) *od* gas (*US*) can; **~tank** *m* petrol tank (*BRIT*), gas tank (*US*); **~uhr** *f* petrol (*BRIT*) *od* gas (*US*) gauge

beobachten [bəˈoːbaxtən] *vt* to observe; **Beobachter (-s, -)** *m* observer; (*eines Unfalls*) witness; (*PRESSE, TV*) correspondent; **Beobachtung** *f* observation

bepacken [bəˈpakən] *vt* to load, to pack

bequem [bəˈkveːm] *adj* comfortable; (*Ausrede*) convenient; (*Person*) lazy, indolent; **~en** *vr:* **sich ~en(, etw zu tun)** to condescend (to do sth); **B~lichkeit** [-ˈlɪçkaɪt] *f* convenience, comfort; (*Faulheit*) laziness, indolence

beraten [bəˈraːtən] (*unreg*) *vt* to advise; (*besprechen*) to discuss, to debate ♦ *vr* to consult; **gut/schlecht ~ sein** to be well/ill advised; **sich ~ lassen** to get advice

Berater (-s, -) *m* adviser

Beratung *f* advice; (*Besprechung*) consultation; **~sstelle** *f* advice centre

berauben [bəˈraʊbən] *vt* to rob

berechenbar [bəˈrɛçənbaːr] *adj* calculable

berechnen [bəˈrɛçnən] *vt* to calculate; (*COMM: anrechnen*) to charge; **~d** *adj* (*Mensch*) calculating, scheming

Berechnung *f* calculation; (*COMM*) charge

berechtigen [bəˈrɛçtɪgən] *vt* to entitle; to authorize; (*fig*) to justify

berechtigt [bəˈrɛçtɪçt] *adj* justifiable, justified

Berechtigung *f* authorization; (*fig*) justification

bereden [bəˈreːdən] *vt* (*besprechen*) to discuss; (*überreden*) to persuade ♦ *vr* to discuss

Bereich [bəˈraɪç] **(-(e)s, -e)** *m* (*Bezirk*) area; (*PHYS*) range; (*Ressort, Gebiet*) sphere

bereichern [bəˈraɪçərn] *vt* to enrich ♦ *vr* to get rich

bereinigen [bəˈraɪnɪgən] *vt* to settle

bereisen [bəˈraɪzən] *vt* (*Land*) to travel through

bereit [bəˈraɪt] *adj* ready, prepared; **zu etw ~ sein** to be ready for sth; **sich ~ erklären** to declare o.s. willing; **~en** *vt* to prepare, to make ready; (*Kummer, Freude*) to cause;

~halten (unreg) vt to keep in readiness; ~legen vt to lay out; ~machen vt, vr to prepare, to get ready; ~s adv already; B~schaft f readiness; (Polizei) alert; B~schaftsdienst m emergency service; ~stehen (unreg) vi (Person) to be prepared; (Ding) to be ready; ~stellen vt (Kisten, Pakete etc) to put ready; (Geld etc) to make available; (Truppen, Maschinen) to put at the ready; ~willig adj willing, ready; B~willigkeit f willingness, readiness

bereuen [bə'rɔʏən] vt to regret

Berg [bɛrk] (-(e)s, -e) m mountain; hill; b~ab adv downhill; ~arbeiter m miner; b~auf adv uphill; ~bahn f mountain railway; ~bau m mining

bergen ['bɛrgən] (unreg) vt (retten) to rescue; (Ladung) to salvage; (enthalten) to contain

Berg- zW: ~führer m mountain guide; ~gipfel m peak, summit; b~ig ['bɛrgɪç] adj mountainous; hilly; ~kette f mountain range; ~mann (pl ~leute) m miner; ~rettungsdienst m mountain rescue team; ~rutsch m landslide; ~steigen nt mountaineering; ~steiger(in) (-s, -) m(f) mountaineer, climber; ~tour f mountain climb

Bergung ['bɛrgʊŋ] f (von Menschen) rescue; (von Material) recovery; (NAUT) salvage

Berg- zW: ~wacht f mountain rescue service; ~wanderung f hike in the mountains; ~werk nt mine

Bericht [bə'rɪçt] (-(e)s, -e) m report, account; b~en vt, vi to report; ~erstatter (-s, -) m reporter; (newspaper) correspondent

berichtigen [bə'rɪçtɪgən] vt to correct; **Berichtigung** f correction

Bernstein ['bɛrnʃtaɪn] m amber

bersten ['bɛrstən] (unreg) vi to burst, to split

berüchtigt [bə'rʏçtɪçt] adj notorious, infamous

berücksichtigen [bə'rʏkzɪçtɪgən] vt to consider, to bear in mind; **Berücksichtigung** f consideration

Beruf [bə'ru:f] (-(e)s, -e) m occupation, profession; (Gewerbe) trade; b~en (unreg)

vt: b~en zu to appoint to ♦ vr: sich auf jdn/etw b~en to refer od appeal to sb/sth ♦ adj competent, qualified; b~lich adj professional

Berufs- zW: ~ausbildung f job training; ~berater m careers adviser; ~beratung f vocational guidance; ~geheimnis nt professional secret; ~leben nt professional life; ~schule f vocational od trade school; ~sportler [-ʃpɔrtlər] m professional (sportsman); b~tätig adj employed; b~unfähig adj unfit for work; ~verkehr m rush-hour traffic

Berufung f vocation, calling; (Ernennung) appointment; (JUR) appeal; ~ einlegen to appeal

beruhen [bə'ru:ən] vi: auf etw dat ~ to be based on sth; etw auf sich ~ lassen to leave sth at that

beruhigen [bə'ru:ɪgən] vt to calm, to pacify, to soothe ♦ vr (Mensch) to calm (o.s.) down; (Situation) to calm down

Beruhigung f soothing; (der Nerven) calming; zu jds ~ (in order) to reassure sb; ~smittel nt sedative

berühmt [bə'ry:mt] adj famous; B~heit f (Ruf) fame; (Mensch) celebrity

berühren [bə'ry:rən] vt to touch; (gefühlsmäßig bewegen) to affect; (flüchtig erwähnen) to mention, to touch on ♦ vr to meet, to touch

Berührung f contact

besagen [bə'za:gən] vt to mean

besänftigen [bə'zɛnftɪgən] vt to soothe, to calm

Besatz [bə'zats] (-es, ⁺e) m trimming, edging

Besatzung f garrison; (NAUT, AVIAT) crew

Besatzungsmacht f occupying power

beschädigen [bə'ʃɛ:dɪgən] vt to damage; **Beschädigung** f damage; (Stelle) damaged spot

beschaffen [bə'ʃafən] vt to get, to acquire ♦ adj: das ist so ~, dass that is such that; B~heit f (von Mensch) constitution, nature

Beschaffung f acquisition

beschäftigen [bə'ʃɛftɪgən] vt to occupy;

(*beruflich*) to employ ♦ *vr* to occupy *od* concern o.s.

beschäftigt *adj* busy, occupied

Beschäftigung *f* (*Beruf*) employment; (*Tätigkeit*) occupation; (*Befassen*) concern

beschämen [bə'ʃɛːmən] *vt* to put to shame; **~d** *adj* shameful; (*Hilfsbereitschaft*) shaming

beschämt *adj* ashamed

Bescheid [bə'ʃaɪt] (**-(e)s, -e**) *m* information; (*Weisung*) directions *pl*; **~ wissen (über** +*akk*) to be well-informed (about); **ich weiß ~** I know; **jdm ~ geben** *od* **sagen** to let sb know

bescheiden [bə'ʃaɪdən] (*unreg*) *vr* to content o.s. ♦ *adj* modest; **B~heit** *f* modesty

bescheinen [bə'ʃaɪnən] (*unreg*) *vt* to shine on

bescheinigen [bə'ʃaɪnɪgən] *vt* to certify; (*bestätigen*) to acknowledge

Bescheinigung *f* certificate; (*Quittung*) receipt

beschenken [bə'ʃɛŋkən] *vt*: **jdn mit etw ~** to give sb sth as a present

bescheren [bə'ʃeːrən] *vt*: **jdm etw ~** to give sb sth as a Christmas present; **jdn ~** to give Christmas presents to sb

Bescherung *f* giving of Christmas presents; (*umg*) mess

beschildern [bə'ʃɪldərn] *vt* to put signs/a sign on

beschimpfen [bə'ʃɪmpfən] *vt* to abuse; **Beschimpfung** *f* abuse; insult

Beschlag [bə'ʃlaːk] (**-(e)s, ⁰e**) *m* (*Metallband*) fitting; (*auf Fenster*) condensation; (*auf Metall*) tarnish; finish; (*Hufeisen*) horseshoe; **jdn/etw in ~ nehmen** *od* **mit ~ belegen** to monopolize sb/sth; **b~en** [bə'ʃlaːgən] (*unreg*) *vt* to cover; (*Pferd*) to shoe ♦ *vi, vr* (*Fenster etc*) to mist over; **b~en sein (in** *od* **auf** +*dat*) to be well versed (in); **b~nahmen** *vt* to seize, to confiscate; to requisition; **~nahmung** *f* confiscation, sequestration

beschleunigen [bə'ʃlɔʏnɪgən] *vt* to accelerate, to speed up ♦ *vi* (*AUT*) to accelerate; **Beschleunigung** *f* acceleration

beschließen [bə'ʃliːsən] (*unreg*) *vt* to decide on; (*beenden*) to end, to close

Beschluss ▲ [bə'ʃlʊs] (**-es, ⁰e**) *m* decision, conclusion; (*Ende*) conclusion, end

beschmutzen [bə'ʃmʊtsən] *vt* to dirty, to soil

beschönigen [bə'ʃøːnɪgən] *vt* to gloss over

beschränken [bə'ʃrɛŋkən] *vt, vr*: **(sich) ~ (auf** +*akk*) to limit *od* restrict (o.s.) (to)

beschränk- *zW*: **~t** *adj* confined, restricted; (*Mensch*) limited, narrow-minded; **B~ung** *f* limitation

beschreiben [bə'ʃraɪbən] (*unreg*) *vt* to describe; (*Papier*) to write on

Beschreibung *f* description

beschriften [bə'ʃrɪftən] *vt* to mark, to label; **Beschriftung** *f* lettering

beschuldigen [bə'ʃʊldɪgən] *vt* to accuse; **Beschuldigung** *f* accusation

Beschuss ▲ [bə'ʃʊs] *m*: **jdn/etw unter ~ nehmen** (*MIL*) to open fire on sb/sth

beschützen [bə'ʃʏtsən] *vt*: **~ (vor** +*dat*) to protect (from); **Beschützer** (**-s, -**) *m* protector

Beschwerde [bə'ʃveːrdə] *f* complaint; (*Mühe*) hardship; **~n** *pl* (*Leiden*) trouble

beschweren [bə'ʃveːrən] *vt* to weight down; (*fig*) to burden ♦ *vr* to complain

beschwerlich *adj* tiring, exhausting

beschwichtigen [bə'ʃvɪçtɪgən] *vt* to soothe, to pacify

beschwindeln [bə'ʃvɪndəln] *vt* (*betrügen*) to cheat; (*belügen*) to fib to

beschwingt [bə'ʃvɪŋt] *adj* in high spirits

beschwipst [bə'ʃvɪpst] (*umg*) *adj* tipsy

beschwören [bə'ʃvøːrən] (*unreg*) *vt* (*Aussage*) to swear to; (*anflehen*) to implore; (*Geister*) to conjure up

beseitigen [bə'zaɪtɪgən] *vt* to remove; **Beseitigung** *f* removal

Besen ['beːzən] (**-s, -**) *m* broom; **~stiel** *m* broomstick

besessen [bə'zɛsən] *adj* possessed

besetz- [bə'zɛts] *zW*: **~en** *vt* (*Haus, Land*) to occupy; (*Platz*) to take, to fill; (*Posten*) to fill; (*Rolle*) to cast; (*mit Edelsteinen*) to set; **~t** *adj* full; (*TEL*) engaged, busy; (*Platz*) taken;

(*WC*) engaged; **B~zeichen** *nt* engaged tone; **B~ung** *f* occupation; filling; (*von Rolle*) casting; (*die Schauspieler*) cast

besichtigen [bə'zɪçtɪgən] *vt* to visit, to have a look at; **Besichtigung** *f* visit

besiegen [bə'zi:gən] *vt* to defeat, to overcome

besinn- [bə'zɪn] *zW*: **~en** (*unreg*) *vr* (*nachdenken*) to think, to reflect; (*erinnern*) to remember; **sich anders ~en** to change one's mind; **B~ung** *f* consciousness; **zur B~ung kommen** to recover consciousness; (*fig*) to come to one's senses; **~ungslos** *adj* unconscious

Besitz [bə'zɪts] (**-es**) *m* possession; (*Eigentum*) property; **b~en** (*unreg*) *vt* to possess, to own; (*Eigenschaft*) to have; **~er(in)** (**-s, -**) *m(f)* owner, proprietor; **~ergreifung** *f* occupation, seizure

besoffen [bə'zɔfən] (*umg*) *adj* drunk, stoned

besohlen [bə'zo:lən] *vt* to sole

Besoldung [bə'zɔldʊŋ] *f* salary, pay

besondere(r, s) [bə'zɔndərə(r, s)] *adj* special; (*eigen*) particular; (*gesondert*) separate; (*eigentümlich*) peculiar

Besonderheit [bə'zɔndərhaɪt] *f* peculiarity

besonders [bə'zɔndərs] *adv* especially, particularly; (*getrennt*) separately

besonnen [bə'zɔnən] *adj* sensible, level-headed

besorg- [bə'zɔrg] *zW*: **~en** *vt* (*beschaffen*) to acquire; (*kaufen auch*) to purchase; (*erledigen: Geschäfte*) to deal with; (*sich kümmern um*) to take care of; **B~nis** (**-, -se**) *f* anxiety, concern; **~t** [bə'zɔrçt] *adj* anxious, worried; **B~ung** *f* acquisition, (*Kauf*) purchase

bespielen [bə'ʃpi:lən] *vt* to record

bespitzeln [bə'ʃpɪtsəln] *vt* to spy on

besprechen [bə'ʃprɛçən] (*unreg*) *vt* to discuss; (*Tonband etc*) to record, to speak onto; (*Buch*) to review ♦ *vr* to discuss, to consult; **Besprechung** *f* meeting, discussion; (*von Buch*) review

besser ['bɛsər] *adj* better; **es geht ihm ~** he is feeling better; **~n** *vt* to make better, to improve ♦ *vr* to improve; (*Menschen*) to

reform; **B~ung** *f* improvement; **gute B~ung!** get well soon!; **B~wisser** (**-s, -**) *m* know-all

Bestand [bə'ʃtant] (**-(e)s, ⁻e**) *m* (*Fortbestehen*) duration, stability; (*Kassenbestand*) amount, balance; (*Vorrat*) stock; **~ haben, von ~ sein** to last long, to endure

beständig [bə'ʃtɛndɪç] *adj* (*ausdauernd: auch fig*) constant; (*Wetter*) settled; (*Stoffe*) resistant; (*Klagen etc*) continual

Bestandsaufnahme [bə'ʃtantsaʊfna:mə] *f* stocktaking

Bestandteil *m* part, component; (*Zutat*) ingredient

bestärken [bə'ʃtɛrkən] *vt*: **jdn in etw** *dat* **~** to strengthen *od* confirm sb in sth

bestätigen [bə'ʃtɛːtɪgən] *vt* to confirm; (*anerkennen, COMM*) to acknowledge; **Bestätigung** *f* confirmation; acknowledgement

bestatten [bə'ʃtatən] *vt* to bury; **Bestattung** *f* funeral; **Bestattungsinstitut** *nt* funeral director's

bestaunen [bə'ʃtaʊnən] *vt* to marvel at, gaze at in wonder

beste(r, s) ['bɛstə(r, s)] *adj* best; **so ist es am ~n** it's best that way; **am ~n gehst du gleich** you'd better go at once; **jdn zum B~n haben** to pull sb's leg; **einen Witz** *etc* **zum B~n geben** to tell a joke *etc*; **aufs B~** *od* **~** in the best possible way; **zu jds B~n** for the benefit of sb

bestechen [bə'ʃtɛçən] (*unreg*) *vt* to bribe; **bestechlich** *adj* corruptible; **Bestechung** *f* bribery, corruption

Besteck [bə'ʃtɛk] (**-(e)s, -e**) *nt* knife, fork and spoon, cutlery; (*MED*) set of instruments

bestehen [bə'ʃte:ən] (*unreg*) *vi* to be; to exist; (*andauern*) to last ♦ *vt* (*Kampf, Probe, Prüfung*) to pass; **~ auf** +*dat* to insist on; **~ aus** to consist of

bestehlen [bə'ʃte:lən] (*unreg*) *vt*: **jdn (um etw) ~** to rob sb (of sth)

besteigen [bə'ʃtaɪgən] (*unreg*) *vt* to climb, to ascend; (*Pferd*) to mount; (*Thron*) to ascend

Bestell- [bə'ʃtɛl] *zW:* **~buch** *nt* order book; **b~en** *vt* to order; (*kommen lassen*) to arrange to see; (*nominieren*) to name; (*Acker*) to cultivate; (*Grüße, Auftrag*) to pass on; **~formular** *nt* order form; **~nummer** *f* order code; **~ung** *f* (*COMM*) order; (*~en*) ordering

bestenfalls ['bɛstən'fals] *adv* at best

bestens ['bɛstəns] *adv* very well

besteuern [bə'ʃtɔyɐrn] *vt* (*jdn, Waren*) to tax

Bestie ['bɛstiə] *f* (*auch fig*) beast

bestimm- [bə'ʃtɪm] *zW:* **~en** *vt* (*Regeln*) to lay down; (*Tag, Ort*) to fix; (*beherrschen*) to characterize; (*vorsehen*) to mean; (*ernennen*) to appoint; (*definieren*) to define; (*veranlassen*) to induce; **~t** *adj* (*entschlossen*) firm; (*gewiss*) certain, definite; (*Artikel*) definite ♦ *adv* (*gewiss*) definitely, for sure; **suchen Sie etwas B~tes?** are you looking for something in particular?; **B~theit** *f* firmness; certainty; **B~ung** *f* (*Verordnung*) regulation; (*Festsetzen*) determining; (*Verwendungszweck*) purpose; (*Schicksal*) fate; (*Definition*) definition; **B~ungsland** *nt* (country of) destination; **B~ungsort** *m* (place of) destination

Bestleistung *f* best performance

bestmöglich *adj* best possible

bestrafen [bə'ʃtraːfən] *vt* to punish; **Bestrafung** *f* punishment

bestrahlen [bə'ʃtraːlən] *vt* to shine on; (*MED*) to treat with X-rays

Bestrahlung *f* (*MED*) X-ray treatment, radiotherapy

Bestreben [bə'ʃtreːbən] (**-s**) *nt* endeavour, effort

bestreiten [bə'ʃtraɪtən] (*unreg*) *vt* (*abstreiten*) to dispute; (*finanzieren*) to pay for, to finance

bestreuen [bə'ʃtrɔyən] *vt* to sprinkle, to dust; (*Straße*) to grit

bestürmen [bə'ʃtʏrmən] *vt* (*mit Fragen, Bitten etc*) to overwhelm, to swamp

bestürzend [bə'ʃtʏrtsənd] *adj* (*Nachrichten*) disturbing

bestürzt [bə'ʃtʏrtst] *adj* dismayed

Bestürzung *f* consternation

Besuch [bə'zuːx] (**-(e)s, -e**) *m* visit; (*Person*) visitor; **einen ~ machen bei jdm** to pay sb a visit *od* call; **~ haben** to have visitors; **bei jdm auf** *od* **zu ~ sein** to be visiting sb; **b~en** *vt* to visit; (*SCH etc*) to attend; **gut b~t** well-attended; **~er(in)** (**-s, -**) *m(f)* visitor, guest; **~szeit** *f* visiting hours *pl*

betätigen [bə'tɛːtɪgən] *vt* (*bedienen*) to work, to operate ♦ *vr* to involve o.s.; **sich als etw ~** to work as sth

Betätigung *f* activity; (*beruflich*) occupation; (*TECH*) operation

betäuben [bə'tɔybən] *vt* to stun; (*fig: Gewissen*) to still; (*MED*) to anaesthetize

Betäubung *f* (*Narkose*): **örtliche ~** local anaesthetic

Betäubungsmittel *nt* anaesthetic

Bete ['beːtə] *f*: **Rote ~** beetroot (*BRIT*), beet (*US*)

beteilig- [bə'taɪlɪg] *zW:* **~en** *vr*: **sich ~en (an +dat)** to take part (in), to participate (in), to share (in); (*an Geschäft: finanziell*) to have a share (in) ♦ *vt*: **jdn ~en (an +dat)** to give sb a share *od* interest (in); **B~te(r)** *f(m)* (*Mitwirkender*) partner; (*finanziell*) shareholder; **B~ung** *f* participation; (*Anteil*) share, interest; (*Besucherzahl*) attendance

beten ['beːtən] *vt, vi* to pray

beteuern [bə'tɔyɐrn] *vt* to assert; (*Unschuld*) to protest

Beton [be'tõː] (**-s, -s**) *m* concrete

betonen [bə'toːnən] *vt* to stress

betonieren [beto'niːrən] *vt* to concrete

Betonung *f* stress, emphasis

betr. *abk* (= *betrifft*) re

Betracht [bə'traxt] *m*: **in ~ kommen** to be considered *od* relevant; **etw in ~ ziehen** to take sth into consideration; **außer ~ bleiben** not to be considered; **b~en** *vt* to look at; (*fig*) to look at, to consider; **~er(in)** (**-s, -**) *m(f)* observer

beträchtlich [bə'trɛçtlɪç] *adj* considerable

Betrachtung *f* (*Ansehen*) examination; (*Erwägung*) consideration

Betrag [bə'traːk] (**-(e)s, ⁻e**) *m* amount; **b~en** (*unreg*) *vt* to amount to ♦ *vr* to behave; **~en** (**-s**) *nt* behaviour

Betreff m: **~ Ihr Schreiben vom ...** re your letter of ...

betreffen [bə'trɛfən] (unreg) vt to concern, to affect; **was mich betrifft** as for me; **~d** adj relevant, in question

betreffs [bə'trɛfs] präp +gen concerning, regarding; (COMM) re

betreiben [bə'traɪbən] (unreg) vt (ausüben) to practise; (Politik) to follow; (Studien) to pursue; (vorantreiben) to push ahead; (TECH: antreiben) to drive

betreten [bə'tre:tən] (unreg) vt to enter; (Bühne auch) to step onto ♦ adj embarrassed; **B~ verboten** keep off/out

Betreuer(in) [bə'trɔʏɐr(ɪn)] (-s, -) m(f) (einer Person) minder; (eines Gebäudes, Arbeitsgebiets) caretaker; (SPORT) coach

Betreuung f care

Betrieb [bə'tri:p] (-(e)s, -e) m (Firma) firm, concern; (Anlage) plant; (Tätigkeit) operation; (Treiben) traffic; **außer ~ sein** to be out of order; **in ~ sein** to be in operation

Betriebs- zW: **~ausflug** m works outing; **b~bereit** adj operational; **b~fähig** adj in working order; **~ferien** pl company holidays (BRIT), company vacation sg (US); **~klima** nt (working) atmosphere; **~kosten** pl running costs; **~rat** m workers' council; **b~sicher** adj safe (to operate); **~störung** f breakdown; **~system** nt (COMPUT) operating system; **~unfall** m industrial accident; **~wirtschaft** f economics

betrinken [bə'trɪŋkən] (unreg) vr to get drunk

betroffen [bə'trɔfən] adj (bestürzt) full of consternation; **von etw ~ werden** od **sein** to be affected by sth

betrüben [bə'try:bən] vt to grieve

betrübt [bə'try:pt] adj sorrowful, grieved

Betrug [bə'tru:k] (-(e)s) m deception; (JUR) fraud

betrügen [bə'try:gən] (unreg) vt to cheat; (JUR) to defraud; (Ehepartner) to be unfaithful to ♦ vr to deceive o.s.

Betrüger (-s, -) m cheat, deceiver; **b~isch** adj deceitful; (JUR) fraudulent

betrunken [bə'trʊŋkən] adj drunk

Bett [bɛt] (-(e)s, -en) nt bed; **ins** od **zu ~ gehen** to go to bed; **~bezug** m duvet cover; **~decke** f blanket; (Daunenbett) quilt; (Überwurf) bedspread

Bettel- ['bɛtəl] zW: **b~arm** adj very poor, destitute; **~ei** [bɛtə'laɪ] f begging; **b~n** vi to beg

bettlägerig ['bɛtlɛːgərɪç] adj bedridden

Bettlaken nt sheet

Bettler(in) ['bɛtlɐr(ɪn)] (-s, -) m(f) beggar

Bett- zW: **~tuch** ▲ nt sheet; **~vorleger** m bedside rug; **~wäsche** f bed linen; **~zeug** nt bed linen pl

beugen ['bɔʏgən] vt to bend; (GRAM) to inflect ♦ vr (sich fügen) to bow

Beule ['bɔʏlə] f bump, swelling

beunruhigen [bə'ʊnru:ɪgən] vt to disturb, to alarm ♦ vr to become worried

Beunruhigung f worry, alarm

beurlauben [bə'u:rlaʊbən] vt to give leave od a holiday to (BRIT), to grant vacation time to (US)

beurteilen [bə'ʊrtaɪlən] vt to judge; (Buch etc) to review

Beurteilung f judgement; review; (Note) mark

Beute ['bɔʏtə] (-) f booty, loot

Beutel (-s, -) m bag; (Geldbeutel) purse; (Tabakbeutel) pouch

Bevölkerung [bə'fœlkərʊŋ] f population

bevollmächtigen [bə'fɔlmɛçtɪgən] vt to authorize

Bevollmächtigte(r) f(m) authorized agent

bevor [bə'fo:r] konj before; **~munden** vt insep to treat like a child; **~stehen** (unreg) vi: **(jdm) ~stehen** to be in store (for sb); **~stehend** adj imminent, approaching; **~zugen** vt insep to prefer

bewachen [bə'vaxən] vt to watch, to guard

Bewachung f (Bewachen) guarding; (Leute) guard, watch

bewaffnen [bə'vafnən] vt to arm

Bewaffnung f (Vorgang) arming; (Ausrüstung) armament, arms pl

bewahren [bə'va:rən] vt to keep; **jdn vor jdm/etw ~** to save sb from sb/sth

bewähren [bə'vɛːrən] *vr* to prove o.s.; (*Maschine*) to prove its worth

bewahrheiten [bə'vaːrhaɪtən] *vr* to come true

bewährt *adj* reliable

Bewährung *f* (*JUR*) probation

bewältigen [bə'vɛltɪgən] *vt* to overcome; (*Arbeit*) to finish; (*Portion*) to manage

bewandert [bə'vandərt] *adj* expert, knowledgeable

bewässern [bə'vɛsərn] *vt* to irrigate

Bewässerung *f* irrigation

bewegen [bə've:gən] *vt, vr* to move; **jdn zu etw ~** to induce sb to do sth; **~d** *adj* touching, moving

Beweg- [bə've:k] *zW:* **~grund** *m* motive; **b~lich** *adj* movable, mobile; (*flink*) quick; **b~t** *adj* (*Leben*) eventful; (*Meer*) rough; (*ergriffen*) touched

Bewegung *f* movement, motion; (*innere*) emotion; (*körperlich*) exercise; **~sfreiheit** *f* freedom of movement; (*fig*) freedom of action; **b~ungslos** *adj* motionless

Beweis [bə'vaɪs] (**-es, -e**) *m* proof; (*Zeichen*) sign; **b~en** [-zən] (*unreg*) *vt* to prove; (*zeigen*) to show; **~mittel** *nt* evidence

Bewerb- [bə'vɛrb] *zW:* **b~en** (*unreg*) *vr* to apply (for); **~er(in)** (**-s, -**) *m(f)* applicant; **~ung** *f* application

bewerkstelligen [bə'vɛrkʃtɛlɪgən] *vt* to manage, to accomplish

bewerten [bə'veːrtən] *vt* to assess

bewilligen [bə'vɪlɪgən] *vt* to grant, to allow

Bewilligung *f* granting

bewirken [bə'vɪrkən] *vt* to cause, to bring about

bewirten [bə'vɪrtən] *vt* to feed, to entertain (to a meal)

bewirtschaften [bə'vɪrtʃaftən] *vt* to manage

Bewirtung *f* hospitality

bewog *etc* [bə'vo:k] *vb siehe* **bewegen**

bewohn- [bə'vo:n] *zW:* **~bar** *adj* habitable; **~en** *vt* to inhabit, to live in; **B~er(in)** (**-s, -**) *m(f)* inhabitant; (*von Haus*) resident

bewölkt [bə'vœlkt] *adj* cloudy, overcast

Bewölkung *f* clouds *pl*

Bewunder- [bə'vʊndər] *zW:* **~er** (**-s, -**) *m* admirer; **b~n** *vt* to admire; **b~nswert** *adj* admirable, wonderful; **~ung** *f* admiration

bewusst ▲ [bə'vʊst] *adj* conscious; (*absichtlich*) deliberate; **sich** *dat* **einer Sache** *gen* **~ sein** to be aware of sth; **~los** *adj* unconscious; **B~losigkeit** *f* unconsciousness; **B~sein** *nt* consciousness; **bei B~sein** conscious

bezahlen [bə'tsaːlən] *vt* to pay for

Bezahlung *f* payment

bezaubern [bə'tsaubərn] *vt* to enchant, to charm

bezeichnen [bə'tsaɪçnən] *vt* (*kennzeichnen*) to mark; (*nennen*) to call; (*beschreiben*) to describe; (*zeigen*) to show, to indicate; **~d** *adj*: **~d (für)** characteristic (of), typical (of)

Bezeichnung *f* (*Zeichen*) mark, sign; (*Beschreibung*) description

bezeugen [bə'tsɔʏgən] *vt* to testify to

Bezichtigung [bə'tsɪçtɪgʊŋ] *f* accusation

beziehen [bə'tsiːən] (*unreg*) *vt* (*mit Überzug*) to cover; (*Bett*) to make; (*Haus, Position*) to move into; (*Standpunkt*) to take up; (*erhalten*) to receive; (*Zeitung*) to subscribe to, to take ♦ *vr* (*Himmel*) to cloud over; **etw auf jdn/etw ~** to relate sth to sb/sth; **sich ~ auf** +*akk* to refer to

Beziehung *f* (*Verbindung*) connection; (*Zusammenhang*) relation; (*Verhältnis*) relationship; (*Hinsicht*) respect; **~en haben** (*vorteilhaft*) to have connections or contacts; **b~sweise** *adv* or; (*genauer gesagt auch*) that is, or rather

Bezirk [bə'tsɪrk] (**-(e)s, -e**) *m* district

Bezug [bə'tsuːk] (**-(e)s, ⁻e**) *m* (*Hülle*) covering; (*COMM*) ordering; (*Gehalt*) income, salary; (*Beziehung*): **~ (zu)** relation(ship) (to); **in ~ auf** +*akk* with reference to; **~ nehmen auf** +*akk* to refer to

bezüglich [bə'tsy:klɪç] *präp* +*gen* concerning, referring to ♦ *adj* (*GRAM*) relative; **auf etw** *akk* **~** relating to sth

bezwecken [bə'tsvɛkən] *vt* to aim at

bezweifeln [bə'tsvaɪfəln] *vt* to doubt, to query

BH *m abk von* **Büstenhalter**

Bhf. *abk* (= *Bahnhof*) station

Bibel ['biːbəl] (**-, -n**) *f* Bible

Biber ['biːbər] (**-s, -**) *m* beaver

Biblio- [biːblio] *zW:* **~grafie** ▲ [-gra'fiː] *f* bibliography; **~thek** [-'teːk] (**-, -en**) *f* library; **~thekar(in)** [-te'kaːr(ɪn)] (**-s, -e**) *m(f)* librarian

biblisch ['biːblɪʃ] *adj* biblical

bieder ['biːdər] *adj* upright, worthy; (*Kleid etc*) plain

bieg- ['biːg] *zW:* **~en** (*unreg*) *vt, vr* to bend ♦ *vi* to turn; **~sam** ['biːk-] *adj* flexible; **B~ung** *f* bend, curve

Biene ['biːnə] *f* bee

Bienenhonig *m* honey

Bienenwachs *nt* beeswax

Bier [biːr] (**-(e)s, -e**) *nt* beer; **~deckel** *m* beer mat; **~garten** *m* beer garden; **~krug** *m* beer mug; **~zelt** *nt* beer tent

Biest [biːst] (**-s, -er**) (*umg: pej*) *nt* (*Tier*) beast, creature; (*Mensch*) beast

bieten ['biːtən] (*unreg*) *vt* to offer; (*bei Versteigerung*) to bid ♦ *vr* (*Gelegenheit*): **sich jdm ~** to present itself to sb; **sich** *dat* **etw ~ lassen** to put up with sth

Bikini [bi'kiːni] (**-s, -s**) *m* bikini

Bilanz [bi'lants] *f* balance; (*fig*) outcome; **~ ziehen (aus)** to take stock (of)

Bild [bɪlt] (**-(e)s, -er**) *nt* (*auch fig*) picture; photo; (*Spiegelbild*) reflection; **~bericht** *m* photographic report

bilden ['bɪldən] *vt* to form; (*erziehen*) to educate; (*ausmachen*) to constitute ♦ *vr* to arise; (*erziehen*) to educate o.s.

Bilderbuch *nt* picture book

Bilderrahmen *m* picture frame

Bild- *zW:* **~fläche** *f* screen; (*fig*) scene; **~hauer** (**-s, -**) *m* sculptor; **b~hübsch** *adj* lovely, pretty as a picture; **b~lich** *adj* figurative; pictorial; **~schirm** *m* television screen; (*COMPUT*) monitor; **~schirmschoner** *m* (*COMPUT*) screen saver; **b~schön** *adj* lovely

Bildung [bɪldʊŋ] *f* formation; (*Wissen, Benehmen*) education

Billard ['bɪljart] (**-s, -e**) *nt* billiards *sg*;

~kugel *f* billiard ball

billig ['bɪlɪç] *adj* cheap; (*gerecht*) fair, reasonable; **~en** ['bɪlɪgən] *vt* to approve of

Binde ['bɪndə] *f* bandage; (*Armbinde*) band; (*MED*) sanitary towel; **~gewebe** *nt* connective tissue; **~glied** *nt* connecting link; **~hautentzündung** *f* conjunctivitis; **b~n** (*unreg*) *vt* to bind, to tie; **~strich** *m* hyphen

Bindfaden ['bɪnt-] *m* string

Bindung *f* bond, tie; (*Skibindung*) binding

binnen ['bɪnən] *präp* (*+dat od gen*) within; **B~hafen** *m* river port; **B~handel** *m* internal trade

Bio- [bio-] *in zW* bio-; **~chemie** *f* biochemistry; **~grafie** ▲ [-gra'fiː] *f* biography; **~laden** *m* wholefood shop; **~loge** [-'loːgə] (**-n, -n**) *m* biologist; **~logie** [-lo'giː] *f* biology; **b~logisch** [-'loːgɪʃ] *adj* biological; **~top** *m od nt* biotope

---

Bioladen

ⓘ A **Bioladen** *is a shop specializing in environmentally-friendly products such as phosphate-free washing powders, recycled paper and organically-grown vegetables.*

Birke ['bɪrkə] *f* birch

Birne ['bɪrnə] *f* pear; (*ELEK*) (light) bulb

SCHLÜSSELWORT

bis [bɪs] *präp +akk, adv* **1** (*zeitlich*) till, until; (*bis spätestens*) by; **Sie haben bis Dienstag Zeit** you have until *od* till Tuesday; **bis Dienstag muss es fertig sein** it must be ready by Tuesday; **bis auf weiteres** until further notice; **bis in die Nacht** into the night; **bis bald/gleich** see you later/soon **2** (*räumlich*) (up) to; **ich fahre bis Köln** I'm going to *od* I'm going as far as Cologne; **bis an unser Grundstück** (right *od* up) to our plot; **bis hierher** this far **3** (*bei Zahlen*) up to; **bis zu** up to **4**: **bis auf etw** *akk* (*außer*) except sth; (*einschließlich*) including sth ♦ *konj* **1** (*mit Zahlen*) to; **10 bis 20** 10 to 20 **2** (*zeitlich*) till, until; **bis es dunkel wird** till

---

od until it gets dark; **von ... bis ...** from ... to ...

Bischof ['bɪʃɔf] (**-s, ⁻e**) *m* bishop; **bischöflich** ['bɪʃøːflɪç] *adj* episcopal

bisher [bɪs'heːr] *adv* till now, hitherto; **~ig** *adj* till now

Biskuit [bɪs'kviːt] (**-(e)s, -s** *od* **-e**) *m od nt* (fatless) sponge

Biss ▲ [bɪs] (**-es, -e**) *m* bite

biss ▲ *etc vb siehe* **beißen**

bisschen ▲ ['bɪsçən] *adj, adv* bit

Bissen ['bɪsən] (**-s, -**) *m* bite, morsel

bissig ['bɪsɪç] *adj* (*Hund*) snappy; (*Bemerkung*) cutting, biting

bist [bɪst] *vb siehe* **sein**

bisweilen [bɪs'vaɪlən] *adv* at times, occasionally

Bitte ['bɪtə] *f* request; **b~** *excl* please; (*wie b~?*) (I beg your) pardon?; ♦ *interj* (*als Antwort auf Dank*) you're welcome; **darf ich? – aber b~!** may I? – please do; **b~ schön!** it was a pleasure; **b~n** (*unreg*) *vt, vi:* **b~n (um)** to ask (for); **b~nd** *adj* pleading, imploring

bitter ['bɪtər] *adj* bitter; **~böse** *adj* very angry; **B~keit** *f* bitterness; **~lich** *adj* bitter

Blähungen ['blɛːʊŋən] *pl* (*MED*) wind *sg*

blamabel [bla'maːbəl] *adj* disgraceful

Blamage [bla'maːʒə] *f* disgrace

blamieren [bla'miːrən] *vr* to make a fool of o.s., to disgrace o.s. ♦ *vt* to let down, to disgrace

blank [blaŋk] *adj* bright; (*unbedeckt*) bare; (*sauber*) clean, polished; (*umg: ohne Geld*) broke; (*offensichtlich*) blatant

blanko ['blaŋko] *adv* blank; **B~scheck** *m* blank cheque

Blase ['blaːzə] *f* bubble; (*MED*) blister; (*ANAT*) bladder; **~balg** (**-(e)s, -bälge**) *m* bellows *pl*; **b~n** (*unreg*) *vt, vi* to blow; **~nentzündung** *f* cystitis

Blas- ['blaːs] *zW:* **~instrument** *nt* wind instrument; **~kapelle** *f* brass band

blass ▲ [blas] *adj* pale

Blässe ['blɛsə] (**-**) *f* paleness, pallor

Blatt [blat] (**-(e)s, ⁻er**) *nt* leaf; (*von Papier*)

sheet; (*Zeitung*) newspaper; (*KARTEN*) hand

blättern ['blɛtərn] *vi:* **in etw** *dat* **~** to leaf through sth

Blätterteig *m* flaky *od* puff pastry

blau [blau] *adj* blue; (*umg*) drunk, stoned; (*KOCH*) boiled; (*Auge*) black; **~er Fleck** bruise; **Fahrt ins B~e** mystery tour; **~äugig** *adj* blue-eyed

Blech [blɛç] (**-(e)s, -e**) *nt* tin, sheet metal; (*Backblech*) baking tray; **~büchse** *f* tin, can; **~dose** *f* tin, can; **b~en** (*umg*) *vt, vi* to fork out; **~schaden** *m* (*AUT*) damage to bodywork

Blei [blaɪ] (**-(e)s, -e**) *nt* lead

Bleibe ['blaɪbə] *f* roof over one's head; **b~n** (*unreg*) *vi* to stay, to remain; **~ lassen** to leave alone; **b~nd** *adj* (*Erinnerung*) lasting; (*Schaden*) permanent

bleich [blaɪç] *adj* faded, pale; **~en** *vt* to bleach

Blei- *zW:* **b~ern** *adj* leaden; **b~frei** *adj* (*Benzin*) lead-free; **~stift** *m* pencil

Blende ['blɛndə] *f* (*PHOT*) aperture; **b~n** *vt* to blind, to dazzle; (*fig*) to hoodwink; **b~nd** (*umg*) *adj* grand; **b~nd aussehen** to look smashing

Blick [blɪk] (**-(e)s, -e**) *m* (*kurz*) glance, glimpse; (*Anschauen*) look; (*Aussicht*) view; **b~en** *vi* to look; **sich b~en lassen** to put in an appearance; **~fang** *m* eye-catcher

blieb *etc* [bliːp] *vb siehe* **bleiben**

blind [blɪnt] *adj* blind; (*Glas etc*) dull; **~er Passagier** stowaway; **B~darm** *m* appendix; **B~darmentzündung** *f* appendicitis; **B~enschrift** ['blɪndən-] *f* Braille; **B~heit** *f* blindness; **~lings** *adv* blindly

blink- ['blɪŋk] *zW:* **~en** *vi* to twinkle, to sparkle; (*Licht*) to flash, to signal; (*AUT*) to indicate ♦ *vt* to flash, to signal; **B~er** (**-s, -**) *m* (*AUT*) indicator; **B~licht** *nt* (*AUT*) indicator; (*an Bahnübergängen usw*) flashing light

blinzeln ['blɪntsəln] *vi* to blink, to wink

Blitz [blɪts] (**-es, -e**) *m* (flash of) lightning; **~ableiter** *m* lightning conductor; **b~en** *vi* (*aufleuchten*) to flash, to sparkle; **es b~t** (*MET*)

Rechtschreibreform: ▲ *neue Schreibung* △ *alte Schreibung (auslaufend)*

(MET) there's a flash of lightning; **~licht** nt flashlight; **b~schnell** adj lightning ♦ adv (as) quick as a flash

Block [blɔk] **(-(e)s, "e)** m block; (von Papier) pad; **~ade** [blɔˈkaːdə] f blockade; **~flöte** f recorder; **b~frei** adj (POL) unaligned; **~haus** nt log cabin; **b~ieren** [blɔˈkiːrən] vt to block ♦ vi (Räder) to jam; **~schrift** f block letters pl

blöd [bløːt] adj silly, stupid; **~eln** [ˈbløːdəln] (umg) vi to act the goat (fam), to fool around; **B~sinn** m nonsense; **~sinnig** adj silly, idiotic

blond [blɔnt] adj blond, fair-haired

SCHLÜSSELWORT

bloß [bloːs] adj 1 (unbedeckt) bare; (nackt) naked; **mit der bloßen Hand** with one's bare hand; **mit bloßem Auge** with the naked eye

2 (alleinig, nur) mere; **der bloße Gedanke** the very thought; **bloßer Neid** sheer envy ♦ adv only, merely; **lass das bloß!** just don't do that!; **wie ist das bloß passiert?** how on earth did that happen?

Blöße [ˈbløːsə] f bareness; nakedness; (fig) weakness

bloßstellen vt to show up

blühen [ˈblyːən] vi to bloom (lit), to be in bloom; (fig) to flourish; **~d** adj (Pflanze) blooming; (Aussehen) blooming, radiant; (Handel) thriving, booming

Blume [ˈbluːmə] f flower; (von Wein) bouquet

Blumen- zW: **~kohl** m cauliflower; **~topf** m flowerpot; **~zwiebel** f bulb

Bluse [ˈbluːzə] f blouse

Blut [bluːt] **(-(e)s)** nt blood; **b~arm** adj anaemic; (fig) penniless; **b~befleckt** adj bloodstained; **b~bild** nt blood count; **~druck** m blood pressure

Blüte [ˈblyːtə] f blossom; (fig) prime

Blut- zW: **b~en** vi to bleed; **~er** m (MED) haemophiliac; **~erguss** ▲ m haemorrhage; (auf Haut) bruise

Blütezeit f flowering period; (fig) prime

Blut- zW: **~gruppe** f blood group; **b~ig** adj bloody; **b~jung** adj very young; **~probe** f blood test; **~spender** m blood donor; **~transfusion** f (MED) blood transfusion; **~ung** f bleeding, haemorrhage; **~vergiftung** f blood poisoning; **~wurst** f black pudding

Bö [bøː] **(-, -en)** f squall

Bock [bɔk] **(-(e)s, "e)** m buck, ram; (Gestell) trestle, support; (SPORT) buck; **~wurst** f type of pork sausage

Boden [ˈboːdən] **(-s, "-)** m ground; (Fußboden) floor; (Meeresboden, Fassboden) bottom; (Speicher) attic; **b~los** adj bottomless; (umg) incredible; **~nebel** m ground mist; **~personal** nt (AVIAT) ground staff; **~schätze** pl mineral resources; **~see** m: **der ~see** Lake Constance; **~turnen** nt floor exercises pl

Böe [ˈbøːə] f squall

Bogen [ˈboːgən] **(-s, -)** m (Biegung) curve; (ARCHIT) arch; (Waffe, MUS) bow; (Papier) sheet

Bohne [ˈboːnə] f bean

bohnern vt to wax, to polish

Bohnerwachs nt floor polish

Bohr- [ˈboːr] zW: **b~en** vt to bore; **~er** **(-s, -)** m drill; **~insel** f oil rig; **~maschine** f drill; **~turm** m derrick

Boiler [ˈbɔylər] **(-s, -)** m (hot-water) tank

Boje [ˈboːjə] f buoy

Bolzen [ˈbɔltsən] **(-s, -)** m bolt

bombardieren [bɔmbarˈdiːrən] vt to bombard; (aus der Luft) to bomb

Bombe [ˈbɔmbə] f bomb

Bombenangriff m bombing raid

Bombenerfolg (umg) m smash hit

Bon [bɔŋ] **(-s, -s)** m voucher, chit

Bonbon [bõˈbõː] **(-s, -s)** m od nt sweet

Boot [boːt] **(-(e)s, -e)** nt boat

Bord [bɔrt] **(-(e)s, -e)** nt (AVIAT, NAUT) board ♦ nt (Brett) shelf; **an ~** on board

Bordell [bɔrˈdɛl] **(-s, -e)** nt brothel

Bordstein m kerb(stone)

borgen [ˈbɔrgən] vt to borrow; **jdm etw ~** to lend sb sth

borniert [bɔrˈniːrt] adj narrow-minded

Börse ['bœːrzə] *f* stock exchange; (*Geldbörse*) purse; **~nmakler** *m* stockbroker

Borte ['bɔrtə] *f* edging; (*Band*) trimming

bös [bøːs] *adj* = **böse**

bösartig ['bøːz-] *adj* malicious

Böschung ['bœʃʊŋ] *f* slope; (*Uferböschung etc*) embankment

böse ['bøːzə] *adj* bad, evil; (*zornig*) angry

boshaft ['boːshaft] *adj* malicious, spiteful

Bosheit *f* malice, spite

Bosnien ['bɔsniən] **(-s)** *nt* Bosnia; **~ und Herzegowina** [-hertsə'goːvina] *nt* Bosnia (and) Herzegovina

böswillig ['bøːsvɪlɪç] *adj* malicious

bot *etc* [boːt] *vb siehe* **bieten**

Botanik [bo'taːnɪk] *f* botany; **botanisch** *adj* botanical

Bot- [boːt] *zW:* **~e (-n, -n)** *m* messenger; **~schaft** *f* message, news; (*POL*) embassy; **~schafter (-s, -)** *m* ambassador

Bottich ['bɔtɪç] **(-(e)s, -e)** *m* vat, tub

Bouillon [bʊ'ljõː] **(-, -s)** *f* consommé

Bowle ['boːlə] *f* punch

Box- ['bɔks] *zW:* **b~en** *vi* to box; **~er (-s, -)** *m* boxer; **~kampf** *m* boxing match

boykottieren [bɔykɔ'tiːrən] *vt* to boycott

brach *etc* [braːx] *vb siehe* **brechen**

brachte *etc* ['braxtə] *vb siehe* **bringen**

Branche ['brãːʃə] *f* line of business

Branchenverzeichnis *nt* Yellow Pages® *pl*

Brand [brant] **(-(e)s, ⁺e)** *m* fire; (*MED*) gangrene; **b~en** ['brandən] *vi* to surge; (*Meer*) to break; **b~marken** *vt* to brand; (*fig*) to stigmatize; **~salbe** *f* ointment for burns; **~stifter** [-ʃtɪftər] *m* arsonist, fire raiser; **~stiftung** *f* arson; **~ung** *f* surf

Branntwein ['brantvaɪn] *m* brandy

Brasilien [bra'ziːliən] *nt* Brazil

Brat- ['braːt] *zW:* **~apfel** *m* baked apple; **b~en** (*unreg*) *vt* to roast; to fry; **~en (-s, -)** *m* roast, joint; **~hähnchen** *nt* roast chicken; **~huhn** *nt* roast chicken; **~kartoffeln** *pl* fried *od* roast potatoes; **~pfanne** *f* frying pan

Bratsche ['braːtʃə] *f* viola

Bratspieß *m* spit

Bratwurst *f* grilled/fried sausage

Brauch [braux] **(-(e)s, Bräuche)** *m* custom; **b~bar** *adj* usable, serviceable; (*Person*) capable; **b~en** *vt* (*bedürfen*) to need; (*müssen*) to have to; (*umg: verwenden*) to use

Braue ['brauə] *f* brow

brauen ['brauən] *vt* to brew

Braue'rei *f* brewery

braun [braun] *adj* brown; (*von Sonne auch*) tanned; **~ gebrannt** tanned

Bräune ['brɔynə] **(-)** *f* brownness; (*Sonnenbräune*) tan; **b~n** *vt* to make brown; (*Sonne*) to tan

Brause ['brauzə] *f* shower bath; (*von Gießkanne*) rose; (*Getränk*) lemonade; **b~n** *vi* to roar; (*auch vr: duschen*) to take a shower

Braut [braut] **(-, Bräute)** *f* bride; (*Verlobte*) fiancée

Bräutigam ['brɔytɪgam] **(-s, -e)** *m* bridegroom; fiancé

Brautpaar *nt* bride and (bride)groom, bridal pair

brav [braːf] *adj* (*artig*) good; (*ehrenhaft*) worthy, honest

bravo ['braːvo] *excl* well done

BRD ['beː'ʔerˈdeː] **(-)** *f abk* = **Bundesrepublik Deutschland**

BRD

---

i The **BRD** (*Bundesrepublik Deutschland*) is the official name for the Federal Republic of Germany. It comprises 16 **Länder** (*see* **Land**). It was formerly the name given to West Germany as opposed to East Germany (the **DDR**). The two Germanies were reunited on 3rd October 1990.

Brech- ['brɛç] *zW:* **~eisen** *nt* crowbar; **b~en** (*unreg*) *vt, vi* to break; (*Licht*) to refract; (*fig: Mensch*) to crush; (*speien*) to vomit; **~reiz** *m* nausea, retching

Brei [braɪ] **(-(e)s, -e)** *m* (*Masse*) pulp; (*KOCH*) gruel; (*Haferbrei*) porridge

breit [braɪt] *adj* wide, broad; **sich ~ machen** to spread o.s. out; **B~e** *f* width; (*bes bei*

Maßangaben) breadth; *(GEOG)* latitude; ~en *vt:* **etw über etw** *akk* ~**en** to spread sth over sth; **B~engrad** *m* degree of latitude; ~**treten** *(unreg) (umg) vt* to go on about

Brems- ['brɛms] *zW:* ~**belag** *m* brake lining; ~**e** [-zə] *f* brake; *(ZOOL)* horsefly; **b~en** [-zən] *vi* to brake ♦ *vt (Auto)* to brake; *(fig)* to slow down; ~**flüssigkeit** *f* brake fluid; ~**licht** *nt* brake light; ~**pedal** *nt* brake pedal; ~**spur** *f* skid mark(s *pl*); ~**weg** *m* braking distance

Brenn- ['brɛn] *zW:* **b~bar** *adj* inflammable; **b~en** *(unreg) vi* to burn, to be on fire; *(Licht, Kerze etc)* to burn ♦ *vt (Holz etc)* to burn; *(Ziegel, Ton)* to fire; *(Kaffee)* to roast; **darauf b~en, etw zu tun** to be dying to do sth; ~**nessel** ▲ *f* stinging nettle; ~**punkt** *m (PHYS)* focal point; *(Mittelpunkt)* focus; ~**stoff** *m* fuel

brenzlig ['brɛntslɪç] *adj (fig)* precarious

Bretagne [bre'tanjə] *f:* **die ~** Brittany

Brett [brɛt] *(-(e)s, -er)* *nt* board, plank; *(Bord)* shelf; *(Spielbrett)* board; ~**er** *pl (SKI)* skis; *(THEAT)* boards; **schwarzes ~** notice board; ~**erzaun** *m* wooden fence; ~**spiel** *nt* board game

Brezel ['bre:tsəl] *(-, -n)* *f* pretzel

brichst *etc* [brɪçst] *vb siehe* **brechen**

Brief [bri:f] *(-(e)s, -e)* *m* letter; ~**freund** *m* penfriend; ~**kasten** *m* letterbox; **b~lich** *adj, adv* by letter; ~**marke** *f* (postage) stamp; ~**papier** *nt* notepaper; ~**tasche** *f* wallet; ~**träger** *m* postman; ~**umschlag** *m* envelope; ~**waage** *f* letter scales; ~**wechsel** *m* correspondence

brief *etc* [bri:t] *vb siehe* **braten**

Brikett [bri'kɛt] *(-s, -s)* *nt* briquette

brillant [brɪl'jant] *adj (fig)* brilliant; **B~** *(-en, -en)* *m* brilliant, diamond

Brille ['brɪlə] *f* spectacles *pl; (Schutzbrille)* goggles *pl; (Toilettenbrille)* (toilet) seat; ~**ngestell** *nt* (spectacle) frames

bringen ['brɪŋən] *(unreg) vt* to bring; *(mitnehmen, begleiten)* to take; *(einbringen: Profit)* to bring in; *(veröffentlichen)* to publish; *(THEAT, CINE)* to show; *(RADIO, TV)* to broadcast; *(in einen Zustand versetzen)* to

get; *(umg: tun können)* to manage; **jdn dazu ~, etw zu tun** to make sb do sth; **jdn nach Hause ~** to take sb home; **jdn um etw ~** to make sb lose sth; **jdn auf eine Idee ~** to give sb an idea

Brise ['bri:zə] *f* breeze

Brit- ['bri:t] *zW:* ~**e** *m* Briton; ~**in** *f* Briton; **b~isch** *adj* British

bröckelig ['brœkəlɪç] *adj* crumbly

Brocken ['brɔkən] *(-s, -)* *m* piece, bit; *(Felsbrocken)* lump of rock

brodeln ['bro:dəln] *vi* to bubble

Brokkoli ['brɔkoli] *pl (BOT)* broccoli

Brombeere ['brɔmbe:rə] *f* blackberry, bramble *(BRIT)*

Bronchien ['brɔnçiən] *pl* bronchia(l tubes) *pl*

Bronchitis [brɔn'çi:tɪs] *(-)* *f* bronchitis

Bronze ['brõ:sə] *f* bronze

Brosche ['brɔʃə] *f* brooch

Broschüre [brɔ'ʃy:rə] *f* pamphlet

Brot [bro:t] *(-(e)s, -e)* *nt* bread; *(Laib)* loaf

Brötchen ['brø:tçən] *nt* roll

Bruch [brʊx] *(-(e)s, ⁺e)* *m* breakage; *(zerbrochene Stelle)* break; *(fig)* split, breach; *(MED: Eingeweidebruch)* rupture, hernia; *(Beinbruch etc)* fracture; *(MATH)* fraction

brüchig ['brʏçɪç] *adj* brittle, fragile; *(Haus)* dilapidated

Bruch- *zW:* ~**landung** *f* crash landing; ~**strich** *m (MATH)* line; ~**stück** *nt* fragment; ~**teil** *m* fraction; ~**zahl** [brʊxtsa:l] *f (MATH)* fraction

Brücke ['brʏkə] *f* bridge; *(Teppich)* rug

Bruder ['bru:dər] *(-s, ⁺)* *m* brother; **brüderlich** *adj* brotherly

Brühe ['bry:ə] *f* broth, stock; *(pej)* muck

brüllen ['brʏlən] *vi* to bellow, to roar

brummen ['brʊmən] *vi (Bär, Mensch etc)* to growl; *(Insekt)* to buzz; *(Motoren)* to roar; *(murren)* to grumble

brünett [brʏ'nɛt] *adj* brunette, dark-haired

Brunnen ['brʊnən] *(-s, -)* *m* fountain; *(tief)* well; *(natürlich)* spring

Brust [brʊst] *(-, ⁺e)* *f* breast; *(Männerbrust)* chest

brüsten ['brʏstən] *vr* to boast

Spelling Reform: ▲ *new spelling* △ *old spelling (to be phased out)*

Brust- *zW:* **~kasten** *m* chest;
~schwimmen *nt* breast-stroke
Brüstung ['brʏstʊŋ] *f* parapet
Brut [bruːt] (-, **-en**) *f* brood; (*Brüten*)
hatching
brutal [bruˈtaːl] *adj* brutal
Brutali'tät *f* brutality
brüten ['bryːtən] *vi* (*auch fig*) to brood
Brutkasten *m* incubator
brutto ['brʊto] *adv* gross; **B~einkommen** *nt*
gross salary; **B~gehalt** *nt* gross salary;
B~gewicht *nt* gross weight; **B~lohn** *m*
gross wages *pl*; **B~sozialprodukt** *nt* gross
national product
BSE *f abk* (= *Bovine Spongiforme
Enzephalopathie*) BSE
Bube ['buːbə] (-**n**, **-n**) *m* (*Schurke*) rogue;
(*KARTEN*) jack
Buch [buːx] (-**(e)s**, **ᵘer**) *nt* book; (*COMM*)
account book; **~binder** *m* bookbinder;
~drucker *m* printer
Buche *f* beech tree
buchen *vt* to book; (*Betrag*) to enter
Bücher- ['byːçər] *zW:* **~brett** *nt* book-
helf; **~ei** [-'rai] *f* library; **~regal** *nt* book-
shelves *pl*, bookcase; **~schrank** *m* bookcase
Buch- *zW:* **~führung** *f* book-keeping,
accounting; **~halter(in)** (-**s**, -) *m(f)* book-
keeper; **~handel** *m* book trade;
~händler(in) *m(f)* bookseller; **~handlung**
f bookshop
Büchse ['bʏksə] *f* tin, can; (*Holzbüchse*) box;
(*Gewehr*) rifle; **~nfleisch** *nt* tinned meat;
~nmilch *f* (*KOCH*) evaporated milk, tinned
milk; **~nöffner** *m* tin *od* can opener
Buchstabe (-**ns**, -**n**) *m* letter (of the
alphabet)
buchstabieren [buːxʃtaˈbiːrən] *vt* to spell
buchstäblich ['buːxʃtɛːplɪç] *adj* literal
Bucht ['bʊxt] (-, **-en**) *f* bay
Buchung ['buːxʊŋ] *f* booking; (*COMM*) entry
Buckel ['bʊkəl] (-**s**, -) *m* hump
bücken ['bʏkən] *vr* to bend
Bude ['buːdə] *f* booth, stall; (*umg*) digs *pl*
(*BRIT*)
Büfett [bʏˈfet] (-**s**, -**s**) *nt* (*Anrichte*) sideboard;

(*Geschirrschrank*) dresser; **kaltes ~** cold
buffet
Büffel ['bʏfəl] (-**s**, -) *m* buffalo
Bug [buːk] (-**(e)s**, **-e**) *m* (*NAUT*) bow; (*AVIAT*)
nose
Bügel ['byːgəl] (-**s**, -) *m* (*Kleider~*) hanger;
(*Steig~*) stirrup; (*Brillen~*) arm; **~brett** *nt*
ironing board; **~eisen** *nt* iron; **~falte** *f*
crease; **b~frei** *adj* crease-resistant, noniron;
b~n *vt*, *vi* to iron
Bühne ['byːnə] *f* stage; **~nbild** *nt* set,
scenery
Buhruf ['buːruːf] *m* boo
buk *etc* [buːk] *vb siehe* **backen**
Bulgarien [bʊlˈgaːriən] *nt* Bulgaria
Bull- ['bʊl] *zW:* **~auge** *nt* (*NAUT*) porthole;
~dogge *f* bulldog; **~dozer** ['bʊldoːzər] (-**s**,
-) *m* bulldozer; **~e** (-**n**, -**n**) *m* bull
Bumerang ['buːməraŋ] (-**s**, -**e**) *m*
boomerang
Bummel ['bʊməl] (-**s**, -) *m* stroll;
(*Schaufensterbummel*) window-shopping;
~ant [-'lant] *m* slowcoach; **~ei** [-'lai] *f*
wandering; dawdling; skiving; **b~n** *vi* to
wander, to stroll; (*trödeln*) to dawdle;
(*faulenzen*) to skive, to loaf around; **~streik**
['bʊməlʃtraik] *m* go-slow
Bund¹ [bʊnt] (-**(e)s**, **ᵘe**) *m*
(*Freundschaftsbund etc*) bond; (*Organisation*)
union; (*POL*) confederacy; (*Hosenbund,
Rockbund*) waistband
Bund² (-**(e)s**, **-e**) *nt* bunch; (*Strohbund*)
bundle
Bündel ['bʏndəl] (-**s**, -) *nt* bundle, bale; **b~n**
vt to bundle
Bundes- ['bʊndəs] *in zW* Federal; **~bürger**
m German citizen; **~hauptstadt** *f* Federal
capital; **~kanzler** *m* Federal Chancellor;
~land *nt* Land; **~liga** *f* football league;
~präsident *m* Federal President; **~rat** *m*
upper house of German Parliament;
~regierung *f* Federal government;
~republik *f* Federal Republic (of
Germany); **~staat** *m* Federal state;
~straße *f* Federal road; **~tag** *m* German
Parliament; **~wehr** *f* German Armed Forces
pl; **b~weit** *adj* nationwide

Bundespräsident
---

i The **Bundespräsident** *is the head of
state of the Federal Republic of
Germany. He is elected every 5 years - no-
one can be elected more than twice - by the
members of the **Bundesversammlung**, a
body formed especially for this purpose. His
role is to represent Germany at home and
abroad. In Switzerland the
Bundespräsident is the head of the
government, known as the **Bundesrat**.
The **Bundesrat** is the Upper House of the
German Parliament whose 68 members are
nominated by the parliaments of the
Länder. Its most important function is to
approve federal laws concerned with the
jurisdiction of the **Länder**; it can raise
objections to other laws, but can be
outvoted by the **Bundestag**. In Austria the
Länder are also represented in the
Bundesrat.*

Bundestag
---

i The **Bundestag** *is the Lower House of
the German Parliament and is elected by
the people by proportional representation.
There are 672 MPs, half of them elected
directly from the first vote (**Erststimme**),
and half from the regional list of
parliamentary candidates resulting from the
second vote (**Zweitstimme**). The
Bundestag exercises parliamentary control
over the government.*

Bündnis ['byntnɪs] **(-ses, -se)** *nt* alliance
bunt [bʊnt] *adj* coloured; (*gemischt*) mixed;
  jdm wird es zu ~ it's getting too much for
  sb;B~**stift** *m* coloured pencil, crayon
Burg [bʊrk] **(-, -en)** *f* castle, fort
Bürge ['byrgə] **(-n, -n)** *m* guarantor;
  b~**n für** to vouch for
Bürger(in) ['byrgər(ɪn)] **(-s, -)** *m(f)* citizen;
  member of the middle class;~**krieg** *m* civil
  war;b~**lich** *adj* (*Rechte*) civil; (*Klasse*)
  middle-class; (*pej*) bourgeois;~**meister** *m*

mayor;~**recht** *nt* civil rights *pl*;~**schaft** *f*
  (*Vertretung*) City Parliament;~**steig** *m*
  pavement
Bürgschaft *f* surety; **~ leisten** to give
  security
Büro [by'ro:] **(-s, -s)** *nt* office;
  ~**angestellte(r)** *f(m)* office worker;
  ~**klammer** *f* paper clip;~**kra'tie** *f*
  bureaucracy;b~'**kratisch** *adj* bureaucratic;
  ~**schluss** ▲ *m* office closing time
Bursche ['bʊrʃə] **(-n, -n)** *m* lad, fellow;
  (*Diener*) servant
Bürste ['byrstə] *f* brush;b~**n** *vt* to brush
Bus [bʊs] **(-ses, -se)** *m* bus;~**bahnhof** *m*
  bus/coach (*BRIT*) station
Busch [bʊʃ] **(-(e)s, ̈e)** *m* bush, shrub
Büschel ['byʃəl] **(-s, -)** *nt* tuft
buschig *adj* bushy
Busen ['bu:zən] **(-s, -)** *m* bosom;
  (*Meerbusen*) inlet, bay
Bushaltestelle *f* bus stop
Buße ['bu:sə] *f* penance; (*Geld*) fine
büßen ['by:sən] *vi* to do penance, to atone
  ♦ *vt* to do penance for, to atone for
Bußgeld ['bu:sgɛlt] *nt* fine;~**bescheid** *m*
  notice of payment due (*for traffic offence
  etc*)
Büste ['bystə] *f* bust;~**nhalter** *m* bra
Butter ['bʊtər] **(-)** *f* butter;~**blume** *f*
  buttercup;~**brot** *nt* (piece of) bread and
  butter; (*umg*) sandwich;~**brotpapier** *nt*
  greaseproof paper;~**dose** *f* butter dish;
  ~**milch** *f* buttermilk;b~**weich** ['bʊtərvaiç]
  adj soft as butter; (*fig, umg*) soft
b. w. *abk* (= *bitte wenden*) p.t.o.
bzgl. *abk* (= *bezüglich*) re
bzw. *abk* = **beziehungsweise**

C, c

ca. [ka] *abk* (= *circa*) approx.
Cabin Crew [kebinkru:] *f* cabin crew
Café [ka'fe:] **(-s, -s)** *nt* café
Cafeteria [kafete'ri:a] **(-, -s)** *f* cafeteria
Camcorder **(-s, -)** *m* camcorder
Camp- ['kɛmp] *zW:*c~**en** *vi* to camp;~**er**

(**-s**, **-**) *m* camper; **~ing** (**-s**) *nt* camping; **~ingführer** *m* camping guide (book); **~ingkocher** *m* camping stove; **~ingplatz** *m* camp(ing) site

CD-Spieler *m* CD (player)

Cello ['tʃɛlo] (**-s**, **-s** *od* **Celli**) *nt* cello

Celsius ['tsɛlziʊs] (**-**) *nt* centigrade

Champagner [ʃam'panjər] (**-s**, **-**) *m* champagne

Champignon ['ʃampinjō] (**-s**, **-s**) *m* button mushroom

Chance ['ʃã:s(ə)] *f* chance, opportunity

Chaos ['ka:ɔs] (**-**, **-**) *nt* chaos; **chaotisch** [ka'o:tiʃ] *adj* chaotic

Charakter [ka'raktər, *pl* karak'te:rə] (**-s**, **-e**) *m* character; **c~fest** *adj* of firm character, strong; **c~i'sieren** *vt* to characterize; **c~istisch** [karakte'ristiʃ] *adj*: **c~istisch (für)** characteristic (of), typical (of); **c~los** *adj* unprincipled; **~losigkeit** *f* lack of principle; **~schwäche** *f* weakness of character; **~stärke** *f* strength of character; **~zug** *m* characteristic, trait

charmant [ʃar'mant] *adj* charming

Charme [ʃarm] (**-s**) *m* charm

Charterflug ['tʃartərflu:k] *m* charter flight

Chauffeur [ʃɔ'fø:r] *m* chauffeur

Chauvinist [ʃovi'nist] *m* chauvinist, jingoist

Chef [ʃɛf] (**-s**, **-s**) *m* head; (*umg*) boss; **~arzt** *m* senior consultant; **~in** (*umg*) *f* boss

Chemie [çe'mi:] (**-**) *f* chemistry; **~faser** *f* man-made fibre

Chemikalie [çemi'ka:liə] *f* chemical

Chemiker ['çe:mikər] (**-s**, **-**) *m* (industrial) chemist

chemisch ['çe:miʃ] *adj* chemical; **~e Reinigung** dry cleaning

Chicorée ['ʃikore:] (**-s**) *m od f* chicory

Chiffre ['ʃifrə] *f* (*Geheimzeichen*) cipher; (*in Zeitung*) box number

Chile ['tʃi:le] *nt* Chile

Chin- ['çi:n] *zW*: **~a** *nt* China; **~akohl** *m* Chinese leaves; **~ese** [-'ne:zə] *m* Chinese; **~esin** *f* Chinese; **c~esisch** *adj* Chinese

Chip [tʃip] (**-s**, **-s**) *m* (*Kartoffelchips*) crisp (*BRIT*), chip (*US*); (*COMPUT*) chip; **~karte** *f* smart card

Chirurg [çi'rʊrg] (**-en**, **-en**) *m* surgeon; **~ie** [-'gi:] *f* surgery; **c~isch** *adj* surgical

Chlor [klo:r] (**-s**) *nt* chlorine; **~o'form** (**-s**) *nt* chloroform

cholerisch [ko'le:riʃ] *adj* choleric

Chor [ko:r] (**-(e)s**, **ᵘe**) *m* choir; (*Musikstück, THEAT*) chorus; **~al** [ko'ra:l] (**-s**, **-äle**) *m* chorale

Choreograf ▲ [koreo'gra:f] (**-en**, **-en**) *m* choreographer

Christ [krist] (**-en**, **-en**) *m* Christian; **~baum** *m* Christmas tree; **~entum** *nt* Christianity; **~in** *f* Christian; **~kind** *nt* ≃ Father Christmas; (*Jesus*) baby Jesus; **c~lich** *adj* Christian; **~us** (**-**) *m* Christ

Chrom [kro:m] (**-s**) *nt* (*CHEM*) chromium; chrome

Chron- ['kro:n] *zW*: **~ik** *f* chronicle; **c~isch** *adj* chronic; **c~ologisch** [-o'lo:giʃ] *adj* chronological

circa ['tsirka] *adv* about, approximately

Clown [klaʊn] (**-s**, **-s**) *m* clown

Cocktail ['kɔkteil] (**-s**, **-s**) *m* cocktail

Cola ['ko:la] (**-**, **-s**) *f* Coke ®

Computer [kɔm'pju:tər] (**-s**, **-**) *m* computer; **~spiel** *nt* computer game

Cord [kɔrt] (**-s**) *m* cord, corduroy

Couch [kaʊtʃ] (**-**, **-es** *od* **-en**) *f* couch

Coupon [ku'põ:] (**-s**, **-s**) *m* = **Kupon**

Cousin [ku'zɛ̃:] (**-s**, **-s**) *m* cousin; **~e** [ku'zi:nə] *f* cousin

Creme [kre:m] (**-**, **-s**) *f* cream; (*Schuhcreme*) polish; (*Zahncreme*) paste; (*KOCH*) mousse; **c~farben** *adj* cream(-coloured)

cremig ['kre:miç] *adj* creamy

Curry ['kari] (**-s**) *m od nt* curry powder; **~pulver** *nt* curry powder; **~wurst** *f* curried sausage

D, d

da [da:] *adv* **1** (*örtlich*) there; (*hier*) here; **da draußen** out there; **da sein** to be there; **da**

bin ich here I am; **da, wo** where; **ist noch Milch da?** is there any milk left?
2 (*zeitlich*) then; (*folglich*) so
3: da haben wir Glück gehabt we were lucky there; **da kann man nichts machen** nothing can be done about it
♦ *konj* (*weil*) as, since

abehalten (*unreg*) *vt* to keep
abei [da'baɪ] *adv* (*räumlich*) close to it; (*noch dazu*) besides; (*zusammen mit*) with them; (*zeitlich*) during this; (*obwohl doch*) but, however; **was ist schon ~?** what of it?; **es ist doch nichts ~, wenn ...** it doesn't matter if ...; **bleiben wir ~** let's leave it at that; **es bleibt ~** that's settled; **das Dumme/Schwierige ~** the stupid/difficult part of it; **er war gerade ~ zu gehen** he was just leaving; **~ sein** (*anwesend*) to be present; (*beteiligt*) to be involved; **~stehen** (*unreg*) *vi* to stand around

ach [dax] **(-(e)s, ⁺er)** *nt* roof; **~boden** *m* attic, loft; **~decker (-s, -)** *m* slater, tiler; **~fenster** *nt* skylight; **~gepäckträger** *m* roof rack; **~luke** *f* skylight; **~pappe** *f* roofing felt; **~rinne** *f* gutter

achs [daks] **(-es, -e)** *m* badger
achte *etc* ['daxtə] *vb siehe* **denken**
ackel ['dakəl] **(-s, -)** *m* dachshund
adurch [da'dʊrç] *adv* (*räumlich*) through it; (*durch diesen Umstand*) thereby, in that way; (*deshalb*) because of that, for that reason
♦ *konj*: **~, dass** because

afür [da'fy:r] *adv* for it; (*anstatt*) instead; **er kann nichts ~** he can't help it; **er ist bekannt ~** he is well-known for that; **was bekomme ich ~?** what will I get for it?

agegen [da'ge:gən] *adv* against it; (*im Vergleich damit*) in comparison with it; (*bei Tausch*) for it/them ♦ *konj* however; **ich habe nichts ~** I don't mind; **ich war ~** I was against it; **~ kann man nichts tun** one can't do anything about it; **~halten** (*unreg*) *vt* (*vergleichen*) to compare with it; (*entgegnen*) to object to it; **~sprechen** (*unreg*) *vi*: **es spricht nichts ~** there's no reason why not

daheim [da'haɪm] *adv* at home; **D~ (-s)** *nt* home
daher [da'he:r] *adv* (*räumlich*) from there; (*Ursache*) from that ♦ *konj* (*deshalb*) that's why
dahin [da'hɪn] *adv* (*räumlich*) there; (*zeitlich*) then; (*vergangen*) gone; **~ gehend** on this matter; **~'gegen** *konj* on the other hand; **~gestellt** *adv*: **~gestellt bleiben** to remain to be seen; **~gestellt sein lassen** to leave open *od* undecided
dahinten [da'hɪntən] *adv* over there
dahinter [da'hɪntər] *adv* behind it; **~ kommen** to get to the bottom of it
dalli ['dali] (*umg*) *adv* chop chop
damalig ['da:ma:lɪç] *adj* of that time, then
damals ['da:ma:ls] *adv* at that time, then
Dame ['da:mə] *f* lady; (*SCHACH, KARTEN*) queen; (*Spiel*) draughts *sg*; **~nbinde** *f* sanitary towel *od* napkin (*US*); **d~nhaft** *adj* ladylike; **~ntoilette** *f* ladies' toilet *od* restroom (*US*); **~nwahl** *f* ladies' excuse-me
damit [da'mɪt] *adv* with it; (*begründend*) by that ♦ *konj* in order that, in order to; **was meint er ~?** what does he mean by that?; **genug ~!** that's enough!
dämlich ['dɛ:mlɪç] (*umg*) *adj* silly, stupid
Damm [dam] **(-(e)s, ⁺e)** *m* dyke; (*Staudamm*) dam; (*Hafendamm*) mole; (*Bahndamm, Straßendamm*) embankment
dämmen ['dɛman] *vt* (*Wasser*) to dam up; (*Schmerzen*) to keep back
dämmer- *zW*: **~ig** *adj* dim, faint; **~n** *vi* (*Tag*) to dawn; (*Abend*) to fall; **D~ung** *f* twilight; (*Morgendämmerung*) dawn; (*Abenddämmerung*) dusk
Dampf [dampf] **(-(e)s, ⁺e)** *m* steam; (*Dunst*) vapour; **d~en** *vi* to steam
dämpfen ['dɛmpfən] *vt* (*KOCH*) to steam; (*bügeln*) to iron with a damp cloth; (*fig*) to dampen, to subdue
Dampf- *zW*: **~schiff** *nt* steamship; **~walze** *f* steamroller
danach [da'na:x] *adv* after that; (*zeitlich*) after that, afterwards; (*gemäß*) accordingly; according to which; according to that; **er sieht ~ aus** he looks it

Spelling Reform: ▲ *new spelling* △ *old spelling (to be phased out)*

Däne ['dɛːnə] **(-n, -n)** *m* Dane

daneben [da'neːbən] *adv* beside it; (*im Vergleich*) in comparison; **~benehmen** (*unreg*) *vr* to misbehave; **~gehen** (*unreg*) *vi* to miss; (*Plan*) to fail

Dänemark ['dɛːnəmark] *nt* Denmark; **Dänin** *f* Dane; **dänisch** *adj* Danish

Dank [daŋk] **(-(e)s)** *m* thanks *pl*; **vielen** *od* **schönen ~** many thanks; **jdm ~ sagen** to thank sb; **d~** *präp* (+*dat od gen*) thanks to; **d~bar** *adj* grateful; (*Aufgabe*) rewarding; **~barkeit** *f* gratitude; **d~e** *excl* thank you, thanks; **d~en** *vi* +*dat* to thank; **d~enswert** *adj* (*Arbeit*) worthwhile; rewarding; (*Bemühung*) kind; **d~sagen** *vi* to express one's thanks

dann [dan] *adv* then; **~ und wann** now and then

daran [da'ran] *adv* on it; (*stoßen*) against it; **es liegt ~, dass ...** the cause of it is that ...; **gut/schlecht ~ sein** to be well-/badly off; **das Beste/Dümmste ~** the best/ stupidest thing about it; **ich war nahe ~ zu ...** I was on the point of ...; **er ist ~ gestorben** he died from it *od* of it; **~gehen** (*unreg*) *vi* to start; **~setzen** *vt* to stake

darauf [da'rauf] *adv* (*räumlich*) on it; (*zielgerichtet*) towards it; (*danach*) afterwards; **es kommt ganz ~ an, ob ...** it depends whether ...; **die Tage ~** the days following *od* thereafter; **am Tag ~** the next day; **~ folgend** (*Tag, Jahr*) next, following; **~ legen** to lay *od* put on top

daraus [da'raus] *adv* from it; **was ist ~ geworden?** what became of it?; **~ geht hervor, dass ...** this means that ...

Darbietung ['darːbiːtuŋ] *f* performance

darf *etc* [darf] *vb siehe* **dürfen**

darin ['daːrɪn] *adv* in (there), in it

darlegen ['darːleːgən] *vt* to explain, to expound, to set forth; **Darlegung** *f* explanation

Darleh(e)n (-s, -) *nt* loan

Darm [darm] **(-(e)s, ⁀e)** *m* intestine; (*Wurstdarm*) skin; **~grippe** *f* (*MED*) gastric influenza *od* flu

darstell- ['darːʃtɛl] *zW*: **~en** *vt* (*abbilden, bedeuten*) to represent; (*THEAT*) to act; (*beschreiben*) to describe ♦ *vr* to appear to be; **D~er(in) (-s, -)** *m(f)* actor (actress); **D~ung** *f* portrayal, depiction

darüber [da'ryːbər] *adv* (*räumlich*) over it, above it; (*fahren*) over it; (*mehr*) more; (*währenddessen*) meanwhile; (*sprechen, streiten*) about it; **~ geht nichts** there's nothing like it

darum [da'rom] *adv* (*räumlich*) round it ♦ *konj* that's why; **er bittet ~** he is pleading for it; **es geht ~, dass ...** the thing is that ...; **er würde viel ~ geben, wenn ...** he would give a lot to ...; **ich tue es ~, weil ...** I am doing it because ...

darunter [da'rontər] *adv* (*räumlich*) under it; (*dazwischen*) among them; (*weniger*) less; **ein Stockwerk ~** one floor below (it); **was verstehen Sie ~?** what do you understand by that?

das [das] *def art* the ♦ *pron* that

Dasein ['daːzaɪn] **(-s)** *nt* (*Leben*) life; (*Anwesenheit*) presence; (*Bestehen*) existence

da sein ▲ *siehe* **da**

dass ▲ [das] *konj* that

dasselbe [das'zɛlbə] *art, pron* the same

dastehen ['daːʃteːən] (*unreg*) *vi* to stand there

Datei [da'taɪ] *f* file

Daten- ['daːtən] *zW*: **~bank** *f* data base; **~schutz** *m* data protection; **~verarbeitung** *f* data processing

datieren [da'tiːrən] *vt* to date

Dativ ['daːtiːf] **(-s, -e)** *m* dative (case)

Dattel ['datəl] **(-, -n)** *f* date

Datum ['daːtum] **(-s, Daten)** *nt* date; **Daten** *pl* (*Angaben*) data *pl*

Dauer ['dauər] **(-, -n)** *f* duration; (*gewisse Zeitspanne*) length; (*Bestand, Fortbestehen*) permanence; **es war nur von kurzer ~** it didn't last long; **auf die ~** in the long run; (*auf längere Zeit*) indefinitely; **~auftrag** *m* standing order; **d~haft** *adj* lasting, durable; **~karte** *f* season ticket; **~lauf** *m* jog(ging); **d~n** *vi* to last; **es hat sehr lang gedauert, bis er ...** it took him a long time to ...;

d~nd *adj* constant; **~parkplatz** *m* long-stay car park; **~welle** *f* perm, permanent wave; **~wurst** *f* German salami; **~zustand** *m* permanent condition

Daumen ['daʊmən] **(-s, -)** *m* thumb

Daune ['daʊnə] *f* down; **~ndecke** *f* down duvet, down quilt

davon [da'fɔn] *adv* of it; (*räumlich*) away; (*weg von*) from it; (*Grund*) because of it; **das kommt ~!** that's what you get; **~ abgesehen** apart from that; **~ sprechen/ wissen** to talk/know of *od* about it; **was habe ich ~?** what's the point?; **~kommen** (*unreg*) *vi* to escape; **~laufen** (*unreg*) *vi* to run away

davor [da'fo:r] *adv* (*räumlich*) in front of it; (*zeitlich*) before (that); **~ warnen** to warn about it

dazu [da'tsu:] *adv* (*legen, stellen*) by it; (*essen, singen*) with it; **und ~ noch** and in addition; **ein Beispiel/seine Gedanken ~** one example for/his thoughts on this; **wie komme ich denn ~?** why should I?; **~ fähig sein** to be capable of it; **sich ~ äußern** to say something on it; **~gehören** *vi* to belong to it; **~kommen** (*unreg*) *vi* (*Ereignisse*) to happen too; (*an einen Ort*) to come along

dazwischen [da'tsvɪʃən] *adv* in between; (*räumlich auch*) between (them); (*zusammen mit*) among them; **~kommen** (*unreg*) *vi* (*hineingeraten*) to get caught in it; **es ist etwas ~gekommen** something cropped up; **~reden** *vi* (*unterbrechen*) to interrupt; (*sich einmischen*) to interfere; **~treten** (*unreg*) *vi* to intervene

DDR

The **DDR** *(Deutsche Demokratische Republik) was the name by which the former Communist German Democratic Republic was known. It was founded in 1949 from the Soviet-occupied zone. After the Berlin Wall was built in 1961 it was virtually sealed off from the West. Mass demonstrations and demands for reform forced the opening of the borders in 1989 and the* **DDR** *merged in 1990 with the* **BRD.**

Debatte [de'batə] *f* debate

Deck [dɛk] **(-(e)s, -s** *od* **-e)** *nt* deck; **an ~ gehen** to go on deck

Decke *f* cover; (*Bettdecke*) blanket; (*Tischdecke*) tablecloth; (*Zimmerdecke*) ceiling; **unter einer ~ stecken** to be hand in glove; **~l (-s, -)** *m* lid; **d~n** *vt* to cover ♦ *vr* to coincide

Deckung *f* (*Schützen*) covering; (*Schutz*) cover; (*SPORT*) defence; (*Übereinstimmen*) agreement

Defekt [de'fɛkt] **(-(e)s, -e)** *m* fault, defect; **d~** *adj* faulty

defensiv [defɛn'si:f] *adj* defensive

definieren [defi'ni:rən] *vt* to define; **Definition** [definitsi'o:n] *f* definition

Defizit ['de:fitsɪt] **(-s, -e)** *nt* deficit

deftig ['dɛftɪç] *adj* (*Essen*) large; (*Witz*) coarse

Degen ['de:gən] **(-s, -)** *m* sword

degenerieren [degene'ri:rən] *vi* to degenerate

dehnbar ['de:nba:r] *adj* elastic; (*fig: Begriff*) loose

dehnen *vt, vr* to stretch

Deich [daɪç] **(-(e)s, -e)** *m* dyke, dike

deichseln (*umg*) *vt* (*fig*) to wangle

dein(e) [daɪn(ə)] *adj* your; **~e(r, s)** *pron* yours; **~er** (*gen von* **du**) *pron* of you; **~erseits** *adv* on your part; **~esgleichen** *pron* people like you; **~etwegen** *adv* (*für dich*) for your sake; (*wegen dir*) on your account; **~etwillen** *adv*: **um ~etwillen** = **deinetwegen; ~ige** *pron*: **der/die/das ~ige** *od* **D~ige** yours

Deklination [deklinatsi'o:n] *f* declension

deklinieren [dekli'ni:rən] *vt* to decline

Dekolleté, Dekolletee ▲ [dekɔl'te:] **(-s, -s)** *nt* low neckline

Deko- [deko] *zW*: **~rateur** [-ra'tø:r] *m* window dresser; **~ration** [-ratsi'o:n] *f* decoration; (*in Laden*) window dressing; **d~rativ** [-ra'ti:f] *adj* decorative; **d~rieren** [-'ri:rən] *vt* to decorate; (*Schaufenster*) to dress

Spelling Reform: ▲ *new spelling* △ *old spelling (to be phased out)*

Delegation [delegatsi'o:n] f delegation

delegieren [dele'gi:rən] vt: ~ **an** +akk (Aufgaben) to delegate to

Delfin ▲ [del'fi:n] **(-s, -e)** m dolphin

delikat [deli'ka:t] adj (zart, heikel) delicate; (köstlich) delicious

Delikatesse [delika'tɛsə] f delicacy; ~n pl (Feinkost) delicatessen food; ~ngeschäft nt delicatessen

Delikt [de'lɪkt] **(-(e)s, -e)** nt (JUR) offence

Delle ['dɛlə] (umg) f dent

Delphin △ [del'fi:n] **(-s, -e)** m = **Delfin**

dem [de(:)m] art dat von **der**

Demagoge [dema'go:gə] **(-n, -n)** m demagogue

dementieren [demɛn'ti:rən] vt to deny

dem- zW: ~**gemäß** adv accordingly; ~**nach** adv accordingly; ~**nächst** adv shortly

Demokrat [demo'kra:t] **(-en, -en)** m democrat; ~**ie** [-'ti:] f democracy; d~**isch** adj democratic; d~**isieren** [-i'zi:rən] vt to democratize

demolieren [demo'li:rən] vt to demolish

Demon- [demɔn] zW: ~**strant(in)** [-'strant(ɪn)] m(f) demonstrator; ~**stration** [-stratsi'o:n] f demonstration; d~**strativ** [-stra'ti:f] adj demonstrative; (Protest) pointed; d~**strieren** [-'stri:rən] vt, vi to demonstrate

Demoskopie [demosko'pi:] f public opinion research

Demut ['de:mu:t] **(-)** f humility

demütig ['de:my:tɪç] adj humble; ~**en** ['de:my:tɪgən] vt to humiliate; **D~ung** f humiliation

demzufolge ['de:mtsu'fɔlgə] adv accordingly

den [de(:)n] art akk von **der**

denen ['de:nən] pron dat pl von **der**; **die**; **das**

Denk- [dɛŋk] zW: d~**bar** adj conceivable; ~**en** **(-s)** nt thinking; d~**en** (unreg) vt, vi to think; d~**faul** adj lazy; ~**fehler** m logical error; ~**mal (-s, ⁻er)** nt monument; ~**malschutz** m protection of historical monuments; **unter ~malschutz stehen** to be classified as a historical monument; d~**würdig** adj memorable; ~**zettel** m: **jdm**

einen ~zettel verpassen to teach sb a lesson

denn [dɛn] konj for ♦ adv then; (nach Komparativ) than; **warum ~?** why?

dennoch ['dɛnnɔx] konj nevertheless

Denunziant [denʊntsi'ant(ɪn)] m informer

Deodorant [de|odo'rant] **(-s, -s od -e)** nt deodorant

Deponie [depo'ni:] f dump

deponieren [depo'ni:rən] vt (COMM) to deposit

Depot [de'po:] **(-s, -s)** nt warehouse; (Busdepot, EISENB) depot; (Bankdepot) strongroom, safe (US)

Depression [deprɛsi'o:n] f depression; **depres'siv** adj depressive

deprimieren [depri'mi:rən] vt to depress

SCHLÜSSELWORT

---

der [de(:)r] (f **die**, nt **das**, gen **des, der, des**, dat **dem, der, dem**, akk **den, die, das**, pl **die**) def art the; **der Rhein** the Rhine; **der Klaus** (umg) Klaus; **die Frau** (im Allgemeinen) women; **der Tod/das Leben** death/life; **der Fuß des Berges** the foot of the hill; **gib es der Frau** give it to the woman; **er hat sich die Hand verletzt** he has hurt his hand

♦ relativ pron (bei Menschen) who, that; (bei Tieren, Sachen) which, that; **der Mann, den ich gesehen habe** the man who od whom od that I saw

♦ demonstrativ pron he/she/it; (jener, dieser) that; (pl) those; **der/die war es** it was him/her; **der mit der Brille** the one with glasses; **ich will den (da)** I want that one

---

derart ['de:r|a:rt] adv so; (solcher Art) such; ~**ig** adj such, this sort of

derb [dɛrp] adj sturdy; (Kost) solid; (grob) coarse

der- zW: ' ~'**gleichen** pron such; ' ~**jenige** pron he; she; it; the one (who); that (which); ' ~'**maßen** adv to such an extent, so; ~'**selbe** art, pron the same; ' ~'**weil(en)** adv in the meantime; ' ~'**zeitig** adj present, current; (damalig) then

des [dɛs] *art gen von* **der**
desertieren [dezɛr'tiːrən] *vi* to desert
desgleichen ['dɛsˈglaiçən] *adv* likewise, also
deshalb ['dɛsˈhalp] *adv* therefore, that's why
Desinfektion [dɛzinfɛktsi'oːn] *f* disinfection; **~smittel** *nt* disinfectant
desinfizieren [dɛzinfi'tsiːrən] *vt* to disinfect
dessen ['dɛsən] *pron gen von* **der; das; ~ ungeachtet** nevertheless, regardless
Dessert [dɛ'seːr] **(-s, -s)** *nt* dessert
destillieren [dɛstɪ'liːrən] *vt* to distil
desto ['dɛsto] *adv* all the, so much the; **~ besser** all the better
deswegen ['dɛsˈveːgən] *konj* therefore, hence
Detail [de'tai] **(-s, -s)** *nt* detail
Detektiv [detɛk'tiːf] **(-s, -e)** *m* detective
deut- ['dɔyt] *zW:* **~en** *vt* to interpret, to explain ♦ *vi:* **~en (auf +**akk**)** to point (to *od* at); **~lich** *adj* clear; (*Unterschied*) distinct; **D~lichkeit** *f* clarity; distinctness
Deutsch [dɔytʃ] *nt* German
deutsch *adj* German; **auf D~** in German; **D~e Demokratische Republik** (*HIST*) German Democratic Republic, East Germany; **~es Beefsteak** ≈ hamburger; **D~e(r)** *mf* German; **ich bin D~er** I am German; **D~land** *nt* Germany
Devise [de'viːzə] *f* motto, device; **~n** *pl* (*FIN*) foreign currency, foreign exchange
Dezember [de'tsɛmbər] **(-s, -)** *m* December
dezent [de'tsɛnt] *adj* discreet
dezimal [detsi'maːl] *adj* decimal; **D~system** *nt* decimal system
d. h. *abk* (= *das heißt*) i.e.
Dia ['diːa] **(-s, -s)** *nt* (*PHOT*) slide, transparency
Diabetes [dia'beːtes] **(-, -)** *m* (*MED*) diabetes
Diagnose [dia'gnoːzə] *f* diagnosis
diagonal [diago'naːl] *adj* diagonal
Dialekt [dia'lɛkt] **(-(e)s, -e)** *m* dialect; **d~isch** *adj* dialectal; (*Logik*) dialectical
Dialog [dia'loːk] **(-(e)s, -e)** *m* dialogue
Diamant [dia'mant] *m* diamond
Diaprojektor ['diːaprojɛktɔr] *m* slide projector
Diät [di'ɛːt] **(-, -en)** *f* diet

dich [dɪç] (*akk von du*) *pron* you; yourself
dicht [dɪçt] *adj* dense; (*Nebel*) thick; (*Gewebe*) close; (*undurchlässig*) (water)tight; (*fig*) concise ♦ *adv:* **~ an/bei** close to; **~ bevölkert** densely *od* heavily populated; **D~e** *f* density; thickness; closeness; (water)tightness; (*fig*) conciseness
dichten *vt* (*dicht machen*) to make watertight, to seal; (*NAUT*) to caulk; (*LITER*) to compose, to write ♦ *vi* to compose, to write
Dichter(in) **(-s, -)** *m(f)* poet; (*Autor*) writer; **d~isch** *adj* poetical
dichthalten (*unreg*) (*umg*) *vi* to keep one's mouth shut
Dichtung *f* (*TECH*) washer; (*AUT*) gasket; (*Gedichte*) poetry; (*Prosa*) (piece of) writing
dick [dɪk] *adj* thick; (*fett*) fat; **durch ~ und dünn** through thick and thin; **D~darm** *m* (*ANAT*) colon; **D~e** *f* thickness; fatness; **~flüssig** *adj* viscous; **D~icht** **(-s, -e)** *nt* thicket; **D~kopf** *m* mule; **D~milch** *f* soured milk
die [diː] *def art siehe* **der**
Dieb(in) [diːp, 'diːbɪn] **(-(e)s, -e)** *m(f)* thief; **d~isch** *adj* thieving; (*umg*) immense; **~stahl** **(-(e)s, -ẹ)** *m* theft; **~stahlversicherung** *f* insurance against theft
Diele ['diːlə] *f* (*Brett*) board; (*Flur*) hall, lobby
dienen ['diːnən] *vi:* **(jdm) ~** to serve (sb)
Diener **(-s, -)** *m* servant; **~in** *f* (maid)servant; **~schaft** *f* servants *pl*
Dienst [diːnst] **(-(e)s, -e)** *m* service; **außer ~** retired; **~ haben** to be on duty; **~ habend** (*Arzt*) on duty
Dienstag ['diːnstaːk] *m* Tuesday; **d~s** *adv* on Tuesdays
Dienst- *zW:* **~bote** *m* servant; **~geheimnis** *nt* official secret; **~gespräch** *nt* business call; **~leistung** *f* service; **d~lich** *adj* official; **~mädchen** *nt* (house)maid; **~reise** *f* business trip; **~stelle** *f* office; **~vorschrift** *f* official regulations *pl*; **~weg** *m* official channels *pl*; **~zeit** *f* working hours *pl*; (*MIL*) period of service

Spelling Reform: ▲ *new spelling* △ *old spelling (to be phased out)*

dies [diːs] pron (demonstrativ: sg) this; (: pl) these; ~**bezüglich** adj (Frage) on this matter; ~**e(r, s)** ['diːzə(r, s)] pron this (one)

Diesel ['diːzəl] m (Kraftstoff) diesel

dieselbe [diːˈzɛlbə] pron, art the same

Dieselmotor m diesel engine

diesig ['diːzɪç] adj drizzly

dies- zW: ~**jährig** adj this year's; ~**mal** adv this time; ~**seits** präp +gen on this side; **D~seits** (-) nt this life

Dietrich ['diːtrɪç] (-s, -e) m picklock

diffamieren [dɪfaˈmiːrən] (pej) vt to defame

Differenz [dɪfəˈrɛnts] (-, -en) f (Unterschied) difference; ~**en** pl (Meinungsverschiedenheit) difference (of opinion); **d~ieren** vt to make distinctions in; **d~iert** adj (Mensch etc) complex

differenzial ▲ [dɪferentsiaːl] adj differential; **D~rechnung** f differential calculus

digital [digiˈtaːl] adj digital; **D~fernsehen** f digital TV

Dikt- [dɪkt] zW: ~**afon**, ~**aphon** [-aˈfoːn] nt dictaphone; ~**at** [-ˈtaːt] (-(e)s, -e) nt dictation; ~**ator** [-ˈtaːtɔr] m dictator; **d~atorisch** [-aˈtoːrɪʃ] adj dictatorial; ~**atur** [-aˈtuːr] f dictatorship; **d~ieren** [-ˈtiːrən] vt to dictate

Dilemma [diˈlɛma] (-s, -s od -ta) nt dilemma

Dilettant [dileˈtant] m dilettante, amateur; **d~isch** adj amateurish, dilettante

Dimension [dimenziˈoːn] f dimension

DIN f abk (= Deutsche Industrie-Norm) German Industrial Standard

Ding [dɪŋ] (-(e)s, -e) nt thing, object; **d~lich** adj real, concrete; ~**s(bums)** ['dɪŋks(bums)] (-) (umg) nt thingummybob

Diplom [diˈploːm] (-(e)s, -e) nt diploma, certificate; ~**at** [-ˈmaːt] (-en, -en) m diplomat; ~**atie** [-aˈtiː] f diplomacy; **d~atisch** [-ˈmaːtɪʃ] adj diplomatic; ~**ingenieur** m qualified engineer

dir [diːr] (dat von du) pron (to) you

direkt [diˈrɛkt] adj direct; **D~flug** m direct flight; **D~or** m director; (SCH) principal, headmaster; **D~übertragung** f live broadcast

Dirigent [diriˈgɛnt(ɪn)] m conductor

dirigieren [diriˈgiːrən] vt to direct; (MUS) to conduct

Diskette [dɪsˈkɛtə] f diskette, floppy disk

Diskont [dɪsˈkɔnt] (-s, -e) m discount; ~**satz** m rate of discount

Diskothek [dɪskoˈteːk] (-, -en) f disco(theque)

diskret [dɪsˈkreːt] adj discreet; **D~ion** f discretion

diskriminieren [dɪskrimiˈniːrən] vt to discriminate against

Diskussion [dɪskusiˈoːn] f discussion; debate; **zur ~ stehen** to be under discussion

diskutieren [dɪskuˈtiːrən] vt, vi to discuss; to debate

Distanz [dɪsˈtants] f distance; **distanˈzieren** vr: **sich von jdm/etw d~ieren** to distance o.s. from sb/sth

Distel ['dɪstəl] (-, -n) f thistle

Disziplin [dɪstsiˈpliːn] f discipline

Dividende [diviˈdɛndə] f dividend

dividieren [diviˈdiːrən] vt: **(durch etw) ~** to divide (by sth)

DM [deːˈʔɛm] abk (HIST = Deutsche Mark) German Mark

D-Mark ['deːmark] f (HIST) D Mark, German Mark

SCHLÜSSELWORT

doch [dɔx] adv 1 (dennoch) after all; (sowieso) anyway; **er kam doch noch** he came after all; **du weißt es ja doch besser** you know better than I do anyway; **und doch ...** and yet ...

2 (als bejahende Antwort) yes I do/it does etc; **das ist nicht wahr - doch!** that's not true - yes it is!

3 (auffordernd): **komm doch** do come; **lass ihn doch** just leave him; **nicht doch!** oh no!

4: **sie ist doch noch so jung** but she's still so young; **Sie wissen doch, wie das ist** you know how it is (, don't you?); **wenn doch** if only

♦ konj (aber) but; (trotzdem) all the same;

---

und doch hat er es getan but still he did it

Docht [dɔxt] **(-(e)s, -e)** *m* wick

Dock [dɔk] **(-s, -s** *od* **-e)** *nt* dock

Dogge ['dɔgə] *f* bulldog

Dogma ['dɔgma] **(-s, -men)** *nt* dogma; **d~tisch** *adj* dogmatic

Doktor ['dɔktɔr, *pl* -'to:rən] **(-s, -en)** *m* doctor

Dokument [doku'mɛnt] *nt* document

Dokumentar- [dokumen'ta:r] *zW:* **~bericht** *m* documentary; **~film** *m* documentary (film); **d~isch** *adj* documentary

Dolch [dɔlç] **(-(e)s, -e)** *m* dagger

dolmetschen ['dɔlmɛtʃən] *vt, vi* to interpret; **Dolmetscher(in) (-s, -)** *m(f)* interpreter

Dom [do:m] **(-(e)s, -e)** *m* cathedral

dominieren [domi'ni:rən] *vt* to dominate ♦ *vi* to predominate

Donau ['do:nau] *f* Danube

Donner ['dɔnər] **(-s, -)** *m* thunder; **d~n** *vi unpers* to thunder

Donnerstag ['dɔnərsta:k] *m* Thursday

doof [do:f] *(umg) adj* daft, stupid

Doppel ['dɔpəl] **(-s, -)** *nt* duplicate; (SPORT) doubles; **~bett** *nt* double bed; **d~deutig** *adj* ambiguous; **~fenster** *nt* double glazing; **~gänger (-s, -)** *m* double; **~punkt** *m* colon; **~stecker** *m* two-way adaptor; **d~t** *adj* double; **in d~ter Ausführung** in duplicate; **~verdiener** *m* person with two incomes; *(pl: Paar)* two-income family; **~zentner** *m* 100 kilograms; **~zimmer** *nt* double room

Dorf [dɔrf] **(-(e)s, ̈er)** *nt* village; **~bewohner** *m* villager

Dorn [dɔrn] **(-(e)s, -en)** *m* (BOT) thorn; **d~ig** *adj* thorny

Dörrobst ['dœro:pst] *nt* dried fruit

Dorsch [dɔrʃ] **(-(e)s, -e)** *m* cod

dort [dɔrt] *adv* there; **~ drüben** over there; **~her** *adv* from there; **~hin** *adv* (to) there; **~ig** *adj* of that place; in that town

Dose ['do:zə] *f* box; *(Blechdose)* tin, can

Dosen *pl von* **Dose; Dosis**

Dosenöffner *m* tin *od* can opener

Dosis ['do:zɪs] **(-, Dosen)** *f* dose

Dotter ['dɔtər] **(-s, -)** *m* (egg) yolk

Drache ['draxə] **(-n, -n)** *m* (Tier) dragon

Drachen (-s, -) *m* kite; **~fliegen (-s)** *nt* hang-gliding

Draht [dra:t] **(-(e)s, ̈e)** *m* wire; **auf ~ sein** to be on the ball; **d~ig** *adj* (Mann) wiry; **~seil** *nt* cable; **~seilbahn** *f* cable railway, funicular

Drama ['dra:ma] **(-s, Dramen)** *nt* drama, play; **~tiker** [-'ma:tikər] **(-s, -)** *m* dramatist; **d~tisch** [-'ma:tɪʃ] *adj* dramatic

dran [dran] *(umg) adv:* **jetzt bin ich ~!** it's my turn now; *siehe* **daran**

Drang [draŋ] **(-(e)s, ̈e)** *m* (Trieb): **~ (nach)** impulse (for), urge (for), desire (for); *(Druck)* pressure

drängeln ['drɛŋəln] *vt, vi* to push, to jostle

drängen ['drɛŋən] *vt (schieben)* to push, to press; *(antreiben)* to urge ♦ *vi (eilig sein)* to be urgent; *(Zeit)* to press; **auf etw** *akk* **~** to press for sth

drastisch ['drastɪʃ] *adj* drastic

drauf [drauf] *(umg) adv =* **darauf; D~gänger (-s, -)** *m* daredevil

draußen ['drausən] *adv* outside

Dreck [drɛk] **(-(e)s)** *m* mud, dirt; **d~ig** *adj* dirty, filthy

Dreh- ['dre:] *zW:* **~arbeiten** *pl* (CINE) shooting *sg;* **~bank** *f* lathe; **~buch** *nt* (CINE) script; **d~en** *vt* to turn, to rotate; *(Zigaretten)* to roll; *(Film)* to shoot ♦ *vi* to turn, to rotate ♦ *vr* to turn; *(handeln von):* **es d~t sich um ...** it's about ...; **~orgel** *f* barrel organ; **~tür** *f* revolving door; **~ung** *f* (Rotation) rotation; *(Umdrehung, Wendung)* turn; **~zahl** *f* rate of revolutions; **~zahlmesser** *m* rev(olution) counter

drei [draɪ] *num* three; **~ viertel** three quarters; **D~eck** *nt* triangle; **~eckig** *adj* triangular; **~einhalb** *num* three and a half; **~erlei** *adj inv* of three kinds; **~fach** *adj* triple, treble ♦ *adv* three times; **~hundert** *num* three hundred; **D~'königsfest** *nt* Epiphany; **~mal** *adv* three times; **~malig** *adj* three times

dreinreden ['draɪnreːdən] *vi*: **jdm ~** (*dazwischenreden*) to interrupt sb; (*sich einmischen*) to interfere with sb

Dreirad *nt* tricycle

dreißig ['draɪsɪç] *num* thirty

dreist [draɪst] *adj* bold, audacious

drei- *zW*: **~viertel** △ *num siehe* **drei**; **D~viertelstunde** *f* three-quarters of an hour; **~zehn** *num* thirteen

dreschen ['drɛʃən] (*unreg*) *vt* (*Getreide*) to thresh; (*umg: verprügeln*) to beat up

dressieren [drɛˈsiːrən] *vt* to train

drillen ['drɪlən] *vt* (*bohren*) to drill, to bore; (*MIL*) to drill; (*fig*) to train

Drilling *m* triplet

drin [drɪn] (*umg*) *adv* = **darin**

dringen ['drɪŋən] (*unreg*) *vi* (*Wasser, Licht, Kälte*): **~ (durch/in** +*akk*) to penetrate (through/into); **auf etw** *akk* **~** to insist on sth

dringend ['drɪŋənt] *adj* urgent

Dringlichkeit *f* urgency

drinnen ['drɪnən] *adv* inside, indoors

dritte(r, s) ['drɪtə(r, s)] *adj* third; **D~ Welt** Third World; **D~s Reich** Third Reich; **D~l** (**-s, -**) *nt* third; **~ns** *adv* thirdly

DRK [deːʔɛrˈkaː] *nt abk* (= *Deutsches Rotes Kreuz*) German Red Cross

droben ['droːbən] *adv* above, up there

Droge ['droːgə] *f* drug

drogen *zW*: **~abhängig** *adj* addicted to drugs; **D~händler** *m* drug pedlar, pusher

Drogerie [droːgəˈriː] *f* chemist's shop

Drogerie

ⓘ The **Drogerie** as opposed to the **Apotheke** sells medicines not requiring a prescription. It tends to be cheaper and also sells cosmetics, perfume and toiletries.

Drogist [droˈgɪst] *m* pharmacist, chemist

drohen ['droːən] *vi*: (**jdm**) **~** to threaten (sb)

dröhnen ['drøːnən] *vi* (*Motor*) to roar; (*Stimme, Musik*) to ring, to resound

Drohung ['droːʊŋ] *f* threat

drollig ['drɔlɪç] *adj* droll

Drossel ['drɔsəl] (**-, -n**) *f* thrush

drüben ['dryːbən] *adv* over there, on the other side

drüber ['dryːbər] (*umg*) *adv* = **darüber**

Druck [drʊk] (**-(e)s, -e**) *m* (*PHYS: Zwang*) pressure; (*TYP: Vorgang*) printing; (: *Produkt*) print; (*fig: Belastung*) burden, weight; **~buchstabe** *m* block letter

drücken ['drʏkən] *vt* (*Knopf, Hand*) to press; (*zu eng sein*) to pinch; (*fig: Preise*) to keep down; (: *belasten*) to oppress, to weigh down ♦ *vi* to press; to pinch ♦ *vr*: **sich vor etw** *dat* **~** to get out of (doing) sth; **~d** *adj* oppressive

Drucker (**-s, -**) *m* printer

Drücker (**-s, -**) *m* button; (*Türdrücker*) handle; (*Gewehrdrücker*) trigger

Druck- *zW*: **~erei** *f* printing works, press; **~erschwärze** *f* printer's ink; **~fehler** *m* misprint; **~knopf** *m* press stud, snap fastener; **~sache** *f* printed matter; **~schrift** *f* block *od* printed letters *pl*

drum [drʊm] (*umg*) *adv* = **darum**

drunten ['drʊntən] *adv* below, down there

Drüse ['dryːzə] *f* gland

Dschungel ['dʒʊŋəl] (**-s, -**) *m* jungle

du [duː] (*nom*) *pron* you; **~ sagen** = **duzen**

Dübel ['dyːbəl] (**-s, -**) *m* Rawlplug ®

ducken ['dʊkən] *vt* (*Kopf, Person*) to duck; (*fig*) to take down a peg or two ♦ *vr* to duck

Duckmäuser ['dʊkmɔʏzər] (**-s, -**) *m* yes man

Dudelsack ['duːdəlzak] *m* bagpipes *pl*

Duell [duˈɛl] (**-s, -e**) *nt* duel

Duft [dʊft] (**-(e)s, ⁼e**) *m* scent, odour; **d~en** *vi* to smell, to be fragrant; **d~ig** *adj* (*Stoff, Kleid*) delicate, diaphanous

dulden ['dʊldən] *vt* to suffer; (*zulassen*) to tolerate ♦ *vi* to suffer

dumm [dʊm] *adj* stupid; (*ärgerlich*) annoying; **der D~e sein** to be the loser; **~erweise** *adv* stupidly; **D~heit** *f* stupidity; (*Tat*) blunder, stupid mistake; **D~kopf** *m* blockhead

dumpf [dʊmpf] *adj* (*Ton*) hollow, dull; (*Luft*)

Rechtschreibreform: ▲ *neue Schreibung* △ *alte Schreibung (auslaufend)*

musty; (*Erinnerung, Schmerz*) vague

Düne ['dy:nə] *f* dune

düngen ['dyŋən] *vt* to manure

Dünger (**-s, -**) *m* dung, manure; (*künstlich*) fertilizer

dunkel ['dʊŋkəl] *adj* dark; (*Stimme*) deep; (*Ahnung*) vague; (*rätselhaft*) obscure; (*verdächtig*) dubious, shady; **im D~n tappen** (*fig*) to grope in the dark

Dunkel- *zW:* **~heit** *f* darkness; (*fig*) obscurity; **~kammer** *f* (*PHOT*) darkroom; **d~n** *vi unpers* to grow dark; **~ziffer** *f estimated number of unreported cases*

dünn [dʏn] *adj* thin; **~flüssig** *adj* watery, thin

Dunst [dʊnst] (**-es, ⁻e**) *m* vapour; (*Wetter*) haze

dünsten ['dʏnstən] *vt* to steam

dunstig ['dʊnstɪç] *adj* vaporous; (*Wetter*) hazy, misty

Duplikat [dupli'ka:t] (**-(e)s, -e**) *nt* duplicate

Dur [du:r] (**-, -**) *nt* (*MUS*) major

SCHLÜSSELWORT

durch [dʊrç] *präp +akk* **1** (*hindurch*) through; **durch den Urwald** through the jungle; **durch die ganze Welt reisen** to travel all over the world

2 (*mittels*) through, by (means of); (*aufgrund*) due to, owing to; **Tod durch Herzschlag/den Strang** death from a heart attack/by hanging; **durch die Post** by post; **durch seine Bemühungen** through his efforts

♦ *adv* **1** (*hindurch*) through; **die ganze Nacht durch** all through the night; **den Sommer durch** during the summer; **8 Uhr durch** past 8 o'clock; **durch und durch** completely

2 (*durchgebraten etc*): **(gut) durch** well-done

---

durch- *zW:* **~arbeiten** *vt, vi* to work through ♦ *vr* to work one's way through; **~'aus** *adv* completely; (*unbedingt*) definitely; **~aus nicht** absolutely not

Durchblick ['dʊrçblɪk] *m* view; (*fig*) comprehension; **d~en** *vi* to look through;

(*umg: verstehen*): **(bei etw) d~en** to understand (sth); **etw d~en lassen** (*fig*) to hint at sth

durchbrechen ['dʊrçbrɛçən] (*unreg*) *vt, vi* to break

durch'brechen ['dʊrçbrɛçən] (*unreg*) *vt insep* (*Schranken*) to break through; (*Schallmauer*) to break; (*Gewohnheit*) to break free from

durchbrennen ['dʊrçbrɛnən] (*unreg*) *vi* (*Draht, Sicherung*) to burn through; (*umg*) to run away

durchbringen (*unreg*) *vt* (*Kranken*) to pull through; (*umg: Familie*) to support; (*durchsetzen: Antrag, Kandidat*) to get through; (*vergeuden: Geld*) to get through, to squander

Durchbruch ['dʊrçbrʊx] *m* (*Öffnung*) opening; (*MIL*) breach; (*von Gefühlen etc*) eruption; (*der Zähne*) cutting; (*fig*) breakthrough; **zum ~ kommen** to break through

durch- *zW:* **~dacht** [-'daxt] *adj* well thought-out; **~'denken** (*unreg*) *vt* to think out; **~'drehen** *vt* (*Fleisch*) to mince ♦ *vi* (*umg*) to crack up

durcheinander [dʊrçʔaɪˈnandər] *adv* in a mess, in confusion; (*umg: verwirrt*) confused; **~ bringen** to mess up; (*verwirren*) to confuse; **~ reden** to talk at the same time; **D~** (**-s**) *nt* (*Verwirrung*) confusion; (*Unordnung*) mess

durch- *zW:* **~fahren** (*unreg*) *vi* (*~ Tunnel usw*) to drive through; (*ohne Unterbrechung*) to drive straight through; (*ohne anzuhalten*): **der Zug fährt bis Hamburg ~** the train runs direct to Hamburg; (*ohne Umsteigen*): **können wir ~fahren?** can we go direct?, can we go non-stop?; **D~fahrt** *f* transit; (*Verkehr*) thoroughfare; **D~fall** *m* (*MED*) diarrhoea; **~fallen** (*unreg*) *vi* to fall through; (*in Prüfung*) to fail; **~finden** (*unreg*) *vr* to find one's way through; **~fragen** *vr* to find one's way by asking

durchführ- ['dʊrçfy:r] *zW:* **~bar** *adj* feasible, practicable; **~en** *vt* to carry out; **D~ung** *f* execution, performance

Spelling Reform: ▲ *new spelling* △ *old spelling (to be phased out)*

Durchgang ['dʊrçgaŋ] m passage(way); (bei Produktion, Versuch) run; (SPORT) round; (bei Wahl) ballot; „**~ verboten**" "no thoroughfare"

Durchgangsverkehr m through traffic

durchgefroren ['dʊrçgəfroːrən] adj (Mensch) frozen stiff

durchgehen ['dʊrçgeːən] (unreg) vt (behandeln) to go over ♦ vi to go through; (ausreißen: Pferd) to break loose; (Mensch) to run away; **mein Temperament ging mit mir durch** my temper got the better of me; **jdm etw ~ lassen** to let sb get away with sth; **~d** adj (Zug) through; (Öffnungszeiten) continuous

durch- zW: **~greifen** (unreg) vi to take strong action; **~halten** (unreg) vi to last out ♦ vt to keep up; **~kommen** (unreg) vi to get through; (überleben) to pull through; **~'kreuzen** vt insep to thwart, to frustrate; **~lassen** (unreg) vt (Person) to let through; (Wasser) to let in; **~lesen** (unreg) vt to read through; **~'leuchten** vt insep to X-ray; **~machen** vt to go through; **die Nacht ~machen** to make a night of it

Durchmesser (-s, -) m diameter

durch- zW: **~'nässen** vt insep to soak (through); **~nehmen** (unreg) vt to go over; **~nummerieren** ▲ vt to number consecutively; **~queren** [dʊrç'kveːrən] vt insep to cross; **D~reise** f transit; **auf der D~reise** passing through; (Güter) in transit; **~ringen** (unreg) vr to reach a decision after a long struggle

durchs [dʊrçs] = **durch das**

Durchsage ['dʊrçzaːgə] f intercom od radio announcement

durchschauen ['dʊrçʃaʊən] vi to look od see through; (Person, Lüge) to see through

durchscheinen ['dʊrçʃaɪnən] (unreg) vi to shine through; **~d** adj translucent

Durchschlag ['dʊrçʃlaːk] m (Doppel) carbon copy; (Sieb) strainer; **d~en** [-gən] (unreg) vt (entzweischlagen) to split (in two); (sieben) to sieve ♦ vi (zum Vorschein kommen) to emerge, to come out ♦ vr to

get by

durchschlagend adj resounding

durchschneiden ['dʊrçʃnaɪdən] (unreg) vt to cut through

Durchschnitt ['dʊrçʃnɪt] m (Mittelwert) average; **über/unter dem ~** above/below average; **im ~** on average; **d~lich** adj average ♦ adv on average

Durchschnittswert m average

durch- zW: **D~schrift** f copy; **~sehen** (unreg) vt to look through; **~setzen** vt to enforce ♦ vr (Erfolg haben) to succeed; (sich behaupten) to get one's way; **seinen Kopf ~setzen** to get one's way; **~'setzen** vt insep to mix

Durchsicht ['dʊrçzɪçt] f looking through, checking; **d~ig** adj transparent

durch- zW: **'~sprechen** (unreg) vt to talk over; **'~stehen** (unreg) vt to live through; **~stellen** vt (an Telefon) to put through; **~stöbern** (auch untr) vt (Kisten) to rummage through, to rifle through; (Haus, Wohnung) to ransack; **'~streichen** (unreg) vt to cross out; **~'suchen** vt insep to search; **D~'suchung** f search; **'~wachsen** adj (Speck) streaky; (fig: mittelmäßig) so-so; **D~wahl** f (TEL) direct dialling; **~weg** adv throughout, completely; **~ziehen** (unreg) vt (Faden) to draw through ♦ vi to pass through; **D~zug** m (Luft) draught; (von Truppen, Vögeln) passage

---
SCHLÜSSELWORT
---

dürfen ['dʏrfən] (unreg) vi 1 (Erlaubnis haben) to be allowed to; **ich darf das** I'm allowed to (do that); **darf ich?** may I?; **darf ich ins Kino?** can od may I go to the cinema?; **es darf geraucht werden** you may smoke

2 (in Verneinungen): **er darf das nicht** he's not allowed to (do that); **das darf nicht geschehen** that must not happen; **da darf sie sich nicht wundern** that shouldn't surprise her

3 (in Höflichkeitsformeln): **darf ich Sie bitten, das zu tun?** may od could I ask you to do that?; **was darf es sein?** what can I do for you?

4 (*können*): **das dürfen Sie mir glauben** you can believe me

5 (*Möglichkeit*): **das dürfte genug sein** that should be enough; **es dürfte Ihnen bekannt sein, dass ...** as you will probably know ...

dürftig ['dʏrftɪç] *adj* (*ärmlich*) needy, poor; (*unzulänglich*) inadequate

dürr [dʏr] *adj* dried-up; (*Land*) arid; (*mager*) skinny, gaunt; **D~e** *f* aridity; (*Zeit*) drought; (*Magerkeit*) skinniness

Durst [dʊrst] (**-(e)s**) *m* thirst; **~ haben** to be thirsty; **d~ig** *adj* thirsty

Dusche ['duʃə] *f* shower; **d~en** *vi, vr* to have a shower

Düse ['dy:zə] *f* nozzle; (*Flugzeugdüse*) jet

Düsen- *zW*: **~antrieb** *m* jet propulsion; **~flugzeug** *nt* jet (plane); **~jäger** *m* jet fighter

Dussel ['dʊsəl] (**-s, -**) (*umg*) *m* twit

düster ['dy:stər] *adj* dark; (*Gedanken, Zukunft*) gloomy

Dutzend ['dʊtsənt] (**-s, -e**) *nt* dozen; **~(e)** *od* **d~(e) Mal(e)** a dozen times

duzen ['du:tsən] *vt*: **(jdn) ~** to use the familiar form of address "du" (to *od* with sb)

---
duzen

ⓘ There are two different forms of address in Germany: du and Sie. **Duzen** means addressing someone as 'du' - used with children, family and close friends - and **siezen** means addressing someone as 'Sie' - used for all grown-ups and older teenagers. Students almost always use 'du' to each other.

Dynamik [dy'na:mɪk] *f* (*PHYS*) dynamics *sg*; (*fig: Schwung*) momentum; (*von Mensch*) dynamism; **dynamisch** *adj* (*auch fig*) dynamic

Dynamit [dyna'mi:t] (**-s**) *nt* dynamite

Dynamo [dy'na:mo] (**-s, -s**) *m* dynamo

DZ *nt abk* = **Doppelzimmer**

D-Zug ['de:tsu:k] *m* through train

E, e

Ebbe ['ɛbə] *f* low tide

eben ['e:bən] *adj* level, flat; (*glatt*) smooth ♦ *adv* just; (*bestätigend*) exactly; **~ deswegen** just because of that; **~bürtig** *adj*: **jdm ~bürtig sein** to be sb's equal; **E~e** *f* plain; (*fig*) level; **~falls** *adv* likewise; **~so** *adv* just as

Eber ['e:bər] (**-s, -**) *m* boar

ebnen ['e:bnən] *vt* to level

Echo ['ɛço] (**-s, -s**) *nt* echo

echt [ɛçt] *adj* genuine; (*typisch*) typical; **E~heit** *f* genuineness

Eck- *zW*: **~ball** *m* corner (kick); **~e** *f* corner; (*MATH*) angle; **e~ig** *adj* angular; **~zahn** *m* eye tooth

ECU [e'ky:] (**-, -s**) *m* (*FIN*) ECU

edel ['e:dəl] *adj* noble; **E~metall** *nt* rare metal; **E~stahl** *m* high-grade steel; **E~stein** *m* precious stone

EDV [e:de:'fau] (**-**) *f abk* (= *elektronische Datenverarbeitung*) electronic data processing

Efeu ['e:fɔy] (**-s**) *m* ivy

Effekt [ɛ'fɛkt] (**-s, -e**) *m* effect

Effekten [ɛ'fɛktən] *pl* stocks

effektiv [ɛfɛk'ti:f] *adj* effective, actual

EG ['e:'ge:] *f abk* (= *Europäische Gemeinschaft*) EC

egal [e'ga:l] *adj* all the same

Ego- [e:go] *zW*: **~ismus** [-'ɪsmʊs] *m* selfishness, egoism; **~ist** [-'ɪst] *m* egoist; **e~istisch** *adj* selfish, egoistic

Ehe ['e:ə] *f* marriage

ehe *konj* before

Ehe- *zW*: **~beratung** *f* marriage guidance (counselling); **~bruch** *m* adultery; **~frau** *f* married woman; wife; **~leute** *pl* married people; **e~lich** *adj* matrimonial; (*Kind*) legitimate

ehemalig *adj* former

ehemals *adv* formerly

Ehe- *zW*: **~mann** *m* married man; husband; **~paar** *nt* married couple

eher ['eːɐr] *adv (früher)* sooner; *(lieber)* rather, sooner; *(mehr)* more

Ehe- *zW:* **~ring** *m* wedding ring; **~schließung** *f* marriage ceremony

eheste(r, s) ['eːəstə(r, s)] *adj (früheste)* first, earliest; **am ~n** *(liebsten)* soonest; *(meist)* most; *(wahrscheinlichst)* most probably

Ehr- ['eːr] *zW:* **e~bar** *adj* honourable, respectable; **~e** *f* honour; **e~en** *vt* to honour

Ehren- ['eːrən] *zW:* **e~amtlich** *adj* honorary; **~gast** *m* guest of honour; **e~haft** *adj* honourable; **~platz** *m* place of honour *od (US)* honor; **~runde** *f* lap of honour; **~sache** *f* point of honour; **e~voll** *adj* honourable; **~wort** *nt* word of honour

Ehr- *zW:* **~furcht** *f* awe, deep respect; **e~fürchtig** *adj* reverent; **~gefühl** *nt* sense of honour; **~geiz** *m* ambition; **e~geizig** *adj* ambitious; **e~lich** *adj* honest; **~lichkeit** *f* honesty; **e~los** *adj* dishonourable; **~ung** *f* honour(ing); **e~würdig** *adj* venerable

Ei [ai] **(-(e)s, -er)** *nt* egg

Eich- *zW:* **~e** ['aiçə] *f* oak (tree); **~l** (-, -n) *f* acorn; **~hörnchen** *nt* squirrel

Eichmaß *nt* standard

Eid [ait] **(-(e)s, -e)** *m* oath

Eidechse ['aidɛksə] *f* lizard

eidesstattlich *adj:* **~e Erklärung** affidavit

Eidgenosse *m* Swiss

Eier- *zW:* **~becher** (-s) *m* eggcup; **~kuchen** *m* omelette; pancake; **~likör** *m* advocaat; **~schale** *f* eggshell; **~stock** *m* ovary; **~uhr** *f* egg timer

Eifer ['aifər] *m* zeal, enthusiasm; **~sucht** *f* jealousy; **e~süchtig** *adj:* **e~süchtig (auf +akk)** jealous (of)

eifrig ['aifriç] *adj* zealous, enthusiastic

Eigelb ['aigɛlp] **(-(e)s, -)** *nt* egg yolk

eigen ['aigən] *adj* own; *(~artig)* peculiar; **mit der / dem ihm ~en ...** with that ... peculiar to him; **sich** *dat* **etw zu E~ machen** to make sth one's own; **E~art** *f* peculiarity; characteristic; **~artig** *adj* peculiar; **E~bedarf** *m:* **zum E~bedarf** for (one's own) personal use/domestic requirements; **der Vermieter machte E~bedarf geltend** the landlord showed he needed the house/flat for himself; **~händig** *adj* with one's own hand; **E~heim** *nt* owner-occupied house; **E~heit** *f* peculiarity; **~mächtig** *adj* high-handed; **E~name** *m* proper name; **~s** *adv* expressly, on purpose; **E~schaft** *f* quality, property, attribute; **E~sinn** *m* obstinacy; **~sinnig** *adj* obstinate; **~tlich** *adj* actual, real ♦ *adv* actually, really; **E~tor** *nt* own goal; **E~tum** *nt* property; **E~tümer(in)** **(-s, -)** *m(f)* owner, proprietor; **~tümlich** *adj* peculiar; **E~tümlichkeit** *f* peculiarity; **E~tumswohnung** *f* freehold flat

eignen ['aignən] *vr* to be suited; **Eignung** *f* suitability

Eil- [ail] *zW:* **~bote** *m* courier; **~brief** *m* express letter; **~e** *f* haste; **es hat keine ~e** there's no hurry; **e~en** *vi (Mensch)* to hurry; *(dringend sein)* to be urgent; **e~ends** *adv* hastily; **e~gut** *nt* express goods *pl*, fast freight *(US)*; **e~ig** *adj* hasty, hurried; *(dringlich)* urgent; **es e~ig haben** to be in a hurry; **~zug** *m* semi-fast train, limited stop train

Eimer ['aimər] **(-s, -)** *m* bucket, pail

ein [ain] *adv:* **nicht ~ noch aus wissen** not to know what to do

ein(e) ['ain(ə)] *num* one ♦ *indef art* a, an

einander [ai'nandər] *pron* one another, each other

einarbeiten ['ain|arbaitən] *vt* to train ♦ *vr:* **sich in etw** *akk* **~** to familiarize o.s. with sth

einatmen ['ain|aːtmən] *vt, vi* to inhale, to breathe in

Einbahnstraße ['ainbaːnʃtrasə] *f* one-way street

Einband ['ainbant] *m* binding, cover

einbauen ['ainbauən] *vt* to build in; *(Motor)* to install, to fit

Einbaumöbel *pl* built-in furniture *sg*

einbegriffen ['ainbəgrifən] *adj* included

einberufen ['ainbəruːfən] *(unreg)* *vt* to convene; *(MIL)* to call up

Einbettzimmer *nt* single room

einbeziehen ['ainbətsiːən] *(unreg)* *vt* to

include

einbiegen ['aɪnbiːɡən] (*unreg*) *vi* to turn

einbilden ['aɪnbɪldən] *vt*: **sich** *dat* **etw ~** to imagine sth

Einbildung *f* imagination; (*Dünkel*) conceit; **~skraft** *f* imagination

Einblick ['aɪnblɪk] *m* insight

einbrechen ['aɪnbrɛçən] (*unreg*) *vi* (*in Haus*) to break in; (*Nacht*) to fall; (*Winter*) to set in; (*durchbrechen*) to break; **~ in** +*akk* (*MIL*) to invade

Einbrecher (**-s, -**) *m* burglar

einbringen ['aɪnbrɪŋən] (*unreg*) *vt* to bring in; (*Geld, Vorteil*) to yield; (*mitbringen*) to contribute

Einbruch ['aɪnbrʊx] *m* (*Hauseinbruch*) break-in, burglary; (*Eindringen*) invasion; (*des Winters*) onset; (*Durchbrechen*) break; (*MET*) approach; (*MIL*) penetration; **(bei/vor) ~ der Nacht** at/before nightfall; **e~sicher** *adj* burglar-proof

einbürgern ['aɪnbʏrɡərn] *vt* to naturalize ♦ *vr* to become adopted

einbüßen ['aɪnbyːsən] *vt* to lose, to forfeit

einchecken ['aɪntʃɛkən] *vt, vi* to check in

eincremen ['aɪnkreːmən] *vt* to put cream on

eindecken ['aɪndɛkən] *vr*: **sich (mit etw) ~** to lay in stocks (of sth); to stock up (with sth)

eindeutig ['aɪndɔʏtɪç] *adj* unequivocal

eindringen ['aɪndrɪŋən] (*unreg*) *vi*: **~ (in** +*akk*) to force one's way in(to); (*in Haus*) to break in(to); (*in Land*) to invade; (*Gas, Wasser*) to penetrate; **(auf jdn) ~** (*mit Bitten*) to pester (sb)

eindringlich *adj* forcible, urgent

Eindringling *m* intruder

Eindruck ['aɪndrʊk] *m* impression

eindrücken ['aɪndrʏkən] *vt* to press in

eindrucksvoll *adj* impressive

eine(r, s) *pron one*; (*jemand*) someone

eineiig ['aɪn|aɪç] *adj* (*Zwillinge*) identical

eineinhalb ['aɪn|aɪn'halp] *num* one and a half

einengen ['aɪn|ɛŋən] *vt* to confine, to restrict

einer- ['aɪnər] *zW*: **'E~lei** (**-s**) *nt* sameness; **'~'lei** *adj* (*gleichartig*) the same kind of; **es ist mir ~lei** it is all the same to me; **~seits** *adv* on the one hand

einfach ['aɪnfax] *adj* simple; (*nicht mehrfach*) single ♦ *adv* simply; **E~heit** *f* simplicity

einfädeln ['aɪnfɛːdəln] *vt* (*Nadel, Faden*) to thread; (*fig*) to contrive

einfahren ['aɪnfaːrən] (*unreg*) *vt* to bring in; (*Barriere*) to knock down; (*Auto*) to run in ♦ *vi* to drive in; (*Zug*) to pull in; (*MIN*) to go down

Einfahrt *f* (*Vorgang*) driving in; pulling in; (*MIN*) descent; (*Ort*) entrance

Einfall ['aɪnfal] *m* (*Idee*) idea, notion; (*Lichteinfall*) incidence; (*MIL*) raid; **e~en** (*unreg*) *vi* (*Licht*) to fall; (*MIL*) to raid; (*einstürzen*) to fall in, to collapse; (*einstimmen*): **(in etw** *akk*) **e~en** to join in (with sth); **etw fällt jdm ein** sth occurs to sb; **das fällt mir gar nicht ein** I wouldn't dream of it; **sich** *dat* **etw e~en lassen** to have a good idea

einfältig ['aɪnfɛltɪç] *adj* simple(-minded)

Einfamilienhaus [aɪnfa'miːliənhaus] *nt* detached house

einfarbig ['aɪnfarbɪç] *adj* all one colour; (*Stoff etc*) self-coloured

einfetten ['aɪnfɛtən] *vt* to grease

einfließen ['aɪnfliːsən] (*unreg*) *vi* to flow in

einflößen ['aɪnfløːsən] *vt*: **jdm etw ~** to give sb sth; (*fig*) to instil sth in sb

Einfluss ▲ ['aɪnflʊs] *m* influence; **~bereich** *m* sphere of influence

einförmig ['aɪnfœrmɪç] *adj* uniform; **E~keit** *f* uniformity

einfrieren ['aɪnfriːrən] (*unreg*) *vi* to freeze (up) ♦ *vt* to freeze

einfügen ['aɪnfyːɡən] *vt* to fit in; (*zusätzlich*) to add

Einfuhr ['aɪnfuːr] (**-**) *f* import; **~beschränkung** *f* import restrictions *pl*; **~bestimmungen** *pl* import regulations

einführen ['aɪnfyːrən] *vt* to bring in; (*Mensch, Sitten*) to introduce; (*Ware*) to import

Einführung *f* introduction

Spelling Reform: ▲ *new spelling* △ *old spelling (to be phased out)*

Eingabe ['aɪngaːbə] f petition; (COMPUT) input

Eingang ['aɪngaŋ] m entrance; (COMM: Ankunft) arrival; (Erhalt) receipt

eingeben ['aɪngeːbən] (unreg) vt (Arznei) to give; (Daten etc) to enter

eingebildet ['aɪngəbɪldət] adj imaginary; (eitel) conceited

Eingeborene(r) ['aɪngəboːrənə(r)] f(m) native

Eingebung f inspiration

eingefleischt ['aɪngəflaɪʃt] adj (Gewohnheit, Vorurteile) deep-rooted

eingehen ['aɪngeːən] (unreg) vi (Aufnahme finden) to come in; (Sendung, Geld) to be received; (Tier, Pflanze) to die; (Firma) to fold; (schrumpfen) to shrink ♦ vt to enter into; (Wette) to make; **auf etw** akk ~ to go into sth; **auf jdn** ~ to respond to sb; **jdm** ~ (verständlich sein) to be comprehensible to sb; ~**d** adj exhaustive, thorough

Eingemachte(s) ['aɪngəmaːxtə(s)] nt preserves pl

eingenommen ['aɪngənɔmən] adj: ~ **(von)** fond (of), partial (to); ~ **(gegen)** prejudiced (against)

eingeschrieben ['aɪngəʃriːbən] adj registered

eingespielt ['aɪngəʃpiːlt] adj: **aufeinander** ~ **sein** to be in tune with each other

Eingeständnis ['aɪngəʃtɛntnɪs] (-ses, -se) nt admission, confession

eingestehen ['aɪngəʃteːən] (unreg) vt to confess

eingestellt ['aɪngəʃtɛlt] adj: **auf etw** ~ **sein** to be prepared for sth

eingetragen ['aɪngətraːgən] adj (COMM) registered

Eingeweide ['aɪngəvaɪdə] (-s, -) nt innards pl, intestines pl

Eingeweihte(r) ['aɪngəvaɪtə(r)] f(m) initiate

eingewöhnen ['aɪngəvøːnən] vr: **sich** ~ **in** +akk to settle (down) in

eingleisig ['aɪnglaɪzɪç] adj single-track

eingreifen ['aɪngraɪfən] (unreg) vi to intervene, to interfere; (Zahnrad) to mesh

Eingriff ['aɪngrɪf] m intervention,

interference; (Operation) operation

einhaken ['aɪnhaːkən] vt to hook in ♦ vr: **sich bei jdm** ~ to link arms with sb ♦ vi (sich einmischen) to intervene

Einhalt ['aɪnhalt] m: ~ **gebieten** +dat to put a stop to; **e~en** (unreg) vt (Regel) to keep ♦ vi to stop

einhändigen ['aɪnhɛndɪgən] vt to hand in

einhängen ['aɪnhɛŋən] vt to hang; (Telefon) to hang up ♦ vi (TEL) to hang up; **sich bei jdm** ~ to link arms with sb

einheimisch ['aɪnhaɪmɪʃ] adj native; **E~e(r)** f(m) local

Einheit ['aɪnhaɪt] f unity; (Maß, MIL) unit; **e~lich** adj uniform; ~**spreis** m standard price

einholen ['aɪnhoːlən] vt (Tau) to haul in; (Fahne, Segel) to lower; (Vorsprung aufholen) to catch up with; (Verspätung) to make up; (Rat, Erlaubnis) to ask ♦ vi (einkaufen) to shop

einhüllen ['aɪnhʏlən] vt to wrap up

einhundert ['aɪn'hʊndərt] num one hundred, a hundred

einig ['aɪnɪç] adj (vereint) united; ~ **gehen** to agree; **sich** dat ~ **sein** to be in agreement; ~ **werden** to agree

einige(r, s) ['aɪnɪgə(r, s)] adj, pron some ♦ pl some; (mehrere) several; ~ **Mal** a few times

einigen vt to unite ♦ vr: **sich** ~ **(auf** +akk) to agree (on)

einigermaßen adv somewhat; (leidlich) reasonably

einig- zW: **E~keit** f unity; (Übereinstimmung) agreement; **E~ung** f agreement; (Vereinigung) unification

einkalkulieren ['aɪnkalkuliːrən] vt to take into account, to allow for

Einkauf ['aɪnkaʊf] m purchase; **e~en** vt to buy ♦ vi to shop; **e~en gehen** to go shopping

Einkaufs- zW: ~**bummel** m shopping spree; ~**korb** m shopping basket; ~**wagen** m shopping trolley; ~**zentrum** nt shopping centre

einklammern ['aɪnklamərn] vt to put in brackets, to bracket

Rechtschreibreform: ▲ *neue Schreibung* △ *alte Schreibung (auslaufend)*

Einklang ['aɪnklaŋ] m harmony

einklemmen ['aɪnklɛmən] vt to jam

einkochen ['aɪnkɔxən] vt to boil down; (Obst) to preserve, to bottle

Einkommen ['aɪnkɔmən] (-s, -) nt income; ~(s)steuer f income tax

Einkünfte ['aɪnkʏnftə] pl income sg, revenue sg

einladen ['aɪnlaːdən] (unreg) vt (Person) to invite; (Gegenstände) to load; **jdn ins Kino ~** to take sb to the cinema

Einladung f invitation

Einlage ['aɪnlaːgə] f (Programmeinlage) interlude; (Spareinlage) deposit; (Schuheinlage) insole; (Fußstütze) support; (Zahneinlage) temporary filling; (KOCH) noodles pl, vegetables pl etc in soup

einlagern ['aɪnlaːgərn] vt to store

Einlass ▲ ['aɪnlas] (-es, ⁱe) m (Zutritt) admission

einlassen ['aɪnlasən] (unreg) vt to let in; (einsetzen) to set in ♦ vr: **sich mit jdm/auf etw** akk ~ to get involved with sb/sth

Einlauf ['aɪnlauf] m arrival; (von Pferden) finish; (MED) enema; **e~en** (unreg) vi to arrive, to come in; (in Hafen) to enter; (SPORT) to finish; (Wasser) to run in; (Stoff) to shrink ♦ vt (Schuhe) to break in ♦ vr (SPORT) to warm up; (Motor, Maschine) to run in; **jdm das Haus e~en** to invade sb's house

einleben ['aɪnleːbən] vr to settle down

einlegen ['aɪnleːgən] vt (einfügen: Blatt, Sohle) to insert; (KOCH) to pickle; (Pause) to have; (Protest) to make; (Veto) to use; (Berufung) to lodge; (AUT: Gang) to engage

einleiten ['aɪnlaɪtən] vt to introduce, to start; (Geburt) to induce; **Einleitung** f introduction; induction

einleuchten ['aɪnlɔʏçtən] vi: **(jdm) ~** to be clear od evident (to sb); ~**d** adj clear

einliefern ['aɪnliːfərn] vt: ~ **(in** +akk) to take (into)

Einlieferungsschein m certificate of posting

Einliegerwohnung ['aɪnliːgərvoːnʊŋ] f self-contained flat; (für Eltern, Großeltern) granny flat

einlösen ['aɪnløːzən] vt (Scheck) to cash; (Schuldschein, Pfand) to redeem; (Versprechen) to keep

einmachen ['aɪnmaxən] vt to preserve

einmal ['aɪnmaːl] adv once; (erstens) first; (zukünftig) sometime; **nehmen wir ~ an** just let's suppose; **noch ~** once more; **nicht ~** not even; **auf ~** all at once; **es war ~** once upon a time there was/were; **E~'eins** nt multiplication tables pl; ~**ig** adj unique; (nur einmal erforderlich) single; (prima) fantastic

Einmarsch ['aɪnmarʃ] m entry; (MIL) invasion; **e~ieren** vi to march in

einmischen ['aɪnmɪʃən] vr: **sich ~ (in** +akk) to interfere (with)

einmütig ['aɪnmyːtɪç] adj unanimous

Einnahme ['aɪnnaːmə] f (von Medizin) taking; (MIL) capture, taking; ~**n** pl (Geld) takings, revenue sg; ~**quelle** f source of income

einnehmen ['aɪnneːmən] (unreg) vt to take; (Stellung, Raum) to take up; ~ **für/gegen** to persuade in favour of/against; ~**d** adj charming

einordnen ['aɪnɔrdnən] vt to arrange, to fit in ♦ vr to adapt; (AUT) to get into lane

einpacken ['aɪnpakən] vt to pack (up)

einparken ['aɪnparkən] vt to park

einpendeln ['aɪnpɛndəln] vr to even out

einpflanzen ['aɪnpflantsən] vt to plant; (MED) to implant

einplanen ['aɪnplaːnən] vt to plan for

einprägen ['aɪnpreːgən] vt to impress, to imprint; (beibringen: **(jdm) ~** to impress (on sb); **sich** dat **etw ~** to memorize sth

einrahmen ['aɪnraːmən] vt to frame

einräumen ['aɪnrɔʏmən] vt (ordnend) to put away; (überlassen: Platz) to give up; (zugestehen) to admit, to concede

einreden ['aɪnreːdən] vt: **jdm/sich etw ~** to talk sb/o.s. into believing sth

einreiben ['aɪnraɪbən] (unreg) vt to rub in

einreichen ['aɪnraɪçən] vt to hand in; (Antrag) to submit

Einreise ['aɪnraɪzə] f entry;

~bestimmungen *pl* entry regulations;
~erlaubnis *f* entry permit;
~genehmigung *f* entry permit; e~n *vi*:
(in ein Land) e~n to enter (a country)

einrichten ['aınrıçtən] *vt* (*Haus*) to furnish;
(*schaffen*) to establish, to set up;
(*arrangieren*) to arrange; (*möglich machen*)
to manage ♦ *vr* (*in Haus*) to furnish one's
house; **sich ~ (auf** +*akk*) (*sich vorbereiten*) to
prepare o.s. (for); (*sich anpassen*) to adapt
(to)

Einrichtung *f* (*Wohnungseinrichtung*)
furnishings *pl*; (*öffentliche Anstalt*)
organization; (*Dienste*) service

einrosten ['aınrɔstən] *vi* to get rusty

einrücken ['aınrʏkən] *vi* (*MIL: in Land*) to
move in

Eins [aıns] (-, -en) *f* one; e~ *num* one; **es ist
mir alles e~** it's all one to me

einsam ['aınza:m] *adj* lonely, solitary;
E~keit *f* loneliness, solitude

einsammeln ['aınzaməln] *vt* to collect

Einsatz ['aınzats] *m* (*Teil*) inset; (*an Kleid*)
insertion; (*Verwendung*) use, employment;
(*Spieleinsatz*) stake; (*Risiko*) risk; (*MIL*)
operation; (*MUS*) entry; **im ~** in action;
e~bereit *adj* ready for action

einschalten ['aınʃaltən] *vt* (*einfügen*) to
insert; (*Pause*) to make; (*ELEK*) to switch on;
(*Anwalt*) to bring in ♦ *vr* (*dazwischentreten*)
to intervene

einschärfen ['aınʃɛrfən] *vt*: **jdm etw ~** to
impress sth (up)on sb

einschätzen ['aınʃɛtsən] *vt* to estimate, to
assess ♦ *vr* to rate o.s.

einschenken ['aınʃɛŋkən] *vt* to pour out

einschicken ['aınʃıkən] *vt* to send in

einschl. *abk* (= *einschließlich*) incl.

einschlafen ['aınʃla:fən] (*unreg*) *vi* to fall
asleep, to go to sleep

einschläfernd ['aınʃlɛ:fərnt] *adj* (*MED*)
soporific; (*langweilig*) boring; (*Stimme*)
lulling

Einschlag ['aınʃla:k] *m* impact; (*fig*:
Beimischung) touch, hint; e~en [-gən]
(*unreg*) *vt* to knock in; (*Fenster*) to smash, to
break; (*Zähne, Schädel*) to smash in; (*AUT*:

Räder) to turn; (*kürzer machen*) to take up;
(*Ware*) to pack, to wrap up; (*Weg, Richtung*)
to take ♦ *vi* to hit; (*sich einigen*) to agree;
(*Anklang finden*) to work, to succeed; **in etw
akk/auf jdn e~en** to hit sth/sb

einschlägig ['aınʃlɛ:gıç] *adj* relevant

einschließen ['aınʃli:sən] (*unreg*) *vt* (*Kind*) to
lock in; (*Häftling*) to lock up; (*Gegenstand*)
to lock away; (*Bergleute*) to cut off;
(*umgeben*) to surround; (*MIL*) to encircle;
(*fig*) to include, to comprise ♦ *vr* to lock
o.s. in

einschließlich *adv* inclusive ♦ *präp* +*gen*
inclusive of, including

einschmeicheln ['aınʃmaıçəln] *vr*: **sich ~
(bei)** to ingratiate o.s. (with)

einschnappen ['aınʃnapən] *vi* (*Tür*) to click
to; (*fig*) to be touchy; **eingeschnappt sein**
to be in a huff

einschneidend ['aınʃnaıdənt] *adj* drastic

Einschnitt ['aınʃnıt] *m* cutting; (*MED*)
incision; (*Ereignis*) decisive point

einschränken ['aınʃrɛŋkən] *vt* to limit, to
restrict; (*Kosten*) to cut down, to reduce
♦ *vr* to cut down on (expenditure);
Einschränkung *f* restriction, limitation;
reduction; (*von Behauptung*) qualification

Einschreib- ['aınʃraıb] *zW*: ~(e)brief *m*
recorded delivery letter; e~en (*unreg*) *vt* to
write in; (*Post*) to send recorded delivery
♦ *vr* to register; (*UNIV*) to enrol; ~en *nt*
recorded delivery letter

einschreiten ['aınʃraıtən] (*unreg*) *vi* to step
in, to intervene; **~ gegen** to take action
against

einschüchtern ['aınʃʏçtərn] *vt* to intimidate

einschulen ['aınʃu:lən] *vt*: **eingeschult
werden** (*Kind*) to start school

einsehen ['aınze:ən] (*unreg*) *vt* (*hineinsehen
in*) to realize; (*Akten*) to have a look at;
(*verstehen*) to see; E~ (-s) *nt*
understanding; **ein E~ haben** to show
understanding

einseitig ['aınzaıtıç] *adj* one-sided

Einsend- ['aınzɛnd] *zW*: e~en (*unreg*) *vt* to
send in; ~er (-s, -) *m* sender, contributor;
~ung *f* sending in

einsetzen ['aɪnzɛtsən] vt to put (in); (in Amt) to appoint, to install; (Geld) to stake; (verwenden) to use; (MIL) to employ ♦ vi (beginnen) to set in; (MUS) to enter, to come in ♦ vr to work hard; **sich für jdn/ etw ~** to support sb/sth

Einsicht ['aɪnzɪçt] f insight; (in Akten) look, inspection; **zu der ~ kommen, dass ...** to come to the conclusion that ...; **e~ig** adj (Mensch) judicious; **e~slos** adj unreasonable; **e~svoll** adj understanding

einsilbig ['aɪnzɪlbɪç] adj (auch fig) monosyllabic; (Mensch) uncommunicative

einspannen ['aɪnʃpanən] vt (Papier) to insert; (Pferde) to harness; (umg: Person) to rope in

Einsparung ['aɪnʃpaːrʊŋ] f economy, saving

einsperren ['aɪnʃpɛrən] vt to lock up

einspielen ['aɪnʃpiːlən] vr (SPORT) to warm up ♦ vt (Film: Geld) to bring in; (Instrument) to play in; **sich aufeinander ~** to become attuned to each other; **gut eingespielt** running smoothly

einsprachig ['aɪnʃpraːxɪç] adj monolingual

einspringen ['aɪnʃprɪŋən] (unreg) vi (aushelfen) to help out, to step into the breach

Einspruch ['aɪnʃprʊx] m protest, objection; **~srecht** nt veto

einspurig ['aɪnʃpuːrɪç] adj (EISENB) single-track; (AUT) single-lane

einst [aɪnst] adv once; (zukünftig) one day, some day

einstecken ['aɪnʃtɛkən] vt to stick in, to insert; (Brief) to post; (ELEK: Stecker) to plug in; (Geld) to pocket; (mitnehmen) to take; (überlegen sein) to put in the shade; (hinnehmen) to swallow

einstehen ['aɪnʃteːən] (unreg) vi: **für jdn/ etw ~** to guarantee sb/sth; (verantworten): **für etw ~** to answer for sth

einsteigen ['aɪnʃtaɪgən] (unreg) vi to get in od on; (in Schiff) to go on board; (sich beteiligen) to come in; (hineinklettern) to climb in

einstellen ['aɪnʃtɛlən] vt (aufhören) to stop; (Geräte) to adjust; (Kamera etc) to focus; (Sender, Radio) to tune in; (unterstellen) to put; (in Firma) to employ, to take on ♦ vi (Firma) to take on staff/workers ♦ vr (anfangen) to set in; (kommen) to arrive; **sich auf jdn ~** to adapt to sb; **sich auf etw** akk **~** to prepare o.s. for sth

Einstellung f (Aufhören) suspension; adjustment; focusing; (von Arbeiter etc) appointment; (Haltung) attitude

Einstieg ['aɪnʃtiːk] (-(e)s, -e) m entry; (fig) approach

einstig ['aɪnstɪç] adj former

einstimmig ['aɪnʃtɪmɪç] adj unanimous; (MUS) for one voice

einstmals adv once, formerly

einstöckig ['aɪnʃtœkɪç] adj two-storeyed

Einsturz ['aɪnʃtʊrts] m collapse

einstürzen ['aɪnʃtʏrtsən] vi to fall in, to collapse

einst- zW: **~weilen** adv meanwhile; (vorläufig) temporarily, for the time being; **~weilig** adj temporary

eintägig ['aɪntɛːgɪç] adj one-day

eintauschen ['aɪntauʃən] vt: **~ (gegen** od **für)** to exchange (for)

eintausend ['aɪn'tauzənt] num one thousand

einteilen ['aɪntaɪlən] vt (in Teile) to divide (up); (Menschen) to assign

einteilig adj one-piece

eintönig ['aɪntøːnɪç] adj monotonous

Eintopf ['aɪntɔpf] m stew

Eintracht ['aɪntraxt] (-) f concord, harmony; **einträchtig** ['aɪntrɛçtɪç] adj harmonious

Eintrag ['aɪntraːk] (-(e)s, **¨e**) m entry; **amtlicher ~** entry in the register; **e~en** [-gən] (unreg) vt (in Buch) to enter; (Profit) to yield ♦ vr to put one's name down

einträglich ['aɪntrɛːklɪç] adj profitable

eintreffen ['aɪntrɛfən] (unreg) vi to happen; (ankommen) to arrive

eintreten ['aɪntreːtən] (unreg) vi to occur; (sich einsetzen) to intercede ♦ vt (Tür) to kick open; **~ in** +akk to enter; (in Klub, Partei) to join

Eintritt ['aɪntrɪt] m (Betreten) entrance; (Anfang) commencement; (in Klub etc)

Spelling Reform: ▲ *new spelling* △ *old spelling (to be phased out)*

joining

Eintritts- *zW:* **~geld** *nt* admission charge; **~karte** *f* (admission) ticket; **~preis** *m* admission charge

einüben ['aɪnˌyːbən] *vt* to practise

Einvernehmen ['aɪnfɛrneːmən] **(-s, -)** *nt* agreement, harmony

einverstanden ['aɪnfɛrʃtandən] *excl* agreed, okay ♦ *adj:* **~ sein** to agree, to be agreed

Einverständnis ['aɪnfɛrʃtɛntnɪs] *nt* understanding; *(gleiche Meinung)* agreement

Einwand ['aɪnvant] **(-(e)s, ⁺e)** *m* objection

Einwand- *zW:* **~erer** ['aɪnvandərər] *m* immigrant; **e~ern** *vi* to immigrate; **~erung** *f* immigration

einwandfrei *adj* perfect ♦ *adv* absolutely

Einweg- ['aɪnveːg-] *zW:* **~flasche** *f* no-deposit bottle; **~spritze** *f* disposable syringe

einweichen ['aɪnvaɪçən] *vt* to soak

einweihen ['aɪnvaɪən] *vt (Kirche)* to consecrate; *(Brücke)* to open; *(Gebäude)* to inaugurate; **~ (in** +akk) *(Person)* to initiate (in); **Einweihung** *f* consecration; opening; inauguration; initiation

einweisen ['aɪnvaɪzən] *(unreg) vt (in Amt)* to install; *(in Arbeit)* to introduce; *(in Anstalt)* to send

einwenden ['aɪnvɛndən] *(unreg) vt:* **etwas ~ gegen** to object to, to oppose

einwerfen ['aɪnvɛrfən] *(unreg) vt* to throw in; *(Brief)* to post; *(Geld)* to put in, to insert; *(Fenster)* to smash; *(äußern)* to interpose

einwickeln ['aɪnvɪkəln] *vt* to wrap up; *(fig: umg)* to outsmart

einwilligen ['aɪnvɪlɪɡən] *vi:* **~ (in** +akk) to consent (to), to agree (to); **Einwilligung** *f* consent

einwirken ['aɪnvɪrkən] *vi:* **auf jdn/etw ~** to influence sb/sth

Einwohner ['aɪnvoːnɐ] **(-s, -)** *m* inhabitant; **~'meldeamt** *nt* registration office; **~schaft** *f* population, inhabitants *pl*

Einwurf ['aɪnvʊrf] *m (Öffnung)* slot; *(von Münze)* insertion; *(von Brief)* posting; *(Einwand)* objection; *(SPORT)* throw-in

Einzahl ['aɪntsaːl] *f* singular; **e~en** *vt* to pay

in; **~ung** *f* paying in; **~ungsschein** *m* paying-in slip, deposit slip

einzäunen ['aɪntsɔynən] *vt* to fence in

Einzel ['aɪntsəl] **(-s, -)** *nt (TENNIS)* singles; **~fahrschein** *m* one-way ticket; **~fall** *m* single instance, individual case; **~handel** *m* retail trade; **~handelspreis** *m* retail price; **~heit** *f* particular, detail; **~kind** *nt* only child; **e~n** *adj* single; *(vereinzelt)* the odd ♦ *adv* singly; **e~n angeben** to specify; **der/die E~ne** the individual; **das E~ne** the particular; **ins E~ne gehen** to go into detail(s); **~teil** *nt* component (part); **~zimmer** *nt* single room; **~zimmerzuschlag** *m* single room supplement

einziehen ['aɪntsiːən] *(unreg) vt* to draw in, to take in; *(Kopf)* to duck; *(Fühler, Antenne, Fahrgestell)* to retract; *(Steuern, Erkundigungen)* to collect; *(MIL)* to draft, to call up; *(aus dem Verkehr ziehen)* to withdraw; *(konfiszieren)* to confiscate ♦ *vi* to move in; *(Friede, Ruhe)* to come; *(Flüssigkeit)* to penetrate

einzig ['aɪntsɪç] *adj* only; *(ohnegleichen)* unique; **das E~e** the only thing; **der/die E~e** the only one; **~artig** *adj* unique

Einzug ['aɪntsuːk] *m* entry, moving in

Eis [aɪs] **(-es, -)** *nt* ice; *(Speiseeis)* ice cream; **~bahn** *f* ice *od* skating rink; **~bär** *m* polar bear; **~becher** *m* sundae; **~bein** *nt* pig's trotters *pl*; **~berg** *m* iceberg; **~café** *nt* ice-cream parlour *(BRIT) od* parlor *(US)*; **~decke** *f* sheet of ice; **~diele** *f* ice-cream parlour

Eisen ['aɪzən] **(-s, -)** *nt* iron

Eisenbahn *f* railway, railroad *(US)*; **~er (-s, -)** *m* railwayman, railway employee, railroader *(US)*; **~schaffner** *m* railway guard; **~wagen** *m* railway carriage

Eisenerz *nt* iron ore

eisern ['aɪzərn] *adj* iron; *(Gesundheit)* robust; *(Energie)* unrelenting; *(Reserve)* emergency

Eis- *zW:* **e~frei** *adj* clear of ice; **~hockey** *nt* ice hockey; **e~ig** ['aɪzɪç] *adj* icy; **e~kalt** *adj* icy cold; **~kunstlauf** *m* figure skating; **~laufen** *nt* ice skating; **~pickel** *m* ice axe; **~schrank** *m* fridge, icebox *(US)*; **~würfel**

Rechtschreibreform: ▲ *neue Schreibung* △ *alte Schreibung (auslaufend)*

m ice cube; **~zapfen** *m* icicle; **~zeit** *f* ice
age

eitel ['aɪtəl] *adj* vain; **E~keit** *f* vanity

Eiter ['aɪtər] **(-s)** *m* pus; **e~ig** *adj*
suppurating; **e~n** *vi* to suppurate

Eiweiß **(-es, -e)** *nt* white of an egg; (*CHEM*)
protein

Ekel[1] ['e:kəl] **(-s, -)** *nt* (*umg: Mensch*)
nauseating person

Ekel[2] ['e:kəl] **(-s)** *m* nausea, disgust; **~
erregend** nauseating, disgusting; **e~haft**
adj nauseating, disgusting; **e~ig** *adj*
nauseating, disgusting; **e~n** *vt* to disgust
♦ *vr*: **sich e~n (vor** +*dat*) to loathe, to be
disgusted (at); **es e~t jdn** *od* **jdm** sb is
disgusted; **eklig** *adj* nauseating, disgusting

Ekstase [ɛk'staːzə] *f* ecstasy

Ekzem [ɛk'tseːm] **(-s, -e)** *nt* (*MED*) eczema

Elan [e'lãː] **(-s)** *m* elan

elastisch [e'lastɪʃ] *adj* elastic

Elastizität [elastitsi'tɛːt] *f* elasticity

Elch [ɛlç] **(-(e)s, -e)** *m* elk

Elefant [ele'fant] *m* elephant

elegant [ele'gant] *adj* elegant

Eleganz [ele'gants] *f* elegance

Elek- [e'lɛk] *zW*: **~triker** [-trikər] **(-s, -)** *m*
electrician; **e~trisch** [-trɪʃ] *adj* electric;
e~trisieren [-tri'ziːrən] *vt* (*auch fig*) to
electrify; (*Mensch*) to give an electric shock
to ♦ *vr* to get an electric shock; **~trizität**
[tritsi'tɛːt] *f* electricity; **~trizitätswerk** *nt*
power station; (*Gesellschaft*) electric power
company

Elektro- [e'lɛktro] *zW*: **~de** [-'troːdə] *f*
electrode; **~gerät** *nt* electrical appliance;
~herd *m* electric cooker; **~n** **(-s, -en)** *nt*
electron; **~nenrechner** [elɛk'troːnən-] *m*
computer; **~nik** *f* electronics *sg*; **e~nisch**
adj electronic; **~rasierer** *m* electric razor;
~technik *f* electrical engineering

Element [ele'mɛnt] **(-s, -e)** *nt* element;
(*ELEK*) cell, battery; **e~ar** [-'taːr] *adj*
elementary; (*naturhaft*) elemental

Elend ['eːlɛnt] **(-(e)s)** *nt* misery; **e~** *adj*
miserable; **~sviertel** *nt* slum

elf [ɛlf] *num* eleven; **E~** **(-, -en)** *f* (*SPORT*)
eleven

Elfe *f* elf

Elfenbein *nt* ivory

Elfmeter *m* (*SPORT*) penalty (kick)

Elite [e'liːtə] *f* elite

Ell- *zW*: **~bogen** *m* elbow; **~e** ['ɛlə] *f* ell;
(*Maß*) yard; **~enbogen** *m* elbow;
~(en)bogenfreiheit *f* (*fig*) elbow room

Elsass ▲ ['ɛlzas] **(- od -es)** *nt*: **das ~** Alsace

Elster ['ɛlstər] **(-, -n)** *f* magpie

Eltern ['ɛltərn] *pl* parents; **~beirat** *m* (*SCH*)
≃ PTA (*BRIT*), parents' council; **~haus** *nt*
home; **e~los** *adj* parentless

E-Mail ['iːmeːl] **(-, -s)** *f* E-mail

Emaille [e'maljə] **(-s, -s)** *nt* enamel

emaillieren [ema'jiːrən] *vt* to enamel

Emanzipation [emantsipatsi'oːn] *f*
emancipation

emanzi'pieren *vt* to emancipate

Embryo ['ɛmbryo] **(-s, -s od Embryonen)** *m*
embryo

Emi- *zW*: **~'grant(in)** *m(f)* emigrant;
~gration *f* emigration; **e~grieren** *vi* to
emigrate

Emissionen [emisi'oːnən] *fpl* emissions

Empfang [ɛm'pfaŋ] **(-(e)s, ˍe)** *m* reception;
(*Erhalten*) receipt; **in ~ nehmen** to receive;
e~en (*unreg*) *vt* to receive ♦ *vi* (*schwanger
werden*) to conceive

Empfäng- [ɛm'pfɛŋ] *zW*: **~er** **(-s, -)** *m*
receiver; (*COMM*) addressee, consignee;
~erabschnitt *m* receipt slip; **e~lich** *adj*
receptive, susceptible; **~nis** **(-, -se)** *f*
conception; **~nisverhütung** *f*
contraception

Empfangs- *zW*: **~bestätigung** *f*
acknowledgement; **~dame** *f* receptionist;
~schein *m* receipt; **~zimmer** *nt* reception
room

empfehlen [ɛm'pfeːlən] (*unreg*) *vt* to
recommend ♦ *vr* to take one's leave;
~swert *adj* recommendable

Empfehlung *f* recommendation

empfiehlst *etc* [ɛm'pfiːlst] *vb siehe*
empfehlen

empfind- [ɛm'pfɪnt] *zW*: **~en** [-dən] (*unreg*)
vt to feel; **~lich** *adj* sensitive; (*Stelle*) sore;
(*reizbar*) touchy; **~sam** *adj* sentimental;

E~ung [-dʊŋ] f feeling, sentiment

empfohlen etc [ɛm'pfoːlən] vb siehe **empfehlen**

empor [ɛm'poːr] adv up, upwards

empören [ɛm'pøːrən] vt to make indignant; to shock ♦ vr to become indignant; ~d adj outrageous

Emporkömmling [ɛm'poːrkœmlɪŋ] m upstart, parvenu

Empörung f indignation

emsig ['ɛmzɪç] adj diligent, busy

End- ['ɛnt] in zW final; ~e (-s, -n) nt end; **am ~e** at the end; (schließlich) in the end; **am ~e sein** to be at the end of one's tether; **~e Dezember** at the end of December; **zu ~e sein** to be finished; e~en vi to end; e~gültig ['ɛnt-] adj final, definite

Endivie [ɛn'diːviə] f endive

End- zW: e~lich adj final; (MATH) finite ♦ adv finally; **e~lich!** at last!; **komm e~lich!** come on!; e~los adj endless, infinite; ~spiel nt final(s); ~spurt m (SPORT) final spurt; ~station f terminus; ~ung f ending

Energie [enɛr'giː] f energy; ~bedarf m energy requirement; e~los adj lacking in energy, weak; ~verbrauch m energy consumption; ~versorgung f supply of energy; ~wirtschaft f energy industry

energisch [e'nɛrgɪʃ] adj energetic

eng [ɛŋ] adj narrow; (Kleidung) tight; (fig: Horizont) narrow, limited; (Freundschaft, Verhältnis) close; **~ an etw** dat close to sth

Engagement [ãgaʒə'mãː] (-s, -s) nt engagement; (Verpflichtung) commitment

engagieren [ãga'ʒiːrən] vt to engage ♦ vr to commit o.s.

Enge ['ɛŋə] f (auch fig) narrowness; (Landenge) defile; (Meerenge) straits pl; **jdn in die ~ treiben** to drive sb into a corner

Engel ['ɛŋəl] (-s, -) m angel; e~haft adj angelic

England ['ɛŋlant] nt England; Engländer(in) m(f) Englishman(-woman); englisch adj English

Engpass ▲ m defile, pass; (fig, Verkehr) bottleneck

en gros [ã'gro] adv wholesale

engstirnig ['ɛŋʃtɪrnɪç] adj narrow-minded

Enkel ['ɛŋkəl] (-s, -) m grandson; ~in f granddaughter; ~kind nt grandchild

enorm [e'nɔrm] adj enormous

Ensemble [ã'sãbəl] (-s, -s) nt company, ensemble

entbehr- [ɛnt'beːr-] zW: ~en vt to do without, to dispense with; ~lich adj superfluous; E~ung f deprivation

entbinden [ɛnt'bɪndən] (unreg) vt (+gen) to release (from); (MED) to deliver ♦ vi (MED) to give birth; Entbindung f release; (MED) confinement; Entbindungsheim nt maternity hospital

entdeck- [ɛnt'dɛk] zW: ~en vt to discover; E~er (-s, -) m discoverer; E~ung f discovery

Ente ['ɛntə] f duck; (fig) canard, false report

enteignen [ɛnt'|aɪgnən] vt to expropriate; (Besitzer) to dispossess

enterben [ɛnt'|ɛrbən] vt to disinherit

entfallen [ɛnt'falən] (unreg) vi to drop, to fall; (wegfallen) to be dropped; **jdm ~** (vergessen) to slip sb's memory; **auf jdn ~** to be allotted to sb

entfalten [ɛnt'faltən] vt to unfold; (Talente) to develop ♦ vr to open; (Mensch) to develop one's potential; Entfaltung f unfolding; (von Talenten) development

entfern- [ɛnt'fɛrn] zW: ~en vt to remove; (hinauswerfen) to expel ♦ vr to go away, to withdraw; ~t adj distant; **weit davon ~t sein, etw zu tun** to be far from doing sth; E~ung f distance; (Wegschaffen) removal

entfremden [ɛnt'frɛmdən] vt to estrange, to alienate; Entfremdung f alienation, estrangement

entfrosten [ɛnt'frɔstən] vt to defrost

Entfroster (-s, -) m (AUT) defroster

entführ- [ɛnt'fyːr] zW: ~en vt to carry off, to abduct; to kidnap; E~er m kidnapper; E~ung f abduction; kidnapping

entgegen [ɛnt'geːgən] präp +dat contrary to, against ♦ adv towards; ~bringen (unreg) vt to bring; **jdm etw ~bringen** (fig) to show sb sth; ~gehen (unreg) vi +dat to go to meet, to go towards; **~gesetzt** *adj* opposite; *(widersprechend)* opposed; **~halten** *(unreg) vt (fig)* to object; **E~kommen** *nt* obligingness; **~kommen** *(unreg) vi +dat* to approach; to meet; *(fig)* to accommodate; **~kommend** *adj* obliging; **~nehmen** *(unreg) vt* to receive, to accept; **~sehen** *(unreg) vt +dat* to await; **~setzen** *vt* to oppose; **~treten** *(unreg) vi +dat* to step up to; *(fig)* to oppose, to counter; **~wirken** *vi +dat* to counteract

entgegnen [ɛnt'geːgnən] *vt* to reply, to retort

entgehen [ɛnt'geːən] *(unreg) vi (fig)*: **jdm ~** to escape sb's notice; **sich** *dat* **etw ~ lassen** to miss sth

Entgelt [ɛnt'gɛlt] **(-(e)s, -e)** *nt* compensation, remuneration

entgleisen [ɛnt'glaɪzən] *vi (EISENB)* to be derailed; *(fig: Person)* to misbehave; **~ lassen** to derail

entgräten [ɛnt'grɛːtən] *vt* to fillet, to bone

Enthaarungscreme [ɛnt'haːrʊŋs-] *f* hair-removing cream

enthalten [ɛnt'haltən] *(unreg) vt* to contain ♦ *vr*: **sich (von etw) ~** to abstain (from sth), to refrain (from sth)

enthaltsam [ɛnt'haltzaːm] *adj* abstinent, abstemious

enthemmen [ɛnt'hɛmən] *vt*: **jdn ~** to free sb from his inhibitions

enthüllen [ɛnt'hʏlən] *vt* to reveal, to unveil

Enthusiasmus [ɛntuzi'asmʊs] *m* enthusiasm

entkommen [ɛnt'kɔmən] *(unreg) vi*: **~ (aus** *od +dat)* to get away (from), to escape (from)

entkräften [ɛnt'krɛftən] *vt* to weaken, to exhaust; *(Argument)* to refute

entladen [ɛnt'laːdən] *(unreg) vt* to unload; *(ELEK)* to discharge ♦ *vr (ELEK: Gewehr)* to discharge; *(Ärger etc)* to vent itself

entlang [ɛnt'laŋ] *adv* along; **~ dem Fluss, den Fluss ~** along the river; **~gehen** *(unreg) vi* to walk along

entlarven [ɛnt'larfən] *vt* to unmask, to expose

entlassen [ɛnt'lasən] *(unreg) vt* to discharge; *(Arbeiter)* to dismiss; **Entlassung** *f* discharge; dismissal

entlasten [ɛnt'lastən] *vt* to relieve; *(Achse)* to relieve the load on; *(Angeklagten)* to exonerate; *(Konto)* to clear

Entlastung *f* relief; *(COMM)* crediting

Entlastungszug *m* relief train

entlegen [ɛnt'leːgən] *adj* remote

entlocken [ɛnt'lɔkən] *vt*: **(jdm etw) ~** to elicit (sth from sb)

entmutigen [ɛnt'muːtɪgən] *vt* to discourage

entnehmen [ɛnt'neːmən] *(unreg) vt (+dat)* to take out (of), to take (from); *(folgern)* to infer (from)

entreißen [ɛnt'raɪsən] *(unreg) vt*: **jdm etw ~** to snatch sth (away) from sb

entrichten [ɛnt'rɪçtən] *vt* to pay

entrosten [ɛnt'rɔstən] *vt* to remove rust from

entrümpeln [ɛnt'rʏmpəln] *vt* to clear out

entrüst- [ɛnt'rʏst] *zW*: **~en** *vt* to incense, to outrage ♦ *vr* to be filled with indignation; **~et** *adj* indignant, outraged; **E~ung** *f* indignation

entschädigen [ɛnt'ʃɛːdɪgən] *vt* to compensate; **Entschädigung** *f* compensation

entschärfen [ɛnt'ʃɛrfən] *vt* to defuse; *(Kritik)* to tone down

Entscheid [ɛnt'ʃaɪt] **(-(e)s, -e)** *m* decision; **e~en** [-dən] *(unreg) vt, vi, vr* to decide; **e~end** *adj* decisive; *(Stimme)* casting; **~ung** *f* decision

entschieden [ɛnt'ʃiːdən] *adj* decided; *(entschlossen)* resolute; **E~heit** *f* firmness, determination

entschließen [ɛnt'ʃliːsən] *(unreg) vr* to decide

entschlossen [ɛnt'ʃlɔsən] *adj* determined, resolute; **E~heit** *f* determination

Entschluss ▲ [ɛnt'ʃlʊs] *m* decision; **e~freudig** *adj* decisive; **~kraft** *f* determination, decisiveness

entschuldigen [ɛnt'ʃʊldɪgən] *vt* to excuse ♦ *vr* to apologize

Entschuldigung *f* apology; *(Grund)*

excuse; **jdn um ~ bitten** to apologize to sb; **~I excuse me;** (*Verzeihung*) sorry

entsetz- [ɛntˈzɛts] *zW:* **~en** *vt* to horrify; (*MIL*) to relieve ♦ *vr* to be horrified *od* appalled; **E~en (-s)** *nt* horror, dismay; **~lich** *adj* dreadful, appalling; **~t** *adj* horrified

Entsorgung [ɛntˈzɔrɡʊŋ] *f* (*von Kraftwerken, Chemikalien*) (waste) disposal

entspannen [ɛntˈʃpanən] *vt, vr* (*Körper*) to relax; (*POL: Lage*) to ease

Entspannung *f* relaxation, rest; (*POL*) détente; **~spolitik** *f* policy of détente

entsprechen [ɛntˈʃprɛçən] (*unreg*) *vi* +*dat* to correspond to; (*Anforderungen, Wünschen*) to meet, to comply with; **~d** *adj* appropriate ♦ *adv* accordingly

entspringen [ɛntˈʃprɪŋən] (*unreg*) *vi* (+*dat*) to spring (from)

entstehen [ɛntˈʃteːən] (*unreg*) *vi:* **~ (aus** *od* **durch)** to arise (from), to result (from)

Entstehung *f* genesis, origin

entstellen [ɛntˈʃtɛlən] *vt* to disfigure; (*Wahrheit*) to distort

entstören [ɛntˈʃtøːrən] *vt* (*RADIO*) to eliminate interference from

enttäuschen [ɛntˈtɔʏʃən] *vt* to disappoint; **Enttäuschung** *f* disappointment

entwaffnen [ɛntˈvafnən] *vt* (*lit, fig*) to disarm

entwässern [ɛntˈvɛsərn] *vt* to drain; **Entwässerung** *f* drainage

entweder [ɛntˈveːdər] *konj* either

entwenden [ɛntˈvɛndən] (*unreg*) *vt* to purloin, to steal

entwerfen [ɛntˈvɛrfən] (*unreg*) *vt* (*Zeichnung*) to sketch; (*Modell*) to design; (*Vortrag, Gesetz etc*) to draft

entwerten [ɛntˈveːrtən] *vt* to devalue; (*stempeln*) to cancel

Entwerter (-s, -) *m* ticket punching machine

entwickeln [ɛntˈvɪkəln] *vt, vr* (*auch PHOT*) to develop; (*Mut, Energie*) to show (o.s.), to display (o.s.)

Entwicklung [ɛntˈvɪklʊŋ] *f* development; (*PHOT*) developing

Entwicklungs- *zW:* **~hilfe** *f* aid for developing countries; **~land** *nt* developing country

entwöhnen [ɛntˈvøːnən] *vt* to wean; (*Süchtige*): **(einer Sache** *dat od* **von etw) ~** to cure (of sth)

Entwöhnung *f* weaning; cure, curing

entwürdigend [ɛntˈvʏrdɪɡənt] *adj* degrading

Entwurf [ɛntˈvʊrf] *m* outline, design; (*Vertragsentwurf, Konzept*) draft

entziehen [ɛntˈtsiːən] (*unreg*) *vt* (+*dat*) to withdraw (from), to take away (from); (*Flüssigkeit*) to draw (from), to extract (from) ♦ *vr* (+*dat*) to escape (from); (*jds Kenntnis*) to be outside *od* beyond; (*der Pflicht*) to shirk

Entziehung *f* withdrawal; **~sanstalt** *f* drug addiction/alcoholism treatment centre; **~skur** *f* treatment for drug addiction/alcoholism

entziffern [ɛntˈtsɪfərn] *vt* to decipher; to decode

entzücken [ɛntˈtsʏkən] *vt* to delight; **E~ (-s)** *nt* delight; **~d** *adj* delightful, charming

entzünden [ɛntˈtsʏndən] *vt* to light, to set light to; (*fig, MED*) to inflame; (*Streit*) to spark off ♦ *vr* (*auch fig*) to catch fire; (*Streit*) to start; (*MED*) to become inflamed

Entzündung *f* (*MED*) inflammation

entzwei [ɛntˈtsvaɪ] *adv* broken; in two; **~brechen** (*unreg*) *vt, vi* to break in two; **~en** *vt* to set at odds ♦ *vr* to fall out; **~gehen** (*unreg*) *vi* to break (in two)

Enzian [ˈɛntsiaːn] *m* gentian

Epidemie [epideˈmiː] *f* epidemic

Epilepsie [epileˈpsiː] *f* epilepsy

Episode [epiˈzoːdə] *f* episode

Epoche [eˈpɔxə] *f* epoch; **~ machend** epoch-making

Epos [ˈeːpɔs] **(-s, Epen)** *nt* epic (poem)

er [eːr] (*nom*) *pron* he; it

erarbeiten [ɛrˈʔarbaɪtən] *vt* to work for, to acquire; (*Theorie*) to work out

erbarmen [ɛrˈbarmən] *vr* (+*gen*) to have pity *od* mercy (on); **E~ (-s)** *nt* pity

erbärmlich [ɛrˈbɛrmlɪç] *adj* wretched,

Rechtschreibreform: ▲ *neue Schreibung* △ *alte Schreibung (auslaufend)*

pitiful; E~keit f wretchedness

erbarmungslos [ɛr'barmʊŋsloːs] adj pitiless, merciless

erbau- [ɛr'bau] zW: ~en vt to build, to erect; (fig) to edify; E~er (-s, -) m builder; ~lich adj edifying

Erbe[1] ['ɛrbə] (-n, -n) m heir

Erbe[2] ['ɛrbə] nt inheritance; (fig) heritage

erben vt to inherit

erbeuten [ɛr'bɔytən] vt to carry off; (MIL) to capture

Erb- [ɛrb] zW: ~faktor m gene; ~folge f (line of) succession; ~in f heiress

erbittern [ɛr'bɪtərn] vt to embitter; (erzürnen) to incense

erbittert [ɛr'bɪtərt] adj (Kampf) fierce, bitter

erblassen [ɛr'blasən] vi to (turn) pale

erblich ['ɛrplɪç] adj hereditary

erblinden [ɛr'blɪndən] vi to go blind

erbrechen [ɛr'brɛçən] (unreg) vt, vr to vomit

Erbschaft f inheritance, legacy

Erbse ['ɛrpsə] f pea

Erbstück nt heirloom

Erd- ['eːrd] zW: ~achse f earth's axis; ~atmosphäre f earth's atmosphere; ~beben nt earthquake; ~beere f strawberry; ~boden m ground; ~e f earth; **zu ebener ~e** at ground level; e~en vt (ELEK) to earth

erdenklich [ɛr'dɛŋklɪç] adj conceivable

Erd- zW: ~gas nt natural gas; ~geschoss ▲ nt ground floor; ~kunde f geography; ~nuss ▲ f peanut; ~öl nt (mineral) oil

erdrosseln [ɛr'drɔsəln] vt to strangle, to throttle

erdrücken [ɛr'drʏkən] vt to crush

Erd- zW: ~rutsch m landslide; ~teil m continent

erdulden [ɛr'dʊldən] vt to endure, to suffer

ereignen [ɛr'|aɪɡnən] vr to happen

Ereignis [ɛr'|aɪɡnɪs] (-ses, -se) nt event; e~los adj uneventful; e~reich adj eventful

ererbt [ɛr'|ɛrpt] adj (Haus) inherited; (Krankheit) hereditary

erfahren [ɛr'faːrən] (unreg) vt to learn, to find out; (erleben) to experience ♦ adj experienced

Erfahrung f experience; e~sgemäß adv according to experience

erfassen [ɛr'fasən] vt to seize; (fig: einbeziehen) to include, to register; (verstehen) to grasp

erfind- [ɛr'fɪnd] zW: ~en (unreg) vt to invent; E~er (-s, -) m inventor; ~erisch adj inventive; E~ung f invention

Erfolg [ɛr'fɔlk] (-(e)s, -e) m success; (Folge) result; ~ versprechend promising; e~en [-ɡən] vi to follow; (sich ergeben) to result; (stattfinden) to take place; (Zahlung) to be effected; e~los adj unsuccessful; ~losigkeit f lack of success; e~reich adj successful

erforderlich adj requisite, necessary

erfordern [ɛr'fɔrdərn] vt to require, to demand

erforschen [ɛr'fɔrʃən] vt (Land) to explore; (Problem) to investigate; (Gewissen) to search; Erforschung f exploration; investigation; searching

erfreuen [ɛr'frɔyən] vr: **sich ~ an** +dat to enjoy ♦ vt to delight; **sich einer Sache** gen ~ to enjoy sth

erfreulich [ɛr'frɔylɪç] adj pleasing, gratifying; ~erweise adv happily, luckily

erfrieren [ɛr'friːrən] (unreg) vi to freeze (to death); (Glieder) to get frostbitten; (Pflanzen) to be killed by frost

erfrischen [ɛr'frɪʃən] vt to refresh; **Erfrischung** f refreshment

Erfrischungs- zW: ~getränk nt (liquid) refreshment; ~raum m snack bar, cafeteria

erfüllen [ɛr'fʏlən] vt (Raum etc) to fill; (fig: Bitte etc) to fulfil ♦ vr to come true

ergänzen [ɛr'ɡɛntsən] vt to supplement, to complete ♦ vr to complement one another; **Ergänzung** f completion; (Zusatz) supplement

ergeben [ɛr'ɡeːbən] (unreg) vt to yield, to produce ♦ vr to surrender; (folgen) to result ♦ adj devoted, humble

Ergebnis [ɛr'ɡeːpnɪs] (-ses, -se) nt result; e~los adj without result, fruitless

ergehen [ɛr'ɡeːən] (unreg) vi to be issued, to go out ♦ vi unpers: **es ergeht ihm gut/**

schlecht he's faring *od* getting on well/badly ♦ *vr*: **sich in etw** *dat* ~ to indulge in sth; **etw über sich ~ lassen** to put up with sth

ergiebig [ɛr'giːbɪç] *adj* productive

Ergonomie [ɛrgono'miː] *f* ergonomics *sg*

Ergonomik [ɛrgo'noːmɪk] *f* = **Ergonomie**

ergreifen [ɛr'graɪfən] (*unreg*) *vt* (*auch fig*) to seize; (*Beruf*) to take up; (*Maßnahmen*) to resort to; (*rühren*) to move; ~**d** *adj* moving, touching

ergriffen [ɛr'grɪfən] *adj* deeply moved

Erguss ▲ [ɛr'gʊs] *m* discharge; (*fig*) outpouring, effusion

erhaben [ɛr'haːbən] *adj* raised, embossed; (*fig*) exalted, lofty; **über etw** *akk* ~ **sein** to be above sth

erhalten [ɛr'haltən] (*unreg*) *vt* to receive; (*bewahren*) to preserve, to maintain; **gut** ~ in good condition

erhältlich [ɛr'hɛltlɪç] *adj* obtainable, available

Erhaltung *f* maintenance, preservation

erhärten [ɛr'hɛrtən] *vt* to harden; (*These*) to substantiate, to corroborate

erheben [ɛr'heːbən] (*unreg*) *vt* to raise; (*Protest, Forderungen*) to make; (*Fakten*) to ascertain, to establish ♦ *vr* to rise (up)

erheblich [ɛr'heːplɪç] *adj* considerable

erheitern [ɛr'haɪtərn] *vt* to amuse, to cheer (up)

Erheiterung *f* exhilaration; **zur allgemeinen** ~ to everybody's amusement

erhitzen [ɛr'hɪtsən] *vt* to heat ♦ *vr* to heat up; (*fig*) to become heated

erhoffen [ɛr'hɔfən] *vt* to hope for

erhöhen [ɛr'høːən] *vt* to raise; (*verstärken*) to increase

erhol- [ɛr'hoːl] *zW*: ~**en** *vr* to recover; (*entspannen*) to have a rest; ~**sam** *adj* restful; **E~ung** *f* recovery; relaxation, rest; ~**ungsbedürftig** *adj* in need of a rest, run-down; **E~ungsgebiet** *nt* ≈ holiday area; **E~ungsheim** *nt* convalescent home

erhören [ɛr'høːrən] *vt* (*Gebet etc*) to hear; (*Bitte etc*) to yield to

erinnern [ɛr'|ɪnərn] *vt*: ~ **(an** +*akk***)** to remind (of) ♦ *vr*: **sich (an** *akk* **etw)** ~ to remember (sth)

Erinnerung *f* memory; (*Andenken*) reminder

erkältet [ɛr'kɛltət] *adj* with a cold; ~ **sein** to have a cold

Erkältung *f* cold

erkennbar *adj* recognizable

erkennen [ɛr'kɛnən] (*unreg*) *vt* to recognize; (*sehen, verstehen*) to see

erkennt- *zW*: ~**lich** *adj*: **sich ~lich zeigen** to show one's appreciation; **E~lichkeit** *f* gratitude; (*Geschenk*) token of one's gratitude; **E~nis (-, -se)** *f* knowledge; (*das Erkennen*) recognition; (*Einsicht*) insight; **zur E~nis kommen** to realize

Erkennung *f* recognition

Erkennungszeichen *nt* identification

Erker ['ɛrkər] **(-s, -)** *m* bay

erklär- [ɛr'klɛːr] *zW*: ~**bar** *adj* explicable; ~**en** *vt* to explain; ~**lich** *adj* explicable; (*verständlich*) understandable; **E~ung** *f* explanation; (*Aussage*) declaration

erkranken [ɛr'kraŋkən] *vi* to fall ill; **Erkrankung** *f* illness

erkund- [ɛr'kʊnd] *zW*: ~**en** *vt* to find out, to ascertain; (*bes* MIL) to reconnoitre, to scout; ~**igen** *vr*: **sich ~igen (nach)** to inquire (about); **E~igung** *f* inquiry; **E~ung** *f* reconnaissance, scouting

erlahmen [ɛr'laːmən] *vi* to tire; (*nachlassen*) to flag, to wane

erlangen [ɛr'laŋən] *vt* to attain, to achieve

Erlass ▲ [ɛr'las] **(-es, ʉe)** *m* decree; (*Aufhebung*) remission

erlassen (*unreg*) *vt* (*Verfügung*) to issue; (*Gesetz*) to enact; (*Strafe*) to remit; **jdm etw** ~ to release sb from sth

erlauben [ɛr'laʊbən] *vt*: **(jdm etw)** ~ to allow *od* permit (sb (to do) sth) ♦ *vr* to permit o.s., to venture

Erlaubnis [ɛr'laʊbnɪs] **(-, -se)** *f* permission; (*Schriftstück*) permit

erläutern [ɛr'lɔʏtərn] *vt* to explain; **Erläuterung** *f* explanation

erleben [ɛr'leːbən] *vt* to experience; (*Zeit*) to live through; (*miterleben*) to witness; (*noch* *miterleben*) to live to see

Erlebnis [ɛrˈleːpnɪs] (**-ses, -se**) *nt* experience

erledigen [ɛrˈleːdɪɡən] *vt* to take care of, to deal with; (*Antrag etc*) to process; (*umg: erschöpfen*) to wear out; (: *ruinieren*) to finish; (: *umbringen*) to do in

erleichtern [ɛrˈlaɪçtərn] *vt* to make easier; (*fig: Last*) to lighten; (*lindern, beruhigen*) to relieve; **Erleichterung** *f* facilitation; lightening; relief

erleiden [ɛrˈlaɪdən] (*unreg*) *vt* to suffer, to endure

erlernen [ɛrˈlɛrnən] *vt* to learn, to acquire

erlesen [ɛrˈleːzən] *adj* select, choice

erleuchten [ɛrˈlɔʏçtən] *vt* to illuminate; (*fig*) to inspire

Erleuchtung *f* (*Einfall*) inspiration

Erlös [ɛrˈløːs] (**-es, -e**) *m* proceeds *pl*

erlösen [ɛrˈløːzən] *vt* to redeem, to save; **Erlösung** *f* release; (*REL*) redemption

ermächtigen [ɛrˈmɛçtɪɡən] *vt* to authorize, to empower; **Ermächtigung** *f* authorization; authority

ermahnen [ɛrˈmaːnən] *vt* to exhort, to admonish; **Ermahnung** *f* admonition, exhortation

ermäßigen [ɛrˈmɛsɪɡən] *vt* to reduce; **Ermäßigung** *f* reduction

ermessen [ɛrˈmɛsən] (*unreg*) *vt* to estimate, to gauge; **E~** (**-s**) *nt* estimation; discretion; **in jds E~ liegen** to lie within sb's discretion

ermitteln [ɛrˈmɪtəln] *vt* to determine; (*Täter*) to trace ♦ *vi*: **gegen jdn ~** to investigate sb

Ermittlung [ɛrˈmɪtlʊŋ] *f* determination; (*Polizeiermittlung*) investigation

ermöglichen [ɛrˈmøːklɪçən] *vt* (+*dat*) to make possible (for)

ermorden [ɛrˈmɔrdən] *vt* to murder

ermüden [ɛrˈmyːdən] *vt, vi* to tire; (*TECH*) to fatigue; **~d** *adj* tiring; (*fig*) wearisome

Ermüdung *f* fatigue

ermutigen [ɛrˈmuːtɪɡən] *vt* to encourage

ernähr- [ɛrˈnɛːr] *zW:* **~en** *vt* to feed, to nourish; (*Familie*) to support ♦ *vr* to support o.s., to earn a living; **sich ~en von** to live

on; **E~er** (**-s, -**) *m* breadwinner; **E~ung** *f* nourishment; nutrition; (*Unterhalt*) maintenance

ernennen [ɛrˈnɛnən] (*unreg*) *vt* to appoint; **Ernennung** *f* appointment

erneu- [ɛrˈnɔʏ] *zW:* **~ern** *vt* to renew; to restore; to renovate; **E~erung** *f* renewal; restoration; renovation; **~t** *adj* renewed, fresh ♦ *adv* once more

ernst [ɛrnst] *adj* serious; **~ gemeint** meant in earnest, serious; **E~** (**-es**) *m* seriousness; **das ist mein E~** I'm quite serious; **im E~** in earnest; **E~ machen mit etw** to put sth into practice; **E~fall** *m* emergency; **~haft** *adj* serious; **E~haftigkeit** *f* seriousness; **~lich** *adj* serious

Ernte [ˈɛrntə] *f* harvest; **e~n** *vt* to harvest; (*Lob etc*) to earn

ernüchtern [ɛrˈnʏçtərn] *vt* to sober up; (*fig*) to bring down to earth

Erober- [ɛrˈoːbər] *zW:* **~er** (**-s, -**) *m* conqueror; **e~n** *vt* to conquer; **~ung** *f* conquest

eröffnen [ɛrˈœfnən] *vt* to open ♦ *vr* to present itself; **jdm etw ~** to disclose sth to sb

Eröffnung *f* opening

erörtern [ɛrˈœrtərn] *vt* to discuss

Erotik [eˈroːtɪk] *f* eroticism; **erotisch** *adj* erotic

erpress- [ɛrˈprɛs] *zW:* **~en** *vt* (*Geld etc*) to extort; (*Mensch*) to blackmail; **E~er** (**-s, -**) *m* blackmailer; **E~ung** *f* extortion; blackmail

erprobt [ɛrˈproːpt] *adj* (*Gerät, Medikamente*) proven, tested

erraten [ɛrˈraːtən] (*unreg*) *vt* to guess

erreg- [ɛrˈreːk] *zW:* **~en** *vt* to excite; (*ärgern*) to infuriate; (*hervorrufen*) to arouse, to provoke ♦ *vr* to get excited *od* worked up; **E~er** (**-s, -**) *m* causative agent; **E~ung** *f* excitement

erreichbar *adj* accessible, within reach

erreichen [ɛrˈraɪçən] *vt* to reach; (*Zweck*) to achieve; (*Zug*) to catch

errichten [ɛrˈrɪçtən] *vt* to erect, to put up; (*gründen*) to establish, to set up

Spelling Reform: ▲ *new spelling* △ *old spelling (to be phased out)*

erringen [ɛrˈrɪŋən] (*unreg*) *vt* to gain, to win

erröten [ɛrˈrøːtən] *vi* to blush, to flush

Errungenschaft [ɛrˈrʊŋənʃaft] *f* achievement; (*umg: Anschaffung*) acquisition

Ersatz [ɛrˈzats] (**-es**) *m* substitute; replacement; (*Schadenersatz*) compensation; (*MIL*) reinforcements *pl*; **~dienst** *m* (*MIL*) alternative service; **~reifen** *m* (*AUT*) spare tyre; **~teil** *nt* spare (part)

erschaffen [ɛrˈʃafən] (*unreg*) *vt* to create

erscheinen [ɛrˈʃaɪnən] (*unreg*) *vi* to appear; **Erscheinung** *f* appearance; (*Geist*) apparition; (*Gegebenheit*) phenomenon; (*Gestalt*) figure

erschießen [ɛrˈʃiːsən] (*unreg*) *vt* to shoot (dead)

erschlagen [ɛrˈʃlaːgən] (*unreg*) *vt* to strike dead

erschöpf- [ɛrˈʃœpf] *zW:* **~en** *vt* to exhaust; **~end** *adj* exhaustive, thorough; **E~ung** *f* exhaustion

erschrecken [ɛrˈʃrɛkən] *vt* to startle, to frighten ♦ *vi* to be frightened *od* startled; **~d** *adj* alarming, frightening

erschrocken [ɛrˈʃrɔkən] *adj* frightened, startled

erschüttern [ɛrˈʃʏtɐn] *vt* to shake; (*fig*) to move deeply; **Erschütterung** *f* shaking; shock

erschweren [ɛrˈʃveːrən] *vt* to complicate

erschwinglich *adj* within one's means

ersetzen [ɛrˈzɛtsən] *vt* to replace; **jdm Unkosten** *etc* **~** to pay sb's expenses *etc*

ersichtlich [ɛrˈzɪçtlɪç] *adj* evident, obvious

ersparen [ɛrˈʃpaːrən] *vt* (*Ärger etc*) to spare; (*Geld*) to save

Ersparnis (**-, -se**) *f* saving

SCHLÜSSELWORT

erst [eːrst] *adv* **1** first; **mach erst mal die Arbeit fertig** finish your work first; **wenn du das erst mal hinter dir hast** once you've got that behind you

2 (*nicht früher als, nur*) only; (*nicht bis*) not till; **erst gestern** only yesterday; **erst morgen** not until tomorrow; **erst als** only when, not until; **wir fahren erst später**

we're not going until later; **er ist (gerade) erst angekommen** he's only just arrived

3: **wäre er doch erst zurück!** if only he were back!

---

erstatten [ɛrˈʃtatən] *vt* (*Kosten*) to (re)pay; **Anzeige** *etc* **gegen jdn ~** to report sb; **Bericht ~** to make a report

Erstattung *f* (*von Kosten*) refund

Erstaufführung [ˈeːrstˈʔaʊffyːrʊŋ] *f* first performance

erstaunen [ɛrˈʃtaʊnən] *vt* to astonish ♦ *vi* to be astonished; **E~** (**-s**) *nt* astonishment

erstaunlich *adj* astonishing

erst- [ˈeːrst] *zW:* **E~ausgabe** *f* first edition; **~beste(r, s)** *adj* first that comes along; **~e(r, s)** *adj* first

erstechen [ɛrˈʃtɛçən] (*unreg*) *vt* to stab (to death)

erstehen [ɛrˈʃteːən] (*unreg*) *vt* to buy ♦ *vi* to (a)rise

erstens [ˈeːrstəns] *adv* firstly, in the first place

ersticken [ɛrˈʃtɪkən] *vt* (*auch fig*) to stifle; (*Mensch*) to suffocate; (*Flammen*) to smother ♦ *vi* (*Mensch*) to suffocate; (*Feuer*) to be smothered; **in Arbeit ~** to be snowed under with work

erst- *zW:* **~klassig** *adj* first-class; **~malig** *adj* first; **~mals** *adv* for the first time

erstrebenswert [ɛrˈʃtreːbənsveːrt] *adj* desirable, worthwhile

erstrecken [ɛrˈʃtrɛkən] *vr* to extend, to stretch

ersuchen [ɛrˈzuːxən] *vt* to request

ertappen [ɛrˈtapən] *vt* to catch, to detect

erteilen [ɛrˈtaɪlən] *vt* to give

Ertrag [ɛrˈtraːk] (**-(e)s, ⁻e**) *m* yield; (*Gewinn*) proceeds *pl*

ertragen [ɛrˈtraːgən] (*unreg*) *vt* to bear, to stand

erträglich [ɛrˈtrɛːklɪç] *adj* tolerable, bearable

ertrinken [ɛrˈtrɪŋkən] (*unreg*) *vi* to drown; **E~** (**-s**) *nt* drowning

erübrigen [ɛrˈyːbrɪgən] *vt* to spare ♦ *vr* to be unnecessary

erwachen [ɛrˈvaxən] *vi* to awake

Rechtschreibreform: ▲ *neue Schreibung* △ *alte Schreibung (auslaufend)*

erwachsen [ɛr'vaksən] *adj* grown-up; E~e(r) *f(m)* adult; **E~enbildung** *f* adult education

erwägen [ɛr'vɛːgən] (*unreg*) *vt* to consider; **Erwägung** *f* consideration

erwähn- [ɛr'vɛːn] *zW:* ~**en** *vt* to mention; ~**enswert** *adj* worth mentioning; **E~ung** *f* mention

erwärmen [ɛr'vɛrmən] *vt* to warm, to heat ♦ *vr* to get warm, to warm up; **sich ~ für** to warm to

Erwarten *nt:* **über meinen/unseren** *usw* ~ beyond my/our *etc* expectations; **wider** ~ contrary to expectations

erwarten [ɛr'vartən] *vt* to expect; (*warten auf*) to wait for; **etw kaum ~ können** to be hardly able to wait for sth

Erwartung *f* expectation

erwartungsgemäß *adv* as expected

erwartungsvoll *adj* expectant

erwecken [ɛr'vɛkən] *vt* to rouse, to awake; **den Anschein ~** to give the impression

Erweis [ɛr'vais] (**-es, -e**) *m* proof; **e~en** (*unreg*) *vt* to prove ♦ *vr:* **sich e~en (als)** to prove (to be); **jdm einen Gefallen/Dienst e~en** to do sb a favour/service

Erwerb [ɛr'vɛrp] (**-(e)s, -e**) *m* acquisition; (*Beruf*) trade; **e~en** [-bən] (*unreg*) *vt* to acquire

erwerbs- *zW:* ~**los** *adj* unemployed; **E~quelle** *f* source of income; ~**tätig** *adj* (gainfully) employed

erwidern [ɛr'viːdərn] *vt* to reply; (*vergelten*) to return

erwischen [ɛr'viʃən] (*umg*) *vt* to catch, to get

erwünscht [ɛr'vʏnʃt] *adj* desired

erwürgen [ɛr'vʏrgən] *vt* to strangle

Erz [eːrts] (**-es, -e**) *nt* ore

erzähl- [ɛr'tsɛːl] *zW:* ~**en** *vt* to tell ♦ *vi:* **sie kann gut ~en** she's a good story-teller; **E~er (-s, -)** *m* narrator; **E~ung** *f* story, tale

Erzbischof *m* archbishop

erzeug- [ɛr'tsɔʏg] *zW:* ~**en** *vt* to produce; (*Strom*) to generate; **E~nis (-ses, -se)** *nt* product, produce; **E~ung** *f* production; generation

erziehen [ɛr'tsiːən] (*unreg*) *vt* to bring up; (*bilden*) to educate, to train; **Erzieher(in) (-s, -)** *m(f)* (*Berufsbezeichnung*) teacher; **Erziehung** *f* bringing up; (*Bildung*) education; **Erziehungsbeihilfe** *f* educational grant; **Erziehungsberechtigte(r)** *f(m)* parent; guardian

erzielen [ɛr'tsiːlən] *vt* to achieve, to obtain; (*Tor*) to score

erzwingen [ɛr'tsvɪŋən] (*unreg*) *vt* to force, to obtain by force

es [ɛs] (*nom, akk*) *pron* it

Esel ['eːzəl] (**-s, -**) *m* donkey, ass

Eskalation [ɛskalatsi'oːn] *f* escalation

ess- ▲ ['ɛs] *zW:* ~**bar** ['ɛsbaːr] *adj* eatable, edible; **E~besteck** *nt* knife, fork and spoon; **E~ecke** *f* dining area

essen ['ɛsən] (*unreg*) *vt, vi* to eat; **E~ (-s, -)** *nt* meal; food

Essig ['ɛsɪç] (**-s, -e**) *m* vinegar

Ess- ▲ *zW:* ~**kastanie** *f* sweet chestnut; ~**löffel** *m* tablespoon; ~**tisch** *m* dining table; ~**waren** *pl* foodstuffs, provisions; ~**zimmer** *nt* dining room

etablieren [eta'bliːrən] *vr* to become established; to set up in business

Etage [e'taːʒə] *f* floor, storey; ~**nbetten** *pl* bunk beds; ~**nwohnung** *f* flat

Etappe [e'tapə] *f* stage

Etat [e'taː] (**-s, -s**) *m* budget

etc *abk* (= *et cetera*) etc

Ethik ['eːtɪk] *f* ethics *sg;* **ethisch** *adj* ethical

Etikett [eti'kɛt] (**-(e)s, -e**) *nt* label; tag; ~**e** *f* etiquette, manners *pl*

etliche ['ɛtlɪçə] *pron pl* some, quite a few; ~**s** *pron* a thing or two

Etui [et'viː] (**-s, -s**) *nt* case

etwa ['ɛtva] *adv* (*ungefähr*) about; (*vielleicht*) perhaps; (*beispielsweise*) for instance; **nicht** ~ by no means; ~**ig** ['ɛtvaɪç] *adj* possible

etwas *pron* something; anything; (*ein wenig*) a little ♦ *adv* a little

euch [ɔʏç] *pron* (*akk von* **ihr**) you; yourselves; (*dat von* **ihr**) (to) you

euer ['ɔʏər] *pron* (*gen von* **ihr**) of you ♦ *adj* your

Spelling Reform: ▲ *new spelling* △ *old spelling (to be phased out)*

Eule ['ɔylə] f owl

eure ['ɔyrə] adj f siehe **euer**

eure(r, s) ['ɔyrə(r, s)] pron yours; **~rseits** adv on your part; **~s** adj nt siehe **euer**; **~sgleichen** pron people like you; **~twegen** adv (für euch) for your sakes; (wegen euch) on your account; **~twillen** adv: **um ~twillen** = euretwegen

eurige ['ɔyrɪgə] pron: **der/die/das ~** od **E~** yours

Euro ['ɔyro:] (-, -s) m (FIN) euro

Euro- zW: **~pa** [ɔy'ro:pa] nt Europe; **~päer(in)** [ɔyro'pɛːər(ɪn)] m(f) European; **e~päisch** adj European; **~pameister** [ɔy'ro:pə-] m European champion; **~paparlament** nt European Parliament; **~scheck** m (FIN) eurocheque

Euter ['ɔytər] (-s, -) nt udder

ev. abk = **evangelisch**

evakuieren [evaku'iːrən] vt to evacuate

evangelisch [evaŋ'geːlɪʃ] adj Protestant

Evangelium [evaŋ'geːliʊm] nt gospel

eventuell [eventu'ɛl] adj possible ♦ adv possibly, perhaps

evtl. abk = **eventuell**

EWG [eːveː'geː] (-) f abk (= Europäische Wirtschaftsgemeinschaft) EEC, Common Market

ewig ['eːvɪç] adj eternal; **E~keit** f eternity

EWU [eːveː'uː] f abk (= Europäische Währungsunion) EMU

exakt [ɛ'ksakt] adj exact

Examen [ɛ'ksaːmən] (-s, - od **Examina**) nt examination

Exemplar [ɛksɛm'plaːr] (-s, -e) nt specimen; (Buchexemplar) copy; **e~isch** adj exemplary

Exil [ɛ'ksiːl] (-s, -e) nt exile

Existenz [ɛksɪs'tɛnts] f existence; (Unterhalt) livelihood, living; (pej: Mensch) character; **~minimum** (-s) nt subsistence level

existieren [ɛksɪs'tiːrən] vi to exist

exklusiv [ɛksklu'ziːf] adj exclusive; **~e** adv exclusive of, not including ♦ präp +gen exclusive of, not including

exotisch [ɛ'ksoːtɪʃ] adj exotic

Expedition [ɛkspeditsi'oːn] f expedition

Experiment [ɛksperi'mɛnt] nt experiment; **~ell** [-'tɛl] adj experimental; **e~ieren** [-'tiːrən] vi to experiment

Experte [ɛks'pɛrtə] (-n, -n) m expert, specialist

Expertin f expert, specialist

explo- [ɛksplo] zW: **~dieren** [-'diːrən] vi to explode; **E~sion** [-zi'oːn] f explosion; **~siv** [-'ziːf] adj explosive

Export [ɛks'pɔrt] (-(e)s, -e) m export; **~eur** [-'tøːr] m exporter; **~handel** m export trade; **e~ieren** [-'tiːrən] vt to export; **~land** nt exporting country

Express- ▲ [ɛks'prɛs] zW: **~gut** nt express goods pl, express freight; **~zug** m express (train)

extra ['ɛkstra] adj inv (umg: gesondert) separate; (besondere) extra ♦ adv (gesondert) separately; (speziell) specially; (absichtlich) on purpose; (vor Adjektiven, zusätzlich) extra; **E~** (-s, -s) nt extra; **E~ausgabe** f special edition; **E~blatt** nt special edition

Extrakt [ɛks'trakt] (-(e)s, -e) m extract

extravagant [ɛkstrava'gant] adj extravagant

extrem [ɛks'treːm] adj extreme; **~istisch** [-'mɪstɪʃ] adj (POL) extremist; **E~itäten** [-mi'tɛːtən] pl extremities

exzentrisch [ɛks'tsɛntrɪʃ] adj eccentric

EZ nt abk = **Einzelzimmer**

F, f

Fa. abk (= Firma) firm; (in Briefen) Messrs

Fabel ['faːbəl] (-, -n) f fable; **f~haft** adj fabulous, marvellous

Fabrik [fa'briːk] f factory; **~ant** [-'kant] m (Hersteller) manufacturer; (Besitzer) industrialist; **~arbeiter** m factory worker; **~at** [-'kaːt] (-(e)s, -e) nt manufacture, product; **~gelände** nt factory site

Fach [fax] (-(e)s, ⁻er) nt compartment; (Sachgebiet) subject; **ein Mann vom ~** an expert; **~arbeiter** m skilled worker; **~arzt** m (medical) specialist; **~ausdruck** m technical term

Fächer ['fɛçər] (-s, -) m fan

Fach- zW: **~geschäft** nt specialist shop;

~**hochschule** f technical college; ~**kraft** f skilled worker, trained employee; **f~kundig** adj expert, specialist; **f~lich** adj professional; expert; ~**mann** (pl -**leute**) m specialist; **f~männisch** adj professional; ~**schule** f technical college; **f~simpeln** vi to talk shop; ~**werk** nt timber frame

Fackel ['fakəl] (-, -n) f torch

fad(e) [faːt, 'faːdə] adj insipid; (langweilig) dull

Faden ['faːdən] (-s, ⁀) m thread; **f~scheinig** adj (auch fig) threadbare

fähig ['fɛːɪç] adj: ~ (**zu** od +gen) capable (of); able (to); **F~keit** f ability

fahnden ['faːndən] vi: ~ **nach** to search for; **Fahndung** f search

Fahndungsliste f list of wanted criminals, wanted list

Fahne ['faːnə] f flag, standard; **eine ~ haben** (umg) to smell of drink; ~**nflucht** f desertion

Fahr- zW: ~**ausweis** m ticket; ~**bahn** f carriageway (BRIT), roadway

Fähre ['fɛːrə] f ferry

fahren ['faːrən] (unreg) vt to drive; (Rad) to ride; (befördern) to drive, to take; (Rennen) to drive in ♦ vi (sich bewegen) to go; (Schiff) to sail; (abfahren) to leave; **mit dem Auto/Zug ~** to go od travel by car/train; **mit der Hand ~ über** +akk to pass one's hand over

Fahr- zW: ~**er(in)** (-s, -) m(f) driver; ~**erflucht** f hit-and-run; ~**gast** m passenger; ~**geld** nt fare; ~**karte** f ticket; ~**kartenausgabe** f ticket office; ~**kartenautomat** m ticket machine; ~**kartenschalter** m ticket office; **f~lässig** adj negligent; **f~lässige Tötung** manslaughter; ~**lehrer** m driving instructor; ~**plan** m timetable; **f~planmäßig** adj scheduled; ~**preis** m fare; ~**prüfung** f driving test; ~**rad** nt bicycle; ~**radweg** m cycle lane; ~**schein** m ticket; ~**scheinentwerter** m (automatic) ticket stamping machine

Fährschiff ['fɛːrʃɪf] nt ferry(boat)

Fahr- zW: ~**schule** f driving school; ~**spur** f lane; ~**stuhl** m lift (BRIT), elevator (US)

Fahrt [faːrt] (-, -en) f journey; (kurz) trip;

(AUT) drive; (Geschwindigkeit) speed; **gute ~!** have a good journey

Fährte ['fɛːrtə] f track, trail

Fahrt- zW: ~**kosten** pl travelling expenses; ~**richtung** f course, direction

Fahrzeit f time for the journey

Fahrzeug nt vehicle; ~**brief** m log book; ~**papiere** pl vehicle documents

fair [fɛːr] adj fair

Fakt [fakt] (-(e)s, -en) m fact

Faktor ['faktɔr] m factor

Fakultät [fakʊl'tɛːt] f faculty

Falke ['falkə] (-n, -n) m falcon

Fall [fal] (-(e)s, ⁀e) m (Sturz) fall; (Sachverhalt, JUR, GRAM) case; **auf jeden ~, auf alle Fälle** in any case; (bestimmt) definitely; **auf keinen ~!** no way!

Falle f trap

fallen (unreg) vi to fall; **etw ~ lassen** to drop sth; (Bemerkung) to make sth; (Plan) to abandon sth, to drop sth

fällen ['fɛlən] vt (Baum) to fell; (Urteil) to pass

fällig ['fɛlɪç] adj due

falls [fals] adv in case, if

Fallschirm m parachute; ~**springer** m parachutist

falsch [falʃ] adj false; (unrichtig) wrong

fälschen ['fɛlʃən] vt to forge

fälsch- zW: ~**lich** adj false; ~**licherweise** adv mistakenly; **F~ung** f forgery

Falte ['faltə] f (Knick) fold, crease; (Hautfalte) wrinkle; (Rockfalte) pleat; **f~n** vt to fold; (Stirn) to wrinkle

faltig ['faltɪç] adj (Hände, Haut) wrinkled; (zerknittert: Rock) creased

familiär [famili'ɛːr] adj familiar

Familie [fa'miːliə] f family

Familien- zW: ~**betrieb** m family business; ~**kreis** m family circle; ~**mitglied** nt member of the family; ~**name** m surname; ~**stand** m marital status

Fanatiker [fa'naːtikər] (-s, -) m fanatic; **fanatisch** adj fanatical

fand etc [fant] vb siehe **finden**

Fang [faŋ] (-(e)s, ⁀e) m catch; (Jagen) hunting; (Kralle) talon, claw; **f~en** (unreg) vt to catch ♦ vr to get caught; (Flugzeug) to level out; (*Mensch: nicht fallen*) to steady o.s.; (*fig*) to compose o.s.; (*in Leistung*) to get back on form

Fantasie ▲ [fanta'zi:] *f* imagination; **f~los** *adj* unimaginative; **f~ren** *vi* to fantasize; **f~voll** *adj* imaginative

fantastisch ▲ [fan'tastɪʃ] *adj* fantastic

Farb- ['farb] *zW:* **~abzug** *m* colour print; **~aufnahme** *f* colour photograph; **~band** *m* typewriter ribbon; **~e** *f* colour; (*zum Malen etc*) paint; (*Stoffarbe*) dye; **f~echt** *adj* colourfast

färben ['fɛrbən] *vt* to colour; (*Stoff, Haar*) to dye

farben- ['farbən] *zW:* **~blind** *adj* colour-blind; **~freudig** *adj* colourful; **~froh** *adj* colourful, gay

Farb- *zW:* **~fernsehen** *nt* colour television; **~film** *m* colour film; **~foto** *nt* colour photograph; **f~ig** *adj* coloured; **~ige(r)** *f(m)* coloured (person); **~kasten** *m* paintbox; **f~lich** *adj* colour; **f~los** *adj* colourless; **~stift** *m* coloured pencil; **~stoff** *m* dye; **~ton** *m* hue, tone

Färbung ['fɛrbʊŋ] *f* colouring; (*Tendenz*) bias

Farn [farn] (-(e)s, -e) *m* fern; bracken

Fasan [fa'za:n] (-(e)s, -e(n)) *m* pheasant

Fasching ['faʃɪŋ] (-s, -e *od* -s) *m* carnival

Faschismus [fa'ʃɪsmʊs] *m* fascism

Faschist *m* fascist

Faser ['fa:zər] (-, -n) *f* fibre; **f~n** *vi* to fray

Fass ▲ [fas] (-es, ᵘer) *nt* vat, barrel; (*für Öl*) drum; **Bier vom ~** draught beer

Fassade [fa'sa:də] *f* façade

fassen ['fasən] *vt* (*ergreifen*) to grasp, to take; (*inhaltlich*) to hold; (*Entschluss etc*) to take; (*verstehen*) to understand; (*Ring etc*) to set; (*formulieren*) to formulate, to phrase ♦ *vr* to calm down; **nicht zu ~** unbelievable

Fassung ['fasʊŋ] *f* (*Umrahmung*) mounting; (*Lampenfassung*) socket; (*Wortlaut*) version; (*Beherrschung*) composure; **jdn aus der ~ bringen** to upset sb; **f~slos** *adj* speechless

fast [fast] *adv* almost, nearly

fasten ['fastən] *vi* to fast; **F~zeit** *f* Lent

Fastnacht *f* Shrove Tuesday; carnival

faszinieren [fastsi'ni:rən] *vt* to fascinate

fatal [fa'ta:l] *adj* fatal; (*peinlich*) embarrassing

faul [faʊl] *adj* rotten; (*Person*) lazy; (*Ausreden*) lame; **daran ist etwas ~** there's something fishy about it; **~en** *vi* to rot; **~enzen** *vi* to idle; **F~enzer** (-s, -) *m* idler, loafer; **F~heit** *f* laziness; **~ig** *adj* putrid

Faust ['faʊst] (-, **Fäuste**) *f* fist; **auf eigene ~** off one's own bat; **~handschuh** *m* mitten

Favorit [favo'ri:t] (-en, -en) *m* favourite

Fax [faks] (-, -(e)) *nt* fax

faxen ['faksən] *vt* to fax; **jdm etw ~** to fax sth to sb

FCKW *m abk* (= *Fluorchlorkohlenwasserstoff*) CFC

Februar ['fe:brua:r] (-(s), -e) *m* February

fechten ['fɛçtən] *vi* to fence

Feder ['fe:dər] (-, -n) *f* feather; (*Schreibfeder*) pen nib; (*TECH*) spring; **~ball** *m* shuttlecock; **~bett** *nt* continental quilt; **~halter** *m* penholder, pen; **f~leicht** *adj* light as a feather; **f~n** *vi* (*nachgeben*) to be springy; (*sich bewegen*) to bounce ♦ *vt* to spring; **~ung** *f* (*AUT*) suspension

Fee [fe:] *f* fairy

fegen ['fe:gən] *vt* to sweep

fehl [fe:l] *adj:* **~ am Platz** *od* **Ort** out of place; **F~betrag** *m* deficit; **~en** *vi* to be wanting *od* missing; (*abwesend sein*) to be absent; **etw ~t jdm** sb lacks sth; **du ~st mir** I miss you; **was ~t ihm?** what's wrong with him?; **F~er** (-s, -) *m* mistake, error; (*Mangel, Schwäche*) fault; **~erfrei** *adj* faultless; without any mistakes; **~erhaft** *adj* incorrect; faulty; **~erlos** *adj* flawless, perfect; **F~geburt** *f* miscarriage; **~gehen** (*unreg*) *vi* to go astray; **F~griff** *m* blunder; **F~konstruktion** *f* badly designed thing; **~schlagen** (*unreg*) *vi* to fail; **F~start** *m* (*SPORT*) false start; **F~zündung** *f* (*AUT*) misfire, backfire

Feier ['faɪər] (-, -n) *f* celebration; **~abend** *m* time to stop work; **~abend machen** to stop, to knock off; **jetzt ist ~abend!** that's enough!; **f~lich** *adj* solemn; **~lichkeit** *f* solemnity; **~lichkeiten** *pl* (*Veranstaltungen*) festivities; **f~n** *vt, vi* to celebrate; **~tag** *m*

holiday
feig(e) [faɪk, 'faɪɡə] *adj* cowardly
Feige ['faɪɡə] *f* fig
Feigheit *f* cowardice
Feigling *m* coward
Feile ['faɪlə] *f* file
feilschen ['faɪlʃən] *vi* to haggle
fein [faɪn] *adj* fine; (*vornehm*) refined; (*Gehör etc*) keen; **~!** great!
Feind [faɪnt] **(-(e)s, -e)** *m* enemy; **f~lich** *adj* hostile; **~schaft** *f* enmity; **f~selig** *adj* hostile
Fein- *zW*: **f~fühlig** *adj* sensitive; **~gefühl** *nt* delicacy, tact; **~heit** *f* fineness; refinement; keenness; **~kostgeschäft** *nt* delicatessen (shop); **~schmecker** **(-s, -)** *m* gourmet; **~wäsche** *f* delicate clothing (*when washing*); **~waschmittel** *nt* mild detergent
Feld [fɛlt] **(-(e)s, -er)** *nt* field; (*SCHACH*) square; (*SPORT*) pitch; **~herr** *m* commander; **~stecher** **(-s, -)** *m* binoculars *pl*; **~weg** *m* path; **~zug** *m* (*fig*) campaign
Felge ['fɛlɡə] *f* (wheel) rim
Fell [fɛl] **(-(e)s, -e)** *nt* fur; coat; (*von Schaf*) fleece; (*von toten Tieren*) skin
Fels [fɛls] **(-en, -en)** *m* rock; (*Klippe*) cliff
Felsen ['fɛlzən] **(-s, -)** *m* = **Fels**; **f~fest** *adj* firm
feminin [femi'ni:n] *adj* feminine
Fenster ['fɛnstər] **(-s, -)** *nt* window; **~bank** *f* windowsill; **~laden** *m* shutter; **~leder** *nt* chamois (leather); **~scheibe** *f* windowpane
Ferien ['fe:rɪən] *pl* holidays, vacation *sg* (*US*); **~ haben** to be on holiday; **~bungalow** [-bʊŋɡalo] **(-s, -s)** *m* holiday bungalow; **~haus** *nt* holiday home; **~kurs** *m* holiday course; **~lager** *nt* holiday camp; **~reise** *f* holiday; **~wohnung** *f* holiday apartment
Ferkel ['fɛrkəl] **(-s, -)** *nt* piglet
fern [fɛrn] *adj, adv* far-off, distant; **~ von hier** a long way (away) from here; **der F~e Osten** the Far East; **~ halten** to keep away; **F~bedienung** *f* remote control; **F~e** *f* distance; **~er** *adj* further ♦ *adv* further; (*weiterhin*) in future; **F~gespräch** *nt* trunk call; **F~glas** *nt* binoculars *pl*; **F~licht** *nt*

(*AUT*) full beam; **F~rohr** *nt* telescope; **F~ruf** *m* (*förmlich*) telephone number; **F~schreiben** *nt* telex; **F~sehapparat** *m* television set; **F~sehen** **(-s)** *nt* television; **im F~sehen** on television; **~sehen** (*unreg*) *vi* to watch television; **F~seher** *m* television; **F~sehturm** *m* television tower; **F~sprecher** *m* telephone; **F~steuerung** *f* remote control; **F~straße** *f* ≃ 'A' road (*BRIT*), highway (*US*); **F~verkehr** *m* long-distance traffic
Ferse ['fɛrzə] *f* heel
fertig ['fɛrtɪç] *adj* (*bereit*) ready; (*beendet*) finished; (*gebrauchsfertig*) ready-made; **~ bringen** (*fähig sein*) to be capable of; **~ machen** (*beenden*) to finish; (*umg: Person*) to finish; (*: körperlich*) to exhaust; (*: moralisch*) to get down; **sich ~ machen** to get ready; **~ stellen** to complete; **F~gericht** *nt* precooked meal; **F~haus** *nt* kit house, prefab; **F~keit** *f* skill
Fessel ['fɛsəl] **(-, -n)** *f* fetter; **f~n** *vt* to bind; (*mit ~n*) to fetter; (*fig*) to spellbind; **f~nd** *adj* fascinating, captivating
Fest **(-(e)s, -e)** *nt* party; festival; **frohes ~!** Happy Christmas!
fest [fɛst] *adj* firm; (*Nahrung*) solid; (*Gehalt*) regular; **~e Kosten** fixed cost ♦ *adv* (*schlafen*) soundly; **~ angestellt** permanently employed; **~binden** (*unreg*) *vt* to tie, to fasten; **~bleiben** (*unreg*) *vi* to stand firm; **F~essen** *nt* banquet; **~halten** (*unreg*) *vt* to seize, to hold fast; (*Ereignis*) to record ♦ *vr*: **sich ~halten (an +dat)** to hold on (to); **~igen** *vt* to strengthen; **F~igkeit** *f* strength; **F~ival** ['fɛstivəl] **(-s, -s)** *nt* festival; **F~land** *nt* mainland; **~legen** *vt* to fix ♦ *vr* to commit o.s.; **~lich** *adj* festive; **~liegen** (*unreg*) *vi* (*~stehen: Termin*) to be confirmed, be fixed; **~machen** *vt* to fasten; (*Termin etc*) to fix; **F~nahme** *f* arrest; **~nehmen** (*unreg*) *vt* to arrest; **F~preis** *m* (*COMM*) fixed price; **F~rede** *f* address; **~setzen** *vt* to fix, to settle; **F~spiele** *pl* (*Veranstaltung*) festival *sg*; **~stehen** (*unreg*) *vi* to be certain; **~stellen** *vt* to establish; (*sagen*) to remark; **F~tag** *m*

feast day, holiday; **F~ung** f fortress;
F~wochen pl festival sg

Fett [fɛt] **(-(e)s, -e)** nt fat, grease

fett adj fat; (Essen etc) greasy; (TYP) bold;
~arm adj low fat; **~en** vt to grease;
F~fleck m grease stain; **~ig** adj greasy,
fatty

Fetzen ['fɛtsən] **(-s, -)** m scrap

feucht [fɔʏçt] adj damp; (Luft) humid;
F~igkeit f dampness; humidity;
F~igkeitscreme f moisturizing cream

Feuer ['fɔʏər] **(-s, -)** nt fire; (zum Rauchen) a
light; (fig: Schwung) spirit; **~alarm** m fire
alarm; **f~fest** adj fireproof; **~gefahr** f
danger of fire; **f~gefährlich** adj
inflammable; **~leiter** f fire escape ladder;
~löscher **(-s, -)** m fire extinguisher;
~melder **(-s, -)** m fire alarm; **f~n** vt, vi
(auch fig) to fire; **~stein** m flint; **~treppe** f
fire escape; **~wehr** **(-, -en)** f fire brigade;
~wehrauto nt fire engine; **~wehrfrau** f
firewoman; **~wehrmann** m fireman;
~werk nt fireworks pl; **~zeug** nt
(cigarette) lighter

Fichte ['fɪçtə] f spruce, pine

Fieber ['fiːbər] **(-s, -)** nt fever, temperature;
f~haft adj feverish; **~thermometer** nt
thermometer; **fiebrig** adj feverish

fiel etc [fiːl] vb siehe **fallen**

fies [fiːs] (umg) adj nasty

Figur [fi'guːr] **(-, -en)** f figure; (Schachfigur)
chessman, chess piece

Filet [fi'leː] **(-s, -s)** nt (KOCH) fillet

Filiale [fili'aːlə] f (COMM) branch

Film [fɪlm] **(-(e)s, -e)** m film; **~aufnahme** f
shooting; **f~en** vt, vi to film; **~kamera** f
cine camera

Filter ['fɪltər] **(-s, -)** m filter; **f~n** vt to filter;
~papier nt filter paper; **~zigarette** f
tipped cigarette

Filz [fɪlts] **(-es, -e)** m felt; **f~en** vt (umg) to
frisk ♦ vi (Wolle) to mat; **~stift** m felt-tip
pen

Finale [fi'naːlə] **(-s, -(s))** nt finale; (SPORT)
final(s)

Finanz [fi'nants] f finance; **~amt** nt Inland
Revenue office; **~beamte(r)** m revenue

officer, **f~iell** [-tsi'ɛl] adj financial; **f~ieren**
[-'tsiːrən] vt to finance; **f~kräftig** adj
financially strong; **~minister** m Chancellor
of the Exchequer (BRIT), Minister of Finance

Find- ['fɪnd] zW: **f~en** (unreg) vt to find;
(meinen) to think ♦ vr to be (found); (sich
fassen) to compose o.s.; **ich f~e nichts
dabei, wenn ...** I don't see what's wrong if
...; **das wird sich f~en** things will work
out; **~er** **(-s, -)** m finder; **~erlohn** m
reward (for sb who finds sth); **f~ig** adj
resourceful

fing etc [fɪŋ] vb siehe **fangen**

Finger ['fɪŋər] **(-s, -)** m finger; **~abdruck** m
fingerprint; **~nagel** m fingernail; **~spitze** f
fingertip

fingiert adj made-up, fictitious

Fink [fɪŋk] **(-en, -en)** m finch

Finn- [fɪn] zW: **~e** **(-n, -n)** m Finn; **~in** f
Finn; **f~isch** adj Finnish; **~land** nt Finland

finster ['fɪnstər] adj dark, gloomy;
(verdächtig) dubious; (verdrossen) grim;
(Gedanke) dark; **F~nis** **(-)** f darkness, gloom

Firma ['fɪrma] **(-, -men)** f firm

Firmen- ['fɪrmən] zW: **~inhaber** m owner
of firm; **~schild** nt (shop) sign; **~wagen**
m company car; **~zeichen** nt trademark

Fisch [fɪʃ] **(-(e)s, -e)** m fish; **~e** pl (ASTROL)
Pisces sg; **f~en** vt, vi to fish; **~er** **(-s, -)** m
fisherman; **~erei** f fishing, fishery; **~fang**
m fishing; **~geschäft** nt fishmonger's
(shop); **~gräte** f fishbone; **~stäbchen**
[-stɛːpçən] nt fish finger (BRIT), fish stick (US)

fit [fɪt] adj fit; **'F~ness** ▲ **(-, -)** f (physical)
fitness

fix [fɪks] adj fixed; (Person) alert, smart; **~ und
fertig** finished; (erschöpft) done in;
F~er(in) m(f) (umg) junkie; **F~erstube** f
(umg) junkies centre; **f~ieren** [fɪ'ksiːrən] vt
to fix; (anstarren) to stare at

flach [flax] adj flat; (Gefäß) shallow

Fläche ['flɛçə] f area; (Oberfläche) surface

Flachland nt lowland

flackern ['flakərn] vi to flare, to flicker

Flagge ['flagə] f flag; **f~n** vi to fly a flag

flämisch ['flɛːmɪʃ] adj (LING) Flemish

Flamme ['flamə] f flame

Flandern ['flandərn] nt Flanders

Flanke ['flaŋkə] f flank; (SPORT: Seite) wing

Flasche ['flaʃə] f bottle; (umg: Versager) wash-out

Flaschen- zW: ~**bier** nt bottled beer; ~**öffner** m bottle opener; ~**zug** m pulley

flatterhaft adj flighty, fickle

flattern ['flatərn] vi to flutter

flau [flau] adj weak, listless; (Nachfrage) slack; **jdm ist** ~ sb feels queasy

Flaum [flaum] (-(e)s) m (Feder) down; (Haare) fluff

flauschig ['flauʃɪç] adj fluffy

Flaute ['flautə] f calm; (COMM) recession

Flechte ['flɛçtə] f plait; (MED) dry scab; (BOT) lichen; f~**n** (unreg) vt to plait; (Kranz) to twine

Fleck [flɛk] (-(e)s, -e) m spot; (Schmutzfleck) stain; (Stofffleck) patch; (Makel) blemish; **nicht vom** ~ **kommen** (auch fig) not to get any further; **vom** ~ **weg** straight away

Flecken (-s, -) m = **Fleck**; f~**los** adj spotless; ~**mittel** nt stain remover; ~**wasser** nt stain remover

fleckig adj spotted; stained

Fledermaus ['fle:dərmaus] f bat

Flegel ['fle:gəl] (-s, -) m (Mensch) lout; f~**haft** adj loutish, unmannerly; ~**jahre** pl adolescence sg

flehen ['fle:ən] vi to implore; ~**tlich** adj imploring

Fleisch [flaiʃ] (-(e)s) nt flesh; (Essen) meat; ~**brühe** f beef tea, meat stock; ~**er** (-s, -) m butcher; ~**e'rei** f butcher's (shop); f~**ig** adj fleshy; f~**los** adj meatless, vegetarian

Fleiß [flais] (-es) m diligence, industry; f~**ig** adj diligent, industrious

fletschen ['flɛtʃən] vt (Zähne) to show

flexibel [flɛ'ksi:bəl] adj flexible

Flicken ['flɪkən] (-s, -) m patch; f~ vt to mend

Flieder ['fli:dər] (-s, -) m lilac

Fliege ['fli:gə] f fly; (Kleidung) bow tie; f~**n** (unreg) vt, vi to fly; **auf jdn/etw f~n** (umg) to be mad about sb/sth; ~**npilz** m toadstool; ~**r** (-s, -) m flier, airman

fliehen ['fli:ən] (unreg) vi to flee

Fliese ['fli:zə] f tile

Fließ- ['fli:s] zW: ~**band** nt production od assembly line; f~**en** (unreg) vi to flow; f~**end** adj flowing; (Rede, Deutsch) fluent; (Übergänge) smooth

flimmern ['flɪmərn] vi to glimmer

flink [flɪŋk] adj nimble, lively

Flinte ['flɪntə] f rifle; shotgun

Flitterwochen pl honeymoon sg

flitzen ['flɪtsən] vi to flit

Flocke ['flɔkə] f flake

flog etc [flo:k] vb siehe **fliegen**

Floh [flo:] (-(e)s, ⁺e) m flea; ~**markt** m flea market

florieren [flo'ri:rən] vi to flourish

Floskel ['flɔskəl] (-, -n) f set phrase

Floß [flo:s] (-es, ⁺e) nt raft, float

floss ▲ etc vb siehe **fließen**

Flosse ['flɔsə] f fin

Flöte ['flø:tə] f flute; (Blockflöte) recorder

flott [flɔt] adj lively; (elegant) smart; (NAUT) afloat; F~**e** f fleet, navy

Fluch [flu:x] (-(e)s, ⁺e) m curse; f~**en** vi to curse, to swear

Flucht [flʊxt] (-, -en) f flight; (Fensterflucht) row; (Zimmerflucht) suite; f~**artig** adj hasty

flücht- ['flʏçt] zW: ~**en** vi, vr to flee, to escape; ~**ig** adj fugitive; (vergänglich) transitory; (oberflächlich) superficial; (eilig) fleeting; F~**igkeitsfehler** m careless slip; F~**ling** m fugitive, refugee

Flug [flu:k] (-(e)s, ⁺e) m flight; ~**blatt** nt pamphlet

Flügel ['fly:gəl] (-s, -) m wing; (MUS) grand piano

Fluggast m airline passenger

Flug- zW: ~**gesellschaft** f airline (company); ~**hafen** m airport; ~**lärm** m aircraft noise; ~**linie** f airline; ~**plan** m flight schedule; ~**platz** m airport; (klein) airfield; ~**reise** f flight; ~**schein** m (Ticket) plane ticket; (Pilotenschein) pilot's licence; ~**steig** [-staik] (-(e)s, -e) m gate; ~**verbindung** f air connection; ~**verkehr** m air traffic; ~**zeug** nt (aero)plane, airplane (US); ~**zeugentführung** f hijacking of a plane; ~**zeughalle** f hangar; ~**zeugträger**

m aircraft carrier

Flunder ['flʊndər] (-, -n) *f* flounder

flunkern ['flʊŋkərn] *vi* to fib, to tell stories

Fluor ['fluːɔr] (-s) *nt* fluorine

Flur [fluːr] (-(e)s, -e) *m* hall; (*Treppenflur*) staircase

Fluss ▲ [flʊs] (-es, ¨e) *m* river; (*Fließen*) flow

flüssig ['flʏsɪç] *adj* liquid; ~ **machen** (*Geld*) to make available; **F~keit** *f* liquid; (*Zustand*) liquidity

flüstern ['flʏstərn] *vt, vi* to whisper

Flut [fluːt] (-, -en) *f* (*auch fig*) flood; (*Gezeiten*) high tide; **f~en** *vi* to flood; **~licht** *nt* floodlight

Fohlen ['foːlən] (-s, -) *nt* foal

Föhn[1] [føːn] (-(e)s, -e) *m* (*warmer Fallwind*) föhn

Föhn[2] (-(e)s, -e) ▲ (*Haartrockner*) hairdryer; **f~en** ▲ *vt* to (blow) dry; **~frisur** ▲ *f* blow-dry hairstyle

Folge ['fɔlgə] *f* series, sequence; (*Fortsetzung*) instalment; (*Auswirkung*) result; **in rascher ~** in quick succession; **etw zur ~ haben** to result in sth; **~n haben** to have consequences; **einer Sache** *dat* **~ leisten** to comply with sth; **f~n** *vi* +*dat* to follow; (*gehorchen*) to obey; **jdm f~n können** (*fig*) to follow od understand sb; **f~nd** *adj* following; **f~ndermaßen** *adv* as follows, in the following way; **f~rn** *vt*: **f~rn (aus)** to conclude (from); **~rung** *f* conclusion

folglich ['fɔlklɪç] *adv* consequently

folgsam ['fɔlkzaːm] *adj* obedient

Folie ['foːliə] *f* foil

Folklore ['fɔlkloːər] *f* folklore

Folter ['fɔltər] (-, -n) *f* torture; (*Gerät*) rack; **f~n** *vt* to torture

Fön [føːn] (-(e)s, -e) ® *m* hair dryer

Fondue [fõdyː] (-s, -s od -, -s) *nt od f* (*KOCH*) fondue

fönen △ *vt siehe* **föhnen**

Fönfrisur △ *f siehe* **Föhnfrisur**

Fontäne [fɔnˈtɛːnə] *f* fountain

Förder- ['fœrdər] *zW*: **~band** *nt* conveyor belt; **~korb** *m* pit cage; **f~lich** *adj* beneficial

fordern ['fɔrdərn] *vt* to demand

fördern ['fœrdərn] *vt* to promote; (*unterstützen*) to help; (*Kohle*) to extract

Forderung ['fɔrdəruŋ] *f* demand

Förderung ['fœrdəruŋ] *f* promotion; help; extraction

Forelle [foˈrɛlə] *f* trout

Form [fɔrm] (-, -en) *f* shape; (*Gestaltung*) form; (*Gussform*) mould; (*Backform*) baking tin; **in ~ sein** to be in good form od shape; **in ~ von** in the shape of

Formali'tät *f* formality

Format [fɔrˈmaːt] (-(e)s, -e) *nt* format; (*fig*) distinction

formbar *adj* malleable

Formblatt *nt* form

Formel (-, -n) *f* formula

formell [fɔrˈmɛl] *adj* formal

formen *vt* to form, to shape

Formfehler *m* faux pas, gaffe; (*JUR*) irregularity

formieren [fɔrˈmiːrən] *vt* to form ♦ *vr* to form up

förmlich ['fœrmlɪç] *adj* formal; (*umg*) real; **F~keit** *f* formality

formlos *adj* shapeless; (*Benehmen etc*) informal

Formular [fɔrmuˈlaːr] (-s, -e) *nt* form

formulieren [fɔrmuˈliːrən] *vt* to formulate

forsch [fɔrʃ] *adj* energetic, vigorous

forsch- *zW*: **~en** *vi*: **~en (nach)** to search (for); (*wissenschaftlich*) to (do) research; **~end** *adj* searching; **F~er** (-s, -) *m* research scientist; (*Naturforscher*) explorer; **F~ung** *f* research

Forst [fɔrst] (-(e)s, -e) *m* forest

Förster ['fœrstər] (-s, -) *m* forester; (*für Wild*) gamekeeper

fort [fɔrt] *adv* away; (*verschwunden*) gone; (*vorwärts*) on; **und so ~** on and on; **in einem ~** on and on; **~bestehen** (*unreg*) *vi* to survive; **~bewegen** *vt, vr* to move away; **~bilden** *vr* to continue one's education; **~bleiben** (*unreg*) *vi* to stay away; **F~dauer** *f* continuance; **~fahren** (*unreg*) *vi* to depart; (*~setzen*) to go on, to continue; **~führen** *vt* to continue, to carry on; **~gehen** (*unreg*) *vi* to go away;

~**geschritten** *adj* advanced; ~**pflanzen** *vr* to reproduce; **F~pflanzung** *f* reproduction

fort- *zW:* ~**schaffen** *vt* to remove; ~**schreiten** *(unreg) vi* to advance

Fortschritt ['fɔrtʃrɪt] *m* advance; ~**e machen** to make progress; **f~lich** *adj* progressive

fort- *zW:* ~**setzen** *vt* to continue; **F~setzung** *f* continuation; *(folgender Teil)* instalment; **F~setzung folgt** to be continued; ~**während** *adj* incessant, continual

Foto ['foːto] *(-s, -s) nt* photo(graph); ~**apparat** *m* camera; ~'**graf** *m* photographer; ~**gra'fie** *f* photography; *(Bild)* photograph; **f~gra'fieren** *vt* to photograph ♦ *vi* to take photographs; ~**kopie** *f* photocopy

Fr. *abk (= Frau)* Mrs, Ms

Fracht [fraxt] *(-, -en) f* freight; *(NAUT)* cargo; *(Preis)* carriage; ~ **zahlt Empfänger** *(COMM)* carriage forward; ~**er** *(-s, -) m* freighter, cargo boat; ~**gut** *nt* freight

Frack [frak] *(-(e)s, ᵘe) m* tails *pl*

Frage ['fraːgə] *(-, -n) f* question; **eine ~ stellen** to ask sb a question, to put a question to sb; *siehe* **infrage**; ~**bogen** *m* questionnaire; **f~n** *vt, vi* to ask; ~**zeichen** *nt* question mark

fraglich *adj* questionable, doubtful

fraglos *adv* unquestionably

Fragment [fra'gmɛnt] *nt* fragment

fragwürdig ['fraːkvʏrdɪç] *adj* questionable, dubious

Fraktion [fraktsi'oːn] *f* parliamentary party

frankieren [fraŋ'kiːrən] *vt* to stamp, to frank

franko ['fraŋko] *adv* post-paid; carriage paid

Frankreich ['fraŋkraɪç] *(-s) nt* France

Franzose [fran'tsoːzə] *m* Frenchman; **Französin** [fran'tsøːzɪn] *f* Frenchwoman; **französisch** *adj* French

fraß *etc* [fras] *vb siehe* **fressen**

Fratze ['fratsə] *f* grimace

Frau [frau] *(-, -en) f* woman; *(Ehefrau)* wife; *(Anrede)* Mrs, Ms; ~ **Doktor** Doctor

Frauen- *zW:* ~**arzt** *m* gynaecologist; ~**bewegung** *f* feminist movement; ~**haus** *nt* women's refuge; ~**zimmer** *nt* female, broad *(US)*

Fräulein ['frɔʏlaɪn] *nt* young lady; *(Anrede)* Miss, Ms

fraulich ['fraʊlɪç] *adj* womanly

frech [frɛç] *adj* cheeky, impudent; **F~heit** *f* cheek, impudence

frei [fraɪ] *adj* free; *(Stelle, Sitzplatz)* free, vacant; *(Mitarbeiter)* freelance; *(unbekleidet)* bare; **von etw ~ sein** to be free of sth; **im F~en** in the open air; ~ **sprechen** to talk without notes; ~ **Haus** *(COMM)* carriage paid; ~**er Wettbewerb** *(COMM)* free competition; **F~bad** *nt* open-air swimming pool; ~**bekommen** *(unreg) vt:* **einen Tag ~bekommen** to get a day off; ~**beruflich** *adj* self-employed; ~**gebig** *adj* generous; ~**halten** *(unreg) vt* to keep free; ~**händig** *adv (fahren)* with no hands; **F~heit** *f* freedom; ~**heitlich** *adj* liberal; **F~heitsstrafe** *f* prison sentence; **F~karte** *f* free ticket; ~**lassen** *(unreg) vt* to (set) free; ~**legen** *vt* to expose; ~**lich** *adv* certainly, admittedly; **ja ~lich** yes of course; **F~lichtbühne** *f* open-air theatre; **F~lichtmuseum** *nt* open-air museum; ~**machen** *vt (Post)* to frank ♦ *vr* to arrange to be free; *(entkleiden)* to undress; **Tage ~machen** to take days off; ~**nehmen** ▲ *(unreg) vt:* **sich** *dat* **einen Tag ~nehmen** to take a day off; ~**sprechen** *(unreg) vt:* ~**sprechen (von)** to acquit (of); **F~spruch** *m* acquittal; ~**stehen** *(unreg) vi:* **es steht dir ~, das zu tun** you're free to do that; *(leer stehen: Wohnung, Haus)* to lie/stand empty; ~**stellen** *vt:* **jdm etw ~stellen** to leave sth (up) to sb; **F~stoß** *m* free kick

Freitag *m* Friday; ~**s** *adv* on Fridays

frei- *zW:* ~**willig** *adj* voluntary; **F~zeit** *f* spare ♦ free time; **F~zeitpark** *m* amusement park; **F~zeitzentrum** *nt* leisure centre; ~**zügig** *adj* liberal, broad-minded; *(mit Geld)* generous

fremd [frɛmt] *adj (unvertraut)* strange; *(ausländisch)* foreign; *(nicht eigen)* someone else's; **etw ist jdm ~** sth is foreign to sb; ~**artig** *adj* strange; **F~enführer** ['frɛmdən-]

m (tourist) guide; **F~enverkehr** *m* tourism; **F~enverkehrsamt** *nt* tourist board; **F~enzimmer** *nt* guest room; **F~körper** *m* foreign body; **~ländisch** *adj* foreign; **F~sprache** *f* foreign language; **F~wort** *nt* foreign word

Frequenz [fre'kvɛnts] *f* (RADIO) frequency

fressen ['frɛsən] (unreg) *vt, vi* to eat

Freude ['frɔydə] *f* joy, delight

freudig *adj* joyful, happy

freuen ['frɔyən] *vt unpers* to make happy *od* pleased ♦ *vr* to be glad *od* happy; **freut mich!** pleased to meet you; **sich auf etw** *akk* **~** to look forward to sth; **sich über etw** *akk* **~** to be pleased about sth

Freund ['frɔynt] (-(e)s, -e) *m* friend; boyfriend; **~in** [-dɪn] *f* friend; girlfriend; **f~lich** *adj* kind, friendly; **f~licherweise** *adv* kindly; **~lichkeit** *f* friendliness, kindness; **~schaft** *f* friendship; **f~schaftlich** *adj* friendly

Frieden ['fri:dən] (-s, -) *m* peace; **im ~** in peacetime

Friedens- *zW:* **~schluss** ▲ *m* peace agreement; **~vertrag** *m* peace treaty; **~zeit** *f* peacetime

fried- ['fri:t] *zW:* **~fertig** *adj* peaceable; **F~hof** *m* cemetery; **~lich** *adj* peaceful

frieren ['fri:rən] (unreg) *vt, vi* to freeze; **ich friere, es friert mich** I'm freezing, I'm cold

Frikadelle [frika'dɛlə] *f* rissole

Frikassee [frika'se:] (-s, -s) *nt* (KOCH) fricassee

frisch [frɪʃ] *adj* fresh; (lebhaft) lively; **~ gestrichen!** wet paint!; **sich ~ machen** to freshen (o.s.) up; **F~e** *f* freshness; liveliness; **F~haltefolie** *f* cling film

Friseur [fri'zø:r] *m* hairdresser

Friseuse [fri'zø:zə] *f* hairdresser

frisieren [fri'zi:rən] *vt* to do (one's hair); (fig: Abrechnung) to fiddle, to doctor ♦ *vr* to do one's hair

Frisiersalon *m* hairdressing salon

frisst ▲ [frɪst] *vb siehe* **fressen**

Frist [frɪst] (-, -en) *f* period; (Termin) deadline; **f~gerecht** *adj* within the stipulated time *od* period; **f~los** *adj*

(Entlassung) instant

Frisur [fri'zu:r] *f* hairdo, hairstyle

frivol [fri'vo:l] *adj* frivolous

froh [fro:] *adj* happy, cheerful; **ich bin ~, dass ...** I'm glad that ...

fröhlich ['frø:lɪç] *adj* merry, happy; **F~keit** *f* merriness, gaiety

fromm [frɔm] *adj* pious, good; (Wunsch) idle; **Frömmigkeit** ['frœmɪçkaɪt] *f* piety

Fronleichnam [fro:n'laɪçna:m] (-(e)s) *m* Corpus Christi

Front [frɔnt] (-, -en) *f* front; **f~al** [frɔn'ta:l] *adj* frontal

fror *etc* [fro:r] *vb siehe* **frieren**

Frosch [frɔʃ] (-(e)s, ⁴e) *m* frog; (Feuerwerk) squib; **~mann** *m* frogman; **~schenkel** *m* frog's leg

Frost [frɔst] (-(e)s, ⁴e) *m* frost; **~beule** *f* chilblain

frösteln ['frœstəln] *vi* to shiver

frostig *adj* frosty

Frostschutzmittel *nt* antifreeze

Frottier(hand)tuch [frɔ'ti:r(hant)tu:x] *nt* towel

Frucht [frʊxt] (-, ⁴e) *f* (auch fig) fruit; (Getreide) corn; **f~bar** *adj* fruitful, fertile; **~barkeit** *f* fertility; **f~ig** *adj* (Geschmack) fruity; **f~los** *adj* fruitless; **~saft** *m* fruit juice

früh [fry:] *adj, adv* early; **heute ~** this morning; **F~aufsteher** (-s, -) *m* early riser; **F~e** *f* early morning; **~er** *adj* earlier; (ehemalig) former ♦ *adv* formerly; **~er war das anders** that used to be different; **~estens** *adv* at the earliest; **F~jahr** *nt*, **F~ling** *m* spring; **~reif** *adj* precocious; **F~stück** *nt* breakfast; **~stücken** *vi* to (have) breakfast; **F~stücksbüfett** *nt* breakfast buffet; **~zeitig** *adj* early; (pej) untimely

frustrieren [frʊs'tri:rən] *vt* to frustrate

Fuchs [fʊks] (-es, ⁴e) *m* fox; **f~en** (umg) *vt* to rile, to annoy; **f~teufelswild** *adj* hopping mad

Fuge ['fu:gə] *f* joint; (MUS) fugue

fügen ['fy:gən] *vt* to place, to join ♦ *vr:* **sich ~ (in** +dat) to be obedient (to); (anpassen) to adapt oneself (to) ♦ *vr unpers* to happen

fühl- *zW:* **~bar** *adj* perceptible, noticeable; **~en** *vt, vi, vr* to feel; **F~er (-s, -)** *m* feeler

fuhr *etc* [fu:r] *vb siehe* **fahren**

führen ['fy:rən] *vt* to lead; (*Geschäft*) to run; (*Name*) to bear; (*Buch*) to keep ♦ *vi* to lead ♦ *vr* to behave

Führer ['fy:rər] **(-s, -)** *m* leader; (*Fremdenführer*) guide; **~schein** *m* driving licence

Führung ['fy:rʊŋ] *f* leadership; (*eines Unternehmens*) management; (*MIL*) command; (*Benehmen*) conduct; (*Museumsführung*) conducted tour; **~szeugnis** *nt* certificate of good conduct

Fülle ['fʏlə] *f* wealth, abundance; **f~n** *vt* to fill; (*KOCH*) to stuff ♦ *vr* to fill (up)

Füll- *zW:* **~er (-s, -)** *m* fountain pen; **~federhalter** *m* fountain pen; **~ung** *f* filling; (*Holzfüllung*) panel

fummeln ['fʊməln] (*umg*) *vi* to fumble

Fund [fʊnt] **(-(e)s, -e)** *m* find

Fundament [fʊnda'mɛnt] *nt* foundation; **fundamen'tal** *adj* fundamental

Fund- *zW:* **~büro** *nt* lost property office, lost and found (*US*); **~grube** *f* (*fig*) treasure trove

fundiert [fʊn'di:rt] *adj* sound

fünf [fʏnf] *num* five; **~hundert** *num* five hundred; **~te(r, s)** *adj* fifth; **F~tel (-s, -)** *nt* fifth; **~zehn** *num* fifteen; **~zig** *num* fifty

Funk [fʊŋk] **(-s)** *m* radio, wireless; **~e -ns, -n)** *m* (*auch fig*) spark; **f~eln** *vi* to sparkle; **~en (-s, -)** *m* (*auch fig*) spark; **f~en** *vi* (*durch Funk*) to signal, to radio; (*umg: richtig funktionieren*) to work ♦ *vt* (*Funken sprühen*) to shower with sparks; **~er (-s, -)** *m* radio operator; **~gerät** *nt* radio set; **~rufempfänger** *m* pager, paging device; **~streife** *f* police radio patrol; **~telefon** *nt* cellphone

Funktion [fʊŋktsi'o:n] *f* function; **f~ieren** [-'ni:rən] *vi* to work, to function

für [fy:r] *präp* +*akk* for; **was ~** what kind *od* sort of; **das F~ und Wider** the pros and cons *pl*; **Schritt ~ Schritt** step by step

Furche ['fʊrçə] *f* furrow

Furcht [fʊrçt] **(-)** *f* fear; **f~bar** *adj* terrible, frightful

fürchten ['fyrçtən] *vt* to be afraid of, to fear ♦ *vr:* **sich ~ (vor** +*dat*) to be afraid (of)

fürchterlich *adj* awful

furchtlos *adj* fearless

füreinander [fy:r|ar'nandər] *adv* for each other

Furnier [fʊr'ni:r] **(-s, -e)** *nt* veneer

fürs [fy:rs] = **für das**

Fürsorge ['fy:rzɔrgə] *f* care; (*Sozialfürsorge*) welfare; **~r(in) (-s, -)** *m(f)* welfare worker; **~unterstützung** *f* social security, welfare benefit (*US*); **fürsorglich** *adj* attentive, caring

Fürsprache *f* recommendation; (*um Gnade*) intercession

Fürsprecher *m* advocate

Fürst [fʏrst] **(-en, -en)** *m* prince; **~entum** *nt* principality; **~in** *f* princess; **f~lich** *adj* princely

Fuß [fu:s] **(-es, ⁻e)** *m* foot; (*von Glas, Säule etc*) base; (*von Möbel*) leg; **zu ~** on foot; **~ball** *m* football; **~ballplatz** *m* football pitch; **~ballspiel** *nt* football match; **~ballspieler** *m* footballer; **~boden** *m* floor; **~bremse** *f* (*AUT*) footbrake; **~ende** *nt* foot; **~gänger(in) (-s, -)** *m(f)* pedestrian; **~gängerzone** *f* pedestrian precinct; **~nagel** *m* toenail; **~note** *f* footnote; **~spur** *f* footprint; **~tritt** *m* kick; (*Spur*) footstep; **~weg** *m* footpath

Futter ['fʊtər] **(-s, -)** *nt* fodder, feed; (*Stoff*) lining; **~al** [-'ra:l] **(-s, -e)** *nt* case

füttern ['fʏtərn] *vt* to feed; (*Kleidung*) to line

Futur [fu'tu:r] **(-s, -e)** *nt* future

G, g

g *abk* = **Gramm**

gab *etc* [ga:p] *vb siehe* **geben**

Gabe ['ga:bə] *f* gift

Gabel ['ga:bəl] **(-, -n)** *f* fork; **~ung** *f* fork

gackern ['gakərn] *vi* to cackle

gaffen ['gafən] *vi* to gape

Gage ['ga:ʒə] *f* fee; salary

gähnen ['gɛ:nən] *vi* to yawn

Spelling Reform: ▲ *new spelling* △ *old spelling (to be phased out)*

Galerie [galə'ri:] *f* gallery

Galgen ['galgən] **(-s, -)** *m* gallows *sg*; **~frist** *f* respite; **~humor** *m* macabre humour

Galle ['galə] *f* gall; (*Organ*) gall bladder; **~nstein** *m* gallstone

gammeln ['gaməln] (*umg*) *vi* to bum around; **Gammler(in) (-s, -)** (*pej*) *m(f)* layabout, loafer (*inf*)

Gämse ▲ ['gɛmzə] *f* chamois

Gang [gaŋ] **(-(e)s, ⁻e)** *m* walk; (*Botengang*) errand; (*~art*) gait; (*Abschnitt eines Vorgangs*) operation; (*Essensgang, Ablauf*) course; (*Flur etc*) corridor; (*Durchgang*) passage; (*TECH*) gear; **in ~ bringen** to start up; (*fig*) to get off the ground; **in ~ sein** to be in operation; (*fig*) to be under way

gang *adj*: **~ und gäbe** usual, normal

gängig ['gɛŋɪç] *adj* common, current; (*Ware*) in demand, selling well

Gangschaltung *f* gears *pl*

Ganove [ga'no:və] **(-n, -n)** (*umg*) *m* crook

Gans [gans] **(-, ⁻e)** *f* goose

Gänse- ['gɛnzə] *zW*: **~blümchen** *nt* daisy; **~füßchen** (*umg*) *pl* (*Anführungszeichen*) inverted commas; **~haut** *f* goose pimples *pl*; **~marsch** *m*: **im ~marsch** in single file; **~rich (-s, -e)** *m* gander

ganz [gants] *adj* whole; (*vollständig*) complete ♦ *adv* quite; (*völlig*) completely; **~ Europa** all Europe; **sein ~es Geld** all his money; **~ und gar nicht** not at all; **es sieht ~ so aus** it really looks like it; **aufs G~e gehen** to go for the lot

gänzlich ['gɛntslɪç] *adj* complete, entire ♦ *adv* completely, entirely

Ganztagsschule *f* all-day school

gar [ga:r] *adj* cooked, done ♦ *adv* quite; **~ nicht/nichts/keiner** not/nothing/nobody at all; **~ nicht schlecht** not bad at all

Garage [ga'ra:ʒə] *f* garage

Garantie [garan'ti:] *f* guarantee; **g~ren** *vt* to guarantee; **er kommt g~rt** he's guaranteed to come

Garbe ['garbə] *f* sheaf

Garde ['gardə] *f* guard

Garderobe [gardə'ro:bə] *f* wardrobe; (*Abgabe*) cloakroom; **~nfrau** *f* cloakroom attendant

Gardine [gar'di:nə] *f* curtain

garen ['ga:rən] *vt, vi* to cook

gären ['gɛ:rən] (*unreg*) *vi* to ferment

Garn [garn] **(-(e)s, -e)** *nt* thread; yarn (*auch fig*)

Garnele [gar'ne:lə] *f* shrimp, prawn

garnieren [gar'ni:rən] *vt* to decorate; (*Speisen, fig*) to garnish

Garnison [garni'zo:n] **(-, -en)** *f* garrison

Garnitur [garni'tu:r] *f* (*Satz*) set; (*Unterwäsche*) set of (matching) underwear; **erste ~** (*fig*) top rank; **zweite ~** (*fig*) second rate

garstig ['garstɪç] *adj* nasty, horrid

Garten ['gartən] **(-s, ⁻)** *m* garden; **~arbeit** *f* gardening; **~gerät** *nt* gardening tool; **~lokal** *nt* beer garden; **~tür** *f* garden gate

Gärtner(in) ['gɛrtnər(ɪn)] **(-s, -)** *m(f)* gardener; **~ei** [-'raɪ] *f* nursery; (*Gemüsegärtnerei*) market garden (*BRIT*), truck farm (*US*)

Gärung ['gɛ:rʊŋ] *f* fermentation

Gas [ga:s] **(-es, -e)** *nt* gas; **~ geben** (*AUT*) to accelerate, to step on the gas; **~hahn** *m* gas tap; **~herd** *m* gas cooker; **~kocher** *m* gas cooker; **~leitung** *f* gas pipe; **~pedal** *nt* accelerator, gas pedal

Gasse ['gasə] *f* lane, alley

Gast [gast] **(-es, ⁻e)** *m* guest; (*in Lokal*) patron; **bei jdm zu ~ sein** to be sb's guest; **~arbeiter(in)** *m(f)* foreign worker

Gäste- ['gɛstə] *zW*: **~buch** *nt* visitors' book, guest book; **~zimmer** *nt* guest *od* spare room

Gast- *zW*: **g~freundlich** *adj* hospitable; **~geber (-s, -)** *m* host; **~geberin** *f* hostess; **~haus** *nt* hotel, inn; **~hof** *m* hotel, inn; **g~ieren** [-'ti:rən] *vi* (*THEAT*) to (appear as a) guest; **g~lich** *adj* hospitable; **~rolle** *f* guest role; **~spiel** *nt* (*THEAT*) guest performance; **~stätte** *f* restaurant; pub; **~wirt** *m* innkeeper; **~wirtschaft** *f* hotel, inn

Gaswerk *nt* gasworks *sg*

Gaszähler *m* gas meter

Gatte ['gatə] **(-n, -n)** *m* husband, spouse

Gattin *f* wife, spouse

Gattung ['gatʊŋ] f genus; kind

Gaudi ['gaʊdi] (umg: SÜDD, ÖSTERR) nt od f fun

Gaul [gaʊl] (-(e)s, Gäule) m horse; nag

Gaumen ['gaʊmən] (-s, -) m palate

Gauner ['gaʊnər] (-s, -) m rogue; ~ei [-'raɪ] f swindle

geb. abk = **geboren**

Gebäck [gə'bɛk] (-(e)s, -e) nt pastry

gebacken [gə'bakən] adj baked; (gebraten) fried

Gebälk [gə'bɛlk] (-(e)s) nt timberwork

Gebärde [gə'bɛːrdə] f gesture; g~n vr to behave

gebären [gə'bɛːrən] (unreg) vt to give birth to, to bear

Gebärmutter f uterus, womb

Gebäude [gə'bɔʏdə] (-s, -) nt building; ~komplex m (building) complex

geben ['geːbən] (unreg) vt, vi to give; (Karten) to deal ♦ vb unpers: **es gibt** there is/are; there will be ♦ vr (sich verhalten) to behave, to act; (aufhören) to abate; **jdm etw ~** to give sb sth od sth to sb; **was gibts?** what's up?; **was gibt es im Kino?** what's on at the cinema?; **sich geschlagen ~** to admit defeat; **das wird sich schon ~** that'll soon sort itself out

Gebet [gə'beːt] (-(e)s, -e) nt prayer

gebeten [gə'beːtən] vb siehe **bitten**

Gebiet [gə'biːt] (-(e)s, -e) nt area; (Hoheitsgebiet) territory; (fig) field; g~en (unreg) vt to command, to demand; g~erisch adj imperious

Gebilde [gə'bɪldə] (-s, -) nt object

gebildet adj cultured, educated

Gebirge [gə'bɪrgə] (-s, -) nt mountain chain

Gebiss [gə'bɪs] (-es, -e) nt teeth pl; (künstlich) dentures pl

gebissen vb siehe **beißen**

geblieben [gə'bliːbən] vb siehe **bleiben**

geblümt [gə'blyːmt] adj (Kleid, Stoff, Tapete) floral

geboren [gə'boːrən] adj born; (Frau) née

geborgen [gə'bɔrgən] adj secure, safe

Gebot [gə'boːt] (-(e)s, -e) nt command; (REL) commandment; (bei Auktion) bid

geboten [gə'boːtən] vb siehe **bieten**

Gebr. abk (= Gebrüder) Bros.

gebracht [gə'braxt] vb siehe **bringen**

gebraten [gə'braːtən] adj fried

Gebrauch [gə'braʊx] (-(e)s, Gebräuche) m use; (Sitte) custom; g~en vt to use

gebräuchlich [gə'brɔʏçlɪç] adj usual, customary

Gebrauchs- zW: ~anweisung f directions pl for use; g~fertig adj ready for use; ~gegenstand m commodity

gebraucht [gə'braʊxt] adj used; G~wagen m secondhand od used car

gebrechlich [gə'brɛçlɪç] adj frail

Gebrüder [gə'bryːdər] pl brothers

Gebrüll [gə'brʏl] (-(e)s) nt roaring

Gebühr [gə'byːr] (-, -en) f charge, fee; **nach ~** fittingly; **über ~** unduly; g~en vi: **jdm g~en** to be sb's due od due to sb ♦ vr to be fitting; g~end adj fitting, appropriate ♦ adv fittingly, appropriately

Gebühren- zW: ~einheit f (TEL) unit; ~erlass ▲ m remission of fees; ~ermäßigung f reduction of fees; g~frei adj free of charge; ~ordnung f scale of charges, tariff; g~pflichtig adj subject to a charge

gebunden [gə'bʊndən] vb siehe **binden**

Geburt [gə'buːrt] (-, -en) f birth

Geburtenkontrolle f birth control

Geburtenregelung f birth control

gebürtig [gə'bʏrtɪç] adj born in, native of; **~e Schweizerin** native of Switzerland

Geburts- zW: ~anzeige f birth notice; ~datum nt date of birth; ~jahr nt year of birth; ~ort m birthplace; ~tag m birthday; ~urkunde f birth certificate

Gebüsch [gə'bʏʃ] (-(e)s, -e) nt bushes pl

gedacht [gə'daxt] vb siehe **denken**

Gedächtnis [gə'dɛçtnɪs] (-ses, -se) nt memory; ~feier f commemoration

Gedanke [gə'daŋkə] (-ns, -n) m thought; **sich über etw** akk **~n machen** to think about sth

Gedanken- zW: ~austausch m exchange of ideas; g~los adj thoughtless; ~strich m dash; ~übertragung f thought transference, telepathy

Gedeck [gə'dɛk] **(-(e)s, -e)** nt cover(ing); (Speisenfolge) menu; **ein ~ auflegen** to lay a place

gedeihen [gə'daɪən] (unreg) vi to thrive, to prosper

Gedenken nt: **zum ~ an jdn** in memory of sb

gedenken [gə'dɛŋkən] (unreg) vi +gen (beabsichtigen) to intend; (sich erinnern) to remember

Gedenk- zW: **~feier** f commemoration; **~minute** f minute's silence; **~stätte** f memorial; **~tag** m remembrance day

Gedicht [gə'dɪçt] **(-(e)s, -e)** nt poem

gediegen [gə'di:gən] adj (good) quality; (Mensch) reliable, honest

Gedränge [gə'drɛŋə] **(-s)** nt crush, crowd

gedrängt adj compressed; **~ voll** packed

gedrückt [gə'drʏkt] adj (deprimiert) low, depressed

gedrungen [gə'drʊŋən] adj thickset, stocky

Geduld [gə'dʊlt] f patience; **g~en** [gə'dʊldən] vr to be patient; **g~ig** adj patient, forbearing; **~sprobe** f trial of (one's) patience

gedurft [gə'dʊrft] vb siehe **dürfen**

geehrt [gə'e:rt] adj: **Sehr ~e Frau X!** Dear Mrs X

geeignet [gə'aɪgnət] adj suitable

Gefahr [gə'fa:r] **(-, -en)** f danger; **~ laufen, etw zu tun** to run the risk of doing sth; **auf eigene ~** at one's own risk

gefährden [gə'fɛ:rdən] vt to endanger

Gefahren- zW: **~quelle** f source of danger; **~zulage** f danger money

gefährlich [gə'fɛ:rlɪç] adj dangerous

Gefährte [gə'fɛ:rtə] **(-n, -n)** m companion; (Lebenspartner) partner

Gefährtin [gə'fɛ:rtɪn] f (female) companion; (Lebenspartner) (female) partner

Gefälle [gə'fɛlə] **(-s, -)** nt gradient, incline

Gefallen¹ [gə'falən] **(-s, -)** m favour

Gefallen² [gə'falən] **(-s)** nt pleasure; **an etw dat ~ finden** to derive pleasure from sth

gefallen pp von **fallen ♦** vi: **jdm ~** to please

sb; **er/es gefällt mir** I like him/it; **das gefällt mir an ihm** that's one thing I like about him; **sich** dat **etw ~ lassen** to put up with sth

gefällig [gə'fɛlɪç] adj (hilfsbereit) obliging; (erfreulich) pleasant; **G~keit** f favour; helpfulness; **etw aus G~keit tun** to do sth out of the goodness of one's heart

gefangen [gə'faŋən] adj captured; (fig) captivated; **~ halten** to keep prisoner; **~ nehmen** to take prisoner; **G~e(r)** f(m) prisoner, captive; **G~nahme** f capture; **G~schaft** f captivity

Gefängnis [gə'fɛŋnɪs] **(-ses, -se)** nt prison; **~strafe** f prison sentence; **~wärter** m prison warder; **~zelle** f prison cell

Gefäß [gə'fɛ:s] **(-es, -e)** nt vessel; (auch ANAT) container

gefasst ▲ [gə'fast] adj composed, calm; **auf etw** akk **~ sein** to be prepared od ready for sth

Gefecht [gə'fɛçt] **(-(e)s, -e)** nt fight; (MIL) engagement

Gefieder [gə'fi:dər] **(-s, -)** nt plumage, feathers pl

gefleckt [gə'flɛkt] adj spotted, mottled

geflogen [gə'flo:gən] vb siehe **fliegen**

geflossen [gə'flɔsən] vb siehe **fließen**

Geflügel [gə'fly:gəl] **(-s)** nt poultry

Gefolgschaft [gə'fɔlkʃaft] f following

gefragt [gə'fra:kt] adj in demand

gefräßig [gə'frɛ:sɪç] adj voracious

Gefreite(r) [gə'fraɪtə(r)] m lance corporal; (NAUT) able seaman; (AVIAT) aircraftman

Gefrierbeutel m freezer bag

gefrieren [gə'fri:rən] (unreg) vi to freeze

Gefrier- zW: **~fach** nt icebox; **~fleisch** nt frozen meat; **g~getrocknet** [-gətrɔknət] freeze-dried; **~punkt** m freezing point; **~schutzmittel** nt antifreeze; **~truhe** f deep-freeze

gefroren [gə'fro:rən] vb siehe **frieren**

Gefühl [gə'fy:l] **(-(e)s, -e)** nt feeling; **etw im ~ haben** to have a feel for sth; **g~los** adj unfeeling

gefühls- zW: **~betont** adj emotional; **G~duselei** [-du:zə'laɪ] f over-sentimentality;

~mäßig adj instinctive

gefüllt [gəˈfʏlt] adj (KOCH) stuffed

gefunden [gəˈfʊndən] vb siehe **finden**

gegangen [gəˈgaŋən] vb siehe **gehen**

gegeben [gəˈgeːbən] vb siehe **geben** ♦ adj given; **zu ~er Zeit** in good time

gegebenenfalls [gəˈgeːbənənfals] adv if need be

SCHLÜSSELWORT

gegen [ˈgeːgən] präp +akk 1 against; **nichts gegen jdn haben** to have nothing against sb; **X gegen Y** (SPORT, JUR) X versus Y; **ein Mittel gegen Schnupfen** something for colds

2 (in Richtung auf) towards; **gegen Osten** to(wards) the east; **gegen Abend** towards evening; **gegen einen Baum fahren** to drive into a tree

3 (ungefähr) round about; **gegen 3 Uhr** around 3 o'clock

4 (gegenüber) towards; (ungefähr) around; **gerecht gegen alle** fair to all

5 (im Austausch für) for; **gegen bar** for cash; **gegen Quittung** against a receipt

6 (verglichen mit) compared with

Gegenangriff m counter-attack

Gegenbeweis m counter-evidence

Gegend [ˈgeːgənt] (-, -en) f area, district

Gegen- zW: **g~ei'nander** adv against one another; **~fahrbahn** f oncoming carriageway; **~frage** f counter-question; **~gewicht** nt counterbalance; **~gift** nt antidote; **~leistung** f service in return; **~maßnahme** f countermeasure; **~mittel** nt antidote, cure; **~satz** m contrast; **~sätze überbrücken** to overcome differences; **g~sätzlich** adj contrary, opposite; (widersprüchlich) contradictory; **g~seitig** adj mutual, reciprocal; **sich g~seitig helfen** to help each other; **~spieler** m opponent; **~sprechanlage** f (two-way) intercom; **~stand** m object; **~stimme** f vote against; **~stoß** m counterblow; **~stück** nt counterpart; **~teil** nt opposite; **im ~teil** on the contrary; **g~teilig** adj opposite, contrary

gegenüber [geːgənˈʔyːbər] präp +dat opposite; (zu) to(wards); (angesichts) in the face of ♦ adv opposite; **G~** (-s, -) nt person opposite; **~liegen** (unreg) vr to face each other; **~stehen** (unreg) vr to be opposed (to each other); **~stellen** vt to confront; (fig) to contrast; **G~stellung** f confrontation; (fig) contrast; **~treten** (unreg) vi +dat to face

Gegen- zW: **~verkehr** m oncoming traffic; **~vorschlag** m counterproposal; **~wart** f present; **g~wärtig** adj present ♦ adv at present; **das ist mir nicht mehr g~wärtig** that has slipped my mind; **~wert** m equivalent; **~wind** m headwind; **g~zeichnen** vt, vi to countersign

gegessen [gəˈgesən] vb siehe **essen**

Gegner [ˈgeːgnər] (-s, -) m opponent; **g~isch** adj opposing

gegr. abk (= gegründet) est.

gegrillt [gəˈgrɪlt] adj grilled

Gehackte(s) [gəˈhaktə(s)] nt mince(d meat)

Gehalt[1] [gəˈhalt] (-(e)s, -e) m content

Gehalt[2] [gəˈhalt] (-(e)s, ꞋꞋer) nt salary

Gehalts- zW: **~empfänger** m salary earner; **~erhöhung** f salary increase; **~zulage** f salary increment

gehaltvoll [gəˈhaltfɔl] adj (nahrhaft) nutritious

gehässig [gəˈhesɪç] adj spiteful, nasty

Gehäuse [gəˈhɔyzə] (-s, -) nt case; casing; (von Apfel etc) core

Gehege [gəˈheːgə] (-s, -) nt reserve; (im Zoo) enclosure

geheim [gəˈhaɪm] adj secret; **~ halten** to keep secret; **G~dienst** m secret service, intelligence service; **G~nis** (-ses, -se) nt secret; mystery; **~nisvoll** adj mysterious; **G~polizei** f secret police

gehemmt [gəˈhemt] adj inhibited, self-conscious

gehen [ˈgeːən] (unreg) vt, vi to go; (zu Fuß ~) to walk ♦ vb unpers: **wie geht es (dir)?** how are you od things?; **~ nach** (Fenster) to face; **mir/ihm geht es gut** I'm/he's (doing) fine; **geht das?** is that possible?; **gehts**

noch? can you manage?; **es geht** not too bad, O.K.; **das geht nicht** that's not on; **es geht um etw** it has to do with sth, it's about sth; **sich ~ lassen** (*unbeherrscht sein*) to lose control (of o.s.); **jdn ~ lassen** to let/leave sb alone; **lass mich ~!** leave me alone!

geheuer [gə'hɔʏər] *adj*: **nicht ~** eerie; (*fragwürdig*) dubious

Gehilfe [gə'hɪlfə] (**-n, -n**) *m* assistant; **Gehilfin** *f* assistant

Gehirn [gə'hɪrn] (**-(e)s, -e**) *nt* brain; **~erschütterung** *f* concussion; **~hautentzündung** *f* meningitis

gehoben [gə'ho:bən] *pp von* **heben** ♦ *adj* (*Position*) elevated; high

geholfen [gə'hɔlfən] *vb siehe* **helfen**

Gehör [gə'hø:r] (**-(e)s**) *nt* hearing; **musikalisches ~** ear; **~ finden** to gain a hearing; **jdm ~ schenken** to give sb a hearing

gehorchen [gə'hɔrçən] *vi +dat* to obey

gehören [gə'hø:rən] *vi* to belong ♦ *vr unpers* to be right *od* proper

gehörig *adj* proper; **~ zu** *od +dat* belonging to; part of

gehörlos *adj* deaf

gehorsam [gə'ho:rza:m] *adj* obedient; **G~** (**-s**) *m* obedience

Geh- ['ge:-] *zW*: **~steig** *m* pavement, sidewalk (*US*); **~weg** *m* pavement, sidewalk (*US*)

Geier ['gaɪər] (**-s, -**) *m* vulture

Geige ['gaɪgə] *f* violin; **~r** (**-s, -**) *m* violinist

geil [gaɪl] *adj* randy (*BRIT*), horny (*US*)

Geisel ['gaɪzəl] (**-, -n**) *f* hostage

Geist [gaɪst] (**-(e)s, -er**) *m* spirit; (*Gespenst*) ghost; (*Verstand*) mind

geisterhaft *adj* ghostly

Geistes- *zW*: **g~abwesend** *adj* absent-minded; **~blitz** *m* brainwave; **~gegenwart** *f* presence of mind; **g~krank** *adj* mentally ill; **~kranke(r)** *f(m)* mentally ill person; **~krankheit** *f* mental illness; **~wissenschaften** *pl* the arts; **~zustand** *m* state of mind

geist- *zW*: **~ig** *adj* intellectual; mental;

(*Getränke*) alcoholic; **~ig behindert** mentally handicapped; **~lich** *adj* spiritual, religious; clerical; **G~liche(r)** *m* clergyman; **G~lichkeit** *f* clergy; **~los** *adj* uninspired, dull; **~reich** *adj* clever; witty; **~voll** *adj* intellectual; (*weise*) wise

Geiz [gaɪts] (**-es**) *m* miserliness, meanness; **g~en** *vi* to be miserly; **~hals** *m* miser; **g~ig** *adj* miserly, mean; **~kragen** *m* miser

gekannt [gə'kant] *vb siehe* **kennen**

gekonnt [gə'kɔnt] *adj* skilful ♦ *vb siehe* **können**

gekünstelt [ge'kʏnstəlt] *adj* artificial, affected

Gel [ge:l] (**-s, -e**) *nt* gel

Gelächter [gə'lɛçtər] (**-s, -**) *nt* laughter

geladen [ge'la:dən] *adj* loaded; (*ELEK*) live; (*fig*) furious

gelähmt [gə'lɛ:mt] *adj* paralysed

Gelände [gə'lɛndə] (**-s, -**) *nt* land, terrain; (*von Fabrik, Sportgelände*) grounds *pl*; (*Bau~*) site; **~lauf** *m* cross-country race

Geländer [gə'lɛndər] (**-s, -**) *nt* railing; (*Treppengeländer*) banister(s)

gelangen [gə'laŋən] *vi*: **~ (an +akk od zu)** to reach; (*erwerben*) to attain; **in jds Besitz** *akk* **~** to come into sb's possession

gelangweilt [gə'laŋvaɪlt] *adj* bored

gelassen [gə'lasən] *adj* calm, composed; **G~heit** *f* calmness, composure

Gelatine [ʒela'ti:nə] *f* gelatine

geläufig [gə'lɔʏfɪç] *adj* (*üblich*) common; **das ist mir nicht ~** I'm not familiar with that

gelaunt [gə'laʊnt] *adj*: **schlecht/gut ~** in a bad/good mood; **wie ist er ~?** what sort of mood is he in?

gelb [gɛlp] *adj* yellow; (*Ampellicht*) amber; **~lich** *adj* yellowish; **G~sucht** *f* jaundice

Geld [gɛlt] (**-(e)s, -er**) *nt* money; **etw zu ~ machen** to sell sth off; **~anlage** *f* investment; **~automat** *m* cash dispenser; **~beutel** *m* purse; **~börse** *f* purse; **~geber** (**-s, -**) *m* financial backer; **g~gierig** *adj* avaricious; **~schein** *m* banknote; **~schrank** *m* safe, strongbox; **~strafe** *f* fine; **~stück** *nt* coin; **~wechsel**

m exchange (of money)

Gelee [ʒe'le:] **(-s, -s)** *nt od m* jelly

gelegen [gə'le:gən] *adj* situated; (*passend*) convenient, opportune ♦ *vb siehe* **liegen**; **etw kommt jdm ~** sth is convenient for sb

Gelegenheit [gə'le:gənhait] *f* opportunity; (*Anlaß*) occasion; **bei jeder ~** at every opportunity; **~arbeit** *f* casual work; **~skauf** *m* bargain

gelegentlich [gə'le:gəntlıç] *adj* occasional ♦ *adv* occasionally; (*bei Gelegenheit*) some time (or other) ♦ *präp +gen* on the occasion of

gelehrt [gə'le:rt] *adj* learned; **G~e(r)** *f(m)* scholar; **G~heit** *f* scholarliness

Geleise [gə'laizə] **(-s, -)** *nt* = **Gleis**

Geleit [gə'lait] **(-(e)s, -e)** *nt* escort; **g~en** *vt* to escort

Gelenk [gə'lɛŋk] **(-(e)s, -e)** *nt* joint; **g~ig** *adj* supple

gelernt [gə'lɛrnt] *adj* skilled

Geliebte(r) [gə'li:ptə(r)] *f(m)* sweetheart, beloved

geliehen [gə'li:ən] *vb siehe* **leihen**

gelind(e) [gə'lɪnd(ə)] *adj* mild, light; (*fig: Wut*) fierce; **~ gesagt** to put it mildly

gelingen [gə'lɪŋən] (*unreg*) *vi* to succeed; **es ist mir gelungen, etw zu tun** I succeeded in doing sth

geloben [gə'lo:bən] *vt, vi* to vow, to swear

gelten ['gɛltən] (*unreg*) *vt* (*wert sein*) to be worth ♦ *vi* (*gültig sein*) to be valid; (*erlaubt sein*) to be allowed ♦ *vb unpers*: **es gilt, etw zu tun** it is necessary to do sth; **jdm viel/ wenig ~** to mean a lot/not to mean much to sb; **was gilt die Wette?** what do you bet?; **etw ~ lassen** to accept sth; **als** *od* **für etw ~** to be considered to be sth; **jdm** *od* **für jdn ~** (*betreffen*) to apply to *od* for sb; **~d** *adj* prevailing; **etw ~d machen** to assert sth; **sich ~d machen** to make itself/ o.s. felt

Geltung ['gɛltʊŋ] *f*: **~ haben** to have validity; **sich/etw** *dat* **~ verschaffen** to establish one's position/the position of sth; **etw zur ~ bringen** to show sth to its best advantage; **zur ~ kommen** to be seen/

heard *etc* to its best advantage

Geltungsbedürfnis *nt* desire for admiration

Gelübde [gə'lʏpdə] **(-s, -)** *nt* vow

gelungen [gə'lʊŋən] *adj* successful

gemächlich [gə'mɛːçlıç] *adj* leisurely

Gemahl [gə'ma:l] **(-(e)s, -e)** *m* husband; **~in** *f* wife

Gemälde [gə'mɛ:ldə] **(-s, -)** *nt* picture, painting

gemäß [gə'mɛ:s] *präp +dat* in accordance with ♦ *adj (+dat)* appropriate (to)

gemäßigt *adj* moderate; (*Klima*) temperate

gemein [gə'main] *adj* common; (*niederträchtig*) mean; **etw ~ haben (mit)** to have sth in common (with)

Gemeinde [gə'maində] *f* district, community; (*Pfarrgemeinde*) parish; (*Kirchengemeinde*) congregation; **~steuer** *f* local rates *pl*; **~verwaltung** *f* local administration; **~wahl** *f* local election

Gemein- *zW*: **g~gefährlich** *adj* dangerous to the public; **~heit** *f* commonness; mean thing to do/to say; **g~nützig** *adj* charitable; **g~nütziger Verein** non-profit-making organization; **g~sam** *adj* joint, common (*AUCH MATH*) ♦ *adv* together, jointly; **g~same Sache mit jdm machen** to be in cahoots with sb; **etw g~sam haben** to have sth in common; **~samkeit** *f* community, having in common; **~schaft** *f* community; **in ~schaft mit** jointly *od* together with; **g~schaftlich** *adj* = **gemeinsam**; **~schaftsarbeit** *f* teamwork; team effort; **~sinn** *m* public spirit

Gemenge [gə'mɛŋə] **(-s, -)** *nt* mixture; (*Handgemenge*) scuffle

gemessen [gə'mɛsən] *adj* measured

Gemetzel [gə'mɛtsəl] **(-s, -)** *nt* slaughter, carnage, butchery

Gemisch [gə'mıʃ] **(-es, -e)** *nt* mixture; **g~t** *adj* mixed

gemocht [gə'mɔxt] *vb siehe* **mögen**

Gemse △ ['gɛmzə] *f siehe* **Gämse**

Gemurmel [gə'mʊrməl] **(-s)** *nt* murmur(ing)

Gemüse [gə'my:zə] **(-s, -)** *nt* vegetables *pl*; **~garten** *m* vegetable garden; **~händler** *m*

Spelling Reform: ▲ *new spelling* △ *old spelling (to be phased out)*

greengrocer

gemusst ▲ [gə'mʊst] *vb siehe* **müssen**

gemustert [gə'mʊstərt] *adj* patterned

Gemüt [gə'my:t] **(-(e)s, -er)** *nt* disposition, nature; person; **sich** *dat* **etw zu ~e führen** (*umg*) to indulge in sth; **die ~er erregen** to arouse strong feelings; **g~lich** *adj* comfortable, cosy; (*Person*) good-natured; **~lichkeit** *f* comfortableness, cosiness; amiability

Gemüts- *zW:* **~mensch** *m* sentimental person; **~ruhe** *f* composure; **~zustand** *m* state of mind

Gen [ge:n] **(-s, -e)** *nt* gene

genannt [gə'nant] *vb siehe* **nennen**

genau [gə'naʊ] *adj* exact, precise ♦ *adv* exactly, precisely; **etw ~ nehmen** to take sth seriously; **~ genommen** strictly speaking; **G~igkeit** *f* exactness, accuracy; **~so** *adv* just the same; **~so gut** just as good

genehm [gə'ne:m] *adj* agreeable, acceptable; **~igen** *vt* to approve, to authorize; **sich** *dat* **etw ~igen** to indulge in sth; **G~igung** *f* approval, authorization; (*Schriftstück*) permit

General [gene'ra:l] **(-s, -e** *od* **¨e)** *m* general; **~direktor** *m* director general; **~konsulat** *nt* consulate general; **~probe** *f* dress rehearsal; **~streik** *m* general strike; **g~überholen** *vt* to overhaul thoroughly; **~versammlung** *f* general meeting

Generation [generatsi'o:n] *f* generation

Generator [gene'ra:tɔr] *m* generator, dynamo

generell [genə'rel] *adj* general

genesen [ge'ne:zən] (*unreg*) *vi* to convalesce, to recover; **Genesung** *f* recovery, convalescence

genetisch [ge'ne:tɪʃ] *adj* genetic

Genf ['genf] *nt* Geneva; **der ~er See** Lake Geneva

genial [geni'a:l] *adj* brilliant

Genick [gə'nɪk] **(-(e)s, -e)** *nt* (back of the) neck

Genie [ʒe'ni:] **(-s, -s)** *nt* genius

genieren [ʒe'ni:rən] *vt* to bother ♦ *vr* to feel

awkward *od* self-conscious

genieß- *zW:* **~bar** *adj* edible; drinkable; **~en** [gə'ni:sən] (*unreg*) *vt* to enjoy; to eat; to drink; **G~er** **(-s, -)** *m* epicure; pleasure lover; **~erisch** *adj* appreciative ♦ *adv* with relish

genmanipuliert ['ge:nmanipuli:rt] *adj* genetically modified

genommen [gə'nɔmən] *vb siehe* **nehmen**

Genosse [gə'nɔsə] **(-n, -n)** *m* (*bes POL*) comrade, companion; **~nschaft** *f* cooperative (association)

Genossin *f* (*bes POL*) comrade, companion

Gentechnik ['ge:ntɛçnɪk] *f* genetic engineering

genug [gə'nu:k] *adv* enough

Genüge [gə'ny:gə] *f:* **jdm/etw ~ tun** *od* **leisten** to satisfy sb/sth; **g~n** *vi* (+*dat*) to be enough (for); **g~nd** *adj* sufficient

genügsam [gə'ny:kza:m] *adj* modest, easily satisfied; **G~keit** *f* moderation

Genugtuung [gə'nu:ktu:ʊŋ] *f* satisfaction

Genuss ▲ [gə'nʊs] **(-es, ¨e)** *m* pleasure; (*Zusichnehmen*) consumption; **in den ~ von etw kommen** to receive the benefit of sth

genüsslich ▲ [gə'nʏslɪç] *adv* with relish

Genussmittel ▲ *pl* (semi-)luxury items

geöffnet [gə'œfnət] *adj* open

Geograf ▲ [geo'gra:f] **(-en, -en)** *m* geographer; **Geografie** ▲ *f* geography; **g~isch** *adj* geographical

Geologe [geo'lo:gə] **(-n, -n)** *m* geologist; **Geologie** *f* geology

Geometrie [geome'tri:] *f* geometry

Gepäck [gə'pɛk] **(-(e)s)** *nt* luggage, baggage; **~abfertigung** *f* luggage office; **~annahme** *f* luggage office; **~aufbewahrung** *f* left-luggage office (*BRIT*), baggage check (*US*); **~aufgabe** *f* luggage office; **~ausgabe** *f* luggage office; (*AVIAT*) luggage reclaim; **~netz** *nt* luggage rack; **~träger** *m* porter; (*Fahrrad*) carrier; **~versicherung** *f* luggage insurance; **~wagen** *m* luggage van (*BRIT*), baggage car (*US*)

gepflegt [gə'pfle:kt] *adj* well-groomed; (*Park etc*) well looked after

Gerade [gə'ra:də] f straight line; **g~'aus** adv straight ahead; **g~he'raus** adv straight out, bluntly; **g~stehen** (unreg) vi: **für jdn/etw g~stehen** to be answerable for sb('s actions)/sth; **g~wegs** adv direct, straight; **g~zu** adv (beinahe) virtually, almost

---

SCHLÜSSELWORT

---

gerade [gə'ra:də] adj straight; (aufrecht) upright; **eine gerade Zahl** an even number

♦ adv **1** (genau) just, exactly; (speziell) especially; **gerade deshalb** that's just od exactly why; **das ist es ja gerade!** that's just it!; **gerade du** you especially; **warum gerade ich?** why me (of all people)?; **jetzt gerade nicht!** not now!; **gerade neben** right next to

2 (eben, soeben) just; **er wollte gerade aufstehen** he was just about to get up; **gerade erst** only just; **gerade noch** (only) just

---

gerannt [gə'rant] vb siehe **rennen**
Gerät [gə'rɛ:t] (-(e)s, -e) nt device; (Werkzeug) tool; (SPORT) apparatus; (Zubehör) equipment no pl
geraten [gə'ra:tən] (unreg) vi (gedeihen) to thrive; (gelingen): **(jdm) ~** to turn out well (for sb); **gut/schlecht ~** to turn out well/badly; **an jdn ~** to come across sb; **in etw akk ~** to get into sth; **nach jdm ~** to take after sb
Geratewohl [gəra:tə'vo:l] nt: **aufs ~** on the off chance; (bei Wahl) at random
geräuchert [gə'rɔʏçərt] adj smoked
geräumig [gə'rɔʏmɪç] adj roomy
Geräusch [gə'rɔʏʃ] (-(e)s, -e) nt sound, noise; **g~los** adj silent
gerben ['gɛrbən] vt to tan
gerecht [gə'rɛçt] adj just, fair; **jdm/etw ~ werden** to do justice to sb/sth; **G~igkeit** f justice, fairness
Gerede [gə're:də] (-s) nt talk, gossip
geregelt [gə're:gəlt] adj (Arbeit) steady, regular; (Mahlzeiten) regular, set

gereizt [gə'raɪtst] adj irritable; **G~heit** f irritation
Gericht [gə'rɪçt] (-(e)s, -e) nt court; (Essen) dish; **mit jdm ins ~ gehen** (fig) to judge sb harshly; **das Jüngste ~** the Last Judgement; **~lich** adj judicial, legal ♦ adv judicially, legally
Gerichts- zW: **~barkeit** f jurisdiction; **~hof** m court (of law); **~kosten** pl (legal) costs; **~medizin** f forensic medicine; **~saal** m courtroom; **~verfahren** nt legal proceedings pl; **~verhandlung** f trial; **~vollzieher** m bailiff
gerieben [gə'ri:bən] adj grated; (umg: schlau) smart, wily ♦ vb siehe **reiben**
gering [gə'rɪŋ] adj slight, small; (niedrig) low; (Zeit) short; **~fügig** adj slight, trivial; **~schätzig** adj disparaging
geringste(r, s) adj slightest, least; **~nfalls** adv at the very least
gerinnen [gə'rɪnən] (unreg) vi to congeal; (Blut) to clot; (Milch) to curdle
Gerippe [gə'rɪpə] (-s, -) nt skeleton
gerissen [gə'rɪsən] adj wily, smart
geritten [gə'rɪtən] vb siehe **reiten**
gern(e) ['gɛrn(ə)] adv willingly, gladly; **~ haben, ~ mögen** to like; **etwas ~ tun** to like doing something; **ich möchte ~ ...** I'd like ...; **ja, ~** yes, please; yes, I'd like to; **~ geschehen** it's a pleasure
gerochen [gə'rɔxən] vb siehe **riechen**
Geröll [gə'rœl] (-(e)s, -e) nt scree
Gerste ['gɛrstə] f barley; **~nkorn** nt (im Auge) stye
Geruch [gə'rʊx] (-(e)s, ¨e) m smell, odour; **g~los** adj odourless
Gerücht [gə'rʏçt] (-(e)s, -e) nt rumour
geruhsam [gə'ru:za:m] adj (Leben) peaceful; (Nacht, Zeit) peaceful, restful; (langsam: Arbeitsweise, Spaziergang) leisurely
Gerümpel [gə'rʏmpəl] (-s) nt junk
Gerüst [gə'rʏst] (-(e)s, -e) nt (Baugerüst) scaffold(ing); frame
gesalzen [gə'zaltsən] pp von **salzen** ♦ adj (umg: Preis, Rechnung) steep
gesamt [gə'zamt] adj whole, entire; (Kosten) total; (Werke) complete; **im G~en** all in all;

Spelling Reform: ▲ *new spelling* △ *old spelling (to be phased out)*

~**deutsch** *adj* all-German; **G~eindruck** *m* general impression; **G~heit** *f* totality, whole; **G~schule** *f* ≈ comprehensive school

---

Gesamtschule

i The **Gesamtschule** *is a comprehensive school for pupils of different abilities. Traditionally pupils go to either a* **Gymnasium,** **Realschule** *or* **Hauptschule,** *depending on ability. The* **Gesamtschule** *seeks to avoid the elitism of many* **Gymnasien.** *However, these schools are still very controversial, with many parents still preferring the traditional education system.*

---

gesandt [gə'zant] *vb siehe* **senden**
Gesandte(r) [gə'zantə(r)] *m* envoy
Gesandtschaft [gə'zantʃaft] *f* legation
Gesang [gə'zaŋ] (-(e)s, "e) *m* song; (*Singen*) singing; ~**buch** *nt* (*REL*) hymn book
Gesäß [gə'zɛːs] (-es, -e) *nt* seat, bottom
Geschäft [gə'ʃɛft] (-(e)s, -e) *nt* business; (*Laden*) shop; (~*sabschluß*) deal; **g~ig** *adj* active, busy; (*pej*) officious; **g~lich** *adj* commercial ♦ *adv* on business
Geschäfts- *zW:* ~**bedingungen** *pl* terms *pl* of business; ~**bericht** *m* financial report; ~**frau** *f* businesswoman; ~**führer** *m* manager; (*Klub*) secretary; ~**geheimnis** *nt* trade secret; ~**jahr** *nt* financial year; ~**lage** *f* business conditions *pl*; ~**mann** *m* businessman; **g~mäßig** *adj* businesslike; ~**partner** *m* business partner; ~**reise** *f* business trip; ~**schluss** ▲ *m* closing time; ~**stelle** *f* office, place of business; **g~tüchtig** *adj* business-minded; ~**viertel** *nt* business quarter; shopping centre; ~**wagen** *m* company car; ~**zeit** *f* business hours *pl*
geschehen [gə'ʃeːən] (*unreg*) *vi* to happen; **es war um ihn ~** that was the end of him
gescheit [gə'ʃaɪt] *adj* clever
Geschenk [gə'ʃɛŋk] (-(e)s, -e) *nt* present, gift
Geschichte [gə'ʃɪçtə] *f* story; (*Sache*) affair;

(*Historie*) history
geschichtlich *adj* historical
Geschick [gə'ʃɪk] (-(e)s, -e) *nt* aptitude; (*Schicksal*) fate; ~**lichkeit** *f* skill, dexterity; **g~t** *adj* skilful
geschieden [gə'ʃiːdən] *adj* divorced
geschienen [gə'ʃiːnən] *vb siehe* **scheinen**
Geschirr [gə'ʃɪr] (-(e)s, -e) *nt* crockery; pots and pans *pl*; (*Pferdegeschirr*) harness; ~**spülmaschine** *f* dishwasher; ~**spülmittel** *nt* washing-up liquid; ~**tuch** *nt* dish cloth
Geschlecht [gə'ʃlɛçt] (-(e)s, -er) *nt* sex; (*GRAM*) gender; (*Gattung*) race; family; **g~lich** *adj* sexual
Geschlechts- *zW:* ~**krankheit** *f* venereal disease; ~**teil** *nt* genitals *pl*; ~**verkehr** *m* sexual intercourse
geschlossen [gə'ʃlɔsən] *adj* shut ♦ *vb siehe* **schließen**
Geschmack [gə'ʃmak] (-(e)s, "e) *m* taste; **nach jds ~** to sb's taste; ~ **finden an etw** *dat* to (come to) like sth; **g~los** *adj* tasteless; (*fig*) in bad taste; ~**ssinn** *m* sense of taste; **g~voll** *adj* tasteful
geschmeidig [gə'ʃmaɪdɪç] *adj* supple; (*formbar*) malleable
Geschnetzelte(s) [gə'ʃnɛtsəltə(s)] *nt* (*KOCH*) strips of meat stewed to produce a thick sauce
geschnitten [gə'ʃnɪtən] *vb siehe* **schneiden**
Geschöpf [gə'ʃœpf] (-(e)s, -e) *nt* creature
Geschoss ▲ [gə'ʃɔs] (-es, -e) *nt* (*MIL*) projectile, missile; (*Stockwerk*) floor
geschossen [gə'ʃɔsən] *vb siehe* **schießen**
geschraubt [gə'ʃraʊpt] *adj* stilted, artificial
Geschrei [gə'ʃraɪ] (-s) *nt* cries *pl*, shouting; (*fig: Aufheben*) noise, fuss
geschrieben [gə'ʃriːbən] *vb siehe* **schreiben**
Geschütz [gə'ʃʏts] (-es, -e) *nt* gun, cannon; **ein schweres ~ auffahren** (*fig*) to bring out the big guns
geschützt *adj* protected
Geschw. *abk siehe* **Geschwister**
Geschwätz [gə'ʃvɛts] (-es) *nt* chatter, gossip; **g~ig** *adj* talkative
geschweige [gə'ʃvaɪgə] *adv:* ~ **(denn)** let

Rechtschreibreform: ▲ *neue Schreibung* △ *alte Schreibung (auslaufend)*

alone, not to mention

geschwind [gə'ʃvɪnt] *adj* quick, swift; **G~igkeit** [-dɪçkaɪt] *f* speed, velocity; **G~igkeitsbeschränkung** *f* speed limit; **G~igkeitsüberschreitung** *f* exceeding the speed limit

Geschwister [gə'ʃvɪstər] *pl* brothers and sisters

geschwommen [gə'ʃvɔmən] *vb siehe* **schwimmen**

Geschworene(r) [gə'ʃvoːrənə(r)] *f(m)* juror; **~n** *pl* jury

Geschwulst [gə'ʃvʊlst] (-, ⁺e) *f* swelling; growth, tumour

geschwungen [gə'ʃvʊŋən] *pp von* **schwingen** ♦ *adj* curved, arched

Geschwür [gə'ʃvyːr] (-(e)s, -e) *nt* ulcer

Gesell- [gə'zɛl] *zW:* ~**e** (-n, -n) *m* fellow; (*Handwerkgeselle*) journeyman; **g~ig** *adj* sociable; ~**igkeit** *f* sociability; ~**schaft** *f* society; (*Begleitung, COMM*) company; (*Abendgesellschaft etc*) party; **g~schaftlich** *adj* social; ~**schaftsordnung** *f* social structure; ~**schaftsschicht** *f* social stratum

gesessen [gə'zɛsən] *vb siehe* **sitzen**

Gesetz [gə'zɛts] (-es, -e) *nt* law; ~**buch** *nt* statute book; ~**entwurf** *m* (draft) bill; ~**gebung** *f* legislation; **g~lich** *adj* legal, lawful; **g~licher Feiertag** statutory holiday; **g~los** *adj* lawless; **g~mäßig** *adj* lawful; **g~t** *adj* (*Mensch*) sedate; **g~widrig** *adj* illegal, unlawful

Gesicht [gə'zɪçt] (-(e)s, -er) *nt* face; **das zweite ~** second sight; **das ist mir nie zu ~ gekommen** I've never laid eyes on that

Gesichts- *zW:* ~**ausdruck** *m* (facial) expression; ~**creme** *f* face cream; ~**farbe** *f* complexion; ~**punkt** *m* point of view; ~**wasser** *nt* face lotion; ~**züge** *pl* features

Gesindel [gə'zɪndəl] (-s) *nt* rabble

gesinnt [gə'zɪnt] *adj* disposed, minded

Gesinnung [gə'zɪnʊŋ] *f* disposition; (*Ansicht*) views *pl*

gesittet [gə'zɪtət] *adj* well-mannered

Gespann [gə'ʃpan] (-(e)s, -e) *nt* team; (*umg*) couple

gespannt *adj* tense, strained; (*begierig*) eager; **ich bin ~, ob** I wonder if *od* whether; **auf etw/jdn ~ sein** to look forward to sth/meeting sb

Gespenst [gə'ʃpɛnst] (-(e)s, -er) *nt* ghost, spectre

gesperrt [gə'ʃpɛrt] *adj* closed off

Gespött [gə'ʃpœt] (-(e)s) *nt* mockery; **zum ~ werden** to become a laughing stock

Gespräch [gə'ʃprɛːç] (-(e)s, -e) *nt* conversation; discussion(s); (*Anruf*) call; **g~ig** *adj* talkative

gesprochen [gə'ʃprɔxən] *vb siehe* **sprechen**

gesprungen [gə'ʃprʊŋən] *vb siehe* **springen**

Gespür [gə'ʃpyːr] (-s) *nt* feeling

Gestalt [gə'ʃtalt] (-, -en) *f* form, shape; (*Person*) figure; **in ~ von** in the form of; **~ annehmen** to take shape; **g~en** *vt* (*formen*) to shape, to form; (*organisieren*) to arrange, to organize ♦ *vr*: **sich g~en (zu)** to turn out (to be); ~**ung** *f* formation; organization

gestanden [gə'ʃtandən] *vb siehe* **stehen**

Geständnis [gə'ʃtɛntnɪs] (-ses, -se) *nt* confession

Gestank [gə'ʃtaŋk] (-(e)s) *m* stench

gestatten [gə'ʃtatən] *vt* to permit, to allow; **~ Sie?** may I?; **sich** *dat* **~, etw zu tun** to take the liberty of doing sth

Geste ['gɛstə] *f* gesture

gestehen [gə'ʃteːən] (*unreg*) *vt* to confess

Gestein [gə'ʃtaɪn] (-(e)s, -e) *nt* rock

Gestell [gə'ʃtɛl] (-(e)s, -e) *nt* frame; (*Regal*) rack, stand

gestern ['gɛstərn] *adv* yesterday; **~ Abend/ Morgen** yesterday evening/morning

Gestirn [gə'ʃtɪrn] (-(e)s, -e) *nt* star; (*Sternbild*) constellation

gestohlen [gə'ʃtoːlən] *vb siehe* **stehlen**

gestorben [gə'ʃtɔrbən] *vb siehe* **sterben**

gestört [gə'ʃtøːrt] *adj* disturbed

gestreift [gə'ʃtraɪft] *adj* striped

gestrichen [gə'ʃtrɪçən] *adj* cancelled

gestrig ['gɛstrɪç] *adj* yesterday's

Gestrüpp [gə'ʃtrʏp] (-(e)s, -e) *nt* undergrowth

Gestüt [gə'ʃtyːt] (-(e)s, -e) *nt* stud farm

Gesuch [gə'zuːx] (-(e)s, -e) *nt* petition;

Spelling Reform: ▲ *new spelling* △ *old spelling (to be phased out)*

(Antrag) application; **g~t** *adj (COMM)* in demand; wanted; *(fig)* contrived

gesund [gə'zʊnt] *adj* healthy; **wieder ~ werden** to get better; **G~heit** *f* health(iness); **G~heit!** bless you!; **~heitlich** *adj* health *attrib*, physical ♦ *adv*: **wie geht es Ihnen ~heitlich?** how's your health?; **~heitsschädlich** *adj* unhealthy; **G~heitswesen** *nt* health service; **G~heitszustand** *m* state of health

gesungen [gə'zʊŋən] *vb siehe* **singen**

getan [gə'taːn] *vb siehe* **tun**

Getöse [gə'tøːzə] **(-s)** *nt* din, racket

Getränk [gə'trɛŋk] **(-(e)s, -e)** *nt* drink; **~ekarte** *f* wine list

getrauen [gə'trauən] *vr* to dare, to venture

Getreide [gə'traidə] **(-s, -)** *nt* cereals *pl*, grain; **~speicher** *m* granary

getrennt [gə'trɛnt] *adj* separate

Getriebe [gə'triːbə] **(-s, -)** *nt (Leute)* bustle; *(AUT)* gearbox

getrieben *vb siehe* **treiben**

getroffen [gə'trɔfən] *vb siehe* **treffen**

getrost [gə'troːst] *adv* without any bother

getrunken [gə'trʊŋkən] *vb siehe* **trinken**

Getue [gə'tuːə] **(-s)** *nt* fuss

geübt [gə'yːpt] *adj* experienced

Gewächs [gə'vɛks] **(-es, -e)** *nt* growth; *(Pflanze)* plant

gewachsen [gə'vaksən] *adj*: **jdm/etw ~ sein** to be sb's equal/equal to sth

Gewächshaus *nt* greenhouse

gewagt [gə'vaːkt] *adj* daring, risky

gewählt [gə'vɛːlt] *adj (Sprache)* refined, elegant

Gewähr [gə'vɛːr] **(-)** *f* guarantee; **keine ~ übernehmen für** to accept no responsibility for; **g~en** *vt* to grant; *(geben)* to provide; **g~leisten** *vt* to guarantee

Gewahrsam [gə'vaːrzaːm] **(-s, -e)** *m* safekeeping; *(Polizeigewahrsam)* custody

Gewalt [gə'valt] **(-, -en)** *f* power; *(große Kraft)* force; *(~taten)* violence; **mit aller ~** with all one's might; **~anwendung** *f* use of force; **g~ig** *adj* tremendous, huge; **~marsch** *m* forced march; **g~sam** *adj* forcible; **g~tätig** *adj* violent

Gewand [gə'vant] **(-(e)s, ⁻er)** *nt* gown, robe

gewandt [gə'vant] *adj* deft, skilful; *(erfahren)* experienced; **G~heit** *f* dexterity, skill

gewann *etc* [gə'vaːn] *vb siehe* **gewinnen**

Gewässer [gə'vɛsər] **(-s, -)** *nt* waters *pl*

Gewebe [gə'veːbə] **(-s, -)** *nt (Stoff)* fabric; *(BIOL)* tissue

Gewehr [gə'veːr] **(-(e)s, -e)** *nt* gun; rifle; **~lauf** *m* rifle barrel

Geweih [gə'vai] **(-(e)s, -e)** *nt* antlers *pl*

Gewerb- [gə'vɛrb] *zW*: **~e (-s, -)** *nt* trade, occupation; **Handel und ~e** trade and industry; **~eschule** *f* technical school; **~ezweig** *m* line of trade

Gewerkschaft [gə'vɛrkʃaft] *f* trade union; **~ler (-s, -)** *m* trade unionist; **~sbund** *m* trade unions federation

gewesen [gə'veːzən] *pp von* **sein**

Gewicht [gə'vɪçt] **(-(e)s, -e)** *nt* weight; *(fig)* importance

gewieft [gə'viːft] *adj* shrewd, cunning

gewillt [gə'vɪlt] *adj* willing, prepared

Gewimmel [gə'vɪməl] **(-s)** *nt* swarm

Gewinde [gə'vɪndə] **(-s, -)** *nt (Kranz)* wreath; *(von Schraube)* thread

Gewinn [gə'vɪn] **(-(e)s, -e)** *m* profit; *(bei Spiel)* winnings *pl*; **~ bringend** profitable; **etw mit ~ verkaufen** to sell sth at a profit; **~- und Verlustrechnung** *(COMM)* profit and loss account; **~beteiligung** *f* profit-sharing; **g~en** *(unreg) vt* to win; *(erwerben)* to gain; *(Kohle, Öl)* to extract ♦ *vi* to win; *(profitieren)* to gain; **an etw** *dat* **g~en** to gain (in) sth; **g~end** *adj (Lächeln, Aussehen)* winning, charming; **~er(in) (-s, -)** *m(f)* winner; **~spanne** *f* profit margin; **~ung** *f* winning; gaining; *(von Kohle etc)* extraction

Gewirr [gə'vɪr] **(-(e)s, -e)** *nt* tangle; *(von Straßen)* maze

gewiss ▲ [gə'vɪs] *adj* certain ♦ *adv* certainly

Gewissen [gə'vɪsən] **(-s, -)** *nt* conscience; **g~haft** *adj* conscientious; **g~los** *adj* unscrupulous

Gewissens- *zW*: **~bisse** *pl* pangs of conscience, qualms; **~frage** *f* matter of conscience; **~konflikt** *m* moral conflict

gewissermaßen [gəvɪsər'maːsən] *adv* more

or less, in a way

Gewissheit ▲ [gə'vɪshaɪt] f certainty

Gewitter [gə'vɪtər] **(-s, -)** nt thunderstorm; **g~n** vi unpers: **es g~t** there's a thunderstorm

gewitzt [gə'vɪtst] adj shrewd, cunning

gewogen [gə'voːgən] adj (+dat) well-disposed (towards)

gewöhnen [gə'vøːnən] vt: **jdn an etw** akk **~** to accustom sb to sth; (erziehen zu) to teach sb sth ♦ vr: **sich an etw** akk **~** to get used od accustomed to sth

Gewohnheit [gə'voːnhaɪt] f habit; (Brauch) custom; **aus ~** from habit; **zur ~ werden** to become a habit

Gewohnheits- zW: **~mensch** m creature of habit; **~recht** nt common law

gewöhnlich [gə'vøːnlɪç] adj usual; ordinary; (pej) common; **wie ~** as usual

gewohnt [gə'voːnt] adj usual; **etw ~ sein** to be used to sth

Gewöhnung f: **~ (an** +akk**)** getting accustomed (to)

Gewölbe [gə'vœlbə] **(-s, -)** nt vault

gewollt [gə'vɔlt] adj affected, artificial

gewonnen [gə'vɔnən] vb siehe **gewinnen**

geworden [gə'vɔrdən] vb siehe **werden**

geworfen [gə'vɔrfən] vb siehe **werfen**

Gewühl [gə'vyːl] **(-(e)s)** nt throng

Gewürz [gə'vyrts] **(-es, -e)** nt spice, seasoning; **g~t** adj spiced

gewusst ▲ [gə'vust] vb siehe **wissen**

Gezeiten [gə'tsaɪtən] pl tides

gezielt [gə'tsiːlt] adj with a particular aim in mind, purposeful; (Kritik) pointed

gezogen [gə'tsoːgən] vb siehe **ziehen**

Gezwitscher [gə'tsvɪtʃər] **(-s)** nt twitter(ing), chirping

gezwungen [gə'tsvuŋən] adj forced; **~ermaßen** adv of necessity

ggf. abk von **gegebenenfalls**

gibst etc [giːpst] vb siehe **geben**

Gicht [gɪçt] **(-)** f gout

Giebel ['giːbəl] **(-s, -)** m gable; **~dach** nt gable(d) roof; **~fenster** nt gable window

Gier [giːr] **(-)** f greed; **g~ig** adj greedy

gießen ['giːsən] (unreg) vt to pour; (Blumen)

to water; (Metall) to cast; (Wachs) to mould

Gießkanne f watering can

Gift [gɪft] **(-(e)s, -e)** nt poison; **g~ig** adj poisonous; (fig: boshaft) venomous; **~müll** m toxic waste; **~stoff** m toxic substance; **~zahn** m fang

ging etc [gɪŋ] vb siehe **gehen**

Gipfel ['gɪpfəl] **(-s, -)** m summit, peak; (fig: Höhepunkt) height; **g~n** vi to culminate; **~treffen** nt summit (meeting)

Gips [gɪps] **(-es, -e)** m plaster; (MED) plaster (of Paris); **~abdruck** m plaster cast; **g~en** vt to plaster; **~verband** m plaster (cast)

Giraffe [gi'rafə] f giraffe

Girlande [gɪr'landə] f garland

Giro ['ʒiːro] **(-s, -s)** nt giro; **~konto** nt current account

Gitarre [gi'tarə] f guitar

Gitter ['gɪtər] **(-s, -)** nt grating, bars pl; (für Pflanzen) trellis; (Zaun) railing(s); **~bett** nt cot; **~fenster** nt barred window; **~zaun** m railing(s)

Glanz [glants] **(-es)** m shine, lustre; (fig) splendour

glänzen ['glɛntsən] vi to shine (also fig), to gleam ♦ vt to polish; **~d** adj shining; (fig) brilliant

Glanz- zW: **~leistung** f brilliant achievement; **g~los** adj dull; **~zeit** f heyday

Glas [glaːs] **(-es, ⁻er)** nt glass; **~er** **(-s, -)** m glazier; **~faser** f fibreglass; **g~ieren** [gla'ziːrən] vt to glaze; **g~ig** adj glassy; **~scheibe** f pane; **~ur** [gla'zuːr] f glaze; (KOCH) icing

glatt [glat] adj smooth; (rutschig) slippery; (Absage) flat; (Lüge) downright; **Glätte** f smoothness; slipperiness

Glatteis nt (black) ice; **jdn aufs ~ führen** (fig) to take sb for a ride

glätten vt to smooth out

Glatze ['glatsə] f bald head; **eine ~ bekommen** to go bald

Glaube ['glaʊbə] **(-ns, -n)** m: **~ (an** +akk**)** faith (in); belief (in); **g~n** vt, vi to believe; to think; **jdm g~n** to believe sb; **an etw** akk **g~n** to believe in sth; **daran g~n müssen**

(umg) to be for it

glaubhaft ['glaʊbhaft] *adj* credible

gläubig ['glɔʏbɪç] *adj (REL)* devout; *(vertrauensvoll)* trustful; **G~e(r)** *f(m)* believer; **die G~en** the faithful; **G~er (-s, -)** *m* creditor

glaubwürdig ['glaʊbvʏrdɪç] *adj* credible; *(Mensch)* trustworthy; **G~keit** *f* credibility; trustworthiness

gleich [glaɪç] *adj* equal; *(identisch)* (the) same, identical ♦ *adv* equally; *(sofort)* straight away; *(bald)* in a minute; **es ist mir ~** it's all the same to me; **~ bleibend** constant; **~ gesinnt** like-minded; **2 mal 2 ~ 4** 2 times 2 is *od* equals 4; **~ groß** the same size; **~ nach/an** right after/at; **~altrig** *adj* of the same age; **~artig** *adj* similar; **~bedeutend** *adj* synonymous; **G~berechtigung** *f* equal rights *pl*; **~en** *(unreg) vi*: **jdm/etw ~en** to be like sb/sth ♦ *vr* to be alike; **~falls** *adv* likewise; **danke ~falls!** the same to you; **G~förmigkeit** *f* uniformity; **G~gewicht** *nt* equilibrium, balance; **~gültig** *adj* indifferent; *(unbedeutend)* unimportant; **G~gültigkeit** *f* indifference; **G~heit** *f* equality; **~kommen** *(unreg) vi +dat* to be equal to; **~mäßig** *adj* even, equal; **~sam** *adv* as it were; **G~schritt** *m*: **im G~schritt gehen** to walk in step; **~stellen** *vt (rechtlich etc)* to treat as (an) equal; **G~strom** *m (ELEK)* direct current; **~tun** *(unreg) vi*: **es jdm ~tun** to match sb; **G~ung** *f* equation; **~viel** *adv* no matter; **~wertig** *adj (Geld)* of the same value; *(Gegner)* evenly matched; **~zeitig** *adj* simultaneous

Gleis [glaɪs] **(-es, -e)** *nt* track, rails *pl*; *(Bahnsteig)* platform

gleiten ['glaɪtən] *(unreg) vi* to glide; *(rutschen)* to slide

Gleitzeit *f* flex(i)time

Gletscher ['glɛtʃər] **(-s, -)** *m* glacier; **~spalte** *f* crevasse

Glied [gli:t] **(-(e)s, -er)** *nt* member; *(Arm, Bein)* limb; *(von Kette)* link; *(MIL)* rank(s); **g~ern** [-dərn] *vt* to organize, to structure; **~erung** *f* structure, organization

glimmen ['glɪmən] *(unreg) vi* to glow, to gleam

glimpflich ['glɪmpflɪç] *adj* mild, lenient; **~ davonkommen** to get off lightly

glitschig ['glɪtʃɪç] *adj (Fisch, Weg)* slippery

glitzern ['glɪtsərn] *vi* to glitter; to twinkle

global [glo'ba:l] *adj* global

Globus ['glo:bʊs] **(- od -ses, Globen** *od* **-se)** *m* globe

Glocke ['glɔkə] *f* bell; **etw an die große ~ hängen** *(fig)* to shout sth from the rooftops

Glocken- *zW*: **~blume** *f* bellflower; **~geläut** *nt* peal of bells; **~spiel** *nt* chime(s); *(MUS)* glockenspiel; **~turm** *m* bell tower

Glosse ['glɔsə] *f* comment

glotzen ['glɔtsən] *(umg) vi* to stare

Glück [glʏk] **(-(e)s)** *nt* luck, fortune; *(Freude)* happiness; **~ haben** to be lucky; **viel ~!** good luck!; **zum ~** fortunately; **g~en** *vi* to succeed; **es g~te ihm, es zu bekommen** he succeeded in getting it

gluckern ['glʊkərn] *vi* to glug

glück- *zW*: **~lich** *adj* fortunate; *(froh)* happy; **~licherweise** *adv* fortunately; **~'selig** *adj* blissful

Glücks- *zW*: **~fall** *m* stroke of luck; **~kind** *nt* lucky person; **~sache** *f* matter of luck; **~spiel** *nt* game of chance

Glückwunsch *m* congratulations *pl*, best wishes *pl*

Glüh- ['gly:] *zW*: **~birne** *f* light bulb; **g~en** *vi* to glow; **~wein** *m* mulled wine; **~würmchen** *nt* glow-worm

Glut [glu:t] **(-, -en)** *f (Röte)* glow; *(Feuersglut)* fire; *(Hitze)* heat; *(fig)* ardour

GmbH [ge:ʔɛmbe:'ha:] *f abk (= Gesellschaft mit beschränkter Haftung)* limited company, Ltd

Gnade ['gna:də] *f (Gunst)* favour; *(Erbarmen)* mercy; *(Milde)* clemency

Gnaden- *zW*: **~frist** *f* reprieve, respite; **g~los** *adj* merciless; **~stoß** *m* coup de grâce

gnädig ['gnɛ:dɪç] *adj* gracious; *(voll Erbarmen)* merciful

Gold [gɔlt] **(-(e)s)** *nt* gold; **g~en** *adj* golden; **~fisch** *m* goldfish; **~grube** *f* goldmine;

g~ig ['gɔldɪç] (*umg*) *adj* (*fig: allerliebst*) sweet, adorable; **~regen** *m* laburnum; **~schmied** *m* goldsmith

Golf¹ [gɔlf] (**-(e)s, -e**) *m* gulf

Golf² [gɔlf] (**-s**) *nt* golf; **~platz** *m* golf course; **~schläger** *m* golf club

Golfstrom *m* Gulf Stream

Gondel ['gɔndəl] (**-, -n**) *f* gondola; (*Seilbahn*) cable car

gönnen ['gœnən] *vt*: **jdm etw ~** not to begrudge sb sth; **sich** *dat* **etw ~** to allow o.s. sth

Gönner (**-s, -**) *m* patron; **g~haft** *adj* patronizing

Gosse ['gɔsə] *f* gutter

Gott [gɔt] (**-es, ⸚er**) *m* god; **mein ~!** for heaven's sake!; **um ~es Willen!** for heaven's sake!; **grüß ~!** hello; **~ sei Dank!** thank God!; **~heit** *f* deity

Göttin ['gœtɪn] *f* goddess

göttlich *adj* divine

gottlos *adj* godless

Götze ['gœtsə] (**-n, -n**) *m* idol

Grab [gra:p] (**-(e)s, ⸚er**) *nt* grave; **g~en** ['gra:bən] (*unreg*) *vt* to dig; **~en** (**-s, ⸚**) *m* ditch; (*MIL*) trench; **~stein** *m* gravestone

Grad [gra:t] (**-(e)s, -e**) *m* degree

Graf [gra:f] (**-en, -en**) *m* count, earl

Grafiker(in) ▲ ['gra:fɪkər(ɪn)] (**-s, -**) *m(f)* graphic designer

grafisch ▲ ['gra:fɪʃ] *adj* graphic

Gram [gra:m] (**-(e)s**) *m* grief, sorrow

grämen ['grɛ:mən] *vr* to grieve

Gramm [gram] (**-s, -e**) *nt* gram(me)

Grammatik [gra'matɪk] *f* grammar

Granat [gra'na:t] (**-(e)s, -e**) *m* (*Stein*) garnet

Granate *f* (*MIL*) shell; (*Handgranate*) grenade

Granit [gra'ni:t] (**-s, -e**) *m* granite

Gras [gra:s] (**-es, ⸚er**) *nt* grass; **g~en** ['gra:zən] *vi* to graze; **~halm** *m* blade of grass

grassieren [gra'si:rən] *vi* to be rampant, to rage

grässlich ▲ ['grɛslɪç] *adj* horrible

Grat [gra:t] (**-(e)s, -e**) *m* ridge

Gräte ['grɛ:tə] *f* fishbone

gratis ['gra:tɪs] *adj, adv* free (of charge);

G~probe *f* free sample

Gratulation [gratulatsi'o:n] *f* congratulation(s)

gratulieren [gratu'li:rən] *vi*: **jdm ~ (zu etw)** to congratulate sb (on sth); **(ich) gratuliere!** congratulations!

grau [grau] *adj* grey

Gräuel ▲ ['grɔyəl] (**-s, -**) *m* horror, revulsion; **etw ist jdm ein ~** sb loathes sth

Grauen (**-s**) *nt* horror; **g~ vi unpers**: **es graut jdm vor etw** sb dreads sth, sb is afraid of sth ♦ *vr*: **sich g~ vor** to dread, to have a horror of; **g~haft** *adj* horrible

grauhaarig *adj* grey-haired

gräulich ▲ ['grɔylɪç] *adj* horrible

grausam ['grauza:m] *adj* cruel; **G~keit** *f* cruelty

Grausen ['grauzən] (**-s**) *nt* horror; **g~ vb** = **grauen**

gravieren [gra'vi:rən] *vt* to engrave; **~d** *adj* grave

graziös [gratsi'ø:s] *adj* graceful

greifbar *adj* tangible, concrete; **in ~er Nähe** within reach

greifen ['graifən] (*unreg*) *vt* to seize; to grip; **nach etw ~** to reach for sth; **um sich ~** (*fig*) to spread; **zu etw ~** (*fig*) to turn to sth

Greis [grais] (**-es, -e**) *m* old man; **g~enhaft** *adj* senile; **~in** *f* old woman

grell [grɛl] *adj* harsh

Grenz- ['grɛnts] *zW*: **~beamte(r)** *m* frontier official; **~e** *f* boundary; (*Staatsgrenze*) frontier; (*Schranke*) limit; **g~en** *vi*: **g~en (an** +*akk*) to border (on); **g~enlos** *adj* boundless; **~fall** *m* borderline case; **~kontrolle** *f* border control; **~übergang** *m* frontier crossing

Greuel △ ['grɔyəl] (**-s, -**) *m siehe* **Gräuel**

greulich △ *adj siehe* **gräulich**

Griech- ['gri:ç] *zW*: **~e** (**-n, -n**) *m* Greek; **~enland** *nt* Greece; **~in** *f* Greek; **g~isch** *adj* Greek

griesgrämig ['gri:sgrɛ:mɪç] *adj* grumpy

Grieß [gri:s] (**-es, -e**) *m* (*KOCH*) semolina

Griff [grɪf] (**-(e)s, -e**) *m* grip; (*Vorrichtung*) handle; **g~bereit** *adj* handy

Grill [grɪl] *m* grill; **~e** *f* cricket; **g~en** *vt* to grill; **~fest** *nt* barbecue party

Grimasse [gri'masə] *f* grimace

grimmig ['grɪmɪç] *adj* furious; (*heftig*) fierce, severe

grinsen ['grɪnzən] *vi* to grin

Grippe ['grɪpə] *f* influenza, flu

grob [gro:p] *adj* coarse, gross; (*Fehler, Verstoß*) gross; **G~heit** *f* coarseness; coarse expression

grölen ['grø:lən] (*pej*) *vt* to bawl, to bellow

Groll [grɔl] **(-(e)s)** *m* resentment; **g~en** *vi* (*Donner*) to rumble; **g~en (mit** *od* +*dat*) to bear ill will (towards)

groß [gro:s] *adj* big, large; (*hoch*) tall; (*fig*) great ♦ *adv* greatly; **im G~en und Ganzen** on the whole; **bei jdm ~ geschrieben werden** to be high on sb's list of priorities; **~artig** *adj* great, splendid; **G~aufnahme** *f* (*CINE*) close-up; **G~britannien** *nt* Great Britain

Größe ['grø:sə] *f* size; (*Höhe*) height; (*fig*) greatness

Groß- *zW:* **~einkauf** *m* bulk purchase; **~eltern** *pl* grandparents; **g~enteils** *adv* mostly; **~format** *nt* large size; **~handel** *m* wholesale trade; **~händler** *m* wholesaler; **~macht** *f* great power; **~mutter** *f* grandmother; **~rechner** *m* mainframe (computer); **g~schreiben** (*unreg*) *vt* (*Wort*) to write in block capitals; *siehe* **groß**; **g~spurig** *adj* pompous; **~stadt** *f* city, large town

größte(r, s) [grø:stə(r, s)] *adj superl von* **groß**; **größtenteils** *adv* for the most part

Groß- *zW:* **g~tun** (*unreg*) *vi* to boast; **~vater** *m* grandfather; **g~ziehen** (*unreg*) *vt* to raise; **g~zügig** *adj* generous; (*Planung*) on a large scale

grotesk [gro'tesk] *adj* grotesque

Grotte ['grɔtə] *f* grotto

Grübchen ['gry:pçən] *nt* dimple

Grube ['gru:bə] *f* pit; mine

grübeln ['gry:bəln] *vi* to brood

Gruft [gruft] **(-, ⁻e)** *f* tomb, vault

grün [gry:n] *adj* green; **der ~e Punkt** green spot symbol on recyclable packaging

---

i The **grüner Punkt** is a green spot which appears on packaging that should be kept separate from normal household refuse to be recycled through the recycling company, **DSD** (Duales System Deutschland). The recycling is financed by licences bought by the packaging manufacturer from **DSD**. These costs are often passed on to the consumer.

Grünanlage *f* park

Grund [grunt] **(-(e)s, ⁻e)** *m* ground; (*von See, Gefäß*) bottom; (*fig*) reason; **im ~e genommen** basically; *siehe* **aufgrund**; **~ausbildung** *f* basic training; **~besitz** *m* land(ed property), real estate; **~buch** *nt* land register

gründen ['gryndən] *vt* to found ♦ *vr*: **sich ~ (auf** +*dat*) to be based (on); **~ auf** +*akk* to base on; **Gründer (-s, -)** *m* founder

Grund- *zW:* **~gebühr** *f* basic charge; **~gesetz** *nt* constitution; **~lage** *f* foundation; **g~legend** *adj* fundamental

gründlich *adj* thorough

Grund- *zW:* **g~los** *adj* groundless; **~regel** *f* basic rule; **~riss** ▲ *m* plan; (*fig*) outline; **~satz** *m* principle; **g~sätzlich** *adj* fundamental; (*Frage*) of principle ♦ *adv* fundamentally; (*prinzipiell*) on principle; **~schule** *f* elementary school; **~stein** *m* foundation stone; **~stück** *nt* estate; plot

Grundwasser *nt* ground water

---

i The **Grundschule** is a primary school which children attend for 4 years from the age of 6 to 10. There are no formal examinations in the **Grundschule** but parents receive a report on their child's progress twice a year. Many children attend a **Kindergarten** from 3-6 years before going to the **Grundschule**, though no formal instruction takes place in the **Kindergarten**.

---

irünstreifen m central reservation

runzen ['grʊntsən] vi to grunt

iruppe ['grʊpə] f group; ~**nermäßigung** f group reduction; **g~nweise** adv in groups

ruppieren [grʊ'piːrən] vt, vr to group

ruselig adj creepy

ruseln ['gruːzəln] vi unpers: **es gruselt jdm vor etw** sth gives sb the creeps ♦ vr to have the creeps

iruß [gruːs] **(-es, ⁻e)** m greeting; (MIL) salute; **viele Grüße** best wishes; **mit freundlichen Grüßen** yours sincerely; **Grüße an** +akk regards to

rüßen ['gryːsən] vt to greet; (MIL) to salute; **jdn von jdm ~** to give sb sb's regards; **jdn ~ lassen** to send sb one's regards

ucken ['gʊkən] vi to look

ültig ['gʏltɪç] adj valid; **G~keit** f validity

iummi ['gʊmi] **(-s, -s)** nt od m rubber; (~harze) gum; ~**band** nt rubber od elastic band; (Hosenband) elastic; ~**bärchen** nt ≈ jelly baby (BRIT); ~**baum** m rubber plant; **g~eren** [gʊ'miːrən] vt to gum; ~**stiefel** m rubber boot

ünstig ['gʏnstɪç] adj convenient; (Gelegenheit) favourable; **das habe ich ~ bekommen** it was a bargain

urgel ['gʊrgəl] **(-, -n)** f throat; **g~n** vi to gurgle; (im Mund) to gargle

urke ['gʊrkə] f cucumber; **saure ~** pickled cucumber, gherkin

urt [gʊrt] **(-(e)s, -e)** m belt

ürtel ['gʏrtəl] **(-s, -)** m belt; (GEOG) zone; ~**reifen** m radial tyre

iUS f abk (= Gemeinschaft unabhängiger Staaten) CIS

iuss ▲ [gʊs] **(-es, ⁻e)** m casting; (Regenguß) downpour; (KOCH) glazing; ~**eisen** nt cast iron

ut adj good; **alles Gute** all the best; **also gut** all right then
♦ adv well; **gut gehen** to work, to come off; **es geht jdm gut** sb's doing fine; **gut gemeint** well meant; **gut schmecken** to

taste good; **jdm gut tun** to do sb good; **gut, aber ...** OK, but ...; **(na) gut, ich komme** all right, I'll come; **gut drei Stunden** a good three hours; **das kann gut sein** that may well be; **lass es gut sein** that'll do

Gut [guːt] **(-(e)s, ⁻er)** nt (Besitz) possession; **Güter** pl (Waren) goods; ~**achten (-s, -)** nt (expert) opinion; ~**achter (-s, -)** m expert; **g~artig** adj good-natured; (MED) benign; **g~bürgerlich** adj (Küche) (good) plain; ~**dünken** nt: **nach ~dünken** at one's discretion

Güte ['gyːtə] f goodness, kindness; (Qualität) quality

Güter- zW: ~**abfertigung** f (EISENB) goods office; ~**bahnhof** m goods station; ~**wagen** m goods waggon (BRIT), freight car (US); ~**zug** m goods train (BRIT), freight train (US)

Gütezeichen nt quality mark; ≈ kite mark

gut- zW: ~**gehen** △ (unreg) vi unpers siehe **gut**; ~**gemeint** △ adj siehe **gut**; ~**gläubig** adj trusting; **G~haben (-s)** nt credit; ~**heißen** (unreg) vt to approve (of)

gütig ['gyːtɪç] adj kind

Gut- zW: **g~mütig** adj good-natured; ~**schein** m voucher; **g~schreiben** (unreg) vt to credit; ~**schrift** f (Betrag) credit; **g~tun** △ (unreg) vi siehe **gut**; **g~willig** adj willing

Gymnasium [gʏm'naːziʊm] nt grammar school (BRIT), high school (US)

Gymnasium

The Gymnasium is a selective secondary school. After nine years of study pupils sit the Abitur so they can go on to higher education. Pupils who successfully complete six years at a Gymnasium automatically gain the mittlere Reife.

Gymnastik [gʏm'nastɪk] f exercises pl, keep fit

H, h

Haag [ha:k] *m:* **Den ~** the Hague

Haar [ha:r] (-(e)s, -e) *nt* hair; **um ein ~** nearly; **an den ~en herbeigezogen** (*umg:* *Vergleich*) very far-fetched; **~bürste** *f* hairbrush; **h~en** *vi, vr* to lose hair; **~esbreite** *f:* **um ~esbreite** by a hair's-breadth; **~festiger** (-s, -) *m* (hair) setting lotion; **h~genau** *adv* precisely; **h~ig** *adj* hairy; (*fig*) nasty; **~klammer** *f* hairgrip; **~nadel** *f* hairpin; **h~scharf** *adv* (*beobachten*) very sharply; (*daneben*) by a hair's breadth; **~schnitt** *m* haircut; **~spange** *f* hair slide; **h~sträubend** *adj* hair-raising; **~teil** *nt* hairpiece; **~waschmittel** *nt* shampoo

Habe ['ha:bə] (-) *f* property

haben ['ha:bən] (*unreg*) *vt, vb aux* to have; **Hunger/Angst ~** to be hungry/afraid; **woher hast du das?** where did you get that from?; **was hast du denn?** what's the matter (with you)?; **du hast zu schweigen** you're to be quiet; **ich hätte gern** I would like; **H~** (-s, -) *nt* credit

Habgier *f* avarice; **h~ig** *adj* avaricious

Habicht ['ha:bɪçt] (-s, -e) *m* hawk

Habseligkeiten ['ha:pze:lɪçkaɪtən] *pl* belongings

Hachse ['haksə] *f* (*KOCH*) knuckle

Hacke ['hakə] *f* hoe; (*Ferse*) heel; **h~n** *vt* to hack, to chop; (*Erde*) to hoe

Hackfleisch *nt* mince, minced meat

Hafen ['ha:fən] (-s, ") *m* harbour, port; **~arbeiter** *m* docker; **~rundfahrt** *f* boat trip round the harbour; **~stadt** *f* port

Hafer ['ha:fər] (-s, -) *m* oats *pl;* **~flocken** *pl* rolled oats; **~schleim** *m* gruel

Haft [haft] (-) *f* custody; **h~bar** *adj* liable, responsible; **~befehl** *m* warrant (for arrest); **h~en** *vi* to stick, to cling; **h~en für** to be liable *od* responsible for; **h~en bleiben (an** +*dat*) to stick (to); **Häftling** *m* prisoner; **~pflicht** *f* liability; **~pflichtversicherung** *f* (*AUT*) third party

insurance; **~schalen** *pl* contact lenses; **~ung** *f* liability; **~ungsbeschränkung** *f* limitation of liability

Hagebutte ['ha:gəbʊtə] *f* rose hip

Hagel ['ha:gəl] (-s) *m* hail; **h~n** *vi unpers* to hail

hager ['ha:gər] *adj* gaunt

Hahn [ha:n] (-(e)s, "e) *m* cock; (*Wasserhahn*) tap, faucet (*US*)

Hähnchen ['hɛ:nçən] *nt* cockerel; (*KOCH*) chicken

Hai(fisch) ['haɪ(fɪʃ)] (-(e)s, -e) *m* shark

häkeln ['hɛ:kəln] *vt* to crochet

Haken ['ha:kən] (-s, -) *m* hook; (*fig*) catch; **~kreuz** *nt* swastika; **~nase** *f* hooked nose

halb [halp] *adj* half; **~ eins** half past twelve; **~ offen** half-open; **ein ~es Dutzend** half a dozen; **H~dunkel** *nt* semi-darkness

halber ['halbər] *präp* +*gen* (*wegen*) on account of; (*für*) for the sake of

Halb- *zW:* **~heit** *f* half-measure; **h~ieren** *vt* to halve; **~insel** *f* peninsula; **~jahr** *nt* six months; (*auch: COMM*) half-year; **h~jährlich** *adj* half-yearly; **~kreis** *m* semicircle; **~leiter** *m* semiconductor; **~mond** *m* half-moon; (*fig*) crescent; **~pension** *f* half-board; **~schuh** *m* shoe; **h~tags** *adv:* **h~tags arbeiten** to work part-time, to work mornings/afternoons; **h~wegs** *adv* halfway; **h~wegs besser** more or less better; **~zeit** *f* (*SPORT*) half; (*Pause*) half-time

Halde ['haldə] *f* (*Kohlen*) heap

half [half] *vb siehe* **helfen**

Hälfte ['hɛlftə] *f* half

Halfter ['halftər] (-s, -) *m od nt* (*für Tiere*) halter

Halle ['halə] *f* hall; (*AVIAT*) hangar; **h~n** *vi* to echo, to resound; **~nbad** *nt* indoor swimming pool

hallo [ha'lo:] *excl* hello

Halluzination [halutsinatsi'o:n] *f* hallucination

Halm ['halm] (-(e)s, -e) *m* blade; stalk

Halogenlampe [halo'ge:nlampə] *f* halogen lamp

Hals [hals] (**-es**, **ᵘe**) m neck; (*Kehle*) throat; **~ über Kopf** in a rush; **~band** nt (*von Hund*) collar; **~kette** f necklace; **~-Nasen-Ohren-Arzt** m ear, nose and throat specialist; **~schmerzen** pl sore throat sg; **~tuch** nt scarf

Halt [halt] (**-(e)s**, **-e**) m stop; (*fester ~*) hold; (*innerer ~*) stability; **~** od **h~!** stop!, halt!; **~ machen** to stop; **h~bar** adj durable; (*Lebensmittel*) non-perishable; (*MIL, fig*) tenable; **~barkeit** f durability; (non-)perishability

halten ['haltən] (*unreg*) vt to keep; (*festhalten*) to hold ♦ vi to hold; (*frisch bleiben*) to keep; (*stoppen*) to stop ♦ vr (*frisch bleiben*) to keep; (*sich behaupten*) to hold out; **~ für** to regard as; **~ von** to think of; **an sich ~** to restrain o.s.; **sich rechts/links ~** to keep to the right/left

Halte- zW: **~stelle** f stop; **~verbot** nt: **hier ist ~verbot** there's no waiting here

Halt- zW: **h~los** adj unstable; **h~machen** △ vi siehe **Halt**; **~ung** f posture; (*fig*) attitude; (*Selbstbeherrschung*) composure

Halunke [ha'luŋkə] (**-n**, **-n**) m rascal

hämisch ['hɛːmɪʃ] adj malicious

Hammel ['haməl] (**-s**, **ᵘ** od **-**) m wether; **~fleisch** nt mutton

Hammer ['hamər] (**-s**, **ᵘ**) m hammer

hämmern ['hɛmɛrn] vt, vi to hammer

Hämorr(ho)iden [hɛmɔro'iːdən, hɛmˈɔriːdn] pl haemorrhoids

Hamster ['hamstər] (**-s**, **-**) m hamster; **~ei** [-'raɪ] f hoarding; **h~n** vi to hoard

Hand [hant] (**-**, **ᵘe**) f hand; **~arbeit** f manual work; (*Nadelarbeit*) needlework; **~ball** m (*SPORT*) handball; **~bremse** f handbrake; **~buch** nt handbook, manual

Händedruck ['hɛndədrʊk] m handshake

Handel ['handəl] (**-s**) m trade; (*Geschäft*) transaction

Handeln ['handəln] (**-s**) nt action

handeln vi to trade; (*agieren*) to act ♦ vr unpers: **sich ~ um** to be a question of, to be about; **~ von** to be about

Handels- zW: **~bilanz** f balance of trade;

~kammer f chamber of commerce; **~reisende(r)** m commercial traveller; **~schule** f business school; **h~üblich** adj customary; (*Preis*) going attrib; **~vertreter** m sales representative

Hand- zW: **~feger** (**-s**, **-**) m hand brush; **h~fest** adj hefty; **h~gearbeitet** adj handmade; **~gelenk** nt wrist; **~gemenge** nt scuffle; **~gepäck** nt hand luggage; **h~geschrieben** adj handwritten; **h~greiflich** adj palpable; **h~greiflich werden** to become violent; **~griff** m flick of the wrist; **h~haben** vt insep to handle

Händler ['hɛndlər] (**-s**, **-**) m trader, dealer

handlich ['hantlɪç] adj handy

Handlung ['handlʊŋ] f act(ion); (*in Buch*) plot; (*Geschäft*) shop

Hand- zW: **~schelle** f handcuff; **~schrift** f handwriting; (*Text*) manuscript; **~schuh** m glove; **~stand** m (*SPORT*) handstand; **~tasche** f handbag; **~tuch** nt towel; **~umdrehen** nt: **im ~umdrehen** in the twinkling of an eye; **~werk** nt trade, craft; **~werker** (**-s**, **-**) m craftsman, artisan; **~werkzeug** nt tools pl

Handy ['hɛndi] (**-s**, **-s**) nt mobile (telephone)

Hanf [hanf] (**-(e)s**) m hemp

Hang [haŋ] (**-(e)s**, **ᵘe**) m inclination; (*Abhang*) slope

Hänge- ['hɛŋə] in zW hanging; **~brücke** f suspension bridge; **~matte** f hammock

hängen ['hɛŋən] (*unreg*) vi to hang ♦ vt: **etw (an etw** akk**) ~** to hang sth (on sth); **~ an** +dat (*fig*) to be attached to; **sich ~ an** +akk to hang on to, to cling to; **~ bleiben** to be caught; (*fig*) to remain, to stick; **~ bleiben an** +dat to catch od get caught on; **~ lassen** (*vergessen*) to leave; **den Kopf ~ lassen** to get downhearted

Hannover [ha'noːfər] (**-s**) nt Hanover

hänseln ['hɛnzəln] vt to tease

Hansestadt ['hanzəʃtat] f Hanse town

hantieren [han'tiːrən] vi to work, to be busy; **mit etw ~** to handle sth

hapern ['haːpərn] vi unpers: **es hapert an etw** dat there is a lack of sth

Happen ['hapən] (**-s, -**) m mouthful
Harfe ['harfə] f harp
Harke ['harkə] f rake; **h~n** vt, vi to rake
harmlos ['harmloːs] adj harmless; **H~igkeit** f harmlessness
Harmonie [harmo'niː] f harmony; **h~ren** vi to harmonize
harmonisch [har'moːnɪʃ] adj harmonious
Harn ['harn] (**-(e)s, -e**) m urine; **~blase** f bladder
Harpune [har'puːnə] f harpoon
harren ['harən] vi: **~ (auf** +akk) to wait (for)
hart [hart] adj hard; (fig) harsh; **~ gekocht** hard-boiled
Härte ['hɛrtə] f hardness; (fig) harshness
hart- zW: **~herzig** adj hard-hearted; **~näckig** adj stubborn
Harz [haːrts] (**-es, -e**) nt resin
Haschee [ha'ʃeː] (**-s, -s**) nt hash
Haschisch ['haʃɪʃ] (**-**) nt hashish
Hase ['haːzə] (**-n, -n**) m hare
Haselnuss ▲ ['haːzəlnʊs] f hazelnut
Hasenscharte f harelip
Hass ▲ [has] (**-es**) m hate, hatred
hassen ['hasən] vt to hate
hässlich ▲ ['hɛslɪç] adj ugly; (gemein) nasty; **H~keit** f ugliness; nastiness
Hast [hast] f haste
hast vb siehe **haben**
hasten vi to rush
hastig adj hasty
hat [hat] vb siehe **haben**
hatte etc ['hatə] vb siehe **haben**
Haube ['haubə] f hood; (Mütze) cap; (AUT) bonnet, hood (US)
Hauch [haux] (**-(e)s, -e**) m breath; (Lufthauch) breeze; (fig) trace; **h~dünn** adj extremely thin
Haue ['hauə] f hoe, pick; (umg) hiding; **h~n** (unreg) vt to hew, to cut; (umg) to thrash
Haufen ['haufən] (**-s, -**) m heap; (Leute) crowd; **ein ~ (x)** (umg) loads od a lot (of x); **auf einem ~** in one heap
häufen ['hɔyfən] vt to pile up ♦ vr to accumulate
haufenweise adv in heaps; in droves; **etw ~ haben** to have piles of sth

häufig ['hɔyfɪç] adj frequent ♦ adv frequently; **H~keit** f frequency
Haupt [haupt] (**-(e)s, Häupter**) nt head; (Oberhaupt) chief ♦ in zW main; **~bahnhof** m central station; **h~beruflich** adv as one's main occupation; **~darsteller(in)** m(f) leading actor (actress); **~fach** nt (SCH, UNIV) main subject, major (US); **~gericht** nt (KOCH) main course
Häuptling ['hɔyptlɪŋ] m chief(tain)
Haupt- zW: **~mann** (pl **-leute**) m (MIL) captain; **~person** f central figure; **~quartier** nt headquarters pl; **~rolle** f leading part; **~sache** f main thing; **h~sächlich** adj chief ♦ adv chiefly; **~saison** f high season, peak season; **~schule** f ≃ secondary school; **~stadt** f capital; **~straße** f main street; **~verkehrszeit** f rush-hour, peak traffic hours pl

---
Hauptschule
---

i The **Hauptschule** is a non-selective school which pupils may attend after the **Grundschule**. They complete five years of study and most go on to do some vocational training.

Haus [haus] (**-es, Häuser**) nt house; **~ halten** (sparen) to economize; **nach ~e** home; **zu ~e** at home; **~apotheke** f medicine cabinet; **~arbeit** f housework; (SCH) homework; **~arzt** m family doctor; **~aufgabe** f (SCH) homework; **~besitzer(in)** m(f) house owner; **~besuch** m (von Arzt) house call; **~durchsuchung** f police raid; **h~eigen** adj belonging to a/ the hotel/firm
Häuser- ['hɔyzər] zW: **~block** m block (of houses); **~makler** m estate agent (BRIT), real estate agent (US)
Haus- zW: **~flur** m hallway; **~frau** f housewife; **h~gemacht** adj home-made; **~halt** m household; (POL) budget; **h~halten** (unreg) vi △ siehe **Haus**; **~hälterin** f housekeeper; **~haltsgeld** nt housekeeping (money); **~haltsgerät** nt

domestic appliance; **~herr** m host; (*Vermieter*) landlord; **h~hoch** adv: **h~hoch verlieren** to lose by a mile

hausieren [hau'zi:rən] vi to peddle

Hausierer (**-s, -**) m pedlar (*BRIT*), peddler (*US*)

häuslich ['hɔʏslɪç] adj domestic

Haus- zW: **~meister** m caretaker, janitor; **~nummer** f street number; **~ordnung** f house rules pl; **~putz** m house cleaning; **~schlüssel** m front door key; **~schuh** m slipper; **~tier** nt pet; **~tür** f front door; **~wirt** m landlord; **~wirtschaft** f domestic science; **~zelt** nt frame tent

Haut [haut] (**-, Häute**) f skin; (*Tierhaut*) hide; **~creme** f skin cream; **h~eng** adj skin-tight; **~farbe** f complexion; **~krebs** m skin cancer

Haxe ['haksə] f = **Hachse**

Hbf. abk = **Hauptbahnhof**

Hebamme ['he:pʔamə] f midwife

Hebel ['he:bəl] (**-s, -**) m lever

heben ['he:bən] (*unreg*) vt to raise, to lift

Hecht [hɛçt] (**-(e)s, -e**) m pike

Heck [hɛk] (**-(e)s, -e**) nt stern; (*von Auto*) rear

Hecke ['hɛkə] f hedge

Heckenschütze m sniper

Heckscheibe f rear window

Heer [he:r] (**-(e)s, -e**) nt army

Hefe ['he:fə] f yeast

Heft ['hɛft] (**-(e)s, -e**) nt exercise book; (*Zeitschrift*) number; (*von Messer*) haft; **h~en** vt: **h~en (an** +*akk*) to fasten (to); (*nähen*) to tack ((on) to); **etw an etw** *akk* **h~en** to fasten sth to sth; **~er** (**-s, -**) m folder

heftig adj fierce, violent; **H~keit** f fierceness, violence

Heft- zW: **~klammer** f paper clip; **~pflaster** nt sticking plaster; **~zwecke** f drawing pin

hegen ['he:gən] vt (*Wild, Bäume*) to care for, to tend; (*fig, geh: empfinden: Wunsch*) to cherish; (: *Misstrauen*) to feel

Hehl [he:l] m od nt: **kein(en) ~ aus etw machen** to make no secret of sth; **~er** (**-s,**

-) m receiver (of stolen goods), fence

Heide[1] ['haidə] (**-n, -n**) m heathen, pagan

Heide[2] ['haidə] f heath, moor; **~kraut** nt heather

Heidelbeere f bilberry

Heidentum nt paganism

Heidin f heathen, pagan

heikel ['haikəl] adj awkward, thorny

Heil [hail] (**-(e)s**) nt well-being; (*Seelenheil*) salvation; **h~** adj in one piece, intact; **~and** (**-(e)s, -e**) m saviour; **h~bar** adj curable; **h~en** vt to cure ♦ vi to heal; **h~froh** adj very relieved

heilig ['hailɪç] adj holy; **~ sprechen** to canonize; **H~abend** m Christmas Eve; **H~e(r)** f(m) saint; **~en** vt to sanctify, to hallow; **H~enschein** m halo; **H~keit** f holiness; **H~tum** nt shrine; (*Gegenstand*) relic

Heil- zW: **h~los** adj unholy; (*fig*) hopeless; **~mittel** nt remedy; **~praktiker(in)** m(f) non-medical practitioner; **h~sam** adj (*fig*) salutary; **~sarmee** f Salvation Army; **~ung** f cure

Heim [haim] (**-(e)s, -e**) nt home; **h~** adv home

Heimat ['haima:t] (**-, -en**) f home (town/ country etc); **~land** nt homeland; **h~lich** adj native, home attrib; (*Gefühle*) nostalgic; **h~los** adj homeless; **~ort** m home town/ area

Heim- zW: **~computer** m home computer; **h~fahren** (*unreg*) vi to drive home; **~fahrt** f journey home; **h~gehen** (*unreg*) vi to go home; (*sterben*) to pass away; **h~isch** adj (*gebürtig*) native; **sich h~isch fühlen** to feel at home; **~kehr** (**-, -en**) f homecoming; **h~kehren** vi to return home; **h~lich** adj secret; **~lichkeit** f secrecy; **~reise** f journey home; **~spiel** nt (*SPORT*) home game; **h~suchen** vt to afflict; (*Geist*) to haunt; **~trainer** m exercise bike; **h~tückisch** adj malicious; **~weg** m way home; **~weh** nt homesickness; **~werker** (**-s, -**) m handyman; **h~zahlen** vt: **jdm etw h~zahlen** to pay sb back for sth

Heirat ['haira:t] (**-, -en**) f marriage; **h~en** vt

to marry ♦ *vi* to marry, to get married ♦ *vr* to get married; **~santrag** *m* proposal

heiser ['haɪzər] *adj* hoarse; **H~keit** *f* hoarseness

heiß [haɪs] *adj* hot; **~e(s) Eisen** (*umg*) hot potato; **~blütig** *adj* hot-blooded

heißen ['haɪsən] (*unreg*) *vi* to be called; (*bedeuten*) to mean ♦ *vt* to command; (*nennen*) to name ♦ *vi unpers*: **es heißt** it says; it is said; **das heißt** that is (to say)

Heiß- *zW*: **~hunger** *m* ravenous hunger; **h~laufen** (*unreg*) *vi, vr* to overheat

heiter ['haɪtər] *adj* cheerful; (*Wetter*) bright; **H~keit** *f* cheerfulness; (*Belustigung*) amusement

Heiz- ['haɪts] *zW*: **h~bar** *adj* heated; (*Raum*) with heating; **h~en** *vt* to heat; **~körper** *m* radiator; **~öl** *nt* fuel oil; **~sonne** *f* electric fire; **~ung** *f* heating

hektisch ['hɛktɪʃ] *adj* hectic

Held [hɛlt] (**-en, -en**) *m* hero; **h~enhaft** *adj* heroic; **~in** *f* heroine

helfen ['hɛlfən] (*unreg*) *vi* to help; (*nützen*) to be of use ♦ *vb unpers*: **es hilft nichts, du musst ...** it's no use, you'll have to ...; **jdm (bei etw) ~** to help sb (with sth); **sich** *dat* **zu ~ wissen** to be resourceful

Helfer (-s, -) *m* helper, assistant; **~shelfer** *m* accomplice

hell [hɛl] *adj* clear, bright; (*Farbe, Bier*) light; **~blau** *adj* light blue; **~blond** *adj* ash blond; **H~e (-)** *f* clearness, brightness; **~hörig** *adj* (*Wand*) paper-thin; **~hörig werden** (*fig*) to prick up one's ears; **H~seher** *m* clairvoyant; **~wach** *adj* wide-awake

Helm ['hɛlm] (**-(e)s, -e**) *m* (*auf Kopf*) helmet

Hemd [hɛmt] (**-(e)s, -en**) *nt* shirt; (*Unterhemd*) vest; **~bluse** *f* blouse

hemmen ['hɛmən] *vt* to check, to hold back; **gehemmt sein** to be inhibited; **Hemmung** *f* check; (*PSYCH*) inhibition; **hemmungslos** *adj* unrestrained, without restraint

Hengst [hɛŋst] (**-es, -e**) *m* stallion

Henkel ['hɛŋkəl] (**-s, -**) *m* handle

Henker (-s, -) *m* hangman

Henne ['hɛnə] *f* hen

SCHLÜSSELWORT
---

her [heːr] *adv* **1** (*Richtung*): **komm her zu mir** come here (to me); **von England her** from England; **von weit her** from a long way away; **her damit!** hand it over!; **wo hat er das her?** where did he get that from?

2 (*Blickpunkt*): **von der Form her** as far as the form is concerned

3 (*zeitlich*): **das ist 5 Jahre her** that was 5 years ago; **wo bist du her?** where do you come from?; **ich kenne ihn von früher her** I know him from before

---

herab [hɛ'rap] *adv* down(ward(s)); **~hängen** (*unreg*) *vi* to hang down; **~lassen** (*unreg*) *vt* to let down ♦ *vr* to condescend; **~lassend** *adj* condescending; **~setzen** *vt* to lower, to reduce; (*fig*) to belittle, to disparage

heran [hɛ'ran] *adv*: **näher ~!** come up closer!; **~ zu mir!** come up to me!; **~bringen** (*unreg*) *vt*: **~bringen (an** +*akk*) to bring up (to); **~fahren** (*unreg*) *vi*: **~fahren (an** +*akk*) to drive up (to); **~kommen** (*unreg*) *vi*: (**an jdn/etw**) **~kommen** to approach (sb/sth), to come near (to sb/sth); **~machen** *vr*: **sich an jdn ~machen** to make up to sb; **~treten** (*unreg*) *vi*: **mit etw an jdn ~treten** to approach sb with sth; **~wachsen** (*unreg*) *vi* to grow up; **~ziehen** (*unreg*) *vt* to pull nearer; (*aufziehen*) to raise; (*ausbilden*) to train; **jdn zu etw ~ziehen** to call upon sb to help in sth

herauf [hɛ'raʊf] *adv* up(ward(s)), up here; **~beschwören** (*unreg*) *vt* to conjure up, to evoke; **~bringen** (*unreg*) *vt* to bring up; **~setzen** *vt* (*Preise, Miete*) to raise, put up

heraus [hɛ'raʊs] *adv* out; **~bekommen** (*unreg*) *vt* to get out; (*fig*) to find *od* figure out; **~bringen** (*unreg*) *vt* to bring out; (*Geheimnis*) to elicit; **~finden** (*unreg*) *vt* to find out; **~fordern** *vt* to challenge; **H~forderung** *f* challenge; provocation; **~geben** (*unreg*) *vt* to hand over, to surrender; (*zurückgeben*) to give back; (*Buch*) to edit; (*veröffentlichen*) to publish; **H~geber (-s, -)** *m* editor; (*Verleger*) publisher; **~gehen** (*unreg*) *vi*: **aus sich ~gehen** to come out of one's shell; **~halten** (*unreg*) *vr*: **sich aus etw ~halten** to keep out of sth; **~hängen**[1] *vt* to hang out; **~hängen**[2] (*unreg*) *vi* to hang out; **~holen** *vt*: **~holen (aus)** to get out (of); **~kommen** (*unreg*) *vi* to come out; **dabei kommt nichts ~** nothing will come of it; **~nehmen** (*unreg*) *vt* to remove (from), take out (of); **sich** *dat* **etw ~nehmen** to take liberties; **~reißen** (*unreg*) *vt* to tear out; to pull out; **~rücken** *vt* (*Geld*) to fork out, to hand over; **mit etw ~rücken** (*fig*) to come out with sth; **~stellen** *vr*: **sich ~stellen (als)** to turn out (to be); **~suchen** *vt*: **sich** *dat* **jdn/etw ~suchen** to pick sb/sth out; **~ziehen** (*unreg*) *vt* to pull out, to extract

herb [herp] *adj* (slightly) bitter, acid; (*Wein*) dry; (*fig: schmerzlich*) bitter

herbei [her'baɪ] *adv* (over) here; **~führen** *vt* to bring about; **~schaffen** *vt* to procure

herbemühen ['he:rbəmy:ən] *vr* to take the trouble to come

Herberge ['hɛrbɛrgə] *f* shelter; hostel, inn

Herbergsmutter *f* warden

Herbergsvater *m* warden

herbitten (*unreg*) *vt* to ask to come (here)

Herbst [herpst] **(-(e)s, -e)** *m* autumn, fall (*US*); **h~lich** *adj* autumnal

Herd [he:rt] **(-(e)s, -e)** *m* cooker; (*fig, MED*) focus, centre

Herde ['he:rdə] *f* herd; (*Schafherde*) flock

herein [he'raɪn] *adv* in (here), here; **~!** come in!; **~bitten** (*unreg*) *vt* to ask in; **~brechen** (*unreg*) *vi* to set in; **~bringen** (*unreg*) *vt* to bring in; **~fallen** (*unreg*) *vi* to be caught, to be taken in; **~fallen auf** +*akk* to fall for; **~kommen** (*unreg*) *vi* to come in; **~lassen** (*unreg*) *vt* to admit; **~legen** *vt*: **jdn ~legen** to take sb in; **~platzen** (*umg*) *vi* to burst in

Her- *zW*: **~fahrt** *f* journey here; **h~fallen** (*unreg*) *vi*: **h~fallen über** +*akk* to fall upon; **~gang** *m* course of events; **h~geben**

(*unreg*) *vt* to give, to hand (over); **sich zu etw h~geben** to lend one's name to sth; **h~gehen** (*unreg*) *vi*: **hinter jdm h~gehen** to follow sb; **es geht hoch h~** there are a lot of goings-on; **h~halten** (*unreg*) *vt* to hold out; **h~halten müssen** (*umg*) to have to suffer; **h~hören** (*unreg*) *vi* to listen

Hering ['he:rɪŋ] **(-s, -e)** *m* herring

her- [her] *zW*: **~kommen** (*unreg*) *vi* to come; **komm mal ~!** come here!; **~kömmlich** *adj* traditional; **H~kunft (-, -künfte)** *f* origin; **H~kunftsland** *nt* country of origin; **H~kunftsort** *m* place of origin; **~laufen** (*unreg*) *vi*: **~laufen hinter** +*dat* to run after

hermetisch [her'me:tɪʃ] *adj* hermetic ♦ *adv* hermetically

her'nach *adv* afterwards

Heroin [hero'i:n] **(-s)** *nt* heroin

Herr [her] **(-(e)n, -en)** *m* master; (*Mann*) gentleman; (*REL*) Lord; (*vor Namen*) Mr.; **mein ~!** sir!; **meine ~en!** gentlemen!

Herren- *zW*: **~haus** *nt* mansion; **~konfektion** *f* menswear; **h~los** *adj* ownerless; **~toilette** *f* men's toilet *od* restroom (*US*)

herrichten ['he:rrɪçtən] *vt* to prepare

Herr- *zW*: **~in** *f* mistress; **h~isch** *adj* domineering; **h~lich** *adj* marvellous, splendid; **~lichkeit** *f* splendour, magnificence; **~schaft** *f* power, rule; (**~ und ~in**) master and mistress; **meine ~schaften!** ladies and gentlemen!

herrschen ['he:rʃən] *vi* to rule; (*bestehen*) to prevail, to be

Herrscher(in) **(-s, -)** *m(f)* ruler

her- *zW*: **~rühren** *vi* to arise, to originate; **~sagen** *vt* to recite; **~stellen** *vt* to make, to manufacture; **H~steller (-s, -)** *m* manufacturer; **H~stellung** *f* manufacture

herüber [he'ry:bər] *adv* over (here), across

herum [he'rum] *adv* about, (a)round; **um etw ~** around sth; **~führen** *vt* to show around; **~gehen** (*unreg*) *vi* to walk about; **um etw ~gehen** to walk *od* go round sth; **~kommen** (*unreg*) *vi* (*um Kurve etc*) to come round, to turn (round); **~kriegen**

(*umg*) *vt* to bring *od* talk around; **~lungern** (*umg*) *vi* to hang about *od* around; **~sprechen** (*unreg*) *vr* to get around, to be spread; **~treiben** *vi*, *vr* to drift about; **~ziehen** *vi*, *vr* to wander about

herunter [hɛ'rʊntər] *adv* downward(s), down (there); **~gekommen** *adj* run-down; **~kommen** (*unreg*) *vi* to come down; (*fig*) to come down in the world; **~machen** *vt* to take down; (*schimpfen*) to have a go at

hervor [hɛr'foːr] *adv* out, forth; **~bringen** (*unreg*) *vt* to produce; (*Wort*) to utter; **~gehen** (*unreg*) *vi* to emerge, to result; **~heben** (*unreg*) *vt* to stress; (*als Kontrast*) to set off; **~ragend** *adj* (*fig*) excellent; **~rufen** (*unreg*) *vt* to cause, to give rise to; **~treten** (*unreg*) *vi* to come out (*from behind/between/below*); (*Adern*) to be prominent

Herz [hɛrts] (**-ens, -en**) *nt* heart; (*KARTEN*) hearts *pl*; **~anfall** *m* heart attack; **~fehler** *m* heart defect; **h~haft** *adj* hearty

herziehen [ˈhɛːrtsiːən] (*unreg*) *vi*: **über jdn/ etw ~** (*umg: auch fig*) to pull sb/sth to pieces (*inf*)

Herz- *zW*: **~infarkt** *m* heart attack; **~klopfen** *nt* palpitation; **h~lich** *adj* cordial; **h~lichen Glückwunsch** congratulations *pl*; **h~liche Grüße** best wishes; **h~los** *adj* heartless

Herzog [ˈhɛrtsoːk] (**-(e)s, ̈e**) *m* duke; **~tum** *nt* duchy

Herz- *zW*: **~schlag** *m* heartbeat; (*MED*) heart attack; **~stillstand** *m* cardiac arrest; **h~zerreißend** *adj* heartrending

Hessen [ˈhɛsən] (**-s**) *nt* Hesse

hessisch *adj* Hessian

Hetze [ˈhɛtsə] *f* (*Eile*) rush; **h~n** *vt* to hunt; (*verfolgen*) to chase ♦ *vi* (*eilen*) to rush; **jdn/etw auf jdn/etw h~n** to set sb/sth on sb/sth; **h~n gegen** to stir up feeling against; **h~n zu** to agitate for

Heu [hɔy] (**-(e)s**) *nt* hay; **Geld wie ~** stacks of money

Heuch- [ˈhɔyç] *zW*: **~elei** [-ə'laɪ] *f* hypocrisy; **h~eln** *vt* to pretend, to feign ♦ *vi* to be hypocritical; **~ler(in)** (**-s, -**) *m(f)* hypocrite; **h~lerisch** *adj* hypocritical

heulen [ˈhɔylən] *vi* to howl; to cry

Heurige(r) [ˈhɔyrɪɡə(r)] *m* new wine

Heu- *zW*: **~schnupfen** *m* hay fever; **'~schrecke** *f* grasshopper; locust

heute [ˈhɔytə] *adv* today; **~ Abend/früh** this evening/morning

heutig [ˈhɔytɪç] *adj* today's

heutzutage [ˈhɔyttsutaːɡə] *adv* nowadays

Hexe [ˈhɛksə] *f* witch; **h~n** *vi* to practise witchcraft; **ich kann doch nicht h~n** I can't work miracles; **~nschuss** ▲ *m* lumbago; **~'rei** *f* witchcraft

Hieb [hiːp] (**-(e)s, -e**) *m* blow; (*Wunde*) cut, gash; (*Stichelei*) cutting remark; **~e bekommen** to get a thrashing

hielt *etc* [hiːlt] *vb siehe* **halten**

hier [hiːr] *adv* here; **~ bleiben** to stay here; **~ lassen** to leave here; **~auf** *adv* thereupon; (*danach*) after that; **~bei** *adv* herewith, enclosed; **~durch** *adv* by this means; (*örtlich*) through here; **~her** *adv* this way, here; **~hin** *adv* here; **~mit** *adv* hereby; **~nach** *adv* hereafter; **~von** *adv* about this, hereof; **~zulande, ~ zu Lande** *adv* in this country

hiesig [ˈhiːzɪç] *adj* of this place, local

hieß *etc* [hiːs] *vb siehe* **heißen**

Hilfe [ˈhɪlfə] *f* help; aid; **erste ~** first aid; **~!** help!

Hilf- *zW*: **h~los** *adj* helpless; **~losigkeit** *f* helplessness; **h~reich** *adj* helpful

Hilfs- *zW*: **~arbeiter** *m* labourer; **h~bedürftig** *adj* needy; **h~bereit** *adj* ready to help; **~kraft** *f* assistant, helper

hilfst [hɪlfst] *vb siehe* **helfen**

Himbeere [ˈhɪmbeːrə] *f* raspberry

Himmel [ˈhɪml] (**-s, -**) *m* sky; (*REL, auch fig*) heaven; **~bett** *nt* four-poster bed; **h~blau** *adj* sky-blue; **~fahrt** *f* Ascension; **~srichtung** *f* direction

himmlisch [ˈhɪmlɪʃ] *adj* heavenly

SCHLÜSSELWORT

hin [hɪn] *adv* **1** (*Richtung*): **hin und zurück** there and back; **hin und her** to and fro; **bis zur Mauer hin** up to the wall; **wo ist**

er hin? where has he gone?; **Geld hin, Geld her** money or no money
2 (*auf ... hin*): **auf meine Bitte hin** at my request; **auf seinen Rat hin** on the basis of his advice
3: mein Glück ist hin my happiness has gone

hinab [hɪˈnap] *adv* down; **~gehen** (*unreg*) *vi* to go down; **~sehen** (*unreg*) *vi* to look down

hinauf [hɪˈnaʊf] *adv* up; **~arbeiten** *vr* to work one's way up; **~steigen** (*unreg*) *vi* to climb

hinaus [hɪˈnaʊs] *adv* out; **~gehen** (*unreg*) *vi* to go out; **~gehen über** +*akk* to exceed; **~laufen** (*unreg*) *vi* to run out; **~laufen auf** +*akk* to come to, to amount to; **~schieben** (*unreg*) *vt* to put off, to postpone; **~werfen** (*unreg*) *vt* (*Gegenstand, Person*) to throw out; **~wollen** *vi* to want to go out; **~wollen auf** +*akk* to drive at, to get at

Hinblick [ˈhɪnblɪk] *m*: **in** *od* **im ~ auf** +*akk* in view of

hinder- [ˈhɪndər] *zW*: **~lich** *adj*: **~lich sein** to be a hindrance *od* nuisance; **~n** *vt* to hinder, to hamper; **jdn an etw** *dat* **~n** to prevent sb from doing sth; **H~nis** (**-ses, -se**) *nt* obstacle; **H~nisrennen** *nt* steeplechase

hindeuten [ˈhɪndɔʏtən] *vi*: **~ auf** +*akk* to point to

hindurch [hɪnˈdʊrç] *adv* through; across; (*zeitlich*) through(out)

hinein [hɪˈnaɪn] *adv* in; **~fallen** (*unreg*) *vi* to fall in; **~fallen in** +*akk* to fall into; **~gehen** (*unreg*) *vi* to go in; **~gehen in** +*akk* to go into, to enter; **~geraten** (*unreg*) *vi*: **~geraten in** +*akk* to get into; **~passen** *vi* to fit into; **~passen in** +*akk* to fit into; (*fig*) to fit in with; **~steigern** *vr* to get worked up; **~versetzen** *vr*: **sich ~versetzen in** +*akk* to put o.s. in the position of; **~ziehen** (*unreg*) *vt* to pull in ♦ *vi* to go in

hin- [ˈhɪn] *zW*: **~fahren** (*unreg*) *vi* to go; to drive ♦ *vt* to take; to drive; **H~fahrt** *f* journey there; **~fallen** (*unreg*) *vi* to fall (down); **~fällig** *adj* frail; (*fig: ungültig*) invalid; **H~flug** *m* outward flight; **H~gabe** *f* devotion; **~geben** (*unreg*) *vr* +*dat* to give o.s. up to, to devote o.s. to; **~gehen** (*unreg*) *vi* to go; (*Zeit*) to pass; **~halten** (*unreg*) *vt* to hold out; (*warten lassen*) to put off, to stall

hinken [ˈhɪŋkən] *vi* to limp; (*Vergleich*) to be unconvincing

hinkommen (*unreg*) *vi* (*an Ort*) to arrive

hin- [ˈhɪn] *zW*: **~legen** *vt* to put down ♦ *vr* to lie down; **~nehmen** (*unreg*) *vt* (*fig*) to put up with, to take; **H~reise** *f* journey out; **~reißen** (*unreg*) *vt* to carry away, to enrapture; **sich ~reißen lassen, etw zu tun** to get carried away and do sth; **~richten** *vt* to execute; **H~richtung** *f* execution; **~setzen** *vt* to put down ♦ *vr* to sit down; **~sichtlich** *präp* +*gen* with regard to; **~stellen** *vt* to put (down) ♦ *vr* to place o.s.

hinten [ˈhɪntən] *adv* at the back; behind; **~herum** *adv* round the back; (*fig*) secretly

hinter [ˈhɪntər] *präp* (+*dat od akk*) behind; (*: nach*) after; **~ jdm her sein** to be after sb; **H~achse** *f* rear axle; **H~bliebene(r)** *f(m)* surviving relative; **~e(r, s)** *adj* rear, back; **~einander** *adv* one after the other; **H~gedanke** *m* ulterior motive; **~gehen** (*unreg*) *vt* to deceive; **H~grund** *m* background; **H~halt** *m* ambush; **~hältig** *adj* underhand, sneaky; **~her** *adv* afterwards, after; **H~hof** *m* backyard; **H~kopf** *m* back of one's head; **~lassen** (*unreg*) *vt* to leave; **~legen** *vt* to deposit; **H~list** *f* cunning, trickery; (*Handlung*) trick, dodge; **~listig** *adj* cunning, crafty; **H~mann** *m* person behind; **H~rad** *nt* back wheel; **H~radantrieb** *m* (*AUT*) rear wheel drive; **~rücks** *adv* from behind; **H~tür** *f* back door; (*fig: Ausweg*) loophole; **~ziehen** (*unreg*) *vt* (*Steuern*) to evade

hinüber [hɪˈnyːbər] *adv* across, over; **~gehen** (*unreg*) *vi* to go over *od* across

hinunter [hɪˈnʊntər] *adv* down; **~bringen** (*unreg*) *vt* to take down; **~schlucken** *vt* *(auch fig)* to swallow; **~steigen** *(unreg)* vi to descend

Hinweg ['hɪnveːk] *m* journey out

hinweghelfen [hɪn'veːk-] *(unreg)* vi: **jdm über etw** *akk* **~** to help sb to get over sth

hinwegsetzen [hɪn'veːk-] *vr*: **sich ~ über** *+akk* to disregard

hin- ['hɪn] *zW*: **H~weis** (-es, -e) *m (Andeutung)* hint; *(Anweisung)* instruction; *(Verweis)* reference; **~weisen** *(unreg)* vi: **~weisen auf** *+akk (anzeigen)* to point to; *(sagen)* to point out, to refer to; **~werfen** *(unreg)* vt to throw down; **~ziehen** *(unreg)* vr *(fig)* to drag on

hinzu [hɪn'tsuː] *adv* in addition; **~fügen** vt to add; **~kommen** *(unreg)* vi *(Mensch)* to arrive, to turn up; *(Umstand)* to ensue

Hirn [hɪrn] (-(e)s, -e) *nt* brain(s); **~gespinst** (-(e)s, -e) *nt* fantasy

Hirsch [hɪrʃ] (-(e)s, -e) *m* stag

Hirt ['hɪrt] (-en, -en) *m* herdsman; *(Schafhirt, fig)* shepherd

hissen ['hɪsən] vt to hoist

Historiker [hɪs'toːrikər] (-s, -) *m* historian

historisch [hɪs'toːrɪʃ] *adj* historical

Hitze ['hɪtsə] (-) *f* heat; **h~beständig** *adj* heat-resistant; **h~frei** *adj*: **h~frei haben** *to have time off school because of excessively hot weather*; **~welle** *f* heat wave

hitzig ['hɪtsɪç] *adj* hot-tempered; *(Debatte)* heated

Hitzkopf *m* hothead

Hitzschlag *m* heatstroke

hl. *abk von* **heilig**

H-Milch ['haːmɪlç] *f* long-life milk

Hobby ['hɔbi] (-s, -s) *nt* hobby

Hobel ['hoːbəl] (-s, -) *m* plane; **~bank** *f* carpenter's bench; **h~n** vt, vi to plane; **~späne** *pl* wood shavings

Hoch (-s, -s) *nt (Ruf)* cheer; *(MET)* anticyclone

hoch [hoːx] *(attrib* **hohe(r, s))** *adj* high;
♦ *adv*: **~ achten** to respect; **~ begabt** extremely gifted; **~ dotiert** highly paid; **H~achtung** *f* respect, esteem; **~achtungsvoll** *adv* yours faithfully; **H~amt** *nt* high mass; **~arbeiten** vr to

work one's way up; **H~betrieb** *m* intense activity; *(COMM)* peak time; **H~burg** *f* stronghold; **H~deutsch** *nt* High German; **H~druck** *m* high pressure; **H~ebene** *f* plateau; **H~form** *f* top form; **H~gebirge** *nt* high mountains *pl*; **H~glanz** *m (PHOT)* high gloss print; **etw auf H~glanz bringen** to make sth sparkle like new; **~halten** *(unreg)* vt to hold up; *(fig)* to uphold, to cherish; **H~haus** *nt* multi-storey building; **~heben** *(unreg)* vt to lift (up); **H~konjunktur** *f* boom; **H~land** *nt* highlands *pl*; **~leben** *(unreg)* vi: **jdn ~leben lassen** to give sb three cheers; **H~mut** *m* pride; **~mütig** *adj* proud, haughty; **~näsig** *adj* stuck-up, snooty; **H~ofen** *m* blast furnace; **~prozentig** *adj (Alkohol)* strong; **H~rechnung** *f* projection; **H~saison** *f* high season; **H~schule** *f* college; university; **H~sommer** *m* middle of summer; **H~spannung** *f* high tension; **H~sprung** *m* high jump

höchst [høːçst] *adv* highly, extremely

Hochstapler ['hoːxʃtaːplər] (-s, -) *m* swindler

höchste(r, s) *adj* highest; *(äußerste)* extreme

Höchst- *zW*: **h~ens** *adv* at the most; **~geschwindigkeit** *f* maximum speed; **h~persönlich** *adv* in person; **~preis** *m* maximum price; **h~wahrscheinlich** *adv* most probably

Hoch- *zW*: **~verrat** *m* high treason; **~wasser** *nt* high water; *(Überschwemmung)* floods *pl*

Hochzeit ['hɔxtsait] (-, -en) *f* wedding; **~sreise** *f* honeymoon

hocken ['hɔkən] vi, vr to squat, to crouch

Hocker (-s, -) *m* stool

Höcker ['hœkər] (-s, -) *m* hump

Hoden ['hoːdən] (-s, -) *m* testicle

Hof [hoːf] (-(e)s, ⁺e) *m (Hinterhof)* yard; *(Bauernhof)* farm; *(Königshof)* court

hoff- ['hɔf] *zW*: **~en** vi: **~en (auf** *+akk***)** to hope (for); **~entlich** *adv* I hope, hopefully; **H~nung** *f* hope

Hoffnungs- *zW*: **h~los** *adj* hopeless;

~losigkeit f hopelessness; h~voll adj
hopeful

höflich ['høːflɪç] adj polite, courteous;
H~keit f courtesy, politeness

hohe(r, s) ['hoːə(r, s)] adj attrib siehe **hoch**

Höhe ['høːə] f height; (Anhöhe) hill

Hoheit ['hoːhaɪt] f (POL) sovereignty; (Titel)
Highness

Hoheits- zW: ~gebiet nt sovereign
territory; ~gewässer nt territorial waters
pl

Höhen- ['høːən] zW: ~luft f mountain air;
~messer (-s, -) m altimeter; ~sonne f
sun lamp; ~unterschied m difference in
altitude

Höhepunkt m climax

höher adj, adv higher

hohl [hoːl] adj hollow

Höhle ['høːlə] f cave, hole; (Mundhöhle)
cavity; (fig, ZOOL) den

Hohlmaß nt measure of volume

Hohn [hoːn] (-(e)s) m scorn

höhnisch adj scornful, taunting

holen ['hoːlən] vt to get, to fetch; (Atem) to
take; **jdn/etw ~ lassen** to send for sb/sth

Holland ['hɔlant] nt Holland; Holländer
['hɔlɛndər] m Dutchman; holländisch adj
Dutch

Hölle ['hœlə] f hell

höllisch ['hœlɪʃ] adj hellish, infernal

holperig ['hɔlpərɪç] adj rough, bumpy

Holunder [ho'lʊndər] (-s, -) m elder

Holz [hɔlts] (-es, ᵘer) nt wood

hölzern ['hœltsərn] adj (auch fig) wooden

Holz- zW: ~fäller (-s, -) m lumberjack,
woodcutter; h~ig adj woody; ~kohle f
charcoal; ~schuh m clog; ~weg m (fig)
wrong track; ~wolle f fine wood shavings
pl

Homöopathie [homøopa'tiː] f homeopathy

homosexuell [homozɛksu'ɛl] adj
homosexual

Honig ['hoːnɪç] (-s, -e) m honey; ~melone
f (BOT, KOCH) honeydew melon; ~wabe f
honeycomb

Honorar [hono'raːr] (-s, -e) nt fee

Hopfen ['hɔpfən] (-s, -) m hops pl

hopsen ['hɔpsən] vi to hop

Hörapparat m hearing aid

hörbar adj audible

horchen ['hɔrçən] vi to listen; (pej) to
eavesdrop

Horde ['hɔrdə] f horde

hör- ['høːr] zW: ~en vt, vi to hear; **Musik/
Radio ~en** to listen to music/the radio;
H~er (-s, -) m hearer; (RADIO) listener;
(UNIV) student; (Telefonhörer) receiver;
H~funk (-s) m radio; ~geschädigt
[-gəʃɛːdɪçt] adj hearing-impaired

Horizont [hori'tsɔnt] (-(e)s, -e) m horizon;
h~al [-'taːl] adj horizontal

Hormon [hɔr'moːn] (-s, -e) nt hormone

Hörmuschel f (TEL) earpiece

Horn [hɔrn] (-(e)s, ᵘer) nt horn; ~haut f
horny skin

Hornisse [hɔr'nɪsə] f hornet

Horoskop [horo'skoːp] (-s, -e) nt horoscope

Hörspiel nt radio play

Hort [hɔrt] (-(e)s, -e) m (SCH) day centre for
schoolchildren whose parents are at work

horten ['hɔrtən] vt to hoard

Hose ['hoːzə] f trousers pl, pants pl (US)

Hosen- zW: ~anzug m trouser suit; ~rock
m culottes pl; ~tasche f (trouser) pocket;
~träger m braces pl (BRIT), suspenders pl
(US)

Hostie ['hɔstiə] f (REL) host

Hotel [ho'tɛl] (-s, -s) nt hotel; ~ier (-s, -s)
[hotɛli'eː] m hotelkeeper, hotelier;
~verzeichnis nt hotel register

Hubraum ['huːp-] m (AUT) cubic capacity

hübsch [hypʃ] adj pretty, nice

Hubschrauber ['huːpʃraubər] (-s, -) m
helicopter

Huf ['huːf] (-(e)s, -e) m hoof; ~eisen nt
horseshoe

Hüft- ['hyft] zW: ~e f hip; ~gürtel m girdle;
~halter (-s, -) m girdle

Hügel ['hyːgəl] (-s, -) m hill; h~ig adj hilly

Huhn [huːn] (-(e)s, ᵘer) nt hen; (KOCH)
chicken

Hühner- ['hyːnər] zW: ~auge nt corn;
~brühe f chicken broth

Hülle ['hʏlə] f cover(ing); wrapping; **in ~**

Spelling Reform: ▲ new spelling △ old spelling (to be phased out)

und Fülle galore; **h~n** *vt*: **h~n (in** +*akk*) to cover (with); to wrap (in)

Hülse ['hʏlzə] *f* husk, shell; **~nfrucht** *f* pulse

human [hu'maːn] *adj* humane; **~i'tär** *adj* humanitarian; **H~i'tät** *f* humanity

Hummel ['hʊməl] (**-, -n**) *f* bumblebee

Hummer ['hʊmər] (**-s, -**) *m* lobster

Humor [hu'moːr] (**-s, -e**) *m* humour; **~ haben** to have a sense of humour; **~ist** [-'rɪst] *m* humorist; **h~voll** *adj* humorous

humpeln ['hʊmpəln] *vi* to hobble

Humpen ['hʊmpən] (**-s, -**) *m* tankard

Hund [hʊnt] (**-(e)s, -e**) *m* dog

Hunde- ['hʊndə] *zW*: **~hütte** *f* (dog) kennel; **h~müde** (*umg*) *adj* dog-tired

hundert ['hʊndərt] *num* hundred; **H~'jahrfeier** *f* centenary; **~prozentig** *adj, adv* one hundred per cent

Hundesteuer *f* dog licence fee

Hündin ['hʏndɪn] *f* bitch

Hunger ['hʊŋər] (**-s**) *m* hunger; **~ haben** to be hungry; **h~n** *vi* to starve; **~snot** *f* famine

hungrig ['hʊŋrɪç] *adj* hungry

Hupe ['huːpə] *f* horn; **h~n** *vi* to hoot, to sound one's horn

hüpfen ['hʏpfən] *vi* to hop; to jump

Hürde ['hʏrdə] *f* hurdle; (*für Schafe*) pen; **~nlauf** *m* hurdling

Hure ['huːrə] *f* whore

hurtig ['hʊrtɪç] *adj* brisk, quick ♦ *adv* briskly, quickly

huschen ['hʊʃən] *vi* to flit; to scurry

Husten ['huːstən] (**-s**) *m* cough; **h~** *vi* to cough; **~anfall** *m* coughing fit; **~bonbon** *m od* n cough drop; **~saft** *m* cough mixture

Hut¹ [huːt] (**-(e)s, ⸚e**) *m* hat

Hut² [huːt] (**-**) *f* care; **auf der ~ sein** to be on one's guard

hüten ['hyːtən] *vt* to guard ♦ *vr* to watch out; **sich ~, zu** to take care not to; **sich ~ (vor)** to beware (of), to be on one's guard (against)

Hütte ['hʏtə] *f* hut; cottage; (*Eisenhütte*) forge

Hütten- *zW*: **~käse** *m* (*KOCH*) cottage

cheese; **~schuh** *m* slipper sock

Hydrant [hy'drant] *m* hydrant

hydraulisch [hy'draʊlɪʃ] *adj* hydraulic

Hygiene [hygi'eːnə] (**-**) *f* hygiene

hygienisch [hygi'eːnɪʃ] *adj* hygienic

Hymne ['hʏmnə] *f* hymn; anthem

Hypno- [hyp'noː] *zW*: **~se** *f* hypnosis; **h~tisch** *adj* hypnotic; **~tiseur** [-ti'zøːr] *m* hypnotist; **h~ti'sieren** *vt* to hypnotize

Hypothek [hypo'teːk] (**-, -en**) *f* mortgage

Hypothese [hypo'teːzə] *f* hypothesis

Hysterie [hyste'riː] *f* hysteria

hysterisch [hys'teːrɪʃ] *adj* hysterical

I, i

ICE [iːtseː'|eː] *m abk* = **Intercity-Expresszug**

Ich (**-(s), -(s)**) *nt* self; (*PSYCH*) ego

ich [ɪç] *pron* I; **~ bins!** it's me!

Ideal [ide'aːl] (**-s, -e**) *nt* ideal; **ideal** *adj* ideal; **idealistisch** [-'lɪstɪʃ] *adj* idealistic

Idee [i'deː, *pl* i'deːən] *f* idea

identifizieren [idɛntifi'tsiːrən] *vt* to identify

identisch [i'dɛntɪʃ] *adj* identical

Identität [idɛnti'tɛːt] *f* identity

Ideo- [ideo] *zW*: **~loge** [-'loːgə] (**-n, -n**) *m* ideologist; **~logie** [-lo'giː] *f* ideology; **ideologisch** [-'loːgɪʃ] *adj* ideological

Idiot [idi'oːt] (**-en, -en**) *m* idiot; **idiotisch** *adj* idiotic

idyllisch [i'dʏlɪʃ] *adj* idyllic

Igel ['iːgəl] (**-s, -**) *m* hedgehog

ignorieren [ɪgno'riːrən] *vt* to ignore

ihm [iːm] (*dat von* **er, es**) *pron* (to) him; (to) it

ihn [iːn] (*akk von* **er, es**) *pron* him; it; **~en** (*dat von* **sie** *pl*) *pron* (to) them; **Ihnen** (*dat von* **Sie** *pl*) *pron* (to) you

---

SCHLÜSSELWORT

ihr [iːr] *pron* 1 (*nom pl*) you; **ihr seid es** it's you

2 (*dat von sie*) to her; **gib es ihr** give it to her; **er steht neben ihr** he is standing beside her

♦ *possessiv pron* 1 (*sg*) her; (: *bei Tieren,*

Dingen) its; **ihr Mann** her husband
2 (*pl*) their; **die Bäume und ihre Blätter**
the trees and their leaves

ihr(e) [iːr] *adj (sg)* her, its; (*pl*) their; **Ihr(e)**
adj your

ihre(r, s) *pron (sg)* hers, its; (*pl*) theirs;
Ihre(r, s) *pron* yours; **~r** (*gen von* **sie** *sg/pl*)
pron of her/them; **Ihrer** (*gen von* **Sie**) *pron*
of you; **~rseits** *adv* for her/their part;
~sgleichen *pron* people like her/them;
(*von Dingen*) others like it; **~twegen** *adv*
(*für sie*) for her/its/their sake; (*wegen ihr*) on
her/its/their account; **~twillen** *adv*: **um
~twillen = ihretwegen**

ihrige [ˈiːrɪɡə] *pron*: **der/die/das ~ od I~**
hers; its; theirs

illegal [ˈɪleɡaːl] *adj* illegal

Illusion [ɪluziˈoːn] *f* illusion

illusorisch [ɪluˈzoːrɪʃ] *adj* illusory

illustrieren [ɪlʊsˈtriːrən] *vt* to illustrate

Illustrierte *f* magazine

im [ɪm] = **in dem**

Imbiss ▲ [ˈɪmbɪs] **(-es, -e)** *m* snack;
~stube *f* snack bar

imitieren [imiˈtiːrən] *vt* to imitate

Imker [ˈɪmkər] **(-s, -)** *m* beekeeper

immatrikulieren [ɪmatrikuˈliːrən] *vi, vr* to
register

immer [ˈɪmər] *adv* always; **~ wieder** again
and again; **~ noch** still; **~ noch nicht** still
not; **für ~** forever; **~ wenn ich ...** every
time I ...; **~ schöner/trauriger** more and
more beautiful/sadder and sadder; **was/
wer (auch) ~** whatever/whoever; **~hin** *adv*
all the same; **~zu** *adv* all the time

Immobilien [ɪmoˈbiːliən] *pl* real estate *sg*;
~makler *m* estate agent (*BRIT*), realtor (*US*)

immun [ɪˈmuːn] *adj* immune; **Immunität**
[-iˈtɛːt] *f* immunity; **Immunsystem** *nt*
immune system

Imperfekt [ˈɪmpɛrfɛkt] **(-s, -e)** *nt* imperfect
(tense)

Impf- [ˈɪmpf] *zW*: **impfen** *vt* to vaccinate;
~stoff *m* vaccine, serum; **~ung** *f*
vaccination

imponieren [ɪmpoˈniːrən] *vi +dat* to impress

Import [ɪmˈpɔrt] **(-(e)s, -e)** *m* import; **~eur**
m importer; **importieren** *vt* to import

imposant [ɪmpoˈzant] *adj* imposing

impotent [ˈɪmpotɛnt] *adj* impotent

imprägnieren [ɪmprɛˈɡniːrən] *vt* to
(water)proof

improvisieren [ɪmproviˈziːrən] *vt, vi* to
improvise

Impuls [ɪmˈpʊls] **(-es, -e)** *m* impulse;
impulsiv [-ˈziːf] *adj* impulsive

imstande, im Stande [ɪmˈʃtandə] *adj*: **~
sein** to be in a position; (*fähig*) to be able

SCHLÜSSELWORT

in [ɪn] *präp +akk* 1 (*räumlich: wohin?*) in, into;
in die Stadt into town; **in die Schule
gehen** to go to school

2 (*zeitlich*): **bis ins 20. Jahrhundert** into *od*
up to the 20th century

♦ *präp +dat* 1 (*räumlich: wo*) in; **in der Stadt**
in town; **in der Schule sein** to be at
school

2 (*zeitlich: wann*): **in diesem Jahr** this year;
(*in jenem Jahr*) in that year; **heute in zwei
Wochen** two weeks today

Inanspruchnahme [ɪnˈʔanʃpruxnaːmə] *f*
(*+gen*) demands *pl* (on)

Inbegriff [ˈɪnbəɡrɪf] *m* embodiment,
personification; **inbegriffen** *adv* included

indem [ɪnˈdeːm] *konj* while; **~ man etw
macht** (*dadurch*) by doing sth

Inder(in) [ˈɪndər(ɪn)] *m(f)* Indian

indes(sen) [ɪnˈdɛs(ən)] *adv* however;
(*inzwischen*) meanwhile ♦ *konj* while

Indianer(in) [ɪndiˈaːnər(ɪn)] **(-s, -)** *m(f)*
American Indian, native American;
indianisch *adj* Red Indian, native

Indien [ˈɪndiən] *nt* India

indirekt [ˈɪndirɛkt] *adj* indirect

indisch [ˈɪndɪʃ] *adj* Indian

indiskret [ˈɪndɪskreːt] *adj* indiscreet

indiskutabel [ˈɪndɪskutaːbəl] *adj* out of the
question

individuell [ɪndividuˈɛl] *adj* individual

Individuum [ɪndiˈviːduʊm] **(-s, -en)** *nt*
individual

Indiz [ɪn'diːts] (**-es, -ien**) nt (JUR) clue; **~ (für)** sign (of)

industrialisieren [ɪndʊstriali'ziːrən] vt to industrialize

Industrie [ɪndʊs'triː] f industry ♦ in zW industrial; **~gebiet** nt industrial area; **~- und Handelskammer** f chamber of commerce; **~zweig** m branch of industry

ineinander [ɪn|aɪ'nandər] adv in(to) one another od each other

Infarkt [ɪn'farkt] (**-(e)s, -e**) m coronary (thrombosis)

Infektion [ɪnfɛktsi'oːn] f infection; **~skrankheit** f infectious disease

Infinitiv ['ɪnfinitiːf] (**-s, -e**) m infinitive

infizieren [ɪnfi'tsiːrən] vt to infect ♦ vr: **sich (bei jdm) ~** to be infected (by sb)

Inflation [ɪnflatsi'oːn] f inflation

inflationär [ɪnflatsio'nɛːr] adj inflationary

infolge [ɪn'fɔlɡə] präp +gen as a result of, owing to; **~dessen** [-'dɛsən] adv consequently

Informatik [ɪnfɔr'maːtɪk] f information studies pl

Information [ɪnfɔrmatsi'oːn] f information no pl

informieren [ɪnfɔr'miːrən] vt to inform ♦ vr: **sich ~ (über +akk)** to find out (about)

infrage, in Frage adv: **~ stellen** to question sth; **nicht ~ kommen** to be out of the question

Ingenieur [ɪnʒeni'øːr] m engineer; **~schule** f school of engineering

Ingwer ['ɪŋvər] (**-s**) m ginger

Inh. abk (= Inhaber) prop.; (= Inhalt) contents

Inhaber(in) ['ɪnhaːbər(ɪn)] (**-s, -**) m(f) owner; (Hausinhaber) occupier; (Lizenzinhaber) licensee, holder; (FIN) bearer

inhaftieren [ɪnhaf'tiːrən] vt to take into custody

inhalieren [ɪnha'liːrən] vt, vi to inhale

Inhalt ['ɪnhalt] (**-(e)s, -e**) m contents pl; (eines Buchs etc) content; (MATH) area; volume; **inhaltlich** adj as regards content

Inhalts- zW: **~angabe** f summary; **~verzeichnis** nt table of contents

inhuman ['ɪnhumaːn] adj inhuman

Initiative [initsia'tiːvə] f initiative

inklusive [ɪnklu'ziːvə] präp +gen inclusive of ♦ adv inclusive

In-Kraft-Treten [ɪn'krafttreːtən] (**-s**) nt coming into force

Inland ['ɪnlant] (**-(e)s**) nt (GEOG) inland; (POL, COMM) home (country); **~flug** m domestic flight

inmitten [ɪn'mɪtən] präp +gen in the middle of; **~ von** amongst

innehaben ['ɪnəhaːbən] (unreg) vt to hold

innen ['ɪnən] adv inside; **Innenarchitekt** m interior designer; **Inneneinrichtung** f (interior) furnishings pl; **Innenhof** m inner courtyard; **Innenminister** m minister of the interior, Home Secretary (BRIT); **Innenpolitik** f domestic policy; **~politisch** adj (Entwicklung, Lage) internal, domestic; **Innenstadt** f town/city centre

inner- ['ɪnər] zW: **~e(r, s)** adj inner; (im Körper, inländisch) internal; **Innere(s)** nt inside; (Mitte) centre; (fig) heart; **Innereien** [-'raɪən] pl innards; **~halb** adv within; (räumlich) inside ♦ präp +gen within; inside; **~lich** adj internal; (geistig) inward; **~ste(r, s)** adj innermost; **Innerste(s)** nt heart

innig ['ɪnɪç] adj (Freundschaft) close

inoffiziell ['ɪn|ɔfitsiɛl] adj unofficial

ins [ɪns] = **in das**

Insasse ['ɪnzasə] (**-n, -n**) m (Anstalt) inmate; (AUT) passenger

Insassenversicherung f passenger insurance

insbesondere [ɪnsbə'zɔndərə] adv (e)specially

Inschrift ['ɪnʃrɪft] f inscription

Insekt [ɪn'zɛkt] (**-(e)s, -en**) nt insect

Insektenschutzmittel nt insect repellent

Insel ['ɪnzəl] (**-, -n**) f island

Inser- zW: **~at** [ɪnze'raːt] (**-(e)s, -e**) nt advertisement; **~ent** [ɪnze'rɛnt] m advertiser; **inserieren** [ɪnze'riːrən] vt, vi to advertise

insgeheim [ɪnsɡə'haɪm] adv secretly

insgesamt [ɪnsɡə'zamt] adv altogether, all in all

insofern [ɪnzo'fɛrn] *adv* in this respect ♦ *konj* if; *(deshalb)* (and) so; ~ **als** in so far as

insoweit [ɪnzo'vaɪt] = **insofern**

Installateur [ɪnstala'tøːr] *m* electrician; plumber

Instandhaltung [ɪn'ʃtanthaltʊŋ] *f* maintenance

inständig [ɪn'ʃtɛndɪç] *adj* urgent

Instandsetzung [ɪn'ʃtant-] *f* overhaul; *(eines Gebäudes)* restoration

Instanz [ɪn'stants] *f* authority; *(JUR)* court

Instinkt [ɪn'stɪŋkt] **(-(e)s, -e)** *m* instinct; **instinktiv** [-'tiːf] *adj* instinctive

Institut [ɪnsti'tuːt] **(-(e)s, -e)** *nt* institute

Instrument [ɪnstru'mɛnt] *nt* instrument

Intell- [ɪntɛl] *zW:* **intellektuell** [-ɛktu'ɛl] *adj* intellectual; **intelligent** [-i'gɛnt] *adj* intelligent; ~**igenz** [-i'gɛnts] *f* intelligence; *(Leute)* intelligentsia *pl*

Intendant [ɪntɛn'dant] *m* director

intensiv [ɪntɛn'ziːf] *adj* intensive; **Intensivstation** *f* intensive care unit

Intercity- [ɪntər'sɪtɪ] *zW:* ~-**Expresszug** ▲ *m* high-speed train; ~-**Zug** *m* intercity (train); ~-**Zuschlag** *m* intercity supplement

Interess- *zW:* **interessant** [ɪntərɛ'sant] *adj* interesting; **interessanterweise** *adv* interestingly enough; ~**e** [ɪntə'rɛsə] **(-s, -n)** *nt* interest; ~**e haben an** +*dat* to be interested in; ~**ent** [ɪntərɛ'sɛnt] *m* interested party; **interessieren** [ɪntərɛ'siːrən] *vt* to interest ♦ *vr:* **sich interessieren für** to be interested in

intern [ɪn'tɛrn] *adj (Angelegenheiten, Regelung)* internal; *(Besprechung)* private

Internat [ɪntər'naːt] **(-(e)s, -e)** *nt* boarding school

inter- [ɪntər] *zW:* ~**national** [-natsio'naːl] *adj* international; **I~net** ['ɪntərnɛt] **(-s)** *nt:* **das I~net** the Internet; **I~net-Café** *nt* Internet café; ~**pretieren** [-pre'tiːrən] *vt* to interpret; **Intervall** [-'val] **(-s, -e)** *nt* interval; **Interview** [-'vjuː] **(-s, -s)** *nt* interview; ~**viewen** [-'vjuːən] *vt* to interview

intim [ɪn'tiːm] *adj* intimate; **Intimität** *f* intimacy

intolerant ['ɪntolerant] *adj* intolerant

Intrige [ɪn'triːgə] *f* intrigue, plot

Invasion [ɪnvazi'oːn] *f* invasion

Inventar [ɪnvɛn'taːr] **(-s, -e)** *nt* inventory

Inventur [ɪnvɛn'tuːr] *f* stocktaking; ~ **machen** to stocktake

investieren [ɪnvɛs'tiːrən] *vt* to invest

inwie- [ɪnvi'] *zW:* ~**fern** *adv* how far, to what extent; ~**weit** *adv* how far, to what extent

inzwischen [ɪn'tsvɪʃən] *adv* meanwhile

Irak [i'raːk] **(-s)** *m:* **der ~** Iraq; **irakisch** *adj* Iraqi

Iran [i'raːn] **(-s)** *m:* **der ~** Iran; **iranisch** *adj* Iranian

irdisch ['ɪrdɪʃ] *adj* earthly

Ire ['iːrə] **(-n, -n)** *m* Irishman

irgend ['ɪrgənt] *adv* at all; **wann/was/wer ~** whenever/whatever/whoever; ~**etwas** *pron* something/anything; ~**jemand** *pron* somebody/anybody; ~**ein(e, s)** *adj* some, any; ~**einmal** *adv* sometime or other; *(fragend)* ever; ~**wann** *adv* sometime; ~**wie** *adv* somehow; ~**wo** *adv* somewhere; anywhere; ~**wohin** *adv* somewhere; anywhere

Irin ['iːrɪn] *f* Irishwoman

Irland ['ɪrlant] **(-s)** *nt* Ireland

Ironie [iro'niː] *f* irony; **ironisch** [i'roːnɪʃ] *adj* ironic(al)

irre ['ɪrə] *adj* crazy, mad; **Irre(r)** *f(m)* lunatic; ~**führen** *vt* to mislead; ~**machen** *vt* to confuse; ~**n** *vi* to be mistaken; *(umherirren)* to wander, to stray ♦ *vr* to be mistaken; **Irrenanstalt** *f* lunatic asylum

Irr- *zW:* ~**garten** *m* maze; **i~ig** ['ɪrɪç] *adj* incorrect, wrong; **i~itieren** [ɪri'tiːrən] *vt (verwirren)* to confuse; *(ärgern)* to irritate; *(stören)* to annoy; **irrsinnig** *adj* mad, crazy; *(umg)* terrific; ~**tum** **(-s, -tümer)** *m* mistake, error; **irrtümlich** *adj* mistaken

Island ['iːslant] **(-s)** *nt* Iceland

Isolation [izolatsi'oːn] *f* isolation; *(ELEK)* insulation

Isolier- [izo'liːr] *zW:* ~**band** *nt* insulating tape; **isolieren** *vt* to isolate; *(ELEK)* to insulate; ~**station** *f (MED)* isolation ward;

~ung f isolation; (ELEK) insulation
Israel ['ɪsraeːl] (-s) nt Israel; ~i (-s, -s) [-'eːli]
m Israeli; **israelisch** adj Israeli
isst ▲ [ɪst] vb siehe **essen**
ist [ɪst] vb siehe **sein**
Italien [i'taːlɪən] (-s) nt Italy; ~er(in) (-s)
m(f) Italian; **italienisch** adj Italian
i. V. abk = **in Vertretung**

J, j

ja [jaː] adv 1 yes; **haben Sie das gesehen? -
ja** did you see it? - yes(, I did); **ich glaube
ja** (yes) I think so
2 (fragend) really?; **ich habe gekündigt -
ja?** I've quit - have you?; **du kommst, ja?**
you're coming, aren't you?
3: **sei ja vorsichtig** do be careful; **Sie
wissen ja, dass ...** as you know, ...; **tu
das ja nicht!** don't do that!; **ich habe es
ja gewusst** I just knew it; **ja, also ...** well
you see ...

Jacht [jaxt] (-, -en) f yacht
Jacke ['jakə] f jacket; (Wolljacke) cardigan
Jackett [ʒa'kɛt] (-s, -s od -e) nt jacket
Jagd [jaːkt] (-, -en) f hunt; (Jagen) hunting;
~beute f kill; ~flugzeug nt fighter;
~hund m hunting dog
jagen ['jaːɡən] vi to hunt; (eilen) to race ♦ vt
to hunt; (wegjagen) to drive (off); (verfolgen)
to chase
Jäger ['jɛːɡər] (-s, -) m hunter; ~schnitzel
nt (KOCH) pork in a spicy sauce with
mushrooms
jäh [jɛː] adj sudden, abrupt; (steil) steep,
precipitous
Jahr [jaːr] (-(e)s, -e) nt year; j~elang adv for
years
Jahres- zW: ~abonnement nt annual
subscription; ~abschluss ▲ m end of the
year; (COMM) annual statement of account;
~beitrag m annual subscription; ~karte f

yearly season ticket; ~tag m anniversary;
~wechsel m turn of the year; ~zahl f
date; year; ~zeit f season
Jahr- zW: ~gang m age group; (von Wein)
vintage; ~'hundert (-s, -e) nt century;
jährlich ['jɛːrlɪç] adj, adv yearly; ~markt m
fair; ~tausend nt millennium; ~'zehnt nt
decade
Jähzorn ['jɛːtsɔrn] m sudden anger; hot
temper; j~ig adj hot-tempered
Jalousie [ʒalu'ziː] f venetian blind
Jammer ['jamər] (-s) m misery; **es ist ein ~,
dass ...** it is a crying shame that ...
jämmerlich ['jɛmərlɪç] adj wretched,
pathetic
jammern vi to wail ♦ vt unpers: **es jammert
jdn** it makes sb feel sorry
Januar ['januaːr] (-(s), -e) m January
Japan ['jaːpan] (-s) nt Japan; ~er(in)
[-'paːnər(ɪn)] (-s) m(f) Japanese; j~isch adj
Japanese
jäten ['jɛːtən] vt: **Unkraut ~** to weed
jauchzen ['jauxtsən] vi to rejoice
jaulen ['jaulən] vi to howl
jawohl [ja'voːl] adv yes (of course)
Jawort ['jaːvɔrt] nt consent
Jazz [dʒɛz] (-) m Jazz

je [jeː] adv 1 (jemals) ever; **hast du so was je
gesehen?** did you ever see anything like
it?
2 (jeweils) every, each; **sie zahlten je 3
Mark** they paid 3 marks each
♦ konj 1: **je nach** depending on; **je
nachdem** it depends; **je nachdem, ob ...**
depending on whether ...
2: **je eher, desto** od **umso besser** the
sooner the better

Jeans [dʒiːnz] pl jeans
jede(r, s) ['jeːdə(r, s)] adj every, each ♦ pron
everybody; (~ Einzelne) each; **~s Mal** every
time, each time; **ohne ~ x** without any x
jedenfalls adv in any case
jedermann pron everyone
jederzeit adv at any time

jedoch [je'dɔx] *adv* however

jeher ['je:he:r] *adv*: **von/seit ~** always

jemals ['je:ma:ls] *adv* ever

jemand ['je:mant] *pron* somebody; anybody

jene(r, s) ['je:nə(r, s)] *adj* that ♦ *pron* that one

jenseits ['je:nzaɪts] *adv* on the other side ♦ *präp +gen* on the other side of, beyond

Jenseits *nt*: **das ~** the hereafter, the beyond

jetzig ['jetsɪç] *adj* present

jetzt [jetst] *adv* now

jeweilig *adj* respective

jeweils *adv*: **~ zwei zusammen** two at a time; **zu ~ 5 Euros** at 5 euros each; **~ das Erste** the first each time

Jh. *abk* = **Jahrhundert**

Job [dʒɔp] (**-s, -s**) *m* (*umg*) job; **j~ben** ['dʒɔbən] *vi* (*umg*) to work

Jockei ['dʒɔke] (**-s, -s**) *m* jockey

Jod [jo:t] (**-(e)s**) *nt* iodine

jodeln ['jo:dəln] *vi* to yodel

joggen ['dʒɔgən] *vi* to jog

Jog(h)urt ['jo:gʊrt] (**-s, -s**) *m od nt* yogurt

Johannisbeere [jo'hanɪsbe:rə] *f* redcurrant; **schwarze ~** blackcurrant

johlen ['jo:lən] *vi* to yell

jonglieren [ʒõ'gli:rən] *vi* to juggle

Journal- [ʒurnal] *zW*: **~ismus** [-'lɪsmʊs] *m* journalism; **~ist(in)** [-'lɪst(ɪn)] *m(f)* journalist; **journa'listisch** *adj* journalistic

Jubel ['ju:bəl] (**-s**) *m* rejoicing; **j~n** *vi* to rejoice

Jubiläum [jubi'lɛ:ʊm] (**-s, Jubiläen**) *nt* anniversary; jubilee

jucken ['jʊkən] *vi* to itch ♦ *vt*: **es juckt mich am Arm** my arm is itching

Juckreiz ['jʊkraɪts] *m* itch

Jude ['ju:də] (**-n, -n**) *m* Jew

Juden- *zW*: **~tum** (**-**) *nt* Judaism; Jewry; **~verfolgung** *f* persecution of the Jews

Jüdin ['jy:dɪn] *f* Jewess

jüdisch ['jy:dɪʃ] *adj* Jewish

Jugend ['ju:gənt] (**-**) *f* youth; **j~frei** *adj* (*CINE*) U (*BRIT*), G (*US*), suitable for children; **~herberge** *f* youth hostel; **~herbergsausweis** *m* youth hostelling

card; **j~lich** *adj* youthful; **~liche(r)** *f(m)* teenager, young person

Jugoslaw- [jugo'sla:v] *zW*: **~ien** (**-s**) *nt* Yugoslavia; **j~isch** *adj* Yugoslavian

Juli ['ju:li] (**-(s), -s**) *m* July

jun. *abk* (= **junior**) jr.

jung [jʊŋ] *adj* young; **J~e** (**-n, -n**) *m* boy, lad ♦ *nt* young animal; **J~en** *pl* (*von Tier*) young *pl*

Jünger ['jʏŋər] (**-s, -**) *m* disciple

jünger *adj* younger

Jung- *zW*: **~frau** *f* virgin; (*ASTROL*) Virgo; **~geselle** *m* bachelor; **~gesellin** *f* unmarried woman

jüngst [jʏŋst] *adv* lately, recently; **~e(r, s)** *adj* youngest; (*neueste*) latest

Juni ['ju:ni] (**-(s), -s**) *m* June

Junior ['ju:niɔr] (**-s, -en**) *m* junior

Jurist [ju'rɪst] *m* jurist, lawyer; **j~isch** *adj* legal

Justiz [jʊs'ti:ts] (**-**) *f* justice; **~beamte(r)** *m* judicial officer; **~irrtum** *m* miscarriage of justice; **~minister** *m* ≈ Lord (High) Chancellor (*BRIT*), ≈ Attorney General (*US*)

Juwel [ju've:l] (**-s, -en**) *nt od m* jewel

Juwelier [juve'li:r] (**-s, -e**) *m* jeweller; **~geschäft** *nt* jeweller's (shop)

Jux [jʊks] (**-es, -e**) *m* joke, lark

K, k

Kabarett [kaba'rɛt] (**-s, -e od -s**) *nt* cabaret; **~ist** [-'tɪst] *m* cabaret artiste

Kabel ['ka:bəl] (**-s, -**) *nt* (*ELEK*) wire; (*stark*) cable; **~fernsehen** *nt* cable television

Kabeljau ['ka:bəljaʊ] (**-s, -e od -s**) *m* cod

Kabine [ka'bi:nə] *f* cabin; (*Zelle*) cubicle

Kabinenbahn *f* cable railway

Kabinett [kabi'nɛt] (**-s, -e**) *nt* (*POL*) cabinet

Kachel ['kaxəl] (**-, -n**) *f* tile; **k~n** *vt* to tile; **~ofen** *m* tiled stove

Käfer ['kɛ:fər] (**-s, -**) *m* beetle

Kaffee ['kafe] (**-s, -s**) *m* coffee; **~haus** *nt* café; **~kanne** *f* coffeepot; **~löffel** *m* coffee spoon

Käfig ['kɛ:fɪç] (**-s, -e**) *m* cage

kahl [ka:l] *adj* bald; **~ geschoren** shaven, shorn; **~köpfig** *adj* bald-headed

Kahn [ka:n] (**-(e)s, ⁻e**) *m* boat, barge

Kai [kaɪ] (**-s, -e** *od* **-s**) *m* quay

Kaiser ['kaɪzər] (**-s, -**) *m* emperor; **~in** *f* empress; **k~lich** *adj* imperial; **~reich** *nt* empire; **~schnitt** *m* (*MED*) Caesarian (section)

Kakao [ka'ka:o] (**-s, -s**) *m* cocoa

Kaktee [kak'te:(ə)] (**-, -n**) *f* cactus

Kaktus ['kaktʊs] (**-, -teen**) *m* cactus

Kalb [kalp] (**-(e)s, ⁻er**) *nt* calf; **k~en** ['kalbən] *vi* to calve; **~fleisch** *nt* veal; **~sleder** *nt* calf(skin)

Kalender [ka'lɛndər] (**-s, -**) *m* calendar; (*Taschenkalender*) diary

Kaliber [ka'li:bər] (**-s, -**) *nt* (*auch fig*) calibre

Kalk [kalk] (**-(e)s, -e**) *m* lime; (*BIOL*) calcium; **~stein** *m* limestone

kalkulieren [kalku'li:rən] *vt* to calculate

Kalorie [kalo'ri:] *f* calorie

kalt [kalt] *adj* cold; **mir ist (es) ~** I am cold; **~ bleiben** (*fig*) to remain unmoved; **~ stellen** to chill; **~blütig** *adj* cold-blooded; (*ruhig*) cool

Kälte ['kɛltə] (**-**) *f* cold; coldness; **~grad** *m* degree of frost *od* below zero; **~welle** *f* cold spell

kalt- *zW:* **~herzig** *adj* cold-hearted; **~schnäuzig** *adj* cold, unfeeling; **~stellen** *vt* (*fig*) to leave out in the cold

kam *etc* [ka:m] *vb siehe* **kommen**

Kamel [ka'me:l] (**-(e)s, -e**) *nt* camel

Kamera ['kaməra] (**-, -s**) *f* camera

Kamerad [kamə'ra:t] (**-en, -en**) *m* comrade, friend; **~schaft** *f* comradeship; **k~schaftlich** *adj* comradely

Kameramann (**-(e)s, -männer**) *m* cameraman

Kamille [ka'mɪlə] *f* camomile; **~ntee** *m* camomile tea

Kamin [ka'mi:n] (**-s, -e**) *m* (*außen*) chimney; (*innen*) fireside, fireplace; **~kehrer** (**-s, -**) *m* chimney sweep

Kamm [kam] (**-(e)s, ⁻e**) *m* comb; (*Bergkamm*) ridge; (*Hahnenkamm*) crest

kämmen ['kɛmən] *vt* to comb ♦ *vr* to comb one's hair

Kammer ['kamər] (**-, -n**) *f* chamber; small bedroom

Kammerdiener *m* valet

Kampagne [kam'panjə] *f* campaign

Kampf [kampf] (**-(e)s, ⁻e**) *m* fight, battle; (*Wettbewerb*) contest; (*fig: Anstrengung*) struggle; **k~bereit** *adj* ready for action

kämpfen ['kɛmpfən] *vi* to fight

Kämpfer (**-s, -**) *m* fighter, combatant

Kampf- *zW:* **~handlung** *f* action; **k~los** *adj* without a fight; **~richter** *m* (*SPORT*) referee; (*TENNIS*) umpire; **~stoff** *m:* **chemischer/biologischer ~stoff** chemical/biological weapon

Kanada ['kanada] (**-s**) *nt* Canada; **Kanadier(in)** (**-s, -**) [ka'na:diər(ɪn)] *m(f)* Canadian; **ka'nadisch** *adj* Canadian

Kanal [ka'na:l] (**-s, Kanäle**) *m* (*Fluss*) canal; (*Rinne, Ärmelkanal*) channel; (*für Abfluss*) drain; **~inseln** *pl* Channel Islands; **~isation** [-izatsi'o:n] *f* sewage system; **~tunnel** *m:* **der ~tunnel** the Channel Tunnel

Kanarienvogel [ka'na:riənfo:gəl] *m* (*ZOOL*) canary

kanarisch [ka'na:rɪʃ] *adj:* **K~e Inseln** Canary Islands, Canaries

Kandi- [kandi] *zW:* **~dat** [-'da:t] (**-en, -en**) *m* candidate; **~datur** [-da'tu:r] *f* candidature, candidacy; **k~dieren** [-'di:rən] *vi* to stand, to run

Kandis(zucker) ['kandɪs(tsʊkər)] (**-**) *m* candy

Känguru ▲ ['kɛŋguru] (**-s, -s**) *nt* kangaroo

Kaninchen [ka'ni:nçən] *nt* rabbit

Kanister [ka'nɪstər] (**-s, -**) *m* can, canister

Kännchen ['kɛnçən] *nt* pot

Kanne ['kanə] *f* (*Krug*) jug; (*Kaffeekanne*) pot; (*Milchkanne*) churn; (*Gießkanne*) can

kannst *etc* [kanst] *vb siehe* **können**

Kanone [ka'no:nə] *f* gun; (*HIST*) cannon; (*fig: Mensch*) ace

Kantate [kan'ta:tə] *f* cantaga

Kante ['kantə] *f* edge

Kantine [kan'ti:nə] *f* canteen

Kanton [kan'to:n] (**-s, -e**) *m* canton

Kanton
---

i **Kanton** is the term for a state or region of Switzerland. Under the Swiss constitution the **Kantone** enjoy considerable autonomy. The Swiss **Kantone** are Aargau, Appenzell, Basel, Bern, Fribourg, Geneva, Glarus, Graubünden, Luzern, Neuchâtel, St. Gallen, Schaffhausen, Schwyz, Solothurn, Ticino, Thurgau, Unterwalden, Uri, Valais, Vaud, Zug and Zürich.

Kanu [ˈkaːnu] (**-s, -s**) *nt* canoe
Kanzel [ˈkantsəl] (**-, -n**) *f* pulpit
Kanzler [ˈkantslər] (**-s, -**) *m* chancellor
Kap [kap] (**-s, -s**) *nt* cape (GEOG)
Kapazität [kapatsiˈtɛːt] *f* capacity; (*Fachmann*) authority
Kapelle [kaˈpɛlə] *f* (*Gebäude*) chapel; (MUS) band
kapieren [kaˈpiːrən] (*umg*) *vt, vi* to get, to understand
Kapital [kapiˈtaːl] (**-s, -e** *od* **-ien**) *nt* capital; **~anlage** *f* investment; **~ismus** [-ˈlɪsmʊs] *m* capitalism; **~ist** [-ˈlɪst] *m* capitalist; **k~istisch** *adj* capitalist
Kapitän [kapiˈtɛːn] (**-s, -e**) *m* captain
Kapitel [kaˈpɪtəl] (**-s, -**) *nt* chapter
Kapitulation [kapitulatsiˈoːn] *f* capitulation
kapitulieren [kapituˈliːrən] *vi* to capitulate
Kappe [ˈkapə] *f* cap; (*Kapuze*) hood
kappen *vt* to cut
Kapsel [ˈkapsəl] (**-, -n**) *f* capsule
kaputt [kaˈpʊt] (*umg*) *adj* kaput, broken; (*Person*) exhausted, finished; **am Auto ist etwas ~** there's something wrong with the car; **~gehen** (*unreg*) *vi* to break; (*Schuhe*) to fall apart; (*Firma*) to go bust; (*Stoff*) to wear out; (*sterben*) to cop it (*umg*); **~machen** *vt* to break; (*Mensch*) to exhaust, to wear out
Kapuze [kaˈpuːtsə] *f* hood
Karamell ▲ [karaˈmɛl] (**-s**) *m* caramel; **~bonbon** *m od nt* toffee
Karate [kaˈraːtə] (**-s**) *nt* karate
Karawane [karaˈvaːnə] *f* caravan

Kardinal [kardiˈnaːl] (**-s, Kardinäle**) *m* cardinal; **~zahl** *f* cardinal number
Karfreitag [kaːrˈfraitaːk] *m* Good Friday
karg [kark] *adj* (*Landschaft, Boden*) barren; (*Lohn*) meagre
kärglich [ˈkɛrklɪç] *adj* poor, scanty
Karibik [kaˈriːbik] (**-**) *f*: **die ~** the Caribbean
karibisch [kaˈriːbɪʃ] *adj*: **K~e Inseln** Caribbean Islands
kariert [kaˈriːrt] *adj* (*Stoff*) checked; (*Papier*) squared
Karies [ˈkaːriɛs] (**-**) *f* caries
Karikatur [karikaˈtuːr] *f* caricature; **~ist** [-ˈrɪst] *m* cartoonist
Karneval [ˈkarnəval] (**-s, -e** *od* **-s**) *m* carnival

Karneval
---

i **Karneval** is the time immediately before Lent when people gather to eat, drink and generally have fun before the fasting begins. **Rosenmontag**, the day before Shrove Tuesday, is the most important day of **Karneval** on the Rhine. Most firms take a day's holiday on that day to enjoy the celebrations. In South Germany and Austria **Karneval** is called **Fasching**.

Karo [ˈkaːro] (**-s, -s**) *nt* square; (KARTEN) diamonds
Karosserie [karɔsəˈriː] *f* (AUT) body(work)
Karotte [kaˈrɔtə] *f* carrot
Karpfen [ˈkarpfən] (**-s, -**) *m* carp
Karre [ˈkarə] *f* cart, barrow
Karren (**-s, -**) *m* cart, barrow
Karriere [kariˈɛːrə] *f* career; **~ machen** to get on, to get to the top; **~macher** (**-s, -**) *m* careerist
Karte [ˈkartə] *f* card; (*Landkarte*) map; (*Speisekarte*) menu; (*Eintrittskarte, Fahrkarte*) ticket; **alles auf eine ~ setzen** to put all one's eggs in one basket
Kartei [karˈtai] *f* card index; **~karte** *f* index card
Kartell [karˈtɛl] (**-s, -e**) *nt* cartel
Karten- *zW*: **~spiel** *nt* card game; pack of cards; **~telefon** *nt* cardphone;

~vorverkauf m advance booking office

Kartoffel [kar'tɔfəl] (-, -n) f potato; ~brei m mashed potatoes pl; ~mus nt mashed potatoes pl; ~püree nt mashed potatoes pl; ~salat m potato salad

Karton [kar'tõː] (-s, -s) m cardboard; (Schachtel) cardboard box; k~iert [karto'niːrt] adj hardback

Karussell [karu'sɛl] (-s, -s) nt roundabout (BRIT), merry-go-round

Karwoche ['kaːrvɔxə] f Holy Week

Käse ['kɛːzə] (-s, -) m cheese; ~glocke f cheese (plate) cover; ~kuchen m cheesecake

Kaserne [ka'zɛrnə] f barracks pl; ~nhof m parade ground

Kasino [ka'ziːno] (-s, -s) nt club; (MIL) officers' mess; (Spielkasino) casino

Kaskoversicherung ['kasko-] f (Teilkasko) ≈ third party, fire and theft insurance; (Vollkasko) ≈ fully comprehensive insurance

Kasse ['kasə] f (Geldkasten) cashbox; (in Geschäft) till, cash register; cash desk, checkout; (Kinokasse, Theaterkasse etc) box office; ticket office; (Krankenkasse) health insurance; (Sparkasse) savings bank; ~ machen to count the money; getrennte ~ führen to pay separately; an der ~ (in Geschäft) at the desk; gut bei ~ sein to be in the money

Kassen- zW: ~arzt m panel doctor (BRIT); ~bestand m cash balance; ~patient m panel patient (BRIT); ~prüfung f audit; ~sturz m: ~sturz machen to check one's money; ~zettel m receipt

Kassette [ka'sɛtə] f small box; (Tonband, PHOT) cassette; (Bücherkassette) case

Kassettenrekorder (-s, -) m cassette recorder

kassieren [ka'siːrən] vt to take ♦ vi: darf ich ~? would you like to pay now?

Kassierer [ka'siːrər] (-s, -) m cashier; (von Klub) treasurer

Kastanie [kas'taːniə] f chestnut; (Baum) chestnut tree

Kasten ['kastən] (-s, ﬞ) m (auch SPORT) box; case; (Truhe) chest

kastrieren [kas'triːrən] vt to castrate

Katalog [kata'loːk] (-(e)s, -e) m catalogue

Katalysator [kataly'zaːtɔr] m catalyst; (AUT) catalytic converter

katastrophal [katastro'faːl] adj catastrophic

Katastrophe [kata'stroːfə] f catastrophe, disaster

Kat-Auto ['kat|auto] nt car fitted with a catalytic converter

Kategorie [katego'riː] f category

kategorisch [kate'goːrɪʃ] adj categorical

Kater ['kaːtər] (-s, -) m tomcat; (umg) hangover

kath. abk (= katholisch) Cath.

Kathedrale [kate'draːlə] f cathedral

Katholik [kato'liːk] (-en, -en) m Catholic

katholisch [ka'toːlɪʃ] adj Catholic

Kätzchen ['kɛtsçən] nt kitten

Katze ['katsə] f cat; für die Katz (umg) in vain, for nothing

Katzen- zW: ~auge nt cat's eye; (Fahrrad) rear light; ~sprung (umg) m stone's throw; short journey

Kauderwelsch ['kaudərvɛlʃ] (-(s)) nt jargon; (umg) double Dutch

kauen ['kauən] vt, vi to chew

kauern ['kauərn] vi to crouch down; (furchtsam) to cower

Kauf [kauf] (-(e)s, Käufe) m purchase, buy; (~en) buying; ein guter ~ a bargain; etw in ~ nehmen to put up with sth; k~en vt to buy

Käufer(in) ['kɔyfər(ɪn)] (-s, -) m(f) buyer

Kauf- zW: ~frau f businesswoman; ~haus nt department store; ~kraft f purchasing power

käuflich ['kɔyflɪç] adj purchasable, for sale; (pej) venal ♦ adv: ~ erwerben to purchase

Kauf- zW: k~lustig adj interested in buying; ~mann (pl -leute) m businessman; shopkeeper; k~männisch adj commercial; k~männischer Angestellter office worker; ~preis m purchase price; ~vertrag m bill of sale

Kaugummi ['kaugumi] m chewing gum

Kaulquappe ['kaulkvapə] f tadpole

kaum [kaum] adv hardly, scarcely

Kaution [kaʊtsi'oːn] f deposit; (JUR) bail

Kauz [kaʊts] (-es, Käuze) m owl; (fig) queer fellow

Kavalier [kava'liːr] (-s, -e) m gentleman, cavalier; ~sdelikt nt peccadillo

Kaviar ['kaːviar] m caviar

keck [kɛk] adj daring, bold

Kegel ['keːgəl] (-s, -) m skittle; (MATH) cone; ~bahn f skittle alley; bowling alley; k~n vi to play skittles

Kehle ['keːlə] f throat

Kehlkopf m larynx

Kehre ['keːrə] f turn(ing), bend; k~n vt, vi (wenden) to turn; (mit Besen) to sweep; **sich an etw** dat **nicht k~n** not to heed sth

Kehricht ['keːrɪçt] (-s) m sweepings pl

Kehrseite f reverse, other side; wrong side; bad side

kehrtmachen vi to turn about, to about-turn

keifen ['kaɪfən] vi to scold, to nag

Keil [kaɪl] (-(e)s, -e) m wedge; (MIL) arrowhead; ~riemen m (AUT) fan belt

Keim [kaɪm] (-(e)s, -e) m bud; (MED, fig) germ; k~en vi to germinate; k~frei adj sterile; ~zelle f (fig) nucleus

kein [kaɪn] adj no, not ... any; ~e(r, s) pron no one, nobody; none; ~erlei adj attrib no ... whatsoever

keinesfalls adv on no account

keineswegs adv by no means

keinmal adv not once

Keks [keːks] (-es, -e) m od nt biscuit

Kelch [kɛlç] (-(e)s, -e) m cup, goblet, chalice

Kelle ['kɛlə] f (Suppenkelle) ladle; (Maurerkelle) trowel

Keller ['kɛlər] (-s, -) m cellar

Kellner(in) ['kɛlnər(ɪn)] (-s, -) m(f) waiter (-tress)

keltern ['kɛltərn] vt to press

kennen ['kɛnən] (unreg) vt to know; ~ **lernen** to get to know; **sich ~ lernen** to get to know each other; (zum ersten Mal) to meet

Kenner (-s, -) m connoisseur

kenntlich adj distinguishable, discernible;

etw ~ machen to mark sth

Kenntnis (-, -se) f knowledge no pl; **etw zur ~ nehmen** to note sth; **von etw ~ nehmen** to take notice of sth; **jdn in ~ setzen** to inform sb

Kenn- zW: ~zeichen nt mark, characteristic; k~zeichnen vt insep to characterize; ~ziffer f reference number

kentern ['kɛntərn] vi to capsize

Keramik [ke'raːmɪk] (-, -en) f ceramics pl, pottery

Kerbe ['kɛrbə] f notch, groove

Kerker ['kɛrkər] (-s, -) m prison

Kerl [kɛrl] (-s, -e) m chap, bloke (BRIT), guy

Kern [kɛrn] (-(e)s, -e) m (Obstkern) pip, stone; (Nusskern) kernel; (Atomkern) nucleus; (fig) heart, core; ~energie f nuclear energy; ~forschung f nuclear research; ~frage f central issue; k~gesund adj thoroughly healthy, fit as a fiddle; k~ig adj (kraftvoll) robust; (Ausspruch) pithy; ~kraftwerk nt nuclear power station; k~los adj seedless, without pips; ~physik f nuclear physics sg; ~spaltung f nuclear fission; ~waffen pl nuclear weapons

Kerze ['kɛrtsə] f candle; (Zündkerze) plug; k~ngerade adj straight as a die; ~nständer m candle holder

kess ▲ [kɛs] adj saucy

Kessel ['kɛsəl] (-s, -) m kettle; (von Lokomotive etc) boiler; (GEOG) depression; (MIL) encirclement

Kette ['kɛtə] f chain; k~n vt to chain; ~nrauchen (-s) nt chain smoking; ~nreaktion f chain reaction

Ketzer ['kɛtsər] (-s, -) m heretic

keuchen ['kɔʏçən] vi to pant, to gasp

Keuchhusten m whooping cough

Keule ['kɔʏlə] f club; (KOCH) leg

keusch [kɔʏʃ] adj chaste; K~heit f chastity

kfm. abk = **kaufmännisch**

Kfz [kaː|ɛf'tseːt] nt abk = **Kraftfahrzeug**

KG [kaː'geː] (-, -s) f abk (= Kommanditgesellschaft) limited partnership

kg abk = **Kilogramm**

kichern ['kɪçərn] vi to giggle

Spelling Reform: ▲ *new spelling* △ *old spelling (to be phased out)*

kidnappen ['kɪtnɛpən] *vt* to kidnap

Kiefer[1] ['ki:fər] (**-s, -**) *m* jaw

Kiefer[2] ['ki:fər] (**-, -n**) *f* pine; **~zapfen** *m* pine cone

Kiel [ki:l] (**-(e)s, -e**) *m* (*Federkiel*) quill; (*NAUT*) keel

Kieme ['ki:mə] *f* gill

Kies [ki:s] (**-es, -e**) *m* gravel

Kilo ['ki:lo] *nt* kilo; **~gramm** [kilo'gram] *nt* kilogram; **~meter** [kilo'me:tər] *m* kilometre; **~meterzähler** *m* milometer

Kind [kɪnt] (**-(e)s, -er**) *nt* child; **von ~ auf** from childhood

Kinder- ['kɪndər] *zW:* **~betreuung** *f* crèche; **~ei** [-'raɪ] *f* childishness; **~garten** *m* nursery school, playgroup; **~gärtnerin** *f* nursery school teacher; **~geld** *nt* child benefit (*BRIT*); **~heim** *nt* children's home; **~krippe** *f* crèche; **~lähmung** *f* poliomyelitis; **k~leicht** *adj* childishly easy; **k~los** *adj* childless; **~mädchen** *nt* nursemaid; **k~reich** *adj* with a lot of children; **~sendung** *f* (*RADIO, TV*) children's programme; **~sicherung** *f* (*AUT*) childproof safety catch; **~spiel** *nt* (*fig*) child's play; **~tagesstätte** *f* day nursery; **~wagen** *m* pram, baby carriage (*US*); **~zimmer** *nt* (*für ~*) children's room; (*für Säugling*) nursery

---

Kindergarten

i A **Kindergarten** is a nursery school for children aged between 3 and 6 years. The children sing and play but do not receive any formal instruction. Most *Kindergärten* are financed by the town or the church with parents paying a monthly contribution towards the cost.

Kind- *zW:* **~heit** *f* childhood; **k~isch** *adj* childish; **k~lich** *adj* childlike

Kinn [kɪn] (**-(e)s, -e**) *nt* chin; **~haken** *m* (*BOXEN*) uppercut

Kino ['ki:no] (**-s, -s**) *nt* cinema; **~besucher** *m* cinema-goer; **~programm** *nt* film programme

Kiosk [ki'ɔsk] (**-(e)s, -e**) *m* kiosk

Kippe ['kɪpə] *f* cigarette end; (*umg*) fag; **auf der ~ stehen** (*fig*) to be touch and go

kippen *vi* to topple over, to overturn ♦ *vt* to tilt

Kirch- ['kɪrç] *zW:* **~e** *f* church; **~enlied** *nt* hymn; **~ensteuer** *f* church tax; **~gänger** (**-s, -**) *m* churchgoer; **~hof** *m* churchyard; **k~lich** *adj* ecclesiastical

Kirmes ['kɪrmɛs] (**-, -sen**) *f* fair

Kirsche ['kɪrʃə] *f* cherry

Kissen ['kɪsən] (**-s, -**) *nt* cushion; (*Kopfkissen*) pillow; **~bezug** *m* pillowslip

Kiste ['kɪstə] *f* box; chest

Kitsch [kɪtʃ] (**-(e)s**) *m* kitsch; **k~ig** *adj* kitschy

Kitt [kɪt] (**-(e)s, -e**) *m* putty

Kittel (**-s, -**) *m* overall, smock

kitten *vt* to putty; (*fig: Ehe etc*) to cement

kitzelig ['kɪtsəlɪç] *adj* (*auch fig*) ticklish

kitzeln *vi* to tickle

Kiwi ['ki:vi] (**-, -s**) *f* (*BOT, KOCH*) kiwi fruit

KKW [ka:ka:'ve:] *nt abk* = **Kernkraftwerk**

Klage ['kla:gə] *f* complaint; (*JUR*) action; **k~n** *vi* (*wehklagen*) to lament, to wail; (*sich beschweren*) to complain; (*JUR*) to take legal action

Kläger(in) ['klɛ:gər(ɪn)] (**-s, -**) *m(f)* plaintiff

kläglich ['klɛ:klɪç] *adj* wretched

klamm [klam] *adj* (*Finger*) numb; (*feucht*) damp

Klammer ['klamər] (**-, -n**) *f* clamp; (*in Text*) bracket; (*Büroklammer*) clip; (*Wäscheklammer*) peg; (*Zahnklammer*) brace; **k~n** *vr:* **sich k~n an** +*akk* to cling to

Klang [klaŋ] (**-(e)s, ⁻e**) *m* sound; **k~voll** *adj* sonorous

Klappe ['klapə] *f* valve; (*Ofenklappe*) damper; (*umg: Mund*) trap; **k~n** *vi* (*Geräusch*) to click; (*Sitz etc*) to tip ♦ *vt* to tip ♦ *vb unpers* to work

Klapper ['klapər] (**-, -n**) *f* rattle; **k~ig** *adj* run-down, worn-out; **k~n** *vi* to clatter, to rattle; **~schlange** *f* rattlesnake; **~storch** *m* stork

Klapp- *zW:* **~messer** *nt* jackknife; **~rad** *nt* collapsible bicycle; **~stuhl** *m* folding chair; **~tisch** *m* folding table

Klaps [klaps] (**-es, -e**) *m* slap

klar [klaːr] *adj* clear; (NAUT) ready for sea; (MIL) ready for action; **sich** *dat* **(über etw** *akk***) ~ werden** to get (sth) clear in one's mind; **sich** *dat* **im K~en sein über** +*akk* to be clear about; **ins K~e kommen** to get clear; **(na) ~!** of course!; **~ sehen** to see clearly

Kläranlage *f* purification plant

klären ['klɛːrən] *vt* (Flüssigkeit) to purify; (Probleme) to clarify ♦ *vr* to clear (itself) up

Klarheit *f* clarity

Klarinette [klari'nɛtə] *f* clarinet

klar- *zW:* **~legen** *vt* to clear up, to explain; **~machen** (Schiff) to get ready for sea; **jdm etw ~machen** to make sth clear to sb; **~sehen** △ (unreg) *vi siehe* **klar**; **K~sichtfolie** *f* transparent film; **~stellen** *vt* to clarify

Klärung ['klɛːrʊŋ] *f* (von Flüssigkeit) purification; (von Probleme) clarification

klarwerden △ (unreg) *vi siehe* **klar**

Klasse ['klasə] *f* class; (SCH) class, form

klasse (umg) *adj* smashing

Klassen- *zW:* **~arbeit** *f* test; **~gesellschaft** *f* class society; **~lehrer** *m* form master; **k~los** *adj* classless; **~sprecher(in)** *m(f)* form prefect; **~zimmer** *nt* classroom

klassifizieren [klasifi'tsiːrən] *vt* to classify

Klassik ['klasɪk] *f* (Zeit) classical period; (Stil) classicism; **~er** (**-s, -**) *m* classic

klassisch *adj* (auch fig) classical

Klatsch [klatʃ] (**-(e)s, -e**) *m* smack, crack; (Gerede) gossip; **~base** *f* gossip, scandalmonger; **~e** (umg) *f* crib; **k~en** *vi* (Geräusch) to clash; (reden) to gossip; (applaudieren) to applaud, to clap ♦ *vt:* **jdm Beifall k~en** to applaud sb; **~mohn** *m* (corn) poppy; **k~nass** ▲ *adj* soaking wet

Klaue ['klauə] *f* claw; (umg: Schrift) scrawl; **k~n** (umg) *vt* to pinch

Klausel ['klauzəl] (**-, -n**) *f* clause

Klausur [klau'zuːr] *f* seclusion; **~arbeit** *f* examination paper

Klavier [kla'viːr] (**-s, -e**) *nt* piano

Kleb- ['kleːb] *zW:* **k~en** ['kleːbən] *vt, vi:*

k~en (an +*akk*) to stick (to); **k~rig** *adj* sticky; **~stoff** *m* glue; **~streifen** *m* adhesive tape

kleckern ['klɛkərn] *vi* to make a mess ♦ *vt* to spill

Klecks [klɛks] (**-es, -e**) *m* blot, stain

Klee [kleː] (**-s**) *m* clover; **~blatt** *nt* cloverleaf; (fig) trio

Kleid [klaɪt] (**-(e)s, -er**) *nt* garment; (Frauenkleid) dress; **~er** *pl* (~ung) clothes; **k~en** ['klaɪdən] *vt* to clothe, to dress; to suit ♦ *vr* to dress

Kleider- ['klaɪdər] *zW:* **~bügel** *m* coat hanger; **~bürste** *f* clothes brush; **~schrank** *m* wardrobe

Kleid- *zW:* **k~sam** *adj* flattering; **~ung** *f* clothing; **~ungsstück** *nt* garment

klein [klaɪn] *adj* little, small; **~ hacken** to chop, to mince; **~ schneiden** to chop up; **K~e(r, s)** *mf* little one; **K~format** *nt* small size; **im K~format** small-scale; **K~geld** *nt* small change; **K~igkeit** *f* trifle; **K~kind** *nt* infant; **K~kram** *m* details *pl*; **~laut** *adj* dejected, quiet; **~lich** *adj* petty, paltry; **K~od** ['klaɪnoːt] (**-s, -odien**) *nt* gem, jewel; treasure; **K~stadt** *f* small town; **~städtisch** *adj* provincial; **~stmöglich** *adj* smallest possible

Kleister ['klaɪstər] (**-s, -**) *m* paste

Klemme ['klɛmə] *f* clip; (MED) clamp; (fig) jam; **k~n** *vt* (festhalten) to jam; (quetschen) to pinch, to nip ♦ *vr* to catch o.s.; (sich hineinzwängen) to squeeze o.s. ♦ *vi* (Tür) to stick, to jam; **sich hinter jdn/etw k~n** to get on to sb/down to sth

Klempner ['klɛmpnər] (**-s, -**) *m* plumber

Klerus ['kleːrʊs] (**-**) *m* clergy

Klette ['klɛtə] *f* burr

Kletter- ['klɛtər] *zW:* **~er** (**-s, -**) *m* climber; **k~n** *vi* to climb; **~pflanze** *f* creeper

Klient(in) [kli'ɛnt(ɪn)] *m(f)* client

Klima ['kliːma] (**-s, -s** *od* **-te**) *nt* climate; **~anlage** *f* air conditioning; **~wechsel** *m* change of air

klimpern ['klɪmpərn] (umg) *vi* (mit Münzen, Schlüsseln) to jingle; (auf Klavier) to plonk (away)

Spelling Reform: ▲ *new spelling* △ *old spelling (to be phased out)*

Klinge ['klɪŋə] f blade; sword
Klingel ['klɪŋəl] (-, -n) f bell; ~beutel m collection bag; k~n vi to ring
klingen ['klɪŋən] (*unreg*) vi to sound; (*Gläser*) to clink
Klinik ['kliːnɪk] f hospital, clinic
Klinke ['klɪŋkə] f handle
Klippe ['klɪpə] f cliff; (*im Meer*) reef; (*fig*) hurdle
klipp und klar ['klɪp|ʊntklaːr] *adj* clear and concise
klirren ['klɪrən] vi to clank, to jangle; (*Gläser*) to clink; ~**de Kälte** biting cold
Klischee [klɪˈʃeː] (-s, -e) nt (*Druckplatte*) plate, block; (*fig*) cliché; ~vorstellung f stereotyped idea
Klo [kloː] (-s, -s) (*umg*) nt loo (*BRIT*), john (*US*)
Kloake [kloˈaːkə] f sewer
klobig ['kloːbɪç] *adj* clumsy
Klopapier (*umg*) nt loo paper (*BRIT*)
klopfen ['klɔpfən] vi to knock; (*Herz*) to thump ♦ vt to beat; **es klopft** somebody's knocking; **jdm auf die Schulter ~** to tap sb on the shoulder
Klopfer (-s, -) m (*Teppichklopfer*) beater; (*Türklopfer*) knocker
Klops [klɔps] (-es, -e) m meatball
Klosett [kloˈzɛt] (-s, -e od -s) nt lavatory, toilet; ~papier nt toilet paper
Kloß [kloːs] (-es, ᵉe) m (*im Hals*) lump; (*KOCH*) dumpling
Kloster ['kloːstər] (-s, ᵉ) nt (*Männerkloster*) monastery; (*Frauenkloster*) convent; **klösterlich** ['kløːstərlɪç] *adj* monastic; convent *cpd*
Klotz [klɔts] (-es, ᵉe) m log; (*Hackklotz*) block; **ein ~ am Bein** (*fig*) a drag, a millstone round (sb's) neck
Klub [klʊp] (-s, -s) m club; ~sessel m easy chair
Kluft [klʊft] (-, ᵉe) f cleft, gap; (*GEOG*) gorge, chasm
klug [kluːk] *adj* clever, intelligent; K~heit f cleverness, intelligence
Klumpen ['klʊmpən] (-s, -) m (*Erdklumpen*) clod; (*Blutklumpen*) clot; (*Goldklumpen*)

nugget; (*KOCH*) lump
km *abk* = **Kilometer**
knabbern ['knabərn] vt, vi to nibble
Knabe ['knaːbə] (-n, -n) m boy
Knäckebrot ['knɛkəbroːt] nt crispbread
knacken ['knakən] vt, vi (*auch fig*) to crack
Knacks [knaks] (-es, -e) m crack; (*fig*) defect
Knall [knal] (-(e)s, -e) m bang; (*Peitschenknall*) crack; ~ **und Fall** (*umg*) unexpectedly; ~bonbon nt cracker; k~en vi to bang; to crack; k~rot *adj* bright red
knapp [knap] *adj* tight; (*Geld*) scarce; (*Sprache*) concise; **eine ~e Stunde** just under an hour; ~ **unter/neben** just under/by; K~heit f tightness; scarcity; conciseness
knarren ['knarən] vi to creak
Knast [knast] (-(e)s) (*umg*) m (*Haftstrafe*) porridge (*inf*), time (*inf*); (*Gefängnis*) slammer (*inf*), clink (*inf*)
knattern ['knatərn] vi to rattle; (*Maschinengewehr*) to chatter
Knäuel ['knɔyəl] (-s, -) m od nt (*Wollknäuel*) ball; (*Menschenknäuel*) knot
Knauf [knauf] (-(e)s, **Knäufe**) m knob; (*Schwertknauf*) pommel
Knebel ['kneːbəl] (-s, -) m gag
kneifen ['knaɪfən] (*unreg*) vt to pinch ♦ vi to pinch; (*sich drücken*) to back out; **vor etw ~** to dodge sth
Kneipe ['knaɪpə] (*umg*) f pub
kneten ['kneːtən] vt to knead; (*Wachs*) to mould
Knick [knɪk] (-(e)s, -e) m (*Sprung*) crack; (*Kurve*) bend; (*Falte*) fold; k~en vt, vi (*springen*) to crack; (*brechen*) to break; (*Papier*) to fold; **geknickt sein** to be downcast
Knicks [knɪks] (-es, -e) m curtsey
Knie [kniː] (-s, -) nt knee; ~beuge f knee bend; ~bundhose m knee breeches; ~gelenk nt knee joint; ~kehle f back of the knee; k~n vi to kneel; ~scheibe f kneecap; ~strumpf m knee-length sock
Kniff [knɪf] (-(e)s, -e) m (*fig*) trick, knack; k~elig *adj* tricky

knipsen ['knɪpsən] *vt* (*Fahrkarte*) to punch; (*PHOT*) to take a snap of, to snap ♦ *vi* to take a snap *od* snaps

Knirps [knɪrps] **(-es, -e)** *m* little chap; (®: *Schirm*) telescopic umbrella

knirschen ['knɪrʃən] *vi* to crunch; **mit den Zähnen ~** to grind one's teeth

knistern ['knɪstərn] *vi* to crackle

Knitter- ['knɪtər] *zW*: **~falte** *f* crease; **k~frei** *adj* non-crease; **k~n** *vi* to crease

Knoblauch ['knoːplaʊx] **(-(e)s)** *m* garlic; **~zehe** *f* (*KOCH*) clove of garlic

Knöchel ['knœçəl] **(-s, -)** *m* knuckle; (*Fußknöchel*) ankle

Knochen ['knɔxən] **(-s, -)** *m* bone; **~bruch** *m* fracture; **~gerüst** *nt* skeleton; **~mark** *nt* bone marrow

knöchern ['knœçərn] *adj* bone

knochig ['knɔxɪç] *adj* bony

Knödel ['knøːdəl] **(-s, -)** *m* dumpling

Knolle ['knɔlə] *f* tuber

Knopf [knɔpf] **(-(e)s, ̈e)** *m* button; (*Kragenknopf*) stud

knöpfen ['knœpfən] *vt* to button

Knopfloch *nt* buttonhole

Knorpel ['knɔrpəl] **(-s, -)** *m* cartilage, gristle; **k~ig** *adj* gristly

Knospe ['knɔspə] *f* bud

Knoten ['knoːtən] **(-s, -)** *m* knot; (*BOT*) node; (*MED*) lump; **k~** *vt* to knot; **~punkt** *m* junction

Knüller ['knʏlər] **(-s, -)** (*umg*) *m* hit; (*Reportage*) scoop

knüpfen ['knʏpfən] *vt* to tie; (*Teppich*) to knot; (*Freundschaft*) to form

Knüppel ['knʏpəl] **(-s, -)** *m* cudgel; (*Polizeiknüppel*) baton, truncheon; (*AVIAT*) (joy)stick

knurren ['knʊrən] *vi* (*Hund*) to snarl, to growl; (*Magen*) to rumble; (*Mensch*) to mutter

knusperig ['knʊspərɪç] *adj* crisp; (*Keks*) crunchy

k. o. [kaːˈoː] *adj* knocked out; (*fig*) done in

Koalition [koalitsiˈoːn] *f* coalition

Kobold ['koːbɔlt] **(-(e)s, -e)** *m* goblin, imp

Koch [kɔx] **(-(e)s, ̈e)** *m* cook; **~buch** *nt* cook(ery) book; **k~en** *vt, vi* to cook; (*Wasser*) to boil; **~er (-s, -)** *m* stove, cooker; **~gelegenheit** *f* cooking facilities *pl*

Köchin ['kœçɪn] *f* cook

Koch- *zW*: **~löffel** *m* kitchen spoon; **~nische** *f* kitchenette; **~platte** *f* hotplate; **~salz** *nt* cooking salt; **~topf** *m* saucepan, pot

Köder ['køːdər] **(-s, -)** *m* bait, lure

ködern *vt* (*Tier*) to trap with bait; (*Person*) to entice, to tempt

Koexistenz [koɛksɪsˈtɛnts] *f* coexistence

Koffein [kɔfeˈiːn] **(-s)** *nt* caffeine; **k~frei** *adj* decaffeinated

Koffer ['kɔfər] **(-s, -)** *m* suitcase; (*Schrankkoffer*) trunk; **~kuli** *m* (luggage) trolley; **~radio** *nt* portable radio; **~raum** *m* (*AUT*) boot (*BRIT*), trunk (*US*)

Kognak ['kɔnjak] **(-s, -s)** *m* brandy, cognac

Kohl [koːl] **(-(e)s, -e)** *m* cabbage

Kohle ['koːlə] *f* coal; (*Holzkohle*) charcoal; (*CHEM*) carbon; **~hydrat (-(e)s, -e)** *nt* carbohydrate

Kohlen- *zW*: **~dioxid (-(e)s, -e)** *nt* carbon dioxide; **~händler** *m* coal merchant, coalman; **~säure** *f* carbon dioxide; **~stoff** *m* carbon

Kohlepapier *nt* carbon paper

Koje ['koːjə] *f* cabin; (*Bett*) bunk

Kokain [kokaˈiːn] **(-s)** *nt* cocaine

kokett [koˈkɛt] *adj* coquettish, flirtatious

Kokosnuss ▲ ['koːkɔsnʊs] *f* coconut

Koks [koːks] **(-es, -e)** *m* coke

Kolben ['kɔlbən] **(-s, -)** *m* (*Gewehrkolben*) rifle butt; (*Keule*) club; (*CHEM*) flask; (*TECH*) piston; (*Maiskolben*) cob

Kolik ['koːlɪk] *f* colic, the gripes *pl*

Kollaps [kɔˈlaps] **(-es, -e)** *m* collapse

Kolleg [kɔˈleːk] **(-s, -s** *od* **-ien)** *nt* lecture course; **~e** [kɔˈleːgə] **(-n, -n)** *m* colleague; **~in** *f* colleague; **~ium** *nt* working party; (*SCH*) staff

Kollekte [kɔˈlɛktə] *f* (*REL*) collection

kollektiv [kɔlɛkˈtiːf] *adj* collective

Köln [kœln] **(-s)** *nt* Cologne

Kolonie [koloˈniː] *f* colony

kolonisieren [koloni'zi:rən] *vt* to colonize

Kolonne [ko'lɔnə] *f* column; (*von Fahrzeugen*) convoy

Koloss ▲ [ko'lɔs] (**-es, -e**) *m* colossus; **kolo'ssal** *adj* colossal

Kölsch [kœlʃ] (**-, -**) *nt* (*Bier*) ≈ (strong) lager

Kombi- ['kɔmbi] *zW:* **~nation** [-natsi'o:n] *f* combination; (*Vermutung*) conjecture; (*Hemdhose*) combinations *pl*; **k~nieren** [-'ni:rən] *vt* to combine ♦ *vi* to deduce, to work out; (*vermuten*) to guess; **~wagen** *m* station wagon; **~zange** *f* (pair of) pliers *pl*

Komet [ko'me:t] (**-en, -en**) *m* comet

Komfort [kɔm'fo:r] (**-s**) *m* luxury

Komik ['ko:mɪk] *f* humour, comedy; **~er** (**-s, -**) *m* comedian

komisch ['ko:mɪʃ] *adj* funny

Komitee [komi'te:] (**-s, -s**) *nt* committee

Komma ['kɔma] (**-s, -s** *od* **-ta**) *nt* comma; **2 ~ 3** 2 point 3

Kommand- [kɔ'mand] *zW:* **~ant** [-'dant] *m* commander, commanding officer; **k~ieren** [-'di:rən] *vt, vi* to command; **~o** (**-s, -s**) *nt* command, order; (*Truppe*) detachment, squad; **auf ~o** to order

kommen ['kɔmən] (*unreg*) *vi* to come; (*näher kommen*) to approach; (*passieren*) to happen; (*gelangen, geraten*) to get; (*Blumen, Zähne, Tränen etc*) to appear; (*in die Schule, das Zuchthaus etc*) to go; **~ lassen** to send for; **das kommt in den Schrank** that goes in the cupboard; **zu sich ~** to come round *od* to; **zu etw ~** to acquire sth; **um etw ~** to lose sth; **nichts auf jdn/etw ~ lassen** to have nothing said against sb/sth; **jdm frech ~** to get cheeky with sb; **auf jeden vierten kommt ein Platz** there's one place for every fourth person; **wer kommt zuerst?** who's first?; **unter ein Auto ~** to be run over by a car; **wie hoch kommt das?** what does that cost?; **komm gut nach Hause!** safe journey (home); **~den Sonntag** next Sunday; **K~** (**-s**) *nt* coming

Kommentar [kɔmɛn'ta:r] *m* commentary; **kein ~** no comment; **k~los** *adj* without comment

Kommentator [kɔmɛn'ta:tɔr] *m* (*TV*) commentator

kommentieren [kɔmɛn'ti:rən] *vt* to comment on

kommerziell [kɔmɛrtsi'ɛl] *adj* commercial

Kommilitone [kɔmili'to:nə] (**-n, -n**) *m* fellow student

Kommissar [kɔmɪ'sa:r] *m* police inspector

Kommission [kɔmɪsi'o:n] *f* (*COMM*) commission; (*Ausschuss*) committee

Kommode [kɔ'mo:də] *f* (chest of) drawers

kommunal [kɔmu'na:l] *adj* local; (*von Stadt auch*) municipal

Kommune [kɔ'mu:nə] *f* commune

Kommunikation [kɔmunɪkatsi'o:n] *f* communication

Kommunion [kɔmuni'o:n] *f* communion

Kommuniqué, Kommunikee ▲ [kɔmyni'ke:] (**-s, -s**) *nt* communiqué

Kommunismus [kɔmu'nɪsmʊs] *m* communism

Kommunist(in) [kɔmu'nɪst(ɪn)] *m(f)* communist; **k~isch** *adj* communist

kommunizieren [kɔmuni'tsi:rən] *vi* to communicate

Komödie [ko'mø:diə] *f* comedy

Kompagnon [kɔmpan'jõ:] (**-s, -s**) *m* (*COMM*) partner

kompakt [kɔm'pakt] *adj* compact

Kompanie [kɔmpa'ni:] *f* company

Kompass ▲ ['kɔmpas] (**-es, -e**) *m* compass

kompatibel [kɔmpa'ti:bəl] *adj* compatible

kompetent [kɔmpe'tɛnt] *adj* competent

Kompetenz *f* competence, authority

komplett [kɔm'plɛt] *adj* complete

Komplex [kɔm'plɛks] (**-es, -e**) *m* (*Gebäudekomplex*) complex

Komplikation [kɔmplikatsi'o:n] *f* complication

Kompliment [kɔmpli'mɛnt] *nt* compliment

Komplize [kɔm'pli:tsə] (**-n, -n**) *m* accomplice

kompliziert [kɔmpli'tsi:rt] *adj* complicated

komponieren [kɔmpo'ni:rən] *vt* to compose

Komponist [kɔmpo'nɪst(ɪn)] *m* composer

Komposition [kɔmpozitsi'o:n] *f* composition

Kompost [kɔm'pɔst] (**-(e)s, -e**) *m* compost

Kompott [kɔm'pɔt] **(-(e)s, -e)** *nt* stewed fruit

Kompromiss ▲ [kɔmpro'mɪs] **(-es, -e)** *m* compromise; **k~bereit** *adj* willing to compromise

Kondens- [kɔn'dɛns] *zW*: **~ation** [kɔndɛnzatsi'o:n] *f* condensation; **k~ieren** [kɔndɛn'zi:rən] *vt* to condense; **~milch** *f* condensed milk

Kondition [kɔndɪtsi'o:n] *f (COMM, FIN)* condition; *(Durchhaltevermögen)* stamina; *(körperliche Verfassung)* physical condition, state of health

Konditionstraining [kɔndɪtsi'o:nstre:nɪŋ] *nt* fitness training

Konditor [kɔn'di:tɔr] *m* pastry cook; **~ei** [-'raɪ] *f* café; cake shop

Kondom [kɔn'do:m] **(-s, -e)** *nt* condom

Konferenz [kɔnfe'rɛnts] *f* conference, meeting

Konfession [kɔnfɛsi'o:n] *f* (religious) denomination; **k~ell** [-'nɛl] *adj* denominational; **k~slos** *adj* non-denominational

Konfirmand [kɔnfɪr'mant] *m* candidate for confirmation

Konfirmation [kɔnfɪrmatsi'o:n] *f (REL)* confirmation

konfirmieren [kɔnfɪr'mi:rən] *vt* to confirm

konfiszieren [kɔnfɪs'tsi:rən] *vt* to confiscate

Konfitüre [kɔnfi'ty:rə] *f* jam

Konflikt [kɔn'flɪkt] **(-(e)s, -e)** *m* conflict

konfrontieren [kɔnfrɔn'ti:rən] *vt* to confront

konfus [kɔn'fu:s] *adj* confused

Kongress ▲ [kɔn'grɛs] **(-es, -e)** *m* congress; **~zentrum** *nt* conference centre

Kongruenz [kɔngru'ɛnts] *f* agreement, congruence

König ['kø:nɪç] **(-(e)s, -e)** *m* king; **~in** ['kø:nɪgɪn] *f* queen; **k~lich** *adj* royal; **~reich** *nt* kingdom

Konjugation [kɔnjugatsi'o:n] *f* conjugation

konjugieren [kɔnju'gi:rən] *vt* to conjugate

Konjunktion [kɔnjuŋktsi'o:n] *f* conjunction

Konjunktiv ['kɔnjuŋkti:f] **(-s, -e)** *m* subjunctive

Konjunktur [kɔnjuŋk'tu:r] *f* economic situation; *(Hochkonjunktur)* boom

konkret [kɔn'kre:t] *adj* concrete

Konkurrent(in) [kɔnkʊ'rɛnt(ɪn)] *m(f)* competitor

Konkurrenz [kɔnkʊ'rɛnts] *f* competition; **k~fähig** *adj* competitive; **~kampf** *m* competition; rivalry, competitive situation

konkurrieren [kɔnkʊ'ri:rən] *vi* to compete

Konkurs [kɔn'kʊrs] **(-es, -e)** *m* bankruptcy

Können **(-s)** *nt* ability

SCHLÜSSELWORT

können ['kœnən] *(pt* **konnte**, *pp* **gekonnt** *od (als Hilfsverb)* **können)** *vt, vi* **1** to be able to; **ich kann es machen** I can do it, I am able to do it; **ich kann es nicht machen** I can't do it, I'm not able to do it; **ich kann nicht ...** I can't ..., I cannot ...; **ich kann nicht mehr** I can't go on

2 *(wissen, beherrschen)* to know; **können Sie Deutsch?** can you speak German?; **er kann gut Englisch** he speaks English well; **sie kann keine Mathematik** she can't do mathematics

3 *(dürfen)* to be allowed to; **kann ich gehen?** can I go?; **könnte ich ...?** could I ...?; **kann ich mit?** *(umg)* can I come with you?

4 *(möglich sein)*: **Sie könnten Recht haben** you may be right; **das kann sein** that's possible; **kann sein** maybe

Könner *m* expert

konnte *etc* ['kɔntə] *vb siehe* **können**

konsequent [kɔnze'kvɛnt] *adj* consistent

Konsequenz [kɔnze'kvɛnts] *f* consistency; *(Folgerung)* conclusion

Konserv- [kɔn'zɛrv] *zW*: **k~ativ** [-a'ti:f] *adj* conservative; **~ative** [-a'ti:və] *f(m) (POL)* conservative; **~e** *f* tinned food; **~enbüchse** *f* tin, can; **k~ieren** [-'vi:rən] *vt* to preserve; **~ierung** *f* preservation; **~ierungsstoff** *m* preservatives

Konsonant [kɔnzo'nant] *m* consonant

konstant [kɔn'stant] *adj* constant

konstru- *zW*: **~ieren** [kɔnstru'i:rən] *vt* to construct; **K~kteur** [kɔnstrʊk'tø:r] *m*

designer; K~ktion [kɔnstrʊktsi'oːn] f
construction; ~ktiv [kɔnstrʊk'tiːf] adj
constructive
Konsul ['kɔnzʊl] (-s, -n) m consul; ~at [-'laːt]
nt consulate
konsultieren [kɔnzʊl'tiːrən] vt to consult
Konsum [kɔn'zuːm] (-s) m consumption;
~artikel m consumer article; ~ent [-'mɛnt]
m consumer; k~ieren [-'miːrən] vt to
consume
Kontakt [kɔn'takt] (-(e)s, -e) m contact;
k~arm adj unsociable; k~freudig adj
sociable; ~linsen pl contact lenses
kontern ['kɔntɐn] vt, vi to counter
Kontinent [kɔnti'nɛnt] m continent
Kontingent [kɔntɪŋ'gɛnt] (-(e)s, -e) nt
quota; (Truppenkontingent) contingent
kontinuierlich [kɔntinu'iːrlɪç] adj
continuous
Konto ['kɔnto] (-s, Konten) nt account;
~auszug m statement (of account);
~inhaber(in) m(f) account holder; ~stand
m balance
Kontra ['kɔntra] (-s, -s) nt (KARTEN) double;
jdm ~ geben (fig) to contradict sb;
~bass ▲ m double bass; ~hent m (COMM)
contracting party; ~punkt m counterpoint
Kontrast [kɔn'trast] (-(e)s, -e) m contrast
Kontroll- [kɔn'trɔl] zW: ~e f control,
supervision; (Passkontrolle) passport control;
~eur [-'løːr] m inspector; k~ieren [-'liːrən]
vt to control, to supervise; (nachprüfen) to
check
Konvention [kɔnvɛntsi'oːn] f convention;
k~ell [-'nɛl] adj conventional
Konversation [kɔnvɛrzatsi'oːn] f
conversation; ~slexikon nt
encyclop(a)edia
Konvoi ['kɔnvɔy] (-s, -s) m convoy
Konzentration [kɔntsɛntratsi'oːn] f
concentration
Konzentrationslager nt concentration
camp
konzentrieren [kɔntsɛn'triːrən] vt, vr to
concentrate
konzentriert adj concentrated ♦ adv
(zuhören, arbeiten) intently

Konzern [kɔn'tsɛrn] (-s, -e) m combine
Konzert [kɔn'tsɛrt] (-(e)s, -e) nt concert;
(Stück) concerto; ~saal m concert hall
Konzession [kɔntsɛsi'oːn] f licence;
(Zugeständnis) concession
Konzil [kɔn'tsiːl] (-s, -e od -ien) nt council
kooperativ [koʔopera'tiːf] adj cooperative
koordinieren [koʔɔrdi'niːrən] vt to
coordinate
Kopf [kɔpf] (-(e)s, ⁺e) m head; ~haut f
scalp; ~hörer m headphones pl; ~kissen
nt pillow; k~los adj panic-stricken;
k~rechnen vi to do mental arithmetic;
~salat m lettuce; ~schmerzen pl
headache sg; ~sprung m header, dive;
~stand m headstand; ~stütze f (im Auto
etc) headrest, head restraint; ~tuch nt
headscarf; ~weh nt headache;
~zerbrechen nt: jdm ~zerbrechen
machen to be a headache for sb
Kopie [ko'piː] f copy; k~ren vt to copy
Kopiergerät nt photocopier
Koppel¹ ['kɔpəl] (-, -n) f (Weide) enclosure
Koppel² ['kɔpəl] (-s, -) nt (Gürtel) belt
koppeln vt to couple
Koppelung f coupling
Koralle [ko'ralə] f coral
Korb [kɔrp] (-(e)s, ⁺e) m basket; jdm einen
~ geben (fig) to turn sb down; ~ball m
basketball; ~stuhl m wicker chair
Kord [kɔrt] (-(e)s, -e) m cord, corduroy
Kordel ['kɔrdəl] (-, -n) f cord, string
Kork [kɔrk] (-(e)s, -e) m cork; ~en (-s, -)
stopper, cork; ~enzieher (-s, -) m
corkscrew
Korn [kɔrn] (-(e)s, ⁺er) nt corn, grain;
(Gewehr) sight
Körper ['kœrper] (-s, -) m body; ~bau m
build; k~behindert adj disabled; ~geruch
m body odour; ~gewicht nt weight;
~größe f height; k~lich adj physical;
~pflege f personal hygiene; ~schaft f
corporation; ~schaftssteuer f corporation
tax; ~teil m part of the body;
~verletzung f bodily od physical injury
korpulent [kɔrpu'lɛnt] adj corpulent
korrekt [ko'rɛkt] adj correct; K~ur [-'tuːr] f

(eines Textes) proofreading; (Text) proof; (SCH) marking, correction

Korrespond- [kɔrɛspɔnd] zW: **~ent(in)** [-'dɛnt(ɪn)] m(f) correspondent; **~enz** [-'dɛnts] f correspondence; **k~ieren** [-'diːrən] vi to correspond

Korridor ['kɔridoːr] (**-s, -e**) m corridor

korrigieren [kɔri'giːrən] vt to correct

Korruption [kɔruptsi'oːn] f corruption

Kose- ['koːzə] zW: **~form** f pet form; **~name** m pet name; **~wort** nt term of endearment

Kosmetik [kɔs'meːtɪk] f cosmetics pl; **~erin** f beautician

kosmetisch adj cosmetic; (Chirurgie) plastic

kosmisch ['kɔsmɪʃ] adj cosmic

Kosmo- [kɔsmo] zW: **~naut** [-'naut] (**-en, -en**) m cosmonaut; **k~politisch** adj cosmopolitan; **~s** (**-**) m cosmos

Kost [kɔst] (**-**) f (Nahrung) food; (Verpflegung) board; **k~bar** adj precious; (teuer) costly, expensive; **~barkeit** f preciousness; costliness, expensiveness; (Wertstück) valuable

Kosten zW: cost(s); (Ausgaben) expenses; **auf ~ von** at the expense of; **k~** vt to cost; (versuchen) to taste ♦ vi to taste; **was kostet ...?** what does ... cost?, how much is ...?; **~anschlag** m estimate; **k~los** adj free (of charge)

köstlich ['kœstlɪç] adj precious; (Einfall) delightful; (Essen) delicious; **sich ~ amüsieren** to have a marvellous time

Kostprobe f taste; (fig) sample

kostspielig adj expensive

Kostüm [kɔs'tyːm] (**-s, -e**) nt costume; (Damenkostüm) suit; **~fest** nt fancy-dress party; **k~ieren** [kɔsty'miːrən] vt, vr to dress up; **~verleih** m costume agency

Kot [koːt] (**-(e)s**) m excrement

Kotelett [kɔtə'lɛt] (**-(e)s, -e** od **-s**) nt cutlet, chop; **~en** pl (Bart) sideboards

Köter ['køːtər] (**-s, -**) m cur

Kotflügel m (AUT) wing

kotzen ['kɔtsən] (umg!) vi to puke (umg), to throw up (umg)

Krabbe ['krabə] f shrimp; **k~ln** vi to crawl

Krach [krax] (**-(e)s, -s** od **-e**) m crash; (andauernd) noise; (umg: Streit) quarrel, argument; **k~en** vi to crash; (beim Brechen) to crack ♦ vr (umg) to argue, to quarrel

krächzen ['krɛçtsən] vi to croak

Kraft [kraft] (**-, ⁿe**) f strength; power; force; (Arbeitskraft) worker; **in ~ treten** to come into force; **k~** präp +gen by virtue of; **~fahrer** m (motor) driver; **~fahrzeug** nt motor vehicle; **~fahrzeugbrief** m logbook; **~fahrzeugsteuer** f ≈ road tax; **~fahrzeugversicherung** f car insurance

kräftig ['krɛftɪç] adj strong; **~en** vt to strengthen

Kraft- zW: **k~los** adj weak; powerless; (JUR) invalid; **~probe** f trial of strength; **~stoff** m fuel; **k~voll** adj vigorous; **~werk** nt power station

Kragen ['kraːgən] (**-s, -**) m collar; **~weite** f collar size

Krähe ['krɛːə] f crow; **k~n** vi to crow

Kralle ['kralə] f claw; (Vogelkralle) talon; **k~n** vt to clutch; (krampfhaft) to claw

Kram [kraːm] (**-(e)s**) m stuff, rubbish; **k~en** vi to rummage; **~laden** (pej) m small shop

Krampf [krampf] (**-(e)s, ⁿe**) m cramp; (zuckend) spasm; **~ader** f varicose vein; **k~haft** adj convulsive; (fig: Versuche) desperate

Kran [kraːn] (**-(e)s, ⁿe**) m crane; (Wasserkran) tap, faucet (US)

krank [kraŋk] adj ill, sick; **K~e(r)** f(m) sick person, invalid; patient; **~en** vi: **an etw** dat **~en** (fig) to suffer from sth

kränken ['krɛŋkən] vt to hurt

Kranken- zW: **~geld** nt sick pay; **~gymnastik** f physiotherapy; **~haus** nt hospital; **~kasse** f health insurance; **~pfleger** m nursing orderly; **~schein** m health insurance card; **~schwester** f nurse; **~versicherung** f health insurance; **~wagen** m ambulance

Krank- zW: **k~haft** adj diseased; (Angst etc) morbid; **~heit** f illness; disease; **~heitserreger** m disease-causing agent

kränklich ['krɛŋklɪç] adj sickly

Kränkung f insult, offence

Kranz [krants] (**-es**, **ꟷe**) *m* wreath, garland

krass ▲ [kras] *adj* crass

Krater ['kra:tər] (**-s**, **-**) *m* crater

Kratz- [krats] *zW:* **~bürste** *f* (*fig*) crosspatch; **k~en** *vt, vi* to scratch; **~er** (**-s**, **-**) *m* scratch; (*Werkzeug*) scraper

Kraul [kraul] (**-s**) *nt* crawl; **~ schwimmen** to do the crawl; **k~en** *vi* (*schwimmen*) to do the crawl ♦ *vt* (*streicheln*) to fondle

kraus [kraus] *adj* crinkly; (*Haar*) frizzy; (*Stirn*) wrinkled

Kraut [kraut] (**-(e)s**, **Kräuter**) *nt* plant; (*Gewürz*) herb; (*Gemüse*) cabbage

Krawall [kra'val] (**-s**, **-e**) *m* row, uproar

Krawatte [kra'vatə] *f* tie

kreativ [krea'ti:f] *adj* creative

Krebs [kre:ps] (**-es**, **-e**) *m* crab; (*MED, ASTROL*) cancer; **k~krank** *adj* suffering from cancer

Kredit [kre'di:t] (**-(e)s**, **-e**) *m* credit; **~institut** *nt* bank; **~karte** *f* credit card

Kreide ['kraidə] *f* chalk; **k~bleich** *adj* as white as a sheet

Kreis [krais] (**-es**, **-e**) *m* circle; (*Stadtkreis etc*) district; **im ~ gehen** (*auch fig*) to go round in circles

kreischen ['kraiʃən] *vi* to shriek, to screech

Kreis- *zW:* **~el** ['kraizəl] (**-s**, **-**) *m* top; (*~verkehr*) roundabout (*BRIT*), traffic circle (*US*); **k~en** ['kraizən] *vi* to spin; **~lauf** *m* (*MED*) circulation; (*fig: der Natur etc*) cycle; **~säge** *f* circular saw; **~stadt** *f* county town; **~verkehr** *m* roundabout traffic

Krematorium [krema'to:riʊm] *nt* crematorium

Kreml ['kre:ml] (**-s**) *m* Kremlin

krepieren [kre'pi:rən] (*umg*) *vi* (*sterben*) to die, to kick the bucket

Krepp [krɛp] (**-s**, **-s** *od* **-e**) *m* crepe; **~papier** ▲ *nt* crepe paper

Kresse ['krɛsə] *f* cress

Kreta ['kre:ta] (**-s**) *nt* Crete

Kreuz [krɔyts] (**-es**, **-e**) *nt* cross; (*ANAT*) small of the back; (*KARTEN*) clubs; **k~en** *vt, vr* to cross ♦ *vi* (*NAUT*) to cruise; **~er** (**-s**, **-**) *m* (*Schiff*) cruiser; **~fahrt** *f* cruise; **~feuer** *nt* (*fig*): **ins ~feuer geraten** to be under fire from all sides; **~gang** *m* cloisters *pl*;

k~igen *vt* to crucify; **~igung** *f* crucifixion; **~ung** *f* (*Verkehrskreuzung*) crossing, junction; (*Züchten*) cross; **~verhör** *nt* cross-examination; **~weg** *m* crossroads; (*REL*) Way of the Cross; **~worträtsel** *nt* crossword puzzle; **~zug** *m* crusade

Kriech- ['kri:ç] *zW:* **k~en** *vi* (*unreg*) to crawl, to creep; (*pej*) to grovel, to crawl; **~er** (**-s**, **-**) *m* crawler; **~spur** *f* crawler lane; **~tier** *nt* reptile

Krieg [kri:k] (**-(e)s**, **-e**) *m* war

kriegen ['kri:ɡən] (*umg*) *vt* to get

Kriegs- *zW:* **~erklärung** *f* declaration of war; **~fuß** *m:* **mit jdm/etw auf ~fuß stehen** to be at loggerheads with sb/to have difficulties with sth; **~gefangene(r)** *m* prisoner of war; **~gefangenschaft** *f* captivity; **~gericht** *nt* court-martial; **~schiff** *nt* warship; **~verbrecher** *m* war criminal; **~versehrte(r)** *m* person disabled in the war; **~zustand** *m* state of war

Krim [krɪm] (**-**) *f* Crimea

Krimi ['kri:mi] (**-s**, **-s**) (*umg*) *m* thriller

Kriminal- [krimi'na:l] *zW:* **~beamte(r)** *m* detective; **~i'tät** *f* criminality; **~'polizei** *f* ≈ Criminal Investigation Department (*BRIT*), Federal Bureau of Investigation (*US*); **~ro'man** *m* detective story

kriminell [krimi'nɛl] *adj* criminal; **K~e(r)** *m* criminal

Krippe ['krɪpə] *f* crib; (*Kinderkrippe*) crèche

Krise ['kri:zə] *f* crisis; **k~ln** *vi:* **es k~lt** there's a crisis

Kristall [krɪs'tal] (**-s**, **-e**) *m* crystal ♦ *nt* (*Glas*) crystal

Kriterium [kri'te:riʊm] *nt* criterion

Kritik [kri'ti:k] *f* criticism; (*Zeitungskritik*) review, write-up; **~er** ['kri:tikər] (**-s**, **-**) *m* critic; **k~los** *adj* uncritical

kritisch ['kri:tɪʃ] *adj* critical

kritisieren [kriti'zi:rən] *vt, vi* to criticize

kritzeln ['krɪtsəln] *vt, vi* to scribble, to scrawl

Kroatien [kro'a:tsiən] *nt* Croatia

Krokodil [kroko'di:l] (**-s**, **-e**) *nt* crocodile

Krokus ['kro:kʊs] (**-**, **-** *od* **-se**) *m* crocus

Krone ['kro:nə] *f* crown; (*Baumkrone*) top

krönen ['krø:nən] *vt* to crown

ron- *zW:* **~korken** *m* bottle top; **~leuchter** *m* chandelier; **~prinz** *m* crown prince

rönung ['krø:nʊŋ] *f* coronation

ropf [krɔpf] **(-(e)s, ⁻e)** *m* (*MED*) goitre; (*von Vogel*) crop

röte ['krø:tə] *f* toad

rücke ['krʏkə] *f* crutch

rug [kru:k] **(-(e)s, ⁻e)** *m* jug; (*Bierkrug*) mug

rümel ['kry:məl] **(-s, -)** *m* crumb; **k~n** *vt, vi* to crumble

rumm [krʊm] *adj* (*auch fig*) crooked; (*kurvig*) curved; **jdm etw ~ nehmen** to take sth amiss; **~beinig** *adj* bandy-legged; **~lachen** (*umg*) *vr* to laugh o.s. silly

rümmung ['krʏmʊŋ] *f* bend, curve

rüppel ['krʏpəl] **(-s, -)** *m* cripple

ruste ['krʊstə] *f* crust

ruzifix [krutsi'fɪks] **(-es, -e)** *nt* crucifix

übel ['ky:bəl] **(-s, -)** *m* tub; (*Eimer*) pail

ubikmeter [ku'bi:kme:tər] *m* cubic metre

üche ['kʏçə] *f* kitchen; (*Kochen*) cooking, cuisine

uchen ['ku:xən] **(-s, -)** *m* cake; **~form** *f* baking tin; **~gabel** *f* pastry fork

üchen- *zW:* **~herd** *m* cooker, stove; **~schabe** *f* cockroach; **~schrank** *m* kitchen cabinet

uckuck ['kʊkʊk] **(-s, -e)** *m* cuckoo; **~suhr** *f* cuckoo clock

ugel ['ku:gəl] **(-, -n)** *f* ball; (*MATH*) sphere; (*MIL*) bullet; (*Erdkugel*) globe; (*SPORT*) shot; **k~förmig** *adj* spherical; **~lager** *nt* ball bearing; **k~rund** *adj* (*Gegenstand*) round; (*umg: Person*) tubby; **~schreiber** *m* ballpoint (pen), Biro ®; **k~sicher** *adj* bulletproof; **~stoßen (-s)** *nt* shot put

uh [ku:] **(-, ⁻e)** *f* cow

ühl [ky:l] *adj* (*auch fig*) cool; **K~anlage** *f* refrigeration plant; **K~e (-)** *f* coolness; **~en** *vt* to cool; **K~er (-s, -)** *m* (*AUT*) radiator; **K~erhaube** *f* (*AUT*) bonnet (*BRIT*), hood (*US*); **K~raum** *m* cold storage chamber; **K~schrank** *m* refrigerator; **K~truhe** *f* freezer; **K~ung** *f* cooling; **K~wasser** *nt* radiator water

ühn [ky:n] *adj* bold, daring; **K~heit** *f* boldness

Kuhstall *m* byre, cattle shed

Küken ['ky:kən] **(-s, -)** *nt* chicken

kulant [ku'lant] *adj* obliging

Kuli ['ku:li] **(-s, -s)** *m* coolie; (*umg: Kugelschreiber*) Biro ®

Kulisse [ku'lɪsə] *f* scenery

kullern ['kʊlərn] *vi* to roll

Kult [kʊlt] **(-(e)s, -e)** *m* worship, cult; **mit etw einen ~ treiben** to make a cult out of sth

kultivieren [kʊlti'vi:rən] *vt* to cultivate

kultiviert *adj* cultivated, refined

Kultur [kʊl'tu:r] *f* culture; civilization; (*des Bodens*) cultivation; **~banause** (*umg*) *m* philistine, low-brow; **~beutel** *m* toilet bag; **k~ell** [-u'rɛl] *adj* cultural; **~ministerium** *nt* ministry of education and the arts

Kümmel ['kʏməl] **(-s, -)** *m* caraway seed; (*Branntwein*) kümmel

Kummer ['kʊmər] **(-s)** *m* grief, sorrow

kümmerlich ['kʏmərlɪç] *adj* miserable, wretched

kümmern ['kʏmərn] *vt* to concern ♦ *vr:* **sich um jdn ~** to look after sb; **das kümmert mich nicht** that doesn't worry me; **sich um etw ~** to see to sth

Kumpel ['kʊmpəl] **(-s, -)** (*umg*) *m* mate

kündbar ['kʏntba:r] *adj* redeemable, recallable; (*Vertrag*) terminable

Kunde¹ ['kʊndə] **(-n, -n)** *m* customer

Kunde² ['kʊndə] *f* (*Botschaft*) news

Kunden- *zW:* **~dienst** *m* after-sales service; **~konto** *nt* charge account; **~nummer** *f* customer number

Kund- *zW:* **k~geben** (*unreg*) *vt* to announce; **~gebung** *f* announcement; (*Versammlung*) rally

Künd- ['kʏnd] *zW:* **k~igen** *vi* to give in one's notice ♦ *vt* to cancel; **jdm k~igen** to give sb his notice; **die Stellung/Wohnung k~igen** to give notice that one is leaving one's job/house; **jdm die Stellung/Wohnung k~igen** to give sb notice to leave his/her job/house; **~igung** *f* notice; **~igungsfrist** *f* period of notice; **~igungsschutz** *m* protection against wrongful dismissal

Kundin f customer

Kundschaft f customers pl, clientele

künftig ['kʏnftɪç] adj future ♦ adv in future

Kunst [kʊnst] (-, ⸚e) f art; (*Können*) skill; **das ist doch keine ~** it's easy; **~dünger** m artificial manure; **~faser** f synthetic fibre; **~fertigkeit** f skilfulness; **~gegenstand** m art object; **~gerecht** adj skilful; **~geschichte** f history of art; **~gewerbe** nt arts and crafts pl; **~griff** m trick, knack; **~händler** m art dealer

Künstler(in) ['kʏnstlər(ɪn)] (-s, -) m(f) artist; **k~isch** adj artistic; **~name** m pseudonym

künstlich ['kʏnstlɪç] adj artificial

Kunst- zW: **~sammler** (-s, -) m art collector; **~seide** f artificial silk; **~stoff** m synthetic material; **~stück** nt trick; **~turnen** nt gymnastics sg; **k~voll** adj artistic; **~werk** nt work of art

kunterbunt ['kʊntərbʊnt] adj higgledy-piggledy

Kupee ▲ [ku'pe:] (-s, -s) nt coupé

Kupfer ['kʊpfər] (-s) nt copper; **k~n** adj copper

Kupon [ku'põ:, ku'pɔŋ] (-s, -s) m coupon; (*Stoff~*) length of cloth

Kuppe ['kʊpə] f (*Bergkuppe*) top; (*Fingerkuppe*) tip

Kuppel (-, -n) f dome; **k~n** vi (*JUR*) to procure; (*AUT*) to declutch ♦ vt to join

Kupplung f coupling; (*AUT*) clutch

Kur [ku:r] (-, -en) f cure, treatment

Kür [ky:r] (-, -en) f (*SPORT*) free exercises pl

Kurbel ['kʊrbəl] (-, -n) f crank, winder; (*AUT*) starting handle; **~welle** f crankshaft

Kürbis ['kʏrbɪs] (-ses, -se) m pumpkin; (*exotisch*) gourd

Kurgast m visitor (to a health resort)

kurieren [ku'ri:rən] vt to cure

kurios [kuri'o:s] adj curious, odd; **K~i'tät** f curiosity

Kurort m health resort

Kurs [kʊrs] (-es, -e) m course; (*FIN*) rate; **~buch** nt timetable; **k~ieren** [kʊr'zi:rən] vi to circulate; **k~iv** [kʊr'zi:f] adv in italics; **~us** ['kʊrzʊs] (-, **Kurse**) m course; **~wagen**

m (*EISENB*) through carriage

Kurtaxe [-taksə] (-, -n) f visitors' tax (at health resort or spa)

Kurve ['kʊrvə] f curve; (*Straßenkurve*) curve, bend; **kurvig** adj (*Straße*) bendy

kurz [kʊrts] adj short; **~ halten** to keep short; **zu ~ kommen** to come off badly; **den Kürzeren ziehen** to get the worst of it; **K~arbeit** f short-time work; **~ärm(e)lig** adj short-sleeved

Kürze ['kʏrtsə] f shortness, brevity; **k~n** vt to cut short; (*in der Länge*) to shorten; (*Gehalt*) to reduce

kurz- zW: **~erhand** adv on the spot; **~fristig** adj short-term; **K~geschichte** f short story; **~halten** △ (*unreg*) vt siehe **kurz**; **~lebig** adj short-lived

kürzlich ['kʏrtslɪç] adv lately, recently

Kurz- zW: **~schluss** ▲ m (*ELEK*) short circuit; **k~sichtig** adj short-sighted

Kürzung f (*eines Textes*) abridgement; (*eines Theaterstück, des Gehalts*) cut

Kurzwelle f short wave

kuscheln ['kʊʃəln] vr to snuggle up

Kusine [ku'zi:nə] f cousin

Kuss ▲ [kʊs] (-es, ⸚e) m kiss

küssen ['kʏsən] vt, vr to kiss

Küste ['kʏstə] f coast, shore

Küstenwache f coastguard

Küster ['kʏstər] (-s, -) m sexton, verger

Kutsche ['kʊtʃə] f coach, carriage; **~r** (-s, -) m coachman

Kutte ['kʊtə] f habit

Kuvert [ku'vert] (-s, -e od -s) nt envelope; cover

KZ nt abk von **Konzentrationslager**

L, l

l. abk = **Liter**

labil [la'bi:l] adj (*MED: Konstitution*) delicate

Labor [la'bo:r] (-s, -e od -s) nt lab; **~ant(in)** m(f) lab(oratory) assistant

Labyrinth [laby'rɪnt] (-s, -e) nt labyrinth

Lache ['laxə] f (*Flüssigkeit*) puddle; (*von Blut, Benzin etc*) pool

ächeln ['lɛçəln] vi to smile; **L~** (**-s**) nt smile

achen ['laxən] vi to laugh

ächerlich ['lɛçərlɪç] adj ridiculous

achgas nt laughing gas

achhaft adj laughable

achs [laks] (**-es, -e**) m salmon

ack [lak] (**-(e)s, -e**) m lacquer, varnish; (von Auto) paint; **l~ieren** [la'ki:rən] vt to varnish; (Auto) to spray; **~ierer** [la'ki:rər] (**-s, -**) m varnisher

aden ['la:dən] (**-s, ̈**) m shop; (Fensterladen) shutter

aden ['la:dən] (unreg) vt (Lasten) to load; (JUR) to summon; (einladen) to invite

aden- zW: **~dieb** m shoplifter; **~diebstahl** m shoplifting; **~schluss** ▲ m closing time; **~tisch** m counter

aderaum m freight space; (AVIAT, NAUT) hold

adung ['la:dʊŋ] f (Last) cargo, load; (Beladen) loading; (JUR) summons; (Einladung) invitation; (Sprengladung) charge

age ['la:gə] f position, situation; (Schicht) layer; **in der ~ sein** to be in a position

ageplan m ground plan

ager ['la:gər] (**-s, -**) nt camp; (COMM) warehouse; (Schlaflager) bed; (von Tier) lair; (TECH) bearing; **~bestand** m stocks pl; **~feuer** nt campfire; **~haus** nt warehouse, store

agern ['la:gərn] vi (Dinge) to be stored; (Menschen) to camp ♦ vt to store; (betten) to lay down; (Maschine) to bed

agune [la'gu:nə] f lagoon

ahm [la:m] adj lame; **~ legen** to paralyse; **~en** vi to be lame

ähmung f paralysis

aib [laip] (**-s, -e**) m loaf

aie ['laiə] (**-n, -n**) m layman; **l~nhaft** adj amateurish

aken ['la:kən] (**-s, -**) nt sheet

akritze [la'krɪtsə] f liquorice

allen ['lalən] vt, vi to slur; (Baby) to babble

amelle [la'mɛlə] f lamella; (ELEK) lamina; (TECH) plate

ametta [la'mɛta] (**-s**) nt tinsel

Lamm [lam] (**-(e)s, ̈er**) nt lamb

Lampe ['lampə] f lamp

Lampen- zW: **~fieber** nt stage fright; **~schirm** m lampshade

Lampion [lampi'õː] (**-s, -s**) m Chinese lantern

Land [lant] (**-(e)s, ̈er**) nt land; (Nation, nicht Stadt) country; (Bundesland) state; **auf dem ~(e)** in the country; siehe **hierzulande**; **~besitz** m landed property; **~ebahn** f runway; **l~en** ['landən] vt, vi to land

---

Land

ⓘ A **Land** (plural **Länder**) is a member state of the **BRD** and of Austria. There are 16 **Länder** in Germany, namely Baden-Württemberg, Bayern, Berlin, Brandenburg, Bremen, Hamburg, Hessen, Mecklenburg-Vorpommern, Niedersachsen, Nordrhein-Westfalen, Rheinland-Pfalz, Saarland, Sachsen, Sachsen-Anhalt, Schleswig-Holstein and Thüringen. Each **Land** has its own parliament and constitution. The 9 **Länder** of Austria are Vorarlberg, Tirol, Salzburg, Oberösterreich, Niederösterreich, Kärnten, Steiermark, Burgenland and Wien.

Landes- ['landəs] zW: **~farben** pl national colours; **~innere(s)** nt inland region; **~sprache** f national language; **l~üblich** adj customary; **~verrat** m high treason; **~währung** f national currency; **l~weit** adj nationwide

Land- zW: **~haus** nt country house; **~karte** f map; **~kreis** m administrative region; **l~läufig** adj customary

ländlich ['lɛntlɪç] adj rural

Land- zW: **~schaft** f countryside; (KUNST) landscape; **~schaftsschutzgebiet** nt nature reserve; **~sitz** m country seat; **~straße** f country road; **~streicher** (**-s, -**) m tramp; **~strich** m region

Landung ['landʊŋ] f landing; **~sbrücke** f jetty, pier

Land- zW: **~weg** m: **etw auf dem ~weg befördern** to transport sth by land; **~wirt**

---

m farmer; **~wirtschaft** *f* agriculture;
~zunge *f* spit

lang [laŋ] *adj* long; (*Mensch*) tall; **~atmig** *adj*
long-winded; **~e** *adv* for a long time;
(*dauern, brauchen*) a long time

Länge ['lɛŋə] *f* length; (*GEOG*) longitude

langen ['laŋən] *vi* (*ausreichen*) to do, to
suffice; (*fassen*): **~ (nach)** to reach (for)
♦ *vt*: **jdm etw ~** to hand *od* pass sb sth; **es
langt mir** I've had enough

Längengrad *m* longitude

Längenmaß *nt* linear measure

lang- *zW*: **~eweile** *f* boredom; **~fristig**
adj long-term; **~jährig** (*Freundschaft,
Gewohnheit*) long-standing; **L~lauf** *m* (*SKI*)
cross-country skiing

länglich *adj* longish

längs [lɛŋs] *präp* (+*gen od dat*) along ♦ *adv*
lengthwise

lang- *zW*: **~sam** *adj* slow; **L~samkeit** *f*
slowness; **L~schläfer(in)** *m(f)* late riser

längst [lɛŋst] *adv*: **das ist ~ fertig** that was
finished a long time ago, that has been
finished for a long time; **~e(r, s)** *adj*
longest

lang- *zW*: **~weilen** *vt* to bore ♦ *vr* to be
bored; **~weilig** *adj* boring, tedious;
L~welle *f* long wave; **~wierig** *adj* lengthy,
long-drawn-out

Lanze ['lantsə] *f* lance

Lappalie [la'pa:liə] *f* trifle

Lappen ['lapən] (**-s, -**) *m* cloth, rag; (*ANAT*)
lobe

läppisch ['lɛpɪʃ] *adj* foolish

Lapsus ['lapsʊs] (**-, -**) *m* slip

Laptop ['lɛptɔp] (**-s, -s**) *m* laptop
(computer)

Lärche ['lɛrçə] *f* larch

Lärm [lɛrm] (**-(e)s**) *m* noise; **l~en** *vi* to be
noisy, to make a noise

Larve ['larfə] *f* (*BIOL*) larva

lasch [laʃ] *adj* slack

Laser ['le:zər] (**-s, -**) *m* laser

SCHLÜSSELWORT

lassen ['lasən] (*pt* **ließ**, *pp* **gelassen** *od* (*als
Hilfsverb*) **lassen**) *vt* **1** (*unterlassen*) to stop;

(*momentan*) to leave; **lass das (sein)!** don't
(do it)!; (*hör auf*) stop it!; **lass mich!** leave
me alone; **lassen wir das!** let's leave it; **er
kann das Trinken nicht lassen** he can't
stop drinking

2 (*zurücklassen*) to leave; **etw lassen, wie
es ist** to leave sth (just) as it is

3 (*überlassen*): **jdn ins Haus lassen** to let
sb into the house

♦ *vi*: **lass mal, ich mache das schon** leave
it, I'll do it

♦ *Hilfsverb* **1** (*veranlassen*): **etw machen
lassen** to have *od* get sth done; **sich** *dat*
etw schicken lassen to have sth sent (to
one)

2 (*zulassen*): **jdn etw wissen lassen** to let
sb know sth; **das Licht brennen lassen** to
leave the light on; **jdn warten lassen** to
keep sb waiting; **das lässt sich machen**
that can be done

3: lass uns gehen let's go

---

lässig ['lɛsɪç] *adj* casual; **L~keit** *f* casualness

Last [last] (**-, -en**) *f* load, burden; (*NAUT,
AVIAT*) cargo; (*meist pl: Gebühr*) charge; **jdm
zur ~ fallen** to be a burden to sb; **~auto**
nt lorry, truck; **l~en** *vi*: **l~en auf** +*dat* to
weigh on; **~enaufzug** *m* goods lift *od*
elevator (*US*)

Laster ['lastər] (**-s, -**) *nt* vice

lästern ['lɛstərn] *vt, vi* (*Gott*) to blaspheme;
(*schlecht sprechen*) to mock

Lästerung *f* jibe; (*Gotteslästerung*)
blasphemy

lästig ['lɛstɪç] *adj* troublesome, tiresome

Last- *zW*: **~kahn** *m* barge; **~kraftwagen**
m heavy goods vehicle; **~schrift** *f* debit;
~wagen *m* lorry, truck; **~zug** *m* articulated
lorry

Latein [la'taɪn] (**-s**) *nt* Latin; **~amerika** *nt*
Latin America

latent [la'tɛnt] *adj* latent

Laterne [la'tɛrnə] *f* lantern; (*Straßenlaterne*)
lamp, light; **~npfahl** *m* lamppost

latschen ['la:tʃən] (*umg*) *vi* (*gehen*) to
wander, to go; (*lässig*) to slouch

Latte ['latə] *f* lath; (*SPORT*) goalpost; (*quer*)

crossbar

Latzhose [ˈlatshoːzə] f dungarees pl

lau [lau] adj (Nacht) balmy; (Wasser) lukewarm

Laub [laup] (-(e)s) nt foliage; ~baum m deciduous tree; ~frosch m tree frog; ~säge f fretsaw

Lauch [laux] (-(e)s, -e) m leek

Lauer [ˈlauər] f: auf der ~ sein od liegen to lie in wait; l~n vi to lie in wait; (Gefahr) to lurk

Lauf [lauf] (-(e)s, Läufe) m run; (Wettlauf) race; (Entwicklung, ASTRON) course; (Gewehrlauf) barrel; einer Sache dat ihren ~ lassen to let sth take its course; ~bahn f career

laufen [ˈlaufən] (unreg) vt, vi to run; (umg: gehen) to walk; ~d adj running; (Monat, Ausgaben) current; auf dem ~den sein/ halten to be/keep up to date; am ~den Band (fig) continuously

Läufer [ˈlɔyfər] (-s, -) m (Teppich, SPORT) runner; (Fußball) half-back; (Schach) bishop

Lauf- zW: ~masche f run, ladder (BRIT); ~pass ▲ m: jdm den ~pass geben (umg) to send sb packing (inf); ~stall m playpen; ~steg m catwalk; ~werk nt (COMPUT) disk drive

Lauge [ˈlaugə] f soapy water; (CHEM) alkaline solution

Laune [ˈlaunə] f mood, humour; (Einfall) caprice; (schlechte) temper; l~nhaft adj capricious, changeable

launisch adj moody; bad-tempered

Laus [laus] (-, Läuse) f louse

lauschen [ˈlaufən] vi to eavesdrop, to listen in

lauschig [ˈlaufıç] adj snug

lausig [ˈlauzıç] (umg: pej) adj measly; (Kälte) perishing

laut [laut] adj loud ♦ adv loudly; (lesen) aloud ♦ präp (+gen od dat) according to; **L~** (-(e)s, -e) m sound

Laute [ˈlautə] f lute

lauten [ˈlautən] vi to say; (Urteil) to be

läuten [ˈlɔytən] vt, vi to ring, to sound

lauter [ˈlautər] adj (Wasser) clear, pure;

(Wahrheit, Charakter) honest ♦ adj inv (Freude, Dummheit etc) sheer ♦ adv nothing but, only

laut- zW: ~hals adv at the top of one's voice; ~los adj noiseless, silent; **L~schrift** f phonetics pl; **L~sprecher** m loudspeaker; ~stark adj vociferous; **L~stärke** f (RADIO) volume

lauwarm [ˈlauvarm] adj (auch fig) lukewarm

Lavendel [laˈvɛndəl] (-s, -) m lavender

Lawine [laˈviːnə] f avalanche; ~ngefahr f danger of avalanches

lax [laks] adj lax

Lazarett [latsaˈrɛt] (-(e)s, -e) nt (MIL) hospital, infirmary

leasen [ˈliːzən] vt to lease

Leben (-s, -) nt life

leben [ˈleːbən] vt, vi to live; ~d adj living; ~dig [leˈbɛndıç] adj living, alive; (lebhaft) lively; **L~digkeit** f liveliness

Lebens- zW: ~art f way of life; ~erwartung f life expectancy; l~fähig adj able to live; ~freude f zest for life; ~gefahr f: **~gefahr!** danger!; in ~gefahr dangerously ill; l~gefährlich adj dangerous; (Verletzung) critical; ~haltungskosten pl cost of living sg; ~jahr nt year of life; l~länglich adj (Strafe) for life; ~lauf m curriculum vitae; ~mittel pl food sg; ~mittelgeschäft nt grocer's (shop); ~mittelvergiftung f (MED) food poisoning; l~müde adj tired of life; ~retter m lifesaver; ~standard m standard of living; ~unterhalt m livelihood; ~versicherung f life insurance; ~wandel m way of life; ~weise f lifestyle, way of life; l~wichtig adj vital, essential; ~zeichen nt sign of life

Leber [ˈleːbər] (-, -n) f liver; ~fleck m mole; ~tran m cod-liver oil; ~wurst f liver sausage

Lebewesen nt creature

leb- [ˈleːp] zW: ~haft adj lively, vivacious; **L~kuchen** m gingerbread; ~los adj lifeless

Leck [lɛk] (-(e)s, -e) nt leak; l~ adj leaky, leaking; l~en vi (Loch haben) to leak; (schlecken) to lick ♦ vt to lick

lecker ['lɛkər] adj delicious, tasty; **L~bissen** m dainty morsel

Leder ['leːdər] (-s, -) nt leather; ~hose f lederhosen; l~n adj leather; ~waren pl leather goods

ledig ['leːdɪç] adj single; **einer Sache** gen ~ **sein** to be free of sth; ~lich adv merely, solely

leer [leːr] adj empty; vacant; ~ **machen** to empty; ~ **stehend** empty; **L~e** (-) f emptiness; ~**en** vt, vr to empty; **L~gewicht** nt weight when empty; **L~gut** nt empties pl; **L~lauf** m neutral; **L~ung** f emptying; (Post) collection

legal [le'gaːl] adj legal, lawful; ~i'sieren vt to legalize

legen ['leːgən] vt to lay, to put, to place; (Ei) to lay ♦ vr to lie down; (fig) to subside

Legende [le'gɛndə] f legend

leger [le'ʒɛːr] adj casual

Legierung [le'giːrʊŋ] f alloy

Legislative [legɪslaˈtiːvə] f legislature

legitim [legi'tiːm] adj legitimate

legitimieren [legiti'miːrən] vt to legitimate ♦ vr to prove one's identity

Lehm [leːm] (-(e)s, -e) m loam; l~ig adj loamy

Lehne ['leːnə] f arm; back; l~n vt, vr to lean

Lehnstuhl m armchair

Lehr- zW: ~amt nt teaching profession; ~buch nt textbook

Lehre ['leːrə] f teaching, doctrine; (beruflich) apprenticeship; (moralisch) lesson; (TECH) gauge; l~n vt to teach

Lehrer(in) (-s, -) m(f) teacher; ~zimmer nt staff room

Lehr- zW: ~gang m course; ~jahre pl apprenticeship sg; ~kraft f (förmlich) teacher; ~ling m apprentice; ~plan m syllabus; l~reich adj instructive; ~stelle f apprenticeship; ~zeit f apprenticeship

Leib [laɪp] (-(e)s, -er) m body; **halt ihn mir vom ~!** keep him away from me!; l~haftig adj personified; (Teufel) incarnate; l~lich adj bodily; (Vater etc) own; ~schmerzen pl stomach pains; ~wache f bodyguard

Leiche ['laɪçə] f corpse; ~nhalle f mortuary;

~nwagen m hearse

Leichnam ['laɪçnaːm] (-(e)s, -e) m corpse

leicht [laɪçt] adj light; (einfach) easy; **jdm ~ fallen** to be easy for sb; **es sich** dat ~ **machen** to make things easy for o.s.; **L~athletik** f athletics sg; ~fertig adj frivolous; ~gläubig adj gullible, credulous; ~hin adv lightly; **L~igkeit** f easiness; **mit L~igkeit** with ease; **L~sinn** m carelessness; ~sinnig adj careless

Leid [laɪt] (-(e)s) nt grief, sorrow; **es tut mir/ihm ~** I am/he is sorry; **er/das tut mir ~** I am sorry for him/it; l~ adj: **etw l~ haben** od **sein** to be tired of sth; l~en (unreg) vt to suffer; (erlauben) to permit ♦ vi to suffer; **jdn/etw nicht l~en können** not to be able to stand sb/sth; **~en** ['laɪdən] (-s, -) nt suffering; (Krankheit) complaint; ~enschaft f passion; l~enschaftlich adj passionate

leider ['laɪdər] adv unfortunately; **ja, ~** yes, I'm afraid so; **~ nicht** I'm afraid not

leidig ['laɪdɪç] adj worrying, troublesome

leidlich [laɪtlɪç] adj tolerable ♦ adv tolerably

Leid- zW: **~tragende** f(m) bereaved; (Benachteiligter) one who suffers; ~wesen nt: **zu jds ~wesen** to sb's disappointment

Leier ['laɪər] (-, -n) f lyre; (fig) old story; ~kasten m barrel organ

Leihbibliothek f lending library

Leihbücherei f lending library

leihen ['laɪən] (unreg) vt to lend; **sich** dat **etw ~** to borrow sth

Leih- zW: ~gebühr f hire charge; ~haus nt pawnshop; ~wagen m hired car

Leim [laɪm] (-(e)s, -e) m glue; l~en vt to glue

Leine ['laɪnə] f line, cord; (Hundeleine) leash, lead

Leinen nt linen; l~ adj linen

Leinwand f (KUNST) canvas; (CINE) screen

leise ['laɪzə] adj quiet; (sanft) soft, gentle

Leiste ['laɪstə] f ledge; (Zierleiste) strip; (ANAT) groin

leisten ['laɪstən] vt (Arbeit) to do; (Gesellschaft) to keep; (Ersatz) to supply; (vollbringen) to achieve; **sich** dat **etw ~**

können to be able to afford sth

Leistung f performance; (gute) achievement; **~sdruck** m pressure; **l~sfähig** adj efficient

Leitartikel m leading article

Leitbild nt model

leiten ['laɪtən] vt to lead; (Firma) to manage; (in eine Richtung) to direct; (ELEK) to conduct

Leiter¹ ['laɪtər] (**-s, -**) m leader, head; (ELEK) conductor

Leiter² ['laɪtər] (**-, -n**) f ladder

Leitfaden m guide

Leitplanke f crash barrier

Leitung f (Führung) direction; (CINE, THEAT etc) production; (von Firma) management; directors pl; (Wasserleitung) pipe; (Kabel) cable; **eine lange ~ haben** to be slow on the uptake

Leitungs- zW: **~draht** m wire; **~rohr** nt pipe; **~wasser** nt tap water

Lektion [lɛktsi'oːn] f lesson

Lektüre [lɛk'tyːrə] f (Lesen) reading; (Lesestoff) reading matter

Lende ['lɛndə] f loin; **~nstück** nt fillet

lenk- ['lɛŋk] zW: **~bar** adj (Fahrzeug) steerable; (Kind) manageable; **~en** vt to steer; (Kind) to guide; (Blick, Aufmerksamkeit): **~en (auf** +akk**)** to direct (at); **L~rad** nt steering wheel; **L~radschloss** ▲ nt steering (wheel) lock; **L~stange** f handlebars pl; **L~ung** f steering

Lepra ['leːpra] (**-**) f leprosy

Lerche ['lɛrçə] f lark

lernbegierig adj eager to learn

lernen ['lɛrnən] vt to learn

lesbar ['leːsbaːr] adj legible

Lesbierin ['lɛsbiərɪn] f lesbian

lesbisch ['lɛsbɪʃ] adj lesbian

Lese ['leːzə] f (Wein) harvest

Lesebrille f reading glasses

Lesebuch nt reading book, reader

lesen (unreg) vt, vi to read; (ernten) to gather, to pick

Leser(in) (**-s, -**) m(f) reader; **~brief** m reader's letter; **l~lich** adj legible

Lesezeichen nt bookmark

Lesung ['leːzʊŋ] f (PARL) reading

letzte(r, s) ['lɛtstə(r, s)] adj last; (neueste) latest; **zum ~n Mal** for the last time; **~ns** adv lately; **~re(r, s)** adj latter

Leuchte ['lɔʏçtə] f lamp, light; **l~n** vi to shine, to gleam; **~r** m candlestick

Leucht- zW: **~farbe** f fluorescent colour; **~rakete** f flare; **~reklame** f neon sign; **~röhre** f strip light; **~turm** m lighthouse

leugnen ['lɔʏɡnən] vt to deny

Leukämie [lɔʏkɛ'miː] f leukaemia

Leukoplast [lɔʏko'plast] (®; **-(e)s, -e**) nt Elastoplast ®

Leumund ['lɔʏmʊnt] (**-(e)s, -e**) m reputation

Leumundszeugnis nt character reference

Leute ['lɔʏtə] pl people pl

Leutnant ['lɔʏtnant] (**-s, -s** od **-e**) m lieutenant

leutselig ['lɔʏtzeːlɪç] adj amiable

Lexikon ['lɛksikɔn] (**-s, Lexiken** od **Lexika**) nt encyclop(a)edia

Libelle [li'bɛlə] f dragonfly; (TECH) spirit level

liberal [libe'raːl] adj liberal; **L~e(r)** f(m) liberal

Licht [lɪçt] (**-(e)s, -er**) nt light; **~bild** nt photograph; (Dia) slide; **~blick** m cheering prospect; **l~empfindlich** adj sensitive to light; **l~en** vt to clear; (Anker) to weigh ♦ vr to clear up; (Haar) to thin; **l~erloh** adv: **l~erloh brennen** to be ablaze; **~hupe** f flashing of headlights; **~jahr** nt light year; **~maschine** f dynamo; **~schalter** m light switch; **~schutzfaktor** m protection factor

Lichtung f clearing, glade

Lid [liːt] (**-(e)s, -er**) nt eyelid; **~schatten** m eyeshadow

lieb [liːp] adj dear; **das ist ~ von dir** that's kind of you; **~ gewinnen** to get fond of; **~ haben** to be fond of; **~äugeln** [li:bɔʏɡəln] vi insep: **mit etw ~äugeln** to have one's eye on sth; **mit dem Gedanken ~äugeln, etw zu tun** to toy with the idea of doing sth

Liebe ['liːbə] f love; **l~bedürftig** adj: **l~bedürftig sein** to need love; **l~n** vt to love; to like

liebens- *zW:* **~wert** *adj* loveable; **~würdig** *adj* kind; **~würdigerweise** *adv* kindly; **L~würdigkeit** *f* kindness

lieber ['li:bər] *adv* rather, preferably; **ich gehe ~ nicht** I'd rather not go; *siehe auch* **gern; lieb**

Liebes- *zW:* **~brief** *m* love letter; **~kummer** *m:* **~kummer haben** to be lovesick; **~paar** *nt* courting couple, lovers *pl*

liebevoll *adj* loving

lieb- [li:p] *zW:* **~gewinnen** △ (*unreg*) *vt siehe* **lieb; ~haben** △ (*unreg*) *vt siehe* **lieb; L~haber (-s, -)** *m* lover; **L~habe'rei** *f* hobby; **~kosen** ['li:pko:zən] *vt insep* to caress; **~lich** *adj* lovely, charming; **L~ling** *m* darling; **L~lings-** *in zW* favourite; **~los** *adj* unloving; **L~schaft** *f* love affair

Lied [li:t] (**-(e)s, -er**) *nt* song; (*REL*) hymn; **~erbuch** ['li:dər-] *nt* songbook; hymn book

liederlich ['li:dərlıç] *adj* slovenly; (*Lebenswandel*) loose, immoral; **L~keit** *f* slovenliness; immorality

lief *etc* [li:f] *vb siehe* **laufen**

Lieferant [li:fə'rant] *m* supplier

Lieferbedingungen *pl* terms of delivery

liefern ['li:fərn] *vt* to deliver; (*versorgen mit*) to supply; (*Beweis*) to produce

Liefer- *zW:* **~schein** *m* delivery note; **~termin** *m* delivery date; **~ung** *f* delivery; supply; **~wagen** *m* van; **~zeit** *f* delivery period

Liege ['li:gə] *f* bed

liegen ['li:gən] (*unreg*) *vi* to lie; (*sich befinden*) to be; **mir liegt nichts/viel daran** it doesn't matter to me/it matters a lot to me; **es liegt bei Ihnen, ob ...** it's up to you whether ...; **Sprachen ~ mir nicht** languages are not my line; **woran liegt es?** what's the cause?; **~ bleiben** (*im Bett*) to stay in bed; (*nicht aufstehen*) to stay lying down; (*vergessen werden*) to be left (behind); **~ lassen** (*vergessen*) to leave behind

Liege- *zW:* **~sitz** *m* (*AUT*) reclining seat; **~stuhl** *m* deck chair; **~wagen** *m* (*EISENB*) couchette

Lift [lıft] (**-(e)s, -e** *od* **-s**) *m* lift

Likör [li'kø:r] (**-s, -e**) *m* liqueur

lila ['li:la] *adj inv* purple, lilac; **L~** (**-s, -s**) *nt* (*Farbe*) purple, lilac

Lilie ['li:liə] *f* lily

Limonade [limo'na:də] *f* lemonade

Limone [li'mo:nə] *f* lime

Linde ['lındə] *f* lime tree, linden

lindern ['lındərn] *vt* to alleviate, to soothe; **Linderung** *f* alleviation

Lineal [line'a:l] (**-s, -e**) *nt* ruler

Linie ['li:niə] *f* line

Linien- *zW:* **~blatt** *nt* ruled sheet; **~flug** *m* scheduled flight; **~richter** *m* linesman

linieren [li'ni:rən] *vt* to line

Linke ['lıŋkə] *f* left side; left hand; (*POL*) left

linkisch *adj* awkward, gauche

links [lıŋks] *adv* left; to *od* on the left; **~ von mir** on *od* to my left; **L~händer(in)** (**-s, -**) *m(f)* left-handed person; **L~kurve** *f* left-hand bend; **L~verkehr** *m* driving on the left

Linoleum [li'no:leʊm] (**-s**) *nt* lino(leum)

Linse ['lınzə] *f* lentil; (*optisch*) lens *sg*

Lippe ['lıpə] *f* lip; **~nstift** *m* lipstick

lispeln ['lıspəln] *vi* to lisp

Lissabon ['lısabon] (**-s**) *nt* Lisbon

List [lıst] (**-, -en**) *f* cunning; trick, ruse

Liste ['lıstə] *f* list

listig ['lıstıç] *adj* cunning, sly

Liter ['li:tər] (**-s, -**) *nt od m* litre

literarisch [lıte'ra:rıʃ] *adj* literary

Literatur [lıtera'tu:r] *f* literature

Litfaßsäule ['lıtfaszɔylə] *f* advertising pillar

Liturgie [lıtʊr'gi:] *f* liturgy

liturgisch [li'tʊrgıʃ] *adj* liturgical

Litze ['lıtsə] *f* braid; (*ELEK*) flex

Lizenz [li'tsents] *f* licence

Lkw [ɛlka:'ve:] (**-(s), -(s)**) *m abk* = **Lastkraftwagen**

Lob [lo:p] (**-(e)s**) *nt* praise

Lobby ['lɔbi] *f* lobby

loben ['lo:bən] *vt* to praise; **~swert** *adj* praiseworthy

löblich ['lø:plıç] *adj* praiseworthy, laudable

Loch [lɔx] (**-(e)s, ~er**) *nt* hole; **l~en** *vt* to punch holes in; **~er** (**-s, -**) *m* punch

öcherig ['lœçərıç] *adj* full of holes

Lochkarte *f* punch card

Lochstreifen *m* punch tape

Locke ['lɔkə] *f* lock, curl; **l~n** *vt* to entice; (*Haare*) to curl; **~nwickler (-s, -)** *m* curler

ocker ['lɔkər] *adj* loose; **~lassen** (*unreg*) *vi*: **nicht ~lassen** not to let up; **~n** *vt* to loosen

ockig ['lɔkıç] *adj* curly

lodern ['lo:dərn] *vi* to blaze

Löffel ['lœfəl] **(-s, -)** *m* spoon

löffeln *vt* to spoon

Loge ['lo:ʒə] *f* (*THEAT*) box; (*Freimaurer*) (masonic) lodge; (*Pförtnerloge*) office

Logik ['lo:gık] *f* logic

logisch ['lo:gıʃ] *adj* logical

Logopäde [logo'pɛ:də] **(-n, -n)** *m* speech therapist

Lohn [lo:n] **(-(e)s, ⁺e)** *m* reward; (*Arbeitslohn*) pay, wages *pl*; **~büro** *nt* wages office; **~empfänger** *m* wage earner

lohnen ['lo:nən] *vr unpers* to be worth it ♦ *vt*: **(jdm etw) ~** to reward (sb for sth); **~d** *adj* worthwhile

Lohn- *zW*: **~erhöhung** *f* pay rise; **~steuer** *f* income tax; **~steuerkarte** *f* (income) tax card; **~streifen** *m* pay slip; **~tüte** *f* pay packet

Lokal [lo'ka:l] **(-(e)s, -e)** *nt* pub(lic house)

lokal *adj* local; **~i'sieren** *vt* to localize

Lokomotive [lokomo'ti:və] *f* locomotive

Lokomotivführer *m* engine driver

Lorbeer ['lɔrbe:r] **(-s, -en)** *m* (*auch fig*) laurel; **~blatt** *nt* (*KOCH*) bay leaf

Los [lo:s] **(-es, -e)** *nt* (*Schicksal*) lot, fate; (*Lotterielos*) lottery ticket

los [lo:s] *adj* (*locker*) loose; **~!** go on!; **etw ~ sein** to be rid of sth; **was ist ~?** what's the matter?; **dort ist nichts/viel ~** there's nothing/a lot going on there; **~binden** (*unreg*) *vt* to untie

Löschblatt ['lœʃblat] *nt* sheet of blotting paper

löschen ['lœʃən] *vt* (*Feuer, Licht*) to put out, to extinguish; (*Durst*) to quench; (*COMM*) to cancel; (*COMPUT*) to delete; (*Tonband*) to erase; (*Fracht*) to unload ♦ *vi* (*Feuerwehr*) to

put out a fire; (*Tinte*) to blot

Lösch- *zW*: **~fahrzeug** *nt* fire engine; fire boat; **~gerät** *nt* fire extinguisher; **~papier** *nt* blotting paper

lose ['lo:zə] *adj* loose

Lösegeld *nt* ransom

losen ['lo:zən] *vi* to draw lots

lösen ['lø:zən] *vt* to loosen; (*Rätsel etc*) to solve; (*Verlobung*) to call off; (*CHEM*) to dissolve; (*Partnerschaft*) to break up; (*Fahrkarte*) to buy ♦ *vr* (*aufgehen*) to come loose; (*Zucker etc*) to dissolve; (*Problem, Schwierigkeit*) to (re)solve itself

los- *zW*: **~fahren** (*unreg*) *vi* to leave; **~gehen** (*unreg*) *vi* to set out; (*anfangen*) to start; (*Bombe*) to go off; **auf jdn ~gehen** to go for sb; **~kaufen** *vt* (*Gefangene, Geißeln*) to pay ransom for; **~kommen** (*unreg*) *vi*: **von etw ~kommen** to get away from sth; **~lassen** (*unreg*) *vt* (*Seil*) to let go of; (*Schimpfe*) to let loose; **~laufen** (*unreg*) *vi* to run off

löslich ['lø:slıç] *adj* soluble; **L~keit** *f* solubility

los- *zW*: **~lösen** *vt*: **(sich) ~lösen** to free (o.s.); **~machen** *vt* to loosen; (*Boot*) to unmoor *vr* to get away; **~schrauben** *vt* to unscrew

Losung ['lo:zʊŋ] *f* watchword, slogan

Lösung ['lø:zʊŋ] *f* (*Lockermachen*) loosening; (*eines Rätsels, CHEM*) solution; **~smittel** *nt* solvent

los- *zW*: **~werden** (*unreg*) *vt* to get rid of; **~ziehen** (*unreg*) (*umg*) *vi* (*sich aufmachen*) to set off

Lot [lo:t] **(-(e)s, -e)** *nt* plumbline; **im ~** vertical; (*fig*) on an even keel

löten ['lø:tən] *vt* to solder

Lothringen ['lo:trıŋən] **(-s)** *nt* Lorraine

Lotse ['lo:tsə] **(-n, -n)** *m* pilot; (*AVIAT*) air traffic controller; **l~n** *vt* to pilot; (*umg*) to lure

Lotterie [lɔtə'ri:] *f* lottery

Lotto ['lɔto] **(-s, -s)** *nt* national lottery; **~zahlen** *pl* winning lottery numbers

Löwe ['lø:və] **(-n, -n)** *m* lion; (*ASTROL*) Leo; **~nanteil** *m* lion's share; **~nzahn** *m*

dandelion

loyal [lɔaˈjaːl] *adj* loyal; **L~ität** *f* loyalty

Luchs [lʊks] **(-es, -e)** *m* lynx

Lücke [ˈlʏkə] *f* gap

Lücken- *zW:* **~büßer (-s, -)** *m* stopgap; **l~haft** *adj* full of gaps; *(Versorgung, Vorräte etc)* inadequate; **l~los** *adj* complete

Luft [lʊft] **(-, ⁔e)** *f* air; *(Atem)* breath; **in der ~ liegen** to be in the air; **jdn wie ~ behandeln** to ignore sb; **~angriff** *m* air raid; **~ballon** *m* balloon; **~blase** *f* air bubble; **l~dicht** *adj* airtight; **~druck** *m* atmospheric pressure

lüften [ˈlʏftən] *vt* to air; *(Hut)* to lift, to raise ♦ *vi* to let some air in

Luft- *zW:* **~fahrt** *f* aviation; **~fracht** *f* air freight; **l~gekühlt** *adj* air-cooled; **~gewehr** *nt* air rifle, airgun; **l~ig** *adj (Ort)* breezy; *(Raum)* airy; *(Kleider)* summery; **~kissenfahrzeug** *nt* hovercraft; **~kurort** *m* health resort; **l~leer** *adj:* **l~leerer Raum** vacuum; **~linie** *f:* **in der ~linie** as the crow flies; **~loch** *nt* air hole; *(AVIAT)* air pocket; **~matratze** *f* Lilo ® *(BRIT)* air mattress; **~pirat** *m* hijacker; **~post** *f* airmail; **~pumpe** *f* air pump; **~röhre** *f (ANAT)* windpipe; **~schlange** *f* streamer; **~schutzkeller** *m* air-raid shelter; **~verkehr** *m* air traffic; **~verschmutzung** *f* air pollution; **~waffe** *f* air force; **~zug** *m* draught

Lüge [ˈlyːgə] *f* lie; **jdn/etw ~n strafen** to give the lie to sb/sth; **l~n** *(unreg) vi* to lie

Lügner(in) **(-s, -)** *m(f)* liar

Luke [ˈluːkə] *f* dormer window; hatch

Lump [lʊmp] **(-en, -en)** *m* scamp, rascal

Lumpen [ˈlʊmpən] **(-s, -)** *m* rag

lumpen [ˈlʊmpən] *vi:* **sich nicht ~ lassen** not to be mean

lumpig [ˈlʊmpɪç] *adj* shabby

Lupe [ˈluːpə] *f* magnifying glass; **unter die ~ nehmen** *(fig)* to scrutinize

Lust [lʊst] **(-, ⁔e)** *f* joy, delight; *(Neigung)* desire; **~ haben zu** *od* **auf etw** *akk* **/etw zu tun** to feel like sth/doing sth

lüstern [ˈlʏstərn] *adj* lustful, lecherous

lustig [ˈlʊstɪç] *adj (komisch)* amusing, funny; *(fröhlich)* cheerful

Lust- *zW:* **~los** *adj* unenthusiastic; **~mord** *m* sex(ual) murder; **~spiel** *nt* comedy

lutschen [ˈlʊtʃən] *vt, vi* to suck; **am Daumen ~** to suck one's thumb

Lutscher **(-s, -)** *m* lollipop

luxuriös [lʊksuriˈøːs] *adj* luxurious

Luxus [ˈlʊksʊs] **(-)** *m* luxury; **~artikel** *pl* luxury goods; **~hotel** *nt* luxury hotel

Luzern [luˈtsɛrn] **(-s)** *nt* Lucerne

Lymphe [ˈlʏmfə] *f* lymph

lynchen [ˈlʏnçən] *vt* to lynch

Lyrik [ˈlyːrɪk] *f* lyric poetry; **~er (-s, -)** *m* lyric poet

lyrisch [ˈlyːrɪʃ] *adj* lyrical

M, m

m *abk* = **Meter**

Machart *f* make

machbar *adj* feasible

SCHLÜSSELWORT
---

machen [ˈmaxən] *vt* **1** to do; *(herstellen, zubereiten)* to make; **was machst du da?** what are you doing (there)?; **das ist nicht zu machen** that can't be done; **das Radio leiser machen** to turn the radio down; **aus Holz gemacht** made of wood

2 *(verursachen, bewirken)* to make; **jdm Angst machen** to make sb afraid; **das macht die Kälte** it's the cold that does that

3 *(ausmachen)* to matter; **das macht nichts** that doesn't matter; **die Kälte macht mir nichts** I don't mind the cold

4 *(kosten, ergeben)* to be; **3 und 5 macht 8** 3 and 5 is *od* are 8; **was** *od* **wie viel macht das?** how much does that make?

5: was macht die Arbeit? how's the work going?; **was macht dein Bruder?** how is your brother doing?; **das Auto machen lassen** to have the car done; **machs gut!** take care!; *(viel Glück)* good luck!

♦ *vi:* **mach schnell!** hurry up!; **Schluss machen** to finish (off); **mach schon!** come on!; **das macht müde** it makes you tired; **in etw** *dat* **machen** to be *od* deal in sth ♦ *vr* to come along (nicely); **sich an etw** *akk* **machen** to set about sth; **sich verständlich machen** to make o.s. understood; **sich** *dat* **viel aus jdm/etw machen** to like sb/sth

Macht [maxt] (-, ¨e) *f* power; **~haber** (-s, -) *m* ruler

mächtig ['mɛçtɪç] *adj* powerful, mighty; (*umg: ungeheuer*) enormous

Macht- *zW*: **m~los** *adj* powerless; **~probe** *f* trial of strength; **~wort** *nt*: **ein ~wort sprechen** to exercise one's authority

Mädchen ['mɛːtçən] *nt* girl; **m~haft** *adj* girlish; **~name** *m* maiden name

Made ['maːdə] *f* maggot

madig ['maːdɪç] *adj* maggoty; **jdm etw ~ machen** to spoil sth for sb

mag *etc* [maːk] *vb siehe* **mögen**

Magazin [maga'tsiːn] (-s, -e) *nt* magazine

Magen ['maːgən] (-s, - *od* ¨) *m* stomach; **~geschwür** *nt* (*MED*) stomach ulcer; **~schmerzen** *pl* stomachache *sg*

mager ['maːgər] *adj* lean; (*dünn*) thin; **M~keit** *f* leanness; thinness

Magie [ma'giː] *f* magic

magisch ['maːgɪʃ] *adj* magical

Magnet [ma'gneːt] (-s *od* -en, -en) *m* magnet; **m~isch** *adj* magnetic; **~nadel** *f* magnetic needle

mähen ['mɛːən] *vt, vi* to mow

Mahl [maːl] (-(e)s, -e) *nt* meal; **m~en** (*unreg*) *vt* to grind; **~zeit** *f* meal ♦ *excl* enjoy your meal

Mahnbrief *m* reminder

Mähne ['mɛːnə] *f* mane

mahn- ['maːn] *zW*: **~en** *vt* to remind; (*warnend*) to warn; (*wegen Schuld*) to demand payment from; **M~mal** *nt* memorial; **M~ung** *f* reminder; admonition, warning

Mai [mai] (-(e)s, -e) *m* May; **~glöckchen** *nt* lily of the valley

Mailand ['mailant] *nt* Milan

mailändisch *adj* Milanese

Mais [mais] (-es, -e) *m* maize, corn (*US*); **~kolben** *m* corncob; **~mehl** *nt* (*KOCH*) corn meal

Majestät [majɛs'tɛːt] *f* majesty; **m~isch** *adj* majestic

Majonäse ▲ [majo'nɛːzə] *f* mayonnaise

Major [ma'joːr] (-s, -e) *m* (*MIL*) major; (*AVIAT*) squadron leader

Majoran [majo'raːn] (-s, -e) *m* marjoram

makaber [ma'kaːbər] *adj* macabre

Makel ['maːkəl] (-s, -) *m* blemish; (*moralisch*) stain; **m~los** *adj* immaculate, spotless

mäkeln ['mɛːkəln] *vi* to find fault

Makler(in) ['maːklər(ɪn)] (-s, -) *m(f)* broker

Makrele [ma'kreːlə] *f* mackerel

Mal [maːl] (-(e)s, -e) *nt* mark, sign; (*Zeitpunkt*) time; **ein für alle ~** once and for all; **m~** *adv* times; (*umg*) *siehe* **einmal** ♦ *suffix*: **-m~** -times

malen *vt, vi* to paint

Maler (-s, -) *m* painter; **Male rei** *f* painting; **m~isch** *adj* picturesque

Malkasten *m* paintbox

Mallorca [ma'jɔrka, ma'lɔrka] (-s) *nt* Majorca

malnehmen (*unreg*) *vt, vi* to multiply

Malz [malts] (-es) *nt* malt; **~bier** *nt* (*KOCH*) malt beer; **~bonbon** *nt* cough drop; **~kaffee** *m* malt coffee

Mama ['mamaː] (-, -s) (*umg*) *f* mum(my) (*BRIT*), mom(my) (*US*)

Mami ['mami] (-, -s) = **Mama**

Mammut ['mamʊt] (-s, -e *od* -s) *nt* mammoth

man [man] *pron* one, you; **~ sagt, ...** they *od* people say ...; **wie schreibt ~ das?** how do you write it?, how is it written?

Manager(in) ['mɛnɪdʒər(ɪn)] (-s, -) *m(f)* manager

manch [manç] (*unver*) *pron* many a

manche(r, s) ['mançə(r, s)] *adj* many a; (*pl: einige*) a number of ♦ *pron* some

mancherlei [mançər'lai] *adj inv* various ♦ *pron inv* a variety of things

manchmal *adv* sometimes

Mandant(in) [man'dant(ɪn)] *m(f)* (*JUR*) client

Mandarine [manda'riːnə] *f* mandarin, tangerine

Mandat [man'da:t] (-(e)s, -e) nt mandate

Mandel ['mandəl] (-, -n) f almond; (ANAT) tonsil; ~entzündung f (MED) tonsillitis

Manege [ma'ne:ʒə] f ring, arena

Mangel ['maŋəl] (-s, ̈) m lack; (Knappheit) shortage; (Fehler) defect, fault; ~ an +dat shortage of; ~erscheinung f deficiency symptom; m~haft adj poor; (fehlerhaft) defective, faulty; m~n vi unpers: es m~t jdm an etw dat sb lacks sth ♦ vt (Wäsche) to mangle

mangels präp +gen for lack of

Manie [ma'ni:] f mania

Manier [ma'ni:r] (-) f manner; style; (pej) mannerism; ~en pl (Umgangsformen) manners; m~lich adj well-mannered

Manifest [mani'fɛst] (-es, -e) nt manifesto

Maniküre [mani'ky:rə] f manicure

manipulieren [manipu'li:rən] vt to manipulate

Manko ['maŋko] (-s, -s) nt deficiency; (COMM) deficit

Mann [man] (-(e)s, ̈er) m man; (Ehemann) husband; (NAUT) hand; **seinen ~ stehen** to hold one's own

Männchen ['mɛnçən] nt little man; (Tier) male

Mannequin [manə'kɛ̃:] (-s, -s) nt fashion model

männlich ['mɛnlıç] adj (BIOL) male; (fig, GRAM) masculine

Mannschaft f (SPORT, fig) team; (AVIAT, NAUT) crew; (MIL) other ranks pl

Manöver [ma'nø:vər] (-s, -) nt manoeuvre

manövrieren [manø'vri:rən] vt, vi to manoeuvre

Mansarde [man'zardə] f attic

Manschette [man'ʃɛtə] f cuff; (TECH) collar; sleeve; ~nknopf m cufflink

Mantel ['mantəl] (-s, ̈) m coat; (TECH) casing, jacket

Manuskript [manu'skrıpt] (-(e)s, -e) nt manuscript

Mappe ['mapə] f briefcase; (Aktenmappe) folder

Märchen ['mɛːrçən] nt fairy tale; m~haft adj fabulous; ~prinz m Prince Charming

Margarine [marga'ri:nə] f margarine

Margerite [marga'ri:tə] f (BOT) marguerite

Marienkäfer [ma'ri:ənkɛːfər] m ladybird

Marine [ma'ri:nə] f navy; m~blau adj navy blue

marinieren [mari'ni:rən] vt to marinate

Marionette [mario'nɛtə] f puppet

Mark¹ [mark] (-, -) f (Münze) mark

Mark² [mark] (-(e)s) nt (Knochenmark) marrow; **jdm durch ~ und Bein gehen** to go right through sb

markant [mar'kant] adj striking

Marke ['markə] f mark; (Warensorte) brand; (Fabrikat) make; (Rabattmarke, Briefmarke) stamp; (Essenmarke) ticket; (aus Metall etc) token, disc

Markenartikel m proprietary article

markieren [mar'ki:rən] vt to mark; (umg) to act ♦ vi (umg) to act it

Markierung f marking

Markise [mar'ki:zə] f awning

Markstück nt one-mark piece

Markt [markt] (-(e)s, ̈e) m market; ~forschung f market research; ~lücke f (COMM) opening, gap in the market; ~platz m market place; m~üblich adj (Preise, Mieten) standard, usual; ~wert m (COMM) market value; ~wirtschaft f market economy

Marmelade [marmə'la:də] f jam

Marmor ['marmɔr] (-s, -e) m marble; m~ieren [-'ri:rən] vt to marble

Marokko [ma'rɔko] (-s) nt Morocco

Marone [ma'ro:nə] (-, -n od **Maroni**) f chestnut

Marotte [ma'rɔtə] f fad, quirk

Marsch¹ [marʃ] (-, -en) f marsh

Marsch² [marʃ] (-(e)s, ̈e) m march ♦ excl march!; ~befehl m marching orders pl; m~bereit adj ready to move; m~ieren [mar'ʃi:rən] vi to march

Märtyrer(in) ['mɛrtyrər(ın)] (-s, -) m(f) martyr

März [mɛrts] (-(es), -e) m March

Marzipan [martsi'pa:n] (-s, -e) nt marzipan

Masche ['maʃə] f mesh; (Strickmasche) stitch; **das ist die neueste ~** that's the latest thing; **~ndraht** m wire mesh; **m~nfest** adj run-resistant

aschine [ma'ʃiːnə] f machine; (Motor) engine; (Schreibmaschine) typewriter; **~schreiben** to type; **m~ll** [maʃi'nel] adj machine(-); mechanical

aschinen- zW: **~bauer** m mechanical engineer; **~gewehr** nt machine gun; **~pistole** f submachine gun; **~schaden** m mechanical fault; **~schlosser** m fitter; **~schrift** f typescript

aschinist [maʃi'nɪst] m engineer

laser ['maːzər] (-, -n) f (von Holz) grain; **~n** pl (MED) measles sg

laske ['maskə] f mask; **~nball** m fancy-dress ball

aaskieren [mas'kiːrən] vt to mask; (verkleiden) to dress up ♦ vr to disguise o.s.; to dress up

laskottchen [mas'kɔtçən] nt (lucky) mascot

aß[1] [maːs] (-es, -e) nt measure; (Mäßigung) moderation; (Grad) degree, extent; **~ halten** to exercise moderation

aß[2] [maːs] (-, -(e)) f litre of beer

lassage [ma'saːʒə] f massage

aßanzug m made-to-measure suit

aßarbeit f (fig) neat piece of work

lasse ['masə] f mass

aßeinheit f unit of measurement

lassen- zW: **~artikel** m mass-produced article; **~grab** nt mass grave; **m~haft** adj loads of; **~medien** pl mass media pl; **~veranstaltung** f mass meeting; **m~weise** adv on a large scale

lasseur [ma'søːr] m masseur; **~in** f masseuse

aßgebend adj authoritative

aßhalten △ (unreg) vi siehe **Maß**[1]

aassieren [ma'siːrən] vt to massage; (MIL) to mass

assig ['masɪç] adj massive; (umg) massive amount of

äßig ['mɛːsɪç] adj moderate; **~en** ['mɛːsɪgən] vt to restrain, to moderate; **M~keit** f moderation

lassiv (-s, -e) nt massif

massiv [ma'siːf] adj solid; (fig) heavy, rough

Maß- zW: **~krug** m tankard; **m~los** adj extreme; **~nahme** f measure, step; **~stab** m rule, measure; (fig) standard; (GEOG) scale; **m~voll** adj moderate

Mast [mast] (-(e)s, -e(n)) m mast; (ELEK) pylon

mästen ['mɛstən] vt to fatten

Material [materi'aːl] (-s, -ien) nt material(s); **~fehler** m material defect; **~ismus** [-'lɪsmʊs] m materialism; **m~istisch** [-'lɪstɪʃ] adj materialistic

Materie [ma'teːriə] f matter, substance

materiell [materi'ɛl] adj material

Mathematik [matema'tiːk] f mathematics sg; **~er(in)** [mate'maːtikər(ɪn)] (-s, -) m(f) mathematician

mathematisch [mate'maːtɪʃ] adj mathematical

Matjeshering ['matjəsheːrɪŋ] m (KOCH) young herring

Matratze [ma'tratsə] f mattress

Matrixdrucker ['maːtrɪks-] m dot-matrix printer

Matrose [ma'troːzə] (-n, -n) m sailor

Matsch [matʃ] (-(e)s) m mud; (Schneematsch) slush; **m~ig** adj muddy; slushy

matt [mat] adj weak; (glanzlos) dull; (PHOT) matt; (SCHACH) mate

Matte ['matə] f mat

Mattscheibe f (TV) screen

Mauer ['mauər] (-, -n) f wall; **m~n** vi to build; to lay bricks ♦ vt to build

Maul [maul] (-(e)s, Mäuler) nt mouth; **m~en** (umg) vi to grumble; **~esel** m mule; **~korb** m muzzle; **~sperre** f lockjaw; **~tasche** f (KOCH) pasta envelopes stuffed and used in soup; **~tier** nt mule; **~wurf** m mole

Maurer ['maurər] (-s, -) m bricklayer

Maus [maus] (-, Mäuse) f (auch COMPUT) mouse

Mause- ['mauzə] zW: **~falle** f mousetrap; **m~n** vi to catch mice ♦ vt (umg) to pinch; **m~tot** adj stone dead

Maut- ['maut] zW: **~gebühr** f toll (charge);

~**straße** f toll road

maximal [maksi'ma:l] adj maximum ♦ adv at most

Mayonnaise [majo'nɛːzə] f mayonnaise

Mechan- [me'çaːn] zW: ~**ik** f mechanics sg; (Getriebe) mechanics pl; ~**iker** (-s, -) m mechanic, engineer; **m~isch** adj mechanical; ~**ismus** m mechanism

meckern ['mɛkərn] vi to bleat; (umg) to moan

Medaille [me'daljə] f medal

Medaillon [medal'jõː] (-s, -s) nt (Schmuck) locket

Medikament [medika'mɛnt] nt medicine

Meditation [meditatsi'oːn] f meditation

meditieren [medi'tiːrən] vi to meditate

Medizin [medi'tsiːn] (-, -en) f medicine; **m~isch** adj medical

Meer [meːr] (-(e)s, -e) nt sea; ~**enge** f straits pl; ~**esfrüchte** pl seafood sg; ~**esspiegel** m sea level; ~**rettich** m horseradish; ~**schweinchen** nt guinea-pig

Mehl [meːl] (-(e)s, -e) nt flour; **m~ig** adj floury; ~**schwitze** f (KOCH) roux; ~**speise** f (KOCH) flummery

mehr [meːr] adj, adv more; ~**deutig** adj ambiguous; ~**ere** adj several; ~**eres** pron several things; ~**fach** adj multiple; (wiederholt) repeated; **M~fahrtenkarte** f multi-journey ticket; **M~heit** f majority; ~**malig** adj repeated; ~**mals** adv repeatedly; ~**stimmig** adj for several voices; ~**stimmig singen** to harmonize; **M~wertsteuer** f value added tax; **M~zahl** f majority; (GRAM) plural

Mehrzweck- in zW multipurpose

meiden ['maɪdən] (unreg) vt to avoid

Meile ['maɪlə] f mile; ~**nstein** m milestone; **m~nweit** adj for miles

mein(e) [maɪn] adj my; ~**e(r, s)** pron mine

Meineid ['maɪnʔaɪt] m perjury

meinen ['maɪnən] vi to think ♦ vt to think; (sagen) to say; (sagen wollen) to mean; **das will ich ~** I should think so

mein- zW: ~**erseits** adv for my part; ~**etwegen** adv (für mich) for my sake; (wegen mir) on my account; (von mir aus) as

far as I'm concerned; I don't care od mind; ~**etwillen** adv: **um ~etwillen** for my sake, on my account

Meinung ['maɪnʊŋ] f opinion; **ganz meine ~** I quite agree; **jdm die ~ sagen** to give sb a piece of one's mind

Meinungs- zW: ~**austausch** m exchange of views; ~**umfrage** f opinion poll; ~**verschiedenheit** f difference of opinion

Meise ['maɪzə] f tit(mouse)

Meißel ['maɪsəl] (-s, -) m chisel

meist [maɪst] adj most ♦ adv mostly; **am ~en** the most; ~**ens** adv generally, usually

Meister ['maɪstər] (-s, -) m master; (SPORT) champion; **m~haft** adj masterly; **m~n** vt (Schwierigkeiten etc) to overcome, conquer; ~**schaft** f mastery; (SPORT) championship; ~**stück** nt masterpiece; ~**werk** nt masterpiece

Melancholie [melaŋko'liː] f melancholy; **melancholisch** [melaŋ'koːlɪʃ] adj melancholy

Melde- ['mɛldə] zW: ~**frist** f registration period; **m~n** vt to report ♦ vr to report; (SCH) to put one's hand up; (freiwillig) to volunteer; (auf etw, am Telefon) to answer; **sich m~n bei** to report to; to register with; **sich zu Wort m~n** to ask to speak; ~**pflicht** f obligation to register with the police; ~**schluss ▲** m closing date; ~**stelle** f registration office

Meldung ['mɛldʊŋ] f announcement; (Bericht) report

meliert [me'liːrt] adj (Haar) greying; (Wolle) flecked

melken ['mɛlkən] (unreg) vt to milk

Melodie [melo'diː] f melody, tune

melodisch [me'loːdɪʃ] adj melodious, tuneful

Melone [me'loːnə] f melon; (Hut) bowler (hat)

Membran [mɛm'braːn] (-, -en) f (TECH) diaphragm

Memoiren [memo'aːrən] pl memoirs

Menge ['mɛŋə] f quantity; (Menschenmenge) crowd; (große Anzahl) lot (of); **m~n** vt to mix ♦ vr: **sich m~n in** +akk to meddle

with; ~lehre f (MATH) set theory;
~nrabatt m bulk discount

Mensch [mɛnʃ] (-en, -en) m human being,
man; person ♦ excl hey!; **kein ~** nobody

Menschen- zW: ~affe m (ZOOL) ape;
m~freundlich adj philanthropical;
~kenner m judge of human nature;
m~leer adj deserted; m~möglich adj
humanly possible; ~rechte pl human
rights; m~unwürdig adj beneath human
dignity; ~verstand m: **gesunder
~verstand** common sense

Mensch- zW: ~heit f humanity, mankind;
m~lich adj human; (human) humane;
~lichkeit f humanity

Menstruation [mɛnstruatsi'oːn] f
menstruation

Mentalität [mɛntali'tɛːt] f mentality

Menü [me'nyː] (-s, -s) nt (auch COMPUT)
menu

Merk- ['mɛrk] zW: ~blatt nt instruction
sheet od leaflet; m~en vt to notice; **sich**
dat **etw m~en** to remember sth; m~lich
adj noticeable; ~mal nt sign, characteristic;
m~würdig adj odd

messbar ▲ ['mɛsbaːr] adj measurable

Messbecher ▲ m measuring jug

Messe ['mɛsə] f fair; (ECCL) mass; ~gelände
nt exhibition centre; ~halle f pavilion at a
fair

messen (unreg) vt to measure ♦ vr to
compete

Messer (-s, -) nt knife; ~spitze f knife
point; (in Rezept) pinch

Messestand m stall at a fair

Messgerät ▲ nt measuring device, gauge

Messing ['mɛsɪŋ] (-s) nt brass

Metall [me'tal] (-s, -e) nt metal; m~isch adj
metallic

Meter ['meːtər] (-s, -) nt od m metre; ~maß
nt tape measure

Methode [me'toːdə] f method;
methodisch adj methodical

Metropole [metro'poːlə] f metropolis

Metzger ['mɛtsgər] (-s, -) m butcher; ~ei
[-'rai] f butcher's (shop)

Meute ['mɔytə] f pack; ~rei f mutiny;

m~rn vi to mutiny

miauen [mi'auən] vi to miaow

mich [mɪç] (akk von ich) pron me; myself

Miene ['miːnə] f look, expression

mies [miːs] (umg) adj lousy

Miet- ['miːt] zW: ~auto nt hired car; ~e f
rent; **zur ~e wohnen** to live in rented
accommodation; m~en vt to rent; (Auto)
to hire; ~er(in) (-s, -) m(f) tenant; ~shaus
nt tenement, block of (rented) flats;
~vertrag m lease

Migräne [mi'grɛːnə] f migraine

Mikro- ['mikro] zW: ~fon, ~phon
[-'foːn] (-s, -e) nt microphone; ~skop
[-'skoːp] (-s, -e) nt microscope;
m~skopisch adj microscopic;
~wellenherd m microwave (oven)

Milch [mɪlç] (-) f milk; ~glas nt frosted
glass; m~ig adj milky; ~kaffee m white
coffee; ~mann (pl -männer) m milkman;
~mixgetränk nt (KOCH) milkshake;
~pulver nt powdered milk; ~straße f
Milky Way; ~zahn m milk tooth

mild [mɪlt] adj mild; (Richter) lenient;
(freundlich) kind, charitable; M~e f
mildness; leniency; m~ern vt to mitigate, to
soften; (Schmerz) to alleviate; **~ernde
Umstände** extenuating circumstances

Milieu [mili'øː] (-s, -s) nt background,
environment; m~geschädigt adj
maladjusted

Mili- [mili] zW: m~tant [-'tant] adj militant;
~tär [-'tɛːr] (-s) nt military, army;
~'tärgericht nt military court; m~'tärisch
adj military

Milli- ['mili] zW: ~ardär [-ar'dɛːr] m
multimillionaire; ~arde [-'ardə] f milliard;
billion (BES US); ~meter m millimetre;
~meterpapier nt graph paper

Million [mili'oːn] (-, -en) f million; ~är
[-o'nɛːr] m millionaire

Milz [mɪlts] (-, -en) f spleen

Mimik ['miːmɪk] f mime

Mimose [mi'moːzə] f mimosa; (fig) sensitive
person

minder ['mɪndər] adj inferior ♦ adv less;
M~heit f minority; ~jährig adj minor;

M~jährige(r) f(m) minor; ~n vt, vr to decrease, to diminish; M~ung f decrease; ~wertig adj inferior; M~wertigkeitskomplex m inferiority complex

Mindest- ['mɪndəst] zW: ~alter nt minimum age; ~betrag m minimum amount; m~e(r, s) adj least; zum ~en od m~en at least; m~ens adv at least; ~haltbarkeitsdatum nt best-before date; ~lohn m minimum wage; ~maß nt minimum

Mine ['miːnə] f mine; (Bleistiftmine) lead; (Kugelschreibermine) refill

Mineral [mine'raːl] (-s, -e od -ien) nt mineral; m~isch adj mineral; ~wasser nt mineral water

Miniatur [minia'tuːr] f miniature

Mini- zW: ~golf ['mɪnɪɡɔlf] nt miniature golf, crazy golf; m~mal [mini'maːl] adj minimal; ~mum ['miːnimʊm] nt minimum; ~rock m miniskirt

Minister [mi'nɪstər] (-s, -) m minister; m~iell adj ministerial; ~ium nt ministry; ~präsident m prime minister

Minus ['miːnʊs] (-, -) nt deficit

minus adv minus; M~zeichen nt minus sign

Minute [mi'nuːtə] f minute

Minze ['mɪntsə] f mint

mir [miːr] (dat von ich) pron (to) me; ~ nichts, dir nichts just like that

Misch- ['mɪʃ] zW: ~brot nt bread made from more than one kind of flour; ~ehe f mixed marriage; m~en vt to mix; ~ling m half-caste; ~ung f mixture

miserabel [mizə'raːbəl] (umg) adj (Essen, Film) dreadful

Miss- ▲ ['mɪs] zW: ~behagen nt discomfort, uneasiness; ~bildung f deformity; m~'billigen vt insep to disapprove of; ~brauch m abuse; (falscher Gebrauch) misuse; m~'brauchen vt insep to abuse; jdn zu od für etw m~brauchen to use sb for od to do sth; ~erfolg m failure; ~fallen (-s) nt displeasure; m~'fallen (unreg) vi insep: jdm m~fallen

to displease sb; ~geschick nt misfortune; m~glücken [mɪs'ɡlʏkən] vi insep to fail; jdm m~glückt etw sb does not succeed with sth; ~griff m mistake; ~gunst f envy; m~günstig adj envious; m~'handeln vt insep to ill-treat; ~'handlung f ill-treatment

Mission [misi'oːn] f mission; ~ar(in) m(f) missionary

Miss- ▲ zW: ~klang m discord; ~kredit m discredit; m~lingen [mɪs'lɪŋən] (unreg) vi insep to fail; ~mut m sullenness; m~mutig adj sullen; m~'raten (unreg) vi insep to turn out badly ♦ adj ill-bred; ~stand m bad state of affairs; abuse; m~'trauen (-s) nt distrust, suspicion; ~trauen (-s) nt mistrust; ~trauensantrag m (POL) motion of no confidence; m~trauisch adj distrustful, suspicious; ~verhältnis nt disproportion; ~verständnis nt misunderstanding; m~verstehen (unreg) vt insep to misunderstand; ~wirtschaft f mismanagement

Mist [mɪst] (-(e)s) m dung; dirt; (umg) rubbish

Mistel (-, -n) f mistletoe

Misthaufen m dungheap

mit [mɪt] präp +dat with; (~tels) by ♦ adv along, too; ~ der Bahn by train; ~ 10 Jahren at the age of 10; wollen Sie ~? do you want to come along?

Mitarbeit ['mɪtarbaɪt] f cooperation; m~en vi to cooperate, to collaborate; ~er(in) m(f) collaborator; co-worker ♦ pl (Personal) staff

Mit- zW: ~bestimmung f participation in decision-making; m~bringen (unreg) vt to bring along

miteinander [mɪtaɪ'nandər] adv together, with one another

miterleben vt to see, to witness

Mitesser ['mɪtɛsər] (-s, -) m blackhead

mitfahr- zW: ~en vi to accompany; (auf Reise auch) to travel with; M~gelegenheit f lift; M~zentrale f agency for arranging lifts

mitfühlend adj sympathetic, compassionate

Mit- zW: **m~geben** (unreg) vt to give; **~gefühl** nt sympathy; **m~gehen** (unreg) vi to go/come along; **m~genommen** adj done in, in a bad way; **~gift** f dowry

Mitglied ['mɪtgliːt] nt member; **~sbeitrag** m membership fee; **~schaft** f membership

Mit- zW: **m~halten** (unreg) vi to keep up; **m~helfen** (unreg) vi to help; **~hilfe** f help, assistance; **m~hören** vt to listen in to; **m~kommen** (unreg) vi to come along; (verstehen) to keep up, to follow; **~läufer** m hanger-on; (POL) fellow traveller

Mitleid nt sympathy; (Erbarmen) compassion; **m~ig** adj sympathetic; **m~slos** adj pitiless, merciless

Mit- zW: **m~machen** vt to join in, to take part in; **~mensch** m fellow man; **m~nehmen** (unreg) vt to take along/away; (anstrengen) to wear out, to exhaust; **zum ~nehmen** to take away; **m~reden** vi: **bei etw m~reden** to have a say in sth; **m~reißen** (unreg) vt to carry away/along; (fig) to thrill, captivate

mitsamt [mɪt'zamt] präp +dat together with

Mitschuld f complicity; **m~ig** adj: **m~ig (an** +dat**)** implicated (in); (an Unfall) partly responsible (for)

Mit- zW: **~schüler(in)** m(f) schoolmate; **m~spielen** vi to join in, to take part; **~spieler(in)** m(f) partner

Mittag ['mɪtaːk] (**-(e)s, -e**) m midday, lunchtime; **(zu) ~ essen** to have lunch; **heute / morgen ~** today/tomorrow at lunchtime od noon; **~essen** nt lunch, dinner

mittags adv at lunchtime od noon; **M~pause** f lunch break; **M~schlaf** m early afternoon nap, siesta

Mittäter(in) ['mɪtɛːtər(ɪn)] m(f) accomplice

Mitte ['mɪtə] f middle; (POL) centre; **aus unserer ~** from our midst

mitteilen ['mɪttaɪlən] vt: **jdm etw ~** to inform sb of sth, to communicate sth to sb

Mitteilung f communication

Mittel ['mɪtəl] (**-s -**) nt means; method; (MATH) average; (MED) medicine; **ein ~ zum Zweck** a means to an end; **~alter** nt

Middle Ages pl; **m~alterlich** adj mediaeval; **~ding** nt cross; **~europa** nt Central Europe; **~gebirge** nt low mountain range; **m~mäßig** adj mediocre, middling; **~mäßigkeit** f mediocrity; **~meer** nt Mediterranean; **~ohrentzündung** f inflammation of the middle ear; **~punkt** m centre; **~stand** m middle class; **~streifen** m central reservation; **~stürmer** m centre-forward; **~weg** m middle course; **~welle** f (RADIO) medium wave

mitten ['mɪtən] adv in the middle; **~ auf der Straße / in der Nacht** in the middle of the street/night

Mitternacht ['mɪtərnaxt] f midnight

mittlere(r, s) ['mɪtlərə(r, s)] adj middle; (durchschnittlich) medium, average; **~ Reife** ≃ O-levels

---
mittlere Reife
---

i The **mittlere Reife** is the standard certificate gained at a **Realschule** or **Gymnasium** on successful completion of 6 years' education there. If a pupil at a **Realschule** attains good results in several subjects he is allowed to enter the 11th class of a **Gymnasium** to study for the **Abitur**.

---

mittlerweile ['mɪtlər'vaɪlə] adv meanwhile

Mittwoch ['mɪtvɔx] (**-(e)s, -e**) m Wednesday; **m~s** adv on Wednesdays

mitunter [mɪt'ʊntər] adv occasionally, sometimes

Mit- zW: **m~verantwortlich** adj jointly responsible; **m~wirken** vi: **m~wirken (bei)** to contribute (to); (THEAT) to take part (in); **~wirkung** f contribution; participation

Mobbing ['mɔbɪŋ] (**-s**) nt workplace bullying

Möbel ['møːbəl] pl furniture sg; **~wagen** m furniture od removal van

mobil [mo'biːl] adj mobile; (MIL) mobilized; **M~iar** [mobili'aːr] (**-s, -e**) nt furnishings pl; **M~machung** f mobilization; **M~telefon** nt mobile phone

möblieren [mø'bliːrən] vt to furnish;

möbliert wohnen to live in furnished accommodation

möchte etc ['mœçtə] vb siehe **mögen**

Mode ['moːdə] f fashion

Modell [mo'dɛl] **(-s, -e)** nt model; **m~ieren** [-'liːrən] vt to model

Modenschau f fashion show

moderig ['moːdərɪç] adj (Keller) musty; (Luft) stale

modern [mo'dɛrn] adj modern; (modisch) fashionable; **~isieren** vt to modernize

Mode- zW: **~schau** f fashion show; **~schmuck** m fashion jewellery; **~schöpfer(in)** m(f) fashion designer; **~wort** nt fashionable word, buzz word

modisch ['moːdɪʃ] adj fashionable

Mofa ['moːfa] **(-s, -s)** nt small moped

mogeln ['moːgəln] (umg) vi to cheat

SCHLÜSSELWORT

mögen ['møːgən] (pt **mochte**, pp **gemocht** od (als Hilfsverb) **mögen**) vt, vi to like; **magst du/mögen Sie ihn?** do you like him?; **ich möchte ... I** would like ..., I'd like ...; **er möchte in die Stadt** he'd like to go into town; **ich möchte nicht, dass du ... I** wouldn't like you to ...; **ich mag nicht mehr** I've had enough

♦ Hilfsverb to like to; (wollen) to want; **möchtest du etwas essen?** would you like something to eat?; **sie mag nicht bleiben** she doesn't want to stay; **das mag wohl sein** that may well be; **was mag das heißen?** what might that mean?; **Sie möchten zu Hause anrufen** could you please call home?

---

möglich ['møːklɪç] adj possible; **~erweise** adv possibly; **M~keit** f possibility; **nach M~keit** if possible; **~st** adv as ... as possible

Mohn [moːn] **(-(e)s, -e)** m (~blume) poppy; (~samen) poppy seed

Möhre ['møːrə] f carrot

Mohrrübe ['moːryːbə] f carrot

mokieren [mo'kiːrən] vr: **sich ~ über** +akk to make fun of

Mole ['moːlə] f (harbour) mole

Molekül [mole'kyːl] **(-s, -e)** nt molecule

Molkerei [mɔlkə'raɪ] f dairy

mollig adj cosy; (dicklich) plump

Moll [mɔl] **(-, -)** nt (MUS) minor (key)

Moment [mo'mɛnt] **(-(e)s, -e)** m moment ♦ nt factor; **im ~** at the moment; **~ (mal)!** just a moment; **m~an** [-'taːn] adj momentary ♦ adv at the moment

Monarch [mo'narç] **(-en, -en)** m monarch; **~ie** [monar'çiː] f monarchy

Monat ['moːnat] **(-(e)s, -e)** m month; **m~elang** adv for months; **m~lich** adj monthly

Monats- zW: **~gehalt** nt: **das dreizehnte ~gehalt** Christmas bonus (of one month's salary); **~karte** f monthly ticket

Mönch [mœnç] **(-(e)s, -e)** m monk

Mond [moːnt] **(-(e)s, -e)** m moon; **~finsternis** f eclipse of the moon; **m~hell** adj moonlit; **~landung** f moon landing; **~schein** m moonlight

Mono- [mono] in zW mono; **~log** [-'loːk] **(-s, -e)** m monologue; **~pol** [-'poːl] **(-s, -e)** nt monopoly; **m~polisieren** [-poli'ziːrən] vt to monopolize; **m~ton** [-'toːn] adj monotonous; **~tonie** [-to'niː] f monotony

Montag ['moːntaːk] **(-(e)s, -e)** m Monday

Montage [mɔn'taːʒə] f (PHOT etc) montage; (TECH) assembly; (Einbauen) fitting

Monteur [mɔn'tøːr] m fitter

montieren [mɔn'tiːrən] vt to assemble

Monument [monu'mɛnt] nt monument; **m~al** [-'taːl] adj monumental

Moor [moːr] **(-(e)s, -e)** nt moor

Moos [moːs] **(-es, -e)** nt moss

Moped ['moːpɛt] **(-s, -s)** nt moped

Moral [mo'raːl] **(-, -en)** f morality; (einer Geschichte) moral; **m~isch** adj moral

Morast [mo'rast] **(-(e)s, -e)** m morass, mire; **m~ig** adj boggy

Mord [mɔrt] **(-(e)s, -e)** m murder; **~anschlag** m murder attempt

Mörder(in) ['mœrdər(ɪn)] **(-s, -)** m(f) murderer (murderess)

mörderisch adj (fig: schrecklich) terrible, dreadful ♦ adv (umg: entsetzlich) terribly, dreadfully

Mord- zW: **~kommission** f murder squad;
~sglück (umg) nt amazing luck;
m~smäßig (umg) adj terrific, enormous;
~verdacht m suspicion of murder; **~waffe**
f murder weapon

morgen ['mɔrgən] adv tomorrow; **~ früh**
tomorrow morning; **M~ (-s, -)** m morning;
M~mantel m dressing gown; **M~rock** m
dressing gown; **M~röte** f dawn; **~s** adv in
the morning

morgig ['mɔrgɪç] adj tomorrow's; **der ~e
Tag** tomorrow

Morphium ['mɔrfiʊm] nt morphine

morsch [mɔrʃ] adj rotten

Morsealphabet ['mɔrzəʔalfabeːt] nt Morse
code

morsen vi to send a message by Morse
code

Mörtel ['mœrtəl] **(-s, -)** m mortar

Mosaik [moza'iːk] **(-s, -en** od **-e)** nt mosaic

Moschee [mɔ'ʃeː] **(-, -n)** f mosque

Moskito [mɔs'kiːto] **(-s, -s)** m mosquito

Most [mɔst] **(-(e)s, -e)** m (unfermented)
fruit juice; (Apfelwein) cider

Motel [mo'tel] **(-s, -s)** nt motel

Motiv [mo'tiːf] **(-s, -e)** nt motive; (MUS)
theme; **~ation** [-vatsi'oːn] f motivation;
m~ieren [moti'viːrən] vt to motivate

Motor ['moːtɔr, pl mo'toːrən] **(-s, -en)** m
engine; (bes ELEK) motor; **~boot** nt
motorboat; **~haube** f (von Auto) bonnet
(BRIT), hood (US); **m~isieren** vt to
motorize; **~öl** nt engine oil; **~rad** nt
motorcycle; **~roller** m (motor) scooter;
~schaden m engine trouble od failure

Motte ['mɔtə] f moth; **~nkugel** f
mothball(s)

Motto ['mɔto] **(-s, -s)** nt motto

Möwe ['møːvə] f seagull

Mücke ['mykə] f midge, gnat; **~nstich** m
midge od gnat bite

müde ['myːdə] adj tired

Müdigkeit ['myːdɪçkaɪt] f tiredness

Muffel (-s, -) m (umg) killjoy, sourpuss

muffig adj (Luft) musty

Mühe ['myːə] f trouble, pains pl; **mit Müh
und Not** with great difficulty; **sich** dat **~**

geben to go to a lot of trouble; **m~los** adj
without trouble, easy; **m~voll** adj
laborious, arduous

Mühle ['myːlə] f mill; (Kaffeemühle) grinder

Müh- zW: **~sal (-, -e)** f tribulation; **m~sam**
adj arduous, troublesome; **m~selig** adj
arduous, laborious

Mulde ['mʊldə] f hollow, depression

Mull [mʊl] **(-(e)s, -e)** m thin muslin

Müll [myl] **(-(e)s)** m refuse; **~abfuhr** f
rubbish disposal; (Leute) dustmen pl;
~abladeplatz m rubbish dump; **~binde** f
gauze bandage; **~eimer** m dustbin,
garbage can (US); **~haufen** m rubbish
heap; **~schlucker (-s, -)** m garbage
disposal unit; **~tonne** f dustbin;
~verbrennungsanlage f incinerator

mulmig ['mʊlmɪç] adj rotten; (umg) dodgy;
jdm ist ~ sb feels funny

multiplizieren [mʊltipli'tsiːrən] vt to
multiply

Mumie ['muːmiə] f mummy

Mumm [mʊm] **(-s)** (umg) m gumption,
nerve

Mumps [mʊmps] **(-)** m od f (MED) mumps

München ['mynçən] **(-s)** nt Munich

Mund [mʊnt] **(-(e)s, ⁺er)** m mouth; **~art** f
dialect

münden ['myndən] vi: **~ in** +akk to flow
into

Mund- zW: **m~faul** adj taciturn; **~geruch**
m bad breath; **~harmonika** f mouth
organ

mündig ['myndɪç] adj of age; **M~keit** f
majority

mündlich ['myntlɪç] adj oral

Mundstück nt mouthpiece;
(Zigarettenmundstück) tip

Mündung ['myndʊŋ] f (von Fluss) mouth;
(Gewehr) muzzle

Mund- zW: **~wasser** nt mouthwash;
~werk nt: **ein großes ~werk haben** to
have a big mouth; **~winkel** m corner of
the mouth

Munition [munitsi'oːn] f ammunition;
~slager nt ammunition dump

munkeln ['mʊŋkəln] vi to whisper, to

mutter

Münster ['mʏnstər] (**-s, -**) nt minster

munter ['mʊntər] adj lively

Münze ['mʏntsə] f coin; **m~n** vt to coin, to mint; **auf jdn gemünzt sein** to be aimed at sb

Münzfernsprecher [mʏntsfɛrnʃpreçər] m callbox (BRIT), pay phone

mürb(e) ['mʏrb(ə)] adj (Gestein) crumbly; (Holz) rotten; (Gebäck) crisp; **jdn ~ machen** to wear sb down; **M~eteig** ['mʏrbətaɪç] m shortcrust pastry

murmeln ['mʊrməln] vt, vi to murmur, to mutter

murren ['mʊrən] vi to grumble, to grouse

mürrisch ['mʏrɪʃ] adj sullen

Mus [muːs] (**-es, -e**) nt purée

Muschel ['mʊʃəl] (**-, -n**) f mussel; (~schale) shell; (Telefonmuschel) receiver

Muse ['muːzə] f muse

Museum [mu'zeːʊm] (**-s, Museen**) nt museum

Musik [mu'ziːk] f music; (Kapelle) band; **m~alisch** [-ka:lɪʃ] adj musical; **~ant(in)** [-'kant(ɪn)] (**-en, -en**) m(f) musician; **~box** f jukebox; **~er** (**-s, -**) m musician; **~hochschule** f college of music; **~instrument** nt musical instrument

musisch ['muːzɪʃ] adj (Mensch) artistic

musizieren [muzi'tsiːrən] vi to make music

Muskat [mʊs'kaːt] (**-(e)s, -e**) m nutmeg

Muskel ['mʊskəl] (**-s, -n**) m muscle; **~kater** m: **~kater haben** to be stiff

Muskulatur [mʊskula'tuːr] f muscular system

muskulös [mʊsku'løːs] adj muscular

Müsli ['myːsli] (**-s, -**) nt (KOCH) muesli

Muss ▲ [mʊs] (**-**) nt necessity, must

Muße ['muːsə] (**-**) f leisure

SCHLÜSSELWORT
---

müssen ['mʏsən] (pt **musste**, pp **gemusst** od (als Hilfsverb) **müssen**) vi 1 (Zwang) must (nur im Präsens), to have to; **ich muss es tun** I must do it, I have to do it; **ich musste es tun** I had to do it; **er muss es**

nicht tun he doesn't have to do it; **muss ich?** must I?, do I have to?; **wann müsst ihr zur Schule?** when do you have to go to school?; **er hat gehen müssen** he (has) had to go; **muss das sein?** is that really necessary?; **ich muss mal** (umg) I need the toilet

2 (sollen): **das musst du nicht tun!** you oughtn't to od shouldn't do that; **Sie hätten ihn fragen müssen** you should have asked him

3: **es muss geregnet haben** it must have rained; **es muss nicht wahr sein** it needn't be true

---

müßig ['myːsɪç] adj idle

Muster ['mʊstər] (**-s, -**) nt model; (Dessin) pattern; (Probe) sample; **m~gültig** adj exemplary; **m~n** vt (Tapete) to pattern; (fig, MIL) to examine; (Truppen) to inspect; **~ung** f (von Stoff) pattern; (MIL) inspection

Mut [muːt] m courage; **nur ~!** cheer up!; **jdm ~ machen** to encourage sb; **m~ig** adj courageous; **m~los** adj discouraged, despondent

mutmaßlich ['muːtmaːslɪç] adj presumed
♦ adv probably

Mutprobe f test od trial of courage

Mutter¹ ['mʊtər] (**-, ̈**) f mother

Mutter² ['mʊtər] (**-, -n**) f (Schraubenmutter) nut

mütterlich ['mʏtərlɪç] adj motherly; **~erseits** adv on the mother's side

Mutter- zW: **~liebe** f motherly love; **~mal** nt birthmark; **~milch** f mother's milk; **~schaft** f motherhood, maternity; **~schutz** m maternity regulations; '~'seelena||llein adj all alone; **~sprache** f native language; **~tag** m Mother's Day

Mutti ['mʊti] (**-, -s**) f mum(my) (BRIT), mom(my) (US)

mutwillig ['muːtvɪlɪç] adj malicious, deliberate

Mütze ['mʏtsə] f cap

MwSt abk (= Mehrwertsteuer) VAT

mysteriös [mʏsteri'øːs] adj mysterious

Mythos ['myːtɔs] (**-, Mythen**) m myth

Rechtschreibreform: ▲ *neue Schreibung* △ *alte Schreibung (auslaufend)*

N, n

na [na] *excl* well; **~ gut** okay then
Nabel ['na:bəl] **(-s, -)** *m* navel; **~schnur** *f* umbilical cord

---
SCHLÜSSELWORT
---

nach [na:x] *präp +dat* **1** (*örtlich*) to; **nach Berlin** to Berlin; **nach links/rechts** (to the) left/right; **nach oben/hinten** up/back
2 (*zeitlich*) after; **einer nach dem anderen** one after the other; **nach Ihnen!** after you!; **zehn (Minuten) nach drei** ten (minutes) past three
3 (*gemäß*) according to; **nach dem Gesetz** according to the law; **dem Namen nach** judging by his/her name; **nach allem, was ich weiß** as far as I know
♦ *adv*: **ihm nach!** after him!; **nach und nach** gradually, little by little; **nach wie vor** still

---

nachahmen ['na:x|a:mən] *vt* to imitate
Nachbar(in) ['naxba:r(ın)] **(-s, -n)** *m(f)* neighbour; **~haus** *nt*: **im ~haus** next door; **n~lich** *adj* neighbourly; **~schaft** *f* neighbourhood; **~staat** *m* neighbouring state
nach- *zW*: **~bestellen** *vt*: **50 Stück ~bestellen** to order another 50; **N~bestellung** *f* (*COMM*) repeat order; **N~bildung** *f* imitation, copy; **~blicken** *vi* to gaze after; **~datieren** *vt* to postdate
nachdem [na:x'de:m] *konj* after; (*weil*) since; **je ~ (ob)** it depends (whether)
nachdenken (*unreg*) *vi*: **~ über** +*akk* to think about; **N~ (-s)** *nt* reflection, meditation
nachdenklich *adj* thoughtful, pensive
Nachdruck ['na:xdrʊk] *m* emphasis; (*TYP*) reprint, reproduction
nachdrücklich ['na:xdrʏklıç] *adj* emphatic
nacheinander [na:x|aı'nandər] *adv* one after the other
nachempfinden ['na:x|ɛmpfındən] (*unreg*)

vt: **jdm etw ~** to feel sth with sb
Nacherzählung ['na:x|ɛrtsɛ:lʊŋ] *f* reproduction (of a story)
Nachfahr ['na:xfa:r] **(-s, -en)** *m* descendant
Nachfolge ['na:xfɔlgə] *f* succession; **n~n** *vi* +*dat* to follow; **~r(in)** (*-s, -*) *m(f)* successor
nachforschen *vt, vi* to investigate
Nachforschung *f* investigation
Nachfrage ['na:xfra:gə] *f* inquiry; (*COMM*) demand; **n~n** *vi* to inquire
nach- *zW*: **~füllen** *vt* to refill; **~geben** (*unreg*) *vi* to give way, to yield; **N~gebühr** *f* (*POST*) excess postage
nachgehen ['na:xge:ən] (*unreg*) *vi* (+*dat*) to follow; (*erforschen*) to inquire (into); (*Uhr*) to be slow
Nachgeschmack ['na:xgəʃmak] *m* aftertaste
nachgiebig ['na:xgi:bıç] *adj* soft, accommodating; **N~keit** *f* softness
nachhaltig ['na:xhaltıç] *adj* lasting; (*Widerstand*) persistent
nachhause *adv* (*österreichisch, schweizerisch*) home
nachhelfen ['na:xhɛlfən] (*unreg*) *vi* +*dat* to assist, to help
nachher [na:x'he:r] *adv* afterwards
Nachhilfeunterricht ['na:xhılfə|ʊntərrıçt] *m* extra tuition
nachholen ['na:xho:lən] *vt* to catch up with; (*Versäumtes*) to make up for
Nachkomme ['na:xkɔmə] **(-, -n)** *m* descendant
nachkommen (*unreg*) *vi* to follow; (*einer Verpflichtung*) to fulfil; **N~schaft** *f* descendants *pl*
Nachkriegszeit *f* postwar period
Nach- *zW*: **~lass** ▲ **(-es, -lässe)** *m* (*COMM*) discount, rebate; (*Erbe*) estate; **n~lassen** (*unreg*) *vt* (*Strafe*) to remit; (*Summe*) to take off; (*Schulden*) to cancel ♦ *vi* to decrease, to ease off; (*Sturm*) to die down, to ease off; (*schlechter werden*) to deteriorate; **er hat n~gelassen** he has got worse; **n~lässig** *adj* negligent, careless
nachlaufen ['na:xlaʊfən] (*unreg*) *vi* +*dat* to run after, to chase

nachlösen ['naːxløːzən] *vi* (*Zuschlag*) to pay on the train, pay at the other end; (*zur Weiterfahrt*) to pay the supplement

nachmachen ['naːxmaxən] *vt* to imitate, to copy; (*fälschen*) to counterfeit

Nachmittag ['naːxmɪtaːk] *m* afternoon; **am ~** in the afternoon; **n~s** *adv* in the afternoon

Nach- *zW*: **~nahme** *f* cash on delivery; **per ~nahme** C.O.D.; **~name** *m* surname; **~porto** *nt* excess postage

nachprüfen ['naːxpryːfən] *vt* to check, to verify

nachrechnen ['naːxrɛçnən] *vt* to check

nachreichen ['naːxraɪçən] *vt* (*Unterlagen*) to hand in later

Nachricht ['naːxrɪçt] (**-, -en**) *f* (*piece of*) news; (*Mitteilung*) message; **~en** *pl* (*Neuigkeiten*) news

Nachrichten- *zW*: **~agentur** *f* news agency; **~dienst** *m* (MIL) intelligence service; **~sprecher(in)** *m(f)* newsreader; **~technik** *f* telecommunications *sg*

Nachruf ['naːxruːf] *m* obituary

nachsagen ['naːxzaːgən] *vt* to repeat; **jdm etw ~** to say sth of sb

Nachsaison ['naːxzɛzõː] *f* off-season

nachschicken ['naːxʃɪkən] *vt* to forward

nachschlagen ['naːxʃlaːgən] (*unreg*) *vt* to look up

Nachschlagewerk *nt* reference book

Nachschlüssel *m* duplicate key

Nachschub ['naːxʃuːp] *m* supplies *pl*; (*Truppen*) reinforcements *pl*

nachsehen ['naːxzeːən] (*unreg*) *vt* (*prüfen*) to check ♦ *vi* (*erforschen*) to look and see; **jdm etw ~** to forgive sb sth; **das N~ haben** to come off worst

Nachsendeantrag *m* application to have one's mail forwarded

nachsenden ['naːxzɛndən] (*unreg*) *vt* to send on, to forward

nachsichtig *adj* indulgent, lenient

nachsitzen ['naːxzɪtsən] (*unreg*) *vi*: **~ (müssen)** (SCH) to be kept in

Nachspeise ['naːxʃpaɪzə] *f* dessert, sweet, pudding

Nachspiel ['naːxʃpiːl] *nt* epilogue; (*fig*) sequel

nachsprechen ['naːxʃprɛçən] (*unreg*) *vt*: **(jdm) ~** to repeat (after sb)

nächst [nɛːçst] *präp +dat* next to; (*außer*) apart from; **~beste(r, s)** *adj* first that comes along; (*zweitbeste*) next best; **N~e(r)** *f(m)* neighbour; **~e(r, s)** *adj* next; (*~gelegen*) nearest

nachstellen ['naːxʃtɛlən] *vt* (TECH: *neu einstellen*) to adjust

nächst *zW*: **N~enliebe** *f* love for one's fellow men; **~ens** *adv* shortly, soon; **~liegend** *adj* nearest; (*fig*) obvious; **~möglich** *adj* next possible

Nacht [naxt] (**-, ⁻e**) *f* night; **~dienst** *m* night shift

Nachteil ['naːxtaɪl] *m* disadvantage; **n~ig** *adj* disadvantageous

Nachthemd *nt* (*Herrennachthemd*) nightshirt; (*Damennachthemd*) nightdress

Nachtigall ['naxtɪgal] (**-, -en**) *f* nightingale

Nachtisch ['naːxtɪʃ] *m* = **Nachspeise**

Nachtklub *m* night club

Nachtleben *nt* nightlife

nächtlich ['nɛçtlɪç] *adj* nightly

Nachtlokal *nt* night club

Nach- *zW*: **~trag** *-(e)s, -träge*) *m* supplement; **n~tragen** (*unreg*) *vt* to carry; (*zufügen*) to add; **jdm etw n~tragen** to hold sth against sb; **n~träglich** *adj* later, subsequent; additional ♦ *adv* later, subsequently; additionally; **n~trauern** *vi*: **jdm/etw n~trauern** to mourn the loss of sb/sth

Nacht- *zW*: **n~s** *adv* at od by night; **~schicht** *f* nightshift; **~schwester** *f* night nurse; **~tarif** *m* off-peak tariff; **~tisch** *m* bedside table; **~wächter** *m* night watchman

Nach- *zW*: **~untersuchung** *f* checkup; **n~wachsen** (*unreg*) *vi* to grow again; **~wahl** *f (POL)* ≈ by-election

Nachweis ['naːxvaɪs] (**-es, -e**) *m* proof; **n~bar** *adj* provable, demonstrable; **n~en** (*unreg*) *vt* to prove; **jdm etw n~en** to point sth out to sb; **n~lich** *adj* evident, demonstrable

nach- *zW:* **~wirken** *vi* to have after-effects; **N~wirkung** *f* aftereffect; **N~wort** *nt* epilogue; **N~wuchs** *m* offspring; *(beruflich etc)* new recruits *pl;* **~zahlen** *vt, vi* to pay extra; **N~zahlung** *f* additional payment; *(zurückdatiert)* back pay; **~ziehen** *(unreg) vt (hinter sich herziehen: Bein)* to drag; **N~zügler (-s, -)** *m* straggler

Nacken ['nakən] **(-s, -)** *m* nape of the neck

nackt [nakt] *adj* naked; *(Tatsachen)* plain, bare; **N~badestrand** *m* nudist beach; **N~heit** *f* nakedness

Nadel ['na:dəl] **(-, -n)** *f* needle; *(Stecknadel)* pin; **~öhr** *nt* eye of a needle; **~wald** *m* coniferous forest

Nagel ['na:gəl] **(-s, ˝)** *m* nail; **~bürste** *f* nailbrush; **~feile** *f* nailfile; **~lack** *m* nail varnish *od* polish *(BRIT);* **n~n** *vt, vi* to nail; **n~neu** *adj* brand-new; **~schere** *f* nail scissors *pl*

nagen ['na:gən] *vt, vi* to gnaw

Nagetier ['na:gəti:r] *nt* rodent

nah(e) ['na:(ə)] *adj (räumlich)* near(by); *(Verwandte)* near; *(Freunde)* close; *(zeitlich)* near, close ♦ *adv* near(by); near, close; *(verwandt)* closely ♦ *präp (+dat)* near (to), close to; **der Nahe Osten** the Near East; **~ gehen** *(+dat)* to grieve; **~ kommen** *(+dat)* to get close (to); **jdm etw ~ legen** to suggest sth to sb; **~ liegen** to be obvious; **~ liegend** obvious; **~ stehen** *(+dat)* to be close (to); **einer Sache ~ stehen** to sympathize with sth; **~ stehend** close; **jdm (zu) ~ treten** to offend sb

Nahaufnahme *f* close-up

Nähe ['nɛ:ə] **(-)** *f* nearness, proximity; *(Umgebung)* vicinity; **in der ~** close by; at hand; **aus der ~** from close to

nahebei *adv* nearby

nahen *vi, vr* to approach, to draw near

nähen ['nɛ:ən] *vt, vi* to sew

näher *adj, adv* nearer; *(Erklärung, Erkundigung)* more detailed; **(sich) ~ kommen** to get closer; **N~e(s)** *nt* details *pl,* particulars *pl*

Naherholungsgebiet *nt* recreational area

(close to a town)

nähern *vr* to approach

nahezu *adv* nearly

Nähgarn *nt* thread

Nahkampf *m* hand-to-hand fighting

Nähkasten *m* sewing basket, workbox

nahm *etc* [na:m] *vb siehe* **nehmen**

Nähmaschine *f* sewing machine

Nähnadel *f* needle

nähren ['nɛ:rən] *vt* to feed ♦ *vr (Person)* to feed o.s.; *(Tier)* to feed

nahrhaft ['na:rhaft] *adj* nourishing, nutritious

Nahrung ['na:rʊŋ] *f* food; *(fig auch)* sustenance

Nahrungs- *zW:* **~mittel** *nt* foodstuffs *pl;* **~mittelindustrie** *f* food industry; **~suche** *f* search for food

Nährwert *m* nutritional value

Naht [na:t] **(-, ˝e)** *f* seam; *(MED)* suture; *(TECH)* join; **n~los** *adj* seamless; **n~los ineinander übergehen** to follow without a gap

Nah- *zW:* **~verkehr** *m* local traffic; **~verkehrszug** *m* local train; **~ziel** *nt* immediate objective

Name ['na:mə] **(-ns, -n)** *m* name; **im ~n von** on behalf of; **n~ns** *adv* by the name of; **~nstag** *m* name day, saint's day; **n~ntlich** *adj* by name ♦ *adv* particularly, especially

Namenstag

In Catholic areas of Germany the **Namenstag** *is often a more important celebration than a birthday. This is the day dedicated to the saint after whom a person is called, and on that day the person receives presents and invites relatives and friends round to celebrate.*

namhaft ['na:mhaft] *adj (berühmt)* famed, renowned; *(beträchtlich)* considerable; **~ machen** to name

nämlich ['nɛ:mlɪç] *adv* that is to say, namely; *(denn)* since

nannte *etc* ['nantə] *vb siehe* **nennen**

Napf [napf] **(-(e)s, ˝e)** *m* bowl, dish

Narbe ['narbə] *f* scar; **narbig** *adj* scarred

Narkose [nar'ko:zə] *f* anaesthetic

Narr [nar] **(-en, -en)** *m* fool; **n~en** *vt* to fool; **Närrin** ['nɛrɪn] *f* fool; **närrisch** *adj* foolish, crazy

Narzisse [nar'tsɪsə] *f* narcissus; daffodil

naschen ['naʃən] *vt*, *vi* to nibble; (*heimlich kosten*) to pinch a bit

naschhaft *adj* sweet-toothed

Nase ['na:zə] *f* nose

Nasen- *zW*: **~bluten (-s)** *nt* nosebleed; **~loch** *nt* nostril; **~tropfen** *pl* nose drops

naseweis *adj* pert, cheeky; (*neugierig*) nosey

Nashorn ['na:shɔrn] *nt* rhinoceros

nass ▲ [nas] *adj* wet

Nässe ['nɛsə] **(-)** *f* wetness; **n~n** *vt* to wet

nasskalt ▲ *adj* wet and cold

Nassrasur ▲ *f* wet shave

Nation [natsi'o:n] *f* nation

national [natsio'na:l] *adj* national; **N~feiertag** *m* national holiday; **N~hymne** *f* national anthem; **~isieren** [-i'zi:rən] *vt* to nationalize; **N~ismus** [-'lɪsmʊs] *m* nationalism; **~istisch** [-'lɪstɪʃ] *adj* nationalistic; **N~i'tät** *f* nationality; **N~mannschaft** *f* national team; **N~sozialismus** *m* national socialism

Natron ['na:trɔn] **(-s)** *nt* soda

Natter ['natər] **(-, -n)** *f* adder

Natur [na'tu:r] *f* nature; (*körperlich*) constitution; **~ell (-es, -e)** *nt* disposition; **~erscheinung** *f* natural phenomenon *od* event; **n~farben** *adj* natural coloured; **n~gemäß** *adj* natural; **~gesetz** *nt* law of nature; **n~getreu** *adj* true to life; **~katastrophe** *f* natural disaster

natürlich [na'ty:rlɪç] *adj* natural ♦ *adv* naturally; **ja, ~!** yes, of course; **N~keit** *f* naturalness

Natur- *zW*: **~park** *m* ≈ national park; **~produkt** *nt* natural product; **n~rein** *adj* natural, pure; **~schutz** *m* nature conservation; **unter ~schutz stehen** to be legally protected; **~schutzgebiet** *nt* nature reserve; **~wissenschaft** *f* natural science; **~wissenschaftler(in)** *m(f)*

scientist

nautisch ['nautɪʃ] *adj* nautical

Nazi ['na:tsi] **(-s, -s)** *m* Nazi

NB *abk* (= *nota bene*) nb

n. Chr. *abk* (= *nach Christus*) A.D.

Nebel ['ne:bəl] **(-s, -)** *m* fog, mist; **n~ig** *adj* foggy, misty; **~scheinwerfer** *m* fog lamp

neben ['ne:bən] *präp* (+*akk od dat*) next to; (+*dat*: *außer*) apart from, besides; **~an** [ne:bən'an] *adv* next door; **N~anschluss** ▲ *m* (*TEL*) extension; **N~ausgang** *m* side exit; **~bei** [ne:bən'bai] *adv* at the same time; (*außerdem*) additionally; (*beiläufig*) incidentally; **N~beruf** *m* second job; **N~beschäftigung** *f* second job; **N~buhler(in) (-s, -)** *m(f)* rival; **~einander** [ne:bən|ar'nandər] *adv* side by side; **~einander legen** to put next to each other; **N~eingang** *m* side entrance; **N~fach** *nt* subsidiary subject; **N~fluss** ▲ *m* tributary; **N~gebäude** *nt* annexe; **N~geräusch** *nt* (*RADIO*) atmospherics *pl*, interference; **~her** [ne:bən'he:r] *adv* (*zusätzlich*) besides; (*gleichzeitig*) at the same time; (*daneben*) alongside; **N~kosten** *pl* extra charges, extras; **N~produkt** *nt* by-product; **N~sache** *f* trifle, side issue; **~sächlich** *adj* minor, peripheral; **N~saison** *f* low season; **N~straße** *f* side street; **N~verdienst** *m* secondary income; **N~wirkung** *f* side effect; **N~zimmer** *nt* adjoining room

neblig ['ne:blɪç] *adj* foggy, misty

Necessaire [nese'sɛ:r] **(-s, -s)** *nt* (*Nähnecessaire*) needlework box; (*Nagelnecessaire*) manicure case

necken ['nɛkən] *vt* to tease

Neckerei [nɛkə'rai] *f* teasing

Neffe ['nɛfə] **(-n, -n)** *m* nephew

negativ ['ne:gati:f] *adj* negative; **N~ (-s, -e)** *nt* (*PHOT*) negative

Neger ['ne:gər] **(-s, -)** *m* negro; **~in** *f* negress

nehmen ['ne:mən] (*unreg*) *vt* to take; **jdn zu sich ~** to take sb in; **sich ernst ~** to take o.s. seriously; **nimm dir doch bitte** please help yourself

Neid [naɪt] **(-(e)s)** *m* envy; **~er (-s, -)** *m* envier; **n~isch** ['naɪdɪʃ] *adj* envious, jealous

neigen ['naɪgən] *vt* to incline, to lean; *(Kopf)* to bow ♦ *vi:* **zu etw ~** to tend to sth

Neigung *f (des Geländes)* slope; *(Tendenz)* tendency, inclination; *(Vorliebe)* liking; *(Zuneigung)* affection

nein [naɪn] *adv* no

Nektarine [nɛktaˈriːnə] *f (Frucht)* nectarine

Nelke ['nɛlkə] *f* carnation, pink; *(Gewürz)* clove

Nenn- [ˈnɛn] *zW:* **n~en** *(unreg) vt* to name; *(mit Namen)* to call; **wie n~t man ...?** what do you call ...?; **n~enswert** *adj* worth mentioning; **~er (-s, -)** *m* denominator; **~wert** *m* nominal value; *(COMM)* par

Neon ['neːɔn] **(-s)** *nt* neon; **~licht** *nt* neon light; **~röhre** *f* neon tube

Nerv [nɛrf] **(-s, -en)** *m* nerve; **jdm auf die ~en gehen** to get on sb's nerves; **n~enaufreibend** *adj* nerve-racking; **~enbündel** *nt* bundle of nerves; **~enheilanstalt** *f* mental home; **n~enkrank** *adj* mentally ill; **~ensäge** *(umg) f* pain (in the neck) *(umg)*; **~ensystem** *nt* nervous system; **~enzusammenbruch** *m* nervous breakdown; **n~lich** *adj (Belastung)* affecting the nerves; **n~ös** [nɛrˈvøːs] *adj* nervous; **~osi'tät** *f* nervousness; **n~tötend** *adj* nerve-racking; *(Arbeit)* soul-destroying

Nerz [nɛrts] **(-es, -e)** *m* mink

Nessel ['nɛsəl] **(-, -n)** *f* nettle

Nessessär ▲ [nesɛˈsɛːr] **(-s, -s)** *nt* = **Necessaire**

Nest [nɛst] **(-(e)s, -er)** *nt* nest; *(umg: Ort)* dump

nett [nɛt] *adj* nice; *(freundlich)* nice, kind; **~erweise** *adv* kindly

netto ['nɛtoː] *adv* net

Netz [nɛts] **(-es, -e)** *nt* net; *(Gepäcknetz)* rack; *(Einkaufsnetz)* string bag; *(Spinnennetz)* web; *(System)* network; **jdm ins ~ gehen** *(fig)* to fall into sb's trap; **~anschluss** ▲ *m* mains connection

Netzhaut *f* retina

neu [nɔy] *adj* new; *(Sprache, Geschichte)* modern; **seit ~estem** (since) recently; **die ~esten Nachrichten** the latest news; **~ schreiben** to rewrite, to write again; **N~anschaffung** *f* new purchase *od* acquisition; **~artig** *adj* new kind of; **N~bau** *m* new building; **N~e(r)** *f(m)* the new man/woman; **~erdings** *adv (kürzlich)* (since) recently; *(von ~em)* again; **N~erscheinung** *f (Buch)* new publication; *(Schallplatte)* new release; **N~erung** *f* innovation, new departure; **N~gier** *f* curiosity; **~gierig** *adj* curious; **N~heit** *f* newness; novelty; **N~igkeit** *f* news *sg*; **N~jahr** *nt* New Year; **~lich** *adv* recently, the other day; **N~ling** *m* novice; **N~mond** *m* new moon

neun [nɔyn] *num* nine; **~zehn** *num* nineteen; **~zig** *num* ninety

neureich *adj* nouveau riche; **N~e(r)** *f(m)* nouveau riche

neurotisch *adj* neurotic

Neuseeland [nɔyˈzeːlant] *nt* New Zealand; **Neuseeländer(in)** [nɔyˈzeːlɛndər(ɪn)] *m(f)* New Zealander

neutral [nɔyˈtraːl] *adj* neutral; **~i'sieren** *vt* to neutralize

Neutrum ['nɔytrʊm] **(-s, -a** *od* **-en)** *nt* neuter

Neu- *zW:* **~wert** *m* purchase price; **n~wertig** *adj* (as) new, not used; **~zeit** *f* modern age; **n~zeitlich** *adj* modern, recent

nicht [nɪçt] *adv* 1 *(Verneinung)* not; **er ist es nicht** it's not him, it isn't him; **er raucht nicht** *(gerade)* he isn't smoking; *(gewöhnlich)* he doesn't smoke; **ich kann das nicht - ich auch nicht** I can't do it - neither *od* nor can I; **es regnet nicht mehr** it's not raining any more; **nicht rostend** stainless

2 *(Bitte, Verbot)*: **nicht!** don't!, no!; **nicht berühren!** do not touch!; **nicht doch!** don't!

3 *(rhetorisch)*: **du bist müde, nicht (wahr)?** you're tired, aren't you?; **das ist schön,**

nicht (wahr)? it's nice, isn't it?
4: was du nicht sagst! the things you say!

Nichtangriffspakt [nɪçt'|angrɪfspakt] *m* non-aggression pact

Nichte ['nɪçtə] *f* niece

nichtig ['nɪçtɪç] *adj* (*ungültig*) null, void; (*wertlos*) futile

Nichtraucher(in) *m(f)* non-smoker

nichts [nɪçts] *pron* nothing; **für ~ und wieder ~** for nothing at all; **~ sagend** meaningless; **N~ (-)** *nt* nothingness; (*pej: Person*) nonentity

Nichtschwimmer *m* non-swimmer

nichts- *zW:* **~desto'weniger** *adv* nevertheless; **N~nutz (-es, -e)** *m* good-for-nothing; **~nutzig** *adj* worthless, useless; **N~tun (-s)** *nt* idleness

Nichtzutreffende(s) *nt:* **~s od nicht Zutreffendes (bitte) streichen!** (please) delete where appropriate

Nickel ['nɪkəl] **(-s)** *nt* nickel

nicken ['nɪkən] *vi* to nod

Nickerchen ['nɪkərçən] *nt* nap

nie [niː] *adv* never; **~ wieder** *od* **mehr** never again; **~ und nimmer** never ever

nieder ['niːdər] *adj* low; (*gering*) inferior
♦ *adv* down; **N~gang** *m* decline; **~gedrückt** *adj* (*deprimiert*) dejected, depressed; **~gehen** (*unreg*) *vi* to descend; (*AVIAT*) to come down; (*Regen*) to fall; (*Boxer*) to go down; **~geschlagen** *adj* depressed, dejected; **N~lage** *f* defeat; **N~lande** *pl* Netherlands; **N~länder(in)** *m(f)* Dutchman(-woman); **~ländisch** *adj* Dutch; **~lassen** (*unreg*) *vr* (*sich setzen*) to sit down; (*an Ort*) to settle (down); (*Arzt, Rechtsanwalt*) to set up a practice; **N~lassung** *f* settlement; (*COMM*) branch; **~legen** *vt* to lay down; (*Arbeit*) to stop; (*Amt*) to resign; **N~sachsen** *nt* Lower Saxony; **N~schlag** *m* (*MET*) precipitation; rainfall; **~schlagen** (*unreg*) *vt* (*Gegner*) to beat down; (*Gegenstand*) to knock down; (*Augen*) to lower; (*Aufstand*) to put down
♦ *vr* (*CHEM*) to precipitate; **~trächtig** *adj* base, mean; **N~trächtigkeit** *f* meanness,

baseness; outrage; **N~ung** *f* (*GEOG*) depression; (*Mündungsgebiet*) flats *pl*

niedlich ['niːtlɪç] *adj* sweet, cute

niedrig ['niːdrɪç] *adj* low; (*Stand*) lowly, humble; (*Gesinnung*) mean

niemals ['niːmaːls] *adv* never

niemand ['niːmant] *pron* nobody, no-one

Niemandsland ['niːmantslant] *nt* no-man's-land

Niere ['niːrə] *f* kidney

nieseln ['niːzəln] *vi* to drizzle

niesen ['niːzən] *vi* to sneeze

Niete ['niːtə] *f* (*TECH*) rivet; (*Los*) blank; (*Reinfall*) flop; (*Mensch*) failure; **n~n** *vt* to rivet

---

St. Nikolaus

On December 6th, **St. Nikolaus** *visits German children to reward those who have been good by filling shoes they have left out with sweets and small presents.*

Nikotin [niko'tiːn] **(-s)** *nt* nicotine

Nilpferd [niːl-] *nt* hippopotamus

Nimmersatt ['nɪmərzat] **(-(e)s, -e)** *m* glutton

nimmst *etc* [nɪmst] *vb siehe* **nehmen**

nippen ['nɪpən] *vt, vi* to sip

nirgend- ['nɪrgənt] *zW:* **~s** *adv* nowhere; **~wo** *adv* nowhere; **~wohin** *adv* nowhere

Nische ['niːʃə] *f* niche

nisten ['nɪstən] *vi* to nest

Niveau [ni'voː] **(-s, -s)** *nt* level

Nixe ['nɪksə] *f* water nymph

nobel ['noːbəl] *adj* (*großzügig*) generous; (*elegant*) posh (*inf*)

SCHLÜSSELWORT

---

noch [nɔx] *adv* **1** (*weiterhin*) still; **noch nicht** not yet; **noch nie** never (yet); **noch immer** *od* **immer noch** still; **bleiben Sie doch noch** stay a bit longer
2 (*in Zukunft*) still, yet; **das kann noch passieren** that might still happen; **er wird noch kommen** he'll come (yet)
3 (*nicht später als*): **noch vor einer Woche** only a week ago; **noch am selben Tag** the

very same day; **noch im 19. Jahrhundert** as late as the 19th century; **noch heute** today

4 (*zusätzlich*): **wer war noch da?** who else was there?; **noch einmal** once more, again; **noch dreimal** three more times; **noch einer** another one

5 (*bei Vergleichen*): **noch größer** even bigger; **das ist noch besser** that's better still; **und wenn es noch so schwer ist** however hard it is

6: **Geld noch und noch** heaps (and heaps) of money; **sie hat noch und noch versucht, ...** she tried again and again to ...

♦ *konj*: **weder A noch B** neither A nor B

noch- *zW*: **~mal** ['nɔxmaːl] *adv* again, once more; **~malig** ['nɔxmaːlɪç] *adj* repeated; **~mals** *adv* again, once more

Nominativ ['noːminatiːf] **(-s, -e)** *m* nominative

nominell [nomi'nɛl] *adj* nominal

Nonne ['nɔnə] *f* nun

Nord(en) ['nɔrd(ən)] **(-s)** *m* north

Nord'irland *nt* Northern Ireland

nordisch *adj* northern

nördlich ['nœrtlɪç] *adj* northerly, northern ♦ *präp +gen* (to the) north of; **~ von** (to the) north of

Nord- *zW*: **~pol** *m* North Pole; **~rhein-Westfalen** *nt* North Rhine-Westphalia; **~see** *f* North Sea; **n~wärts** *adv* northwards

nörgeln ['nœrgəln] *vi* to grumble; **Nörgler (-s, -)** *m* grumbler

Norm [nɔrm] **(-, -en)** *f* norm; (*Größenvorschrift*) standard; **n~al** [nɔr'maːl] *adj* normal; **~al(benzin)** *nt* ≈ 2-star petrol (*BRIT*), regular petrol (*US*); **n~alerweise** *adv* normally; **n~ali'sieren** *vt* to normalize ♦ *vr* to return to normal

normen *vt* to standardize

Norwegen ['nɔrveːgən] *nt* Norway; **norwegisch** *adj* Norwegian

Nostalgie [nɔstal'giː] *f* nostalgia

Not [noːt] **(-, ⁺e)** *f* need; (*Mangel*) want; (*Mühe*) trouble; (*Zwang*) necessity; **~leidend** needy; **zur ~** if necessary; (*gerade noch*) just about

Notar [no'taːr] **(-s, -e)** *m* notary; **n~i'ell** *adj* notarial

Not- *zW*: **~arzt** *m* emergency doctor; **~ausgang** *m* emergency exit; **~behelf (-s, -e)** *m* makeshift; **~bremse** *f* emergency brake; **~dienst** *m* (*Bereitschaftsdienst*) emergency service; **n~dürftig** *adj* scanty; (*behelfsmäßig*) makeshift

Note ['noːtə] *f* note; (*SCH*) mark (*BRIT*), grade (*US*)

Noten- *zW*: **~blatt** *nt* sheet of music; **~schlüssel** *m* clef; **~ständer** *m* music stand

Not- *zW*: **~fall** *m* (case of) emergency; **n~falls** *adv* if need be; **n~gedrungen** *adj* necessary, unavoidable; **etw n~gedrungen machen** to be forced to do sth

notieren [no'tiːrən] *vt* to note; (*COMM*) to quote

Notierung *f* (*COMM*) quotation

nötig ['nøːtɪç] *adj* necessary; **etw ~ haben** to need sth; **~en** [-gən] *vt* to compel, to force; **~enfalls** *adv* if necessary

Notiz [no'tiːts] **(-, -en)** *f* note; (*Zeitungsnotiz*) item; **~ nehmen** to take notice; **~block** *m* notepad; **~buch** *nt* notebook

Not- *zW*: **~lage** *f* crisis, emergency; **n~landen** *vi* to make a forced *od* emergency landing; **n~leidend** △ *adj siehe* **Not**; **~lösung** *f* temporary solution; **~lüge** *f* white lie

notorisch [no'toːrɪʃ] *adj* notorious

Not- *zW*: **~ruf** *m* emergency call; **~rufsäule** *f* emergency telephone; **~stand** *m* state of emergency; **~unterkunft** *f* emergency accommodation; **~verband** *m* emergency dressing; **~wehr (-)** *f* self-defence; **n~wendig** *adj* necessary; **~wendigkeit** *f* necessity

Novelle [no'vɛlə] *f* short novel; (*JUR*) amendment

November [no'vɛmbər] **(-s, -)** *m* November

Nu [nuː] *m*: **im ~** in an instant

Spelling Reform: ▲ *new spelling* △ *old spelling (to be phased out)*

Nuance [ny'ã:sə] *f* nuance

nüchtern ['nyçtərn] *adj* sober; (*Magen*) empty; (*Urteil*) prudent; **N~heit** *f* sobriety

Nudel ['nu:dəl] (-, -n) *f* noodle; **~n** *pl* (*Teigwaren*) pasta *sg*; (*in Suppe*) noodles

Null [nʊl] (-, -en) *f* nought, zero; (*pej: Mensch*) washout; **n~** *num* zero; (*Fehler*) no; **n~ Uhr** midnight; **n~ und nichtig** null and void; **~punkt** *m* zero; **auf dem ~punkt** at zero

numerisch [nu'me:rɪʃ] *adj* numerical

Nummer ['nʊmər] (-, -n) *f* number; (*Größe*) size; **n~ieren** ▲ *vt* to number; **~nschild** *nt* (*AUT*) number *od* license (*US*) plate

nun [nu:n] *adv* now ♦ *excl* well; **das ist ~ mal so** that's the way it is

nur [nu:r] *adv* just, only; **wo bleibt er ~?** (just) where is he?

Nürnberg ['nʏrnbɛrk] (-s) *nt* Nuremberg

Nuss ▲ [nʊs] (-, ⁓e) *f* nut; **~baum** *m* walnut tree; **~knacker** (-s, -) *m* nutcracker

nutz [nʊts] *adj*: **zu nichts ~ sein** to be no use for anything; **~bringend** *adj* (*Verwendung*) profitable

nütze ['nʏtsə] *adj* = **nutz**

Nutzen (-s) *m* usefulness; (*Gewinn*) profit; **von ~** useful; **n~** *vi* to be of use ♦ *vt*: **etw zu etw n~** to use sth for sth; **was nutzt es?** what's the use?, what use is it?

nützen *vi, vt* = **nutzen**

nützlich ['nʏtslɪç] *adj* useful; **N~keit** *f* usefulness

Nutz- *zW*: **n~los** *adj* useless; **~losigkeit** *f* uselessness; **~nießer** (-s, -) *m* beneficiary

Nylon ['naɪlɔn] (-(s)) *nt* nylon

O, o

Oase [o'a:zə] *f* oasis

ob [ɔp] *konj* if, whether; **~ das wohl wahr ist?** can that be true?; **und ~!** you bet!

obdachlos *adj* homeless

Obdachlose(r) *f(m)* homeless person; **~nasyl** *nt* shelter for the homeless

Obduktion [ɔpdʊktsi'o:n] *f* post-mortem

obduzieren [ɔpdu'tsi:rən] *vt* to do a post-

mortem on

O-Beine ['o:baɪnə] *pl* bow *od* bandy legs

oben ['o:bən] *adv* above; (*in Haus*) upstairs; **~ erwähnt, ~ gennant** above-mentioned; **nach ~** up; **von ~** down; **~ ohne** topless; **jdn von ~ bis unten ansehen** to look sb up and down; **~an** *adv* at the top; **~auf** *adv* up above, on the top ♦ *adj* (*munter*) in form; **~drein** *adv* into the bargain

Ober ['o:bər] (-s, -) *m* waiter; **die ~en** *pl* (*umg*) the bosses; (*ECCL*) the superiors; **~arm** *m* upper arm; **~arzt** *m* senior physician; **~aufsicht** *f* supervision; **~bayern** *nt* Upper Bavaria; **~befehl** *m* supreme command; **~befehlshaber** *m* commander-in-chief; **~bekleidung** *f* outer clothing; **~'bürgermeister** *m* lord mayor; **~deck** *nt* upper *od* top deck; **o~e(r, s)** *adj* upper; **~fläche** *f* surface; **o~flächlich** *adj* superficial; **~geschoss** ▲ *nt* upper storey; **o~halb** *adv* above ♦ *präp +gen* above; **~haupt** *nt* head, chief; **~haus** *nt* (*POL*) upper house, House of Lords (*BRIT*); **~hemd** *nt* shirt; **~herrschaft** *f* supremacy, sovereignty; **~in** *f* matron; (*ECCL*) Mother Superior; **~kellner** *m* head waiter; **~kiefer** *m* upper jaw; **~körper** *m* upper part of body; **~leitung** *f* direction; (*ELEK*) overhead cable; **~licht** *nt* skylight; **~lippe** *f* upper lip; **~schenkel** *m* thigh; **~schicht** *f* upper classes *pl*; **~schule** *f* grammar school (*BRIT*), high school (*US*); **~schwester** *f* (*MED*) matron

Oberst ['o:bərst] (-en *od* -s, -en *od* -e) *m* colonel; **o~e(r, s)** *adj* very top, top-most

Ober- *zW*: **~stufe** *f* upper school; **~teil** *nt* upper part; **~weite** *f* bust/chest measurement

obgleich [ɔp'glaɪç] *konj* although

Obhut ['ɔphu:t] (-) *f* care, protection; **in jds ~ sein** to be in sb's care

obig ['o:bɪç] *adj* above

Objekt [ɔp'jɛkt] (-(e)s, -e) *nt* object; **~iv** [-'ti:f] (-s, -e) *nt* lens; **o~iv** *adj* objective; **~ivi'tät** *f* objectivity

Oblate [o'bla:tə] *f* (*Gebäck*) wafer; (*ECCL*) host

bligatorisch [obligaˈtoːrɪʃ] adj compulsory, obligatory

brigkeit [ˈoːbrɪçkaɪt] f (Behörden) authorities pl, administration; (Regierung) government

bschon [ɔpˈʃoːn] konj although

bservatorium [ɔpzɛrvaˈtoːriʊm] nt observatory

bskur [ɔpsˈkuːr] adj obscure; (verdächtig) dubious

bst [oːpst] (-(e)s) nt fruit; ~baum m fruit tree; ~garten m orchard; ~händler m fruiterer, fruit merchant; ~kuchen m fruit tart

bszön [ɔpsˈtsøːn] adj obscene; O~i'tät f obscenity

bwohl [ɔpˈvoːl] konj although

chse [ˈɔksə] (-n, -n) m ox; o~n (umg) vt, vi to cram, to swot (BRIT)

chsenschwanzsuppe f oxtail soup

chsenzunge f oxtongue

d(e) [ˈøːd(ə)] adj (Land) waste, barren; (fig) dull; O~ f desert, waste(land); (fig) tedium

der [ˈoːdər] konj or; das stimmt, ~? that's right, isn't it?

fen [ˈoːfən] (-s, ") m oven; (Heizofen) fire, heater; (Kohlenofen) stove; (Hochofen) furnace; (Herd) cooker, stove; ~rohr nt stovepipe

ffen [ˈɔfən] adj open; (aufrichtig) frank; (Stelle) vacant; ~ bleiben (Fenster) to stay open; (Frage, Entscheidung) to remain open; ~ halten to keep open; ~ lassen to leave open; ~ stehen to be open; (Rechnung) to be unpaid; es steht Ihnen ~, es zu tun you are at liberty to do it; ~ gesagt to be honest; ~bar adj obvious; ~baren [ɔfənˈbaːrən] vt to reveal, to manifest; O~'barung f (REL) revelation; O~heit f candour, frankness; ~herzig adj candid, frank; (Kleid) revealing; ~kundig adj well-known; (klar) evident; ~sichtlich adj evident, obvious

ffensiv [ɔfɛnˈziːf] adj offensive; O~e [-ˈziːvə] f offensive

ffentlich [ˈœfəntlɪç] adj public; Ö~keit f (Leute) public; (einer Versammlung etc) public nature; in aller Ö~keit in public; an die Ö~keit dringen to reach the public ear

offiziell [ɔfitsiˈɛl] adj official

Offizier [ɔfiˈtsiːr] (-s, -e) m officer; ~skasino nt officers' mess

öffnen [ˈœfnən] vt, vr to open; jdm die Tür ~ to open the door for sb

Öffner [ˈœfnər] (-s, -) m opener

Öffnung [ˈœfnʊŋ] f opening; ~szeiten pl opening times

oft [ɔft] adv often

öfter [ˈœftər] adv more often od frequently; ~s adv often, frequently

oh [oː] excl oh; ~ je! oh dear

OHG abk (= Offene Handelsgesellschaft) general partnership

ohne [ˈoːnə] präp +akk without ♦ konj without; das ist nicht ~ (umg) it's not bad; ~ weiteres without a second thought; (sofort) immediately; ~ zu fragen without asking; ~ dass er es wusste without him knowing it; ~dies [oːnəˈdiːs] adv anyway; ~gleichen [oːnəˈglaɪçən] adj unsurpassed, without equal; ~hin [oːnəˈhɪn] adv anyway, in any case

Ohnmacht [ˈoːnmaxt] f faint; (fig) impotence; in ~ fallen to faint

ohnmächtig [ˈoːnmɛçtɪç] adj in a faint, unconscious; (fig) weak, impotent; sie ist ~ she has fainted

Ohr [oːr] (-(e)s, -en) nt ear

Öhr [øːr] (-(e)s, -e) nt eye

Ohren- zW: ~arzt m ear specialist; o~betäubend adj deafening; ~schmalz nt earwax; ~schmerzen pl earache sg

Ohr- zW: ~feige f slap on the face; box on the ears; o~feigen vt: jdn o~feigen to slap sb's face; to box sb's ears; ~läppchen nt ear lobe; ~ring m earring; ~wurm m earwig; (MUS) catchy tune

Öko- [øko] zW: ~laden m wholefood shop; ö~logisch [-ˈloːgɪʃ] adj ecological; ö~nomisch [-ˈnoːmɪʃ] adj economical

Oktober [ɔkˈtoːbər] (-s, -) m October; ~fest nt Munich beer festival

---

Oktoberfest

i *The annual beer festival, the* **Oktoberfest**, *takes place in Munich at the end of September in a huge area where beer tents and various amusements are set up. People sit at long wooden tables, drink beer from enormous beer mugs, eat pretzels and listen to brass bands. It is a great attraction for tourists and locals alike.*

ökumenisch [øku'me:nɪʃ] *adj* ecumenical
Öl [øːl] (-(e)s, -e) *nt* oil; **~baum** *m* olive tree; **ö~en** *vt* to oil; (*TECH*) to lubricate; **~farbe** *f* oil paint; **~feld** *nt* oilfield; **~film** *m* film of oil; **~heizung** *f* oil-fired central heating; **ö~ig** *adj* oily; **~industrie** *f* oil industry
oliv [o'liːf] *adj* olive-green; **O~e** *f* olive
Öl- *zW:* **~messstab** ▲ *m* dipstick; **~sardine** *f* sardine; **~stand** *m* oil level; **~standanzeiger** *m* (*AUT*) oil gauge; **~tanker** *m* oil tanker; **~ung** *f* lubrication; oiling; (*ECCL*) anointment; **die Letzte ~ung** Extreme Unction; **~wechsel** *m* oil change
Olymp- [o'lymp] *zW:* **~iade** [olympi'aːdə] *f* Olympic Games *pl*; **~iasieger(in)** [-iazi:gər(ɪn)] *m(f)* Olympic champion; **~iateilnehmer(in)** *m(f)* Olympic competitor; **o~isch** *adj* Olympic
Ölzeug *nt* oilskins *pl*
Oma ['oːma] (-, -s) (*umg*) *f* granny
Omelett [ɔm(ə)'lɛt] (-(e)s, -s) *nt* omelet(te)
ominös [omi'nøːs] *adj* (*unheilvoll*) ominous
Onanie [ona'niː] *f* masturbation; **o~ren** *vi* to masturbate
Onkel ['ɔŋkəl] (-s, -) *m* uncle
Opa ['oːpa] (-s, -s) (*umg*) *m* grandpa
Oper ['oːpər] (-, -n) *f* opera; opera house
Operation [operatsi'oːn] *f* operation; **~ssaal** *m* operating theatre
Operette [opə'rɛta] *f* operetta
operieren [ope'riːrən] *vt* to operate on ♦ *vi* to operate
Opern- *zW:* **~glas** *nt* opera glasses *pl*; **~haus** *nt* opera house
Opfer ['ɔpfər] (-s, -) *nt* sacrifice; (*Mensch*) victim; **o~n** *vt* to sacrifice; **~ung** *f* sacrifice
opponieren [ɔpo'niːrən] *vi*: **gegen jdn/etw ~** to oppose sb/sth
Opportunist [ɔpɔrtu'nɪst] *m* opportunist
Opposition [ɔpozitsi'oːn] *f* opposition; **o~ell** *adj* opposing
Optik ['ɔptɪk] *f* optics *sg*; **~er** (-s, -) *m* optician
optimal [ɔpti'maːl] *adj* optimal, optimum
Optimismus [ɔpti'mɪsmʊs] *m* optimism
Optimist [ɔpti'mɪst] *m* optimist; **o~isch** *adj* optimistic
optisch ['ɔptɪʃ] *adj* optical
Orakel [o'raːkal] (-s, -) *nt* oracle
oral [o'raːl] *adj* (*MED*) oral
Orange [o'rãːʒə] *f* orange; **o~** *adj* orange; **~ade** [orã'ʒaːdə] *f* orangeade; **~at** [orã'ʒaːt] (-s, -e) *nt* candied peel
Orchester [ɔr'kɛstər] (-s, -) *nt* orchestra
Orchidee [ɔrçi'deːə] *f* orchid
Orden ['ɔrdən] (-s, -) *m* (*ECCL*) order; (*MIL*) decoration; **~sschwester** *f* nun
ordentlich ['ɔrdəntlɪç] *adj* (*anständig*) decent, respectable; (*geordnet*) tidy, neat; (*umg: annehmbar*) not bad; (: *tüchtig*) real, proper ♦ *adv* properly; **~er Professor** (full) professor; **O~keit** *f* respectability; tidiness, neatness
ordinär [ɔrdi'nɛːr] *adj* common, vulgar
ordnen ['ɔrdnən] *vt* to order, to put in order
Ordner (-s, -) *m* steward; (*COMM*) file
Ordnung *f* order; (*Ordnen*) ordering; (*Geordnetsein*) tidiness; **~ machen** to tidy up; **in ~!** okay!
Ordnungs- *zW:* **o~gemäß** *adj* proper, according to the rules; **o~liebend** *adj* orderly, methodical; **~strafe** *f* fine; **o~widrig** *adj* contrary to the rules, irregular; **~widrigkeit** [-vɪdrɪçkaɪt] *f* infringement (*of law or rule*); **~zahl** *f* ordinal number
Organ [ɔr'gaːn] (-s, -e) *nt* organ; (*Stimme*) voice; **~isation** [-izatsi'oːn] *f* organization; **~isator** [i'zaːtɔr] *m* organizer; **o~isch** *adj* organic; **o~isieren** [-i'ziːrən] *vt* to organize, to arrange; (*umg: beschaffen*) to acquire ♦ *vr* to organize; **~ismus** [-'nɪsmʊs] *m*

Rechtschreibreform: ▲ *neue Schreibung* △ *alte Schreibung (auslaufend)*

organism; **~ist** [-'nɪst] *m* organist;
~spende *f* organ donation;
~spenderausweis *m* donor card
Orgasmus [ɔr'gasmʊs] *m* orgasm
Orgel ['ɔrgəl] **(-, -n)** *f* organ
Orgie ['ɔrgiə] *f* orgy
Orient ['o:riɛnt] **(-s)** *m* Orient, east;
o~alisch [-'ta:lɪʃ] *adj* oriental
orientier- *zW:* **~en** [-'ti:rən] *vt (örtlich)* to
locate; *(fig)* to inform ♦ *vr* to find one's way
od bearings; to inform o.s.; **O~ung** [-'ti:rʊŋ]
f orientation; *(fig)* information;
O~ungssinn *m* sense of direction;
O~ungsstufe *f* period during which pupils
are selected for different schools

Orientierungsstufe

ℹ The **Orientierungsstufe** is the name
given to the first two years spent in a
Realschule or **Gymnasium**, during which
a child is assessed as to his or her
suitability for that type of school. At the
end of two years it may be decided to
transfer the child to a school more suited to
his or her ability.

---

original [origi'na:l] *adj* original; **O~ (-s, -e)**
nt original; **O~fassung** *f* original version;
O~i'tät *f* originality
originell [origi'nɛl] *adj* original
Orkan [ɔr'ka:n] **(-(e)s, -e)** *m* hurricane;
o~artig *adj (Wind)* gale-force; *(Beifall)*
thunderous
Ornament [ɔrna'mɛnt] *nt* decoration,
ornament; **o~al** [-'ta:l] *adj* decorative,
ornamental
Ort [ɔrt] **(-(e)s, -e** *od* **⁼er)** *m* place; **an ~ und
Stelle** on the spot; **o~en** *vt* to locate
ortho- [ɔrto] *zW:* **~dox** [-'dɔks] *adj* orthodox;
O~grafie ▲ [-gra:'fi:] *f* spelling,
orthography; **~'grafisch** ▲ *adj*
orthographic; **O~päde** [-'pɛ:də] *m*
orthopaedist; **O~pädie** [-pe'di:] *f*
orthopaedics *sg;* **~'pädisch** *adj*
orthopaedic
örtlich ['œrtlɪç] *adj* local; **Ö~keit** *f* locality
ortsansässig *adj* local

Ortschaft *f* village, small town
Orts- *zW:* **o~fremd** *adj* non-local;
~gespräch *nt* local (phone)call; **~name**
m place name; **~netz** *nt (TEL)* local
telephone exchange area; **~tarif** *m (TEL)*
tariff for local calls; **~zeit** *f* local time
Ortung *f* locating
Öse ['ø:zə] *f* loop, eye
Ost'asien [ɔs'ta:ziən] *nt* Eastern Asia
Osten ['ɔstən] **(-s)** *m* east
Oster- ['o:stər] *zW:* **~ei** *nt* Easter egg; **~fest**
nt Easter; **~glocke** *f* daffodil; **~hase** *m*
Easter bunny; **~montag** *m* Easter Monday;
~n (-s, -) *nt* Easter
Österreich ['ø:stəraɪç] **(-s)** *nt* Austria;
~er(in) (-s, -) *m(f)* Austrian; **ö~isch** *adj*
Austrian
Ostküste *f* east coast
östlich ['œstlɪç] *adj* eastern, easterly
Ostsee *f:* **die ~** the Baltic (Sea)
Ouvertüre [uver'ty:rə] *f* overture
oval [o'va:l] *adj* oval
Ovation [ovatsi'o:n] *f* ovation
Oxid, Oxyd [ɔ'ksy:t] **(-(e)s, -e)** *nt* oxide;
o~ieren *vt, vi* to oxidize; **~ierung** *f*
oxidization
Ozean ['o:tsea:n] **(-s, -e)** *m* ocean;
~dampfer *m* (ocean-going) liner
Ozon [o'tso:n] **(-s)** *nt* ozone; **~loch** *nt* ozone
hole; **~schicht** *f* ozone layer

P, p

Paar [pa:r] **(-(e)s, -e)** *nt* pair; *(Ehepaar)*
couple; **ein p~** a few; **ein p~ Mal** a few
times; **p~en** *vt, vr* to couple; *(Tiere)* to
mate; **~lauf** *m* pair skating; **~ung** *f*
combination; mating; **p~weise** *adv* in
pairs; in couples
Pacht [paxt] **(-, -en)** *f* lease; **p~en** *vt* to
lease
Pächter ['pɛçtər] **(-s, -)** *m* leaseholder,
tenant
Pack¹ [pak] **(-(e)s, -e** *od* **⁼e)** *m* bundle,
pack
Pack² [pak] **(-(e)s)** *nt (pej)* mob, rabble

Spelling Reform: ▲ *new spelling* △ *old spelling (to be phased out)*

Päckchen ['pɛkçən] *nt* small package; (*Zigaretten*) packet; (*Postpäckchen*) small parcel

Pack- *zW:* **p~en** *vt* to pack; (*fassen*) to grasp, to seize; (*umg: schaffen*) to manage; (*fig: fesseln*) to grip; **~en** (*-s, -*) *m* bundle; (*fig: Menge*) heaps of; **~esel** *m* (*auch fig*) packhorse; **~papier** *nt* brown paper, wrapping paper; **~ung** *f* packet; (*Pralinenpackung*) box; (*MED*) compress; **~ungsbeilage** *f* enclosed instructions *pl* for use

Pädagog- [pɛda'go:g] *zW:* **~e** (*-n, -n*) *m* teacher; **~ik** *f* education; **p~isch** *adj* educational, pedagogical

Paddel ['padəl] (*-s, -*) *nt* paddle; **~boot** *nt* canoe; **p~n** *vi* to paddle

Page ['pa:ʒə] (*-n, -n*) *m* page

Paket [pa'ke:t] (*-(e)s, -e*) *nt* packet; (*Postpaket*) parcel; **~karte** *f* dispatch note; **~post** *f* parcel post; **~schalter** *m* parcels counter

Pakt [pakt] (*-(e)s, -e*) *m* pact

Palast [pa'last] (*-es, Paläste*) *m* palace

Palästina [palɛ'sti:na] (*-s*) *nt* Palestine

Palme ['palmə] *f* palm (tree)

Pampelmuse ['pampəlmu:zə] *f* grapefruit

panieren [pa'ni:rən] *vt* (*KOCH*) to bread

Paniermehl [pa'ni:rme:l] *nt* breadcrumbs *pl*

Panik ['pa:nɪk] *f* panic

panisch ['pa:nɪʃ] *adj* panic-stricken

Panne ['panə] *f* (*AUT etc*) breakdown; (*Missgeschick*) slip; **~nhilfe** *f* breakdown service

panschen ['panʃən] *vi* to splash about ♦ *vt* to water down

Pantoffel [pan'tɔfəl] (*-s, -n*) *m* slipper

Pantomime [panto'mi:mə] *f* mime

Panzer ['pantsər] (*-s, -*) *m* armour; (*Platte*) armour plate; (*Fahrzeug*) tank; **~glas** *nt* bulletproof glass; **p~n** *vt* to armour ♦ *vr* (*fig*) to arm o.s.

Papa [pa'pa:] (*-s, -s*) (*umg*) *m* dad, daddy

Papagei [papa'gaɪ] (*-s, -en*) *m* parrot

Papier [pa'pi:r] (*-s, -e*) *nt* paper; (*Wertpapier*) security; **~fabrik** *f* paper mill; **~geld** *nt* paper money; **~korb** *m* wastepaper basket;

~taschentuch *nt* tissue

Papp- ['pap] *zW:* **~deckel** *m* cardboard; **~e** *f* cardboard; **~el** (*-, -n*) *f* poplar; **p~en** (*umg*) *vt, vi* to stick; **p~ig** *adj* sticky

Paprika ['paprika] (*-s, -s*) *m* (*Gewürz*) paprika; (*~schote*) pepper

Papst [pa:pst] (*-(e)s, ᵛe*) *m* pope

päpstlich ['pɛ:pstlɪç] *adj* papal

Parabel [pa'ra:bəl] (*-, -n*) *f* parable; (*MATH*) parabola

Parabolantenne [parabo:lantɛnə] *f* satellite dish

Parade [pa'ra:də] *f* (*MIL*) parade, review; (*SPORT*) parry

Paradies [para'di:s] (*-es, -e*) *nt* paradise; **p~isch** *adj* heavenly

Paradox [para'dɔks] (*-es, -e*) *nt* paradox; **p~** *adj* paradoxical

Paragraf ▲ [para'gra:f] (*-en, -en*) *m* paragraph; (*JUR*) section

parallel [para'le:l] *adj* parallel; **P~e** *f* parallel

Parasit [para'zi:t] (*-en, -en*) *m* (*auch fig*) parasite

parat [pa'ra:t] *adj* ready

Pärchen ['pɛ:rçən] *nt* couple

Parfüm [par'fy:m] (*-s, -s* *od* *-e*) *nt* perfume; **~erie** [-ə'ri:] *f* perfumery; **p~frei** *adj* nonperfumed; **p~ieren** *vt* to scent, to perfume

parieren [pa'ri:rən] *vt* to parry ♦ *vi* (*umg*) to obey

Paris [pa'ri:s] (*-*) *nt* Paris; **~er** *adj* Parisian ♦ *m* Parisian; **~erin** *f* Parisian

Park [park] (*-s, -s*) *m* park; **~anlage** *f* park; (*um Gebäude*) grounds *pl*; **p~en** *vt, vi* to park; **~ett** (*-(e)s, -e*) *nt* parquet (floor); (*THEAT*) stalls *pl*; **~gebühr** *f* parking fee; **~haus** *nt* multi-storey car park; **~lücke** *f* parking space; **~platz** *m* parking place; car park, parking lot (*US*); **~scheibe** *f* parking disc; **~schein** *m* car park ticket; **~uhr** *f* parking meter; **~verbot** *nt* parking ban

Parlament [parla'mɛnt] *nt* parliament; **~arier** [-'ta:riər] (*-s, -*) *m* parliamentarian; **p~arisch** [-'ta:rɪʃ] *adj* parliamentary

Parlaments- *zW:* **~beschluss** ▲ *m* vote of parliament; **~mitglied** *nt* member of parliament; **~sitzung** *f* sitting (of parliament)

Parodie [paro'di:] f parody; **p~ren** vt to parody

Parole [pa'ro:lə] f password; (Wahlspruch) motto

Partei [par'taɪ] f party; **~ ergreifen für jdn** to take sb's side; **p~isch** adj partial, bias(s)ed; **p~los** adj neutral, impartial; **~mitglied** nt party member; **~programm** nt (party) manifesto; **~tag** m party conference

Parterre [par'tɛr] (**-s, -s**) nt ground floor; (THEAT) stalls pl

Partie [par'ti:] f part; (Spiel) game; (Ausflug) outing; (Mann, Frau) catch; (COMM) lot; **mit von der ~ sein** to join in

Partizip [parti'tsi:p] (**-s, -ien**) nt participle

Partner(in) ['partnər(ɪn)] (**-s, -**) m(f) partner; **~schaft** f partnership; (von Städten) twinning; **p~schaftlich** adj as partners; **~stadt** f twin town

Party ['pa:rti] (**-, -s**) f party

Pass ▲ [pas] (**-es, ⁻e**) m pass; (Ausweis) passport

passabel [pa'sa:bəl] adj passable, reasonable

Passage [pa'sa:ʒə] f passage

Passagier [pasa'ʒi:r] (**-s, -e**) m passenger; **~flugzeug** nt airliner

Passamt ▲ nt passport office

Passant [pa'sant] m passer-by

Passbild ▲ nt passport photograph

passen ['pasən] vi to fit; (Farbe) to go; (auf Frage, KARTEN, SPORT) to pass; **das passt mir nicht** that doesn't suit me; **~ zu** (Farbe, Kleider) to go with; **er passt nicht zu dir** he's not right for you; **~d** adj suitable; (zusammenpassend) matching; (angebracht) fitting; (Zeit) convenient

passier- [pa'si:r] zW: **~bar** adj passable; **~en** vt to pass; (durch Sieb) to strain ♦ vi to happen; **P~schein** m pass, permit

Passion [pasi'o:n] f passion; **p~iert** [-'ni:rt] adj enthusiastic, passionate; **~sspiel** nt Passion Play

passiv ['pasi:f] adj passive; **P~** (**-s, -e**) nt passive; **P~a** pl (COMM) liabilities; **P~i'tät** f

passiveness; **P~rauchen** nt passive smoking

Pass- ▲ zW: **~kontrolle** f passport control; **~stelle** f passport office; **~straße** f (mountain) pass

Paste ['pastə] f paste

Pastete [pas'te:tə] f pie

pasteurisieren [pastøri'zi:rən] vt to pasteurize

Pastor ['pastɔr] m vicar; pastor, minister

Pate ['pa:tə] (**-n, -n**) m godfather; **~nkind** nt godchild

Patent [pa'tɛnt] (**-(e)s, -e**) nt patent; (MIL) commission; **p~** adj clever; **~amt** nt patent office

Patentante f godmother

patentieren [patɛn'ti:rən] vt to patent

Patentinhaber m patentee

pathetisch [pa'te:tɪʃ] adj emotional; bombastic

Pathologe [pato'lo:gə] (**-n, -n**) m pathologist

pathologisch adj pathological

Pathos ['pa:tɔs] (**-**) nt emotiveness, emotionalism

Patient(in) [patsi'ɛnt(ɪn)] m(f) patient

Patin ['pa:tɪn] f godmother

Patriot [patri'o:t] (**-en, -en**) m patriot; **p~isch** adj patriotic; **~ismus** [-'tɪsmʊs] m patriotism

Patrone [pa'tro:nə] f cartridge

Patrouille [pa'trʊljə] f patrol

patrouillieren [patrʊl'ji:rən] vi to patrol

patsch [patʃ] excl splash; **P~e** (umg) f (Bedrängnis) mess, jam; **~en** vi to smack, to slap; (im Wasser) to splash; **~nass** ▲ adj soaking wet

patzig ['patsɪç] (umg) adj cheeky, saucy

Pauke ['paʊkə] f kettledrum; **auf die ~ hauen** to live it up

pauken vt (intensiv lernen) to swot up (inf) ♦ vi to swot (inf), cram (inf)

pausbäckig ['paʊsbɛkɪç] adj chubby-cheeked

pauschal [paʊ'ʃa:l] adj (Kosten) inclusive; (Urteil) sweeping; **P~e** f flat rate; **P~gebühr** f flat rate; **P~preis** m all-in price; **P~reise** f package tour; **P~summe** f lump sum

Pause ['pauzə] f break; (THEAT) interval; (Innehalten) pause; (Kopie) tracing

pausen vt to trace; **~los** adj non-stop; **P~zeichen** nt call sign; (MUS) rest

Pauspapier ['pauspapiːr] nt tracing paper

Pavillon ['paviljõ] (**-s, -s**) m pavilion

Pazif- [pa'tsiːf] zW: **~ik** (**-s**) m Pacific; **p~istisch** adj pacifist

Pech [pɛç] (**-s, -e**) nt pitch; (fig) bad luck; **~ haben** to be unlucky; **p~schwarz** adj pitch-black; **~strähne** (umg) f unlucky patch; **~vogel** (umg) m unlucky person

Pedal [pe'daːl] (**-s, -e**) nt pedal

Pedant [pe'dant] m pedant; **~e'rie** f pedantry; **p~isch** adj pedantic

Pediküre [pedi'kyːrə] f (Fußpflege) pedicure

Pegel ['peːɡəl] (**-s, -**) m water gauge; **~stand** m water level

peilen ['pailən] vt to get a fix on

Pein [pain] (**-**) f agony, pain; **p~igen** vt to torture; (plagen) to torment; **p~lich** adj (unangenehm) embarrassing, awkward, painful; (genau) painstaking

Peitsche ['paitʃə] f whip; **p~n** vt to whip; (Regen) to lash

Pelle ['pɛlə] f skin; **p~n** vt to skin, to peel

Pellkartoffeln pl jacket potatoes

Pelz [pɛlts] (**-es, -e**) m fur

Pendel ['pɛndəl] (**-s, -**) nt pendulum; **p~n** vi (Zug, Fähre etc) to operate a shuttle service; (Mensch) to commute; **~verkehr** m shuttle traffic; (für Pendler) commuter traffic

Pendler ['pɛndlər] (**-s, -**) m commuter

penetrant [pene'trant] adj sharp; (Person) pushing

Penis ['peːnɪs] (**-, -se**) m penis

pennen ['pɛnən] (umg) vi to kip

Penner (umg: pej) m (Landstreicher) tramp

Pension [penzi'oːn] f (Geld) pension; (Ruhestand) retirement; (für Gäste) boarding od guesthouse; **~är(in)** [-'nɛːr(ɪn)] (**-s, -e**) m(f) pensioner; **p~ieren** vt to pension off; **p~iert** adj retired; **~ierung** f retirement; **~sgast** m boarder, paying guest

Pensum ['pɛnzʊm] (**-s, Pensen**) nt quota;

(SCH) curriculum

per [pɛr] präp +akk by, per; (pro) per; (bis) by

Perfekt ['pɛrfɛkt] (**-(e)s, -e**) nt perfect; **p~** adj perfect

perforieren [pɛrfo'riːrən] vt to perforate

Pergament [pɛrɡa'mɛnt] nt parchment; **~papier** nt greaseproof paper

Periode [peri'oːdə] f period; **periodisch** adj periodic; (dezimal) recurring

Perle ['pɛrlə] f (auch fig) pearl; **p~n** vi to sparkle; (Tropfen) to trickle

Perl- ['pɛrl] zW: **~mutt** (**-s**) nt mother-of-pearl; **~wein** m sparkling wine

perplex [pɛr'plɛks] adj dumbfounded

Person [pɛr'zoːn] (**-, -en**) f person; **ich für meine ~ ...** personally I ...

Personal [pɛrzo'naːl] (**-s**) nt personnel; (Bedienung) servants pl; **~ausweis** m identity card; **~computer** m personal computer; **~ien** [-iən] pl particulars; **~mangel** m undermanning; **~pronomen** nt personal pronoun

personell [pɛrzo'nɛl] adj (Veränderungen) personnel

Personen- zW: **~aufzug** m lift, elevator (US); **~kraftwagen** m private motorcar; **~schaden** m injury to persons; **~zug** m stopping train; passenger train

personifizieren [pɛrzonifi'tsiːrən] vt to personify

persönlich [pɛr'zøːnlɪç] adj personal ♦ adv in person; personally; **P~keit** f personality

Perspektive [pɛrspɛk'tiːvə] f perspective

Perücke [pe'rʏkə] f wig

pervers [pɛr'vɛrs] adj perverse

Pessimismus [pɛsi'mɪsmʊs] m pessimism

Pessimist [pɛsi'mɪst] m pessimist; **p~isch** adj pessimistic

Pest [pɛst] (**-**) f plague

Petersilie [petɛr'ziːliə] f parsley

Petroleum [pe'troːleʊm] (**-s**) nt paraffin, kerosene (US)

Pfad [pfaːt] (**-(e)s, -e**) m path; **~finder** (**-s, -**) m boy scout; **~finderin** f girl guide

Pfahl [pfaːl] (**-(e)s, ¨e**) m post, stake

Pfand [pfant] (**-(e)s, ¨er**) nt pledge, security; (Flaschenpfand) deposit; (im Spiel) forfeit;

~brief m bond

fänden ['pfɛndən] vt to seize, to distrain

fänderspiel nt game of forfeits

fandflasche f returnable bottle

fandschein m pawn ticket

fändung ['pfɛnduŋ] f seizure, distraint

fanne ['pfanə] f (frying) pan

fannkuchen m pancake; (Berliner) doughnut

farr- ['pfar] zW: ~ei f parish; ~er (-s, -) m priest; (evangelisch) vicar; minister; ~haus nt vicarage; manse

fau [pfau] (-(e)s), **-en** m peacock; ~enauge nt peacock butterfly

feffer ['pfɛfər] (-s, -) m pepper; ~kuchen m gingerbread; ~minz (-es, -e) nt peppermint; ~mühle f pepper mill; p~n vt to pepper; (umg: werfen) to fling; **gepfefferte Preise/Witze** steep prices/ spicy jokes

feife ['pfaɪfə] f whistle; (Tabakpfeife, Orgelpfeife) pipe; p~n (unreg) vt, vi to whistle; ~r (-s, -) m piper

feil [pfaɪl] (-(e)s, -e) m arrow

feiler ['pfaɪlər] (-s, -) m pillar, prop; (Brückenpfeiler) pier

fennig ['pfɛnɪç] (-(e)s, -e) m (HIST) pfennig (hundredth part of a mark)

ferd [pfe:rt] (-(e)s, -e) nt horse

Pferde- ['pfe:rdə] zW: ~rennen nt horse race; horse racing; ~schwanz m (Frisur) ponytail; ~stall m stable

Pfiff [pfɪf] (-(e)s, -e) m whistle

Pfifferling ['pfɪfərlɪŋ] m yellow chanterelle (mushroom); **keinen ~ wert** not worth a thing

pfiffig adj sly, sharp

Pfingsten ['pfɪŋstən] (-, -) nt Whitsun (BRIT), Pentecost

Pfirsich ['pfɪrzɪç] (-s, -e) m peach

Pflanz- ['pflants] zW: ~e f plant; p~en vt to plant; ~enfett nt vegetable fat; p~lich adj vegetable; ~ung f plantation

Pflaster ['pflastər] (-s, -) nt plaster; (Straße) pavement; p~n vt to pave; ~stein m paving stone

Pflaume ['pflaumə] f plum

Pflege ['pfle:gə] f care; (von Idee) cultivation; (Krankenpflege) nursing; **in ~ sein** (Kind) to be fostered out; p~bedürftig adj needing care; ~eltern pl foster parents; ~heim nt nursing home; ~kind nt foster child; p~leicht adj easy-care; ~mutter f foster mother; p~n vt to look after; (Kranke) to nurse; (Beziehungen) to foster; ~r (-s, -) m orderly; male nurse; ~rin f nurse, attendant; ~vater m foster father

Pflicht [pflɪçt] (-, -en) f duty; (SPORT) compulsory section; p~bewusst ▲ adj conscientious; ~fach nt (SCH) compulsory subject; ~gefühl nt sense of duty; p~gemäß adj dutiful ♦ adv as in duty bound; ~versicherung f compulsory insurance

pflücken ['pflʏkən] vt to pick; (Blumen) to pick, to pluck

Pflug [pflu:k] (-(e)s, ᵘe) m plough

pflügen ['pfly:gən] vt to plough

Pforte ['pfɔrtə] f gate; door

Pförtner ['pfœrtnər] (-s, -) m porter, doorkeeper, doorman

Pfosten ['pfɔstən] (-s, -) m post

Pfote ['pfo:tə] f paw; (umg: Schrift) scrawl

Pfropfen (-s, -) m (Flaschenpfropfen) stopper; (Blutpfropfen) clot

pfui [pfui] excl ugh!

Pfund [pfunt] (-(e)s, -e) nt pound

pfuschen ['pfuʃən] (umg) vi to be sloppy; **jdm ins Handwerk ~** to interfere in sb's business

Pfuscher ['pfuʃər] (-s, -) (umg) m sloppy worker; (Kurpfuscher) quack; ~ei (umg) f sloppy work; quackery

Pfütze ['pfʏtsə] f puddle

Phänomen [feno'me:n] (-s, -e) nt phenomenon

phänomenal [-'na:l] adj phenomenal

Phantasie etc [fanta'zi:] f = **Fantasie** etc

phantastisch [fan'tastɪʃ] adj = **fantastisch**

Phase ['fa:zə] f phase

Philologie [filolo'gi:] f philology

Philosoph [filo'zo:f] (-en, -en) m philosopher; ~ie [-'fi:] f philosophy; p~isch adj philosophical

phlegmatisch [fle'gma:tɪʃ] *adj* lethargic

Phonetik [fo'ne:tɪk] *f* phonetics *sg*

phonetisch *adj* phonetic

Phosphor ['fɔsfɔr] (**-s**) *m* phosphorus

Photo *etc* ['fo:to] (**-s, -s**) *nt* = **Foto** *etc*

Phrase ['fra:zə] *f* phrase; (*pej*) hollow phrase

pH-Wert [pe:'ha:ve:rt] *m* pH-value

Physik [fy'zi:k] *f* physics *sg*; **p~alisch** [-'ka:lɪʃ] *adj* of physics; **~er(in)** ['fy:zɪkər(ɪn)] (**-s, -**) *m(f)* physicist

Physiologie [fyziolo'gi:] *f* physiology

physisch ['fy:zɪʃ] *adj* physical

Pianist(in) [pia'nɪst(ɪn)] *m(f)* pianist

Pickel ['pɪkəl] (**-s, -**) *m* pimple; (*Werkzeug*) pickaxe; (*Bergpickel*) ice axe; **p~ig** *adj* pimply, spotty

picken ['pɪkən] *vi* to pick, to peck

Picknick ['pɪknɪk] (**-s, -e** *od* **-s**) *nt* picnic; **~ machen** to have a picnic

piepen ['pi:pən] *vi* to chirp

piepsen ['pi:psən] *vi* to chirp

Piepser (*umg*) *m* pager, paging device

Pier [pi:ər] (**-s, -s** *od* **-e**) *m od f* pier

Pietät [pie'tɛ:t] *f* piety, reverence; **p~los** *adj* impious, irreverent

Pigment [pɪg'mɛnt] *nt* pigment

Pik [pi:k] (**-s, -s**) *nt* (*KARTEN*) spades

pikant [pi'kant] *adj* spicy, piquant; (*anzüglich*) suggestive

Pilger ['pɪlgər] (**-s, -**) *m* pilgrim; **~fahrt** *f* pilgrimage

Pille ['pɪlə] *f* pill

Pilot [pi'lo:t] (**-en, -en**) *m* pilot

Pilz [pɪlts] (**-es, -e**) *m* fungus; (*essbar*) mushroom; (*giftig*) toadstool; **~krankheit** *f* fungal disease

Pinguin ['pɪŋgui:n] (**-s, -e**) *m* penguin

Pinie ['pi:niə] *f* pine

pinkeln ['pɪŋkəln] (*umg*) *vi* to pee

Pinnwand ['pɪnvant] *f* noticeboard

Pinsel ['pɪnzəl] (**-s, -**) *m* paintbrush

Pinzette [pɪn'tsɛtə] *f* tweezers *pl*

Pionier [pio'ni:r] (**-s, -e**) *m* pioneer; (*MIL*) sapper, engineer

Pirat [pi'ra:t] (**-en, -en**) *m* pirate

Piste ['pɪstə] *f* (*SKI*) run, piste; (*AVIAT*) runway

Pistole [pɪs'to:lə] *f* pistol

Pizza ['pɪtsa] (**-, -s**) *f* pizza

Pkw [pe:ka:'ve:] (**-(s), -(s)**) *m abk* = **Personenkraftwagen**

plädieren [plɛ'di:rən] *vi* to plead

Plädoyer [plɛdoa'je:] (**-s, -s**) *nt* speech for the defence; (*fig*) plea

Plage ['pla:gə] *f* plague; (*Mühe*) nuisance; **~geist** *m* pest, nuisance; **p~n** *vt* to torment ♦ *vr* to toil, to slave

Plakat [pla'ka:t] (**-(e)s, -e**) *nt* placard; poster

Plan [pla:n] (**-(e)s, ⁀e**) *m* plan; (*Karte*) map

Plane *f* tarpaulin

planen *vt* to plan; (*Mord etc*) to plot

Planer (**-s, -**) *m* planner

Planet [pla'ne:t] (**-en, -en**) *m* planet

planieren [pla'ni:rən] *vt* to plane, to level

Planke ['plaŋkə] *f* plank

plan- ['pla:n] *zW:* **~los** *adj* (*Vorgehen*) unsystematic; (*Umherlaufen*) aimless; **~mäßig** *adj* according to plan; systematic; (*EISENB*) scheduled

Plansoll (**-s**) *nt* output target

Plantage [plan'ta:ʒə] *f* plantation

Plan(t)schbecken ['plan(t)ʃbɛkən] *nt* paddling pool

plan(t)schen ['plan(t)ʃən] *vi* to splash

Planung *f* planning

Planwirtschaft *f* planned economy

plappern ['plapərn] *vi* to chatter

plärren ['plɛrən] *vi* (*Mensch*) to cry, to whine; (*Radio*) to blare

Plasma ['plasma] (**-s, Plasmen**) *nt* plasma

Plastik¹ ['plastɪk] *f* sculpture

Plastik² ['plastɪk] (**-s**) *nt* (*Kunststoff*) plastic; **~beutel** *m* plastic bag, carrier bag; **~folie** *f* plastic film

plastisch ['plastɪʃ] *adj* plastic; **stell dir das ~ vor!** just picture it!

Platane [pla'ta:nə] *f* plane (tree)

Platin [pla'ti:n] (**-s**) *nt* platinum

platonisch [pla'to:nɪʃ] *adj* platonic

platsch [platʃ] *excl* splash; **~en** *vi* to splash

plätschern ['plɛtʃərn] *vi* to babble

platschnass ▲ *adj* drenched

platt [plat] *adj* flat; (*umg: überrascht*) flabbergasted; (*fig: geistlos*) flat, boring; **~deutsch** *adj* low German; **P~e** *f*

(*Speisenplatte, PHOT, TECH*) plate; (*Steinplatte*) flag; (*Kachel*) tile; (*Schallplatte*) record; **P~enspieler** *m* record player; **P~enteller** *m* turntable

Platz [plats] (**-es, ⸚e**) *m* place; (*Sitzplatz*) seat; (*Raum*) space, room; (*in Stadt*) square; (*Sportplatz*) playing field; **~ nehmen** to take a seat; **jdm ~ machen** to make room for sb; **~angst** *f* claustrophobia; **~anweiser(in)** (**-s, -**) *m(f)* usher(ette)

Plätzchen ['plɛtsçən] *nt* spot; (*Gebäck*) biscuit

platzen *vi* to burst; (*Bombe*) to explode; **vor Wut p~en** (*umg*) to be bursting with anger

platzieren ▲ [pla'tsi:rən] *vt* to place ♦ *vr* (*SPORT*) to be placed; (*TENNIS*) to be seeded

Platz- *zW*: **~karte** *f* seat reservation; **~mangel** *m* lack of space; **~patrone** *f* blank cartridge; **~regen** *m* downpour; **~reservierung** [-rezɛrvi:rʊŋ] *f* seat reservation; **~wunde** *f* cut

Plauderei [plaʊdə'raɪ] *f* chat, conversation; (*RADIO*) talk

plaudern ['plaʊdərn] *vi* to chat, to talk

plausibel [plaʊ'zi:bəl] *adj* plausible

plazieren △ [pla'tsi:rən] *vt, vr siehe* **platzieren**

Pleite ['plaɪtə] *f* bankruptcy; (*umg: Reinfall*) flop; **~ machen** to go bust; **p~** (*umg*) *adj* broke

Plenum ['ple:nʊm] (**-s**) *nt* plenum

Plombe ['plɔmbə] *f* lead seal; (*Zahnplombe*) filling

plombieren [plɔm'bi:rən] *vt* to seal; (*Zahn*) to fill

plötzlich ['plœtslɪç] *adj* sudden ♦ *adv* suddenly

plump [plʊmp] *adj* clumsy; (*Hände*) coarse; (*Körper*) shapeless; **~sen** (*umg*) *vi* to plump down, to fall

Plunder ['plʊndər] (**-s**) *m* rubbish

plündern ['plʏndərn] *vt* to plunder; (*Stadt*) to sack ♦ *vi* to plunder; **Plünderung** *f* plundering, sack, pillage

Plural ['plu:ra:l] (**-s, -e**) *m* plural; **p~istisch** *adj* pluralistic

Plus [plʊs] (**-, -**) *nt* plus; (*FIN*) profit; (*Vorteil*) advantage; **p~** *adv* plus

Plüsch [ply:ʃ] (**-(e)s, -e**) *m* plush

Plus- [plʊs] *zW*: **~pol** *m* (*ELEK*) positive pole; **~punkt** *m* point; (*fig*) point in sb's favour

Plutonium [plu'to:niʊm] (**-s**) *nt* plutonium

PLZ *abk* = **Postleitzahl**

Po [po:] (**-s, -s**) (*umg*) *m* bottom, bum

Pöbel ['pø:bəl] (**-s**) *m* mob, rabble; **~ei** *f* vulgarity; **p~haft** *adj* low, vulgar

pochen ['pɔxən] *vi* to knock; (*Herz*) to pound; **auf etw** *akk* **~** (*fig*) to insist on sth

Pocken ['pɔkən] *pl* smallpox *sg*

Podium ['po:diʊm] *nt* podium; **~sdiskussion** *f* panel discussion

Poesie [poe'zi:] *f* poetry

Poet [po'e:t] (**-en, -en**) *m* poet; **p~isch** *adj* poetic

Pointe [po'ɛ̃:tə] *f* point

Pokal [po'ka:l] (**-s, -e**) *m* goblet; (*SPORT*) cup; **~spiel** *nt* cup tie

pökeln ['pø:kəln] *vt* to pickle, to salt

Poker ['po:kər] (**-s**) *nt od m* poker

Pol [po:l] (**-s, -e**) *m* pole; **p~ar** *adj* polar; **~arkreis** *m* Arctic circle

Pole ['po:lə] (**-n, -n**) *m* Pole

polemisch [po:le:mɪʃ] *adj* polemical

Polen ['po:lən] (**-s**) *nt* Poland

Police [po'li:s(ə)] *f* insurance policy

Polier [po'li:r] (**-s, -e**) *m* foreman

polieren *vt* to polish

Poliklinik [poli'kli:nɪk] *f* outpatients (department) *sg*

Polin *f* Pole

Politik [poli'ti:k] *f* politics *sg*; (*eine bestimmte*) policy; **~er(in)** [poli'ti:kər(ɪn)] (**-s, -**) *m(f)* politician

politisch [po'li:tɪʃ] *adj* political

Politur [poli'tu:r] *f* polish

Polizei [poli'tsaɪ] *f* police; **~beamte(r)** *m* police officer; **p~lich** *adj* police; **sich p~lich melden** to register with the police; **~revier** *nt* police station; **~staat** *m* police state; **~streife** *f* police patrol; **~stunde** *f* closing time; **~wache** *f* police station

Polizist(in) [poli'tsɪst(ɪn)] (**-en, -en**) *m(f)* policeman(-woman)

Pollen ['pɔlən] (**-s, -**) *m* pollen; **~flug** *m* pollen count

polnisch ['pɔlnɪʃ] *adj* Polish

Polohemd ['poːlohɛmt] *nt* polo shirt

Polster ['pɔlstər] (**-s, -**) *nt* cushion; (*~ung*) upholstery; (*in Kleidung*) padding; (*fig: Geld*) reserves *pl;* **~er** (**-s, -**) *m* upholsterer; **~möbel** *pl* upholstered furniture *sg;* **p~n** *vt* to upholster; to pad

Polterabend ['pɔltəraːbənt] *m* party on eve of wedding

poltern *vi* (*Krach machen*) to crash; (*schimpfen*) to rant

Polyp [po'lyːp] (**-en, -en**) *m* polyp; (*umg*) cop; **~en** *pl* (*MED*) adenoids

Pomade [po'maːdə] *f* pomade

Pommes frites [pɔm'frɪt] *pl* chips, French fried potatoes

Pomp [pɔmp] (**-(e)s**) *m* pomp; **p~ös** [pɔm'pøːs] *adj* (*Auftritt, Fest, Haus*) ostentatious, showy

Pony ['pɔni] (**-s, -s**) *nt* (*Pferd*) pony ♦ *m* (*Frisur*) fringe

Popmusik ['pɔpmuziːk] *f* pop music

Popo [po'poː] (**-s, -s**) (*umg*) *m* bottom, bum

poppig ['pɔpɪç] *adj* (*Farbe etc*) gaudy

populär [popu'lɛːr] *adj* popular

Popularität [populari'tɛːt] *f* popularity

Pore ['poːrə] *f* pore

Pornografie ▲ [pɔrnogra'fiː] *f* pornography; **pornografisch** ▲ [pɔrno'graːfɪʃ] *adj* pornographic

porös [po'røːs] *adj* porous

Porree ['pɔre] (**-s, -s**) *m* leek

Portefeuille [pɔrt(ə)'føːj] *nt* (*POL, FIN*) portfolio

Portemonnaie [pɔrtmɔ'neː] (**-s, -s**) *nt* purse

Portier [pɔrti'eː] (**-s, -s**) *m* porter

Portion [pɔrtsi'oːn] *f* portion, helping; (*umg: Anteil*) amount

Portmonee ▲ [pɔrtmɔ'neː] (**-s, -s**) *nt* = **Portemonnaie**

Porto ['pɔrto] (**-s, -s**) *nt* postage; **p~frei** *adj* post-free, (postage) prepaid

Portrait [pɔr'trɛː] (**-s, -s**) *nt* = **Porträt;** **p~ieren** *vt* = **porträtieren**

Porträt [pɔr'trɛː] (**-s, -s**) *nt* portrait; **p~ieren** *vt* to paint, to portray

Portugal ['pɔrtugal] (**-s**) *nt* Portugal; **Portugiese** [pɔrtu'giːzə] (**-n, -n**) *m* Portuguese; **Portu'giesin** *f* Portuguese; **portu'giesisch** *adj* Portuguese

Porzellan [pɔrtse'laːn] (**-s, -e**) *nt* china, porcelain; (*Geschirr*) china

Posaune [po'zaunə] *f* trombone

Pose ['poːzə] *f* pose

Position [pozitsi'oːn] *f* position

positiv ['poːzitiːf] *adj* positive; **P~** (**-s, -e**) *nt* (*PHOT*) positive

possessiv ['pɔsesiːf] *adj* possessive; **P~pronomen** (**-s, -e**) *nt* possessive pronoun

possierlich [pɔ'siːrlɪç] *adj* funny

Post [pɔst] (**-, -en**) *f* post (office); (*Briefe*) mail; **~amt** *nt* post office; **~anweisung** *f* postal order, money order; **~bote** *m* postman; **~en** (**-s, -**) *m* post, position; (*COMM*) item; (*auf Liste*) entry; (*MIL*) sentry; (*Streikposten*) picket; **~er** (**-s, -(s)**) *nt* poster; **~fach** *nt* post office box; **~karte** *f* postcard; **p~lagernd** *adv* poste restante (*BRIT*), general delivery (*US*); **~leitzahl** *f* postal code; **~scheckkonto** *nt* postal giro account; **~sparbuch** *nt* post office savings book; **~sparkasse** *f* post office savings bank; **~stempel** *m* postmark; **p~wendend** *adv* by return of post; **~wertzeichen** *nt* postage stamp

potent [po'tɛnt] *adj* potent

Potential △ [potɛntsi'aːl] (**-s, -e**) *nt* siehe **Potenzial**

potentiell △ [potɛntsi'el] *adj* siehe **potenziell**

Potenz [po'tɛnts] *f* power; (*eines Mannes*) potency

Potenzial ▲ [potɛn'tsiaːl] (**-s, -e**) *nt* potential

potenziell ▲ [potɛn'tsiel] *adj* potential

Pracht [praxt] (**-**) *f* splendour, magnificence; **prächtig** ['prɛçtɪç] *adj* splendid

Prachtstück *nt* showpiece

prachtvoll *adj* splendid, magnificent

Prädikat [predi'kaːt] (**-(e)s, -e**) *nt* title;

(GRAM) predicate; (Zensur) distinction

prägen ['prɛːgən] vt to stamp; (Münze) to mint; (Ausdruck) to coin; (Charakter) to form

prägnant [prɛ'gnant] adj precise, terse

Prägung ['prɛːgʊŋ] f minting; forming; (Eigenart) character, stamp

prahlen ['praːlən] vi to boast, to brag; **Prahle'rei** f boasting

Praktik ['praktɪk] f practice; **p~abel** [-'kaːbəl] adj practicable; **~ant(in)** [-'kant(ɪn)] m(f) trainee; **~um (-s, Praktika** od **Praktiken)** nt practical training

praktisch ['praktɪʃ] adj practical, handy; **~er Arzt** general practitioner

praktizieren [prakti'tsiːrən] vt, vi to practise

Praline [pra'liːnə] f chocolate

prall [pral] adj firmly rounded; (Segel) taut; (Arme) plump; (Sonne) blazing; **~en** vi to bounce, to rebound; (Sonne) to blaze

Prämie ['prɛːmiə] f premium; (Belohnung) award, prize; **p~ren** vt to give an award to

Präparat [prɛpa'raːt] **(-(e)s, -e)** nt (BIOL) preparation; (MED) medicine

Präposition [prɛpozitsi'oːn] f preposition

Prärie [prɛ'riː] f prairie

Präsens ['prɛːzɛns] **(-)** nt present tense

präsentieren [prɛzɛn'tiːrən] vt to present

Präservativ [prɛzɛrva'tiːf] **(-s, -e)** nt contraceptive

Präsident(in) [prɛzi'dɛnt(ɪn)] m(f) president; **~schaft** f presidency

Präsidium [prɛ'ziːdiʊm] nt presidency, chair(manship); (Polizeipräsidium) police headquarters pl

prasseln ['prasəln] vi (Feuer) to crackle; (Hagel) to drum; (Wörter) to rain down

Praxis ['praksɪs] **(-, Praxen)** f practice; (Behandlungsraum) surgery; (von Anwalt) office

Präzedenzfall [prɛtse'dɛnts-] m precedent

präzis [prɛ'tsiːs] adj precise; **P~ion** [prɛtsizi'oːn] f precision

predigen ['preːdɪgən] vt, vi to preach; **Prediger (-s, -)** m preacher

Predigt ['preːdɪçt] **(-, -en)** f sermon

Preis [praɪs] **(-es, -e)** m price; (Siegespreis) prize; **um keinen ~** not at any price;

p~bewusst ▲ adj price-conscious

Preiselbeere f cranberry

preis- ['praɪz] zW: **~en (unreg)** vi to praise; **~geben (unreg)** vt to abandon; (opfern) to sacrifice; (zeigen) to expose; **~gekrönt** adj prizewinning; **P~gericht** nt jury; **~günstig** adj inexpensive; **P~lage** f price range; **~lich** adj (Lage, Unterschied) price, in price; **P~liste** f price list; **P~richter** m judge (in a competition); **P~schild** nt price tag; **P~träger(in)** m(f) prizewinner; **~wert** adj inexpensive

Prell- [prɛl] zW: **~bock** m buffers pl; **p~en** vt to bump; (fig) to cheat, to swindle; **~ung** f bruise

Premiere [prəmi'ɛːrə] f premiere

Premierminister [prəmi'eːmɪnɪstər] m prime minister, premier

Presse ['prɛsə] f press; **~agentur** f press agency; **~freiheit** f freedom of the press; **p~n** vt to press

Pressluft ▲ ['prɛslʊft] f compressed air; **~bohrer** m pneumatic drill

Prestige [prɛs'tiːʒə] **(-s)** nt prestige

prickeln ['prɪkəln] vt, vi to tingle; to tickle

Priester ['priːstər] **(-s, -)** m priest

prima adj inv first-class, excellent

primär [pri'mɛːr] adj primary

Primel ['priːməl] **(-, -n)** f primrose

primitiv [primi'tiːf] adj primitive

Prinz [prɪnts] **(-en, -en)** m prince; **~essin** f princess

Prinzip [prɪn'tsiːp] **(-s, -ien)** nt principle; **p~iell** [-i'ɛl] adj, adv on principle; **p~ienlos** adj unprincipled

Priorität [priori'tɛːt] f priority

Prise ['priːzə] f pinch

Prisma ['prɪsma] **(-s, Prismen)** nt prism

privat [pri'vaːt] adj private; **P~besitz** m private property; **P~fernsehen** nt commercial television; **P~patient(in)** m(f) private patient; **P~schule** f public school

Privileg [privi'leːk] **(-(e)s, -ien)** nt privilege

Pro [proː] **(-)** nt pro

pro präp +akk per

Probe ['proːbə] f test; (Teststück) sample; (THEAT) rehearsal; **jdn auf die ~ stellen** to put sb to the test; **~exemplar** *nt* specimen copy; **~fahrt** *f* test drive; **p~n** *vt* to try; (*THEAT*) to rehearse; **p~weise** *adv* on approval; **~zeit** *f* probation period

probieren [pro'biːrən] *vt* to try; (*Wein, Speise*) to taste, to sample ♦ *vi* to try; to taste

Problem [pro'bleːm] (**-s, -e**) *nt* problem; **~atik** [-'maːtɪk] *f* problem; **p~atisch** [-'maːtɪʃ] *adj* problematic; **p~los** *adj* problem-free

Produkt [pro'dʊkt] (**-(e)s, -e**) *nt* product; (*AGR*) produce *no pl*; **~ion** [prodʊktsi'oːn] *f* production; output; **p~iv** [-'tiːf] *adj* productive; **~ivität** *f* productivity

Produzent [produ'tsɛnt] *m* manufacturer; (*Film*) producer

produzieren [produ'tsiːrən] *vt* to produce

Professor [pro'fɛsɔr] *m* professor

Profi ['proːfi] (**-s, -s**) *m* (*umg, SPORT*) pro

Profil [pro'fiːl] (**-s, -e**) *nt* profile; (*fig*) image

Profit [pro'fiːt] (**-(e)s, -e**) *m* profit; **p~ieren** *vi*: **p~ieren (von)** to profit (from)

Prognose [pro'gnoːzə] *f* prediction, prognosis

Programm [pro'gram] (**-s, -e**) *nt* programme; (*COMPUT*) program; **p~ieren** [-'miːrən] *vt* to programme; (*COMPUT*) to program; **~ierer(in)** (**-s, -**) *m(f)* programmer

progressiv [progrɛ'siːf] *adj* progressive

Projekt [pro'jɛkt] (**-(e)s, -e**) *nt* project; **~or** [pro'jɛktɔr] *m* projector

proklamieren [prokla'miːrən] *vt* to proclaim

Prokurist(in) [proku'rɪst(ɪn)] *m(f)* ≃ company secretary

Prolet [pro'leːt] (**-en, -en**) *m* prole, pleb; **~arier** [-'taːriər] (**-s, -**) *m* proletarian

Prolog [pro'loːk] (**-(e)s, -e**) *m* prologue

Promenade [promə'naːdə] *f* promenade

Promille [pro'mɪlə] (**-(s), -**) *nt* alcohol level

prominent [promi'nɛnt] *adj* prominent

Prominenz [promi'nɛnts] *f* VIPs *pl*

Promotion [promotsi'oːn] *f* doctorate, Ph.D.

promovieren [promo'viːrən] *vi* to do a doctorate *od* Ph.D.

prompt [prɔmpt] *adj* prompt

Pronomen [pro'noːmɛn] (**-s, -**) *nt* pronoun

Propaganda [propa'ganda] (**-**) *f* propaganda

Propeller [pro'pɛlər] (**-s, -**) *m* propeller

Prophet [pro'feːt] (**-en, -en**) *m* prophet

prophezeien [profe'tsaɪən] *vt* to prophesy; **Prophezeiung** *f* prophecy

Proportion [proportsi'oːn] *f* proportion; **p~al** [-'naːl] *adj* proportional

proportioniert [proportsio'niːrt] *adj*: **gut/ schlecht ~** well-/badly-proportioned

Prosa ['proːza] (**-**) *f* prose; **p~isch** [pro'zaːɪʃ] *adj* prosaic

prosit ['proːzɪt] *excl* cheers

Prospekt [pro'spɛkt] (**-(e)s, -e**) *m* leaflet, brochure

prost [proːst] *excl* cheers

Prostituierte [prostitu'iːrtə] *f* prostitute

Prostitution [prostitutsi'oːn] *f* prostitution

Protest [pro'tɛst] (**-(e)s, -e**) *m* protest; **~ant(in)** [protɛs'tant(ɪn)] *m(f)* Protestant; **p~antisch** [protɛs'tantɪʃ] *adj* Protestant; **p~ieren** [protɛs'tiːrən] *vi* to protest

Prothese [pro'teːzə] *f* artificial limb; (*Zahnprothese*) dentures *pl*

Protokoll [proto'kɔl] (**-s, -e**) *nt* register; (*von Sitzung*) minutes *pl*; (*diplomatisch*) protocol; (*Polizeiprotokoll*) statement; **p~ieren** [-'liːrən] *vt* to take down in the minutes

protzen ['prɔtsən] *vi* to show off

Proviant [provi'ant] (**-s, -e**) *m* provisions *pl*, supplies *pl*

Provinz [pro'vɪnts] (**-, -en**) *f* province; **p~iell** *adj* provincial

Provision [provizi'oːn] *f* (*COMM*) commission

provisorisch [provi'zoːrɪʃ] *adj* provisional

Provokation [provokatsi'oːn] *f* provocation

provozieren [provo'tsiːrən] *vt* to provoke

Prozedur [protse'duːr] *f* procedure; (*pej*) carry-on

Prozent [pro'tsɛnt] (**-(e)s, -e**) *nt* per cent, percentage; **~satz** *m* percentage; **p~ual** [-u'aːl] *adj* percentage *cpd*; as a percentage

Prozess ▲ [pro'tsɛs] (**-es, -e**) *m* trial, case

Prozession [protsesi'oːn] *f* procession

prüde ['pryːdə] *adj* prudish; **P~rie** [-'riː] *f* prudery

Prüf- ['pry:f] *zW:* **p~en** *vt* to examine, to test; *(nachprüfen)* to check; **~er (-s, -)** *m* examiner; **~ling** *m* examinee; **~ung** *f* examination; checking; **~ungsausschuss** ▲ *m* examining board

Prügel ['pry:gəl] **(-s, -)** *m* cudgel ♦ *pl (Schläge)* beating; **~ei** [-'laɪ] *f* fight; **p~n** *vt* to beat ♦ *vr* to fight; **~strafe** *f* corporal punishment

Prunk [proŋk] **(-(e)s)** *m* pomp, show; **p~voll** *adj* splendid, magnificent

PS [pe:'ɛs] *abk (= Pferdestärke)* H.P.

Psych- ['psyç] *zW:* **~iater** [-i'a:tər] **(-s, -)** *m* psychiatrist; **p~iatrisch** *adj (MED)* psychiatric; **p~isch** *adj* psychological; **~oanalyse** [-o|ana'ly:zə] *f* psychoanalysis; **~ologe (-n, -n)** *m* psychologist; **~olo'gie** *f* psychology; **p~ologisch** *adj* psychological; **~otherapeut(in) (-en, -en)** *m(f)* psychotherapist

Pubertät [puber'tɛ:t] *f* puberty

Publikum ['pu:blikum] **(-s)** *nt* audience; *(SPORT)* crowd

publizieren [publi'tsi:rən] *vt* to publish, to publicize

Pudding ['pudɪŋ] **(-s, -e** *od* **-s)** *m* blancmange

Pudel ['pu:dəl] **(-s)** *m* poodle

Puder ['pu:dər] **(-s, -)** *m* powder; **~dose** *f* powder compact; **p~n** *vt* to powder; **~zucker** *m* icing sugar

Puff¹ [puf] **(-s, -e)** *m (Wäschepuff)* linen basket; *(Sitzpuff)* pouf

Puff² [puf] **(-s, ⁺e)** *(umg) m (Stoß)* push

Puff³ [puf] **(-s, -)** *(umg) m od nt (Bordell)* brothel

Puffer (-s, -) *m* buffer

Pullover [pu'lo:vər] **(-s, -)** *m* pullover, jumper

Puls [puls] **(-es, -e)** *m* pulse; **~ader** *f* artery; **p~ieren** *vi* to throb, to pulsate

Pult [pult] **(-(e)s, -e)** *nt* desk

Pulver ['pulfər] **(-s, -)** *nt* powder; **p~ig** *adj* powdery; **~schnee** *m* powdery snow

pummelig ['pumlɪç] *adj* chubby

Pumpe ['pumpə] *f* pump; **p~n** *vt* to pump; *(umg)* to lend; to borrow

Punkt [puŋkt] **(-(e)s, -e)** *m* point; *(bei Muster)* dot; *(Satzzeichen)* full stop; **p~ieren** [-'ti:rən] *vt* to dot; *(MED)* to aspirate

pünktlich ['pyŋktlɪç] *adj* punctual; **P~keit** *f* punctuality

Punktsieg *m* victory on points

Punktzahl *f* score

Punsch [punʃ] **(-(e)s, -e)** *m* punch

Pupille [pu'pɪlə] *f* pupil

Puppe ['pupə] *f* doll; *(Marionette)* puppet; *(Insektenpuppe)* pupa, chrysalis

Puppen- *zW:* **~spieler** *m* puppeteer; **~stube** *f* doll's house; **~theater** *nt* puppet theatre

pur [pu:r] *adj* pure; *(völlig)* sheer; *(Whisky)* neat

Püree [py're:] **(-s, -s)** *nt* mashed potatoes *pl*

Purzelbaum ['purtsəlbaum] *m* somersault

purzeln ['purtsəln] *vi* to tumble

Puste ['pu:stə] **(-)** *(umg) f* puff; *(fig)* steam; **p~n** *vi* to puff, to blow

Pute ['pu:tə] *f* turkey hen; **~r (-s, -)** *m* turkey cock

Putsch [putʃ] **(-(e)s, -e)** *m* revolt, putsch

Putz [puts] **(-es)** *m (Mörtel)* plaster, roughcast

putzen *vt* to clean; *(Nase)* to wipe, to blow ♦ *vr* to clean o.s.; to dress o.s. up

Putz- *zW:* **~frau** *f* charwoman; **p~ig** *adj* quaint, funny; **~lappen** *m* cloth

Puzzle ['pasəl] **(-s, -s)** *nt* jigsaw

PVC *nt abk* PVC

Pyjama [pi'dʒa:ma] **(-s, -s)** *m* pyjamas *pl*

Pyramide [pyra'mi:də] *f* pyramid

Pyrenäen [pyre'nɛ:ən] *pl* Pyrenees

Q, q

Quacksalber ['kvakzalbər] **(-s, -)** *m* quack (doctor)

Quader ['kva:dər] **(-s, -)** *m* square stone; *(MATH)* cuboid

Quadrat [kva'dra:t] **(-(e)s, -e)** *nt* square; **q~isch** *adj* square; **~meter** *m* square metre

quaken ['kva:kən] *vi* to croak; *(Ente)* to

quack
quäken ['kvɛːkən] *vi* to screech
Qual [kvaːl] (-, -en) *f* pain, agony; (*seelisch*) anguish; **q~en** *vt* to torment ♦ *vr* to struggle; (*geistig*) to torment o.s.; ~erei *f* torture, torment
Qualifikation [kvalifikatsi'oːn] *f* qualification
qualifizieren [kvalifi'tsiːrən] *vt* to qualify; (*einstufen*) to label ♦ *vr* to qualify
Qualität [kvali'tɛːt] *f* quality; ~sware *f* article of high quality
Qualle ['kvalə] *f* jellyfish
Qualm [kvalm] (-(e)s) *m* thick smoke; **q~en** *vt, vi* to smoke
qualvoll ['kvaːlfɔl] *adj* excruciating, painful, agonizing
Quant- ['kvant] *zW:* ~ität [-i'tɛːt] *f* quantity; **q~itativ** [-ita'tiːf] *adj* quantitative; ~um (-s) *nt* quantity, amount
Quarantäne [karan'tɛːnə] *f* quarantine
Quark [kvark] (-s) *m* curd cheese
Quartal [kvar'taːl] (-s, -e) *nt* quarter (year)
Quartier [kvar'tiːr] (-s, -e) *nt* accommodation; (*MIL*) quarters *pl*; (*Stadtquartier*) district
Quarz [kvaːrts] (-es, -e) *m* quartz
quasseln ['kvasəln] (*umg*) *vi* to natter
Quatsch [kvatʃ] (-es) *m* rubbish; **q~en** *vi* to chat, to natter
Quecksilber ['kvɛkzɪlbər] *nt* mercury
Quelle ['kvɛlə] *f* spring; (*eines Flusses*) source; **q~n** (*unreg*) *vi* (*hervorquellen*) to pour *od* gush forth; (*schwellen*) to swell
quer [kveːr] *adv* crossways, diagonally; (*rechtwinklig*) at right angles; ~ **auf dem Bett** across the bed; **Q~balken** *m* crossbeam; **Q~flöte** *f* flute; **Q~format** *nt* (*PHOT*) oblong format; **Q~schnitt** *m* cross-section; ~**schnittsgelähmt** *adj* paralysed below the waist; **Q~straße** *f* intersecting road
quetschen ['kvɛtʃən] *vt* to squash, to crush; (*MED*) to bruise
Quetschung *f* bruise, contusion
quieken ['kviːkən] *vi* to squeak
quietschen ['kviːtʃən] *vi* to squeak
Quintessenz ['kvɪntɛsɛnts] *f* quintessence

Quirl [kvɪrl] (-(e)s, -e) *m* whisk
quitt [kvɪt] *adj* quits, even
Quitte *f* quince
quittieren [kvɪ'tiːrən] *vt* to give a receipt for; (*Dienst*) to leave
Quittung *f* receipt
Quiz [kvɪs] (-, -) *nt* quiz
quoll *etc* [kvɔl] *vb siehe* **quellen**
Quote ['kvoːtə] *f* number, rate

R, r

Rabatt [ra'bat] (-(e)s, -e) *m* discount
Rabattmarke *f* trading stamp
Rabe ['raːbə] (-n, -n) *m* raven
rabiat [rabi'aːt] *adj* furious
Rache ['raxə] (-) *f* revenge, vengeance
Rachen (-s, -) *m* throat
rächen ['rɛçən] *vt* to avenge, to revenge ♦ *vr* to take (one's) revenge; **das wird sich ~** you'll pay for that
Rad [raːt] (-(e)s, ⁺er) *nt* wheel; (*Fahrrad*) bike; ~ **fahren** to cycle
Radar ['raːdaːr] (-s) *m od nt* radar; ~falle *f* speed trap; ~kontrolle *f* radar-controlled speed trap
Radau [ra'dau] (-s) (*umg*) *m* row
radeln ['raːdəln] (*umg*) *vi* to cycle
Radfahr- *zW:* **r~en** △ (*unreg*) *vi siehe* **Rad**; ~**er(in)** *m(f)* cyclist; ~weg *m* cycle track *od* path
Radier- [ra'diːr] *zW:* **r~en** *vt* to rub out, to erase; (*KUNST*) to etch; ~gummi *m* rubber, eraser; ~ung *f* etching
Radieschen [ra'diːsçən] *nt* radish
radikal [radi'kaːl] *adj* radical
Radio ['raːdio] (-s, -s) *nt* radio, wireless; **r~ak'tiv** *adj* radioactive; ~aktivi'tät *f* radioactivity; ~apparat *m* radio, wireless set
Radius ['raːdius] (-, **Radien**) *m* radius
Rad- *zW:* ~kappe *f* (*AUT*) hub cap; ~**ler(in)** (*umg*) *m(f)* cyclist; ~rennen *nt* cycle race; cycle racing; ~sport *m* cycling; ~weg *m* cycleway
raffen ['rafən] *vt* to snatch, to pick up; (*Stoff*)

to gather (up); (Geld) to pile up, to rake in

affi'niert adj crafty, cunning

agen ['ra:gən] vi to tower, to rise

ahm [ra:m] (-s) m cream

ahmen (-s, -) m frame(work); **im ~ des Möglichen** within the bounds of possibility; r~ vt to frame

äkeln ['rɛ:kln] vr = **rekeln**

akete [ra'ke:tə] f rocket; ~**nstützpunkt** m missile base

ammen ['ramən] vt to ram

ampe ['rampə] f ramp; ~**nlicht** nt (THEAT) footlights pl

amponieren [rampo'ni:rən] (umg) vt to damage

amsch [ramʃ] (-(e)s, -e) m junk

an [ran] (umg) adv = **heran**

and [rant] (-(e)s, ⁺er) m edge; (von Brille, Tasse etc) rim; (Hutrand) brim; (auf Papier) margin; (Schmutzrand, unter Augen) ring; (fig) verge, brink; **außer ~ und Band** wild; **am ~e bemerkt** mentioned in passing

andalieren [randa'li:rən] vi to (go on the) rampage

ang [raŋ] (-(e)s, ⁺e) m rank; (Stand) standing; (Wert) quality; (THEAT) circle

Rangier- [rãʒi:r] zW: ~**bahnhof** m marshalling yard; r~**en** vt (EISENB) to shunt, to switch (US) ♦ vi to rank, to be classed; ~**gleis** nt siding

anke ['raŋkə] f tendril, shoot

anzig ['rantsɪç] adj rancid

appen ['rapən] m (FIN) rappen, centime

ar [ra:r] adj rare; **sich ~ machen** (umg) to keep o.s. to o.s.; R~**i'tät** f rarity; (Sammelobjekt) curio

asant [ra'zant] adj quick, rapid

asch [raʃ] adj quick

aschein vi to rustle

asen ['ra:zən] (-s, -) m lawn; grass

asen to rave; (schnell) to race; ~**d** adj furious; ~**de Kopfschmerzen** a splitting headache

Rasenmäher (-s, -) m lawnmower

Rasier- [ra'zi:r] zW: ~**apparat** m shaver; ~**creme** f shaving cream; r~**en** vt, vr to shave; ~**klinge** f razor blade; ~**messer** nt

razor; ~**pinsel** m shaving brush; ~**schaum** m shaving foam; ~**seife** f shaving soap od stick; ~**wasser** nt shaving lotion

Rasse ['rasə] f race; (Tierrasse) breed; ~**hund** m thoroughbred dog

rasseln ['rasəln] vi to clatter

Rassen- zW: ~**hass** ▲ m race od racial hatred; ~**trennung** f racial segregation

Rassismus [ra'sɪsmʊs] m racism

Rast [rast] (-, -en) f rest; r~**en** vi to rest; ~**hof** m (AUT) service station; r~**los** adj tireless; (unruhig) restless; ~**platz** m (AUT) layby; ~**stätte** f (AUT) service station

Rasur [ra'zu:r] f shaving

Rat [ra:t] (-(e)s, -schläge) m advice no pl; **ein ~** a piece of advice; **keinen ~ wissen** not to know what to do; siehe **zurate**

Rate f instalment

raten (unreg) vt, vi to guess; (empfehlen): **jdm ~** to advise sb

Ratenzahlung f hire purchase

Ratgeber (-s, -) m adviser

Rathaus nt town hall

ratifizieren [ratifi'tsi:rən] vt to ratify

Ration [ratsi'o:n] f ration; r~**al** [-'na:l] adj rational; r~**ali'sieren** vt to rationalize; r~**ell** [-'nɛl] adj efficient; r~**ieren** [-'ni:rən] vt to ration

Rat- zW: r~**los** adj at a loss, helpless; r~**sam** adj advisable; ~**schlag** m (piece of) advice

Rätsel ['rɛ:tsəl] (-s, -) nt puzzle; (Worträtsel) riddle; r~**haft** adj mysterious; **es ist mir r~haft** it's a mystery to me

Ratte ['ratə] f rat; ~**nfänger** (-s, -) m ratcatcher

rattern ['ratərn] vi to rattle, to clatter

rau ▲ [rau] adj rough, coarse; (Wetter) harsh

Raub [raup] (-(e)s, -) m robbery; (Beute) loot, booty; ~**bau** m ruthless exploitation; r~**en** ['rauben] vt to rob; (Mensch) to kidnap, to abduct

Räuber ['rɔybər] (-s, -) m robber

Raub- zW: ~**mord** m robbery with murder; ~**tier** nt predator; ~**überfall** m robbery with violence; ~**vogel** m bird of prey

Rauch [raux] (-(e)s) m smoke; r~**en** vt, vi to

smoke; ~**er(in)** (**-s, -**) *m(f)* smoker;
~**erabteil** *nt* (*EISENB*) smoker; **räuchern** *vt*
to smoke, to cure; ~**fleisch** *nt* smoked
meat; **r~ig** *adj* smoky

rauf [rauf] (*umg*) *adv* = **herauf; hinauf**

raufen *vt* (*Haare*) to pull out ♦ *vi, vr* to fight;
Raufe'rei *f* brawl, fight

rauh △ *etc* [rau] *adj siehe* **rau** *etc*

Raum [raum] (**-(e)s, Räume**) *m* space;
(*Zimmer, Platz*) room; (*Gebiet*) area

räumen ['rɔymən] *vt* to clear; (*Wohnung,
Platz*) to vacate; (*wegbringen*) to shift, to
move; (*in Schrank etc*) to put away

Raum- *zW:* ~**fähre** *f* space shuttle; ~**fahrt** *f*
space travel; ~**inhalt** *m* cubic capacity,
volume

räumlich ['rɔymlıç] *adj* spatial; **R~keiten** *pl*
premises

Raum- *zW:* ~**pflegerin** *f* cleaner; ~**schiff**
nt spaceship; ~**schifffahrt** ▲ *f* space
travel

Räumung ['rɔymuŋ] *f* vacating, evacuation;
clearing (away)

Räumungs- *zW:* ~**arbeiten** *pl* clearance
operations; ~**verkauf** *m* clearance sale; (*bei
Geschäftsaufgabe*) closing down sale

raunen ['raunən] *vt, vi* to whisper

Raupe ['raupə] *f* caterpillar; (~*nkette*)
(caterpillar) track

Raureif ▲ ['raurarf] *m* hoarfrost

raus [raus] (*umg*) *adv* = **heraus; hinaus**

Rausch [rauʃ] (**-(e)s, Räusche**) *m*
intoxication

rauschen *vi* (*Wasser*) to rush; (*Baum*) to
rustle; (*Radio etc*) to hiss; (*Mensch*) to
sweep, to sail; ~**d** *adj* (*Beifall*) thunderous;
(*Fest*) sumptuous

Rauschgift *nt* drug; ~**süchtige(r)** *f(m)*
drug addict

räuspern ['rɔyspərn] *vr* to clear one's throat

Razzia ['ratsia] (**-, Razzien**) *f* raid

Reagenzglas [rea'gɛntsglaːs] *nt* test tube

reagieren [rea'giːrən] *vi:* ~ (**auf** +*akk*) to
react (to)

Reakt- *zW:* ~**ion** [reaktsi'oːn] *f* reaction;
r~io'när *adj* reactionary; ~**or** [re'aktɔr] *m*
reactor

real [re'aːl] *adj* real, material

reali'sieren *vt* (*verwirklichen: Pläne*) to carry
out

Realismus [rea'lɪsmus] *m* realism

rea'listisch *adj* realistic

Realschule *f* secondary school

Realschule

ℹ️ The **Realschule** is one of the secondary
schools a German schoolchild may
attend after the **Grundschule**. On the
successful completion of six years of
schooling in the **Realschule** pupils gain the
mittlere Reife and usually go on to
vocational training or further education.

Rebe ['reːbə] *f* vine

rebellieren [rebe'liːrən] *vi* to rebel;
Rebelli'on *f* rebellion; **re'bellisch** *adj*
rebellious

Rebhuhn ['rɛphuːn] *nt* (*KOCH, ZOOL*)
partridge

Rechen ['rɛçən] (**-s, -**) *m* rake

Rechen- *zW:* ~**fehler** *m* miscalculation;
~**maschine** *f* calculating machine;
~**schaft** *f* account; **für etw ~schaft
ablegen** to account for sth; ~**schieber** *m*
slide rule

Rech- [rɛç] *zW:* **r~nen** *vt, vi* to calculate;
jdn/etw r~nen zu to count sb/sth among;
r~nen mit to reckon with; **r~nen auf** +*akk*
to count on; ~**nen** *nt* arithmetic; ~**ner** (**-s,
-**) *m* calculator; (*COMPUT*) computer; ~**nung**
f calculation(s); (*COMM*) bill, check (*US*);
jdm/etw ~nung tragen to take sb/sth into
account; ~**nungsbetrag** *m* total amount
of a bill/invoice; ~**nungsjahr** *nt* financial
year; ~**nungsprüfer** *m* auditor

Recht [rɛçt] (**-(e)s, -e**) *nt* right; (*JUR*) law;
mit ~ rightly, justly; **R~ haben** to be right;
jdm R~ geben to agree with sb; **von ~s
wegen** by rights

recht *adj* right ♦ *adv* (*vor Adjektiv*) really,
quite; **das ist mir ~** that suits me; **jetzt
erst ~** now more than ever

Rechte *f* right (hand); (*POL*) Right; **r~(r, s)**
adj right; (*POL*) right-wing; **ein ~r** a right-

winger; ~(s) nt right thing; **etwas/nichts ~s** something/nothing proper

recht- zW: ~eckig adj rectangular; ~fertigen vt insep to justify ♦ vr insep to justify o.s.; R~fertigung f justification; ~haberisch (pej) adj (Mensch) opinionated; ~lich adj (gesetzlich: Gleichstellung, Anspruch) legal; ~los adj with no rights; ~mäßig adj legal, lawful

rechts [reçts] adv on/to the right; R~anwalt m lawyer, barrister; R~anwältin f lawyer, barrister

Rechtschreibung f spelling

Rechts- zW: ~fall m (law) case; ~händer (-s, -) m right-handed person; r~kräftig adj valid, legal; ~kurve f right-hand bend; r~verbindlich adj legally binding; ~verkehr m driving on the right; r~widrig adj illegal; ~wissenschaft f jurisprudence

rechtwinklig adj right-angled

rechtzeitig adj timely ♦ adv in time

Reck [rɛk] (-(e)s, -e) nt horizontal bar; r~en vt, vr to stretch

recyceln [riːˈsaɪkəln] vt to recycle; **Recycling** [riːˈsaɪklɪŋ] (-s) nt recycling

Redakteur [redakˈtøːr] m editor

Redaktion [redaktsiˈoːn] f editing; (Leute) editorial staff; (Büro) editorial office(s)

Rede [ˈreːdə] f speech; (Gespräch) talk; **jdn zur ~ stellen** to take sb to task; ~freiheit f freedom of speech; r~gewandt adj eloquent; r~n vi to talk, to speak ♦ vt to say; (Unsinn etc) to talk; ~nsart f set phrase

redlich [ˈreːtlɪç] adj honest

Redner (-s, -) m speaker, orator

redselig [ˈreːtzeːlɪç] adj talkative, loquacious

reduzieren [reduˈtsiːrən] vt to reduce

Reede [ˈreːdə] f protected anchorage; ~r (-s, -) m shipowner; ~ˈrei f shipping line od firm

reell [reˈɛl] adj fair, honest; (MATH) real

Refer- zW: ~at [refeˈraːt] (-(e)s, -e) nt report; (Vortrag) paper; (Gebiet) section; ~ent [refeˈrɛnt] m speaker; (Berichterstatter) reporter; (Sachbearbeiter) expert; r~ieren [refeˈriːrən] vi: **r~ieren über** +akk to speak od talk on

reflektieren [reflɛkˈtiːrən] vt (Licht) to reflect

Reflex [reˈflɛks] (-es, -e) m reflex; r~iv [-ˈksiːf] adj (GRAM) reflexive

Reform [reˈfɔrm] (-, -en) f reform; ~atiˈon f reformation; ~ationstag m Reformation Day; ~haus nt health food shop; r~ieren [-ˈmiːrən] vt to reform

Regal [reˈgaːl] (-s, -e) nt (book)shelves pl, bookcase; stand, rack

rege [ˈreːgə] adj (lebhaft: Treiben) lively; (wach, lebendig: Geist) keen

Regel [ˈreːgəl] (-, -n) f rule; (MED) period; r~mäßig adj regular; ~mäßigkeit f regularity; r~n vt to regulate, to control; (Angelegenheit) to settle ♦ vr: **sich von selbst r~n** to take care of itself; r~recht adj regular, proper, thorough; ~ung f regulation; settlement; r~widrig adj irregular, against the rules

Regen [ˈreːgən] (-s, -) m rain; ~bogen m rainbow; ~bogenpresse f tabloids pl

regenerierbar [regeneˈriːrbaːr] adj renewable

Regen- zW: ~mantel m raincoat, mac(kintosh); ~schauer m shower (of rain); ~schirm m umbrella; ~wald m (GEOG) rainforest; ~wurm m earthworm; ~zeit f rainy season

Regie [reˈʒiː] f (Film etc) direction; (THEAT) production

Regier- [reˈgiːr] zW: r~en vt, vi to govern, to rule; ~ung f government; (Monarchie) reign; ~ungssitz m seat of government; ~ungswechsel m change of government; ~ungszeit f period in government; (von König) reign

Regiment [regiˈmɛnt] (-s, -er) nt regiment

Region [regiˈoːn] f region

Regisseur [reʒɪˈsøːr] m director; (THEAT) (stage) producer

Register [reˈgɪstər] (-s, -) nt register; (in Buch) table of contents, index

registrieren [regɪsˈtriːrən] vt to register

Regler [ˈreːglər] (-s, -) m regulator, governor

reglos [ˈreːkloːs] adj motionless

regnen [ˈreːgnən] vi unpers to rain

regnerisch adj rainy

regulär [regu'lɛːr] adj regular

regulieren [regu'liːrən] vt to regulate; (COMM) to settle

Regung ['reːgʊŋ] f motion; (Gefühl) feeling, impulse; **r~slos** adj motionless

Reh [reː] (-(e)s, -e) nt deer, roe; **~bock** m roebuck; **~kitz** nt fawn

Reib- ['raɪb] zW: **~e** f grater; **~eisen** nt grater; **r~en** (unreg) vt to rub; (KOCH) to grate; **~fläche** f rough surface; **~ung** f friction; **r~ungslos** adj smooth

Reich (-(e)s, -e) nt empire, kingdom; (fig) realm; **das Dritte R~** the Third Reich

reich [raɪç] adj rich

reichen vi to reach; (genügen) to be enough od sufficient ♦ vt to hold out; (geben) to pass, to hand; (anbieten) to offer; **jdm ~** to be enough od sufficient for sb

reich- zW: **~haltig** adj ample, rich; **~lich** adj ample, plenty of; **R~tum** (-s) m wealth; **R~weite** f range

Reif (-(e)s, -e) m (Ring) ring, hoop

reif [raɪf] adj ripe; (Mensch, Urteil) mature

Reife (-) f ripeness; maturity; **r~n** vi to mature; to ripen

Reifen (-s, -) m ring, hoop; (Fahrzeugreifen) tyre; **~druck** m tyre pressure; **~panne** f puncture

Reihe ['raɪə] f row; (von Tagen etc, umg: Anzahl) series sg; **der ~ nach** in turn; **er ist an der ~** it's his turn; **an die ~ kommen** to have one's turn

Reihen- zW: **~folge** f sequence; **alphabetische ~folge** alphabetical order; **~haus** nt terraced house

reihum [raɪ'ʊm] adv: **es geht/wir machen das ~** we take turns

Reim [raɪm] (-(e)s, -e) m rhyme; **r~en** vt to rhyme

rein¹ [raɪn] (umg) adv = **herein; hinein**

rein² [raɪn] adj pure; (sauber) clean ♦ adv purely; **etw ins R~e schreiben** to make a fair copy of sth; **etw ins R~e bringen** to clear up sth; **R~fall** (umg) m let-down; **R~gewinn** m net profit; **R~heit** f purity; cleanness; **~igen** vt to clean; (Wasser) to

purify; **R~igung** f cleaning; purification; (Geschäft) cleaner's; **chemische R~igung** dry cleaning; dry cleaner's; **R~igungsmittel** nt cleansing agent; **~rassig** adj pedigree; **R~schrift** f fair copy

Reis [raɪs] (-es, -e) m rice

Reise ['raɪzə] f journey; (Schiffsreise) voyage; **~n** pl (Herumreisen) travels; **gute ~!** have a good journey; **~apotheke** f first-aid kit; **~büro** nt travel agency; **r~fertig** adj ready to start; **~führer** m guide(book); (Mensch) travel guide; **~gepäck** nt luggage; **~gesellschaft** f party of travellers; **~kosten** pl travelling expenses; **~leiter** m courier; **~lektüre** f reading matter for the journey; **r~n** vi to travel; **r~n to go to**; **~nde(r)** f(m) traveller; **~pass** ▲ m passport; **~proviant** m food and drink for the journey; **~route** f route, itinerary; **~ruf** m personal message; **~scheck** m traveller's cheque; **~veranstalter** m tour operator; **~versicherung** f travel insurance; **~ziel** nt destination

Reißbrett nt drawing board

reißen ['raɪsən] (unreg) vt to tear; (ziehen) to pull, to drag; (Witz) to crack ♦ vi to tear; to pull, to drag; **etw an sich ~** to snatch sth up; (fig) to take over sth; **sich um etw ~** to scramble for sth; **~d** adj (Fluss) raging; (WIRTS: Verkauf) rapid

Reiß- zW: **~verschluss** ▲ m zip(per), zip fastener; **~zwecke** m drawing pin (BRIT), thumbtack (US)

Reit- ['raɪt] zW: **r~en** (unreg) vt, vi to ride; **~er** (-s, -) m rider; (MIL) cavalryman, trooper; **~erin** f rider; **~hose** f riding breeches pl; **~pferd** nt saddle horse; **~stiefel** m riding boot; **~weg** n bridle path; **~zeug** nt riding outfit

Reiz [raɪts] (-es, -e) m stimulus; (angenehm) charm; (Verlockung) attraction; **r~bar** adj irritable; **~barkeit** f irritability; **r~en** vt to stimulate; (unangenehm) to irritate; (verlocken) to appeal to, to attract; **r~end** adj charming; **r~voll** adj attractive

rekeln ['reːkəln] vr to stretch out; (lümmeln)

to lounge *od* loll about
Reklamation [reklamatsi'oːn] *f* complaint
Reklame [re'klaːmə] *f* advertising;
advertisement; **~ machen für etw** to
advertise sth
rekonstruieren [rekɔnstru'iːrən] *vt* to
reconstruct
Rekord [re'kɔrt] **(-(e)s, -e)** *m* record;
~leistung *f* record performance
Rektor ['rɛktɔr] *m* (UNIV) rector, vice-
chancellor; (SCH) headteacher (BRIT),
principal (US); **~at** [-'raːt] **(-(e)s, -e)** *nt*
rectorate, vice-chancellorship; headship;
(Zimmer) rector's *etc* office
Relais [rə'lɛː] **(-, -)** *nt* relay
relativ [rela'tiːf] *adj* relative; **R~ität**
[relativi'tɛːt] *f* relativity
relevant [rele'vant] *adj* relevant
Relief [reli'ɛf] **(-s, -s)** *nt* relief
Religion [religi'oːn] *f* religion
religiös [religi'øːs] *adj* religious
Reling ['reːlɪŋ] **(-, -s)** *f* (NAUT) rail
Remoulade [remu'laːdə] *f* remoulade
Rendezvous [rãde'vuː] **(-, -)** *nt* rendezvous
Renn- ['rɛn] *zW:* **~bahn** *f* racecourse; (AUT)
circuit, race track; **r~en** (unreg) *vt, vi* to
run, to race; **~en** **(-s, -)** *nt* running;
(Wettbewerb) race; **~fahrer** *m* racing driver;
~pferd *nt* racehorse; **~wagen** *m* racing
car
renommiert [renɔ'miːrt] *adj* renowned
renovieren [reno'viːrən] *vt* to renovate;
Renovierung *f* renovation
rentabel [rɛn'taːbəl] *adj* profitable, lucrative
Rentabilität [rɛntabili'tɛːt] *f* profitability
Rente ['rɛntə] *f* pension
Rentenversicherung *f* pension scheme
rentieren [rɛn'tiːrən] *vr* to pay, to be
profitable
Rentner(in) ['rɛntnər(ɪn)] **(-s, -)** *m(f)*
pensioner
Reparatur [repara'tuːr] *f* repairing; repair;
~werkstatt *f* repair shop; (AUT) garage
reparieren [repa'riːrən] *vt* to repair
Reportage [repɔr'taːʒə] *f* (on-the-spot)
report; (TV, RADIO) live commentary *od*
coverage

Reporter [re'pɔrtər] **(-s, -)** *m* reporter,
commentator
repräsentativ [reprɛzɛnta'tiːf] *adj*
(stellvertretend, typisch: Menge, Gruppe)
representative; (beeindruckend: Haus, Auto
etc) impressive
repräsentieren [reprɛzɛn'tiːrən] *vt* (Staat,
Firma) to represent; (darstellen: Wert) to
constitute ♦ *vi* (gesellschaftlich) to perform
official duties
Repressalie [reprɛ'saːliə] *f* reprisal
Reprivatisierung [reprivati'ziːrʊŋ] *f*
denationalization
Reproduktion [reprodʊktsi'oːn] *f*
reproduction
reproduzieren [reprodu'tsiːrən] *vt* to
reproduce
Reptil [rɛp'tiːl] **(-s, -ien)** *nt* reptile
Republik [repu'bliːk] *f* republic; **r~anisch**
adj republican
Reservat [rezɛr'vaːt] **(-(e)s, -e)** *nt*
reservation
Reserve [re'zɛrvə] *f* reserve; **~rad** *nt* (AUT)
spare wheel; **~spieler** *m* reserve; **~tank** *m*
reserve tank
reservieren [rezɛr'viːrən] *vt* to reserve
Reservoir [rezɛrvo'aːr] **(-s, -e)** *nt* reservoir
Residenz [rezi'dɛnts] *f* residence, seat
resignieren [rezi'gniːrən] *vi* to resign
resolut [rezo'luːt] *adj* resolute
Resonanz [rezo'nants] *f* resonance; (fig)
response
Resozialisierung [rezotsiali'ziːrʊŋ] *f*
rehabilitation
Respekt [rɛ'spɛkt] **(-(e)s)** *m* respect;
r~ieren [-'tiːrən] *vt* to respect; **r~los** *adj*
disrespectful; **r~voll** *adj* respectful
Ressort [rɛ'soːr] **(-s, -s)** *nt* department
Rest [rɛst] **(-(e)s, -e)** *m* remainder, rest;
(Überrest) remains *pl*
Restaurant [rɛsto'rãː] **(-s, -s)** *nt* restaurant
restaurieren [rɛstau'riːrən] *vt* to restore
Rest- *zW:* **~betrag** *m* remainder,
outstanding sum; **r~lich** *adj* remaining;
r~los *adj* complete
Resultat [rezʊl'taːt] **(-(e)s, -e)** *nt* result
Retorte [re'tɔrtə] *f* retort

Spelling Reform: ▲ *new spelling* △ *old spelling (to be phased out)*

Retouren [re'tu:rən] *pl* (*COMM*) returns

retten ['retən] *vt* to save, to rescue

Retter(in) *m(f)* rescuer

Rettich ['retɪç] (**-s, -e**) *m* radish

Rettung *f* rescue; (*Hilfe*) help; **seine letzte ~** his last hope

Rettungs- *zW*: **~boot** *nt* lifeboat; **~dienst** *m* rescue service; **r~los** *adj* hopeless; **~ring** *m* lifebelt, life preserver (*US*); **~wagen** *m* ambulance

retuschieren [retu'ʃi:rən] *vt* (*PHOT*) to retouch

Reue ['rɔyə] (**-**) *f* remorse; (*Bedauern*) regret; **r~n** *vt*: **es reut ihn** he regrets (it) *od* is sorry (about it)

Revanche [re'vã:ʃə] *f* revenge; (*SPORT*) return match

revanchieren [revã'ʃi:rən] *vr* (*sich rächen*) to get one's own back, to have one's revenge; (*erwidern*) to reciprocate, to return the compliment

Revier [re'vi:r] (**-s, -e**) *nt* district; (*Jagdrevier*) preserve; (*Polizeirevier*) police station; beat

Revolte [re'vɔltə] *f* revolt

revol'tieren *vi* (*gegen jdn/etw*) to rebel

Revolution [revolutsi'o:n] *f* revolution; **~är** [-'nɛ:r] (**-s, -e**) *m* revolutionary; **r~ieren** [-'ni:rən] *vt* to revolutionize

Rezept [re'tsept] (**-(e)s, -e**) *nt* recipe; (*MED*) prescription; **r~frei** *adj* available without prescription; **~ion** *f* reception; **r~pflichtig** *adj* available only on prescription

R-Gespräch ['ɛrgəʃprɛːç] *nt* reverse charge call (*BRIT*), collect call (*US*)

Rhabarber [ra'barbər] (**-s**) *m* rhubarb

Rhein [raɪn] (**-s**) *m* Rhine; **r~isch** *adj* Rhenish

Rheinland-Pfalz *nt* (*GEOG*) Rheinland-Pfalz, Rhineland-Palatinate

Rhesusfaktor ['re:zusfaktor] *m* rhesus factor

rhetorisch [re'to:rɪʃ] *adj* rhetorical

Rheuma ['rɔyma] (**-s**) *nt* rheumatism; **r~tisch** [-'ma:tɪʃ] *adj* rheumatic

rhythmisch ['rʏtmɪʃ] *adj* rhythmical

Rhythmus ['rʏtmʊs] *m* rhythm

richt- ['rɪçt] *zW*: **~en** *vt* to direct; (*Waffe*) to aim; (*einstellen*) to adjust; (*instandsetzen*) to repair; (*zurechtmachen*) to prepare; (*bestrafen*) to pass judgement on ♦ *vr*: **sich ~en nach** to go by; **~en an** +*akk* to direct at; (*fig*) to direct to; **~en auf** +*akk* to aim at; **R~er(in)** (**-s, -**) *m(f)* judge; **~erlich** *adj* judicial; **R~geschwindigkeit** *f* recommended speed

richtig *adj* right, correct; (*echt*) proper ♦ *adv* (*umg: sehr*) really; **bin ich hier ~?** am I in the right place?; **der/die R~e** the right one/person; **das R~e** the right thing; **etw ~ stellen** to correct sth; **R~keit** *f* correctness

Richt- *zW*: **~linie** *f* guideline; **~preis** *m* recommended price

Richtung *f* direction; tendency, orientation

rieb *etc* [ri:p] *vb siehe* **reiben**

riechen ['ri:çən] (*unreg*) *vt, vi* to smell; **an etw** *dat* **~** to smell sth; **nach etw ~** to smell of sth; **ich kann das/ihn nicht ~** (*umg*) I can't stand it/him

rief *etc* [ri:f] *vb siehe* **rufen**

Riegel ['ri:gəl] (**-s, -**) *m* bolt; (*Schokolade usw*) bar

Riemen ['ri:mən] (**-s, -**) *m* strap; (*Gürtel, TECH*) belt; (*NAUT*) oar

Riese ['ri:zə] (**-n, -n**) *m* giant

rieseln *vi* to trickle; (*Schnee*) to fall gently

Riesen- *zW*: **~erfolg** *m* enormous success; **r~groß** *adj* colossal, gigantic, huge; **~rad** *nt* big wheel

riesig ['ri:zɪç] *adj* enormous, huge, vast

riet *etc* [ri:t] *vb siehe* **raten**

Riff [rɪf] (**-(e)s, -e**) *nt* reef

Rille ['rɪlə] *f* groove

Rind [rɪnt] (**-(e)s, -er**) *nt* ox; cow; cattle *pl*; (*KOCH*) beef

Rinde ['rɪndə] *f* rind; (*Baumrinde*) bark; (*Brotrinde*) crust

Rind- ['rɪnt] *zW*: **~fleisch** *nt* beef; **~vieh** *nt* cattle *pl*; (*umg*) blockhead, stupid oaf

Ring [rɪŋ] (**-(e)s, -e**) *m* ring; **~buch** *nt* ring binder; **r~en** (*unreg*) *vi* to wrestle; **~en** (**-s**) *nt* wrestling; **~finger** *m* ring finger; **~kampf** *m* wrestling bout; **~richter** *m* referee; **r~s** *adv*: **r~s um** round; **r~sherum** *adv* round about; **~straße** *f* ring road; **r~sum** adv (rundherum) round about; (überall) all round; **r~sumher =** **ringsum**

inn- ['rɪn] zW: **~e** f gutter, drain; **r~en** (unreg) vi to run, to trickle; **~stein** m gutter

ippchen ['rɪpçən] nt small rib; cutlet

ippe ['rɪpə] f rib

isiko ['riːziko] (-s, -s od Risiken) nt risk

iskant [rɪs'kant] adj risky, hazardous

iskieren [rɪs'kiːrən] vt to risk

iss ▲ [rɪs] (-es, -e) m tear; (in Mauer, Tasse etc) crack; (in Haut) scratch; (TECH) design

issig ['rɪsɪç] adj torn; cracked; scratched

itt [rɪt] (-(e)s, -e) m ride

itt etc vb siehe **reiten**

itter (-s, -) m knight; **r~lich** adj chivalrous

itze ['rɪtsə] f crack, chink

ivale [ri'vaːlə] (-n, -n) m rival

ivalität [rivali'tɛːt] f rivalry

obbe ['rɔbə] f seal

oboter ['rɔbɔtər] (-s, -) m robot

obust [ro'bʊst] adj (kräftig: Mensch, Gesundheit) robust

och etc [rɔx] vb siehe **riechen**

ock [rɔk] (-(e)s, ⁓e) m skirt; (Jackett) jacket; (Uniformrock) tunic

odel ['roːdəl] (-s, -) m toboggan; **~bahn** f toboggan run; **r~n** vi to toboggan

ogen ['roːgən] (-s, -) m roe, spawn

oggen ['rɔgən] (-s, -) m rye; **~brot** nt (KOCH) rye bread

oh [roː] adj raw; (Mensch) coarse, crude; **R~bau** m shell of a building; **R~material** nt raw material; **R~öl** nt crude oil

ohr [roːr] (-(e)s, -e) nt pipe, tube; (BOT) cane; (Schilf) reed; (Gewehrrohr) barrel; **~bruch** m burst pipe

öhre ['røːrə] f tube, pipe; (RADIO etc) valve; (Backröhre) oven

ohr- zW: **~leitung** f pipeline; **~zucker** m cane sugar

ohstoff m raw material

okoko ['rɔkoko] (-s) nt rococo

olladen △ m siehe **Rollladen**

ollbahn ['rɔlbaːn] f (AVIAT) runway

olle ['rɔlə] f roll; (THEAT, soziologisch) role; (Garnrolle etc) reel, spool; (Walze) roller;

(Wäscherolle) mangle; **keine ~ spielen** not to matter; **eine (wichtige) ~ spielen bei** to play a (major) part od role in; **r~n** vt, vi to roll; (AVIAT) to taxi; **~r (-s, -)** m scooter; (Welle) roller

Roll- zW: **~kragen** m rollneck, polo neck; **~laden** ▲ m shutter; **~mops** m pickled herring; **~schuh** m roller skate; **~stuhl** m wheelchair; **~stuhlfahrer(in)** m(f) wheelchair user; **~treppe** f escalator

Rom [roːm] (-s) nt Rome

Roman [ro'maːn] (-s, -e) m novel; **~tik** f romanticism; **~tiker** [ro'mantɪkər] (-s, -) m romanticist; **r~tisch** [ro'mantɪʃ] adj romantic; **~ze** [ro'mantsə] f romance

Römer ['røːmər] (-s, -) m wineglass; (Mensch) Roman

römisch ['røːmɪʃ] adj Roman; **~-katholisch** adj (REL) Roman Catholic

röntgen ['rœntgən] vt to X-ray; **R~bild** nt X-ray; **R~strahlen** pl X-rays

rosa ['roːza] adj inv pink, rose(-coloured)

Rose ['roːzə] f rose

Rosen- zW: **~kohl** m Brussels sprouts pl; **~kranz** m rosary; **~montag** m Monday before Ash Wednesday

rosig ['roːzɪç] adj rosy

Rosine [ro'ziːnə] f raisin, currant

Ross ▲ [rɔs] (-es, -e) nt horse, steed; **~kastanie** f horse chestnut

Rost [rɔst] (-(e)s, -e) m rust; (Gitter) grill, gridiron; (Bettrost) springs pl; **r~braten** m roast(ed) meat, roast; **r~en** vi to rust

rösten ['røːstən] vt to roast; to toast; to grill

Rost- zW: **r~frei** adj rust-free; rustproof; stainless; **r~ig** adj rusty; **~schutz** m rust-proofing

rot [roːt] adj red; **in den ~en Zahlen** in the red

Röte ['røːtə] (-) f redness; **~ln** pl German measles sg; **r~n** vt, vr to redden

rothaarig adj red-haired

rotieren [ro'tiːrən] vi to rotate

Rot- zW: **~kehlchen** nt robin; **~stift** m red pencil; **~wein** m red wine

Rouge [ruːʒ] nt blusher

Roulade [ru'laːdə] f (KOCH) beef olive

Route ['ru:tə] f route

Routine [ru'ti:nə] f experience; routine

Rübe ['ry:bə] f turnip; **Gelbe ~** carrot; **Rote ~** beetroot (BRIT), beet (US)

rüber ['ry:bər] (umg) adv = **herüber; hinüber**

Rubrik [ru'bri:k] f heading; (Spalte) column

Ruck [rʊk] (-(e)s, -e) m jerk, jolt

Rück- ['rʏk] zW: **~antwort** f reply, answer; **r~bezüglich** adj reflexive

Rücken ['rʏkən] (-s, -) m back; (Bergrücken) ridge

rücken vt, vi to move

Rücken- zW: **~mark** nt spinal cord; **~schwimmen** nt backstroke

Rück- zW: **~erstattung** f return, restitution; **~fahrkarte** f return (ticket); **~fahrt** f return journey; **~fall** m relapse; **r~fällig** adj relapsing; **r~fällig werden** to relapse; **~flug** m return flight; **~frage** f question; **r~fragen** vi to check, to inquire (further); **~gabe** f return; **~gaberecht** nt right of return; **~gang** m decline, fall; **r~gängig** adj: **etw r~gängig machen** to cancel sth; **~grat** (-(e)s, -e) nt spine, backbone; **~halt** m (Unterstützung) backing, support; **~kehr** (-, -en) f return; **~licht** nt back light; **r~lings** adv from behind; backwards; **~nahme** f taking back; **~porto** nt return postage; **~reise** f return journey; (NAUT) home voyage; **~reiseverkehr** m homebound traffic; **~ruf** m recall

Rucksack ['rʊkzak] m rucksack; **~tourist(in)** m(f) backpacker

Rück- zW: **~schau** f reflection; **~schlag** m (plötzliche Verschlechterung) setback; **~schluss ▲** m conclusion; **~schritt** m retrogression; **r~schrittlich** adj reactionary; retrograde; **~seite** f back; (von Münze etc) reverse; **~sicht** f consideration; **~sicht nehmen auf** +akk to show consideration for; **r~sichtslos** adj inconsiderate; (Fahren) reckless; (unbarmherzig) ruthless; **r~sichtsvoll** adj considerate; **~sitz** m back seat; **~spiegel** m (AUT) rear-view mirror; **~spiel** nt return match; **~sprache** f further discussion od talk; **~stand** m arrears pl; **r~ständig** adj

backward, out-of-date; (Zahlungen) in arrears; **~strahler** (-s, -) m rear reflector; **~tritt** m resignation; **~trittbremse** f pedal brake; **~vergütung** f repayment; (COMM) refund; **~versicherung** f reinsurance; **r~wärtig** adj rear; **r~wärts** adv backward(s), back; **~wärtsgang** m (AUT) reverse gear; **~weg** m return journey, way back; **r~wirkend** adj retroactive; **~wirkung** f reaction; retrospective effect; **~zahlung** f repayment; **~zug** m retreat

Rudel ['ru:dəl] (-s, -) nt pack; herd

Ruder ['ru:dər] (-s, -) nt oar; (Steuer) rudder; **~boot** nt rowing boat; **r~n** vt, vi to row

Ruf [ru:f] (-(e)s, -e) m call, cry; (Ansehen) reputation; **r~en** (unreg) vt, vi to call; to cry; **~name** m usual (first) name; **~nummer** f (tele)phone number; **~säule** f (an Autobahn) emergency telephone; **~zeichen** nt (RADIO) call sign; (TEL) ringing tone

rügen ['ry:gən] vt to rebuke

Ruhe ['ru:ə] (-) f rest; (Ungestörtheit) peace, quiet; (Gelassenheit, Stille) calm; (Schweigen) silence; **jdn in ~ lassen** to leave sb alone; **sich zur ~ setzen** to retire; **~!** be quiet!, silence!; **r~n** vi to rest; **~pause** f break; **~stand** m retirement; **~stätte** f: **letzte ~stätte** final resting place; **~störung** f breach of the peace; **~tag** m (von Geschäft) closing day

ruhig ['ru:ɪç] adj quiet; (bewegungslos) still; (Hand) steady; (gelassen, friedlich) calm; (Gewissen) clear; **kommen Sie ~ herein** just come on in; **tu das ~** feel free to do that

Ruhm [ru:m] (-(e)s) m fame, glory

rühmen ['ry:mən] vt to praise ♦ vr to boast

Rühr- [ry:r] zW: **~ei** nt scrambled egg; **r~en** vt, vr (auch fig) to move, to stir ♦ vi: **r~en von** to come od stem from; **r~en an** +akk to touch; (fig) to touch on; **r~end** adj touching, moving; **r~selig** adj sentimental, emotional; **~ung** f emotion

Ruin [ru'i:n] (-s, -e) m ruin; **~e** f ruin; **r~ieren** [-'ni:rən] vt to ruin

rülpsen ['rʏlpsən] vi to burp, to belch

Rum [rʊm] (-s, -s) m rum

Rechtschreibreform: ▲ *neue Schreibung* △ *alte Schreibung (auslaufend)*

Rumän- [ru'mɛːn] zW: **~ien (-s)** nt Ro(u)mania; **r~isch** adj Ro(u)manian

Rummel ['rʊməl] **(-s)** (umg) m hubbub; (Jahrmarkt) fair; **~platz** m fairground, fair

Rumpf [rʊmpf] **(-(e)s, ̈e)** m trunk, torso; (AVIAT) fuselage; (NAUT) hull

rümpfen ['rʏmpfən] vt (Nase) to turn up

rund [rʊnt] adj round ♦ adv (etwa) around; **~ um etw** round sth; **R~brief** m circular; **R~e** ['rʊndə] f round; (in Rennen) lap; (Gesellschaft) circle; **R~fahrt** f (round) trip

Rundfunk ['rʊntfʊŋk] **(-(e)s)** m broadcasting; **im ~** on the radio; **~gerät** nt wireless set; **~sendung** f broadcast, radio programme

Rund- zW: **r~heraus** adv straight out, bluntly; **r~herum** adv round about; all round; **r~lich** adj plump, rounded; **~reise** f round trip; **~schreiben** nt (COMM) circular; **~(wander)weg** m circular path od route

runter ['rʊntər] (umg) adv = **herunter; hinunter**

Runzel ['rʊntsəl] **(-, -n)** f wrinkle; **r~ig** adj wrinkled; **r~n** vt to wrinkle; **die Stirn r~n** to frown

rupfen ['rʊpfən] vt to pluck

ruppig ['rʊpɪç] adj rough, gruff

Rüsche ['ryːʃə] f frill

Ruß [ruːs] **(-es)** m soot

Russe ['rʊsə] **(-n, -n)** m Russian

Rüssel ['rʏsəl] **(-s, -)** m snout; (Elefantenrüssel) trunk

rußig ['ruːsɪç] adj sooty

Russin ['rʊsɪn] f Russian

russisch adj Russian

Russland ▲ ['rʊslant] **(-s)** nt Russia

rüsten ['rʏstən] vt to prepare ♦ vi to prepare; (MIL) to arm ♦ vr to prepare (o.s.); to arm o.s.

rüstig ['rʏstɪç] adj sprightly, vigorous

Rüstung ['rʏstʊŋ] f preparation; arming; (Ritterrüstung) armour; (Waffen etc) armaments pl; **~skontrolle** f arms control

Rute ['ruːtə] f rod

Rutsch [rʊtʃ] **(-(e)s, -e)** m slide; (Erdrutsch) landslide; **~bahn** f slide; **r~en** vi to slide;

(ausrutschen) to slip; **r~ig** adj slippery

rütteln ['rʏtəln] vt, vi to shake, to jolt

S, s

S. abk (= Seite) p.; = **Schilling**

s. abk (= siehe) see

Saal [zaːl] **(-(e)s, Säle)** m hall; room

Saarland ['zaːrlant] nt: **das ~** the Saar(land)

Saat [zaːt] **(-, -en)** f seed; (Pflanzen) crop; (Säen) sowing

Säbel ['zɛːbəl] **(-s, -)** m sabre, sword

Sabotage [zabo'taːʒə] f sabotage

Sach- ['zax] zW: **~bearbeiter** m specialist; **s~dienlich** adj relevant, helpful; **~e** f thing; (Angelegenheit) affair, business; (Frage) matter; (Pflicht) task; **zur ~e** to the point; **s~kundig** adj expert; **s~lich** adj matter-of-fact; objective; (Irrtum, Angabe) factual

sächlich ['zɛxlɪç] adj neuter

Sachschaden m material damage

Sachsen ['zaksən] **(-s)** nt Saxony

sächsisch ['zɛksɪʃ] adj Saxon

sacht(e) ['zaxt(ə)] adv softly, gently

Sachverständige(r) f(m) expert

Sack [zak] **(-(e)s, ̈e)** m sack; **~gasse** f cul-de-sac, dead-end street (US)

Sadismus [za'dɪsmʊs] m sadism

Sadist [za'dɪst] m sadist

säen ['zɛːən] vt, vi to sow

Safersex ▲, **Safer Sex** m safe sex

Saft [zaft] **(-(e)s, ̈e)** m juice; (BOT) sap; **s~ig** adj juicy; **s~los** adj dry

Sage ['zaːgə] f saga

Säge ['zɛːgə] f saw; **~mehl** nt sawdust

sagen ['zaːgən] vt, vi to say; (mitteilen): **jdm ~ to tell sb; ~ Sie ihm, dass ...** tell him ...

sägen vt, vi to saw

sagenhaft adj legendary; (umg) great, smashing

sah etc [zaː] vb siehe **sehen**

Sahne ['zaːnə] **(-)** f cream

Saison [zɛ'zõː] **(-, -s)** f season

Saite ['zaɪtə] f string

Sakko ['zako] **(-s, -s)** m od nt jacket

Sakrament [zakra'mɛnt] nt sacrament

Sakristei [zakrıs'taı] f sacristy

Salat [za'la:t] **(-(e)s, -e)** m salad; (Kopfsalat) lettuce; ~**soße** f salad dressing

Salbe ['zalbə] f ointment

Salbei ['zalbaı] **(-s** od **-)** m od f sage

Saldo ['zaldo] **(-s, Salden)** m balance

Salmiak [zalmi'ak] **(-s)** m sal ammoniac; ~**geist** m liquid ammonia

Salmonellenvergiftung [zalmo'nɛlən-] f salmonella (poisoning)

salopp [za'lɔp] adj casual

Salpeter [zal'pe:tər] **(-s)** m saltpetre; ~**säure** f nitric acid

Salz [zalts] **(-es, -e)** nt salt; **s~en** (unreg) vt to salt; **s~ig** adj salty; ~**kartoffeln** pl boiled potatoes; ~**säure** f hydrochloric acid; ~**streuer** m salt cellar; ~**wasser** nt (Meerwasser) salt water

Samen ['za:mən] **(-s, -)** m seed; (ANAT) sperm

Sammel- ['zaməl] zW: ~**band** m anthology; ~**fahrschein** m multi-journey ticket; (für mehrere Personen) group ticket

sammeln ['zaməln] vt to collect ♦ vr to assemble, to gather; (konzentrieren) to concentrate

Sammlung ['zamlʊŋ] f collection; assembly, gathering; concentration

Samstag ['zamsta:k] m Saturday; **s~s** adv (on) Saturdays

Samt [zamt] **(-(e)s, -e)** m velvet; ~ präp +dat (along) with, together with; ~ **und sonders** each and every one (of them)

sämtlich ['zɛmtlıç] adj all (the), entire

Sand [zant] **(-(e)s, -e)** m sand

Sandale [zan'da:lə] f sandal

Sand- zW: ~**bank** f sandbank; **s~ig** ['zandıç] adj sandy; ~**kasten** m sandpit; ~**kuchen** m Madeira cake; ~**papier** nt sandpaper; ~**stein** m sandstone; **s~strahlen** vt, vi insep to sandblast; ~**strand** m sandy beach

sandte etc ['zantə] vb siehe **senden**

sanft [zanft] adj soft, gentle; ~**mütig** adj gentle, meek

sang etc [zaŋ] vb siehe **singen**

Sänger(in) ['zɛŋər(ın)] **(-s, -)** m(f) singer

Sani- zW: **s~eren** [za'ni:rən] vt to redevelop; (Betrieb) to make financially sound ♦ vr to line one's pockets; to become financially sound; **s~tär** [zani'tɛ:r] adj sanitary; **s~täre Anlagen** sanitation sg; ~**täter** [zani'tɛ:tər] **(-s, -)** m first-aid attendant; (MIL) (medical) orderly

sanktionieren [zaŋktsio'ni:rən] vt to sanction

Sardelle [zar'dɛlə] f anchovy

Sardine [zar'di:nə] f sardine

Sarg [zark] **(-(e)s, -̈e)** m coffin

Sarkasmus [zar'kasmʊs] m sarcasm

saß etc [za:s] vb siehe **sitzen**

Satan ['za:tan] **(-s, -e)** m Satan; devil

Satellit [zate'li:t] **(-en, -en)** m satellite; ~**enfernsehen** nt satellite television

Satire [za'ti:rə] f satire; **satirisch** adj satirical

satt [zat] adj full; (Farbe) rich, deep; **jdn/etw ~ sein** od **haben** to be fed up with sb/sth; **sich ~ hören/sehen an** +dat to hear/see enough of sth; **sich ~ essen** to eat one's fill; ~ **machen** to be filling

Sattel ['zatəl] **(-s, -̈)** m saddle; (Berg) ridge; **s~n** vt to saddle; ~**schlepper** m articulated lorry

sättigen ['zɛtıgən] vt to satisfy; (CHEM) to saturate

Satz [zats] **(-es, -̈e)** m (GRAM) sentence; (Nebensatz, Adverbialsatz) clause; (Theorem) theorem; (MUS) movement; (TENNIS: Briefmarken etc) set; (Kaffee) grounds pl; (COMM) rate; (Sprung) jump; ~**teil** m part of a sentence; ~**ung** f (Statut) statute, rule; ~**zeichen** nt punctuation mark

Sau [zau] **(-, Säue)** f sow; (umg) dirty pig

sauber ['zaubər] adj clean; (ironisch) fine; ~ **halten** to keep clean; **S~keit** f cleanness; (einer Person) cleanliness

säuberlich ['zɔybərlıç] adv neatly

säubern vt to clean; (POL etc) to purge; **Säuberung** f cleaning; purge

Sauce ['zo:sə] f sauce, gravy

sauer ['zauər] adj sour; (CHEM) acid; (umg)

cross; **saurer Regen** acid rain; **S~braten** m braised beef marinated in vinegar

Sauerei [zaʊə'raɪ] (umg) f rotten state of affairs, scandal; (Schmutz etc) mess; (Unanständigkeit) obscenity

Sauerkraut nt sauerkraut, pickled cabbage

säuerlich ['zɔʏɐlɪç] adj (Geschmack) sour; (missvergnügt: Gesicht) dour

Sauer- zW: **~milch** f sour milk; **~rahm** m (KOCH) sour cream; **~stoff** m oxygen; **~teig** m leaven

saufen ['zaʊfən] (unreg) (umg) vt, vi to drink, to booze; **Säufer** ['zɔʏfɐ] (-s, -) (umg) m boozer

saugen ['zaʊɡən] (unreg) vt, vi to suck

säugen ['zɔʏɡən] vt to suckle

Sauger ['zaʊɡɐ] (-s, -) m dummy, comforter (US); (auf Flasche) teat

Säugetier ['zɔʏɡə-] nt mammal

Säugling m infant, baby

Säule ['zɔʏlə] f column, pillar

Saum [zaʊm] (-(e)s, Säume) m hem; (Naht) seam

säumen ['zɔʏmən] vt to hem; to seam ♦ vi to delay, to hesitate

Sauna ['zaʊna] (-, -s) f sauna

Säure ['zɔʏrə] f acid

sausen ['zaʊzən] vi to blow; (umg: eilen) to rush; (Ohren) to buzz; **etw ~ lassen** (umg) not to bother with sth

Saxofon, Saxophon [zakso'fo:n] (-s, -e) nt saxophone

SB abk = **Selbstbedienung**

S-Bahn f abk (= Schnellbahn) high speed railway; (= Stadtbahn) suburban railway

schaben ['ʃa:bən] vt to scrape

schäbig ['ʃe:bɪç] adj shabby

Schablone [ʃa'blo:nə] f stencil; (Muster) pattern; (fig) convention

Schach [ʃax] (-s, -s) nt chess; (Stellung) check; **~brett** nt chessboard; **~figur** f chessman; **'~'matt** adj checkmate; **~spiel** nt game of chess

Schacht [ʃaxt] (-(e)s, -e) m shaft

Schachtel (-, -n) f box

schade ['ʃa:də] adj a pity od shame ♦ excl: **(wie) ~!** (what a) pity od shame; **sich** dat

zu ~ sein für etw to consider o.s. too good for sth

Schädel ['ʃe:dəl] (-s, -) m skull; **~bruch** m fractured skull

Schaden ['ʃa:dən] (-s, ⁴) m damage; (Verletzung) injury; (Nachteil) disadvantage; **s~** vi +dat to hurt; **einer Sache s~** to damage sth; **~ersatz** m compensation, damages pl; **~freude** f malicious glee; **s~froh** adj (Mensch, Lachen) gloating; **~sfall** m: **im ~sfall** in the event of a claim

schadhaft ['ʃa:thaft] adj faulty, damaged

schäd- ['ʃe:t] zW: **~igen** ['ʃe:dɪɡən] vt to damage; (Person) to do harm to, to harm; **~lich** adj: **~lich (für)** harmful (to); **S~lichkeit** f harmfulness; **S~ling** m pest

Schadstoff ['ʃa:tʃtɔf] m harmful substance; **s~arm** adj: **s~arm sein** to contain a low level of harmful substances

Schaf [ʃa:f] (-(e)s, -e) nt sheep

Schäfer ['ʃe:fɐ] (-s, -e) m shepherd; **~hund** m Alsatian (dog) (BRIT), German shepherd (dog) (US)

Schaffen ['ʃafən] (-s) nt (creative) activity

schaffen¹ ['ʃafən] (unreg) vt to create; (Platz) to make

schaffen² ['ʃafən] vt (erreichen) to manage, to do; (erledigen) to finish; (Prüfung) to pass; (transportieren) to take ♦ vi (umg: arbeiten) to work; **sich** dat **etw ~** to get o.s. sth; **sich an etw** dat **zu ~ machen** to busy o.s. with sth

Schaffner(in) ['ʃafnɐ(ɪn)] (-s, -) m(f) (Busschaffner) conductor(-tress); (EISENB) guard

Schaft [ʃaft] (-(e)s, ⁴e) m shaft; (von Gewehr) stock; (von Stiefel) leg; (BOT) stalk; tree trunk

Schal [ʃa:l] (-s, -e od -s) m scarf

schal adj flat; (fig) insipid

Schälchen ['ʃe:lçən] nt cup, bowl

Schale ['ʃa:lə] f skin; (abgeschält) peel; (Nussschale, Muschelschale, Eischale) shell; (Geschirr) dish, bowl

schälen ['ʃe:lən] vt to peel; to shell ♦ vr to peel

Schall [ʃal] (-(e)s, -e) m sound; **~dämpfer** (-s, -) m (AUT) silencer; **s~dicht** adj

soundproof; **s~en** *vi* to (re)sound; **s~end**
adj resounding, loud; **~mauer** *f* sound
barrier; **~platte** *f* (gramophone) record
Schalt- [ʃalt] *zW:* **~bild** *nt* circuit diagram;
~brett *nt* switchboard; **s~en** *vt* to switch,
to turn ♦ *vi* (AUT) to change (gear); (*umg:
begreifen*) to catch on; **~er** (**-s, -**) *m*
counter; (*an Gerät*) switch; **~erbeamte(r)**
m counter clerk; **~erstunden** *pl* hours of
business; **~hebel** *m* switch; (AUT) gear
lever; **~jahr** *nt* leap year; **~ung** *f* switching;
(ELEK) circuit; (AUT) gear change
Scham [ʃaːm] (**-**) *f* shame; (*~gefühl*)
modesty; (*Organe*) private parts *pl*
schämen ['ʃɛːmən] *vr* to be ashamed
schamlos *adj* shameless
Schande ['ʃandə] (**-**) *f* disgrace
schändlich ['ʃɛntlıç] *adj* disgraceful,
shameful
Schändung ['ʃɛnduŋ] *f* violation, defilement
Schanze ['ʃantsə] *f* (*Sprungschanze*) ski jump
Schar [ʃaːr] (**-, -en**) *f* band, company;
(*Vögel*) flock; (*Menge*) crowd; **in ~en** in
droves; **s~en** *vr* to assemble, to rally
scharf [ʃarf] *adj* sharp; (*Essen*) hot, spicy;
(*Munition*) live; **~ nachdenken** to think
hard; **auf etw** *akk* **~ sein** (*umg*) to be keen
on sth
Schärfe ['ʃɛrfə] *f* sharpness; (*Strenge*) rigour;
s~n *vt* to sharpen
Scharf- *zW:* **s~machen** (*umg*) *vt* to stir up;
~richter *m* executioner; **~schütze** *m*
marksman, sharpshooter; **s~sinnig** *adj*
astute, shrewd
Scharlach ['ʃarlax] (**-s, -e**) *m* (*~fieber*)
scarlet fever
Scharnier [ʃarˈniːr] (**-s, -e**) *nt* hinge
scharren ['ʃarən] *vt, vi* to scrape, to scratch
Schaschlik ['ʃaʃlık] (**-s, -s**) *m od nt* (shish)
kebab
Schatten ['ʃatən] (**-s, -**) *m* shadow;
~riss ▲ *m* silhouette; **~seite** *f* shady side,
dark side
schattieren [ʃaˈtiːrən] *vt, vi* to shade
schattig ['ʃatıç] *adj* shady
Schatulle [ʃaˈtulə] *f* casket; (*Geldschatulle*)
coffer

Schatz [ʃats] (**-es, ²e**) *m* treasure; (*Person*)
darling
schätz- [ʃɛts] *zW:* **~bar** *adj* assessable;
S~chen *nt* darling, love; **~en** *vt*
(*abschätzen*) to estimate; (*Gegenstand*) to
value; (*würdigen*) to value, to esteem;
(*vermuten*) to reckon; **S~ung** *f* estimate;
estimation; valuation; **nach meiner S~ung
...** I reckon that ...
Schau [ʃau] (**-**) *f* show; (*Ausstellung*) display,
exhibition; **etw zur ~ stellen** to make a
show of sth, to show sth off; **~bild** *nt*
diagram
Schauder ['ʃaudər] (**-s, -s**) *m* shudder;
(*wegen Kälte*) shiver; **s~haft** *adj* horrible;
s~n *vi* to shudder; to shiver
schauen ['ʃauən] *vi* to look
Schauer ['ʃauər] (**-s, -**) *m* (*Regenschauer*)
shower; (*Schreck*) shudder; **~geschichte** *f*
horror story; **s~lich** *adj* horrific, spine-
chilling
Schaufel ['ʃaufəl] (**-, -n**) *f* shovel; (NAUT)
paddle; (TECH) scoop; **s~n** *vt* to shovel, to
scoop
Schau- *zW:* **~fenster** *nt* shop window;
~fensterbummel *m* window shopping
(expedition); **~kasten** *m* showcase
Schaukel ['ʃaukəl] (**-, -n**) *f* swing; **s~n** *vi* to
swing, to rock; **~pferd** *nt* rocking horse;
~stuhl *m* rocking chair
Schaulustige(r) ['ʃaulustıgə(r)] *f(m)*
onlooker
Schaum [ʃaum] (**-(e)s, Schäume**) *m* foam;
(*Seifenschaum*) lather; **~bad** *nt* bubble bath
schäumen ['ʃɔymən] *vi* to foam
Schaum- *zW:* **~festiger** (**-s, -**) *m* mousse;
~gummi *m* foam (rubber); **s~ig** *adj* frothy,
foamy; **~stoff** *m* foam material; **~wein** *m*
sparkling wine
Schauplatz *m* scene
schaurig ['ʃaurıç] *adj* horrific, dreadful
Schauspiel *nt* spectacle; (THEAT) play;
~er(in) *m(f)* actor (actress); **s~ern** *vi insep*
to act; **Schauspielhaus** *nt* theatre
Scheck [ʃɛk] (**-s, -s**) *m* cheque; **~gebühr** *f*
encashment fee; **~heft** *m* cheque book;
~karte *f* cheque card

scheffeln ['ʃɛfəln] vt to amass

Scheibe ['ʃaɪbə] f disc; (Brot etc) slice; (Glasscheibe) pane; (MIL) target

Scheiben- zW: **~bremse** f (AUT) disc brake; **~wischer** m (AUT) windscreen wiper

Scheide ['ʃaɪdə] f sheath; (Grenze) boundary; (ANAT) vagina; **s~n** (unreg) vt to separate; (Ehe) to dissolve ♦ vi to depart; to part; **sich s~n lassen** to get a divorce

Scheidung f (Ehescheidung) divorce

Schein [ʃaɪn] **(-(e)s, -e)** m light; (Anschein) appearance; (Geld) (bank)note; (Bescheinigung) certificate; **zum ~** in pretence; **s~bar** adj apparent; **s~en** (unreg) vi to shine; (Anschein haben) to seem; **s~heilig** adj hypocritical; **~werfer** **(-s, -)** m floodlight; spotlight; (Suchscheinwerfer) searchlight; (AUT) headlamp

Scheiß- ['ʃaɪs] (umg) in zW bloody

Scheiße ['ʃaɪsə] **(-)** (umg) f shit

Scheitel ['ʃaɪtəl] **(-s, -)** m top; (Haarscheitel) parting; **s~n** vt to part

scheitern ['ʃaɪtərn] vi to fail

Schelle ['ʃɛlə] f small bell; **s~n** vi to ring

Schellfisch ['ʃɛlfɪʃ] m haddock

Schelm [ʃɛlm] **(-(e)s, -e)** m rogue; **s~isch** adj mischievous, roguish

Schelte ['ʃɛltə] f scolding; **s~n** (unreg) vt to scold

Schema ['ʃeːma] **(-s, -s** od **-ta)** nt scheme, plan; (Darstellung) schema; **nach ~** quite mechanically; **s~tisch** [ʃeˈmaːtɪʃ] adj schematic; (pej) mechanical

Schemel ['ʃeːməl] **(-s, -)** m (foot)stool

Schenkel ['ʃɛŋkəl] **(-s, -)** m thigh

schenken ['ʃɛŋkən] vt (auch fig) to give; (Getränk) to pour; **sich** dat **etw ~** (umg) to skip sth; **das ist geschenkt!** (billig) that's a giveaway!; (nichts wert) that's worthless!

Scherbe ['ʃɛrbə] f broken piece, fragment; (archäologisch) potsherd

Schere ['ʃeːrə] f scissors pl; (groß) shears pl; **s~n** (unreg) vt to cut; (Schaf) to shear; (kümmern) to bother ♦ vr to care; **scher dich zum Teufel!** get lost!; **~'rei** (umg) f bother, trouble

Scherz [ʃɛrts] **(-es, -e)** m joke; fun; **~frage** f conundrum; **s~haft** adj joking, jocular

Scheu [ʃɔy] **(-)** f shyness; (Angst) fear; (Ehrfurcht) awe; **s~** adj shy; **s~en** vr: **sich s~en vor** +dat to be afraid of, to shrink from ♦ vt to shun ♦ vi (Pferd) to shy

scheuern ['ʃɔyərn] vt to scour, to scrub

Scheune ['ʃɔynə] f barn

Scheusal ['ʃɔyzaːl] **(-s, -e)** nt monster

scheußlich ['ʃɔyslɪç] adj dreadful, frightful

Schi [ʃiː] m = **Ski**

Schicht [ʃɪçt] **(-, -en)** f layer; (Klasse) class, level; (in Fabrik etc) shift; **~arbeit** f shift work; **s~en** vt to layer, to stack

schick [ʃɪk] adj stylish, chic

schicken vt to send ♦ vr: **sich ~ (in** +akk) to resign o.s. (to) ♦ vb unpers (anständig sein) to be fitting

schicklich adj proper, fitting

Schicksal **(-s, -e)** nt fate; **~sschlag** m great misfortune, blow

Schieb- ['ʃiːb] zW: **~edach** nt (AUT) sun roof; **s~en** (unreg) vt (auch Drogen) to push; (Schuld) to put ♦ vi to push; **~etür** f sliding door; **~ung** f fiddle

Schieds- ['ʃiːts] zW: **~gericht** nt court of arbitration; **~richter** m referee; umpire; (Schlichter) arbitrator

schief [ʃiːf] adj crooked; (Ebene) sloping; (Turm) leaning; (Winkel) oblique; (Blick) funny; (Vergleich) distorted ♦ adv crooked(ly); (ansehen) askance; **etw ~ stellen** to slope sth; **~ gehen** (umg) to go wrong

Schiefer ['ʃiːfər] **(-s, -)** m slate

schielen ['ʃiːlən] vi to squint; **nach etw ~** (fig) to eye sth

schien etc [ʃiːn] vb siehe **scheinen**

Schienbein nt shinbone

Schiene ['ʃiːnə] f rail; (MED) splint; **s~n** vt to put in splints

schier [ʃiːr] adj (fig) sheer ♦ adv nearly, almost

Schieß- ['ʃiːs] zW: **~bude** f shooting gallery; **s~en** (unreg) vt to shoot; (Ball) to kick; (Geschoss) to fire ♦ vi to shoot; (Salat etc) to run to seed; **s~en auf** +akk to shoot at; **~e'rei** f shooting incident, shoot-out; **~pulver** nt gunpowder; **~scharte** f embrasure

Schiff [ʃɪf] **(-(e)s, -e)** nt ship, vessel; (*Kirchenschiff*) nave; **s~bar** adj (*Fluß*) navigable; **~bruch** m shipwreck; **s~brüchig** adj shipwrecked; **~chen** nt small boat; (*Weben*) shuttle; (*Mütze*) forage cap; **~er (-s, -)** m bargeman, boatman; **~fahrt** ▲ f shipping; (*Reise*) voyage

Schikane [ʃi'kaːnə] f harassment; dirty trick; **mit allen ~n** with all the trimmings

schikanieren [ʃika'niːrən] vt to harass, to torment

Schikoree ▲ ['ʃikoreː] **(-s)** m od f = **Chicorée**

Schild¹ [ʃɪlt] **(-(e)s, -e)** m shield; **etw im ~e führen** to be up to sth

Schild² [ʃɪlt] **(-(e)s, -er)** nt sign; nameplate; (*Etikett*) label

Schilddrüse f thyroid gland

schildern ['ʃɪldərn] vt to depict, to portray

Schildkröte f tortoise; (*Wasserschildkröte*) turtle

Schilf [ʃɪlf] **(-(e)s, -e)** nt (*Pflanze*) reed; (*Material*) reeds pl, rushes pl; **~rohr** nt (*Pflanze*) reed

schillern ['ʃɪlərn] vi to shimmer; **~d** adj iridescent

Schilling ['ʃɪlɪŋ] m schilling

Schimmel ['ʃɪməl] **(-s, -)** m mould; (*Pferd*) white horse; **s~ig** adj mouldy; **s~n** vi to get mouldy

Schimmer ['ʃɪmər] **(-s)** m (*Lichtsein*) glimmer; (*Glanz*) shimmer; **s~n** vi to glimmer, to shimmer

Schimpanse [ʃɪm'panzə] **(-n, -n)** m chimpanzee

schimpfen ['ʃɪmpfən] vt to scold ♦ vi to curse, to complain; to scold

Schimpfwort nt term of abuse

schinden ['ʃɪndən] (*unreg*) vt to maltreat, to drive too hard ♦ vr: **sich ~ (mit)** to sweat and strain (at); **Eindruck ~** (*umg*) to create an impression

Schinde'rei f grind, drudgery

Schinken ['ʃɪŋkən] **(-s, -)** m ham

Schirm [ʃɪrm] **(-(e)s, -e)** m (*Regenschirm*) umbrella; (*Sonnenschirm*) parasol, sunshade; (*Wandschirm, Bildschirm*) screen; (*Lampenschirm*) (lamp)shade; (*Mützenschirm*) peak; (*Pilzschirm*) cap; **~mütze** f peaked cap; **~ständer** m umbrella stand

schizophren [ʃitso'freːn] adj schizophrenic

Schlacht [ʃlaxt] **(-, -en)** f battle; **s~en** vt to slaughter, to kill; **~er (-s, -)** m butcher; **~feld** nt battlefield; **~hof** m slaughterhouse, abattoir; **~schiff** nt battleship; **~vieh** nt animals kept for meat; beef cattle

Schlaf [ʃlaːf] **(-(e)s)** m sleep; **~anzug** m pyjamas pl

Schläfe f (ANAT) temple

schlafen ['ʃlaːfən] (*unreg*) vi to sleep; **~ gehen** to go to bed; **S~szeit** f bedtime

schlaff [ʃlaf] adj slack; (*energielos*) limp; (*erschöpft*) exhausted

Schlaf- zW: **~gelegenheit** f sleeping accommodation; **~lied** nt lullaby; **s~los** adj sleepless; **~losigkeit** f sleeplessness, insomnia; **~mittel** nt sleeping pill

schläfrig ['ʃlɛːfrɪç] adj sleepy

Schlaf- zW: **~saal** m dormitory; **~sack** m sleeping bag; **~tablette** f sleeping pill; **~wagen** m sleeping car, sleeper; **s~wandeln** vi insep to sleepwalk; **~zimmer** nt bedroom

Schlag [ʃlaːk] **(-(e)s, ⁺e)** m (*auch fig*) blow; (*auch MED*) stroke; (*Pulsschlag, Herzschlag*) beat; (*ELEK*) shock; (*Blitzschlag*) bolt, stroke; (*Autotür*) car door; (*umg: Portion*) helping; (*Art*) kind, type; **Schläge** pl (*Tracht Prügel*) beating sg; **mit einem ~** all at once; **~ auf ~** in rapid succession; **~ader** f artery; **~anfall** m stroke; **s~artig** adj sudden, without warning; **~baum** m barrier

Schlägel ['ʃlɛːgəl] **(-s, -)** m (*drum*)stick; (*Hammer*) mallet, hammer

schlagen ['ʃlaːgən] (*unreg*) vt, vi to strike, to hit; (*wiederholt ~, besiegen*) to beat; (*Glocke*) to ring; (*Stunde*) to strike; (*Sahne*) to whip; (*Schlacht*) to fight ♦ vr to fight; **nach jdm ~** (*fig*) to take after sb; **sich gut ~** (*fig*) to do well; **Schlager** ['ʃlaːgər] **(-s, -)**

m (auch fig) hit

chläger ['ʃlɛːgər] *m* brawler; *(SPORT)* bat; *(TENNIS etc)* racket; *(GOLF)* club; hockey stick; *(Waffe)* rapier; **Schläge'rei** *f* fight, punch-up

chlagersänger(in) *m(f)* pop singer

chlag- *zW:* **s~fertig** *adj* quick-witted; **~fertigkeit** *f* ready wit, quickness of repartee; **~loch** *nt* pothole; **~obers** *(ÖSTERR) nt* = **Schlagsahne; ~sahne** *f* (whipped) cream; **~seite** *f (NAUT)* list; **~wort** *nt* slogan, catch phrase; **~zeile** *f* headline; **~zeug** *nt* percussion; drums *pl*; **~zeuger (-s, -)** *m* drummer

chlamassel [ʃlaˈmasəl] **(-s, -)** *(umg) m* mess

chlamm [ʃlam] **(-(e)s, -e)** *m* mud; **s~ig** *adj* muddy

chlamp- [ˈʃlamp] *zW:* **~e** *(umg) f* slut; **s~en** *(umg) vi* to be sloppy; **~e'rei** *(umg) f* disorder, untidiness; sloppy work; **s~ig** *(umg) adj (Mensch, Arbeit)* sloppy, messy

chlange [ˈʃlaŋə] *f* snake; *(Menschenschlange)* queue *(BRIT)*, line-up *(US)*; **~ stehen** to (form a) queue, to line up

chlängeln [ˈʃlɛŋəln] *vr (Schlange)* to wind; *(Weg)* to wind, twist; *(Fluss)* to meander

chlangen- *zW:* **~biss** ▲ *m* snake bite; **~gift** *nt* snake venom; **~linie** *f* wavy line

chlank [ʃlaŋk] *adj* slim, slender; **S~heit** *f* slimness, slenderness; **S~heitskur** *f* diet

chlapp [ʃlap] *adj* limp; *(locker)* slack; **S~e** *(umg) f* setback

chlaraffenland [ʃlaˈrafənlant] *nt* land of milk and honey

chlau [ʃlaʊ] *adj* crafty, cunning

chlauch [ʃlaʊx] **(-(e)s, Schläuche)** *m* hose; *(in Reifen)* inner tube; *(umg: Anstrengung)* grind; **~boot** *nt* rubber dinghy; **s~en** *(umg) vt* to tell on, to exhaust

chläue [ˈʃlɔʏə] **(-)** *f* cunning

chlaufe [ˈʃlaʊfə] *f* loop; *(Aufhänger)* hanger

chlauheit *f* cunning

chlecht [ʃlɛçt] *adj* bad ♦ *adv* badly; **~ gelaunt** in a bad mood; **~ und recht** after

a fashion; **jdm ist ~** sb feels sick *od* bad; **jdm geht es ~** sb is in a bad way; **~ machen** to run down; **S~igkeit** *f* badness; bad deed

schlecken [ˈʃlɛkən] *vt, vi* to lick

Schlegel [ˈʃleːgəl] **(-s, -)** *m (KOCH)* leg; *siehe* **Schlägel**

schleichen [ˈʃlaɪçən] *(unreg) vi* to creep, to crawl; **~d** *adj* gradual; creeping

Schleichwerbung *f (COMM)* plug

Schleier [ˈʃlaɪər] **(-s, -)** *m* veil; **s~haft** *(umg) adj:* **jdm s~haft sein** to be a mystery to sb

Schleif- [ʃlaɪf] *zW:* **~e** *f* loop; *(Band)* bow; **s~en¹** *vt, vi* to drag; **s~en²** *(unreg) vt* to grind; *(Edelstein)* to cut; **~stein** *m* grindstone

Schleim [ʃlaɪm] **(-(e)s, -e)** *m* slime; *(MED)* mucus; *(KOCH)* gruel; **~haut** *f (ANAT)* mucous membrane; **s~ig** *adj* slimy

Schlemm- [ˈʃlɛm] *zW:* **s~en** *vi* to feast; **~er (-s, -)** *m* gourmet; **~e'rei** *f* gluttony, feasting

schlendern [ˈʃlɛndərn] *vi* to stroll

schlenkern [ˈʃlɛŋkərn] *vt, vi* to swing, to dangle

Schlepp- [ʃlɛp] *zW:* **~e** *f* train; **s~en** *vt* to drag; *(Auto, Schiff)* to tow; *(tragen)* to lug; **s~end** *adj* dragging, slow; **~er (-s, -)** *m* tractor; *(Schiff)* tug

Schlesien [ˈʃleːziən] **(-s)** *nt* Silesia

Schleuder [ˈʃlɔʏdər] **(-, -n)** *f* catapult; *(Wäscheschleuder)* spin-drier; *(Butterschleuder etc)* centrifuge; **~gefahr** *f* risk of skidding; **„Achtung ~gefahr"** "slippery road ahead"; **s~n** *vt* to hurl; *(Wäsche)* to spin-dry ♦ *vi (AUT)* to skid; **~preis** *m* give-away price; **~sitz** *m (AVIAT)* ejector seat; *(fig)* hot seat; **~ware** *f* cheap *od* cut-price goods *pl*

schleunigst [ˈʃlɔʏnɪçst] *adv* straight away

Schleuse [ˈʃlɔʏzə] *f* lock; *(~ntor)* sluice

schlicht [ʃlɪçt] *adj* simple, plain; **~en** *vt (glätten)* to smooth, to dress; *(Streit)* to settle; **S~er (-s, -)** *m* mediator, arbitrator; **S~ung** *f* settlement; arbitration

Schlick [ʃlɪk] **(-(e)s, -e)** *m* mud; *(Ölschlick)* slick

schlief *etc* [ʃliːf] *vb siehe* **schlafen**

Schließ- [ˈʃliːs] zW: **s~en** (unreg) vt to close, to shut; (beenden) to close; (Freundschaft, Bündnis, Ehe) to enter into; (folgern): **s~en (aus)** to infer (from) ♦ vi, vr to close, to shut; **etw in sich s~en** to include sth; **~fach** nt locker; **s~lich** adv finally; **s~lich doch** after all

Schliff [ʃlɪf] (-(e)s, -e) m cut(ting); (fig) polish

schlimm [ʃlɪm] adj bad; **~er** adj worse; **~ste(r, s)** adj worst; **~stenfalls** adv at (the) worst

Schlinge [ˈʃlɪŋə] f loop; (bes Henkersschlinge) noose; (Falle) snare; (MED) sling; **s~n** (unreg) vt to wind; (essen) to bolt, to gobble ♦ vi (essen) to bolt one's food, to gobble

schlingern vi to roll

Schlips [ʃlɪps] (-es, -e) m tie

Schlitten [ˈʃlɪtən] (-s, -) m sledge, sleigh; **~fahren** (-s) nt tobogganing

schlittern [ˈʃlɪtərn] vi to slide

Schlittschuh [ˈʃlɪtʃuː] m skate; **~ laufen** to skate; **~bahn** f skating rink; **~läufer(in)** m(f) skater

Schlitz [ʃlɪts] (-es, -e) m slit; (für Münze) slot; (Hosenschlitz) flies pl; **s~äugig** adj slant-eyed

Schloss ▲ [ʃlɔs] (-es, ▀er) nt lock; (an Schmuck etc) clasp; (Bau) castle; chateau

schloss ▲ etc vb siehe **schließen**

Schlosser [ˈʃlɔsər] (-s, -) m (Autoschlosser) fitter; (für Schlüssel etc) locksmith

Schlosserei [-ˈraɪ] f metal (working) shop

Schlot [ʃloːt] (-(e)s, -e) m chimney; (NAUT) funnel

schlottern [ˈʃlɔtərn] vi to shake, to tremble; (Kleidung) to be baggy

Schlucht [ʃluxt] (-, -en) f gorge, ravine

schluchzen [ˈʃluxtsən] vi to sob

Schluck [ʃlʊk] (-(e)s, -e) m swallow; (Menge) drop; **~auf** (-s, -s) m hiccups pl; **s~en** vt, vi to swallow

schludern [ˈʃluːdərn] vi to skimp, to do sloppy work

schlug etc [ʃluːk] vb siehe **schlagen**

Schlummer [ˈʃlʊmər] (-s) m slumber; **s~n** vi to slumber

Schlund [ʃlʊnt] (-(e)s, ▀e) m gullet; (fig) jaw

schlüpfen [ˈʃlʏpfən] vi to slip; (Vogel etc) to hatch (out)

Schlüpfer [ˈʃlʏpfər] (-s, -) m panties pl, knickers pl

schlüpfrig [ˈʃlʏpfrɪç] adj slippery; (fig) lewd; **S~keit** f slipperiness; (fig) lewdness

schlurfen [ˈʃlʊrfən] vi to shuffle

schlürfen [ˈʃlʏrfən] vt, vi to slurp

Schluss ▲ [ʃlʊs] (-es, ▀e) m end; (~folgerung) conclusion; **am ~** at the end; **~ machen mit** to finish with

Schlüssel [ˈʃlʏsəl] (-s, -) m (auch fig) key; (Schraubenschlüssel) spanner, wrench; (MUS) clef; **~bein** nt collarbone; **~blume** f cowslip, primrose; **~bund** m bunch of keys; **~dienst** m key cutting service; **~loch** nt keyhole; **~position** f key position; **~wort** nt keyword

schlüssig [ˈʃlʏsɪç] adj conclusive

Schluss- ▲ zW: **~licht** nt taillight; (fig) tailender; **~strich** m (fig) final stroke; **~verkauf** m clearance sale

schmächtig [ˈʃmɛçtɪç] adj slight

schmackhaft [ˈʃmakhaft] adj tasty

schmal [ʃmaːl] adj narrow; (Person, Buch etc) slender, slim; (karg) meagre

schmälern [ˈʃmɛːlərn] vt to diminish; (fig) to belittle

Schmalfilm m cine film

Schmalz [ʃmalts] (-es, -e) nt dripping, lard; (fig) sentiment, schmaltz; **s~ig** adj (fig) schmaltzy

schmarotzen [ʃmaˈrɔtsən] vi to sponge; (BOT) to be parasitic; **Schmarotzer** (-s, -) m parasite; sponger

Schmarren [ˈʃmarən] (-s, -) m (ÖSTERR) small piece of pancake; (fig) rubbish, tripe

schmatzen [ˈʃmatsən] vi to smack one's lips; to eat noisily

schmecken [ˈʃmɛkən] vt, vi to taste; **es schmeckt ihm** he likes it

Schmeichel- [ˈʃmaɪçəl] zW: **~ei** [-ˈlaɪ] f flattery; **s~haft** adj flattering; **s~n** vi to flatter

schmeißen [ˈʃmaɪsən] (unreg) (umg) vt to

throw, to chuck

Schmelz [ʃmɛlts] **(-es, -e)** m enamel; (Glasur) glaze; (von Stimme) melodiousness; **s~en** (unreg) vt to melt; (Erz) to smelt ♦ vi to melt; **~punkt** m melting point; **~wasser** nt melted snow

Schmerz [ʃmɛrts] **(-es, -en)** m pain; (Trauer) grief; **s~empfindlich** adj sensitive to pain; **s~en** vt, vi to hurt; **~ensgeld** nt compensation; **s~haft** adj painful; **s~lich** adj painful; **s~los** adj painless; **~mittel** nt painkiller; **~tablette** f painkiller

Schmetterling [ʃmɛtərlɪŋ] m butterfly

schmettern [ʃmɛtərn] vt (werfen) to hurl; (TENNIS: Ball) to smash; (singen) to belt out (inf)

Schmied [ʃmiːt] **(-(e)s, -e)** m blacksmith; **~e** [ʃmiːdə] f smithy, forge; **~eeisen** nt wrought iron; **s~en** vt to forge; (Pläne) to devise, to concoct

schmiegen [ʃmiːgən] vt to press, to nestle ♦ vr: **sich ~ (an** +akk) to cuddle up (to), to nestle (up to)

Schmier- [ʃmiːr] zW: **~e** f grease; (THEAT) greasepaint, make-up; **s~en** vt to smear; (ölen) to lubricate, to grease; (bestechen) to bribe; (schreiben) to scrawl ♦ vi (schreiben) to scrawl; **~fett** nt grease; **~geld** nt bribe; **s~ig** adj greasy; **~seife** f soft soap

Schminke [ʃmɪŋkə] f make-up; **s~n** vt, vr to make up

schmirgeln [ʃmɪrgəln] vt to sand (down)

Schmirgelpapier nt emery paper

schmollen [ʃmɔlən] vi to sulk, to pout

Schmorbraten m stewed od braised meat

schmoren [ʃmoːrən] vt to stew, to braise

Schmuck [ʃmʊk] **(-(e)s, -e)** m jewellery; (Verzierung) decoration

schmücken [ʃmʏkən] vt to decorate

Schmuck- zW: **s~los** adj unadorned, plain; **~sachen** pl jewels, jewellery sg

Schmuggel [ʃmʊgəl] **(-s)** m smuggling; **s~n** vt, vi to smuggle

Schmuggler **(-s, -)** m smuggler

schmunzeln [ʃmʊntsəln] vi to smile benignly

schmusen [ʃmuːzən] (umg) vi (zärtlich sein)

to cuddle, to canoodle (inf)

Schmutz [ʃmʊts] **(-es)** m dirt, filth; **~fink** m filthy creature; **~fleck** m stain; **s~ig** adj dirty

Schnabel [ʃnaːbəl] **(-s, ")** m beak, bill; (Ausguss) spout

Schnalle [ʃnalə] f buckle, clasp; **s~n** vt to buckle

Schnapp- [ʃnap] zW: **s~en** vt to grab, to catch ♦ vi to snap; **~schloss** ▲ nt spring lock; **~schuss** ▲ m (PHOT) snapshot

Schnaps [ʃnaps] **(-es, "e)** m spirits pl; schnapps

schnarchen [ʃnarçən] vi to snore

schnattern [ʃnatərn] vi (Gänse) to gabble; (Ente) to quack

schnauben [ʃnaʊbən] vi to snort ♦ vr to blow one's nose

schnaufen [ʃnaʊfən] vi to puff, to pant

Schnauze f snout, muzzle; (Ausguss) spout; (umg) gob

schnäuzen ▲ [ʃnɔytsən] vr to blow one's nose

Schnecke [ʃnɛkə] f snail; **~nhaus** nt snail's shell

Schnee [ʃneː] **(-s)** m snow; (Eischnee) beaten egg white; **~ball** m snowball; **~flocke** f snowflake; **s~frei** adj free of snow; **~gestöber** nt snowstorm; **~glöckchen** nt snowdrop; **~grenze** f snow line; **~kette** f (AUT) snow chain; **~mann** m snowman; **~pflug** m snowplough; **~regen** m sleet; **~schmelze** f thaw; **~wehe** f snowdrift

Schneide [ʃnaɪdə] f edge; (Klinge) blade; **s~n** (unreg) vt to cut; (kreuzen) to cross, to intersect ♦ vr to cut o.s.; to cross, to intersect; **s~nd** adj cutting; **~r (-s, -)** m tailor; **~rei** f (Geschäft) tailor's; **~rin** f dressmaker; **s~rn** vt to make ♦ vi to be a tailor; **~zahn** m incisor

schneien [ʃnaɪən] vi unpers to snow

Schneise [ʃnaɪzə] f clearing

schnell [ʃnɛl] adj quick, fast ♦ adv quick, quickly, fast; **S~hefter (-s, -)** m loose-leaf binder; **S~igkeit** f speed; **S~imbiss** ▲ m (Lokal) snack bar; **S~kochtopf** m

Spelling Reform: ▲ new spelling △ old spelling (to be phased out)

(*Dampfkochtopf*) pressure cooker;
S~**reinigung** *f* dry cleaner's; ~**stens** *adv*
as quickly as possible; S~**straße** *f*
expressway; S~**zug** *m* fast *od* express train
schneuzen △ ['ʃnɔʏtsən] *vr siehe*
schnäuzen

schnippeln ['ʃnɪpəln] (*umg*) *vt*: ~ (**an** +*dat*)
to snip (at)
schnippisch ['ʃnɪpɪʃ] *adj* sharp-tongued
Schnitt (-(**e**)**s**, -**e**) *m* cut(ting); (~**punkt**)
intersection; (*Querschnitt*) (cross) section;
(*Durchschnitt*) average; (~**muster**) pattern;
(*an Buch*) edge; (*umg*: *Gewinn*) profit
schnitt *etc vb siehe* **schneiden**
Schnitt- *zW*: ~**blumen** *pl* cut flowers; ~**e** *f*
slice; (*belegt*) sandwich; ~**fläche** *f* section;
~**lauch** *m* chive; ~**punkt** *m* (point of)
intersection; ~**stelle** *f* (*COMPUT*) interface;
~**wunde** *f* cut
Schnitz- ['ʃnɪts] *zW*: ~**arbeit** *f* wood
carving; ~**el** (-**s**, -) *nt* chip; (*KOCH*)
escalope; **s~en** *vt* to carve; ~**er** (-**s**, -) *m*
carver; (*umg*) blunder; ~**e'rei** *f* carving;
carved woodwork
schnodderig ['ʃnɔdərɪç] (*umg*) *adj* snotty
Schnorchel ['ʃnɔrçəl] (-**s**, -) *m* snorkel
Schnörkel ['ʃnœrkəl] (-**s**, -) *m* flourish;
(*ARCHIT*) scroll
schnorren ['ʃnɔrən] *vt, vi* to cadge
schnüffeln ['ʃnʏfəln] *vi* to sniff
Schnüffler (-**s**, -) *m* snooper
Schnuller ['ʃnʊlər] (-**s**, -) *m* dummy,
comforter (*US*)
Schnupfen ['ʃnʊpfən] (-**s**, -) *m* cold
schnuppern ['ʃnʊpərn] *vi* to sniff
Schnur [ʃnuːr] (-, **ꞏe**) *f* string, cord; (*ELEK*)
flex
schnüren ['ʃnyːrən] *vt* to tie
schnurgerade *adj* straight (as a die)
Schnurrbart ['ʃnʊrbaːrt] *m* moustache
schnurren ['ʃnʊrən] *vi* to purr; (*Kreisel*) to
hum
Schnürschuh *m* lace-up (shoe)
Schnürsenkel *m* shoelace
schnurstracks *adv* straight (away)
Schock [ʃɔk] (-(**e**)**s**, -**e**) *m* shock; **s~ieren**
[ʃɔ'kiːrən] *vt* to shock, to outrage

Schöffe ['ʃœfə] (-**n**, -**n**) *m* lay magistrate;
Schöffin *f* lay magistrate
Schokolade [ʃoko'laːdə] *f* chocolate
Scholle ['ʃɔlə] *f* clod; (*Eisscholle*) ice floe;
(*Fisch*) plaice

SCHLÜSSELWORT

schon [ʃoːn] *adv* 1 (*bereits*) already; **er ist
schon da** he's there already, he's already
there; **ist er schon da?** is he there yet?;
warst du schon einmal da? have you ever
been there?; **ich war schon einmal da** I've
been there before; **das war schon immer
so** that has always been the case; **schon
oft** often; **hast du schon gehört?** have
you heard?
2 (*bestimmt*) all right; **du wirst schon
sehen** you'll see (all right); **das wird
schon noch gut** that'll be OK
3 (*bloß*) just; **allein schon das Gefühl ...**
just the very feeling ...; **schon der
Gedanke** the very thought; **wenn ich das
schon höre** I only have to hear that
4 (*einschränkend*): **ja schon, aber ...** yes
(well), but ...
5: **schon möglich** possible; **schon gut!**
OK!; **du weißt schon** you know; **komm
schon!** come on!

schön [ʃøːn] *adj* beautiful; (*nett*) nice; ~**e
Grüße** best wishes; ~**e Ferien** have a nice
holiday; ~**en Dank** (many) thanks; **sich ~
machen** to make o.s. look nice
schonen ['ʃoːnən] *vt* to look after ♦ *vr* to
take it easy; ~**d** *adj* careful, gentle
Schön- *zW*: ~**heit** *f* beauty; ~**heitsfehler**
m blemish, flaw; ~**heitsoperation** *f*
cosmetic surgery
Schonkost (-) *f* light diet; (*Spezialdiät*)
special diet
Schon- *zW*: ~**ung** *f* good care; (*Nachsicht*)
consideration; (*Forst*) plantation of young
trees; **s~ungslos** *adj* unsparing, harsh;
~**zeit** *f* close season
Schöpf- ['ʃœpf] *zW*: **s~en** *vt* to scoop, to
ladle; (*Mut*) to summon up; (*Luft*) to
breathe in; ~**er** (-**s**, -) *m* creator; **s~erisch**

adj creative; ~**kelle** *f* ladle; ~**ung** *f* creation

Schorf [ʃɔrf] **(-(e)s, -e)** *m* scab

Schornstein ['ʃɔrnʃtam] *m* chimney; (*NAUT*) funnel; ~**feger (-s, -)** *m* chimney sweep

Schoß [ʃoːs] **(-es, ⁻e)** *m* lap

Schoss ▲ *etc vb siehe* **schießen**

Schoßhund *m* pet dog, lapdog

Schote ['ʃoːtə] *f* pod

Schotte ['ʃɔtə] *m* Scot, Scotsman

Schotter ['ʃɔtər] **(-s)** *m* broken stone, road metal; (*EISENB*) ballast

Schott- [ʃɔt] *zW:* ~**in** *f* Scot, Scotswoman; **s~isch** *adj* Scottish, Scots; ~**land** *nt* Scotland

schraffieren [ʃraˈfiːrən] *vt* to hatch

schräg [ʃrɛːk] *adj* slanting, not straight; **etw ~ stellen** to put sth at an angle; ~ **gegenüber** diagonally opposite; **S~e** ['ʃrɛːgə] *f* slant; **S~strich** *m* oblique stroke

Schramme ['ʃramə] *f* scratch; **s~n** *vt* to scratch

Schrank [ʃraŋk] **(-(e)s, ⁻e)** *m* cupboard; (*Kleiderschrank*) wardrobe; ~**e** *f* barrier; ~**koffer** *m* trunk

Schraube ['ʃraubə] *f* screw; **s~n** *vt* to screw; ~**nschlüssel** *m* spanner; ~**nzieher (-s, -)** *m* screwdriver

Schraubstock ['ʃraupʃtɔk] *m* (*TECH*) vice

Schreck [ʃrɛk] **(-(e)s, -e)** *m* terror; fright; ~**en (-s, -)** *m* terror; fright; **s~en** *vt* to frighten, to scare; ~**gespenst** *nt* spectre, nightmare; **s~haft** *adj* jumpy, easily frightened; **s~lich** *adj* terrible, dreadful

Schrei [ʃrai] **(-(e)s, -e)** *m* scream; (*Ruf*) shout

Schreib- ['ʃraib] *zW:* ~**block** *m* writing pad; **s~en** (*unreg*) *vt, vi* to write; (*buchstabieren*) to spell; ~**en (-s, -)** *nt* letter, communication; **s~faul** *adj* bad about writing letters; ~**kraft** *f* typist; ~**maschine** *f* typewriter; ~**papier** *nt* notepaper; ~**tisch** *m* desk; ~**ung** *f* spelling; ~**waren** *pl* stationery *sg*; ~**weise** *f* spelling; way of writing; ~**zentrale** *f* typing pool; ~**zeug** *nt* writing materials *pl*

schreien ['ʃraiən] (*unreg*) *vt, vi* to scream; (*rufen*) to shout; ~**d** *adj* (*fig*) glaring; (*Farbe*) loud

Schrein [ʃrain] **(-(e)s, -e)** *m* shrine

Schreiner ['ʃrainər] **(-s, -)** *m* joiner; (*Zimmermann*) carpenter; (*Möbelschreiner*) cabinetmaker; ~**ei** [-'rai] *f* joiner's workshop

schreiten ['ʃraitən] (*unreg*) *vi* to stride

schrieb *etc* [ʃriːp] *vb siehe* **schreiben**

Schrift [ʃrift] **(-, -en)** *f* writing; handwriting; (~*art*) script; (*Gedrucktes*) pamphlet, work; ~**deutsch** *nt* written German; ~**führer** *m* secretary; **s~lich** *adj* written ♦ *adv* in writing; ~**sprache** *f* written language; ~**steller(in)** **(-s, -)** *m(f)* writer; ~**stück** *nt* document; ~**wechsel** *m* correspondence

schrill [ʃril] *adj* shrill

Schritt [ʃrit] **(-(e)s, -e)** *m* step; (*Gangart*) walk; (*Tempo*) pace; (*von Hose*) crutch; ~ **fahren** to drive at walking pace; ~**macher (-s, -)** *m* pacemaker; ~**tempo** ▲ *nt:* **im ~tempo** at a walking pace

schroff [ʃrɔf] *adj* steep; (*zackig*) jagged; (*fig*) brusque

schröpfen ['ʃrœpfən] *vt* (*fig*) to fleece

Schrot [ʃroːt] **(-(e)s, -e)** *m od nt* (*Blei*) (small) shot; (*Getreide*) coarsely ground grain, groats *pl*; ~**flinte** *f* shotgun

Schrott [ʃrɔt] **(-(e)s, -e)** *m* scrap metal; ~**haufen** *m* scrap heap; **s~reif** *adj* ready for the scrap heap

schrubben ['ʃrubən] *vt* to scrub

Schrubber (-s, -) *m* scrubbing brush

schrumpfen ['ʃrumpfən] *vi* to shrink; (*Apfel*) to shrivel

Schub- ['ʃuːb] *zW:* ~**fach** *nt* drawer; ~**karren** *m* wheelbarrow; ~**lade** *f* drawer

Schubs [ʃuːps] **(-es, -e)** *m* (*umg*) shove (*inf*), push

schüchtern ['ʃʏçtərn] *adj* shy; **S~heit** *f* shyness

Schuft [ʃuft] **(-(e)s, -e)** *m* scoundrel

schuften (*umg*) *vi* to graft, to slave away

Schuh [ʃuː] **(-(e)s, -e)** *m* shoe; ~**band** *nt* shoelace; ~**creme** *f* shoe polish; ~**größe** *f* shoe size; ~**löffel** *m* shoehorn; ~**macher (-s, -)** *m* shoemaker

Schul- *zW:* ~**arbeit** *f* homework (*no pl*); ~**aufgaben** *pl* homework *sg*; ~**besuch** *m*

school attendance; ~**buch** *nt* school book

Schuld [ʃʊlt] (-, **-en**) *f* guilt; (*FIN*) debt; (*Verschulden*) fault; ~ **haben** (**an** +*dat*) to be to blame (for); **er hat ~ it's** his fault; **jdm ~ geben** to blame sb; *siehe* **zuschulden**; s~ *adj*: **s~ sein** (**an** +*dat*) to be to blame (for); **er ist s~** it's his fault; **s~en** [ʃʊldən] *vt* to owe; **s~enfrei** *adj* free from debt; ~**gefühl** *nt* feeling of guilt; **s~ig** *adj* guilty; (*gebührend*) due; **s~ig an etw** *dat* **sein** to be guilty of sth; **jdm etw s~ig sein** to owe sb sth; **jdm etw s~ig bleiben** not to provide sb with sth; **s~los** *adj* innocent, without guilt; ~**ner** (**-s, -**) *m* debtor; ~**schein** *m* promissory note, IOU

Schule [ʃuːlə] *f* school; **s~n** *vt* to train, to school

Schüler(in) [ʃyːlər(ɪn)] (**-s, -**) *m(f)* pupil; ~**austausch** *m* school *od* exchange; ~**ausweis** *m* (school) student card

Schul- *zW*: ~**ferien** *pl* school holidays; **s~frei** *adj*: **s~freier Tag** holiday; **s~frei sein** to be a holiday; ~**hof** *m* playground; ~**jahr** *nt* school year; ~**kind** *nt* schoolchild; **s~pflichtig** *adj* of school age; ~**schiff** *nt* (*NAUT*) training ship; ~**stunde** *f* period, lesson; ~**tasche** *f* school bag

Schulter [ʃʊltər] (**-, -n**) *f* shoulder; ~**blatt** *nt* shoulder blade; **s~n** *vt* to shoulder

Schulung *f* education, schooling

Schulzeugnis *nt* school report

Schund [ʃʊnt] (**-(e)s**) *m* trash, garbage

Schuppe [ʃʊpə] *f* scale; ~**n** *pl* (*Haarschuppen*) dandruff *sg*

Schuppen (**-s, -**) *m* shed

schuppig [ʃʊpɪç] *adj* scaly

Schur [ʃuːr] (**-, -en**) *f* shearing

schüren [ʃyːrən] *vt* to rake; (*fig*) to stir up

schürfen [ʃʏrfən] *vt, vi* to scrape, to scratch; (*MIN*) to prospect

Schurke [ʃʊrkə] (**-n, -n**) *m* rogue

Schurwolle *f*: „**reine ~**" "pure new wool"

Schürze [ʃʏrtsə] *f* apron

Schuss ▲ [ʃʊs] (**-es, ⁺e**) *m* shot; (*WEBEN*) woof; ~**bereich** *m* effective range

Schüssel [ʃʏsəl] (**-, -n**) *f* bowl

Schuss- ▲ *zW*: ~**linie** *f* line of fire; ~**verletzung** *f* bullet wound; ~**waffe** *f* firearm

Schuster [ʃuːstər] (**-s, -**) *m* cobbler, shoemaker

Schutt [ʃʊt] (**-(e)s**) *m* rubbish; (*Bauschutt*) rubble

Schüttelfrost *m* shivering

schütteln [ʃʏtəln] *vt, vr* to shake

schütten [ʃʏtən] *vt* to pour; (*Zucker, Kies etc*) to tip; (*verschütten*) to spill ♦ *vi unpers* to pour (down)

Schutthalde *f* dump

Schutthaufen *m* heap of rubble

Schutz [ʃʊts] (**-es**) *m* protection; (*Unterschlupf*) shelter; **jdn in ~ nehmen** to stand up for sb; ~**anzug** *m* overalls *pl*; ~**blech** *nt* mudguard

Schütze [ʃʏtsə] (**-n, -n**) *m* gunman; (*Gewehrschütze*) rifleman; (*Scharfschütze, Sportschütze*) marksman; (*ASTROL*) Sagittarius

schützen [ʃʏtsən] *vt* to protect; ~ **vor** +*dat od* **gegen** to protect from

Schützenfest *nt* fair featuring shooting matches

Schutz- *zW*: ~**engel** *m* guardian angel; ~**gebiet** *nt* protectorate; (*Naturschutzgebiet*) reserve; ~**hütte** *f* shelter, refuge; ~**impfung** *f* immunisation

Schützling [ʃʏtslɪŋ] *m* protégé(e); (*bes Kind*) charge

Schutz- *zW*: **s~los** *adj* defenceless; ~**mann** *m* policeman; ~**patron** *m* patron saint

Schwaben [ʃvaːbən] *nt* Swabia; **schwäbisch** *adj* Swabian

schwach [ʃvax] *adj* weak, feeble

Schwäche [ʃvɛçə] *f* weakness; **s~n** *vt* to weaken

Schwachheit *f* weakness

schwächlich *adj* weakly, delicate

Schwächling *m* weakling

Schwach- *zW*: ~**sinn** *m* imbecility; **s~sinnig** *adj* mentally deficient; (*Idee*) idiotic; ~**strom** *m* weak current

Schwächung [ʃvɛçʊŋ] *f* weakening

Schwager [ʃvaːgər] (**-s, ⁺**) *m* brother-in-law;

Schwägerin [ʃvɛːgərɪn] *f* sister-in-law

Schwalbe ['ʃvalbə] f swallow

Schwall [ʃval] (-(e)s, -e) m surge; (*Worte*) flood, torrent

Schwamm [ʃvam] (-(e)s, ⁺e) m sponge; (*Pilz*) fungus

schwamm *etc vb siehe* **schwimmen**

schwammig *adj* spongy; (*Gesicht*) puffy

Schwan [ʃvaːn] (-(e)s, ⁺e) m swan

schwanger ['ʃvaŋər] *adj* pregnant; **S~schaft** f pregnancy

schwanken *vi* to sway; (*taumeln*) to stagger, to reel; (*Preise, Zahlen*) to fluctuate; (*zögern*) to hesitate, to vacillate

Schwankung f fluctuation

Schwanz [ʃvants] (-es, ⁺e) m tail

schwänzen ['ʃvɛntsən] (*umg*) vt to skip, to cut ♦ vi to play truant

Schwarm [ʃvarm] (-(e)s, ⁺e) m swarm; (*umg*) heart-throb, idol

schwärm- ['ʃvɛrm] zW: **~en** vi to swarm; **~en für** to be mad *od* wild about; **S~erei** [-ə'raɪ] f enthusiasm; **~erisch** *adj* impassioned, effusive

Schwarte ['ʃvartə] f hard skin; (*Speckschwarte*) rind

schwarz [ʃvarts] *adj* black; **~es Brett** notice board; **ins S~e treffen** (*auch fig*) to hit the bull's eye; **in den ~en Zahlen** in the black; **~ sehen** (*umg*) to see the gloomy side of things; **S~arbeit** f illicit work, moonlighting; **S~brot** nt black bread; **S~e(r)** f(m) (man/woman)

Schwärze ['ʃvɛrtsə] f blackness; (*Farbe*) blacking; (*Druckerschwärze*) printer's ink; **s~n** vt to blacken

Schwarz- zW: **s~fahren** (*unreg*) vi to travel without paying; to drive without a licence; **~handel** m black market (trade); **~markt** m black market; **~wald** m Black Forest; **s~weiß, s~-weiß** *adj* black and white

schwatzen ['ʃvatsən] vi to chatter

schwätzen ['ʃvɛtsən] vi to chatter

Schwätzer ['ʃvɛtsər] (-s, -) m gasbag

schwatzhaft *adj* talkative, gossipy

Schwebe ['ʃveːbə] f: **in der ~** (*fig*) in abeyance; **~bahn** f overhead railway; **s~n** vi to drift, to float; (*hoch*) to soar

Schwed- ['ʃveːd] zW: **~e** m Swede; **~en** nt Sweden; **~in** f Swede; **s~isch** *adj* Swedish

Schwefel ['ʃveːfəl] (-s) m sulphur; **s~ig** *adj* sulphurous; **~säure** f sulphuric acid

Schweig- ['ʃvaɪg] zW: **~egeld** nt hush money; **~en** (-s) nt silence; **s~en** (*unreg*) vi to be silent; to stop talking; **~epflicht** f pledge of secrecy; (*von Anwalt*) requirement of confidentiality; **s~sam** ['ʃvaɪkzaːm] *adj* silent, taciturn; **~samkeit** f taciturnity, quietness

Schwein [ʃvaɪn] (-(e)s, -e) nt pig; (*umg*) (good) luck

Schweine- zW: **~fleisch** nt pork; **~'rei** f mess; (*Gemeinheit*) dirty trick; **~stall** m pigsty

schweinisch *adj* filthy

Schweinsleder nt pigskin

Schweiß [ʃvaɪs] (-es) m sweat, perspiration; **s~en** vt, vi to weld; **~er** (-s, -) m welder; **~füße** pl sweaty feet; **~naht** f weld

Schweiz [ʃvaɪts] f Switzerland; **~er(in)** m(f) Swiss; **s~erisch** *adj* Swiss

schwelgen ['ʃvɛlgən] vi to indulge

Schwelle ['ʃvɛlə] f (*auch fig*) threshold; doorstep; (*EISENB*) sleeper (*BRIT*), tie (*US*)

schwellen (*unreg*) vi to swell

Schwellung f swelling

Schwemme ['ʃvɛmə] f (*WIRTS*: *Überangebot*) surplus

Schwenk- ['ʃvɛŋk] zW: **s~bar** *adj* swivel-mounted; **s~en** vt to swing; (*Fahne*) to wave; (*abspülen*) to rinse ♦ vi to turn, to swivel; (*MIL*) to wheel; **~ung** f turn; wheel

schwer [ʃveːr] *adj* heavy; (*schwierig*) difficult, hard; (*schlimm*) serious, bad ♦ *adv* (*sehr*) very (much); (*verletzt etc*) seriously, badly; **~ erziehbar** difficult (to bring up); **jdm ~ fallen** to be difficult for sb; **jdm/sich etw ~ machen** to make sth difficult for sb/o.s.; **~ nehmen** to take to heart; **sich** *dat od akk* **~ tun** to have difficulties; **~ verdaulich** indigestible, heavy; **~ wiegend** weighty, important; **S~arbeiter** m manual worker, labourer; **S~behinderte(r)** f(m) seriously handicapped person; **S~e** f weight, heaviness; *(PHYS)* gravity; **~elos** adj weightless; *(Kammer)* zero-G; **~fällig** adj ponderous; **S~gewicht** nt heavyweight; *(fig)* emphasis; **~hörig** adj hard of hearing; **S~industrie** f heavy industry; **S~kraft** f gravity; **S~kranke(r)** f(m) person who is seriously ill; **~lich** adv hardly; **~mütig** adj melancholy; **S~punkt** m centre of gravity; *(fig)* emphasis, crucial point

Schwert [fveːrt] **(-(e)s, -er)** nt sword; **~lilie** f iris

schwer- zW: **S~verbrecher(in)** m(f) criminal, serious offender; **S~verletzte(r)** f(m) serious casualty; *(bei Unfall usw auch)* seriously injured person

Schwester ['fvɛstər] **(-, -n)** f sister; *(MED)* nurse; **s~lich** adj sisterly

Schwieger- ['fviːgər] zW: **~eltern** pl parents-in-law; **~mutter** f mother-in-law; **~sohn** m son-in-law; **~tochter** f daughter-in-law; **~vater** m father-in-law

schwierig ['fviːrɪç] adj difficult, hard; **S~keit** f difficulty

Schwimm- ['fvɪm] zW: **~bad** nt swimming baths pl; **~becken** nt swimming pool; **s~en** *(unreg)* vi to swim; *(treiben, nicht sinken)* to float; *(fig: unsicher sein)* to be all at sea; **~er** **(-s, -)** m swimmer; *(Angeln)* float; **~erin** f (female) swimmer; **~lehrer** m swimming instructor; **~weste** f life jacket

Schwindel ['fvɪndəl] **(-s)** m giddiness; dizzy spell; *(Betrug)* swindle, fraud; *(Zeug)* stuff; **s~frei** adj: **s~frei sein** to have a good head for heights; **s~n** *(umg)* vi *(lügen)* to fib; **jdm s~t es** sb feels dizzy

schwinden ['fvɪndən] *(unreg)* vi to disappear; *(sich verringern)* to decrease; *(Kräfte)* to decline

Schwindler ['fvɪndlər] m swindler; *(Lügner)* liar

schwindlig adj dizzy; **mir ist ~** I feel dizzy

Schwing- ['fvɪŋ] zW: **s~en** *(unreg)* vt to swing; *(Waffe etc)* to brandish ♦ vi to swing; *(vibrieren)* to vibrate; *(klingen)* to sound; **~tür** f swing door(s); **~ung** f vibration;

(PHYS) oscillation

Schwips [fvɪps] **(-es, -e)** m: **einen ~ haben** to be tipsy

schwirren ['fvɪrən] vi to buzz

schwitzen ['fvɪtsən] vi to sweat, to perspire

schwören ['fvøːrən] *(unreg)* vt, vi to swear

schwul [fvuːl] *(umg)* adj gay, queer

schwül [fvyːl] adj sultry, close; **S~e** **(-)** f sultriness

Schwule(r) *(umg)* f(m) gay (man/woman)

Schwung [fvʊŋ] **(-(e)s, ᵉe)** m swing; *(Triebkraft)* momentum; *(fig: Energie)* verve, energy; *(umg: Menge)* batch; **s~haft** adj brisk, lively; **s~voll** adj vigorous

Schwur [fvuːr] **(-(e)s, ᵉe)** m oath; **~gericht** nt court with a jury

sechs [zɛks] num six; **~hundert** num six hundred; **~te(r, s)** adj sixth; **S~tel** **(-s, -)** nt sixth

sechzehn ['zɛçtseːn] num sixteen

sechzig ['zɛçtsɪç] num sixty

See¹ [zeː] **(-, -n)** f sea

See² [zeː] **(-s, -n)** m lake

See- [zeː] zW: **~bad** nt seaside resort; **~hund** m seal; **~igel** ['zeːiːgəl] m sea urchin; **s~krank** adj seasick; **~krankheit** f seasickness; **~lachs** m rock salmon

Seele ['zeːlə] f soul; **s~nruhig** adv calmly

Seeleute ['zeːlɔytə] pl seamen

Seel- zW: **s~isch** adj mental; **~sorge** f pastoral duties pl; **~sorger** **(-s, -)** m clergyman

See- zW: **~macht** f naval power; **~mann** (pl **-leute**) m seaman, sailor; **~meile** f nautical mile; **~möwe** f *(ZOOL)* seagull; **~not** f distress; **~räuber** m pirate; **~rose** f water lily; **~stern** m starfish; **s~tüchtig** adj seaworthy; **~weg** m sea route; **auf dem ~weg** by sea; **~zunge** f sole

Segel ['zeːgəl] **(-s, -)** nt sail; **~boot** nt yacht; **~fliegen** **(-s)** nt gliding; **~flieger** m glider pilot; **~flugzeug** nt glider; **s~n** vt, vi to sail; **~schiff** nt sailing vessel; **~sport** m sailing; **~tuch** nt canvas

Segen ['zeːgən] **(-s, -)** m blessing

Segler ['zeːglər] **(-s, -)** m sailor, yachtsman

segnen ['zeːgnən] vt to bless

eh- ['ze:] zW: **s~behindert** adj partially
sighted; **s~en** (unreg) vt, vi to see; (in
bestimmte Richtung) to look; **mal s~en(, ob
...)** let's see (if ...); **siehe Seite 5** see page
5; **s~enswert** adj worth seeing;
~enswürdigkeiten pl sights (of a town);
~fehler m sight defect

ehne ['ze:nə] f sinew; (an Bogen) string

ehnen vr: **sich ~ nach** to long od yearn
for

ehnig adj sinewy

ehn- zW: **s~lich** adj ardent; **~sucht** f
longing; **s~süchtig** adj longing

ehr [ze:r] adv very; (mit Verben) a lot, (very)
much; **zu ~** too much; **~ geehrte(r) ...**
dear ...

eicht [zaiçt] adj (auch fig) shallow

eide ['zaidə] f silk; **s~n** adj silk; **~npapier**
nt tissue paper

eidig ['zaidiç] adj silky

eife ['zaifə] f soap

eifen- zW: **~lauge** f soapsuds pl;
~schale f soap dish; **~schaum** m lather

eihen ['zaiən] vt to strain, to filter

eil [zail] (-(e)s, -e) nt rope; cable; **~bahn** f
cable railway; **~hüpfen** (-s) nt skipping;
~springen (-s) nt skipping; **~tänzer(in)**
m(f) tightrope walker

SCHLÜSSELWORT

ein [zain] (pt **war**, pp **gewesen**) vi **1** to be;
ich bin I am; **du bist** you are; **er/sie/es
ist** he/she/it is; **wir sind/ihr seid/sie sind**
we/you/they are; **wir waren** we were; **wir
sind gewesen** we have been

2: seien Sie nicht böse don't be angry;
sei so gut und ... be so kind as to ...; **das
wäre gut** that would od that'd be a good
thing; **wenn ich Sie wäre** if I were od was
you; **das wärs** that's all, that's it; **morgen
bin ich in Rom** tomorrow I'll od I will od I
shall be in Rome; **waren Sie mal in Rom?**
have you ever been to Rome?

3: wie ist das zu verstehen? how is that
to be understood?; **er ist nicht zu
ersetzen** he cannot be replaced; **mit ihr
ist nicht zu reden** you can't talk to her

4: mir ist kalt I'm cold; **was ist?** what's
the matter?, what is it?; **ist was?** is
something the matter?; **es sei denn, dass
...** unless ...; **wie dem auch sei** be that as
it may; **wie wäre es mit ...?** how od what
about ...?; **lass das sein!** stop that!

---

sein(e) ['zain(ə)] adj his; its; **~e(r, s)** pron
his; its; **~er** (gen von **er**) pron of him;
~erseits adv for his part; **~erzeit** adv in
those days, formerly; **~esgleichen** pron
people like him; **~etwegen** adv (für ihn)
for his sake; (wegen ihm) on his account;
(von ihm aus) as far as he is concerned;
~etwillen adv: **um ~etwillen** =
seinetwegen; ~ige pron: **der/die/das
~ige** od **S~ige** his

seit [zait] präp +dat since ♦ konj since; **er ist
~ einer Woche hier** he has been here for a
week; **~ langem** for a long time; **~dem**
[zait'de:m] adv, konj since

Seite ['zaitə] f side; (Buchseite) page; (MIL)
flank

Seiten- zW: **~ansicht** f side view; **~hieb** m
(fig) passing shot, dig; **s~s** präp +gen on
the part of; **~schiff** nt aisle; **~sprung** m
extramarital escapade; **~stechen** nt (a)
stitch; **~straße** f side road; **~streifen** m
verge; (der Autobahn) hard shoulder

seither [zait'he:r] adv, konj since (then)

seit- zW: **~lich** adj on one od the side; side
cpd; **~wärts** adv sidewards

Sekretär [zekre'tɛ:r] m secretary; (Möbel)
bureau

Sekretariat [zekretari'a:t] (-(e)s, -e) nt
secretary's office, secretariat

Sekretärin f secretary

Sekt [zɛkt] (-(e)s, -e) m champagne

Sekte ['zɛktə] f sect

Sekunde [ze'kʊndə] f second

selber ['zɛlbər] = **selbst**

Selbst [zɛlpst] (-) nt self

SCHLÜSSELWORT

selbst [zɛlpst] pron **1**: **ich/er/wir selbst** I
myself/he himself/we ourselves; **sie ist die
Tugend selbst** she's virtue itself; **er braut**

Spelling Reform: ▲ *new spelling* △ *old spelling (to be phased out)*

sein Bier selbst he brews his own beer;
wie gehts? - gut, und selbst? how are
things? - fine, and yourself?
2 (*ohne Hilfe*) alone, on my/his/one's *etc*
own; **von selbst** by itself; **er kam von
selbst** he came of his own accord; **selbst
gemacht** home-made
♦ *adv* even; **selbst wenn** even if; **selbst
Gott** even God (himself)

selbständig *etc* ['zɛlpʃtɛndɪç] = **selbstständig** *etc*
Selbst- *zW*: **~auslöser** *m* (*PHOT*) delayed-
action shutter release; **~bedienung** *f* self-
service; **~befriedigung** *f* masturbation;
~beherrschung *f* self-control;
~bestimmung *f* (*POL*) self-determination;
~beteiligung *f* (*VERSICHERUNG: bei Kosten*)
(voluntary) excess; **s~bewusst** ▲ *adj*
(self-)confident; **~bewusstsein** ▲ *nt* self-
confidence; **~erhaltung** *f* self-preservation;
~erkenntnis *f* self-knowledge; **s~gefällig**
adj smug, self-satisfied; **~gespräch** *nt*
conversation with o.s.; **~kostenpreis** *m*
cost price; **s~los** *adj* unselfish, selfless;
~mord *m* suicide; **~mörder(in)** *m(f)*
suicide; **s~mörderisch** *adj* suicidal;
s~sicher *adj* self-assured; **s~ständig** ▲
adj independent; **~ständigkeit** ▲ *f*
independence; **s~süchtig** *adj* (*Mensch*)
selfish; **~versorger (-s, -)** *m* (*im Urlaub etc*)
self-caterer; **s~verständlich**
['zɛlpstfɛrʃtɛntlɪç] *adj* obvious ♦ *adv* naturally;
ich halte das für s~verständlich I take
that for granted; **~verteidigung** *f* self-
defence; **~vertrauen** *nt* self-confidence;
~verwaltung *f* autonomy, self-
government

selig ['ze:lɪç] *adj* happy, blissful; (*REL*)
blessed; (*tot*) late; **S~keit** *f* bliss
Sellerie ['zɛləri:] **(-s, -(s)** *od* **-, -)** *m od f*
celery
selten ['zɛltən] *adj* rare ♦ *adv* seldom, rarely;
S~heit *f* rarity
Selterswasser ['zɛltərsvasər] *nt* soda water
seltsam ['zɛltza:m] *adj* strange, curious;
S~keit *f* strangeness

Semester [ze'mɛstər] **(-s, -)** *nt* semester;
~ferien *pl* vacation *sg*
Semi- [zemi] *in zW* semi-; **~kolon** [-'ko:lɔn]
(-s, -s) *nt* semicolon
Seminar [zemi'na:r] **(-s, -e)** *nt* seminary;
(*Kurs*) seminar; (*UNIV: Ort*) department
building
Semmel ['zɛməl] **(-, -n)** *f* roll
Senat [ze'na:t] **(-(e)s, -e)** *m* senate, council
Sende- ['zɛndə] *zW*: **~bereich** *m*
transmission range; **~folge** *f* (*Serie*) series;
s~n (*unreg*) *vt* to send; (*RADIO, TV*) to
transmit, to broadcast ♦ *vi* to transmit, to
broadcast; **~r (-s, -)** *m* station; (*Anlage*)
transmitter; **~reihe** *f* series (of broadcasts)
Sendung ['zɛndʊŋ] *f* consignment;
(*Aufgabe*) mission; (*RADIO, TV*) transmission;
(*Programm*) programme
Senf [zɛnf] **(-(e)s, -e)** *m* mustard
senil [ze'ni:l] (*pej*) *adj* senile
Senior(in) ['ze:niɔr(ɪn)] **(-s, -en)** *m(f)*
(*Mensch im Rentenalter*) (old age) pensioner
Seniorenheim [zeni'o:rənhaɪm] *nt* old
people's home
Senk- ['zɛŋk] *zW*: **~blei** *nt* plumb; **~e** *f*
depression; **s~en** *vt* to lower ♦ *vr* to sink,
to drop gradually; **s~recht** *adj* vertical,
perpendicular; **~rechte** *f* perpendicular;
~rechtstarter *m* (*AVIAT*) vertical take-off
plane; (*fig*) high-flyer
Sensation [zɛnzatsi'o:n] *f* sensation; **s~ell**
[-'nɛl] *adj* sensational
sensibel [zɛn'zi:bəl] *adj* sensitive
sentimental [zɛntimɛn'ta:l] *adj* sentimental;
S~i'tät *f* sentimentality
separat [zepa'ra:t] *adj* separate
September [zɛp'tɛmbər] **(-(s), -)** *m*
September
Serie ['ze:riə] *f* series
serien- *zW*: **~mäßig** *adj* standard;
S~mörder(in) *m(f)* serial killer; **~weise**
adv in series
seriös [zeri'ø:s] *adj* serious, bona fide
Service¹ [zɛr'vi:s] **(-(s), -)** *nt* (*Geschirr*) set,
service
Service² **(-, -s)** *m* service
servieren [zɛr'vi:rən] *vt, vi* to serve

Serviererin [zɛr'viːrərɪn] f waitress
Serviette [zɛrvi'ɛtə] f napkin, serviette
Servo- ['zɛrvo] zW: **~bremse** f (AUT) servo(-assisted) brake; **~lenkung** f (AUT) power steering
Sessel ['zɛsəl] **(-s, -)** m armchair; **~lift** m chairlift
sesshaft ▲ ['zɛshaft] adj settled; (ansässig) resident
setzen ['zɛtsən] vt to put, to set; (Baum etc) to plant; (Segel, TYP) to set ♦ vr to settle; (Person) to sit down ♦ vi (springen) to leap; (wetten) to bet
Setz- ['zɛts] zW: **~er (-s, -)** m (TYP) compositor; **~ling** m young plant
Seuche ['zɔʏçə] f epidemic; **~ngebiet** nt infected area
seufzen ['zɔʏftsən] vt, vi to sigh
Seufzer ['zɔʏftsɐ] **(-s, -)** m sigh
Sex [zɛks] **(-(es))** m sex; **~ualität** [-uali'tɛt] f sex, sexuality; **~ualkunde** [zɛksu'a:l-] f (SCH) sex education; **s~uell** [-u'ɛl] adj sexual
Shampoo [ʃam'puː] **(-s, -s)** nt shampoo
Sibirien [zi'biːriən] nt Siberia

sich [zɪç] pron 1 (akk): **er/sie/es ... sich** he/she/it ... himself/herself/itself; **sie** pl/ **man ... sich** they/one ... themselves/ oneself; **Sie ... sich** you ... yourself/ yourselves pl; **sich wiederholen** to repeat oneself/itself
2 (dat): **er/sie/es ... sich** he/she/it ... himself/herself/itself; **sie** pl/**man ... sich** they/one ... to themselves/oneself; **Sie ... sich** you ... to yourself/yourselves pl; **sie hat sich einen Pullover gekauft** she bought herself a jumper; **sich die Haare waschen** to wash one's hair
3 (mit Präposition): **haben Sie Ihren Ausweis bei sich?** do you have your pass on you?; **er hat nichts bei sich** he's got nothing on him; **sie bleiben gern unter sich** they keep themselves to themselves
4 (einander) each other, one another; **sie bekämpfen sich** they fight each other od

one another
5: **dieses Auto fährt sich gut** this car drives well; **hier sitzt es sich gut** it's good to sit here

Sichel ['zɪçəl] **(-, -n)** f sickle; (Mondsichel) crescent
sicher ['zɪçɐ] adj safe; (gewiss) certain; (zuverlässig) secure, reliable; (selbstsicher) confident; **vor jdm/etw ~ sein** to be safe from sb/sth; **ich bin nicht ~** I'm not sure od certain; **~ nicht** surely not; **aber ~!** of course!; **~gehen** (unreg) vi to make sure
Sicherheit ['zɪçɐhaɪt] f safety; (auch FIN) security; (Gewissheit) certainty; (Selbstsicherheit) confidence
Sicherheits- zW: **~abstand** m safe distance; **~glas** nt safety glass; **~gurt** m safety belt; **s~halber** adv for safety; to be on the safe side; **~nadel** f safety pin; **~schloss** ▲ nt safety lock; **~vorkehrung** f safety precaution
sicher- zW: **~lich** adv certainly, surely; **~n** vt to secure; (schützen) to protect; (Waffe) to put the safety catch on; **jdm etw ~n** to secure sth for sb; **sich** dat **etw ~n** to secure sth (for o.s.); **~stellen** vt to impound; (COMPUT) to save; **S~ung** f (S~n) securing; (Vorrichtung) safety device; (an Waffen) safety catch; (ELEK) fuse; **S~ungskopie** f back-up copy
Sicht [zɪçt] **(-)** f sight; (Aussicht) view; **auf** od **nach ~** (FIN) at sight; **auf lange ~** on a long-term basis; **s~bar** adj visible; **s~en** vt to sight; (auswählen) to sort out; **s~lich** adj evident, obvious; **~verhältnisse** pl visibility sg; **~vermerk** m visa; **~weite** f visibility
sickern ['zɪkɐn] vi to trickle, to seep
Sie [ziː] **(-, -)** (nom, akk) pron you
sie [ziː] pron (sg: nom) she, it; (: akk) her, it; (pl: nom) they; (: akk) them
Sieb [ziːp] **(-(e)s, -e)** nt sieve; (KOCH) strainer; **s~en**[1] ['ziːbən] vt to sift; (Flüssigkeit) to strain
sieben[2] num seven; **~hundert** num seven hundred; **S~sachen** pl belongings

siebte(r, s) ['ziːptə(r, s)] *adj* seventh; **S~l**
(-s, -) *nt* seventh

siebzehn ['ziːptseːn] *num* seventeen

siebzig ['ziːptsɪç] *num* seventy

siedeln ['ziːdəln] *vi* to settle

sieden ['ziːdən] *vt, vi* to boil, to simmer

Siedepunkt *m* boiling point

Siedler (-s, -) *m* settler

Siedlung *f* settlement; *(Häusersiedlung)*
housing estate

Sieg [ziːk] **(-(e)s, -e)** *m* victory

Siegel ['ziːgəl] **(-s, -)** *nt* seal; **~ring** *m* signet
ring

Sieg- *zW:* **s~en** *vi* to be victorious; *(SPORT)*
to win; **~er (-s, -)** *m* victor; *(SPORT etc)*
winner; **s~reich** *adj* victorious

siehe *etc* ['ziːə] *vb siehe* **sehen**

siezen ['ziːtsən] *vt* to address as "Sie"

Signal [zɪ'gnaːl] **(-s, -e)** *nt* signal

Silbe ['zɪlbə] *f* syllable

Silber ['zɪlbər] **(-s)** *nt* silver; **~hochzeit** *f*
silver wedding (anniversary); **s~n** *adj* silver;
~papier *nt* silver paper

Silvester [zɪl'vɛstər] **(-s, -)** *nt* New Year's
Eve, Hogmanay (*SCOTTISH*); **~abend** *m* =
Silvester

Silvester

> 🛈 **Silvester** is the German word for New
> Year's Eve. Although not an official
> holiday most businesses close early and
> shops shut at midday. Most Germans
> celebrate in the evening, and at midnight
> they let off fireworks and rockets; the revelry
> usually lasts until the early hours of the
> morning.

---

simpel ['zɪmpəl] *adj* simple

Sims [zɪms] **(-es, -e)** *nt od m (Kaminsims)*
mantelpiece; *(Fenstersims)* (window)sill

simsen ['zɪmzn] *vti* to text

simulieren [zimu'liːrən] *vt* to simulate;
(vortäuschen) to feign ♦ *vi* to feign illness

simultan [zimʊl'taːn] *adj* simultaneous

Sinfonie [zɪnfo'niː] *f* symphony

singen ['zɪŋən] *(unreg)* *vt, vi* to sing

Singular ['zɪŋgulaːr] *m* singular

Singvogel ['zɪŋfoːgəl] *m* songbird

sinken ['zɪŋkən] *(unreg)* *vi* to sink; *(Preise etc)*
to fall, to go down

Sinn [zɪn] **(-(e)s, -e)** *m* mind;
(Wahrnehmungssinn) sense; *(Bedeutung)*
sense, meaning; **~ für etw** sense of sth;
von ~en sein to be out of one's mind; **es**
hat keinen ~ there's no point; **~bild** *nt*
symbol; **s~en** *(unreg)* *vi* to ponder; **auf**
etw *akk* **s~en** to contemplate sth;
~estäuschung *f* illusion; **s~gemäß** *adj*
faithful; *(Wiedergabe)* in one's own words;
s~ig *adj* clever; **s~lich** *adj* sensual,
sensuous; *(Wahrnehmung)* sensory;
~lichkeit *f* sensuality; **s~los** *adj* senseless;
meaningless; **~losigkeit** *f* senselessness;
meaninglessness; **s~voll** *adj* meaningful;
(vernünftig) sensible

Sintflut ['zɪntfluːt] *f* Flood

Sippe ['zɪpə] *f* clan, kin

Sippschaft ['zɪpʃaft] *(pej)* *f* relations *pl*,
tribe; *(Bande)* gang

Sirene [zi'reːnə] *f* siren

Sirup ['ziːrʊp] **(-s, -e)** *m* syrup

Sitt- ['zɪt] *zW:* **~e** *f* custom; **~en** *pl (~lichkeit)*
morals; **~enpolizei** *f* vice squad; **s~sam**
adj modest, demure

Situation [zituatsi'oːn] *f* situation

Sitz [zɪts] **(-es, -e)** *m* seat; **der Anzug hat**
einen guten ~ the suit is a good fit; **s~en**
(unreg) *vi* to sit; *(Bemerkung, Schlag)* to strike
home, to tell; *(Gelerntes)* to have sunk in;
s~en bleiben to remain seated; *(SCH)* to
have to repeat a year; **auf etw** *dat* **s~en**
bleiben to be lumbered with sth; **s~en**
lassen *(SCH)* to make (sb) repeat a year;
(Mädchen) to jilt; *(Wartenden)* to stand up;
etw auf sich *dat* **s~en lassen** to take sth
lying down; **s~end** *adj (Tätigkeit)*
sedentary; **~gelegenheit** *f* place to sit
down; **~platz** *m* seat; **~streik** *m* sit-down
strike; **~ung** *f* meeting

Sizilien [zi'tsiːliən] *nt* Sicily

Skala ['skaːla] **(-, Skalen)** *f* scale

Skalpell [skal'pɛl] **(-s, -e)** *nt* scalpel

Skandal [skan'daːl] **(-s, -e)** *m* scandal; **s~ös**
[-'løːs] *adj* scandalous

Skandinav- [skandi'na:v] zW: **~ien** nt Scandinavia; **~ier(in)** m(f) Scandinavian; **s~isch** adj Scandinavian

Skelett [ske'lɛt] **(-(e)s, -e)** nt skeleton

Skepsis ['skɛpsɪs] **(-)** f scepticism

skeptisch ['skɛptɪʃ] adj sceptical

Ski [ʃiː] **(-s, -er)** m ski; **~ laufen** od **fahren** to ski; **~fahrer** m skier; **~gebiet** nt ski(ing) area; **~läufer** m skier; **~lehrer** m ski instructor; **~lift** m ski-lift; **~springen** nt ski-jumping; **~stock** m ski-pole

Skizze ['skɪtsə] f sketch

skizzieren [skɪ'tsiːrən] vt, vi to sketch

Sklave ['skla:və] **(-n, -n)** m slave; **~rei** f slavery; **Sklavin** f slave

Skorpion [skɔrpi'oːn] **(-s, -e)** m scorpion; (ASTROL) Scorpio

Skrupel ['skru:pəl] **(-s, -)** m scruple; **s~los** adj unscrupulous

Skulptur [skʊlp'tuːr] f (Gegenstand) sculpture

Slip [slɪp] **(-s, -s)** m (under)pants; **~einlage** f panty liner

Slowakei [slova'kai] f: **die ~** Slovakia

Slowenien [slo've:niən] nt Slovenia

Smaragd [sma'rakt] **(-(e)s, -e)** m emerald

Smoking ['smo:kɪŋ] **(-s, -s)** m dinner jacket

SMS abbr (= Short Message Service) text message

Snowboarding ['sno:bɔːbdɪŋ] nt snowboarding

---

so [zo:] adv **1** (so sehr) so; **so groß/schön etc** so big/nice etc; **so groß/schön wie ...** as big/nice as ...; **so viel (wie)** as much as; **rede nicht so viel** don't talk so much; **so weit sein** to be ready; **so weit wie** od **als möglich** as far as possible; **ich bin so weit zufrieden** by and large I'm quite satisfied; **so wenig (wie)** as little (as); **das hat ihn so geärgert, dass ...** that annoyed him so much that ...; **so einer wie ich** somebody like me; **na so was!** well, well!

2 (auf diese Weise) like this; **mach es nicht so** don't do it like that; **so oder so** in one way or the other; **und so weiter** and so on; **... oder so was** ... or something like

that; **das ist gut so** that's fine; **so genannt** so-called

3 (umg: umsonst): **ich habe es so bekommen** I got it for nothing

♦ konj: **so dass, sodass** so that; **so wie es jetzt ist** as things are at the moment

♦ excl: **so?** really?; **so, das wärs** so, that's it then

---

s. o. abk = **siehe oben**

Socke ['zɔkə] f sock

Sockel ['zɔkəl] **(-s, -)** m pedestal, base

sodass ▲ [zo'das] konj so that

Sodawasser ['zo:davasər] nt soda water

Sodbrennen ['zo:tbrɛnən] **(-s, -)** nt heartburn

soeben [zo'e:bən] adv just (now)

Sofa ['zo:fa] **(-s, -s)** nt sofa

sofern [zo'fɛrn] konj if, provided (that)

sofort [zo'fɔrt] adv immediately, at once; **~ig** adj immediate

Sog [zo:k] **(-(e)s, -e)** m (Strömung) undertow

sogar [zo'ga:r] adv even

sogleich [zo'glaiç] adv straight away, at once

Sohle ['zo:lə] f sole; (Talsohle etc) bottom; (MIN) level

Sohn [zo:n] **(-(e)s, ⁺e)** m son

Solar- [zo'la:r] in zW solar; **~zelle** f solar cell

solch [zɔlç] pron such; **ein ~e(r, s) ...** such a ...

Soldat [zɔl'da:t] **(-en, -en)** m soldier

Söldner ['zœldnər] **(-s, -)** m mercenary

solidarisch [zoli'da:rɪʃ] adj in od with solidarity; **sich ~ erklären** to declare one's solidarity

Solidari'tät f solidarity

solid(e) [zo'li:d(ə)] adj solid; (Leben, Person) respectable

Solist(in) [zo'lɪst(ɪn)] m(f) soloist

Soll [zɔl] **(-s, (s))** nt (FIN) debit (side); (Arbeitsmenge) quota, target

---

sollen ['zɔlən] (pt **sollte**, pp **gesollt** od (als Hilfsverb) **sollen**) Hilfsverb **1** (Pflicht, Befehl) to be supposed to; **du hättest nicht gehen**

---

sollen you shouldn't have gone, you oughtn't to have gone; **soll ich?** shall I?; **soll ich dir helfen?** shall I help you?; **sag ihm, er soll warten** tell him he's to wait; **was soll ich machen?** what should I do? 2 (*Vermutung*): **sie soll verheiratet sein** she's said to be married; **was soll das heißen?** what's that supposed to mean?; **man sollte glauben, dass ...** you would think that ...; **sollte das passieren, ...** if that should happen ...
♦ *vt, vi*: **was soll das?** what's all this?; **das sollst du nicht** you shouldn't do that; **was solls?** what the hell!

Solo ['zo:lo] (**-s, -s** *od* **Soli**) *nt* solo
somit [zo'mɪt] *konj* and so, therefore
Sommer ['zɔmər] (**-s, -**) *m* summer; **s~lich** *adj* summery; summer; **~reifen** *m* normal tyre; **~schlussverkauf** ▲ *m* summer sale; **~sprossen** *pl* freckles
Sonde ['zɔndə] *f* probe
Sonder- ['zɔndər] *in zW* special; **~angebot** *nt* special offer; **s~bar** *adj* strange, odd; **~fahrt** *f* special trip; **~fall** *m* special case; **s~lich** *adj* particular; (*außergewöhnlich*) remarkable; (*eigenartig*) peculiar; **~marke** *f* special issue stamp; **s~n** *konj* but ♦ *vt* to separate; **nicht nur ..., s~n auch** not only ..., but also; **~preis** *m* special reduced price; **~zug** *m* special train
Sonnabend ['zɔn|a:bənt] *m* Saturday
Sonne ['zɔnə] *f* sun; **s~n** *vr* to sun o.s.
Sonnen- *zW*: **~aufgang** *m* sunrise; **s~baden** *vi* to sunbathe; **~brand** *m* sunburn; **~brille** *f* sunglasses *pl*; **~creme** *f* suntan lotion; **~energie** *f* solar energy, solar power; **~finsternis** *f* solar eclipse; **~kollektor** *m* solar panel; **~schein** *m* sunshine; **~schirm** *m* parasol, sunshade; **~schutzfaktor** *m* protection factor; **~stich** *m* sunstroke; **~uhr** *f* sundial; **~untergang** *m* sunset; **~wende** *f* solstice
sonnig ['zɔnɪç] *adj* sunny
Sonntag ['zɔnta:k] *m* Sunday
sonst [zɔnst] *adv* otherwise; (*mit pron, in Fragen*) else; (*zu anderer Zeit*) at other times,

normally ♦ *konj* otherwise; **~ noch etwas?** anything else?; **~ nichts** nothing else; **~ jemand** anybody (at all); **~ wo** somewhere else; **~ woher** from somewhere else; **~ wohin** somewhere else; **~ig** *adj* other
sooft [zo'ɔft] *konj* whenever
Sopran [zo'pra:n] (**-s, -e**) *m* soprano
Sorge ['zɔrgə] *f* care, worry
sorgen *vi*: **für jdn ~** to look after sb ♦ *vr*: **sich ~ (um)** to worry (about); **für etw ~** to take care of *od* see to sth; **~frei** *adj* carefree; **~voll** *adj* troubled, worried
Sorgerecht *nt* custody (of a child)
Sorg- [zɔrk] *zW*: **~falt** (**-**) *f* care(fulness); **s~fältig** *adj* careful; **s~los** *adj* careless; (*ohne ~en*) carefree; **s~sam** *adj* careful
Sorte ['zɔrtə] *f* sort; (*Warensorte*) brand; **~n** *pl* (FIN) foreign currency *sg*
sortieren [zɔr'ti:rən] *vt* to sort (out)
Sortiment [zɔrti'mɛnt] *nt* assortment
sosehr [zo'ze:r] *konj* as much as
Soße ['zo:sə] *f* sauce; (*Bratensoße*) gravy
soufflieren [zu'fli:rən] *vt, vi* to prompt
Souterrain [zute'rɛ̃:] (**-s, -s**) *nt* basement
souverän [zuvə'rɛ:n] *adj* sovereign; (*überlegen*) superior
so- *zW*: **~viel** [zo'fi:l] *konj*: **~viel ich weiß** as far as I know; *siehe* **so**; **~weit** [zo'vaɪt] *konj* as far as; *siehe* **so**; **~wenig** [zo've:nɪç] *konj* little as; *siehe* **so**; **~wie** [zo'vi:] *konj* (*~bald*) as soon as; (*ebenso*) as well as; **~wieso** [zovi'zo:] *adv* anyway
sowjetisch [zɔ'vjɛtɪʃ] *adj* Soviet
Sowjetunion *f* Soviet Union
sowohl [zo'vo:l] *konj*: **~ ... als** *od* **wie auch** both ... and
sozial [zotsi'a:l] *adj* social; **S~abgaben** *pl* national insurance contributions; **S~arbeiter(in)** *m(f)* social worker; **S~demokrat** *m* social democrat; **~demokratisch** *adj* social democratic; **S~hilfe** *f* income support (BRIT), welfare (aid) (US); **~i'sieren** *vt* to socialize; **S~ismus** [-'lɪsmʊs] *m* socialism; **S~ist** [-'lɪst] *m* socialist; **~istisch** *adj* socialist; **S~politik** *f* social welfare policy; **S~produkt** *nt* (net) national product;

S~staat m welfare state;
S~versicherung f national insurance (BRIT), social security (US); S~wohnung f council flat

soziologisch [zotsio'lo:gɪʃ] adj sociological

sozusagen [zotsu'za:gən] adv so to speak

Spachtel ['ʃpaxtəl] (-s, -) m spatula

spähen ['ʃpɛːən] vi to peep, to peek

Spalier [ʃpa'liːr] (-s, -e) nt (Gerüst) trellis; (Leute) guard of honour

Spalt [ʃpalt] (-(e)s, -e) m crack; (Türspalt) chink; (fig: Kluft) split; ~e f crack, fissure; (Gletscherspalte) crevasse; (in Text) column; s~en vt, vr (auch fig) to split; ~ung f splitting

Span [ʃpaːn] (-(e)s, ⁺e) m shaving

Spanferkel nt sucking pig

Spange ['ʃpaŋə] f clasp; (Haarspange) hair slide; (Schnalle) buckle

Spanien ['ʃpaːniən] nt Spain; **Spanier(in)** m(f) Spaniard; **spanisch** adj Spanish

Spann- ['ʃpan] zW: ~beton m prestressed concrete; ~betttuch ▲ nt fitted sheet; ~e f (Zeitspanne) space; (Differenz) gap; s~en vt (straffen) to tighten, to tauten; (befestigen) to brace ♦ vi to be tight; s~end adj exciting, gripping; ~ung f tension; (ELEK) voltage; (fig) suspense; (unangenehm) tension

Spar- ['ʃpaːr] zW: ~buch nt savings book; ~büchse f money box; s~en vt, vi to save; **sich** dat **etw s~en** to save o.s. sth; (Bemerkung) to keep sth to o.s.; **mit etw s~en** to be sparing with sth; **an etw** dat **s~en** to economize on sth; ~er (-s, -) m saver

Spargel ['ʃpargəl] (-s, -) m asparagus

Sparkasse f savings bank

Sparkonto nt savings account

spärlich ['ʃpɛːrlɪç] adj meagre; (Bekleidung) scanty

Spar- zW: ~preis m economy price; s~sam adj economical, thrifty; ~samkeit f thrift, economizing; ~schwein nt piggy bank

Sparte ['ʃpartə] f field; line of business; (PRESSE) column

Spaß [ʃpaːs] (-es, ⁺e) m joke; (Freude) fun; **jdm ~ machen** to be fun (for sb); **viel ~!** have fun!; s~en vi to joke; **mit ihm ist nicht zu s~en** you can't take liberties with him; s~haft adj funny, droll; s~ig adj funny, droll

spät [ʃpɛːt] adj, adv late; **wie ~ ist es?** what's the time?

Spaten ['ʃpaːtən] (-s, -) m spade

später adj, adv later

spätestens adv at the latest

Spätvorstellung f late show

Spatz [ʃpats] (-en, -en) m sparrow

spazier- [ʃpa'tsiːr] zW: ~en vi to stroll, to walk; ~en fahren to go for a drive; ~en gehen to go for a walk; S~gang m walk; S~stock m walking stick; S~weg m path, walk

Specht [ʃpɛçt] (-(e)s, -e) m woodpecker

Speck [ʃpɛk] (-(e)s, -e) m bacon

Spediteur [ʃpedi'tøːr] m carrier; (Möbelspediteur) furniture remover

Spedition [ʃpeditsi'oːn] f carriage; (~sfirma) road haulage contractor; removal firm

Speer [ʃpeːr] (-(e)s, -e) m spear; (SPORT) javelin

Speiche ['ʃpaɪçə] f spoke

Speichel ['ʃpaɪçəl] (-s) m saliva, spit(tle)

Speicher ['ʃpaɪçər] (-s, -) m storehouse; (Dachspeicher) attic, loft; (Kornspeicher) granary; (Wasserspeicher) tank; (TECH) store; (COMPUT) memory; s~n vt to store; (COMPUT) to save

speien ['ʃpaɪən] (unreg) vt, vi to spit; (erbrechen) to vomit; (Vulkan) to spew

Speise ['ʃpaɪzə] f food; ~eis [-|aɪs] nt ice-cream; ~kammer f larder, pantry; ~karte f menu; s~n vt to feed; to eat ♦ vi to dine; ~röhre f gullet, oesophagus; ~saal m dining room; ~wagen m dining car

Speku- [ʃpeku] zW: ~lant m speculator; ~lation [-latsi'oːn] f speculation; s~lieren [-'liːrən] vi (fig) to speculate; **auf etw** akk **s~lieren** to have hopes of sth

Spelunke [ʃpe'luŋka] f dive

Spende ['ʃpɛndə] f donation; s~n vt to donate, to give; ~r (-s, -) m donor, donator

spendieren [ʃpɛnˈdiːrən] *vt* to pay for, to buy; **jdm etw ~** to treat sb to sth, to stand sb sth

Sperling [ˈʃpɛrlɪŋ] *m* sparrow

Sperma [ˈʃpɛrma] **(-s, Spermen)** *nt* sperm

Sperr- [ˈʃpɛr] *zW:* **~e** *f* barrier; (*Verbot*) ban; **s~en** *vt* to block; (*SPORT*) to suspend, to bar; (*vom Ball*) to obstruct; (*einschließen*) to lock; (*verbieten*) to ban ♦ *vr* to baulk, to jib(e); **~gebiet** *nt* prohibited area; **~holz** *nt* plywood; **s~ig** *adj* bulky; **~müll** *m* bulky refuse; **~sitz** *m* (*THEAT*) stalls *pl*; **~stunde** *f* closing time

Spesen [ˈʃpeːzən] *pl* expenses

Spezial- [ʃpetsiˈaːl] *in zW* special; **~gebiet** *nt* specialist field; **s~iˈsieren** *vr* to specialize; **~iˈsierung** *f* specialization; **~iˈst** [-ˈlɪst] *m* specialist; **~iˈtät** *f* speciality

speziell [ʃpetsiˈɛl] *adj* special

spezifisch [ʃpeˈtsiːfɪʃ] *adj* specific

Sphäre [ˈsfɛːrə] *f* sphere

Spiegel [ˈʃpiːgəl] **(-s, -)** *m* mirror; (*Wasserspiegel*) level; (*MIL*) tab; **~bild** *nt* reflection; **s~bildlich** *adj* reversed; **~ei** *nt* fried egg; **s~n** *vt* to mirror, to reflect ♦ *vr* to be reflected ♦ *vi* to gleam; (*widerspiegeln*) to be reflective; **~ung** *f* reflection

Spiel [ʃpiːl] **(-(e)s, -e)** *nt* game; (*Schauspiel*) play; (*Tätigkeit*) play(ing); (*KARTEN*) deck; (*TECH*) (free) play; **s~en** *vt, vi* to play; (*um Geld*) to gamble; (*THEAT*) to perform, to act; **s~end** *adv* easily; **~er (-s, -)** *m* player; (*um Geld*) gambler; **~eˈrei** *f* trifling pastime; **~feld** *nt* pitch, field; **~film** *m* feature film; **~kasino** *nt* casino; **~plan** *m* (*THEAT*) programme; **~platz** *m* playground; **~raum** *m* room to manoeuvre, scope; **~regel** *f* rule; **~sachen** *pl* toys; **~uhr** *f* musical box; **~verderber (-s, -)** *m* spoilsport; **~waren** *pl* toys; **~zeug** *nt* toy(s)

Spieß [ʃpiːs] **(-es, -e)** *m* spear; (*Bratspieß*) spit; **~bürger** *m* bourgeois; **~er (-s, -)** (*umg*) *m* bourgeois; **s~ig** (*pej*) *adj* (petit) bourgeois

Spinat [ʃpiˈnaːt] **(-(e)s, -e)** *m* spinach

Spind [ʃpɪnt] **(-(e)s, -e)** *m od nt* locker

Spinn- [ˈʃpɪn] *zW:* **~e** *f* spider; **s~en** (*unreg*) *vt, vi* to spin; (*umg*) to talk rubbish; (*verrückt sein*) to be crazy od mad; **~eˈrei** *f* spinning mill; **~rad** *nt* spinning wheel; **~webe** *f* cobweb

Spion [ʃpiˈoːn] **(-s, -e)** *m* spy; (*in Tür*) spyhole; **~age** [ʃpioˈnaːʒə] *f* espionage; **s~ieren** [ʃpioˈniːrən] *vi* to spy; **~in** *f* (female) spy

Spirale [ʃpiˈraːlə] *f* spiral

Spirituosen [ʃpirituˈoːzən] *pl* spirits

Spiritus [ˈʃpiːrɪtʊs] **(-, -se)** *m* (methylated) spirit

Spital [ʃpiˈtaːl] **(-s, ⁿer)** *nt* hospital

spitz [ʃpɪts] *adj* pointed; (*Winkel*) acute; (*fig: Zunge*) sharp; (: *Bemerkung*) caustic

Spitze *f* point, tip; (*Bergspitze*) peak; (*Bemerkung*) taunt, dig; (*erster Platz*) lead, top; (*meist pl: Gewebe*) lace

Spitzel (-s, -) *m* police informer

spitzen *vt* to sharpen

Spitzenmarke *f* brand leader

spitzfindig *adj* (over)subtle

Spitzname *m* nickname

Splitter [ˈʃplɪtər] **(-s, -)** *m* splinter

sponsern [ˈʃpɔnzərn] *vt* to sponsor

spontan [ʃpɔnˈtaːn] *adj* spontaneous

Sport [ʃpɔrt] **(-(e)s, -e)** *m* sport; (*fig*) hobby; **~lehrer(in)** *m(f)* games od P.E. teacher; **~ler(in) (-s, -)** *m(f)* sportsman(-woman); **s~lich** *adj* sporting; (*Mensch*) sporty; **~platz** *m* playing od sports field; **~schuh** *m* (*Turnschuh*) training shoe, trainer; **~stadion** *nt* sports stadium; **~verein** *m* sports club; **~wagen** *m* sports car

Spott [ʃpɔt] **(-(e)s)** *m* mockery, ridicule; **s~billig** *adj* dirt-cheap; **s~en** *vi* to mock; **s~en (über** +*akk*) to mock (at), to ridicule

spöttisch [ˈʃpœtɪʃ] *adj* mocking

sprach *etc* [ʃpraːx] *vb siehe* **sprechen**

Sprach- *zW:* **s~begabt** *adj* good at languages; **~e** *f* language; **~enschule** *f* language school; **~fehler** *m* speech defect; **~führer** *m* phrasebook; **~gefühl** *nt* feeling for language; **~kenntnisse** *pl* linguistic proficiency *sg*; **~kurs** *m* language course; **~labor** *nt* language laboratory; **s~lich** *adj* linguistic; **s~los** adj speechless

sprang etc [ʃpraŋ] vb siehe **springen**

Spray [spreː] (**-s, -s**) m od nt spray

Sprech- ['ʃprɛç] zW: **~anlage** f intercom; **s~en** (unreg) vi to speak, to talk ♦ vt to say; (Sprache) to speak; (Person) to speak to; **mit jdm s~en** to speak to sb; **das spricht für ihn** that's a point in his favour; **~er(in)** (**-s, -**) m(f) speaker; (für Gruppe) spokesman(-woman); (RADIO, TV) announcer; **~stunde** f consultation (hour); (doctor's) surgery; **~stundenhilfe** f (doctor's) receptionist; **~zimmer** nt consulting room, surgery, office (US)

spreizen ['ʃpraɪtsən] vt (Beine) to open, to spread; (Finger, Flügel) to spread

Spreng- ['ʃprɛŋ] zW: **~en** vt to sprinkle; (mit ~stoff) to blow up; (Gestein) to blast; (Versammlung) to break up; **~stoff** m explosive(s)

sprichst etc [ʃprɪçst] vb siehe **sprechen**

Sprichwort nt proverb; **sprichwörtlich** adj proverbial

Spring- ['ʃprɪŋ] zW: **~brunnen** m fountain; **s~en** (unreg) vi to jump; (Glas) to crack; (mit Kopfsprung) to dive; **~er** (**-s, -**) m jumper; (Schach) knight

Sprit [ʃprɪt] (**-(e)s, -e**) (umg) m juice, gas

Spritz- ['ʃprɪts] zW: **~e** f syringe; injection; (an Schlauch) nozzle; **s~en** vt to spray; (MED) to inject ♦ vi to splash; (herausspritzen) to spurt; (MED) to give injections; **~pistole** f spray gun; **~tour** f (umg) spin

spröde ['ʃprøːdə] adj brittle; (Person) reserved, coy

Sprosse ['ʃprɔsə] f rung

Sprössling ▲ ['ʃprœslɪŋ] (umg) m (Kind) offspring (pl inv)

Spruch [ʃprʊx] (**-(e)s, ⁼e**) m saying, maxim; (JUR) judgement

Sprudel ['ʃpruːdəl] (**-s, -**) m mineral water; lemonade; **s~n** vi to bubble; **~wasser** nt (KOCH) sparkling od fizzy mineral water

Sprüh- ['ʃpryː] zW: **~dose** f aerosol (can); **s~en** vi to spray; (fig) to sparkle ♦ vt to spray; **~regen** m drizzle

Sprung [ʃprʊŋ] (**-(e)s, ⁼e**) m jump; (Riss) crack; **~brett** nt springboard; **s~haft** adj erratic; (Aufstieg) rapid; **~schanze** f ski jump

Spucke ['ʃpʊkə] (**-**) f spit; **s~n** vt, vi to spit

Spuk [ʃpuːk] (**-(e)s, -e**) m haunting; (fig) nightmare; **s~en** vi (Geist) to walk; **hier s~t es** this place is haunted

Spülbecken ['ʃpyːlbɛkən] nt (in Küche) sink

Spule ['ʃpuːlə] f spool; (ELEK) coil

Spül- ['ʃpyːl] zW: **~e** f (kitchen) sink; **s~en** vt, vi to rinse; (Geschirr) to wash up; (Toilette) to flush; **~maschine** f dishwasher; **~mittel** nt washing-up liquid; **~stein** m sink; **~ung** f rinsing; flush; (MED) irrigation

Spur [ʃpuːr] (**-, -en**) f trace; (Fußspur, Radspur, Tonbandspur) track; (Fährte) trail; (Fahrspur) lane

spürbar adj noticeable, perceptible

spüren ['ʃpyːrən] vt to feel

spurlos adv without (a) trace

Spurt [ʃpʊrt] (**-(e)s, -s** od **-e**) m spurt; **s~en** vi to spurt

sputen ['ʃpuːtən] vr to make haste

St. abk = **Stück** (= Sankt) St.

Staat [ʃtaːt] (**-(e)s, -en**) m state; (Prunk) show; (Kleidung) finery; **s~enlos** adj stateless; **s~lich** adj state(-); state-run

Staats- zW: **~angehörige(r)** f(m) national; **~angehörigkeit** f nationality; **~anwalt** m public prosecutor; **~bürger** m citizen; **~dienst** m civil service; **~examen** nt (UNIV) state exam(ination); **s~feindlich** adj subversive; **~mann** (pl **-männer**) m statesman; **~oberhaupt** nt head of state

Stab [ʃtaːp] (**-(e)s, ⁼e**) m rod; (Gitterstab) bar; (Menschen) staff; **~hochsprung** m pole vault

stabil [ʃtaˈbiːl] adj stable; (Möbel) sturdy; **~i'sieren** vt to stabilize

Stachel ['ʃtaxəl] (**-s, -n**) m spike; (von Tier) spine; (von Insekten) sting; **~beere** f gooseberry; **~draht** m barbed wire; **s~ig** adj prickly; **~schwein** nt porcupine

Stadion ['ʃtaːdiɔn] (**-s, Stadien**) nt stadium

Stadium ['ʃtaːdiʊm] nt stage, phase

Spelling Reform: ▲ *new spelling* △ *old spelling (to be phased out)*

Stadt [ʃtat] **(-, ⁼e)** f town; **~autobahn** f urban motorway; **~bahn** f suburban railway; **~bücherei** f municipal library

Städt- [ˈʃtɛːt] zW: **~ebau** m town planning; **~epartnerschaft** f town twinning; **~er(in) (-s, -)** m(f) town dweller; **s~isch** adj municipal; (*nicht ländlich*) urban

Stadt- zW: **~kern** m town centre, city centre; **~mauer** f city wall(s); **~mitte** f town centre; **~plan** m street map; **~rand** m outskirts pl; **~rat** m (*Behörde*) town council, city council; **~rundfahrt** f tour of a/the city; **~teil** m district, part of town; **~zentrum** nt town centre

Staffel [ˈʃtafəl] **(-, -n)** f rung; (*SPORT*) relay (team); (*AVIAT*) squadron; **~lauf** m (*SPORT*) relay (race); **s~n** vt to graduate

Stahl [ʃtaːl] **(-(e)s, ⁼e)** m steel

stahl etc vb siehe **stehlen**

stak etc [staːk] vb siehe **stecken**

Stall [ʃtal] **(-(e)s, ⁼e)** m stable; (*Kaninchenstall*) hutch; (*Schweinestall*) sty; (*Hühnerstall*) henhouse

Stamm [ʃtam] **(-(e)s, ⁼e)** m (*Baumstamm*) trunk; (*Menschenstamm*) tribe; (*GRAM*) stem; **~baum** m family tree; (*von Tier*) pedigree; **s~eln** vt, vi to stammer; **s~en** vi: **s~en von** od **aus** to come from; **~gast** m regular (customer)

stämmig [ˈʃtɛmɪç] adj sturdy; (*Mensch*) stocky

Stammtisch [ˈʃtamtɪʃ] m table for the regulars

stampfen [ˈʃtampfən] vt, vi to stamp; (*stapfen*) to tramp; (*mit Werkzeug*) to pound

Stand [ʃtant] **(-(e)s, ⁼e)** m position; (*Wasserstand, Benzinstand etc*) level; (*Stehen*) standing position; (*Zustand*) state; (*Spielstand*) score; (*Messestand etc*) stand; (*Klasse*) class; (*Beruf*) profession; siehe **imstande, zustande**

stand etc vb siehe **stehen**

Standard [ˈʃtandart] **(-s, -s)** m standard

Ständer [ˈʃtɛndər] **(-s, -)** m stand

Standes- [ˈʃtandəs] zW: **~amt** nt registry office; **~beamte(r)** m registrar; **s~gemäß** adj, adv according to one's social position;

~unterschied m social difference

Stand- zW: **s~haft** adj steadfast; **s~halten** (*unreg*) vi: **(jdm/etw) s~halten** to stand firm (against sb/sth), to resist (sb/sth)

ständig [ˈʃtɛndɪç] adj permanent; (*ununterbrochen*) constant, continual

Stand- zW: **~licht** nt sidelights pl, parking lights pl (*US*); **~ort** m location; (*MIL*) garrison; **~punkt** m standpoint; **~spur** f hard shoulder

Stange [ˈʃtaŋə] f stick; (*Stab*) pole, bar; rod; (*Zigaretten*) carton; **von der ~** (*COMM*) off the peg; **eine ~ Geld** (*umg*) quite a packet

Stängel ▲ [ˈʃtɛŋəl] **(-s, -)** m stalk

Stapel [ˈʃtaːpəl] **(-s, -)** m pile; (*NAUT*) stocks pl; **~lauf** m launch; **s~n** vt to pile (up)

Star¹ [ʃtaːr] **(-(e)s, -e)** m starling; (*MED*) cataract

Star² [staːr] **(-s, -s)** m (*Filmstar etc*) star

starb etc [ʃtarp] vb siehe **sterben**

stark [ʃtark] adj strong; (*heftig, groß*) heavy; (*Maßangabe*) thick

Stärke [ˈʃtɛrkə] f strength; heaviness; thickness; (*KOCH: Wäschestärke*) starch; **s~n** vt to strengthen; (*Wäsche*) to starch

Starkstrom m heavy current

Stärkung [ˈʃtɛrkʊŋ] f strengthening; (*Essen*) refreshment

starr [ʃtar] adj stiff; (*unnachgiebig*) rigid; (*Blick*) staring; **~en** vi to stare; **~en vor** od **von** to be covered in; (*Waffen*) to be bristling with; **S~heit** f rigidity; **~köpfig** adj stubborn; **S~sinn** m obstinacy

Start [ʃtart] **(-(e)s, -e)** m start; (*AVIAT*) takeoff; **~automatik** f (*AUT*) automatic choke; **~bahn** f runway; **s~en** vt to start ◆ vi to start; to take off; **~er (-s, -)** m starter; **~erlaubnis** f takeoff clearance; **~hilfekabel** nt jump leads pl

Station [ʃtatsiˈoːn] f station; hospital ward; **s~är** [ʃtatsioˈnɛːr] adj (*MED*) in-patient attr; **s~ieren** [-ˈniːrən] vt to station

Statist [ʃtaˈtɪst] m extra, supernumerary

Statistik f statistics sg; **~er (-s, -)** m statistician

statistisch adj statistical

Stativ [ʃtaˈtiːf] **(-s, -e)** nt tripod

statt [ʃtat] *konj* instead of ♦ *präp (+gen od dat)* instead of

Stätte ['ʃtɛtə] *f* place

statt- *zW:* **~finden** *(unreg) vi* to take place; **~haft** *adj* admissible; **~lich** *adj* imposing, handsome

Statue ['ʃta:tuə] *f* statue

Status ['ʃta:tʊs] **(-, -)** *m* status

Stau [ʃtaʊ] **(-(e)s, -e)** *m* blockage; *(Verkehrsstau)* (traffic) jam

Staub [ʃtaʊp] **(-(e)s)** *m* dust; **~ saugen** to vacuum, to hoover®; **s~en** ['ʃtaʊbən] *vi* to be dusty; **s~ig** *adj* dusty; **s~saugen** *vi* to vacuum, to hoover ®; **~sauger** *m* vacuum cleaner; **~tuch** *nt* duster

Staudamm *m* dam

Staude ['ʃtaʊdə] *f* shrub

stauen ['ʃtaʊən] *vt (Wasser)* to dam up; *(Blut)* to stop the flow of ♦ *vr (Wasser)* to become dammed up; *(MED: Verkehr)* to become congested; *(Menschen)* to collect; *(Gefühle)* to build up

staunen ['ʃtaʊnən] *vi* to be astonished; **S~ (-s)** *nt* amazement

Stausee ['ʃtaʊze:] **(-s, -n)** *m* reservoir, man-made lake

Stauung ['ʃtaʊʊŋ] *f (von Wasser)* damming-up; *(von Verkehr)* congestion

Std. *abk (= Stunde)* hr.

Steak [ʃte:k] *nt* steak

Stech- ['ʃtɛç] *zW:* **s~en** *(unreg) vt (mit Nadel etc)* to prick; *(mit Messer)* to stab; *(mit Finger)* to poke; *(Biene etc)* to sting; *(Mücke)* to bite; *(Sonne)* to burn; *(KARTEN)* to take; *(ART)* to engrave; *(Torf, Spargel)* to cut; **in See s~en** to put to sea; **~en (-s, -)** *nt (SPORT)* play-off; jump-off; **s~end** *adj* piercing, stabbing; *(Geruch)* pungent; **~palme** *f* holly; **~uhr** *f* time clock

Steck- [ʃtɛk] *zW:* **~brief** *m* "wanted" poster; **~dose** *f* (wall) socket; **s~en** *vt* to put, to insert; *(Nadel)* to stick; *(Pflanzen)* to plant; *(beim Nähen)* to pin ♦ *vi (auch unreg)* to be; *(festsitzen)* to be stuck; *(Nadeln)* to stick; **s~en bleiben** to get stuck; **s~en lassen** to leave in; **~enpferd** *nt* hobby-horse; **~er (-s, -)** *m* plug; **~nadel** *f* pin

Steg [ʃte:k] **(-(e)s, -e)** *m* small bridge; *(Anlegesteg)* landing stage; **~reif** *m:* **aus dem ~reif** just like that

stehen ['ʃte:ən] *(unreg) vi* to stand; *(sich befinden)* to be; *(in Zeitung)* to say; *(stillstehen)* to have stopped ♦ *vi unpers:* **es steht schlecht um jdn/etw** things are bad for sb/sth; **zu jdm/etw ~** to stand by sb/sth; **jdm ~** to suit sb; **wie stehts?** how are things?; *(SPORT)* what's the score?; **~ bleiben** to remain standing; *(Uhr)* to stop; *(Fehler)* to stay as it is; **~ lassen** to leave; *(Bart)* to grow

Stehlampe ['ʃte:lampə] *f* standard lamp

stehlen ['ʃte:lən] *(unreg) vt* to steal

Stehplatz ['ʃte:plats] *m* standing place

steif [ʃtaɪf] *adj* stiff; **S~heit** *f* stiffness

Steig- [ʃtaɪk] *zW:* **~bügel** *m* stirrup; **s~en** ['ʃtaɪgən] *(unreg) vi* to rise; *(klettern)* to climb; **s~en in** *+akk/* **auf** *+akk* to get in/on; **s~ern** *vt* to raise; *(GRAM)* to compare ♦ *vi (Auktion)* to bid ♦ *vr* to increase; **~erung** *f* raising; *(GRAM)* comparison; **~ung** *f* incline, gradient, rise

steil [ʃtaɪl] *adj* steep; **S~küste** *f* steep coast; *(Klippen)* cliffs *pl*

Stein [ʃtaɪn] **(-(e)s, -e)** *m* stone; *(in Uhr)* jewel; **~bock** *m (ASTROL)* Capricorn; **~bruch** *m* quarry; **s~ern** *adj* (made of) stone; *(fig)* stony; **~gut** *nt* stoneware; **s~ig** ['ʃtaɪnɪç] *adj* stony; **s~igen** *vt* to stone; **~kohle** *f* mineral coal; **~zeit** *f* Stone Age

Stelle ['ʃtɛlə] *f* place; *(Arbeit)* post, job; *(Amt)* office; **an Ihrer/meiner ~** in your/my place; *siehe* **anstelle**

stellen *vt* to put; *(Uhr etc)* to set; *(zur Verfügung ~)* to supply; *(fassen: Dieb)* to apprehend ♦ *vr (sich aufstellen)* to stand; *(sich einfinden)* to present o.s.; *(bei Polizei)* to give o.s. up; *(vorgeben)* to pretend (to be); **sich zu etw ~** to have an opinion of sth

Stellen- *zW:* **~angebot** *nt* offer of a post; *(in Zeitung)* "vacancies"; **~anzeige** *f* job advertisement; **~gesuch** *nt* application for a post; **~vermittlung** *f* employment agency

Stell- *zW:* **~ung** *f* position; (*MIL*) line; **~ung nehmen zu** to comment on; **~ungnahme** *f* comment; **s~vertretend** *adj* deputy, acting; **~vertreter** *m* deputy

Stelze ['ʃtɛltsə] *f* stilt

stemmen ['ʃtɛmən] *vt* to lift (up); (*drücken*) to press; **sich ~ gegen** (*fig*) to resist, to oppose

Stempel ['ʃtɛmpəl] (**-s, -**) *m* stamp; (*BOT*) pistil; **~kissen** *nt* ink pad; **s~n** *vt* to stamp; (*Briefmarke*) to cancel; **s~n gehen** (*umg*) to be *od* go on the dole

Stengel △ ['ʃtɛŋəl] (**-s, -**) *m* = **Stängel**

Steno- [ʃteno] *zW:* **~gramm** [-'gram] *nt* shorthand report; **~grafie** ▲ [-gra'fiː] *f* shorthand; **s~grafieren** [-gra'fiːrən] *vt, vi* to write (in) shorthand; **~typist(in)** [-ty'pɪst(ɪn)] *m(f)* shorthand typist

Stepp- ['ʃtɛp] *zW:* **~decke** *f* quilt; **~e** *f* prairie; steppe; **s~en** *vt* to stitch ♦ *vi* to tap-dance

Sterb- ['ʃtɛrb] *zW:* **~efall** *m* death; **~ehilfe** *f* euthanasia; **s~en** (*unreg*) *vi* to die; **s~lich** ['ʃtɛrplɪç] *adj* mortal; **~lichkeit** *f* mortality; **~lichkeitsziffer** *f* death rate

stereo- ['ʃtereo] *in zW* stereo(-); **S~anlage** *f* stereo (system); **~typ** [ʃtereo'tyːp] *adj* stereotype

steril [ʃteˈriːl] *adj* sterile; **~i'sieren** *vt* to sterilize; **S~i'sierung** *f* sterilization

Stern [ʃtɛrn] (**-(e)s, -e**) *m* star; **~bild** *nt* constellation; **~schnuppe** *f* meteor, falling star; **~stunde** *f* historic moment; **~zeichen** *nt* sign of the zodiac

stet [ʃteːt] *adj* steady; **~ig** *adj* constant, continual; **~s** *adv* continually, always

Steuer¹ ['ʃtɔyər] (**-s, -**) *nt* (*NAUT*) helm; (*~ruder*) rudder; (*AUT*) steering wheel

Steuer² ['ʃtɔyər] (**-, -n**) *f* tax; **~berater(in)** *m(f)* tax consultant

Steuerbord *nt* (*NAUT, AVIAT*) starboard

Steuer- ['ʃtɔyər] *zW:* **~erklärung** *f* tax return; **s~frei** *adj* tax-free; **~freibetrag** *m* tax allowance; **~klasse** *f* tax group; **~knüppel** *m* control column; (*AVIAT, COMPUT*) joystick; **~mann** (*pl* **-männer** *od* **-leute**) *m* helmsman; **s~n** *vt, vi* to steer;

(*Flugzeug*) to pilot; (*Entwicklung, Tonstärke*) to control; **s~pflichtig** [-pflɪçtɪç] *adj* taxable; **~rad** *nt* steering wheel; **~ung** *f* (*auch AUT*) steering; piloting; control; (*Vorrichtung*) controls *pl*; **~zahler** (**-s, -**) *m* taxpayer

Steward ['stjuːərt] (**-s, -s**) *m* steward; **~ess** ▲ ['stjuːərdɛs] (**-, -en**) *f* stewardess; air hostess

Stich [ʃtɪç] (**-(e)s, -e**) *m* (*Insektenstich*) sting; (*Messerstich*) stab; (*beim Nähen*) stitch; (*Färbung*) tinge; (*KARTEN*) trick; (*ART*) engraving; **jdn im ~ lassen** to leave sb in the lurch; **s~eln** *vi* (*fig*) to jibe; **s~haltig** *adj* sound, tenable; **~probe** *f* spot check; **~straße** *f* cul-de-sac; **~wahl** *f* final ballot; **~wort** *nt* cue; (*in Wörterbuch*) headword; (*für Vortrag*) note

sticken ['ʃtɪkən] *vt, vi* to embroider

Sticke'rei *f* embroidery

stickig *adj* stuffy, close

Stickstoff *m* nitrogen

Stief- ['ʃtiːf] *in zW* step

Stiefel ['ʃtiːfəl] (**-s, -**) *m* boot

Stief- *zW:* **~kind** *nt* stepchild; (*fig*) Cinderella; **~mutter** *f* stepmother; **~mütterchen** *nt* pansy; **s~mütterlich** *adj* (*fig*): **jdn/etw s~mütterlich behandeln** to pay little attention to sb/sth; **~vater** *m* stepfather

stiehlst *etc* [ʃtiːlst] *vb siehe* **stehlen**

Stiel [ʃtiːl] (**-(e)s, -e**) *m* handle; (*BOT*) stalk

Stier (**-(e)s, -e**) *m* bull; (*ASTROL*) Taurus

stieren *vi* to stare

Stierkampf *m* bullfight

Stierkämpfer *m* bullfighter

Stift [ʃtɪft] (**-(e)s, -e**) *m* peg; (*Nagel*) tack; (*Farbstift*) crayon; (*Bleistift*) pencil ♦ *nt* (*charitable*) foundation; (*ECCL*) religious institution; **s~en** *vt* to found; (*Unruhe*) to cause; (*spenden*) to contribute; **~er(in)** (**-s, -**) *m(f)* founder; **~ung** *f* donation; (*Organisation*) foundation; **~zahn** *m* post crown

Stil [ʃtiːl] (**-(e)s, -e**) *m* style

still [ʃtɪl] *adj* quiet; (*unbewegt*) still; (*heimlich*) secret; **S~er Ozean** Pacific; **~ halten** to keep still; **~ stehen** to stand still; **S~e** *f* stillness, quietness; **in aller S~e** quietly; ~**en** vt to stop; (befriedigen) to satisfy; (Säugling) to breast-feed; ~**legen** ▲ vt to close down; ~**schweigen** (unreg) vi to be silent; **S~schweigen** nt silence; ~**schweigend** adj silent; (Einverständnis) tacit ♦ adv silently; tacitly; **S~stand** m standstill

imm- ['ʃtɪm] zW: ~**bänder** pl vocal cords; **s~berechtigt** adj entitled to vote; ~**e** f voice; (Wahlstimme) vote; **s~en** vt (MUS) to tune ♦ vi to vote; **das s~te ihn traurig** that made him feel sad; **s~en für/gegen** to vote for/against; **s~t so!** that's right; ~**enmehrheit** f majority (of votes); ~**enthaltung** f abstention; ~**gabel** f tuning fork; ~**recht** nt right to vote; ~**ung** f mood; atmosphere; **s~ungsvoll** adj enjoyable; full of atmosphere; ~**zettel** m ballot paper

inken ['ʃtɪŋkən] (unreg) vi to stink

ipendium [ʃtiˈpɛndiʊm] nt grant

irbst etc ['ʃtɪrpst] vb siehe **sterben**

irn [ʃtɪrn] (-, -en) f forehead, brow; (Frechheit) impudence; ~**band** nt headband; ~**höhle** f sinus

öbern ['ʃtøːbərn] vi to rummage

ochern ['ʃtɔxərn] vi to poke (about)

tock[1] [ʃtɔk] (-(e)s, ⁺e) m stick; (BOT) stock

tock[2] [ʃtɔk] (-(e)s, - od Stockwerke) m storey

ocken vi to stop, to pause; ~**d** adj halting

tockung f stoppage

tockwerk nt storey, floor

toff [ʃtɔf] (-(e)s, -e) m (Gewebe) material, cloth; (Materie) matter; (von Buch etc) subject (matter); **s~lich** adj material; ~**tier** nt soft toy; ~**wechsel** m metabolism

öhnen ['ʃtøːnən] vi to groan

tollen ['ʃtɔlən] (-s, -) m (MIN) gallery; (KOCH) cake eaten at Christmas; (von Schuhen) stud

olpern ['ʃtɔlpərn] vi to stumble, to trip

tolz [ʃtɔlts] (-es) m pride; **s~** adj proud; **s~ieren** [ʃtɔlˈtsiːrən] vi to strut

opfen ['ʃtɔpfən] vt (hineinstopfen) to stuff; (voll stopfen) to fill (up); (nähen) to darn ♦ vi

(MED) to cause constipation

Stopfgarn nt darning thread

Stoppel ['ʃtɔpəl] (-, -n) f stubble

Stopp- ['ʃtɔp] zW: **s~en** vt to stop; (mit Uhr) to time ♦ vi to stop; ~**schild** nt stop sign; ~**uhr** f stopwatch

Stöpsel ['ʃtœpsəl] (-s, -) m plug; (für Flaschen) stopper

Storch [ʃtɔrç] (-(e)s, ⁺e) m stork

Stör- ['ʃtøːr] zW: **s~en** vt to disturb; (behindern, RADIO) to interfere with ♦ vr: **sich an etw** dat **s~en** to let sth bother one; **s~end** adj disturbing, annoying; ~**enfried** (-(e)s, -e) m troublemaker

stornieren [ʃtɔrˈniːrən] vt (Auftrag) to cancel; (Buchung) to reverse

Stornogebühr ['ʃtɔrno-] f cancellation fee

störrisch ['ʃtœrɪʃ] adj stubborn, perverse

Störung f disturbance; interference

Stoß [ʃtoːs] (-es, ⁺e) m (Schub) push; (Schlag) blow; knock; (mit Schwert) thrust; (mit Fuß) kick; (Erdstoß) shock; (Haufen) pile; ~**dämpfer** (-s, -) m shock absorber; **s~en** (unreg) vt (mit Druck) to shove, to push; (mit Schlag) to knock, to bump; (mit Fuß) to kick; (Schwert etc) to thrust; (anstoßen: Kopf etc) to bump ♦ vr to get a knock ♦ vi: **s~en an** od **auf** +akk to bump into; (finden) to come across; (angrenzen) to be next to; **sich s~en an** +dat (fig) to take exception to; ~**stange** f (AUT) bumper

stottern ['ʃtɔtərn] vt, vi to stutter

Str. abk (= Straße) St.

Straf- ['ʃtraːf] zW: ~**anstalt** f penal institution; ~**arbeit** f (SCH) punishment; lines pl; **s~bar** adj punishable; ~**e** f punishment; (JUR) penalty; (Gefängnisstrafe) sentence; (Geldstrafe) fine; **s~en** vt to punish

straff [ʃtraf] adj tight; (streng) strict; (Stil etc) concise; (Haltung) erect; ~**en** vt to tighten, to tauten

Strafgefangene(r) f(m) prisoner, convict

Strafgesetzbuch nt penal code

sträflich ['ʃtrɛːflɪç] adj criminal

Sträfling m convict

Straf- zW: ~**porto** nt excess postage

Spelling Reform: ▲ new spelling △ old spelling (to be phased out)

(charge); ~**predigt** f telling-off; ~**raum** m (SPORT) penalty area; ~**recht** nt criminal law; ~**stoß** m (SPORT) penalty (kick); ~**tat** f punishable act; ~**zettel** m ticket

Strahl [ʃtraːl] (-s, -en) m ray, beam; (Wasserstrahl) jet; s~**en** vi to radiate; (fig) to beam; ~**ung** f radiation

Strähne [ˈʃtrɛːnə] f strand

stramm [ʃtram] adj tight; (Haltung) erect; (Mensch) robust

strampeln [ˈʃtrampəln] vi to kick (about), to fidget

Strand [ʃtrant] (-(e)s, ⁻e) m shore; (mit Sand) beach; ~**bad** nt open-air swimming pool, lido; s~**en** [ˈʃtrandən] vi to run aground; (fig: Mensch) to fail; ~**gut** nt flotsam; ~**korb** m beach chair

Strang [ʃtraŋ] (-(e)s, ⁻e) m cord, rope; (Bündel) skein

Strapaz- zW: ~**e** [ʃtraˈpaːtsə] f strain, exertion; s~**ieren** [ʃtrapaˈtsiːrən] vt (Material) to treat roughly, to punish; (Mensch, Kräfte) to wear out, to exhaust; s~**ierfähig** adj hard-wearing; s~**iös** [ʃtrapatsiˈøːs] adj exhausting, tough

Straße [ˈʃtraːsə] f street, road

Straßen- zW: ~**bahn** f tram, streetcar (US); ~**glätte** f slippery road surface; ~**karte** f road map; ~**kehrer** (-s, -) m roadsweeper; ~**sperre** f roadblock; ~**verkehr** m (road) traffic; ~**verkehrsordnung** f highway code

Strateg- [ʃtraˈteːg] zW: ~**e** (-n, -n) m strategist; ~**ie** [ʃtrateˈgiː] f strategy; s~**isch** adj strategic

sträuben [ˈʃtrɔybən] vt to ruffle ♦ vr to bristle; (Mensch): **sich (gegen etw) ~** to resist (sth)

Strauch [ʃtraux] (-(e)s, Sträucher) m bush, shrub

Strauß¹ [ʃtraus] (-es, Sträuße) m bunch; bouquet

Strauß² [ʃtraus] (-es, -e) m ostrich

Streb- [ˈʃtreːb] zW: s~**en** vi to strive, to endeavour; s~**en nach** to strive for; ~**er** (-s, -) (pej) m pusher, climber; (SCH) swot (BRIT)

Strecke [ˈʃtrɛkə] f stretch; (Entfernung) distance; (EISENB, MATH) line; s~**n** vt to stretch; (Waffen) to lay down; (KOCH) to eke out ♦ vr to stretch (o.s.)

Streich [ʃtraiç] (-(e)s, -e) m trick, prank; (Hieb) blow; s~**eln** vt to stroke; s~**en** (unreg) vt (berühren) to stroke; (auftragen) to spread; (anmalen) to paint; (durchstreichen) to delete; (nicht genehmigen) to cancel ♦ vi (berühren) to brush; (schleichen) to prowl; ~**holz** nt match; ~**instrument** nt string instrument

Streif- [ˈʃtraif] zW: ~**e** f patrol; s~**en** vt (leicht berühren) to brush against, to graze; (Blick) to skim over; (Thema, Problem) to touch on; (abstreifen) to take off ♦ vi (gehen) to roam; ~**en** (-s, -) m (Linie) stripe; (Stück) strip; (Film) film; ~**enwagen** m patrol car; ~**schuss** ▲ m graze, grazing shot; ~**zug** m scouting trip

Streik [ʃtraik] (-(e)s, -s) m strike; ~**brecher** (-s, -) m blackleg, strikebreaker; s~**en** vi to strike; ~**posten** m (strike) picket

Streit [ʃtrait] (-(e)s, -e) m argument; dispute; s~**en** (unreg) vi, vr to argue; to dispute; ~**frage** f point at issue; s~**ig** adj: **jdm etw s~ig machen** to dispute sb's right to sth; ~**igkeiten** pl quarrel sg, dispute sg; ~**kräfte** pl (MIL) armed forces

streng [ʃtrɛŋ] adj severe; (Lehrer, Maßnahme) strict; (Geruch etc) sharp; ~ **genommen** strictly speaking; S~**e** (-) f severity, strictness, sharpness; ~**gläubig** adj orthodox, strict; ~**stens** adv strictly

Stress ▲ [ʃtrɛs] (-es, -e) m stress

stressen vt to put under stress

streuen [ˈʃtrɔyən] vt to strew, to scatter, to spread

Strich [ʃtriç] (-(e)s, -e) m (Linie) line; (Federstrich, Pinselstrich) stroke; (von Geweben) nap; (von Fell) pile; **auf den ~ gehen** (umg) to walk the streets; **jdm gegen den ~ gehen** to rub sb up the wrong way; **einen ~ machen durch** to cross out; (fig) to foil; ~**kode** m (auf Waren) bar code; ~**mädchen** nt streetwalker; s~**weise** adv here and there

Strick [ʃtrɪk] (**-(e)s**, **-e**) m rope; **s~en** vt, vi to knit; **~jacke** f cardigan; **~leiter** f rope ladder; **~nadel** f knitting needle; **~waren** pl knitwear sg

strikt [strɪkt] adj strict

strittig [ˈʃtrɪtɪç] adj disputed, in dispute

Stroh [ʃtroː] (**-(e)s**, **-e**) nt straw; **~blume** f everlasting flower; **~dach** nt thatched roof; **~halm** m (drinking) straw

Strom [ʃtroːm] (**-(e)s**, **ⁱe**) m river; (fig) stream; (ELEK) current; **s~abwärts** adv downstream; **s~aufwärts** adv upstream; **~ausfall** m power failure

strömen [ˈʃtrøːmən] vi to stream, to pour

Strom- zW: **~kreis** m circuit; **s~linienförmig** adj streamlined; **~sperre** f power cut

Strömung [ˈʃtrøːmʊŋ] f current

Strophe [ˈʃtroːfə] f verse

strotzen [ˈʃtrɔtsən] vi: **~ vor** od **von** to abound in, to be full of

Strudel [ˈʃtruːdəl] (**-s**, **-**) m whirlpool, vortex; (KOCH) strudel

Struktur [ʃtrʊkˈtuːr] f structure

Strumpf [ʃtrʊmpf] (**-(e)s**, **ⁱe**) m stocking; **~band** nt garter; **~hose** f (pair of) tights

Stube [ˈʃtuːbə] f room

Stuben- zW: **~arrest** m confinement to one's room; (MIL) confinement to quarters; **~hocker** (umg) m stay-at-home; **s~rein** adj house-trained

Stuck [ʃtʊk] (**-(e)s**) m stucco

Stück [ʃtʏk] (**-(e)s**, **-e**) nt piece; (etwas) bit; (THEAT) play; **~chen** nt little piece; **~lohn** m piecework wages pl; **s~weise** adv bit by bit, piecemeal; (COMM) individually

Student(in) [ʃtuˈdɛnt(ɪn)] m(f) student; **s~isch** adj student, academic

Studie [ˈʃtuːdiə] f study

Studienfahrt f study trip

studieren [ʃtuˈdiːrən] vt, vi to study

Studio [ˈʃtuːdio] (**-s**, **-s**) nt studio

Studium [ˈʃtuːdiʊm] nt studies pl

Stufe [ˈʃtuːfə] f step; (Entwicklungsstufe) stage; **s~nweise** adv gradually

Stuhl [ʃtuːl] (**-(e)s**, **ⁱe**) m chair; **~gang** m bowel movement

stülpen [ˈʃtʏlpən] vt (umdrehen) to turn upside down; (bedecken) to put

stumm [ʃtʊm] adj silent; (MED) dumb

Stummel [ˈʃtʊməl] (**-s**, **-**) m stump; (Zigarettenstummel) stub

Stummfilm m silent film

Stümper [ˈʃtʏmpər] (**-s**, **-**) m incompetent, duffer; **s~haft** adj bungling, incompetent; **s~n** vi to bungle

Stumpf [ʃtʊmpf] (**-(e)s**, **ⁱe**) m stump; **s~** adj blunt; (teilnahmslos, glanzlos) dull; (Winkel) obtuse; **~sinn** m tediousness; **s~sinnig** adj dull

Stunde [ˈʃtʊndə] f hour; (SCH) lesson

stunden vt: **jdm etw ~** to give sb time to pay sth; **S~geschwindigkeit** f average speed per hour; **S~kilometer** pl kilometres per hour; **~lang** adj for hours; **S~lohn** m hourly wage; **S~plan** m timetable; **~weise** adj by the hour; every hour

stündlich [ˈʃtʏntlɪç] adj hourly

Stups [ʃtʊps] (**-es**, **-e**) (umg) m push; **~nase** f snub nose

stur [ʃtuːr] adj obstinate, pigheaded

Sturm [ʃtʊrm] (**-(e)s**, **ⁱe**) m storm, gale; (MIL etc) attack, assault

stürm- [ˈʃtʏrm] zW: **~en** vi (Wind) to blow hard, to rage; (rennen) to storm ♦ vt (MIL, fig) to storm ♦ vb unpers: **es ~t** there's a gale blowing; **S~er** (**-s**, **-**) m (SPORT) forward, striker; **~isch** adj stormy

Sturmwarnung f gale warning

Sturz [ʃtʊrts] (**-es**, **ⁱe**) m fall; (POL) overthrow

stürzen [ˈʃtʏrtsən] vt (werfen) to hurl; (POL) to overthrow; (umkehren) to overturn ♦ vr to rush; (hineinstürzen) to plunge ♦ vi to fall; (AVIAT) to dive; (rennen) to dash

Sturzflug m nose dive

Sturzhelm m crash helmet

Stute [ˈʃtuːtə] f mare

Stützbalken m brace, joist

Stütze [ˈʃtʏtsə] f support; help

stutzen [ˈʃtʊtsən] vt to trim; (Ohr, Schwanz) to dock; (Flügel) to clip ♦ vi to hesitate; to become suspicious

stützen vt (auch fig) to support; (Ellbogen

etc) to prop up

stutzig *adj* perplexed, puzzled; (*misstrauisch*) suspicious

Stützpunkt *m* point of support; (*von Hebel*) fulcrum; (*MIL, fig*) base

Styropor [ʃtyroˈpoːr] (®; **-s**) *nt* polystyrene s. u. *abk* = **siehe unten**

Subjekt [zʊpˈjɛkt] (**-(e)s, -e**) *nt* subject; **s~iv** [-ˈtiːf] *adj* subjective; **~ivi'tät** *f* subjectivity

Subsidiarität *f* subsidiarity

Substantiv [zʊpstanˈtiːf] (**-s, -e**) *nt* noun

Substanz [zʊpˈstants] *f* substance

subtil [zʊpˈtiːl] *adj* subtle

subtrahieren [zʊptraˈhiːrən] *vt* to subtract

subtropisch [zʊpˈtroːpɪʃ] *adj* subtropical

Subvention [zʊpvɛntsiˈoːn] *f* subsidy; **s~ieren** *vt* to subsidize

Such- [ˈzuːx] *zW:* **~aktion** *f* search; **~e** *f* search; **s~en** *vt* to look (for), to seek; (*versuchen*) to try ♦ *vi* to seek, to search; **~er** (**-s, -**) *m* seeker, searcher; (*PHOT*) viewfinder; **~maschine** *f* (*COMPUT*) search engine

Sucht [zʊxt] (**-, ⁻e**) *f* mania; (*MED*) addiction, craving

süchtig [ˈzʏçtɪç] *adj* addicted; **S~e(r)** *f(m)* addict

Süd- [zyːt] *zW:* **~en** [ˈzyːdən] (**-s**) *m* south; **~früchte** *pl* Mediterranean fruit *sg*; **s~lich** *adj* southern; **s~lich von** (to the) south of; **~pol** *m* South Pole; **s~wärts** *adv* southwards

süffig [ˈzʏfɪç] *adj* (*Wein*) pleasant to the taste

süffisant [zʏfiˈzant] *adj* smug

suggerieren [zʊɡeˈriːrən] *vt* to suggest

Sühne [ˈzyːnə] *f* atonement, expiation; **s~n** *vt* to atone for, to expiate

Sultan [ˈzʊltan] (**-s, -e**) *m* sultan; **~ine** [zʊltaˈniːnə] *f* sultana

Sülze [ˈzʏltsə] *f* brawn

Summe [ˈzʊmə] *f* sum, total

summen *vt, vi* to buzz; (*Lied*) to hum

Sumpf [zʊmpf] (**-(e)s, ⁻e**) *m* swamp, marsh; **s~ig** *adj* marshy

Sünde [ˈzʏndə] *f* sin; **~nbock** (*umg*) *m* scapegoat; **~r(in)** (**-s, -**) *m(f)* sinner; **sündigen** *vi* to sin

Super [ˈzuːpər] (**-s**) *nt* (*Benzin*) four star (petrol) (*BRIT*), premium (*US*); **~lativ** [-latiːf] (**-s, -e**) *m* superlative; **~macht** *f* superpower; **~markt** *m* supermarket

Suppe [ˈzʊpə] *f* soup; **~nteller** *m* soup plate

süß [zyːs] *adj* sweet; **S~e(-)** *f* sweetness; **~en** *vt* to sweeten; **S~igkeit** *f* sweetness; (*Bonbon etc*) sweet (*BRIT*), candy (*US*); **~lich** *adj* sweetish; (*fig*) sugary; **~sauer** *adj* (*Gurke*) pickled; (*Sauce etc*) sweet-and-sour; **S~speise** *f* pudding, sweet; **S~stoff** *m* sweetener; **S~waren** *pl* confectionery (*sing*); **S~wasser** *nt* fresh water

Symbol [zʏmˈboːl] (**-s, -e**) *nt* symbol; **s~isch** *adj* symbolic(al)

Symmetrie [zʏmeˈtriː] *f* symmetry

symmetrisch [zʏˈmeːtrɪʃ] *adj* symmetrical

Sympathie [zʏmpaˈtiː] *f* liking, sympathy; **sympathisch** [zʏmˈpaːtɪʃ] *adj* likeable; **er ist mir sympathisch** I like him; **sympathi'sieren** *vi* to sympathize

Symphonie [zʏmfoˈniː] *f* (*MUS*) symphony

Symptom [zʏmpˈtoːm] (**-s, -e**) *nt* symptom; **s~atisch** [zʏmptoˈmaːtɪʃ] *adj* symptomatic

Synagoge [zʏnaˈɡoːɡə] *f* synagogue

synchron [zʏnˈkroːn] *adj* synchronous; **~i'sieren** *vt* to synchronize; (*Film*) to dub

Synonym [zʏnoˈnyːm] (**-s, -e**) *nt* synonym; **s~** *adj* synonymous

Synthese [zʏnˈteːzə] *f* synthesis

synthetisch *adj* synthetic

System [zʏsˈteːm] (**-s, -e**) *nt* system; **s~atisch** *adj* systematic; **s~ati'sieren** *vt* to systematize

Szene [ˈstseːnə] *f* scene; **~rie** [stsenəˈriː] *f* scenery

T, t

t *abk* (= *Tonne*) t

Tabak [ˈtaːbak] (**-s, -e**) *m* tobacco

Tabell- [taˈbɛl] *zW:* **t~arisch** [tabeˈlaːrɪʃ] *adj* tabular; **~e** *f* table

Tablett [taˈblɛt] *nt* tray; **~e** *f* tablet, pill

Tabu [taˈbuː] *nt* taboo; **t~** *adj* taboo

Tachometer [taxoˈmeːtər] (**-s, -**) *m* (*AUT*)

speedometer

Tadel ['ta:dəl] **(-s, -)** m censure; scolding; (Fehler) fault, blemish; t~los adj faultless, irreproachable; t~n vt to scold

Tafel ['ta:fəl] **(-, -n)** f (auch MATH) table; (Anschlag~) board; (Wand~) blackboard; (Schiefer~) slate; (Gedenk~) plaque; (Illustration) plate; (Schalt~) panel; (Schokolade etc) bar

Tag [ta:k] **(-(e)s, -e)** m day; daylight; **unter/über ~** (MIN) underground/on the surface; **an den ~ kommen** to come to light; **guten ~!** good morning/afternoon!; siehe **zutage**; t~aus adv: **t~aus, ~ein** day in, day out; ~dienst m day duty

Tage- ['ta:gə] zW: ~buch ['ta:gəbu:x] nt diary, journal; ~geld nt daily allowance; t~lang adv for days; t~n vi to sit, to meet ♦ vb unpers: **es tagt** dawn is breaking

Tages- zW: ~ablauf m course of the day; ~anbruch m dawn; ~fahrt f day trip; ~karte f menu of the day; (Fahrkarte) day ticket; ~licht nt daylight; ~ordnung f agenda; ~zeit f time of day; ~zeitung f daily (paper)

täglich ['tɛːklɪç] adj, adv daily

tagsüber ['ta:ks|yːbər] adv during the day

Tagung f conference

Taille ['taljə] f waist

Takt [takt] **(-(e)s, -e)** m tact; (MUS) time; ~gefühl nt tact

Taktik f tactics pl; taktisch adj tactical

Takt- zW: t~los adj tactless; ~losigkeit f tactlessness; ~stock m (conductor's) baton; t~voll adj tactful

Tal [ta:l] **(-(e)s, ˝er)** nt valley

Talent [ta'lɛnt] **(-(e)s, -e)** nt talent; t~iert [talɛn'tiːrt] adj talented, gifted

Talisman ['ta:lɪsman] **(-s, -e)** m talisman

Talkshow ['tɔːkʃoː] f chat show

Talsohle f bottom of a valley

Talsperre f dam

Tampon ['tampɔn] **(-s, -s)** m tampon

Tang [taŋ] **(-(e)s, -e)** m seaweed

Tank [taŋk] **(-s, -s)** m tank; ~anzeige f fuel gauge; t~en vi to fill up with petrol (BRIT) od gas (US); (AVIAT) to (re)fuel; ~er **(-s, -)** m tanker; ~schiff nt tanker; ~stelle f petrol (BRIT) od gas (US) station; ~wart m petrol pump (BRIT) od gas station (US) attendant

Tanne ['tanə] f fir

Tannen- zW: ~baum m fir tree; ~zapfen m fir cone

Tante ['tantə] f aunt

Tanz [tants] **(-es, ˝e)** m dance; t~en vt, vi to dance

Tänzer(in) ['tɛntsər(ɪn)] **(-s, -)** m(f) dancer

Tanzfläche f (dance) floor

Tanzschule f dancing school

Tapete [ta'peːtə] f wallpaper; ~nwechsel m (fig) change of scenery

tapezieren [tapeˈtsiːrən] vt to (wall)paper; **Tapezierer** [tapeˈtsiːrər] **(-s, -)** m (interior) decorator

tapfer ['tapfər] adj brave; T~keit f courage, bravery

Tarif [ta'riːf] **(-s, -e)** m tariff, (scale of) fares od charges; ~lohn m standard wage rate; ~verhandlungen pl wage negotiations; ~zone f fare zone

Tarn- ['tarn] zW: t~en vt to camouflage; (Person, Absicht) to disguise; ~ung f camouflaging; disguising

Tasche ['taʃə] f pocket; handbag

Taschen- in zW pocket; ~buch nt paperback; ~dieb m pickpocket; ~geld nt pocket money; ~lampe f (electric) torch, flashlight (US); ~messer nt penknife; ~tuch nt handkerchief

Tasse ['tasə] f cup

Tastatur [tasta'tuːr] f keyboard

Taste ['tastə] f push-button control; (an Schreibmaschine) key; t~n vt to feel, to touch ♦ vi to feel, to grope ♦ vr to feel one's way

Tat [ta:t] **(-, -en)** f act, deed, action; **in der ~** indeed, as a matter of fact; t~ etc vb siehe **tun**; ~bestand m facts pl of the case; t~enlos adj inactive

Tät- ['tɛːt] zW: ~er(in) **(-s, -)** m(f) perpetrator, culprit; t~ig adj active; **in einer Firma t~ig sein** to work for a firm; ~igkeit f activity; (Beruf) occupation; t~lich adj violent; ~lichkeit f violence; **~lichkeiten** pl (Schläge) blows

tätowieren [tɛto'viːrən] *vt* to tattoo
Tatsache *f* fact
tatsächlich *adj* actual ♦ *adv* really
Tau[1] [tau] **(-(e)s, -e)** *nt* rope
Tau[2] [tau] **(-(e)s)** *m* dew
taub [taup] *adj* deaf; (*Nuss*) hollow
Taube ['taubə] *f* dove; pigeon; **~nschlag** *m* dovecote; **hier geht es zu wie in einem ~nschlag** it's a hive of activity here
taub- *zW*: **T~heit** *f* deafness; **~stumm** *adj* deaf-and-dumb
Tauch- ['taux] *zW*: **t~en** *vt* to dip ♦ *vi* to dive; (*NAUT*) to submerge; **~er (-s, -)** *m* diver; **~eranzug** *m* diving suit; **~erbrille** *f* diving goggles *pl*; **~sieder (-s, -)** *m* immersion coil (*for boiling water*)
tauen ['tauən] *vt, vi* to thaw ♦ *vb unpers*: **es taut** it's thawing
Tauf- ['tauf] *zW*: **~becken** *nt* font; **~e** *f* baptism; **t~en** *vt* to christen, to baptize; **~pate** *m* godfather; **~patin** *f* godmother; **~schein** *nt* certificate of baptism
taug- ['taug] *zW*: **~en** *vi* to be of use; **~en für** to do for, to be good for; **nicht ~en** to be no good *od* useless; **T~enichts (-es, -e)** *m* good-for-nothing; **~lich** ['tauklıç] *adj* suitable; (*MIL*) fit (*for service*)
Taumel ['tauməl] **(-s)** *m* dizziness; (*fig*) frenzy; **t~n** *vi* to reel, to stagger
Tausch [tauʃ] **(-(e)s, -e)** *m* exchange; **t~en** *vt* to exchange, to swap
täuschen ['tɔyʃən] *vt* to deceive ♦ *vi* to be deceptive ♦ *vr* to be wrong; **~d** *adj* deceptive
Tauschhandel *m* barter
Täuschung *f* deception; (*optisch*) illusion
tausend ['tauzənt] *num* (a) thousand
Tauwetter *nt* thaw
Taxi ['taksi] **(-(s), -(s))** *nt* taxi; **~fahrer** *m* taxi driver; **~stand** *m* taxi rank
Tech- ['tɛç] *zW*: **~nik** *f* technology; (*Methode, Kunstfertigkeit*) technique; **~niker (-s, -)** *m* technician; **t~nisch** *adj* technical; **~nologie** *f* technology; **t~no'logisch** *adj* technological
Tee [teː] **(-s, -s)** *m* tea; **~beutel** *m* tea bag; **~kanne** *f* teapot; **~löffel** *m* teaspoon

Teer [teːr] **(-(e)s, -e)** *m* tar; **t~en** *vt* to tar
Teesieb *nt* tea strainer
Teich [taıç] **(-(e)s, -e)** *m* pond
Teig [taık] **(-(e)s, -e)** *m* dough; **t~ig** ['taıgıç] *adj* doughy; **~waren** *pl* pasta *sg*
Teil [taıl] **(-(e)s, -e)** *m od nt* part; (*Anteil*) share; (*Bestandteil*) component; **zum ~** partly; **t~bar** *adj* divisible; **~betrag** *m* instalment; **~chen** *nt* (atomic) particle; **t~en** *vt, vr* to divide; (*mit jdm*) to share; **t~haben** (*unreg*) *vi*: **t~haben an** +*dat* to share in; **~haber (-s, -)** *m* partner; **~kaskoversicherung** *f* third party, fire and theft insurance; **t~möbliert** *adj* partially furnished; **~nahme** *f* participation; (*Mitleid*) sympathy *f*; **t~nahmslos** *adj* disinterested, apathetic; **t~nehmen** (*unreg*) *vi*: **t~nehmen an** +*dat* to take part in; **~nehmer (-s, -)** *m* participant; **t~s** *adv* partly; **~ung** *f* division; **t~weise** *adv* partially, in part; **~zahlung** *f* payment by instalments; **~zeitarbeit** *f* part-time work
Teint [tɛ̃ː] **(-s, -s)** *m* complexion
Telearbeit ['teːleˌarbaıt] *f* teleworking
Telefax ['teːlefaks] *nt* fax
Telefon [tele'foːn] **(-s, -e)** *nt* telephone; **~anruf** *m* (tele)phone call; **~at** [telefo'naːt] **(-(e)s, -e)** *nt* (tele)phone call; **~buch** *nt* telephone directory; **~hörer** *m* (telephone) receiver; **t~ieren** *vi* to telephone; **t~isch** [-ıʃ] *adj* telephone; (*Benachrichtigung*) by telephone; **~ist(in)** [telefo'nıst(ın)] *m(f)* telephonist; **~karte** *f* phonecard; **~nummer** *f* (tele)phone number; **~zelle** *f* telephone kiosk, callbox; **~zentrale** *f* telephone exchange
Telegraf [tele'graːf] **(-en, -en)** *m* telegraph; **~enmast** *m* telegraph pole; **~ie** [-'fiː] *f* telegraphy; **t~ieren** [-'fiːrən] *vt, vi* to telegraph, to wire
Telegramm [tele'gram] **(-s, -e)** *nt* telegram, cable; **~adresse** *f* telegraphic address
Tele- *zW*: **~objektiv** ['teːlɔpjɛktiːf] *nt* telephoto lens; **t~pathisch** [tele'paːtıʃ] *adj* telepathic; **~skop** [tele'skoːp] **(-s, -e)** *nt* telescope

Teller ['tɛlər] **(-s, -)** *m* plate; **~gericht** *nt* (KOCH) one-course meal

Tempel ['tɛmpəl] **(-s, -)** *m* temple

Temperament [tempəra'mɛnt] *nt* temperament; (Schwung) vivacity, liveliness; **t~voll** adj high-spirited, lively

Temperatur [tempəra'tuːr] *f* temperature

Tempo¹ ['tɛmpo] **(-s, Tempi)** *nt* (MUS) tempo

Tempo² ['tɛmpo] **(-s, -s)** *nt* speed, pace; **~!** get a move on!; **~limit** [-lɪmɪt] **(-s, -s)** *nt* speed limit; **~taschentuch** ⓡ *nt* tissue

Tendenz [tɛn'dɛnts] *f* tendency; (Absicht) intention; **t~iös** [-i'øːs] adj biased, tendentious

tendieren [tɛn'diːrən] vi: **~ zu** to show a tendency to, to incline towards

Tennis ['tɛnɪs] **(-)** *nt* tennis; **~ball** *m* tennis ball; **~platz** *m* tennis court; **~schläger** *m* tennis racket; **~schuh** *m* tennis shoe; **~spieler(in)** *m(f)* tennis player

Tenor [te'noːr] **(-s, ᵘe)** *m* tenor

Teppich ['tɛpɪç] **(-s, -e)** *m* carpet; **~boden** *m* wall-to-wall carpeting

Termin [tɛr'miːn] **(-s, -e)** *m* (Zeitpunkt) date; (Frist) time limit, deadline; (Arzttermin etc) appointment; **~kalender** *m* diary, appointments book; **~planer** *m* personal organizer

Terrasse [tɛ'rasə] *f* terrace

Terrine [tɛ'riːnə] *f* tureen

territorial [tɛritori'aːl] adj territorial

Territorium [tɛri'toːriʊm] *nt* territory

Terror ['tɛrɔr] **(-s)** *m* terror; reign of terror; **t~isieren** [tɛrori'ziːrən] vt to terrorize; **~ismus** [-'rɪsmʊs] *m* terrorism; **~ist** [-'rɪst] *m* terrorist

Tesafilm ['teːzafɪlm] ⓡ *m* Sellotape ⓡ (BRIT), Scotch tape (US)

Tessin [tɛ'siːn] **(-s)** *nt*: **das ~** Ticino

Test [tɛst] **(-s, -s)** *m* test

Testament [tɛsta'mɛnt] *nt* will, testament; (REL) Testament; **t~arisch** [-'taːrɪʃ] adj testamentary

Testamentsvollstrecker *m* executor (of a will)

testen vt to test

Tetanus ['teːtanʊs] **(-)** *m* tetanus; **~impfung** *f* (anti-)tetanus injection

teuer ['tɔyər] adj dear, expensive; **T~ung** *f* increase in prices; **T~ungszulage** *f* cost of living bonus

Teufel ['tɔyfəl] **(-s, -)** *m* devil; **teuflisch** ['tɔyflɪʃ] adj fiendish, diabolical

Text [tɛkst] **(-(e)s, -e)** *m* text; (Liedertext) words *pl*; **t~en** vi to write the words

textil [tɛks'tiːl] adj textile; **T~ien** *pl* textiles; **T~industrie** *f* textile industry; **T~waren** *pl* textiles

Textverarbeitung *f* word processing

Theater [te'aːtər] **(-s, -)** *nt* theatre; (umg) fuss; **~ spielen** (auch fig) to playact; **~besucher** *m* playgoer; **~kasse** *f* box office; **~stück** *nt* (stage) play

Theke ['teːkə] *f* (Schanktisch) bar; (Ladentisch) counter

Thema ['teːma] **(-s, Themen** od **-ta)** *nt* theme, topic, subject

Themse ['tɛmzə] *f* Thames

Theo- [teo] zW: **~loge** [-'loːgə] **(-n, -n)** *m* theologian; **~logie** [-lo'giː] *f* theology; **t~logisch** [-'loːgɪʃ] adj theological; **~retiker** [-'reːtikər] **(-s, -)** *m* theorist; **t~retisch** [-'reːtɪʃ] adj theoretical; **~rie** [-'riː] *f* theory

Thera- [tera] zW: **~peut** [-'pɔyt] **(-en, -en)** *m* therapist; **t~peutisch** [-'pɔytɪʃ] adj therapeutic; **~pie** [-'piː] *f* therapy

Therm- zW: **~albad** [tɛr'maːlbaːt] *nt* thermal bath; thermal spa; **~odrucker** [tɛrmo-] *m* thermal printer; **~ometer** [tɛrmo'meːtər] **(-s, -)** *nt* thermometer; **~osflasche** ['tɛrmɔsflaʃə] ⓡ *f* Thermos ⓡ flask

These ['teːzə] *f* thesis

Thrombose [trɔm'boːzə] *f* thrombosis

Thron [troːn] **(-(e)s, -e)** *m* throne; **t~en** vi to sit enthroned; (fig) to sit in state; **~folge** *f* succession (to the throne); **~folger(in)** **(-s, -)** *m(f)* heir to the throne

Thunfisch ['tuːnfɪʃ] *m* tuna

Thüringen ['tyːrɪŋən] **(-s)** *nt* Thuringia

Thymian ['tyːmiaːn] **(-s, -e)** *m* thyme

Tick [tɪk] **(-(e)s, -s)** *m* tic; (Eigenart) quirk;

Spelling Reform: ▲ *new spelling* △ *old spelling (to be phased out)*

(*Fimmel*) craze

ticken *vi* to tick

tief [tiːf] *adj* deep; (~*sinnig*) profound; (*Ausschnitt, Preis, Ton*) low; **~ greifend** far-reaching; **~ schürfend** profound; **T~** (**-s, -s**) *nt* (MET) depression; **T~druck** *m* low pressure; **T~e** *f* depth; **T~ebene** *f* plain; **T~enschärfe** *f* (PHOT) depth of focus; **T~garage** *f* underground garage; **~gekühlt** *adj* frozen; **T~kühlfach** *nt* deepfreeze compartment; **T~kühlkost** *f* (deep) frozen food; **T~kühltruhe** *f* deepfreeze, freezer; **T~punkt** *m* low point; (*fig*) low ebb; **T~schlag** *m* (BOXEN, *fig*) blow below the belt; **T~see** *f* deep sea; **~sinnig** *adj* profound; melancholy; **T~stand** *m* low level; **T~stwert** *m* minimum *od* lowest value

Tier [tiːr] (**-(e)s, -e**) *nt* animal; **~arzt** *m* vet(erinary surgeon); **~garten** *m* zoo(logical gardens *pl*); **~heim** *nt* cat/dog home; **t~isch** *adj* animal; (*auch fig*) brutish; (*fig: Ernst etc*) deadly; **~kreis** *m* zodiac; **~kunde** *f* zoology; **t~liebend** *adj* fond of animals; **~park** *m* zoo; **~quälerei** [-kvɛːləˈraɪ] *f* cruelty to animals; **~schutzverein** *m* society for the prevention of cruelty to animals

Tiger(in) [ˈtiːɡər(ɪn)] (**-s, -**) *m(f)* tiger(-gress)

tilgen [ˈtɪlɡən] *vt* to erase; (*Sünden*) to expiate; (*Schulden*) to pay off

Tinte [ˈtɪntə] *f* ink

Tintenfisch *m* cuttlefish

Tipp ▲ [tɪp] *m* tip; **t~en** *vt, vi* to tap, to touch; (*umg: schreiben*) to type; (*im Lotto etc*) to bet (on); **auf jdn t~en** (*umg: raten*) to tip sb, to put one's money on sb (*fig*)

Tipp- [tɪp] *zW:* **~fehler** (*umg*) *m* typing error; **t~topp** (*umg*) *adj* tip-top; **~zettel** *m* (pools) coupon

Tirol [tiˈroːl] *nt* the Tyrol; **~er(in)** *m(f)* Tyrolean; **t~isch** *adj* Tyrolean

Tisch [tɪʃ] (**-(e)s, -e**) *m* table; **bei ~** at table; **vor/nach ~** before/after eating; **unter den ~ fallen** (*fig*) to be dropped; **~decke** *f* tablecloth; **~ler** (**-s, -**) *m* carpenter, joiner; **~lerei** *f* joiner's workshop; (*Arbeit*)

carpentry, joinery; **t~lern** *vi* to do carpentry *etc*; **~rede** *f* after-dinner speech; **~tennis** *nt* table tennis; **~tuch** *nt* tablecloth

Titel [ˈtiːtəl] (**-s, -**) *m* title; **~bild** *nt* cover (picture); (*von Buch*) frontispiece; **~rolle** *f* title role; **~seite** *f* cover; (*Buchtitelseite*) title page; **~verteidiger** *m* defending champion, title holder

Toast [toːst] (**-(e)s, -s** *od* **-e**) *m* toast; **~brot** *nt* bread for toasting; **~er** (**-s, -**) *m* toaster

tob- [toːp] *zW:* **~en** *vi* to rage; (*Kinder*) to romp about; **~süchtig** *adj* maniacal

Tochter [ˈtɔxtər] (**-, ⁴**) *f* daughter; **~gesellschaft** *f* subsidiary (company)

Tod [toːt] (**-(e)s, -e**) *m* death; **t~ernst** *adj* deadly serious ♦ *adv* in dead earnest

Todes- [ˈtoːdəs] *zW:* **~angst** [-aŋst] *f* mortal fear; **~anzeige** *f* obituary (notice); **~fall** *m* death; **~strafe** *f* death penalty; **~ursache** *f* cause of death; **~urteil** *nt* death sentence; **~verachtung** *f* utter disgust

todkrank *adj* dangerously ill

tödlich [ˈtøːtlɪç] *adj* deadly, fatal

tod- *zW:* **~müde** *adj* dead tired; **~schick** (*umg*) *adj* dead smart, classy; **~sicher** (*umg*) *adj* absolutely *od* dead certain; **T~sünde** *f* deadly sin

Toilette [toaˈlɛtə] *f* toilet, lavatory; (*Frisiertisch*) dressing table

Toiletten- *zW:* **~artikel** *pl* toiletries, toilet articles; **~papier** *nt* toilet paper; **~tisch** *m* dressing table

toi, toi, toi [ˈtɔyˈtɔyˈtɔy] *excl* touch wood

tolerant [toleˈrant] *adj* tolerant

Toleranz [toleˈrants] *f* tolerance

tolerieren [toleˈriːrən] *vt* to tolerate

toll [tɔl] *adj* mad; (*Treiben*) wild; (*umg*) terrific; **~en** *vi* to romp; **T~kirsche** *f* deadly nightshade; **~kühn** *adj* daring; **T~wut** *f* rabies

Tomate [toˈmaːtə] *f* tomato; **~nmark** *nt* tomato purée

Ton¹ [toːn] (**-(e)s, -e**) *m* (*Erde*) clay

Ton² [toːn] (**-(e)s, ⁴e**) *m* (*Laut*) sound; (MUS) note; (*Redeweise*) tone; (*Farbton, Nuance*) shade; (*Betonung*) stress;

t~**angebend** adj leading; ~**art** f (musical) key; ~**band** nt tape; ~**bandgerät** nt tape recorder

tönen ['tøːnən] vi to sound ♦ vt to shade; (Haare) to tint

tönern ['tøːnərn] adj clay

Ton- zW: ~**fall** m intonation; ~**film** m sound film; ~**leiter** f (MUS) scale; t~**los** adj soundless

Tonne ['tɔnə] f barrel; (Maß) ton

Ton- zW: ~**taube** f clay pigeon; ~**waren** pl pottery sg, earthenware sg

Topf [tɔpf] (-(e)s, ⁺e) m pot; ~**blume** f pot plant

Töpfer ['tœpfər] (-s, -) m potter; ~**ei** [-'raɪ] f piece of pottery, potter's workshop; ~**scheibe** f potter's wheel

topografisch ▲ [topo'graːfɪʃ] adj topographic

Tor¹ [toːr] (-en, -en) m fool

Tor² [toːr] (-(e)s, -e) nt gate; (SPORT) goal; ~**bogen** m archway

Torf [tɔrf] (-(e)s) m peat

Torheit f foolishness; foolish deed

töricht ['tøːrɪçt] adj foolish

torkeln ['tɔrkəln] vi to stagger, to reel

Torte ['tɔrtə] f cake; (Obsttorte) flan, tart

Tortur [tɔr'tuːr] f ordeal

Torwart (-(e)s, -e) m goalkeeper

tosen ['toːzən] vi to roar

tot [toːt] adj dead; ~ **geboren** stillborn; **sich ~ stellen** to pretend to be dead

total [to'taːl] adj total; ~**itär** [totali'tɛːr] adj totalitarian; **T~schaden** m (AUT) complete write-off

Tote(r) f(m) dead person

töten ['tøːtən] vt, vi to kill

Toten- zW: ~**bett** nt death bed; t~**blass** ▲ adj deathly pale, white as a sheet; ~**kopf** m skull; ~**schein** m death certificate; ~**stille** f deathly silence

tot- zW: ~**fahren** (unreg) vt to run over; ~**geboren** △ adj siehe **tot**; ~**lachen** (umg) vr to laugh one's head off

Toto [to'toː] (-s, -s) m od nt pools pl; ~**schein** m pools coupon

tot- zW: **T~schlag** m manslaughter;

~**schlagen** (unreg) vt (auch fig) to kill; ~**schweigen** (unreg) vt to hush up; ~**stellen** △ vr siehe **tot**

Tötung ['tøːtʊŋ] f killing

Toupet [tu'peː] (-s, -s) nt toupee

toupieren [tu'piːrən] vt to backcomb

Tour [tuːr] (-, -en) f tour; (Umdrehung) revolution; (Verhaltensart) way; **in einer ~** incessantly; ~**enzähler** m rev counter; ~**ismus** [tu'rɪsmʊs] m tourism; ~**ist** [tu'rɪst] m tourist; ~**istenklasse** f tourist class; ~**nee** [tʊr'neː] (-, -n) f (THEAT etc) tour; **auf ~nee gehen** to go on tour

Trab [traːp] (-(e)s) m trot

Trabantenstadt f satellite town

traben ['traːbən] vi to trot

Tracht [traxt] (-, -en) f (Kleidung) costume, dress; **eine ~ Prügel** a sound thrashing; t~**en** vi: t~**en (nach)** to strive (for); **jdm nach dem Leben t~en** to seek to kill sb; **danach t~en, etw zu tun** to strive od endeavour to do sth

trächtig ['trɛçtɪç] adj (Tier) pregnant

Tradition [traditsi'oːn] f tradition; t~**ell** [-'nɛl] adj traditional

traf etc [traːf] vb siehe **treffen**

Tragbahre f stretcher

tragbar adj (Gerät) portable; (Kleidung) wearable; (erträglich) bearable

träge ['trɛːgə] adj sluggish, slow; (PHYS) inert

tragen ['traːgən] (unreg) vt to carry; (Kleidung, Brille) to wear; (Namen, Früchte) to bear; (erdulden) to endure ♦ vi (schwanger sein) to be pregnant; (Eis) to hold; **sich mit einem Gedanken ~** to have an idea in mind; **zum T~ kommen** to have an effect

Träger ['trɛːgər] (-s, -) m carrier; wearer; bearer; (Ordensträger) holder; (an Kleidung) (shoulder) strap; (Körperschaft etc) sponsor

Tragetasche f carrier bag

Tragfläche f (AVIAT) wing

Tragflügelboot nt hydrofoil

Trägheit ['trɛːkhaɪt] f laziness; (PHYS) inertia

Tragik ['traːgɪk] f tragedy; **tragisch** adj tragic

Tragödie [tra'gøːdiə] f tragedy

Tragweite f range; (fig) scope

Spelling Reform: ▲ *new spelling* △ *old spelling (to be phased out)*

Train- ['tre:n] zW: **~er** (**-s, -**) m (SPORT) trainer, coach; (Fußball) manager; **t~ieren** [trɛ'ni:rən] vt, vi to train; (Mensch) to train, to coach; (Übung) to practise; **~ing** (**-s, -s**) nt training; **~ingsanzug** m track suit

Traktor ['traktɔr] m tractor; (von Drucker) tractor feed

trällern ['trɛlərn] vt, vi to trill, to sing

Tram [tram] (**-, -s**) f tram

trampeln ['trampəln] vt, vi to trample, to stamp

trampen ['trɛmpən] vi to hitch-hike

Tramper(in) [trɛmpər(ɪn)] (**-s, -**) m(f) hitch-hiker

Tran [tra:n] (**-(e)s, -e**) m train oil, blubber

tranchieren [trã'ʃi:rən] vt to carve

Träne ['trɛ:nə] f tear; **t~n** vi to water; **~ngas** nt teargas

trank etc [traŋk] vb siehe **trinken**

tränken ['trɛŋkən] vt (Tiere) to water

transchieren ▲ [tran'ʃi:rən] vt to carve

Trans- zW: **~formator** [transfɔr'ma:tɔr] m transformer; **~istor** [tran'zistɔr] m transistor; **~itverkehr** [tran'zit:ferke:r] m transit traffic; **~itvisum** nt transit visa; **t~parent** adj transparent; **~parent** (**-(e)s, -e**) nt (Bild) transparency; (Spruchband) banner; **~plantation** [transplantatsi'o:n] f transplantation; (Hauttransplantation) graft(ing)

Transport [trans'pɔrt] (**-(e)s, -e**) m transport; **t~ieren** [transpɔr'ti:rən] vt to transport; **~kosten** pl transport charges, carriage sg; **~mittel** nt means sg of transportation; **~unternehmen** nt carrier

Traube ['traubə] f grape; bunch (of grapes); **~nzucker** m glucose

trauen ['trauən] vi: **jdm/etw ~** to trust sb/sth ♦ vr to dare ♦ vt to marry

Trauer ['trauər] (**-**) f sorrow; (für Verstorbenen) mourning; **~fall** m death, bereavement; **~feier** f funeral service; **~kleidung** f mourning; **t~n** vi to mourn; **um jdn t~n** to mourn (for) sb; **~rand** m black border; **~spiel** nt tragedy

traulich ['traulıç] adj cosy, intimate

Traum [traum] (**-(e)s, Träume**) m dream

Trauma (**-s, -men**) nt trauma

träum- ['trɔym] zW: **~en** vt, vi to dream; **T~er** (**-s, -**) m dreamer; **T~e'rei** f dreaming; **~erisch** adj dreamy

traumhaft adj dreamlike; (fig) wonderful

traurig ['trauriç] adj sad; **T~keit** f sadness

Trau- ['trau] zW: **~ring** m wedding ring; **~schein** m marriage certificate; **~ung** f wedding ceremony; **~zeuge** m witness (to a marriage); **~zeugin** f witness (to a marriage)

treffen ['trefən] (unreg) vt to strike, to hit; (Bemerkung) to hurt; (begegnen) to meet; (Entscheidung etc) to make; (Maßnahmen) to take ♦ vi to hit ♦ vr to meet; **er hat es gut getroffen** he did well; **~ auf** +akk to come across, to meet with; **es traf sich, dass ...** it so happened that ...; **es trifft sich gut** it's convenient; **wie es so trifft** as these things happen; **T~** (**-s, -**) nt meeting; **~d** adj pertinent, apposite

Treffer (**-s, -**) m hit; (Tor) goal; (Los) winner

Treffpunkt m meeting place

Treib- ['traib] zW: **~eis** nt drift ice; **t~en** (unreg) vt to drive; (Studien etc) to pursue; (Sport) to do, to go in for ♦ vi (Schiff etc) to drift; (Pflanzen) to sprout; (KOCH: aufgehen) to rise; (Tee, Kaffee) to be diuretic; **~haus** nt greenhouse; **~hauseffekt** m greenhouse effect; **~hausgas** nt greenhouse gas; **~stoff** m fuel

trenn- ['tren] zW: **~bar** adj separable; **~en** vt to separate; (teilen) to divide ♦ vr to separate; **sich ~en von** to part with; **T~ung** f separation; **T~wand** f partition (wall)

Trepp- ['trep] zW: **t~ab** adv downstairs; **t~auf** adv upstairs; **~e** f stair(case); **~engeländer** nt banister; **~enhaus** nt staircase

Tresor [tre'zo:r] (**-s, -e**) m safe

Tretboot nt pedalo, pedal boat

treten ['tre:tən] (unreg) vi to step; (Tränen, Schweiß) to appear ♦ vt (mit Fußtritt) to kick; (niedertreten) to tread, to trample; **~ nach** to kick at; **~ in** +akk to step in(to); **in Verbindung ~** to get in contact; **in**

Erscheinung ~ to appear

treu [trɔy] adj faithful, true; **T~e** (-) f loyalty, faithfulness; **T~händer** (**-s, -**) m trustee; **T~handanstalt** f trustee organization; **T~handgesellschaft** f trust company; **~herzig** adj innocent; **~los** adj faithless

---
Treuhandanstalt

i *The Treuhandanstalt was the organization set up in 1990 to take over the nationally-owned companies of the former DDR, break them down into smaller units and privatize them. It was based in Berlin and had nine branches. Many companies were closed down by the Treuhandanstalt because of their outdated equipment and inability to compete with Western firms which resulted in rising unemployment. Having completed its initial task, the Treuhandanstalt was closed down in 1995.*

Tribüne [tri'by:nə] f grandstand; (Rednertribüne) platform

Trichter ['trɪçtər] (**-s, -**) m funnel; (in Boden) crater

Trick [trɪk] (**-s, -e** od **-s**) m trick; **~film** m cartoon

Trieb [tri:p] (**-(e)s, -e**) m urge, drive; (Neigung) inclination; (an Baum etc) shoot; **t~** etc vb siehe **treiben**; **~kraft** f (fig) drive; **~täter** m sex offender; **~werk** nt engine

triefen ['tri:fən] vi to drip

triffst etc ['trɪfst] vb siehe **treffen**

triftig ['trɪftɪç] adj good, convincing

Trikot [tri'ko:] (**-s**) nt vest; (SPORT) shirt

Trimester [tri'mɛstər] (**-s, -**) nt term

trimmen ['trɪmən] vr to do keep fit exercises

trink- ['trɪŋk] zW: **~bar** adj drinkable; **~en** (unreg) vt, vi to drink; **T~er** (**-s, -**) m drinker; **T~geld** nt tip; **T~halle** f refreshment kiosk; **T~wasser** nt drinking water

Tripper ['trɪpər] (**-s, -**) m gonorrhoea

Tritt [trɪt] (**-(e)s, -e**) m step; (Fußtritt) kick; **~brett** nt (EISENB) step; (AUT) running board

Triumph [tri'ʊmf] (**-(e)s, -e**) m triumph; **~bogen** m triumphal arch; **t~ieren** [triʊm'fi:rən] vi to triumph; (jubeln) to exult

trocken ['trɔkən] adj dry; **T~element** nt dry cell; **T~haube** f hair dryer; **T~heit** f dryness; **~legen** vt (Sumpf) to drain; (Kind) to put a clean nappy on; **T~milch** f dried milk; **T~rasur** f dry shave, electric shave

trocknen ['trɔknən] vt, vi to dry

Trödel ['trø:dəl] (**-s**) (umg) m junk; **~markt** m flea market; **t~n** (umg) vi to dawdle

Trommel ['trɔməl] (**-, -n**) f drum; **~fell** nt eardrum; **t~n** vt, vi to drum

Trompete [trɔm'pe:tə] f trumpet; **~r** (**-s, -**) m trumpeter

Tropen ['tro:pən] pl tropics; **~helm** m sun helmet

tröpfeln ['trœpfəln] vi to drop, to trickle

Tropfen ['trɔpfən] (**-s, -**) m drop; **t~** vt, vi to drip ♦ vb unpers: **es tropft** a few raindrops are falling; **t~weise** adv in drops

Tropfsteinhöhle f stalactite cave

tropisch ['tro:pɪʃ] adj tropical

Trost [tro:st] (**-es**) m consolation, comfort

trösten ['trø:stən] vt to console, to comfort

trost- zW: **~los** adj bleak; (Verhältnisse) wretched; **T~preis** m consolation prize; **~reich** adj comforting

Trott [trɔt] (**-(e)s, -e**) m trot; (Routine) routine; **~el** (**-s, -**) (umg) m fool, dope; **t~en** vi to trot

Trotz [trɔts] (**-es**) m pigheadedness; **etw aus ~ tun** to do sth just to show them; **jdm zum ~** in defiance of sb; **t~** präp (+gen od dat) in spite of; **t~dem** adv nevertheless, all the same ♦ konj although; **t~en** vi (+dat) to defy; (der Kälte, Klima etc) to withstand; (der Gefahr) to brave; (t~ig sein) to be awkward; **t~ig** adj defiant, pig-headed; **~kopf** m obstinate child

trüb [try:p] adj dull; (Flüssigkeit, Glas) cloudy; (fig) gloomy

Trubel ['tru:bəl] (**-s**) m hurly-burly

trüb- zW: **~en** ['try:bən] vt to cloud ♦ vr to become clouded; **T~heit** f dullness; cloudiness; gloom; **T~sal** (**-, -e**) f distress; **~selig** adj sad, melancholy; **T~sinn** m depression; ~**sinnig** *adj* depressed, gloomy

Trüffel ['trʏfəl] (**-, -n**) *f* truffle

trug *etc* [truːk] *vb siehe* **tragen**

trügen ['tryːgən] (*unreg*) *vt* to deceive ♦ *vi* to be deceptive

trügerisch *adj* deceptive

Trugschluss ▲ ['truːgʃlʊs] *m* false conclusion

Truhe ['truːə] *f* chest

Trümmer ['trʏmər] *pl* wreckage *sg*; (*Bautrümmer*) ruins; ~**haufen** *m* heap of rubble

Trumpf [trʊmpf] (**-(e)s, ¨e**) *m* (*auch fig*) trump; **t~en** *vt*, *vi* to trump

Trunk [trʊŋk] (**-(e)s, ¨e**) *m* drink; **t~en** *adj* intoxicated; ~**enheit** *f* intoxication; ~**enheit am Steuer** drunken driving; ~**sucht** *f* alcoholism

Trupp [trʊp] (**-s, -s**) *m* troop; ~**e** *f* troop; (*Waffengattung*) force; (*Schauspieltruppe*) troupe; ~**en** *pl* (*MIL*) troops; ~**enübungsplatz** *m* training area

Truthahn ['truːthaːn] *m* turkey

Tschech- ['tʃɛç] *zW*: ~**e** *m* Czech; ~**ien** (**-s**) *nt* the Czech Republic; ~**in** *f* Czech; **t~isch** *adj* Czech; ~**oslowakei** [-oslova'kaɪ] *f*: **die ~oslowakei** Czechoslovakia; **t~oslowakisch** [-oslo'vaːkɪʃ] *adj* Czechoslovak(ian)

tschüs(s) [tʃʏs] *excl* cheerio

T-Shirt ['tiːʃəːt] *nt* T-shirt

Tube ['tuːbə] *f* tube

Tuberkulose [tuberku'loːzə] *f* tuberculosis

Tuch [tuːx] (**-(e)s, ¨er**) *nt* cloth; (*Halstuch*) scarf; (*Kopftuch*) headscarf; (*Handtuch*) towel

tüchtig ['tʏçtɪç] *adj* efficient, (*cap*)able; (*umg*: *kräftig*) good, sound; **T~keit** *f* efficiency, ability

Tücke ['tʏkə] *f* (*Arglist*) malice; (*Trick*) trick; (*Schwierigkeit*) difficulty, problem

tückisch ['tʏkɪʃ] *adj* treacherous; (*böswillig*) malicious

Tugend ['tuːgənt] (**-, -en**) *f* virtue; **t~haft** *adj* virtuous

Tülle *f* spout

Tulpe ['tʊlpə] *f* tulip

Tumor ['tuːmɔr] (**-s, -e**) *m* tumour

Tümpel ['tʏmpəl] (**-s, -**) *m* pool, pond

Tumult [tu'mʊlt] (**-(e)s, -e**) *m* tumult

tun [tuːn] (*unreg*) *vt* (*machen*) to do; (*legen*) to put ♦ *vi* to act ♦ *vr*: **es tut sich etwas/viel** something/a lot is happening; **jdm etw ~** (*antun*) to do sth to sb; **etw tut es auch** sth will do; **das tut nichts** that doesn't matter; **das tut nichts zur Sache** that's neither here nor there; **so ~ als ob** to act as if

tünchen ['tʏnçən] *vt* to whitewash

Tunfisch ▲ ['tuːnfɪʃ] *m* = **Thunfisch**

Tunke ['tʊŋkə] *f* sauce; **t~n** *vt* to dip, to dunk

tunlichst ['tuːnlɪçst] *adv* if at all possible; ~**bald** as soon as possible

Tunnel ['tʊnəl] (**-s, -s** *od* **-**) *m* tunnel

Tupfen ['tʊpfən] (**-s, -**) *m* dot, spot; **t~** *vt*, *vi* to dab; (*mit Farbe*) to dot

Tür [tyːr] (**-, -en**) *f* door

Turbine [tʊr'biːnə] *f* turbine

Türk- [tʏrk] *zW*: ~**e** *m* Turk; ~**ei** [tʏr'kaɪ] *f*: **die ~ei** Turkey; ~**in** *f* Turk

Türkis [tʏr'kiːs] (**-es, -e**) *m* turquoise; **t~** *adj* turquoise

türkisch ['tʏrkɪʃ] *adj* Turkish

Türklinke *f* doorknob, door handle

Turm [tʊrm] (**-(e)s, ¨e**) *m* tower; (*Kirchturm*) steeple; (*Sprungturm*) diving platform; (*SCHACH*) castle, rook

türmen ['tʏrmən] *vr* to tower up ♦ *vt* to heap up ♦ *vi* (*umg*) to scarper, to bolt

Turn- ['tʊrn] *zW*: **t~en** *vi* to do gymnastic exercises ♦ *vt* to perform; ~**en** (**-s**) *nt* gymnastics; (*SCH*) physical education, P.E.; ~**er(in)** (**-s, -**) *m(f)* gymnast; ~**halle** *f* gym(nasium); ~**hose** *f* gym shorts *pl*

Turnier [tʊr'niːr] (**-s, -e**) *nt* tournament

Turn- *zW*: ~**schuh** *m* gym shoe; ~**verein** *m* gymnastics club; ~**zeug** *nt* gym things *pl*

Tusche ['tʊʃə] *f* Indian ink

tuscheln ['tʊʃəln] *vt*, *vi* to whisper

Tuschkasten *m* paintbox

Tüte ['tyːtə] *f* bag

tuten ['tuːtən] *vi* (*AUT*) to hoot (*BRIT*), to honk (*US*)

TÜV [tyf] (**-s, -s**) m abk (= Technischer Überwachungs-Verein) ≃ MOT

Typ [ty:p] (**-s, -en**) m type; **~e** f (TYP) type

Typhus ['ty:fʊs] (**-**) m typhoid (fever)

typisch ['ty:pɪʃ] adj: **~ (für)** typical (of)

Tyrann [ty'ran] (**-en, -en**) m tyrant; **~ei** [-'naɪ] f tyranny; **t~isch** adj tyrannical; **t~i'sieren** vt to tyrannize

U, u

u. a. abk = unter anderem

U-Bahn ['u:ba:n] f underground, tube

übel ['y:bəl] adj bad; (moralisch) bad, wicked; **jdm ist ~** sb feels sick; **~ gelaunt** bad-tempered; **jdm eine Bemerkung** etc **~ nehmen** to be offended at sb's remark etc; **Ü~ (-s, -)** nt evil; (Krankheit) disease; **Ü~keit** f nausea

üben ['y:bən] vt, vi to exercise, to practise

SCHLÜSSELWORT

über ['y:bər] präp +dat **1** (räumlich) over, above; **zwei Grad über null** two degrees above zero

2 (zeitlich) over; **über der Arbeit einschlafen** to fall asleep over one's work
♦ präp +akk **1** (räumlich) over; (hoch über auch) above; (quer über auch) across

2 (zeitlich) over; **über Weihnachten** over Christmas; **über kurz oder lang** sooner or later

3 (mit Zahlen): **Kinder über 12 Jahren** children over od above 12 years of age; **ein Scheck über 200 Mark** a cheque for 200 marks

4 (auf dem Wege) via; **nach Köln über Aachen** to Cologne via Aachen; **ich habe es über die Auskunft erfahren** I found out from information

5 (betreffend) about; **ein Buch über ...** a book about od on ...; **über jdn/etw lachen** to laugh about od at sb/sth

6: Macht über jdn haben to have power over sb; **sie liebt ihn über alles** she loves him more than everything

♦ adv over; **über und über** over and over; **den ganzen Tag über** all day long; **jdm in etw** dat **über sein** to be superior to sb in sth

---

überall [y:bər'al] adv everywhere; **~'hin** adv everywhere

überanstrengen [y:bər'anʃtrɛŋən] vt insep to overexert ♦ vr insep to overexert o.s.

überarbeiten [y:bər'arbaɪtən] vt insep to revise, to rework ♦ vr insep to overwork (o.s.)

überaus ['y:bəraʊs] adv exceedingly

überbelichten ['y:bərbəlɪçtən] vt (PHOT) to overexpose

über'bieten (unreg) vt insep to outbid; (übertreffen) to surpass; (Rekord) to break

Überbleibsel ['y:bərblaɪpsəl] (**-s, -**) nt residue, remainder

Überblick ['y:bərblɪk] m view; (fig: Darstellung) survey, overview; (Fähigkeit): **~ (über** +akk) grasp (of), overall view (of); **ü~en** [-'blɪkən] vt insep to survey

überbring- [y:bər'brɪŋ] zW: **~en** (unreg) vt insep to deliver, to hand over; **Ü~er (-s, -)** m bearer

überbrücken [y:bər'brʏkən] vt insep to bridge (over)

überbuchen ['y:bərbu:xən] vt insep to overbook

über'dauern vt insep to outlast

über'denken (unreg) vt insep to think over

überdies [y:bər'di:s] adv besides

überdimensional ['y:bərdimɛnziona:l] adj oversize

Überdruss ▲ ['y:bərdrʊs] (**-es**) m weariness; **bis zum ~** ad nauseam

überdurchschnittlich ['y:bərdʊrçʃnɪtlɪç] adj above-average ♦ adv exceptionally

übereifrig ['y:bəraɪfrɪç] adj over-keen

übereilt [y:bər'aɪlt] adj (over)hasty, premature

überein- [y:bər'aɪn] zW: **~ander** [y:bəraɪn'andər] adv one upon the other; (sprechen) about each other; **~kommen** (unreg) vi to agree; **Ü~kunft (-, -künfte)** f agreement; **~stimmen** vi to agree;

Ü~**stimmung** f agreement

überempfindlich [ˈyːbərˌɛmpfɪntlɪç] adj hypersensitive

überfahren [yːbərˈfaːrən] (unreg) vt insep (AUT) to run over; (fig) to walk all over

Überfahrt [ˈyːbərfaːrt] f crossing

Überfall [ˈyːbərfal] m (Banküberfall, MIL) raid; (auf jdn) assault; ü~**en** [-ˈfalən] (unreg) vt insep to attack; (Bank) to raid; (besuchen) to drop in on, to descend on

überfällig [ˈyːbərfɛlɪç] adj overdue

überfliegen (unreg) vt insep to fly over, to overfly; (Buch) to skim through

Überfluss ▲ [ˈyːbərflʊs] m: ~ **(an** +dat) (super)abundance (of), excess (of)

überflüssig [ˈyːbərflʏsɪç] adj superfluous

überfordern vt insep to demand too much of; (Kräfte etc) to overtax

überführen vt insep (Leiche etc) to transport; (Täter) to have convicted

Überführung f transport; conviction; (Brücke) bridge, overpass

überfüllt adj (Schulen, Straßen) overcrowded; (Kurs) oversubscribed

Übergabe [ˈyːbərgaːbə] f handing over; (MIL) surrender

Übergang [ˈyːbərgaŋ] m crossing; (Wandel, Überleitung) transition

Übergangs- zW: ~**lösung** f provisional solution, stopgap; ~**zeit** f transitional period

übergeben (unreg) vt insep to hand over; (MIL) to surrender ♦ vr insep to be sick

übergehen [ˈyːbərgeːən] (unreg) vi (Besitz) to pass; (zum Feind etc) to go over, to defect; ~ **in** +akk to turn into; **über'gehen** (unreg) vt insep to pass over, to omit

Übergewicht [ˈyːbərgəvɪçt] nt excess weight; (fig) preponderance

überglücklich [ˈyːbərglʏklɪç] adj overjoyed

Übergröße [ˈyːbərgrøːsə] f oversize

überhaupt [yːbərˈhaupt] adv at all; (im Allgemeinen) in general; (besonders) especially; ~ **nicht/keine** not/none at all

überheblich [yːbərˈheːplɪç] adj arrogant; Ü~**keit** f arrogance

überholen vt insep to overtake; (TECH) to overhaul

überholt adj out-of-date, obsolete

Überholverbot [yːbərˈhoːlfɛrboːt] nt restriction on overtaking

überhören vt insep not to hear; (absichtlich) to ignore

überirdisch [ˈyːbərˌɪrdɪʃ] adj supernatural, unearthly

überladen (unreg) vt insep to overload ♦ adj (fig) cluttered

überlassen (unreg) vt insep: **jdm etw ~** to leave sth to sb ♦ vr insep: **sich einer Sache** dat ~ to give o.s. over to sth

überlasten vt insep to overload; (Mensch) to overtax

überlaufen [ˈyːbərlaufən] (unreg) vi (Flüssigkeit) to flow over; (zum Feind etc) to go over, to defect; ~ **sein** to be inundated od besieged; **über'laufen** (unreg) vt insep (Schauer etc) to come over

überleben vt insep to survive; **Über'lebende(r)** f(m) survivor

überlegen vt insep to consider ♦ adj superior; **ich muss es mir ~** I'll have to think about it; **Über'legenheit** f superiority

Überlegung f consideration, deliberation

überliefern vt insep to hand down, to transmit

Überlieferung f tradition

überlisten [yːbərˈlɪstən] vt insep to outwit

überm [ˈyːbərm] = **über dem**

Übermacht [ˈyːbərmaxt] f superior force, superiority; **übermächtig** [ˈyːbərmɛçtɪç] adj superior (in strength); (Gefühl etc) overwhelming

übermäßig [ˈyːbərmɛːsɪç] adj excessive

Übermensch [ˈyːbərmɛnʃ] m superman; ü~**lich** adj superhuman

übermitteln [yːbərˈmɪtəln] vt insep to convey

übermorgen [ˈyːbərmɔrgən] adv the day after tomorrow

Übermüdung [yːbərˈmyːdʊŋ] f fatigue, overtiredness

Übermut [ˈyːbərmuːt] m exuberance

übermütig [ˈyːbərmyːtɪç] adj exuberant,

high-spirited; **~ werden** to get overconfident

übernächste(r, s) ['y:bɐrnɛːçstə(r, s)] *adj* (*Jahr*) next but one

übernacht- [y:bɐr'naxt] *zW:* **~en** *vi insep:* **(bei jdm) ~en** to spend the night (at sb's place); **Ü~ung** *f* overnight stay; **Ü~ung mit Frühstück** bed and breakfast; **Ü~ungsmöglichkeit** *f* overnight accommodation *no pl*

Übernahme ['y:bɐrnaːmə] *f* taking over *od* on, acceptance

über'nehmen (*unreg*) *vt insep* to take on, to accept; (*Amt, Geschäft*) to take over ♦ *vr insep* to take on too much

über'prüfen *vt insep* to examine, to check

überqueren [y:bɐr'kveːrən] *vt insep* to cross

überragen [y:bɐr'raːgən] *vt insep* to tower above; (*fig*) to surpass

überraschen [y:bɐr'raʃən] *vt insep* to surprise

Überraschung *f* surprise

überreden [y:bɐr'reːdən] *vt insep* to persuade

überreichen [y:bɐr'raiçən] *vt insep* to present, to hand over

'Überrest *m* remains, remnants

überrumpeln [y:bɐr'rʊmpəln] *vt insep* to take by surprise

überrunden [y:bɐr'rʊndən] *vt insep* to lap

übers ['y:bɐrs] = **über das**

Überschall- ['y:bɐrʃal] *zW:* **~flugzeug** *nt* supersonic jet; **~geschwindigkeit** *f* supersonic speed

über'schätzen *vt insep* to overestimate

'überschäumen *vi* (*Bier*) to foam over, bubble over; (*Temperament*) to boil over

Überschlag ['y:bɐrʃlaːk] *m* (*FIN*) estimate; (*SPORT*) somersault; **ü~en** [-'ʃlaːgən] (*unreg*) *vt insep* (*berechnen*) to estimate; (*auslassen: Seite*) to omit ♦ *vr insep* to somersault; (*Stimme*) to crack; (*AVIAT*) to loop the loop; **'überschlagen** (*unreg*) *vt insep* (*Beine*) to cross ♦ *vi* (*Wellen*) to break; (*Funken*) to flash

überschnappen ['y:bɐrʃnapən] *vi* (*Stimme*) to crack; (*umg: Mensch*) to flip one's lid

über'schneiden (*unreg*) *vr insep* (*auch fig*)

to overlap; (*Linien*) to intersect

über'schreiben (*unreg*) *vt insep* to provide with a heading; **jdm etw ~** to transfer *od* make over sth to sb

über'schreiten (*unreg*) *vt insep* to cross over; (*fig*) to exceed; (*verletzen*) to transgress

Überschrift ['y:bɐrʃrɪft] *f* heading, title

Überschuss ▲ ['y:bɐrʃʊs] *m:* **~ (an** +*dat*) surplus (of); **überschüssig** ['y:bɐrʃʏsɪç] *adj* surplus, excess

über'schütten *vt insep:* **jdn/etw mit etw ~** to pour sth over sb/sth; **jdn mit etw ~** (*fig*) to shower sb with sth

überschwänglich ▲ ['y:bɐrʃvɛŋlɪç] *adj* effusive

überschwemmen [y:bɐr'ʃvɛmən] *vt insep* to flood

Überschwemmung *f* flood

Übersee ['y:bɐrzeː] *f:* **nach/in ~** overseas; **ü~isch** *adj* overseas

über'sehen (*unreg*) *vt insep* to look (out) over; (*fig: Folgen*) to see, to get an overall view of; (: *nicht beachten*) to overlook

über'senden (*unreg*) *vt insep* to send, to forward

übersetz- *zW:* **~en** [y:bɐr'zɛtsən] *vt insep* to translate; **'übersetzen** *vi* to cross; **Ü~er(in)** [-'zɛtsɐr(ɪn)] (**-s, -**) *m(f)* translator; **Ü~ung** [-'zɛtsʊŋ] *f* translation; (*TECH*) gear ratio

Übersicht ['y:bɐrzɪçt] *f* overall view; (*Darstellung*) survey; **ü~lich** *adj* clear; (*Gelände*) open; **~lichkeit** *f* clarity, lucidity

übersiedeln ['y:bɐrziːdəln] *vi sep* to move; **über'siedeln** *vi* to move

über'spannt *adj* eccentric; (*Idee*) wild, crazy

überspitzt [y:bɐr'ʃpɪtst] *adj* exaggerated

über'springen (*unreg*) *vt insep* to jump over; (*fig*) to skip

überstehen [y:bɐr'ʃteːən] (*unreg*) *vt insep* to overcome, to get over; (*Winter etc*) to survive, to get through; **'überstehen** (*unreg*) *vi* to project

über'steigen (*unreg*) *vt insep* to climb over; (*fig*) to exceed

über'stimmen vt insep to outvote

Überstunden ['y:bərʃtʊndən] pl overtime sg

über'stürzen vt insep to rush ♦ vr insep to follow (one another) in rapid succession

überstürzt adj (over)hasty

Übertrag ['y:bərtra:k] (-(e)s, -träge) m (COMM) amount brought forward; **ü~bar** [-'tra:kba:r] adj transferable; (MED) infectious; **ü~en** [-'tra:gən] (unreg) vt insep to transfer; (RADIO) to broadcast; (übersetzen) to render; (Krankheit) to transmit ♦ vr insep to spread ♦ adj figurative; **ü~en auf** +akk to transfer to; **jdm etw ü~en** to assign sth to sb; **sich ü~en auf** +akk to spread to; **~ung** [-'tra:gʊŋ] f transfer(ence); (RADIO) broadcast; rendering; transmission

über'treffen (unreg) vt insep to surpass

über'treiben (unreg) vt insep to exaggerate; **Übertreibung** f exaggeration

übertreten [y:bər'tre:tən] (unreg) vt insep to cross; (Gebot etc) to break; '**übertreten** (unreg) vi (über Linie, Gebiet) to step (over); (SPORT) to overstep; (zu anderem Glauben) to be converted; '**übertreten (in** +akk) (POL) to go over (to)

Über'tretung f violation, transgression

übertrieben [y:bər'tri:bən] adj exaggerated, excessive

übervölkert [y:bər'fœlkərt] adj overpopulated

übervoll ['y:bərfɔl] adj overfull

übervorteilen [y:bər'fɔrtailən] vt insep to dupe, to cheat

über'wachen vt insep to supervise; (Verdächtigen) to keep under surveillance; **Überwachung** f supervision; surveillance

überwältigen [y:bər'vɛltɪgən] vt insep to overpower; **~d** adj overwhelming

überweisen [y:bər'vaizən] (unreg) vt insep to transfer

Überweisung f transfer; **~sauftrag** m (credit) transfer order

über'wiegen (unreg) vi insep to predominate; **~d** adj predominant

über'winden (unreg) vt insep to overcome ♦ vr insep to make an effort, to bring o.s. (to do sth)

Überwindung f effort, strength of mind

Überzahl ['y:bərtsa:l] f superiority, superior numbers pl; **in der ~ sein** to be numerically superior

überzählig ['y:bərtse:lɪç] adj surplus

über'zeugen vt insep to convince; **~d** adj convincing

Überzeugung f conviction

überziehen ['y:bərtsi:ən] (unreg) vt to put on; **über'ziehen** (unreg) vt insep to cover; (Konto) to overdraw

Überziehungskredit m overdraft provision

Überzug ['y:bərtsu:k] m cover; (Belag) coating

üblich ['y:plɪç] adj usual

U-Boot ['u:bo:t] nt submarine

übrig ['y:brɪç] adj remaining; **für jdn etwas ~ haben** (umg) to be fond of sb; **die Ü~en** the others; **das Ü~e** the rest; **im Ü~en** besides; **~ bleiben** to remain, to be left (over); **~ lassen** to leave (over); **~ens** ['y:brɪgəns] adv besides; (nebenbei bemerkt) by the way

Übung ['y:bʊŋ] f practice; (Turnübung, Aufgabe etc) exercise; **~ macht den Meister** practice makes perfect

Ufer ['u:fər] (-s, -) nt bank; (Meeresufer) shore

Uhr [u:r] (-, -en) f clock; (Armbanduhr) watch; **wie viel ~ ist es?** what time is it?; **1 ~** 1 o'clock; **20 ~** 8 o'clock, 20.00 (twenty hundred) hours; **~(arm)band** nt watch strap; **~band** nt watch strap; **~macher** (-s, -) m watchmaker; **~werk** nt clockwork; works of a watch; **~zeiger** m hand; **~zeigersinn** m: **im ~zeigersinn** clockwise; **entgegen dem ~zeigersinn** anticlockwise; **~zeit** f time of (day)

Uhu ['u:hu] (-s, -s) m eagle owl

UKW [u:ka:'ve:] abk (= Ultrakurzwelle) VHF

ulkig ['ʊlkɪç] adj funny

Ulme ['ʊlmə] f elm

Ultimatum [ʊlti'ma:tʊm] (-s, Ultimaten) nt ultimatum

Ultra- ['ʊltra] zW: **~schall** m (PHYS) ultrasound; **u~violett** adj ultraviolet

m [ʊm] *präp +akk* **1** (*um herum*) (a)round; **um Weihnachten** around Christmas; **er schlug um sich** he hit about him
2 (*mit Zeitangabe*) at; **um acht (Uhr)** at eight (o'clock)
3 (*mit Größenangabe*) by; **etw um 4 cm kürzen** to shorten sth by 4 cm; **um 10% teurer** 10% more expensive; **um vieles besser** better by far; **um nichts besser** not in the least bit better
4: **der Kampf um den Titel** the battle for the title; **um Geld spielen** to play for money; **Stunde um Stunde** hour after hour; **Auge um Auge** an eye for an eye
♦ *präp +gen*: **um ... willen** for the sake of ...; **um Gottes willen** for goodness *od* (*stärker*) God's sake
♦ *konj*: **um ... zu** (in order) to ...; **zu klug, um zu ...** too clever to ...; *siehe* **umso**
♦ *adv* **1** (*ungefähr*) about; **um (die) 30 Leute** about *od* around 30 people
2 (*vorbei*): **die 2 Stunden sind um** the two hours are up

mändern ['ʊm|ɛndərn] *vt* to alter
mänderung *f* alteration
marbeiten ['ʊm|arbaɪtən] *vt* to remodel; (*Buch etc*) to revise, to rework
marmen [ʊm'|armən] *vt insep* to embrace
mbau ['ʊmbaʊ] **(-(e)s, -e** *od* **-ten)** *m* reconstruction, alteration(s); **u~en** *vt* to rebuild, to reconstruct
mbilden ['ʊmbɪldən] *vt* to reorganize; (*POL: Kabinett*) to reshuffle
mbinden ['ʊmbɪndən] (*unreg*) *vt* (*Krawatte etc*) to put on
mblättern ['ʊmblɛtərn] *vt* to turn over
mblicken ['ʊmblɪkən] *vr* to look around
mbringen ['ʊmbrɪŋən] (*unreg*) *vt* to kill
mbuchen ['ʊmbuːxən] *vi* to change one's reservation/flight *od* ♦ *vt* to change
mdenken ['ʊmdɛŋkən] (*unreg*) *vi* to adjust one's views
mdrehen ['ʊmdreːən] *vt* to turn (round); (*Hals*) to wring ♦ *vr* to turn (round)

Um'drehung *f* revolution; rotation
umeinander [ʊm|aɪ'nandər] *adv* round one another; (*füreinander*) for one another
umfahren ['ʊmfaːrən] (*unreg*) *vt* to run over; **um'fahren** (*unreg*) *vt insep* to drive round; to sail round
umfallen ['ʊmfalən] (*unreg*) *vi* to fall down *od* over
Umfang ['ʊmfaŋ] *m* extent; (*von Buch*) size; (*Reichweite*) range; (*Fläche*) area; (*MATH*) circumference; **u~reich** *adj* extensive; (*Buch etc*) voluminous
um'fassen *vt insep* to embrace; (*umgeben*) to surround; (*enthalten*) to include; **um'fassend** *adj* comprehensive, extensive
umformen ['ʊmfɔrmən] *vt* to transform
Umfrage ['ʊmfraːgə] *f* poll
umfüllen ['ʊmfʏlən] *vt* to transfer; (*Wein*) to decant
umfunktionieren ['ʊmfʊŋktsioniːrən] *vt* to convert, to transform
Umgang ['ʊmgaŋ] *m* company; (*mit jdm*) dealings *pl*; (*Behandlung*) way of behaving
umgänglich ['ʊmgɛŋlɪç] *adj* sociable
Umgangs- *zW*: **~formen** *pl* manners; **~sprache** *f* colloquial language
umgeben [ʊm'geːbən] (*unreg*) *vt insep* to surround
Umgebung *f* surroundings *pl*; (*Milieu*) environment; (*Personen*) people in one's circle
umgehen ['ʊmgeːən] (*unreg*) *vi* to go (a)round; **im Schlosse ~** to haunt the castle; **mit jdm grob** *etc* **~** to treat sb roughly *etc*; **mit Geld sparsam ~** to be careful with one's money; **um'gehen** *vt insep* to bypass; (*MIL*) to outflank; (*Gesetz etc*) to circumvent; (*vermeiden*) to avoid; **'umgehend** *adj* immediate
Um'gehung *f* bypassing; outflanking; circumvention; avoidance; **~sstraße** *f* bypass
umgekehrt ['ʊmgəkeːrt] *adj* reverse(d); (*gegenteilig*) opposite ♦ *adv* the other way around; **und ~** and vice versa
umgraben ['ʊmgraːbən] (*unreg*) *vt* to dig up
Umhang ['ʊmhaŋ] *m* wrap, cape

Spelling Reform: ▲ *new spelling* △ *old spelling (to be phased out)*

umhauen ['ʊmhaʊən] *vt* to fell; (*fig*) to bowl over

umher [ʊm'heːr] *adv* about, around; ~**gehen** (*unreg*) *vi* to walk about; ~**ziehen** (*unreg*) *vi* to wander from place to place

umhinkönnen [ʊm'hɪnkœnən] (*unreg*) *vi*: **ich kann nicht umhin, das zu tun** I can't help doing it

umhören ['ʊmhøːrən] *vr* to ask around

Umkehr ['ʊmkeːr] (-) *f* turning back; (*Änderung*) change; **u~en** *vi* to turn back ♦ *vt* to turn round, to reverse; (*Tasche etc*) to turn inside out; (*Gefäß etc*) to turn upside down

umkippen ['ʊmkɪpən] *vt* to tip over ♦ *vi* to overturn; (*umg: Mensch*) to keel over; (*fig: Meinung ändern*) to change one's mind

Umkleide- ['ʊmklaɪdə] *zW*: ~**kabine** *f* (*im Schwimmbad*) (changing) cubicle; ~**raum** *m* changing *od* dressing room

umkommen ['ʊmkɔmən] (*unreg*) *vi* to die, to perish; (*Lebensmittel*) to go bad

Umkreis ['ʊmkraɪs] *m* neighbourhood; **im ~ von** within a radius of

Umlage ['ʊmlaːgə] *f* share of the costs

Umlauf ['ʊmlaʊf] *m* (*Geldumlauf*) circulation; (*von Gestirn*) revolution; ~**bahn** *f* orbit

Umlaut ['ʊmlaʊt] *m* umlaut

umlegen ['ʊmleːgən] *vt* to put on; (*verlegen*) to move, to shift; (*Kosten*) to share out; (*umkippen*) to tip over; (*umg: töten*) to bump off

umleiten ['ʊmlaɪtən] *vt* to divert

Umleitung *f* diversion

umliegend ['ʊmliːgənt] *adj* surrounding

um'randen *vt insep* to border, to edge

umrechnen ['ʊmrɛçnən] *vt* to convert

Umrechnung *f* conversion; ~**skurs** *m* rate of exchange

um'reißen (*unreg*) *vt insep* to outline, to sketch

Umriss ▲ ['ʊmrɪs] *m* outline

umrühren ['ʊmryːrən] *vt*, *vi* to stir

ums [ʊms] = **um das**

Umsatz ['ʊmzats] *m* turnover; ~**steuer** *f* sales tax

umschalten ['ʊmʃaltən] *vt* to switch

umschauen *vr* to look round

Umschlag ['ʊmʃlaːk] *m* cover; (*Buchumschlag auch*) jacket; (*MED*) compress; (*Briefumschlag*) envelope; (*Wechsel*) change; (*von Hose*) turn-up; **u~en** [-gən] (*unreg*) *vi* to change; (*NAUT*) to capsize ♦ *vt* to knock over; (*Ärmel*) to turn up; (*Seite*) to turn over; (*Waren*) to transfer; ~**platz** *m* (*COMM*) distribution centre

umschreiben ['ʊmʃraɪbən] (*unreg*) *vt* (*neu schreiben*) to rewrite; (*übertragen*) to transfer; ~ **auf** +*akk* to transfer to; **um'schreiben** (*unreg*) *vt insep* to paraphrase; (*abgrenzen*) to define

umschulen ['ʊmʃuːlən] *vt* to retrain; (*Kind*) to send to another school

Umschweife ['ʊmʃvaɪfə] *pl*: **ohne ~** without beating about the bush, straight out

Umschwung ['ʊmʃvʊŋ] *m* change (around), revolution

umsehen ['ʊmzeːən] (*unreg*) *vr* to look around *od* about; (*suchen*): **sich ~ (nach)** to look out (for)

umseitig ['ʊmzaɪtɪç] *adv* overleaf

umsichtig ['ʊmzɪçtɪç] *adj* cautious, prudent

umso ▲ ['ʊmzo] *konj*: ~ **besser/schlimmer** so much the better/worse

umsonst [ʊm'zɔnst] *adv* in vain; (*gratis*) for nothing

umspringen ['ʊmʃprɪŋən] (*unreg*) *vi* to change; (*Wind auch*) to veer; **mit jdm ~** to treat sb badly

Umstand ['ʊmʃtant] *m* circumstance; **Umstände** *pl* (*fig: Schwierigkeiten*) fuss; **in anderen Umständen sein** to be pregnant; **Umstände machen** to go to a lot of trouble; **unter Umständen** possibly

umständlich ['ʊmʃtɛntlɪç] *adj* (*Methode*) cumbersome, complicated; (*Ausdrucksweise, Erklärung*) long-winded; (*Mensch*) ponderous

Umstandskleid *nt* maternity dress

Umstehende(n) ['ʊmʃteːəndə(n)] *pl* bystanders

umsteigen ['ʊmʃtaɪgən] (*unreg*) *vi* (*EISENB*) to change

umstellen ['ʊmʃtɛlən] *vt* (*an anderen Ort*) to

change round, to rearrange; (TECH) to convert ♦ vr to adapt (o.s.); **sich auf etw** akk ~ to adapt to sth; um'stellen vt insep to surround

Umstellung ['ʊmʃtɛlʊŋ] f change; (Umgewöhnung) adjustment; (TECH) conversion

umstimmen ['ʊmʃtɪmən] vt (MUS) to retune; **jdn** ~ to make sb change his mind

umstoßen ['ʊmʃtoːsən] (unreg) vt to overturn; (Plan etc) to change, to upset

umstritten [ʊm'ʃtrɪtən] adj disputed

Umsturz ['ʊmʃtʊrts] m overthrow

umstürzen ['ʊmʃtʏrtsən] vt (umwerfen) to overturn ♦ vi to collapse, to fall down; (Wagen) to overturn

Umtausch ['ʊmtaʊʃ] m exchange; **u~en** vt to exchange

Umverpackung ['ʊmfɛrpakʊŋ] f packaging

umwandeln ['ʊmvandəln] vt to change, to convert; (ELEK) to transform

umwechseln ['ʊmvɛksəln] vt to change

Umweg ['ʊmveːk] m detour, roundabout way

Umwelt ['ʊmvɛlt] f environment; u~freundlich adj not harmful to the environment, environment-friendly; u~schädlich adj ecologically harmful; ~schutz m environmental protection; ~schützer m environmentalist; ~verschmutzung f environmental pollution

umwenden ['ʊmvɛndən] (unreg) vt, vr to turn (round)

umwerfen ['ʊmvɛrfən] (unreg) vt to upset, to overturn; (fig: erschüttern) to upset, to throw; ~d (umg) adj fantastic

umziehen ['ʊmtsiːən] (unreg) vt, vr to change ♦ vi to move

Umzug ['ʊmtsuːk] m procession; (Wohnungsumzug) move, removal

unab- ['ʊn|ap] zW: ~änderlich adj irreversible, unalterable; ~hängig adj independent; U~hängigkeit f independence; ~kömmlich adj indispensable; **zur Zeit ~kömmlich** not free at the moment; ~lässig adj incessant,

constant; ~sehbar adj immeasurable; (Folgen) unforeseeable; (Kosten) incalculable; ~sichtlich adj unintentional; ~'wendbar adj inevitable

unachtsam ['ʊn|axtzaːm] adj careless; U~keit f carelessness

unan- ['ʊn|an] zW: ~'fechtbar adj indisputable; ~gebracht adj uncalled-for; ~gemessen adj inadequate; ~genehm adj unpleasant; U~nehmlichkeit f inconvenience; **U~nehmlichkeiten** pl (Ärger) trouble sg; ~sehnlich adj unsightly; ~ständig adj indecent, improper

unappetitlich ['ʊn|apetiːtlɪç] adj unsavoury

Unart ['ʊn|aːrt] f bad manners pl; (Angewohnheit) bad habit; u~ig adj naughty, badly behaved

unauf- ['ʊn|aʊf] zW: ~fällig adj unobtrusive; (Kleidung) inconspicuous; ~'findbar adj not to be found; ~gefordert adj unasked ♦ adv spontaneously; ~haltsam adj irresistible; ~'hörlich adj incessant, continuous; ~merksam adj inattentive; ~richtig adj insincere

unaus- ['ʊn|aʊs] zW: ~geglichen adj unbalanced; ~'sprechlich adj inexpressible; ~'stehlich adj intolerable

unbarmherzig ['ʊnbarmhɛrtsɪç] adj pitiless, merciless

unbeabsichtigt ['ʊnbə|apzɪçtɪçt] adj unintentional

unbeachtet ['ʊnbə|axtət] adj unnoticed, ignored

unbedenklich ['ʊnbədɛŋklɪç] adj (Plan) unobjectionable

unbedeutend ['ʊnbədɔʏtənt] adj insignificant, unimportant; (Fehler) slight

unbedingt ['ʊnbədɪŋt] adj unconditional ♦ adv absolutely; **musst du ~ gehen?** do you really have to go?

unbefangen ['ʊnbəfaŋən] adj impartial, unprejudiced; (ohne Hemmungen) uninhibited; U~heit f impartiality; uninhibitedness

unbefriedigend ['ʊnbəfriːdɪgənd] adj unsatisfactory

unbefriedigt ['ʊnbəfriːdɪçt] adj unsatisfied,

dissatisfied

unbefugt ['ʊnbəfuːkt] *adj* unauthorized

unbegreiflich [ʊnbə'ɡraɪflɪç] *adj* inconceivable

unbegrenzt ['ʊnbəɡrɛntst] *adj* unlimited

unbegründet ['ʊnbəɡryndət] *adj* unfounded

Unbehagen ['ʊnbəhaːɡən] *nt* discomfort; **unbehaglich** ['ʊnbəhaːklɪç] *adj* uncomfortable; *(Gefühl)* uneasy

unbeholfen ['ʊnbəhɔlfən] *adj* awkward, clumsy

unbekannt ['ʊnbəkant] *adj* unknown

unbekümmert ['ʊnbəkymərt] *adj* unconcerned

unbeliebt ['ʊnbəliːpt] *adj* unpopular

unbequem ['ʊnbəkveːm] *adj* (*Stuhl*) uncomfortable; *(Mensch)* bothersome; *(Regelung)* inconvenient

unberechenbar [ʊnbə'reçənbaːr] *adj* incalculable; *(Mensch, Verhalten)* unpredictable

unberechtigt ['ʊnbəreçtɪçt] *adj* unjustified; *(nicht erlaubt)* unauthorized

unberührt ['ʊnbəryːrt] *adj* untouched, intact; **sie ist noch ~** she is still a virgin

unbescheiden ['ʊnbəʃaɪdən] *adj* presumptuous

unbeschreiblich [ʊnbə'ʃraɪplɪç] *adj* indescribable

unbeständig ['ʊnbəʃtɛndɪç] *adj* (*Mensch*) inconstant; *(Wetter)* unsettled; *(Lage)* unstable

unbestechlich [ʊnbə'ʃteçlɪç] *adj* incorruptible

unbestimmt ['ʊnbəʃtɪmt] *adj* indefinite; *(Zukunft auch)* uncertain

unbeteiligt [ʊnbə'taɪlɪçt] *adj* unconcerned, indifferent

unbeweglich ['ʊnbəveːklɪç] *adj* immovable

unbewohnt ['ʊnbəvoːnt] *adj* uninhabited; *(Wohnung)* unoccupied

unbewusst ▲ ['ʊnbəvʊst] *adj* unconscious

unbezahlt ['ʊnbətsaːlt] *adj* (*Rechnung*) outstanding, unsettled; *(Urlaub)* unpaid

unbrauchbar ['ʊnbrauxbaːr] *adj* (*Arbeit*) useless; *(Gerät auch)* unusable

und [ʊnt] *konj* and; **~ so weiter** and so on

Undank ['ʊndaŋk] *m* ingratitude; **u~bar** *adj* ungrateful

undefinierbar [ʊndefi'niːrbaːr] *adj* indefinable

undenkbar [ʊn'dɛŋkbaːr] *adj* inconceivable

undeutlich ['ʊndɔʏtlɪç] *adj* indistinct

undicht ['ʊndɪçt] *adj* leaky

Unding ['ʊndɪŋ] *nt* absurdity

undurch- ['ʊndʊrç] *zW:* **~führbar** [-'fyːrbaːr] *adj* impracticable; **~lässig** [-'lɛsɪç] *adj* waterproof, impermeable; **~sichtig** [-'zɪçtɪç] *adj* opaque; *(fig)* obscure

uneben ['ʊn|eːbən] *adj* uneven

unecht ['ʊn|eçt] *adj* (*Schmuck*) fake; *(vorgetäuscht: Freundlichkeit)* false

unehelich ['ʊn|eːəlɪç] *adj* illegitimate

uneinig ['ʊn|aɪnɪç] *adj* divided; **~ sein** to disagree; **U~keit** *f* discord, dissension

uneins ['ʊn|aɪns] *adj* at variance, at odds

unempfindlich ['ʊn|ɛmpfɪntlɪç] *adj* insensitive; *(Stoff)* practical

unendlich [ʊn'|ɛntlɪç] *adj* infinite

unent- [ʊn'|ɛnt] *zW:* **~behrlich** [-'beːrlɪç] *adj* indispensable; **~geltlich** [-ɡɛltlɪç] *adj* free (of charge); **~schieden** [-ʃiːdən] *adj* undecided; **~schieden enden** *(SPORT)* to end in a draw; **~schlossen** [-ʃlɔsən] *adj* undecided; irresolute; **~wegt** [-'veːkt] *adj* unswerving; *(unaufhörlich)* incessant

uner- ['ʊn|er] *zW:* **~bittlich** [-'bɪtlɪç] *adj* unyielding, inexorable; **~fahren** [-fa:rən] *adj* inexperienced; **~freulich** [-frɔʏlɪç] *adj* unpleasant; **~gründlich** *adj* unfathomable; **~hört** [-høːrt] *adj* unheard-of; *(Bitte)* outrageous; **~lässlich** ▲ [-'lɛslɪç] *adj* indispensable; **~laubt** *adj* unauthorized; **~messlich** ▲ *adj* immeasurable, immense; **~reichbar** *adj* (*Ziel*) unattainable; *(Ort)* inaccessible; *(telefonisch)* unobtainable; **~schöpflich** [-'ʃœpflɪç] *adj* inexhaustible; **~schwinglich** [-'ʃvɪŋlɪç] *adj* (*Preis*) exorbitant; too expensive; **~träglich** [-'trɛːklɪç] *adj* unbearable; *(Frechheit)* insufferable; **~wartet** *adj* unexpected; **~wünscht** *adj* undesirable, unwelcome

unfähig ['ʊnfɛːɪç] *adj* incapable, incompetent; **zu etw ~ sein** to be incapable of sth; **U~keit** *f* incapacity; incompetence

unfair ['ʊnfɛːr] *adj* unfair

Unfall ['ʊnfal] *m* accident; **~flucht** *f* hit-and-run (driving); **~schaden** *m* damages *pl*; **~station** *f* emergency ward; **~stelle** *f* scene of the accident; **~versicherung** *f* accident insurance

unfassbar ▲ [ʊn'fasbaːr] *adj* inconceivable

unfehlbar [ʊn'feːlbaːr] *adj* infallible ♦ *adv* inevitably; **U~keit** *f* infallibility

unförmig ['ʊnfœrmɪç] *adj* (*formlos*) shapeless

unfrei ['ʊnfraɪ] *adj* not free, unfree; (*Paket*) unfranked; **~willig** *adj* involuntary, against one's will

unfreundlich ['ʊnfrɔʏntlɪç] *adj* unfriendly; **U~keit** *f* unfriendliness

Unfriede(n) ['ʊnfriːdə(n)] *m* dissension, strife

unfruchtbar ['ʊnfrʊxtbaːr] *adj* infertile; (*Gespräche*) unfruitful; **U~keit** *f* infertility; unfruitfulness

Unfug ['ʊnfuːk] **(-s)** *m* (*Benehmen*) mischief; (*Unsinn*) nonsense; **grober ~** (*JUR*) gross misconduct; malicious damage

Ungar(in) ['ʊngar(ɪn)] *m(f)* Hungarian; **u~isch** *adj* Hungarian; **~n** *nt* Hungary

ungeachtet ['ʊngəˌaxtət] *präp* +*gen* notwithstanding

ungeahnt ['ʊngəˌaːnt] *adj* unsuspected, undreamt-of

ungebeten ['ʊngəbeːtən] *adj* uninvited

ungebildet ['ʊngəbɪldət] *adj* uneducated; uncultured

ungedeckt ['ʊngədɛkt] *adj* (*Scheck*) uncovered

Ungeduld ['ʊngədʊlt] *f* impatience; **u~ig** [-dɪç] *adj* impatient

ungeeignet ['ʊngəˌaɪgnət] *adj* unsuitable

ungefähr ['ʊngəfɛːr] *adj* rough, approximate; **das kommt nicht von ~** that's hardly surprising

ungefährlich ['ʊngəfɛːrlɪç] *adj* not dangerous, harmless

ungehalten ['ʊngəhaltən] *adj* indignant

ungeheuer ['ʊngəhɔʏər] *adj* huge ♦ *adv* (*umg*) enormously; **U~** **(-s, -)** *nt* monster;

~lich [-'hɔʏərlɪç] *adj* monstrous

ungehörig ['ʊngəhøːrɪç] *adj* impertinent, improper

ungehorsam ['ʊngəhoˌrzaːm] *adj* disobedient; **U~** *m* disobedience

ungeklärt ['ʊngəklɛːrt] *adj* not cleared up; (*Rätsel*) unsolved

ungeladen ['ʊngəlaːdən] *adj* not loaded; (*Gast*) uninvited

ungelegen ['ʊngəleːgən] *adj* inconvenient

ungelernt ['ʊngəlɛrnt] *adj* unskilled

ungelogen ['ʊngəloːgən] *adv* really, honestly

ungemein ['ʊngəmaɪn] *adj* uncommon

ungemütlich ['ʊngəmyːtlɪç] *adj* uncomfortable; (*Person*) disagreeable

ungenau ['ʊngənaʊ] *adj* inaccurate; **U~igkeit** *f* inaccuracy

ungenießbar ['ʊngəniːsbaːr] *adj* inedible; undrinkable; (*umg*) unbearable

ungenügend ['ʊngənyːgənt] *adj* insufficient, inadequate

ungepflegt ['ʊngəpfleːkt] *adj* (*Garten etc*) untended; (*Person*) unkempt; (*Hände*) neglected

ungerade ['ʊngəraːdə] *adj* uneven, odd

ungerecht ['ʊngərɛçt] *adj* unjust; **~fertigt** *adj* unjustified; **U~igkeit** *f* injustice, unfairness

ungern ['ʊngɛrn] *adv* unwillingly, reluctantly

ungeschehen ['ʊngəʃeːən] *adj*: **~ machen** to undo

Ungeschicklichkeit ['ʊngəˌʃɪklɪçkaɪt] *f* clumsiness

ungeschickt *adj* awkward, clumsy

ungeschminkt ['ʊngəʃmɪŋkt] *adj* without make-up; (*fig*) unvarnished

ungesetzlich ['ʊngəzɛtslɪç] *adj* illegal

ungestört ['ʊngəʃtøːrt] *adj* undisturbed

ungestraft ['ʊngəʃtraːft] *adv* with impunity

ungestüm ['ʊngəʃtyːm] *adj* impetuous; tempestuous

ungesund ['ʊngəzʊnt] *adj* unhealthy

ungetrübt ['ʊngətryːpt] *adj* clear; (*fig*) untroubled; (*Freude*) unalloyed

Ungetüm ['ʊngətyːm] **(-(e)s, -e)** *nt* monster

ungewiss ▲ ['ʊngəvɪs] *adj* uncertain;

U~heit *f* uncertainty
ungewöhnlich ['ʊngəvøːnlɪç] *adj* unusual
ungewohnt ['ʊngəvoːnt] *adj* unaccustomed
Ungeziefer ['ʊngətsiːfər] (**-s**) *nt* vermin
ungezogen ['ʊngətsoːgən] *adj* rude,
impertinent; U~heit *f* rudeness,
impertinence
ungezwungen ['ʊngətsvʊŋən] *adj* natural,
unconstrained
unglaublich [ʊn'glaʊplɪç] *adj* incredible
ungleich ['ʊnglaɪç] *adj* dissimilar; unequal
♦ *adv* incomparably; ~**artig** *adj* different;
U~heit *f* dissimilarity; inequality; ~**mäßig**
adj irregular, uneven
Unglück ['ʊnglʏk] (**-(e)s, -e**) *nt* misfortune;
(*Pech*) bad luck; (~*sfall*) calamity, disaster;
(*Verkehrsunglück*) accident; u~**lich** *adj*
unhappy; (*erfolglos*) unlucky; (*unerfreulich*)
unfortunate; u~**licherweise** [-'vaɪzə] *adv*
unfortunately; ~**sfall** *m* accident, calamity
ungültig ['ʊngʏltɪç] *adj* invalid; U~**keit** *f*
invalidity
ungünstig ['ʊngʏnstɪç] *adj* unfavourable
ungut ['ʊnguːt] *adj* (*Gefühl*) uneasy; **nichts
für ~** no offence
unhaltbar ['ʊnhaltbaːr] *adj* untenable
Unheil ['ʊnhaɪl] *nt* evil; (*Unglück*) misfortune;
~ **anrichten** to cause mischief; u~**bar** *adj*
incurable
unheimlich ['ʊnhaɪmlɪç] *adj* weird, uncanny
♦ *adv* (*umg*) tremendously
unhöflich ['ʊnhøːflɪç] *adj* impolite; U~**keit** *f*
impoliteness
unhygienisch ['ʊnhygieːnɪʃ] *adj* unhygienic
Uni ['ʊni] (**-, -s**) (*umg*) *f* university
Uniform [uni'fɔrm] *f* uniform; u~**iert**
[-'miːrt] *adj* uniformed
uninteressant ['ʊn|ɪnteresant] *adj*
uninteresting
Uni- *zW*: ~**versität** [univerziˈtɛːt] *f* university;
~**versum** [uni'verzʊm] (**-s**) *nt* universe
unkenntlich ['ʊnkɛntlɪç] *adj* unrecognizable
Unkenntnis ['ʊnkɛntnɪs] *f* ignorance
unklar ['ʊnklaːr] *adj* unclear; **im U~en sein
über** +*akk* to be in the dark about; U~**heit**
f unclarity; (*Unentschiedenheit*) uncertainty
unklug ['ʊnkluːk] *adj* unwise

Unkosten ['ʊnkɔstən] *pl* expense(s);
~**beitrag** *m* contribution to costs *od*
expenses
Unkraut ['ʊnkraʊt] *nt* weed; weeds *pl*
unkündbar ['ʊnkʏntbaːr] *adj* (*Stelle*)
permanent; (*Vertrag*) binding
unlauter ['ʊnlaʊtər] *adj* unfair
unleserlich ['ʊnleːzərlɪç] *adj* illegible
unlogisch ['ʊnloːgɪʃ] *adj* illogical
unlösbar [ʊn'løːsbaːr] *adj* insoluble
Unlust ['ʊnlʊst] *f* lack of enthusiasm
Unmenge ['ʊnmɛŋə] *f* tremendous number,
hundreds *pl*
Unmensch ['ʊnmɛnʃ] *m* ogre, brute;
u~**lich** *adj* inhuman, brutal; (*ungeheuer*)
awful
unmerklich [ʊn'mɛrklɪç] *adj* imperceptible
unmissverständlich ▲ ['ʊnmɪsfɛrʃtɛntlɪç]
adj unmistakable
unmittelbar ['ʊnmɪtəlbaːr] *adj* immediate
unmodern ['ʊnmodɛrn] *adj* old-fashioned
unmöglich ['ʊnmøːklɪç] *adj* impossible;
U~**keit** *f* impossibility
unmoralisch ['ʊnmoraːlɪʃ] *adj* immoral
Unmut ['ʊnmuːt] *m* ill humour
unnachgiebig ['ʊnnaːxgiːbɪç] *adj* unyielding
unnahbar [ʊn'naːbaːr] *adj* unapproachable
unnötig ['ʊnnøːtɪç] *adj* unnecessary
unnütz ['ʊnnʏts] *adj* useless
unordentlich ['ʊn|ɔrdəntlɪç] *adj* untidy
Unordnung ['ʊn|ɔrdnʊŋ] *f* disorder
unparteiisch ['ʊnpartaɪʃ] *adj* impartial;
U~**e(r)** *f(m)* umpire; (*FUSSBALL*) referee
unpassend ['ʊnpasənt] *adj* inappropriate;
(*Zeit*) inopportune
unpässlich ▲ ['ʊnpɛslɪç] *adj* unwell
unpersönlich ['ʊnperzøːnlɪç] *adj* impersonal
unpolitisch ['ʊnpoliːtɪʃ] *adj* apolitical
unpraktisch ['ʊnpraktɪʃ] *adj* unpractical
unpünktlich ['ʊnpʏŋktlɪç] *adj* unpunctual
unrationell ['ʊnratsionɛl] *adj* inefficient
unrealistisch ['ʊnrealɪstɪʃ] *adj* unrealistic
unrecht ['ʊnrɛçt] *adj* wrong; U~ *nt* wrong;
zu U~ wrongly; U~ **haben** to be wrong;
~**mäßig** *adj* unlawful, illegal
unregelmäßig ['ʊnreːgəlmɛːsɪç] *adj*
irregular; U~**keit** *f* irregularity

reif ['ʊnraɪf] adj (Obst) unripe; (fig) immature

rentabel ['ʊnrɛntaːbəl] adj unprofitable

richtig ['ʊnrɪçtɪç] adj incorrect, wrong

ruhe ['ʊnruːə] f unrest; **~stifter** m troublemaker

ruhig ['ʊnruːɪç] adj restless

ns [ʊns] (akk, dat von **wir**) pron us; ourselves

nsachlich ['ʊnzaxlɪç] adj not to the point, irrelevant

nsagbar [ʊn'zaːkbaːr] adj indescribable

nsanft ['ʊnzanft] adj rough

nsauber ['ʊnzaʊbər] adj unclean, dirty; (fig) crooked; (MUS) fuzzy

nschädlich ['ʊnʃɛːtlɪç] adj harmless; **jdn/ etw ~ machen** to render sb/sth harmless

nscharf ['ʊnʃarf] adj indistinct; (Bild etc) out of focus, blurred

nscheinbar ['ʊnʃaɪnbaːr] adj insignificant; (Aussehen, Haus etc) unprepossessing

nschlagbar [ʊn'ʃlaːkbaːr] adj invincible

nschön ['ʊnʃøːn] adj (hässlich: Anblick) ugly, unattractive; (unfreundlich: Benehmen) unpleasant, ugly

nschuld ['ʊnʃʊlt] f innocence; **u~ig** [-dɪç] adj innocent

nselbst(st)ändig ['ʊnzɛlpʃtɛndɪç] adj dependent, over-reliant on others

nser(e) ['ʊnzər(ə)] adj our; **~e(r, s)** pron ours; **~einer** pron people like us; **~eins** pron = **unsereiner**; **~erseits** adv on our part; **~twegen** adv (für uns) for our sake; (wegen uns) on our account; **~twillen** adv: **um ~twillen = unsertwegen**

nsicher ['ʊnzɪçər] adj uncertain; (Mensch) insecure; **U~heit** f uncertainty; insecurity

nsichtbar ['ʊnzɪçtbaːr] adj invisible

nsinn ['ʊnzɪn] m nonsense; **u~ig** adj nonsensical

nsitte ['ʊnzɪtə] f deplorable habit

nsozial ['ʊnzotsiaːl] adj (Verhalten) antisocial

nsportlich ['ʊnʃpɔrtlɪç] adj not sporty; unfit; (Verhalten) unsporting

nsre ['ʊnzrə] = **unsere**

nsterblich ['ʊnʃtɛrplɪç] adj immortal

Unstimmigkeit ['ʊnʃtɪmɪçkaɪt] f inconsistency; (Streit) disagreement

unsympathisch ['ʊnzʏmpaːtɪʃ] adj unpleasant; **er ist mir ~** I don't like him

untätig ['ʊntɛːtɪç] adj idle

untauglich ['ʊntaʊklɪç] adj unsuitable; (MIL) unfit

unteilbar [ʊn'taɪlbaːr] adj indivisible

unten ['ʊntən] adv below; (im Haus) downstairs; (an der Treppe etc) at the bottom; **nach ~** down; **~ am Berg** etc at the bottom of the mountain etc; **ich bin bei ihm ~ durch** (umg) he's through with me

---

SCHLÜSSELWORT

---

unter ['ʊntər] präp +dat 1 (räumlich, mit Zahlen) under; (drunter) underneath, below; **unter 18 Jahren** under 18 years
2 (zwischen) among(st); **sie waren unter sich** they were by themselves; **einer unter ihnen** one of them; **unter anderem** among other things
♦ präp +akk under, below

Unterarm ['ʊntər|arm] m forearm

unter- zW: **~belichten** vt (PHOT) to underexpose; **U~bewusstsein** ▲ nt subconscious; **~bezahlt** adj underpaid

unterbieten [ʊntər'biːtən] (unreg) vt insep (COMM) to undercut; (Rekord) to lower

unterbrechen [ʊntər'brɛçən] (unreg) vt insep to interrupt

Unterbrechung f interruption

unterbringen ['ʊntərbrɪŋən] (unreg) vt (in Koffer) to stow; (in Zeitung) to place; (Person: in Hotel etc) to accommodate, to put up

unterdessen [ʊntər'dɛsən] adv meanwhile

Unterdruck ['ʊntərdrʊk] m low pressure

unterdrücken [ʊntər'drʏkən] vt insep to suppress; (Leute) to oppress

untere(r, s) ['ʊntərə(r, s)] adj lower

untereinander [ʊntər|aɪ'nandər] adv with each other; among themselves etc

unterentwickelt ['ʊntər|ɛntvɪkəlt] adj underdeveloped

Spelling Reform: ▲ *new spelling* △ *old spelling (to be phased out)*

unterernährt ['ʊntərʔɛrnɛːrt] *adj*
undernourished, underfed

Unterernährung *f* malnutrition

Unter'führung *f* subway, underpass

Untergang ['ʊntərgaŋ] *m* (down)fall,
decline; (*NAUT*) sinking; (*von Gestirn*) setting

unter'geben *adj* subordinate

untergehen ['ʊntərgeːən] (*unreg*) *vi* to go
down; (*Sonne auch*) to set; (*Staat*) to fall;
(*Volk*) to perish; (*Welt*) to come to an end;
(*im Lärm*) to be drowned

Untergeschoss ▲ ['ʊntərgəʃɔs] *nt*
basement

'Untergewicht *nt* underweight

unter'gliedern *vt insep* to subdivide

Untergrund ['ʊntərgrʊnt] *m* foundation;
(*POL*) underground; **~bahn** *f* underground,
tube, subway (*US*)

unterhalb ['ʊntərhalp] *präp +gen* below
♦ *adv* below; **~ von** below

Unterhalt ['ʊntərhalt] *m* maintenance;
u~en (*unreg*) *vt insep* to maintain;
(*belustigen*) to entertain ♦ *vr insep* to talk;
(*sich belustigen*) to enjoy o.s.; **u~sam** *adj*
(*Abend, Person*) entertaining, amusing;
~ung *f* maintenance; (*Belustigung*)
entertainment, amusement; (*Gespräch*) talk

Unterhändler ['ʊntərhɛntlər] *m* negotiator

Unter- *zW*: **~hemd** *nt* vest, undershirt (*US*);
~hose *f* underpants *pl*; **~kiefer** *m* lower
jaw

unterkommen ['ʊntərkɔmən] (*unreg*) *vi* to
find shelter; to find work; **das ist mir noch
nie untergekommen** I've never met with
that

unterkühlt [ʊntər'kyːlt] *adj* (*Körper*) affected
by hypothermia

Unterkunft ['ʊntərkʊnft] (**-, -künfte**) *f*
accommodation

Unterlage ['ʊntərlaːgə] *f* foundation; (*Beleg*)
document; (*Schreibunterlage etc*) pad

unter'lassen (*unreg*) *vt insep* (*versäumen*) to
fail to do; (*sich enthalten*) to refrain from

unterlaufen [ʊntər'laʊfən] (*unreg*) *vi insep* to
happen ♦ *adj*: **mit Blut ~** suffused with
blood; (*Augen*) bloodshot

unterlegen ['ʊntərleːgən] *vt* to lay *od* put

under; **unter'legen** *adj* inferior; (*besiegt*)
defeated

Unterleib ['ʊntərlaip] *m* abdomen

unter'liegen (*unreg*) *vi insep* (+*dat*) to be
defeated *od* overcome (by); (*unterworfen
sein*) to be subject (to)

Untermiete ['ʊntərmiːtə] *f*: **zur ~ wohnen**
to be a subtenant *od* lodger; **~r(in)** *m(f)*
subtenant, lodger

unter'nehmen (*unreg*) *vt insep* to
undertake; **Unter'nehmen** (**-s, -**) *nt*
undertaking, enterprise (*auch COMM*)

Unternehmer [ʊntər'neːmər] (**-s, -**) *m*
entrepreneur, businessman

'unterordnen ['ʊntərɔrdnən] *vr +dat* to
submit o.s. (to), to give o.s. second place
to

Unterredung [ʊntər'reːdʊŋ] *f* discussion,
talk

Unterricht ['ʊntərrɪçt] (**-(e)s, -e**) *m*
instruction, lessons *pl*; **u~en** [ʊntər'rɪçtən] *vt
insep* to instruct; (*SCH*) to teach ♦ *vr insep*:
sich u~en (über +*akk*) to inform o.s.
(about), to obtain information (about);
~sfach *nt* subject (on school *etc*)
curriculum

Unterrock ['ʊntərrɔk] *m* petticoat, slip

unter'sagen *vt insep* to forbid; **jdm etw ~**
to forbid sb to do sth

Untersatz ['ʊntərzats] *m* coaster, saucer

unter'schätzen *vt insep* to underestimate

unter'scheiden (*unreg*) *vt insep* to
distinguish ♦ *vr insep* to differ

Unter'scheidung *f* (*Unterschied*)
distinction; (*Unterscheiden*) differentiation

Unterschied ['ʊntərʃiːt] *m* (**-(e)s, -e**) *m*
difference, distinction; **im ~ zu** as distinct
from; **u~lich** *adj* varying, differing;
(*diskriminierend*) discriminatory

unterschiedslos *adv* indiscriminately

unter'schlagen (*unreg*) *vt insep* to
embezzle; (*verheimlichen*) to suppress

Unter'schlagung *f* embezzlement

Unterschlupf ['ʊntərʃlʊpf] (**-(e)s,
-schlüpfe**) *m* refuge

unter'schreiben (*unreg*) *vt insep* to sign

Unterschrift ['ʊntərʃrɪft] *f* signature

Unterseeboot ['ʊntərze:bo:t] *nt* submarine

Untersetzer ['ʊntərzɛtsər] *m* tablemat; *(für Gläser)* coaster

untersetzt [ʊntər'zɛtst] *adj* stocky

unterste(r, s) ['ʊntərstə(r, s)] *adj* lowest, bottom

unterstehen [ʊntər'ʃte:ən] *(unreg) vi insep (+dat)* to be under ♦ *vr insep* to dare; '**unterstehen** *(unreg) vi* to shelter

unterstellen [ʊntər'ʃtɛlən] *vt insep* to subordinate; *(fig)* to impute ♦ *vt (Auto)* to garage, to park ♦ *vr* to take shelter

unter'streichen *(unreg) vt insep (auch fig)* to underline

Unterstufe ['ʊntərʃtu:fə] *f* lower grade

unter'stützen *vt insep* to support

Unter'stützung *f* support, assistance

unter'suchen *vt insep (MED)* to examine; *(Polizei)* to investigate

Unter'suchung *f* examination, investigation, inquiry; **~sausschuss** ▲ *m* committee of inquiry; **~shaft** *f* imprisonment on remand

Untertasse ['ʊntərtasə] *f* saucer

untertauchen ['ʊntərtauxən] *vi* to dive; *(fig)* to disappear, to go underground

Unterteil ['ʊntərtail] *nt od m* lower part, bottom; **u~en** [ʊntər'tailən] *vt insep* to divide up

Untertitel ['ʊntərti:təl] *m* subtitle

Unterwäsche ['ʊntərvɛʃə] *f* underwear

unterwegs [ʊntər've:ks] *adv* on the way

unter'werfen *(unreg) vt insep* to subject; *(Volk)* to subjugate ♦ *vr insep (+dat)* to submit (to)

unter'zeichnen *vt insep* to sign

unter'ziehen *(unreg) vt insep* to subject ♦ *vr insep (+dat)* to undergo; *(einer Prüfung)* to take

untragbar [ʊn'tra:kba:r] *adj* unbearable, intolerable

untreu ['ʊntrɔy] *adj* unfaithful; **U~e** *f* unfaithfulness

untröstlich [ʊn'trø:stlɪç] *adj* inconsolable

unüberlegt ['ʊn|y:bərle:kt] *adj* ill-considered ♦ *adv* without thinking

unübersichtlich *adj (Gelände)* broken;

(Kurve) blind

unumgänglich [ʊn|ʊm'gɛŋlɪç] *adj* indispensable, vital; absolutely necessary

ununterbrochen ['ʊn|ʊntərbrɔxən] *adj* uninterrupted

unver- ['ʊnfer] *zW:* **~änderlich** [-'ɛndərlɪç] *adj* unchangeable; **~antwortlich** [-'antvɔrtlɪç] *adj* irresponsible; *(unentschuldbar)* inexcusable; **~besserlich** *adj* incorrigible; **~bindlich** *adj* not binding; *(Antwort)* curt ♦ *adv (COMM)* without obligation; **~bleit** *adj (Benzin usw)* unleaded; **ich fahre ~bleit** I use unleaded; **~blümt** [-'bly:mt] *adj* plain, blunt ♦ *adv* plainly, bluntly; **~daulich** *adj* indigestible; **~einbar** *adj* incompatible; **~fänglich** [-'fɛŋlɪç] *adj* harmless; **~froren** *adj* impudent; **~gesslich** ▲ *adj (Tag, Erlebnis)* unforgettable; **~hofft** [-'hɔft] *adj* unexpected; **~meidlich** [-'maitlɪç] *adj* unavoidable; **~mutet** *adj* unexpected; **~nünftig** [-'nʏnftɪç] *adj* foolish; **~schämt** *adj* impudent; **U~schämtheit** *f* impudence, insolence; **~sehrt** *adj* uninjured; **~söhnlich** [-'zø:nlɪç] *adj* irreconcilable; **~ständlich** [-'ʃtɛntlɪç] *adj* unintelligible; **~träglich** *adj* quarrelsome; *(Meinungen, MED)* incompatible; **~zeihlich** *adj* unpardonable; **~züglich** [-'tsy:klɪç] *adj* immediate

unvollkommen ['ʊnfɔlkɔmən] *adj* imperfect

unvollständig *adj* incomplete

unvor- ['ʊnfo:r] *zW:* **~bereitet** *adj* unprepared; **~eingenommen** *adj* unbiased; **~hergesehen** [-he:rgeze:ən] *adj* unforeseen; **~sichtig** [-zɪçtɪç] *adj* careless, imprudent; **~stellbar** [-'ʃtelba:r] *adj* inconceivable; **~teilhaft** *adj* disadvantageous

unwahr ['ʊnva:r] *adj* untrue; **~scheinlich** *adj* improbable, unlikely ♦ *adv (umg)* incredibly

unweigerlich [ʊn'vaigərlɪç] *adj* unquestioning ♦ *adv* without fail

Unwesen ['ʊnve:zən] *nt* nuisance; *(Unfug)* mischief; **sein ~ treiben** to wreak havoc

unwesentlich *adj* inessential, unimportant; **~ besser** marginally better

Unwetter ['ʊnvɛtər] *nt* thunderstorm
unwichtig ['ʊnvɪçtɪç] *adj* unimportant
unwider- ['ʊnviːdər] *zW:* ~**legbar** *adj* irrefutable; ~**ruflich** *adj* irrevocable; ~**stehlich** *adj* irresistible
unwill- ['ʊnvɪl] *zW:* **U~e(n)** (*m*) indignation; ~**ig** *adj* indignant; (*widerwillig*) reluctant; ~**kürlich** [-kyːrlɪç] *adj* involuntary ♦ *adv* instinctively; (*lachen*) involuntarily
unwirklich ['ʊnvɪrklɪç] *adj* unreal
unwirksam ['ʊnvɪrkzaːm] *adj* (*Mittel, Methode*) ineffective
unwirtschaftlich ['ʊnvɪrtʃaftlɪç] *adj* uneconomical
unwissen- ['ʊnvɪsən] *zW:* ~**d** *adj* ignorant; **U~heit** *f* ignorance; ~**tlich** *adv* unknowingly, unwittingly
unwohl ['ʊnvoːl] *adj* unwell, ill; **U~sein** (**-s**) *nt* indisposition
unwürdig ['ʊnvʏrdɪç] *adj* unworthy
unzählig [ʊn'tsɛːlɪç] *adj* innumerable, countless
unzer- [ʊntsɛr] *zW:* ~**brechlich** *adj* unbreakable; ~**störbar** *adj* indestructible; ~**trennlich** *adj* inseparable
Unzucht ['ʊntsʊxt] *f* sexual offence
unzüchtig ['ʊntsʏçtɪç] *adj* immoral; lewd
unzu- ['ʊntsu] *zW:* ~**frieden** *adj* dissatisfied; **U~friedenheit** *f* discontent; ~**länglich** *adj* inadequate; ~**lässig** *adj* inadmissible; ~**rechnungsfähig** *adj* irresponsible; ~**treffend** *adj* incorrect; ~**verlässig** *adj* unreliable
unzweideutig ['ʊntsvaɪdɔʏtɪç] *adj* unambiguous
üppig ['ʏpɪç] *adj* (*Frau*) curvaceous; (*Busen*) full, ample; (*Essen*) sumptuous; (*Vegetation*) luxuriant, lush
Ur- ['uːr] *in zW* original
uralt ['uːr|alt] *adj* ancient, very old
Uran [u'raːn] (**-s**) *nt* uranium
Ur- *zW:* ~**aufführung** *f* first performance; ~**einwohner** *m* original inhabitant; ~**eltern** *pl* ancestors; ~**enkel(in)** *m(f)* great-grandchild, great-grandson (-daughter); ~**großeltern** *pl* great-grandparents; ~**heber** (**-s**, **-**) *m* originator;

(*Autor*) author; ~**heberrecht** *nt* copyright
Urin [u'riːn] (**-s**, **-e**) *m* urine
Urkunde ['uːrkʊndə] *f* document, deed
Urlaub ['uːrlaup] (**-(e)s**, **-e**) *m* holiday(s *pl*) (*BRIT*), vacation (*US*); (*MIL etc*) leave; ~**er** [-'laʊbər] (**-s**, **-**) *m* holiday-maker (*BRIT*), vacationer (*US*); ~**sort** *m* holiday resort; ~**szeit** *f* holiday season
Urne ['ʊrnə] *f* urn
Ursache ['uːrzaxə] *f* cause; **keine ~** that's all right
Ursprung ['uːrʃprʊŋ] *m* origin, source; (*von Fluss*) source
ursprünglich ['uːrʃprʏŋlɪç] *adj* original ♦ *adv* originally
Ursprungsland *nt* country of origin
Urteil ['ʊrtaɪl] (**-s**, **-e**) *nt* opinion; (*JUR*) sentence, judgement; **u~en** *vi* to judge; ~**sspruch** *m* sentence, verdict
Urwald *m* jungle
Urzeit *f* prehistoric times *pl*
USA [uː'ɛs'|aː] *pl abk* (= *Vereinigte Staaten von Amerika*) USA
usw. *abk* (= *und so weiter*) etc
Utensilien [uten'ziːliən] *pl* utensils
Utopie [uto'piː] *f* pipe dream
utopisch [u'toːpɪʃ] *adj* utopian

V, v

vag(e) [vaːk, 'vaːgə] *adj* vague
Vagina [va'giːna] (**-, Vaginen**) *f* vagina
Vakuum ['vaːkuʊm] (**-s, Vakua** *od* **Vakuen**) *nt* vacuum
Vampir [vam'piːr] (**-s**, **-e**) *m* vampire
Vanille [va'nɪljə] (**-**) *f* vanilla
Variation [variatsi'oːn] *f* variation
variieren [vari'iːrən] *vt*, *vi* to vary
Vase ['vaːzə] *f* vase
Vater ['faːtər] (**-s**, **ʸ**) *m* father; ~**land** *nt* native country; Fatherland
väterlich ['fɛːtərlɪç] *adj* fatherly
Vaterschaft *f* paternity
Vaterunser (**-s**, **-**) *nt* Lord's prayer
Vati ['faːti] *m* daddy
v. Chr. *abk* (= *vor Christus*) B.C.

Rechtschreibreform: ▲ *neue Schreibung* △ *alte Schreibung (auslaufend)*

Vegetarier(in) [vege'ta:riər(ɪn)] **(-s, -)** *m(f)*
vegetarian

vegetarisch [vege'ta:rɪʃ] *adj* vegetarian

Veilchen ['faɪlçən] *nt* violet

Vene ['ve:nə] *f* vein

Ventil [vɛn'ti:l] **(-s, -e)** *nt* valve

Ventilator [vɛntila'to:r] *m* ventilator

verab- [fer'|ap] *zW:* **~reden** *vt* to agree, to
arrange ♦ *vr:* **sich mit jdm ~reden** to
arrange to meet sb; **mit jdm ~redet sein**
to have arranged to meet sb; **V~redung** *f*
arrangement; (*Treffen*) appointment;
~scheuen *vt* to detest, to abhor;
~schieden *vt* (*Gäste*) to say goodbye to;
(*entlassen*) to discharge; (*Gesetz*) to pass
♦ *vr* to take one's leave; **V~schiedung** *f*
leave-taking; discharge; passing

ver- [fer] *zW:* **~achten** *vt* to despise;
~ächtlich [-'|ɛçtlɪç] *adj* contemptuous;
(*~achtenswert*) contemptible; **jdn ~ächtlich
machen** to run sb down; **V~achtung** *f*
contempt

verallgemeinern [fer|algə'maɪnərn] *vt* to
generalize; **Verallgemeinerung** *f*
generalization

veralten [fer'|altən] *vi* to become obsolete
od out-of-date

Veranda [ve'randa] **(-, Veranden)** *f* veranda

veränder- [fer'|ɛndər] *zW:* **~lich** *adj*
changeable; **~n** *vt, vr* to change, to alter;
V~ung *f* change, alteration

veran- [fer'|an] *zW:* **~lagt** *adj* with a ...
nature; **V~lagung** *f* disposition; **~lassen**
vt to cause; **Maßnahmen ~lassen** to take
measures; **sich ~lasst sehen** to feel
prompted; **~schaulichen** *vt* to illustrate;
~schlagen *vt* to estimate; **~stalten** *vt* to
organize, to arrange; **V~stalter (-s, -)** *m*
organizer; **V~staltung** *f* (*V~stalten*)
organizing; (*Konzert etc*) event, function

verantwort- [fer'|antvɔrt] *zW:* **~en** *vt* to
answer for ♦ *vr* to justify o.s.; **~lich** *adj*
responsible; **V~ung** *f* responsibility;
~ungsbewusst ▲ *adj* responsible;
~ungslos *adj* irresponsible

verarbeiten [fer'|arbaɪtən] *vt* to process;
(*geistig*) to assimilate; **etw zu etw ~** to
make sth into sth; **Verarbeitung** *f*
processing; assimilation

verärgern [fer'|ɛrgərn] *vt* to annoy

verausgaben [fer'|ausga:bən] *vr* to run out
of money; (*fig*) to exhaust o.s.

Verb [vɛrp] **(-s, -en)** *nt* verb

Verband [fer'bant] **(-(e)s, ⁼e)** *m* (*MED*)
bandage, dressing; (*Bund*) association,
society; (*MIL*) unit; **~kasten** *m* medicine
chest, first-aid box; **~zeug** *nt* bandage

verbannen [fer'banən] *vt* to banish

verbergen [fer'bergən] (*unreg*) *vt, vr:* **(sich)
~ (vor** +*dat*) to hide (from)

verbessern [fer'besərn] *vt, vr* to improve;
(*berichtigen*) to correct (o.s.)

Verbesserung *f* improvement; correction

verbeugen [fer'bɔygən] *vr* to bow

Verbeugung *f* bow

ver'biegen (*unreg*) *vi* to bend

ver'bieten (*unreg*) *vt* to forbid; **jdm etw ~**
to forbid sb to do sth

verbilligen [fer'bɪlɪgən] *vt* to reduce the
cost of; (*Preis*) to reduce

ver'binden (*unreg*) *vt* to connect;
(*kombinieren*) to combine; (*MED*) to
bandage ♦ *vr* (*auch CHEM*) to combine, to
join; **jdm die Augen ~** to blindfold sb

verbindlich [fer'bɪntlɪç] *adj* binding;
(*freundlich*) friendly

Ver'bindung *f* connection;
(*Zusammensetzung*) combination; (*CHEM*)
compound; (*UNIV*) club

verbissen [fer'bɪsən] *adj* (*Kampf*) bitter;
(*Gesichtsausdruck*) grim

ver'bitten (*unreg*) *vt:* **sich** *dat* **etw ~** not to
tolerate sth, not to stand for sth

Verbleib [fer'blaɪp] **(-(e)s)** *m* whereabouts;
v~en (*unreg*) *vi* to remain

verbleit [fer'blaɪt] *adj* (*Benzin*) leaded

verblüffen [fer'blʏfən] *vt* to stagger, to
amaze; **Verblüffung** *f* stupefaction

ver'blühen *vi* to wither, to fade

ver'bluten *vi* to bleed to death

verborgen [fer'bɔrgən] *adj* hidden

Verbot [fer'bo:t] **(-(e)s, -e)** *nt* prohibition,
ban; **v~en** *adj* forbidden; **Rauchen v~en!**
no smoking; **~sschild** *nt* prohibitory sign

Verbrauch [fɛrˈbraʊx] **(-(e)s)** *m*
consumption; **v~en** *vt* to use up; **~er (-s,
-)** *m* consumer; **v~t** *adj* used up, finished;
(*Luft*) stale; (*Mensch*) worn-out

Verbrechen [fɛrˈbrɛçən] **(-s, -)** *nt* crime

Verbrecher [fɛrˈbrɛçɔr] **(-s, -)** *m* criminal;
v~isch *adj* criminal

ver'breiten *vt, vr* to spread; **sich über etw**
akk **~** to expound on sth

verbreitern [fɛrˈbraɪtərn] *vt* to broaden

Verbreitung *f* spread(ing), propagation

verbrenn- [fɛrˈbrɛn] *zW:* **~bar** *adj*
combustible; **~en (-s)** *vt* to burn;
(*Leiche*) to cremate; **V~ung** *f* burning; (*in
Motor*) combustion; (*von Leiche*) cremation;
V~ungsmotor *m* internal combustion
engine

verbringen [fɛrˈbrɪŋən] (*unreg*) *vt* to spend

verbrühen [fɛrˈbryːən] *vt* to scald

verbuchen [fɛrˈbuːxən] *vt* (*FIN*) to register;
(*Erfolg*) to enjoy; (*Misserfolg*) to suffer

verbunden [fɛrˈbʊndən] *adj* connected; **jdm
~ sein** to be obliged *od* indebted to sb;
„falsch ~" (*TEL*) "wrong number"

verbünden [fɛrˈbyndən] *vr* to ally o.s.;
Verbündete(r) *f(m)* ally

ver'bürgen *vr:* **sich ~ für** to vouch for

ver'büßen *vt:* **eine Strafe ~** to serve a
sentence

Verdacht [fɛrˈdaxt] **(-(e)s)** *m* suspicion

verdächtig [fɛrˈdɛçtɪç] *adj* suspicious,
suspect; **~en** [fɛrˈdɛçtɪɡən] *vt* to suspect

verdammen [fɛrˈdamən] *vt* to damn, to
condemn; **verdammt!** damn!

verdammt (*umg*) *adj, adv* damned; **~ noch
mal!** dammit!, dammit!

ver'dampfen *vt* to vaporize, to evaporate

ver'danken *vt:* **jdm etw ~** to owe sb sth

verdau- [fɛrˈdaʊ] *zW:* **~en** *vt* (*auch fig*) to
digest; **~lich** *adj* digestible; **das ist schwer
~lich** that is hard to digest; **V~ung** *f*
digestion

Verdeck [fɛrˈdɛk] **(-(e)s, -e)** *nt* (*AUT*) hood;
(*NAUT*) deck; **v~en** *vt* to cover (up);
(*verbergen*) to hide

Verderb- [fɛrˈdɛrp] *zW:* **~en** [-ˈdɛrbən] **(-s)**
nt ruin; **v~en** (*unreg*) *vt* to spoil; (*schädigen*)

to ruin; (*moralisch*) to corrupt ♦ *vi* (*Essen*) to
spoil, to rot; (*Mensch*) to go to the bad; **es
mit jdm v~en** to get into sb's bad books;
v~lich *adj* (*Einfluss*) pernicious;
(*Lebensmittel*) perishable

verdeutlichen [fɛrˈdɔʏtlɪçən] *vt* to make
clear

ver'dichten *vt, vr* to condense

ver'dienen *vt* to earn; (*moralisch*) to
deserve

Ver'dienst (-(e)s, -e) *m* earnings *pl* ♦ *nt*
merit; (*Leistung*) **~ (um)** service (to)

verdient [fɛrˈdiːnt] *adj* well-earned; (*Person*)
deserving of esteem; **sich um etw ~
machen** to do a lot for sth

verdoppeln [fɛrˈdɔpəln] *vt* to double

verdorben [fɛrˈdɔrbən] *adj* spoilt;
(*geschädigt*) ruined; (*moralisch*) corrupt

verdrängen [fɛrˈdrɛŋən] *vt* to oust, to
displace (*auch PHYS*); (*PSYCH*) to repress

ver'drehen *vt* (*auch fig*) to twist; (*Augen*) to
roll; **jdm den Kopf ~** (*fig*) to turn sb's
head

verdrießlich [fɛrˈdriːslɪç] *adj* peevish,
annoyed

Verdruss ▲ [fɛrˈdrʊs] **(-es, -e)** *m*
annoyance, worry

verdummen [fɛrˈdʊmən] *vt* to make stupid
♦ *vi* to grow stupid

verdunkeln [fɛrˈdʊŋkəln] *vt* to darken; (*fig*)
to obscure ♦ *vr* to darken

Verdunk(e)lung *f* blackout; (*fig*) obscuring

verdünnen [fɛrˈdʏnən] *vt* to dilute

verdunsten [fɛrˈdʊnstən] *vi* to evaporate

verdursten [fɛrˈdʊrstən] *vi* to die of thirst

verdutzt [fɛrˈdʊtst] *adj* nonplussed, taken
aback

verehr- [fɛrˈʔeːr] *zW:* **~en** *vt* to venerate, to
worship (*auch REL*); **jdm etw ~en** to present
sb with sth; **V~er(in) (-s, -)** *m(f)* admirer,
worshipper (*auch REL*); **~t** *adj* esteemed;
V~ung *f* respect; (*REL*) worship

Verein [fɛrˈʔaɪn] **(-(e)s, -e)** *m* club,
association; **v~bar** *adj* compatible;
v~baren *vt* to agree upon; **~barung** *f*
agreement; **v~en** *vt* (*Menschen, Länder*) to
unite; (*Prinzipien*) to reconcile; **mit v~ten**

Kräften having pooled resources, having joined forces; **~te Nationen** United Nations; **v~fachen** vt to simplify; **v~heitlichen** [-haɪtlɪçən] vt to standardize; **v~igen** vt, vr to unite; **~igung** f union; (Verein) association; **v~t** adj united; **v~zelt** adj isolated

ver'eitern vi to suppurate, to fester

verengen [fɛr'ɛŋən] vr to narrow

vererb- [fɛr'ɛrb] zW: **~en** vt to bequeath; (BIOL) to transmit ♦ vr to be hereditary; **V~ung** f bequeathing; (BIOL) transmission; (Lehre) heredity

verewigen [fɛr'e:vɪgən] vt to immortalize ♦ vr (umg) to immortalize o.s.

ver'fahren (unreg) vi to act ♦ vr to get lost ♦ adj tangled; **~ mit** to deal with; **Ver'fahren (-s, -)** nt procedure; (TECH) process; (JUR) proceedings pl

Verfall [fɛr'fal] **(-(e)s)** m decline; (von Haus) dilapidation; (FIN) expiry; **v~en** (unreg) vi to decline; (Haus) to be falling down; (FIN) to lapse; **v~en in** +akk to lapse into; **v~en auf** +akk to hit upon; **einem Laster v~en sein** to be addicted to a vice; **~sdatum** nt expiry date; (der Haltbarkeit) sell-by date

ver'färben vr to change colour

verfassen [fɛr'fasən] vt (Rede) to prepare, work out

Verfasser(in) [fɛr'fasər(ɪn)] **(-s, -)** m(f) author, writer

Verfassung f (auch POL) constitution

Verfassungs- zW: **~gericht** nt constitutional court; **v~widrig** adj unconstitutional

ver'faulen vi to rot

ver'fehlen vt to miss; **etw für verfehlt halten** to regard sth as mistaken

verfeinern [fɛr'faɪnərn] vt to refine

ver'filmen vt to film

verflixt [fɛr'flɪkst] (umg) adj damned, damn

ver'fluchen vt to curse

verfolg- [fɛr'fɔlg] zW: **~en** vt to pursue; (gerichtlich) to prosecute; (grausam, bes POL) to persecute; **V~er (-s, -)** m pursuer; **V~ung** f pursuit; prosecution; persecution

verfrüht [fɛr'fry:t] adj premature

verfüg- [fɛr'fy:g] zW: **~bar** adj available; **~en** vt to direct, to order ♦ vr to proceed ♦ vi: **~en über** +akk to have at one's disposal; **V~ung** f direction, order; **zur V~ung** at one's disposal; **jdm zur V~ung stehen** to be available to sb

verführ- [fɛr'fy:r] zW: **~en** vt to tempt; (sexuell) to seduce; **V~er** m tempter; seducer; **~erisch** adj seductive; **V~ung** f seduction; (Versuchung) temptation

ver'gammeln (umg) vi to go to seed; (Nahrung) to go off

vergangen [fɛr'gaŋən] adj past; **V~heit** f past

vergänglich [fɛr'gɛŋlɪç] adj transitory

vergasen [fɛr'ga:zən] vt (töten) to gas

Vergaser (-s, -) m (AUT) carburettor

vergaß etc [fɛr'ga:s] vb siehe **vergessen**

vergeb- [fɛr'ge:b] zW: **~en** (unreg) vt (verzeihen) to forgive; (weggeben) to give away; **jdm etw ~en** to forgive sb (for) sth; **~ens** adv in vain; **~lich** [fɛr'ge:plɪç] adv in vain ♦ adj vain, futile; **V~ung** f forgiveness

ver'gehen (unreg) vi to pass by od away ♦ vr to commit an offence; **jdm vergeht etw** sb loses sth; **sich an jdm ~** to (sexually) assault sb; **Ver'gehen (-s, -)** nt offence

ver'gelten (unreg) vt: **jdm etw ~** to pay sb back for sth, to repay sb for sth

Ver'geltung f retaliation, reprisal

vergessen [fɛr'gɛsən] (unreg) vt to forget; **V~heit** f oblivion

vergesslich ▲ [fɛr'gɛslɪç] adj forgetful; **V~keit** f forgetfulness

vergeuden [fɛr'gɔʏdən] vt to squander, to waste

vergewaltigen [fɛrgə'valtɪgən] vt to rape; (fig) to violate

Vergewaltigung f rape

vergewissern [fɛrgə'vɪsərn] vr to make sure

ver'gießen (unreg) vt to shed

vergiften [fɛr'gɪftən] vt to poison

Vergiftung f poisoning

Vergissmeinnicht ▲ [fɛr'gɪsmaɪnnɪçt] **(-(e)s, -e)** nt forget-me-not

vergisst ▲ etc [fɛr'gɪst] vb siehe **vergessen**

Vergleich [fɛrˈglaɪç] (-(e)s, -e) *m*
comparison; (*JUR*) settlement; **im ~ mit** *od*
zu compared with *od* to; **v~bar** *adj*
comparable; **v~en** (*unreg*) *vt* to compare
♦ *vr* to reach a settlement

vergnügen [fɛrˈgnyːgən] *vr* to enjoy *od*
amuse o.s.; **V~** (-s, -) *nt* pleasure; **viel V~!**
enjoy yourself!

vergnügt [fɛrˈgnyːkt] *adj* cheerful

Vergnügen *f* pleasure, amusement;
~spark *m* amusement park

vergolden [fɛrˈgɔldən] *vt* to gild

ver'graben *vt* to bury

ver'greifen (*unreg*) *vr*: **sich an jdm ~** to lay
hands on sb; **sich an etw ~** to
misappropriate sth; **sich im Ton ~** to say
the wrong thing

vergriffen [fɛrˈgrɪfən] *adj* (*Buch*) out of print;
(*Ware*) out of stock

vergrößern [fɛrˈgrøːsərn] *vt* to enlarge;
(*mengenmäßig*) to increase; (*Lupe*) to
magnify

Vergrößerung *f* enlargement; increase;
magnification; **~sglas** *nt* magnifying glass

Vergünstigung [fɛrˈgʏnstɪgʊŋ] *f*
concession, privilege

Vergütung *f* compensation

verhaften [fɛrˈhaftən] *vt* to arrest

Verhaftung *f* arrest

ver'halten (*unreg*) *vr* to be, to stand; (*sich
benehmen*) to behave ♦ *vt* to hold *od* keep
back; (*Schritt*) to check; **sich ~ (zu)** (*MATH*)
to be in proportion (to); **Ver'halten** (-s) *nt*
behaviour

Verhältnis [fɛrˈhɛltnɪs] (-ses, -se) *nt*
relationship; (*MATH*) proportion, ratio; **~se**
pl (*Umstände*) conditions; **über seine ~se
leben** to live beyond one's means;
v~mäßig *adj* relative, comparative ♦ *adv*
relatively, comparatively

verhandeln [fɛrˈhandəln] *vi* to negotiate;
(*JUR*) to hold proceedings ♦ *vt* to discuss;
(*JUR*) to hear; **über etw** *akk* **~** to negotiate
sth *od* about sth

Verhandlung *f* negotiation; (*JUR*)
proceedings *pl*; **~sbasis** *f* (*FIN*) basis for
negotiations

ver'hängen *vt* (*fig*) to impose, to inflict

Verhängnis [fɛrˈhɛŋnɪs] (-ses, -se) *nt* fate,
doom; **jdm zum ~ werden** to be sb's
undoing; **v~voll** *adj* fatal, disastrous

verharmlosen [fɛrˈharmloːzən] *vt* to make
light of, to play down

verhärten [fɛrˈhɛrtən] *vr* to harden

verhasst ▲ [fɛrˈhast] *adj* odious, hateful

verhauen [fɛrˈhaʊən] (*unreg*; *umg*) *vt*
(*verprügeln*) to beat up

verheerend [fɛrˈheːrənt] *adj* disastrous,
devastating

verheimlichen [fɛrˈhaɪmlɪçən] *vt*: **jdm etw
~** to keep sth secret from sb

verheiratet [fɛrˈhaɪraːtət] *adj* married

ver'helfen (*unreg*) *vi*: **jdm ~ zu** to help sb
to get

ver'hindern *vt* to prevent; **verhindert sein**
to be unable to make it

verhöhnen [fɛrˈhøːnən] *vt* to mock, to
sneer at

Verhör [fɛrˈhøːr] (-(e)s, -e) *nt* interrogation;
(*gerichtlich*) (cross-)examination; **v~en** *vt* to
interrogate; to (cross-)examine ♦ *vr* to
misunderstand, to mishear

ver'hungern *vi* to starve, to die of hunger

ver'hüten *vt* to prevent, to avert

Ver'hütung *f* prevention; **~smittel** *nt*
contraceptive

verirren [fɛrˈʔɪrən] *vr* to go astray

ver'jagen *vt* to drive away *od* out

verkalken [fɛrˈkalkən] *vi* to calcify; (*umg*) to
become senile

Verkauf [fɛrˈkaʊf] *m* sale; **v~en** *vt* to sell

Verkäufer(in) [fɛrˈkɔʏfər(ɪn)] (-s, -) *m(f)*
seller; salesman(-woman); (*in Laden*) shop
assistant

verkaufsoffen *adj*: **~er Samstag** *Saturday
when the shops stay open all day*

Verkehr [fɛrˈkeːr] (-s, -e) *m* traffic; (*Umgang,
bes sexuell*) intercourse; (*Umlauf*) circulation;
v~en *vi* (*Fahrzeug*) to ply, to run ♦ *vt*, *vr* to
turn, to transform; **v~en mit** to associate
with; **bei jdm v~en** (*besuchen*) to visit sb
regularly

Verkehrs- *zW*: **~ampel** *f* traffic lights *pl*;
~aufkommen *nt* volume of traffic;

~**beruhigung** f traffic calming; ~**delikt** nt traffic offence; ~**funk** m radio traffic service; v~**günstig** adj convenient; ~**mittel** nt means of transport; ~**schild** nt road sign; ~**stauung** f traffic jam, stoppage; ~**unfall** m traffic accident; ~**verein** m tourist information office; ~**zeichen** nt traffic sign

er'kehrt adj wrong; (umgekehrt) the wrong way round

er'kennen (unreg) vt to misjudge, not to appreciate

er'klagen vt to take to court

erkleiden [fɛr'klaɪdən] vr to disguise (o.s.); (sich kostümieren) to get dressed up ♦ vt (Wand) to cover

erkleidung f disguise; (ARCHIT) wainscoting

erkleinern [fɛr'klaɪnərn] vt to make smaller, to reduce in size

er'kneifen (umg) vt: **sich** dat **etw ~** (Lachen) to stifle sth; (Schmerz) to hide sth; (sich versagen) to do without sth

erknüpfen [fɛr'knypfən] vt to tie (up), to knot; (fig) to connect

er'kommen (unreg) vi to deteriorate, to decay; (Mensch) to go downhill, to come down in the world ♦ adj (moralisch) dissolute, depraved

erkörpern [fɛr'kœrpərn] vt to embody, to personify

erkraften [fɛr'kraftən] vt to cope with

er'kriechen (unreg) vr to creep away, to creep into a corner

erkrüppelt [fɛr'krypəlt] adj crippled

er'kühlen vr to get a chill

er'kümmern vi to waste away

erkünden [fɛr'kyndən] vt to proclaim; (Urteil) to pronounce

erkürzen [fɛr'kyrtsən] vt to shorten; (Wort) to abbreviate; **sich** dat **die Zeit ~** to while away the time

/erkürzung f shortening; abbreviation

erladen [fɛr'la:dən] (unreg) vt (Waren, Vieh) to load; (Truppen: auf Schiff) to embark, (auf Zug) to entrain, (auf Flugzeug) to enplane

erlag [fɛr'la:k] **(-(e)s, -e)** m publishing firm

verlangen [fɛr'laŋən] vt to demand; to desire ♦ vi: ~ **nach** to ask for, to desire; ~ **Sie Herrn X** ask for Mr X; V~ **(-s, -)** nt: V~ **(nach)** desire (for); **auf jds V~ (hin)** at sb's request

verlängern [fɛr'lɛŋərn] vt to extend; (länger machen) to lengthen

Verlängerung f extension; (SPORT) extra time; ~**sschnur** f extension cable

verlangsamen [fɛr'laŋza:mən] vt, vr to decelerate, to slow down

Verlass ▲ [fɛr'las] m: **auf ihn/das ist kein ~** he/it cannot be relied upon

ver'lassen (unreg) vt to leave ♦ vr: **sich ~ auf** +akk to depend on ♦ adj desolate; (Mensch) abandoned

verlässlich ▲ [fɛr'lɛslɪç] adj reliable

Verlauf [fɛr'laʊf] m course; v~**en** (unreg) vi (zeitlich) to pass; (Farben) to run ♦ vr to get lost; (Menschenmenge) to disperse

ver'lauten vi: **etw ~ lassen** to disclose sth; **wie verlautet** as reported

ver'legen vt to move; (verlieren) to mislay; (Buch) to publish ♦ vr: **sich auf etw** akk ~ to take up od to sth ♦ adj embarrassed; **nicht ~ um** never at a loss for; **Ver'legenheit** f embarrassment; (Situation) difficulty, scrape

Verleger [fɛr'le:gər] **(-s, -)** m publisher

Verleih [fɛr'laɪ] **(-(e)s, -e)** m hire service; v~**en** (unreg) vt to lend; (Kraft, Anschein) to confer, to bestow; (Preis, Medaille) to award; ~**ung** f lending; bestowal; award

ver'leiten vt to lead astray; ~ **zu** to talk into, to tempt into

ver'lernen vt to forget, to unlearn

ver'lesen (unreg) vt to read out; (aussondern) to sort out ♦ vr to make a mistake in reading

verletz- [fɛr'lɛts] zW: ~**en** vt (auch fig) to injure, to hurt; (Gesetz etc) to violate; ~**end** adj (fig: Worte) hurtful; ~**lich** adj vulnerable, sensitive; V~**te(r)** f(m) injured person; V~**ung** f injury; (Verstoß) violation, infringement

verleugnen [fɛr'lɔygnən] vt (Herkunft, Glauben) to belie; (Menschen) to disown

verleumden [fɛrˈlɔymdən] *vt* to slander; **Verleumdung** *f* slander, libel

verˈlieben *vr*: **sich ~ (in** *+akk*) to fall in love (with)

verliebt [fɛrˈliːpt] *adj* in love

verlieren [fɛrˈliːrən] *(unreg) vt, vi* to lose ♦ *vr* to get lost

Verlierer *m* loser

verlob- [fɛrˈloːb] *zW*: **~en** *vr*: **sich ~en (mit)** to get engaged (to); **V~te(r)** [fɛrˈloːptə(r)] *f(m)* fiancé *m*, fiancée *f*; **V~ung** *f* engagement

verˈlocken *vt* to entice, to lure

Verˈlockung *f* temptation, attraction

verlogen [fɛrˈloːgən] *adj* untruthful

verlor *etc vb siehe* **verlieren**

verloren [fɛrˈloːrən] *adj* lost; *(Eier)* poached ♦ *vb siehe* **verlieren**; **etw ~ geben** to give sth up for lost; **~ gehen** to get lost

verlosen [fɛrˈloːzən] *vt* to raffle, to draw lots for; **Verlosung** *f* raffle, lottery

Verlust [fɛrˈlʊst] **(-(e)s, -e)** *m* loss; *(MIL)* casualty

verˈmachen *vt* to bequeath, to leave

Vermächtnis [fɛrˈmɛçtnɪs] **(-ses, -se)** *nt* legacy

Vermählung [fɛrˈmɛːlʊŋ] *f* wedding, marriage

vermarkten [fɛrˈmarktən] *vt (COMM: Artikel)* to market

vermehren [fɛrˈmeːrən] *vt, vr* to multiply; *(Menge)* to increase

Vermehrung *f* multiplying; increase

verˈmeiden *(unreg) vt* to avoid

vermeintlich [fɛrˈmaɪntlɪç] *adj* supposed

Vermerk [fɛrˈmɛrk] **(-(e)s, -e)** *m* note; *(in Ausweis)* endorsement; **v~en** *vt* to note

verˈmessen *(unreg) vt* to survey ♦ *adj* presumptuous, bold; **Verˈmessenheit** *f* presumptuousness; recklessness

Verˈmessung *f* survey(ing)

vermiet- [fɛrˈmiːt] *zW*: **verˈmieten** *vt* to let, to rent (out); *(Auto)* to hire out, to rent; **Verˈmieter(in) (-s, -)** *m(f)* landlord(-lady); **Verˈmietung** *f* letting, renting (out); *(von Autos)* hiring (out)

vermindern [fɛrˈmɪndərn] *vt, vr* to lessen, to decrease; *(Preise)* to reduce

Verminderung *f* reduction

verˈmischen *vt, vr* to mix, to blend

vermissen [fɛrˈmɪsən] *vt* to miss

vermitt- [fɛrˈmɪt] *zW*: **~eln** *vi* to mediate ♦ *vt (Gespräch)* to connect; **jdm etw ~eln** to help sb to obtain sth; **V~ler (-s, -)** *m (Schlichter)* agent, mediator; **V~lung** *f* procurement; *(Stellenvermittlung)* agency; *(TEL)* exchange; *(Schlichtung)* mediation; **V~lungsgebühr** *f* commission

verˈmögen *(unreg) vt* to be capable of; **~ zu** to be able to; **Verˈmögen (-s, -)** *nt* wealth; *(Fähigkeit)* ability; **ein V~ kosten** to cost a fortune; **verˈmögend** *adj* wealthy

vermuten [fɛrˈmuːtən] *vt* to suppose, to guess; *(argwöhnen)* to suspect

vermutlich *adj* supposed, presumed ♦ *adv* probably

Vermutung *f* supposition; suspicion

vernachlässigen [fɛrˈnaːxlɛsɪgən] *vt* to neglect

verˈnehmen *(unreg) vt* to perceive, to hear; *(erfahren)* to learn; *(JUR)* to (cross-)examine; **dem V~ nach** from what I/we *etc* hear

Vernehmung *f* (cross-)examination

verneigen [fɛrˈnaɪgən] *vr* to bow

verneinen [fɛrˈnaɪnən] *vt (Frage)* to answer in the negative; *(ablehnen)* to deny; *(GRAM)* to negate; **~d** *adj* negative

Verneinung *f* negation

vernichten [fɛrˈnɪçtən] *vt* to annihilate, to destroy; **~d** *adj (fig)* crushing; *(Blick)* withering; *(Kritik)* scathing

Vernunft [fɛrˈnʊnft] **(-)** *f* reason, understanding

vernünftig [fɛrˈnʏnftɪç] *adj* sensible, reasonable

veröffentlichen [fɛrˈʔœfəntlɪçən] *vt* to publish; **Veröffentlichung** *f* publication

verordnen [fɛrˈʔɔrdnən] *vt (MED)* to prescribe

Verordnung *f* order, decree; *(MED)* prescription

verˈpachten *vt* to lease (out)

verˈpacken *vt* to pack

Verˈpackung *f* packing, wrapping;

~smaterial *nt* packing, wrapping

er'passen *vt* to miss; **jdm eine Ohrfeige ~** (*umg*) to give sb a clip round the ear

erpfänden [fɛrˈpfɛndən] *vt* (*Besitz*) to mortgage

er'pflanzen *vt* to transplant

er'pflegen *vt* to feed, to cater for

er'pflegung *f* feeding, catering; (*Kost*) food; (*in Hotel*) board

erpflichten [fɛrˈpflɪçtən] *vt* to oblige, to bind; (*anstellen*) to engage ♦ *vr* to undertake; (*MIL*) to sign on ♦ *vi* to carry obligations; **jdm zu Dank verpflichtet sein** to be obliged to sb

erpflichtung *f* obligation, duty

erpönt [fɛrˈpøːnt] *adj* disapproved (of), taboo

er'prügeln (*umg*) *vt* to beat up, to do over

erputz [fɛrˈpʊts] *m* plaster, roughcast; v~en *vt* to plaster; (*umg: Essen*) to put away

errat [fɛrˈraːt] (-(e)s) *m* treachery; (*POL*) treason; v~en (*unreg*) *vt* to betray; (*Geheimnis*) to divulge ♦ *vr* to give o.s. away

erräter [fɛrˈrɛːtər] (-s, -) *m* traitor(-tress); v~isch *adj* treacherous

er'rechnen *vt*: **~ mit** to set off against ♦ *vr* to miscalculate

errechnungsscheck [fɛrˈrɛçnʊŋsʃɛk] *m* crossed cheque

erregnet [fɛrˈreːgnət] *adj* spoilt by rain, rainy

er'reisen *vi* to go away (on a journey)

errenken [fɛrˈrɛŋkən] *vt* to contort; (*MED*) to dislocate; **sich** *dat* **den Knöchel ~** to sprain one's ankle

er'richten *vt* to do, to perform

erriegeln [fɛrˈriːgəln] *vt* to bolt up, to lock

erringern [fɛrˈrɪŋərn] *vt* to reduce ♦ *vr* to diminish

erringerung *f* reduction; lessening

er'rinnen (*unreg*) *vi* to run out *od* away; (*Zeit*) to elapse

er'rosten *vi* to rust

errotten [fɛrˈrɔtən] *vi* to rot

ver'rücken *vt* to move, to shift

verrückt [fɛrˈrʏkt] *adj* crazy, mad; V~e(r) *f(m)* lunatic; V~heit *f* madness, lunacy

Verruf [fɛrˈruːf] *m*: **in ~ geraten/bringen** to fall/bring into disrepute; v~en *adj* notorious, disreputable

Vers [fɛrs] (-es, -e) *m* verse

ver'sagen *vt*: **jdm/sich etw ~** to deny sb/o.s. sth ♦ *vi* to fail; Ver'sagen (-s) *nt* failure

ver'salzen (*unreg*) *vt* to put too much salt in; (*fig*) to spoil

ver'sammeln *vt, vr* to assemble, to gather

Ver'sammlung *f* meeting, gathering

Versand [fɛrˈzant] (-(e)s) *m* forwarding; dispatch; (~abteilung) dispatch department; ~haus *nt* mail-order firm

versäumen [fɛrˈzɔʏmən] *vt* to miss; (*unterlassen*) to neglect, to fail

ver'schaffen *vt*: **jdm/sich etw ~** to get *od* procure sth for sb/o.s.

verschämt [fɛrˈʃɛːmt] *adj* bashful

verschandeln [fɛrˈʃandəln] (*umg*) *vt* to spoil

verschärfen [fɛrˈʃɛrfən] *vt* to intensify; (*Lage*) to aggravate ♦ *vr* to intensify; to become aggravated

ver'schätzen *vr* to be out in one's reckoning

ver'schenken *vt* to give away

verscheuchen [fɛrˈʃɔʏçən] *vt* (*Tiere*) to chase off *od* away

ver'schicken *vt* to send off

ver'schieben (*unreg*) *vt* to shift; (*EISENB*) to shunt; (*Termin*) to postpone

verschieden [fɛrˈʃiːdən] *adj* different; (*pl: mehrere*) various; **sie sind ~ groß** they are of different sizes; ~tlich *adv* several times

verschimmeln [fɛrˈʃɪməln] *vi* (*Nahrungsmittel*) to go mouldy

verschlafen [fɛrˈʃlaːfən] (*unreg*) *vt* to sleep through; (*fig: versäumen*) to miss ♦ *vi, vr* to oversleep ♦ *adj* sleepy

Verschlag [fɛrˈʃlaːk] *m* shed; v~en [-gən] (*unreg*) *vt* to board up ♦ *adj* cunning; **jdm den Atem v~en** to take sb's breath away; **an einen Ort v~en werden** to wind up in a place

verschlechtern [fɛrˈʃlɛçtərn] *vt* to make worse ♦ *vr* to deteriorate, to get worse; **Verschlechterung** *f* deterioration

Verschleiß [fɛrˈʃlaɪs] **(-es, -e)** *m* wear and tear; **v~en** (*unreg*) *vt* to wear out

verˈschleppen *vt* to carry off, to abduct; (*Krankheit*) to protract; (*zeitlich*) to drag out

verˈschleudern *vt* to squander; (*COMM*) to sell dirt-cheap

verschließbar *adj* lockable

verschließen [fɛrˈʃliːsən] (*unreg*) *vt* to close; to lock ♦ *vr*: **sich einer Sache** *dat* **~** to close one's mind to sth

verschlimmern [fɛrˈʃlɪmərn] *vt* to make worse, to aggravate ♦ *vr* to get worse, to deteriorate

verschlingen [fɛrˈʃlɪŋən] (*unreg*) *vt* to devour, to swallow up; (*Fäden*) to twist

verschlossen [fɛrˈʃlɔsən] *adj* locked; (*fig*) reserved; **V~heit** *f* reserve

verˈschlucken *vt* to swallow ♦ *vr* to choke

Verschluss ▲ [fɛrˈʃlʊs] *m* lock; (*von Kleid etc*) fastener; (*PHOT*) shutter; (*Stöpsel*) plug

verschlüsseln [fɛrˈʃlʏsəln] *vt* to encode

verschmieren [fɛrˈʃmiːrən] *vt* (*verstreichen: Gips, Mörtel*) to apply, spread on; (*schmutzig machen: Wand etc*) to smear

verschmutzen [fɛrˈʃmʊtsən] *vt* to soil; (*Umwelt*) to pollute

verschneit [fɛrˈʃnaɪt] *adj* snowed up, covered with snow

verschollen [fɛrˈʃɔlən] *adj* lost, missing

verˈschonen *vt*: **jdn mit etw ~** to spare sb sth

verschönern [fɛrˈʃøːnərn] *vt* to decorate; (*verbessern*) to improve

verˈschreiben (*unreg*) *vt* (*MED*) to prescribe ♦ *vr* to make a mistake (in writing); **sich einer Sache** *dat* **~** to devote o.s. to sth

verschreibungspflichtig *adj* (*Medikament*) available on prescription only

verschrotten [fɛrˈʃrɔtən] *vt* to scrap

verschuld- [fɛrˈʃʊld] *zW*: **~en** *vt* to be guilty of; **V~en (-s)** *nt* fault, guilt; **~et** *adj* in debt; **V~ung** *f* fault; (*Geld*) debts *pl*

verˈschütten *vt* to spill; (*zuschütten*) to fill; (*unter Trümmer*) to bury

verˈschweigen (*unreg*) *vt* to keep secret; **jdm etw ~** to keep sth from sb

verschwend- [fɛrˈʃvɛnd] *zW*: **~en** *vt* to squander; **V~er (-s, -)** *m* spendthrift; **~erisch** *adj* wasteful, extravagant; **V~ung** *f* waste; extravagance

verschwiegen [fɛrˈʃviːgən] *adj* discreet; (*Ort*) secluded; **V~heit** *f* discretion; seclusion

verˈschwimmen (*unreg*) *vi* to grow hazy, to become blurred

verˈschwinden (*unreg*) *vi* to disappear, to vanish; **Verˈschwinden (-s)** *nt* disappearance

verschwitzt [fɛrˈʃvɪtst] *adj* (*Mensch*) sweaty

verschwommen [fɛrˈʃvɔmən] *adj* hazy, vague

verschwör- [fɛrˈʃvøːr] *zW*: **~en** (*unreg*) *vr* to plot, to conspire; **V~ung** *f* conspiracy, plot

verˈsehen (*unreg*) *vt* to supply, to provide; (*Pflicht*) to carry out; (*Amt*) to fill; (*Haushalt*) to keep ♦ *vr* (*fig*) to make a mistake; **ehe er (es) sich ~ hatte ...** before he knew it ...; **Verˈsehen (-s, -)** *nt* oversight; **aus V~** by mistake; **~tlich** *adv* by mistake

Versehrte(r) [fɛrˈzeːrtə(r)] *f(m)* disabled person

verˈsenden (*unreg*) *vt* to forward, to dispatch

verˈsenken *vt* to sink ♦ *vr*: **sich ~ in** +*akk* to become engrossed in

versessen [fɛrˈzɛsən] *adj*: **~ auf** +*akk* mad about

verˈsetzen *vt* to transfer; (*verpfänden*) to pawn; (*umg*) to stand up ♦ *vr*: **sich in jdn** *od* **in jds Lage ~** to put o.s. in sb's place; **jdm einen Tritt/Schlag ~** to kick/hit sb; **etw mit etw ~** to mix sth with sth; **jdn in gute Laune ~** to put sb in a good mood

Verˈsetzung *f* transfer

verseuchen [fɛrˈzɔʏçən] *vt* to contaminate

versichern [fɛrˈzɪçərn] *vt* to assure; (*mit Geld*) to insure

Versicherung *f* assurance; insurance

Versicherungs- *zW*: **~gesellschaft** *f* insurance company; **~karte** *f* insurance card; **die grüne ~karte** the green card;

~police f insurance policy

ver'sinken (unreg) vi to sink

ver'söhnen [fɛr'zøːnən] vt to reconcile ♦ vr to become reconciled

Ver'söhnung f reconciliation

ver'sorgen vt to provide, to supply; (Familie etc) to look after

Ver'sorgung f provision; (Unterhalt) maintenance; (Altersversorgung etc) benefit, assistance

ver'späten [fɛr'ʃpɛːtən] vr to be late

ver'spätet adj (Zug, Abflug, Ankunft) late; (Glückwünsche) belated

Ver'spätung f delay; ~ **haben** to be late

ver'sperren vt to bar, to obstruct

ver'spielt [fɛr'ʃpiːlt] adj (Kind, Tier) playful

ver'spotten vt to ridicule, to scoff at

ver'sprechen (unreg) vt to promise; **sich** dat **etw von etw ~** to expect sth from sth; **Ver'sprechen** (-s, -) nt promise

ver'staatlichen [fɛr'ʃtaːtlɪçən] vt to nationalize

Ver'stand [fɛr'ʃtant] m intelligence; mind; **den ~ verlieren** to go out of one's mind; **über jds ~ gehen** to go beyond sb

ver'ständig [fɛr'ʃtɛndɪç] adj sensible; **~en** [fɛr'ʃtɛndɪgən] vt to inform ♦ vr to communicate; (sich einigen) to come to an understanding; **V~ung** f communication; (Benachrichtigung) informing; (Einigung) agreement

ver'ständ- [fɛr'ʃtɛnt] zW: **~lich** adj understandable, comprehensible; **V~lichkeit** f clarity, intelligibility; **V~nis** (-ses, -se) nt understanding; **~nislos** adj uncomprehending; **~nisvoll** adj understanding, sympathetic

ver'stärk- [fɛr'ʃtɛrk] zW: **~en** vt to strengthen; (Ton) to amplify; (erhöhen) to intensify ♦ vr to intensify; **V~er** (-s, -) m amplifier; **V~ung** f strengthening; (Hilfe) reinforcements pl; (von Ton) amplification

ver'stauchen [fɛr'ʃtauxən] vt to sprain

ver'stauen [fɛr'ʃtauən] vt to stow away

Ver'steck [fɛr'ʃtɛk] (-(e)s, -e) nt hiding (place); **v~en** vt, vr to hide; **v~t** adj hidden

ver'stehen (unreg) vt to understand ♦ vr to

get on; **das versteht sich (von selbst)** that goes without saying

ver'steigern [fɛr'ʃtaɪgərn] vt to auction; **Versteigerung** f auction

verstell- [fɛr'ʃtɛl] zW: **~bar** adj adjustable, variable; **~en** vt to move, to shift; (Uhr) to adjust; (versperren) to block; (fig) to disguise ♦ vr to pretend, to put on an act; **V~ung** f pretence

ver'steuern [fɛr'ʃtɔyərn] vt to pay tax on

ver'stimmt [fɛr'ʃtɪmt] adj out of tune; (fig) cross, put out; (Magen) upset

ver'stopfen vt to block, to stop up; (MED) to constipate

Ver'stopfung f obstruction; (MED) constipation

ver'storben [fɛr'ʃtɔrbən] adj deceased, late

ver'stört [fɛr'ʃtøːrt] adj (Mensch) distraught

Ver'stoß [fɛr'ʃtoːs] m: **~ (gegen)** infringement (of), violation (of); **v~en** (unreg) vt to disown, to reject ♦ vi: **v~en gegen** to offend against

ver'streichen (unreg) vt to spread ♦ vi to elapse

ver'streuen vt to scatter (about)

ver'stümmeln [fɛr'ʃtʏməln] vt to maim, to mutilate (auch fig)

ver'stummen [fɛr'ʃtomən] vi to go silent; (Lärm) to die away

Ver'such [fɛr'zuːx] (-(e)s, -e) m attempt; (SCI) experiment; **v~en** vt to try; (verlocken) to tempt ♦ vr: **sich an etw** dat **v~en** to try one's hand at sth; **~skaninchen** nt (fig) guinea-pig; **~ung** f temptation

ver'tagen [fɛr'taːgən] vt, vi to adjourn

ver'tauschen vt to exchange; (versehentlich) to mix up

verteidig- [fɛr'taɪdɪç] zW: **~en** vt to defend; **V~er** (-s, -) m defender; (JUR) defence counsel; **V~ung** f defence

ver'teilen vt to distribute; (Rollen) to assign; (Salbe) to spread

Ver'teilung f distribution, allotment

ver'tiefen [fɛr'tiːfən] vt to deepen ♦ vr: **sich in etw** akk **~** to become engrossed od absorbed in sth

Ver'tiefung f depression

vertikal [vɛrti'kaːl] *adj* vertical

vertilgen [fɛr'tɪlgən] *vt* to exterminate; (*umg*) to eat up, to consume

vertonen [fɛr'toːnən] *vt* to set to music

Vertrag [fɛr'traːk] (**-(e)s, ⸚e**) *m* contract, agreement; (*POL*) treaty; **v~en** [-gən] (*unreg*) *vt* to tolerate, to stand ♦ *vr* to get along; (*sich aussöhnen*) to become reconciled; **v~lich** *adj* contractual

verträglich [fɛr'trɛːklɪç] *adj* good-natured, sociable; (*Speisen*) easily digested; (*MED*) easily tolerated; **V~keit** *f* sociability; good nature; digestibility

Vertrags- *zW*: **~bruch** *m* breach of contract; **~händler** *m* appointed retailer; **~partner** *m* party to a contract; **~werkstatt** *f* appointed repair shop; **v~widrig** *adj* contrary to contract

vertrauen [fɛr'travən] *vi*: **jdm ~** to trust sb; **~ auf** +*akk* to rely on; **V~ (-s)** *nt* confidence; **V~ erweckend** inspiring trust; **~svoll** *adj* trustful; **~swürdig** *adj* trustworthy

vertraulich [fɛr'travlɪç] *adj* familiar; (*geheim*) confidential

vertraut [fɛr'travt] *adj* familiar; **V~heit** *f* familiarity

ver'treiben (*unreg*) *vt* to drive away; (*aus Land*) to expel; (*COMM*) to sell; (*Zeit*) to pass

vertret- [fɛr'treːt] *zW*: **~en** (*unreg*) *vt* to represent; (*Ansicht*) to hold, to advocate; **sich** *dat* **die Beine ~en** to stretch one's legs; **V~er (-s, -)** *m* representative; (*Verfechter*) advocate; **V~ung** *f* representation; advocacy

Vertrieb [fɛr'triːp] (**-(e)s, -e**) *m* marketing (department)

ver'trocknen *vi* to dry up

ver'trösten *vt* to put off

vertun [fɛr'tuːn] (*unreg*) *vt* to waste ♦ *vr* (*umg*) to make a mistake

vertuschen [fɛr'tʊʃən] *vt* to hush *od* cover up

verübeln [fɛr'|yːbəln] *vt*: **jdm etw ~** to be cross *od* offended with sb on account of sth

verüben [fɛr'|yːbən] *vt* to commit

verun- [fɛr'|ʊn] *zW*: **~glimpfen** *vt* to disparage; **~glücken** *vi* to have an accident; **tödlich ~glücken** to be killed in an accident; **~reinigen** *vt* to soil; (*Umwelt*) to pollute; **~sichern** *vt* to rattle; **~treuen** [-trɔyən] *vt* to embezzle

verur- [fɛr'|uːr] *zW*: **~sachen** *vt* to cause; **~teilen** [-taılən] *vt* to condemn; **V~teilung** *f* condemnation; (*JUR*) sentence

verviel- [fɛr'fiːl] *zW*: **~fachen** *vt* to multiply; **~fältigen** [-fɛltɪgən] *vt* to duplicate, to copy; **V~fältigung** *f* duplication, copying

vervollkommnen [fɛr'fɔlkɔmnən] *vt* to perfect

vervollständigen [fɛr'fɔlʃtɛndɪgən] *vt* to complete

ver'wackeln *vt* (*Foto*) to blur

ver'wählen *vr* (*TEL*) to dial the wrong number

verwahren [fɛr'vaːrən] *vt* to keep, to lock away ♦ *vr* to protest

verwalt- [fɛr'valt] *zW*: **~en** *vt* to manage; to administer; **V~er (-s, -)** *m* manager; (*Vermögensverwalter*) trustee; **V~ung** *f* administration; management

ver'wandeln *vt* to change, to transform ♦ *vr* to change; to be transformed; **Ver'wandlung** *f* change, transformation

verwandt [fɛr'vant] *adj*: **~ (mit)** related (to); **V~e(r)** *f(m)* relative, relation; **V~schaft** *f* relationship; (*Menschen*) relations *pl*

ver'warnen *vt* to caution

Ver'warnung *f* caution

ver'wechseln *vt*: **~ mit** to confuse with; to mistake for; **zum V~ ähnlich** as like as two peas

Ver'wechslung *f* confusion, mixing up

Verwehung [fɛr'veːʊŋ] *f* snowdrift; sand drift

verweichlicht [fɛr'vaıçlıçt] *adj* effeminate, soft

ver'weigern *vt*: **jdm etw ~** to refuse sb sth; **den Gehorsam/die Aussage ~** to refuse to obey/testify

Ver'weigerung *f* refusal

Verweis [fɛr'vaıs] (**-es, -e**) *m* reprimand,

rebuke; (Hinweis) reference; **v~en** (unreg) vt to refer; **jdn von der Schule v~en** to expel sb (from school); **jdn des Landes v~en** to deport od expel sb

er'welken vi to fade

erwend- [fɛr'vɛnd] zW: **~bar** [-'vɛntbaːr] adj usable; **ver'wenden** (unreg) vt to use; (Mühe, Zeit, Arbeit) to spend ♦ vr to intercede; **Ver'wendung** f use

er'werfen (unreg) vt to reject

erwerflich [fɛr'vɛrflɪç] adj reprehensible

er'werten vt to utilize

er'wertung f utilization

erwesen [fɛr'veːzən] vi to decay

erwickeln vt to tangle (up); (fig) to involve ♦ vr to get tangled (up); **jdn in etw** akk **~** to involve sb in sth; **sich in etw** akk **~** to get involved in sth

erwickelt [fɛr'vɪkəlt] adj (Situation, Fall) difficult, complicated

erwildern [fɛr'vɪldərn] vi to run wild

erwirklichen [fɛr'vɪrklɪçən] vt to realize, to put into effect

erwirklichung f realization

erwirren [fɛr'vɪrən] vt to tangle (up); (fig) to confuse

erwirrung f confusion

erwittern [fɛr'vɪtərn] vi to weather

erwitwet [fɛr'vɪtvət] adj widowed

erwöhnen [fɛr'vøːnən] vt to spoil

erworren [fɛr'vɔrən] adj confused

erwundbar [fɛr'vʊntbaːr] adj vulnerable

erwunden [fɛr'vʊndən] vt to wound

erwunder- [fɛr'vʊndər] zW: **~lich** adj surprising; **V~ung** f astonishment

erwundete(r) f(m) injured person

erwundung f wound, injury

er'wünschen vt to curse

erwüsten [fɛr'vyːstən] vt to devastate

erzagen [fɛr'tsaːgən] vi to despair

erzählen vt to miscount

erzehren [fɛr'tseːrən] vt to consume

er'zeichnen vt to list; (Niederlage, Verlust) to register

erzeichnis [fɛr'tsaɪçnɪs] (**-ses, -se**) nt list, catalogue; (in Buch) index

erzeih- [fɛr'tsaɪ] zW: **~en** (unreg) vt, vi to

forgive; **jdm etw ~en** to forgive sb for sth; **~lich** adj pardonable; **V~ung** f forgiveness, pardon; **V~ung!** sorry!, excuse me!

verzichten [fɛr'tsɪçtən] vi: **~ auf** +akk to forgo, to give up

ver'ziehen (unreg) vi to move ♦ vt to put out of shape; (Kind) to spoil; (Pflanzen) to thin out ♦ vr to go out of shape; (Gesicht) to contort; (verschwinden) to disappear; **das Gesicht ~** to pull a face

verzieren [fɛr'tsiːrən] vt to decorate, to ornament

Verzierung f decoration

verzinsen [fɛr'tsɪnzən] vt to pay interest on

ver'zögern vt to delay

Ver'zögerung f delay, time lag; **~staktik** f delaying tactics pl

verzollen [fɛr'tsɔlən] vt to pay duty on

Verzug [fɛr'tsuːk] m delay

verzweif- [fɛr'tsvaɪf] zW: **~eln** vi to despair; **~elt** adj desperate; **V~lung** f despair

Veto ['veːto] (**-s, -s**) nt veto

Vetter ['fɛtɐ] (**-s, -n**) m cousin

vgl. abk (= vergleiche) cf.

v. H. abk (= vom Hundert) p.c.

vibrieren [vi'briːrən] vi to vibrate

Video ['viːdeo] nt video; **~gerät** nt video recorder; **~rekorder** m video recorder

Vieh [fiː] (**-(e)s**) nt cattle pl; **v~isch** adj bestial

viel [fiːl] adj a lot of, much ♦ adv a lot, much; **~ sagend** significant; **~ versprechend** promising; **~e** pron pl a lot of, many; **~ zu wenig** much too little; **~erlei** adj a great variety of; **~es** pron a lot; **~fach** adj, adv many times; **auf ~fachen Wunsch** at the request of many people; **V~falt** (**-**) f variety; **~fältig** adj varied, many-sided

vielleicht [fi'laɪçt] adv perhaps

viel- zW: **~mal(s)** adv many times; **danke ~mals** many thanks; **~mehr** adv rather, on the contrary; **~seitig** adj many-sided

vier [fiːr] num four; **V~eck** (**-(e)s, -e**) nt four-sided figure; (gleichseitig) square; **~eckig** adj four-sided; square; **V~takt-motor** m four-stroke engine; **~te(r, s)**

['fi:rtə(r, s)] *adj* fourth; **V~tel** ['fɪrtəl] (**-s, -**) *nt* quarter; **V~teljahr** *nt* quarter; **~teljährlich** *adj* quarterly; **~teln** *vt* to divide into four; (*Kuchen usw*) to divide into quarters; **V~telstunde** *f* quarter of an hour; **~zehn** ['fɪrtse:n] *num* fourteen; **in ~zehn Tagen** in a fortnight; **~zehntägig** *adj* fortnightly; **~zig** ['fɪrtsɪç] *num* forty

Villa ['vɪla] (**-, Villen**) *f* villa

violett [vio'lɛt] *adj* violet

Violin- [vio'li:n] *zW:* **~e** *f* violin; **~schlüssel** *m* treble clef

virtuell [vɪrtu'ɛl] *adj* (COMPUT) virtual; **~e Realität** virtual reality

Virus ['vi:rʊs] (**-, Viren**) *m od nt* (*auch* COMPUT) virus

Visa ['vi:za] *pl von* **Visum**

vis-a-vis ▲, **vis-à-vis** [viza'vi:] *adv* opposite

Visen ['vi:zən] *pl von* **Visum**

Visier [vi'zi:r] (**-s, -e**) *nt* gunsight; (*am Helm*) visor

Visite [vi'zi:tə] *f* (MED) visit; **~nkarte** *f* visiting card

Visum ['vi:zʊm] (**-s, Visa od Visen**) *nt* visa

vital [vi'ta:l] *adj* lively, full of life, vital

Vitamin [vita'mi:n] (**-s, -e**) *nt* vitamin

Vogel ['fo:gəl] (**-s, ·**) *m* bird; **einen ~ haben** (*umg*) to have bats in the belfry; **jdm den ~ zeigen** (*umg*) to tap one's forehead (*meaning that one thinks sb stupid*); **~bauer** *nt* birdcage; **~perspektive** *f* bird's-eye view; **~scheuche** *f* scarecrow

Vokabel [vo'ka:bəl] (**-, -n**) *f* word

Vokabular [vokabu'la:r] (**-s, -e**) *nt* vocabulary

Vokal [vo'ka:l] (**-s, -e**) *m* vowel

Volk [fɔlk] (**-(e)s, ·er**) *nt* people; nation

Völker- ['fœlkər] *zW:* **~recht** *nt* international law; **v~rechtlich** *adj* according to international law; **~verständigung** *f* international understanding

---
Volkshochschule

ⓘ The **Volkshochschule** (*VHS*) is an institution which offers Adult Education classes. No set qualifications are necessary

to attend. For a small fee adults can attend both vocational and non-vocational classes in the day-time or evening.

Volks- *zW:* **~entscheid** *m* referendum; **~fest** *nt* fair; **~hochschule** *f* adult education classes *pl*; **~lied** *nt* folksong; **~republik** *f* people's republic; **~schule** *f* elementary school; **~tanz** *m* folk dance; **~vertreter(in)** *m(f)* people's representative; **~wirtschaft** *f* economics *sg*

voll [fɔl] *adj* full; **etw ~ machen** to fill sth up; **~ tanken** to fill up; **~ und ganz** completely; **jdn für ~ nehmen** (*umg*) to take sb seriously; **~auf** *adv* amply; **V~bart** *m* full beard; **V~beschäftigung** *f* full employment; **~'bringen** (*unreg*) *vt insep* to accomplish; **~'enden** *vt insep* to finish, to complete; **~endet** *adj* (*~kommen*) completed; **~ends** ['fɔlɛnts] *adv* completely; **V~'endung** *f* completion

Volleyball ['vɔlibal] *m* volleyball

völlig ['fœlɪç] *adj* complete ♦ *adv* completely

voll- *zW:* **~jährig** *adj* of age; **V~kaskoversicherung** ['fɔlkaskoferzɪçərʊŋ] *f* fully comprehensive insurance; **~'kommen** *adj* perfect; **V~'kommenheit** *f* perfection; **V~kornbrot** *nt* wholemeal bread; **V~macht** (**-, -en**) *f* authority, full powers *pl*; **V~milch** *f* (KOCH) full-cream milk; **V~mond** *m* full moon; **V~pension** *f* full board; **~ständig** ['fɔlʃtɛndɪç] *adj* complete; **~'strecken** *vt insep* to execute; **~tanken** △ *vt, vi siehe* **voll**; **V~waschmittel** *nt* detergent; **V~wertkost** *f* wholefood; **~zählig** ['fɔlsɛ:lɪç] *adj* complete; in full number; **~'ziehen** (*unreg*) *vt insep* to carry out ♦ *vr insep* to happen; **V~'zug** *m* execution

Volumen [vo'lu:mən] (**-s, - od Volumina**) *nt* volume

vom [fɔm] = **von dem**

SCHLÜSSELWORT
---

von [fɔn] *präp +dat* **1** (*Ausgangspunkt*) from;

von from ... to; **von morgens bis abends** from morning till night; **von ... nach ...** from ... to ...; **von ... an** from ...; **von ... aus** from ...; **von dort aus** from there; **etw von sich aus tun** to do sth of one's own accord; **von mir aus** (umg) if you like, I don't mind; **von wo/wann ...?** where/when ... from?

2 (Ursache, im Passiv) by; **ein Gedicht von Schiller** a poem by Schiller; **von etw müde** tired from sth

3 (als Genitiv) of; **ein Freund von mir** a friend of mine; **nett von dir** nice of you; **jeweils zwei von zehn** two out of every ten

4 (über) about; **er erzählte vom Urlaub** he talked about his holiday

5: **von wegen!** (umg) no way!

voneinander adv from each other

⎯⎯⎯⎯⎯⎯⎯⎯⎯
│ SCHLÜSSELWORT │
⎯⎯⎯⎯⎯⎯⎯⎯⎯

vor [foːr] präp +dat 1 (räumlich) in front of; **vor der Kirche links abbiegen** turn left before the church

2 (zeitlich) before; **ich war vor ihm da** I was there before him; **vor 2 Tagen** 2 days ago; **5 (Minuten) vor 4** 5 (minutes) to 4; **vor kurzem** a little while ago

3 (Ursache) with; **vor Wut/Liebe** with rage/love; **vor Hunger sterben** to die of hunger; **vor lauter Arbeit** because of work

4: **vor allem, vor allen Dingen** most of all

♦ präp +akk (räumlich) in front of

♦ adv: **vor und zurück** backwards and forwards

Vorabend ['foːr|aːbənt] m evening before, eve

voran [fo'ran] adv before, ahead; **mach ~!** get on with it!; **~gehen** (unreg) vi to go ahead; **einer Sache** dat **~gehen** to precede sth; **~kommen** (unreg) vi to come along, to make progress

Voranschlag ['foːr|anʃlaːk] m estimate

Vorarbeiter ['foːr|arbaitər] m foreman

voraus [fo'raus] adv ahead; (zeitlich) in advance; **jdm ~ sein** to be ahead of sb; **im V~** in advance; **~gehen** (unreg) vi to go (on) ahead; (fig) to precede; **~haben** (unreg) vt: **jdm etw ~haben** to have the edge on sb in sth; **V~sage** f prediction; **~sagen** vt to predict; **~sehen** (unreg) vt to foresee; **~setzen** vt to assume; **~gesetzt, dass ...** provided that ...; **V~setzung** f requirement, prerequisite; **V~sicht** f foresight; **aller V~sicht nach** in all probability; **~sichtlich** adv probably

Vorbehalt ['foːrbəhalt] (-(e)s, -e) m reservation, proviso; **v~en** (unreg) vt: **sich/jdm etw v~en** to reserve sth (for o.s.)/for sb; **v~los** adj unconditional ♦ adv unconditionally

vorbei [foːr'bai] adv by, past; **das ist ~** that's over; **~gehen** (unreg) vi to pass by, to go past; **~kommen** (unreg) vi: **bei jdm ~kommen** to drop in od call in on sb

vor- zW: **~belastet** ['foːrbəlastət] adj (fig) handicapped; **~bereiten** vt to prepare; **V~bereitung** f preparation; **V~bestellung** f advance order; (von Platz, Tisch etc) advance booking; **~bestraft** ['foːrbəʃtraːft] adj previously convicted, with a record

vorbeugen ['foːrbɔygən] vt, vr to lean forward ♦ vi +dat to prevent; **~d** adj preventive

Vorbeugung f prevention; **zur ~ gegen** for the prevention of

Vorbild ['foːrbɪlt] nt model; **sich** dat **jdn zum ~ nehmen** to model o.s. on sb; **v~lich** adj model, ideal

vorbringen ['foːrbrɪŋən] (unreg) vt to advance, to state

Vorder- ['fɔrdər] zW: **~achse** f front axle; **v~e(r, s)** adj front; **~grund** m foreground; **~mann** (pl -**männer**) m man in front; **jdn auf ~mann bringen** (umg) to get sb to shape up; **~seite** f front (side); **v~ste(r, s)** adj front

vordrängen ['foːrdrɛŋən] vr to push to the front

voreilig ['foːr|ailɪç] adj hasty, rash

voreinander [foːr|ai'nandər] adv (räumlich)

in front of each other

voreingenommen ['foːɐ|aɪngənɔmən] *adj* biased; **V~heit** *f* bias

vorenthalten ['foːɐ|ɛnthaltən] (*unreg*) *vt*: **jdm etw ~** to withhold sth from sb

vorerst ['foːɐ|eːrst] *adv* for the moment *od* present

Vorfahr ['foːɐfaːr] (**-en, -en**) *m* ancestor

vorfahren (*unreg*) *vi* to drive (on) ahead; (*vors Haus etc*) to drive up

Vorfahrt *f* (*AUT*) right of way; **~ achten!** give way!

Vorfahrts- *zW:* **~regel** *f* right of way; **~schild** *nt* give way sign; **~straße** *f* major road

Vorfall ['foːɐfal] *m* incident; **v~en** (*unreg*) *vi* to occur

vorfinden ['foːɐfɪndən] (*unreg*) *vt* to find

Vorfreude ['foːɐfrɔʏdə] *f* (joyful) anticipation

vorführen ['foːɐfyːrən] *vt* to show, to display; **dem Gericht ~** to bring before the court

Vorgabe ['foːɐgaːbə] *f* (*SPORT*) start, handicap ♦ *in zW* (*COMPUT*) default

Vorgang ['foːɐgaŋ] *m* course of events; (*bes SCI*) process

Vorgänger(in) ['foːɐgɛŋər(ɪn)] (**-s, -**) *m(f)* predecessor

vorgeben ['foːɐgeːbən] (*unreg*) *vt* to pretend, to use as a pretext; (*SPORT*) to give an advantage *od* a start of

vorgefertigt ['foːɐgəfɛrtɪçt] *adj* prefabricated

vorgehen ['foːɐgeːən] (*unreg*) *vi* (*voraus*) to go (on) ahead; (*nach vorn*) to go up front; (*handeln*) to act, to proceed; (*Uhr*) to be fast; (*Vorrang haben*) to take precedence; (*passieren*) to go on

Vorgehen (**-s**) *nt* action

Vorgeschichte ['foːɐgəʃɪçtə] *f* past history

Vorgeschmack ['foːɐgəʃmak] *m* foretaste

Vorgesetzte(r) ['foːɐgəzɛtstə(r)] *f(m)* superior

vorgestern ['foːɐgɛstərn] *adv* the day before yesterday

vorhaben ['foːɐhaːbən] (*unreg*) *vt* to intend; **hast du schon was vor?** have you got anything on?; **V~** (**-s, -**) *nt* intention

vorhalten ['foːɐhaltən] (*unreg*) *vt* to hold *od* put up ♦ *vi* to last; **jdm etw ~** (*fig*) to reproach sb for sth

vorhanden [foːɐ'handən] *adj* existing; (*erhältlich*) available

Vorhang ['foːɐhaŋ] *m* curtain

Vorhängeschloss ▲ ['foːɐhɛŋəʃlɔs] *nt* padlock

vorher [foːɐ'heːr] *adv* before(hand); **~bestimmen** *vt* (*Schicksal*) to preordain; **~gehen** (*unreg*) *vi* to precede; **~ig** *adj* previous

Vorherrschaft ['foːɐhɛrʃaft] *f* predominance, supremacy

vorherrschen ['foːɐhɛrʃən] *vi* to predominate

vorher- [foːɐ'heːr] *zW:* **V~sage** *f* forecast; **~sagen** *vt* to forecast, to predict; **~sehbar** *adj* predictable; **~sehen** (*unreg*) *vt* to foresee

vorhin [foːɐ'hɪn] *adv* not long ago, just now; **V~ein** ▲ *adv:* **im V~ein** beforehand

vorig ['foːrɪç] *adj* previous, last

Vorkämpfer(in) ['foːɐkɛmpfər(ɪn)] *m(f)* pioneer

Vorkaufsrecht ['foːɐkaʊfsrɛçt] *nt* option to buy

Vorkehrung ['foːɐkeːrʊŋ] *f* precaution

vorkommen ['foːɐkɔmən] (*unreg*) *vi* to come forward; (*geschehen, sich finden*) to occur; (*scheinen*) to seem (to be); **sich** *dat* **dumm** *etc* **~** to feel stupid *etc*; **V~** (**-s, -**) *nt* occurrence

Vorkriegs- ['foːɐkriːks] *in zW* prewar

Vorladung ['foːɐlaːdʊŋ] *f* summons *sg*

Vorlage ['foːɐlaːgə] *f* model, pattern; (*Gesetzesvorlage*) bill; (*SPORT*) pass

vorlassen ['foːɐlasən] (*unreg*) *vt* to admit; (*vorgehen lassen*) to allow to go in front

vorläufig ['foːɐlɔʏfɪç] *adj* temporary, provisional

vorlaut ['foːɐlaʊt] *adj* impertinent, cheeky

vorlesen ['foːɐleːzən] (*unreg*) *vt* to read (out)

Vorlesung *f* (*UNIV*) lecture

vorletzte(r, s) ['foːɐlɛtstə(r, s)] *adj* last but one

vorlieb [foːɐ'liːp] *adv:* **~ nehmen mit** to

make do with

Vorliebe ['foːrliːbə] f preference, partiality

vorliegen ['foːrliːgən] (unreg) vi to be (here); **etw liegt jdm vor** sb has sth; **~d** adj present, at issue

vormachen ['foːrmaxən] vt: **jdm etw ~** to show sb how to do sth; (fig) to fool sb; to have sb on

Vormachtstellung ['foːrmaxtʃtɛlʊŋ] f supremacy, hegemony

Vormarsch ['foːrmarʃ] m advance

vormerken ['foːrmɛrkən] vt to book

Vormittag ['foːrmɪtaːk] m morning; **v~s** adv in the morning, before noon

vorn [fɔrn] adv in front; **von ~ anfangen** to start at the beginning; **nach ~** to the front

Vorname ['foːrnaːmə] m first name, Christian name

vorne ['fɔrnə] adv = **vorn**

vornehm ['foːrneːm] adj distinguished; refined; elegant

vornehmen (unreg) vt (fig) to carry out; **sich** dat **etw ~** to start on sth; (beschließen) to decide to do sth; **sich** dat **jdn ~** to tell sb off

vornherein ['fɔrnhɛraɪn] adv: **von ~** from the start

Vorort ['foːrʔɔrt] m suburb

Vorrang ['foːrraŋ] m precedence, priority; **v~ig** adj of prime importance, primary

Vorrat ['foːrraːt] m stock, supply

vorrätig ['foːrrɛːtɪç] adj in stock

Vorratskammer f pantry

Vorrecht ['foːrrɛçt] nt privilege

Vorrichtung ['foːrrɪçtʊŋ] f device, contrivance

vorrücken ['foːrrʏkən] vi to advance ♦ vt to move forward

Vorsaison ['foːrzɛzõː] f early season

Vorsatz ['foːrzats] m intention; (JUR) intent; **einen ~ fassen** to make a resolution

vorsätzlich ['foːrzɛtslɪç] adj intentional; (JUR) premeditated ♦ adv intentionally

Vorschau ['foːrʃaʊ] f (RADIO, TV) (programme) preview; (Film) trailer

Vorschlag ['foːrʃlaːk] m suggestion, proposal; **v~en** (unreg) vt to suggest, to propose

vorschreiben ['foːrʃraɪbən] (unreg) vt to prescribe, to specify

Vorschrift ['foːrʃrɪft] f regulation(s); rule(s); (Anweisungen) instruction(s); **Dienst nach ~** work-to-rule; **v~smäßig** adj as per regulations/instructions

Vorschuss ▲ ['foːrʃʊs] m advance

vorsehen ['foːrzeːən] (unreg) vt to provide for, to plan ♦ vr to take care, to be careful ♦ vi to be visible

Vorsehung f providence

Vorsicht ['foːrzɪçt] f caution, care; **~!** look out!, take care!; (auf Schildern) caution!, danger!; **~, Stufe!** mind the step!; **v~ig** adj cautious, careful; **v~shalber** adv just in case

Vorsilbe ['foːrzɪlbə] f prefix

vorsingen ['foːrzɪŋən] vt (vor Zuhörern) to sing (to); (in Prüfung, für Theater etc) to audition (for) ♦ vi to sing

Vorsitz ['foːrzɪts] m chair(manship); **~ende(r)** f(m) chairman(-woman)

Vorsorge ['foːrzɔrgə] f precaution(s), provision(s); **v~n** vi: **v~n für** to make provision(s) for; **~untersuchung** f check-up

vorsorglich ['foːrzɔrklɪç] adv as a precaution

Vorspeise ['foːrʃpaɪzə] f hors d'oeuvre, appetizer

Vorspiel ['foːrʃpiːl] nt prelude

vorspielen vt: **jdm etw ~** (MUS) to play sth for od to sb ♦ vi (zur Prüfung etc) to play for od to sb

vorsprechen ['foːrʃprɛçən] (unreg) vt to say out loud, to recite ♦ vi: **bei jdm ~** to call on sb

Vorsprung ['foːrʃprʊŋ] m projection, ledge; (fig) advantage, start

Vorstadt ['foːrʃtat] f suburbs pl

Vorstand ['foːrʃtant] m executive committee; (COMM) board (of directors); (Person) director, head

vorstehen ['foːrʃteːən] (unreg) vi to project; **einer Sache** dat **~** (fig) to be the head of sth

vorstell- ['foːrʃtɛl] zW: **~bar** adj

conceivable; **~en** *vt* to put forward; (*bekannt machen*) to introduce; (*darstellen*) to represent; **~en vor** +*akk* to put in front of; **sich** *dat* **etw ~en** to imagine sth; **V~ung** *f* (*Bekanntmachen*) introduction; (*THEAT etc*) performance; (*Gedanke*) idea, thought

vorstoßen ['foːrʃtoːsən] (*unreg*) *vi* (*ins Unbekannte*) to venture (forth)

Vorstrafe ['foːrʃtraːfə] *f* previous conviction

Vortag ['foːrtaːk] *m*: **am ~ einer Sache** *gen* on the day before sth

vortäuschen ['foːrtɔʏʃən] *vt* to feign, to pretend

Vorteil ['foːrtaɪl] (**-s, -e**) *m*: **~ (gegenüber)** advantage (over); **im ~ sein** to have the advantage; **v~haft** *adj* advantageous

Vortrag ['foːrtraːk] (**-(e)s, Vorträge**) *m* talk, lecture; **v~en** [-ɡən] (*unreg*) *vt* to carry forward; (*fig*) to recite; (*Rede*) to deliver; (*Lied*) to perform; (*Meinung etc*) to express

vortreten ['foːrtreːtən] (*unreg*) *vi* to step forward; (*Augen etc*) to protrude

vorüber [fo'ryːbər] *adv* past, over; **~gehen** (*unreg*) *vi* to pass (by); **~gehen an** +*dat* (*fig*) to pass over; **~gehend** *adj* temporary, passing

Vorurteil ['foːrʔʊrtaɪl] *nt* prejudice

Vorverkauf ['foːrfɛrkaʊf] *m* advance booking

Vorwahl ['foːrvaːl] *f* preliminary election; (*TEL*) dialling code

Vorwand ['foːrvant] (**-(e)s, Vorwände**) *m* pretext

vorwärts ['foːrvɛrts] *adv* forward; **~ gehen** to progress; **V~gang** *m* (*AUT etc*) forward gear; **~ kommen** to get on, to make progress

Vorwäsche *f* prewash

vorweg [foːr'vɛk] *adv* in advance; **~nehmen** (*unreg*) *vt* to anticipate

vorweisen ['foːrvaɪzən] (*unreg*) *vt* to show, to produce

vorwerfen ['foːrvɛrfən] (*unreg*) *vt*: **jdm etw ~** to reproach sb for sth, to accuse sb of sth; **sich** *dat* **nichts vorzuwerfen haben** to have nothing to reproach o.s. with

vorwiegend ['foːrviːɡənt] *adj* predominant
♦ *adv* predominantly

vorwitzig ['foːrvɪtsɪç] *adj* (*Mensch, Bemerkung*) cheeky

Vorwort ['foːrvɔrt] (**-(e)s, -e**) *nt* preface

Vorwurf ['foːrvʊrf] *m* reproach; **jdm/sich Vorwürfe machen** to reproach sb/o.s.; **v~svoll** *adj* reproachful

vorzeigen ['foːrtsaɪɡən] *vt* to show, to produce

vorzeitig ['foːrtsaɪtɪç] *adj* premature

vorziehen ['foːrtsiːən] (*unreg*) *vt* to pull forward; (*Gardinen*) to draw; (*lieber haben*) to prefer

Vorzimmer ['foːrtsɪmər] *nt* (*Büro*) outer office

Vorzug ['foːrtsuːk] *m* preference; (*gute Eigenschaft*) merit, good quality; (*Vorteil*) advantage

vorzüglich [foːr'tsyːklɪç] *adj* excellent

Vorzugspreis *m* special discount price

vulgär [vʊl'ɡɛːr] *adj* vulgar

Vulkan [vʊl'kaːn] (**-s, -e**) *m* volcano

W, w

Waage ['vaːɡə] *f* scales *pl*; (*ASTROL*) Libra; **w~recht** *adj* horizontal

Wabe ['vaːbə] *f* honeycomb

wach [vax] *adj* awake; (*fig*) alert; **W~e** *f* guard, watch; **W~e halten** to keep watch; **W~e stehen** to stand guard; **~en** *vi* to be awake; (*Wache halten*) to guard

Wachs [vaks] (**-es, -e**) *nt* wax

wachsam ['vaxzaːm] *adj* watchful, vigilant, alert

wachsen (*unreg*) *vi* to grow

Wachstuch ['vakstuːx] *nt* oilcloth

Wachstum ['vakstuːm] (**-s**) *nt* growth

Wächter ['vɛçtər] (**-s, -**) *m* guard, warden, keeper; (*Parkplatzwächter*) attendant

wackel- ['vakəl] *zW*: **~ig** *adj* shaky, wobbly; **W~kontakt** *m* loose connection; **~n** *vi* to shake; (*fig: Position*) to be shaky

wacker ['vakər] *adj* valiant, stout ♦ *adv* well, bravely

Wade ['vaːdə] f (ANAT) calf

Waffe ['vafə] f weapon

Waffel ['vafəl] (-, -n) f waffle; wafer

Waffen- zW: **~schein** m gun licence; **~stillstand** m armistice, truce

Wagemut ['vaːgəmuːt] m daring

wagen ['vaːgən] vt to venture, to dare

Wagen ['vaːgən] (-s, -) m vehicle; (AUTO) car; (EISENB) carriage; (Pferdewagen) cart; **~heber** (-s, -) m jack

Waggon [va'gõː] (-s, -s) m carriage; (Güterwaggon) goods van, freight truck (US)

Wagnis ['vaːknis] (-ses, -se) nt risk

Wagon ▲ [va'gõː, va'goːn] (-s, -s) m = **Waggon**

Wahl [vaːl] (-, -en) f choice; (POL) election; **zweite** (-) (COMM) seconds pl

wähl- ['veːl] zW: **~bar** adj eligible; **~en** vt, vi to choose; (POL) to elect, to vote (for); (TEL) to dial; **W~er(in)** (-s, -) m(f) voter; **~erisch** adj fastidious, particular

Wahl- zW: **~fach** nt optional subject; **~gang** m ballot; **~kabine** f polling booth; **~kampf** m election campaign; **~kreis** m constituency; **~lokal** nt polling station; **w~los** adv at random; **~recht** nt franchise; **~spruch** m motto; **~urne** f ballot box

Wahn [vaːn] (-(e)s) m delusion; folly; **~sinn** m madness; **w~sinnig** adj insane, mad ♦ adv (umg) incredibly

wahren [vaːr] adj true

wahren ['vaːrən] vt to maintain, to keep

während ['veːrənt] präp +gen during ♦ konj while; **~dessen** adv meanwhile

wahr- zW: **~haben** (unreg) vt: **etw nicht ~haben wollen** to refuse to admit sth; **~haft** adv (tatsächlich) truly; **~haftig** [vaːr'haftɪç] adj true, real ♦ adv really; **W~heit** f truth; **~nehmen** (unreg) vt to perceive, to observe; **W~nehmung** f perception; **~sagen** vi to prophesy, to tell fortunes; **W~sager(in)** (-s, -) m(f) fortune teller; **~scheinlich** [vaːr'ʃaɪnlɪç] adj probable ♦ adv probably; **W~'scheinlichkeit** f probability; **aller W~scheinlichkeit nach** in all probability

Währung ['veːrʊŋ] f currency

Wahrzeichen nt symbol

Waise ['vaɪzə] f orphan; **~nhaus** nt orphanage

Wald [valt] (-(e)s, ⁻er) m wood(s); (groß) forest; **~brand** m forest fire; **~sterben** nt trees dying due to pollution

Wales [weɪlz] (-) nt Wales

Wal(fisch) ['vaːl(fɪʃ)] (-(e)s, -e) m whale

Waliser [va'liːzər] (-s, -) m Welshman; **Waliserin** [va'liːzərɪn] f Welsh woman; **walisisch** [va'liːzɪʃ] adj Welsh

Walkman ['wɔːkmən] (®; -s, **Walkmen**) m Walkman ®, personal stereo

Wall [val] (-(e)s, ⁻e) m embankment; (Bollwerk) rampart

Wallfahr- zW: **~er(in)** m(f) pilgrim; **~t** f pilgrimage

Walnuss ▲ ['valnʊs] f walnut

Walross ▲ ['valrɔs] nt walrus

Walze ['valtsə] f (Gerät) cylinder; (Fahrzeug) roller; **w~n** vt to roll (out)

wälzen ['vɛltsən] vt to roll (over); (Bücher) to hunt through; (Probleme) to deliberate on ♦ vr to wallow; (vor Schmerzen) to roll about; (im Bett) to toss and turn

Walzer ['valtsər] (-s, -) m waltz

Wand [vant] (-, ⁻e) f wall; (Trennwand) partition; (Bergwand) precipice

Wandel ['vandəl] (-s) m change; **w~bar** adj changeable, variable; **w~n** vt, vr to change ♦ vi (gehen) to walk

Wander- ['vandər] zW: **~er** (-s, -) m hiker, rambler; **~karte** f map of country walks; **w~n** vi to hike; (Blick) to wander; (Gedanken) to stray; **~schaft** f travelling; **~ung** f walk, hike; **~weg** m trail, walk

Wandlung f change, transformation

Wange ['vaŋə] f cheek

wanken ['vaŋkən] vi to stagger; (fig) to waver

wann [van] adv when

Wanne ['vanə] f tub

Wanze ['vantsə] f bug

Wappen ['vapən] (-s, -) nt coat of arms, crest; **~kunde** f heraldry

war etc [vaːr] vb siehe **sein**

Ware ['vaːrə] f ware

Waren- *zW:* **~haus** *nt* department store;
~lager *nt* stock, store; **~muster** *nt* trade
sample; **~probe** *f* sample; **~sendung** *f*
trade sample *(sent by post)*; **~zeichen** *nt:*
(eingetragenes) ~zeichen (registered)
trademark

warf *etc* [varf] *vb siehe* **werfen**

warm [varm] *adj* warm; *(Essen)* hot

Wärm- ['vɛrm] *zW:* **~e** *f* warmth; **w~en** *vt,*
vr to warm (up), to heat (up); **~flasche** *f*
hot-water bottle

Warn- ['varn] *zW:* **~blinkanlage** *f (AUT)*
hazard warning lights *pl*; **~dreieck** *nt*
warning triangle; **w~en** *vt* to warn; **~ung** *f*
warning

warten ['vartən] *vi:* **~ (auf** +*akk)* to wait
(for); **auf sich ~ lassen** to take a long time

Wärter(in) ['vɛrtər(ɪn)] **(-s, -)** *m(f)* attendant

Warte- ['vartə] *zW:* **~saal** *m (EISENB)* waiting
room; **~zimmer** *nt* waiting room

Wartung *f* servicing; service; **~ und
Instandhaltung** maintenance

warum [va'rʊm] *adv* why

Warze ['vartsə] *f* wart

was [vas] *pron* what; *(umg: etwas)*
something; **~ für (ein) ...** what sort of ...

waschbar *adj* washable

Waschbecken *nt* washbasin

Wäsche ['vɛʃə] *f* wash(ing); *(Bettwäsche)*
linen; *(Unterwäsche)* underclothing

waschecht *adj* colourfast; *(fig)* genuine

Wäsche- *zW:* **~klammer** *f* clothes peg
(BRIT), clothespin *(US)*; **~leine** *f* washing
line *(BRIT)*

waschen ['vaʃən] *(unreg) vt, vi* to wash ♦ *vr*
to (have a) wash; **sich** *dat* **die Hände ~** to
wash one's hands

Wäsche'rei *f* laundry

Wasch- *zW:* **~gelegenheit** *f* washing
facilities; **~küche** *f* laundry room;
~lappen *m* face flannel, washcloth *(US)*;
(umg) sissy; **~maschine** *f* washing
machine; **~mittel** *nt* detergent, washing
powder; **~pulver** *nt* detergent, washing
powder; **~raum** *m* washroom; **~salon** *m*
Launderette ®

Wasser ['vasər] **(-s, -)** *nt* water; **~ball** *m*

water polo; **w~dicht** *adj* waterproof; **~fall**
m waterfall; **~farbe** *f* watercolour; **~hahn**
m tap, faucet *(US)*; **~kraftwerk** *nt*
hydroelectric power station; **~leitung** *f*
water pipe; **~mann** *n (ASTROL)* Aquarius

wässern ['vɛsərn] *vt, vi* to water

Wasser- *zW:* **w~scheu** *adj* afraid of (the)
water; **~ski** ['vasərʃiː] *nt* water-skiing;
~stoff *m* hydrogen; **~waage** *f* spirit level;
~zeichen *nt* watermark

wässrig ▲ ['vɛsrɪç] *adj* watery

Watt [vat] **(-(e)s, -en)** *nt* mud flats *pl*

Watte *f* cotton wool, absorbent cotton *(US)*

WC ['veː'tseː] **(-s, -s)** *nt abk (= water closet)*
W.C.

Web- ['veːb] *zW:* **w~en** *(unreg) vt* to weave;
~er (-s, -) *m* weaver; **~e'rei** *f (Betrieb)*
weaving mill; **~stuhl** *m* loom

Wechsel ['vɛksəl] **(-s, -)** *m* change; *(COMM)*
bill of exchange; **~geld** *nt* change; **w~haft**
adj (Wetter) variable; **~jahre** *pl* change of
life *sg*; **~kurs** *m* rate of exchange; **w~n** *vt*
to change; *(Blicke)* to exchange ♦ *vi* to
change; to vary; *(Geldwechseln)* to have
change; **~strom** *m* alternating current;
~stube *f* bureau de change; **~wirkung** *f*
interaction

Weck- ['vɛk] *zW:* **~dienst** *m* alarm call
service; **w~en** *vt* to wake (up); to call; **~er**
(-s, -) *m* alarm clock

wedeln ['veːdəln] *vi (mit Schwanz)* to wag;
(mit Fächer etc) to wave

weder ['veːdər] *konj* neither; **~ ... noch ...**
neither ... nor ...

Weg [veːk] **(-(e)s, -e)** *m* way; *(Pfad)* path;
(Route) route; **sich auf den ~ machen** to
be on one's way; **jdm aus dem ~ gehen**
to keep out of sb's way; *siehe* **zuwege**

weg [vɛk] *adv* away, off; **über etw** *akk* **~
sein** to be over sth; **er war schon ~** he
had already left; **Finger ~!** hands off!

wegbleiben *(unreg) vi* to stay away

wegen ['veːgən] *präp* +*gen (umg: +dat)*
because of

weg- ['vɛk] *zW:* **~fallen** *(unreg) vi* to be left
out; *(Ferien, Bezahlung)* to be cancelled;
(aufhören) to cease; **~gehen** *(unreg) vi* to

go away; to leave; ~**lassen** (*unreg*) *vt* to leave out; ~**laufen** (*unreg*) *vi* to run away *od* off; ~**legen** *vt* to put aside; ~**machen** (*umg*) *vt* to get rid of; ~**müssen** (*unreg*; *umg*) *vi* to have to go; ~**nehmen** (*unreg*) *vt* to take away; ~**tun** (*unreg*) *vt* to put away; **W~weiser** (**-s, -**) *m* road sign, signpost; ~**werfen** (*unreg*) *vt* to throw away

weh [ve:] *adj* sore; ~(**e**) *excl*: ~(**e**), **wenn du ...** woe betide you if ...; **o ~!** oh dear!; ~**e!** just you dare!

wehen *vt, vi* to blow; (*Fahnen*) to flutter

weh- *zW*: ~**leidig** *adj* whiny, whining; ~**mütig** *adj* melancholy

Wehr [ve:r] (**-, -en**) *f*: **sich zur ~ setzen** to defend o.s.; ~**dienst** *m* military service; ~**dienstverweigerer** *m* ≈ conscientious objector; **w~en** *vr* to defend o.s.; **w~los** *adj* defenceless; ~**pflicht** *f* compulsory military service; **w~pflichtig** *adj* liable for military service

wehtun ▲ ['ve:tu:n] (*unreg*) *vt* to hurt, to be sore; **jdm/sich ~** to hurt sb/o.s.

Weib [vaɪp] (**-(e)s, -er**) *nt* woman, female; wife; ~**chen** *nt* female; **w~lich** *adj* feminine

weich [vaɪç] *adj* soft; **W~e** *f* (*EISENB*) points *pl*; ~**en** (*unreg*) *vi* to yield, to give way; **W~heit** *f* softness; ~**lich** *adj* soft, namby-pamby

Weide ['vaɪdə] *f* (*Baum*) willow; (*Gras*) pasture; **w~n** *vi* to graze ♦ *vr*: **sich an etw** *dat* **w~n** to delight in sth

weigern ['vaɪgərn] *vr* to refuse

Weigerung ['vaɪgərʊŋ] *f* refusal

Weihe ['vaɪə] *f* consecration; (*Priesterweihe*) ordination; **w~n** *vt* to consecrate; to ordain

Weihnacht- *zW*: ~**en** (**-**) *nt* Christmas; **w~lich** *adj* Christmas *cpd*

Weihnachts- *zW*: ~**abend** *m* Christmas Eve; ~**lied** *nt* Christmas carol; ~**mann** *m* Father Christmas, Santa Claus; ~**markt** *m* Christmas fair; ~**tag** *m* Christmas Day; **zweiter ~tag** Boxing Day

Weihwasser *nt* holy water

weil [vaɪl] *konj* because

Weile ['vaɪlə] (**-**) *f* while, short time

Wein [vaɪn] (**-(e)s, -e**) *m* wine; (*Pflanze*) vine; ~**bau** *m* cultivation of vines; ~**berg** *m* vineyard; ~**bergschnecke** *f* snail; ~**brand** *m* brandy

weinen *vt, vi* to cry; **das ist zum W~** it's enough to make you cry *od* weep

Wein- *zW*: ~**glas** *nt* wine glass; ~**karte** *f* wine list; ~**lese** *f* vintage; ~**probe** *f* wine-tasting; ~**rebe** *f* vine; **w~rot** *adj* burgundy, claret, wine-red; ~**stock** *m* vine; ~**stube** *f* wine bar; ~**traube** *f* grape

weise ['vaɪzə] *adj* wise

Weise *f* manner, way; (*Lied*) tune; **auf diese ~** in this way

weisen (*unreg*) *vt* to show

Weisheit ['vaɪshaɪt] *f* wisdom; ~**szahn** *m* wisdom tooth

weiß [vaɪs] *adj* white ♦ *vb siehe* **wissen**; **W~bier** *nt* weissbier (*light, fizzy beer made using top-fermentation yeast*); **W~brot** *nt* white bread; ~**en** *vt* to whitewash; **W~glut** *f* (*TECH*) incandescence; **jdn bis zur W~glut bringen** (*fig*) to make sb see red; **W~kohl**

m (white) cabbage; **W~wein** *m* white wine; **W~wurst** *f* veal sausage

weit [vaɪt] *adj* wide; (*Begriff*) broad; (*Reise, Wurf*) long ♦ *adv* far; **wie ~ ist es ...?** how far is it ...?; **in ~er Ferne** in the far distance; **~ blickend** far-seeing; **~ reichend** long-range; (*fig*) far-reaching; **~ verbreitet** widespread; **das geht zu ~** that's going too far; **~aus** *adv* by far; **~blickend** *adj* far-seeing; **W~e** *f* width; (*Raum*) space; (*von Entfernung*) distance; **~en** *vt, vr* to widen

weiter ['vaɪtər] *adj* wider; broader; farther (away); (*zusätzlich*) further ♦ *adv* further; **ohne ~es** without further ado; just like that; **~ nichts/niemand** nothing/nobody else; **~arbeiten** *vi* to go on working; **~bilden** *vr* to continue one's education; **~empfehlen** (*unreg*) *vt* to recommend (to others); **W~fahrt** *f* continuation of the journey; **~führen** *vi* (*Straße*) to lead on (to) ♦ *vt* (*fortsetzen*) to continue, carry on; **~gehen** (*unreg*) *vi* to go on; **~hin** *adv*: **etw ~hin tun** to go on doing sth; **~kommen** (*unreg*) *vi* (*fig*: *mit Arbeit*) to make progress; **~leiten** *vt* to pass on; **~machen** *vt, vi* to continue

weit- *zW*: **~gehend** *adj* considerable ♦ *adv* largely; **~läufig** *adj* (*Gebäude*) spacious; (*Erklärung*) lengthy; (*Verwandter*) distant; **~reichend** *adj* long-range; (*fig*) far-reaching; **~schweifig** *adj* long-winded; **~sichtig** *adj* (*MED*) long-sighted; (*fig*) far-sighted; **W~sprung** *m* long jump; **~verbreitet** *adj* widespread

Weizen ['vaɪtsən] (**-s, -**) *m* wheat

welche(r, s) *interrogativ pron* which; **welcher von beiden?** which (one) of the two?; **welchen hast du genommen?** which (one) did you take?; **welche eine ...!** what a ...!; **welche Freude!** what joy! ♦ *indef pron* some; (*in Fragen*) any; **ich habe welche** I have some; **haben Sie welche?** do you have any?
♦ *relativ pron* (*bei Menschen*) who; (*bei Sachen*) which, that; **welche(r, s) auch immer** whoever/whichever/whatever

welk [vɛlk] *adj* withered; **~en** *vi* to wither

Welle ['vɛlə] *f* wave; (*TECH*) shaft

Wellen- *zW*: **~bereich** *m* waveband; **~länge** *f* (*auch fig*) wavelength; **~linie** *f* wavy line; **~sittich** *m* budgerigar

Welt [vɛlt] (**-, -en**) *f* world; **~all** *nt* universe; **~anschauung** *f* philosophy of life; **w~berühmt** *adj* world-famous; **~krieg** *m* world war; **w~lich** *adj* worldly; (*nicht kirchlich*) secular; **~macht** *f* world power; **~meister** *m* world champion; **~raum** *m* space; **~reise** *f* trip round the world; **~stadt** *f* metropolis; **w~weit** *adj* worldwide

wem [veːm] (*dat von* **wer**) *pron* to whom

wen [veːn] (*akk von* **wer**) *pron* whom

Wende ['vɛndə] *f* turn; (*Veränderung*) change; **~kreis** *m* (*GEOG*) tropic; (*AUT*) turning circle; **~ltreppe** *f* spiral staircase; **w~n** (*unreg*) *vt, vi, vr* to turn; **sich an jdn w~n** to go/come to sb

wendig ['vɛndɪç] *adj* (*Auto etc*) manœuvrable; (*fig*) agile

Wendung *f* turn; (*Redewendung*) idiom

wenig ['veːnɪç] *adj, adv* little; **~e** *pron pl* few *pl*; **~er** *adj* less; (*mit pl*) fewer ♦ *adv* less; **~ste(r, s)** *adj* least; **am ~sten** least; **~stens** *adv* at least

wenn [vɛn] *konj* **1** (*falls, bei Wünschen*) if; **wenn auch ..., selbst wenn ...** even if ...; **wenn ich doch ...** if only I ...
2 (*zeitlich*) when; **immer wenn** whenever

wennschon ['vɛnʃoːn] *adv*: **na ~** so what?; **~, dennschon!** in for a penny, in for a pound

wer [veːr] *pron* who

Werbe- ['vɛrbə] *zW*: **~fernsehen** *nt* commercial television; **~geschenk** *nt* gift (*from company*); (*zu Gekauftem*) free gift; **w~n** (*unreg*) *vt* to win; (*Mitglied*) to recruit ♦ *vi* to advertise; **um jdn/etw w~n** to try to win sb/sth; **für jdn/etw w~n** to promote sb/sth

Werbung f advertising; (von Mitgliedern) recruitment; **~ um jdn/etw** promotion of sb/sth

Werdegang ['ve:rdəgaŋ] m (Laufbahn) development; (beruflich) career

---
SCHLÜSSELWORT
---

werden ['ve:rdən] (pt **wurde**, pp **geworden** od (bei Passiv) **worden**) vi to become; **was ist aus ihm/aus der Sache geworden?** what became of him/it?; **es ist nichts/gut geworden** it came to nothing/turned out well; **es wird Nacht/Tag** it's getting dark/light; **mir wird kalt** I'm getting cold; **mir wird schlecht** I feel ill; **Erster werden** to come od be first; **das muss anders werden** that'll have to change; **rot/zu Eis werden** to turn red/to ice; **was willst du (mal) werden?** what do you want to be?; **die Fotos sind gut geworden** the photos have come out nicely

♦ als Hilfsverb **1** (bei Futur): **er wird es tun** he will od he'll do it; **er wird das nicht tun** he will not od he won't do it; **es wird gleich regnen** it's going to rain

2 (bei Konjunktiv): **ich würde ...** I would ...; **er würde gern ...** he would od he'd like to ...; **ich würde lieber ...** I would od I'd rather ...

3 (bei Vermutung): **sie wird in der Küche sein** she will be in the kitchen

4 (bei Passiv): **gebraucht werden** to be used; **er ist erschossen worden** he has od he's been shot; **mir wurde gesagt, dass ...** I was told that ...

---

werfen ['vɛrfən] (unreg) vt to throw

Werft [vɛrft] (-, -en) f shipyard, dockyard

Werk [vɛrk] (-(e)s, -e) nt work; (Tätigkeit) job; (Fabrik, Mechanismus) works pl; **ans ~ gehen** to set to work; **~statt** (-, **-stätten**) f workshop; (AUT) garage; **~tag** m working day; **w~tags** adv on working days; **w~tätig** adj working; **~zeug** nt tool

Wermut ['ve:rmu:t] (-(e)s) m wormwood;

(Wein) vermouth

Wert [ve:rt] (-(e)s, -e) m worth; (FIN) value; **~ legen auf** +akk to attach importance to; **es hat doch keinen ~** it's useless; **w~** adj worth; (geschätzt) dear; worthy; **das ist nichts/viel w~** it's not worth anything/it's worth a lot; **das ist es/er mir w~** it's/he's worth that to me; **~angabe** f declaration of value; **~brief** m registered letter (containing sth of value); **w~en** vt to rate; **~gegenstände** mpl valuables; **w~los** adj worthless; **~papier** nt security; **w~voll** adj valuable

Wesen ['ve:zən] (-s, -) nt (Geschöpf) being; (Natur, Charakter) nature; **w~tlich** adj significant; (beträchtlich) considerable

weshalb [vɛs'halp] adv why

Wespe ['vɛspə] f wasp

wessen ['vɛsən] (gen von **wer**) pron whose

Weste ['vɛstə] f waistcoat, vest (US); (Wollweste) cardigan

West- zW: **~en** (-s) m west; **~europa** nt Western Europe; **w~lich** adj western ♦ adv to the west

weswegen [vɛs've:gən] adv why

wett [vɛt] adj even; **W~bewerb** m competition; **W~e** f bet, wager; **~en** vt, vi to bet

Wetter ['vɛtər] (-s, -) nt weather; **~bericht** m weather report; **~dienst** m meteorological service; **~lage** f (weather) situation; **~vorhersage** f weather forecast; **~warte** f weather station

Wett- zW: **~kampf** m contest; **~lauf** m race; **w~machen** vt to make good

wichtig ['vɪçtɪç] adj important; **W~keit** f importance

wickeln ['vɪkəln] vt to wind; (Haare) to set; (Kind) to change; **jdn/etw in etw** akk **~** to wrap sb/sth in sth

Wickelraum m mothers' (and babies') room

Widder ['vɪdər] (-s, -) m ram; (ASTROL) Aries

wider ['vi:dər] präp +akk against; **~'fahren** (unreg) vi to happen; **~'legen** vt to refute

widerlich ['vi:dərlɪç] adj disgusting, repulsive

Spelling Reform: ▲ new spelling △ old spelling (to be phased out)

wider- ['vi:dər] *zW:* **~rechtlich** *adj* unlawful; **W~rede** *f* contradiction; **~'rufen** (*unreg*) *vt insep* to retract; (*Anordnung*) to revoke; (*Befehl*) to countermand; **~'setzen** *vr insep:* **sich jdm/etw ~setzen** to oppose sb/sth

widerspenstig ['vi:dərʃpɛnstɪç] *adj* wilful

wider- ['vi:dər] *zW:* **~spiegeln** *vt* (*Entwicklung, Erscheinung*) to mirror, reflect ♦ *vr* to be reflected; **~'sprechen** (*unreg*) *vi insep:* **jdm ~sprechen** to contradict sb

Widerspruch ['vi:dərʃprʊx] *m* contradiction; **w~slos** *adv* without arguing

Widerstand ['vi:dərʃtant] *m* resistance

Widerstands- *zW:* **~bewegung** *f* resistance (movement); **w~fähig** *adj* resistant, tough; **w~los** *adj* unresisting

wider'stehen (*unreg*) *vi insep:* **jdm/etw ~** to withstand sb/sth

wider- ['vi:dər] *zW:* **~wärtig** *adj* nasty, horrid; **W~wille** *m:* **W~wille (gegen)** aversion (to); **~willig** *adj* unwilling, reluctant

widmen ['vɪtmən] *vt* to dedicate; to devote ♦ *vr* to devote o.s.

widrig ['vi:drɪç] *adj* (*Umstände*) adverse

SCHLÜSSELWORT

---

wie [vi:] *adv* how; **wie groß/schnell?** how big/fast?; **wie wärs?** how about it?; **wie ist er?** what's he like?; **wie gut du das kannst!** you're very good at it; **wie bitte?** pardon?; (*entrüstet*) I beg your pardon!; **und wie!** and how!; **wie viel** how much; **wie viel Menschen** how many people; **wie weit** to what extent

♦ *konj* 1 (*bei Vergleichen*): **so schön wie ...** as beautiful as ...; **wie ich schon sagte** as I said; **wie du** like you; **singen wie ein ...** to sing like a ...; **wie (zum Beispiel)** such as (for example)

2 (*zeitlich*): **wie er das hörte, ging er** when he heard that he left; **er hörte, wie der Regen fiel** he heard the rain falling

---

wieder ['vi:dər] *adv* again; **~ da sein** to be back (again); **~ aufbereiten** to recycle; **~**

aufnehmen to resume; **~ erkennen** to recognize; **~ gutmachen** to make up for; (*Fehler*) to put right; **~ herstellen** (*Ruhe, Frieden etc*) to restore; **~ vereinigen** to reunite; (*POL*) to reunify; **~ verwerten** to recycle; **gehst du schon ~?** are you off again?; **~ ein(e) ...** another ...; **W~aufbau** *m* rebuilding; **~bekommen** (*unreg*) *vt* to get back; **W~gabe** *f* reproduction; **~geben** (*unreg*) *vt* (*zurückgeben*) to return; (*Erzählung etc*) to repeat; (*Gefühle etc*) to convey; **W~'gutmachung** *f* reparation; **~'herstellen** *vt* (*Gesundheit, Gebäude*) to restore; **~'holen** *vt insep* to repeat; **W~'holung** *f* repetition; **W~hören** *nt:* **auf W~hören** (*TEL*) goodbye; **W~kehr** (-) *f* return; (*von Vorfall*) repetition, recurrence; **~sehen** (*unreg*) *vt* to see again; **auf W~sehen** goodbye; **~um** *adv* again; (*andererseits*) on the other hand; **W~vereinigung** *f* (*POL*) reunification; **W~wahl** *f* re-election

Wiege ['vi:gə] *f* cradle; **w~n**[1] *vt* (*schaukeln*) to rock

wiegen[2] (*unreg*) *vt, vi* (*Gewicht*) to weigh

Wien [vi:n] *nt* Vienna

Wiese ['vi:zə] *f* meadow

Wiesel ['vi:zəl] (**-s, -**) *nt* weasel

wieso [vi:'zo:] *adv* why

wieviel △ [vi:'fi:l] *adj siehe* **wie**

wievielmal [vi:'fi:lma:l] *adv* how often

wievielte(r, s) *adj:* **zum ~n Mal?** how many times?; **den W~n haben wir?** what's the date?; **an ~r Stelle?** in what place?; **der ~ Besucher war er?** how many visitors were there before him?

wild [vɪlt] *adj* wild; **W~ (-(e)s)** *nt* game; **W~e(r)** ['vɪldə(r)] *f(m)* savage; **~ern** *vi* to poach; **~'fremd** (*umg*) *adj* quite strange *od* unknown; **W~heit** *f* wildness; **W~leder** *nt* suede; **W~nis (-, -se)** *f* wilderness; **W~schwein** *nt* (wild) boar

will *etc* [vɪl] *vb siehe* **wollen**

Wille ['vɪlə] (**-ns, -n**) *m* will; **w~n** *präp +gen:* **um ... w~n** for the sake of ...; **w~nsstark** *adj* strong-willed

will- *zW:* **~ig** *adj* willing; **W~kommen**

[vɪl'kɔmən] (-s, -) nt welcome; ~kommen adj welcome; **jdn ~kommen heißen** to welcome sb; ~kürlich adj arbitrary; (Bewegung) voluntary

wimmeln ['vɪməln] vi: ~ **(von)** to swarm (with)

wimmern ['vɪmərn] vi to whimper

Wimper ['vɪmpər] (-, -n) f eyelash

Wimperntusche f mascara

Wind [vɪnt] (-(e)s, -e) m wind; ~beutel m cream puff; (fig) rake; ~e f (TECH) winch, windlass; (BOT) bindweed; ~el ['vɪndəl] (-, -n) f nappy, diaper (US); w~en vi unpers to be windy ♦ vt (unreg) to wind; (Kranz) to weave; (entwinden) to twist ♦ vr (unreg) to wind; (Person) to writhe; ~energie f wind energy; w~ig ['vɪndɪç] adj windy; (fig) dubious; ~jacke f windcheater; ~mühle f windmill; ~pocken pl chickenpox sg; ~schutzscheibe f (AUT) windscreen (BRIT), windshield (US); ~stärke f wind force; w~still adj (Tag) still, windless; (Platz) sheltered; ~stille f calm; ~stoß m gust of wind

Wink [vɪŋk] (-(e)s, -e) m (mit Hand) wave; (mit Kopf) nod; (Hinweis) hint

Winkel ['vɪŋkəl] (-s, -) m (MATH) angle; (Gerät) set square; (in Raum) corner

winken ['vɪŋkən] vt, vi to wave

winseln ['vɪnzəln] vi to whine

Winter ['vɪntər] (-s, -) m winter; w~fest adj (Pflanze) hardy; ~garten m conservatory; w~lich adj wintry; ~reifen m winter tyre; ~sport m winter sports pl

Winzer ['vɪntsər] (-s, -) m vine grower

winzig ['vɪntsɪç] adj tiny

Wipfel ['vɪpfəl] (-s, -) m treetop

wir [viːr] pron we; ~ **alle** all of us, we all

Wirbel ['vɪrbəl] (-s, -) m whirl, swirl; (Trubel) hurly-burly; (Aufsehen) fuss; (ANAT) vertebra; w~n vi to whirl, to swirl; ~säule f spine

wird [vɪrt] vb siehe **werden**

wirfst etc [vɪrfst] vb siehe **werfen**

wirken ['vɪrkən] vi to have an effect; (erfolgreich sein) to work; (scheinen) to seem ♦ vt (Wunder) to work

wirklich ['vɪrklɪç] adj real ♦ adv really;

W~keit f reality

wirksam ['vɪrkzaːm] adj effective

Wirkstoff m (biologisch, chemisch, pflanzlich) active substance

Wirkung ['vɪrkʊŋ] f effect; w~slos adj ineffective; **w~slos bleiben** to have no effect; w~svoll adj effective

wirr [vɪr] adj confused, wild; W~warr (-s) m disorder, chaos

wirst [vɪrst] vb siehe **werden**

Wirt(in) [vɪrt(ɪn)] (-(e)s, -e) m(f) landlord(lady); ~schaft f (Gaststätte) pub; (Haushalt) housekeeping; (eines Landes) economy; (umg: Durcheinander) mess; w~schaftlich adj economical; (POL) economic

Wirtschafts- zW: ~krise f economic crisis; ~politik f economic policy; ~prüfer m chartered accountant; ~wunder nt economic miracle

Wirtshaus nt inn

wischen ['vɪʃən] vt to wipe

Wischer (-s, -) m (AUT) wiper

Wissbegier(de) ▲ ['vɪsbəgiːr(də)] f thirst for knowledge; **wissbegierig** ▲ adj inquisitive, eager for knowledge

wissen ['vɪsən] (unreg) vt to know; **was weiß ich!** I don't know!; W~ (-s) nt knowledge; W~schaft f science; W~schaftler(in) (-s, -) m(f) scientist; ~schaftlich adj scientific; ~swert adj worth knowing

wittern ['vɪtərn] vt to scent; (fig) to suspect

Witterung f weather; (Geruch) scent

Witwe ['vɪtvə] f widow; ~r (-s, -) m widower

Witz [vɪts] (-(e)s, -e) m joke; ~bold (-(e)s, -e) m joker, wit; w~ig adj funny

wo [voː] adv where; (umg: irgendwo) somewhere; **im Augenblick, ~ ...** the moment (that) ...; **die Zeit, ~ ...** the time when ...; ~anders [voːʔandərs] adv elsewhere; ~bei [-'baɪ] adv (relativ) by/with which; (interrogativ) what ... in/by/with

Woche ['vɔxə] f week

Wochen- zW: ~ende nt weekend; w~lang adj, adv for weeks; ~markt m weekly market; ~schau f newsreel

wöchentlich ['vœçəntlɪç] *adj, adv* weekly
wodurch [vo'dʊrç] *adv (relativ)* through
which; *(interrogativ)* what ... through
wofür [vo'fy:r] *adv (relativ)* for which;
(interrogativ) what ... for
wog *etc* [vo:k] *vb siehe* **wiegen**
wo- [vo:] *zW:* **~'gegen** *adv (relativ)* against
which; *(interrogativ)* what ... against; **~her**
[-'he:r] *adv* where ... from; **~hin** [-'hɪn] *adv*
where ... to

SCHLÜSSELWORT
---

wohl [vo:l] *adv* **1**: **sich wohl fühlen**
(zufrieden) to feel happy; *(gesundheitlich)* to
feel well; **jdm wohl tun** to do sb good;
wohl oder übel whether one likes it or not
2 *(wahrscheinlich)* probably; *(gewiss)*
certainly; *(vielleicht)* perhaps; **sie ist wohl
zu Hause** she's probably at home; **das ist
doch wohl nicht dein Ernst!** surely you're
not serious!; **das mag wohl sein** that may
well be; **ob das wohl stimmt?** I wonder if
that's true; **er weiß das sehr wohl** he
knows that perfectly well

Wohl [vo:l] **(-(e)s)** *nt* welfare; **zum ~!**
cheers!; **w~auf** *adv* well; **~behagen** *nt*
comfort; **~fahrt** *f* welfare; **~fahrtsstaat** *m*
welfare state; **w~habend** *adj* wealthy;
w~ig *adj* contented, comfortable;
w~schmeckend *adj* delicious; **~stand** *m*
prosperity; **~standsgesellschaft** *f*
affluent society; **~tat** *f* relief; act of charity;
~täter(in) *m(f)* benefactor; **w~tätig** *adj*
charitable; **~tätigkeits-** *zW* charity,
charitable; **w~tun** *(unreg) vi* △ *siehe* **wohl**;
w~verdient *adj* well-earned, well-
deserved; **w~weislich** *adv* prudently;
~wollen (-s) *nt* good will; **w~wollend** *adj*
benevolent
wohn- ['vo:n] *zW:* **~en** *vi* to live;
W~gemeinschaft *f (Menschen)* people
sharing a flat; **~haft** *adj* resident; **W~heim**
nt (für Studenten) hall of residence; *(für
Senioren)* home; *(bes für Arbeiter)* hostel;
~lich *adj* comfortable; **W~mobil (-s, -e)**
nt camper; **W~ort** *m* domicile; **W~sitz** *m*

place of residence; **W~ung** *f* house;
(Etagenwohnung) flat, apartment *(US)*;
W~wagen *m* caravan; **W~zimmer** *nt*
living room
wölben ['vœlbən] *vt, vr* to curve
Wolf [vɔlf] **(-(e)s, -e)** *m* wolf
Wolke ['vɔlkə] *f* cloud; **~nkratzer** *m*
skyscraper; **wolkig** ['vɔlkɪç] *adj* cloudy
Wolle ['vɔlə] *f* wool; **w~n¹** *adj* woollen

SCHLÜSSELWORT
---

wollen² ['vɔlən] *(pt* **wollte**, *pp* **gewollt** *od
(als Hilfsverb)* **wollen)** *vt, vi* to want; **ich
will nach Hause** I want to go home; **er
will nicht** he doesn't want to; **er wollte
das nicht** he didn't want it; **wenn du
willst** if you like; **ich will, dass du mir
zuhörst** I want you to listen to me
♦ *Hilfsverb*: **er will ein Haus kaufen** he
wants to buy a house; **ich wollte, ich wäre
...** I wish I were ...; **etw gerade tun wollen**
to be going to do sth

---

wollüstig ['vɔlʏstɪç] *adj* lusty, sensual
wo- *zW:* **~mit** *adv (relativ)* with which;
(interrogativ) what ... with; **~möglich** *adv*
probably, I suppose; **~nach** *adv (relativ)*
after/for which; *(interrogativ)* what ... for/
after; **~ran** *adv (relativ)* on/at which;
(interrogativ) what ... on/at; **~rauf** *adv
(relativ)* on which; *(interrogativ)* what ... on;
~raus *adv (relativ)* from/out of which;
(interrogativ) what ... from/out of; **~rin** *adv
(relativ)* in which; *(interrogativ)* what ... in
Wort [vɔrt] **(-(e)s, ⁺er** *od* **-e)** *nt* word; **jdn
beim ~ nehmen** to take sb at his word;
mit anderen ~en in other words;
w~brüchig *adj* not true to one's word
Wörterbuch ['vœrtərbu:x] *nt* dictionary
Wort- *zW:* **~führer** *m* spokesman; **w~karg**
adj taciturn; **~laut** *m* wording
wörtlich ['vœrtlɪç] *adj* literal
Wort- *zW:* **~los** *adj* mute; **w~reich** *adj*
wordy, verbose; **~schatz** *m* vocabulary;
~spiel *nt* play on words, pun
wo- *zW:* **~rüber** *adv (relativ)* over/about
which; *(interrogativ)* what ... over/about;

Rechtschreibreform: ▲ *neue Schreibung* △ *alte Schreibung (auslaufend)*

~rum adv (relativ) about/round which; (interrogativ) what ... about/round; ~runter adv (relativ) under which; (interrogativ) what ... under; ~von adv (relativ) from which; (interrogativ) what ... from; ~vor adv (relativ) in front of/before which; (interrogativ) in front of/before what; of what; ~zu adv (relativ) to/for which; (interrogativ) what ... for/to; (warum) why

Wrack [vrak] **(-(e)s, -s)** nt wreck

Wucher ['vu:xər] **(-s)** m profiteering; ~er **(-s, -)** m profiteer; w~isch adj profiteering; w~n vi (Pflanzen) to grow wild; ~ung f (MED) growth, tumour

Wuchs [vu:ks] **(-es)** m (Wachstum) growth; (Statur) build

Wucht [vuxt] **(-)** f force

wühlen ['vy:lən] vi to scrabble; (Tier) to root; (Maulwurf) to burrow; (umg: arbeiten) to slave away ♦ vt to dig

Wulst [vulst] **(-es, ̈e)** m bulge; (an Wunde) swelling

wund [vunt] adj sore, raw; W~e f wound

Wunder ['vundər] **(-s, -)** nt miracle; es ist kein ~ it's no wonder; w~bar adj wonderful, marvellous; ~kerze f sparkler; ~kind nt infant prodigy; w~lich adj odd, peculiar; w~n vr to be surprised ♦ vt to surprise; sich w~n über +akk to be surprised at; w~schön adj beautiful; w~voll adj wonderful

Wundstarrkrampf ['vuntʃtarkrampf] m tetanus, lockjaw

Wunsch [vunʃ] **(-(e)s, ̈e)** m wish

wünschen ['vynʃən] vt to wish; sich dat etw ~ to want sth, to wish for sth; ~swert adj desirable

wurde etc ['vurdə] vb siehe **werden**

Würde ['vyrdə] f dignity; (Stellung) honour; w~voll adj dignified

würdig ['vyrdɪç] adj worthy; (würdevoll) dignified; ~en vt to appreciate

Wurf [vurf] **(-s, ̈e)** m throw; (Junge) litter

Würfel ['vyrfəl] **(-s, -)** m dice; (MATH) cube; ~becher m (dice) cup; w~n vi to play dice ♦ vt to dice; ~zucker m lump sugar

würgen ['vyrgən] vt, vi to choke

Wurm [vurm] **(-(e)s, ̈er)** m worm; w~stichig adj worm-ridden

Wurst [vurst] **(-, ̈e)** f sausage; das ist mir ~ (umg) I don't care, I don't give a damn

Würstchen ['vyrstçən] nt sausage

Würze ['vyrtsə] f seasoning, spice

Wurzel ['vurtsəl] **(-, -n)** f root

würzen ['vyrtsən] vt to season, to spice

würzig adj spicy

wusch etc [vuʃ] vb siehe **waschen**

wusste ▲ etc ['vustə] vb siehe **wissen**

wüst [vy:st] adj untidy, messy; (ausschweifend) wild; (öde) waste; (umg: heftig) terrible; W~e f desert

Wut [vu:t] **(-)** f rage, fury; ~anfall m fit of rage

wüten ['vy:tən] vi to rage; ~d adj furious, mad

X, x

X-Beine ['ɪksbaɪnə] pl knock-knees

x-beliebig [ɪksbə'li:bɪç] adj any (whatever)

xerokopieren [kseroko'pi:rən] vt to xerox, to photocopy

x-mal ['ɪksma:l] adv any number of times, n times

Xylofon ▲, **Xylophon** [ksylo'fo:n] **(-s, -e)** nt xylophone

---

Y, y

Yacht **(-, -en)** f siehe **Jacht**

Ypsilon ['ypsilɔn] **(-(s), -s)** nt the letter Y

Z, z

Zacke ['tsakə] f point; (Bergzacke) jagged peak; (Gabelzacke) prong; (Kammzacke) tooth

zackig ['tsakɪç] adj jagged; (umg) smart; (Tempo) brisk

zaghaft ['tsa:khaft] adj timid

zäh [tsɛ:] adj tough; (Mensch) tenacious;

Spelling Reform: ▲ new spelling △ old spelling (to be phased out)

(*Flüssigkeit*) thick; (*schleppend*) sluggish; **Z~igkeit** *f* toughness; tenacity

Zahl [tsaːl] (**-, -en**) *f* number; **z~bar** *adj* payable; **z~en** *vt, vi* to pay; **z~en bitte!** the bill please!

zählen ['tsɛːlən] *vt, vi* to count; **~ auf** +*akk* to count on; **~ zu** to be numbered among

Zahlenschloss ▲ *nt* combination lock

Zähler ['tsɛːlər] (**-s, -**) *m* (*TECH*) meter; (*MATH*) numerator

Zahl- *zW*: **z~los** *adj* countless; **z~reich** *adj* numerous; **~tag** *m* payday; **~ung** *f* payment; **~ungsanweisung** *f* giro transfer order; **z~ungsfähig** *adj* solvent; **~wort** *nt* numeral

zahm [tsaːm] *adj* tame

zähmen ['tsɛːmən] *vt* to tame; (*fig*) to curb

Zahn [tsaːn] (**-(e)s, ⁻e**) *m* tooth; **~arzt** *m* dentist; **~ärztin** *f* (female) dentist; **~bürste** *f* toothbrush; **~fleisch** *nt* gums *pl*; **~pasta** *f* toothpaste; **~rad** *nt* cog(wheel); **~schmerzen** *pl* toothache *sg*; **~stein** *m* tartar; **~stocher** (**-s, -**) *m* toothpick

Zange ['tsaŋə] *f* pliers *pl*; (*Zuckerzange etc*) tongs *pl*; (*Beißzange, ZOOL*) pincers *pl*; (*MED*) forceps *pl*

zanken ['tsaŋkən] *vi, vr* to quarrel

zänkisch ['tsɛŋkɪʃ] *adj* quarrelsome

Zäpfchen ['tsɛpfçən] *nt* (*ANAT*) uvula; (*MED*) suppository

Zapfen ['tsapfən] (**-s, -**) *m* plug; (*BOT*) cone; (*Eiszapfen*) icicle

zappeln ['tsapəln] *vi* to wriggle; to fidget

zart [tsart] *adj* (*weich, leise*) soft; (*Fleisch*) tender; (*fein, schwächlich*) delicate; **Z~heit** *f* softness; tenderness; delicacy

zärtlich ['tsɛːrtlɪç] *adj* tender, affectionate

Zauber ['tsaubər] (**-s, -**) *m* magic; (*~bann*) spell; **~ei** [-'raɪ] *f* magic; **~er** (**-s, -**) *m* magician; conjuror; **z~haft** *adj* magical, enchanting; **~künstler** *m* conjuror; **~kunststück** *nt* conjuring trick; **z~n** *vi* to conjure, to practise magic

zaudern ['tsaudərn] *vi* to hesitate

Zaum [tsaum] (**-(e)s, Zäume**) *m* bridle; **etw im ~ halten** to keep sth in check

Zaun [tsaun] (**-(e)s, Zäune**) *m* fence

z. B. *abk* (= *zum Beispiel*) e.g.

Zebra ['tseːbra] *nt* zebra; **~streifen** *m* zebra crossing

Zeche ['tsɛçə] *f* (*Rechnung*) bill; (*Bergbau*) mine

Zeh [tseː] (**-s, -en**) *m* toe

Zehe [tseːə] *f* toe; (*Knoblauchzehe*) clove

zehn [tseːn] *num* ten; **~te(r, s)** *adj* tenth; **Z~tel** (**-s, -**) *nt* tenth (part)

Zeich- ['tsaɪç] *zW*: **~en** (**-s, -**) *nt* sign; **z~nen** *vt* to draw; (*kennzeichnen*) to mark; (*unterzeichnen*) to sign ♦ *vi* to draw; to sign; **~ner** (**-s, -**) *m* artist; **technischer ~ner** draughtsman; **~nung** *f* drawing; (*Markierung*) markings *pl*

Zeige- ['tsaɪgə] *zW*: **~finger** *m* index finger; **z~n** *vt* to show ♦ *vi* to point ♦ *vr* to show o.s.; **z~n auf** +*akk* to point to; to point at; **es wird sich z~n** time will tell; **es zeigte sich, dass ...** it turned out that ...; **~r** (**-s, -**) *m* pointer; (*Uhrzeiger*) hand

Zeile ['tsaɪlə] *f* line; (*Häuserzeile*) row

Zeit [tsaɪt] (**-, -en**) *f* time; (*GRAM*) tense; **sich** *dat* **~ lassen** to take one's time; **von ~ zu ~** from time to time; **siehe zurzeit**; **~alter** *nt* age; **~ansage** *f* (*TEL*) speaking clock; **~arbeit** *f* (*COMM*) temporary job; **z~gemäß** *adj* in keeping with the times; **~genosse** *m* contemporary; **z~ig** *adj* early; **z~lich** *adj* temporal; **~lupe** *f* slow motion; **z~raubend** *adj* time-consuming; **~raum** *m* period; **~rechnung** *f* time, era; **nach/vor unserer ~rechnung** A.D./B.C.; **~schrift** *f* periodical; **~ung** *f* newspaper; **~vertreib** *m* pastime, diversion; **z~weilig** *adj* temporary; **z~weise** *adv* for a time; **~wort** *nt* verb

Zelle ['tsɛlə] *f* cell; (*Telefonzelle*) callbox

Zellstoff *m* cellulose

Zelt [tsɛlt] (**-(e)s, -e**) *nt* tent; **z~en** *vi* to camp; **~platz** *m* camp site

Zement [tse'mɛnt] (**-(e)s, -e**) *m* cement; **z~ieren** *vt* to cement

zensieren [tsɛn'ziːrən] *vt* to censor; (*SCH*) to mark

Zensur [tsɛn'zuːr] *f* censorship; (*SCH*) mark

entimeter [tsɛnti'meːtər] *m od nt* centimetre

entner ['tsɛntnər] **(-s, -)** *m* hundredweight

entral [tsɛn'traːl] *adj* central; **Z~e** *f* central office; (*TEL*) exchange; **Z~heizung** *f* central heating

entrum ['tsɛntrʊm] **(-s, Zentren)** *nt* centre

erbrechen [tsɛr'brɛçən] (*unreg*) *vt, vi* to break

erbrechlich *adj* fragile

er'drücken *vt* to squash, to crush; (*Kartoffeln*) to mash

eremonie [tseremo'niː] *f* ceremony

erfall [tsɛr'fal] *m* decay; **z~en** (*unreg*) *vi* to disintegrate, to decay; (*sich gliedern*): **z~en (in** +*akk*) to fall (into)

er'gehen (*unreg*) *vi* to melt, to dissolve

erkleinern [tsɛr'klainərn] *vt* to reduce to small pieces

erlegbar [tsɛr'leːkbaːr] *adj* able to be dismantled

erlegen [tsɛr'leːgən] *vt* to take to pieces; (*Fleisch*) to carve; (*Satz*) to analyse

ermürben [tsɛr'myrbən] *vt* to wear down

erquetschen [tsɛr'kvɛtʃən] *vt* to squash

er'reißen (*unreg*) *vt* to tear to pieces ♦ *vi* to tear, to rip

erren ['tsɛran] *vt* to drag ♦ *vi*: **~ (an** +*dat*) to tug (at)

er'rinnen (*unreg*) *vi* to melt away

errissen [tsɛr'rɪsən] *adj* torn, tattered; **Z~heit** *f* tattered state; (*POL*) disunion, discord; (*innere Z~heit*) disintegration

errung *f* (*MED*): **eine ~** pulled muscle

errütten [tsɛr'rytən] *vt* to wreck, to destroy

er'schlagen (*unreg*) *vt* to shatter, to smash ♦ *vr* to fall through

er'schneiden (*unreg*) *vt* to cut up

er'setzen *vt, vr* to decompose, to dissolve

er'springen (*unreg*) *vt* to shatter, to burst

erstäuber [tsɛr'ʃtɔybər] **(-s, -)** *m* atomizer

erstören [tsɛr'ʃtøːrən] *vt* to destroy

erstörung *f* destruction

erstreu- [tsɛr'ʃtrɔy] *zW:* **~en** *vt* to disperse, to scatter; (*unterhalten*) to divert; (*Zweifel etc*) to dispel ♦ *vr* to disperse, to scatter; to be dispelled; **~t** *adj* scattered; (*Mensch*)

absent-minded; **Z~theit** *f* absent-mindedness; **Z~ung** *f* dispersion; (*Ablenkung*) diversion

zerstückeln [tsɛr'ʃtykəln] *vt* to cut into pieces

zer'teilen *vt* to divide into parts

Zertifikat [tsɛrtifi'kaːt] **(-(e)s, -e)** *nt* certificate

zer'treten (*unreg*) *vt* to crush underfoot

zertrümmern [tsɛr'trymərn] *vt* to shatter; (*Gebäude etc*) to demolish

Zettel ['tsɛtəl] **(-s, -)** *m* piece of paper, slip; (*Notizzettel*) note; (*Formular*) form

Zeug [tsɔyk] **(-(e)s, -e)** (*umg*) *nt* stuff; (*Ausrüstung*) gear; **dummes ~** (stupid) nonsense; **das ~ haben zu** to have the makings of; **sich ins ~ legen** to put one's shoulder to the wheel

Zeuge ['tsɔygə] **(-n, -n)** *m* witness; **z~n** *vi* to bear witness, to testify ♦ *vt* (*Kind*) to father; **es zeugt von ...** it testifies to ...; **~naussage** *f* evidence; **Zeugin** ['tsɔygin] *f* witness

Zeugnis ['tsɔyknis] **(-ses, -se)** *nt* certificate; (*SCH*) report; (*Referenz*) reference; (*Aussage*) evidence, testimony; **~ geben von** to be evidence of, to testify to

z. H(d). *abk* (= *zu Händen*) attn.

Zickzack ['tsiktsak] **(-(e)s, -e)** *m* zigzag

Ziege ['tsiːgə] *f* goat

Ziegel ['tsiːgəl] **(-s, -)** *m* brick; (*Dachziegel*) tile

ziehen ['tsiːən] (*unreg*) *vt* to draw; (*zerren*) to pull; (*SCHACH etc*) to move; (*züchten*) to rear ♦ *vi* to draw; (*umziehen, wandern*) to move; (*Rauch, Wolke etc*) to drift; (*reißen*) to pull ♦ *vb unpers*: **es zieht** there is a draught, it's draughty ♦ *vr* (*Gummi*) to stretch; (*Grenze etc*) to run; (*Gespräche*) to be drawn out; **etw nach sich ~** to lead to sth, to entail sth

Ziehung ['tsiːʊŋ] *f* (*Losziehung*) drawing

Ziel [tsiːl] **(-(e)s, -e)** *nt* (*einer Reise*) destination; (*SPORT*) finish; (*MIL*) target; (*Absicht*) goal; **z~bewusst** ▲ *adj* decisive; **z~en** *vi*: **z~en (auf** +*akk*) to aim (at); **z~los** *adj* aimless; **~scheibe** *f* target; **z~strebig**

adj purposeful

ziemlich ['tsiːmlɪç] *adj* quite a; fair ♦ *adv* rather; quite a bit

zieren ['tsiːrən] *vr* to act coy

zierlich ['tsiːrlɪç] *adj* dainty

Ziffer ['tsɪfər] (-, -n) *f* figure, digit; ~**blatt** *nt* dial, clock-face

zig [tsɪk] (*umg*) *adj* umpteen

Zigarette [tsiga'rɛtə] *f* cigarette

Zigaretten- *zW:* ~**automat** *m* cigarette machine; ~**schachtel** *f* cigarette packet; ~**spitze** *f* cigarette holder

Zigarre [tsi'garə] *f* cigar

Zigeuner(in) [tsi'gɔʏnər(ɪn)] (-s, -) *m(f)* gipsy

Zimmer ['tsɪmər] (-s, -) *nt* room; ~**lautstärke** *f* reasonable volume; ~**mädchen** *nt* chambermaid; ~**mann** *m* carpenter; **z~n** *vt* to make (from wood); ~**nachweis** *m* accommodation office; ~**pflanze** *f* indoor plant; ~**service** *m* room service

zimperlich ['tsɪmpərlɪç] *adj* squeamish; (*pingelig*) fussy, finicky

Zimt [tsɪmt] (-(e)s, -e) *m* cinnamon

Zink [tsɪŋk] (-(e)s) *nt* zinc

Zinn [tsɪn] (-(e)s) *nt* (*Element*) tin; (*in ~waren*) pewter; ~**soldat** *m* tin soldier

Zins [tsɪns] (-es, -en) *m* interest; ~**eszins** *m* compound interest; ~**fuß** *m* rate of interest; **z~los** *adj* interest-free; ~**satz** *m* rate of interest

Zipfel ['tsɪpfəl] (-s, -) *m* corner; (*spitz*) tip; (*Hemdzipfel*) tail; (*Wurstzipfel*) end

zirka ['tsɪrka] *adv* (round) about

Zirkel ['tsɪrkəl] (-s, -) *m* circle; (*MATH*) pair of compasses

Zirkus ['tsɪrkʊs] (-, -se) *m* circus

zischen ['tsɪʃən] *vi* to hiss

Zitat [tsi'taːt] (-(e)s, -e) *nt* quotation, quote

zitieren [tsi'tiːrən] *vt* to quote

Zitrone [tsi'troːnə] *f* lemon; ~**nlimonade** *f* lemonade; ~**nsaft** *m* lemon juice

zittern ['tsɪtərn] *vi* to tremble

zivil [tsi'viːl] *adj* civil; (*Preis*) moderate; **Z~** (-s) *nt* plain clothes *pl*; (*MIL*) civilian clothing; **Z~courage** *f* courage of one's convictions;

Z~dienst *m* community service;

Z~isation [tsivilizatsi'oːn] *f* civilization;

Z~isationskrankheit *f* disease peculiar to civilization; ~**i'sieren** *vt* to civilize

---

Zivildienst

i A young German has to complete his 13 months' **Zivildienst** or service to the community if he has opted out of military service as a conscientious objector. This is usually done in a hospital or old people's home. About 18% of young Germans choose to do this as an alternative to the **Wehrdienst**.

Zivilist [tsivi'lɪst] *m* civilian

zögern ['tsøːgərn] *vi* to hesitate

Zoll [tsɔl] (-(e)s, ⁺e) *m* customs *pl*; (*Abgabe*) duty; ~**abfertigung** *f* customs clearance; ~**amt** *nt* customs office; ~**beamte(r)** *m* customs official; ~**erklärung** *f* customs declaration; **z~frei** *adj* duty-free; ~**kontrolle** *f* customs check; **z~pflichtig** *adj* liable to duty, dutiable

Zone ['tsoːnə] *f* zone

Zoo [tsoː] (-s, -s) *m* zoo; ~**loge** [tsoo'loːgə] (-n, -n) *m* zoologist; ~**lo'gie** *f* zoology; **z~'logisch** *adj* zoological

Zopf [tsɔpf] (-(e)s, ⁺e) *m* plait; pigtail; **alter** ~ antiquated custom

Zorn [tsɔrn] (-(e)s) *m* anger; **z~ig** *adj* angry

zottig ['tsɔtɪç] *adj* shaggy

z. T. *abk* = **zum Teil**

SCHLÜSSELWORT

zu [tsuː] *präp +dat* **1** (*örtlich*) to; **zum Bahnhof/Arzt gehen** to go to the station/doctor; **zur Schule/Kirche gehen** to go to school/church; **sollen wir zu euch gehen?** shall we go to your place?; **sie sah zu ihm hin** she looked towards him; **zum Fenster herein** through the window; **zu meiner Linken** to *od* on my left

2 (*zeitlich*) at; **zu Ostern** at Easter; **bis zum 1. Mai** until May 1st; (*nicht später als*) by May 1st; **zu meiner Zeit** in my time

3 (*Zusatz*) with; **Wein zum Essen trinken**

Rechtschreibreform: ▲ *neue Schreibung* △ *alte Schreibung (auslaufend)*

to drink wine with one's meal; **sich zu jdm setzen** to sit down beside sb; **setz dich doch zu uns** (come and) sit with us; **Anmerkungen zu etw** notes on sth
4 (Zweck) for; **Wasser zum Waschen** water for washing; **Papier zum Schreiben** paper to write on; **etw zum Geburtstag bekommen** to get sth for one's birthday
5 (Veränderung) into; **zu etw werden** to turn into sth; **jdn zu etw machen** to make sb (into) sth; **zu Asche verbrennen** to burn to ashes
6 (mit Zahlen): **3 zu 2** (SPORT) 3-2; **das Stück zu 2 Mark** at 2 marks each; **zum ersten Mal** for the first time
7: **zu meiner Freude** etc to my joy etc; **zum Glück** luckily; **zu Fuß** on foot; **es ist zum Weinen** it's enough to make you cry
♦ konj to; **etw zu essen** sth to eat; **um besser sehen zu können** in order to see better; **ohne es zu wissen** without knowing it; **noch zu bezahlende Rechnungen** bills that are still to be paid
♦ adv 1 (allzu) too; **zu sehr** too much; **zu viel** too much; **zu wenig** too little
2 (örtlich) toward(s); **er kam auf mich zu** he came up to me
3 (geschlossen) shut, closed; **die Geschäfte haben zu** the shops are closed; **„auf/zu"** (Wasserhahn etc) "on/off"
4 (umg: los): **nur zu!** just keep on!; **mach zu!** hurry up!

zualler- [tsu'ʔalər] zW: **~erst** [-'ʔe:rst] adv first of all; **~letzt** [-'lɛtst] adv last of all
Zubehör ['tsu:bəhø:r] (-(e)s, -e) nt accessories pl
zubereiten ['tsu:bərartən] vt to prepare
zubilligen ['tsu:bɪlɪɡən] vt to grant
zubinden ['tsu:bɪndən] (unreg) vt to tie up
zubringen ['tsu:brɪŋən] (unreg) vt (Zeit) to spend
Zubringer (-s, -) m (Straße) approach od slip road
Zucchini [tsu'ki:ni:] pl (BOT, KOCH) courgette (BRIT), zucchini (US)
Zucht [tsʊxt] (-, -en) f (von Tieren) breeding;

(von Pflanzen) cultivation; (Rasse) breed; (Erziehung) raising; (Disziplin) discipline
züchten ['tsʏçtən] vt (Tiere) to breed; (Pflanzen) to cultivate, to grow; **Züchter** (-s, -) m breeder; grower
Zuchthaus nt prison, penitentiary (US)
züchtigen ['tsʏçtɪɡən] vt to chastise
Züchtung f (Zuchtart, Sorte: von Tier) breed; (: von Pflanze) variety
zucken ['tsʊkən] vi to jerk, to twitch; (Strahl etc) to flicker ♦ vt (Schultern) to shrug
Zucker ['tsʊkər] (-s, -) m sugar; (MED) diabetes; **~guss** ▲ m icing; **z~krank** adj diabetic; **~krankheit** f (MED) diabetes; **z~n** vt to sugar; **~rohr** nt sugar cane; **~rübe** f sugar beet
Zuckung ['tsʊkʊŋ] f convulsion, spasm; (leicht) twitch
zudecken ['tsu:dɛkən] vt to cover (up)
zudem [tsu'de:m] adv in addition (to this)
zudringlich ['tsu:drɪŋlɪç] adj forward, pushing, obtrusive
zudrücken ['tsu:drʏkən] vt to close; **ein Auge ~** to turn a blind eye
zueinander [tsuʔar'nandər] adv to one other; (in Verbindung) together
zuerkennen ['tsu:ʔɛrkɛnən] (unreg) vt to award; **jdm etw ~** to award sth to sb, to award sb sth
zuerst [tsu'ʔe:rst] adv first; (zu Anfang) at first; **~ einmal** first of all
Zufahrt ['tsu:fa:rt] f approach; **~straße** f approach road; (von Autobahn etc) slip road
Zufall ['tsu:fal] m chance; (Ereignis) coincidence; **durch ~** by accident; **so ein ~** what a coincidence; **z~en** (unreg) vi to close, to shut; (Anteil, Aufgabe) to fall
zufällig ['tsu:fɛlɪç] adj chance ♦ adv by chance; (in Frage) by any chance
Zuflucht ['tsu:flʊxt] f recourse; (Ort) refuge
zufolge [tsu'fɔlɡə] präp (+dat od gen) judging by; (laut) according to
zufrieden [tsu'fri:dən] adj content(ed), satisfied; **~ geben** to be content od satisfied (with); **~ stellen** to satisfy
zufrieren ['tsu:fri:rən] (unreg) vi to freeze up od over

Spelling Reform: ▲ *new spelling* △ *old spelling (to be phased out)*

zufügen ['tsu:fy:gən] vt to add; (Leid etc): **(jdm) etw ~** to cause (sb) sth

Zufuhr ['tsu:fu:r] (-, -en) f (Herbeibringen) supplying; (MET) influx

Zug [tsu:k] (-(e)s, ⁺e) m (EISENB) train; (Luftzug) draught; (Ziehen) pull(ing); (Gesichtszug) feature; (SCHACH etc) move; (Schriftzug) stroke; (Atemzug) breath; (Charakterzug) trait; (an Zigarette) puff, pull, drag; (Schluck) gulp; (Menschengruppe) procession; (von Vögeln) flight; (MIL) platoon; **etw in vollen Zügen genießen** to enjoy sth to the full

Zu- ['tsu:] zW: **~gabe** f extra; (in Konzert etc) encore; **~gang** m access, approach; **z~gänglich** adj accessible; (Mensch) approachable

zugeben ['tsu:ge:bən] (unreg) vt (beifügen) to add, to throw in; (zugestehen) to admit; (erlauben) to permit

zugehen ['tsu:ge:ən] (unreg) vi (schließen) to shut; **es geht dort seltsam zu** there are strange goings-on there; **auf jdn/etw ~** to walk towards sb/sth; **dem Ende ~** to be finishing

Zugehörigkeit ['tsu:gəhø:rɪçkaɪt] f: **~ (zu)** membership (of), belonging (to)

Zügel ['tsy:gəl] (-s, -) m rein(s); (fig) curb; **z~n** vt to curb; (Pferd) to rein in

zuge- ['tsu:gə] zW: **Z~ständnis** (-ses, -se) nt concession; **~stehen** (unreg) vt to admit; (Rechte) to concede

Zugführer m (EISENB) guard

zugig ['tsu:gɪç] adj draughty

zügig ['tsy:gɪç] adj speedy, swift

zugreifen ['tsu:graɪfən] (unreg) vi to seize od grab at; (helfen) to help; (beim Essen) to help o.s.

Zugrestaurant nt dining car

zugrunde, zu Grunde [tsu'grʊndə] adv: **~ gehen** to collapse; (Mensch) to perish; **einer Sache** dat **etw ~ legen** to base sth on sth; **einer Sache** dat **~ liegen** to be based on sth; **~ richten** to ruin, to destroy

zugunsten, zu Gunsten [tsu'gʊnstən] präp (+gen od dat) in favour of

zugute [tsu'gu:tə] adv: **jdm etw ~ halten** to concede sth to sb; **jdm ~ kommen** to be of assistance to sb

Zugvogel m migratory bird

zuhalten ['tsu:haltən] (unreg) vt to keep closed ♦ vi: **auf jdn/etw ~** to make a beeline for sb/sth

Zuhälter ['tsu:hɛltər] (-s, -) m pimp

Zuhause [tsu'hauzə] (-) nt home

zuhause [tsu'hauzə] adv (österreichisch, schweizerisch) at home

zuhören ['tsu:hø:rən] vi to listen

Zuhörer (-s, -) m listener

zukleben [tsu:kle:bən] vt to paste up

zukommen ['tsu:kɔmən] (unreg) vi to come up; **auf jdn ~** to come up to sb; **jdm etw ~ lassen** to give sb sth; **etw auf sich ~ lassen** to wait and see; **jdm ~** (sich gehören) to be fitting for sb

Zukunft ['tsu:kʊnft] (-, Zukünfte) f future; **zukünftig** ['tsu:kʏnftɪç] adj future ♦ adv in future; **mein zukünftiger Mann** my husband to be

Zulage ['tsu:la:gə] f bonus

zulassen ['tsu:lasən] (unreg) vt (hereinlassen) to admit; (erlauben) to permit; (Auto) to license; (umg: nicht öffnen) to (keep) shut

zulässig ['tsu:lɛsɪç] adj permissible, permitted

Zulassung f (amtlich) authorization; (von Kfz) licensing

zulaufen ['tsu:laufən] (unreg) vi (subj: Mensch): **~ auf jdn/etw** to run up to sb/sth; (: Straße): **~ auf** to lead towards

zuleide, zu Leide [tsu'laɪdə] adv: **jdm etw ~ tun** to hurt od harm sb

zuletzt [tsu'lɛtst] adv finally, at last

zuliebe [tsu'li:bə] adv: **jdm ~** to please sb

zum [tsʊm] = zu dem; **~ dritten Mal** for the third time; **~ Scherz** as a joke; **~ Trinken** for drinking

zumachen ['tsu:maxən] vt to shut; (Kleidung) to do up, to fasten ♦ vi to shut; (umg) to hurry up

zu- zW: **~mal** [tsu'ma:l] konj especially (as); **~meist** [tsu'maɪst] adv mostly; **~mindest** [tsu'mɪndəst] adv at least

zumutbar ['tsu:mu:tba:r] *adj* reasonable

zumute, zu Mute [tsu'mu:tə] *adv*: **wie ist ihm ~?** how does he feel?

zumuten ['tsu:mu:tən] *vt*: **(jdm) etw ~** to expect *od* ask sth (of sb)

Zumutung ['tsu:mu:tʊŋ] *f* unreasonable expectation *od* demand, impertinence

zunächst [tsu'nɛ:çst] *adv* first of all; **~ einmal** to start with

Zunahme ['tsu:na:mə] *f* increase

Zuname ['tsu:na:mə] *m* surname

Zünd- [tsʏnd] *zW*: **z~en** *vi* (*Feuer*) to light, to ignite; (*Motor*) to fire; (*begeistern*): **bei jdm z~en** to fire sb (with enthusiasm); **z~end** *adj* fiery; **~er (-s, -)** *m* fuse; (*MIL*) detonator; **~holz** ['tsʏnt] *nt* match; **~kerze** *f* (*AUT*) spark(ing) plug; **~schloss** ▲ *nt* ignition lock; **~schlüssel** *m* ignition key; **~schnur** *f* fuse wire; **~stoff** *m* (*fig*) inflammatory stuff; **~ung** *f* ignition

zunehmen ['tsu:ne:mən] (*unreg*) *vi* to increase, to grow; (*Mensch*) to put on weight

Zuneigung ['tsu:naɪgʊŋ] *f* affection

Zunft [tsʊnft] (**-, ⁼e**) *f* guild

zünftig ['tsʏnftɪç] *adj* proper, real; (*Handwerk*) decent

Zunge ['tsʊŋə] *f* tongue

zunichte [tsu'nɪçtə] *adv*: **~ machen** to ruin, to destroy; **~ werden** to come to nothing

zunutze, zu Nutze [tsu'nʊtsə] *adv*: **sich** *dat* **etw ~ machen** to make use of sth

zuoberst [tsu'|o:bərst] *adv* at the top

zupfen ['tsʊpfən] *vt* to pull, to pick, to pluck; (*Gitarre*) to pluck

zur [tsu:r] = **zu der**

zurate, zu Rate [tsu'ra:tə] *adv*: **jdn ~ ziehen** to consult sb

zurechnungsfähig ['tsu:rɛçnʊŋsfɛ:ɪç] *adj* responsible, accountable

zurecht- [tsu:'rɛçt] *zW*: **~finden** (*unreg*) *vr* to find one's way (about); **~kommen** (*unreg*) *vi* to (be able to) cope, to manage; **~legen** *vt* to get ready; (*Ausrede etc*) to have ready; **~machen** *vt* to prepare ♦ *vr* to get ready; **~weisen** (*unreg*) *vt* to reprimand

zureden ['tsu:re:dən] *vi*: **jdm ~** to persuade *od* urge sb

zurück [tsu'rʏk] *adv* back; **~behalten** (*unreg*) *vt* to keep back; **~bekommen** (*unreg*) *vt* to get back; **~bleiben** (*unreg*) *vi* (*Mensch*) to remain behind; (*nicht nachkommen*) to fall behind, to lag; (*Schaden*) to remain; **~bringen** (*unreg*) *vt* to bring back; **~fahren** (*unreg*) *vi* to travel back; (*vor Schreck*) to recoil, to start ♦ *vt* to drive back; **~finden** (*unreg*) *vi* to find one's way back; **~fordern** *vt* to demand back; **~führen** *vt* to lead back; **etw auf etw** *akk* **~führen** to trace sth back to sth; **~geben** (*unreg*) *vt* to give back; (*antworten*) to retort with; **~geblieben** *adj* retarded; **~gehen** (*unreg*) *vi* to go back; (*fallen*) to go down, to fall; (*zeitlich*): **~gehen (auf** +*akk*) to date back (to); **~gezogen** *adj* retired, withdrawn; **~halten** (*unreg*) *vt* to hold back; (*Mensch*) to restrain; (*hindern*) to prevent ♦ *vr* (*reserviert sein*) to be reserved; (*im Essen*) to hold back; **~haltend** *adj* reserved; **Z~haltung** *f* reserve; **~kehren** *vi* to return; **~kommen** (*unreg*) *vi* to come back; **auf etw** *akk* **~kommen** to return to sth; **~lassen** (*unreg*) *vt* to leave behind; **~legen** *vt* to put back; (*Geld*) to put by; (*reservieren*) to keep back; (*Strecke*) to cover; **~nehmen** (*unreg*) *vt* to take back; **~stellen** *vt* to put back, to replace; (*aufschieben*) to put off, to postpone; (*Interessen*) to defer; (*Ware*) to keep; **~treten** (*unreg*) *vi* to step back; (*vom Amt*) to retire; **gegenüber etw** *od* **hinter etw** *dat* **~treten** to diminish in importance in view of sth; **~weisen** (*unreg*) *vt* to turn down; (*Mensch*) to reject; **~zahlen** *vt* to repay, to pay back; **~ziehen** (*unreg*) *vt* to pull back; (*Angebot*) to withdraw ♦ *vr* to retire

Zuruf ['tsu:ru:f] *m* shout, cry

zurzeit [tsʊr'tsaɪt] *adv* at the moment

Zusage ['tsu:za:gə] *f* promise; (*Annahme*) consent; **z~n** *vt* to promise ♦ *vi* to accept; **jdm z~n** (*gefallen*) to agree with *od* please sb

zusammen [tsu'zamən] *adv* together;

Z~arbeit f cooperation; ~arbeiten vi to cooperate; ~beißen (unreg) vt (Zähne) to clench; ~brechen (unreg) vi to collapse; (Mensch auch) to break down; ~bringen (unreg) vt to bring od get together; (Geld) to get; (Sätze) to put together; Z~bruch m collapse; ~fassen vt to summarize; (vereinigen) to unite; Z~fassung f summary, résumé; ~fügen vt to join (together), to unite; ~halten (unreg) vi to stick together; Z~hang m connection; **im/aus dem Z~hang** in/out of context; ~hängen (unreg) vi to be connected od linked; ~kommen (unreg) vi to meet, to assemble; (sich ereignen) to occur at once od together; ~legen vt to put together; (stapeln) to pile up; (falten) to fold; (verbinden) to combine, to unite; (Termine, Fest) to amalgamate; (Geld) to collect; ~nehmen (unreg) vt to summon up ♦ vr to pull o.s. together; **alles ~genommen** all in all; ~passen vi to go well together, to match; ~schließen (unreg) vt, vr to join (together); Z~schluss ▲ m amalgamation; ~schreiben (unreg) vt to write as one word; (Bericht) to put together; Z~sein (-s) nt get-together; ~setzen vt to put together ♦ vr (Stoff) to be composed of; (Menschen) to get together; Z~setzung f composition; ~stellen vt to put together; to compile; Z~stoß m collision; ~stoßen (unreg) vi to collide; ~treffen (unreg) vi to coincide; (Menschen) to meet; Z~treffen nt coincidence; meeting; ~zählen vt to add up; ~ziehen (unreg) vt (verengern) to draw together; (vereinigen) to bring together; (addieren) to add up ♦ vr to shrink; (sich bilden) to form, to develop

zusätzlich ['tsu:zɛtslɪç] adj additional ♦ adv in addition

zuschauen ['tsu:ʃauən] vi to watch, to look on; Zuschauer(in) (-s, -) m(f) spectator ♦ pl (THEAT) audience sg

zuschicken ['tsu:ʃɪkən] vt: **(jdm etw)** ~ to send od to forward (sth to sb)

Zuschlag ['tsu:ʃla:k] m extra charge,

surcharge; z~en (unreg) vt (Tür) to slam; (Ball) to hit; (bei Auktion) to knock down; (Steine etc) to knock into shape ♦ vi (Fenster, Tür) to shut; (Mensch) to hit, to punch; ~karte f (EISENB) surcharge ticket; z~pflichtig adj subject to surcharge

zuschneiden ['tsu:ʃnaidən] (unreg) vt to cut out; to cut to size

zuschrauben ['tsu:ʃrauben] vt to screw down od up

zuschreiben ['tsu:ʃraibən] (unreg) vt (fig) to ascribe, to attribute; (COMM) to credit

Zuschrift ['tsu:ʃrɪft] f letter, reply

zuschulden, zu Schulden [tsu:'ʃʊldən] adv: **sich** dat **etw ~ kommen lassen** to make o.s. guilty of sth

Zuschuss ▲ ['tsu:ʃʊs] m subsidy, allowance

zusehen ['tsu:ze:ən] (unreg) vi to watch; (dafür sorgen) to take care; **jdm/etw ~** to watch sb/sth; ~ds adv visibly

zusenden ['tsu:zendən] (unreg) vt to forward, to send on

zusichern ['tsu:zɪçərn] vt: **jdm etw ~** to assure sb of sth

zuspielen ['tsu:ʃpi:lən] vt, vi to pass

zuspitzen ['tsu:ʃpɪtsən] vt to sharpen ♦ vr (Lage) to become critical

zusprechen ['tsu:ʃprɛçən] (unreg) vt (zuerkennen) to award ♦ vi to speak; **jdm etw ~** to award sb sth od sth to sb; **jdm Trost ~** to comfort sb; **dem Essen/ Alkohol ~** to eat/drink a lot

Zustand ['tsu:ʃtant] m state, condition

zustande, zu Stande [tsu:'ʃtandə] adv: **~ bringen** to bring about; **~ kommen** to come about

zuständig ['tsu:ʃtɛndɪç] adj responsible; Z~keit f competence, responsibility

zustehen ['tsu:ʃte:ən] (unreg) vi: **jdm ~** to be sb's right

zustellen ['tsu:ʃtɛlən] vt (verstellen) to block; (Post etc) to send

Zustellung f delivery

zustimmen ['tsu:ʃtɪmən] vi to agree

Zustimmung f agreement, consent

zustoßen ['tsu:ʃto:sən] (unreg) vi (fig) to happen

Rechtschreibreform: ▲ *neue Schreibung* △ *alte Schreibung (auslaufend)*

zutage, zu Tage [tsu'ta:gə] adv: ~ **bringen** to bring to light; ~ **treten** to come to light

Zutaten ['tsu:ta:tən] pl ingredients

zuteilen ['tsu:taɪlən] vt (Arbeit, Rolle) to designate, assign; (Aktien, Wohnung) to allocate

zutiefst [tsu'ti:fst] adv deeply

zutragen ['tsu:tra:gən] (unreg) vt to bring; (Klatsch) to tell ♦ vr to happen

zutrau- ['tsu:trau] zW: **Z~en (-s)** nt: **Z~en (zu)** trust (in); **~en** vt: **jdm etw ~en** to credit sb with sth; **~lich** adj trusting, friendly

zutreffen ['tsu:trɛfən] (unreg) vi to be correct; to apply; **~d** adj (richtig) accurate; **Z~des bitte unterstreichen** please underline where applicable

Zutritt ['tsu:trɪt] m access, admittance

Zutun ['tsu:tu:n] (-s) nt assistance

zuverlässig ['tsu:fɛrlɛsɪç] adj reliable; **Z~keit** f reliability

zuversichtlich ['tsu:fɛrzɪçtlɪç] adj confident

zuvor [tsu'fo:r] adv before, previously; **~kommen** (unreg) vi +dat to anticipate; **jdm ~kommen** to beat sb to it; **~kommend** adj obliging, courteous

Zuwachs ['tsu:vaks] (-es) m increase, growth; (umg) addition; **z~en** (unreg) vi to become overgrown; (Wunde) to heal (up)

zuwege, zu Wege [tsu've:gə] adv: **etw ~ bringen** to accomplish sth

zuweilen [tsu'vaɪlən] adv at times, now and then

zuweisen ['tsu:vaɪzən] (unreg) vt to assign, to allocate

zuwenden ['tsu:vɛndən] (unreg) vt (+dat) to turn (towards) ♦ vr: **sich jdm/etw ~** to devote o.s. to sb/sth; to turn to sb/sth

zuwider [tsu'vi:dər] adv: **etw ist jdm ~** sb loathes sth, sb finds sth repugnant; **~handeln** vi: **einer Sache** dat **~handeln** to act contrary to sth; **einem Gesetz ~handeln** to contravene a law

zuziehen ['tsu:tsi:ən] (unreg) vt (schließen: Vorhang) to draw, to close; (herbeirufen: Experten) to call in ♦ vi to move in, to

come; **sich** dat **etw ~** (Krankheit) to catch sth; (Zorn) to incur sth

zuzüglich ['tsu:tsy:klɪç] präp +gen plus, with the addition of

Zwang [tsvaŋ] **(-(e)s, ᵁe)** m compulsion, coercion

zwängen ['tsvɛŋən] vt, vr to squeeze

zwanglos adj informal

Zwangs- zW: **~arbeit** f forced labour; (Strafe) hard labour; **~lage** f predicament, tight corner; **z~läufig** adj necessary, inevitable

zwanzig ['tsvantsɪç] num twenty

zwar [tsva:r] adv to be sure, indeed; **das ist ~ ..., aber ...** that may be ... but ...; **und ~ am Sonntag** on Sunday to be precise; **und ~ so schnell, dass ...** in fact so quickly that ...

Zweck [tsvɛk] **(-(e)s, -e)** m purpose, aim; **es hat keinen ~** there's no point; **z~dienlich** adj practical; expedient

Zwecke f hobnail; (Heftzwecke) drawing pin, thumbtack (US)

Zweck- zW: **z~los** adj pointless; **z~mäßig** adj suitable, appropriate; **z~s** präp +gen for the purpose of

zwei [tsvaɪ] num two; **Z~bettzimmer** nt twin room; **~deutig** adj ambiguous; (unanständig) suggestive; **~erlei** adj: **~erlei Stoff** two different kinds of material; **~erlei Meinung** of differing opinions; **~fach** adj double

Zweifel ['tsvaɪfəl] **(-s, -)** m doubt; **z~haft** adj doubtful, dubious; **z~los** adj doubtless; **z~n** vi: **(an etw** dat**) z~n** to doubt (sth)

Zweig [tsvaɪk] **(-(e)s, -e)** m branch; **~stelle** f branch (office)

zwei- zW: **~hundert** num two hundred; **~mal** adv twice; **~sprachig** adj bilingual; **~spurig** adj (AUT) two-lane; **~stimmig** adj for two voices

zweit [tsvaɪt] adv: **zu ~** together; (bei mehreren Paaren) in twos

zweitbeste(r, s) adj second best

zweite(r, s) adj second

zweiteilig ['tsvaɪtaɪlɪç] adj (Gruppe) two-piece; (Fernsehfilm) two-part; (Kleidung)

Spelling Reform: ▲ *new spelling* △ *old spelling (to be phased out)*

two-piece

zweit- zW: ~ens adv secondly; ~größte(r, s) adj second largest; ~klassig adj second-class; ~letzte(r, s) adj last but one, penultimate; ~rangig adj second-rate

Zwerchfell ['tsverçfɛl] nt diaphragm

Zwerg [tsverk] (-(e)s, -e) m dwarf

Zwetsch(g)e ['tsvetʃ(g)ə] f plum

Zwieback ['tsviːbak] (-(e)s, -e) m rusk

Zwiebel ['tsviːbəl] (-, -n) f onion; (Blumenzwiebel) bulb

Zwie- ['tsviː] zW: z~lichtig adj shady, dubious; z~spältig adj (Gefühle) conflicting; (Charakter) contradictory; ~tracht f discord, dissension

Zwilling ['tsvɪlɪŋ] (-s, -e) m twin; ~e pl (ASTROL) Gemini

zwingen ['tsvɪŋən] (unreg) vt to force; ~d adj (Grund etc) compelling

zwinkern ['tsvɪŋkərn] vi to blink; (absichtlich) to wink

Zwirn [tsvɪrn] (-(e)s, -e) m thread

zwischen ['tsvɪʃən] präp (+akk od dat)

between; Z~bemerkung f (incidental) remark; Z~ding nt cross; ~durch adv in between; (räumlich) here and there; Z~ergebnis nt intermediate result; Z~fall m incident; Z~frage f question; Z~handel m middlemen pl; middleman's trade; Z~landung f (AVIAT) stopover; ~menschlich adj interpersonal; Z~raum m space; Z~ruf m interjection; Z~stecker m adaptor (plug); Z~zeit f interval; in der Z~zeit in the interim, meanwhile

zwitschern ['tsvɪtʃərn] vt, vi to twitter, to chirp

zwo [tsvoː] num two

zwölf [tsvœlf] num twelve

Zyklus ['tsyːklʊs] (-, Zyklen) m cycle

Zylinder [tsiˈlɪndər] (-s, -) m cylinder; (Hut) top hat

Zyniker ['tsyːnikər] (-s, -) m cynic

zynisch ['tsyːnɪʃ] adj cynical

Zypern ['tsyːpərn] nt Cyprus

Zyste ['tsystə] f cyst

zz., zzt. abk = zurzeit

PUZZLES AND
WORDGAMES

PUZZLES AND WORDGAMES

Introduction

We are delighted that you have decided to invest in this Collins German Dictionary! Whether you intend to use it in school, at home, on holiday or at work, we are sure that you will find it very useful.

In the pages which follow you will find explanations and wordgames (not too difficult!) designed to give you practice in exploring the dictionary's contents and in retrieving information for a variety of purposes. Answers are provided at the end. If you spend a little time on these pages you should be able to use your dictionary more efficiently and effectively. Have fun!

Supplement by
Roy Simon
reproduced by kind permission of
Tayside Region Education Department

HOW INFORMATION IS PRESENTED IN YOUR DICTIONARY

A great deal of information is packed into your Collins German Dictionary using colour, various typefaces, sizes of type, symbols, abbreviations and brackets. The purpose of this section is to acquaint you with the conventions used in presenting information.

Headwords

A headword is the word you look up in a dictionary. Headwords are listed in alphabetical order throughout the dictionary. They are printed in colour so that they stand out clearly from all the other words on the dictionary page.

Note that at the top of each page a headword appears. This is a guide to the alphabetical order of words on the page. It is there to help you scan through the dictionary more quickly to find the word you want.

The German alphabet consists of the same 26 letters as the English alphabet, plus the letter ß. Although certain letters in the German alphabet take umlaut (ä, ö, ü), this does not affect the order of words in the German-English section of the dictionary.

A Dictionary Entry

An entry is made up of a headword and all the information about that headword. Entries will be short or long depending on how frequently a word is used in either English or German and how many meanings it has. Inevitably, the fuller the dictionary entry the more care is needed in sifting through it to find the information you require.

Meanings

The translations of a headword are given in ordinary type. Where there is more than one meaning or usage, a semi-colon separates one from the other.

abladen ['apla:dən] (*unreg*) *vt* to unload
Ablage ['apla:gə] *f* (*für Akten*) tray; (*für Kleider*) cloakroom
ablassen ['aplasən] (*unreg*) *vt* (*Wasser, Dampf*) to let off; (*vom Preis*) to knock off
♦ *vi*: **von etw ~** to give sth up, to abandon sth

brünett [bry'nɛt] *adj* brunette, dark-haired
Brunnen ['brʊnən] (**-s, -**) *m* fountain; (*tief*)

Bude ['bu:də] *f* booth, stall; (*umg*) digs *pl* (*BRIT*)

Ohnmacht ['o:nmaxt] *f* faint; (*fig*) impotence; **in ~ fallen** to faint
ohnmächtig ['o:nmɛçtɪç] *adj* in a faint, unconscious; (*fig*) weak, impotent; **sie ist ~** she has fainted
Ohr [o:r] (**-(e)s, -en**) *nt* ear
Öhr [ø:r] (**-(e)s, -e**) *nt* eye

Gurt [gʊrt] (**-(e)s, -e**) *m* belt

klar- *zW*: **~legen** *vt* to clear up, to explain; **~machen** *vt* (*Schiff*) to get ready for sea; **jdm etw ~machen** to make sth clear to sb; **~sehen** △ (*unreg*) *vi siehe* **klar**; **K~sichtfolie** *f* transparent film; **~stellen** *vt* to clarify

Zug [tsu:k] (**-(e)s, ⁻e**) *m* (*EISENB*) train; (*Luftzug*) draught; (*Ziehen*) pull(ing); (*Gesichtszug*) feature; (*SCHACH etc*) move; (*Schriftzug*) stroke; (*Atemzug*) breath; (*Charakterzug*) trait; (*an Zigarette*) puff, pull, drag; (*Schluck*) gulp; (*Menschengruppe*) procession; (*von Vögeln*) flight; (*MIL*) platoon; **etw in vollen Zügen genießen** to enjoy sth to the full

In addition, you will often find other words appearing in *italics* in brackets before the translations. These either give some notion of the contexts in which the headword might appear (as with 'scharf' opposite – 'scharfes Essen', 'scharfe Munition', etc.) or else they provide synonyms (as with 'fremd' opposite – 'unvertraut', 'ausländisch', etc.).

Phonetic Spellings

In square brackets immediately after most headwords you will find the phonetic spelling of the word – i.e. its pronunciation. The phonetic transcription of German and English vowels and consonants is given on page xii near the front of your dictionary.

Additional Information About Headwords

Information about the usage or form of certain headwords is given in brackets between the phonetics and the translation or translations. Have a look at the entries for 'KG', 'Filiale', 'löschen' and 'Bruch' opposite.

This information is usually given in abbreviated form. A helpful list of abbreviations is given on pages viii to x at the front of your dictionary.

You should be particularly careful with colloquial words or phrases. Words labelled '(*umg*)' would not normally be used in formal speech, while those labelled '(*umg!*)' would be considered offensive.

Careful consideration of such style labels will provide indications as to the degree of formality and appropriateness of a word and could help you avoid many an embarrassing situation when using German!

Expressions in which the Headword Appears

An entry will often feature certain common expressions in which the headword appears. These expressions are in **bold** type but in black as opposed to colour. A swung dash (~) is used instead of repeating a headword in an entry. 'Schikane' and 'man' opposite illustrate this point.

Related Words

In the German Dictionary words related to certain headwords are sometimes given at the end of an entry, as with 'Lohn' and 'accept' opposite. These are easily picked out as they are also in colour. To help you find these words, they are placed in alphabetical order after the headword to which they belong – see 'acceptable', 'acceptance' etc. opposite.

scharf [ʃarf] *adj* sharp; *(Essen)* hot, spicy; *(Munition)* live; **~ nachdenken** to think hard; **auf etw** *akk* **~ sein** *(umg)* to be keen on sth

fremd [frɛmt] *adj (unvertraut)* strange; *(ausländisch)* foreign; *(nicht eigen)* someone else's; **etw ist jdm ~** sth is foreign to sb; **~artig** *adj* strange; **F~enführer** ['frɛmdən-]

KG [kaːˈɡeː] (-, -s) *f abk (= Kommanditgesellschaft)* limited partnership

Filiale [filiˈaːlə] *f (COMM)* branch

löschen ['lœʃən] *vt (Feuer, Licht)* to put out, to extinguish; *(Durst)* to quench; *(COMM)* to cancel; *(COMPUT)* to delete; *(Tonband)* to erase; *(Fracht)* to unload ♦ *vi (Feuerwehr)* to put out a fire; *(Tinte)* to blot

Bruch [brʊx] (-(e)s, ⁻e) *m* breakage; *(zerbrochene Stelle)* break; *(fig)* split, breach; *(MED: Eingeweidebruch)* rupture, hernia; *(Beinbruch etc)* fracture; *(MATH)* fraction

Schikane [ʃiˈkaːnə] *f* harassment; dirty trick; **mit allen ~n** with all the trimmings

man [man] *pron* one, you; **~ sagt, ...** they *od* people say ...; **wie schreibt ~ das?** how do you write it?, how is it written?

gänzlich ['ɡɛntslɪç] *adj* complete, entire ♦ *adv* completely, entirely

Teufel ['tɔyfəl] (-s, -) *m* devil; **teuflisch** ['tɔyflɪʃ] *adj* fiendish, diabolical

schenken ['ʃɛŋkən] *vt (auch fig)* to give; *(Getränk)* to pour; **sich** *dat* **etw ~** *(umg)* to skip sth; **das ist geschenkt!** *(billig)* that's a giveaway!; *(nichts wert)* that's worthless!

Bombenerfolg *(umg)* *m* smash hit

Arsch [arʃ] (-es, ⁻e) *(umg!)* *m* arse *(BRIT!)*, ass *(US!)*

Lohn [loːn] (-(e)s, ⁻e) *m* reward; *(Arbeitslohn)* pay, wages *pl*; **~büro** *nt* wages office; **~empfänger** *m* wage earner

accept [əkˈsɛpt] *vt (take)* annehmen; *(agree to)* akzeptieren; **~able** *adj* annehmbar; **~ance** *n* Annahme *f*

'Key' Words

Your Collins German Dictionary gives special status to certain German and English words which can be looked on as 'key' words in each language. These are words which have many different usages. 'werden', 'alle(r, s)' and 'sich' opposite are typical examples in German. You are likely to become familiar with them in your day-to-day language studies.

There will be occasions, however, when you want to check on a particular usage. Your dictionary can be very helpful here. Note how different parts of speech and different usages are clearly indicated by a combination of lozenges (♦) and numbers. In addition, further guides to usage are given in italics in brackets in the language of the user who needs them.

werden ['veːrdən] (*pt* **wurde**, *pp* **geworden** *od* (*bei Passiv*) **worden**) *vi* to become; **was ist aus ihm/aus der Sache geworden?** what became of him/it?; **es ist nichts/gut geworden** it came to nothing/turned out well; **es wird Nacht/Tag** it's getting dark/light; **mir wird kalt** I'm getting cold; **mir wird schlecht** I feel ill; **Erster werden** to come *od* be first; **das muss anders werden** that'll have to change; **rot/zu Eis werden** to turn red/to ice; **was willst du (mal) werden?** what do you want to be?; **die Fotos sind gut geworden** the photos have come out nicely

♦ *als Hilfsverb* **1** (*bei Futur*): **er wird es tun** he will *od* he'll do it; **er wird das nicht tun** he will not *od* he won't do it; **es wird gleich regnen** it's going to rain

2 (*bei Konjunktiv*): **ich würde ...** I would ...; **er würde gern ...** he would *od* he'd like to ...; **ich würde lieber ...** I would *od* I'd rather ...

3 (*bei Vermutung*): **sie wird in der Küche sein** she will be in the kitchen

4 (*bei Passiv*): **gebraucht werden** to be used; **er ist erschossen worden** he has *od* he's been shot; **mir wurde gesagt, dass ... ** I was told that ...

alle(r, s) ['alə(r,s)] *adj* **1** (*sämtliche*) all; **wir alle** all of us; **alle Kinder waren da** all the children were there; **alle Kinder mögen ...** all children like ...; **alle beide** both of us/them; **sie kamen alle** they all came; **alles Gute** all the best; **alles in allem** all in all **2** (*mit Zeit- oder Maßangaben*) every; **alle vier Jahre** every four years; **alle fünf Meter** every five metres

♦ *pron* (*zu Ende, aufgebraucht*) everything; **alles was er sagt** everything he says, all that he says

♦ *adv* (*zu Ende, aufgebraucht*) finished; **die Milch ist alle** the milk's all gone, there's no milk left; **etw alle machen** to finish sth up

sich [zɪç] *pron* **1** (*akk*): **er/sie/es ... sich** he/she/it ... himself/herself/itself; **sie** *pl*/**man ... sich** they/one ... themselves/oneself; **Sie ... sich** you ... yourself/yourselves *pl*; **sich wiederholen** to repeat oneself/itself

2 (*dat*): **er/sie/es ... sich** he/she/it ... to himself/herself/itself; **sie** *pl*/**man ... sich** they/one ... to themselves/oneself; **Sie ... sich** you ... to yourself/yourselves *pl*; **sie hat sich einen Pullover gekauft** she bought herself a jumper; **sich die Haare waschen** to wash one's hair

3 (*mit Präposition*): **haben Sie Ihren Ausweis bei sich?** do you have your pass on you?; **er hat nichts bei sich** he's got nothing on him; **sie bleiben gern unter sich** they keep themselves to themselves

4 (*einander*) each other, one another; **sie bekämpfen sich** they fight each other *od* one another

5: **dieses Auto fährt sich gut** this car drives well; **hier sitzt es sich gut** it's good to sit here

WORDGAME 1
HEADWORDS

Study the following sentences. In each sentence a wrong word spelt very similarly to the correct word has deliberately been put in and the sentence doesn't make sense. This word is shaded each time. Write out the correct word, which you will find in your dictionary near the wrong word.

Example   Raufen verboten

['Raufen' (= 'to pull out') is the wrong word and should be replaced by 'rauchen' (= 'to smoke')]

1. Hast du das Buch schon gekonnt?

2. Ich habe ein paar VW-Akten gekauft.

3. Wir waren gestern im Kilo.

4. Sollen wir die Theaterkarten schon kauen?

5. Unser Nachbar hat einen kleinen schwarzen Puder.

6. Ich zähle heute die Rechnung.

7. Der Student muss sich für den Kurs einschreiten.

8. Das neue Restaurant ist gar nicht über.

9. Gans viele Leute standen am Unfallort.

10. Ich habe meiner Tanne einen Brief geschrieben.

WORDGAME 2

DICTIONARY ENTRIES

Complete the crossword below by looking up the English words in the list and finding the correct German translations. There is a slight catch, however! All the English words can be translated several ways into German, but only one translation will fit correctly into each part of the crossword. So look carefully through the entries in the English-German section of your dictionary.

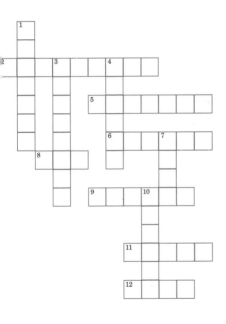

1. FAIR

2. CATCH

3. LEARN

4. FALL

5. HIT

6. HARD

7. CALF

8. PLACE

9. HOLD

10. PLACE

11. TRACK

12. HOME

WORDGAME 3

FINDING MEANINGS

In this list there are eight pairs of words that have some sort of connection with each other. For example, 'Diplom' (= 'diploma') and 'Student' (='student') are linked. Find the other pairs by looking up the words in your dictionary.

1. Morgenrock
2. Handtasche
3. Bett
4. Kirche
5. Fisch
6. Nest
7. Diplom
8. Lederwaren
9. Hausschuhe
10. Glockengeläut
11. Student
12. Decke
13. Elster
14. Buch
15. Schuppe
16. Regal

WORDGAME 4
SYNONYMS

Complete the crossword by supplying synonyms of the words below. You will sometimes find the words you are looking for in italics in brackets in the entries for the words in the list. Sometimes you will have to turn to the English-German section for help.

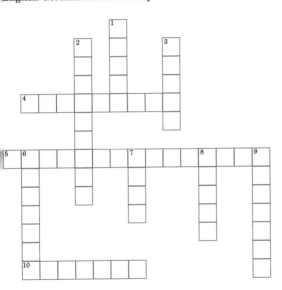

1. Art
2. probieren
3. Feuer
4. sich ereignen
5. Arroganz

6. namhaft
7. Ladung
8. Plan
9. begegnen
10. Neigung

WORDGAME 5

SPELLING

You will often use your dictionary to check spellings. The person who has compiled this list of ten German words has made <u>three</u> spelling mistakes. Find the three words which have been misspelt and write them out correctly.

1. nachsehen
2. nacht
3. Nagetier
4. Name
5. Nature
6. neuriech
7. Nickerchen
8. Nimmersatt
9. nördlich
10. nötig

WORDGAME 6

ANTONYMS

Complete the crossword by supplying ANTONYMS (i.e. opposites) in German of the words below. Use your dictionary to help.

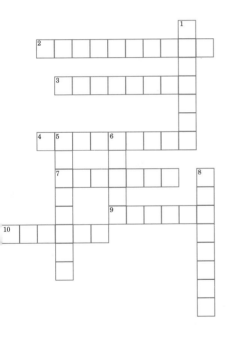

1. gestehen
2. enthüllen
3. unschuldig
4. kaufen
5. verbieten
6. Reichtum
7. ruhig
8. ankommen
9. ängstlich
10. schmutzig

WORDGAME 7

PHONETIC SPELLINGS

The phonetic transcriptions of ten German words are given below. If you study page xii near the front of your dictionary you should be able to work out what the words are.

1. frika'dɛlə

2. ʃpuːr

3. faın

4. 'lyːgə

5. 'ʃtaxəl

6. 'naʊtɪʃ

7. gə'vœlbə

8. 'kɔʏçən

9. 'møːgən

10. 'glaʊbvʏrdɪç

WORDGAME 8

EXPRESSIONS IN WHICH THE HEADWORD APPEARS

If you look up the headword 'Satz' in the German-English section of your dictionary you will find that the word can have many meanings. Study the entry carefully and translate the following sentences into English.

1. Der Satz ist viel zu lang.

2. Unterstreicht jeden Satz, der mit einer Konjunktion beginnt.

3. Den Satz von Pythagoras kennt jeder.

4. Das Orchester hat den letzten Satz ganz ausgezeichnet gespielt.

5. Steffi Graf hat in der Meisterschaft keinen Satz verloren.

6. Der ganze Satz war in der Tasse.

7. Bei Lieferungen ins Ausland gilt ein anderer Satz.

8. Sie hat vor lauter Begeisterung einen großen Satz gemacht.

WORDGAME 9

RELATED WORDS

Fill in the blanks in the pairs of sentences below. The missing words are related to the headwords on the left. Choose the correct "relative" each time. You will find it in your dictionary near the headword provided.

HEADWORD	RELATED WORDS
Stellung	1. Ich habe die Uhr auf halb sechs _____. 2. Das Auto steht an der gleichen_____.
Hoffnung	3. _____bleibt das Wetter so. 4. Sie_____, dass sie bald wieder gesund ist.
Betrug	5. Von ihm lassen wir uns nicht mehr_____. 6. Er ist als_____bekannt.
sprechen	7. Hat er schon mit seiner Mutter_____? 8. Das Buch wurde in fünf _____übersetzt.
Student	9. Er hat letztes Semester mit dem_____ begonnen. 10. Sie _____Medizin.
kurz	11. Ich habe_____noch mit ihm gesprochen. 12. Der Rock muss_____werden.

WORDGAME 10

'KEY' WORDS

Study carefully the entry 'machen' in your dictionary and find translations for the following:

1. what are you doing (there)?

2. it's the cold that does that

3. that doesn't matter

4. I don't mind the cold

5. 3 and 5 are 8

6. to have the car done

7. how's the work going?

8. hurry up!

9. to set about sth

10. to turn the radio down

THE DICTIONARY AND GRAMMAR

While it is true that a dictionary can never be a substitute for a detailed grammar book, it nevertheless provides a great deal of grammatical information. If you know how to extract this information you will be able to use German more accurately both in speech and in writing.

The Collins German Dictionary presents grammatical information as follows.

Parts of Speech

Parts of speech are given in italics immediately after the phonetic spellings of headwords. Abbreviated forms are used. Abbreviations can be checked on pages viii to x.

Changes in parts of speech within an entry – for example, from adjective to pronoun to adverb, or from noun to intransitive verb to transitive verb – are indicated by means of lozenges (♦), as with the German 'alle(r, s)' and the English 'fast' opposite.

German Nouns

The gender of each noun in the German-English section of the dictionary is indicated in the following way:

> m = Maskulinum
> f = Femininum
> nt = Neutrum

You will occasionally see 'm od nt' or 'm od f' beside an entry. This indicates that the noun can be either masculine or neuter (see 'Knäuel' opposite or masculine or feminine (see 'Sellerie' opposite).

Feminine forms of nouns are shown, as with 'Schaffner(in)' opposite. This is marked $m(f)$ to show that the feminine form has the ending '-in'. Nouns which have the ending '-(r)', like 'Angeklagte(r)' opposite, are formed from adjectives and are marked $f(m)$ to show that they can be either masculine or feminine. Their spelling changes in the same way as adjectives, depending on their article and position in the sentence.

prosit [ˈproːzɪt] *excl* cheers

leiten [ˈlaɪtən] *vt* to lead; (*Firma*) to manage; (*in eine Richtung*) to direct; (*ELEK*) to conduct

---

SCHLÜSSELWORT

alle(r, s) [ˈalə(r,s)] *adj* **1** (*sämtliche*) all; **wir alle** all of us; **alle Kinder waren da** all the children were there; **alle Kinder mögen ...** all children like ...; **alle beide** both of us/ them; **sie kamen alle** they all came; **alles Gute** all the best; **alles in allem** all in all **2** (*mit Zeit- oder Maßangaben*) every; **alle vier Jahre** every four years; **alle fünf Meter** every five metres
♦ *pron* everything; **alles was er sagt** everything he says, all that he says
♦ *adv* (*zu Ende, aufgebraucht*) finished; **die Milch ist alle** the milk's all gone, there's no milk left; **etw alle machen** to finish sth up

---

fast [faːst] *adj* schnell; (*firm*) fest ♦ *adv* schnell; fest ♦ *n* Fasten *nt* ♦ *vi* fasten; **to be ~** (*clock*) vorgehen

Knäuel [ˈknɔʏəl] **(-s, -)** *m od nt* (*Wollknäuel*) ball; (*Menschenknäuel*) knot

Sellerie [ˈzɛləriː] **(-s, -(s)** *od* **-, -)** *m od f* celery

Schaffner(in) [ˈʃafnər(ɪn)] **(-s, -)** *m(f)* (*Busschaffner*) conductor(-tress); (*EISENB*) guard

Angeklagte(r) [ˈangəklaːktə(r)] *f(m)* accused

295

So many things depend on you knowing the correct gender of a German noun – whether you use 'er', 'sie' or 'es' to translate 'it'; whether you use 'er' or 'es' to translate 'he', 'sie' or 'es' to translate 'she'; the spelling of adjectives etc. If you are in any doubt as to the gender of a noun, it is always best to check it in your dictionary.

Genitive singular and nominative plural forms of many nouns are also given (see 'Bube' and 'Scheitel' opposite). A list of regular noun endings is given on page xi and nouns which have these forms will not show genitive singular and nominative plural at the headword (see 'Rasur' and 'Forelle' opposite). Nouns formed from two or more words do not have genitive singular and nominative plural shown if the last element appears in the dictionary as a headword. For example, if you want to know how to decline 'Backenzahn', you will find the necessary information at 'Zahn'.

Adjectives

Adjectives are given in the form used when they come after a verb. If the adjective comes before a noun, the spelling changes, depending on the gender of the noun and on the article (if any), which comes before the adjective. Compare 'der Hund ist schwarz' with 'der schwarze Hund'. If you find an unfamiliar adjective in a text and want to look it up in the dictionary, you will have to decide what spelling changes have been made before you can know how it will appear in the dictionary.

Some adjectives are never used after a verb. In these cases, the dictionary shows all the possible nominative singular endings.

Adverbs

German adverbs come in three main types.

Some are just adjectives in their after-verb form, used as adverbs. Sometimes the meaning is similar to the meaning of the adjective (see 'laut'), sometimes it is rather different (see 'richtig').

Some adverbs are formed by adding '-weise', '-sweise' or '-erweise' to the adjective.

Other adverbs are not considered to be derived from particular adjectives.

In your dictionary, adjective-adverbs may be shown by a change of part of speech or by the mention 'adj, adv' at the beginning of the entry.

Fuß [fuːs] (**-es**, **⁻e**) *m* foot; (*von Glas, Säule etc*) base; (*von Möbel*) leg; **zu ~** on foot;

Stube [ˈʃtuːbə] *f* room

Mädchen [ˈmɛːtçən] *nt* girl; **m~haft** *adj* girlish; **~name** *m* maiden name

Rasur [raˈzuːr] *f* shaving

Forelle [foˈrɛlə] *f* trout

schwarz [ʃvarts] *adj* black; **~es Brett** notice board; **ins S~e treffen** (*auch fig*) to hit the bull's eye; **in den ~en Zahlen** in the black; **~ sehen** (*umg*) to see the gloomy side of things; **S~arbeit** *f* illicit work, moonlighting; **S~brot** *nt* black bread; **S~e(r)** *f(m)* black (man/woman)

laut [laʊt] *adj* loud ♦ *adv* loudly; (*lesen*) aloud ♦ *präp* (*+gen od dat*) according to; **L~** (**-(e)s**, **-e**) *m* sound

richtig *adj* right, correct; (*echt*) proper ♦ *adv* (*umg: sehr*) really; **bin ich hier ~?** am I in the right place?; **der/die R~e** the right one/person; **das R~e** the right thing; **etw ~ stellen** to correct sth; **R~keit** *f* correctness

leider [ˈlaɪdər] *adv* unfortunately; **ja, ~** yes, I'm afraid so; **~ nicht** I'm afraid not

oben [ˈoːbən] *adv* above; (*in Haus*) upstairs; **~ erwähnt**, **~ genannt** above-mentioned; **nach ~** up; **von ~** down; **~ ohne** topless;

Bube [ˈbuːbə] (**-n**, **-n**) *m* (*Schurke*) rogue; (*KARTEN*) jack

Scheitel [ˈʃaɪtəl] (**-s**, **-**) *m* top; (*Haarscheitel*) parting; **s~n** *vt* to part

Backenzahn *m* molar

Zahn [tsaːn] (**-(e)s**, **⁻e**) *m* tooth; **~arzt** *m* dentist; **~ärztin** *f* (female) dentist; **~bürste** *f* toothbrush; **~fleisch** *nt* gums *pl*; **~pasta** *f* toothpaste; **~rad** *nt* cog(wheel); **~schmerzen** *pl* toothache *sg*; **~stein** *m* tartar; **~stocher** (**-s**, **-**) *m* toothpick

besondere(r, s) [bəˈzɔndərə(r, s)] *adj* special; (*eigen*) particular; (*gesondert*) separate; (*eigentümlich*) peculiar

letzte(r, s) [ˈlɛtstə(r, s)] *adj* last; (*neueste*) latest; **zum ~n Mal** for the last time; **~ns** *adv* lately; **~re(r, s)** *adj* latter

nett [nɛt] *adj* nice; (*freundlich*) nice, kind; **~erweise** *adv* kindly

glück- *zW:* **~lich** *adj* fortunate; (*froh*) happy; **~licherweise** *adv* fortunately; **~ˈselig** *adj* blissful

Adjective-plus-ending adverbs will usually appear as subentries.

Adverbs like 'oben' and 'leider' will usually appear as separate headwords.

Where a word in your text seems to be an adverb but does not appear in the dictionary, you should be able to work out a translation from the word it is related to, once you have found that in the dictionary.

Information about Verbs

A major problem facing language learners is that the form of a verb will change according to the subject and/or the tense being used. A typical German verb can take on many different forms – too many to list in a dictionary entry.

Yet, although verbs are listed in your dictionary in their infinitive forms only, this does not mean that the dictionary is of limited value when it comes to handling the verb system of the German language. On the contrary, it contains much valuable information.

First of all, your dictionary will help you with the meanings of unfamiliar verbs. If you came across the word 'füllt' in a text and looked it up in your dictionary you wouldn't find it. What you must do is assume that it is part of a verb and look for the infinitive form. Thus you will deduce that 'füllt' is a form of the verb 'füllen'. You now have the basic meaning of the word you are concerned with – something to do with English verb 'fill' – and this should be enough to help you understand the text you are reading.

It is usually an easy task to make the connection between the form of a verb and the infinitive. For example, 'füllten', 'füllst', 'füllte' and 'gefüllt' are all recognizable as parts of the infinitive 'füllen'. However, sometimes it is less obvious – for example, 'hilft', 'halfen' and 'geholfen' are all parts of 'helfen'. The only real solution to this problem is to learn the various forms of the main German irregular verbs.

And this is the second source of help offered by your dictionary as far as verbs are concerned. The irregular verb lists on pages 609 to 613 at the back of the Collins German Dictionary provide the main forms of the main tenses of the basic irregular verbs. (Verbs which consist of a basic verb with prefix usually follow the rules for the basic verb.) Consider the verb 'sehen' below where the following information is given:

infinitive	present indicative (2nd, 3rd sg)	imperfect	past participle
sehen	siehst, sieht	sah	gesehen

In order to make maximum use of the information contained in these pages, a good working knowledge of the various rules affecting German verbs is required. You will acquire this in the course of your German studies and your Collins dictionary will serve as a useful 'aide-mémoire'. If you happen to forget how to form the second person singular form of the Past Tense of 'sehen' (i.e. how to translate 'You saw'), there will be no need to panic – your dictionary contains the information!

In addition, the main parts of the most common irregular verbs are listed in the body of the dictionary.

WORDGAME 11
PARTS OF SPEECH

In each sentence below a word has been shaded. Put a tick in the appropriate box to indicate the **part of speech** each time.

SENTENCE	Noun	Adj	Adv	Verb
1. Das Essen ist fertig.				
2. Er hat kein Recht dazu.				
3. Warum fahren wir nicht in die Stadt zum Essen?				
4. Ich gehe nicht mit essen.				
5. Rauchen ist strengstens verboten.				
6. Gehen Sie geradeaus und dann die erste Straße links.				
7. Das war aber ein interessanter Vortrag.				
8. Die Schauspielerin trug ein herrliches Kleid.				
9. Hast du schon von deiner Freundin gehört?				
10. Es ist immer noch recht sommerlich.				

WORDGAME 12

MEANING CHANGING WITH GENDER

ome German nouns change meaning according to their gender. Look at
he pairs of sentences below and fill in the blanks with either 'ein, einen,
ine' or 'der, den, die, das'.

. Ist das _____ erste Band der Schillerausgabe?

_____ Band ist nicht lang genug.

. _____ Mark ist in letzter Zeit wieder gestiegen.

Der Metzger löst _____ Mark aus den Knochen.

. Was kostet _____ Bund Petersilie?

_____ Bund an der Hose ist zu weit.

. _____ Tau lag noch auf den Wiesen.

Der Mann konnte _____ Tau nicht heben.

. Wie steht mir _____ Hut?

Wir müssen wirklich auf _____ Hut sein.

. Hinter dem Haus steht _____ Kiefer.

Er hat sich _____ Kiefer gebrochen.

WORDGAME 13
ADJECTIVES

Try to work out how the adjectives in the following phrases will appear in the dictionary. Write your answer beside the phrase, then check in the dictionary.

1. ein englisches Buch

2. der rote Traktor

3. letzte Nacht

4. mein kleiner Bruder

5. eine lange Reise

6. guter Käse

7. das alte Trikot

8. schwarzes Brot

9. die große Kommode

10. ein heftiger Schlag

11. der siebte Sohn

12. die neuen Nachbarn

WORDGAME 14

VERB TENSES

Use your dictionary to help you fill in the blanks in the table below.
(Remember the important pages at the back of your dictionary.)

INFINITIVE	PRESENT TENSE	IMPERFECT	PERFECT TENSE
sehen		ich	
schlafen	du		
sein			ich
schlagen		ich	
anrufen			ich
abfahren	er		
studieren			ich
haben		ich	
anfangen	du		
waschen	er		
werden		ich	
nehmen			ich

WORDGAME 15

PAST PARTICIPLES

Use your dictionary to find the past participle of these verbs.

INFINITIVE	PAST PARTICIPLE
singen	
beißen	
bringen	
frieren	
reiben	
gewinnen	
helfen	
geschehen	
liegen	
lügen	
schneiden	
kennen	
mögen	
wissen	
können	

WORDGAME 16

IDENTIFYING INFINITIVES

In the sentences below you will see various German verbs shaded. Use your dictionary to help you find the INFINITIVE form of each verb.

1. Leider habe ich Ihren Namen vergessen.

2. Bitte ruf mich doch morgen früh mal an.

3. Er ist um 16 Uhr angekommen.

4. Sie hielt an ihrem Argument fest.

5. Wir waren im Sommer in Italien.

6. Ich würde gerne kommen, wenn ich nur könnte.

7. Die Maschine flog über den Nordpol.

8. Ich würde es ja machen, aber ich habe keine Zeit.

9. Wohin fährst du diesen Winter zum Skilaufen?

10. Wen habt ihr sonst noch eingeladen?

11. Er hat deinen Brief erst gestern bekommen.

12. Liest du das Buch nicht zu Ende?

13. Meine Mutter ist letztes Jahr gestorben.

14. Er hat den Zettel aus Versehen weggeworfen.

15. Ich nahm ihn jeden Tag mit nach Hause.

MORE ABOUT MEANING

In this section we will consider some of the problems associated with using a bilingual dictionary.

Overdependence on your dictionary

That the dictionary is an invaluable tool for the language learner is beyond dispute. Nevertheless, it is possible to become overdependent on your dictionary, turning to it in an almost automatic fashion every time you come up against a new German word or phrase. Tackling an unfamiliar text in this way will turn reading in German into an extremely tedious activity. If you stop to look up every new word you may actually be *hindering* your ability to read in German – you are so concerned with the individual words that you pay no attention to the text as a whole and to the context which gives them meaning. It is therefore important to develop appropriate reading skills – using clues such as titles, headlines, illustrations, etc., understanding relations within a sentence, etc. to predict or infer what a text is about.

A detailed study of the development of reading skills is not within the scope of this supplement; we are concerned with knowing how to use a dictionary, which is only one of several important skills involved in reading. Nevertheless, it may be instructive to look at one example. You see the following text in a German newspaper and are interested in working out what it is about.

Contextual clues here include the word in large type which you would probably recognize as a German name, something that looks like a date below, and the name and address at the bottom. Some 'form' words such as 'wir', 'sind', 'und' and 'Tochter' will be familiar to you from your general studies in German. Given that we are dealing with

> *Wir sind glücklich*
> *über die Geburt*
> *unserer Tochter*
>
> # Julia
>
> am 5. Juni 1999
>
> *Christine und Artur Landgraf*
> *Vacher Straße 50 B, Köln*

a newspaper, you will probably have worked out by now that this could be an announcement placed in the 'Personal Column'.

So you have used a series of cultural, contextual and word-formation clues to get you to the point where you have understood that Christine and Artur Landgraf have placed this notice in the 'Personal Column' of the newspaper and that something happened to Julia on 5 November 1997. And you have reached this point *without* opening your dictionary once. Common sense and your knowledge of newspaper contents in this country might suggest that this must be an announcement of someone's birth or death. Thus 'glücklich' ('happy') and 'Geburt' ('birth') become the only words that you might have to look up in order to confirm that this is indeed a birth announcement.

When learning German we are helped by the fact that some German and English words look and sound alike and have exactly the same meaning. Such words are called 'COGNATES' i.e. words derived from the same root. Many words come from a common Latin root. Other words are the same or nearly the same in both languages because the German language has borrowed a word from English or vice versa. The dictionary should not be necessary where cognates are concerned – provided you know the English word that the German word resembles!

Words With More Than One Meaning

The need to examine with care *all* the information contained in a dictionary entry must be stressed. This is particularly important with the many German words which have more than one meaning. For example, the German 'Zeit' can mean 'grammatical tense' as well as 'time'. How you translated the word would depend on the context in which you found it.

Similarly, if you were trying to translate a phrase such as 'sich vor etwas drücken', you would have to look through the whole entry for 'drücken' to get the right translation. If you restricted your search to the first couple of lines of the entry and saw that the first meaning given is 'press', you might be tempted to assume that the idiom meant 'to press o.s. in front of sth'. But if you examined the entry closely you would see that 'sich vor etwas drücken' means 'to get out of (doing) sth', as in the sentence 'Sie drückt sich immer vor dem Abwasch'.

The same need for care applies when you are using the English-German section of your dictionary to translate a word from English into German. Watch out in particular for the lozenges indicating changes in parts of speech.

If you want to translate 'You can't fool me', the capital letters at 'Narr' and 'Närrin' will remind you that these words are nouns. But watch what you are doing with the verbs or you could end up with a mistranslation like 'Sie können mich nicht herumalbern'!

Phrasal Verbs

Another potential source of difficulty is English phrasal verbs. These consist of a common verb ('go', 'make', etc.) plus an adverb and/or a preposition to give English expressions such as 'to take after', 'to make out', etc. Entries for such verbs tend to be fairly full; therefore close examination of the contents is required. Note how these verbs appear in colour within the entry.

False Friends

fool [fuːl] n Narr m, Närrin f ♦ vt (deceive) hereinlegen ♦ vi (also: ~ **around**) (herum)albern; ~**hardy** adj tollkühn; ~**ish** adj albern; ~**proof** adj idiotensicher

make [meɪk] (pt, pp **made**) vt machen; (appoint) ernennen (zu); (cause to do sth) veranlassen; (reach) erreichen; (in time) schaffen; (earn) verdienen ♦ n Marke f; **to ~ sth happen** etw geschehen lassen; **to ~ it** es schaffen; **what time do you ~ it?** wie spät hast du es?; **to ~ do with** auskommen mit; ~ **for** vi gehen/fahren nach; ~ **out** vt (write out) ausstellen; (understand) verstehen; ~ **up** vt machen; (face) schminken; (quarrel) beilegen; (story etc) erfinden ♦ vi sich versöhnen; ~ **up for** vt wieder gutmachen; ~**believe** n Fantasie f; ~**r** n (COMM) Hersteller m; ~**shift** adj behelfsmäßig, Not-; ~**-up** n Schminke f, Make-up nt; ~**up remover** n Make-up-Entferner m; **making** n: **in the making** im Entstehen; **to have the makings of** das Zeug haben zu

Some German and English words have similar forms *and* meanings. There are, however, German words which *look* like English words but have a completely *different* meaning. For example, 'blank' in German means 'bright'; 'Probe' means 'rehearsal'; 'bilden' means 'to educate'. This can easily lead to serious mistranslations.

Sometimes the meaning of the German word is close to the English. For example, 'die Chips' are 'potato crisps' rather than 'chips'; 'der Hund' means a dog of any sort, not just a 'hound'. But some German words have two meanings, one the same as the English, the other completely different! 'Golf' can mean 'gulf' as well as 'golf'; 'senden' can mean 'to send' but can also mean 'to transmit/broadcast'.

Such words are often referred to as 'false friends'. You will have to look at the context in which they appear in order to arrive at the correct meaning. If they seem to fit with the sense of the passage as a whole, it will probably not be necessary to look them up. If they don't make sense, however, you may be dealing with 'false friends'.

WORDGAME 17

WORDS IN CONTEXT

Study the sentences below. Translations of the underlined words are given at the bottom. Match the number of the sentence and the letter of the translation correctly each time.

1. Sprich bitte lauter, ich kann dich nicht hören.

2. Er hört den ganzen Tag Radio.

3. Kannst du das Licht ausmachen, wenn du ins Bett gehst?

4. Können wir heute schon einen Termin ausmachen?

5. Seine Frau saß am Steuer, als der Unfall passierte.

6. Ich muss dieses Jahr viel Steuern nachzahlen.

7. Die Nachfrage nach japanischen Autos ist groß.

8. Aufgrund meiner Nachfrage konnte ich dann doch etwas erfahren.

9. Das Haus wird auf meinen Namen umgeschrieben.

10. Das Referat musst du völlig umschreiben.

11. Sind die Äpfel schon reif?

12. Für ihr Alter wirkt sie schon ziemlich reif.

a.	demand	e.	ripe	i.	steering wheel
b.	transferred	f.	inquiry	j.	listens to
c.	turn off	g.	mature	k.	agree
d.	hear	h.	rewrite	l.	tax

WORDGAME 18

FALSE FRIENDS

Look at the advertisements below. The words which have been shaded
resemble English words but have different meanings here. Find a correct
translation for each word in the context.

Reformhaus
Neustr. 23
Sonderangebot:
Vollkornbrot 2, 78 DM

1

2

Hotel Olympia

Alle Zimmer mit Dusche/WC
Gemütliche Atmosphäre
Bitte Prospekt anfordern

Heinrichstraße 51 –
7000 STUTTGART 25
Tel. 0711/21 56 93

3

KP-Chef Italiens fliegt
morgen nach New York

4

W. Meinzer   Lebensmittel
Heute Chips
im
Sonderangebot

5

Der Mann im Smoking

6

Clinton
will wieder
Präsident der
USA werden

7

Nach der
Jahrtausendwende
erst mit 65 in
Rente

8

Europaparlament

Fraktions-Flanke abdecken

9

**Reise sorgenfrei
mit diesen Drei**

**Reisescheck
Devisen
Sparkassenbuch**

BEZIRKSSPARKASSE HAUSACH
Hauptstr. 14

WORDGAME 19

WORDS WITH MORE THAN ONE MEANING

Look at the advertisements and headlines below. The words which have
been shaded can have more than one meaning. Use your dictionary to
help you work out the correct translation in the context.

1

Landespräsident
tritt
zurück

2

Vermögen:

Vom kleinen zum
großen Geld

3

Ich weiß, wie ich
Schmerzen schnell los werde

Parazetamol
Aus Ihrer Apotheke

4

**Heinrich Wohnmobile
GmbH**

Spezialisten bieten
günstige Preise

5

Hotel Restaurant Seeberger

Alle Preise inklusive
Bedienung

Marktplatz 12
Loßburg   Telefon (07165) 33 14

6

Müsli – Riegel

von Cadbury
– gibt Kraft und Energie!

7

Hotel - Pension Miramar

Behagliche Atmosphäre
Günstige Nachsaisonpreise

Strandstr. 6,
24340 Eckernförde
Telefon (04269) 29 51

8

Das Blatt
Finanz- und
Wirtschaftszeitung

HAVE FUN WITH YOUR DICTIONARY

Here are some word games for you to try. You will find your dictionary helpful as you attempt the activities.

WORDGAME 20
CODED WORDS

In the boxes below the letters of eight German words have been replaced by numbers. A number represents the same letter each time.

Try to crack the code and find the eight words. If you need help, use your dictionary.

Here is a clue: all the words you are looking for have something to do with TRANSPORT.

1 | W¹ | A² | G³ | 4 | 5 |

2 | 10 | 8 | 11 | 11 | 4 | 10 |

3 | 12 | 2 | 13 | 14 |

4 | 9 | 2 | 7 | 10 | 10 | 2 | 19 |

5 | 9 | 11 | 16 | 3 | 15 | 4 | 16 | 3 |

6 | 6 | 2 | 7 | 5 | 7 | 8 | 9 |

7 | 15 | 16 | 3 |

8 | 11 | 2 | 18 | 12 | 1 | 2 | 3 | 4 | 5 |

314

WORDGAME 21

BEHEADED WORDS

If you 'behead' certain German words, i.e. take away their first letter, you are left with another German word. For example, if you behead 'Kleider' (= 'clothes'), you get 'leider' (= 'unfortunately'), and 'dort' (= 'there') gives 'Ort' (= 'place').

The following words have their heads chopped off, i.e. the first letter has been removed. Use your dictionary to help you form a new German word by adding one letter to the start of each word below. Write down the new German word and its meaning.

1. ragen (= to tower)

2. tollen (= to romp)

3. nie (= never)

4. Rand (= edge)

5. oben (= above)

6. ich (= I)

7. Rad (= wheel)

8. innen (= inside)

9. raten (= to guess)

10. indisch (= Indian)

11. eigen (=own)

12. eben (= level)

13. Ohr (= ear)

14. pur (= pure)

WORDGAME 22

CROSSWORD

Complete this crossword by looking up the words listed below in the English-German section of your dictionary. Remember to read through the entry carefully to find the word that will fit.

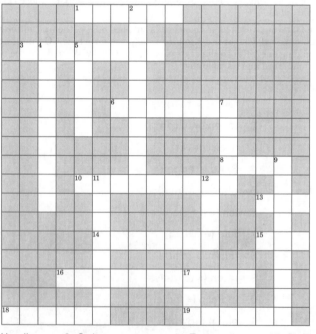

1. Heavily	6. Sad
2. Tearful	7. Smooth
3. Meal	8. Deaf
4. To record	9. To reassure
5. Mood	10. (A piece of) news

11. To start up (a car)	15. Clock
12. Tap	16. To dirty
13. Place	17. Day
14. To withdraw	18. To fold
	19. Profit

WORDGAME 23

There are twelve German words hidden in the grid below. Each word is made up of five letters but has been split into two parts.

Find the German words. Each group of letters can only be used once.

Use your dictionary to help you.

Re	ten	cke	er	Lad	Na
rbe	Sch	tr	Sip	eh	wei
unt	en	He	am	ank	pe
ren	be	ne	cht	se	ben

WORDGAME 24

Here is a list of German words for things you will find in the kitchen. Unfortunately, they have all been jumbled up. Try to work out what each word is and put the word in the boxes on the right. You will see that there are six shaded boxes below. With the six letters in the shaded boxes make up <u>another</u> German word for an object you can find in the kitchen.

1. CSIHT Die Kinder decken den_____

2. DERH Die Kasserolle steht auf dem

_____

3. RSNAHKC Ist die Kaffeekanne in diesem _____ ?

4. SAETS Sie gießt den Tee in die_____

5. SRIGHCRE Das_____ liegt im Spülbecken

6. HKRÜHNSKCLA Hol die Milch aus dem _____ heraus

The word you are looking for is:

WORDGAME 25

Take the four letters given each time and put them in the four empty boxes in the centre of each grid. Arrange them in such a way that you form four six-letter words. Use your dictionary to check the words.

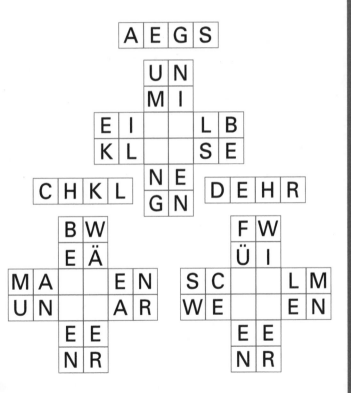

ANSWERS

WORDGAME 1

1	gekannt	6	zahle
2	Aktien	7	einschreiben
3	Kino	8	übel
4	kaufen	9	Ganz
5	Pudel	10	Tante

WORDGAME 2

1	gerecht	7	Wade
2	erreichen	8	Ort
3	erfahren	9	fassen
4	Herbst	10	Stelle
5	treffen	11	Gleis
6	schwer	12	Heim

WORDGAME 3

Morgenrock+Hausschuhe
Handtasche+Lederwaren
Bett+Decke
Kirchturm+Glockengeläut
Fisch+Schuppe
Nest+Elster
Diplom+Student
Buch+Regal

WORDGAME 4

1	Weise *or* Sorte	6	berühmt
2	versuchen	7	Last
3	Brand	8	Karte
4	passieren	9	treffen
5	Überheblichkeit	10	Tendenz

WORDGAME 5

2 Nacht	5 Natur	6 neureich

WORDGAME 6

1	leugnen	6	Armut
2	verstecken	7	lärmend
3	schuldig	8	abreisen
4	verkaufen	9	tapfer
5	erlauben	10	sauber

WORDGAME 7

1	Frikadelle	6	nautisch
2	Spur	7	Gewölbe
3	fein	8	keuchen
4	Lüge	9	mögen
5	Stachel	10	glaubwürdig

WORDGAME 8

1 The sentence is much too long.
2 Underline every clause which starts with a conjunction.
3 Everybody knows Pythagoras' theorem.
4 The orchestra performed the last movement really well.
5 Steffi Graf hasn't lost a set in the championships.
6 All the grounds were in the cup.
7 For deliveries abroad there is a different rate.
8 She jumped for joy.

WORDGAME 9

1	gestellt	7	gesprochen
2	Stelle	8	Sprachen
3	hoffentlich	9	Studium
4	hofft	10	studiert
5	betrügen	11	kürzlich
6	Betrüger	12	gekürzt

WORDGAME 11

1	adj	6	adv
2	noun	7	adj
3	noun	8	verb
4	verb	9	verb
5	adv	10	adj

WORDGAME 12

1 der/das
2 die/das
3 das (*or* ein)/der
4 der/das
5 der/der
6 eine/den

WORDGAME 13

1	englisch	7	alt
2	rot	8	schwarz
3	letzte(r, s)	9	groß
4	klein	10	heftig
5	lang	11	siebte(r, s)
6	gut	12	neu

WORDGAME 14

ich sah
du schläfst
ich bin gewesen
ich schlug
ich habe angerufen
er fährt ab
ich habe studiert
ich hatte
du fängst an
er wäscht
ich wurde
ich habe genommen

WORDGAME 15

gesungen	gelegen
gebissen	gelogen
gebracht	geschnitten
gefroren	gekannt
gerieben	gemocht
gewonnen	gewusst
geholfen	gekonnt
geschehen	

WORDGAME 16

1	vergessen	9	fahren
2	anrufen	10	einladen
3	ankommen	11	bekommen
4	festhalten	12	lesen
5	sein	13	sterben
6	können	14	wegwerfen
7	fliegen	15	mitnehmen
8	werden		

WORDGAME 17

1	d	5	i	9	b
2	j	6	l	10	h
3	c	7	a	11	e
4	k	8	f	12	g

WORDGAME 18

1. health food shop
2. brochure
3. boss
4. crisps
5. dinner jacket
6. wants
7. pension
8. parliamentary party
9. foreign currency

WORDGAME 19

1. resigns
2. wealth
3. know
4. offer
5. service
6. bar
7. guesthouse
8. newspaper

WORDGAME 20

1. Wagen
2. Roller
3. Taxi
4. Fahrrad
5. Flugzeug
6. Bahnhof
7. Zug
8. Lastwagen

WORDGAME 21

1. tragen (= to carry); fragen (= to ask)
2. Stollen (= gallery)
3. Knie (= knee)
4. Brand (= fire)
5. loben (= to praise)
6. dich (= you); sich (= oneself);

mich (= me)
7. Grad (= degree)
8. sinnen (= to ponder); rinnen (= to trickle)
9. braten (= to roast)
10. kindisch (= childish)
11. zeigen (= to show); neigen (= to incline)
12. geben (= to give); leben (= to live); neben (= next to); beben (= to tremble); heben (= to raise); weben (= to weave)
13. Rohr (= pipe, tube)
14. Spur (= race)

WORDGAME 22

1. schwer
2. weinerlich
3. Mahlzeit
4. aufnehmen
5. Laune
6. traurig
7. glatt
8. taub
9. beruhigen
10. Nachricht
11. anlassen
12. Hahn
13. Ort
14. abheben
15. Uhr
16. beschmutzen
17. Tag
18. falten
19. Gewinn

WORDGAME 23

1. Recht
2. Laden
3. Hecke
4. ehren
5. beten
6. Narbe
7. neben
8. Sippe
9. unter
10. Scham
11. weise
12. trank

WORDGAME 24

1. Tisch
2. Herd
3. Schrank
4. Tasse
5. Geschirr
6. Kühlschrank

Hidden word – KESSEL

WORDGAME 25

ENGLISH – GERMAN
ENGLISCH – DEUTSCH

A, a

A [eɪ] *n* (*MUS*) A *nt*; **~ road** Hauptverkehrsstraße *f*

a [eɪ, ə] (*before vowel or silent h: an*) *indef art* 1 ein; eine; **a woman** eine Frau; **a book** ein Buch; **an eagle** ein Adler; **she's a doctor** sie ist Ärztin
2 (*instead of the number "one"*) ein, eine; **a year ago** vor einem Jahr; **a hundred/thousand** *etc* **pounds** (ein) hundert/(ein) tausend *etc* Pfund
3 (*in expressing ratios, prices etc*) pro; **3 a day/week** 3 pro Tag/Woche, 3 am Tag/in der Woche; **10 km an hour** 10 km pro Stunde/in der Stunde

A.A. *n abbr* = **Alcoholics Anonymous**; (*BRIT*) = **Automobile Association**
A.A.A. (*US*) *n abbr* = **American Automobile Association**
aback [əˈbæk] *adv*: **to be taken ~** verblüfft sein
abandon [əˈbændən] *vt* (*give up*) aufgeben; (*desert*) verlassen ♦ *n* Hingabe *f*
abate [əˈbeɪt] *vi* nachlassen, sich legen
abattoir [ˈæbətwɑː*r*] (*BRIT*) *n* Schlachthaus *nt*
abbey [ˈæbɪ] *n* Abtei *f*
abbot [ˈæbət] *n* Abt *m*
abbreviate [əˈbriːvɪeɪt] *vt* abkürzen; **abbreviation** [əbriːvɪˈeɪʃən] *n* Abkürzung *f*
abdicate [ˈæbdɪkeɪt] *vt* aufgeben ♦ *vi* abdanken
abdomen [ˈæbdəmen] *n* Unterleib *m*
abduct [æbˈdʌkt] *vt* entführen
aberration [æbəˈreɪʃən] *n* (geistige) Verwirrung *f*
abet [əˈbet] *vt see* **aid**
abeyance [əˈbeɪəns] *n*: **in ~** in der Schwebe; (*disuse*) außer Kraft

abide [əˈbaɪd] *vt* vertragen; leiden; **~ by** *vt* sich halten an +*acc*
ability [əˈbɪlɪtɪ] *n* (*power*) Fähigkeit *f*; (*skill*) Geschicklichkeit *f*
abject [ˈæbdʒekt] *adj* (*liar*) übel; (*poverty*) größte(r, s); (*apology*) zerknirscht
ablaze [əˈbleɪz] *adj* in Flammen
able [ˈeɪbl] *adj* geschickt, fähig; **to be ~ to do sth** etw tun können; **~-bodied** [ˈeɪblˈbɒdɪd] *adj* kräftig; (*seaman*) Voll-; **ably** [ˈeɪblɪ] *adv* geschickt
abnormal [æbˈnɔːməl] *adj* regelwidrig, abnorm
aboard [əˈbɔːd] *adv*, *prep* an Bord +*gen*
abode [əˈbəʊd] *n*: **of no fixed ~** ohne festen Wohnsitz
abolish [əˈbɒlɪʃ] *vt* abschaffen; **abolition** [æbəˈlɪʃən] *n* Abschaffung *f*
abominable [əˈbɒmɪnəbl] *adj* scheußlich
aborigine [æbəˈrɪdʒɪnɪ] *n* Ureinwohner *m*
abort [əˈbɔːt] *vt* abtreiben; fehlgebären; **~ion** [əˈbɔːʃən] *n* Abtreibung *f*; (*miscarriage*) Fehlgeburt *f*; **~ive** *adj* misslungen
abound [əˈbaʊnd] *vi* im Überfluss vorhanden sein; **to ~ in** Überfluss haben an +*dat*

about [əˈbaʊt] *adv* 1 (*approximately*) etwa, ungefähr; **about a hundred/thousand** *etc* etwa hundert/tausend *etc*; **at about 2 o'clock** etwa um 2 Uhr; **I've just about finished** ich bin gerade fertig
2 (*referring to place*) herum, umher; **to leave things lying about** Sachen herumliegen lassen; **to run/walk** *etc* **about** herumrennen/gehen *etc*
3: **to be about to do sth** im Begriff sein, etw zu tun; **he was about to go to bed** er wollte gerade ins Bett gehen
♦ *prep* 1 (*relating to*) über +*acc*; **a book**

about London ein Buch über London; **what is it about?** worum geht es?; (*book etc*) wovon handelt es?; **we talked about it** wir haben darüber geredet; **what** or **how about doing this?** wollen wir das machen? 2 (*referring to place*) um (... herum;) **to walk about the town** in der Stadt herumgehen; **her clothes were scattered about the room** ihre Kleider waren über das ganze Zimmer verstreut

about-turn [ə'baut'təːn] *n* Kehrtwendung *f*
above [ə'bʌv] *adv* oben ♦ *prep* über; **~ all** vor allem; **~ board** *adj* offen, ehrlich
abrasive [ə'breɪzɪv] *adj* Abschleif-; (*personality*) zermürbend, aufreibend
abreast [ə'brɛst] *adv* nebeneinander; **to keep ~ of** Schritt halten mit
abroad [ə'brɔːd] *adv* (*be*) im Ausland; (*go*) ins Ausland
abrupt [ə'brʌpt] *adj* (*sudden*) abrupt, jäh; (*curt*) schroff; **~ly** *adv* abrupt
abscess ['æbsɪs] *n* Geschwür *nt*
abscond [əb'skɔnd] *vi* flüchten, sich davonmachen
abseil ['æbseɪl] *vi* (*also:* **~ down**) sich abseilen
absence ['æbsəns] *n* Abwesenheit *f*
absent ['æbsənt] *adj* abwesend, nicht da; (*lost in thought*) geistesabwesend; **~-minded** *adj* zerstreut
absolute ['æbsəluːt] *adj* absolut; (*power*) unumschränkt; (*rubbish*) vollkommen, rein; **~ly** [æbsə'luːtlɪ] *adv* absolut, vollkommen; **~ly!** ganz bestimmt!
absolve [əb'zɔlv] *vt* entbinden; freisprechen
absorb [əb'zɔːb] *vt* aufsaugen, absorbieren; (*fig*) ganz in Anspruch nehmen, fesseln; **to be ~ed in a book** in ein Buch vertieft sein; **~ent cotton** (*US*) *n* Verbandwatte *f*; **~ing** *adj* aufsaugend; (*fig*) packend; **absorption** [əb'sɔːpʃən] *n* Aufsaugung *f*, Absorption *f*; (*fig*) Versunkenheit *f*
abstain [əb'steɪn] *vi* (*in vote*) sich enthalten; **to ~ from** (*keep from*) sich enthalten +*gen*
abstemious [əb'stiːmɪəs] *adj* enthaltsam
abstinence ['æbstɪnəns] *n* Enthaltsamkeit *f*

abstract ['æbstrækt] *adj* abstrakt
absurd [əb'sɜːd] *adj* absurd
abundance [ə'bʌndəns] *n*: **~ (of)** Überfluss *m* (an +*dat*); **abundant** [ə'bʌndənt] *adj* reichlich
abuse [*n* ə'bjuːs, *vb* ə'bjuːz] *n* (*rude language*) Beschimpfung *f*; (*ill usage*) Missbrauch *m*; (*bad practice*) (Amts)missbrauch *m* ♦ *vt* (*misuse*) missbrauchen; **abusive** [ə'bjuːsɪv] *adj* beleidigend, Schimpf-
abysmal [ə'bɪzməl] *adj* scheußlich; (*ignorance*) bodenlos
abyss [ə'bɪs] *n* Abgrund *m*
AC *abbr* (= *alternating current*) Wechselstrom *m*
academic [ækə'dɛmɪk] *adj* akademisch; (*theoretical*) theoretisch ♦ *n* Akademiker(in) *m(f)*
academy [ə'kædəmɪ] *n* (*school*) Hochschule *f*; (*society*) Akademie *f*
accelerate [æk'sɛləreɪt] *vi* schneller werden; (*AUT*) Gas geben ♦ *vt* beschleunigen; **acceleration** [æksɛlə'reɪʃən] *n* Beschleunigung *f*; **accelerator** [æk'sɛləreɪtər] *n* Gas(pedal) *nt*
accent ['æksɛnt] *n* Akzent *m*, Tonfall *m*; (*mark*) Akzent *m*; (*stress*) Betonung *f*
accept [ək'sɛpt] *vt* (*take*) annehmen; (*agree to*) akzeptieren; **~able** *adj* annehmbar; **~ance** *n* Annahme *f*
access ['æksɛs] *n* Zugang *m*; **~ible** [æk'sɛsəbl] *adj* (*easy to approach*) zugänglich; (*within reach*) (leicht) erreichbar
accessory [æk'sɛsərɪ] *n* Zubehörteil *nt*; **toilet accessories** Toilettenartikel *pl*
accident ['æksɪdənt] *n* Unfall *m*; (*coincidence*) Zufall *m*; **by ~** zufällig; **~al** [æksɪ'dɛntl] *adj* unbeabsichtigt; **~ally** [æksɪ'dɛntəlɪ] *adv* zufällig; **~ insurance** *n* Unfallversicherung *f*; **~-prone** *adj*: **to be ~-prone** zu Unfällen neigen
acclaim [ə'kleɪm] *vt* zujubeln +*dat* ♦ *n* Beifall *m*
acclimatize [ə'klaɪmətaɪz] *vt*: **to become ~d (to)** sich gewöhnen (an +*acc*), sich akklimatisieren (in +*dat*)
accommodate [ə'kɔmədeɪt] *vt*

unterbringen; (*hold*) Platz haben für; (*oblige*) (aus)helfen +*dat*

accommodating [ə'kɔmədeıtıŋ] *adj* entgegenkommend

accommodation [əkɔmə'deıʃən] (*US* **accommodations**) *n* Unterkunft *f*

accompany [ə'kʌmpənı] *vt* begleiten

accomplice [ə'kʌmplıs] *n* Helfershelfer *m*, Komplize *m*

accomplish [ə'kʌmplıʃ] *vt* (*fulfil*) durchführen; (*finish*) vollenden; (*aim*) erreichen; **~ed** *adj* vollendet, ausgezeichnet; **~ment** *n* (*skill*) Fähigkeit *f*; (*completion*) Vollendung *f*; (*feat*) Leistung *f*

accord [ə'kɔ:d] *n* in Übereinstimmung *f* ♦ *vt* gewähren; **of one's own ~** freiwillig; **~ing to** nach, laut +*gen*; **~ance** *n*: **in ~ance with** in Übereinstimmung mit; **~ingly** *adv* danach, dementsprechend

accordion [ə'kɔ:dıən] *n* Akkordeon *nt*

accost [ə'kɔst] *vt* ansprechen

account [ə'kaunt] *n* (*bill*) Rechnung *f*; (*narrative*) Bericht *m*; (*report*) Rechenschaftsbericht *m*; (*in bank*) Konto *nt*; (*importance*) Geltung *f*; **~s** *npl* (*FIN*) Bücher *pl*; **on ~** auf Rechnung; **of no ~** ohne Bedeutung; **on no ~** keinesfalls; **on ~ of** wegen; **to take into ~** berücksichtigen; **~ for** *vt fus* (*expenditure*) Rechenschaft ablegen für; **how do you ~ for that?** wie erklären Sie (sich) das?; **~able** *adj* verantwortlich; **~ancy** [ə'kauntənsı] *n* Buchhaltung *f*; **~ant** [ə'kauntənt] *n* Wirtschaftsprüfer(in) *m(f)*; **~ number** *n* Kontonummer *f*

accumulate [ə'kju:mjuleıt] *vt* ansammeln ♦ *vi* sich ansammeln

accuracy ['ækjurəsı] *n* Genauigkeit *f*

accurate ['ækjurıt] *adj* genau; **~ly** *adv* genau, richtig

accusation [ækju'zeıʃən] *n* Anklage *f*, Beschuldigung *f*

accuse [ə'kju:z] *vt* anklagen, beschuldigen; **~d** *n* Angeklagte(r) *f(m)*

accustom [ə'kʌstəm] *vt*: **to ~ sb (to sth)** jdn (an etw *acc*) gewöhnen; **~ed** *adj* gewohnt

ace [eıs] *n* Ass *nt*; (*inf*) Ass *nt*, Kanone *f*

ache [eık] *n* Schmerz *m* ♦ *vi* (*be sore*) schmerzen, wehtun

achieve [ə'tʃi:v] *vt* zustande *or* zu Stande bringen; (*aim*) erreichen; **~ment** *n* Leistung *f*; (*act*) Erreichen *nt*

acid ['æsıd] *n* Säure *f* ♦ *adj* sauer, scharf; **~ rain** *n* saure(r) Regen *m*

acknowledge [ək'nɔlıdʒ] *vt* (*receipt*) bestätigen; (*admit*) zugeben; **~ment** *n* Anerkennung *f*; (*letter*) Empfangsbestätigung *f*

acne ['æknı] *n* Akne *f*

acorn ['eıkɔ:n] *n* Eichel *f*

acoustic [ə'ku:stık] *adj* akustisch; **~s** *npl* Akustik *f*

acquaint [ə'kweınt] *vt* vertraut machen; **to be ~ed with sb** mit jdm bekannt sein; **~ance** *n* (*person*) Bekannte(r) *f(m)*; (*knowledge*) Kenntnis *f*

acquire [ə'kwaıər] *vt* erwerben; **acquisition** [ækwı'zıʃən] *n* Errungenschaft *f*; (*act*) Erwerb *m*

acquit [ə'kwıt] *vt* (*free*) freisprechen; **to ~ o.s. well** sich bewähren; **~tal** *n* Freispruch *m*

acre ['eıkər] *n* Morgen *m*

acrid ['ækrıd] *adj* (*smell, taste*) bitter; (*smoke*) beißend

acrobat ['ækrəbæt] *n* Akrobat *m*

across [ə'krɔs] *prep* über +*acc* ♦ *adv* hinüber, herüber; **he lives ~ the river** er wohnt auf der anderen Seite des Flusses; **ten metres ~** zehn Meter breit; **he lives ~ from us** er wohnt uns gegenüber; **to run/swim ~** hinüberlaufen/schwimmen

acrylic [ə'krılık] *adj* Acryl-

act [ækt] *n* (*deed*) Tat *f*; (*JUR*) Gesetz *nt*; (*THEAT*) Akt *m*; (: *turn*) Nummer *f* ♦ *vi* (*take -ion*) handeln; (*behave*) sich verhalten; (*pretend*) vorgeben; (*THEAT*) spielen ♦ *vt* (*in play*) spielen; **to ~ as** fungieren als; **~ing** *adj* stellvertretend ♦ *n* Schauspielkunst *f*; (*performance*) Aufführung *f*

action ['ækʃən] *n* (*deed*) Tat *f*; Handlung *f*; (*motion*) Bewegung *f*; (*way of working*) Funktionieren *nt*; (*battle*) Einsatz *m*, Gefecht *nt*; (*lawsuit*) Klage *f*, Prozess *m*; **out of ~**

(*person*) nicht einsatzfähig; (*thing*) außer Betrieb; **to take ~** etwas unternehmen; **~ replay** n (TV) Wiederholung f

activate ['æktɪveɪt] vt (*mechanism*) betätigen; (CHEM, PHYS) aktivieren

active ['æktɪv] adj (*brisk*) rege, tatkräftig; (*working*) aktiv; (GRAM) aktiv, Tätigkeits-; **~ly** adv aktiv; (*dislike*) offen

activity [æk'tɪvɪtɪ] n Aktivität f; (*doings*) Unternehmungen pl; (*occupation*) Tätigkeit f; **~ holiday** n Aktivurlaub m

actor ['æktə*] n Schauspieler m

actress ['æktrɪs] n Schauspielerin f

actual ['æktjʊəl] adj wirklich; **~ly** adv tatsächlich; **~ly no** eigentlich nicht

acumen ['ækjʊmən] n Scharfsinn m

acute [ə'kjuːt] adj (*severe*) heftig, akut; (*keen*) scharfsinnig

ad [æd] n abbr = **advertisement**

A.D. adv abbr (= *Anno Domini*) n. Chr.

adamant ['ædəmənt] adj eisern; hartnäckig

adapt [ə'dæpt] vt anpassen ♦ vi: **to ~ (to)** sich anpassen (an +acc); **~able** adj anpassungsfähig; **~ation** [ædæp'teɪʃən] n (THEAT etc) Bearbeitung f; (*adjustment*) Anpassung f; **~er**, **~or** (ELEC) Zwischenstecker m

add [æd] vt (*join*) hinzufügen; (*numbers: also:* **~ up**) addieren; **~ up** vi (*make sense*) stimmen; **~ up to** vt fus ausmachen

adder ['ædə*] n Kreuzotter f, Natter f

addict ['ædɪkt] n Süchtige(r) f(m); **~ed** [ə'dɪktɪd] adj: **~ed to** -süchtig; **~ion** [ə'dɪkʃən] n Sucht f; **~ive** [ə'dɪktɪv] adj: **to be ~ive** süchtig machen

addition [ə'dɪʃən] n Anhang m, Addition f; (MATH) Addition f, Zusammenzählen nt; **in ~** zusätzlich, außerdem; **~al** adj zusätzlich, weiter

additive ['ædɪtɪv] n Zusatz m

address [ə'drɛs] n Adresse f; (*speech*) Ansprache f ♦ vt (*letter*) adressieren; (*speak to*) ansprechen; (*make speech to*) eine Ansprache halten an +acc

adept ['ædɛpt] adj geschickt; **to be ~ at** gut sein in +dat

adequate ['ædɪkwɪt] adj angemessen

adhere [əd'hɪə*] vi: **to ~ to** haften an +dat; (*fig*) festhalten an +dat

adhesive [əd'hiːzɪv] adj klebend; Kleb(e)- ♦ n Klebstoff m; **~ tape** n (BRIT) Klebestreifen m; (US) Heftpflaster nt

ad hoc [æd'hɔk] adj (*decision, committee*) Ad-hoc- ♦ adv ad hoc

adjacent [ə'dʒeɪsənt] adj benachbart; **~ to** angrenzend an +acc

adjective ['ædʒɛktɪv] n Adjektiv nt, Eigenschaftswort nt

adjoining [ə'dʒɔɪnɪŋ] adj benachbart, Neben-

adjourn [ə'dʒɜːn] vt vertagen ♦ vi abbrechen

adjudicate [ə'dʒuːdɪkeɪt] vi entscheiden, ein Urteil fällen

adjust [ə'dʒʌst] vt (*alter*) anpassen; (*put right*) regulieren, richtig stellen ♦ vi sich anpassen; **~able** adj verstellbar

ad-lib [æd'lɪb] vt, vi improvisieren ♦ adv: **ad lib** aus dem Stegreif

administer [əd'mɪnɪstə*] vt (*manage*) verwalten; (*dispense*) ausüben; (*justice*) sprechen; (*medicine*) geben; **administration** [ədmɪnɪs'treɪʃən] n Verwaltung f; (POL) Regierung f; **administrative** [əd'mɪnɪstrətɪv] adj Verwaltungs-; **administrator** [əd'mɪnɪstreɪtə*] n Verwaltungsbeamte(r) f(m)

Admiralty ['ædmərəltɪ] (BRIT) n Admiralität f

admiration [ædmə'reɪʃən] n Bewunderung f

admire [əd'maɪə*] vt (*respect*) bewundern; (*love*) verehren; **~r** n Bewunderer m

admission [əd'mɪʃən] n (*entrance*) Einlass m; (*fee*) Eintritt(spreis m) m; (*confession*) Geständnis nt; **~ charge** n Eintritt(spreis) m

admit [əd'mɪt] vt (*let in*) einlassen; (*confess*) gestehen; (*accept*) anerkennen; **~tance** n Zulassung f; **~tedly** adv zugegebenermaßen

admonish [əd'mɔnɪʃ] vt ermahnen

ad nauseam [æd'nɔːsɪæm] adv (*repeat, talk*) endlos

ado [ə'duː] n: **without more ~** ohne weitere Umstände

adolescence [ædəʊ'lesns] *n* Jugendalter *nt*; **adolescent** [ædəʊ'lesnt] *adj* jugendlich ♦ *n* Jugendliche(r) *f(m)*

adopt [ə'dɒpt] *vt* (*child*) adoptieren; (*idea*) übernehmen; **~ion** [ə'dɒpʃən] *n* Adoption *f*; Übernahme *f*

adore [ə'dɔːʳ] *vt* anbeten; verehren

adorn [ə'dɔːn] *vt* schmücken

Adriatic [eɪdrɪ'ætɪk] *n*: **the ~ (Sea)** die Adria

adrift [ə'drɪft] *adv* Wind und Wellen preisgegeben

adult [ˈædʌlt] *n* Erwachsene(r) *f(m)*

adultery [ə'dʌltərɪ] *n* Ehebruch *m*

advance [əd'vɑːns] *n* (*progress*) Vorrücken *nt*; (*money*) Vorschuss *m* ♦ *vt* (*move forward*) vorrücken; (*money*) vorschießen; (*argument*) vorbringen ♦ *vi* vorwärts gehen; **in ~** im Voraus; **~ booking** *n* Vorverkauf *m*; **~d** *adj* (*ahead*) vorgerückt; (*modern*) fortgeschritten; (*study*) für Fortgeschrittene

advantage [əd'vɑːntɪdʒ] *n* Vorteil *m*; **to have an ~ over sb** jdm gegenüber im Vorteil sein; **to take ~ of** (*misuse*) ausnutzen; (*profit from*) Nutzen ziehen aus; **~ous** [ædvən'teɪdʒəs] *adj* vorteilhaft

advent ['ædvənt] *n* Ankunft *f*; **A~** Advent *m*

adventure [əd'ventʃəʳ] *n* Abenteuer *nt*; **adventurous** [əd'ventʃərəs] *adj* abenteuerlich, waghalsig

adverb ['ædvɜːb] *n* Adverb *nt*, Umstandswort *nt*

adversary ['ædvəsərɪ] *n* Gegner *m*

adverse ['ædvɜːs] *adj* widrig; **adversity** [əd'vɜːsɪtɪ] *n* Widrigkeit *f*, Missgeschick *nt*

advert ['ædvɜːt] *n* Anzeige *f*; **~ise** ['ædvətaɪz] *vt* werben für ♦ *vi* annoncieren; **to ~ise for sth** etw (per Anzeige) suchen; **~isement** [əd'vɜːtɪsmənt] *n* Anzeige *f*, Inserat *nt*; **~iser** *n* (*in newspaper etc*) Inserent *m*; **~ising** *n* Werbung *f*

advice [əd'vaɪs] *n* Rat(schlag) *m*

advisable [əd'vaɪzəbl] *adj* ratsam

advise [əd'vaɪz] *vt*: **to ~ (sb)** (jdm) raten; **~dly** [əd'vaɪzɪdlɪ] *adv* (*deliberately*) bewusst; **~r** *n* Berater *m*; **advisory** [əd'vaɪzərɪ] *adj* beratend, Beratungs-

advocate [*vb* 'ædvəkeɪt, *n* 'ædvəkət] *vt* vertreten ♦ *n* Befürworter(in) *m(f)*

Aegean [iː'dʒiːən] *n*: **the ~ (Sea)** die Ägäis

aerial ['ɛərɪəl] *n* Antenne *f* ♦ *adj* Luft-

aerobics [ɛə'rəʊbɪks] *n* Aerobic *nt*

aerodynamic ['ɛərəʊdaɪ'næmɪk] *adj* aerodynamisch

aeroplane ['ɛərəpleɪn] *n* Flugzeug *nt*

aerosol ['ɛərəsɒl] *n* Aerosol *nt*; Sprühdose *f*

aesthetic [iːs'θetɪk] *adj* ästhetisch

afar [ə'fɑːʳ] *adv*: **from ~** aus der Ferne

affable ['æfəbl] *adj* umgänglich

affair [ə'fɛəʳ] *n* (*concern*) Angelegenheit *f*; (*event*) Ereignis *nt*; (*love ~*) Verhältnis *nt*; **~s** *npl* (*business*) Geschäfte *pl*

affect [ə'fekt] *vt* (*influence*) (ein)wirken auf +*acc*; (*move deeply*) bewegen; **this change doesn't ~ us** diese Änderung betrifft uns nicht; **~ed** *adj* affektiert, gekünstelt

affection [ə'fekʃən] *n* Zuneigung *f*; **~ate** *adj* liebevoll

affiliated [ə'fɪlɪeɪtɪd] *adj* angeschlossen

affinity [ə'fɪnɪtɪ] *n* (*attraction*) gegenseitige Anziehung *f*; (*relationship*) Verwandtschaft *f*

affirmative [ə'fɜːmətɪv] *adj* bestätigend

afflict [ə'flɪkt] *vt* quälen, heimsuchen

affluence ['æfluəns] *n* (*wealth*) Wohlstand *m*; **affluent** *adj* wohlhabend, Wohlstands-

afford [ə'fɔːd] *vt* sich *dat* leisten; (*yield*) bieten, einbringen

afield [ə'fiːld] *adv*: **far ~** weit fort

afloat [ə'fləʊt] *adj*: **to be ~** schwimmen

afoot [ə'fʊt] *adv* im Gang

afraid [ə'freɪd] *adj* ängstlich; **to be ~ of** Angst haben vor +*dat*; **to be ~ to do sth** sich scheuen, etw zu tun; **I am ~ I have ...** ich habe leider ...; **I'm ~ so/not** leider/ leider nicht; **I am ~ that ...** ich fürchte(, dass) ...

afresh [ə'freʃ] *adv* von neuem

Africa ['æfrɪkə] *n* Afrika *nt*; **~n** *adj* afrikanisch ♦ *n* Afrikaner(in) *m(f)*

after ['ɑːftəʳ] *prep* nach; (*following, seeking*) hinter ... *dat* ... her; (*in imitation*) nach, im Stil von ♦ *adv*: **soon ~** bald danach ♦ *conj* nachdem; **what are you ~?** was wollen Sie?; **~ he left** nachdem er gegangen war; **~ you!** nach Ihnen!; **~ all** letzten Endes; **~ having shaved** als er sich rasiert hatte;

~**effects** *npl* Nachwirkungen *pl*; ~**math** *n* Auswirkungen *pl*; ~**noon** *n* Nachmittag *m*; ~**s** (*inf*) *n* (*dessert*) Nachtisch *m*; ~**sales service** (*BRIT*) *n* Kundendienst *m*; ~**shave** (**lotion**) *n* Rasierwasser *nt*; ~**sun** *n* Aftersunlotion *f*; ~**thought** *n* nachträgliche(r) Einfall *m*; ~**wards** *adv* danach, nachher

again [əˈɡɛn] *adv* wieder, noch einmal; (*besides*) außerdem, ferner; ~ **and** ~ immer wieder

against [əˈɡɛnst] *prep* gegen

age [eɪdʒ] *n* (*of person*) Alter *nt*; (*in history*) Zeitalter *nt* ♦ *vi* altern, alt werden ♦ *vt* älter machen; **to come of** ~ mündig werden; **20 years of** ~ 20 Jahre alt; **it's been** ~**s since** ... es ist ewig her, seit ...

aged[1] [eɪdʒd] *adj* ... Jahre alt, -jährig

aged[2] [eɪdʒɪd] *adj* (*elderly*) betagt ♦ *npl*: **the** ~ die Alten *pl*

age group *n* Altersgruppe *f*

age limit *n* Altersgrenze *f*

agency [ˈeɪdʒənsɪ] *n* Agentur *f*; Vermittlung *f*; (*CHEM*) Wirkung *f*; **through** *or* **by the** ~ **of** ... mithilfe *or* mit Hilfe von ...

agenda [əˈdʒɛndə] *n* Tagesordnung *f*

agent [ˈeɪdʒənt] *n* (*COMM*) Vertreter *m*; (*spy*) Agent *m*

aggravate [ˈæɡrəveɪt] *vt* (*make worse*) verschlimmern; (*irritate*) reizen

aggregate [ˈæɡrɪɡɪt] *n* Summe *f*

aggression [əˈɡrɛʃən] *n* Aggression *f*; **aggressive** [əˈɡrɛsɪv] *adj* aggressiv

aghast [əˈɡɑːst] *adj* entsetzt

agile [ˈædʒaɪl] *adj* flink; agil; (*mind*) rege

agitate [ˈædʒɪteɪt] *vt* rütteln; **to** ~ **for** sich stark machen für

AGM *n abbr* (= *annual general meeting*) JHV *f*

ago [əˈɡəʊ] *adv*: **two days** ~ vor zwei Tagen; **not long** ~ vor kurzem; **it's so long** ~ es ist schon so lange her

agog [əˈɡɒɡ] *adj* gespannt

agonizing [ˈæɡənaɪzɪŋ] *adj* quälend

agony [ˈæɡənɪ] *n* Qual *f*; **to be in** ~ Qualen leiden

agree [əˈɡriː] *vt* (*date*) vereinbaren ♦ *vi* (*have same opinion, correspond*) übereinstimmen;

(*consent*) zustimmen; (*be in harmony*) sich vertragen; **to** ~ **to sth** einer Sache *dat* zustimmen; **to** ~ **that** ... (*admit*) zugeben, dass ...; **to** ~ **to do sth** sich bereit erklären, etw zu tun; **garlic doesn't** ~ **with me** Knoblauch vertrage ich nicht; **I** ~ einverstanden, ich stimme zu; **to** ~ **on sth** sich auf etw *acc* einigen; ~**able** *adj* (*pleasing*) liebenswürdig; (*willing to consent*) einverstanden; ~**d** *adj* vereinbart; ~**ment** *n* (~*ing*) Übereinstimmung *f*; (*contract*) Vereinbarung *f*, Vertrag *m*; **to be in** ~**ment** übereinstimmen

agricultural [æɡrɪˈkʌltʃərəl] *adj* landwirtschaftlich, Landwirtschafts-

agriculture [ˈæɡrɪkʌltʃər] *n* Landwirtschaft *f*

aground [əˈɡraʊnd] *adv*: **to run** ~ auf Grund laufen

ahead [əˈhɛd] *adv* vorwärts; **to be** ~ voraus sein; ~ **of time** der Zeit voraus; **go right** *or* **straight** ~ gehen Sie geradeaus; fahren Sie geradeaus

aid [eɪd] *n* (*assistance*) Hilfe *f*, Unterstützung *f*; (*person*) Hilfe *f*; (*thing*) Hilfsmittel *nt* ♦ *vt* unterstützen, helfen +*dat*; **in** ~ **of** zugunsten *or* zu Gunsten +*gen*; **to** ~ **and abet sb** jdm Beihilfe leisten

aide [eɪd] *n* (*person*) Gehilfe *m*; (*MIL*) Adjutant *m*

AIDS [eɪdz] *n abbr* (= *acquired immune deficiency syndrome*) Aids *nt*; **AIDS-related** aidsbedingt

ailing [ˈeɪlɪŋ] *adj* kränkelnd

ailment [ˈeɪlmənt] *n* Leiden *nt*

aim [eɪm] *vt* (*gun, camera*) richten ♦ *vi* (*with gun: also:* **take** ~) zielen; (*intend*) beabsichtigen ♦ *n* (*intention*) Absicht *f*, Ziel *nt*; (*pointing*) Zielen *nt*, Richten *nt*; **to** ~ **at sth** auf etw *dat* richten; (*fig*) etw anstreben; **to** ~ **to do sth** vorhaben, etw zu tun; ~**less** *adj* ziellos; ~**lessly** *adv* ziellos

ain't [eɪnt] (*inf*) = **am not**; **are not**; **is not**; **has not**; **have not**

air [eər] *n* Luft *f*; (*manner*) Miene *f*, Anschein *m*; (*MUS*) Melodie *f* ♦ *vt* lüften; (*fig*) an die Öffentlichkeit bringen ♦ *cpd* Luft-; **by** ~ (*travel*) auf dem Luftweg; **to be on the** ~

(*RADIO, TV*: *programme*) gesendet werden;
~**bed** (*BRIT*) *n* Luftmatratze *f*; ~-
conditioned *adj* mit Klimaanlage; ~-
conditioning *n* Klimaanlage *f*; ~**craft** *n*
Flugzeug *nt*, Maschine *f*; ~**craft carrier** *n*
Flugzeugträger *m*; ~**field** *n* Flugplatz *m*; ~
force *n* Luftwaffe *f*; ~ **freshener** *n*
Raumspray *nt*; ~**gun** *n* Luftgewehr *nt*; ~
hostess (*BRIT*) *n* Stewardess *f*; ~ **letter**
(*BRIT*) *n* Luftpostbrief *m*; ~**lift** *n* Luftbrücke
f; ~**line** *n* Luftverkehrsgesellschaft *f*; ~**liner**
n Verkehrsflugzeug *nt*; ~**lock** *n* Luftblase *f*;
~**mail** *n*: **by ~mail** mit Luftpost; ~ **miles**
npl ≃ Flugkilometer *pl*; ~**plane** (*US*) *n*
Flugzeug *nt*; ~**port** *n* Flughafen *m*,
Flugplatz *m*; ~ **raid** *n* Luftangriff *m*; ~**sick**
adj luftkrank; ~**space** *n* Luftraum *m*;
~**strip** *n* Landestreifen *m*; ~ **terminal** *n*
Terminal *m*; ~**tight** *adj* luftdicht; ~ **traffic**
controller *n* Fluglotse *m*; ~**y** *adj* luftig;
(*manner*) leichtfertig

aisle [aɪl] *n* Gang *m*; ~ **seat** *n* Sitz *m* am
Gang

ajar [əˈdʒɑːʳ] *adv* angelehnt; einen Spalt offen

alarm [əˈlɑːm] *n* (*warning*) Alarm *m*; (*bell etc*)
Alarmanlage *f*; (*anxiety*) Sorge *f* ♦ *vt*
erschrecken; ~ **call** *n* (*in hotel etc*) Weckruf
m; ~ **clock** *n* Wecker *m*

Albania [ælˈbeɪnɪə] *n* Albanien *nt*

albeit [ɔːlˈbiːɪt] *conj* obgleich

album [ˈælbəm] *n* Album *nt*

alcohol [ˈælkəhɒl] *n* Alkohol *m*; ~-**free** *adj*
alkoholfrei; ~**ic** [ælkəˈhɒlɪk] *adj* (*drink*)
alkoholisch ♦ *n* Alkoholiker(in) *m(f)*; ~**ism** *n*
Alkoholismus *m*

alert [əˈlɜːt] *adj* wachsam ♦ *n* Alarm *m* ♦ *vt*
alarmieren; **to be on the ~** wachsam sein

Algeria [ælˈdʒɪərɪə] *n* Algerien *nt*

alias [ˈeɪlɪəs] *adv* alias ♦ *n* Deckname *m*

alibi [ˈælɪbaɪ] *n* Alibi *nt*

alien [ˈeɪlɪən] *n* Ausländer *m* ♦ *adj* (*foreign*)
ausländisch; (*strange*) fremd; ~ **to** fremd
+*dat*; ~**ate** *vt* entfremden

alight [əˈlaɪt] *adj* brennend; (*of building*) in
Flammen ♦ *vi* (*descend*) aussteigen; (*bird*)
sich setzen

align [əˈlaɪn] *vt* ausrichten

alike [əˈlaɪk] *adj* gleich, ähnlich ♦ *adv* gleich,
ebenso; **to look ~** sich *dat* ähnlich sehen

alimony [ˈælɪmənɪ] *n* Unterhalt *m*, Alimente
pl

alive [əˈlaɪv] *adj* (*living*) lebend; (*lively*)
lebendig, aufgeweckt; ~ **(with)** (*full of*) voll
(von), wimmelnd (von)

KEYWORD

all [ɔːl] *adj* alle(r, s); **all day / night** den
ganzen Tag/die ganze Nacht; **all men are**
equal alle Menschen sind gleich; **all five**
came alle fünf kamen; **all the books / food**
die ganzen Bücher/das ganze Essen; **all the**
time die ganze Zeit (über); **all his life** sein
ganzes Leben (lang)
♦ *pron* 1 alles; **I ate it all, I ate all of it** ich
habe alles gegessen; **all of us / the boys**
went wir gingen alle/alle Jungen gingen;
we all sat down wir setzten uns alle
2 (*in phrases*): **above all** vor allem; **after all**
schließlich; **at all: not at all** (*in answer to*
question) überhaupt nicht; (*in answer to*
thanks) gern geschehen; **I'm not at all**
tired ich bin überhaupt nicht müde;
anything at all will do es ist egal, welche(r,
s); **all in all** alles in allem
♦ *adv* ganz; **all alone** ganz allein; **it's not**
as hard as all that so schwer ist es nun
auch wieder nicht; **all the more / the**
better umso mehr/besser; **all but** fast; **the**
score is 2 all es steht 2 zu 2

---

allay [əˈleɪ] *vt* (*fears*) beschwichtigen

all clear *n* Entwarnung *f*

allegation [ælɪˈgeɪʃən] *n* Behauptung *f*

allege [əˈledʒ] *vt* (*declare*) behaupten;
(*falsely*) vorgeben; ~**dly** *adv* angeblich

allegiance [əˈliːdʒəns] *n* Treue *f*

allergic [əˈlɜːdʒɪk] *adj*: ~ **(to)** allergisch
(gegen)

allergy [ˈælədʒɪ] *n* Allergie *f*

alleviate [əˈliːvɪeɪt] *vt* lindern

alley [ˈælɪ] *n* Gasse *f*, Durchgang *m*

alliance [əˈlaɪəns] *n* Bund *m*, Allianz *f*

allied [ˈælaɪd] *adj* vereinigt; (*powers*) alliiert; ~
(to) verwandt (mit)

all: ~-**in** (*BRIT*) *adj, adv* (*charge*) alles inbegriffen, Gesamt-; ~-**in wrestling** *n* Freistilringen *nt*; ~-**night** *adj* (*café, cinema*) die ganze Nacht geöffnet, Nacht-

allocate ['æləkeɪt] *vt* zuteilen

allot [ə'lɒt] *vt* zuteilen; ~**ment** *n* (*share*) Anteil *m*; (*plot*) Schrebergarten *m*

all-out ['ɔːlaut] *adj* total; **all out** *adv* mit voller Kraft

allow [ə'lau] *vt* (*permit*) erlauben, gestatten; (*grant*) bewilligen; (*deduct*) abziehen; (*concede*): **to** ~ **that** ... annehmen, dass ...; **to** ~ **sb sth** jdm etw erlauben, jdm etw gestatten; **to** ~ **sb to do sth** jdm erlauben *or* gestatten, etw zu tun; ~ **for** *vt fus* berücksichtigen, einplanen; ~**ance** *n* Beihilfe *f*; **to make** ~**ances for** berücksichtigen

alloy ['ælɔɪ] *n* Metalllegierung *f*

all: ~ **right** *adv* (*well*) gut; (*correct*) richtig; (*as answer*) okay; ~-**round** *adj* (*sportsman*) allseitig, Allround-; (*view*) Rundum-; ~-**time** *adj* (*record, high*) ... aller Zeiten, Höchst-

allude [ə'luːd] *vi*: **to** ~ **to** hinweisen auf +*acc*, anspielen auf +*acc*

alluring [ə'ljuərɪŋ] *adj* verlockend

ally [*n* 'ælaɪ, *vb* ə'laɪ] *n* Verbündete(r) *f(m)*; (*POL*) Alliierte(r) *f(m)* ♦ *vr*: **to** ~ **o.s. with** sich verbünden mit

almighty [ɔːl'maɪtɪ] *adj* allmächtig

almond ['ɑːmənd] *n* Mandel *f*

almost ['ɔːlməust] *adv* fast, beinahe

alms [ɑːmz] *npl* Almosen *nt*

alone [ə'ləun] *adj, adv* allein; **to leave sth** ~ etw sein lassen; **let** ~ ... geschweige denn ...

along [ə'lɒŋ] *prep* entlang, längs ♦ *adv* (*onward*) vorwärts, weiter; ~ **with** zusammen mit; **he was limping** ~ humpelte einher; **all** ~ (*all the time*) die ganze Zeit; ~**side** *adv* (*walk*) nebenher; (*come*) nebendran; (*be*) daneben ♦ *prep* (*walk, compared with*) neben +*dat*; (*come*) neben +*acc*; (*be*) entlang, neben +*dat*; (*of ship*) längsseits +*gen*

aloof [ə'luːf] *adj* zurückhaltend ♦ *adv* fern; **to stand** ~ abseits stehen

aloud [ə'laud] *adv* laut

alphabet ['ælfəbet] *n* Alphabet *nt*; ~**ical** [ælfə'betɪkl] *adj* alphabetisch

alpine ['ælpaɪn] *adj* alpin, Alpen-

Alps [ælps] *npl*: **the** ~ die Alpen *pl*

already [ɔːl'redɪ] *adv* schon, bereits

alright ['ɔːl'raɪt] (*BRIT*) *adv* = **all right**

Alsatian [æl'seɪʃən] *n* (*dog*) Schäferhund *m*

also ['ɔːlsəu] *adv* auch, außerdem

altar ['ɔːltə*] *n* Altar *m*

alter ['ɔːltə*] *vt* ändern; (*dress*) umändern; ~**ation** [ɔːltə'reɪʃən] *n* Änderung *f*; Umänderung *f*; (*to building*) Umbau *m*

alternate [*adj* ɔl'tɜːnɪt, *vb* 'ɔːltɜːneɪt] *adj* abwechselnd ♦ *vi* abwechseln; **on** ~ **days** jeden zweiten Tag

alternating ['ɔːltɜːneɪtɪŋ] *adj*: ~ **current** Wechselstrom *m*; **alternative** [ɔl'tɜːnətɪv] *adj* andere(r, s) ♦ *n* Alternative *f*; **alternative medicine** Alternativmedizin *f*; **alternatively** *adv* im anderen Falle; **alternatively one could** ... oder man könnte ...; **alternator** ['ɔːltɜːneɪtə*] *n* (*AUT*) Lichtmaschine *f*

although [ɔːl'ðəu] *conj* obwohl

altitude ['æltɪtjuːd] *n* Höhe *f*

alto ['æltəu] *n* Alt *m*

altogether [ɔːltə'geðə*] *adv* (*on the whole*) im Ganzen genommen; (*entirely*) ganz und gar

aluminium [ælju'mɪnɪəm] (*BRIT*) *n* Aluminium *nt*

aluminum [ə'luːmɪnəm] (*US*) *n* Aluminium *nt*

always ['ɔːlweɪz] *adv* immer

Alzheimer's (disease) ['æltshaɪməz-] *n* (*MED*) Alzheimerkrankheit *f*

AM *n abbr* (= *Assembly Member*) Mitglied *nt* der walisischen Versammlung

am [æm] *see* **be**

a.m. *adv abbr* (= *ante meridiem*) vormittags

amalgamate [ə'mælgəmeɪt] *vi* (*combine*) sich vereinigen ♦ *vt* (*mix*) amalgamieren

amass [ə'mæs] *vt* anhäufen

amateur ['æmətə*] *n* Amateur *m*; (*pej*) Amateur *m*, Stümper *m*; ~**ish** (*pej*) *adj* dilettantisch, stümperhaft

amaze [ə'meɪz] *vt* erstaunen; **to be** ~**d (at)** erstaunt sein (über); ~**ment** *n* höchste(s)

Erstaunen nt; **amazing** adj höchst erstaunlich

mazon ['æməzən] n (GEOG) Amazonas m

mbassador [æm'bæsədər] n Botschafter m

mber ['æmbər] n Bernstein m; **at ~** (BRIT: AUT) auf Gelb, gelb

mbiguous [æm'bɪgjuəs] adj zweideutig; (not clear) unklar

mbition [æm'bɪʃən] n Ehrgeiz m; **ambitious** adj ehrgeizig

mble ['æmbl] vi (usu: ~ along) schlendern

mbulance ['æmbjuləns] n Krankenwagen m; ~ **man** (irreg) n Sanitäter m

mbush ['æmbuʃ] n Hinterhalt m ♦ vt (aus dem Hinterhalt) überfallen

menable [ə'miːnəbl] adj gefügig; **~ (to)** (reason) zugänglich (+dat); (flattery) empfänglich (für)

mend [ə'mend] vt (law etc) abändern, ergänzen; **to make ~s** etw wieder gutmachen; ~**ment** n Abänderung f

menities [ə'miːnɪtɪz] npl Einrichtungen pl

merica [ə'merɪkə] n Amerika nt; ~**n** adj amerikanisch ♦ n Amerikaner(in) m(f)

miable ['eɪmɪəbl] adj liebenswürdig

micable ['æmɪkəbl] adj freundschaftlich; (settlement) gütlich

mid(st) [ə'mɪd(st)] prep mitten in or unter +dat

miss [ə'mɪs] adv: **to take sth ~** etw übel nehmen; **there's something ~** da stimmt irgendetwas nicht

mmonia [ə'məunɪə] n Ammoniak nt

mmunition [æmju'nɪʃən] n Munition f

mnesia [æm'niːzɪə] n Gedächtnisverlust m

mnesty ['æmnɪstɪ] n Amnestie f

mok [ə'mɔk] adv: **to run ~** Amok laufen

mong(st) [ə'mʌŋ(st)] prep unter

moral [æ'mɔrəl] adj unmoralisch

morous ['æmərəs] adj verliebt

mount [ə'maunt] n (of money) Betrag m; (of water, sand) Menge f ♦ vi: **to ~ to** (total) sich belaufen auf +acc; **a great ~ of time/energy** ein großer Aufwand an Zeit/Energie (dat); **this ~s to treachery** das kommt Verrat gleich; **he won't ~ to much** aus ihm wird nie was

amp(ere) [æmp(ɛər)] n Ampere nt

amphibian [æm'fɪbɪən] n Amphibie f

ample ['æmpl] adj (portion) reichlich; (dress) weit, groß; **~ time** genügend Zeit

amplifier ['æmplɪfaɪər] n Verstärker m

amuse [ə'mjuːz] vt (entertain) unterhalten; (make smile) belustigen; ~**ment** n (feeling) Unterhaltung f; (recreation) Zeitvertreib m; ~**ment arcade** n Spielhalle f; ~**ment park** n Vergnügungspark m

an [æn, ən] see **a**

anaemia [ə'niːmɪə] n Anämie f; **anaemic** adj blutarm

anaesthetic [ænɪs'θetɪk] n Betäubungsmittel nt; **under ~** unter Narkose; **anaesthetist** [æ'niːsθɪtɪst] n Anästhesist(in) m(f)

analgesic [ænæl'dʒiːsɪk] n schmerzlindernde(s) Mittel nt

analog(ue) ['ænəlɔg] adj Analog-

analogy [ə'nælədʒɪ] n Analogie f

analyse ['ænəlaɪz] (BRIT) vt analysieren

analyses [ə'næləsiːz] (BRIT) npl of **analysis**

analysis [ə'næləsɪs] (pl **analyses**) n Analyse f

analyst ['ænəlɪst] n Analytiker(in) m(f)

analytic(al) [ænə'lɪtɪk(l)] adj analytisch

analyze ['ænəlaɪz] (US) vt = **analyse**

anarchy ['ænəkɪ] n Anarchie f

anatomy [ə'nætəmɪ] n (structure) anatomische(r) Aufbau m; (study) Anatomie f

ancestor ['ænsɪstər] n Vorfahr m

anchor ['æŋkər] n Anker m ♦ vi (also: **to drop ~**) ankern, vor Anker gehen ♦ vt verankern; **to weigh ~** den Anker lichten

anchovy ['æntʃəvɪ] n Sardelle f

ancient ['eɪnʃənt] adj alt; (car etc) uralt

ancillary [æn'sɪlərɪ] adj Hilfs-

and [ænd] conj und; **~ so on** und so weiter; **try ~ come** versuche zu kommen; **better ~ better** immer besser

Andes ['ændiːz] npl: **the ~** die Anden pl

anemia etc [ə'niːmɪə] (US) n = **anaemia** etc

anesthetic etc [ænɪs'θetɪk] (US) n = **anaesthetic** etc

anew [ə'njuː] adv von neuem

angel ['eɪndʒəl] n Engel m

anger ['æŋgər] n Zorn m ♦ vt ärgern

angina [æn'dʒaɪnə] *n* Angina *f*

angle ['æŋgl] *n* Winkel *m*; (*point of view*) Standpunkt *m*

angler ['æŋglə'] *n* Angler *m*

Anglican ['æŋglɪkən] *adj* anglikanisch ♦ *n* Anglikaner(in) *m(f)*

angling ['æŋglɪŋ] *n* Angeln *nt*

angrily ['æŋgrɪlɪ] *adv* ärgerlich, böse

angry ['æŋgrɪ] *adj* ärgerlich, ungehalten, böse; (*wound*) entzündet; **to be ~ with sb** auf jdn böse sein; **to be ~ at sth** über etw *acc* verärgert sein

anguish ['æŋgwɪʃ] *n* Qual *f*

angular ['æŋgjulə'] *adj* eckig, winkelförmig; (*face*) kantig

animal ['ænɪməl] *n* Tier *nt*; (*living creature*) Lebewesen *nt* ♦ *adj* tierisch

animate [*vb* 'ænɪmeɪt, *adj* 'ænɪmɪt] *vt* beleben ♦ *adj* lebhaft; **~d** *adj* lebendig; (*film*) Zeichentrick-

animosity [ænɪ'mɔsɪtɪ] *n* Feindseligkeit *f*, Abneigung *f*

aniseed ['ænɪsiːd] *n* Anis *m*

ankle ['æŋkl] *n* (Fuß)knöchel *m*; **~ sock** *n* Söckchen *nt*

annex [*n* 'æneks, *vb* ə'neks] *n* (*BRIT: also:* **~e**) Anbau *m* ♦ *vt* anfügen; (*POL*) annektieren, angliedern

annihilate [ə'naɪəleɪt] *vt* vernichten

anniversary [ænɪ'vɜːsərɪ] *n* Jahrestag *m*

announce [ə'nauns] *vt* ankündigen, anzeigen; **~ment** *n* Ankündigung *f*; (*official*) Bekanntmachung *f*; **~r** *n* Ansager(in) *m(f)*

annoy [ə'nɔɪ] *vt* ärgern; **don't get ~ed!** reg dich nicht auf!; **~ance** *n* Ärgernis *nt*, Störung *f*; **~ing** *adj* ärgerlich; (*person*) lästig

annual ['ænjuəl] *adj* jährlich; (*salary*) Jahres- ♦ *n* (*plant*) einjährige Pflanze *f*; (*book*) Jahrbuch *nt*; **~ly** *adv* jährlich

annul [ə'nʌl] *vt* aufheben, annullieren

annum ['ænəm] *n see* **per**

anonymous [ə'nɔnɪməs] *adj* anonym

anorak ['ænəræk] *n* Anorak *m*, Windjacke *f*

anorexia [ænə'reksɪə] *n* (*MED*) Magersucht *f*

another [ə'nʌðə'] *adj, pron* (*different*) ein(e) andere(r, s); (*additional*) noch eine(r, s); *see*

also **one**

answer ['ɑːnsə'] *n* Antwort *f* ♦ *vi* antworten; (*on phone*) sich melden ♦ *vt* (*person*) antworten +*dat*; (*letter, question*) beantworten; (*telephone*) gehen an +*acc*, abnehmen; (*door*) öffnen; **in ~ to your letter** in Beantwortung Ihres Schreibens; **to ~ the phone** ans Telefon gehen; **to ~ the bell** *or* **the door** aufmachen; **~ back** *vi* frech sein; **~ for** *vt fus*: **to ~ for sth** für etw verantwortlich sein; **~able** *adj*: **to be ~able to sb for sth** jdm gegenüber für etw verantwortlich sein; **~ing machine** *n* Anrufbeantworter *m*

ant [ænt] *n* Ameise *f*

antagonism [æn'tægənɪzəm] *n* Antagonismus *m*

antagonize [æn'tægənaɪz] *vt* reizen

Antarctic [ænt'ɑːktɪk] *adj* antarktisch ♦ *n*: **the ~** die Antarktis

antelope ['æntɪləup] *n* Antilope *f*

antenatal ['æntɪ'neɪtl] *adj* vor der Geburt; **~ clinic** *n* Sprechstunde *f* für werdende Mütter

antenna [æn'tenə] *n* (*BIOL*) Fühler *m*; (*RAD*) Antenne *f*

antennae [æn'teniː] *npl of* **antenna**

anthem ['ænθəm] *n* Hymne *f*; **national ~** Nationalhymne *f*

anthology [æn'θɔlədʒɪ] *n* Gedichtsammlung *f*, Anthologie *f*

anti- ['ænti] *prefix* Gegen-, Anti-

anti-aircraft ['æntɪ'eəkrɑːft] *adj* Flugabwehr-

antibiotic ['æntɪbaɪ'ɔtɪk] *n* Antibiotikum *nt*

antibody ['æntɪbɔdɪ] *n* Antikörper *m*

anticipate [æn'tɪsɪpeɪt] *vt* (*expect: trouble, question*) erwarten, rechnen mit; (*look forward to*) sich freuen auf +*acc*; (*do first*) vorwegnehmen; (*foresee*) ahnen, vorhersehen; **anticipation** [æntɪsɪ'peɪʃən] *n* Erwartung *f*; (*foreshadowing*) Vorwegnahme *f*

anticlimax ['æntɪ'klaɪmæks] *n* Ernüchterung *f*

anticlockwise ['æntɪ'klɔkwaɪz] *adv* entgegen dem Uhrzeigersinn

antics ['æntɪks] *npl* Possen *pl*

ti: **~cyclone** *n* Hoch *nt*, Hochdruckgebiet *nt*; **~depressant** *n* Antidepressivum *nt*; **~dote** *n* Gegenmittel *nt*; **~freeze** *n* Frostschutzmittel *nt*; **~histamine** *n* Antihistamin *nt*

tiquated ['æntɪkweɪtɪd] *adj* antiquiert

tique [æn'tiːk] *n* Antiquität *f* ♦ *adj* antik; (*old-fashioned*) altmodisch; **~ shop** *n* Antiquitätenladen *m*; **antiquity** [æn'tɪkwɪtɪ] *n* Altertum *nt*

tiseptic [æntɪ'septɪk] *n* Antiseptikum *nt* ♦ *adj* antiseptisch

tisocial ['æntɪ'səʊʃəl] *adj* (*person*) ungesellig; (*law*) unsozial

tlers ['æntləz] *npl* Geweih *nt*

nus ['eɪnəs] *n* After *m*

nvil ['ænvɪl] *n* Amboss *m*

nxiety [æŋ'zaɪətɪ] *n* Angst *f*; (*worry*) Sorge *f*; **anxious** ['æŋkʃəs] *adj* ängstlich; (*worried*) besorgt; **to be anxious to do sth** etw unbedingt tun wollen

<u>*EYWORD*</u>

ny ['enɪ] *adj* 1 (*in questions etc*): **have you any butter?** haben Sie (etwas) Butter?; **have you any children?** haben Sie Kinder?; **if there are any tickets left** falls noch Karten da sind
2 (*with negative*): **I haven't any money/ books** ich habe kein Geld/keine Bücher
3 (*no matter which*) jede(r, s) (beliebige); **any colour (at all)** jede beliebige Farbe; **choose any book you like** nehmen Sie ein beliebiges Buch
4 (*in phrases*): **in any case** in jedem Fall; **any day now** jeden Tag; **at any moment** jeden Moment; **at any rate** auf jeden Fall
♦ *pron* 1 (*in questions etc*): **have you got any?** haben Sie welche?; **can any of you sing?** kann (irgend)einer von euch singen?
2 (*with negative*): **I haven't any (of them)** ich habe keinen/keines (davon)
3 (*no matter which one(s)*): **take any of those books (you like)** nehmen Sie irgendeines dieser Bücher
♦ *adv* 1 (*in questions etc*): **do you want any more soup/sandwiches?** möchten Sie

noch Suppe/Brote?; **are you feeling any better?** fühlen Sie sich etwas besser?
2 (*with negative*): **I can't hear him any more** ich kann ihn nicht mehr hören

anybody ['enɪbɔdɪ] *pron* (*no matter who*) jede(r); (*in questions etc*) (irgend)jemand, (irgend)eine(r); (*with negative*): **I can't see** ~ ich kann niemanden sehen
anyhow ['enɪhaʊ] *adv* (*at any rate*): **I shall go** ~ ich gehe sowieso; (*haphazardly*): **do it** ~ machen Sie es, wie Sie wollen
anyone ['enɪwʌn] *pron* = **anybody**

<u>*KEYWORD*</u>

anything ['enɪθɪŋ] *pron* 1 (*in questions etc*) (irgend)etwas; **can you see anything?** können Sie etwas sehen?
2 (*with negative*): **I can't see anything** ich kann nichts sehen
3 (*no matter what*): **you can say anything you like** Sie können sagen, was Sie wollen; **anything will do** irgendetwas (wird genügen), irgendeine(r, s) (wird genügen); **he'll eat anything** er isst alles

anyway ['enɪweɪ] *adv* (*at any rate*) auf jeden Fall; (*besides*): **~, I couldn't come even if I wanted to** jedenfalls könnte ich nicht kommen, selbst wenn ich wollte; **why are you phoning, ~?** warum rufst du überhaupt an?
anywhere ['enɪweə] *adv* (*in questions etc*) irgendwo; (: *with direction*) irgendwohin; (*no matter where*) überall; (: *with direction*) überallhin; (*with negative*): **I can't see him** ~ ich kann ihn nirgendwo *or* nirgends sehen; **can you see him ~?** siehst du ihn irgendwo?; **put the books down ~** leg die Bücher irgendwohin
apart [ə'pɑːt] *adv* (*parted*) auseinander; (*away*) beiseite, abseits; **10 miles ~** 10 Meilen auseinander; **to take ~** auseinander nehmen; **~ from** *prep* außer
apartheid [ə'pɑːteɪt] *n* Apartheid *f*
apartment [ə'pɑːtmənt] (*US*) *n* Wohnung *f*; **~ building** (*US*) *n* Wohnhaus *nt*
apathy ['æpəθɪ] *n* Teilnahmslosigkeit *f*,

Apathie f

ape [eɪp] n (Menschen)affe m ♦ vt nachmachen

aperitif [əˈperɪtiːf] n Aperitif m

aperture [ˈæpətʃʊər] n Öffnung f; (PHOT) Blende f

APEX [ˈeɪpeks] n abbr (AVIAT: = advance purchase excursion) APEX (im Voraus reservierte(r) Fahrkarte/Flugschein zu reduzierten Preisen)

apex [ˈeɪpeks] n Spitze f

apiece [əˈpiːs] adv pro Stück; (per person) pro Kopf

apologetic [əpɒləˈdʒetɪk] adj entschuldigend; **to be ~** sich sehr entschuldigen

apologize [əˈpɒlədʒaɪz] vi: **to ~ (for sth to sb)** sich (für etw bei jdm) entschuldigen; **apology** n Entschuldigung f

apostle [əˈpɒsl] n Apostel m

apostrophe [əˈpɒstrəfɪ] n Apostroph m

appal [əˈpɔːl] vt erschrecken; **~ling** adj schrecklich

apparatus [æpəˈreɪtəs] n Gerät nt

apparel [əˈpærəl] (US) n Kleidung f

apparent [əˈpærənt] adj offenbar; **~ly** adv anscheinend

apparition [æpəˈrɪʃən] n (ghost) Erscheinung f, Geist m

appeal [əˈpiːl] vi dringend ersuchen; (JUR) Berufung einlegen ♦ n Aufruf m; (JUR) Berufung f; **to ~ for** dringend bitten um; **to ~ to** sich wenden an +acc; (to public) appellieren an +acc; **it doesn't ~ to me** es gefällt mir nicht; **~ing** adj ansprechend

appear [əˈpɪər] vi (come into sight) erscheinen; (be seen) auftauchen; (seem) scheinen; **it would ~ that ...** anscheinend ...; **~ance** n (coming into sight) Erscheinen nt; (outward show) Äußere(s) nt

appease [əˈpiːz] vt beschwichtigen

appendices [əˈpendɪsiːz] npl of **appendix**

appendicitis [əpendɪˈsaɪtɪs] n Blinddarmentzündung f

appendix [əˈpendɪks] (pl **appendices**) n (in book) Anhang m; (MED) Blinddarm m

appetite [ˈæpɪtaɪt] n Appetit m; (fig) Lust f

appetizer [ˈæpɪtaɪzər] n Appetitanreger m; **appetizing** [ˈæpɪtaɪzɪŋ] adj appetitanregend

applaud [əˈplɔːd] vi Beifall klatschen, applaudieren ♦ vt Beifall klatschen +dat; **applause** [əˈplɔːz] n Beifall m, Applaus m

apple [ˈæpl] n Apfel m; **~ tree** n Apfelbaum m

appliance [əˈplaɪəns] n Gerät nt

applicable [əˈplɪkəbl] adj anwendbar; (in forms) zutreffend

applicant [ˈæplɪkənt] n Bewerber(in) m(f)

application [æplɪˈkeɪʃən] n (request) Antrag m; (for job) Bewerbung f; (putting into practice) Anwendung f; (hard work) Fleiß m; **~ form** n Bewerbungsformular nt

applied [əˈplaɪd] adj angewandt

apply [əˈplaɪ] vi (be suitable) zutreffen; (ask): **to ~ (to)** sich wenden an (+acc); (request): **to ~ for** sich melden für +acc ♦ vt (place on) auflegen; (cream) auftragen; (put into practice) anwenden; **to ~ for sth** sich um etw bewerben; **to ~ o.s. to sth** sich bei etw anstrengen

appoint [əˈpɔɪnt] vt (to office) ernennen, berufen; (settle) festsetzen; **~ment** n (meeting) Verabredung f; (at hairdresser etc) Bestellung f; (in business) Termin m; (choice for a position) Ernennung f; (UNIV) Berufung f

appraisal [əˈpreɪzl] n Beurteilung f

appreciable [əˈpriːʃəbl] adj (perceptible) merklich; (able to be estimated) abschätzbar

appreciate [əˈpriːʃɪeɪt] vt (value) zu schätzen wissen; (understand) einsehen ♦ vi (increase in value) im Wert steigen; **appreciation** [əpriːʃɪˈeɪʃən] n Wertschätzung f; (COMM) Wertzuwachs m; **appreciative** [əˈpriːʃɪətɪv] adj (showing thanks) dankbar; (showing liking) anerkennend

apprehend [æprɪˈhend] vt (arrest) festnehmen; (understand) erfassen

apprehension [æprɪˈhenʃən] n Angst f

apprehensive [æprɪˈhensɪv] adj furchtsam

apprentice [əˈprentɪs] n Lehrling m; **~ship** n Lehrzeit f

approach [əˈprəʊtʃ] vi sich nähern ♦ vt herantreten an +acc; (problem) herangehen

ın +*acc* ♦ *n* Annäherung *f*; (*to problem*)
Ansatz *m*; (*path*) Zugang *m*, Zufahrt *f*;
~**able** *adj* zugänglich

propriate [*adj* ə'prəuprı1t, *vb* ə'prəuprıeıt]
adj angemessen; (*remark*) angebracht ♦ *vt*
take for o.s.) sich aneignen; (*set apart*)
bereitstellen

proval [ə'pru:vəl] *n* (*show of satisfaction*)
Beifall *m*; (*permission*) Billigung *f*; **on ~**
COMM) bei Gefallen

prove [ə'pru:v] *vt*, *vi* billigen; **I don't ~ of**
t/him ich halte nichts davon/von ihm; ~**d**
school (*BRIT*) *n* Erziehungsheim *nt*

proximate [*adj* ə'prɒksımıt, *vb*
ə'prɒksımeıt] *adj* annähernd, ungefähr ♦ *vt*
ıahe kommen +*dat*; ~**ly** *adv* rund,
ungefähr

ricot ['eıprıkɒt] *n* Aprikose *f*

pril ['eıprəl] *n* April *m*; ~ **Fools' Day** in der
erste April

ron ['eıprən] *n* Schürze *f*

t [æpt] *adj* (*suitable*) passend; (*able*)
begabt; (*likely*): **to be ~ to do sth** dazu
neigen, etw zu tun

titude ['æptıtju:d] *n* Begabung *f*

qualung ['ækwəlʌŋ] *n*
Unterwasseratmungsgerät *nt*

quarium [ə'kwɛərıəm] *n* Aquarium *nt*

quarius [ə'kwɛərıəs] *n* Wassermann *m*

quatic [ə'kwætık] *adj* Wasser-

~**ab** ['ærəb] *n* Araber(in) *m(f)*

~**abia** [ə'reıbıə] *n* Arabien *nt*; ~**n** *adj*
arabisch

~**abic** ['ærəbık] *adj* arabisch ♦ *n* Arabisch *nt*

able ['ærəbl] *adj* bebaubar, Kultur-

bitrary ['ɑ:bıtrərı] *adj* willkürlich

bitration [ɑ:bı'treıʃən] *n* Schlichtung *f*

c [ɑ:k] *n* Bogen *m*

cade [ɑ:'keıd] *n* Säulengang *m*; (*with video*
games) Spielhalle *f*

ch [ɑ:tʃ] *n* Bogen *m* ♦ *vt* überwölben;
back) krumm machen

chaeologist [ɑ:kı'ɒlədʒıst] *n* Archäologe
m

chaeology [ɑ:kı'ɒlədʒı] *n* Archäologie *f*

chaic [ɑ:'keıık] *adj* altertümlich

chbishop [ɑ:tʃ'bıʃəp] *n* Erzbischof *m*

archenemy ['ɑ:tʃ'enəmı] *n* Erzfeind *m*

archeology *etc* [ɑ:kı'ɒlədʒı] (*US*) =
archaeology *etc*

archery ['ɑ:tʃərı] *n* Bogenschießen *nt*

architect ['ɑ:kıtekt] *n* Architekt(in) *m(f)*;
~**ural** [ɑ:kı'tektʃərəl] *adj* architektonisch;
~**ure** *n* Architektur *f*

archives ['ɑ:kaıvz] *npl* Archiv *nt*

archway ['ɑ:tʃweı] *n* Bogen *m*

Arctic ['ɑ:ktık] *adj* arktisch ♦ *n*: **the ~** die
Arktis

ardent ['ɑ:dənt] *adj* glühend

arduous ['ɑ:djuəs] *adj* mühsam

are [ɑ:ʳ] *see* **be**

area ['ɛərıə] *n* Fläche *f*; (*of land*) Gebiet *nt*;
(*part of sth*) Teil *m*, Abschnitt *m*

arena [ə'ri:nə] *n* Arena *f*

aren't [ɑ:nt] = **are not**

Argentina [ɑ:dʒən'ti:nə] *n* Argentinien *nt*;
Argentinian [ɑ:dʒən'tınıən] *adj*
argentinisch ♦ *n* Argentinier(in) *m(f)*

arguably ['ɑ:gjuəblı] *adv* wohl

argue ['ɑ:gju:] *vi* diskutieren; (*angrily*)
streiten; **argument** *n* (*theory*) Argument *nt*;
(*reasoning*) Argumentation *f*; (*row*)
Auseinandersetzung *f*, Streit *m*; **to have an
argument** sich streiten; **argumentative**
[ɑ:gju'mentətıv] *adj* streitlustig

aria ['ɑ:rıə] *n* Arie *f*

Aries ['ɛəri:z] *n* Widder *m*

arise [ə'raız] (*pt* **arose**, *pp* **arisen**) *vi*
aufsteigen; (*get up*) aufstehen; (*difficulties
etc*) entstehen; (*case*) vorkommen; **to ~
from sth** herrühren von etw; ~**n** [ə'rızn] *pp*
of **arise**

aristocracy [ærıs'tɒkrəsı] *n* Adel *m*,
Aristokratie *f*; **aristocrat** ['ærıstəkræt] *n*
Adlige(r) *f(m)*, Aristokrat(in) *m(f)*

arithmetic [ə'rıθmətık] *n* Rechnen *nt*,
Arithmetik *f*

arm [ɑ:m] *n* Arm *m*; (*branch of military service*)
Zweig *m* ♦ *vt* bewaffnen; ~**s** *npl* (*weapons*)
Waffen *pl*

armaments ['ɑ:məmənts] *npl* Ausrüstung *f*

armchair ['ɑ:mtʃɛəʳ] *n* Lehnstuhl *m*

armed [ɑ:md] *adj* (*forces*) Streit-, bewaffnet;
~ **robbery** *n* bewaffnete(r) Raubüberfall *m*

armistice [ˈɑːmɪstɪs] n Waffenstillstand m

armour [ˈɑːməʳ] (US **armor**) n (knight's) Rüstung f; (MIL) Panzerplatte f; **~ed car** n Panzerwagen m

armpit [ˈɑːmpɪt] n Achselhöhle f

armrest [ˈɑːmrest] n Armlehne f

army [ˈɑːmɪ] n Armee f, Heer nt; (host) Heer nt

aroma [əˈrəumə] n Duft m, Aroma nt; **~therapy** [ərəuməˈθerəpɪ] n Aromatherapie f; **~tic** [ærəˈmætɪk] adj aromatisch, würzig

arose [əˈrəuz] pt of **arise**

around [əˈraund] adv ringsherum; (almost) ungefähr ♦ prep um ... herum; **is he ~?** ist er hier?

arrange [əˈreɪndʒ] vt (time, meeting) festsetzen; (holidays) festlegen; (flowers, hair, objects) anordnen; **I ~d to meet him** ich habe mit ihm ausgemacht, ihn zu treffen; **it's all ~d** es ist alles arrangiert; **~ment** n (order) Reihenfolge f; (agreement) Vereinbarung f; **~ments** npl (plans) Pläne pl

array [əˈreɪ] n (collection) Ansammlung f

arrears [əˈrɪəz] npl (of debts) Rückstand m; (of work) Unerledigte(s) nt; **in ~** im Rückstand

arrest [əˈrest] vt (person) verhaften; (stop) aufhalten ♦ n Verhaftung f; **under ~** in Haft

arrival [əˈraɪvl] n Ankunft f

arrive [əˈraɪv] vi ankommen; **to ~ at** ankommen in +dat, ankommen bei

arrogance [ˈærəgəns] n Überheblichkeit f, Arroganz f; **arrogant** [ˈærəgənt] adj überheblich, arrogant

arrow [ˈærəu] n Pfeil m

arse [ɑːs] (inf!) n Arsch m (!)

arsenal [ˈɑːsɪnl] n Waffenlager nt, Zeughaus nt

arsenic [ˈɑːsnɪk] n Arsen nt

arson [ˈɑːsn] n Brandstiftung f

art [ɑːt] n Kunst f; **A~s** npl (UNIV) Geisteswissenschaften pl

artery [ˈɑːtərɪ] n Schlagader f, Arterie f

art gallery n Kunstgalerie f

arthritis [ɑːˈθraɪtɪs] n Arthritis f

artichoke [ˈɑːtɪtʃəuk] n Artischocke f;

Jerusalem ~ Erdartischocke f

article [ˈɑːtɪkl] n (PRESS, GRAM) Artikel m; (thing) Gegenstand m, Artikel m; (clause) Abschnitt m, Paragraf m; **~ of clothing** Kleidungsstück nt

articulate [adj ɑːˈtɪkjulɪt, vb ɑːˈtɪkjuleɪt] adj (able to express o.s.) redegewandt; (speaking clearly) deutlich, verständlich ♦ vt (connect) zusammenfügen, gliedern; **to be ~** sich gut ausdrücken können; **~d vehicle** n Sattelschlepper m

artificial [ɑːtɪˈfɪʃəl] adj künstlich, Kunst-; **~ respiration** n künstliche Atmung f

artisan [ˈɑːtɪzæn] n gelernte(r) Handwerker m

artist [ˈɑːtɪst] n Künstler(in) m(f); **~ic** [ɑːˈtɪstɪk] adj künstlerisch; **~ry** n künstlerische(s) Können nt

art school n Kunsthochschule f

⎡ KEYWORD ⎤

as [æz] conj 1 (referring to time) als; **as the years went by** mit den Jahren; **he came in as I was leaving** als er hereinkam, ging ich gerade; **as from tomorrow** ab morgen
2 (in comparisons): **as big as** so groß wie; **twice as big as** zweimal so groß wie; **as much/many as** so viel/so viele wie; **as soon as** sobald
3 (since, because) da; **he left early as he had to be home by 10** er ging früher, da er um 10 zu Hause sein musste
4 (referring to manner, way) wie; **do as you wish** mach was du willst; **as she said** wie sie sagte
5 (concerning): **as for** or **to that** was das betrifft or angeht
6: **as if** or **though** als ob
♦ prep als; see also **long**; **he works as a driver** er arbeitet als Fahrer; see also **such**; **he gave it to me as a present** er hat es mir als Geschenk gegeben; see also **well**

a.s.a.p. abbr = **as soon as possible**

asbestos [æzˈbestəs] n Asbest m

ascend [əˈsend] vi aufsteigen ♦ vt besteigen; **ascent** n Aufstieg m; Besteigung f

scertain [æsə'teɪn] vt feststellen

scribe [ə'skraɪb] vt: **to ~ sth to sth /sth to sb** etw einer Sache/jdm etw zuschreiben

sh [æʃ] n Asche f; (tree) Esche f

shamed [ə'ʃeɪmd] adj beschämt; **to be ~ of sth** sich für etw schämen

shen ['æʃən] adj (pale) aschfahl

shore [ə'ʃɔːr] adv an Land

shtray ['æʃtreɪ] n Aschenbecher m

sh Wednesday n Aschermittwoch m

sia ['eɪʃə] n Asien nt; **~n** adj asiatisch ♦ n Asiat(in) m(f)

side [ə'saɪd] adv beiseite

sk [ɑːsk] vt fragen; (permission) bitten um; **~ him his name** frage ihn nach seinem Namen; **he ~ed to see you** er wollte dich sehen; **to ~ sb to do sth** jdn bitten, etw zu tun; **to ~ sb about sth** jdn nach etw fragen; **to ~ (sb) a question** (jdn) etwas fragen; **to ~ sb out to dinner** jdn zum Essen einladen; **~ after** vt fus fragen nach; **~ for** vt fus bitten um

skance [ə'skɑːns] adv: **to look ~ at sb** jdn schief ansehen

sking price ['ɑːskɪŋ-] n Verkaufspreis m

sleep [ə'sliːp] adj: **to be ~** schlafen; **to fall ~** einschlafen

sparagus [əs'pærəgəs] n Spargel m

spect ['æspɛkt] n Aspekt m

spersions [əs'pɜːʃənz] npl: **to cast ~ on sb/sth** sich abfällig über jdn/etw äußern

sphyxiation [æsfɪksɪ'eɪʃən] n Erstickung f

spirations [æspə'reɪʃənz] npl: **to have ~ towards sth** etw anstreben

spire [ə'spaɪər] vi: **to ~ to** streben nach

spirin ['æsprɪn] n Aspirin nt

ss [æs] n (also fig) Esel m; (US: inf!) Arsch m (!)

ssailant [ə'seɪlənt] n Angreifer m

ssassin [ə'sæsɪn] n Attentäter(in) m(f); **~ate** vt ermorden; **~ation** [əsæsɪ'neɪʃən] n (geglückte(s)) Attentat nt

ssault [ə'sɔːlt] n Angriff m ♦ vt überfallen; (woman) herfallen über +acc

ssemble [ə'sɛmbl] vt versammeln; (parts) zusammensetzen ♦ vi sich versammeln; **assembly** n (meeting) Versammlung f;

(construction) Zusammensetzung f, Montage f; **assembly line** n Fließband nt

assent [ə'sɛnt] n Zustimmung f

assert [ə'sɜːt] vt erklären; **~ion** n Behauptung f

assess [ə'sɛs] vt schätzen; **~ment** n Bewertung f, Einschätzung f; **~or** n Steuerberater m

asset ['æsɛt] n Vorteil m, Wert m; **~s** npl (FIN) Vermögen nt; (estate) Nachlass m

assign [ə'saɪn] vt zuweisen; **~ment** n Aufgabe f, Auftrag m

assimilate [ə'sɪmɪleɪt] vt sich aneignen, aufnehmen

assist [ə'sɪst] vt beistehen +dat; **~ance** n Unterstützung f, Hilfe f; **~ant** n Assistent(in) m(f), Mitarbeiter(in) m(f); (BRIT: also: **shop ~ant**) Verkäufer(in) m(f)

associate [n ə'səʊʃɪɪt, vb ə'səʊʃɪeɪt] n (partner) Kollege m, Teilhaber m; (member) außerordentliche(s) Mitglied nt ♦ vt verbinden ♦ vi (keep company) verkehren; **association** [əsəʊsɪ'eɪʃən] n Verband m, Verein m; (PSYCH) Assoziation f; (link) Verbindung f

assorted [ə'sɔːtɪd] adj gemischt

assortment [ə'sɔːtmənt] n Sammlung f; (COMM): **~ (of)** Sortiment nt (von), Auswahl f (an +dat)

assume [ə'sjuːm] vt (take for granted) annehmen; (put on) annehmen, sich geben; **~d name** n Deckname m

assumption [ə'sʌmpʃən] n Annahme f

assurance [ə'ʃʊərəns] n (firm statement) Versicherung f; (confidence) Selbstsicherheit f; (insurance) (Lebens)versicherung f

assure [ə'ʃʊər] vt (make sure) sicherstellen; (convince) versichern +dat; (life) versichern

asterisk ['æstərɪsk] n Sternchen nt

asthma ['æsmə] n Asthma nt

astonish [ə'stɒnɪʃ] vt erstaunen; **~ment** n Erstaunen nt

astound [ə'staʊnd] vt verblüffen

astray [ə'streɪ] adv in die Irre; auf Abwege; **to go ~** (go wrong) sich vertun; **to lead ~** irreführen

astride [ə'straɪd] adv rittlings ♦ prep rittlings

auf
astrologer [əs'trɒlədʒəʳ] *n* Astrologe *m*,
Astrologin *f*; **astrology** *n* Astrologie *f*
astronaut ['æstrənɔːt] *n* Astronaut(in) *m(f)*
astronomer [əs'trɒnəməʳ] *n* Astronom *m*
astronomical [æstrə'nɒmɪkl] *adj*
astronomisch; (*success*) riesig
astronomy [əs'trɒnəmɪ] *n* Astronomie *f*
astute [əs'tjuːt] *adj* scharfsinnig; schlau,
gerissen
asylum [ə'saɪləm] *n* (*home*) Heim *nt*; (*refuge*)
Asyl *nt*

| KEYWORD |
---

at [æt] *prep* 1 (*referring to position, direction*) an
+*dat*, bei +*dat*; (*with place*) in +*dat*; **at the
top** an der Spitze; **at home/school** zu
Hause/in der Schule; **at the baker's** beim
Bäcker; **to look at sth** auf etw *acc* blicken;
to throw sth at sb etw nach jdm werfen
2 (*referring to time*): **at 4 o'clock** um 4 Uhr;
at night bei Nacht; **at Christmas** zu
Weihnachten; **at times** manchmal
3 (*referring to rates, speed etc*): **at £1 a kilo**
zu £1 pro Kilo; **two at a time** zwei auf
einmal; **at 50 km/h** mit 50 km/h
4 (*referring to manner*): **at a stroke** mit
einem Schlag; **at peace** in Frieden
5 (*referring to activity*): **to be at work** bei
der Arbeit sein; **to play at cowboys**
Cowboy spielen; **to be good at sth** gut in
etw *dat* sein
6 (*referring to cause*): **shocked/surprised/
annoyed at sth** schockiert/überrascht/
verärgert über etw *acc*; **I went at his
suggestion** ich ging auf seinen Vorschlag
hin

---

ate [eɪt] *pt of* **eat**
atheist ['eɪθɪɪst] *n* Atheist(in) *m(f)*
Athens ['æθɪnz] *n* Athen *nt*
athlete ['æθliːt] *n* Athlet *m*, Sportler *m*
athletic [æθ'letɪk] *adj* sportlich, athletisch;
~s *n* Leichtathletik *f*
Atlantic [ət'læntɪk] *adj* atlantisch ♦ *n*: **the ~
(Ocean)** der Atlantik
atlas ['ætləs] *n* Atlas *m*

ATM *abbr* (= *automated teller machine*)
Geldautomat *m*
atmosphere ['ætməsfɪəʳ] *n* Atmosphäre *f*
atom ['ætəm] *n* Atom *nt*; (*fig*) bisschen *nt*;
~ic [ə'tɒmɪk] *adj* atomar, Atom-; **~(ic)
bomb** *n* Atombombe *f*
atomizer ['ætəmaɪzəʳ] *n* Zerstäuber *m*
atone [ə'təʊn] *vi* sühnen; **to ~ for sth** etw
sühnen
atrocious [ə'trəʊʃəs] *adj* grässlich
atrocity [ə'trɒsɪtɪ] *n* Scheußlichkeit *f*; (*deed*)
Gräueltat *f*
attach [ə'tætʃ] *vt* (*fasten*) befestigen; **to be
~ed to sb/sth** an jdm/etw hängen; **to ~
importance** *etc* **to sth** Wichtigkeit *etc* auf
etw *acc* legen, einer Sache *dat* Wichtigkeit
etc beimessen
attaché case [ə'tæʃeɪ] *n* Aktenkoffer *m*
attachment [ə'tætʃmənt] *n* (*tool*)
Zubehörteil *nt*; (*love*): **~ (to sb)** Zuneigung
f (zu jdm)
attack [ə'tæk] *vt* angreifen ♦ *n* Angriff *m*;
(*MED*) Anfall *m*; **~er** *n* Angreifer(in) *m(f)*
attain [ə'teɪn] *vt* erreichen; **~ments** *npl*
Kenntnisse *pl*
attempt [ə'tempt] *n* Versuch *m* ♦ *vt*
versuchen; **~ed murder** Mordversuch *m*
attend [ə'tend] *vt* (*go to*) teilnehmen (an
+*dat*); (*lectures*) besuchen; **to ~ to** (*needs*)
nachkommen +*dat*; (*person*) sich kümmern
um; **~ance** *n* (*presence*) Anwesenheit *f*;
(*people present*) Besucherzahl *f*; **good ~ance**
gute Teilnahme; **~ant** *n* (*companion*)
Begleiter(in) *m(f)*; Gesellschafter(in) *m(f)*; (*in
car park etc*) Wächter(in) *m(f)*; (*servant*)
Bedienstete(r) *mf* ♦ *adj* begleitend; (*fig*)
damit verbunden
attention [ə'tenʃən] *n* Aufmerksamkeit *f*;
(*care*) Fürsorge *f*; (*for machine etc*) Pflege *f*
♦ *excl* (*MIL*) Achtung!; **for the ~ of ...** zu
Händen (von) ...
attentive [ə'tentɪv] *adj* aufmerksam
attic ['ætɪk] *n* Dachstube *f*, Mansarde *f*
attitude ['ætɪtjuːd] *n* (*mental*) Einstellung *f*
attorney [ə'tɜːnɪ] *n* (*solicitor*) Rechtsanwalt
m; **A~ General** *n* Justizminister *m*
attract [ə'trækt] *vt* anziehen; (*attention*)

erregen; ~ion n Anziehungskraft f; (thing) Attraktion f; ~ive adj attraktiv

attribute [n 'ætrɪbjuːt, vb ə'trɪbjuːt] n Eigenschaft f, Attribut nt ♦ vt zuschreiben

attrition [ə'trɪʃən] n: **war of ~** Zermürbungskrieg m

aubergine ['əubəʒiːn] n Aubergine f

auburn ['ɔːbən] adj kastanienbraun

auction ['ɔːkʃən] n (also: **sale by ~**) Versteigerung f, Auktion f ♦ vt versteigern; ~**eer** [ɔːkʃə'nɪə*] n Versteigerer m

audacity [ɔː'dæsɪtɪ] n (boldness) Wagemut m; (impudence) Unverfrorenheit f

audible ['ɔːdɪbl] adj hörbar

audience ['ɔːdɪəns] n Zuhörer pl, Zuschauer pl; (with queen) Audienz f

audiotypist ['ɔːdɪəu'taɪpɪst] n Phonotypistin f, Fonotypistin f

audiovisual ['ɔːdɪəu'vɪzjuəl] adj audiovisuell

audit ['ɔːdɪt] vt prüfen

audition [ɔː'dɪʃən] n Probe f

auditor ['ɔːdɪtə*] n (accountant) Rechnungsprüfer(in) m(f), Buchprüfer m

auditorium [ɔːdɪ'tɔːrɪəm] n Zuschauerraum m

augment [ɔːg'mɛnt] vt vermehren

augur ['ɔːgə*] vi bedeuten, voraussagen; **this ~s well** das ist ein gutes Omen

August ['ɔːgəst] n August m

aunt [ɑːnt] n Tante f; ~**ie** n Tantchen nt; ~**y** n = **auntie**

au pair ['əu'pεə*] n (also: ~ **girl**) Aupairmädchen nt, Au-pair-Mädchen nt

aura ['ɔːrə] n Nimbus m

auspicious [ɔːs'pɪʃəs] adj günstig; verheißungsvoll

austere [ɔs'tɪə*] adj streng; (room) nüchtern; **austerity** [ɔs'tɛrɪtɪ] n Strenge f; (POL) wirtschaftliche Einschränkung f

Australia [ɔs'treɪlɪə] n Australien nt; ~**n** adj australisch ♦ n Australier(in) m(f)

Austria ['ɔstrɪə] n Österreich nt; ~**n** adj österreichisch ♦ n Österreicher(in) m(f)

authentic [ɔː'θɛntɪk] adj echt, authentisch

author ['ɔːθə*] n Autor m, Schriftsteller m; (beginner) Urheber m, Schöpfer m

authoritarian [ɔːθɔrɪ'tεərɪən] adj autoritär

authoritative [ɔː'θɔrɪtətɪv] adj (account) maßgeblich; (manner) herrisch

authority [ɔː'θɔrɪtɪ] n (power) Autorität f; (expert) Autorität f, Fachmann m; **the authorities** npl (ruling body) die Behörden pl

authorize ['ɔːθəraɪz] vt bevollmächtigen; (permit) genehmigen

auto ['ɔːtəu] (US) n Auto nt, Wagen m

autobiography [ɔːtəbaɪ'ɔgrəfɪ] n Autobiografie f

autograph ['ɔːtəgrɑːf] n (of celebrity) Autogramm nt ♦ vt mit Autogramm versehen

automatic [ɔːtə'mætɪk] adj automatisch ♦ n (gun) Selbstladepistole f; (car) Automatik m; ~**ally** adv automatisch

automation [ɔːtə'meɪʃən] n Automatisierung f

automobile ['ɔːtəməbiːl] (US) n Auto(mobil) nt

autonomous [ɔː'tɔnəməs] adj autonom; **autonomy** n Autonomie f

autumn ['ɔːtəm] n Herbst m

auxiliary [ɔːg'zɪlɪərɪ] adj Hilfs-

Av. abbr = **avenue**

avail [ə'veɪl] vt: **to ~ o.s. of sth** sich einer Sache gen bedienen ♦ n: **to no ~** nutzlos

availability [əveɪlə'bɪlɪtɪ] n Erhältlichkeit f, Vorhandensein nt

available [ə'veɪləbl] adj erhältlich; zur Verfügung stehend; (person) erreichbar, abkömmlich

avalanche ['ævəlɑːnʃ] n Lawine f

Ave. abbr = **avenue**

avenge [ə'vɛndʒ] vt rächen, sühnen

avenue ['ævənjuː] n Allee f

average ['ævərɪdʒ] n Durchschnitt m ♦ adj durchschnittlich, Durchschnitts- ♦ vt (figures) den Durchschnitt nehmen von; (perform) durchschnittlich leisten; (in car etc) im Schnitt fahren; **on ~** durchschnittlich, im Durchschnitt; ~ **out** vi: **to ~ out at** im Durchschnitt betragen

averse [ə'vɜːs] adj: **to be ~ to doing sth** eine Abneigung dagegen haben, etw zu tun

avert [ə'vɜːt] vt (turn away) abkehren; (prevent) abwehren
aviary ['eɪvɪərɪ] n Vogelhaus nt
aviation [eɪvɪ'eɪʃən] n Luftfahrt f, Flugwesen nt
avid ['ævɪd] adj: ~ **(for)** gierig (auf +acc)
avocado [ævə'kɑːdəʊ] n (BRIT: also: ~ **pear**) Avocado(birne) f
avoid [ə'vɔɪd] vt vermeiden
await [ə'weɪt] vt erwarten, entgegensehen +dat
awake [ə'weɪk] (pt **awoke**, pp **awoken** or **awaked**) adj wach ♦ vt (auf)wecken ♦ vi aufwachen; **to be ~** wach sein; **~ning** n Erwachen nt
award [ə'wɔːd] n (prize) Preis m ♦ vt: **to ~ (sb sth)** (jdm etw) zuerkennen
aware [ə'weər] adj bewusst; **to be ~** sich bewusst sein; **~ness** n Bewusstsein nt
awash [ə'wɒʃ] adj überflutet
away [ə'weɪ] adv weg, fort; **two hours ~ by car** zwei Autostunden entfernt; **the holiday was two weeks ~** es war noch zwei Wochen bis zum Urlaub; **two kilometres ~** zwei Kilometer entfernt; **~ match** n (SPORT) Auswärtsspiel nt
awe [ɔː] n Ehrfurcht f; **~-inspiring** adj Ehrfurcht gebietend; **~some** adj Ehrfurcht gebietend
awful ['ɔːfəl] adj (very bad) furchtbar; **~ly** adv furchtbar, sehr
awhile [ə'waɪl] adv eine Weile
awkward ['ɔːkwəd] adj (clumsy) ungeschickt, linkisch; (embarrassing) peinlich
awning ['ɔːnɪŋ] n Markise f
awoke [ə'wəʊk] pt of **awake**; **~n** pp of **awake**
awry [ə'raɪ] adv schief; (plans) schief gehen
axe [æks] (US **ax**) n Axt f, Beil nt ♦ vt (end suddenly) streichen
axes¹ ['æksɪz] npl of **axe**
axes² ['æksiːz] npl of **axis**
axis ['æksɪs] (pl **axes**) n Achse f
axle ['æksl] n Achse f
ay(e) [aɪ] excl (yes) ja
azalea [ə'zeɪlɪə] n Azalee f

B, b

B [biː] n (MUS) H nt; **~ road** (BRIT) Landstraße f
B.A. n abbr = **Bachelor of Arts**
babble ['bæbl] vi schwätzen
baby ['beɪbɪ] n Baby nt; **~ carriage** (US) n Kinderwagen m; **~ food** n Babynahrung f; **~-sit** vi Kinder hüten, babysitten; **~-sitter** n Babysitter m; **~-sitting** n Babysitten nt, Babysitting nt; **~ wipe** n Ölpflegetuch nt
bachelor ['bætʃələr] n Junggeselle m; **B~ of Arts** Bakkalaureus m der philosophischen Fakultät; **B~ of Science** Bakkalaureus m der Naturwissenschaften
back [bæk] n (of person, horse) Rücken m; (of house) Rückseite f; (of train) Ende nt; (FOOTBALL) Verteidiger m ♦ vt (support) unterstützen; (wager) wetten auf +acc; (car) rückwärts fahren ♦ vi (go ~wards) rückwärts gehen or fahren ♦ adj hintere(r, s) ♦ adv zurück; (to the rear) nach hinten; **~ down** vi zurückstecken; **~ out** vi sich zurückziehen; (inf) kneifen; **~ up** vt (support) unterstützen; (car) zurücksetzen; (COMPUT) eine Sicherungskopie machen von; **~ache** n Rückenschmerzen pl; **~bencher** (BRIT) n Parlamentarier(in) m(f); **~bone** n Rückgrat nt; (support) Rückhalt m; **~cloth** n Hintergrund m; **~date** vt rückdatieren; **~drop** n (THEAT) = **backcloth**; (~ground) Hintergrund m; **~fire** vi (plan) fehlschlagen; (TECH) fehlzünden; **~ground** n Hintergrund m; (person's education) Vorbildung f; **family ~ground** Familienverhältnisse pl; **~hand** n (TENNIS: also: **~hand stroke**) Rückhand f; **~hander** (BRIT) n (bribe) Schmiergeld nt; **~ing** n (support) Unterstützung f; **~lash** n (fig) Gegenschlag m; **~log** n (of work) Rückstand m; **~ number** n (PRESS) alte Nummer f; **~pack** n Rucksack m; **~packer** n Rucksacktourist(in) m(f); **~ pain** n Rückenschmerzen pl; **~ pay** n (Gehalts- or Lohn)nachzahlung f; **~ payments** npl

Zahlungsrückstände pl; ~ seat n (AUT) Rücksitz m; ~side (inf) n Hintern m; ~stage adv hinter den Kulissen; ~stroke n Rückenschwimmen nt; ~up adj (COMPUT) Sicherungs- ♦ n (COMPUT) Sicherungskopie f; ~ward adj (less developed) zurückgeblieben; (primitive) rückständig; ~wards adv rückwärts; ~water n (fig) Kaff nt; ~yard n Hinterhof m

bacon ['beɪkən] n Schinkenspeck m

bacteria [bæk'tɪərɪə] npl Bakterien pl

bad [bæd] adj schlecht, schlimm; **to go ~** schlecht werden

bade [bæd] pt of **bid**

badge [bædʒ] n Abzeichen nt

badger ['bædʒər] n Dachs m

badly ['bædlɪ] adv schlecht, schlimm; **~ wounded** schwer verwundet; **he needs it ~** er braucht es dringend; **to be ~ off (for money)** dringend Geld nötig haben

badminton ['bædmɪntən] n Federball m, Badminton nt

bad-tempered ['bæd'tempəd] adj schlecht gelaunt

baffle ['bæfl] vt (puzzle) verblüffen

bag [bæg] n (sack) Beutel m; (paper) Tüte f; (handbag) Tasche f; (suitcase) Koffer m; (inf: old woman) alte Schachtel f ♦ vt (put in sack) in einen Sack stecken; (hunting) erlegen; **~s of** (inf: lots of) eine Menge +acc; **~gage** ['bægɪdʒ] n Gepäck nt; **~ allowance** n Freigepäck nt; **~ reclaim** n Gepäckausgabe f; **~gy** ['bægɪ] adj bauschig, sackartig

bagpipes ['bægpaɪps] npl Dudelsack m

bail [beɪl] n (money) Kaution f ♦ vt (prisoner: usu: grant ~ to) gegen Kaution freilassen; (boat: also: ~ out) ausschöpfen; **on ~** (prisoner) gegen Kaution freigelassen; **to ~ sb out** die Kaution für jdn stellen; see also **bale**

bailiff ['beɪlɪf] n Gerichtsvollzieher(in) m(f)

bait [beɪt] n Köder m ♦ vt mit einem Köder versehen; (fig) ködern

bake [beɪk] vt, vi backen; **~d beans** gebackene Bohnen pl; **~d potatoes** npl in der Schale gebackene Kartoffeln pl; **~r** n

Bäcker m; **~ry** n Bäckerei f; **baking** n Backen nt; **baking powder** n Backpulver nt

balance ['bæləns] n (scales) Waage f; (equilibrium) Gleichgewicht nt; (FIN: state of account) Saldo m; (difference) Bilanz f; (amount remaining) Restbetrag m ♦ vt (weigh) wägen; (make equal) ausgleichen; **~ of trade/payments** Handels-/Zahlungsbilanz f; **~d** adj ausgeglichen; **~ sheet** n Bilanz f, Rechnungsabschluss m

balcony ['bælkənɪ] n Balkon m

bald [bɔːld] adj kahl; (statement) knapp

bale [beɪl] n Ballen m; **bale out** vi (from a plane) abspringen

ball [bɔːl] n Ball m; **~ bearing** n Kugellager nt

ballet ['bæleɪ] n Ballett nt; **~ dancer** n Balletttänzer(in) m(f); **~ shoe** n Ballettschuh m

balloon [bə'luːn] n (Luft)ballon m

ballot ['bælət] n (geheime) Abstimmung f

ballpoint (pen) ['bɔːlpɔɪnt-] n Kugelschreiber m

ballroom ['bɔːlrum] n Tanzsaal m

Baltic ['bɔːltɪk] n: **the ~ (Sea)** die Ostsee

bamboo [bæm'buː] n Bambus m

ban [bæn] n Verbot nt ♦ vt verbieten

banana [bə'nɑːnə] n Banane f

band [bænd] n Band nt; (group) Gruppe f; (of criminals) Bande f; (MUS) Kapelle f, Band f; **~ together** vi sich zusammentun

bandage ['bændɪdʒ] n Verband m; (elastic) Bandage f ♦ vt (cut) verbinden; (broken limb) bandagieren

Bandaid ['bændeɪd] (®) (US) n Heftpflaster nt

bandit ['bændɪt] n Bandit m, Räuber m

bandwagon ['bændwægən] n: **to jump on the ~** (fig) auf den fahrenden Zug aufspringen

bandy ['bændɪ] vt wechseln; **~-legged** adj o-beinig, O-beinig

bang [bæŋ] n (explosion) Knall m; (blow) Hieb m ♦ vt, vi knallen

Bangladesh [bæŋglə'deʃ] n Bangladesch nt

bangle ['bæŋgl] n Armspange f

bangs [bæŋz] (US) npl (fringe) Pony m

banish [ˈbænɪʃ] *vt* verbannen
banister(s) [ˈbænɪstə(z)] *n(pl)* (Treppen)geländer *nt*
bank [bæŋk] *n* (raised ground) Erdwall *m*; (of lake etc) Ufer *nt*; (FIN) Bank *f* ♦ *vt* (tilt: AVIAT) in die Kurve bringen; (money) einzahlen; **~ on** *vt fus*: **to ~ on sth** mit etw rechnen; **~ account** *n* Bankkonto *nt*; **~ card** *n* Scheckkarte *f*; **~er** *n* Bankier *m*; **~er's card** (BRIT) *n* = **bank card**; **B~ holiday** (BRIT) *n* gesetzliche(r) Feiertag *m*; **~ing** *n* Bankwesen *nt*; **~note** *n* Banknote *f*; **~ rate** *n* Banksatz *m*

| bank holiday |
---

i Als **bank holiday** wird in Großbritannien ein gesetzlicher Feiertag bezeichnet, an dem die Banken geschlossen sind. Die meisten dieser Feiertage, abgesehen von Weihnachten und Ostern, fallen auf Montage im Mai und August. An diesen langen Wochenenden (bank holiday weekends) fahren viele Briten in Urlaub, so dass dann auf den Straßen, Flughäfen und bei der Bahn sehr viel Betrieb ist.

---

bankrupt [ˈbæŋkrʌpt] *adj*: **to be ~** bankrott sein; **to go ~** Bankrott machen; **~cy** *n* Bankrott *m*
bank statement *n* Kontoauszug *m*
banned [bænd] *adj*: **he was ~ from driving** (BRIT) ihm wurde Fahrverbot erteilt
banner [ˈbænər] *n* Banner *nt*
banns [bænz] *npl* Aufgebot *nt*
baptism [ˈbæptɪzəm] *n* Taufe *f*
baptize [bæpˈtaɪz] *vt* taufen
bar [baː*] *n* (rod) Stange *f*; (obstacle) Hindernis *nt*; (of chocolate) Tafel *f*; (of soap) Stück *nt*; (for food, drink) Buffet *nt*, Bar *f*; (pub) Wirtschaft *f*; (MUS) Takt(strich) *m* ♦ *vt* (fasten) verriegeln; (hinder) versperren; (exclude) ausschließen; **behind ~s** hinter Gittern; **the B~**: **to be called to the B~** als Anwalt zugelassen werden; **~ none** ohne Ausnahme
barbaric [baːˈbærɪk] *adj* primitiv, unkultiviert
barbecue [ˈbaːbɪkjuː] *n* Barbecue *nt*

barbed wire [ˈbaːbd-] *n* Stacheldraht *m*
barber [ˈbaːbər] *n* Herrenfriseur *m*
bar code *n* (COMM) Registrierkode *f*
bare [beər] *adj* nackt; (trees, country) kahl; (mere) bloß ♦ *vt* entblößen; **~back** *adv* ungesattelt; **~faced** *adj* unverfroren; **~foot** *adj, adv* barfuß; **~ly** *adv* kaum, knapp
bargain [ˈbaːgɪn] *n* (sth cheap) günstiger Kauf; (agreement: written) Kaufvertrag *m*; (: oral) Geschäft *nt*; **into the ~** obendrein; **~ for** *vt*: **he got more than he ~ed for** er erlebte sein blaues Wunder
barge [baːdʒ] *n* Lastkahn *m*; **~ in** *vi* hereinplatzen; **~ into** *vt* rennen gegen
bark [baːk] *n* (of tree) Rinde *f*; (of dog) Bellen *nt* ♦ *vi* (dog) bellen
barley [ˈbaːlɪ] *n* Gerste *f*; **~ sugar** *n* Malzbonbon *nt*
bar: **~maid** *n* Bardame *f*; **~man** (irreg) *n* Barkellner *m*; **~ meal** *n* einfaches Essen in einem Pub
barn [baːn] *n* Scheune *f*
barometer [bəˈrɒmɪtər] *n* Barometer *nt*
baron [ˈbærən] *n* Baron *m*; **~ess** *n* Baronin *f*
barracks [ˈbærəks] *npl* Kaserne *f*
barrage [ˈbæraːʒ] *n* (gunfire) Sperrfeuer *nt*; (dam) Staudamm *m*; Talsperre *f*
barrel [ˈbærəl] *n* Fass *nt*; (of gun) Lauf *m*
barren [ˈbærən] *adj* unfruchtbar
barricade [bærɪˈkeɪd] *n* Barrikade *f* ♦ *vt* verbarrikadieren
barrier [ˈbærɪər] *n* (obstruction) Hindernis *nt*; (fence) Schranke *f*
barring [ˈbaːrɪŋ] *prep* außer im Falle +gen
barrister [ˈbærɪstər] (BRIT) *n* Rechtsanwalt *m*
barrow [ˈbærəʊ] *n* (cart) Schubkarren *m*
bartender [ˈbaːtendər] (US) *n* Barmann *or* -kellner *m*
barter [ˈbaːtər] *vt* handeln
base [beɪs] *n* (bottom) Boden *m*, Basis *f*; (MIL) Stützpunkt *m* ♦ *vt* gründen; (opinion, theory): **to be ~d on** basieren auf +dat ♦ *adj* (low) gemein; **I'm ~d in London** ich wohne in London; **~ball** [ˈbeɪsbɔːl] *n* Baseball *nt*; **~ment** [ˈbeɪsmənt] *n* Kellergeschoss *nt*
bases[1] [ˈbeɪsɪz] *npl of* **base**
bases[2] [ˈbeɪsiːz] *npl of* **basis**

ash [bæʃ] (inf) vt (heftig) schlagen

ashful ['bæʃful] adj schüchtern

asic ['beɪsɪk] adj grundlegend; **~s** npl: **the ~s** das Wesentliche sg; **~ally** adv im Grunde

asil ['bæzl] n Basilikum nt

asin ['beɪsn] n (dish) Schüssel f; (for washing, also valley) Becken nt; (dock) (Trocken)becken nt

asis ['beɪsɪs] (pl **bases**) n Basis f, Grundlage f

ask [bɑːsk] vi: **to ~ in the sun** sich sonnen

asket ['bɑːskɪt] n Korb m; **~ball** n Basketball m

ass [beɪs] n (MUS, also instrument) Bass m; (voice) Bassstimme f; **~ drum** n große Trommel

assoon [bə'suːn] n Fagott nt

astard ['bɑːstəd] n Bastard m; (inf!) Arschloch nt (!)

at [bæt] n (SPORT) Schlagholz nt; Schläger m; (ZOOL) Fledermaus f ♦ vt: **he didn't ~ an eyelid** er hat nicht mit der Wimper gezuckt

atch [bætʃ] n (of letters) Stoß m; (of samples) Satz m

ated ['beɪtɪd] adj: **with ~ breath** mit angehaltenem Atem

ath [bɑːθ] n Bad nt; (~ tub) Badewanne f ♦ vt baden; **to have a ~** baden; see also **baths**

athe [beɪð] vt, vi baden; **~r** n Badende(r) f(m)

athing ['beɪðɪŋ] n Baden nt; **~ cap** n Badekappe f; **~ costume** n Badeanzug m; **~ suit** (US) n Badeanzug m; **~ trunks** (BRIT) npl Badehose f

ath: **~robe** n Bademantel m; **~room** n Bad(ezimmer nt) nt; **~s** npl (Schwimm)bad nt; **~ towel** n Badetuch nt

aton ['bætən] n (of police) Gummiknüppel m; (MUS) Taktstock m

atter ['bætə*] vt verprügeln ♦ n Schlagteig m; (for cake) Biskuitteig m; **~ed** adj (hat, pan) verbeult

attery ['bætərɪ] n (ELEC) Batterie f; (MIL) Geschützbatterie f

attery farming n (Hühner- etc)batterien

pl

battle ['bætl] n Schlacht f; (small) Gefecht nt ♦ vi kämpfen; **~field** n Schlachtfeld nt; **~ship** n Schlachtschiff nt

Bavaria [bə'veərɪə] n Bayern nt; **~n** adj bay(e)risch ♦ n (person) Bayer(in) m(f)

bawdy ['bɔːdɪ] adj unflätig

bawl [bɔːl] vi brüllen

bay [beɪ] n (of sea) Bucht f ♦ vi bellen; **to keep at ~** unter Kontrolle halten; **~ window** n Erkerfenster nt

bazaar [bə'zɑː*] n Basar m

B. & B. abbr = **bed and breakfast**

BBC n abbr (= British Broadcasting Corporation) BBC f or m

B.C. adv abbr (= before Christ) v. Chr.

KEYWORD

---

be [biː] (pt **was, were**, pp **been**) aux vb
1 (with present participle: forming continuous tenses): **what are you doing?** was machst du (gerade)?; **it is raining** es regnet; **I've been waiting for you for hours** ich warte schon seit Stunden auf dich
2 (with pp: forming passives): **to be killed** getötet werden; **the thief was nowhere to be seen** der Dieb war nirgendwo zu sehen
3 (in tag questions): **it was fun, wasn't it?** es hat Spaß gemacht, nicht wahr?
4 (+to +infin): **the house is to be sold** das Haus soll verkauft werden; **he's not to open it** er darf es nicht öffnen
♦ vb +complement **1** (usu) sein; **I'm tired** ich bin müde; **I'm hot/cold** mir ist heiß/kalt; **he's a doctor** er ist Arzt; **2 and 2 are 4** 2 und 2 ist or sind 4; **she's tall/pretty** sie ist groß/hübsch; **be careful/quiet** sei vorsichtig/ruhig
2 (of health): **how are you?** wie geht es dir?; **he's very ill** er ist sehr krank; **I'm fine now** jetzt geht es mir gut
3 (of age): **how old are you?** wie alt bist du?; **I'm sixteen (years old)** ich bin sechzehn (Jahre alt)
4 (cost): **how much was the meal?** was or wie viel hat das Essen gekostet?; **that'll be £5.75, please** das macht £5.75, bitte

♦ *vi* 1 (*exist, occur etc*) sein; **is there a God?** gibt es einen Gott?; **be that as it may** wie dem auch sei; **so be it** also gut
2 (*referring to place*) sein; **I won't be here tomorrow** iche werde morgen nicht hier sein
3 (*referring to movement*): **where have you been?** wo bist du gewesen?; **I've been in the garden** ich war im Garten
♦ *impers vb* 1 (*referring to time, distance, weather*) sein; **it's 5 o'clock** es ist 5 Uhr; **it's 10 km to the village** es sind 10 km bis zum Dorf; **it's too hot/cold** es ist zu heiß/kalt
2 (*emphatic*): **it's me** ich bins; **it's the postman** es ist der Briefträger

beach [biːtʃ] *n* Strand *m* ♦ *vt* (*ship*) auf den Strand setzen
beacon ['biːkən] *n* (*signal*) Leuchtfeuer *nt*; (*traffic* ~) Bake *f*
bead [biːd] *n* Perle *f*; (*drop*) Tropfen *m*
beak [biːk] *n* Schnabel *m*
beaker ['biːkə^r] *n* Becher *m*
beam [biːm] *n* (*of wood*) Balken *m*; (*of light*) Strahl *m*; (*smile*) strahlende(s) Lächeln *nt* ♦ *vi* strahlen
bean [biːn] *n* Bohne *f*; (*also:* **baked ~s**) gebackene Bohnen *pl*; ~ **sprouts** *npl* Sojasprossen *pl*
bear [bɛə^r] (*pt* **bore**, *pp* **borne**) *n* Bär *m* ♦ *vt* (*weight, crops*) tragen; (*tolerate*) ertragen; (*young*) gebären ♦ *vi*: **to** ~ **right/left** sich rechts/links halten; ~ **out** *vt* (*suspicions etc*) bestätigen; ~ **up** *vi* sich halten
beard [biəd] *n* Bart *m*; ~**ed** *adj* bärtig
bearer ['bɛərə^r] *n* Träger *m*
bearing ['bɛərɪŋ] *n* (*posture*) Haltung *f*; (*relevance*) Relevanz *f*; (*relation*) Bedeutung *f*; (*TECH*) Kugellager *nt*; ~**s** *npl* (*direction*) Orientierung *f*; (*also:* **ball ~s**) (Kugel)lager *nt*
beast [biːst] *n* Tier *nt*, Vieh *nt*; (*person*) Biest *nt*
beat [biːt] (*pt* **beat**, *pp* **beaten**) *n* (*stroke*) Schlag *m*; (*pulsation*) (Herz)schlag *m*; (*police round*) Runde *f*; Revier *nt*; (*MUS*) Takt *m*;

Beat *m* ♦ *vt, vi* schlagen; **to** ~ **it** abhauen; **off the ~en track** abgelegen; ~ **off** *vt* abschlagen; ~ **up** *vt* zusammenschlagen; ~**en** *pp of* **beat**; ~**ing** *n* Prügel *pl*
beautiful ['bjuːtɪful] *adj* schön; ~**ly** *adv* ausgezeichnet
beauty ['bjuːtɪ] *n* Schönheit *f*; ~ **salon** *n* Schönheitssalon *m*; ~ **spot** *n* Schönheitsfleck *m*; (*BRIT: TOURISM*) (besonders) schöne(r) Ort *m*
beaver ['biːvə^r] *n* Biber *m*
became [bɪ'keɪm] *pt of* **become**
because [bɪ'kɒz] *conj* weil ♦ *prep*: ~ **of** wegen +*gen*, wegen +*dat* (*inf*)
beck [bɛk] *n*: **to be at the** ~ **and call of sb** nach jds Pfeife tanzen
beckon ['bɛkən] *vt, vi*: **to** ~ **sb** jdm ein Zeichen geben
become [bɪ'kʌm] (*irreg: like* **come**) *vi* werden ♦ *vt* werden; (*clothes*) stehen +*dat*
becoming [bɪ'kʌmɪŋ] *adj* (*suitable*) schicklich; (*clothes*) kleidsam
bed [bɛd] *n* Bett *nt*; (*of river*) Flussbett *nt*; (*foundation*) Schicht *f*; (*in garden*) Beet *nt*; **to go to** ~ zu Bett gehen; ~ **and breakfast** *n* Übernachtung *f* mit Frühstück; ~**clothes** *npl* Bettwäsche *f*; ~**ding** *n* Bettzeug *nt*

Bed and Breakfast

ⓘ **Bed and Breakfast** *bedeutet „Übernachtung mit Frühstück", wobei sich dies in Großbritannien nicht auf Hotels, sondern auf kleinere Pensionen, Privathäuser und Bauernhöfe bezieht, wo man wesentlich preisgünstiger übernachten kann als in Hotels. Oft wird für Bed and Breakfast, auch B & B genannt, durch ein entsprechendes Schild im Garten oder an der Einfahrt geworben.*

---

bedlam ['bɛdləm] *n* (*uproar*) tolle(s) Durcheinander *nt*
bed linen *n* Bettwäsche *f*
bedraggled [bɪ'dræɡld] *adj* ramponiert
bed: ~**ridden** *adj* bettlägerig; ~**room** *n* Schlafzimmer *nt*; ~**side** *n*: **at the** ~**side** am Bett; ~**sit(ter)** (*BRIT*) *n* Einzimmerwohnung

f, möblierte(s) Zimmer nt; ~**spread** n Tagesdecke f; ~**time** n Schlafenszeit f

bee [bi:] n Biene f

beech [bi:tʃ] n Buche f

beef [bi:f] n Rindfleisch nt; **roast ~** Roastbeef nt; ~**burger** n Hamburger m

beehive ['bi:haɪv] n Bienenstock m

beeline ['bi:laɪn] n: **to make a ~ for** schnurstracks zugehen auf +acc

been [bi:n] pp of **be**

beer [bɪəʳ] n Bier nt

beet [bi:t] n (vegetable) Rübe f; (US: also: **red ~**) Rote Bete f or Rübe f

beetle ['bi:tl] n Käfer m

beetroot ['bi:tru:t] (BRIT) n Rote Bete f

before [bɪ'fɔ:ʳ] prep vor ♦ conj bevor ♦ adv (of time) zuvor; früher; **the week ~** die Woche zuvor or vorher; **I've done it ~** das hab ich schon mal getan; ~ **going** bevor er/sie etc geht/ging; ~ **she goes** bevor sie geht; ~**hand** adv im Voraus

beg [beg] vt, vi (implore) dringend bitten; (alms) betteln

began [bɪ'gæn] pt of **begin**

beggar ['begəʳ] n Bettler(in) m(f)

begin [bɪ'gɪn] (pt **began**, pp **begun**) vt, vi anfangen, beginnen; (found) gründen; **to ~ doing** or **to do sth** anfangen or beginnen, etw zu tun; **to ~ with** zunächst (einmal); ~**ner** n Anfänger m; ~**ning** n Anfang m

begun [bɪ'gʌn] pp of **begin**

behalf [bɪ'hɑ:f] n: **on ~ of** im Namen +gen; **on my ~** für mich

behave [bɪ'heɪv] vi sich benehmen; **behaviour** [bɪ'heɪvjəʳ] (US **behavior**) n Benehmen nt

beheld [bɪ'held] pt, pp of **behold**

behind [bɪ'haɪnd] prep hinter ♦ adv (late) im Rückstand; (in the rear) hinten ♦ n (inf) Hinterteil nt; ~ **the scenes** (fig) hinter den Kulissen

behold [bɪ'həʊld] (irreg: like **hold**) vt erblicken

beige [beɪʒ] adj beige

Beijing ['beɪ'dʒɪŋ] n Peking nt

being ['bi:ɪŋ] n (existence) (Da)sein nt; (person) Wesen nt; **to come into ~**

entstehen

Belarus [belə'rus] n Weißrussland nt

belated [bɪ'leɪtɪd] adj verspätet

belch [beltʃ] vi rülpsen ♦ vt (smoke) ausspeien

belfry ['belfrɪ] n Glockenturm m

Belgian ['beldʒən] adj belgisch ♦ n Belgier(in) m(f)

Belgium ['beldʒəm] n Belgien nt

belie [bɪ'laɪ] vt Lügen strafen +acc

belief [bɪ'li:f] n Glaube m; (conviction) Überzeugung f; ~ **in sb/sth** Glaube an jdn/etw

believe [bɪ'li:v] vt glauben +dat; (think) glauben, meinen, denken ♦ vi (have faith) glauben; **to ~ in sth** an etw acc glauben; ~**r** n Gläubige(r) f(m)

belittle [bɪ'lɪtl] vt herabsetzen

bell [bel] n Glocke f

belligerent [bɪ'lɪdʒərənt] adj (person) streitsüchtig; (country) Krieg führend

bellow ['beləʊ] vt, vi brüllen

bellows ['beləʊz] npl (TECH) Gebläse nt; (for fire) Blasebalg m

belly ['belɪ] n Bauch m

belong [bɪ'lɒŋ] vi gehören; **to ~ to sb** jdm gehören; **to ~ to a club** etc einem Klub etc angehören; ~**ings** npl Habe f

beloved [bɪ'lʌvɪd] adj innig geliebt ♦ n Geliebte(r) f(m)

below [bɪ'ləʊ] prep unter ♦ adv unten

belt [belt] n (band) Riemen m; (round waist) Gürtel m ♦ vt (fasten) mit Riemen befestigen; (inf: beat) schlagen; ~**way** (US) n (AUT: ring road) Umgehungsstraße f

bemused [bɪ'mju:zd] adj verwirrt

bench [bentʃ] n (seat) Bank f; (workshop) Werkbank f; (judge's seat) Richterbank f; (judges) Richter pl

bend [bend] (pt, pp **bent**) vt (curve) biegen; (stoop) beugen ♦ vi sich biegen; sich beugen ♦ n Biegung f; (BRIT: in road) Kurve f; ~ **down** or **over** vi sich bücken

beneath [bɪ'ni:θ] prep unter ♦ adv darunter

benefactor ['benɪfæktəʳ] n Wohltäter(in) m(f)

beneficial [benɪ'fɪʃəl] adj vorteilhaft; (to

health) heilsam

benefit ['benɪfɪt] n (*advantage*) Nutzen m ♦ vt fördern ♦ vi: **to ~ (from)** Nutzen ziehen (aus)

Benelux ['benɪlʌks] n Beneluxstaaten pl

benevolent [bɪ'nevələnt] adj wohlwollend

benign [bɪ'naɪn] adj (*person*) gütig; (*climate*) mild

bent [bent] pt, pp of **bend** ♦ n (*inclination*) Neigung f ♦ adj (*inf: dishonest*) unehrlich; **to be ~ on** versessen sein auf +acc

bequest [bɪ'kwest] n Vermächtnis nt

bereaved [bɪ'riːvd] npl: **the ~** die Hinterbliebenen pl

beret ['bereɪ] n Baskenmütze f

Berlin [bəː'lɪn] n Berlin nt

berm [bɑːm] (US) n (AUT) Seitenstreifen m

berry ['berɪ] n Beere f

berserk [bə'səːk] adj: **to go ~** wild werden

berth [bəːθ] n (*for ship*) Ankerplatz m; (*in ship*) Koje f; (*in train*) Bett nt ♦ vt am Kai festmachen ♦ vi anlegen

beseech [bɪ'siːtʃ] (pt, pp **besought**) vt anflehen

beset [bɪ'set] (pt, pp **beset**) vt bedrängen

beside [bɪ'saɪd] prep neben, bei; (*except*) außer; **to be ~ o.s. (with)** außer sich sein (vor +dat); **that's ~ the point** das tut nichts zur Sache

besides [bɪ'saɪdz] prep außer, neben ♦ adv außerdem

besiege [bɪ'siːdʒ] vt (MIL) belagern; (*surround*) umlagern, bedrängen

besought [bɪ'sɔːt] pt, pp of **beseech**

best [best] adj beste(r, s) ♦ adv am besten; **the ~ part of** (*quantity*) das meiste +gen; **at ~** höchstens; **to make the ~ of it** das Beste daraus machen; **to do one's ~** sein Bestes tun; **to the ~ of my knowledge** meines Wissens; **to the ~ of my ability** so gut ich kann; **for the ~** zum Besten; **~-before date** n Mindesthaltbarkeitsdatum nt; **~ man** n Trauzeuge m

bestow [bɪ'stəu] vt verleihen

bet [bet] (pt, pp **bet** or **betted**) n Wette f ♦ vt, vi wetten

betray [bɪ'treɪ] vt verraten

better ['betər] adj, adv besser ♦ vt verbessern ♦ n: **to get the ~ of sb** jdn überwinden; **he thought ~ of it** er hat sich eines Besseren besonnen; **you had ~ leave** Sie gehen jetzt wohl besser; **to get ~** (MED) gesund werden; **~ off** adj (*richer*) wohlhabender

betting ['betɪŋ] n Wetten nt; **~ shop** (BRIT) n Wettbüro nt

between [bɪ'twiːn] prep zwischen; (*among*) unter ♦ adv dazwischen

beverage ['bevərɪdʒ] n Getränk nt

bevy ['bevɪ] n Schar f

beware [bɪ'weər] vt, vi sich hüten vor +dat; **"~ of the dog"** „Vorsicht, bissiger Hund!"

bewildered [bɪ'wɪldəd] adj verwirrt

beyond [bɪ'jɔnd] prep (*place*) jenseits +gen; (*time*) über ... hinaus; (*out of reach*) außerhalb +gen ♦ adv darüber hinaus; **~ doubt** ohne Zweifel; **~ repair** nicht mehr zu reparieren

bias ['baɪəs] n (*slant*) Neigung f; (*prejudice*) Vorurteil nt; **~(s)ed** adj voreingenommen

bib [bɪb] n Latz m

Bible ['baɪbl] n Bibel f

bicarbonate of soda [baɪ'kɑːbənɪt-] n Natron nt

bicker ['bɪkər] vi zanken

bicycle ['baɪsɪkl] n Fahrrad nt

bid [bɪd] (pt **bade** or **bid**, pp **bid(den)**) n (*offer*) Gebot nt; (*attempt*) Versuch m ♦ vt, vi (*offer*) bieten; **to ~ farewell** Lebewohl sagen; **~der** n (*person*) Steigerer m; **the highest ~der** der Meistbietende; **~ding** n (*command*) Geheiß nt

bide [baɪd] vt: **to ~ one's time** abwarten

bifocals [baɪ'fəuklz] npl Bifokalbrille f

big [bɪg] adj groß; **~ dipper** [-'dɪpər] n Achterbahn f; **~headed** ['bɪg'hedɪd] adj eingebildet

bigot ['bɪgət] n Frömmler m; **~ed** adj bigott; **~ry** n Bigotterie f

big top n Zirkuszelt nt

bike [baɪk] n Rad nt

bikini [bɪ'kiːnɪ] n Bikini m

bile [baɪl] n (BIOL) Galle f

bilingual [baɪ'lɪŋgwəl] adj zweisprachig

bill [bɪl] n (*account*) Rechnung f; (POL)

Gesetzentwurf m; (US: FIN) Geldschein m; **to fit** or **fill the ~** fig) der/die/das Richtige sein; **"post no ~s"** „Plakate ankleben verboten"; **~board** ['bɪlbɔːd] n Reklameschild nt

illet ['bɪlɪt] n Quartier nt

illfold ['bɪlfəʊld] (US) n Geldscheintasche f

illiards ['bɪljədz] n Billard nt

illion ['bɪljən] n (BRIT) Billion f; (US) Milliarde f

imbo ['bɪmbəʊ] (inf: pej) n Puppe f, Häschen nt

in [bɪn] n Kasten m; (dustbin) (Abfall)eimer m

ind [baɪnd] (pt, pp **bound**) vt (tie) binden; (tie together) zusammenbinden; (oblige) verpflichten; **~ing** n (Buch)einband m ♦ adj verbindlich

inge [bɪndʒ] (inf) n Sauferei f

ingo ['bɪŋgəʊ] n Bingo nt

inoculars [bɪ'nɒkjʊləz] npl Fernglas nt

io... [baɪəʊ] prefix: **~chemistry** n Biochemie f; **~degradable** adj biologisch abbaubar; **~graphy** n Biografie f; **~logical** [baɪə'lɒdʒɪkl] adj biologisch; **~logy** [baɪ'ɒlədʒɪ] n Biologie f

irch [bɜːtʃ] n Birke f

ird [bɜːd] n Vogel m; (BRIT: inf: girl) Mädchen nt; **~'s-eye view** n Vogelschau f; **~ watcher** n Vogelbeobachter(in) m(f); **~ watching** n Vogelbeobachten nt

iro ['baɪərəʊ] ® n Kugelschreiber m

irth [bɜːθ] n Geburt f; **to give ~ to** zur Welt bringen; **~ certificate** n Geburtsurkunde f; **~ control** n Geburtenkontrolle f; **~day** n Geburtstag m; **~day card** n Geburtstagskarte f; **~place** n Geburtsort m; **~ rate** n Geburtenrate f

iscuit ['bɪskɪt] n Keks m

isect [baɪ'sekt] vt halbieren

ishop ['bɪʃəp] n Bischof m

it [bɪt] pt of **bite** ♦ n bisschen, Stückchen nt; (horse's) Gebiss nt; (COMPUT) Bit nt; **a ~ tired** etwas müde

itch [bɪtʃ] n (dog) Hündin f; (unpleasant woman) Weibsstück nt

ite [baɪt] (pt **bit**, pp **bitten**) vt, vi beißen ♦ n

Biss m; (mouthful) Bissen m; **to ~ one's nails** Nägel kauen; **let's have a ~ to eat** lass uns etwas essen

bitten ['bɪtn] pp of **bite**

bitter ['bɪtər] adj bitter; (memory etc) schmerzlich; (person) verbittert ♦ n (BRIT: beer) dunkle(s) Bier nt; **~ness** n Bitterkeit f

blab [blæb] vi klatschen ♦ vt (also: **~ out**) ausplaudern

black [blæk] adj schwarz; (night) finster ♦ vt schwärzen; (shoes) wichsen; (eye) blau schlagen; (BRIT: INDUSTRY) boykottieren; **to give sb a ~ eye** jdm ein blaues Auge schlagen; **in the ~** (bank account) in den schwarzen Zahlen; **~ and blue** adj grün und blau; **~berry** n Brombeere f; **~bird** n Amsel f; **~board** n (Wand)tafel f; **~ coffee** n schwarze(r) Kaffee m; **~currant** n schwarze Johannisbeere f; **~en** vt schwärzen; (fig) verunglimpfen; **B~ Forest** n Schwarzwald m; **~ ice** n Glatteis nt; **~leg** (BRIT) n Streikbrecher(in) m(f); **~list** n schwarze Liste f; **~mail** n Erpressung f ♦ vt erpressen; **~ market** n Schwarzmarkt m; **~out** n Verdunklung f; (MED): **to have a ~out** bewusstlos werden; **~ pudding** n ≈ Blutwurst f; **B~ Sea** n: **the B~ Sea** das Schwarze Meer; **~ sheep** n schwarze(s) Schaf nt; **~smith** n Schmied m; **~ spot** n (AUT) Gefahrenstelle f; (for unemployment etc) schwer betroffene(s) Gebiet nt

bladder ['blædər] n Blase f

blade [bleɪd] n (of weapon) Klinge f; (of grass) Halm m; (of oar) Ruderblatt nt

blame [bleɪm] n Tadel m, Schuld f ♦ vt Vorwürfe machen +dat; **to ~ sb for sth** jdm die Schuld an etw dat geben; **he is to ~** er ist daran schuld

bland [blænd] adj mild

blank [blæŋk] adj leer, unbeschrieben; (look) verdutzt; (verse) Blank- ♦ n (space) Lücke f; Zwischenraum m; (cartridge) Platzpatrone f; **~ cheque** n Blankoscheck m; (fig) Freibrief m

blanket ['blæŋkɪt] n (Woll)decke f

blare [bleər] vi (radio) plärren; (horn) tuten; (MUS) schmettern

blasé [ˈblɑːzeɪ] *adj* blasiert

blast [blɑːst] *n* Explosion *f*; (*of wind*) Windstoß *m* ♦ *vt* (*blow up*) sprengen; **~!** (*inf*) verflixt!; **~off** *n* (*SPACE*) (Raketen)abschuss *m*

blatant [ˈbleɪtənt] *adj* offenkundig

blaze [bleɪz] *n* (*fire*) lodernde(s) Feuer *nt* ♦ *vi* lodern ♦ *vt*: **to ~ a trail** Bahn brechen

blazer [ˈbleɪzər] *n* Blazer *m*

bleach [bliːtʃ] *n* (*also:* **household ~**) Bleichmittel *nt* ♦ *vt* bleichen; **~ed** *adj* gebleicht

bleachers [ˈbliːtʃəz] (*US*) *npl* (*SPORT*) unüberdachte Tribüne *f*

bleak [bliːk] *adj* kahl, rau; (*future*) trostlos

bleary-eyed [ˈblɪərˈaɪd] *adj* triefäugig; (*on waking up*) mit verschlafenen Augen

bleat [bliːt] *vi* blöken; (*fig: complain*) meckern

bled [bled] *pt, pp of* **bleed**

bleed [bliːd] (*pt, pp* **bled**) *vi* bluten ♦ *vt* (*draw blood*) zur Ader lassen; **to ~ to death** verbluten

bleeper [ˈbliːpər] *n* (*of doctor etc*) Funkrufempfänger *m*

blemish [ˈblemɪʃ] *n* Makel *m* ♦ *vt* verunstalten

blend [blend] *n* Mischung *f* ♦ *vt* mischen ♦ *vi* sich mischen; **~er** *n* Mixer *m*, Mixgerät *nt*

bless [bles] (*pt, pp* **blessed**) *vt* segnen; (*give thanks*) preisen; (*make happy*) glücklich machen; **~ you!** Gesundheit!; **~ing** *n* Segen *m*; (*at table*) Tischgebet *nt*; (*happiness*) Wohltat *f*; Segen *m*; (*good wish*) Glück *nt*

blew [bluː] *pt of* **blow**

blimey [ˈblaɪmɪ] (*BRIT: inf*) *excl* verflucht

blind [blaɪnd] *adj* blind; (*corner*) unübersichtlich ♦ *n* (*for window*) Rouleau *nt* ♦ *vt* blenden; **~ alley** *n* Sackgasse *f*; **~fold** *n* Augenbinde *f* ♦ *adj, adv* mit verbundenen Augen ♦ *vt*: **to ~fold sb** jdm die Augen verbinden; **~ly** *adv* blind; (*fig*) blindlings; **~ness** *n* Blindheit *f*; **~ spot** *n* (*AUT*) tote(r) Winkel *m*; (*fig*) schwache(r) Punkt *m*

blink [blɪŋk] *vi* blinzeln; **~ers** *npl* Scheuklappen *pl*

bliss [blɪs] *n* (Glück)seligkeit *f*

blister [ˈblɪstər] *n* Blase *f* ♦ *vi* Blasen werfen

blitz [blɪts] *n* Luftkrieg *m*

blizzard [ˈblɪzəd] *n* Schneesturm *m*

bloated [ˈbləʊtɪd] *adj* aufgedunsen; (*inf: full*) nudelsatt

blob [blɒb] *n* Klümpchen *nt*

bloc [blɒk] *n* (*POL*) Block *m*

block [blɒk] *n* (*of wood*) Block *m*, Klotz *m*; (*of houses*) Häuserblock *m* ♦ *vt* hemmen; **~ade** [blɒˈkeɪd] *n* Blockade *f* ♦ *vt* blockieren; **~age** *n* Verstopfung *f*; **~buster** *n* Knüller *m*; **~ letters** *npl* Blockbuchstaben *pl*; **~ of flats** (*BRIT*) *n* Häuserblock *m*

bloke [bləʊk] (*BRIT: inf*) *n* Kerl *m*, Typ *m*

blond(e) [blɒnd] *adj* blond ♦ *n* Blondine *f*

blood [blʌd] *n* Blut *nt*; **~ donor** *n* Blutspender *m*; **~ group** *n* Blutgruppe *f*; **~ poisoning** *n* Blutvergiftung *f*; **~ pressure** *n* Blutdruck *m*; **~shed** *n* Blutvergießen *nt*; **~shot** *adj* blutunterlaufen; **~ sports** *npl* Jagdsport, Hahnenkampf *etc*; **~stained** *adj* blutbefleckt; **~stream** *n* Blut *nt*, Blutkreislauf *m*; **~ test** *n* Blutprobe *f*; **~thirsty** *adj* blutrünstig; **~ vessel** *n* Blutgefäß *nt*; **~y** *adj* blutig; (*BRIT: inf*) verdammt; **~y-minded** (*BRIT: inf*) *adj* stur

bloom [bluːm] *n* Blüte *f*; (*freshness*) Glanz *m* ♦ *vi* blühen

blossom [ˈblɒsəm] *n* Blüte *f* ♦ *vi* blühen

blot [blɒt] *n* Klecks *m* ♦ *vt* beklecksen; (*ink*) (ab)löschen; **~ out** *vt* auslöschen

blotchy [ˈblɒtʃɪ] *adj* fleckig

blotting paper [ˈblɒtɪŋ-] *n* Löschpapier *nt*

blouse [blaʊz] *n* Bluse *f*

blow [bləʊ] (*pt* **blew**, *pp* **blown**) *n* Schlag *m* ♦ *vi* blasen ♦ *vi* (*wind*) wehen; **to ~ one's nose** sich *dat* die Nase putzen; **~ away** *vt* wegblasen; **~ down** *vt* umwehen; **~ off** *vt* wegwehen ♦ *vi* wegfliegen; **~ out** *vi* ausgehen; **~ over** *vi* vorübergehen; **~ up** *vi* explodieren ♦ *vt* sprengen; **~-dry** *n*: **to have a ~-dry** sich föhnen lassen ♦ *vt* föhnen; **~lamp** (*BRIT*) *n* Lötlampe *f*; **~n** *pp of* **blow**; **~-out** *n* (*AUT*) geplatzte(r) Reifen *m*; **~torch** *n* = **blowlamp**

blue [bluː] *adj* blau; (*inf: unhappy*) niedergeschlagen; (*obscene*) pornografisch;

(joke) anzüglich ♦ *n*: **out of the ~** *(fig)* aus heiterem Himmel; **to have the ~s** traurig sein; **~bell** *n* Glockenblume *f*; **~bottle** *n* Schmeißfliege *f*; **~ film** *n* Pornofilm *m*; **~print** *n (fig)* Entwurf *m*

bluff [blʌf] *vi* bluffen, täuschen ♦ *n (deception)* Bluff *m*; **to call sb's ~** es darauf ankommen lassen

blunder ['blʌndə*r*] *n* grobe(r) Fehler *m*, Schnitzer *m* ♦ *vi* einen groben Fehler machen

blunt [blʌnt] *adj (knife)* stumpf; *(talk)* unverblümt ♦ *vt* abstumpfen

blur [blə:*r*] *n* Fleck *m* ♦ *vt* verschwommen machen

blurb [blə:b] *n* Waschzettel *m*

blush [blʌʃ] *vi* erröten

blustery ['blʌstəri] *adj* stürmisch

boar [bɔ:*r*] *n* Keiler *m*, Eber *m*

board [bɔ:d] *n (of wood)* Brett *nt*; *(of card)* Pappe *f*; *(committee)* Ausschuss *m*; *(of firm)* Aufsichtsrat *m*; *(SCH)* Direktorium *nt* ♦ *vt (train)* einsteigen in +*acc*; *(ship)* an Bord gehen +*gen*; **on ~** *(AVIAT, NAUT)* an Bord; **~ and lodging** Unterkunft *f* und Verpflegung; **full/half ~** *(BRIT)* Voll-/Halbpension *f*; **to go by the ~** flachfallen, über Bord gehen; **~ up** *vt* mit Brettern vernageln; **~er** *n* Kostgänger *m*; *(SCH)* Internatsschüler(in) *m(f)*; **~ game** *n* Brettspiel *nt*; **~ing card** *n (AVIAT, NAUT)* Bordkarte *f*; **~ing house** *n* Pension *f*; **~ing school** *n* Internat *nt*; **~ room** *n* Sitzungszimmer *nt*

boast [bəust] *vi* prahlen ♦ *vt* sich rühmen +*gen* ♦ *n* Großtuerei *f*; Prahlerei *f*; **to ~ about** *or* **of sth** mit etw prahlen

boat [bəut] *n* Boot *nt*; *(ship)* Schiff *nt*; **~er** *n (hat)* Kreissäge *f*; **~swain** *n* = **bosun**; **~ train** *n* Zug *m* mit Fährenanschluss

bob [bɔb] *vi* sich auf und nieder bewegen; **~ up** *vi* auftauchen

bobbin ['bɔbin] *n* Spule *f*

bobby ['bɔbi] *(BRIT: inf)* *n* Bobby *m*

bobsleigh ['bɔbslei] *n* Bob *m*

bode [bəud] *vi*: **to ~ well/ill** ein gutes/ schlechtes Zeichen sein

bodily ['bɔdili] *adj, adv* körperlich

body ['bɔdi] *n* Körper *m*; *(dead)* Leiche *f*; *(group)* Mannschaft *f*; *(AUT)* Karosserie *f*; *(trunk)* Rumpf *m*; **~ building** *n* Bodybuilding *nt*; **~guard** *n* Leibwache *f*; **~work** *n* Karosserie *f*

bog [bɔg] *n* Sumpf *m* ♦ *vt*: **to get ~ged down** sich festfahren

boggle ['bɔgl] *vi* stutzen; **the mind ~s** es ist kaum auszumalen

bog-standard *adj* stinknormal *(inf)*

bogus ['bəugəs] *adj* unecht, Schein-

boil [bɔil] *vt, vi* kochen ♦ *n (MED)* Geschwür *nt*; **to come to the** *(BRIT)* or **a** *(US)* **~** zu kochen anfangen; **to ~ down to** *(fig)* hinauslaufen auf +*acc*; **~ over** *vi* überkochen; **~ed egg** *n* (weich) gekochte(s) Ei *nt*; **~ed potatoes** *npl* Salzkartoffeln *pl*; **~er** *n* Boiler *m*; **~er suit** *(BRIT)* *n* Arbeitsanzug *m*; **~ing point** *n* Siedepunkt *m*

boisterous ['bɔistərəs] *adj* ungestüm

bold [bəuld] *adj (fearless)* unerschrocken; *(handwriting)* fest und klar

bollard ['bɔləd] *n (NAUT)* Poller *m*; *(BRIT: AUT)* Pfosten *m*

bolt [bəult] *n* Bolzen *m*; *(lock)* Riegel *m* ♦ *adv*: **~ upright** kerzengerade ♦ *vt* verriegeln; *(swallow)* verschlingen ♦ *vi (horse)* durchgehen

bomb [bɔm] *n* Bombe *f* ♦ *vt* bombardieren; **~ard** [bɔm'ba:d] *vt* bombardieren; **~ardment** [bɔm'ba:dmənt] *n* Beschießung *f*; **~ disposal** *n*: **~ disposal unit** Bombenräumkommando *nt*; **~er** *n* Bomber *m*; *(terrorist)* Bombenattentäter(in) *m(f)*; **~ing** *n* Bomben *nt*; **~shell** *n (fig)* Bombe *f*

bona fide ['bəunə'faidi] *adj* echt

bond [bɔnd] *n (link)* Band *nt*; *(FIN)* Schuldverschreibung *f*

bondage ['bɔndidʒ] *n* Sklaverei *f*

bone [bəun] *n* Knochen *m*; *(of fish)* Gräte *f*; *(piece of ~)* Knochensplitter *m* ♦ *vt* die Knochen herausnehmen +*dat*; *(fish)* entgräten; **~ dry** *adj (inf)* knochentrocken; **~ idle** *adj* stinkfaul; **~ marrow** *n (ANAT)* Knochenmark *nt*

bonfire ['bɔnfaiə*r*] *n* Feuer *nt* im Freien

bonnet ['bɔnɪt] *n* Haube *f*; (*for baby*) Häubchen *nt*; (*BRIT: AUT*) Motorhaube *f*

bonus ['bəunəs] *n* Bonus *m*; (*annual ~*) Prämie *f*

bony ['bəunɪ] *adj* knochig, knochendürr

boo [bu:] *vt* auspfeifen

booby trap ['bu:bɪ-] *n* Falle *f*

book [buk] *n* Buch *nt* ♦ *vt* (*ticket etc*) vorbestellen; (*person*) verwarnen; **~s** *npl* (*COMM*) Bücher *pl*; **~case** *n* Bücherregal *nt*, Bücherschrank *m*; **~ing office** (*BRIT*) *n* (*RAIL*) Fahrkartenschalter *m*; (*THEAT*) Vorverkaufsstelle *f*; **~keeping** *n* Buchhaltung *f*; **~let** *n* Broschüre *f*; **~maker** *n* Buchmacher *m*; **~seller** *n* Buchhändler *m*; **~shelf** *n* Bücherbord *nt*; **~shop** ['bukʃɔp], **~store** *n* Buchhandlung *f*

boom [bu:m] *n* (*noise*) Dröhnen *nt*; (*busy period*) Hochkonjunktur *f* ♦ *vi* dröhnen

boon [bu:n] *n* Wohltat *f*, Segen *m*

boost [bu:st] *n* Auftrieb *m*; (*fig*) Reklame *f* ♦ *vt* Auftrieb geben; **~er** *n* (*MED*) Wiederholungsimpfung *f*

boot [bu:t] *n* Stiefel *m*; (*BRIT: AUT*) Kofferraum *m* ♦ *vt* (*kick*) einen Fußtritt geben; (*COMPUT*) laden; **to ~** (*in addition*) obendrein

booth [bu:ð] *n* (*at fair*) Bude *f*; (*telephone ~*) Zelle *f*; (*voting ~*) Kabine *f*

booze [bu:z] (*inf*) *n* Alkohol *m*, Schnaps *m* ♦ *vi* saufen

border ['bɔ:dər] *n* Grenze *f*; (*edge*) Kante *f*; (*in garden*) (Blumen)rabatte *f* ♦ *adj* Grenz-; **the B~s** *Grenzregion zwischen England und Schottland*; **~ on** *vt* grenzen an +*acc*; **~line** *n* Grenze *f*; **~line case** *n* Grenzfall *m*

bore [bɔ:r] *pt of* **bear** ♦ *vt* bohren; (*weary*) langweilen ♦ *n* (*person*) Langweiler *m*; (*thing*) langweilige Sache *f*; (*of gun*) Kaliber *nt*; **I am ~d** ich langweile mich; **~dom** *n* Langeweile *f*

boring ['bɔ:rɪŋ] *adj* langweilig

born [bɔ:n] *adj*: **to be ~** geboren werden

borne [bɔ:n] *pp of* **bear**

borough ['bʌrə] *n* Stadt(gemeinde) *f*, Stadtbezirk *m*

borrow ['bɔrəu] *vt* borgen

Bosnia (and) Herzegovina ['bɔznɪə (ənd) hə:tsəgəu'vi:nə] *n* Bosnien und Herzegowina *nt*; **~n** *n* Bosnier(in) *m(f)* ♦ *adj* bosnisch

bosom ['buzəm] *n* Busen *m*

boss [bɔs] *n* Chef *m*, Boss *m* ♦ *vt*: **to ~ around** *or* **about** herumkommandieren; **~y** *adj* herrisch

bosun ['bəusn] *n* Bootsmann *m*

botany ['bɔtənɪ] *n* Botanik *f*

botch [bɔtʃ] *vt* (*also: ~ up*) verpfuschen

both [bəuθ] *adj* beide(s) ♦ *pron* beide(s) ♦ *adv*: **~ X and Y** sowohl X wie *or* als auch Y; **~ (of) the books** beide Bücher; **~ of us went, we ~ went** wir gingen beide

bother ['bɔðər] *vt* (*pester*) quälen ♦ *vi* (*fuss*) sich aufregen ♦ *n* Mühe *f*, Umstand *m*; **to ~ doing sth** sich *dat* die Mühe machen, etw zu tun; **what a ~!** wie ärgerlich!

bottle ['bɔtl] *n* Flasche *f* ♦ *vt* (*in Flaschen*) abfüllen; **~ up** *vt* aufstauen; **~ bank** *n* Altglascontainer *m*; **~d beer** *n* Flaschenbier *nt*; **~d water** *n* in Flaschen abgefülltes Wasser; **~neck** (*also fig*) Engpass *m*; **~ opener** *n* Flaschenöffner *m*

bottom ['bɔtəm] *n* Boden *m*; (*of person*) Hintern *m*; (*riverbed*) Flussbett *nt* ♦ *adj* unterste(r, s)

bough [bau] *n* Zweig *m*, Ast *m*

bought [bɔ:t] *pt*, *pp of* **buy**

boulder ['bəuldər] *n* Felsbrocken *m*

bounce [bauns] *vi* (*person*) herumhüpfen; (*ball*) hochspringen; (*cheque*) platzen ♦ *vt* (*auf*)springen lassen ♦ *n* (*rebound*) Aufprall *m*; **~r** *n* Rausschmeißer *m*

bound [baund] *pt*, *pp of* **bind** ♦ *n* Grenze *f*; (*leap*) Sprung *m* ♦ *vi* (*spring, leap*) (*auf*)springen ♦ *adj* (*obliged*) gebunden, verpflichtet; (*out of ~s*) Zutritt verboten; **to be ~ to do sth** verpflichtet sein, etw zu tun; **it's ~ to happen** es muss so kommen; **to be ~ for ...** nach ... fahren

boundary ['baundrɪ] *n* Grenze *f*

bouquet ['bukeɪ] *n* Strauß *m*; (*of wine*) Blume *f*

bourgeois ['buəʒwɑ:] *adj* kleinbürgerlich, bourgeois ♦ *n* Spießbürger(in) *m(f)*

bout [baut] *n* (*of illness*) Anfall *m*; (*of contest*) ampf *m*

w¹ [bəu] *n* (*ribbon*) Schleife *f*; (*weapon, MUS*) Bogen *m*

w² [bau] *n* (*with head, body*) Verbeugung (*of ship*) Bug *m* ♦ *vi* sich verbeugen; *submit*): **to ~ to** sich beugen +*dat*

wels ['bauəlz] *npl* (*ANAT*) Darm *m*

wl [bəul] *n* (*basin*) Schüssel *f*; (*of pipe*) Pfeifen)kopf *m*; (*wooden ball*) (Holz)kugel *f* ♦ *vt, vi* (die Kugel) rollen

w-legged ['bəu'legɪd] *adj* o-beinig, O-beinig

wler ['bəulə*ʳ*] *n* Werfer *m*; (*BRIT: also:* ~ **at**) Melone *f*

wling ['bəulɪŋ] *n* Kegeln *nt*; ~ **alley** *n* Kegelbahn *f*; ~ **green** *n* Rasen *m* zum owlingspiel

wls *n* (*game*) Bowlsspiel *nt*

w tie [bəu-] *n* Fliege *f*

x [bɔks] *n* (*also:* **cardboard ~**) Schachtel *f*; *bigger*) Kasten *m*; (*THEAT*) Loge *f* ♦ *vt* inpacken ♦ *vi* boxen; ~**er** *n* Boxer *m*; ~**er shorts** (*BRIT*) *npl* Boxershorts *pl*; ~**ing** *n* SPORT) Boxen *nt*; **B~ing Day** (*BRIT*) *n* weite(r) Weihnachtsfeiertag *m*; ~**ing gloves** *npl* Boxhandschuhe *pl*; ~**ing ring** Boxring *m*; ~ **office** *n* (Theater)kasse *f*; **room** *n* Rumpelkammer *f*

Boxing Day

● **Boxing Day** *(26.12.)* ist ein Feiertag in Großbritannien. Wenn Weihnachten auf *n* Wochenende fällt, wird der Feiertag am *ichsten darauf folgenden Wochentag achgeholt. Der Name geht auf einen alten rauch zurück; früher erhielten Händler und eferanten an diesem Tag ein Geschenk, e so genannte Christmas Box.*

y [bɔɪ] *n* Junge *m*

ycott ['bɔɪkɔt] *n* Boykott *m* ♦ *vt* oykottieren

yfriend ['bɔɪfrend] *n* Freund *m*

yish ['bɔɪʃ] *adj* jungenhaft

R. *n abbr* = **British Rail**

a [brɑː] *n* BH *m*

ace [breɪs] *n* (*TECH*) Stütze *f*; (*MED*)

Klammer *f* ♦ *vt* stützen; ~**s** *npl* (*BRIT*) Hosenträger *pl*; **to ~ o.s. for sth** (*fig*) sich auf etw *acc* gefasst machen

bracelet ['breɪslɪt] *n* Armband *nt*

bracing ['breɪsɪŋ] *adj* kräftigend

bracken ['brækən] *n* Farnkraut *nt*

bracket ['brækɪt] *n* Halter *m*, Klammer *f*; (*in punctuation*) Klammer *f*; (*group*) Gruppe *f* ♦ *vt* einklammern; (*fig*) in dieselbe Gruppe einordnen

brag [bræg] *vi* sich rühmen

braid [breɪd] *n* (*hair*) Flechte *f*; (*trim*) Borte *f*

Braille [breɪl] *n* Blindenschrift *f*

brain [breɪn] *n* (*ANAT*) Gehirn *nt*; (*intellect*) Intelligenz *f*, Verstand *m*; (*person*) kluge(r) Kopf *m*; ~**s** *npl* (*intelligence*) Verstand *m*; ~**child** *n* Erfindung *f*; ~**wash** *vt* eine Gehirnwäsche vornehmen bei; ~**wave** *n* Geistesblitz *m*; ~**y** *adj* gescheit

braise [breɪz] *vt* schmoren

brake [breɪk] *n* Bremse *f* ♦ *vt, vi* bremsen; ~ **fluid** *n* Bremsflüssigkeit *f*; ~ **light** *n* Bremslicht *nt*

bramble ['bræmbl] *n* Brombeere *f*

bran [bræn] *n* Kleie *f*; (*food*) Frühstücksflocken *pl*

branch [brɑːntʃ] *n* Ast *m*; (*division*) Zweig *m* ♦ *vi* (*also:* ~ **out**: *road*) sich verzweigen

brand [brænd] *n* (*COMM*) Marke *f*, Sorte *f*; (*on cattle*) Brandmal *nt* ♦ *vt* brandmarken; (*COMM*) ein Warenzeichen geben +*dat*

brandish ['brændɪʃ] *vt* (*drohend*) schwingen

brand-new ['brænd'njuː] *adj* funkelnagelneu

brandy ['brændɪ] *n* Weinbrand *m*, Kognak *m*

brash [bræʃ] *adj* unverschämt

brass [brɑːs] *n* Messing *nt*; **the ~** (*MUS*) das Blech; ~ **band** *n* Blaskapelle *f*

brassière ['bræsɪə*ʳ*] *n* Büstenhalter *m*

brat [bræt] *n* Gör *nt*

bravado [brə'vɑːdəu] *n* Tollkühnheit *f*

brave [breɪv] *adj* tapfer ♦ *vt* die Stirn bieten +*dat*; ~**ry** *n* Tapferkeit *f*

brawl [brɔːl] *n* Rauferei *f*

brawn [brɔːn] *n* (*ANAT*) Muskeln *pl*; (*strength*) Muskelkraft *f*

bray [breɪ] *vi* schreien

brazen ['breɪzn] *adj* (*shameless*) unverschämt

♦ vt: to ~ it out sich mit Lügen und Betrügen durchsetzen

brazier ['breɪzɪəʳ] n (of workmen) offene(r) Kohlenofen m

Brazil [brə'zɪl] n Brasilien nt; **~ian** adj brasilianisch ♦ n Brasilianer(in) m(f)

breach [briːtʃ] n (gap) Lücke f; (MIL) Durchbruch m; (of discipline) Verstoß m (gegen die Disziplin); (of faith) Vertrauensbruch m ♦ vt durchbrechen; ~ **of contract** Vertragsbruch m; ~ **of the peace** öffentliche Ruhestörung f

bread [bred] n Brot nt; ~ **and butter** Butterbrot nt; **~bin** n Brotkasten m; ~ **box** (US) n Brotkasten m; **~crumbs** npl Brotkrumen pl; (COOK) Paniermehl nt; **~line** n: **to be on the ~line** sich gerade so durchschlagen

breadth [bretθ] n Breite f

breadwinner ['bredwɪnəʳ] n Ernährer m

break [breɪk] (pt **broke**, pp **broken**) vt (destroy) (ab- or zer)brechen; (promise) brechen, nicht einhalten ♦ vi (fall apart) auseinander brechen; (collapse) zusammenbrechen; (dawn) anbrechen ♦ n (gap) Lücke f; (chance) Chance f, Gelegenheit f; (fracture) Bruch m; (rest) Pause f; ~ **down** vt (figures, data) aufschlüsseln; (undermine) überwinden ♦ vi (car) eine Panne haben; (person) zusammenbrechen; ~ **even** vi die Kosten decken; ~ **free** vi sich losreißen; ~ **in** vt (horse) zureiten ♦ vi (burglar) einbrechen; ~ **into** vt fus (house) einbrechen in +acc; ~ **loose** vi sich losreißen; ~ **off** vi abbrechen; ~ **open** vt (door etc) aufbrechen; ~ **out** vi ausbrechen; **to ~ out in spots** Pickel bekommen; ~ **up** vi zerbrechen; (fig) sich zerstreuen; (BRIT: SCH) in die Ferien gehen ♦ vt brechen; **~age** n Bruch m, Beschädigung f; **~down** n (TECH) Panne f; (MED: also: **nervous ~down**) Zusammenbruch m; **~down van** (BRIT) n Abschleppwagen m; **~er** n Brecher m

breakfast ['brekfəst] n Frühstück nt

break: **~-in** n Einbruch m; **~ing** n: **~ing and entering** (JUR) Einbruch m; **~through**

n Durchbruch m; **~water** n Wellenbrecher m

breast [brest] n Brust f; **~-feed** (irreg: like **feed**) vt, vi stillen; **~-stroke** n Brustschwimmen nt

breath [breθ] n Atem m; **out of ~** außer Atem; **under one's ~** flüsternd

Breathalyzer ['breθəlaɪzəʳ] ® n Röhrchen nt

breathe [briːð] vt, vi atmen; ~ **in** vt, vi einatmen; ~ **out** vt, vi ausatmen; **~r** n Verschnaufpause f; **breathing** n Atmung f

breathless ['breθlɪs] adj atemlos

breathtaking ['breθteɪkɪŋ] adj atemberaubend

bred [bred] pt, pp of **breed**

breed [briːd] (pt, pp **bred**) vi sich vermehren ♦ vt züchten ♦ n (race) Rasse f, Zucht f; **~ing** n Züchtung f; (upbringing) Erziehung f

breeze [briːz] n Brise f; **breezy** adj windig; (manner) munter

brevity ['brevɪtɪ] n Kürze f

brew [bruː] vt (beer) brauen ♦ vi (storm) sich zusammenziehen; **~ery** n Brauerei f

bribe [braɪb] n Bestechungsgeld nt, Bestechungsgeschenk nt ♦ vt bestechen; **~ry** ['braɪbərɪ] n Bestechung f

bric-a-brac ['brɪkəbræk] n Nippes pl

brick [brɪk] n Backstein m; **~layer** n Maurer m; **~works** n Ziegelei f

bridal ['braɪdl] adj Braut-

bride [braɪd] n Braut f; **~groom** n Bräutigam m; **~smaid** n Brautjungfer f

bridge [brɪdʒ] n Brücke f; (NAUT) Kommandobrücke f; (CARDS) Bridge nt; (ANAT) Nasenrücken m ♦ vt eine Brücke schlagen über +acc; (fig) überbrücken

bridle ['braɪdl] n Zaum m ♦ vt (fig) zügeln; (horse) aufzäumen; ~ **path** n Reitweg m

brief [briːf] adj kurz ♦ n (JUR) Akten pl ♦ vt instruieren; **~s** npl (underwear) Schlüpfer m, Slip m; **~case** n Aktentasche f; **~ing** n (genaue) Anweisung f; **~ly** adv kurz

brigadier [brɪgə'dɪəʳ] n Brigadegeneral m

bright [braɪt] adj hell; (cheerful) heiter; (idea) klug; **~en (up)** ['braɪtn-] vt aufhellen; (person) aufheitern ♦ vi sich aufheitern

brilliance ['brɪljəns] n Glanz m; (of person)

Scharfsinn m

brilliant ['brɪljənt] adj glänzend

brim [brɪm] n Rand m

brine [braɪn] n Salzwasser nt

bring [brɪŋ] (pt, pp **brought**) vt bringen; **~ about** vt zustande or zu Stande bringen; **~ back** vt zurückbringen; **~ down** vt (price) senken; **~ forward** vt (meeting) vorverlegen; (COMM) übertragen; **~ in** vt hereinbringen; (harvest) einbringen; **~ off** vt davontragen; (success) erzielen; **~ out** vt (object) herausbringen; **~ round** or **to** vt wieder zu sich bringen; **~ up** vt aufziehen; (question) zur Sprache bringen

brink [brɪŋk] n Rand m

brisk [brɪsk] adj lebhaft

bristle ['brɪsl] n Borste f ♦ vi sich sträuben; **bristling with** strotzend vor +dat

Britain ['brɪtən] n (also: **Great ~**) Großbritannien nt

British ['brɪtɪʃ] adj britisch ♦ npl: **the ~** die Briten pl; **~ Isles** npl: **the ~ Isles** die Britischen Inseln pl; **~ Rail** n die Britischen Eisenbahnen

Briton ['brɪtən] n Brite m, Britin f

Brittany ['brɪtənɪ] n die Bretagne

brittle ['brɪtl] adj spröde

broach [brəʊtʃ] vt (subject) anschneiden

broad [brɔːd] adj breit; (hint) deutlich; (general) allgemein; (accent) stark; **in ~ daylight** am helllichten Tag; **~band** n Breitband nt; **~cast** (pt, pp **broadcast**) n Rundfunkübertragung f ♦ vt, vi übertragen, senden; **~en** vt erweitern ♦ vi sich erweitern; **~ly** adv allgemein gesagt; **~-minded** adj tolerant

broccoli ['brɔkəlɪ] n Brokkoli pl

brochure ['brəʊʃjʊə'] n Broschüre f

broil [brɔɪl] vt (grill) grillen

broke [brəʊk] pt of **break** ♦ adj (inf) pleite

broken ['brəʊkn] pp of **break** ♦ adj: **~ leg** gebrochenes Bein; **in ~ English** in gebrochenem Englisch; **~-hearted** adj untröstlich

broker ['brəʊkə'] n Makler m

brolly ['brɔlɪ] (BRIT: inf) n Schirm m

bronchitis [brɔŋ'kaɪtɪs] n Bronchitis f

bronze [brɔnz] n Bronze f

brooch [brəʊtʃ] n Brosche f

brood [bruːd] n Brut f ♦ vi brüten

brook [bruk] n Bach m

broom [brum] n Besen m

Bros. abbr = **Brothers**

broth [brɔθ] n Suppe f, Fleischbrühe f

brothel ['brɔθl] n Bordell nt

brother ['brʌðə'] n Bruder m; **~-in-law** n Schwager m

brought [brɔːt] pt, pp of **bring**

brow [brau] n (eyebrow) (Augen)braue f; (forehead) Stirn f; (of hill) Bergkuppe f

brown [braun] adj braun ♦ n Braun nt ♦ vt bräunen; **~ bread** n Mischbrot nt; **B~ie** n Wichtel m; **~ paper** n Packpapier nt

browse [brauz] vi (in books) blättern; (in shop) schmökern, herumschauen; **~r** n (COMPUT) Browser m

bruise [bruːz] n Bluterguss m, blaue(r) Fleck m ♦ vt einen blauen Fleck geben ♦ vi einen blauen Fleck bekommen

brunt [brʌnt] n volle Wucht f

brush [brʌʃ] n Bürste f; (for sweeping) Handbesen m; (for painting) Pinsel m; (fight) kurze(r) Kampf m; (MIL) Scharmützel nt; (fig) Auseinandersetzung f ♦ vt (clean) bürsten; (sweep) fegen; (usu. ~ past, ~ against) streifen; **~ aside** vt abtun; **~ up** vt (knowledge) auffrischen; **~wood** n Gestrüpp nt

brusque [bruːsk] adj schroff

Brussels ['brʌslz] n Brüssel nt; **~ sprout** n Rosenkohl m

brutal ['bruːtl] adj brutal

brute [bruːt] n (person) Scheusal nt ♦ adj: **by ~ force** mit roher Kraft

B.Sc. n abbr = **Bachelor of Science**

BSE n abbr (= bovine spongiform encephalopathy) BSE f

bubble ['bʌbl] n (Luft)blase f ♦ vi sprudeln; (with joy) übersprudeln; **~ bath** n Schaumbad nt; **~ gum** n Kaugummi m or nt

buck [bʌk] n Bock m; (US: inf) Dollar m ♦ vi bocken; **to pass the ~ (to sb)** die Verantwortung (auf jdn) abschieben; **~ up** (inf) vi sich zusammenreißen

bucket [ˈbʌkɪt] n Eimer m

Buckingham Palace

ℹ️ **Buckingham Palace** *ist die offizielle Londoner Residenz der britischen Monarchen und liegt am St James Park. Der Palast wurde 1703 für den Herzog von Buckingham erbaut, 1762 von George III. gekauft, zwischen 1821 und 1836 von John Nash umgebaut, und Anfang des 20. Jahrhunderts teilweise neu gestaltet. Teile des Buckingham Palace sind heute der Öffentlichkeit zugänglich.*

buckle [ˈbʌkl] n Schnalle f ♦ vt (an- or zusammen)schnallen ♦ vi (bend) sich verziehen

bud [bʌd] n Knospe f ♦ vi knospen, keimen

Buddhism [ˈbudɪzəm] n Buddhismus m; **Buddhist** adj buddhistisch ♦ n Buddhist(in) m(f)

budding [ˈbʌdɪŋ] adj angehend

buddy [ˈbʌdɪ] (inf) n Kumpel m

budge [bʌdʒ] vt, vi (sich) von der Stelle rühren

budgerigar [ˈbʌdʒərɪgɑːr] n Wellensittich m

budget [ˈbʌdʒɪt] n Budget nt; (POL) Haushalt m ♦ vi: **to ~ for sth** etw einplanen

budgie [ˈbʌdʒɪ] n = **budgerigar**

buff [bʌf] adj (colour) lederfarben ♦ n (enthusiast) Fan m

buffalo [ˈbʌfələu] (pl ~ or ~es) n (BRIT) Büffel m; (US: bison) Bison m

buffer [ˈbʌfər] n Puffer m; (COMPUT) Pufferspeicher m; ~ **zone** n Pufferzone f

buffet¹ [ˈbʌfɪt] n (blow) Schlag m ♦ vt (herum)stossen

buffet² [ˈbufeɪ] (BRIT) n (bar) Imbissraum m, Erfrischungsraum m; (food) (kaltes) Büfett nt; ~ **car** (BRIT) n Speisewagen m

bug [bʌg] n (also fig) Wanze f ♦ vt verwanzen; **the room is bugged** das Zimmer ist verwanzt

bugle [ˈbjuːgl] n Jagdhorn nt; (MIL: MUS) Bügelhorn nt

build [bɪld] (pt, pp **built**) vt bauen ♦ n Körperbau m; ~ **up** vt aufbauen; ~**er** n

Bauunternehmer m; ~**ing** n Gebäude nt; ~**ing society** (BRIT) n Bausparkasse f

built [bɪlt] pt, pp of **build**; ~-**in** adj (cupboard) eingebaut; ~-**up area** n Wohngebiet nt

bulb [bʌlb] n (BOT) (Blumen)zwiebel f; (ELEC) Glühlampe f, Birne f

Bulgaria [bʌlˈgeərɪə] n Bulgarien nt; ~**n** adj bulgarisch ♦ n Bulgare m, Bulgarin f; (LING) Bulgarisch nt

bulge [bʌldʒ] n Wölbung f ♦ vi sich wölben

bulk [bʌlk] n Größe f, Masse f; (greater part) Großteil m; **in** ~ (COMM) en gros; **the ~ of** der größte Teil +gen; ~**head** n Schott nt; ~**y** adj (sehr) umfangreich; (goods) sperrig

bull [bul] n Bulle m; (cattle) Stier m; ~**dog** n Bulldogge f

bulldozer [ˈbuldəuzər] n Planierraupe f

bullet [ˈbulɪt] n Kugel f

bulletin [ˈbulɪtɪn] n Bulletin nt, Bekanntmachung f

bulletproof [ˈbulɪtpruːf] adj kugelsicher

bullfight [ˈbulfaɪt] n Stierkampf m; ~**er** n Stierkämpfer m; ~**ing** n Stierkamp m

bullion [ˈbuljən] n Barren m

bullock [ˈbulək] n Ochse m

bullring [ˈbulrɪŋ] n Stierkampfarena f

bull's-eye [ˈbulzaɪ] n Zentrum nt

bully [ˈbulɪ] n Raufbold m ♦ vt einschüchtern

bum [bʌm] n (inf: backside) Hintern m; (tramp) Landstreicher m

bumblebee [ˈbʌmblbiː] n Hummel f

bump [bʌmp] n (blow) Stoß m; (swelling) Beule f ♦ vt, vi stoßen, prallen; ~ **into** vt fus stoßen gegen ♦ vt (person) treffen; ~**er** n (AUT) Stoßstange f ♦ adj (edition) dick; (harvest) Rekord-

bumpy [ˈbʌmpɪ] adj holprig

bun [bʌn] n Korinthenbrötchen nt

bunch [bʌntʃ] n (of flowers) Strauß m; (of keys) Bund m; (of people) Haufen m; ~**es** npl (in hair) Zöpfe pl

bundle [ˈbʌndl] n Bündel nt ♦ vt (also: ~ **up**) bündeln

bungalow [ˈbʌŋgələu] n einstöckige(s) Haus nt, Bungalow m

bungle [ˈbʌŋgl] vt verpfuschen

bunion [ˈbʌnjən] n entzündete(r) Fußballen m

unk [bʌŋk] n Schlafkoje f; **~ beds** npl Etagenbett nt

unker ['bʌŋkəʳ] n (coal store) Kohlenbunker m; (GOLF) Sandloch nt

unny ['bʌnɪ] n (also: **~ rabbit**) Häschen nt

unting ['bʌntɪŋ] n Fahnentuch nt

uoy [bɔɪ] n Boje f; (lifebuoy) Rettungsboje f; **~ant** adj (floating) schwimmend; (fig) heiter

urden ['bɜːdn] n (weight) Ladung f, Last f; (fig) Bürde f ♦ vt belasten

ureau ['bjuərəu] n (pl **~x**) n (BRIT: writing desk) Sekretär m; (US: chest of drawers) Kommode f; (for information etc) Büro nt

ureaucracy [bjuə'rɔkrəsɪ] n Bürokratie f

ureaucrat ['bjuərəkræt] n Bürokrat(in) m(f)

ureaux ['bjuərəuz] npl of **bureau**

urglar ['bɜːgləʳ] n Einbrecher m; **~ alarm** n Einbruchssicherung f; **~y** n Einbruch m

urial ['bɛrɪəl] n Beerdigung f

urly ['bɜːlɪ] adj stämmig

urma ['bɜːmə] n Birma nt

urn [bɜːn] (pt, pp **burned** or **burnt**) vt verbrennen ♦ vi brennen ♦ n Brandwunde f; **~ down** vt, vi abbrennen; **~er** n Brenner m; **~ing** adj brennend; **~t** [bɜːnt] pt, pp of **burn**

urrow ['bʌrəu] n (of fox) Bau m; (of rabbit) Höhle f ♦ vt eingraben

ursar ['bɜːsəʳ] n Kassenverwalter m, Quästor m; **~y** (BRIT) n Stipendium nt

urst [bɜːst] (pt, pp **burst**) vt zerbrechen ♦ vi platzen ♦ n Explosion f; (outbreak) Ausbruch m; (in pipe) Bruch(stelle f) m; **to ~ into flames** in Flammen aufgehen; **to ~ into tears** in Tränen ausbrechen; **to ~ out laughing** in Gelächter ausbrechen; **~ into** vt fus (room etc) platzen in +acc; **~ open** vi aufbrechen

ury ['bɛrɪ] vt vergraben; (in grave) beerdigen

us [bʌs] n (Auto)bus m, Omnibus m

ush [buʃ] n Busch m; **to beat about the ~** wie die Katze um den heißen Brei herumgehen; **~y** ['buʃɪ] adj buschig

usily ['bɪzɪlɪ] adv geschäftig

usiness ['bɪznɪs] n Geschäft nt; (concern)

Angelegenheit f; **it's none of your ~** es geht dich nichts an; **to mean ~** es ernst meinen; **to be away on ~** geschäftlich verreist sein; **it's my ~ to ...** es ist meine Sache, zu ...; **~like** adj geschäftsmäßig; **~man** (irreg) n Geschäftsmann m; **~ trip** n Geschäftsreise f; **~woman** (irreg) n Geschäftsfrau f

busker ['bʌskəʳ] n (BRIT) Straßenmusikant m

bus: ~ shelter n Wartehäuschen nt; **~ station** n Busbahnhof m; **~ stop** n Bushaltestelle f

bust [bʌst] n Büste f ♦ adj (broken) kaputt(gegangen); (business) pleite; **to go ~** Pleite machen

bustle ['bʌsl] n Getriebe nt ♦ vi hasten

bustling ['bʌslɪŋ] adj geschäftig

busy ['bɪzɪ] adj beschäftigt; (road) belebt ♦ vt: **to ~ o.s.** sich beschäftigen; **~body** n Übereifrige(r) mf; **~ signal** (US) n (TEL) Besetztzeichen nt

KEYWORD

but [bʌt] conj 1 (yet) aber; **not X but Y** nicht X sondern Y

2 (however): **I'd love to come, but I'm busy** ich würde gern kommen, bin aber beschäftigt

3 (showing disagreement, surprise etc): **but that's fantastic!** (aber) das ist ja fantastisch!

♦ prep (apart from, except): **nothing but trouble** nichts als Ärger; **no-one but him can do it** niemand außer ihn kann es machen; **but for you/your help** ohne dich/deine Hilfe; **anything but that** alles, nur das nicht

♦ adv (just, only): **she's but a child** sie ist noch ein Kind; **had I but known** wenn ich es nur gewusst hätte; **I can but try** ich kann es immerhin versuchen; **all but finished** so gut wie fertig

butcher ['butʃəʳ] n Metzger m; (murderer) Schlächter m ♦ vt schlachten; (kill) abschlachten; **~'s (shop)** n Metzgerei f

butler ['bʌtləʳ] n Butler m

butt [bʌt] n (cask) große(s) Fass nt; (BRIT: fig: target) Zielscheibe f; (of gun) Kolben m; (of cigarette) Stummel m ♦ vt (mit dem Kopf) stoßen; ~ **in** vi sich einmischen

butter ['bʌtəʳ] n Butter f ♦ vt buttern; ~ **bean** n Wachsbohne f; ~**cup** n Butterblume f

butterfly ['bʌtəflaɪ] n Schmetterling m; (SWIMMING: also: ~ **stroke**) Butterflystil m

buttocks ['bʌtəks] npl Gesäß nt

button ['bʌtn] n Knopf m ♦ vt, vi (also: ~ **up**) zuknöpfen

buttress ['bʌtrɪs] n Strebepfeiler m; Stützbogen m

buxom ['bʌksəm] adj drall

buy [baɪ] (pt, pp **bought**) vt kaufen ♦ n Kauf m; **to ~ sb a drink** jdm einen Drink spendieren; ~**er** n Käufer(in) m(f)

buzz [bʌz] n Summen nt ♦ vi summen; ~**er** ['bʌzəʳ] n Summer m; ~ **word** n Modewort nt

by [baɪ] prep 1 (referring to cause, agent) of, durch; **killed by lightning** vom Blitz getötet; **a painting by Picasso** ein Gemälde von Picasso
2 (referring to method, manner): **by bus/car/train** mit dem Bus/Auto/Zug; **to pay by cheque** per Scheck bezahlen; **by moonlight** bei Mondschein; **by saving hard, he ...** indem er eisern sparte, ... er ...
3 (via, through) über +acc; **he came in by the back door** er kam durch die Hintertür herein
4 (close to, past) bei, an +dat; **a holiday by the sea** ein Urlaub am Meer; **she rushed by me** sie eilte an mir vorbei
5 (not later than): **by 4 o'clock** bis 4 Uhr; **by this time tomorrow** morgen um diese Zeit; **by the time I got here it was too late** als ich hier ankam, war es zu spät
6 (during): **by day** bei Tag
7 (amount): **by the kilo/metre** kiloweise/meterweise; **paid by the hour** stundenweise bezahlt
8 (MATH, measure): **to divide by 3** durch 3

teilen; **to multiply by 3** mit 3 malnehmen; **a room 3 metres by 4** ein Zimmer 3 mal 4 Meter; **it's broader by a metre** es ist (um) einem Meter breiter
9 (according to) nach; **it's all right by me** von mir aus gern
10: **(all) by oneself** etc ganz allein
11: **by the way** übrigens
♦ adv 1 see **go**; **pass** etc
2: **by and by** irgendwann; (with past tenses) nach einiger Zeit; **by and large** (on the whole) im Großen und Ganzen

bye(-bye) ['baɪ('baɪ)] excl (auf) Wiedersehen

by(e)-law ['baɪlɔː] n Verordnung f

by-election ['baɪɪlekʃən] (BRIT) n Nachwahl f

bygone ['baɪɡɒn] adj vergangen ♦ n: **let ~s be ~s** lass(t) das Vergangene vergangen sein

bypass ['baɪpɑːs] n Umgehungsstraße f ♦ vt umgehen

by-product ['baɪprɒdʌkt] n Nebenprodukt nt

bystander ['baɪstændəʳ] n Zuschauer m

byte [baɪt] n (COMPUT) Byte nt

byword ['baɪwəːd] n Inbegriff m

C, c

C [siː] n (MUS) C nt

C. abbr (= centigrade) C

C.A. abbr = **chartered accountant**

cab [kæb] n Taxi nt; (of train) Führerstand m; (of truck) Führersitz m

cabaret ['kæbəreɪ] n Kabarett nt

cabbage ['kæbɪdʒ] n Kohl(kopf) m

cabin ['kæbɪn] n Hütte f; (NAUT) Kajüte f; (AVIAT) Kabine f; ~ **crew** n (AVIAT) Flugbegleitpersonal nt; ~ **cruiser** n Motorjacht f

cabinet ['kæbɪnɪt] n Schrank m; (for china) Vitrine f; (POL) Kabinett nt; ~~**maker** n Kunsttischler m

cable ['keɪbl] n Drahtseil nt, Tau nt; (TEL) (Leitungs)kabel nt; (telegram) Kabel nt ♦ vt kabeln, telegrafieren; ~ **car** n Seilbahn f; ~ **television** n Kabelfernsehen nt

cache [kæʃ] n geheime(s) (Waffen)lager nt; geheime(s) (Proviant)lager nt

cackle ['kækl] vi gackern

cacti ['kæktaɪ] npl of **cactus**

cactus ['kæktəs] (pl **cacti**) n Kaktus m, Kaktee f

caddie ['kædɪ] n (GOLF) Golfjunge m; **caddy** ['kædɪ] n = **caddie**

cadet [kə'dɛt] n Kadett m

cadge [kædʒ] vt schmarotzen

Caesarean [sɪ'zɛərɪən] adj: ~ **(section)** Kaiserschnitt m

café ['kæfeɪ] n Café nt, Restaurant nt

cafeteria [kæfɪ'tɪərɪə] n Selbstbedienungsrestaurant nt

caffein(e) ['kæfi:n] n Koffein nt

cage [keɪdʒ] n Käfig m ♦ vt einsperren

cagey ['keɪdʒɪ] adj geheimnistuerisch, zurückhaltend

cagoule [kə'gu:l] n Windhemd nt

Cairo ['kaɪərəu] n Kairo nt

cajole [kə'dʒəul] vt überreden

cake [keɪk] n Kuchen m; (of soap) Stück nt; ~**d** adj verkrustet

calamity [kə'læmɪtɪ] n Unglück nt, (Schicksals)schlag m

calcium ['kælsɪəm] n Kalzium nt

calculate ['kælkjuleɪt] vt berechnen, kalkulieren; **calculating** adj berechnend; **calculation** [kælkju'leɪʃən] n Berechnung f; **calculator** n Rechner m

calendar ['kæləndə'] n Kalender m; ~ **month** n Kalendermonat m

calf [kɑ:f] (pl **calves**) n Kalb nt; (also: ~**skin**) Kalbsleder nt; (ANAT) Wade f

calibre ['kælɪbə'] (US **caliber**) n Kaliber nt

call [kɔ:l] vt rufen; (name) nennen; (meeting) einberufen; (awaken) wecken; (TEL) anrufen ♦ vi (shout) rufen; (visit: also: ~ **in**, ~ **round**) vorbeikommen ♦ n (shout) Ruf m; (TEL) Anruf m; **to be ~ed** heißen; **on** ~ in Bereitschaft; ~ **back** vi (return) wiederkommen; (TEL) zurückrufen; ~ **for** vt fus (demand) erfordern, verlangen; (fetch) abholen; ~ **off** vt (cancel) absagen; ~ **on** vt fus (visit) besuchen; (turn to) bitten; ~ **out** vi rufen; ~ **up** vt (MIL) einberufen;

~**box** (BRIT) n Telefonzelle f; ~ **centre** n Telefoncenter nt, Callcenter nt; ~**er** n Besucher(in) m(f); (TEL) Anrufer m; ~ **girl** n Callgirl nt; ~-**in** (US) n (phone-in) Phone-in nt; ~**ing** n (vocation) Berufung f; ~**ing card** (US) n Visitenkarte f

callous ['kæləs] adj herzlos

calm [kɑ:m] n Ruhe f; (NAUT) Flaute f ♦ vt beruhigen ♦ adj ruhig; (person) gelassen; ~ **down** vi sich beruhigen ♦ vt beruhigen

Calor gas ['kælə'-] ® n Propangas nt

calorie ['kælərɪ] n Kalorie f

calves [kɑ:vz] npl of **calf**

Cambodia [kæm'bəudɪə] n Kambodscha nt

camcorder ['kæmkɔ:də'] n Camcorder m

came [keɪm] pt of **come**

cameo ['kæmɪəu] n Kamee f

camera ['kæmərə] n Fotoapparat m; (CINE, TV) Kamera f; **in** ~ unter Ausschluss der Öffentlichkeit; ~**man** (irreg) n Kameramann m; ~**phone** n Fotohandy nt

camouflage ['kæməflɑ:ʒ] n Tarnung f ♦ vt tarnen

camp [kæmp] n Lager nt ♦ vi zelten, campen ♦ adj affektiert

campaign [kæm'peɪn] n Kampagne f; (MIL) Feldzug m ♦ vi (MIL) Krieg führen; (fig) werben, Propaganda machen; (POL) den Wahlkampf führen

camp: ~ **bed** ['kæmp'bed] (BRIT) n Campingbett nt; ~**er** ['kæmpə'] n Camper(in) m(f); (vehicle) Campingwagen m; ~**ing** ['kæmpɪŋ] n: **to go** ~**ing** zelten, Camping machen; ~**ing gas** (US) n Campinggas nt; ~**site** ['kæmpsaɪt] n Campingplatz m

campus ['kæmpəs] n Universitätsgelände nt, Campus m

can¹ [kæn] n Büchse f, Dose f; (for water) Kanne f ♦ vt konservieren, in Büchsen einmachen

---

KEYWORD

can² [kæn] (negative **cannot**, **can't**, conditional **could**) aux vb **1** (be able to, know how to) können; **I can see you tomorrow, if you like** ich könnte Sie morgen sehen, wenn Sie wollen; **I can swim** ich kann schwimmen; **can you speak German?** sprechen Sie Deutsch?

2 (*may*) können, dürfen; **could I have a word with you?** könnte ich Sie kurz sprechen?

Canada ['kænədə] n Kanada nt; **Canadian** [kə'neɪdɪən] adj kanadisch ♦ n Kanadier(in) m(f)

canal [kə'næl] n Kanal m

canapé ['kænəpeɪ] n Cocktail- or Appetithappen m

canary [kə'neərɪ] n Kanarienvogel m

cancel ['kænsəl] vt absagen; (*delete*) durchstreichen; (*train*) streichen; **~lation** [kænsə'leɪʃən] n Absage f; Streichung f

cancer ['kænsər] n (ASTROL: C~) Krebs m

candid ['kændɪd] adj offen, ehrlich

candidate ['kændɪdeɪt] n Kandidat(in) m(f)

candle ['kændl] n Kerze f; **~light** n Kerzenlicht nt; **~stick** n (*also: ~ holder*) Kerzenhalter m

candour ['kændər] (US **candor**) n Offenheit f

candy ['kændɪ] n Kandis(zucker) m; (US) Bonbons pl; **~floss** [BRIT] n Zuckerwatte f

cane [keɪn] n (BOT) Rohr nt; (*stick*) Stock m ♦ vt (BRIT: *beat*) schlagen

canine ['keɪnaɪn] adj Hunde-

canister ['kænɪstər] n Blechdose f

cannabis ['kænəbɪs] n Hanf m, Haschisch nt

canned [kænd] adj Büchsen-, eingemacht

cannon ['kænən] n (pl ~ or ~s) Kanone f

cannot ['kænɒt] = **can not**

canny ['kænɪ] adj schlau

canoe [kə'nuː] n Kanu nt; **~ing** n Kanusport m, Kanufahren nt

canon ['kænən] n (*clergyman*) Domherr m; (*standard*) Grundsatz m

can-opener ['kænəʊpnər] n Büchsenöffner m

canopy ['kænəpɪ] n Baldachin m

can't [kænt] = **can not**

cantankerous [kæn'tæŋkərəs] adj zänkisch, mürrisch

canteen [kæn'tiːn] n Kantine f; (BRIT: *of cutlery*) Besteckkasten m

canter ['kæntər] n Kanter m ♦ vi in kurzem Galopp reiten

canvas ['kænvəs] n Segeltuch nt; (*sail*) Segel nt; (*for painting*) Leinwand f; **under ~** (*camping*) in Zelten

canvass ['kænvəs] vi um Stimmen werben; **~ing** n Wahlwerbung f

canyon ['kænjən] n Felsenschlucht f

cap [kæp] n Mütze f; (*of pen*) Kappe f; (*of bottle*) Deckel m ♦ vt (*surpass*) übertreffen; (SPORT); (*put limit on*) einen Höchstsatz festlegen für

capability [keɪpə'bɪlɪtɪ] n Fähigkeit f

capable ['keɪpəbl] adj fähig

capacity [kə'pæsɪtɪ] n Fassungsvermögen nt; (*ability*) Fähigkeit f; (*position*) Eigenschaft f

cape [keɪp] n (*garment*) Cape nt, Umhang m; (GEOG) Kap nt

caper ['keɪpər] n (COOK: *usu: ~s*) Kaper f; (*prank*) Kapriole f

capital ['kæpɪtl] n (~ *city*) Hauptstadt f; (FIN) Kapital nt; (~ *letter*) Großbuchstabe m; **~ gains tax** n Kapitalertragssteuer f; **~ism** n Kapitalismus m; **~ist** adj kapitalistisch ♦ n Kapitalist(in) m(f); **~ize** vi: **to ~ize on** Kapital schlagen aus; **~ punishment** n Todesstrafe f

---

Capitol

ⓘ **Capitol** ist das Gebäude in Washington auf dem Capitol Hill, in dem der Kongress der USA zusammentritt. Die Bezeichnung wird in vielen amerikanischen Bundesstaaten auch für das Parlamentsgebäude des jeweiligen Staates verwendet.

Capricorn ['kæprɪkɔːn] n Steinbock m

capsize [kæp'saɪz] vt, vi kentern

capsule ['kæpsjuːl] n Kapsel f

captain ['kæptɪn] n Kapitän m; (MIL) Hauptmann m ♦ vt anführen

caption ['kæpʃən] n (*heading*) Überschrift f; (*to picture*) Unterschrift f

captivate ['kæptɪveɪt] vt fesseln

captive ['kæptɪv] n Gefangene(r) f(m) ♦ adj gefangen (gehalten); **captivity** [kæp'tɪvɪtɪ] *n* Gefangenschaft *f*

apture ['kæptʃər] *vt* gefangen nehmen; (*place*) erobern; (*attention*) erregen ♦ *n* Gefangennahme *f*; (*data ~*) Erfassung *f*

ar [kɑːr] *n* Auto *nt*, Wagen *m*; (*RAIL*) Wagen *m*

aramel ['kærəməl] *n* Karamelle *f*, Karamellbonbon *m or nt*; (*burnt sugar*) Karamell *m*

arat ['kærət] *n* Karat *nt*

aravan ['kærəvæn] *n* (*BRIT*) Wohnwagen *m*; (*in desert*) Karawane *f*; ~**ning** *n* Caravaning *nt*, Urlaub *m* im Wohnwagen; ~ **site** (*BRIT*) *n* Campingplatz *m* für Wohnwagen

arbohydrate [kɑːbəʊ'haɪdreɪt] *n* Kohlenhydrat *nt*

arbon ['kɑːbən] *n* Kohlenstoff *m*; ~ **copy** *n* Durchschlag *m*; ~ **dioxide** *n* Kohlendioxyd *nt*; ~ **monoxide** *n* Kohlenmonoxid *nt*; ~ **paper** *n* Kohlepapier *nt*

ar boot sale *n* auf einem Parkplatz *stattfindender Flohmarkt mit dem Kofferraum als Auslage*

arburettor [kɑːbju'retər] (*US* **carburetor**) *n* Vergaser *m*

arcass ['kɑːkəs] *n* Kadaver *m*

ard [kɑːd] *n* Karte *f*; ~**board** *n* Pappe *f*; ~ **game** *n* Kartenspiel *nt*

ardiac ['kɑːdɪæk] *adj* Herz-

ardigan ['kɑːdɪgən] *n* Strickjacke *f*

ardinal ['kɑːdɪnl] *adj*: ~ **number** Kardinalzahl *f* ♦ *n* (*REL*) Kardinal *m*

ard index *n* Kartei *f*; (*in library*) Katalog *m*

ardphone *n* Kartentelefon *nt*

are [keər] *n* (*of teeth, car etc*) Pflege *f*; (*of children*) Fürsorge *f*; (*~fulness*) Sorgfalt *f*; (*worry*) Sorge *f* ♦ *vi*: **to ~ about** sich kümmern um; ~ **of** bei; **in sb's** ~ in jds Obhut; **I don't** ~ das ist mir egal; **I couldn't** ~ **less** es ist mir doch völlig egal; **to take** ~ aufpassen; **to take** ~ **of** sorgen für; **to take** ~ **to do sth** sich bemühen, etw zu tun; ~ **for** *vt* sorgen für; (*like*) mögen

areer [kə'rɪər] *n* Karriere *f*, Laufbahn *f* ♦ *vi* (*also*: ~ **along**) rasen; ~ **woman** (*irreg*) *n* Karrierefrau *f*

are: ~**free** *adj* sorgenfrei; ~**ful** *adj*

sorgfältig; **(be)** ~**ful!** pass auf!; ~**fully** *adv* vorsichtig; (*methodically*) sorgfältig; ~**less** *adj* nachlässig; ~**lessness** *n* Nachlässigkeit *f*; ~**r** *n* (*MED*) Betreuer(in) *m(f)*

caress [kə'res] *n* Liebkosung *f* ♦ *vt* liebkosen

caretaker ['keəteɪkər] *n* Hausmeister *m*

car ferry *n* Autofähre *f*

cargo ['kɑːgəʊ] (*pl* ~**es**) *n* Schiffsladung *f*

car hire *n* Autovermietung *f*

Caribbean [kærɪ'biːən] *n*: **the** ~ **(Sea)** die Karibik

caricature ['kærɪkətjʊər] *n* Karikatur *f*

caring ['keərɪŋ] *adj* (*society, organization*) sozial eingestellt; (*person*) liebevoll

carnage ['kɑːnɪdʒ] *n* Blutbad *nt*

carnation [kɑː'neɪʃən] *n* Nelke *f*

carnival ['kɑːnɪvl] *n* Karneval *m*, Fasching *m*; (*US: fun fair*) Kirmes *f*

carnivorous [kɑː'nɪvərəs] *adj* Fleisch fressend

carol ['kærəl] *n*: **(Christmas)** ~ (Weihnachts)lied *nt*

carp [kɑːp] *n* (*fish*) Karpfen *m*

car park (*BRIT*) *n* Parkplatz *m*; (*covered*) Parkhaus *nt*

carpenter ['kɑːpɪntər] *n* Zimmermann *m*; **carpentry** ['kɑːpɪntrɪ] *n* Zimmerei *f*

carpet ['kɑːpɪt] *n* Teppich *m* ♦ *vt* mit einem Teppich auslegen; ~ **bombing** *n* Flächenbombardierung *f*; ~ **slippers** *npl* Pantoffeln *pl*; ~ **sweeper** ['kɑːpɪtswiːpər] *n* Teppichkehrer *m*

car phone *n* (*TEL*) Autotelefon *nt*

car rental (*US*) *n* Autovermietung *f*

carriage ['kærɪdʒ] *n* Kutsche *f*; (*RAIL, of typewriter*) Wagen *m*; (*of goods*) Beförderung *f*; (*bearing*) Haltung *f*; ~ **return** *n* (*on typewriter*) Rücklauftaste *f*; ~**way** (*BRIT*) *n* (*part of road*) Fahrbahn *f*

carrier ['kærɪər] *n* Träger(in) *m(f)*; (*COMM*) Spediteur *m*; ~ **bag** (*BRIT*) *n* Tragetasche *m*

carrot ['kærət] *n* Möhre *f*, Karotte *f*

carry ['kærɪ] *vt, vi* tragen; **to get carried away** (*fig*) sich nicht mehr bremsen können; ~ **on** *vi* (*continue*) weitermachen; (*inf: complain*) Theater machen; ~ **out** *vt* (*orders*) ausführen; (*investigation*) durchführen; ~cot (BRIT) n Babytragetasche f; ~-on (inf) n (fuss) Theater nt

cart [kɑːt] n Wagen m, Karren m ♦ vt schleppen

cartilage ['kɑːtɪlɪdʒ] n Knorpel m

carton ['kɑːtən] n Karton m; (of milk) Tüte f

cartoon [kɑːˈtuːn] n (PRESS) Karikatur f; (comic strip) Comics pl; (CINE) (Zeichen)trickfilm m

cartridge ['kɑːtrɪdʒ] n Patrone f

carve [kɑːv] vt (wood) schnitzen; (stone) meißeln; (meat) (vor)schneiden; ~ **up** vt aufschneiden; **carving** ['kɑːvɪŋ] n Schnitzerei f; **carving knife** n Tran(s)chiermesser nt

car wash n Autowäsche f

cascade [kæsˈkeɪd] n Wasserfall m ♦ vi kaskadenartig herabfallen

case [keɪs] n (box) Kasten m; (BRIT: also: **suitcase**) Koffer m; (JUR, matter) Fall m; **in** ~ falls, im Falle; **in any** ~ jedenfalls, auf jeden Fall

cash [kæʃ] n (Bar)geld nt ♦ vt einlösen; ~ **on delivery** per Nachnahme; ~ **book** n Kassenbuch nt; ~ **card** n Scheckkarte f; ~ **desk** (BRIT) n Kasse f; ~ **dispenser** n Geldautomat m

cashew [kæˈʃuː] n (also: ~ **nut**) Cashewnuss f

cash flow n Cashflow m

cashier [kæˈʃɪər] n Kassierer(in) m(f)

cashmere ['kæʃmɪər] n Kaschmirwolle f

cash register n Registrierkasse f

casing ['keɪsɪŋ] n Gehäuse nt

casino [kəˈsiːnəu] n Kasino nt

casket ['kɑːskɪt] n Kästchen nt; (US: coffin) Sarg m

casserole ['kæsərəul] n Kasserolle f; (food) Auflauf m

cassette [kæˈset] n Kassette f; ~ **player** n Kassettengerät nt

cast [kɑːst] (pt, pp **cast**) vt werfen; (horns) verlieren; (metal) gießen; (THEAT) besetzen; (vote) abgeben ♦ n (THEAT) Besetzung f; (also: **plaster** ~) Gipsverband m; ~ **off** vi (NAUT) losmachen

castaway ['kɑːstəweɪ] n Schiffbrüchige(r) f(m)

caste [kɑːst] n Kaste f

caster sugar ['kɑːstə-] (BRIT) n Raffinade f

casting vote ['kɑːstɪŋ-] (BRIT) n entscheidende Stimme f

cast iron n Gusseisen nt

castle ['kɑːsl] n Burg f; Schloss nt; (CHESS) Turm m

castor ['kɑːstər] n (wheel) Laufrolle f

castor oil n Rizinusöl nt

castrate [kæsˈtreɪt] vt kastrieren

casual ['kæʒjul] adj (attitude) nachlässig; (dress) leger; (meeting) zufällig; (work) Gelegenheits-; ~**ly** adv (dress) zwanglos, leger; (remark) beiläufig

casualty ['kæʒjultɪ] n Verletzte(r) f(m); (dead) Tote(r) f(m); (also: ~ **department**) Unfallstation f

cat [kæt] n Katze f

catalogue ['kætəlɔg] (US **catalog**) n Katalog m ♦ vt katalogisieren

catalyst ['kætəlɪst] n Katalysator m

catalytic converter [kætəˈlɪtɪk kənˈvɜːtər] n Katalysator m

catapult ['kætəpʌlt] n Schleuder f

cataract ['kætərækt] n (MED) graue(r) Star m

catarrh [kəˈtɑːr] n Katarr(h) m

catastrophe [kəˈtæstrəfɪ] n Katastrophe f

catch [kætʃ] (pt, pp **caught**) vt fangen; (arrest) fassen; (train) erreichen; (person: by surprise) ertappen; (also: ~ **up**) einholen ♦ vi (fire) in Gang kommen; (in branches etc) hängen bleiben ♦ n (fish etc) Fang m; (trick) Haken m; (of lock) Sperrhaken m; **to** ~ **an illness** sich dat eine Krankheit holen; **to** ~ **fire** Feuer fangen; ~ **on** vi (understand) begreifen; (grow popular) ankommen; ~ **up** vi (fig) aufholen; ~**ing** ['kætʃɪŋ] adj ansteckend; ~**ment area** ['kætʃmənt-] (BRIT) n Einzugsgebiet nt; ~ **phrase** n Slogan m; ~**y** ['kætʃɪ] adj (tune) eingängig

categoric(al) [kætɪˈgɔrɪk(l)] adj kategorisch

category ['kætɪgəri] n Kategorie f

cater ['keɪtər] vi versorgen; ~ **for** (BRIT) vt fus (party) ausrichten; (needs) eingestellt sein auf +acc; ~**er** n Lieferant(in) m(f) von Speisen und Getränken; ~**ing** n

icory ['tʃɪkərɪ] n (in coffee) Zichorie f; (plant) Chicorée f, Schikoree f

hief [tʃi:f] n (of tribe) Häuptling m; (COMM) Chef m ♦ adj Haupt-; ~ **executive** n Geschäftsführer(in) m(f); ~**ly** adv hauptsächlich

chilblain ['tʃɪlbleɪn] n Frostbeule f

child [tʃaɪld] (pl ~**ren**) n Kind nt; ~**birth** n Entbindung f; ~**hood** n Kindheit f; ~**ish** adj kindisch; ~**like** adj kindlich; ~ **minder** (BRIT) n Tagesmutter f; ~**ren** ['tʃɪldrən] npl of **child**; ~ **seat** n Kindersitz m

Chile ['tʃɪlɪ] n Chile nt; ~**an** adj chilenisch

chill [tʃɪl] n Kühle f; (MED) Erkältung f ♦ vt (CULIN) kühlen

chilli ['tʃɪlɪ] n Peperoni pl; (meal, spice) Chili m

chilly ['tʃɪlɪ] adj kühl, frostig

chime [tʃaɪm] n Geläut nt ♦ vi ertönen

chimney ['tʃɪmnɪ] n Schornstein m; ~ **sweep** n Schornsteinfeger(in) m(f)

chimpanzee [tʃɪmpæn'zi:] n Schimpanse m

chin [tʃɪn] n Kinn nt

China ['tʃaɪnə] n China nt

china ['tʃaɪnə] n Porzellan nt

Chinese [tʃaɪ'ni:z] adj chinesisch ♦ n (inv) Chinese m, Chinesin f; (LING) Chinesisch nt

chink [tʃɪŋk] n (opening) Ritze f; (noise) Klirren nt

chip [tʃɪp] n (of wood etc) Splitter m; (in poker etc; US: crisp) Chip m ♦ vt absplittern; ~**s** npl (BRIT: COOK) Pommes frites pl; ~ **in** vi Zwischenbemerkungen machen

---

Chip shop

Chip shop, auch *fish-and-chip shop*, ist die traditionelle britische Imbissbude, in der vor allem fritierte Fischfilets und Pommes frites, aber auch andere einfache Mahlzeiten angeboten werden. Früher wurde das Essen zum Mitnehmen in Zeitungspapier verpackt. Manche chip shops haben auch einen Essraum.

---

chiropodist [kɪ'rɔpədɪst] (BRIT) n Fußpfleger(in) m(f)

chirp [tʃə:p] vi zwitschern

chisel ['tʃɪzl] n Meißel m

chit [tʃɪt] n Notiz f

chivalrous ['ʃɪvəlrəs] adj ritterlich; **chivalry** ['ʃɪvəlrɪ] n Ritterlichkeit f

chives [tʃaɪvz] npl Schnittlauch m

chlorine ['klɔ:ri:n] n Chlor nt

chock-a-block ['tʃɔkə'blɔk] adj voll gepfropft

chock-full [tʃɔk'ful] adj voll gepfropft

chocolate ['tʃɔklɪt] n Schokolade f

choice [tʃɔɪs] n Wahl f; (of goods) Auswahl f ♦ adj Qualitäts-

choir ['kwaɪər] n Chor m; ~**boy** n Chorknabe m

choke [tʃəuk] vi ersticken ♦ vt erdrosseln; (block) (ab)drosseln ♦ n (AUT) Starterklappe f

cholera ['kɔlərə] n Cholera f

cholesterol [kə'lestərɔl] n Cholesterin nt

choose [tʃu:z] (pt **chose**, pp **chosen**) vt wählen; **choosy** ['tʃu:zɪ] adj wählerisch

chop [tʃɔp] vt (wood) spalten; (COOK: also: ~ **up**) (zer)hacken ♦ n Hieb m; (COOK) Kotelett nt; ~**s** npl (jaws) Lefzen pl

chopper ['tʃɔpər] n (helicopter) Hubschrauber m

choppy ['tʃɔpɪ] adj (sea) bewegt

chopsticks ['tʃɔpstɪks] npl (Ess)stäbchen pl

choral ['kɔ:rəl] adj Chor-

chord [kɔ:d] n Akkord m

chore [tʃɔ:r] n Pflicht f; ~**s** npl (housework) Hausarbeit f

choreographer [kɔrɪ'ɔgrəfər] n Choreograf(in) m(f)

chorister ['kɔrɪstər] n Chorsänger(in) m(f)

chortle ['tʃɔ:tl] vi glucksen

chorus ['kɔ:rəs] n Chor m; (in song) Refrain m

chose [tʃəuz] pt of **choose**

chosen ['tʃəuzn] pp of **choose**

chowder ['tʃaudər] (US) n sämige Fischsuppe f

Christ [kraɪst] n Christus m

christen ['krɪsn] vt taufen; ~**ing** n Taufe f

Christian ['krɪstɪən] adj christlich ♦ n Christ(in) m(f); ~**ity** [krɪstɪ'ænɪtɪ] n Christentum nt; ~ **name** n Vorname m

Gastronomie f

caterpillar ['kætəpɪlər] n Raupe f; ~ **track** ® n Gleiskette f

cathedral [kə'θi:drəl] n Kathedrale f, Dom m

Catholic ['kæθəlɪk] adj (REL) katholisch ♦ n Katholik(in) m(f); **c~** adj (tastes etc) vielseitig

CAT scan [kæt-] n Computertomografie f

Catseye ['kæts'aɪ] (BRIT: ®) n (AUT) Katzenauge nt

cattle ['kætl] npl Vieh nt

catty ['kætɪ] adj gehässig

caucus ['kɔ:kəs] n (POL) Gremium nt; (US: meeting) Sitzung f

caught [kɔ:t] pt, pp of **catch**

cauliflower ['kɔlɪflauər] n Blumenkohl m

cause [kɔ:z] n Ursache f; (purpose) Sache f ♦ vt verursachen

causeway ['kɔ:zweɪ] n Damm m

caustic ['kɔ:stɪk] adj ätzend; (fig) bissig

caution ['kɔ:ʃən] n Vorsicht f; (warning) Verwarnung f ♦ vt verwarnen; **cautious** ['kɔ:ʃəs] adj vorsichtig

cavalry ['kævəlrɪ] n Kavallerie f

cave [keɪv] n Höhle f; ~ **in** vi einstürzen; ~**man** (irreg) n Höhlenmensch m

cavern ['kævən] n Höhle f

caviar(e) ['kævɪɑ:r] n Kaviar m

cavity ['kævɪtɪ] n Loch nt

cavort [kə'vɔ:t] vi umherspringen

C.B. n abbr (= Citizens' Band (Radio)) CB

C.B.I. n abbr (= Confederation of British Industry) ≃ BDI m

cc n abbr = **carbon copy**; **cubic centimetres**

CCTV n abbr (= closed-circuit television) Videoüberwachung f

CD n abbr (= compact disc) CD f

CDI n abbr (= Compact Disk Interactive) CD-I f

CD player n CD-Spieler m

CD-ROM n abbr (= compact disc read-only memory) CD-Rom f

cease [si:s] vi aufhören ♦ vt beenden; ~**fire** n Feuereinstellung f; ~**less** adj unaufhörlich

cedar ['si:dər] n Zeder f

ceiling ['si:lɪŋ] n Decke f; (fig) Höchstgrenze f

celebrate ['selɪbreɪt] vt, vi feiern; ~**d** adj gefeiert; **celebration** [selɪ'breɪʃən] n Feier f

celebrity [sɪ'lebrɪtɪ] n gefeierte Persönlichkeit f

celery ['selərɪ] n Sellerie m or f

celibacy ['selɪbəsɪ] n Zölibat nt or m

cell [sel] n Zelle f; (ELEC) Element nt

cellar ['selər] n Keller m

cello ['tʃeləu] n Cello nt

Cellophane ['seləfeɪn] ® n Cellophan nt ®

cellphone ['selfəun] n Funktelefon nt

cellular ['seljulər] adj zellular

cellulose ['seljuləus] n Zellulose f

Celt [kelt, selt] n Kelte m, Keltin f; ~**ic** ['keltɪk, 'seltɪk] adj keltisch

cement [sə'ment] n Zement m ♦ vt zementieren; ~ **mixer** n Betonmischmaschine f

cemetery ['semɪtrɪ] n Friedhof m

censor ['sensər] n Zensor m ♦ vt zensieren; ~**ship** n Zensur f

censure ['senʃər] vt rügen

census ['sensəs] n Volkszählung f

cent [sent] n (coin) Cent m; see also **per cent**

centenary [sen'ti:nərɪ] n Jahrhundertfeier f

center ['sentər] (US) n = **centre**

centigrade ['sentɪgreɪd] adj Celsius

centimetre ['sentɪmi:tər] (US **centimeter**) n Zentimeter nt

centipede ['sentɪpi:d] n Tausendfüßler m

central ['sentrəl] adj zentral; **C~ America** n Mittelamerika nt; ~ **heating** n Zentralheizung f; ~**ize** vt zentralisieren; ~ **reservation** (BRIT) n (AUT) Mittelstreifen m

centre ['sentər] (US **center**) n Zentrum nt ♦ vt zentrieren; ~**-forward** n (SPORT) Mittelstürmer m; ~**-half** n (SPORT) Stopper m

century ['sentʃurɪ] n Jahrhundert nt

ceramic [sɪ'ræmɪk] adj keramisch; ~**s** npl Keramiken pl

cereal ['sɪərɪəl] n (grain) Getreide nt; (at breakfast) Getreideflocken pl

cerebral ['serɪbrəl] adj zerebral; (intellectual) geistig

ceremony ['serɪmənɪ] n Zeremonie f; **to**

stand on ~ förmlich sein
certain ['sɜːtən] *adj* sicher; *(particular)*
gewiss; **for** ~ ganz bestimmt; **~ly** *adv*
sicher, bestimmt; **~ty** *n* Gewissheit *f*
certificate [sə'tɪfɪkɪt] *n* Bescheinigung *f*;
(SCH etc) Zeugnis *nt*
certified mail ['sɜːtɪfaɪd-] *(US) n*
Einschreiben *nt*
certified public accountant ['sɜːtɪfaɪd-]
(US) n geprüfte(r) Buchhalter *m*
certify ['sɜːtɪfaɪ] *vt* bescheinigen
cervical ['sɜːvɪkl] *adj (smear, cancer)*
Gebärmutterhals-
cervix ['sɜːvɪks] *n* Gebärmutterhals *m*
cf. *abbr* (= *compare*) vgl.
CFC *n abbr* (= *chlorofluorocarbon*) FCKW *m*
ch. *abbr* (= *chapter*) Kap.
chafe [tʃeɪf] *vt* scheuern
chaffinch ['tʃæfɪntʃ] *n* Buchfink *m*
chain [tʃeɪn] *n* Kette *f* ♦ *vt (also:* ~ **up)**
anketten; ~ **reaction** *n* Kettenreaktion *f*;
~-smoke *vi* kettenrauchen; ~ **store** *n*
Kettenladen *m*
chair [tʃeəʳ] *n* Stuhl *m; (armchair)* Sessel *m;*
(UNIV) Lehrstuhl *m* ♦ *vt (meeting)* den
Vorsitz führen bei; **~lift** *n* Sessellift *m;*
~man *(irreg) n* Vorsitzende(r) *m*
chalet ['ʃæleɪ] *n* Chalet *nt*
chalk [tʃɔːk] *n* Kreide *f*
challenge ['tʃælɪndʒ] *n* Herausforderung *f*
♦ *vt* herausfordern; *(contest)* bestreiten;
challenging *adj (tone)* herausfordernd;
(work) anspruchsvoll
chamber ['tʃeɪmbəʳ] *n* Kammer *f;* ~ **of**
commerce Handelskammer *f;* **~maid** *n*
Zimmermädchen *nt;* ~ **music** *n*
Kammermusik *f*
chamois ['ʃæmwɑː] *n* Gämse *f*
champagne [ʃæm'peɪn] *n* Champagner *m,*
Sekt *m*
champion ['tʃæmpɪən] *n (SPORT)* Meister(in)
m(f); (of cause) Verfechter(in) *m(f);* **~ship** *n*
Meisterschaft *f*
chance [tʃɑːns] *n (luck)* Zufall *m; (possibility)*
Möglichkeit *f; (opportunity)* Gelegenheit *f,*
Chance *f; (risk)* Risiko *nt* ♦ *adj* zufällig ♦ *vt:*
to ~ **it** es darauf ankommen lassen; **by** ~

zufällig; **to take a** ~ ein Risiko eingehen
chancellor ['tʃɑːnsələʳ] *n* Kanzler *m;* **C~ of**
the Exchequer *(BRIT) n* Schatzkanzler *m*
chandelier [ʃændə'lɪəʳ] *n* Kronleuchter *m*
change [tʃeɪndʒ] *vt* ändern; *(replace, COMM:*
money) wechseln; *(exchange)* umtauschen;
(transform) verwandeln ♦ *vi* sich ändern; *(~*
trains) umsteigen; *(~ clothes)* sich umziehen
♦ *n* Veränderung *f; (money returned)*
Wechselgeld *nt; (coins)* Kleingeld *nt;* **to** ~
one's mind es sich *dat* anders überlegen;
to ~ **into sth** *(be transformed)* sich in etw
acc verwandeln; **for a** ~ zur Abwechslung;
~able *adj (weather)* wechselhaft; ~
machine *n* Geldwechselautomat *m;*
~over *n* Umstellung *f*
changing ['tʃeɪndʒɪŋ] *adj* veränderlich; ~
room *(BRIT) n* Umkleideraum *m*
channel ['tʃænl] *n (stream)* Bachbett *nt;*
(NAUT) Straße *f; (TV)* Kanal *m; (fig)* Weg *m*
♦ *vt (efforts)* lenken; **the (English) C~** der
Ärmelkanal; **~-hopping** *n (TV)* ständiges
Umschalten; **C~ Islands** *npl:* **the C~**
Islands die Kanalinseln *pl;* **C~ Tunnel** *n:*
the C~ Tunnel der Kanaltunnel
chant [tʃɑːnt] *n* Gesang *m; (of fans)*
Sprechchor *m* ♦ *vt* intonieren
chaos ['keɪɒs] *n* Chaos *nt*
chap [tʃæp] *(inf) n* Kerl *m*
chapel ['tʃæpl] *n* Kapelle *f*
chaperon ['ʃæpərəʊn] *n* Anstandsdame *f*
chaplain ['tʃæplɪn] *n* Kaplan *m*
chapped [tʃæpt] *adj (skin, lips)* spröde
chapter ['tʃæptəʳ] *n* Kapitel *nt*
char [tʃɑːʳ] *vt (burn)* verkohlen
character ['kærɪktəʳ] *n* Charakter *m,* Wesen
nt; (in novel, film) Figur *f;* **~istic**
[kærɪktə'rɪstɪk] *adj:* **~istic (of sb/ sth)** (für
jdn/etw) charakteristisch ♦ *n* Kennzeichen
nt; **~ize** *vt* charakterisieren, kennzeichnen
charade [ʃə'rɑːd] *n* Scharade *f*
charcoal ['tʃɑːkəʊl] *n* Holzkohle *f*
charge [tʃɑːdʒ] *n (cost)* Preis *m; (JUR)*
Anklage *f; (explosive)* Ladung *f; (attack)*
Angriff *m* ♦ *vt (gun, battery)* laden; *(price)*
verlangen; *(JUR)* anklagen; *(MIL)* angreifen
♦ *vi (rush)* (an)stürmen; **bank ~s**

Bankgebühren *pl;* **free of** ~ kostenlos; **to**
reverse the ~s *(TEL)* ein R-Gespräch
führen; **to be in** ~ **of** verantwortlich sein
für; **to take** ~ (die Verantwortung)
übernehmen; **to** ~ **sth (up) to sb's**
account jdm etw in Rechnung stellen; ~
card *n* Kundenkarte *f*
charitable ['tʃærɪtəbl] *adj* wohltätig; *(lenient)*
nachsichtig
charity ['tʃærɪtɪ] *n (institution)* Hilfswerk *nt;*
(attitude) Nächstenliebe *f*
charm [tʃɑːm] *n* Charme *m; (spell)* Bann *m;*
(object) Talisman *m* ♦ *vt* bezaubern; **~ing**
adj reizend
chart [tʃɑːt] *n* Tabelle *f; (NAUT)* Seekarte *f*
♦ *vt (course)* abstecken
charter ['tʃɑːtəʳ] *vt* chartern ♦ *n* Schutzbrief
m; **~ed accountant** *n* Wirtschafts-
prüfer(in) *m(f);* ~ **flight** *n* Charterflug *m*
chase [tʃeɪs] *vt* jagen, verfolgen ♦ *n* Jagd *f*
chasm ['kæzəm] *n* Kluft *f*
chassis ['ʃæsɪ] *n* Fahrgestell *nt*
chat [tʃæt] *vi (also:* **have a ~)** plaudern ♦ *n*
Plauderei *f;* ~ **show** *(BRIT) n* Talkshow *f*
chatter ['tʃætəʳ] *vi* schwatzen; *(teeth)*
klappern ♦ *n* Geschwätz *nt;* **~box** *n*
Quasselstrippe *f*
chatty ['tʃætɪ] *adj* geschwätzig
chauffeur ['ʃəʊfəʳ] *n* Chauffeur *m*
chauvinist ['ʃəʊvɪnɪst] *n (male ~)* Chauvi *m*
(inf)
cheap [tʃiːp] *adj, adv* billig; ~ **day return** *n*
Tagesrückfahrkarte *f (zu einem günstigeren*
Tarif); **~ly** *adv* billig
cheat [tʃiːt] *vt, vi* betrügen; *(SCH)* mogeln
♦ *n* Betrüger(in) *m(f)*
check [tʃek] *vt (examine)* prüfen; *(make sure)*
nachsehen; *(control)* kontrollieren; *(restrain)*
zügeln; *(stop)* anhalten ♦ *n (examination,*
restraint) Kontrolle *f; (bill)* Rechnung *f;*
(pattern) Karo(muster) *nt; (US)* = **cheque**
♦ *adj (pattern, cloth)* kariert; ~ **in** *vi (in*
hotel, airport) einchecken ♦ *vt (luggage)*
abfertigen lassen; ~ **out** *vi (of hotel)*
abreisen; ~ **up** *vi* nachschauen; ~ **up on**
vt kontrollieren; **~ered** *(US) adj* =

chequered; ~ers *(US) n (draughts)*
Damespiel *nt;* **~-in (desk)** *n* Abfert...
~ing account *(US) n (current accoun...*
Girokonto *nt;* **~mate** *n* Schachmatt ...
~out *n* Kasse *f;* **~point** *n* Kontrollpun...
~ **room** *(US) n (left-luggage office)*
Gepäckaufbewahrung *f;* **~up** *n*
(Nach)prüfung *f; (MED)* (ärztliche)
Untersuchung *f*
cheek [tʃiːk] *n* Backe *f; (fig)* Frechheit *f;*
~bone *n* Backenknochen *m;* **~y** *adj* frech
cheep [tʃiːp] *vi* piepsen
cheer [tʃiəʳ] *n (usu pl)* Hurra- *or* Beifallsruf *m*
♦ *vt* zujubeln; *(encourage)* aufmuntern ♦ *vi*
jauchzen; **~s!** Prost!; ~ **up** *vi* bessere Laune
bekommen ♦ *vt* aufmuntern; ~ **up!** nun
lach doch mal!; **~ful** *adj* fröhlich
cheerio [tʃɪərɪ'əʊ] *(BRIT) excl* tschüss!
cheese [tʃiːz] *n* Käse *m;* **~board** *n*
(gemischte) Käseplatte *f*
cheetah ['tʃiːtə] *n* Gepard *m*
chef [ʃef] *n* Küchenchef *m*
chemical ['kemɪkl] *adj* chemisch ♦ *n*
Chemikalie *f*
chemist ['kemɪst] *n (BRIT: pharmacist)*
Apotheker *m,* Drogist *m; (scientist)*
Chemiker *m;* **~ry** *n* Chemie *f;* **~'s (shop)**
(BRIT) n Apotheke *f,* Drogerie *f*
cheque [tʃek] *(BRIT) n* Scheck *m;* **~book** *n*
Scheckbuch *nt;* ~ **card** *n* Scheckkarte *f*
chequered ['tʃekəd] *adj (fig)* bewegt
cherish ['tʃerɪʃ] *vt (person)* lieben; *(hope)*
hegen
cherry ['tʃerɪ] *n* Kirsche *f*
chess [tʃes] *n* Schach *nt;* **~board** *n*
Schachbrett *nt;* **~man** *(irreg) n* Schachfigur
f
chest [tʃest] *n (ANAT)* Brust *f; (box)* Kiste *f;* ~
of drawers Kommode *f*
chestnut ['tʃesnʌt] *n* Kastanie *f*
chew [tʃuː] *vt, vi* kauen; **~ing gum** *n*
Kaugummi *m*
chic [ʃiːk] *adj* schick, elegant
chick [tʃɪk] *n* Küken *nt; (US: inf: girl)* Biene *f*
chicken ['tʃɪkɪn] *n* Huhn *nt; (food)*
Hähnchen *nt;* ~ **out** *(inf) vi* kneifen
chickenpox ['tʃɪkɪnpɒks] *n* Windpocken *pl*

hristmas ['krɪsməs] n Weihnachten pl; **Happy** or **Merry ~!** frohe or fröhliche Weihnachten!; **~ card** n Weihnachtskarte f; **~ Day** n der erste Weihnachtstag; **~ Eve** n Heiligabend m; **~ tree** n Weihnachtsbaum m

hrome [krəʊm] n Verchromung f

hromium ['krəʊmɪəm] n Chrom nt

hronic ['krɔnɪk] adj chronisch

hronicle ['krɔnɪkl] n Chronik f

hronological [krɔnə'lɔdʒɪkl] adj chronologisch

hubby ['tʃʌbɪ] adj rundlich

huck [tʃʌk] vt werfen; (BRIT: also: **~ up**) hinwerfen; **~ out** vt (person) rauswerfen; (old clothes etc) wegwerfen

huckle ['tʃʌkl] vi in sich hineinlachen

hug [tʃʌg] vi tuckern

hunk [tʃʌŋk] n Klumpen m; (of food) Brocken m

hurch [tʃɜːtʃ] n Kirche f; **~yard** n Kirchhof m

hurn [tʃɜːn] n (for butter) Butterfass nt; (for milk) Milchkanne f; **~ out** (inf) vt produzieren

hute [ʃuːt] n Rutsche f; (rubbish ~) Müllschlucker m

hutney ['tʃʌtnɪ] n Chutney nt

IA (US) n abbr (= Central Intelligence Agency) CIA m

ID (BRIT) n abbr (= Criminal Investigation Department) ≃ Kripo f

der ['saɪdər] n Apfelwein m

igar [sɪ'gɑːr] n Zigarre f

igarette [sɪgə'ret] n Zigarette f; **~ case** n Zigarettenetui nt; **~ end** n Zigarettenstummel m

inderella [sɪndə'relə] n Aschenbrödel nt

inders ['sɪndəz] npl Asche f

ine camera ['sɪnɪ-] (BRIT) n Filmkamera f

ine film (BRIT) n Schmalfilm m

inema ['sɪnəmə] n Kino nt

innamon ['sɪnəmən] n Zimt m

ircle ['sɜːkl] n Kreis m; (in cinema etc) Rang m ♦ vi kreisen ♦ vt (surround) umgeben; (move round) kreisen um

ircuit ['sɜːkɪt] n (track) Rennbahn f; (lap)

Runde f; (ELEC) Stromkreis m

circular ['sɜːkjʊlər] adj rund ♦ n Rundschreiben nt

circulate ['sɜːkjʊleɪt] vi zirkulieren ♦ vt in Umlauf setzen; **circulation** [sɜːkjʊ'leɪʃən] n (of blood) Kreislauf m; (of newspaper) Auflage f; (of money) Umlauf m

circumcise ['sɜːkəmsaɪz] vt beschneiden

circumference [sə'kʌmfərəns] n (Kreis)umfang m

circumspect ['sɜːkəmspekt] adj umsichtig

circumstances ['sɜːkəmstənsɪz] npl Umstände pl; (financial) Verhältnisse pl

circumvent [sɜːkəm'vent] vt umgehen

circus ['sɜːkəs] n Zirkus m

CIS n abbr (= Commonwealth of Independent States) GUS f

cistern ['sɪstən] n Zisterne f; (of W.C.) Spülkasten m

cite [saɪt] vt zitieren, anführen

citizen ['sɪtɪzn] n Bürger(in) m(f); **~ship** n Staatsbürgerschaft f

citrus fruit ['sɪtrəs-] n Zitrusfrucht f

city ['sɪtɪ] n Großstadt f; **the C~** die City, das Finanzzentrum Londons

city technology college n ≃ Technische Fachschule f

civic ['sɪvɪk] adj (of town) städtisch; (of citizen) Bürger-; **~ centre** (BRIT) n Stadtverwaltung f

civil ['sɪvɪl] adj bürgerlich; (not military) zivil; (polite) höflich; **~ engineer** n Bauingenieur m; **~ian** [sɪ'vɪlɪən] n Zivilperson f ♦ adj zivil, Zivil-

civilization [sɪvɪlaɪ'zeɪʃən] n Zivilisation f

civilized ['sɪvɪlaɪzd] adj zivilisiert

civil: ~ law n Zivilrecht nt; **~ servant** n Staatsbeamte(r) m; **C~ Service** n Staatsdienst m; **~ war** n Bürgerkrieg m

clad [klæd] adj: **~ in** gehüllt in +acc

claim [kleɪm] vt beanspruchen; (have opinion) behaupten ♦ vi (for insurance) Ansprüche geltend machen ♦ n (demand) Forderung f; (right) Anspruch m; (pretension) Behauptung f; **~ant** n Antragsteller(in) m(f)

clairvoyant [kleə'vɔɪənt] n Hellseher(in) m(f)

clam [klæm] n Venusmuschel f

clamber ['klæmbəʳ] *vi* kraxeln

clammy ['klæmɪ] *adj* klamm

clamour ['klæməʳ] *vi*: **to ~ for sth** nach etw verlangen

clamp [klæmp] *n* Schraubzwinge *f* ♦ *vt* einspannen; (*AUT: wheel*) krallen; ~ **down on** *vt fus* Maßnahmen ergreifen gegen

clan [klæn] *n* Clan *m*

clandestine [klæn'dɛstɪn] *adj* geheim

clang [klæŋ] *vi* scheppern

clap [klæp] *vi* klatschen ♦ *vt* Beifall klatschen +*dat* ♦ *n* (*of hands*) Klatschen *nt*; (*of thunder*) Donnerschlag *m*; ~**ping** *n* Klatschen *nt*

claret ['klærət] *n* rote(r) Bordeaux(wein) *m*

clarify ['klærɪfaɪ] *vt* klären, erklären

clarinet [klærɪ'nɛt] *n* Klarinette *f*

clarity ['klærɪtɪ] *n* Klarheit *f*

clash [klæʃ] *n* (*fig*) Konflikt *m* ♦ *vi* zusammenprallen; (*colours*) sich beißen; (*argue*) sich streiten

clasp [klɑːsp] *n* Griff *m*; (*on jewels, bag*) Verschluss *m* ♦ *vt* umklammern

class [klɑːs] *n* Klasse *f* ♦ *vt* einordnen; ~-**conscious** *adj* klassenbewusst

classic ['klæsɪk] *n* Klassiker *m* ♦ *adj* klassisch; ~**al** *adj* klassisch

classified ['klæsɪfaɪd] *adj* (*information*) Geheim-; ~ **advertisement** *n* Kleinanzeige *f*

classify ['klæsɪfaɪ] *vt* klassifizieren

classmate ['klɑːsmeɪt] *n* Klassenkamerad(in) *m(f)*

classroom ['klɑːsrʊm] *n* Klassenzimmer *nt*

clatter ['klætəʳ] *vi* klappern; (*feet*) trappeln

clause [klɔːz] *n* (*JUR*) Klausel *f*; (*GRAM*) Satz *m*

claustrophobia [klɔːstrə'fəʊbɪə] *n* Platzangst *f*

claw [klɔː] *n* Kralle *f* ♦ *vt* (zer)kratzen

clay [kleɪ] *n* Lehm *m*; (*for pots*) Ton *m*

clean [kliːn] *adj* sauber ♦ *vt* putzen; (*clothes*) reinigen; ~ **out** *vt* gründlich putzen; ~ **up** *vt* aufräumen; ~-**cut** *adj* (*person*) adrett; (*clear*) klar; ~**er** *n* (*person*) Putzfrau *f*; ~**er's** *n* (*also*: **dry ~er's**) Reinigung *f*; ~**ing** *n* Putzen *nt*; (*clothes*) Reinigung *f*; ~**liness** ['klɛnlɪnɪs] *n* Reinlichkeit *f*

cleanse [klɛnz] *vt* reinigen; ~**r** *n* (*for face*) Reinigungsmilch *f*

clean-shaven ['kliːn'ʃeɪvn] *adj* glatt rasiert

cleansing department ['klɛnzɪŋ-] (*BRIT*) *n* Stadtreinigung *f*

clear [klɪəʳ] *adj* klar; (*road*) frei ♦ *vt* (*road etc*) freimachen; (*obstacle*) beseitigen; (*JUR: suspect*) freisprechen ♦ *vi* klar werden; (*fog*) sich lichten ♦ *adv*: ~ **of** von ... entfernt; **to ~ the table** den Tisch abräumen; ~ **up** *vt* aufräumen; (*solve*) aufklären; ~**ance** ['klɪərəns] *n* (*removal*) Räumung *f*; (*free space*) Lichtung *f*; (*permission*) Freigabe *f*; ~-**cut** *adj* (*case*) eindeutig; ~**ing** *n* Lichtung *f*; ~**ing bank** (*BRIT*) *n* Clearingbank *f*; ~**ly** *adv* klar; (*obviously*) eindeutig; ~**way** (*BRIT*) *n* (Straße *f* mit) Halteverbot *nt*

cleaver ['kliːvəʳ] *n* Hackbeil *nt*

cleft [klɛft] *n* (*in rock*) Spalte *f*

clementine ['klɛməntaɪn] *n* (*fruit*) Klementine *f*

clench [klɛntʃ] *vt* (*teeth*) zusammenbeißen; (*fist*) ballen

clergy ['klɜːdʒɪ] *n* Geistliche(n) *pl*; ~**man** (*irreg*) *n* Geistliche(r) *m*

clerical ['klɛrɪkl] *adj* (*office*) Schreib-, Büro-; (*REL*) geistlich

clerk [klɑːk, (*US*) klɜːrk] *n* (*in office*) Büroangestellte(r) *mf*; (*US: sales person*) Verkäufer(in) *m(f)*

clever ['klɛvəʳ] *adj* klug; (*crafty*) schlau

cliché ['kliːʃeɪ] *n* Klischee *nt*

click [klɪk] *vt* (*tongue*) schnalzen mit; (*heels*) zusammenklappen; ~ **on** *vt* (*COMPUT*) anklicken

client ['klaɪənt] *n* Klient(in) *m(f)*; ~**ele** [kliːɑ̃ːn'tɛl] *n* Kundschaft *f*

cliff [klɪf] *n* Klippe *f*

climate ['klaɪmɪt] *n* Klima *nt*

climax ['klaɪmæks] *n* Höhepunkt *m*

climb [klaɪm] *vt* besteigen ♦ *vi* steigen, klettern ♦ *n* Aufstieg *m*; ~-**down** *n* Abstieg *m*; ~**er** *n* Bergsteiger(in) *m(f)*; ~**ing** *n* Bergsteigen *nt*

clinch [klɪntʃ] *vt* (*decide*) entscheiden; (*deal*) festmachen

cling [klɪŋ] (*pt, pp* **clung**) *vi* (*clothes*) eng anliegen; **to ~ to** sich festklammern an +*dat*

clinic ['klɪnɪk] *n* Klinik *f*; ~**al** *adj* klinisch

ink [klɪŋk] vi klimpern

ip [klɪp] n Spange f; (also: **paper ~**) Klammer f ♦ vt (papers) heften; (hair, hedge) stutzen; ~**pers** npl (for hedge) Heckenschere f; (for hair) Haarschneidemaschine f; ~**ping** n Ausschnitt m

oak [kləuk] n Umhang m ♦ vt hüllen; ~**room** n (for coats) Garderobe f; (BRIT: W.C.) Toilette f

ock [klɔk] n Uhr f; ~ **in** or **on** vi stempeln; ~ **off** or **out** vi stempeln; ~**wise** adv im Uhrzeigersinn; ~**work** n Uhrwerk nt ♦ adj zum Aufziehen

og [klɔg] n Holzschuh m ♦ vt verstopfen

oister [ˈklɔɪstər] n Kreuzgang m

one [kləun] n Klon m ♦ vt klonen

ose¹ [kləus] adj (near) in der Nähe; (friend, connection, print) eng; (relative) nahe; (result) knapp; (examination) eingehend; (weather) schwül; (room) stickig ♦ adv nahe, dicht; ~ **by** in der Nähe; ~ **at hand** in der Nähe; **to have a ~ shave** (fig) mit knapper Not davonkommen

ose² [kləuz] vt (shut) schließen; (end) beenden ♦ vi (shop etc) schließen; (door etc) sich schließen ♦ n Ende nt; ~ **down** vi schließen; ~**d** adj (shop etc) geschlossen; ~**d shop** n Gewerkschaftszwang m

ose-knit [ˈkləusˈnɪt] adj eng zusammengewachsen

osely [ˈkləuslɪ] adv eng; (carefully) genau

oset [ˈklɔzɪt] n Schrank m

ose-up [ˈkləuszʌp] n Nahaufnahme f

osure [ˈkləuʒər] n Schließung f

ot [klɔt] n (of blood) Blutgerinnsel nt; (fool) Blödmann m ♦ vi gerinnen

oth [klɔθ] n (material) Tuch nt; (rag) Lappen m

othe [kləuð] vt kleiden

othes [kləuðz] npl Kleider pl; ~ **brush** n Kleiderbürste f; ~ **line** n Wäscheleine f; ~ **peg**, ~ **pin** (US) n Wäscheklammer f

othing [ˈkləuðɪŋ] n Kleidung f

otted cream [ˈklɔtɪd-] (BRIT) n Sahne aus erhitzter Milch

oud [klaud] n Wolke f; ~**burst** n Wolkenbruch m; ~**y** adj bewölkt; (liquid) trüb

clout [klaut] vt hauen

clove [kləuv] n Gewürznelke f; ~ **of garlic** Knoblauchzehe f

clover [ˈkləuvər] n Klee m

clown [klaun] n Clown m ♦ vi (also: ~ **about**, ~ **around**) kaspern

cloying [ˈklɔɪɪŋ] adj (taste, smell) übersüß

club [klʌb] n (weapon) Knüppel m; (society) Klub m; (also: **golf ~**) Golfschläger m ♦ vt prügeln ♦ vi: **to ~ together** zusammenlegen; ~**s** npl (CARDS) Kreuz nt; ~ **car** (US) n (RAIL) Speisewagen m; ~ **class** n (AVIAT) Club-Klasse f; ~**house** n Klubhaus nt

cluck [klʌk] vi glucken

clue [klu:] n Anhaltspunkt m; (in crosswords) Frage f; **I haven't a ~** (ich hab) keine Ahnung

clump [klʌmp] n Gruppe f

clumsy [ˈklʌmzɪ] adj (person) unbeholfen; (shape) unförmig

clung [klʌŋ] pt, pp of **cling**

cluster [ˈklʌstər] n (of trees etc) Gruppe f ♦ vi sich drängen, sich scharen

clutch [klʌtʃ] n Griff m; (AUT) Kupplung f ♦ vt sich festklammern an +dat

clutter [ˈklʌtər] vt voll pfropfen; (desk) übersäen

CND n abbr = **Campaign for Nuclear Disarmament**

Co. abbr = **county**; **company**

c/o abbr (= care of) c/o

coach [kəutʃ] n (bus) Reisebus m; (horse-drawn) Kutsche f; (RAIL) (Personen)wagen m; (trainer) Trainer m ♦ vt (SCH) Nachhilfeunterricht geben +dat; (SPORT) trainieren; ~ **trip** n Busfahrt f

coal [kəul] n Kohle f; ~ **face** n Streb m

coalition [kəuəˈlɪʃən] n Koalition f

coalman [ˈkəulmæn] (irreg) n Kohlenhändler m

coal mine n Kohlenbergwerk nt

coarse [kɔ:s] adj grob; (fig) ordinär

coast [kəust] n Küste f ♦ vi dahinrollen; (AUT) im Leerlauf fahren; ~**al** adj Küsten-;

~**guard** n Küstenwache f; ~**line** n
Küste(nlinie) f
coat [kəut] n Mantel m; (on animals) Fell nt;
(of paint) Schicht f ♦ vt überstreichen;
~**hanger** n Kleiderbügel m; ~**ing** n
Überzug m; (of paint) Schicht f; ~ **of arms**
n Wappen nt
coax [kəuks] vt beschwatzen
cob [kɔb] n see **corn**
cobbler [ˈkɔblə⁺] n Schuster m
cobbles [ˈkɔblz] npl Pflastersteine pl
cobweb [ˈkɔbwɛb] n Spinnennetz nt
cocaine [kəˈkeɪn] n Kokain nt
cock [kɔk] n Hahn m ♦ vt (gun) entsichern;
~**erel** [ˈkɔkərl] n junge(r) Hahn m; ~**eyed**
adj (fig) verrückt
cockle [ˈkɔkl] n Herzmuschel f
cockney [ˈkɔknɪ] n echte(r) Londoner m
cockpit [ˈkɔkpɪt] n (AVIAT) Pilotenkanzel f
cockroach [ˈkɔkrəutʃ] n Küchenschabe f
cocktail [ˈkɔkteɪl] n Cocktail m; ~ **cabinet** n
Hausbar f; ~ **party** n Cocktailparty f
cocoa [ˈkəukəu] n Kakao m
coconut [ˈkəukənʌt] n Kokosnuss f
cocoon [kəˈkuːn] n Kokon m
cod [kɔd] n Kabeljau m
C.O.D. abbr = **cash on delivery**
code [kəud] n Kode m; (JUR) Kodex m
cod-liver oil [ˈkɔdlɪvə-] n Lebertran m
coercion [kəuˈɜːʃən] n Zwang m
coffee [ˈkɔfɪ] n Kaffee m; ~ **bar** (BRIT) n Café
nt; ~ **bean** n Kaffeebohne f; ~ **break** n
Kaffeepause f; ~**pot** n Kaffeekanne f; ~
table n Couchtisch m
coffin [ˈkɔfɪn] n Sarg m
cog [kɔg] n (Rad)zahn m
cognac [ˈkɔnjæk] n Kognak m
coherent [kəuˈhɪərənt] adj
zusammenhängend; (person) verständlich
coil [kɔɪl] n Rolle f; (ELEC) Spule f;
(contraceptive) Spirale f ♦ vt aufwickeln
coin [kɔɪn] n Münze f ♦ vt prägen; ~**age**
[ˈkɔɪnɪdʒ] n (word) Prägung f; ~ **box** (BRIT) n
Münzfernsprecher m
coincide [kəuɪnˈsaɪd] vi (happen together)
zusammenfallen; (agree) übereinstimmen;
~**nce** [kəuˈɪnsɪdəns] n Zufall m

coinphone [ˈkɔɪnfəun] n Münzfernsprecher
m
Coke [kəuk] ® n (drink) Coca-Cola ® f
coke [kəuk] n Koks m
colander [ˈkɔləndə⁺] n Durchschlag m
cold [kəuld] adj kalt ♦ n Kälte f; (MED)
Erkältung f; **I'm** ~ mir ist kalt; **to catch** ~
sich erkälten; **in** ~ **blood** kaltblütig; **to give
sb the** ~ **shoulder** jdm die kalte Schulter
zeigen; ~**ly** adv kalt; ~-**shoulder** vt die
kalte Schulter zeigen +dat; ~ **sore** n
Erkältungsbläschen nt
coleslaw [ˈkəulslɔː] n Krautsalat m
colic [ˈkɔlɪk] n Kolik f
collaborate [kəˈlæbəreɪt] vi zusammenarbeiten
collapse [kəˈlæps] vi (people)
zusammenbrechen; (things) einstürzen ♦ n
Zusammenbruch m; Einsturz m;
collapsible adj zusammenklappbar,
Klapp-
collar [ˈkɔlə⁺] n Kragen m; ~**bone** n
Schlüsselbein nt
collateral [kɔˈlætərl] n (zusätzliche)
Sicherheit f
colleague [ˈkɔliːg] n Kollege m, Kollegin f
collect [kəˈlekt] vt sammeln; (BRIT: call and
pick up) abholen ♦ vi sich sammeln ♦ adv:
to call ~ (US: TEL) ein R-Gespräch führen;
~**ion** [kəˈlekʃən] n Sammlung f; (REL)
Kollekte f; (of post) Leerung f; ~**ive**
[kəˈlektɪv] adj gemeinsam; (POL) kollektiv;
~**or** [kəˈlektə⁺] n Sammler m; (tax ~or)
(Steuer)einnehmer m
college [ˈkɔlɪdʒ] n (UNIV) College nt; (TECH)
Fach-, Berufsschule f
collide [kəˈlaɪd] vi zusammenstoßen
collie [ˈkɔlɪ] n Collie m
colliery [ˈkɔlɪərɪ] (BRIT) n Zeche f
collision [kəˈlɪʒən] n Zusammenstoß m
colloquial [kəˈləukwɪəl] adj
umgangssprachlich
colon [ˈkəulən] n Doppelpunkt m; (MED)
Dickdarm m
colonel [ˈkɜːnl] n Oberst m
colonial [kəˈləunɪəl] adj Kolonial-
colonize [ˈkɔlənaɪz] vt kolonisieren

●lony ['kɔlənɪ] n Kolonie f

●lour ['kʌləʳ] (US **color**) n Farbe f ♦ vt (also
fig) färben ♦ vi sich verfärben; **~s** npl (of
club) Fahne f; ~ **bar** n Rassenschranke f;
~-blind adj farbenblind; **~ed** adj farbig; ~
film n Farbfilm m; **~ful** adj bunt;
(*personality*) schillernd; **~ing** n (*complexion*)
Gesichtsfarbe f; (*substance*) Farbstoff m; ~
scheme n Farbgebung f; ~ **television** n
Farbfernsehen nt

●lt [kəʊlt] n Fohlen nt

●lumn ['kɔləm] n Säule f; (MIL) Kolonne f;
(*of print*) Spalte f; **~ist** ['kɔləmnɪst] n
Kolumnist m

●ma ['kəʊmə] n Koma nt

●mb [kəʊm] n Kamm m ♦ vt kämmen;
(*search*) durchkämmen

●mbat ['kɔmbæt] n Kampf m ♦ vt
bekämpfen

●mbination [kɔmbɪ'neɪʃən] n Kombination
f

●mbine [vb kəm'baɪn, n 'kɔmbaɪn] vt
verbinden ♦ vi sich vereinigen ♦ n (COMM)
Konzern m; ~ (**harvester**) n Mähdrescher
m

●mbustion [kəm'bʌstʃən] n Verbrennung f

●me [kʌm] (pt **came**, pp **come**) vi
kommen; ~ **to undone** aufgehen; ~
about vi geschehen; ~ **across** vt fus
(*find*) stoßen auf +acc; ~ **away** vi (*person*)
weggehen; (*handle etc*) abgehen; ~ **back**
vi zurückkommen; ~ **by** vt fus (*find*): **to ~
by sth** zu etw kommen; ~ **down** vi (*price*)
fallen; ~ **forward** vi (*volunteer*) sich
melden; ~ **from** vt fus (*result*) kommen
von; **where do you ~ from?** wo kommen
Sie her?; **I ~ from London** ich komme aus
London; ~ **in** vi hereinkommen; (*train*)
einfahren; ~ **in for** vt fus abkriegen; ~
into vt fus (*inherit*) erben; ~ **off** vi (*handle*)
abgehen; (*succeed*) klappen; ~ **on** vi
(*progress*) vorankommen; ~ **on!** komm!;
(*hurry*) beeil dich!; ~ **out** vi
herauskommen; ~ **round** vi (MED) wieder
zu sich kommen; ~ **to** vi (MED) wieder zu
sich kommen ♦ vt fus (*bill*) sich belaufen auf
+acc; ~ **up** vi hochkommen; (*sun*)

aufgehen; (*problem*) auftauchen; ~ **up
against** vt fus (*resistance, difficulties*)
stoßen auf +acc; ~ **upon** vt fus stoßen auf
+acc; ~ **up with** vt fus sich einfallen lassen

comedian [kə'miːdɪən] n Komiker m;
comedienne [kəmi:dɪ'en] n Komikerin f

comedown ['kʌmdaʊn] n Abstieg m

comedy ['kɔmɪdɪ] n Komödie f

comet ['kɔmɪt] n Komet m

comeuppance [kʌm'ʌpəns] n: **to get
one's ~** seine Quittung bekommen

comfort ['kʌmfət] n Komfort m; (*consolation*)
Trost m ♦ vt trösten; **~able** adj bequem;
~ably adv (*sit etc*) bequem; (*live*)
angenehm; ~ **station** (US) n öffentliche
Toilette f

comic ['kɔmɪk] n Comic(heft) nt; (*comedian*)
Komiker m ♦ adj (also: **~al**) komisch; ~
strip n Comicstrip m

coming ['kʌmɪŋ] n Kommen nt; **~(s) and
going(s)** n(pl) Kommen und Gehen nt

comma ['kɔmə] n Komma nt

command [kə'mɑːnd] n Befehl m; (*control*)
Führung f; (MIL) Kommando nt; (*mastery*)
Beherrschung f ♦ vt befehlen +dat; (MIL)
kommandieren; (*be able to get*) verfügen
über +acc; **~eer** [kɔmən'dɪəʳ] vt requirieren;
~er n Kommandant m; **~ment** n (REL)
Gebot nt

commando [kə'mɑːndəʊ] n
Kommandotruppe nt; (*person*) Mitglied nt
einer Kommandotruppe

commemorate [kə'meməreɪt] vt gedenken
+gen

commence [kə'mens] vt, vi beginnen

commend [kə'mend] vt (*recommend*)
empfehlen; (*praise*) loben

commensurate [kə'menʃərɪt] adj: **~ with
sth** einer Sache dat entsprechend

comment ['kɔment] n Bemerkung f ♦ vi: **to
~ (on)** sich äußern (zu); **~ary** n
Kommentar m; **~ator** n Kommentator m;
(TV) Reporter(in) m(f)

commerce ['kɔmə:s] n Handel m

commercial [kə'mə:ʃəl] adj kommerziell,
geschäftlich; (*training*) kaufmännisch ♦ n
(TV) Fernsehwerbung f; ~ **break** n

Werbespot *m*; **~ize** *vt* kommerzialisieren

commiserate [kəˈmɪzəreɪt] *vi*: **to ~ with** Mitleid haben mit

commission [kəˈmɪʃən] *n* (*act*) Auftrag *m*; (*fee*) Provision *f*; (*body*) Kommission *f* ♦ *vt* beauftragen; (*MIL*) zum Offizier ernennen; (*work of art*) in Auftrag geben; **out of ~** außer Betrieb; **~er** *n* (*POLICE*) Polizeipräsident *m*

commit [kəˈmɪt] *vt* (*crime*) begehen; (*entrust*) anvertrauen; **to ~ o.s.** sich festlegen; **~ment** *n* Verpflichtung *f*

committee [kəˈmɪtɪ] *n* Ausschuss *m*

commodity [kəˈmɒdɪtɪ] *n* Ware *f*

common [ˈkɒmən] *adj* (*cause*) gemeinsam; (*pej*) gewöhnlich; (*widespread*) üblich, häufig ♦ *n* Gemeindeland *nt*; **C~s** *npl* (*BRIT*): **the C~s** das Unterhaus; **~er** *n* Bürgerliche(r) *mf*; **~ law** *n* Gewohnheitsrecht *nt*; **~ly** *adv* gewöhnlich; **C~ Market** *n* Gemeinsame(r) Markt *m*; **~place** *adj* alltäglich; **~ room** *n* Gemeinschaftsraum *m*; **~ sense** *n* gesunde(r) Menschenverstand *m*; **C~wealth** *n*: **the C~wealth** das Commonwealth

commotion [kəˈməʊʃən] *n* Aufsehen *nt*

communal [ˈkɒmjuːnl] *adj* Gemeinde-; Gemeinschafts-

commune [*n* ˈkɒmjuːn, *vb* kəˈmjuːn] *n* Kommune *f* ♦ *vi*: **to ~ with** sich mitteilen +*dat*

communicate [kəˈmjuːnɪkeɪt] *vt* (*transmit*) übertragen ♦ *vi* (*be in touch*) in Verbindung stehen; (*make self understood*) sich verständigen; **communication** [kəmjuːnɪˈkeɪʃən] *n* (*message*) Mitteilung *f*; (*making understood*) Kommunikation *f*; **communication cord** (*BRIT*) *n* Notbremse *f*

communion [kəˈmjuːnɪən] *n* (*also*: **Holy C~**) Abendmahl *nt*, Kommunion *f*

communism [ˈkɒmjunɪzəm] *n* Kommunismus *m*; **communist** [ˈkɒmjunɪst] *n* Kommunist(in) *m(f)* ♦ *adj* kommunistisch

community [kəˈmjuːnɪtɪ] *n* Gemeinschaft *f*; **~ centre** *n* Gemeinschaftszentrum *nt*; **~ chest** (*US*) *n* Wohltätigkeitsfonds *m*; **~ home** (*BRIT*) *n* Erziehungsheim *nt*

commutation ticket [kɒmjuˈteɪʃən-] (*US*) *n* Zeitkarte *f*

commute [kəˈmjuːt] *vi* pendeln ♦ *vt* umwandeln; **~r** *n* Pendler *m*

compact [*adj* kəmˈpækt, *n* ˈkɒmpækt] *adj* kompakt ♦ *n* (*for make-up*) Puderdose *f*; **~ disc** *n* Compactdisc *f*, Compact Disc *f*; **~ disc player** *n* CD-Spieler *m*

companion [kəmˈpænjən] *n* Begleiter(in) *m(f)*; **~ship** *n* Gesellschaft *f*

company [ˈkʌmpənɪ] *n* Gesellschaft *f*; (*COMM*) Firma *f*, Gesellschaft *f*; **to keep sb ~** jdm Gesellschaft leisten; **~ secretary** (*BRIT*) *n* ≈ Prokurist(in) *m(f)*

comparable [ˈkɒmpərəbl] *adj* vergleichbar

comparative [kəmˈpærətɪv] *adj* (*relative*) relativ; **~ly** *adv* verhältnismäßig

compare [kəmˈpeər] *vt* vergleichen ♦ *vi* sich vergleichen lassen; **comparison** [kəmˈpærɪsn] *n* Vergleich *m*; **in comparison (with)** im Vergleich (mit *or* zu)

compartment [kəmˈpɑːtmənt] *n* (*RAIL*) Abteil *nt*; (*in drawer*) Fach *n*

compass [ˈkʌmpəs] *n* Kompass *m*; **~es** *npl* (*MATH etc*: *also*: **pair of ~es**) Zirkel *m*

compassion [kəmˈpæʃən] *n* Mitleid *nt*; **~ate** *adj* mitfühlend

compatible [kəmˈpætɪbl] *adj* vereinbar; (*COMPUT*) kompatibel

compel [kəmˈpel] *vt* zwingen

compensate [ˈkɒmpənseɪt] *vt* entschädigen ♦ *vi*: **to ~ for** Ersatz leisten für; **compensation** [kɒmpənˈseɪʃən] *n* Entschädigung *f*

compère [ˈkɒmpeər] *n* Conférencier *m*

compete [kəmˈpiːt] *vi* (*take part*) teilnehmen; (*vie with*) konkurrieren

competent [ˈkɒmpɪtənt] *adj* kompetent

competition [kɒmpɪˈtɪʃən] *n* (*contest*) Wettbewerb *m*; (*COMM, rivalry*) Konkurrenz *f*; **competitive** [kəmˈpetɪtɪv] *adj* Konkurrenz-; (*COMM*) konkurrenzfähig; **competitor** [kəmˈpetɪtər] *n* (*COMM*) Konkurrent(in) *m(f)*; (*participant*) Teilnehmer(in) *m(f)*

compile [kəm'paɪl] vt zusammenstellen

complacency [kəm'pleɪsnsɪ] n Selbstzufriedenheit f

complacent [kəm'pleɪsnt] adj selbstzufrieden

complain [kəm'pleɪn] vi sich beklagen; (formally) sich beschweren; ~t n Klage f; (formal ~t) Beschwerde f; (MED) Leiden nt

complement [n 'kɒmplɪmənt, vb 'kɒmplɪment] n Ergänzung f; (ship's crew etc) Bemannung f ♦ vt ergänzen; ~ary [kɒmplɪ'mentərɪ] adj (sich) ergänzend

complete [kəm'pliːt] adj (full) vollkommen, ganz; (finished) fertig ♦ vt vervollständigen; (finish) beenden; (fill in: form) ausfüllen; ~ly adv ganz; completion [kəm'pliːʃən] n Fertigstellung f; (of contract etc) Abschluss m

complex ['kɒmpleks] adj kompliziert

complexion [kəm'plekʃən] n Gesichtsfarbe f; (fig) Aspekt m

complexity [kəm'pleksɪtɪ] n Kompliziertheit f

compliance [kəm'plaɪəns] n Fügsamkeit f, Einwilligung f; in ~ with sth einer Sache dat gemäß

complicate ['kɒmplɪkeɪt] vt komplizieren; ~d adj kompliziert; complication [kɒmplɪ'keɪʃən] n Komplikation f

compliment [n 'kɒmplɪmənt, vb 'kɒmplɪment] n Kompliment nt ♦ vt ein Kompliment machen +dat; ~s npl (greetings) Grüße pl; to pay sb a ~ jdm ein Kompliment machen; ~ary [kɒmplɪ'mentərɪ] adj schmeichelhaft; (free) Frei-, Gratis-

comply [kəm'plaɪ] vi: to ~ with erfüllen +acc; entsprechen +dat

component [kəm'pəunənt] adj Teil- ♦ n Bestandteil m

compose [kəm'pəuz] vt (music) komponieren; (poetry) verfassen; to ~ o.s. sich sammeln; ~d adj gefasst; ~r n Komponist(in) m(f); composition ['kɒmpə'zɪʃən] n (MUS) Komposition f; (SCH) Aufsatz m; (structure) Zusammensetzung f, Aufbau m

composure [kəm'pəuʒəʳ] n Fassung f

compound ['kɒmpaund] n (CHEM) Verbindung f; (enclosure) Lager nt; (LING) Kompositum nt ♦ adj zusammengesetzt; (fracture) kompliziert; ~ interest n Zinseszins m

comprehend [kɒmprɪ'hend] vt begreifen; comprehension n Verständnis nt

comprehensive [kɒmprɪ'hensɪv] adj umfassend ♦ n = comprehensive school; ~ insurance n Vollkasko nt; ~ school (BRIT) n Gesamtschule f

compress [vb kəm'pres, n 'kɒmpres] vt komprimieren ♦ n (MED) Kompresse f

comprise [kəm'praɪz] vt (also: be ~d of) umfassen, bestehen aus

compromise ['kɒmprəmaɪz] n Kompromiss m ♦ vt kompromittieren ♦ vi einen Kompromiss schließen

compulsion [kəm'pʌlʃən] n Zwang m; compulsive [kəm'pʌlsɪv] adj zwanghaft; compulsory [kəm'pʌlsərɪ] adj obligatorisch

computer [kəm'pjuːtəʳ] n Computer m, Rechner m; ~ game n Computerspiel nt; ~-generated adj computergeneriert; ~ize vt (information) computerisieren; (company, accounts) auf Computer umstellen; ~ programmer n Programmierer(in) m(f); ~ programming n Programmieren nt; ~ science n Informatik f; computing [kəm'pjuːtɪŋ] n (science) Informatik f; (work) Computerei f

comrade ['kɒmrɪd] n Kamerad m; (POL) Genosse m

con [kɒn] vt hereinlegen ♦ n Schwindel nt

concave ['kɒnkeɪv] adj konkav

conceal [kən'siːl] vt (secret) verschweigen; (hide) verbergen

concede [kən'siːd] vt (grant) gewähren; (point) zugeben ♦ vi (admit defeat) nachgeben

conceit [kən'siːt] n Einbildung f; ~ed adj eingebildet

conceivable [kən'siːvəbl] adj vorstellbar

conceive [kən'siːv] vt (idea) ausdenken; (imagine) sich vorstellen; (baby) empfangen ♦ vi empfangen

concentrate ['kɒnsəntreɪt] vi sich konzentrieren ♦ vt konzentrieren; to ~ on sth sich auf etw acc konzentrieren;

concentration [kɒnsən'treɪʃən] n Konzentration f; **concentration camp** n Konzentrationslager nt, KZ nt

concept ['kɒnsept] n Begriff m

conception [kən'sepʃən] n (idea) Vorstellung f; (BIOL) Empfängnis f

concern [kən'sɜːn] n (affair) Angelegenheit f; (COMM) Unternehmen nt; (worry) Sorge f ♦ vt (interest) angehen; (be about) handeln von; (have connection with) betreffen; **to be ~ed (about)** sich Sorgen machen (um); **~ing** prep hinsichtlich +gen

concert ['kɒnsət] n Konzert nt

concerted [kən'sɜːtɪd] adj gemeinsam

concert hall n Konzerthalle f

concertina [kɒnsə'tiːnə] n Handharmonika f

concerto [kən'tʃɜːtəʊ] n Konzert nt

concession [kən'seʃən] n (yielding) Zugeständnis nt; **tax ~** Steuerkonzession f

conciliation [kənsɪlɪ'eɪʃən] n Versöhnung f; (official) Schlichtung f

concise [kən'saɪs] adj präzis

conclude [kən'kluːd] vt (end) beenden; (treaty) (ab)schließen; (decide) schließen, folgern; **conclusion** [kən'kluːʒən] n (Ab)schluss m; (deduction) Schluss m; **conclusive** [kən'kluːsɪv] adj schlüssig

concoct [kən'kɒkt] vt zusammenbrauen; **~ion** [kən'kɒkʃən] n Gebräu nt

concourse ['kɒŋkɔːs] n (Bahnhofs)halle f, Vorplatz m

concrete ['kɒŋkriːt] n Beton m ♦ adj konkret

concur [kən'kɜː] vi übereinstimmen

concurrently [kən'kʌrntlɪ] adv gleichzeitig

concussion [kən'kʌʃən] n (Gehirn)erschütterung f

condemn [kən'dem] vt (JUR) verurteilen; (building) abbruchreif erklären

condensation [kɒndɛn'seɪʃən] n Kondensation f

condense [kən'dens] vi (CHEM) kondensieren ♦ vt (fig) zusammendrängen; **~d milk** n Kondensmilch f

condescending [kɒndɪ'sendɪŋ] adj herablassend

condition [kən'dɪʃən] n (state) Zustand m; (presupposition) Bedingung f ♦ vt (hair etc)

behandeln; (accustom) gewöhnen; **~s** npl (circumstances) Verhältnisse pl; **on ~ that ...** unter der Bedingung, dass ...; **~al** adj bedingt; **~er** n (for hair) Spülung f; (for fabrics) Weichspüler m

condolences [kən'dəʊlənsɪz] npl Beileid nt

condom ['kɒndəm] n Kondom nt or m

condominium [kɒndə'mɪnɪəm] (US) n Eigentumswohnung f; (block) Eigentumsblock m

condone [kən'dəʊn] vt gutheißen

conducive [kən'djuːsɪv] adj: **~ to** dienlich +dat

conduct [n 'kɒndʌkt, vb kən'dʌkt] n (behaviour) Verhalten nt; (management) Führung f ♦ vt führen; (MUS) dirigieren; **~ed tour** n Führung f; **~or** [kən'dʌktə] n (of orchestra) Dirigent m; (in bus, US: on train) Schaffner m; (ELEC) Leiter m; **~ress** [kən'dʌktrɪs] n (in bus) Schaffnerin f

cone [kəʊn] n (MATH) Kegel m; (for ice cream) (Waffel)tüte f; (BOT) Tannenzapfen m

confectioner's (shop) [kən'fekʃənəz-] n Konditorei f; **~y** [kən'fekʃənrɪ] n Süßigkeiten pl

confederation [kənfedə'reɪʃən] n Bund m

confer [kən'fɜː] vt (degree) verleihen ♦ vi (discuss) konferieren, verhandeln; **~ence** ['kɒnfərəns] n Konferenz f

confess [kən'fes] vt, vi gestehen; (ECCL) beichten; **~ion** [kən'feʃən] n Geständnis nt; (ECCL) Beichte f; **~ional** n Beichtstuhl m

confide [kən'faɪd] vi: **to ~ in** (sich) anvertrauen +dat

confidence ['kɒnfɪdns] n Vertrauen nt; (assurance) Selbstvertrauen nt; (secret) Geheimnis nt; **in ~** (speak, write) vertraulich; **~ trick** n Schwindel m

confident ['kɒnfɪdənt] adj (sure) überzeugt; (self-assured) selbstsicher

confidential [kɒnfɪ'denʃəl] adj vertraulich

confine [kən'faɪn] vt (limit) beschränken; (lock up) einsperren; **~d** adj (space) eng; **~ment** n (in prison) Haft f; (MED) Wochenbett nt; **~s** ['kɒnfaɪnz] npl Grenzen pl

confirm [kən'fɜːm] vt bestätigen; **~ation**

kɔnfəˈmeɪʃən] n Bestätigung f; (REL)
Konfirmation f; ~ed adj unverbesserlich;
bachelor) eingefleischt

nfiscate [ˈkɔnfɪskeɪt] vt beschlagnahmen

nflict [n ˈkɔnflɪkt, vb kənˈflɪkt] n Konflikt m
♦ vi im Widerspruch stehen; ~ing
kənˈflɪktɪŋ] adj widersprüchlich

nform [kənˈfɔːm] vi: **to ~ (to)** (*things*)
entsprechen +dat; (*people*) sich anpassen
+dat; (*to rules*) sich richten (nach)

nfound [kənˈfaund] vt verblüffen;
confuse) durcheinander bringen

nfront [kənˈfrʌnt] vt (*enemy*)
entgegentreten +dat; (*problems*) sich stellen
+dat; **to ~ sb with sth** jdn mit etw
konfrontieren; ~**ation** [kɔnfrənˈteɪʃən] n
Konfrontation f

nfuse [kənˈfjuːz] vt verwirren; (*sth with
sth*) verwechseln; ~**d** adj verwirrt;
confusing adj verwirrend; **confusion**
kənˈfjuːʒən] n (*perplexity*) Verwirrung f;
mixing up) Verwechslung f; (*tumult*) Aufruhr
m

ngeal [kənˈdʒiːl] vi (*freeze*) gefrieren; (*clot*)
gerinnen

ngested [kənˈdʒestɪd] adj überfüllt

ngestion [kənˈdʒestʃən] n Stau m

nglomerate [kənˈglɔmərɪt] n (COMM,
GEOL) Konglomerat nt

nglomeration [kənglɔməˈreɪʃən] n
Anhäufung f

ngratulate [kənˈgrætjuleɪt] vt: **to ~ sb
(on sth)** jdn (zu etw) beglückwünschen;
congratulations [kəngrætjuˈleɪʃənz] npl
Glückwünsche pl; **congratulations!**
gratuliere!, herzlichen Glückwunsch!

ngregate [ˈkɔŋgrɪgeɪt] vi sich
versammeln; **congregation** [kɔŋgrɪˈgeɪʃən]
n Gemeinde f

ngress [ˈkɔŋgres] n Kongress m; C~man
(*irreg: US*) n Mitglied nt des amerikanischen
Repräsentantenhauses

nifer [ˈkɔnɪfər] n Nadelbaum m

njunction [kənˈdʒʌŋkʃən] n Verbindung f;
(GRAM) Konjunktion f

njunctivitis [kəndʒʌŋktɪˈvaɪtɪs] n
Bindehautentzündung f

conjure [ˈkʌndʒər] vi zaubern; ~ **up** vt
heraufbeschwören; ~**r** n Zauberkünstler(in)
m(f)

conk out [kɔŋk-] (*inf*) vi den Geist aufgeben

con man (*irreg*) n Schwindler m

connect [kəˈnekt] vt verbinden; (ELEC)
anschließen; **to be ~ed with** eine
Beziehung haben zu; (*be related to*)
verwandt sein mit; ~**ion** [kəˈnekʃən] n
Verbindung f; (*relation*) Zusammenhang m;
(ELEC, TEL, RAIL) Anschluss m

connive [kəˈnaɪv] vi: **to ~ at** stillschweigend
dulden

connoisseur [kɔnɪˈsəːr] n Kenner m

conquer [ˈkɔŋkər] vt (*feelings*) überwinden;
(*enemy*) besiegen; (*country*) erobern; ~**or** n
Eroberer m

conquest [ˈkɔŋkwest] n Eroberung f

cons [kɔnz] npl see **convenience**; **pro**

conscience [ˈkɔnʃəns] n Gewissen nt

conscientious [kɔnʃɪˈenʃəs] adj
gewissenhaft

conscious [ˈkɔnʃəs] adj bewusst; (MED) bei
Bewusstsein; ~**ness** n Bewusstsein nt

conscript [ˈkɔnskrɪpt] n Wehrpflichtige(r) m;
~**ion** [kənˈskrɪpʃən] n Wehrpflicht f

consecutive [kənˈsekjutɪv] adj aufeinander
folgend

consensus [kənˈsensəs] n allgemeine
Übereinstimmung f

consent [kənˈsent] n Zustimmung f ♦ vi
zustimmen

consequence [ˈkɔnsɪkwəns] n (*importance*)
Bedeutung f; (*effect*) Folge f

consequently [ˈkɔnsɪkwəntlɪ] adv folglich

conservation [kɔnsəˈveɪʃən] n Erhaltung f;
(*nature ~*) Umweltschutz m

conservative [kənˈsəːvətɪv] adj konservativ;
C~ adj (BRIT) adj konservativ ♦ n
Konservative(r) mf

conservatory [kənˈsəːvətrɪ] n (*room*)
Wintergarten m

conserve [kənˈsəːv] vt erhalten

consider [kənˈsɪdər] vt überlegen; (*take into
account*) in Betracht ziehen; (*regard as*)
halten für; **to ~ doing sth** daran denken,
etw zu tun; ~**able** [kənˈsɪdərəbl] adj

beträchtlich; **~ably** *adv* beträchtlich; **~ate** *adj* rücksichtsvoll; **~ation** [kənsıdə'reıʃən] *n* Rücksicht(nahme) *f*; (*thought*) Erwägung *f*; **~ing** *prep* in Anbetracht +*gen*

consign [kən'saın] *vt* übergeben; **~ment** *n* Sendung *f*

consist [kən'sıst] *vi*: **to ~ of** bestehen aus

consistency [kən'sıstənsı] *n* (*of material*) Konsistenz *f*; (*of argument, person*) Konsequenz *f*

consistent [kən'sıstənt] *adj* (*person*) konsequent; (*argument*) folgerichtig

consolation [kɒnsə'leıʃən] *n* Trost *m*

console[1] [kən'səul] *vt* trösten

console[2] ['kɒnsəul] *n* Kontroll(pult) *nt*

consolidate [kən'sɒlıdeıt] *vt* festigen

consommé [kən'sɒmeı] *n* Fleischbrühe *f*

consonant ['kɒnsənənt] *n* Konsonant *m*, Mitlaut *m*

conspicuous [kən'spıkjuəs] *adj* (*prominent*) auffällig; (*visible*) deutlich sichtbar

conspiracy [kən'spırəsı] *n* Verschwörung *f*

conspire [kən'spaıəʳ] *vi* sich verschwören

constable ['kʌnstəbl] (*BRIT*) *n* Polizist(in) *m(f)*; **chief ~** Polizeipräsident *m*; **constabulary** [kən'stæbjulərı] *n* Polizei *f*

constant ['kɒnstənt] *adj* (*continuous*) ständig; (*unchanging*) konstant; **~ly** *adv* ständig

constellation [kɒnstə'leıʃən] *n* Sternbild *nt*

consternation [kɒnstə'neıʃən] *n* Bestürzung *f*

constipated ['kɒnstıpeıtıd] *adj* verstopft; **constipation** [kɒnstı'peıʃən] *n* Verstopfung *f*

constituency [kən'stıtjuənsı] *n* Wahlkreis *m*

constituent [kən'stıtjuənt] *n* (*person*) Wähler *m*; (*part*) Bestandteil *m*

constitute ['kɒnstıtju:t] *vt* (*make up*) bilden; (*amount to*) darstellen

constitution [kɒnstı'tju:ʃən] *n* Verfassung *f*; **~al** *adj* Verfassungs-

constraint [kən'streınt] *n* Zwang *m*; (*shyness*) Befangenheit *f*

construct [kən'strʌkt] *vt* bauen; **~ion** [kən'strʌkʃən] *n* Konstruktion *f*; (*building*) Bau *m*; **~ive** *adj* konstruktiv

construe [kən'stru:] *vt* deuten

consul ['kɒnsl] *n* Konsul *m*; **~ate** *n* Konsulat *nt*

consult [kən'sʌlt] *vt* um Rat fragen; (*doctor*) konsultieren; (*book*) nachschlagen in +*dat*; **~ant** *n* (*MED*) Facharzt *m*; (*other specialist*) Gutachter *m*; **~ation** [kɒnsəl'teıʃən] *n* Beratung *f*; (*MED*) Konsultation *f*; **~ing room** *n* Sprechzimmer *nt*

consume [kən'sju:m] *vt* verbrauchen; (*food*) konsumieren; **~r** *n* Verbraucher *m*; **~r goods** *npl* Konsumgüter *pl*; **~rism** *n* Konsum *m*; **~r society** *n* Konsumgesellschaft *f*

consummate ['kɒnsʌmeıt] *vt* (*marriage*) vollziehen

consumption [kən'sʌmpʃən] *n* Verbrauch *m*; (*of food*) Konsum *m*

cont. *abbr* (= *continued*) Forts.

contact ['kɒntækt] *n* (*touch*) Berührung *f*; (*connection*) Verbindung *f*; (*person*) Kontakt *m* ♦ *vt* sich in Verbindung setzen mit; **~ lenses** *npl* Kontaktlinsen *pl*

contagious [kən'teıdʒəs] *adj* ansteckend

contain [kən'teın] *vt* enthalten; **to ~ o.s.** sich zügeln; **~er** *n* Behälter *m*; (*transport*) Container *m*

contaminate [kən'tæmıneıt] *vt* verunreinigen

cont'd *abbr* (= *continued*) Forts.

contemplate ['kɒntəmpleıt] *vt* (*look at*) (nachdenklich) betrachten; (*think about*) überdenken; (*plan*) vorhaben

contemporary [kən'tempərərı] *adj* zeitgenössisch ♦ *n* Zeitgenosse *m*

contempt [kən'tempt] *n* Verachtung *f*; **~ of court** (*JUR*) Missachtung *f* des Gerichts; **~ible** *adj* verachtenswert; **~uous** *adj* verächtlich

contend [kən'tend] *vt* (*argue*) behaupten ♦ *vi* kämpfen; **~er** *n* (*for post*) Bewerber(in) *m(f)*; (*SPORT*) Wettkämpfer(in) *m(f)*

content [*adj, vb* kən'tent, *n* 'kɒntent] *adj* zufrieden ♦ *vt* befriedigen ♦ *n* (*also*: **~s**) Inhalt *m*; **~ed** *adj* zufrieden

contention [kən'tenʃən] *n* (*dispute*) Streit *m*; (*argument*) Behauptung *f*

contentment [kən'tentmənt] *n* Zufriedenheit *f*

contest [*n* 'kɔntest, *vb* kən'test] *n*
(Wett)kampf *m* ♦ *vt* (*dispute*) bestreiten;
(*JUR*) anfechten; (*POL*) kandidieren in +*dat*;
~ant [kən'testənt] *n* Bewerber(in) *m(f)*

context ['kɔntekst] *n* Zusammenhang *m*

continent ['kɔntɪnənt] *n* Kontinent *m*; **the
C~** (*BRIT*) das europäische Festland; **~al**
[kɔntɪ'nentl] *adj* kontinental; **~al breakfast**
n kleines Frühstück *nt*; **~al quilt** (*BRIT*) *n*
Federbett *nt*

contingency [kən'tɪndʒənsɪ] *n* Möglichkeit *f*

contingent [kən'tɪndʒənt] *n* Kontingent *nt*

continual [kən'tɪnjuəl] *adj* (*endless*)
fortwährend; (*repeated*) immer
wiederkehrend; **~ly** *adv* immer wieder

continuation [kəntɪnju'eɪʃən] *n* Fortsetzung
f

continue [kən'tɪnju:] *vi* (*person*)
weitermachen; (*thing*) weitergehen ♦ *vt*
fortsetzen

continuity [kɔntɪ'nju:ɪtɪ] *n* Kontinuität *f*

continuous [kən'tɪnjuəs] *adj*
ununterbrochen; **~ stationery** *n*
Endlospapier *nt*

contort [kən'tɔ:t] *vt* verdrehen; **~ion**
[kən'tɔ:ʃən] *n* Verzerrung *f*

contour ['kɔntuər] *n* Umriss *m*; (*also*: **~ line**)
Höhenlinie *f*

contraband ['kɔntrəbænd] *n*
Schmuggelware *f*

contraception [kɔntrə'sepʃən] *n*
Empfängnisverhütung *f*

contraceptive [kɔntrə'septɪv] *n*
empfängnisverhütende(s) Mittel *nt* ♦ *adj*
empfängnisverhütend

contract [*n* 'kɔntrækt, *vb* kən'trækt] *n* Vertrag
m ♦ *vi* (*muscle, metal*) sich zusammenziehen
♦ *vt* zusammenziehen; **to ~ to do sth**
(*COMM*) sich vertraglich verpflichten, etw zu
tun; **~ion** [kən'trækʃən] *n* (*shortening*)
Verkürzung *f*; **~or** [kən'træktər] *n*
Unternehmer *m*

contradict [kɔntrə'dɪkt] *vt* widersprechen
+*dat*; **~ion** [kɔntrə'dɪkʃən] *n* Widerspruch *m*

contraflow ['kɔntrəfləʊ] *n* (*AUT*)
Gegenverkehr *m*

contraption [kən'træpʃən] (*inf*) *n* Apparat *m*

contrary[1] ['kɔntrərɪ] *adj* (*opposite*)
entgegengesetzt ♦ *n* Gegenteil *nt*; **on the ~**
im Gegenteil

contrary[2] [kən'trɛərɪ] *adj* (*obstinate*)
widerspenstig

contrast [*n* 'kɔntrɑ:st, *vb* kən'trɑ:st] *n*
Kontrast *m* ♦ *vt* entgegensetzen; **~ing**
[kən'trɑ:stɪŋ] *adj* Kontrast-

contravene [kɔntrə'vi:n] *vt* verstoßen
gegen

contribute [kən'trɪbju:t] *vt, vi*: **to ~ to**
beitragen zu; **contribution** [kɔntrɪ'bju:ʃən]
n Beitrag *m*; **contributor** [kən'trɪbjutər] *n*
Beitragende(r) *f(m)*

contrive [kən'traɪv] *vt* ersinnen ♦ *vi*: **to ~ to
do sth** es schaffen, etw zu tun

control [kən'trəʊl] *vt* (*direct, test*)
kontrollieren ♦ *n* Kontrolle *f*; **~s** *npl* (*of
vehicle*) Steuerung *f*; (*of engine*) Schalttafel *f*;
to be in ~ of (*business, office*) leiten; (*group
of children*) beaufsichtigen; **out of ~** außer
Kontrolle; **under ~** unter Kontrolle; **~led
substance** *n* verschreibungspflichtiges
Medikament; **~ panel** *n* Schalttafel *f*; **~
room** *n* Kontrollraum *m*; **~ tower** *n* (*AVIAT*)
Kontrollturm *m*

controversial [kɔntrə'və:ʃl] *adj* umstritten;
controversy ['kɔntrəvə:sɪ] *n* Kontroverse *f*

conurbation [kɔnə'beɪʃən] *n* Ballungsgebiet
nt

convalesce [kɔnvə'les] *vi* genesen;
convalescence [kɔnvə'lesns] *n* Genesung *f*

convector [kən'vektər] *n* Heizlüfter *m*

convene [kən'vi:n] *vt* zusammenrufen ♦ *vi*
sich versammeln

convenience [kən'vi:nɪəns] *n*
Annehmlichkeit *f*; **all modern ~s** *or* (*BRIT*)
mod cons mit allem Komfort; **at your ~**
wann es Ihnen passt

convenient [kən'vi:nɪənt] *adj* günstig

convent ['kɔnvənt] *n* Kloster *nt*

convention [kən'venʃən] *n* Versammlung *f*;
(*custom*) Konvention *f*; **~al** *adj*
konventionell

convent school *n* Klosterschule *f*

converge [kən'və:dʒ] *vi* zusammenlaufen

conversant [kən'vɜːsnt] *adj*: **to be ~ with** bewandert sein in +*dat*

conversation [kɔnvə'seɪʃən] *n* Gespräch *nt*; **~al** *adj* Unterhaltungs-

converse [*n* 'kɔnvɜːs, *vb* kən'vɜːs] *n* Gegenteil *nt* ♦ *vi* sich unterhalten

conversion [kən'vɜːʃən] *n* Umwandlung *f*; (*REL*) Bekehrung *f*

convert [*vb* kən'vɜːt, *n* 'kɔnvɜːt] *vt* (*change*) umwandeln; (*REL*) bekehren ♦ *n* Bekehrte(r) *mf*; Konvertit(in) *m(f)*; **~ible** *n* (*AUT*) Kabriolett *nt* ♦ *adj* umwandelbar; (*FIN*) konvertierbar

convex ['kɔnvɛks] *adj* konvex

convey [kən'veɪ] *vt* (*carry*) befördern; (*feelings*) vermitteln; **~or belt** *n* Fließband *nt*

convict [*vb* kən'vɪkt, *n* 'kɔnvɪkt] *vt* verurteilen ♦ *n* Häftling *m*; **~ion** [kən'vɪkʃən] *n* (*verdict*) Verurteilung *f*; (*belief*) Überzeugung *f*

convince [kən'vɪns] *vt* überzeugen; **~d** *adj*: **~d that** überzeugt davon, dass; **convincing** *adj* überzeugend

convoluted ['kɔnvəluːtɪd] *adj* verwickelt; (*style*) gewunden

convoy ['kɔnvɔɪ] *n* (*of vehicles*) Kolonne *f*; (*protected*) Konvoi *m*

convulse [kən'vʌls] *vt* zusammenzucken lassen; **to be ~d with laughter** sich vor Lachen krümmen; **convulsion** [kən'vʌlʃən] *n* (*esp MED*) Zuckung *f*, Krampf *m*

coo [kuː] *vi* gurren

cook [kuk] *vt*, *vi* kochen ♦ *n* Koch *m*, Köchin *f*; ~ **book** *n* Kochbuch *nt*; **~er** *n* Herd *m*; **~ery** *n* Kochkunst *f*; **~ery book** (*BRIT*) *n* = **cook book**; **~ie** (*US*) *n* Plätzchen *nt*; **~ing** *n* Kochen *nt*

cool [kuːl] *adj* kühl ♦ *vt*, *vi* (ab)kühlen; ~ **down** *vt*, *vi* (*fig*) (sich) beruhigen; **~ness** *n* Kühle *f*; (*of temperament*) kühle(r) Kopf *m*

coop [kuːp] *n* Hühnerstall *m* ♦ *vt*: ~ **up** (*fig*) einpferchen

cooperate [kəu'ɔpəreɪt] *vi* zusammenarbeiten; **cooperation** [kəuɔpə'reɪʃən] *n* Zusammenarbeit *f*

cooperative [kəu'ɔpərətɪv] *adj* hilfsbereit; (*COMM*) genossenschaftlich ♦ *n* (*of farmers*) Genossenschaft *f*; (~ *store*) Konsumladen *m*

coordinate [*vb* kəu'ɔːdɪneɪt, *n* kəu'ɔːdɪnət] *vt* koordinieren ♦ *n* (*MATH*) Koordinate *f*; **~s** *npl* (*clothes*) Kombinationen *pl*; **coordination** [kəuɔːdɪ'neɪʃən] *n* Koordination *f*

cop [kɔp] (*inf*) *n* Polyp *m*, Bulle *m*

cope [kəup] *vi*: **to ~ with** fertig werden mit

copious ['kəupɪəs] *adj* reichhaltig

copper ['kɔpər] *n* (*metal*) Kupfer *nt*; (*inf*: *policeman*) Polyp *m*, Bulle *m*; ~**s** *npl* (*money*) Kleingeld *nt*

copse [kɔps] *n* Unterholz *nt*

copy ['kɔpɪ] *n* (*imitation*) Kopie *f*; (*of book etc*) Exemplar *nt*; (*of newspaper*) Nummer *f* ♦ *vt* kopieren, abschreiben; **~right** *n* Copyright *nt*

coral ['kɔrəl] *n* Koralle *f*; ~ **reef** *n* Korallenriff *nt*

cord [kɔːd] *n* Schnur *f*; (*ELEC*) Kabel *nt*

cordial ['kɔːdɪəl] *adj* herzlich ♦ *n* Fruchtsaft *m*

cordon ['kɔːdn] *n* Absperrkette *f*; ~ **off** *vt* abriegeln

corduroy ['kɔːdərɔɪ] *n* Kord(samt) *m*

core [kɔːr] *n* Kern *m* ♦ *vt* entkernen

cork [kɔːk] *n* (*bark*) Korkrinde *f*; (*stopper*) Korken *m*; **~screw** *n* Korkenzieher *m*

corn [kɔːn] *n* (*BRIT*: *wheat*) Getreide *nt*, Korn *nt*; (*US*: *maize*) Mais *m*; (*on foot*) Hühnerauge *nt*; ~ **on the cob** Maiskolben *m*

corned beef ['kɔːnd-] *n* Cornedbeef *nt*, Corned Beef *nt*

corner ['kɔːnər] *n* Ecke *f*; (*on road*) Kurve *f* ♦ *vt* in die Enge treiben; (*market*) monopolisieren ♦ *vi* (*AUT*) in die Kurve gehen; **~stone** *n* Eckstein *m*

cornet ['kɔːnɪt] *n* (*MUS*) Kornett *nt*; (*BRIT*: *of ice cream*) Eistüte *f*

corn: ~**flakes** ['kɔːnfleɪks] *npl* Cornflakes *pl* ®; ~**flour** ['kɔːnflauər] (*BRIT*) *n* Maizena *nt* ®; ~**starch** ['kɔːnstɑːtʃ] (*US*) *n* Maizena *nt* ®

corny ['kɔːnɪ] *adj* (*joke*) blöd(e)

coronary ['kɔrənərɪ] *n* (*also*: ~ **thrombosis**) Herzinfarkt *m*

coronation [kɔrə'neɪʃən] n Krönung f

coroner ['kɔrənər] n Untersuchungsrichter m

corporal ['kɔːpərl] n Obergefreite(r) m ♦ adj: **~ punishment** Prügelstrafe f

corporate ['kɔːpərɪt] adj gemeinschaftlich, korporativ

corporation [kɔːpə'reɪʃən] n (of town) Gemeinde f; (COMM) Körperschaft f, Aktiengesellschaft f

corps [kɔːr] (pl **~**) n (Armee)korps nt

corpse [kɔːps] n Leiche f

corral [kə'rɑːl] n Pferch m, Korral m

correct [kə'rekt] adj (accurate) richtig; (proper) korrekt ♦ vt korrigieren; **~ion** [kə'rekʃən] n Berichtigung f

correlation [kɔrɪ'leɪʃən] n Wechselbeziehung f

correspond [kɔrɪs'pɔnd] vi (agree) übereinstimmen; (exchange letters) korrespondieren; **~ence** n (similarity) Entsprechung f; (letters) Briefwechsel m, Korrespondenz f; **~ence course** n Fernkurs m; **~ent** n (PRESS) Berichterstatter m

corridor ['kɔrɪdɔːr] n Gang m

corroborate [kə'rɔbəreɪt] vt bestätigen

corrode [kə'rəud] vt zerfressen ♦ vi rosten

corrosion [kə'rəuʒən] n Korrosion f

corrugated ['kɔrəgeɪtɪd] adj gewellt; **~ iron** n Wellblech nt

corrupt [kə'rʌpt] adj korrupt ♦ vt verderben; (bribe) bestechen; **~ion** [kə'rʌpʃən] n Verdorbenheit f; (bribery) Bestechung f

Corset ['kɔːsɪt] n Korsett nt

Corsica ['kɔːsɪkə] n Korsika f

cosmetics [kɔz'metɪks] npl Kosmetika pl

cosmic ['kɔzmɪk] adj kosmisch

cosmonaut ['kɔzmənɔːt] n Kosmonaut(in) m(f)

cosmopolitan [kɔzmə'pɔlɪtn] adj international; (city) Welt-

cosmos ['kɔzmɔs] n Kosmos m

cost [kɔst] (pt, pp **cost**) n Kosten pl, Preis m ♦ vt, vi kosten; **~s** npl (JUR) Kosten pl; **how much does it ~?** wie viel kostet das?; **at all ~s** um jeden Preis

co-star ['kəustɑːr] n zweite(r) or weitere(r) Hauptdarsteller(in) m(f)

cost: ~-effective adj rentabel; **~ly** ['kɔstlɪ] adj kostspielig; **~-of-living** ['kɔstəv'lɪvɪŋ] adj (index) Lebenshaltungskosten-; **~ price** (BRIT) n Selbstkostenpreis m

costume ['kɔstjuːm] n Kostüm nt; (fancy dress) Maskenkostüm nt; (BRIT: also: **swimming ~**) Badeanzug m; **~ jewellery** n Modeschmuck m

cosy ['kəuzɪ] (BRIT) adj behaglich; (atmosphere) gemütlich

cot [kɔt] n (BRIT: child's) Kinderbett(chen) nt; (US: camp bed) Feldbett nt

cottage ['kɔtɪdʒ] n kleine(s) Haus nt; **~ cheese** n Hüttenkäse m; **~ industry** n Heimindustrie f; **~ pie** n Auflauf mit Hackfleisch und Kartoffelbrei

cotton ['kɔtn] n Baumwolle f; (thread) Garn nt; **~ on to** (inf) vt kapieren; **~ candy** (US) n Zuckerwatte f; **~ wool** (BRIT) n Watte f

couch [kautʃ] n Couch f

couchette [kuː'ʃet] n (on train, boat) Liegewagenplatz m

cough [kɔf] vi husten ♦ n Husten m; **~ drop** n Hustenbonbon nt

could [kud] pt of **can²**

couldn't ['kudnt] = **could not**

council ['kaunsl] n (of town) Stadtrat m; **~ estate** (BRIT) n Siedlung f des sozialen Wohnungsbaus; **~ house** (BRIT) n Haus nt des sozialen Wohnungsbaus; **~lor** ['kaunslər] n Stadtrat m/-rätin f

counsel ['kaunsl] n (barrister) Anwalt m; (advice) Rat(schlag) m ♦ vt beraten; **~lor** ['kaunslər] n Berater m

count [kaunt] vt, vi zählen ♦ n (reckoning) Abrechnung f; (nobleman) Graf m; **~ on** vt zählen auf +acc

countenance ['kauntɪnəns] n (old) Antlitz nt ♦ vt (tolerate) gutheißen

counter ['kauntər] n (in shop) Ladentisch m; (in café) Theke f; (in bank, post office) Schalter m ♦ vt entgegnen

counteract ['kauntər'ækt] vt entgegenwirken +dat

counterfeit ['kauntəfɪt] n Fälschung f ♦ vt fälschen ♦ adj gefälscht

counterfoil ['kauntəfɔıl] n
(Kontroll)abschnitt m

counterpart ['kauntəpɑːt] n (object)
Gegenstück nt; (person) Gegenüber nt

counterproductive ['kauntəprə'dʌktɪv] adj
destruktiv

countersign ['kauntəsaın] vt gegenzeichnen

countess ['kauntıs] n Gräfin f

countless ['kauntlıs] adj zahllos, unzählig

country ['kʌntrɪ] n Land nt; ~ **dancing**
(BRIT) n Volkstanz m; ~ **house** n Landhaus
nt; ~**man** (irreg) n (national) Landsmann m;
(rural) Bauer m; ~**side** n Landschaft f

county ['kauntı] n Landkreis m; (BRIT)
Grafschaft f

coup [kuː] n (pl ~**s**) n Coup m; (also: ~ **d'état**)
Staatsstreich m, Putsch m

couple ['kʌpl] n Paar nt ♦ vt koppeln; **a ~ of**
ein paar

coupon ['kuːpɔn] n Gutschein m

coups [kuː] npl of **coup**

courage ['kʌrıdʒ] n Mut m; ~**ous**
[kə'reıdʒəs] adj mutig

courgette [kuə'ʒet] (BRIT) n Zucchini f or pl

courier ['kurıər] n (for holiday) Reiseleiter m;
(messenger) Kurier m

course [kɔːs] n (race) Bahn f; (of stream) Lauf
m; (golf ~) Platz m; (NAUT, SCH) Kurs m; (in
meal) Gang m; **of** ~ natürlich

court [kɔːt] n (royal) Hof m; (JUR) Gericht nt
♦ vt (woman) gehen mit; (danger)
herausfordern; **to take to** ~ vor Gericht
bringen

courteous ['kɔːtıəs] adj höflich

courtesy ['kɔːtəsı] n Höflichkeit f

courtesy bus, courtesy coach n
gebührenfreier Bus m

court: ~ **house** (US) n Gerichtsgebäude nt;
~**ier** ['kɔːtıər] n Höfling m; ~ **martial**
['kɔːt'mɑːʃəl] (pl ~**s martial**) n Kriegsgericht
nt ♦ vt vor ein Kriegsgericht stellen; ~**room**
n Gerichtssaal m; ~**s martial** npl of **court
martial**; ~**yard** ['kɔːtjɑːd] n Hof m

cousin ['kʌzn] n Cousin m, Vetter m; Kusine
f

cove [kəuv] n kleine Bucht f

covenant ['kʌvənənt] n (ECCL) Bund m; (JUR)
Verpflichtung f

cover ['kʌvər] vt (spread over) bedecken;
(shield) abschirmen; (include) sich erstrecken
über +acc; (protect) decken; (distance)
zurücklegen; (report on) berichten über +acc
♦ n (lid) Deckel m; (for bed) Decke f; (MIL)
Bedeckung f; (of book) Einband m; (of
magazine) Umschlag m; (insurance)
Versicherung f; **to take** ~ (from rain) sich
unterstellen; (MIL) in Deckung gehen;
under ~ (indoors) drinnen; **under** ~ **of** im
Schutze +gen; **under separate** ~ (COMM)
mit getrennter Post; **to** ~ **up for sb** jdn
decken; ~**age** n (PRESS: reports)
Berichterstattung f; (distribution)
Verbreitung f; ~ **charge** n Bedienungsgeld
nt; ~**ing** n Bedeckung f; ~**ing letter** (US ~
letter) n Begleitbrief m; ~ **note** n
(INSURANCE) vorläufige(r)
Versicherungsschein m

covert ['kʌvət] adj geheim

cover-up ['kʌvərʌp] n Vertuschung f

cow [kau] n Kuh f ♦ vt einschüchtern

coward ['kauəd] n Feigling m; ~**ice**
['kauədıs] n Feigheit f; ~**ly** adj feige

cower ['kauər] vi kauern

coy [kɔı] adj schüchtern

coyote [kɔı'əutı] n Präriewolf m

cozy ['kauzı] (US) adj = **cosy**

CPA (US) n abbr = **certified public
accountant**

crab [kræb] n Krebs m

crab apple n Holzapfel m

crack [kræk] n Riss m, Sprung m; (noise)
Knall m; (drug) Crack nt ♦ vt (break)
springen lassen; (joke) reißen; (nut, safe)
knacken; (whip) knallen lassen ♦ vi springen
♦ adj erstklassig; (troops) Elite-; ~ **down** vi:
to ~ **down (on)** hart durchgreifen (bei); ~
up vi (fig) zusammenbrechen

cracked [krækt] adj (glass, plate, ice)
gesprungen; (rib, bone) gebrochen,
angeknackst (umg); (broken) gebrochen;
(surface, walls) rissig; (inf: mad)
übergeschnappt

cracker ['krækər] n (firework) Knallkörper m,
Kracher m; (biscuit) Keks m; (Christmas ~)

Knallbonbon nt

crackle ['krækl] vi knistern; (fire) prasseln

cradle ['kreɪdl] n Wiege f

craft [krɑːft] n (skill) (Hand- or Kunst)fertigkeit f; (trade) Handwerk nt; (NAUT) Schiff nt; **~sman** (irreg) n Handwerker m; **~smanship** n (quality) handwerkliche Ausführung f; (ability) handwerkliche(s) Können nt

crafty ['krɑːftɪ] adj schlau

crag [kræg] n Klippe f

cram [kræm] vt voll stopfen ♦ vi (learn) pauken; **to ~ sth into sth** etw in etw acc stopfen

cramp [kræmp] n Krampf m ♦ vt (limit) einengen; (hinder) hemmen; **~ed** adj (position) verkrampft; (space) eng

crampon ['kræmpən] n Steigeisen nt

cranberry ['krænbərɪ] n Preiselbeere f

crane [kreɪn] n (machine) Kran m; (bird) Kranich m

crank [kræŋk] n (lever) Kurbel f; (person) Spinner m; **~shaft** n Kurbelwelle f

cranny ['krænɪ] n see **nook**

crash [kræʃ] n (noise) Krachen nt; (with cars) Zusammenstoß m; (with plane) Absturz m; (COMM) Zusammenbruch m ♦ vt (plane) abstürzen mit ♦ vi (cars) zusammenstoßen; (plane) abstürzen; (economy) zusammenbrechen; (noise) knallen; **~ course** n Schnellkurs m; **~ helmet** n Sturzhelm m; **~ landing** n Bruchlandung f

crass [kræs] adj krass

crate [kreɪt] n (also fig) Kiste f

crater ['kreɪtər] n Krater m

cravat(e) [krə'væt] n Halstuch nt

crave [kreɪv] vt verlangen nach

crawl [krɔːl] vi kriechen; (baby) krabbeln ♦ n Kriechen nt; (swim) Kraul m

crayfish ['kreɪfɪʃ] n inv (freshwater) Krebs m; (saltwater) Languste f

crayon ['kreɪən] n Buntstift m

craze [kreɪz] n Fimmel m

crazy ['kreɪzɪ] adj verrückt

creak [kriːk] vi knarren

cream [kriːm] n (from milk) Rahm m, Sahne f; (polish, cosmetic) Creme f; (fig: people)

Elite f ♦ adj cremefarbig; **~ cake** n Sahnetorte f; **~ cheese** n Rahmquark m; **~y** adj sahnig

crease [kriːs] n Falte f ♦ vt falten; (wrinkle) zerknittern ♦ vi (wrinkle up) knittern; **~d** adj zerknittert, faltig

create [kriː'eɪt] vt erschaffen; (cause) verursachen; **creation** [kriː'eɪʃən] n Schöpfung f; **creative** adj kreativ; **creator** n Schöpfer m

creature ['kriːtʃər] n Geschöpf nt

crèche [kreʃ] n Krippe f

credence ['kriːdns] n: **to lend** or **give ~ to sth** etw dat Glauben schenken

credentials [krɪ'denʃlz] npl Beglaubigungsschreiben pl

credibility [kredɪ'bɪlɪtɪ] n Glaubwürdigkeit f

credible ['kredɪbl] adj (person) glaubwürdig; (story) glaubhaft

credit ['kredɪt] n (also COMM) Kredit m ♦ vt Glauben schenken +dat; (COMM) gutschreiben; **~s** npl (of film) Mitwirkenden pl; **~able** adj rühmlich; **~ card** n Kreditkarte f; **~or** n Gläubiger m

creed [kriːd] n Glaubensbekenntnis nt

creek [kriːk] n (inlet) kleine Bucht f; (US: river) kleine(r) Wasserlauf m

creep [kriːp] (pt, pp **crept**) vi kriechen; **~er** n Kletterpflanze f; **~y** adj (frightening) gruselig

cremate [krɪ'meɪt] vt einäschern; **cremation** [krɪ'meɪʃən] n Einäscherung f; **crematorium** [kremə'tɔːrɪəm] n Krematorium nt

crêpe [kreɪp] n Krepp m; **~ bandage** (BRIT) n Elastikbinde f

crept [krept] pt, pp of **creep**

crescent ['kresnt] n (of moon) Halbmond m

cress [kres] n Kresse f

crest [krest] n (of cock) Kamm m; (of wave) Wellenkamm m; (coat of arms) Wappen nt; **crestfallen** ['krestfɔːlən] adj niedergeschlagen

Crete [kriːt] n Kreta nt

crevice ['krevɪs] n Riss m

crew [kruː] n Besatzung f, Mannschaft f; **~-cut** n Bürstenschnitt m; **~ neck** n runde(r)

Ausschnitt m

crib [krɪb] n (bed) Krippe f ♦ vt (inf) spicken

crick [krɪk] n Muskelkrampf m

cricket ['krɪkɪt] n (insect) Grille f; (game) Kricket nt

crime [kraɪm] n Verbrechen nt

criminal ['krɪmɪnl] n Verbrecher m ♦ adj kriminell; (act) strafbar

crimson ['krɪmzn] adj leuchtend rot

cringe [krɪndʒ] vi sich ducken

crinkle ['krɪŋkl] vt zerknittern

cripple ['krɪpl] n Krüppel m ♦ vt lahm legen; (MED) verkrüppeln

crisis ['kraɪsɪs] (pl **crises**) n Krise f

crisp [krɪsp] adj knusprig; **~s** (BRIT) npl Chips pl

crisscross ['krɪskrɔs] adj gekreuzt, Kreuz-

criteria [kraɪ'tɪərɪə] npl of **criterion**

criterion [kraɪ'tɪərɪən] (pl **criteria**) n Kriterium nt

critic ['krɪtɪk] n Kritiker(in) m(f); **~al** adj kritisch; **~ally** adv kritisch; (ill) gefährlich; **~ism** ['krɪtɪsɪzəm] n Kritik f; **~ize** ['krɪtɪsaɪz] vt kritisieren

croak [krəuk] vi krächzen; (frog) quaken

Croatia [krəu'eɪʃə] n Kroatien nt

crochet ['krəuʃeɪ] n Häkelei f

crockery ['krɔkərɪ] n Geschirr nt

crocodile ['krɔkədaɪl] n Krokodil nt

crocus ['krəukəs] n Krokus m

croft [krɔft] (BRIT) n kleine(s) Pachtgut nt

crony ['krəunɪ] (inf) n Kumpel m

crook [kruk] n (criminal) Gauner m; (stick) Hirtenstab m

crooked ['krukɪd] adj krumm

crop [krɔp] n (harvest) Ernte f; (riding ~) Reitpeitsche f ♦ vt ernten; **~ up** vi passieren

croquet ['krəukeɪ] n Krocket nt

croquette [krə'kɛt] n Krokette f

cross [krɔs] n Kreuz nt ♦ vt (road) überqueren; (legs) übereinander legen; kreuzen ♦ adj (annoyed) böse; **~ out** vt streichen; **~ over** vi hinübergehen; **~bar** n Querstange f; **~-country (race)** n Geländelauf m; **~-examine** vt ins Kreuzverhör nehmen; **~-eyed** adj: **to be**

~-eyed schielen; **~fire** n Kreuzfeuer nt; **~ing** n (~roads) (Straßen)kreuzung f; (of ship) Überfahrt f; (for pedestrians) Fußgängerüberweg m; **~ing guard** (US) n Schülerlotse m; **~ purposes** npl: **to be at ~ purposes** aneinander vorbeireden; **~-reference** n Querverweis m; **~roads** n Straßenkreuzung f; (fig) Scheideweg m; **~ section** n Querschnitt m; **~walk** (US) n Fußgängerüberweg m; **~wind** n Seitenwind m; **~word (puzzle)** n Kreuzworträtsel m

crotch [krɔtʃ] n Zwickel m; (ANAT) Unterleib nt

crouch [krautʃ] vi hocken

crow [krəu] n (bird) Krähe f; (of cock) Krähen nt ♦ vi krähen

crowbar ['krəubɑː] n Stemmeisen nt

crowd [kraud] n Menge f ♦ vt (fill) überfüllen ♦ vi drängen; **~ed** adj überfüllt

crown [kraun] n Krone f; (of head, hat) Kopf m ♦ vt krönen; **~ jewels** npl Kronjuwelen pl; **~ prince** n Kronprinz m

crow's-feet ['krəuzfiːt] npl Krähenfüße pl

crucial ['kruːʃl] adj entscheidend

crucifix ['kruːsɪfɪks] n Kruzifix nt; **~ion** [kruːsɪ'fɪkʃən] n Kreuzigung f

crude [kruːd] adj (raw) roh; (humour, behaviour) grob; (basic) primitiv; **~ (oil)** n Rohöl nt

cruel ['kruəl] adj grausam; **~ty** n Grausamkeit f

cruise [kruːz] n Kreuzfahrt f ♦ vi kreuzen; **~r** n (MIL) Kreuzer m

crumb [krʌm] n Krume f

crumble ['krʌmbl] vt, vi zerbröckeln; **crumbly** adj krümelig

crumpet ['krʌmpɪt] n Tee(pfann)kuchen m

crumple ['krʌmpl] vt zerknittern

crunch [krʌntʃ] n: **the ~** (fig) der Knackpunkt ♦ vt knirschen; **~y** adj knusprig

crusade [kruː'seɪd] n Kreuzzug m

crush [krʌʃ] n Gedränge nt ♦ vt zerdrücken; (rebellion) unterdrücken

crust [krʌst] n Kruste f

crutch [krʌtʃ] n Krücke f

crux [krʌks] n springende(r) Punkt m

ry [kraɪ] vi (*shout*) schreien; (*weep*) weinen ♦ n (*call*) Schrei m; ~ **off** vi (plötzlich) absagen

rypt [krɪpt] n Krypta f

ryptic ['krɪptɪk] adj hintergründig

rystal ['krɪstl] n Kristall m; (*glass*) Kristallglas nt; (*mineral*) Bergkristall m; ~-**clear** adj kristallklar

rystallize ['krɪstəlaɪz] vt, vi kristallisieren; (*fig*) klären

SA n abbr (= Child Support Agency) Amt zur Regelung von Unterhaltszahlungen für Kinder

TC (*BRIT*) n abbr = **city technology college**

ub [kʌb] n Junge(s) nt; (*also*: **C~ scout**) Wölfling m

uba ['kju:bə] n Kuba nt; ~**n** adj kubanisch ♦ n Kubaner(in) m(f)

ubbyhole ['kʌbɪhəul] n Eckchen nt

ube [kju:b] n Würfel m ♦ vt (*MATH*) hoch drei nehmen

ubic ['kju:bɪk] adj würfelförmig; (*centimetre etc*) Kubik-; ~ **capacity** n Fassungsvermögen nt

ubicle ['kju:bɪkl] n Kabine f

uckoo ['kuku:] n Kuckuck m; ~ **clock** n Kuckucksuhr f

ucumber ['kju:kʌmbə'] n Gurke f

uddle ['kʌdl] vt, vi herzen, drücken (*inf*)

ue [kju:] n (*THEAT*) Stichwort nt; (*snooker ~*) Billardstock m

uff [kʌf] n (*BRIT*: *of shirt, coat etc*) Manschette f; Aufschlag m; (*US*) = **turn-up**; **off the** ~ aus dem Handgelenk; ~**link** n Manschettenknopf m

uisine [kwɪ'zi:n] n Kochkunst f, Küche f

ul-de-sac ['kʌldəsæk] n Sackgasse f

ulinary ['kʌlɪnərɪ] adj Koch-

ull [kʌl] vt (*select*) auswählen

ulminate ['kʌlmɪneɪt] vi gipfeln; **culmination** [kʌlmɪ'neɪʃən] n Höhepunkt m

ulottes [kju:'lɔts] npl Hosenrock m

ulpable ['kʌlpəbl] adj schuldig

ulprit ['kʌlprɪt] n Täter m

ult [kʌlt] n Kult m

ultivate ['kʌltɪveɪt] vt (*AGR*) bebauen; (*mind*) bilden; **cultivation** [kʌltɪ'veɪʃən] n

(*AGR*) Bebauung f; (*of person*) Bildung f

cultural ['kʌltʃərəl] adj kulturell, Kultur-

culture ['kʌltʃər] n Kultur f; ~**d** adj gebildet

cumbersome ['kʌmbəsəm] adj (*object*) sperrig

cumulative ['kju:mjulətɪv] adj gehäuft

cunning ['kʌnɪŋ] n Verschlagenheit f ♦ adj schlau

cup [kʌp] n Tasse f; (*prize*) Pokal m

cupboard ['kʌbəd] n Schrank m

cup tie (*BRIT*) n Pokalspiel nt

curate ['kjuərɪt] n (*Catholic*) Kurat m; (*Protestant*) Vikar m

curator [kjuə'reɪtər] n Kustos m

curb [kə:b] vt zügeln ♦ n (*on spending etc*) Einschränkung f; (*US*) Bordstein m

curdle ['kə:dl] vi gerinnen

cure [kjuər] n Heilmittel nt; (*process*) Heilverfahren nt ♦ vt heilen

curfew ['kə:fju:] n Ausgangssperre f; Sperrstunde f

curio ['kjuəriəu] n Kuriosität f

curiosity [kjuəri'ɔsɪtɪ] n Neugier f

curious ['kjuəriəs] adj neugierig; (*strange*) seltsam

curl [kə:l] n Locke f ♦ vt locken ♦ vi sich locken; ~ **up** vi sich zusammenrollen; (*person*) sich ankuscheln; ~**er** n Lockenwickler m; ~**y** ['kə:lɪ] adj lockig

currant ['kʌrnt] n Korinthe f

currency ['kʌrnsɪ] n Währung f; **to gain** ~ an Popularität gewinnen

current ['kʌrnt] n Strömung f ♦ adj (*expression*) gängig, üblich; (*issue*) neueste; ~ **account** (*BRIT*) n Girokonto nt; ~ **affairs** npl Zeitgeschehen nt; ~**ly** adv zurzeit

curricula [kə'rɪkjulə] npl of **curriculum**

curriculum [kə'rɪkjuləm] (*pl* ~**s** or **curricula**) n Lehrplan m; ~ **vitae** [-'vi:taɪ] n Lebenslauf m

curry ['kʌrɪ] n Currygericht nt ♦ vt: **to** ~ **favour with** sich einschmeicheln bei; ~ **powder** n Curry(pulver) nt

curse [kə:s] vi (*swear*): **to** ~ **(at)** fluchen (auf or über +acc) ♦ vt (*insult*) verwünschen ♦ n Fluch m

cursor ['kə:sər] n (*COMPUT*) Cursor m

cursory ['kə:sərɪ] *adj* flüchtig

curt [kə:t] *adj* schroff

curtail [kə:'teɪl] *vt* abkürzen; *(rights)* einschränken

curtain ['kə:tn] *n* Vorhang *m*

curts(e)y ['kə:tsɪ] *n* Knicks *m* ♦ *vi* knicksen

curve [kə:v] *n* Kurve *f*; *(of body, vase etc)* Rundung *f* ♦ *vi* sich biegen; *(hips, breasts)* sich runden; *(road)* einen Bogen machen

cushion ['kuʃən] *n* Kissen *nt* ♦ *vt* dämpfen

custard ['kʌstəd] *n* Vanillesoße *f*

custodian [kʌs'təudɪən] *n* Kustos *m*, Verwalter(in) *m(f)*

custody ['kʌstədɪ] *n* Aufsicht *f*; *(police ~)* Haft *f*; **to take into ~** verhaften

custom ['kʌstəm] *n* *(tradition)* Brauch *m*; *(COMM)* Kundschaft *f*; **~ary** *adj* üblich

customer ['kʌstəmə*] *n* Kunde *m*, Kundin *f*

customized ['kʌstəmaɪzd] *adj* *(car etc)* mit Spezialausrüstung

custom-made ['kʌstəm'meɪd] *adj* speziell angefertigt

customs ['kʌstəmz] *npl* Zoll *m*; **~ duty** *n* Zollabgabe *f*; **~ officer** *n* Zollbeamte(r) *m*, Zollbeamtin *f*

cut [kʌt] *(pt, pp* **cut***)* *vt* schneiden; *(wages)* kürzen; *(prices)* heruntersetzen ♦ *vi* schneiden; *(intersect)* sich schneiden ♦ *n* Schnitt *m*; *(wound)* Schnittwunde *f*; *(in income etc)* Kürzung *f*; *(share)* Anteil *m*; **to ~ a tooth** zahnen; **~ down** *vt* *(tree)* fällen; *(reduce)* einschränken; **~ off** *vt* *(also fig)* abschneiden; *(allowance)* sperren; **~ out** *vt* *(shape)* ausschneiden; *(delete)* streichen; **~ up** *vt* *(meat)* aufschneiden; **~back** *n* Kürzung *f*

cute [kju:t] *adj* niedlich

cuticle ['kju:tɪkl] *n* Nagelhaut *f*

cutlery ['kʌtlərɪ] *n* Besteck *nt*

cutlet ['kʌtlɪt] *n* *(pork)* Kotelett *nt*; *(veal)* Schnitzel *nt*

cut: ~out *n* *(cardboard ~out)* Ausschneidemodell *nt*; **~-price**, **~-rate** *(US)* *adj* verbilligt; **~throat** *n* Verbrechertyp *m* ♦ *adj* mörderisch

cutting ['kʌtɪŋ] *adj* schneidend ♦ *n* *(BRIT: PRESS)* Ausschnitt *m*; *(: RAIL)* Durchstich *m*

CV *n abbr* = **curriculum vitae**

cwt *abbr* = **hundredweight(s)**

cyanide ['saɪənaɪd] *n* Zyankali *nt*

cybercafé ['saɪbəkæfeɪ] *n* Internet-Café *nt*

cyberspace ['saɪbəspeɪs] *n* Cyberspace *m*

cycle ['saɪkl] *n* Fahrrad *nt*; *(series)* Reihe *f* ♦ *vi* Rad fahren; **~ hire** *n* Fahrradverleih *m*; **~ lane**, **~ path** *n* (Fahr)radweg *m*; **cycling** *n* Radfahren *nt*; **cyclist** *n* Radfahrer(in) *m(f)*

cyclone ['saɪkləun] *n* Zyklon *m*

cygnet ['sɪgnɪt] *n* junge(r) Schwan *m*

cylinder ['sɪlɪndə*] *n* Zylinder *m*; *(TECH)* Walze *f*

cymbals ['sɪmblz] *npl* Becken *nt*

cynic ['sɪnɪk] *n* Zyniker(in) *m(f)*; **~al** *adj* zynisch; **~ism** ['sɪnɪsɪzəm] *n* Zynismus *m*

cypress ['saɪprɪs] *n* Zypresse *f*

Cyprus ['saɪprəs] *n* Zypern *nt*

cyst [sɪst] *n* Zyste *f*

cystitis [sɪs'taɪtɪs] *n* Blasenentzündung *f*

czar [zɑ:*] *n* Zar *m*

Czech [tʃek] *adj* tschechisch ♦ *n* Tscheche *m*, Tschechin *f*

Czechoslovakia [tʃekəslə'vækɪə] *(HIST)* *n* die Tschechoslowakei; **~n** *adj* tschechoslowakisch ♦ *n* Tschechoslowake *m*, Tschechoslowakin *f*

D, d

D [di:] *n* *(MUS)* D *nt*

dab [dæb] *vt* *(wound, paint)* betupfen ♦ *n* *(little bit)* bisschen *nt*; *(of paint)* Tupfer *m*

dabble ['dæbl] *vi*: **to ~ in sth** in etw *dat* machen

dad [dæd] *n* Papa *m*, Vati *m*; **~dy** ['dædɪ] *n* Papa *m*, Vati *m*; **~dy-long-legs** *n* Weberknecht *m*

daffodil ['dæfədɪl] *n* Osterglocke *f*

daft [dɑ:ft] *(inf)* *adj* blöd(e), doof

dagger ['dægə*] *n* Dolch *m*

daily ['deɪlɪ] *adj* täglich ♦ *n* *(PRESS)* Tageszeitung *f*; *(BRIT: cleaner)* Haushaltshilfe *f* ♦ *adv* täglich

dainty ['deɪntɪ] *adj* zierlich

dairy ['deərɪ] *n* *(shop)* Milchgeschäft *nt*; *(on*

farm) Molkerei *f* ♦ *adj* Milch-; ~ **farm** *n* Hof *m* mit Milchwirtschaft; ~ **produce** *n* Molkereiprodukte *pl*; ~ **products** *npl* Milchprodukte *pl*, Molkereiprodukte *pl*; ~ **store** (*US*) *n* Milchgeschäft *nt*

ais ['deɪs] *n* Podium *nt*

aisy ['deɪzɪ] *n* Gänseblümchen *nt*

ale [deɪl] *n* Tal *nt*

am [dæm] *n* (Stau)damm *m* ♦ *vt* stauen

amage ['dæmɪdʒ] *n* Schaden *m* ♦ *vt* beschädigen; ~**s** *npl* (*JUR*) Schaden(s)ersatz *m*

amn [dæm] *vt* verdammen ♦ *n* (*inf*): **I don't give a ~** das ist mir total egal ♦ *adj* (*inf*: *also*: ~**ed**) verdammt; ~ **it!** verflucht!; ~**ing** *adj* vernichtend

amp [dæmp] *adj* feucht ♦ *n* Feuchtigkeit *f* ♦ *vt* (*also*: ~**en**) befeuchten; (*discourage*) dämpfen

amson ['dæmzən] *n* Damaszenerpflaume *f*

ance [dɑːns] *n* Tanz *m* ♦ *vi* tanzen; ~ **hall** *n* Tanzlokal *nt*; ~**r** *n* Tänzer(in) *m(f)*; **dancing** *n* Tanzen *nt*

andelion ['dændɪlaɪən] *n* Löwenzahn *m*

andruff ['dændrəf] *n* (Kopf)schuppen *pl*

ane [deɪn] *n* Däne *m*, Dänin *f*

anger ['deɪndʒəʳ] *n* Gefahr *f*; ~! (*sign*) Achtung!; **to be in ~ of doing sth** Gefahr laufen, etw zu tun; ~**ous** *adj* gefährlich

angle ['dæŋgl] *vi* baumeln ♦ *vt* herabhängen lassen

anish ['deɪnɪʃ] *adj* dänisch ♦ *n* Dänisch *nt*

are [dɛəʳ] *vt* herausfordern ♦ *vi*: **to ~ (to) do sth** es wagen, etw zu tun; **I ~ say** ich würde sagen; **daring** ['dɛərɪŋ] *adj* (*audacious*) verwegen; (*bold*) wagemutig; (*dress*) gewagt ♦ *n* Mut *m*

ark [dɑːk] *adj* dunkel; (*fig*) düster, trübe; (*deep colour*) dunkel- ♦ *n* Dunkelheit *f*; **to be left in the ~ about** im Dunkeln sein über +*acc*; **after ~** nach Anbruch der Dunkelheit; ~**en** *vt*, *vi* verdunkeln; ~ **glasses** *npl* Sonnenbrille *f*; ~**ness** *n* Finsternis *nt*; ~**room** *n* Dunkelkammer *f*

arling ['dɑːlɪŋ] *n* Liebling *m* ♦ *adj* lieb

arn [dɑːn] *vt* stopfen

art [dɑːt] *n* (*weapon*) Pfeil *m*; (*in sewing*)

Abnäher *m* ♦ *vi* sausen; ~**s** *n* (*game*) Pfeilwerfen *nt*; ~**board** *n* Zielscheibe *f*

dash [dæʃ] *n* Sprung *m*; (*mark*) (Gedanken)strich *m*; (*small amount*) bisschen *nt* ♦ *vt* (*hopes*) zunichte machen ♦ *vi* stürzen; ~ **away** *vi* davonstürzen; ~ **off** *vi* davonstürzen

dashboard ['dæʃbɔːd] *n* Armaturenbrett *nt*

dashing ['dæʃɪŋ] *adj* schneidig

data ['deɪtə] *npl* Einzelheiten *pl*, Daten *pl*; ~**base** *n* Datenbank *f*; ~ **processing** *n* Datenverarbeitung *f*

date [deɪt] *n* Datum *nt*; (*for meeting etc*) Termin *m*; (*with person*) Verabredung *f*; (*fruit*) Dattel *f* ♦ *vt* (*letter etc*) datieren; (*person*) gehen mit; ~ **of birth** Geburtsdatum *nt*; **to ~** bis heute; **out of ~** überholt; **up to ~** (*clothes*) modisch; (*report*) up-to-date; (*with news*) auf dem Laufenden; ~**d** *adj* altmodisch; ~ **rape** *n* Vergewaltigung *f* nach einem Rendezvous

daub [dɔːb] *vt* beschmieren; (*paint*) schmieren

daughter ['dɔːtəʳ] *n* Tochter *f*; ~**-in-law** *n* Schwiegertochter *f*

daunting ['dɔːntɪŋ] *adj* entmutigend

dawdle ['dɔːdl] *vi* trödeln

dawn [dɔːn] *n* Morgendämmerung *f* ♦ *vi* dämmern; (*fig*): **it ~ed on him that ...** es dämmerte ihm, dass ...

day [deɪ] *n* Tag *m*; **the ~ before/after** am Tag zuvor/danach; **the ~ after tomorrow** übermorgen; **the ~ before yesterday** vorgestern; **by ~** am Tage; ~**break** *n* Tagesanbruch *m*; ~**dream** *vi* mit offenen Augen träumen; ~**light** *n* Tageslicht *nt*; ~ **return** (*BRIT*) *n* Tagesrückfahrkarte *f*; ~**time** *n* Tageszeit *f*; ~**-to-~** *adj* alltäglich

daze [deɪz] *vt* betäuben ♦ *n* Betäubung *f*; **in a ~** benommen

dazzle ['dæzl] *vt* blenden

DC *abbr* (= *direct current*) Gleichstrom *m*

D-day ['diːdeɪ] *n* (*HIST*) *Tag der Invasion durch die Alliierten (6.6.44)*; (*fig*) der Tag X

deacon ['diːkən] *n* Diakon *m*

dead [dɛd] *adj* tot; (*without feeling*) gefühllos ♦ *adv* ganz; (*exactly*) genau ♦ *npl*: **the ~** die

Toten *pl*; **to shoot sb ~** jdn erschießen; **~ tired** todmüde; **to stop ~** abrupt stehen bleiben; **~en** *vt (pain)* abtöten; *(sound)* ersticken; **~ end** *n* Sackgasse *f*; **~ heat** *n* totes Rennen *nt*; **~line** *n* Stichtag *m*; **~lock** *n* Stillstand *m*; **~ loss** *(inf) n*: **to be a ~ loss** ein hoffnungsloser Fall sein; **~ly** *adj* tödlich; **~pan** *adj* undurchdringlich; **D~ Sea** *n*: **the D~ Sea** das Tote Meer

deaf [dɛf] *adj* taub; **~en** *vt* taub machen; **~ening** *adj (noise)* ohrenbetäubend; *(noise)* lautstark; **~-mute** *n* Taubstumme(r) *mf*; **~ness** *n* Taubheit *f*

deal [diːl] *(pt, pp* **dealt)** *n* Geschäft *nt ♦ vt* austeilen; *(CARDS)* geben; **a great ~ of** sehr viel; **~ in** *vt fus* handeln mit; **~ with** *vt fus (person)* behandeln; *(subject)* sich befassen mit; *(problem)* in Angriff nehmen; **~er** *n (COMM)* Händler *m*; *(CARDS)* Kartengeber *m*; **~ings** *npl (FIN)* Geschäfte *pl*; *(relations)* Beziehungen *pl*; **~t** [dɛlt] *pt, pp of* **deal**

dean [diːn] *n (Protestant)* Superintendent *m*; *(Catholic)* Dechant *m*; *(UNIV)* Dekan *m*

dear [dɪəʳ] *adj* lieb; *(expensive)* teuer ♦ *n* Liebling *m ♦ excl*: **~ me!** du liebe Zeit!; **D~ Sir** Sehr geehrter Herr!; **D~ John** Lieber John!; **~ly** *adv (love)* herzlich; *(pay)* teuer

death [dɛθ] *n* Tod *m*; *(statistic)* Todesfall *m*; **~ certificate** *n* Totenschein *m*; **~ly** *adj* totenähnlich, Toten-; **~ penalty** *n* Todesstrafe *f*; **~ rate** *n* Sterblichkeitsziffer *f*

debar [dɪˈbɑːʳ] *vt* ausschließen

debase [dɪˈbeɪs] *vt* entwerten

debatable [dɪˈbeɪtəbl] *adj* anfechtbar

debate [dɪˈbeɪt] *n* Debatte *f ♦ vt* debattieren, diskutieren; *(consider)* überlegen

debilitating [dɪˈbɪlɪteɪtɪŋ] *adj* schwächend

debit [ˈdɛbɪt] *n* Schuldposten *m ♦ vt* belasten

debris [ˈdɛbriː] *n* Trümmer *pl*

debt [dɛt] *n* Schuld *f*; **to be in ~** verschuldet sein; **~or** *n* Schuldner *m*

debunk [diːˈbʌŋk] *vt* entlarven

decade [ˈdɛkeɪd] *n* Jahrzehnt *nt*

decadence [ˈdɛkədəns] *n* Dekadenz *f*

decaff [ˈdiːkæf] *(inf) n* koffeinfreier Kaffee

decaffeinated [dɪˈkæfɪneɪtɪd] *adj* koffeinfrei

decanter [dɪˈkæntəʳ] *n* Karaffe *f*

decay [dɪˈkeɪ] *n* Verfall *m*; *(tooth ~)* Karies *m ♦ vi* verfallen; *(teeth, meat etc)* faulen; *(leaves etc)* verrotten

deceased [dɪˈsiːst] *adj* verstorben

deceit [dɪˈsiːt] *n* Betrug *m*; **~ful** *adj* falsch

deceive [dɪˈsiːv] *vt* täuschen

December [dɪˈsɛmbəʳ] *n* Dezember *m*

decency [ˈdiːsənsɪ] *n* Anstand *m*

decent [ˈdiːsənt] *adj (respectable)* anständig; *(pleasant)* annehmbar

deception [dɪˈsɛpʃən] *n* Betrug *m*

deceptive [dɪˈsɛptɪv] *adj* irreführend

decibel [ˈdɛsɪbɛl] *n* Dezibel *nt*

decide [dɪˈsaɪd] *vt* entscheiden ♦ *vi* sich entscheiden; **to ~ on sth** etw beschließen; **~d** *adj* entschieden; **~dly** [dɪˈsaɪdɪdlɪ] *adv* entschieden

deciduous [dɪˈsɪdjuəs] *adj* Laub-

decimal [ˈdɛsɪməl] *adj* dezimal ♦ *n* Dezimalzahl *f*; **~ point** *n* Komma *nt*

decipher [dɪˈsaɪfəʳ] *vt* entziffern

decision [dɪˈsɪʒən] *n* Entscheidung *f*, Entschluss *m*

decisive [dɪˈsaɪsɪv] *adj* entscheidend; *(person)* entschlossen

deck [dɛk] *n (NAUT)* Deck *nt*; *(of cards)* Pack *m*; **~chair** *n* Liegestuhl *m*

declaration [dɛkləˈreɪʃən] *n* Erklärung *f*

declare [dɪˈklɛəʳ] *vt* erklären; *(CUSTOMS)* verzollen

decline [dɪˈklaɪn] *n (decay)* Verfall *m*; *(lessening)* Rückgang *m ♦ vt (invitation)* ablehnen ♦ *vi (say no)* ablehnen; *(of strength)* nachlassen

decode [diːˈkəud] *vt* entschlüsseln; **~r** *n (TV)* Decoder *m*

decompose [diːkəmˈpəuz] *vi* (sich) zersetzen

décor [ˈdeɪkɔːʳ] *n* Ausstattung *f*

decorate [ˈdɛkəreɪt] *vt (room: paper)* tapezieren; *(: paint)* streichen; *(adorn)* (aus)schmücken; *(cake)* verzieren; *(honour)* auszeichnen; **decoration** [dɛkəˈreɪʃən] *n (of house)* (Wand)dekoration *f*; *(medal)* Orden *m*; **decorator** [ˈdɛkəreɪtəʳ] *n* Maler *m*, Anstreicher *m*

decorum [dɪˈkɔːrəm] *n* Anstand *m*

coy ['dɪːkɔɪ] n Lockvogel m

crease [n 'diːkriːs, vb diːˈkriːs] n Abnahme *f* ♦ vt vermindern ♦ vi abnehmen

cree [dɪˈkriː] n Erlass m; ~ **nisi** n

vorläufige(s) Scheidungsurteil nt

crepit [dɪˈkrepɪt] adj hinfällig

dicate ['dedɪkeɪt] vt widmen; ~**d** adj hingebungsvoll, engagiert; (COMPUT) dediziert; **dedication** [dedɪˈkeɪʃən] n (devotion) Ergebenheit f; (in book) Widmung f

duce [dɪˈdjuːs] vt: **to ~ sth (from sth)** etw (aus etw) ableiten, etw (aus etw) schließen

duct [dɪˈdʌkt] vt abziehen; ~**ion** [dɪˈdʌkʃən] n (of money) Abzug m; (conclusion) (Schluss)folgerung f

ed [diːd] n Tat f; (document) Urkunde f

eem [diːm] vt: **to ~ sb/sth (to be) sth** jdn/etw für etw halten

eep [diːp] adj tief ♦ adv: **the spectators stood 20 ~** die Zuschauer standen in 20 Reihen hintereinander; **to be 4m ~** 4 Meter tief sein; ~**en** vt vertiefen ♦ vi (darkness) tiefer werden; ~ **end** n: **the ~ end** (of swimming pool) das Tiefe; ~**-freeze** n Tiefkühlung f; ~**-fry** vt frittieren; ~**ly** adv tief; ~**-sea diving** n Tiefseetauchen nt; ~**-seated** adj tief sitzend

eer [dɪər] n Reh nt; ~**skin** n Hirsch-/ Rehleder nt

eface [dɪˈfeɪs] vt entstellen

efamation [defəˈmeɪʃən] n Verleumdung f

efault [dɪˈfɔːlt] n Versäumnis nt; (COMPUT) Standardwert m ♦ vi versäumen; **by ~** durch Nichterscheinen

efeat [dɪˈfiːt] n Niederlage f ♦ vt schlagen; ~**ist** adj defätistisch ♦ n Defätist m

efect [n 'diːfekt, vb dɪˈfekt] n Fehler m ♦ vi überlaufen; ~**ive** [dɪˈfektɪv] adj fehlerhaft

efence [dɪˈfens] n Verteidigung f; ~**less** adj wehrlos

efend [dɪˈfend] vt verteidigen; ~**ant** n Angeklagte(r) m; ~**er** n Verteidiger m

efense [dɪˈfens] (US) n = **defence**

efensive [dɪˈfensɪv] adj defensiv ♦ n: **on the ~** in der Defensive

efer [dɪˈfɜːr] vt verschieben

deference ['defərəns] n Rücksichtnahme f

defiance [dɪˈfaɪəns] n Trotz m, Unnachgiebigkeit f; **in ~ of sth** einer Sache dat zum Trotz

defiant [dɪˈfaɪənt] adj trotzig, unnachgiebig

deficiency [dɪˈfɪʃənsɪ] n (lack) Mangel m; (weakness) Schwäche f

deficient [dɪˈfɪʃənt] adj mangelhaft

deficit ['defɪsɪt] n Defizit nt

defile [vb dɪˈfaɪl, n 'diːfaɪl] vt beschmutzen ♦ n Hohlweg m

define [dɪˈfaɪn] vt bestimmen; (explain) definieren

definite ['defɪnɪt] adj (fixed) definitiv; (clear) eindeutig; ~**ly** adv bestimmt

definition [defɪˈnɪʃən] n Definition f

deflate [diːˈfleɪt] vt die Luft ablassen aus

deflect [dɪˈflekt] vt ablenken

deformity [dɪˈfɔːmɪtɪ] n Missbildung f

defraud [dɪˈfrɔːd] vt betrügen

defrost [diːˈfrɒst] vt (fridge) abtauen; (food) auftauen; ~**er** (US) n (demister) Gebläse nt

deft [deft] adj geschickt

defunct [dɪˈfʌŋkt] adj verstorben

defuse [diːˈfjuːz] vt entschärfen

defy [dɪˈfaɪ] vt (disobey) sich widersetzen +dat; (orders, death) trotzen +dat; (challenge) herausfordern

degenerate [v dɪˈdʒenəreɪt, adj dɪˈdʒenərɪt] vi degenerieren ♦ adj degeneriert

degrading [dɪˈɡreɪdɪŋ] adj erniedrigend

degree [dɪˈɡriː] n Grad m; (UNIV) Universitätsabschluss m; **by ~s** allmählich; **to some ~** zu einem gewissen Grad

dehydrated [diːhaɪˈdreɪtɪd] adj (person) ausgetrocknet

de-ice ['diːˈaɪs] vt enteisen

deign [deɪn] vi sich herablassen

deity ['diːɪtɪ] n Gottheit f

dejected [dɪˈdʒektɪd] adj niedergeschlagen

delay [dɪˈleɪ] vt (hold back) aufschieben ♦ vi (linger) sich aufhalten ♦ n Aufschub m, Verzögerung f; (of train etc) Verspätung f; **to be ~ed** (train) Verspätung haben; **without ~** unverzüglich

delectable [dɪˈlektəbl] adj köstlich; (fig) reizend

delegate [n ˈdɛlɪgɪt, vb ˈdɛlɪgeɪt] n Delegierte(r) mf ♦ vt delegieren
delete [dɪˈliːt] vt (aus)streichen
deliberate [adj dɪˈlɪbərɪt, vb dɪˈlɪbəreɪt] adj (intentional) absichtlich; (slow) bedächtig ♦ vi (consider) überlegen; (debate) sich beraten; ~ly adv absichtlich
delicacy [ˈdɛlɪkəsɪ] n Zartheit f; (weakness) Anfälligkeit f; (food) Delikatesse f
delicate [ˈdɛlɪkɪt] adj (fine) fein; (fragile) zart; (situation) heikel; (MED) empfindlich
delicatessen [dɛlɪkəˈtɛsn] n Feinkostgeschäft nt
delicious [dɪˈlɪʃəs] adj lecker
delight [dɪˈlaɪt] n Wonne f ♦ vt entzücken; **to take ~ in sth** Freude an etw dat haben; ~ed adj: ~**ed (at** or **with sth)** entzückt (über +acc etw); ~**ed to do sth** etw sehr gern tun; ~**ful** adj entzückend, herrlich
delinquency [dɪˈlɪŋkwənsɪ] n Kriminalität f
delinquent [dɪˈlɪŋkwənt] n Straffällige(r) mf ♦ adj straffällig
delirious [dɪˈlɪrɪəs] adj im Fieberwahn
deliver [dɪˈlɪvəʳ] vt (goods) (ab)liefern; (letter) zustellen; (speech) halten; ~**y** n (Ab)lieferung f; (of letter) Zustellung f; (of speech) Vortragsweise f; (MED) Entbindung f; **to take ~y of** im Empfang nehmen
delude [dɪˈluːd] vt täuschen
deluge [ˈdɛljuːdʒ] n Überschwemmung f; (fig) Flut f ♦ vt (fig) überfluten
delusion [dɪˈluːʒən] n (Selbst)täuschung f
de luxe [dəˈlʌks] adj Luxus-
delve [dɛlv] vi: **to ~ into** sich vertiefen in +acc
demand [dɪˈmɑːnd] vt verlangen ♦ n (request) Verlangen nt; (COMM) Nachfrage f; **in ~** gefragt; **on ~** auf Verlangen; ~**ing** adj anspruchsvoll
demean [dɪˈmiːn] vt: **to ~ o.s.** sich erniedrigen
demeanour [dɪˈmiːnəʳ] (US **demeanor**) n Benehmen nt
demented [dɪˈmɛntɪd] adj wahnsinnig
demister [diːˈmɪstəʳ] n (AUT) Gebläse nt
demo [ˈdɛməu] (inf) n abbr (= demonstration) Demo f

democracy [dɪˈmɔkrəsɪ] n Demokratie f
democrat [ˈdɛməkræt] n Demokrat m; **democratic** [dɛməˈkrætɪk] adj demokratisch
demolish [dɪˈmɔlɪʃ] vt abreißen; (fig) vernichten
demolition [dɛməˈlɪʃən] n Abbruch m
demon [ˈdiːmən] n Dämon m
demonstrate [ˈdɛmənstreɪt] vt, vi demonstrieren; **demonstration** [dɛmənˈstreɪʃən] n Demonstration f; **demonstrator** [ˈdɛmənstreɪtəʳ] n (POL) Demonstrant(in) m(f)
demote [dɪˈməut] vt degradieren
demure [dɪˈmjuəʳ] adj ernst
den [dɛn] n (of animal) Höhle f; (study) Bude f
denatured alcohol [diːˈneɪtʃəd-] (US) n ungenießbar gemachte(r) Alkohol m
denial [dɪˈnaɪəl] n Leugnung f; **official ~** Dementi nt
denim [ˈdɛnɪm] adj Denim-; ~**s** npl Denimjeans pl
Denmark [ˈdɛnmɑːk] n Dänemark nt
denomination [dɪnɔmɪˈneɪʃən] n (ECCL) Bekenntnis nt; (type) Klasse f; (FIN) Wert m
denote [dɪˈnəut] vt bedeuten
denounce [dɪˈnauns] vt brandmarken
dense [dɛns] adj dicht; (stupid) schwer von Begriff; ~**ly** adv dicht; **density** [ˈdɛnsɪtɪ] n Dichte f; **single/double density disk** Diskette f mit einfacher/doppelter Dichte
dent [dɛnt] n Delle f ♦ vt (also: **make a ~ in**) einbeulen
dental [ˈdɛntl] adj Zahn-; **~ surgeon** n = **dentist**
dentist [ˈdɛntɪst] n Zahnarzt(ärztin) m(f)
dentures [ˈdɛntʃəz] npl Gebiss nt
deny [dɪˈnaɪ] vt leugnen; (officially) dementieren; (help) abschlagen
deodorant [diːˈəudərənt] n Deodorant nt
depart [dɪˈpɑːt] vi abfahren; **to ~ from** (fig: differ from) abweichen von
department [dɪˈpɑːtmənt] n (COMM) Abteilung f; (UNIV) Seminar nt; (POL) Ministerium nt; **~ store** n Warenhaus nt
departure [dɪˈpɑːtʃəʳ] n (of person) Abreise f; (of train) Abfahrt f; (of plane) Abflug m; **new**

~ Neuerung *f*; ~ **lounge** *n* (*at airport*)
Abflughalle *f*

pend [dɪ'pɛnd] *vi*: **to ~ on** abhängen von;
(*rely on*) angewiesen sein auf +*acc*; **it ~s** es
kommt darauf an; **~ing on the result ...**
abhängend vom Resultat ...; **~able** *adj*
zuverlässig; **~ant** *n* Angehörige(r) *f(m)*;
~ence *n* Abhängigkeit *f*; **~ent** *adj*
abhängig ♦ *n* = **dependant**; **~ent on**
abhängig von

pict [dɪ'pɪkt] *vt* schildern

pleted [dɪ'pliːtɪd] *adj* aufgebraucht

plorable [dɪ'plɔːrəbl] *adj* bedauerlich

ploy [dɪ'plɔɪ] *vt* einsetzen

population ['diːpɔpjʊ'leɪʃən] *n*
Entvölkerung *f*

port [dɪ'pɔːt] *vt* deportieren; **~ation**
[diːpɔː'teɪʃən] *n* Abschiebung *f*

portment [dɪ'pɔːtmənt] *n* Betragen *nt*

posit [dɪ'pɔzɪt] *n* (*in bank*) Guthaben *nt*;
(*down payment*) Anzahlung *f*; (*security*)
Kaution *f*; (*CHEM*) Niederschlag *m* ♦ *vt* (*in
bank*) deponieren; (*put down*) niederlegen;
~ account *n* Sparkonto *nt*

pot ['dɛpəʊ] *n* Depot *nt*

praved [dɪ'preɪvd] *adj* verkommen

preciate [dɪ'priːʃeɪt] *vi* im Wert sinken;
depreciation [dɪpriːʃi'eɪʃən] *n*
Wertminderung *f*

press [dɪ'prɛs] *vt* (*press down*)
niederdrücken; (*in mood*) deprimieren; **~ed**
adj deprimiert; **~ion** [dɪ'prɛʃən] *n* (*mood*)
Depression *f*; (*in trade*) Wirtschaftskrise *f*;
(*hollow*) Vertiefung *f*; (*MET*)
Tief(druckgebiet) *nt*

privation [dɛprɪ'veɪʃən] *n* Not *f*

prive [dɪ'praɪv] *vt*: **to ~ sb of sth** jdn
einer Sache *gen* berauben; **~d** *adj* (*child*)
sozial benachteiligt; (*area*) unterentwickelt

pth [dɛpθ] *n* Tiefe *f*; **in the ~s of despair**
in tiefster Verzweiflung

putation [dɛpjʊ'teɪʃən] *n* Abordnung *f*

putize ['dɛpjʊtaɪz] *vi*: **to ~ (for sb)** (jdn)
vertreten

puty ['dɛpjʊtɪ] *adj* stellvertretend ♦ *n*
(Stell)vertreter *m*; **~ head** (*BRIT: SCOL*) *n*
Konrektor(in) *m(f)*

derail [dɪ'reɪl] *vt*: **to be ~ed** entgleisen;
~ment *n* Entgleisung *f*

deranged [dɪ'reɪndʒd] *adj* verrückt

derby ['dɑːrbɪ] (*US*) *n* Melone *f*

derelict ['dɛrɪlɪkt] *adj* verlassen

deride [dɪ'raɪd] *vt* auslachen

derisory [dɪ'raɪsərɪ] *adj* spöttisch

derivative [dɪ'rɪvətɪv] *n* Derivat *nt* ♦ *adj*
abgeleitet

derive [dɪ'raɪv] *vt* (*get*) gewinnen; (*deduce*)
ableiten ♦ *vi* (*come from*) abstammen

dermatitis [dɜːmə'taɪtɪs] *n* Hautentzündung
f

derogatory [dɪ'rɔgətərɪ] *adj* geringschätzig

derrick ['dɛrɪk] *n* Drehkran *m*

descend [dɪ'sɛnd] *vt, vi* hinuntersteigen; **to
~ from** abstammen von; **~ant** *n*
Nachkomme *m*; **descent** [dɪ'sɛnt] *n*
(*coming down*) Abstieg *m*; (*origin*)
Abstammung *f*

describe [dɪs'kraɪb] *vt* beschreiben

description [dɪs'krɪpʃən] *n* Beschreibung *f*;
(*sort*) Art *f*

descriptive [dɪs'krɪptɪv] *adj* beschreibend;
(*word*) anschaulich

desecrate ['dɛsɪkreɪt] *vt* schänden

desert [*n* 'dɛzət, *vb* dɪ'zɜːt] *n* Wüste *f* ♦ *vt*
verlassen; (*temporarily*) im Stich lassen ♦ *vi*
(*MIL*) desertieren; **~s** *npl* (*what one deserves*):
to get one's just ~s seinen gerechten
Lohn bekommen; **~er** *n* Deserteur *m*; **~ion**
[dɪ'zɜːʃən] *n* (*of wife*) Verlassen *nt*; (*MIL*)
Fahnenflucht *f*; **~ island** *n* einsame Insel *f*

deserve [dɪ'zɜːv] *vt* verdienen; **deserving**
adj verdienstvoll

design [dɪ'zaɪn] *n* (*plan*) Entwurf *m*;
(*planning*) Design *n* ♦ *vt* entwerfen

designate [*vb* 'dɛzɪgneɪt, *adj* 'dɛzɪgnɪt] *vt*
bestimmen ♦ *adj* designiert

designer [dɪ'zaɪnəʳ] *n* Designer(in) *m(f)*;
(*TECH*) Konstrukteur(in) *m(f)*; (*fashion* ~)
Modeschöpfer(in) *m(f)*

desirable [dɪ'zaɪərəbl] *adj* wünschenswert

desire [dɪ'zaɪəʳ] *n* Wunsch *m*, Verlangen *nt*
♦ *vt* (*lust*) begehren; (*ask for*) wollen

desk [dɛsk] *n* Schreibtisch *m*; (*BRIT: in shop,
restaurant*) Kasse *f*; **~top publishing** *n*

Desktop-Publishing nt

desolate ['desəlɪt] adj öde; (sad) trostlos; **desolation** [desə'leɪʃən] n Trostlosigkeit f

despair [dɪs'peəʳ] n Verzweiflung f ♦ vi: **to ~ (of)** verzweifeln (an +dat)

despatch [dɪs'pætʃ] n, vt = **dispatch**

desperate ['despərɪt] adj verzweifelt; **~ly** adv verzweifelt; **desperation** [despə'reɪʃən] n Verzweiflung f

despicable [dɪs'pɪkəbl] adj abscheulich

despise [dɪs'paɪz] vt verachten

despite [dɪs'paɪt] prep trotz +gen

despondent [dɪs'pɔndənt] adj mutlos

dessert [dɪ'zɜːt] n Nachtisch m; **~spoon** n Dessertlöffel m

destination [destɪ'neɪʃən] n (of person) (Reise)ziel nt; (of goods) Bestimmungsort m

destiny ['destɪnɪ] n Schicksal nt

destitute ['destɪtjuːt] adj Not leidend

destroy [dɪs'trɔɪ] vt zerstören; **~er** n (NAUT) Zerstörer m

destruction [dɪs'trʌkʃən] n Zerstörung f

destructive [dɪs'trʌktɪv] adj zerstörend

detach [dɪ'tætʃ] vt loslösen; **~able** adj abtrennbar; **~ed** adj (attitude) distanziert; (house) Einzel-; **~ment** n (fig) Abstand m; (MIL) Sonderkommando nt

detail ['diːteɪl] n Einzelheit f, Detail n ♦ vt (relate) ausführlich berichten; (appoint) abkommandieren; **in ~** im Detail; **~ed** adj detailliert

detain [dɪ'teɪn] vt aufhalten; (imprison) in Haft halten

detect [dɪ'tekt] vt entdecken; **~ion** [dɪ'tekʃən] n Aufdeckung f; **~ive** n Detektiv m; **~ive story** n Kriminalgeschichte f, Krimi m

détente [deɪ'tɑːnt] n Entspannung f

detention [dɪ'tenʃən] n Haft f; (SCH) Nachsitzen nt

deter [dɪ'tɜːʳ] vt abschrecken

detergent [dɪ'tɜːdʒənt] n Waschmittel nt

deteriorate [dɪ'tɪərɪəreɪt] vi sich verschlechtern; **deterioration** [dɪtɪərɪə'reɪʃən] n Verschlechterung f

determination [dɪtɜːmɪ'neɪʃən] n Entschlossenheit f

determine [dɪ'tɜːmɪn] vt bestimmen; **~d** adj entschlossen

deterrent [dɪ'terənt] n Abschreckungsmittel nt

detest [dɪ'test] vt verabscheuen

detonate ['detəneɪt] vt explodieren lassen ♦ vi detonieren

detour ['diːtuəʳ] n Umweg m; (US: AUT: diversion) Umleitung f ♦ vt (US: AUT: traffic) umleiten

detract [dɪ'trækt] vi: **to ~ from** schmälern

detriment ['detrɪmənt] n: **to the ~ of** zum Schaden +gen; **~al** [detrɪ'mentl] adj schädlich

devaluation [diːvælju'eɪʃən] n Abwertung f

devastate ['devəsteɪt] vt verwüsten; (fig: shock): **to be ~d by** niedergeschmettert sein von; **devastating** adj verheerend

develop [dɪ'veləp] vt entwickeln; (resources) erschließen ♦ vi sich entwickeln; **~ing country** n Entwicklungsland nt; **~ment** n Entwicklung f

deviate ['diːvɪeɪt] vi abweichen

device [dɪ'vaɪs] n Gerät nt

devil ['devl] n Teufel m

devious ['diːvɪəs] adj (means) krumm; (person) verschlagen

devise [dɪ'vaɪz] vt entwickeln

devoid [dɪ'vɔɪd] adj: **~ of** ohne

devolution [diːvə'luːʃən] n (POL) Dezentralisierung f

devote [dɪ'vəut] vt: **to ~ sth (to sth)** etw (einer Sache dat) widmen; **~d** adj ergeben; **~e** [devəu'tiː] n Anhänger(in) m(f), Verehrer(in) m(f); **devotion** [dɪ'vəuʃən] n (piety) Andacht f; (loyalty) Ergebenheit f, Hingabe f

devour [dɪ'vauəʳ] vt verschlingen

devout [dɪ'vaut] adj andächtig

dew [djuː] n Tau m

dexterity [deks'terɪtɪ] n Geschicklichkeit f

DHSS (BRIT) n abbr = **Department of Health and Social Security**

diabetes [daɪə'biːtiːz] n Zuckerkrankheit f

diabetic [daɪə'betɪk] adj zuckerkrank; (food) Diabetiker- ♦ n Diabetiker m

diabolical [daɪə'bɔlɪkl] (inf) adj (weather, behaviour) saumäßig

agnose [daɪəg'nəuz] vt diagnostizieren

agnoses [daɪəg'nəusi:z] npl of **diagnosis**

agnosis [daɪəg'nəusɪs] n Diagnose f

agonal [daɪ'ægənl] adj diagonal ♦ n
Diagonale f

agram [daɪəgræm] n Diagramm nt,
Schaubild nt

al ['daɪəl] n (TEL) Wählscheibe f; (of clock)
Zifferblatt nt ♦ vt wählen

alect ['daɪəlekt] n Dialekt m

alling code ['daɪəlɪŋ-] n Vorwahl f

alling tone n Amtszeichen nt

alogue ['daɪəlɔg] n Dialog m

ial tone (US) n = **dialling tone**

iameter [daɪ'æmɪtər] n Durchmesser m

iamond ['daɪəmənd] n Diamant m; **~s** npl
(CARDS) Karo nt

iaper ['daɪəpər] (US) n Windel f

iaphragm ['daɪəfræm] n Zwerchfell nt

iarrhoea [daɪə'ri:ə] (US **diarrhea**) n
Durchfall m

iary ['daɪərɪ] n Taschenkalender m; (account)
Tagebuch nt

ice [daɪs] n Würfel pl ♦ vt in Würfel
schneiden

ictate [dɪk'teɪt] vt diktieren; **~s** ['dɪkteɪts]
npl Gebote pl; **dictation** [dɪk'teɪʃən] n
Diktat nt

ictator [dɪk'teɪtər] n Diktator m; **~ship**
[dɪk'teɪtəʃɪp] n Diktatur f

ictionary ['dɪkʃənrɪ] n Wörterbuch nt

id [dɪd] pt of **do**

idn't ['dɪdnt] = **did not**

ie [daɪ] vi sterben; **to be dying for sth** etw
unbedingt haben wollen; **to be dying to
do sth** darauf brennen, etw zu tun; **~
away** vi schwächer werden; **~ down** vi
nachlassen; **~ out** vi aussterben

iesel ['di:zl] n (car) Diesel m; **~ engine** n
Dieselmotor m; **~ oil** n Dieselkraftstoff m

iet ['daɪət] n Nahrung f; (special food) Diät f;
(slimming) Abmagerungskur f ♦ vi (also: **be
on a ~**) eine Abmagerungskur machen

iffer ['dɪfər] vi sich unterscheiden; (disagree)
anderer Meinung sein; **~ence** n
Unterschied m; **~ent** adj anders; (two
things) verschieden; **~entiate** [dɪfə'renʃɪeɪt]

vt, vi unterscheiden; **~ently** adv anders;
(from one another) unterschiedlich

difficult ['dɪfɪkəlt] adj schwierig; **~y** n
Schwierigkeit f

diffident ['dɪfɪdənt] adj schüchtern

diffuse [adj dɪ'fju:s, vb dɪ'fju:z] adj langatmig
♦ vt verbreiten

dig [dɪg] (pt, pp **dug**) vt graben ♦ n (prod)
Stoß m; (remark) Spitze f; (archaeological)
Ausgrabung f; **~ in** vi (MIL) sich eingraben;
~ into vt fus (savings) angreifen; **~ up** vt
ausgraben; (fig) aufgabeln

digest [vb daɪ'dʒest, n 'daɪdʒest] vt verdauen
♦ n Auslese f; **~ion** [dɪ'dʒestʃən] n
Verdauung f

digit ['dɪdʒɪt] n Ziffer f; (ANAT) Finger m; **~al**
adj digital, Digital-; **~al camera** n
Digitalkamera f; **~al TV** n Digitalfernsehen nt

dignified ['dɪgnɪfaɪd] adj würdevoll

dignity ['dɪgnɪtɪ] n Würde f

digress [daɪ'gres] vi abschweifen

digs [dɪgz] (BRIT: inf) npl Bude f

dilapidated [dɪ'læpɪdeɪtɪd] adj baufällig

dilate [daɪ'leɪt] vt weiten ♦ vi sich weiten

dilemma [daɪ'lemə] n Dilemma nt

diligent ['dɪlɪdʒənt] adj fleißig

dilute [daɪ'lu:t] vt verdünnen

dim [dɪm] adj trübe; (stupid) schwer von
Begriff ♦ vt verdunkeln; **to ~ one's
headlights** (esp US) abblenden

dime [daɪm] (US) n Zehncentstück nt

dimension [daɪ'menʃən] n Dimension f

diminish [dɪ'mɪnɪʃ] vt, vi verringern

diminutive [dɪ'mɪnjutɪv] adj winzig ♦ n
Verkleinerungsform f

dimmer ['dɪmər] (US) n (AUT)
Abblendschalter m; **~s** npl Abblendlicht nt;
(sidelights) Begrenzungsleuchten pl

dimple ['dɪmpl] n Grübchen nt

din [dɪn] n Getöse nt

dine [daɪn] vi speisen; **~r** n Tischgast m;
(RAIL) Speisewagen m

dinghy ['dɪŋgɪ] n Dingi nt; **rubber ~**
Schlauchboot nt

dingy ['dɪndʒɪ] adj armselig

dining car (BRIT) n Speisewagen m

dining room ['daɪnɪŋ-] n Esszimmer nt; (in

hotel) Speisezimmer *nt*

dinner ['dɪnəʳ] *n* (*lunch*) Mittagessen *nt*; (*evening*) Abendessen *nt*; (*public*) Festessen *nt*; ~ **jacket** *n* Smoking *m*; ~ **party** *n* Tischgesellschaft *f*; ~ **time** *n* Tischzeit *f*

dinosaur ['daɪnəsɔːʳ] *n* Dinosaurier *m*

dint [dɪnt] *n*: **by** ~ **of** durch

diocese ['daɪəsɪs] *n* Diözese *f*

dip [dɪp] *n* (*hollow*) Senkung *f*; (*bathe*) kurze(s) Baden *nt* ♦ *vt* eintauchen; (*BRIT*: *AUT*) abblenden ♦ *vi* (*slope*) sich senken, abfallen

diploma [dɪ'pləumə] *n* Diplom *nt*

diplomacy [dɪ'pləuməsɪ] *n* Diplomatie *f*

diplomat ['dɪpləmæt] *n* Diplomat(in) *m(f)*; ~**ic** [dɪplə'mætɪk] *adj* diplomatisch

dip stick *n* Ölmessstab *m*

dipswitch ['dɪpswɪtʃ] (*BRIT*) *n* (*AUT*) Abblendschalter *m*

dire [daɪəʳ] *adj* schrecklich

direct [daɪ'rɛkt] *adj* direkt ♦ *vt* leiten; (*film*) die Regie führen +*gen*; (*aim*) richten; (*order*) anweisen; **can you ~ me to ...?** können Sie mir sagen, wo ich zu ... komme?; ~ **debit** *n* (*BRIT*) Einzugsauftrag *m*; (*transaction*) automatische Abbuchung *f*

direction [dɪ'rɛkʃən] *n* Richtung *f*; (*CINE*) Regie *f*; Leitung *f*; ~**s** *npl* (*for use*) Gebrauchsanleitung *f*; (*orders*) Anweisungen *pl*; **sense of** ~ Orientierungssinn *m*

directly [dɪ'rɛktlɪ] *adv* direkt; (*at once*) sofort

director [dɪ'rɛktəʳ] *n* Direktor *m*; (*of film*) Regisseur *m*

directory [dɪ'rɛktərɪ] *n* (*TEL*) Telefonbuch *nt*; ~ **enquiries**, ~ **assistance** (*US*) *n* (Fernsprech)auskunft *f*

dirt [dɜːt] *n* Schmutz *m*, Dreck *m*; ~~**cheap** *adj* spottbillig; ~**y** *adj* schmutzig ♦ *vt* beschmutzen; ~**y trick** *n* gemeine(r) Trick *m*

disability [dɪsə'bɪlɪtɪ] *n* Körperbehinderung *f*

disabled [dɪs'eɪbld] *adj* körperbehindert

disadvantage [dɪsəd'vɑːntɪdʒ] *n* Nachteil *m*

disagree [dɪsə'griː] *vi* nicht übereinstimmen; (*quarrel*) (sich) streiten; (*food*): **to** ~ **with sb** jdm nicht bekommen; ~**able** *adj*

unangenehm; ~**ment** *n* (*between persons*) Streit *m*; (*between things*) Widerspruch *m*

disallow ['dɪsə'lau] *vt* nicht zulassen

disappear [dɪsə'pɪəʳ] *vi* verschwinden; ~**ance** *n* Verschwinden *nt*

disappoint [dɪsə'pɔɪnt] *vt* enttäuschen; ~**ed** *adj* enttäuscht; ~**ment** *n* Enttäuschung *f*

disapproval [dɪsə'pruːvəl] *n* Missbilligung *f*

disapprove [dɪsə'pruːv] *vi*: **to ~ of** missbilligen

disarm [dɪs'ɑːm] *vt* entwaffnen; (*POL*) abrüsten; ~**ament** *n* Abrüstung *f*

disarray [dɪsə'reɪ] *n*: **to be in ~** (*army*) in Auflösung (begriffen) sein; (*clothes*) in unordentlichen Zustand sein

disaster [dɪ'zɑːstəʳ] *n* Katastrophe *f*; **disastrous** [dɪ'zɑːstrəs] *adj* verhängnisvoll

disband [dɪs'bænd] *vt* auflösen ♦ *vi* auseinander gehen

disbelief ['dɪsbə'liːf] *n* Ungläubigkeit *f*

disc [dɪsk] *n* Scheibe *f*; (*record*) (Schall)platte *f*; (*COMPUT*) = **disk**

discard [dɪs'kɑːd] *vt* ablegen

discern [dɪ'sɜːn] *vt* erkennen; ~**ing** *adj* scharfsinnig

discharge [*vb* dɪs'tʃɑːdʒ, *n* 'dɪstʃɑːdʒ] *vt* (*ship*) entladen; (*duties*) nachkommen +*dat*; (*dismiss*) entlassen; (*gun*) abschießen; (*JUR*) freisprechen ♦ *n* (*of ship, ELEC*) Entladung *f*; (*dismissal*) Entlassung *f*; (*MED*) Ausfluss *m*

disciple [dɪ'saɪpl] *n* Jünger *m*

discipline ['dɪsɪplɪn] *n* Disziplin *f* ♦ *vt* (*train*) schulen; (*punish*) bestrafen

disc jockey *n* Diskjockey *m*

disclaim [dɪs'kleɪm] *vt* nicht anerkennen

disclose [dɪs'kləuz] *vt* enthüllen; **disclosure** [dɪs'kləuʒəʳ] *n* Enthüllung *f*

disco ['dɪskəu] *n abbr* = **discotheque**

discoloured [dɪs'kʌləd] (*US* **discolored**) *adj* verfärbt

discomfort [dɪs'kʌmfət] *n* Unbehagen *nt*

disconcert [dɪskən'sɜːt] *vt* aus der Fassung bringen

disconnect [dɪskə'nɛkt] *vt* abtrennen

discontent [dɪskən'tɛnt] *n* Unzufriedenheit *f*; ~**ed** *adj* unzufrieden

discontinue [dɪskən'tɪnjuː] *vt* einstellen

iscord ['dɪskɔːd] n Zwietracht f; (noise) Dissonanz f

iscotheque ['dɪskəʊtek] n Diskothek f

iscount [n 'dɪskaʊnt, vb dɪs'kaʊnt] n Rabatt m ♦ vt außer Acht lassen

iscourage [dɪs'kʌrɪdʒ] vt entmutigen; (prevent) abraten

iscourteous [dɪs'kɜːtɪəs] adj unhöflich

iscover [dɪs'kʌvəʳ] vt entdecken; ~y n Entdeckung f

iscredit [dɪs'kredɪt] vt in Verruf bringen

iscreet [dɪs'kriːt] adj diskret

iscrepancy [dɪs'krepənsɪ] n Diskrepanz f

iscriminate [dɪs'krɪmɪneɪt] vi unterscheiden; **to ~ against** diskriminieren; **discriminating** adj anspruchsvoll; **discrimination** [dɪskrɪmɪ'neɪʃən] n Urteilsvermögen nt; (pej) Diskriminierung f

iscuss [dɪs'kʌs] vt diskutieren, besprechen; ~ion [dɪs'kʌʃən] n Diskussion f, Besprechung f

isdain [dɪs'deɪn] n Verachtung f

isease [dɪ'ziːz] n Krankheit f

isembark [dɪsɪm'bɑːk] vi von Bord gehen

isenchanted ['dɪsɪn'tʃɑːntɪd] adj desillusioniert

isengage [dɪsɪn'geɪdʒ] vt (AUT) auskuppeln

isentangle [dɪsɪn'tæŋgl] vt entwirren

isfigure [dɪs'fɪgəʳ] vt entstellen

isgrace [dɪs'greɪs] n Schande f ♦ vt Schande bringen über +acc; ~ful adj unerhört

isgruntled [dɪs'grʌntld] adj verärgert

isguise [dɪs'gaɪz] vt verkleiden; (feelings) verhehlen ♦ n Verkleidung f; **in ~** verkleidet, maskiert

isgust [dɪs'gʌst] n Abscheu f ♦ vt anwidern; ~ed adj angeekelt; (at sb's behaviour) empört; ~ing adj widerlich

ish [dɪʃ] n Schüssel f; (food) Gericht nt; **to do** or **wash the ~es** abwaschen; ~ **up** vt auftischen; ~ **cloth** n Spüllappen m

ishearten [dɪs'hɑːtn] vt entmutigen

ishevelled [dɪ'ʃevəld] adj (hair) zerzaust; (clothing) ungepflegt

ishonest [dɪs'ɒnɪst] adj unehrlich

ishonour [dɪs'ɒnəʳ] (US **dishonor**) n Unehre f; ~able adj unehrenhaft

dishtowel ['dɪʃtaʊəl] n Geschirrtuch nt

dishwasher ['dɪʃwɒʃəʳ] n Geschirrspülmaschine f

disillusion [dɪsɪ'luːʒən] vt enttäuschen, desillusionieren

disincentive [dɪsɪn'sentɪv] n Entmutigung f

disinfect [dɪsɪn'fekt] vt desinfizieren; ~ant n Desinfektionsmittel nt

disintegrate [dɪs'ɪntɪgreɪt] vi sich auflösen

disinterested [dɪs'ɪntrəstɪd] adj uneigennützig; (inf) uninteressiert

disjointed [dɪs'dʒɔɪntɪd] adj unzusammenhängend

disk [dɪsk] n (COMPUT) Diskette f; **single/ double sided ~** einseitige/beidseitige Diskette; ~ **drive** n Diskettenlaufwerk nt; ~**ette** [dɪs'ket] (US) n = **disk**

dislike [dɪs'laɪk] n Abneigung f ♦ vt nicht leiden können

dislocate ['dɪsləkeɪt] vt auskugeln

dislodge [dɪs'lɒdʒ] vt verschieben; (MIL) aus der Stellung werfen

disloyal [dɪs'lɔɪəl] adj treulos

dismal ['dɪzml] adj trostlos, trübe

dismantle [dɪs'mæntl] vt demontieren

dismay [dɪs'meɪ] n Bestürzung f ♦ vt bestürzen

dismiss [dɪs'mɪs] vt (employee) entlassen; (idea) von sich weisen; (send away) wegschicken; (JUR) abweisen; ~al n Entlassung f

dismount [dɪs'maʊnt] vi absteigen

disobedience [dɪsə'biːdɪəns] n Ungehorsam m; **disobedient** adj ungehorsam

disobey [dɪsə'beɪ] vt nicht gehorchen +dat

disorder [dɪs'ɔːdəʳ] n (confusion) Verwirrung f; (commotion) Aufruhr m; (MED) Erkrankung f

disorderly [dɪs'ɔːdəlɪ] adj (untidy) unordentlich; (unruly) ordnungswidrig

disorganized [dɪs'ɔːgənaɪzd] adj unordentlich

disorientated [dɪs'ɔːrɪenteɪtɪd] adj (person: after journey) verwirrt

disown [dɪs'əʊn] vt (child) verstoßen

disparaging [dɪs'pærɪdʒɪŋ] adj

geringschätzig

dispassionate [dɪsˈpæʃənət] adj objektiv

dispatch [dɪsˈpætʃ] vt (goods) abschicken, abfertigen ♦ n Absendung f; (esp MIL) Meldung f

dispel [dɪsˈpɛl] vt zerstreuen

dispensary [dɪsˈpɛnsərɪ] n Apotheke f

dispense [dɪsˈpɛns] vt verteilen, austeilen; ~ **with** vt fus verzichten auf +acc; ~r n (container) Spender m; **dispensing** adj: **dispensing chemist** (BRIT) Apotheker m

dispersal [dɪsˈpəːsl] n Zerstreuung f

disperse [dɪsˈpəːs] vt zerstreuen ♦ vi sich verteilen

dispirited [dɪsˈpɪrɪtɪd] adj niedergeschlagen

displace [dɪsˈpleɪs] vt verschieben; ~d **person** n Verschleppte(r) mf

display [dɪsˈpleɪ] n (of goods) Auslage f; (of feeling) Zurschaustellung f ♦ vt zeigen; (ostentatiously) vorführen; (goods) ausstellen

displease [dɪsˈpliːz] vt missfallen +dat

displeasure [dɪsˈplɛʒəʳ] n Missfallen nt

disposable [dɪsˈpəuzəbl] adj Wegwerf-; ~ **nappy** n Papierwindel f

disposal [dɪsˈpəuzl] n (of property) Verkauf m; (throwing away) Beseitigung f; **to be at one's** ~ einem zur Verfügung stehen

dispose [dɪsˈpəuz] vi: **to** ~ **of** loswerden; ~d adj geneigt

disposition [dɪspəˈzɪʃən] n Wesen nt

disproportionate [dɪsprəˈpɔːʃənət] adj unverhältnismäßig

disprove [dɪsˈpruːv] vt widerlegen

dispute [dɪsˈpjuːt] n Streit m; (also: **industrial** ~) Arbeitskampf m ♦ vt bestreiten

disqualify [dɪsˈkwɒlɪfaɪ] vt disqualifizieren

disquiet [dɪsˈkwaɪət] n Unruhe f

disregard [dɪsrɪˈgɑːd] vt nicht (be)achten

disrepair [ˈdɪsrɪˈpɛəʳ] n: **to fall into** ~ verfallen

disreputable [dɪsˈrɛpjutəbl] adj verrufen

disrespectful [dɪsrɪˈspɛktful] adj respektlos

disrupt [dɪsˈrʌpt] vt stören; (service) unterbrechen; ~**ion** n [dɪsˈrʌpʃən] n Störung f; Unterbrechung f

dissatisfaction [dɪssætɪsˈfækʃən] n Unzufriedenheit f; **dissatisfied** [dɪsˈsætɪsfaɪd] adj unzufrieden

dissect [dɪˈsɛkt] vt zerlegen, sezieren

dissent [dɪˈsɛnt] n abweichende Meinung f

dissertation [dɪsəˈteɪʃən] n wissenschaftliche Arbeit f; (Ph.D.) Doktorarbeit f

disservice [dɪsˈsəːvɪs] n: **to do sb a** ~ jdm einen schlechten Dienst erweisen

dissident [ˈdɪsɪdnt] adj anders denkend ♦ n Dissident m

dissimilar [dɪˈsɪmɪləʳ] adj: ~ **(to sb/sth)** (jdm/etw) unähnlich

dissipate [ˈdɪsɪpeɪt] vt (waste) verschwenden; (scatter) zerstreuen

dissociate [dɪˈsəuʃɪeɪt] vt trennen

dissolve [dɪˈzɒlv] vt auflösen ♦ vi sich auflösen

dissuade [dɪˈsweɪd] vt: **to** ~ **sb from doing sth** jdn davon abbringen, etw zu tun

distance [ˈdɪstns] n Entfernung f; **in the** ~ in der Ferne; **distant** adj entfernt, fern; (with time) fern

distaste [dɪsˈteɪst] n Abneigung f; ~**ful** adj widerlich

distended [dɪsˈtɛndɪd] adj (stomach) aufgebläht

distil [dɪsˈtɪl] vt destillieren; ~**lery** n Brennerei f

distinct [dɪsˈtɪŋkt] adj (separate) getrennt; (clear) klar, deutlich; **as** ~ **from** im Unterschied zu; ~**ion** [dɪsˈtɪŋkʃən] n Unterscheidung f; (eminence) Auszeichnung f; ~**ive** adj bezeichnend

distinguish [dɪsˈtɪŋgwɪʃ] vt unterscheiden; ~**ed** adj (eminent) berühmt; ~**ing** adj bezeichnend

distort [dɪsˈtɔːt] vt verdrehen; (misrepresent) entstellen; ~**ion** [dɪsˈtɔːʃən] n Verzerrung f

distract [dɪsˈtrækt] vt ablenken; ~**ing** adj verwirrend; ~**ion** [dɪsˈtrækʃən] n (distress) Raserei f; (diversion) Zerstreuung f

distraught [dɪsˈtrɔːt] adj bestürzt

distress [dɪsˈtrɛs] n Not f; (suffering) Qual f ♦ vt quälen; ~**ing** adj erschütternd; ~ **signal** n Notsignal nt

distribute [dɪsˈtrɪbjuːt] vt verteilen; **distribution** [dɪstrɪˈbjuːʃən] n Verteilung f;

distributor *n* Verteiler *m*

district ['dɪstrɪkt] *n* (*of country*) Kreis *m*; (*of town*) Bezirk *m*; ~ **attorney** (*US*) *n* Oberstaatsanwalt *m*; ~ **nurse** *n* Kreiskrankenschwester *f*

distrust [dɪs'trʌst] *n* Misstrauen *nt* ♦ *vt* misstrauen +*dat*

disturb [dɪs'tɜːb] *vt* stören; (*agitate*) erregen; ~**ance** *n* Störung *f*; ~**ed** *adj* beunruhigt; **emotionally ~ed** emotional gestört; ~**ing** *adj* beunruhigend

disuse [dɪs'juːs] *n*: **to fall into ~** außer Gebrauch kommen; ~**d** [dɪs'juːzd] *adj* außer Gebrauch; (*mine, railway line*) stillgelegt

ditch [dɪtʃ] *n* Graben *m* ♦ *vt* (*person*) loswerden; (*plan*) fallen lassen

dither ['dɪðər] *vi* verdattert sein

ditto ['dɪtəu] *adv* dito, ebenfalls

divan [dɪ'væn] *n* Liegesofa *nt*

dive [daɪv] *n* (*into water*) Kopfsprung *m*; (*AVIAT*) Sturzflug *m* ♦ *vi* tauchen; ~**r** *n* Taucher *m*

diverge [daɪ'vɜːdʒ] *vi* auseinander gehen

diverse [daɪ'vɜːs] *adj* verschieden

diversion [daɪ'vɜːʃən] *n* Ablenkung *f*; (*BRIT: AUT*) Umleitung *f*

diversity [daɪ'vɜːsɪtɪ] *n* Vielfalt *f*

divert [daɪ'vɜːt] *vt* ablenken; (*traffic*) umleiten

divide [dɪ'vaɪd] *vt* teilen ♦ *vi* sich teilen; ~**d highway** (*US*) *n* Schnellstraße *f*

divine [dɪ'vaɪn] *adj* göttlich

diving ['daɪvɪŋ] *n* (*SPORT*) Turmspringen *nt*; (*underwater ~*) Tauchen *nt*; ~ **board** *n* Sprungbrett *nt*

divinity [dɪ'vɪnɪtɪ] *n* Gottheit *f*; (*subject*) Religion *f*

division [dɪ'vɪʒən] *n* Teilung *f*; (*MIL*) Division *f*; (*part*) Abteilung *f*; (*in opinion*) Uneinigkeit *f*; (*BRIT: POL*) Abstimmung *f* durch Hammelsprung *f*

divorce [dɪ'vɔːs] *n* (*Ehe*)scheidung *f* ♦ *vt* scheiden; ~**d** *adj* geschieden; ~**e** [dɪvɔː'siː] *n* Geschiedene(r) *f(m)*

divulge [daɪ'vʌldʒ] *vt* preisgeben

DIY (*BRIT*) *n abbr* = **do-it-yourself**

dizzy ['dɪzɪ] *adj* schwindlig

DJ *n abbr* = **disc jockey**

DNA fingerprinting *n* genetische Fingerabdrücke *pl*

KEYWORD

do [duː] (*pt* **did**, *pp* **done**) *n* (*inf: party etc*) Fete *f*

♦ *aux vb* **1** (*in negative constructions and questions*): **I don't understand** ich verstehe nicht; **didn't you know?** wusstest du das nicht?; **what do you think?** was meinen Sie?

2 (*for emphasis, in polite phrases*): **she does seem rather tired** sie scheint wirklich sehr müde zu sein; **do sit down/help yourself** setzen Sie sich doch hin/greifen Sie doch zu

3 (*used to avoid repeating vb*): **she swims better than I do** sie schwimmt besser als ich; **she lives in Glasgow - so do I** sie wohnt in Glasgow - ich auch

4 (*in tag questions*): **you like him, don't you?** du magst ihn doch, oder?

♦ *vt* **1** (*carry out, perform etc*) tun, machen; **what are you doing tonight?** was machst du heute Abend?; **I've got nothing to do** ich habe nichts zu tun; **to do one's hair/ nails** sich die Haare/Nägel machen

2 (*AUT etc*) fahren

♦ *vi* **1** (*act, behave*): **do as I do** mach es wie ich

2 (*get on, fare*): **he's doing well/badly at school** er ist gut/schlecht in der Schule; **how do you do?** guten Tag

3 (*be suitable*) gehen; (*be sufficient*) reichen; **to make do (with)** auskommen mit

do away with *vt* (*kill*) umbringen; (*abolish: law etc*) abschaffen

do up *vt* (*laces, dress, buttons*) zumachen; (*room, house*) renovieren

do with *vt* (*need*) brauchen; (*be connected*) zu tun haben mit

do without *vt, vi* auskommen ohne

docile ['dəusaɪl] *adj* gefügig

dock [dɔk] *n* Dock *nt*; (*JUR*) Anklagebank *f* ♦ *vi* ins Dock gehen; ~**er** *n* Hafenarbeiter *m*; ~**yard** *n* Werft *f*

doctor ['dɔktər] n Arzt m, Ärztin f; (UNIV) Doktor m ♦ vt (fig) fälschen; (drink etc) etw beimischen +dat; D~ of Philosophy n Doktor m der Philosophie

document ['dɔkjumənt] n Dokument nt; ~ary [dɔkju'mentəri] n Dokumentarbericht m; (film) Dokumentarfilm m ♦ adj dokumentarisch; ~ation [dɔkjumən'teɪʃən] n dokumentarische(r) Nachweis m

dodge [dɔdʒ] n Kniff m ♦ vt ausweichen +dat

dodgems ['dɔdʒəmz] (BRIT) npl Autoskooter m

doe [dəu] n (roe deer) Ricke f; (red deer) Hirschkuh f; (rabbit) Weibchen nt

does [dʌz] vb see **do**; ~n't = **does not**

dog [dɔg] n Hund m; ~ **collar** n Hundehalsband nt; (ECCL) Kragen m des Geistlichen; ~-eared adj mit Eselsohren

dogged ['dɔgɪd] adj hartnäckig

dogsbody ['dɔgzbɔdɪ] n Mädchen nt für alles

doings ['duːɪŋz] npl (activities) Treiben nt

do-it-yourself ['duːɪtjɔː'self] n Do-it-yourself nt

doldrums ['dɔldrəmz] npl: **to be in the ~** (business) Flaute haben; (person) deprimiert sein

dole [dəul] (BRIT) n Stempelgeld nt; **to be on the ~** stempeln gehen; ~ **out** vt ausgeben, austeilen

doleful ['dəulful] adj traurig

doll [dɔl] n Puppe f ♦ vt: **to ~ o.s. up** sich aufdonnern

dollar ['dɔlər] n Dollar m

dolphin ['dɔlfɪn] n Delfin m, Delphin m

dome [dəum] n Kuppel f

domestic [də'mestɪk] adj häuslich; (within country) Innen-, Binnen-; (animal) Haus-; ~ated adj (person) häuslich; (animal) zahm

dominant ['dɔmɪnənt] adj vorherrschend

dominate ['dɔmɪneɪt] vt beherrschen

domineering [dɔmɪ'nɪərɪŋ] adj herrisch

dominion [də'mɪnɪən] n (rule) Regierungsgewalt f; (land) Staatsgebiet nt mit Selbstverwaltung

domino ['dɔmɪnəu] (pl **-es**) n Dominostein m; ~es n (game) Domino(spiel) nt

don [dɔn] (BRIT) n akademische(r) Lehrer m

donate [də'neɪt] vt (blood, money) spenden; (lot of money) stiften; **donation** [də'neɪʃən] n Spende f

done [dʌn] pp of **do**

donkey ['dɔŋkɪ] n Esel m

donor ['dəunər] n Spender m; ~ **card** n Organspenderausweis m

don't [dəunt] = **do not**

doodle ['duːdl] vi kritzeln

doom [duːm] n böse(s) Geschick nt; (downfall) Verderben nt ♦ vt: **to be ~ed** zum Untergang verurteilt sein; ~sday n der Jüngste Tag

door [dɔːr] n Tür f; ~bell n Türklingel f; ~ **handle** n Türklinke f; ~man (irreg) n Türsteher m; ~mat n Fußmatte f; ~step n Türstufe f; ~way n Türöffnung f

dope [dəup] n (drug) Aufputschmittel nt ♦ vt (horse) dopen

dopey ['dəupɪ] (inf) adj bekloppt

dormant ['dɔːmənt] adj latent

dormitory ['dɔːmɪtrɪ] n Schlafsaal m

dormouse ['dɔːmaus] (pl **-mice**) n Haselmaus f

DOS [dɔs] n abbr (= disk operating system) DOS nt

dosage ['dəusɪdʒ] n Dosierung f

dose [dəus] n Dosis f

dosh [dɔʃ] (inf) n (money) Moos nt, Knete f

doss house ['dɔs-] (BRIT) n Bleibe f

dot [dɔt] n Punkt m; ~ted with übersät mit; **on the ~** pünktlich

dote [dəut]: **to ~ on** vt fus vernarrt sein in +acc

dotted line ['dɔtɪd-] n punktierte Linie f

double ['dʌbl] adj, adv doppelt ♦ n Doppelgänger m ♦ vt verdoppeln ♦ vi sich verdoppeln; ~s npl (TENNIS) Doppel nt; **on** or **at the ~** im Laufschritt; ~ **bass** n Kontrabass m; ~ **bed** n Doppelbett nt; ~ **bend** (BRIT) n S-Kurve f; ~-breasted adj zweireihig; ~-cross vt hintergehen; ~-decker n Doppeldecker m; ~ **glazing** (BRIT) n Doppelverglasung f; ~ **room** n Doppelzimmer nt

doubly ['dʌblɪ] adv doppelt

ubt [daut] n Zweifel m ♦ vt bezweifeln; **~ful** adj zweifelhaft; **~less** adv ohne Zweifel

ugh [dəu] n Teig m; **~nut** n Berliner m

use [dauz] vt (drench) mit Wasser begießen, durchtränken; (extinguish) ausmachen

ve [dʌv] n Taube f

vetail ['dʌvteɪl] vi (plans) übereinstimmen

wdy ['daudɪ] adj unmodern

wn [daun] n (fluff) Flaum m; (hill) Hügel m ♦ adv unten; (motion) herunter; hinunter ♦ prep: **to go ~ the street** die Straße hinuntergehen ♦ vt niederschlagen; **~ with X!** nieder mit X!; **~-and-out** n Tramp m; **~-at-heel** adj schäbig; **~cast** adj niedergeschlagen; **~fall** n Sturz m; **~hearted** adj niedergeschlagen; **~hill** adv ergab; **~ payment** n Anzahlung f; **~pour** n Platzregen m; **~right** adj ausgesprochen; **~size** vi (ECON: company) sich verkleinern

---

Downing Street ist die Straße in London, die von Whitehall zum St James Park führt und in der sich der offizielle Wohnsitz des Premierministers (Nr. 10) und des Finanzministers (Nr. 11) befindet. Im weiteren Sinne bezieht sich der Begriff Downing Street auf die britische Regierung.

---

own's syndrome [daunz-] n (MED) Down-Syndrom nt

own: **~stairs** adv unten; (motion) nach unten; **~stream** adv flussabwärts; **~-to-earth** adj praktisch; **~town** adv in der Innenstadt; (motion) in die Innenstadt; **~ under** (BRIT: inf) adv in/nach Australien/Neuseeland; **~ward** adj Abwärts-, nach unten ♦ adv abwärts, nach unten; **~wards** adv abwärts, nach unten

owry ['dauɪ] n Mitgift f

oz. abbr (= dozen) Dtzd.

oze [dəuz] vi dösen; **~ off** vi einnicken

ozen ['dʌzn] n Dutzend nt; **a ~ books** ein Dutzend Bücher; **~s of** dutzende or Dutzende von

Dr. abbr = **doctor**; **drive**

drab [dræb] adj düster, eintönig

draft [drɑːft] n Entwurf m; (FIN) Wechsel m; (US: MIL) Einberufung f ♦ vt skizzieren; see also **draught**

draftsman ['drɑːftsmən] (US: irreg) n = **draughtsman**

drag [dræg] vt schleppen; (river) mit einem Schleppnetz absuchen ♦ vi sich (dahin)schleppen ♦ n (bore) etwas Blödes; **in ~** als Tunte; **a man in ~** eine Tunte; **~ on** vi sich in die Länge ziehen; **~ and drop** vt (COMPUT) Drag & Drop nt

dragon ['drægn] n Drache m; **~fly** ['drægənflaɪ] n Libelle f

drain [dreɪn] n Abfluss m; (fig: burden) Belastung f ♦ vt ableiten; (exhaust) erschöpfen ♦ vi (of water) abfließen; **~age** n Kanalisation f; **~ing board** (US **~board**) n Ablaufbrett nt; **~pipe** n Abflussrohr nt

dram [dræm] n Schluck m

drama ['drɑːmə] n Drama nt; **~tic** [drə'mætɪk] adj dramatisch; **~tist** ['dræmətɪst] n Dramatiker m; **~tize** ['dræmətaɪz] vt (events) dramatisieren; (for TV etc) bearbeiten

drank [dræŋk] pt of **drink**

drape [dreɪp] vt drapieren; **~s** (US) npl Vorhänge pl

drastic ['dræstɪk] adj drastisch

draught [drɑːft] (US **draft**) n Zug m; (NAUT) Tiefgang m; **~s** n Damespiel nt; **on ~** (beer) vom Fass; **~ beer** n Bier nt vom Fass; **~board** (BRIT) n Zeichenbrett nt

draughtsman ['drɑːftsmən] (irreg) n technische(r) Zeichner m

draw [drɔː] (pt **drew**, pp **drew**) vt ziehen; (crowd) anlocken; (picture) zeichnen; (money) abheben; (water) schöpfen ♦ vi (SPORT) unentschieden spielen ♦ n (SPORT) Unentschieden nt; (lottery) Ziehung f; **~ near** vi näher rücken; **~ out** vi (train) ausfahren; (lengthen) sich hinziehen; **~ up** vi (stop) halten ♦ vt (document) aufsetzen

drawback ['drɔːbæk] n Nachteil m

drawbridge ['drɔːbrɪdʒ] n Zugbrücke f

drawer [drɔːʳ] *n* Schublade *f*

drawing ['drɔːɪŋ] *n* Zeichnung *f*; Zeichnen *nt*; ~ **board** *n* Reißbrett *nt*; ~ **pin** *(BRIT) n* Reißzwecke *f*; ~ **room** *n* Salon *m*

drawl [drɔːl] *n* schleppende Sprechweise *f*

drawn [drɔːn] *pp of* **draw**

dread [drɛd] *n* Furcht *f* ♦ *vt* fürchten; ~**ful** *adj* furchtbar

dream [driːm] *(pt, pp* **dreamed** *or* **dreamt)** *n* Traum *m* ♦ *vt* träumen ♦ *vi*: **to ~ (about)** träumen (von); ~**er** *n* Träumer *m*; ~**t** [drɛmt] *pt, pp of* **dream**; ~**y** *adj* verträumt

dreary ['drɪərɪ] *adj* trostlos, öde

dredge [drɛdʒ] *vt* ausbaggern

dregs [drɛgz] *npl* Bodensatz *m*; *(fig)* Abschaum *m*

drench [drɛntʃ] *vt* durchnässen

dress [drɛs] *n* Kleidung *f*; *(garment)* Kleid *nt* ♦ *vt* anziehen; *(MED)* verbinden; **to get ~ed** sich anziehen; ~ **up** *vi* sich fein machen; ~ **circle** *(BRIT) n* erste(r) Rang *m*; ~**er** *n (furniture)* Anrichte *f*; ~**ing** *n (MED)* Verband *m*; *(COOK)* Soße *f*; ~**ing gown** *(BRIT) n* Morgenrock *m*; ~**ing room** *n (THEAT)* Garderobe *f*; *(SPORT)* Umkleideraum *m*; ~**ing table** *n* Toilettentisch *m*; ~**maker** *n* Schneiderin *f*; ~ **rehearsal** *n* Generalprobe *f*

drew [druː] *pt of* **draw**

dribble ['drɪbl] *vi* sabbern ♦ *vt (ball)* dribbeln

dried [draɪd] *adj* getrocknet; *(fruit)* Dörr-, gedörrte(r, s); ~ **milk** *n* Milchpulver *nt*

drier ['draɪəʳ] *n* = **dryer**

drift [drɪft] *n* Strömung *f*; *(snowdrift)* Schneewehe *f*; *(fig)* Richtung *f* ♦ *vi* sich treiben lassen; ~**wood** *n* Treibholz *nt*

drill [drɪl] *n* Bohrer *m*; *(MIL)* Drill *m* ♦ *vt* bohren; *(MIL)* ausbilden ♦ *vi*: **to ~ (for)** bohren (nach)

drink [drɪŋk] *(pt* **drank**, *pp* **drunk)** *n* Getränk *nt*; *(spirits)* Drink *m* ♦ *vt, vi* trinken; **to have a ~** etwas trinken; ~**er** *n* Trinker *m*; ~**ing water** *n* Trinkwasser *nt*

drip [drɪp] *n* Tropfen *m* ♦ *vi* tropfen; ~**-dry** *adj* bügelfrei; ~**ping** *n* Bratenfett *nt*

drive [draɪv] *(pt* **drove**, *pp* **driven)** *n* Fahrt *f*; *(road)* Einfahrt *f*; *(campaign)* Aktion *f*; *(energy)* Schwung *m*; *(SPORT)* Schlag *m*;

(also: **disk ~)** Diskettenlaufwerk *nt* ♦ *vt (car)* fahren; *(animals, people, objects)* treiben; *(power)* antreiben ♦ *vi* fahren; **left-/right-hand ~** Links-/Rechtssteuerung *f*; **to ~ sb mad** jdn verrückt machen; ~**-by shooting** *n* Schusswaffenangriff *m* aus einem *vorbeifahrenden Wagen*

drivel ['drɪvl] *n* Faselei *f*

driven ['drɪvn] *pp of* **drive**

driver ['draɪvəʳ] *n* Fahrer *m*; ~**'s license** *(US) n* Führerschein *m*

driveway ['draɪvweɪ] *n* Auffahrt *f*; *(longer)* Zufahrtsstraße *f*

driving ['draɪvɪŋ] *adj (rain)* stürmisch; ~ **instructor** *n* Fahrlehrer *m*; ~ **lesson** *n* Fahrstunde *f*; ~ **licence** *(BRIT) n* Führerschein *m*; ~ **school** *n* Fahrschule *f*; ~ **test** *n* Fahrprüfung *f*

drizzle ['drɪzl] *n* Nieselregen *m* ♦ *vi* nieseln

droll [drəul] *adj* drollig

drone [drəun] *n (sound)* Brummen *nt*; *(bee)* Drohne *f*

drool [druːl] *vi* sabbern

droop [druːp] *vi (schlaff)* herabhängen

drop [drɔp] *n (of liquid)* Tropfen *m*; *(fall)* Fall *m* ♦ *vt* fallen lassen; *(lower)* senken; *(abandon)* fallen lassen ♦ *vi (fall)* herunterfallen; ~**s** *npl (MED)* Tropfen *pl*; ~ **off** *vi (sleep)* einschlafen ♦ *vt (passenger)* absetzen; ~ **out** *vi (withdraw)* ausscheiden; ~**-out** *n* Aussteiger *m*; ~**per** *n* Pipette *f*; ~**pings** *npl* Kot *m*

drought [draut] *n* Dürre *f*

drove [drəuv] *pt of* **drive**

drown [draun] *vt* ertränken; *(sound)* übertönen ♦ *vi* ertrinken

drowsy ['drauzɪ] *adj* schläfrig

drudgery ['drʌdʒərɪ] *n* Plackerei *f*

drug [drʌg] *n (MED)* Arznei *f*; *(narcotic)* Rauschgift *nt* ♦ *vt* betäuben; ~ **addict** *n* Rauschgiftsüchtige(r) *f(m)*; ~**gist** *(US) n* Drogist(in) *m(f)*; ~**store** *(US) n* Drogerie *f*

drum [drʌm] *n* Trommel *f* ♦ *vi* trommeln; ~**s** *npl (MUS)* Schlagzeug *nt*; ~**mer** *n* Trommler *m*

drunk [drʌŋk] *pp of* **drink** ♦ *adj* betrunken ♦ *n (also:* ~**ard)** Trinker(in) *m(f)*; ~**en** *adj* etrunken

y [draɪ] *adj* trocken ♦ *vt* (ab)trocknen ♦ *vi*
rocknen; **~ up** *vi* austrocknen ♦ *vt* (*dishes*)
btrocknen; **~ cleaner's** *n* chemische
einigung *f*; **~ cleaning** *n* chemische
einigung *f*; **~er** *n* Trockner *m*; (*US: spin-
ryer*) (Wäsche)schleuder *f*; **~ goods store**
US) *n* Kurzwarengeschäft *nt*; **~ness** *n*
rockenheit *f*; **~ rot** *n* Hausschwamm *m*
S (*BRIT*) *n abbr* (= *Department of Social
ecurity*) ≈ Sozialministerium *nt*
P *n abbr* (= *desktop publishing*) DTP *nt*
al ['dʒuəl] *adj* doppelt; **~ carriageway**
BRIT) *n* zweispurige Fahrbahn *f*; **~
ationality** *n* doppelte Staatsangehörigkeit
; **~-purpose** *adj* Mehrzweck-
bbed [dʌbd] *adj* (*film*) synchronisiert
bious ['dʒuːbɪəs] *adj* zweifelhaft
chess ['dʌtʃɪs] *n* Herzogin *f*
ck [dʌk] *n* Ente *f* ♦ *vi* sich ducken; **~ling** *n*
ntchen *nt*
ct [dʌkt] *n* Röhre *f*
d [dʌd] *n* Niete *f* ♦ *adj* (*cheque*) ungedeckt
e [dʒuː] *adj* fällig; (*fitting*) angemessen ♦ *n*
Gebühr *f*; (*right*) Recht *nt* ♦ *adv* (*south etc*)
jenau; **~s** *npl* (*for club*) Beitrag *m*; (*NAUT*)
Gebühren *pl*; **~ to** wegen +*gen*
el ['dʒuəl] *n* Duell *nt*
et [dʒuː'et] *n* Duett *nt*
ffel ['dʌfl] *adj*: **~ bag** Matchbeutel *m*,
Matchsack *m*
g [dʌg] *pt, pp of* **dig**
ke [dʒuːk] *n* Herzog *m*
ll [dʌl] *adj* (*colour, weather*) trübe; (*stupid*)
chwer von Begriff; (*boring*) langweilig ♦ *vt*
abstumpfen
ly ['dʒuːlɪ] *adv* ordnungsgemäß
mb [dʌm] *adj* stumm; (*inf: stupid*) doof,
blöde; **~founded** [dʌm'faundɪd] *adj*
verblüfft
mmy ['dʌmɪ] *n* Schneiderpuppe *f*;
(*substitute*) Attrappe *f*; (*BRIT: for baby*)
Schnuller *m* ♦ *adj* Schein-
mp [dʌmp] *n* Abfallhaufen *m*; (*MIL*)
Stapelplatz *m*; (*inf: place*) Nest *nt* ♦ *vt*
abladen, auskippen; **~ing** *n* (*COMM*)
Schleuderexport *m*; (*of rubbish*)

Schuttabladen *nt*
dumpling ['dʌmplɪŋ] *n* Kloß *m*, Knödel *m*
dumpy ['dʌmpɪ] *adj* pummelig
dunce [dʌns] *n* Dummkopf *m*
dune [dʒuːn] *n* Düne *f*
dung [dʌŋ] *n* Dünger *m*
dungarees [dʌŋgə'riːz] *npl* Latzhose *f*
dungeon ['dʌndʒən] *n* Kerker *m*
dupe [dʒuːp] *n* Gefoppte(r) *f(m)* ♦ *vt*
hintergehen, anführen
duplex ['dʒuːpleks] (*US*) *n* zweistöckige
Wohnung *f*
duplicate [*n* 'dʒuːplɪkət, *vb* 'dʒuːplɪkeɪt] *n*
Duplikat *nt* ♦ *vt* verdoppeln; (*make copies*)
kopieren; **in ~** in doppelter Ausführung
duplicity [dʒuː'plɪsɪtɪ] *n* Doppelspiel *nt*
durable ['dʒuərəbl] *adj* haltbar
duration [dʒuə'reɪʃən] *n* Dauer *f*
duress [dʒuə'res] *n*: **under ~** unter Zwang
during ['dʒuərɪŋ] *prep* während +*gen*
dusk [dʌsk] *n* Abenddämmerung *f*
dust [dʌst] *n* Staub *m* ♦ *vt* abstauben;
(*sprinkle*) bestäuben; **~bin** (*BRIT*) *n*
Mülleimer *m*; **~er** *n* Staubtuch *nt*; **~ jacket**
n Schutzumschlag *m*; **~man** (*BRIT: irreg*) *n*
Müllmann *m*; **~y** *adj* staubig
Dutch [dʌtʃ] *adj* holländisch, niederländisch
♦ *n* (*LING*) Holländisch *nt*, Niederländisch
nt; **the ~** *npl* (*people*) die Holländer *pl*, die
Niederländer *pl*; **to go ~** getrennte Kasse
machen; **~man/woman** (*irreg*) *n*
Holländer(in) *m(f)*, Niederländer(in) *m(f)*
dutiful ['dʒuːtɪful] *adj* pflichtbewusst
duty ['dʒuːtɪ] *n* Pflicht *f*; (*job*) Aufgabe *f*; (*tax*)
Einfuhrzoll *m*; **on ~** im Dienst; **~
chemist's** *n* Apotheke *f* im
Bereitschaftsdienst; **~-free** *adj* zollfrei
duvet ['duːveɪ] (*BRIT*) *n* Daunendecke *nt*
DVD *n abbr* (= *digital video disc*) DVD *f*
dwarf [dwɔːf] (*pl* **dwarves**) *n* Zwerg *m* ♦ *vt*
überragen
dwell [dwel] (*pt, pp* **dwelt**) *vi* wohnen; **~ on**
vt fus verweilen bei; **~ing** *n* Wohnung *f*
dwelt [dwelt] *pt, pp of* **dwell**
dwindle ['dwɪndl] *vi* schwinden
dye [daɪ] *n* Farbstoff *m* ♦ *vt* färben
dying ['daɪɪŋ] *adj* (*person*) sterbend;

(*moments*) letzt

dyke [daɪk] (*BRIT*) n (*channel*) Kanal m; (*barrier*) Deich m, Damm m

dynamic [daɪˈnæmɪk] adj dynamisch

dynamite [ˈdaɪnəmaɪt] n Dynamit nt

dyslexia [dɪsˈleksɪə] n Legasthenie f

E, e

E [iː] n (*MUS*) E nt

each [iːtʃ] adj jeder/jede/jedes ♦ pron (ein) jeder/(eine) jede/(ein) jedes; **~ other** einander, sich; **they have two books ~** sie haben je zwei Bücher

eager [ˈiːgəʳ] adj eifrig

eagle [ˈiːgl] n Adler m

ear [ɪəʳ] n Ohr nt; (*of corn*) Ähre f; **~ache** n Ohrenschmerzen pl; **~drum** n Trommelfell nt

earl [əːl] n Graf m

earlier [ˈəːlɪəʳ] adj, adv früher; **I can't come any ~** ich kann nicht früher or eher kommen

early [ˈəːlɪ] adj, adv früh; **~ retirement** n vorzeitige Pensionierung

earmark [ˈɪəmɑːk] vt vorsehen

earn [əːn] vt verdienen

earnest [ˈəːnɪst] adj ernst; **in ~** im Ernst

earnings [ˈəːnɪŋz] npl Verdienst m

ear: ~phones [ˈɪəfəunz] npl Kopfhörer pl; **~ring** [ˈɪərɪŋ] n Ohrring m; **~shot** [ˈɪəʃɔt] n Hörweite f

earth [əːθ] n Erde f; (*BRIT*: *ELEC*) Erdung f ♦ vt erden; **~enware** n Steingut nt; **~quake** n Erdbeben nt; **~y** adj roh

earwig [ˈɪəwɪg] n Ohrwurm m

ease [iːz] n (*simplicity*) Leichtigkeit f; (*social*) Ungezwungenheit f ♦ vt (*pain*) lindern; (*burden*) erleichtern; **at ~** ungezwungen; (*MIL*) rührt euch!; **~ off** or **up** vi nachlassen

easel [ˈiːzl] n Staffelei f

easily [ˈiːzɪlɪ] adv leicht

east [iːst] n Osten m ♦ adj östlich ♦ adv nach Osten

Easter [ˈiːstəʳ] n Ostern nt; **~ egg** n Osterei

nt

east: ~erly adj östlich, Ost-; **~ern** adj östlich; **~ward(s)** adv ostwärts

easy [ˈiːzɪ] adj (*task*) einfach; (*life*) bequem; (*manner*) ungezwungen, natürlich ♦ adv leicht; **~ chair** n Sessel m; **~-going** adj gelassen; (*lax*) lässig

eat [iːt] (*pt* **ate**, *pp* **eaten**) vt essen; (*animals*) fressen; (*destroy*) (zer)fressen ♦ vi essen; fressen; **~ away** vt zerfressen; **~ into** vt *fus* zerfressen; **~en** *pp* of **eat**

eau de Cologne [ˈəudəkəˈləun] n Kölnischwasser nt

eaves [iːvz] npl Dachrand m

eavesdrop [ˈiːvzdrɔp] vi lauschen; **to ~ on sb** jdn belauschen

ebb [eb] n Ebbe f ♦ vi (*fig*: *also*: **~ away**) (ab)ebben

ebony [ˈebənɪ] n Ebenholz nt

EC n abbr (= *European Community*) EG f

ECB n abbr (= *European Central Bank*) EZB f

eccentric [ɪkˈsentrɪk] adj exzentrisch ♦ n Exzentriker(in) m(f)

ecclesiastical [ɪkliːzɪˈæstɪkl] adj kirchlich

echo [ˈekəu] (*pl* **~es**) n Echo nt ♦ vt zurückwerfen; (*fig*) nachbeten ♦ vi widerhallen

eclipse [ɪˈklɪps] n Finsternis f ♦ vt verfinstern

ecology [ɪˈkɔlədʒɪ] n Ökologie f

e-commerce [ˈiːkɔməːs] n Onlinehandel m

economic [iːkəˈnɔmɪk] adj wirtschaftlich; **~al** adj wirtschaftlich; (*person*) sparsam; **~ refugee** n Wirtschaftsflüchtling m; **~s** n Volkswirtschaft f

economist [ɪˈkɔnəmɪst] n Volkswirt(schaftler) m

economize [ɪˈkɔnəmaɪz] vi sparen

economy [ɪˈkɔnəmɪ] n (*thrift*) Sparsamkeit f; (*of country*) Wirtschaft f; **~ class** n Touristenklasse f

ecstasy [ˈekstəsɪ] n Ekstase f; (*drug*) Ecstasy nt; **ecstatic** [eksˈtætɪk] adj hingerissen

ECU [ˈeɪkjuː] n abbr (= *European Currency Unit*) ECU m

eczema [ˈeksɪmə] n Ekzem nt

edge [edʒ] n Rand m; (*of knife*) Schneide f ♦ vt (*SEWING*) einfassen; **on ~** (*fig*) = **edgy**;

to ~ away from langsam abrücken von;
~ways *adv*: **he couldn't get a word in
~ways** er kam überhaupt nicht zu Wort

lgy ['edʒɪ] *adj* nervös

lible ['edɪbl] *adj* essbar

lict ['iːdɪkt] *n* Erlass *m*

lit ['edɪt] *vt* redigieren; **~ion** [ɪ'dɪʃən] *n*
Ausgabe *f*; **~or** *n* (*of newspaper*) Redakteur
m; (*of book*) Lektor *m*; **~orial** [edɪ'tɔːrɪəl] *adj*
Redaktions- **♦** *n* Leitartikel *m*

lucate ['edjukeɪt] *vt* erziehen, (aus)bilden;
~d *adj* gebildet; **education** [edju'keɪʃən] *n*
(*teaching*) Unterricht *m*; (*system*)
Schulwesen *nt*; (*schooling*) Erziehung *f*;
Bildung *f*; **educational** *adj* pädagogisch

~l [iːl] *n* Aal *m*

rie ['ɪərɪ] *adj* unheimlich

fect [ɪ'fekt] *n* Wirkung *f* **♦** *vt* bewirken; **~s**
npl (*sound, visual*) Effekte *pl*; **in ~** in der Tat;
to take ~ (*law*) in Kraft treten; (*drug*)
wirken; **~ive** *adj* wirksam, effektiv; **~ively**
adv wirksam, effektiv

feminate [ɪ'femɪnɪt] *adj* weibisch

fervescent [efə'vesnt] *adj* (*also fig*)
sprudelnd

ficiency [ɪ'fɪʃənsɪ] *n* Leistungsfähigkeit *f*

ficient [ɪ'fɪʃənt] *adj* tüchtig; (*TECH*)
leistungsfähig; (*method*) wirksam

figy ['efɪdʒɪ] *n* Abbild *nt*

fort ['efət] *n* Anstrengung *f*; **~less** *adj*
mühelos

fusive [ɪ'fjuːsɪv] *adj* überschwänglich

g. *adv abbr* (= *exempli gratia*) z. B.

galitarian [ɪgælɪ'teərɪən] *adj* Gleichheits-,
egalitär

lg [eg] *n* Ei *nt*; **~ on** *vt* anstacheln; **~cup** *n*
Eierbecher *m*; **~plant** (*esp US*) *n* Aubergine
f; **~shell** *n* Eierschale *f*

lo ['iːgəu] *n* Ich *nt*, Selbst *nt*; **~tism**
['egəutɪzəm] *n* Ichbezogenheit *f*; **~tist**
['egəutɪst] *n* Egozentriker *m*

lypt ['iːdʒɪpt] *n* Ägypten *nt*; **~ian** [ɪ'dʒɪpʃən]
adj ägyptisch **♦** *n* Ägypter(in) *m(f)*

derdown ['aɪdədaun] *n* Daunendecke *f*

ght [eɪt] *num* acht; **~een** *num* achtzehn;
~h [eɪtθ] *adj* achte(r, s) **♦** *n* Achtel *nt*; **~y**
num achtzig

Eire ['eərə] *n* Irland *nt*

either ['aɪðə] *conj*: **~ ... or** entweder ... oder
♦ *pron*: **~ of the two** eine(r, s) von beiden
♦ *adj*: **on ~ side** auf beiden Seiten **♦** *adv*: **I
don't ~** ich auch nicht; **I don't want ~** ich
will keins von beiden

eject [ɪ'dʒekt] *vt* ausstoßen, vertreiben

eke [iːk] *vt*: **to ~ out** strecken

elaborate [*adj* ɪ'læbərɪt, *vb* ɪ'læbəreɪt] *adj*
sorgfältig ausgearbeitet, ausführlich **♦** *vt*
sorgfältig ausarbeiten **♦** *vi* ausführlich
darstellen

elapse [ɪ'læps] *vi* vergehen

elastic [ɪ'læstɪk] *n* Gummiband *nt* **♦** *adj*
elastisch; **~ band** (*BRIT*) *n* Gummiband *nt*

elated [ɪ'leɪtɪd] *adj* froh

elation [ɪ'leɪʃən] *n* gehobene Stimmung *f*

elbow ['elbəu] *n* Ellbogen *m*

elder ['eldə] *adj* älter **♦** *n* Ältere(r) *f(m)*; **~ly**
adj ältere(r, s) **♦** *npl*: **the ~ly** die Älteren *pl*;
eldest ['eldɪst] *adj* älteste(r, s) **♦** *n* Älteste(r)
f(m)

elect [ɪ'lekt] *vt* wählen **♦** *adj* zukünftig; **~ion**
[ɪ'lekʃən] *n* Wahl *f*; **~ioneering** [ɪlekʃə'nɪərɪŋ]
n Wahlpropaganda *f*; **~or** *n* Wähler *m*;
~oral *adj* Wahl-; **~orate** *n* Wähler *pl*,
Wählerschaft *f*

electric [ɪ'lektrɪk] *adj* elektrisch, Elektro-; **~al**
adj elektrisch; **~ blanket** *n* Heizdecke *f*; **~
chair** *n* elektrische(r) Stuhl *m*; **~ fire** *n*
elektrische(r) Heizofen *m*

electrician [ɪlek'trɪʃən] *n* Elektriker *m*

electricity [ɪlek'trɪsɪtɪ] *n* Elektrizität *f*

electrify [ɪ'lektrɪfaɪ] *vt* elektrifizieren; (*fig*)
elektrisieren

electrocute [ɪ'lektrəkjuːt] *vt* durch
elektrischen Strom töten

electronic [ɪlek'trɒnɪk] *adj* elektronisch,
Elektronen-; **~ mail** *n* E-Mail *f*; **~s** *n*
Elektronik *f*

elegance ['elɪgəns] *n* Eleganz *f*; **elegant**
['elɪgənt] *adj* elegant

element ['elɪmənt] *n* Element *nt*; **~ary**
[elɪ'mentərɪ] *adj* einfach; (*primary*) Grund-

elephant ['elɪfənt] *n* Elefant *m*

elevate ['elɪveɪt] *vt* emporheben; **elevation**
[elɪ'veɪʃən] *n* (*height*) Erhebung *f*; (*ARCHIT*)

(Quer)schnitt m; **elevator** (*US*) n Fahrstuhl m, Aufzug m

eleven [ɪ'lɛvn] num elf; **~ses** (*BRIT*) npl ≃ zweite(s) Frühstück nt; **~th** adj elfte(r, s)

elicit [ɪ'lɪsɪt] vt herausbekommen

eligible ['ɛlɪdʒəbl] adj wählbar; **to be ~ for a pension** pensionsberechtigt sein

eliminate [ɪ'lɪmɪneɪt] vt ausschalten

elite [eɪ'liːt] n Elite f

elm [ɛlm] n Ulme f

elocution [ɛlə'kjuːʃən] n Sprecherziehung f

elongated ['iːlɒŋɡeɪtɪd] adj verlängert

elope [ɪ'ləup] vi entlaufen

eloquence ['ɛləkwəns] n Beredsamkeit f; **eloquent** adj redegewandt

else [ɛls] adv sonst; **who ~?** wer sonst?; **somebody ~** jemand anders; **or ~** sonst; **~where** adv anderswo, woanders

elude [ɪ'luːd] vt entgehen +dat

elusive [ɪ'luːsɪv] adj schwer fassbar

emaciated [ɪ'meɪsɪeɪtɪd] adj abgezehrt

e-mail ['iːmeɪl] n abbr (= electronic mail) E-Mail f ♦ vti mailen

emancipation [ɪmænsɪ'peɪʃən] n Emanzipation f; Freilassung f

embankment [ɪm'bæŋkmənt] n (of river) Uferböschung f; (of road) Straßendamm m

embargo [ɪm'bɑːɡəu] (pl **~es**) n Embargo nt

embark [ɪm'bɑːk] vi sich einschiffen; **~ on** vt fus unternehmen; **~ation** [ɛmbɑː'keɪʃən] n Einschiffung f

embarrass [ɪm'bærəs] vt in Verlegenheit bringen; **~ed** adj verlegen; **~ing** adj peinlich; **~ment** n Verlegenheit f

embassy ['ɛmbəsɪ] n Botschaft f

embed [ɪm'bed] vt einbetten

embellish [ɪm'belɪʃ] vt verschönern

embers ['ɛmbəz] npl Glut(asche) f

embezzle [ɪm'bezl] vt unterschlagen; **~ment** n Unterschlagung f

embitter [ɪm'bɪtər] vt verbittern

embody [ɪm'bɒdɪ] vt (ideas) verkörpern; (new features) (in sich) vereinigen

embossed [ɪm'bɒst] adj geprägt

embrace [ɪm'breɪs] vt umarmen; (include) einschließen ♦ vi sich umarmen ♦ n Umarmung f

embroider [ɪm'brɔɪdər] vt (be)sticken; (story) ausschmücken; **~y** n Stickerei f

emerald ['ɛmərəld] n Smaragd m

emerge [ɪ'mɜːdʒ] vi auftauchen; (truth) herauskommen; **~nce** n Erscheinen nt

emergency [ɪ'mɜːdʒənsɪ] n Notfall m; **~ cord** (*US*) n Notbremse f; **~ exit** n Notausgang m; **~ landing** n Notlandung f; **~ services** npl Notdienste pl

emery board ['ɛmərɪ-] n Papiernagelfeile f

emigrant ['ɛmɪɡrənt] n Auswanderer m

emigrate ['ɛmɪɡreɪt] vi auswandern; **emigration** [ɛmɪ'ɡreɪʃən] n Auswanderung f

eminence ['ɛmɪnəns] n hohe(r) Rang m

eminent ['ɛmɪnənt] adj bedeutend

emission [ɪ'mɪʃən] n Ausströmen nt; **~s** npl Emissionen fpl

emit [ɪ'mɪt] vt von sich dat geben

emotion [ɪ'məuʃən] n Emotion f, Gefühl nt; **~al** adj (person) emotional; (scene) ergreifend

emotive [ɪ'məutɪv] adj gefühlsbetont

emperor ['ɛmpərər] n Kaiser m

emphases ['ɛmfəsiːz] npl of **emphasis**

emphasis ['ɛmfəsɪs] n (*LING*) Betonung f; (fig) Nachdruck m; **emphasize** ['ɛmfəsaɪz] vt betonen

emphatic [ɛm'fætɪk] adj nachdrücklich; **~ally** adv nachdrücklich

empire ['ɛmpaɪər] n Reich nt

empirical [ɛm'pɪrɪkl] adj empirisch

employ [ɪm'plɔɪ] vt (hire) anstellen; (use) verwenden; **~ee** [ɪmplɔɪ'iː] n Angestellte(r) f(m); **~er** n Arbeitgeber(in) m(f); **~ment** n Beschäftigung f; **~ment agency** n Stellenvermittlung f

empower [ɪm'pauər] vt: **to ~ sb to do sth** jdn ermächtigen, etw zu tun

empress ['ɛmprɪs] n Kaiserin f

emptiness ['ɛmptɪnɪs] n Leere f

empty ['ɛmptɪ] adj leer ♦ n (bottle) Leergut nt ♦ vt (contents) leeren; (container) ausleeren ♦ vi (water) abfließen; (river) münden; (house) sich leeren; **~-handed** adj mit leeren Händen

EMU ['iːmjuː] n abbr (= economic and monetary union) EWU f

ᵃulate ['emjʊleɪt] vt nacheifern +dat

ᵃulsion [ɪ'mʌlʃən] n Emulsion f

ᵃable [ɪ'neɪbl] vt: **to ~ sb to do sth** es jdm
ᵉrmöglichen, etw zu tun

ᵃact [ɪ'nækt] vt (law) erlassen; (play)
ᵃufführen; (role) spielen

ᵃamel [ɪ'næməl] n Email nt; (of teeth)
(Zahn)schmelz m

ᵃcased [ɪn'keɪst] adj: **~ in** (enclosed)
ᵃingeschlossen in +dat; (covered) verkleidet
ᵃit

ᵃchant [ɪn'tʃɑːnt] vt bezaubern; **~ing** adj
ᵉntzückend

ᵃcircle [ɪn'sɜːkl] vt umringen

ᵃcl. abbr (= enclosed) Anl.

ᵃclose [ɪn'kləʊz] vt einschließen; **to ~ sth
ᵃin or with a letter)** etw (einem Brief)
ᵇeilegen; **~d** (in letter) beiliegend, anbei;

ᵃnclosure [ɪn'kləʊʒəʳ] n Einfriedung f; (in
ᵉtter) Anlage f

ᵃcompass [ɪn'kʌmpəs] vt (include)
ᵃmfassen

ᵃcore [ɒŋ'kɔːʳ] n Zugabe f

ᵃcounter [ɪn'kaʊntəʳ] n Begegnung f; (MIL)
Zusammenstoß m ♦ vt treffen; (resistance)
ᵗoßen auf +acc

ᵃcourage [ɪn'kʌrɪdʒ] vt ermutigen; **~ment**
ᶰ Ermutigung f, Förderung f;
ᵃncouraging adj ermutigend, viel
ᵛersprechend

ᵃcroach [ɪn'krəʊtʃ] vi: **to ~ (up)on**
ᵉindringen in +acc; (time) in Anspruch
ᵃehmen

ᵃcrusted [ɪn'krʌstɪd] adj: **~ with** besetzt
ᵃit

ᵃcyclop(a)edia [ensaɪkləʊ'piːdɪə] n
ᴷonversationslexikon nt

ᵃd [end] n Ende nt, Schluss m; (purpose)
ᶻweck m ♦ vt (also: **bring to an ~, put an ~
ᵗo**) beenden ♦ vi zu Ende gehen; **in the ~**
ᶻum Schluss; **on ~** (object) hochkant; **to
ᵃtand on ~** (hair) zu Berge stehen; **for
ᵃours on ~** stundenlang; **~ up** vi landen

ᵃdanger [ɪn'deɪndʒəʳ] vt gefährden; **~ed
ᵃpecies** n eine vom Aussterben bedrohte
ᴬrt

ᵃdearing [ɪn'dɪərɪŋ] adj gewinnend

endeavour [ɪn'devəʳ] (US **endeavor**) n
Bestrebung f ♦ vi sich bemühen

ending ['endɪŋ] n Ende nt

endless ['endlɪs] adj endlos

endorse [ɪn'dɔːs] vt unterzeichnen; (approve)
unterstützen; **~ment** n (AUT) Eintrag m

endow [ɪn'daʊ] vt: **to ~ sb with sth** jdm etw
verleihen; (with money) jdm etw stiften

endurance [ɪn'djʊərəns] n Ausdauer f

endure [ɪn'djʊəʳ] vt ertragen ♦ vi (last)
(fort)dauern

enemy ['enəmɪ] n Feind m ♦ adj feindlich

energetic [enə'dʒetɪk] adj tatkräftig

energy ['enədʒɪ] n Energie f

enforce [ɪn'fɔːs] vt durchsetzen

engage [ɪn'geɪdʒ] vt (employ) einstellen; (in
conversation) verwickeln; (TECH) einschalten
♦ vi (TECH) ineinander greifen; (clutch)
fassen; **to ~ in** sich beteiligen an +dat; **~d**
adj verlobt; (BRIT: TEL, toilet) besetzt; (: busy)
beschäftigt; **to get ~d** sich verloben; **~d
tone** (BRIT) n (TEL) Besetztzeichen nt;
~ment n (appointment) Verabredung f; (to
marry) Verlobung f; (MIL) Gefecht nt;
~ment ring n Verlobungsring m;
engaging adj gewinnend

engender [ɪn'dʒendəʳ] vt hervorrufen

engine ['endʒɪn] n (AUT) Motor m; (RAIL)
Lokomotive f; **~ driver** n
Lok(omotiv)führer(in) m(f)

engineer [endʒɪ'nɪəʳ] n Ingenieur m; (US:
RAIL) Lok(omotiv)führer(in) m(f); **~ing**
[endʒɪ'nɪərɪŋ] n Technik f

England ['ɪŋglənd] n England nt

English ['ɪŋglɪʃ] adj englisch ♦ n (LING)
Englisch nt; **the ~** npl (people) die
Engländer pl; **~ Channel** n: **the ~
Channel** der Ärmelkanal m; **~man /
woman** (irreg) n Engländer(in) m(f)

engraving [ɪn'greɪvɪŋ] n Stich m

engrossed [ɪn'grəʊst] adj vertieft

engulf [ɪn'gʌlf] vt verschlingen

enhance [ɪn'hɑːns] vt steigern, heben

enigma [ɪ'nɪgmə] n Rätsel nt; **~tic**
[enɪg'mætɪk] adj rätselhaft

enjoy [ɪn'dʒɔɪ] vt genießen; (privilege)
besitzen; **to ~ o.s.** sich amüsieren; **~able**

adj erfreulich; **~ment** *n* Genuss *m*, Freude *f*

enlarge [ɪn'lɑːdʒ] *vt* erweitern; (*PHOT*) vergrößern ♦ *vi*: **to ~ on sth** etw weiter ausführen; **~ment** *n* Vergrößerung *f*

enlighten [ɪn'laɪtn] *vt* aufklären; **~ment** *n*: **the E~ment** (*HIST*) die Aufklärung

enlist [ɪn'lɪst] *vt* gewinnen ♦ *vi* (*MIL*) sich melden

enmity ['ɛnmɪtɪ] *n* Feindschaft *f*

enormity [ɪ'nɔːmɪtɪ] *n* Ungeheuerlichkeit *f*

enormous [ɪ'nɔːməs] *adj* ungeheuer

enough [ɪ'nʌf] *adj, adv* genug; **funnily ~** komischerweise

enquire [ɪn'kwaɪər] *vt, vi* = **inquire**

enrage [ɪn'reɪdʒ] *vt* wütend machen

enrich [ɪn'rɪtʃ] *vt* bereichern

enrol [ɪn'rəul] *vt* einschreiben ♦ *vi* (*register*) sich anmelden; **~ment** *n* (*for course*) Anmeldung *f*

en route [ɒn'ruːt] *adv* unterwegs

ensign ['ɛnsaɪn, 'ɛnsən] *n* (*NAUT*) Flagge *f*; (*MIL*) Fähnrich *m*

enslave [ɪn'sleɪv] *vt* versklaven

ensue [ɪn'sjuː] *vi* folgen, sich ergeben

en suite [ɒnswiːt] *adj*: **room with ~ bathroom** Zimmer *nt* mit eigenem Bad

ensure [ɪn'ʃuər] *vt* garantieren

entail [ɪn'teɪl] *vt* mit sich bringen

entangle [ɪn'tæŋgl] *vt* verwirren, verstricken; **~d** *adj*: **to become ~d (in)** (*in net, rope etc*) sich verfangen (in +*dat*)

enter ['ɛntər] *vt* eintreten in +*dat*, betreten; (*club*) beitreten +*dat*; (*in book*) eintragen ♦ *vi* hereinkommen, hineingehen; **~ for** *vt fus* sich beteiligen an +*dat*; **~ into** *vt fus* (*agreement*) eingehen; (*plans*) eine Rolle spielen bei; **~ (up)on** *vt fus* beginnen

enterprise ['ɛntəpraɪz] *n* (*in person*) Initiative *f*; (*COMM*) Unternehmen *nt*; **enterprising** ['ɛntəpraɪzɪŋ] *adj* unternehmungslustig

entertain [ɛntə'teɪn] *vt* (*guest*) bewirten; (*amuse*) unterhalten; **~er** *n* Unterhaltungskünstler(in) *m(f)*; **~ing** *adj* unterhaltsam; **~ment** *n* Unterhaltung *f*

enthralled [ɪn'θrɔːld] *adj* gefesselt

enthusiasm [ɪn'θuːzɪæzəm] *n* Begeisterung *f*

enthusiast [ɪn'θuːzɪæst] *n* Enthusiast *m*; **~ic** [ɪnθuːzɪ'æstɪk] *adj* begeistert

entice [ɪn'taɪs] *vt* verleiten, locken

entire [ɪn'taɪər] *adj* ganz; **~ly** *adv* ganz, völlig; **~ty** [ɪn'taɪərətɪ] *n*: **in its ~ty** in seiner Gesamtheit

entitle [ɪn'taɪtl] *vt* (*allow*) berechtigen; (*name*) betiteln; **~d** *adj* (*book*) mit dem Titel; **to be ~d to sth** das Recht auf etw *acc* haben; **to be ~d to do sth** das Recht haben, etw zu tun

entity ['ɛntɪtɪ] *n* Ding *nt*, Wesen *nt*

entourage [ɒntu'rɑːʒ] *n* Gefolge *nt*

entrails ['ɛntreɪlz] *npl* Eingeweide *pl*

entrance [*n* 'ɛntrns, *vb* ɪn'trɑːns] *n* Eingang *m*; (*entering*) Eintritt *m* ♦ *vt* hinreißen; **~ examination** *n* Aufnahmeprüfung *f*; **~ fee** *n* Eintrittsgeld *nt*; **~ ramp** (*US*) *n* (*AUT*) Einfahrt *f*

entrant ['ɛntrnt] *n* (*for exam*) Kandidat *m*; (*in race*) Teilnehmer *m*

entreat [ɛn'triːt] *vt* anflehen

entrenched [ɛn'trɛntʃt] *adj* (*fig*) verwurzelt

entrepreneur ['ɒntrəprə'nɜːr] *n* Unternehmer(in) *m(f)*

entrust [ɪn'trʌst] *vt*: **to ~ sb with sth** *or* **sth to sb** jdm etw anvertrauen

entry ['ɛntrɪ] *n* Eingang *m*; (*THEAT*) Auftritt *m*; (*in account*) Eintragung *f*; (*in dictionary*) Eintrag *m*; **"no ~"** „Eintritt verboten"; (*for cars*) „Einfahrt verboten"; **~ form** *n* Anmeldeformular *nt*; **~ phone** *n* Sprechanlage *f*

enumerate [ɪ'njuːməreɪt] *vt* aufzählen

enunciate [ɪ'nʌnsɪeɪt] *vt* aussprechen

envelop [ɪn'vɛləp] *vt* einhüllen

envelope ['ɛnvələup] *n* Umschlag *m*

enviable ['ɛnvɪəbl] *adj* beneidenswert

envious ['ɛnvɪəs] *adj* neidisch

environment [ɪn'vaɪərnmənt] *n* Umgebung *f*; (*ECOLOGY*) Umwelt *f*; **~al** [ɪnvaɪərn'mɛntl] *adj* Umwelt-; **~-friendly** *adj* umweltfreundlich

envisage [ɪn'vɪzɪdʒ] *vt* sich *dat* vorstellen

envoy ['ɛnvɔɪ] *n* Gesandte(r) *mf*

envy ['ɛnvɪ] *n* Neid *m* ♦ *vt*: **to ~ sb sth** jdn um etw beneiden

enzyme ['ɛnzaɪm] *n* Enzym *nt*

pic ['epɪk] n Epos nt ♦ adj episch
pidemic [epɪ'demɪk] n Epidemie f
pilepsy ['epɪlepsɪ] n Epilepsie f; **epileptic** [epɪ'leptɪk] adj epileptisch ♦ n Epileptiker(in) m(f)
pisode ['epɪsəud] n (incident) Vorfall m; (story) Episode f
pitaph ['epɪtɑːf] n Grabinschrift f
pitomize [ɪ'pɪtəmaɪz] vt verkörpern
quable ['ekwəbl] adj ausgeglichen
qual ['iːkwl] adj gleich ♦ n Gleichgestellte(r) mf ♦ vt gleichkommen +dat; **~ to the task** der Aufgabe gewachsen; **equality** [iː'kwɔlɪtɪ] n Gleichheit f; (equal rights) Gleichberechtigung f; **~ize** vi gleichmachen ♦ vi (SPORT) ausgleichen; **~izer** n (SPORT) Ausgleich(streffer) m; **~ly** adv gleich
quanimity [ekwə'nɪmɪtɪ] n Gleichmut m
quate [ɪ'kweɪt] vt gleichsetzen
quation [ɪ'kweɪʃən] n Gleichung f
quator [ɪ'kweɪtəʳ] n Äquator m
questrian [ɪ'kwestrɪən] adj Reit-
quilibrium [iːkwɪ'lɪbrɪəm] n Gleichgewicht nt
quinox ['iːkwɪnɔks] n Tagundnachtgleiche f
quip [ɪ'kwɪp] vt ausrüsten; **to be well ~ped** gut ausgerüstet sein; **~ment** n Ausrüstung f; (TECH) Gerät nt
quitable ['ekwɪtəbl] adj gerecht, billig
quities ['ekwɪtɪz] (BRIT) npl (FIN) Stammaktien pl
quivalent [ɪ'kwɪvələnt] adj gleichwertig, entsprechend ♦ n Äquivalent nt; (in money) Gegenwert m; **~ to** gleichwertig +dat, entsprechend +dat
quivocal [ɪ'kwɪvəkl] adj zweideutig
ra ['ɪərə] n Epoche f, Ära f
radicate [ɪ'rædɪkeɪt] vt ausrotten
rase [ɪ'reɪz] vt ausradieren; (tape) löschen; **~r** n Radiergummi m
rect [ɪ'rekt] adj aufrecht ♦ vt errichten; **~ion** [ɪ'rekʃən] n Errichtung f; (ANAT) Erektion f
ERM n abbr (= Exchange Rate Mechanism) Wechselkursmechanismus m
rode [ɪ'rəud] vt zerfressen; (land)

auswaschen
erotic [ɪ'rɔtɪk] adj erotisch
err [əːʳ] vi sich irren
errand ['erənd] n Besorgung f
erratic [ɪ'rætɪk] adj unberechenbar
erroneous [ɪ'rəunɪəs] adj irrig
error ['erəʳ] n Fehler m
erupt [ɪ'rʌpt] vi ausbrechen; **~ion** [ɪ'rʌpʃən] n Ausbruch m
escalate ['eskəleɪt] vi sich steigern
escalator ['eskəleɪtəʳ] n Rolltreppe f
escape [ɪs'keɪp] n Flucht f; (of gas) Entweichen nt ♦ vi entkommen; (prisoners) fliehen; (leak) entweichen ♦ vt entkommen +dat; **escapism** n Flucht f (vor der Wirklichkeit)
escort [n 'eskɔːt, vb ɪs'kɔːt] n (person accompanying) Begleiter m; (guard) Eskorte f ♦ vt (lady) begleiten; (MIL) eskortieren
Eskimo ['eskɪməu] n Eskimo(frau) m(f)
especially [ɪs'peʃlɪ] adv besonders
espionage ['espɪɑnɑːʒ] n Spionage f
esplanade [esplə'neɪd] n Promenade f
Esquire [ɪs'kwaɪəʳ] n: **J. Brown ~** Herrn J. Brown
essay ['eseɪ] n Aufsatz m; (LITER) Essay m
essence ['esns] n (quality) Wesen nt; (extract) Essenz f
essential [ɪ'senʃl] adj (necessary) unentbehrlich; (basic) wesentlich ♦ n Allernötigste(s) nt; **~ly** adv eigentlich
establish [ɪs'tæblɪʃ] vt (set up) gründen; (prove) nachweisen; **~ed** adj anerkannt; (belief, laws etc) herrschend; **~ment** n (setting up) Einrichtung f
estate [ɪs'teɪt] n Gut nt; (BRIT: housing ~) Siedlung f; (will) Nachlass m; **~ agent** (BRIT) n Grundstücksmakler m; **~ car** (BRIT) n Kombiwagen m
esteem [ɪs'tiːm] n Wertschätzung f
esthetic [ɪs'θetɪk] (US) adj = **aesthetic**
estimate [n 'estɪmət, vb 'estɪmeɪt] n Schätzung f; (of price) (Kosten)voranschlag m ♦ vt schätzen; **estimation** [estɪ'meɪʃən] n Einschätzung f; (esteem) Achtung f
estranged [ɪs'treɪndʒd] adj entfremdet
estuary ['estjuərɪ] n Mündung f

etc *abbr* (= *et cetera*) usw.

etching ['etʃɪŋ] *n* Kupferstich *m*

eternal [ɪ'tɜːnl] *adj* ewig

eternity [ɪ'tɜːnɪtɪ] *n* Ewigkeit *f*

ether ['iːθəʳ] *n* Äther *m*

ethical ['eθɪkl] *adj* ethisch

ethics ['eθɪks] *n* Ethik *f* ♦ *npl* Moral *f*

Ethiopia [iːθɪ'əupɪə] *n* Äthiopien *nt*

ethnic ['eθnɪk] *adj* Volks-, ethnisch; ~ minority *n* ethnische Minderheit *f*

ethos ['iːθɔs] *n* Gesinnung *f*

e-ticket ['iːtɪkɪt] *n* E-Ticket *nt*

etiquette ['etɪket] *n* Etikette *f*

EU *n* (= *European Union*) EU *f*

euphemism ['juːfəmɪzəm] *n* Euphemismus *m*

euro ['juərəu] *n* (*FIN*) Euro *m*

Eurocheque ['juərəutʃek] *n* Euroscheck *m*

Euroland ['juərəulænd] *n* Eurozone *f*, Euroland *nt*

Europe ['juərəp] *n* Europa *nt*; ~an [juərə'piːən] *adj* europäisch ♦ *n* Europäer(in) *m(f)*; ~an Community *n*: the ~an Community die Europäische Gemeinschaft

Euro-sceptic ['juərəuskeptɪk] *n* Kritiker der Europäischen Gemeinschaft

evacuate [ɪ'vækjueɪt] *vt* (*place*) räumen; (*people*) evakuieren; evacuation [ɪvækju'eɪʃən] *n* Räumung *f*; Evakuierung *f*

evade [ɪ'veɪd] *vt* (*escape*) entkommen +*dat*; (*avoid*) meiden; (*duty*) sich entziehen +*dat*

evaluate [ɪ'væljueɪt] *vt* bewerten; (*information*) auswerten

evaporate [ɪ'væpəreɪt] *vi* verdampfen ♦ *vt* verdampfen lassen; ~d milk *n* Kondensmilch *f*

evasion [ɪ'veɪʒən] *n* Umgehung *f*

evasive [ɪ'veɪsɪv] *adj* ausweichend

eve [iːv] *n*: on the ~ of am Vorabend +*gen*

even ['iːvn] *adj* eben; gleichmäßig; (*score etc*) unentschieden; (*number*) gerade ♦ *adv*: ~ you sogar du; to get ~ with sb jdm heimzahlen; ~ if selbst wenn; ~ so dennoch; ~ though obwohl; ~ more sogar noch mehr; ~ out *vi* sich ausgleichen

evening ['iːvnɪŋ] *n* Abend *m*; in the ~ abends, am Abend; ~ class *n* Abendschule *f*; ~ dress *n* (*man's*) Gesellschaftsanzug *m*;

(*woman's*) Abendkleid *nt*

event [ɪ'vent] *n* (*happening*) Ereignis *nt*; (*SPORT*) Disziplin *f*; in the ~ of im Falle +*gen*; ~ful *adj* ereignisreich

eventual [ɪ'ventʃuəl] *adj* (*final*) schließlich; ~ity [ɪventʃu'ælɪtɪ] *n* Möglichkeit *f*; ~ly *adv* am Ende; (*given time*) schließlich

ever ['evəʳ] *adv* (*always*) immer; (*at any time*) je(mals) ♦ *conj* seit; ~ since seitdem; have you ~ seen it? haben Sie es je gesehen?; ~green *n* Immergrün *nt*; ~lasting *adj* immer während

every ['evrɪ] *adj* jede(r, s); ~ other/third day jeden zweiten/dritten Tag; ~ one of them alle; they ~ confidence in him ich habe uneingeschränktes Vertrauen in ihn; we wish you ~ success wir wünschen Ihnen viel Erfolg; he's ~ bit as clever as his brother er ist genauso klug wie sein Bruder; ~ now and then ab und zu; ~body *pron* = everyone; ~day *adj* (*daily*) täglich; (*commonplace*) alltäglich, Alltags-; ~one *pron* jeder, alle *pl*; ~thing *pron* alles; ~where *adv* überall(hin); (*wherever*) wohin; ~where you go wohin du auch gehst

evict [ɪ'vɪkt] *vt* ausweisen; ~ion [ɪ'vɪkʃən] *n* Ausweisung *f*

evidence ['evɪdns] *n* (*sign*) Spur *f*; (*proof*) Beweis *m*; (*testimony*) Aussage *f*

evident ['evɪdnt] *adj* augenscheinlich; ~ly *adv* offensichtlich

evil ['iːvl] *adj* böse ♦ *n* Böse *nt*

evocative [ɪ'vɔkətɪv] *adj*: to be ~ of sth an etw *acc* erinnern

evoke [ɪ'vəuk] *vt* hervorrufen

evolution [iːvə'luːʃən] *n* Entwicklung *f*; (*of life*) Evolution *f*

evolve [ɪ'vɔlv] *vt* entwickeln ♦ *vi* sich entwickeln

ewe [juː] *n* Mutterschaf *nt*

ex- [eks] *prefix* Ex-, Alt-, ehemalig

exacerbate [eks'æsəbeɪt] *vt* verschlimmern

exact [ɪg'zækt] *adj* genau ♦ *vt* (*demand*) verlangen; ~ing *adj* anspruchsvoll; ~ly *adv* genau

exaggerate [ɪg'zædʒəreɪt] *vt*, *vi* übertreiben; exaggeration [ɪgzædʒə'reɪʃən] *n*

Übertreibung f

xalted [ɪgˈzɔːltɪd] adj (position, style) hoch; (person) exaltiert

xam [ɪgˈzæm] n abbr (SCH) = **examination**

xamination [ɪgzæmɪˈneɪʃən] n Untersuchung f; (SCH) Prüfung f, Examen nt; (customs) Kontrolle f

xamine [ɪgˈzæmɪn] vt untersuchen; (SCH) prüfen; (consider) erwägen; ~ **r** n Prüfer m

xample [ɪgˈzɑːmpl] n Beispiel nt; **for ~** zum Beispiel

xasperate [ɪgˈzɑːspəreɪt] vt zur Verzweiflung bringen; **exasperating** adj ärgerlich, zum Verzweifeln bringend; **exasperation** [ɪgzɑːspəˈreɪʃən] n Verzweiflung f

xcavate [ˈekskəveɪt] vt ausgraben; **excavation** [ekskəˈveɪʃən] n Ausgrabung f

xceed [ɪkˈsiːd] vt überschreiten; (hopes) übertreffen; **~ingly** adv äußerst

xcel [ɪkˈsel] vi sich auszeichnen; **~lence** [ˈeksələns] n Vortrefflichkeit f; **E~lency** [ˈeksələnsɪ] n: **His E~lency** Seine Exzellenz f; **~lent** [ˈeksələnt] adj ausgezeichnet

xcept [ɪkˈsept] prep (also: **~ for, ~ing**) außer +dat ♦ vt ausnehmen; **~ion** [ɪkˈsepʃən] n Ausnahme f; **to take ~ion to** Anstoß nehmen an +dat; **~ional** [ɪkˈsepʃənl] adj außergewöhnlich

xcerpt [ˈeksəːpt] n Auszug m

xcess [ɪkˈses] n Übermaß nt; **an ~ of** ein Übermaß an +dat; **~ baggage** n Mehrgepäck nt; **~ fare** n Nachlösegebühr f; **~ive** adj übermäßig

xchange [ɪksˈtʃeɪndʒ] n Austausch m; (also: **telephone ~**) Zentrale f ♦ vt (goods) tauschen; (greetings) austauschen; (money, blows) wechseln; **~ rate** n Wechselkurs m

xchequer [ɪksˈtʃekər] (BRIT) n: **the ~** das Schatzamt

xcise [ˈeksaɪz] n Verbrauchssteuer f

xcite [ɪkˈsaɪt] vt erregen; **to get ~d** sich aufregen; **~ment** n Aufregung f; **exciting** adj spannend

xclaim [ɪksˈkleɪm] vi ausrufen

xclamation [ekskləˈmeɪʃən] n Ausruf m; **~ mark** n Ausrufezeichen nt

exclude [ɪksˈkluːd] vt ausschließen

exclusion [ɪksˈkluːʒən] n Ausschluss m; **~ zone** n Sperrzone f

exclusive [ɪksˈkluːsɪv] adj (select) exklusiv; (sole) ausschließlich, Allein-; **~ of** exklusive +gen; **~ly** adv nur, ausschließlich

excrement [ˈekskrəmənt] n Kot m

excruciating [ɪksˈkruːʃieɪtɪŋ] adj qualvoll

excursion [ɪksˈkəːʃən] n Ausflug m

excusable [ɪksˈkjuːzəbl] adj entschuldbar

excuse [n ɪksˈkjuːs, vb ɪksˈkjuːz] n Entschuldigung f ♦ vt entschuldigen; **~ me!** entschuldigen Sie!

ex-directory [ˈeksdɪˈrektərɪ] (BRIT) adj: **to be ~** nicht im Telefonbuch stehen

execute [ˈeksɪkjuːt] vt (carry out) ausführen; (kill) hinrichten; **execution** [eksɪˈkjuːʃən] n Ausführung f; (killing) Hinrichtung f; **executioner** [eksɪˈkjuːʃnər] n Scharfrichter m

executive [ɪgˈzekjutɪv] n (COMM) Geschäftsführer m; (POL) Exekutive f ♦ adj Exekutiv-, ausführend

executor [ɪgˈzekjutər] n Testamentsvollstrecker m

exemplary [ɪgˈzemplərɪ] adj musterhaft

exemplify [ɪgˈzemplɪfaɪ] vt veranschaulichen

exempt [ɪgˈzempt] adj befreit ♦ vt befreien; **~ion** [ɪgˈzempʃən] n Befreiung f

exercise [ˈeksəsaɪz] n Übung f ♦ vt (power) ausüben; (muscle, patience) üben; (dog) ausführen ♦ vi Sport treiben; **~ bike** n Heimtrainer m; **~ book** n (Schul)heft nt

exert [ɪgˈzəːt] vt (influence) ausüben; **to ~ o.s.** sich anstrengen; **~ion** [ɪgˈzəːʃən] n Anstrengung f

exhale [eksˈheɪl] vt, vi ausatmen

exhaust [ɪgˈzɔːst] n (fumes) Abgase pl; (pipe) Auspuffrohr nt ♦ vt erschöpfen; **~ed** adj erschöpft; **~ion** [ɪgˈzɔːstʃən] n Erschöpfung f; **~ive** adj erschöpfend

exhibit [ɪgˈzɪbɪt] n (JUR) Beweisstück nt; (ART) Ausstellungsstück nt ♦ vt ausstellen; **~ion** [eksɪˈbɪʃən] n (ART) Ausstellung f; (of temper etc) Zurschaustellung f; **~ionist** [eksɪˈbɪʃənɪst] n Exhibitionist m

exhilarating [ɪgˈzɪləreɪtɪŋ] adj erhebend

ex-husband n Ehemann m

exile ['eksaıl] n Exil nt; (*person*) Verbannte(r) f(m) ♦ vt verbannen

exist [ıg'zıst] vi existieren; ~**ence** n Existenz f; ~**ing** adj bestehend

exit ['eksıt] n Ausgang m; (*THEAT*) Abgang m ♦ vi (*THEAT*) abtreten; (*COMPUT*) aus einem Programm herausgehen; ~ **poll** n bei Wahlen unmittelbar nach Verlassen der Wahllokale durchgeführte Umfrage; ~ **ramp** (*US*) n (*AUT*) Ausfahrt f

exodus ['eksədəs] n Auszug m

exonerate [ıg'zɒnəreıt] vt entlasten

exorbitant [ıg'zɔːbıtnt] adj übermäßig; (*price*) Fantasie-

exotic [ıg'zɒtık] adj exotisch

expand [ıks'pænd] vt ausdehnen ♦ vi sich ausdehnen

expanse [ıks'pæns] n Fläche f

expansion [ıks'pænʃən] n Erweiterung f

expatriate [eks'pætrıət] n Ausländer(in) m(f)

expect [ıks'pekt] vt erwarten; (*suppose*) annehmen ♦ vi: **to be ~ing** ein Kind erwarten; ~**ancy** n Erwartung f; ~**ant mother** n werdende Mutter f; ~**ation** [ekspek'teıʃən] n Hoffnung f

expedient [ıks'piːdıənt] adj zweckdienlich ♦ n (Hilfs)mittel nt

expedition [ekspə'dıʃən] n Expedition f

expel [ıks'pel] vt ausweisen; (*student*) (ver)weisen

expend [ıks'pend] vt (*effort*) aufwenden; ~**iture** n Ausgaben pl

expense [ıks'pens] n Kosten pl; ~**s** npl (*COMM*) Spesen pl; **at the ~ of** auf Kosten von; ~ **account** n Spesenkonto nt; **expensive** [ıks'pensıv] adj teuer

experience [ıks'pıərıəns] n (*incident*) Erlebnis nt; (*practice*) Erfahrung f ♦ vt erleben; ~**d** adj erfahren

experiment [ıks'perımənt] n Versuch m, Experiment nt ♦ vi experimentieren; ~**al** [ıksperı'mentl] adj experimentell

expert ['ekspɔːt] n Fachmann m; (*official*) Sachverständige(r) m ♦ adj erfahren; ~**ise** [ekspɔː'tiːz] n Sachkenntnis f

expire [ıks'paıər] vi (*end*) ablaufen; (*ticket*)

verfallen; (*die*) sterben; **expiry** n Ablauf m

explain [ıks'pleın] vt erklären

explanation [eksplə'neıʃən] n Erklärung f; **explanatory** [ıks'plænətrı] adj erklärend

explicit [ıks'plısıt] adj ausdrücklich

explode [ıks'pləud] vi explodieren ♦ vt (*bomb*) sprengen

exploit [n 'eksplɔıt, vb ıks'plɔıt] n (Helden)tat f ♦ vt ausbeuten; ~**ation** [eksplɔı'teıʃən] n Ausbeutung f

exploration [eksplə'reıʃən] n Erforschung f

exploratory [ıks'plɔrətrı] adj Probe-

explore [ıks'plɔː] vt (*travel*) erforschen; (*search*) untersuchen; ~**r** n Erforscher(in) m(f)

explosion [ıks'pləuʒən] n Explosion f; (*fig*) Ausbruch m

explosive [ıks'pləusıv] adj explosiv, Spreng- ♦ n Sprengstoff m

export [vb eks'pɔːt, n 'ekspɔːt] vt exportieren ♦ n Export m ♦ cpd (*trade*) Export-; ~**er** [eks'pɔːtər] n Exporteur m

expose [ıks'pəuz] vt (*to danger etc*) aussetzen; (*impostor*) entlarven; **to ~ sb to sth** jdn einer Sache dat aussetzen; ~**d** adj (*position*) exponiert; **exposure** [ıks'pəuʒər] n (*MED*) Unterkühlung f; (*PHOT*) Belichtung f; **exposure meter** n Belichtungsmesser m

express [ıks'pres] adj ausdrücklich, (*speedy*) Express-, Eil- ♦ n (*RAIL*) Schnellzug m ♦ adv (*send*) per Express ♦ vt ausdrücken; **to ~ o.s.** sich ausdrücken; ~**ion** [ıks'preʃən] n Ausdruck m; ~**ive** adj ausdrucksvoll; ~**ly** adv ausdrücklich; ~**way** (*US*) n (*urban motorway*) Schnellstraße f

expulsion [ıks'pʌlʃən] n Ausweisung f

exquisite [eks'kwızıt] adj erlesen

extend [ıks'tend] vt (*visit etc*) verlängern; (*building*) ausbauen; (*hand*) ausstrecken; (*welcome*) bieten ♦ vi (*land*) sich erstrecken

extension [ıks'tenʃən] n Erweiterung f; (*of building*) Anbau m; (*TEL*) Apparat m

extensive [ıks'tensıv] adj (*knowledge*) umfassend; (*use*) weitgehend, weit gehend

extent [ıks'tent] n Ausdehnung f; (*fig*) Ausmaß nt; **to a certain ~** bis zu einem

gewissen Grade; **to such an ~ that ...**
dermaßen, dass ...; **to what ~?** inwieweit?

extenuating [ɪksˈtenjueɪtɪŋ] *adj* mildernd

exterior [eksˈtɪərɪər] *adj* äußere(r, s), Außen-
♦ *n* Äußere(s) *nt*

exterminate [ɪksˈtɜːmɪneɪt] *vt* ausrotten

external [eksˈtɜːnl] *adj* äußere(r, s), Außen-

extinct [ɪksˈtɪŋkt] *adj* ausgestorben; **~ion**
[ɪksˈtɪŋkʃən] *n* Aussterben *nt*

extinguish [ɪksˈtɪŋgwɪʃ] *vt* (aus)löschen

extort [ɪksˈtɔːt] *vt* erpressen; **~ion** [ɪksˈtɔːʃən]
n Erpressung *f*; **~ionate** [ɪksˈtɔːʃnɪt] *adj*
überhöht, erpresserisch

extra [ˈekstrə] *adj* zusätzlich ♦ *adv* besonders
♦ *n* (for car etc) Extra *nt*; (charge) Zuschlag
m; (THEAT) Statist *m* ♦ *prefix* außer...

extract [*v* ɪksˈtrækt, *n* ˈekstrækt] *vt*
(heraus)ziehen ♦ *n* (from book etc) Auszug
m; (COOK) Extrakt *m*

extracurricular [ˈekstrəkəˈrɪkjulər] *adj*
außerhalb des Stundenplans

extradite [ˈekstrədaɪt] *vt* ausliefern

extramarital [ˈekstrəˈmærɪtl] *adj*
außerehelich

extramural [ˈekstrəˈmjuərl] *adj* (course)
Volkshochschul-

extraordinary [ɪksˈtrɔːdnrɪ] *adj*
außerordentlich; (amazing) erstaunlich

extravagance [ɪksˈtrævəgəns] *n*
Verschwendung *f*; (lack of restraint)
Zügellosigkeit *f*; (an ~) Extravaganz *f*

extravagant [ɪksˈtrævəgənt] *adj* extravagant

extreme [ɪksˈtriːm] *adj* (edge) äußerste(r, s),
hinterste(r, s); (cold) äußerste(r, s);
(behaviour) außergewöhnlich, übertrieben
♦ *n* Extrem *nt*; **~ly** *adv* äußerst, höchst;
extremist *n* Extremist(in) *m(f)*

extremity [ɪksˈtremɪtɪ] *n* (end) Spitze *f*,
äußerste(s) Ende *nt*; (hardship) bitterste Not
f; (ANAT) Hand *f*; Fuß *m*

extricate [ˈekstrɪkeɪt] *vt* losmachen, befreien

extrovert [ˈekstrəvɜːt] *n* extrovertierte(r)
Mensch *m*

exuberant [ɪgˈzjuːbərnt] *adj* ausgelassen

exude [ɪgˈzjuːd] *vt* absondern

eye [aɪ] *n* Auge *nt*; (of needle) Öhr *nt* ♦ *vt*
betrachten; (up and down) mustern; **to**

keep an ~ on aufpassen
Augapfel *m*; **~bath** *n* A[...]
n Augenbraue *f*; **~brow** [...]
Augenbrauenstift *m*; **~c**[...]
Augentropfen *pl*; **~las**[...]
~lid *n* Augenlid *nt*; **~li**[...]
opener *n*: **that was an ~-opener** das hat
mir/ihm *etc* die Augen geöffnet; **~shadow**
n Lidschatten *m*; **~sight** *n* Sehkraft *f*;
~sore *n* Schandfleck *m*; **~ witness** *n*
Augenzeuge *m*

F, f

F [ef] *n* (MUS) F *nt*

F. *abbr* (= Fahrenheit) F

fable [ˈfeɪbl] *n* Fabel *f*

fabric [ˈfæbrɪk] *n* Stoff *m*; (fig) Gefüge *nt*

fabrication [fæbrɪˈkeɪʃən] *n* Erfindung *f*

fabulous [ˈfæbjuləs] *adj* sagenhaft

face [feɪs] *n* Gesicht *nt*; (surface) Oberfläche
f; (of clock) Zifferblatt *nt* ♦ *vt* (point towards)
liegen nach; (situation, difficulty) sich stellen
+*dat*; **~ down** (person) mit dem Gesicht
nach unten; (card) mit der Vorderseite nach
unten; **to make** *or* **pull a ~** das Gesicht
verziehen; **in the ~ of** angesichts +*gen*; **on
the ~ of it** so, wie es aussieht; **~ to ~** Auge
in Auge; **to ~ up to sth** einer Sache *dat* ins
Auge sehen; **~ cloth** (BRIT) *n* Waschlappen
m; **~ cream** *n* Gesichtscreme *f*; **~ lift** *n*
Facelifting *nt*; **~ powder** *n* (Gesichts)puder
m

facet [ˈfæsɪt] *n* Aspekt *m*; (of gem) Facette *f*,
Fassette *f*

facetious [fəˈsiːʃəs] *adj* witzig

face value *n* Nennwert *m*; **to take sth at
(its) ~** (fig) etw für bare Münze nehmen

facial [ˈfeɪʃl] *adj* Gesichts-

facile [ˈfæsaɪl] *adj* (easy) leicht

facilitate [fəˈsɪlɪteɪt] *vt* erleichtern

facilities [fəˈsɪlɪtɪz] *npl* Einrichtungen *pl*;
credit ~ Kreditmöglichkeiten *pl*

facing [ˈfeɪsɪŋ] *adj* zugekehrt ♦ *prep*
gegenüber

facsimile [fækˈsɪmɪlɪ] *n* Faksimile *nt*;

...) Telekopierer *m*

...kt] *n* Tatsache *f*; **in ~** in der Tat

...on ['fækʃən] *n* Splittergruppe *f*

...ctor ['fæktə*r*] *n* Faktor *m*

...actory ['fæktəri] *n* Fabrik *f*

factual ['fæktjuəl] *adj* sachlich

faculty ['fækəltı] *n* Fähigkeit *f*; (*UNIV*) Fakultät *f*; (*US: teaching staff*) Lehrpersonal *nt*

fad [fæd] *n* Tick *m*; (*fashion*) Masche *f*

fade [feɪd] *vi* (*lose colour*) verblassen; (*dim*) nachlassen; (*sound, memory*) schwächer werden; (*wilt*) verwelken

fag [fæg] (*inf*) *n* (*cigarette*) Kippe *f*

fail [feɪl] *vt* (*exam*) nicht bestehen; (*student*) durchfallen lassen; (*courage*) verlassen; (*memory*) im Stich lassen ♦ *vi* (*supplies*) zu Ende gehen; (*student*) durchfallen; (*eyesight*) nachlassen; (*light*) schwächer werden; (*crop*) fehlschlagen; (*remedy*) nicht wirken; **to ~ to do sth** (*neglect*) es unterlassen, etw zu tun; (*be unable*) es nicht schaffen, etw zu tun; **without ~** unbedingt; **~ing** *n* Schwäche *f* ♦ *prep* mangels +*gen*; **~ure** ['feɪljə*r*] *n* (*person*) Versager *m*; (*act*) Versagen *nt*; (*TECH*) Defekt *m*

faint [feɪnt] *adj* schwach ♦ *n* Ohnmacht *f* ♦ *vi* ohnmächtig werden

fair [feə*r*] *adj* (*just*) gerecht, fair; (*hair*) blond; (*skin*) hell; (*weather*) schön; (*not very good*) mittelmäßig; (*sizeable*) ansehnlich ♦ *adv* (*play*) fair ♦ *n* (*COMM*) Messe *f*; (*BRIT: funfair*) Jahrmarkt *m*; **~ly** *adv* (*honestly*) gerecht, fair; (*rather*) ziemlich; **~ness** *n* Fairness *f*

fairy ['feəri] *n* Fee *f*; **~ tale** *n* Märchen *nt*

faith [feɪθ] *n* Glaube *m*; (*trust*) Vertrauen *nt*; (*sect*) Bekenntnis *nt*; **~ful** *adj* treu; **~fully** *adv* treu; **yours ~fully** (*BRIT*) hochachtungsvoll

fake [feɪk] *n* (*thing*) Fälschung *f*; (*person*) Schwindler *m* ♦ *adj* vorgetäuscht ♦ *vt* fälschen

falcon ['fɔ:lkən] *n* Falke *m*

fall [fɔ:l] (*pt* **fell**, *pp* **fallen**) *n* Fall *m*, Sturz *m*; (*decrease*) Fallen *nt*; (*of snow*) (Schnee)fall *m*; (*US: autumn*) Herbst *m* ♦ *vi* (*also fig*) fallen; (*night*) hereinbrechen; **~s** *npl* (*waterfall*) Fälle *pl*; **to ~ flat** platt hinfallen;

(*joke*) nicht ankommen; **~ back** *vi* zurückweichen; **~ back on** *vt fus* zurückgreifen auf +*acc*; **~ behind** *vi* zurückbleiben; **~ down** *vi* (*person*) hinfallen; (*building*) einstürzen; **~ for** *vt fus* (*trick*) hereinfallen auf +*acc*; (*person*) sich verknallen in +*acc*; **~ in** *vi* (*roof*) einstürzen; **~ off** *vi* herunterfallen; (*diminish*) sich vermindern; **~ out** *vi* sich streiten; (*MIL*) wegtreten; **~ through** *vi* (*plan*) ins Wasser fallen

fallacy ['fæləsı] *n* Trugschluss *m*

fallen ['fɔ:lən] *pp of* **fall**

fallible ['fæləbl] *adj* fehlbar

fallout ['fɔ:laut] *n* radioaktive(r) Niederschlag *m*; **~ shelter** *n* Atombunker *m*

fallow ['fæləu] *adj* brach(liegend)

false [fɔ:ls] *adj* falsch; (*artificial*) künstlich; **under ~ pretences** unter Vorspiegelung falscher Tatsachen; **~ alarm** *n* Fehlalarm *m*; **~ teeth** (*BRIT*) *npl* Gebiss *nt*

falter ['fɔ:ltə*r*] *vi* schwanken; (*in speech*) stocken

fame [feɪm] *n* Ruhm *m*

familiar [fə'mɪlɪə*r*] *adj* bekannt; (*intimate*) familiär; **to be ~ with** vertraut sein mit; **~ize** *vt* vertraut machen

family ['fæmɪlı] *n* Familie *f*; (*relations*) Verwandtschaft *f*; **~ business** *n* Familienunternehmen *nt*; **~ doctor** *n* Hausarzt *m*

famine ['fæmɪn] *n* Hungersnot *f*

famished ['fæmɪʃt] *adj* ausgehungert

famous ['feɪməs] *adj* berühmt

fan [fæn] *n* (*folding*) Fächer *m*; (*ELEC*) Ventilator *m*; (*admirer*) Fan *m* ♦ *vt* fächeln; **~ out** *vi* sich (fächerförmig) ausbreiten

fanatic [fə'nætɪk] *n* Fanatiker(in) *m(f)*

fan belt *n* Keilriemen *m*

fanciful ['fænsıful] *adj* (*odd*) seltsam; (*imaginative*) fantasievoll

fancy ['fænsı] *n* (*liking*) Neigung *f*; (*imagination*) Einbildung *f* ♦ *adj* schick ♦ *vt* (*like*) gern haben; wollen; (*imagine*) sich einbilden; **he fancies her** er mag sie; **~ dress** *n* Maskenkostüm *nt*; **~-dress ball** *n* Maskenball *m*

fang [fæŋ] n Fangzahn m; (of snake) Giftzahn m

fantastic [fæn'tæstɪk] adj fantastisch

fantasy ['fæntəsɪ] n Fantasie f

far [fɑːʳ] adj weit ♦ adv weit entfernt; (very much) weitaus; **by ~** bei weitem; **so ~** so weit; bis jetzt; **go as ~ as the station** gehen Sie bis zum Bahnhof; **as ~ as I know** soweit or soviel ich weiß; **~away** adj weit entfernt

farce [fɑːs] n Farce f; **farcical** ['fɑːsɪkl] adj lächerlich

fare [fɛəʳ] n Fahrpreis m; Fahrgeld nt; (food) Kost f; **half/full ~** halber/voller Fahrpreis m

Far East n: **the ~** der Ferne Osten

farewell [fɛə'wɛl] n Abschied(sgruß) m ♦ excl lebe wohl!

farm [fɑːm] n Bauernhof m, Farm f ♦ vt bewirtschaften; **~er** n Bauer m, Landwirt m; **~hand** n Landarbeiter m; **~house** n Bauernhaus nt; **~ing** n Landwirtschaft f; **~land** n Ackerland nt; **~yard** n Hof m

far-reaching ['fɑː'riːtʃɪŋ] adj (reform, effect) weitreichend, weit reichend

fart [fɑːt] (inf!) n Furz m ♦ vi furzen

farther ['fɑːðəʳ] adv weiter; **farthest** ['fɑːðɪst] adj fernste(r, s) ♦ adv am weitesten

fascinate ['fæsɪneɪt] vt faszinieren; **fascinating** adj faszinierend; **fascination** [fæsɪ'neɪʃən] n Faszination f

fascism ['fæʃɪzəm] n Faschismus m

fashion ['fæʃən] n (of clothes) Mode f; (manner) Art f (und Weise f) ♦ vt machen; **in ~** in Mode; **out of ~** unmodisch; **~able** adj (clothes) modisch; (place) elegant; **~ show** n Mode(n)schau f

fast [fɑːst] adj schnell; (firm) fest ♦ adv schnell; fest ♦ n Fasten nt ♦ vi fasten; **to be ~** (clock) vorgehen

fasten ['fɑːsn] vt (attach) befestigen; (with rope) zuschnüren; (seat belt) festmachen; (coat) zumachen ♦ vi sich schließen lassen; **~er** n Verschluss m; **~ing** n Verschluss m

fast food n Fastfood nt, Fast Food nt

fastidious [fæs'tɪdɪəs] adj wählerisch

fat [fæt] adj dick ♦ n Fett nt

fatal ['feɪtl] adj tödlich; (disastrous) verhängnisvoll; **~ity** [fə'tælɪtɪ etc) Todesopfer nt; **~ly** etc

fate [feɪt] n Schicksal nt; schicksalsschwer; (impo

father ['fɑːðəʳ] n Vater m in-law n Schwiegervat väterlich

fathom ['fæðəm] n Klafter m ♦ vt ausloten; (fig) ergründen

fatigue [fə'tiːg] n Ermüdung f

fatten ['fætn] vt dick machen; (animals) mästen ♦ vi dick werden

fatty ['fætɪ] adj fettig ♦ n (inf) Dickerchen nt

fatuous ['fætjʊəs] adj albern, affig

faucet ['fɔːsɪt] (US) n Wasserhahn m

fault [fɔːlt] n (defect) Defekt m; (ELEC) Störung f; (blame) Schuld f; (GEOG) Verwerfung f; **it's your ~** du bist daran schuld; **to find ~ with (sth/sb)** etwas auszusetzen haben an (etw/jdm); **at ~** im Unrecht; **~less** adj tadellos; **~y** adj fehlerhaft, defekt

fauna ['fɔːnə] n Fauna f

favour ['feɪvəʳ] (US **favor**) n (approval) Wohlwollen nt; (kindness) Gefallen m ♦ vt (prefer) vorziehen; **in ~ of** für; zugunsten or zu Gunsten +gen; **to find ~ with sb** bei jdm Anklang finden; **~able** adj (favourable) günstig; **~ite** ['feɪvrɪt] adj Lieblings- ♦ n (child) Liebling m; (SPORT) Favorit m

fawn [fɔːn] adj rehbraun ♦ n (animal) (Reh)kitz nt ♦ vi: **to ~ (up)on** (fig) katzbuckeln vor +dat

fax [fæks] n (document) Fax nt; (machine) Telefax nt ♦ vt: **to ~ sth to sb** jdm etw faxen

FBI (US) n abbr (= Federal Bureau of Investigation) FBI nt

fear [fɪəʳ] n Furcht f ♦ vt fürchten; **~ful** adj (timid) furchtsam; (terrible) fürchterlich; **~less** adj furchtlos

feasible ['fiːzəbl] adj durchführbar

feast [fiːst] n Festmahl nt; (REL: also: **~ day**) Feiertag m ♦ vi: **to ~ (on)** sich gütlich tun (an +dat)

feat [fiːt] n Leistung f

feather ['fɛðəʳ] n Feder f

feature ['fiːtʃəʳ] n (Gesichts)zug m;

...t part) Grundzug m; (CINE, PRESS) ...nt ♦ vt darstellen; (advertising etc) ... herausbringen ♦ vi vorkommen; **...eaturing** X mit X; **~ film** n Spielfilm m

February ['februəri] n Februar m

fed [fed] pt, pp of **feed**

federal ['fedərəl] adj Bundes-

federation [fedə'reɪʃən] n (society) Verband m; (of states) Staatenbund m

fed up adj: **to be ~ with sth** etw satt haben; **I'm ~** ich habe die Nase voll

fee [fiː] n Gebühr f

feeble ['fiːbl] adj (person) schwach; (excuse) lahm

feed [fiːd] (pt, pp **fed**) n (for animals) Futter nt ♦ vt füttern; (support) ernähren; (data) eingeben; **to ~ on** fressen; **~back** n (information) Feed-back nt, Feedback nt; **~ing bottle** (BRIT) n Flasche f

feel [fiːl] (pt, pp **felt**) n: **it has a soft ~** es fühlt sich weich an ♦ vt (sense) fühlen; (touch) anfassen; (think) meinen ♦ vi (person) sich fühlen; (thing) sich anfühlen; **to get the ~ of sth** sich an etw acc gewöhnen; **I ~ cold** mir ist kalt; **I ~ like a cup of tea** ich habe Lust auf eine Tasse Tee; **~ about** or **around** vi herumsuchen; **~er** n Fühler m; **~ing** n Gefühl nt; (opinion) Meinung f

feet [fiːt] npl of **foot**

feign [feɪn] vt vortäuschen

feline ['fiːlaɪn] adj katzenartig

fell [fel] pt of **fall** ♦ vt (tree) fällen

fellow ['feləu] n (man) Kerl m; **~ citizen** n Mitbürger(in) m(f); **~ countryman** (irreg) n Landsmann m; **~ men** npl Mitmenschen pl; **~ship** n (group) Körperschaft f; (friendliness) Kameradschaft f; (scholarship) Forschungsstipendium nt; **~ student** n Kommilitone m, Kommilitonin f

felony ['feləni] n schwere(s) Verbrechen nt

felt [felt] pt, pp of **feel** ♦ n Filz m; **~-tip pen** n Filzstift m

female ['fiːmeɪl] n (of animals) Weibchen nt ♦ adj weiblich

feminine ['feminin] adj (LING) weiblich; (qualities) fraulich

feminist ['feminist] n Feminist(in) m(f)

fence [fens] n Zaun m ♦ vt (also: **~ in**) einzäunen ♦ vi fechten; **fencing** ['fensɪŋ] n Zaun m; (SPORT) Fechten nt

fend [fend] vi: **to ~ for o.s.** sich (allein) durchschlagen; **~ off** vt abwehren

fender ['fendə] n Kaminvorsetzer m; (US: AUT) Kotflügel m

ferment [vb fə'ment, n 'fɜːment] vi (CHEM) gären ♦ n (unrest) Unruhe f

fern [fɜːn] n Farn m

ferocious [fə'rəuʃəs] adj wild, grausam

ferret ['ferit] n Frettchen nt ♦ vt: **to ~ out** aufspüren

ferry ['feri] n Fähre f ♦ vt übersetzen

fertile ['fɜːtaɪl] adj fruchtbar

fertilize ['fɜːtɪlaɪz] vt (AGR) düngen; (BIOL) befruchten; **~r** n (Kunst)dünger m

fervent ['fɜːvənt] adj (admirer) glühend; (hope) innig

fervour ['fɜːvə] (US **fervor**) n Leidenschaft f

fester ['festə] vi eitern

festival ['festivəl] n (REL etc) Fest nt; (ART, MUS) Festspiele pl

festive ['festiv] adj festlich; **the ~ season** (Christmas) die Festzeit; **festivities** [fes'tivitiz] npl Feierlichkeiten pl

festoon [fes'tuːn] vt: **to ~ with** schmücken mit

fetch [fetʃ] vt holen; (in sale) einbringen

fetching ['fetʃɪŋ] adj reizend

fête [feit] n Fest nt

fetus ['fiːtəs] (esp US) n = **foetus**

feud [fjuːd] n Fehde f

feudal ['fjuːdl] adj Feudal-

fever ['fiːvə] n Fieber nt; **~ish** adj (MED) fiebrig; (fig) fieberhaft

few [fjuː] adj wenig; **a ~** einige; **~er** adj weniger; **~est** adj wenigste(r,s)

fiancé [fɪ'ɒːnseɪ] n Verlobte(r) m; **~e** n Verlobte f

fib [fib] n Flunkerei f ♦ vi flunkern

fibre ['faibə] (US **fiber**) n Faser f; **~glass** n Glaswolle f

fickle ['fikl] adj unbeständig

fiction ['fikʃən] n (novels) Romanliteratur f; (story) Erdichtung f; **~al** adj erfunden

fictitious [fɪkˈtɪʃəs] *adj* erfunden, fingiert

fiddle [ˈfɪdl] *n* Geige *f*; (*trick*) Schwindelei *f*
♦ *vt* (*BRIT*: *accounts*) frisieren; ~ **with** *vt fus*
herumfummeln an +*dat*

fidelity [fɪˈdelɪtɪ] *n* Treue *f*

fidget [ˈfɪdʒɪt] *vi* zappeln

field [fiːld] *n* Feld *nt*; (*range*) Gebiet *nt*; ~
marshal *n* Feldmarschall *m*; ~**work** *n*
Feldforschung *f*

fiend [fiːnd] *n* Teufel *m*

fierce [fɪəs] *adj* wild

fiery [ˈfaɪərɪ] *adj* (*person*) hitzig

fifteen [fɪfˈtiːn] *num* fünfzehn

fifth [fɪfθ] *adj* fünfte(r, s) ♦ *n* Fünftel *nt*

fifty [ˈfɪftɪ] *num* fünfzig; ~**-fifty** *adj*, *adv*
halbe-halbe, fifty-fifty (*inf*)

fig [fɪg] *n* Feige *f*

fight [faɪt] (*pt*, *pp* **fought**) *n* Kampf *m*; (*brawl*)
Schlägerei *f*; (*argument*) Streit *m* ♦ *vt*
kämpfen gegen; sich schlagen mit; (*fig*)
bekämpfen ♦ *vi* kämpfen; sich schlagen;
streiten; ~**er** *n* Kämpfer(in) *m(f)*; (*plane*)
Jagdflugzeug *nt*; ~**ing** *n* Kämpfen *nt*; (*war*)
Kampfhandlungen *pl*

figment [ˈfɪgmənt] *n*: ~ **of the imagination**
reine Einbildung *f*

figurative [ˈfɪgjurətɪv] *adj* bildlich

figure [ˈfɪgər] *n* (*of person*) Figur *f*; (*person*)
Gestalt *f*; (*number*) Ziffer *f* ♦ *vt* (*US*: *imagine*)
glauben ♦ *vi* (*appear*) erscheinen; ~ **out** *vt*
herausbekommen; ~**head** *n* (*NAUT*, *fig*)
Galionsfigur *f*; ~ **of speech** *n* Redensart *f*

file [faɪl] *n* (*tool*) Feile *f*; (*dossier*) Akte *f*;
(*folder*) Aktenordner *m*; (*COMPUT*) Datei *f*;
(*row*) Reihe *f* ♦ *vt* (*metal*, *nails*) feilen;
(*papers*) abheften; (*claim*) einreichen ♦ *vi*: **to
~ in/out** hintereinander hereinkommen/
hinausgehen; **to ~ past** vorbeimarschieren;
filing [ˈfaɪlɪŋ] *n* Ablage *f*; **filing cabinet** *n*
Aktenschrank *m*

fill [fɪl] *vt* füllen; (*occupy*) ausfüllen; (*satisfy*)
sättigen ♦ *n*: **to eat one's ~** sich richtig
satt essen; ~ **in** *vt* (*hole*) (auf)füllen; (*form*)
ausfüllen; ~ **up** *vt* (*container*) auffüllen;
(*form*) ausfüllen ♦ *vt* (*AUT*) tanken

fillet [ˈfɪlɪt] *n* Filet *nt*; ~ **steak** *n* Filetsteak *nt*

filling [ˈfɪlɪŋ] *n* (*COOK*) Füllung *f*; (*for tooth*)

(*Zahn*)plombe *f*; ~ **station** *n* Tankstelle *f*

film [fɪlm] *n* Film *m* ♦ *vt* (*scene*) filmen; ~
star *n* Filmstar *m*

filter [ˈfɪltər] *n* Filter *m* ♦ *vt* filtern; ~ **lane**
n (*BRIT*) *n* Abbiegespur *f*; ~**-tipped** *adj* Filter-

filth [fɪlθ] *n* Dreck *m*; ~**y** *adj* dreckig;
(*weather*) scheußlich

fin [fɪn] *n* Flosse *f*

final [ˈfaɪnl] *adj* letzte(r, s); End-; (*conclusive*)
endgültig ♦ *n* (*FOOTBALL etc*) Endspiel *nt*; ~**s**
npl (*UNIV*) Abschlussexamen *nt*; (*SPORT*)
Schlussrunde *f*

finale [fɪˈnɑːlɪ] *n* (*MUS*) Finale *nt*

final: ~**ist** *n* (*SPORT*) Schluss-
rundenteilnehmer *m*; ~**ize** *vt* endgültige
Form geben +*dat*; abschließen; ~**ly** *adv*
(*lastly*) zuletzt; (*eventually*) endlich;
(*irrevocably*) endgültig

finance [faɪˈnæns] *n* Finanzwesen *nt* ♦ *vt*
finanzieren; ~**s** *npl* (*funds*) Finanzen *pl*;
financial [faɪˈnænʃəl] *adj* Finanz-; finanziell

find [faɪnd] (*pt*, *pp* **found**) *vt* finden ♦ *n* Fund
m; **to ~ sb guilty** jdn für schuldig erklären;
~ **out** *vt* herausfinden; ~**ings** *npl* (*JUR*)
Ermittlungsergebnis *nt*; (*of report*) Befund *m*

fine [faɪn] *adj* fein; (*good*) gut; (*weather*)
schön ♦ *adv* (*well*) gut; (*small*) klein ♦ *n* (*JUR*)
Geldstrafe *f* ♦ *vt* (*JUR*) mit einer Geldstrafe
belegen; ~ **arts** *npl* schöne(n) Künste *pl*

finger [ˈfɪŋgər] *n* Finger *m* ♦ *vt* befühlen;
~**nail** *n* Fingernagel *m*; ~**print** *n*
Fingerabdruck *m*; ~**tip** *n* Fingerspitze *f*

finicky [ˈfɪnɪkɪ] *adj* pingelig

finish [ˈfɪnɪʃ] *n* Ende *nt*; (*SPORT*) Ziel *nt*; (*of
object*) Verarbeitung *f*; (*of paint*)
Oberflächenwirkung *f* ♦ *vt* beenden; (*book*)
zu Ende lesen ♦ *vi* aufhören; (*SPORT*) ans
Ziel kommen; **to be ~ed with sth** fertig
sein mit etw; **to ~ doing sth** mit etw fertig
werden; ~ **off** *vt* (*complete*) fertig machen;
(*kill*) den Gnadenstoß geben +*dat*; (*knock
out*) erledigen (*umg*); ~ **up** *vt* (*food*)
aufessen; (*drink*) austrinken ♦ *vi* (*end up*)
enden; ~**ing line** *n* Ziellinie *f*; ~**ing
school** *n* Mädchenpensionat *nt*

finite [ˈfaɪnaɪt] *adj* endlich, begrenzt

Finland [ˈfɪnlənd] *n* Finnland *nt*

Finn [fɪn] *n* Finne *m*, Finnin *f*; **~ish** *adj*
finnisch ♦ *n* (*LING*) Finnisch *nt*

fir [fəːʳ] *n* Tanne *f*

fire ['faɪəʳ] *n* Feuer *nt*; (*in house etc*) Brand *m*
♦ *vt* (*gun*) abfeuern; (*imagination*)
entzünden; (*dismiss*) hinauswerfen ♦ *vi*
(*AUT*) zünden; **to be on ~** brennen; **~
alarm** *n* Feueralarm *m*; **~arm** *n*
Schusswaffe *f*; **~ brigade** (*BRIT*) *n*
Feuerwehr *f*; **~ department** (*US*) *n*
Feuerwehr *f*; **~ engine** *n* Feuerwehrauto
nt; **~ escape** *n* Feuerleiter *f*; **~
extinguisher** *n* Löschgerät *nt*; **~man**
(*irreg*) *n* Feuerwehrmann *m*; **~place** *n*
Kamin *m*; **~side** *n* Kamin *m*; **~ station** *n*
Feuerwehrwache *f*; **~wood** *n* Brennholz *nt*;
~works *npl* Feuerwerk *nt*; **~ squad** *n*
Exekutionskommando *nt*

firm [fəːm] *adj* fest ♦ *n* Firma *f*; **~ly**
adv (*grasp, speak*) fest; (*push, tug*) energisch;
(*decide*) endgültig

first [fəːst] *adj* erste(r, s) ♦ *adv* zuerst; (*arrive*)
als Erste(r); (*happen*) zum ersten Mal ♦ *n*
(*person: in race*) Erste(r) *mf*; (*UNIV*) Eins *f*;
(*AUT*) erste(r) Gang *m*; **at ~** zuerst; **~ of all**
zuallererst; **~ aid** *n* erste Hilfe *f*; **~-aid kit** *n*
Verbandskasten *m*; **~-class** *adj* erstklassig;
(*travel*) erster Klasse; **~-hand** *adj* aus erster
Hand; **~ lady** (*US*) *n* First Lady *f*; **~ly** *adv*
erstens; **~ name** *n* Vorname *m*; **~-rate** *adj*
erstklassig

fiscal ['fɪskl] *adj* Finanz-

fish [fɪʃ] *n inv* Fisch *m* ♦ *vi* fischen; angeln; **to
go ~ing** angeln gehen; (*in sea*) fischen
gehen; **~erman** (*irreg*) *n* Fischer *m*; **~ farm**
n Fischzucht *f*; **~ fingers** (*BRIT*) *npl*
Fischstäbchen *pl*; **~ing boat** *n* Fischerboot
nt; **~ing line** *n* Angelschnur *f*; **~ing rod** *n*
Angel(rute) *f*; **~ing tackle** *n* (*for sport*)
Angelgeräte *pl*; **~monger's (shop)** *n*
Fischhändler *m*; **~ slice** *n*
Fischvorlegemesser *nt*; **~ sticks** (*US*) *npl* =
fish fingers

fishy ['fɪʃɪ] (*inf*) *adj* (*suspicious*) faul

fission ['fɪʃən] *n* Spaltung *f*

fissure ['fɪʃəʳ] *n* Riss *m*

fist [fɪst] *n* Faust *f*

fit [fɪt] *adj* (*MED*) gesund; (*SPORT*) in Form, fit;
(*suitable*) geeignet ♦ *vt* passen +*dat*; (*insert,
attach*) einsetzen ♦ *vi* passen; (*in space, gap*)
hineinpassen ♦ *n* (*of clothes*) Sitz *m*; (*MED, of
anger*) Anfall *m*; (*of laughter*) Krampf *m*; **by
~s and starts** (*move*) ruckweise; (*work*)
unregelmäßig; **~ in** *vi* hineinpassen; (*fig:
person*) passen; **~ out** *vt* (*also:* **~ up**)
ausstatten; **~ful** *adj* (*sleep*) unruhig; **~ment**
n Einrichtungsgegenstand *m*; **~ness** *n*
(*suitability*) Eignung *f*; (*MED*) Gesundheit *f*;
(*SPORT*) Fitness *f*; **~ted carpet** *n*
Teppichboden *m*; **~ted kitchen** *n*
Einbauküche *f*; **~ter** *n* (*TECH*) Monteur *m*;
~ting *adj* passend ♦ *n* (*of dress*) Anprobe *f*;
(*piece of equipment*) (Ersatz)teil *nt*; **~tings**
npl (*equipment*) Zubehör *nt*; **~ting room** *n*
Anproberaum *m*

five [faɪv] *num* fünf; **~r** (*inf*) *n* (*BRIT*)
Fünfpfundnote *f*; (*US*) Fünfdollarnote *f*

fix [fɪks] *vt* befestigen; (*settle*) festsetzen;
(*repair*) reparieren ♦ *n*: **in a ~** in der
Klemme; **~ up** *vt* (*meeting*) arrangieren; **to
~ sb up with sth** jdm etw *acc* verschaffen;
~ation [fɪk'seɪʃən] *n* Fixierung *f*; **~ed** [fɪkst]
adj fest; **~ture** ['fɪkstʃəʳ] *n* Installationsteil *m*;
(*SPORT*) Spiel *nt*

fizzy ['fɪzɪ] *adj* Sprudel-, sprudelnd

flabbergasted ['flæbəgɑːstɪd] (*inf*) *adj* platt

flabby ['flæbɪ] *adj* wabbelig

flag [flæg] *n* Fahne *f* ♦ *vi* (*strength*)
nachlassen; (*spirit*) erlahmen; **~ down** *vt*
anhalten; **~pole** ['flægpəul] *n* Fahnenstange
f

flair [flɛəʳ] *n* Talent *nt*

flak [flæk] *n* Flakfeuer *nt*

flake [fleɪk] *n* (*of snow*) Flocke *f*; (*of rust*)
Schuppe *f* ♦ *vi* (*also:* **~ off**) abblättern

flamboyant [flæm'bɔɪənt] *adj* extravagant

flame [fleɪm] *n* Flamme *f*

flamingo [flə'mɪŋgəu] *n* Flamingo *m*

flammable ['flæməbl] *adj* brennbar

flan [flæn] (*BRIT*) *n* Obsttorte *f*

flank [flæŋk] *n* Flanke *f* ♦ *vt* flankieren

flannel ['flænl] *n* Flanell *m*; (*BRIT: also:* **face
~**) Waschlappen *m*; (: *inf*) Geschwafel *nt*;
~s *npl* (*trousers*) Flanellhose *f*

flap [flæp] n Klappe f ♦ vt (wings) schlagen mit ♦ vi flattern

flare [fleəʳ] n (signal) Leuchtsignal nt; (in skirt etc) Weite f; ~ **up** vi aufflammen; (fig) aufbrausen; (revolt) (plötzlich) ausbrechen

flash [flæʃ] n Blitz m; (also: **news ~**) Kurzmeldung f; (PHOT) Blitzlicht nt ♦ vt aufleuchten lassen ♦ vi aufleuchten; **in a ~** im Nu; ~ **by** or **past** vi vorbeirasen; ~**back** n Rückblende f; ~**bulb** n Blitzlichtbirne f; ~ **cube** n Blitzwürfel m; ~**light** n Blitzlicht nt

flashy ['flæʃɪ] (pej) adj knallig

flask [flɑːsk] n (CHEM) Kolben m; (also: **vacuum ~**) Thermosflasche f ®

flat [flæt] adj flach; (dull) matt; (MUS) erniedrigt; (beer) schal; (tyre) platt ♦ n (BRIT: rooms) Wohnung f; (MUS) b nt; (AUT) Platte(r) m; **to work ~ out** auf Hochtouren arbeiten; ~**ly** adv glatt; ~**screen** adj (TV, COMPUT) mit flachem Bildschirm; ~**ten** vt (also: ~**ten out**) ebnen

flatter ['flætəʳ] vt schmeicheln +dat; ~**ing** adj schmeichelhaft; ~**y** n Schmeichelei f

flatulence ['flætjʊləns] n Blähungen pl

flaunt [flɔːnt] vt prunken mit

flavour ['fleɪvəʳ] (US **flavor**) n Geschmack m ♦ vt würzen; ~**ed** adj: **strawberry-~ed** mit Erdbeergeschmack; ~**ing** n Würze f

flaw [flɔː] n Fehler m; ~**less** adj einwandfrei

flax [flæks] n Flachs m; ~**en** adj flachsfarben

flea [fliː] n Floh m

fleck [flek] n (mark) Fleck m; (pattern) Tupfen m

fled [fled] pt, pp of **flee**

flee [fliː] (pt, pp **fled**) vi fliehen ♦ vt fliehen vor +dat; (country) fliehen aus

fleece [fliːs] n Vlies nt ♦ vt (inf) schröpfen

fleet [fliːt] n Flotte f

fleeting ['fliːtɪŋ] adj flüchtig

Flemish ['flemɪʃ] adj flämisch

flesh [fleʃ] n Fleisch nt; ~ **wound** n Fleischwunde f

flew [fluː] pt of **fly**

flex [fleks] n Kabel nt ♦ vt beugen; ~**ibility** [fleksɪ'bɪlɪtɪ] n Biegsamkeit f; (fig) Flexibilität

f; ~**ible** adj biegsam; (plans) flexibel

flick [flɪk] n leichte(r) Schlag m ♦ vt leicht schlagen; ~ **through** vt fus durchblättern

flicker ['flɪkəʳ] n Flackern nt ♦ vi flackern

flier ['flaɪəʳ] n Flieger m

flight [flaɪt] n Flug m; (fleeing) Flucht f; (also: ~ **of steps**) Treppe f; **to take ~** die Flucht ergreifen; ~ **attendant** (US) n Steward(ess) m(f); ~ **deck** n Flugdeck nt

flimsy ['flɪmzɪ] adj (thin) hauchdünn; (excuse) fadenscheinig

flinch [flɪntʃ] vi: **to ~ (away from)** zurückschrecken (vor +dat)

fling [flɪŋ] (pt, pp **flung**) vt schleudern

flint [flɪnt] n Feuerstein m

flip [flɪp] vt werfen

flippant ['flɪpənt] adj schnippisch

flipper ['flɪpəʳ] n Flosse f

flirt [flɜːt] vi flirten ♦ n: **he/she is a ~** er/sie flirtet gern

flit [flɪt] vi flitzen

float [fləʊt] n (FISHING) Schwimmer m; (esp in procession) Plattformwagen m ♦ vi schwimmen; (in air) schweben ♦ vt (COMM) gründen; (currency) floaten

flock [flɔk] n (of sheep, REL) Herde f; (of birds) Schwarm m

flog [flɔg] vt prügeln; (inf: sell) verkaufen

flood [flʌd] n Überschwemmung f; (fig) Flut f ♦ vt überschwemmen; ~**ing** n Überschwemmung f; ~**light** n Flutlicht nt

floor [flɔːʳ] n (Fuß)boden m; (storey) Stock m ♦ vt (person) zu Boden schlagen; **ground ~** (BRIT) Erdgeschoss nt; **first ~** (BRIT) erste(r) Stock m; (US) Erdgeschoss nt; ~**board** n Diele f; ~ **show** n Kabarettvorstellung f

flop [flɔp] n Plumps m; (failure) Reinfall m ♦ vi (fail) durchfallen

floppy ['flɔpɪ] adj hängend; ~ (**disk**) n (COMPUT) Diskette f

flora ['flɔːrə] n Flora f; ~**l** adj Blumen-

florist ['flɔrɪst] n Blumenhändler(in) m(f); ~**'s (shop)** n Blumengeschäft nt

flotation [fləʊ'teɪʃən] n (FIN) Auflegung f

flounce [flaʊns] n Volant m

flounder ['flaʊndəʳ] vi (fig) ins Schleudern kommen ♦ n (ZOOL) Flunder f

flour ['flauə^r] n Mehl nt

flourish ['flʌrɪʃ] vi blühen; gedeihen ♦ n (waving) Schwingen nt; (of trumpets) Tusch m, Fanfare f

flout [flaut] vt missachten

flow [fləu] n Fließen nt; (of sea) Flut f ♦ vi fließen; ~ **chart** n Flussdiagramm nt

flower ['flauə^r] n Blume f ♦ vi blühen; ~ **bed** n Blumenbeet nt; ~**pot** n Blumentopf m; ~**y** adj (style) blumenreich

flown [fləun] pp of **fly**

flu [fluː] n Grippe f

fluctuate ['flʌktjueɪt] vi schwanken; **fluctuation** [flʌktju'eɪʃən] n Schwankung f

fluency ['fluːənsɪ] n Flüssigkeit f

fluent ['fluːənt] adj fließend; ~**ly** adv fließend

fluff [flʌf] n Fussel f; ~**y** adj flaumig

fluid ['fluːɪd] n Flüssigkeit f ♦ adj flüssig; (fig: plans) veränderbar

fluke [fluːk] (inf) n Dusel m

flung [flʌŋ] pt, pp of **fling**

fluoride ['fluəraɪd] n Fluorid nt; ~ **toothpaste** n Fluorzahnpasta f

flurry ['flʌrɪ] n (of snow) Gestöber nt; (of activity) Aufregung f

flush [flʌʃ] n Erröten nt; (excited) Glühen nt ♦ vt (aus)spülen ♦ vi erröten ♦ adj glatt; ~ **out** vt aufstöbern; ~**ed** adj rot

flustered ['flʌstəd] adj verwirrt

flute [fluːt] n Querflöte f

flutter ['flʌtə^r] n Flattern nt ♦ vi flattern

flux [flʌks] n: **in a state of ~** im Fluss

fly [flaɪ] (pt **flew**, pp **flown**) n (insect) Fliege f; (on trousers: also: **flies**) (Hosen)schlitz m ♦ vt fliegen ♦ vi fliegen; (flee) fliehen; (flag) wehen; ~ **away** or **off** vi (bird, insect) wegfliegen; ~-**drive** n: ~-**drive holiday** Fly & Drive-Urlaub m; ~**ing** n Fliegen nt ♦ adj: **with ~ing colours** mit fliegenden Fahnen; ~**ing start** gute(r) Start m; ~**ing visit** Stippvisite f; ~**ing saucer** n fliegende Untertasse f; ~**over** (BRIT) n Überführung f; ~**sheet** n (for tent) Regendach nt

foal [fəul] n Fohlen nt

foam [fəum] n Schaum m ♦ vi schäumen; ~ **rubber** n Schaumgummi m

fob [fɔb] vt: **to ~ sb off with sth** jdm etw andrehen; (with promise) jdn mit etw abspeisen

focal ['fəukl] adj Brenn-; ~ **point** n (of room, activity) Mittelpunkt m

focus ['fəukəs] (pl ~**es**) n Brennpunkt m ♦ vt (attention) konzentrieren; (camera) scharf einstellen ♦ vi: **to ~ (on)** sich konzentrieren (auf +acc); **in ~** scharf eingestellt; **out of ~** unscharf

fodder ['fɔdə^r] n Futter nt

foe [fəu] n Feind m

foetus ['fiːtəs] (US **fetus**) n Fötus m

fog [fɔg] n Nebel m; ~**gy** adj neblig; ~ **lamp** (BRIT), ~ **light** (US) n (AUT) Nebelscheinwerfer m

foil [fɔɪl] vt vereiteln ♦ n (metal, also fig) Folie f; (FENCING) Florett nt

fold [fəuld] n (bend, crease) Falte f; (AGR) Pferch m ♦ vt falten; ~ **up** vt (map etc) zusammenfalten ♦ vi (business) eingehen; ~**er** n Schnellhefter m; ~**ing** adj (chair etc) Klapp-

foliage ['fəulɪɪdʒ] n Laubwerk nt

folk [fəuk] npl Leute pl ♦ adj Volks-; ~**s** npl (family) Leute pl; ~**lore** ['fəuklɔː^r] n (study) Volkskunde f; (tradition) Folklore f; ~ **song** n Volkslied nt; (modern) Folksong m

follow ['fɔləu] vt folgen +dat; (fashion) mitmachen ♦ vi folgen; ~ **up** vt verfolgen; ~**er** n Anhänger(in) m(f); ~**ing** adj folgend ♦ n (people) Gefolgschaft f; ~-**on call** n weiteres Gespräch in einer Telefonzelle um Guthaben zu verbrauchen

folly ['fɔlɪ] n Torheit f

fond [fɔnd] adj: **to be ~ of** gern haben

fondle ['fɔndl] vt streicheln

font [fɔnt] n Taufbecken nt

food [fuːd] n Essen nt; (fodder) Futter nt; ~ **mixer** n Küchenmixer m; ~ **poisoning** n Lebensmittelvergiftung f; ~ **processor** n Küchenmaschine f; ~**stuffs** npl Lebensmittel pl

fool [fuːl] n Narr m, Närrin f ♦ vt (deceive) hereinlegen ♦ vi (also: ~ **around**) (herum)albern; ~**hardy** adj tollkühn; ~**ish** adj albern; ~**proof** adj idiotensicher

foot [fut] (pl **feet**) n Fuß m ♦ vt (bill)

bezahlen; **on ~** zu Fuß

footage ['futɪdʒ] n (CINE) Filmmaterial nt

football ['futbɔːl] n Fußball m; (game: BRIT) Fußball m; (: US) Football m; **~ player** n (BRIT: also: **~er**) Fußballspieler m, Fußballer m; (US) Footballer m

---

Football Pools

i Football Pools, umgangssprachlich auch the pools genannt, ist das in Großbritannien sehr beliebte Fußballtoto, bei dem auf die Ergebnisse der samstäglichen Fußballspiele gewettet wird. Teilnehmer schicken ihren ausgefüllten Totoschein vor den Spielen an die Totogesellschaft und vergleichen nach den Spielen die Ergebnisse mit ihrem Schein. Die Gewinne können sehr hoch sein und gelegentlich Millionen von Pfund betragen.

---

foot: **~brake** n Fußbremse f; **~bridge** n Fußgängerbrücke f; **~hills** npl Ausläufer pl; **~hold** n Halt m; **~ing** n Halt m; (fig) Verhältnis nt; **~lights** npl Rampenlicht nt; **~man** (irreg) n Bedienstete(r) m; **~note** n Fußnote f; **~path** n Fußweg m; **~print** n Fußabdruck m; **~sore** adj fußkrank; **~step** n Schritt m; **~wear** n Schuhzeug nt

---

for [fɔː] prep **1** für; **is this for me?** ist das für mich?; **the train for London** der Zug nach London; **he went for the paper** er ging die Zeitung holen; **give it to me - what for?** gib es mir – warum?

2 (because of) wegen; **for this reason** aus diesem Grunde

3 (referring to distance): **there are roadworks for 5 km** die Baustelle ist 5 km lang; **we walked for miles** wir sind meilenweit gegangen

4 (referring to time) seit; (: with future sense) für; **he was away for 2 years** er war zwei Jahre lang weg

5 (+infin clauses): **it is not for me to decide** das kann ich nicht entscheiden; **for this to be possible ...** damit dies möglich wird/

wurde ...

6 (in spite of) trotz +gen or (inf) dat ; **for all his complaints** obwohl er sich ständig beschwert

♦ conj denn

---

forage ['fɒrɪdʒ] n (Vieh)futter nt

foray ['fɒreɪ] n Raubzug m

forbad(e) [fə'bæd] pt of **forbid**

forbid [fə'bɪd] (pt **forbad(e)**, pp **forbidden**) vt verbieten; **~ding** adj einschüchternd

force [fɔːs] n Kraft f; (compulsion) Zwang m ♦ vt zwingen; (lock) aufbrechen; **the F~s** npl (BRIT) die Streitkräfte npl; **in ~** (rule) gültig; (group) in großer Stärke; **~d** adj (smile) gezwungen; (landing) Not-; **~-feed** vt zwangsernähren; **~ful** adj (speech) kraftvoll; (personality) resolut

forceps ['fɔːseps] npl Zange f

forcibly ['fɔːsəblɪ] adv zwangsweise

ford [fɔːd] n Furt f ♦ vt durchwaten

fore [fɔː] n: **to the ~** in den Vordergrund; **~arm** ['fɔːrɑːm] n Unterarm m; **~boding** [fɔː'bəʊdɪŋ] n Vorahnung f; **~cast** ['fɔːkɑːst] (irreg: like **cast**) n Vorhersage f ♦ vt voraussagen; **~court** ['fɔːkɔːt] n (of garage) Vorplatz m; **~fathers** ['fɔːfɑːðəz] npl Vorfahren pl; **~finger** ['fɔːfɪŋgə] n Zeigefinger m; **~front** ['fɔːfrʌnt] n Spitze f

forego [fɔː'gəʊ] (irreg: like **go**) vt verzichten auf +acc

fore: **~gone** ['fɔːgɒn] adj: **it's a ~gone conclusion** es steht von vornherein fest; **~ground** ['fɔːgraʊnd] n Vordergrund m; **~head** ['fɒrɪd] n Stirn f

foreign ['fɒrɪn] adj Auslands-; (accent) ausländisch; (trade) Außen-; (body) Fremd-; **~er** n Ausländer(in) m(f); **~ exchange** n Devisen pl; **F~ Office** (BRIT) n Außenministerium nt; **F~ Secretary** (BRIT) n Außenminister m

fore ['fɔː-]: **~leg** n Vorderbein nt; **~man** (irreg) n Vorarbeiter m; **~most** adj erste(r, s) ♦ adv: **first and ~most** vor allem

forensic [fə'rensɪk] adj gerichtsmedizinisch

fore ['fɔː-]: **~runner** n Vorläufer m; **~see** [fɔː'siː] (irreg: like **see**) vt vorhersehen;

~seeable adj absehbar; **~shadow** [fɔ:'ʃædəu] vt andeuten; **~sight** ['fɔ:saɪt] n Voraussicht f

forest ['fɒrɪst] n Wald m

forestall [fɔ:'stɔ:l] vt zuvorkommen +dat

forestry ['fɒrɪstrɪ] n Forstwirtschaft f

foretaste ['fɔ:teɪst] n Vorgeschmack m

foretell [fɔ:'tel] (irreg: like **tell**) vt vorhersagen

forever [fə'revə*] adv für immer

foreword ['fɔ:wə:d] n Vorwort nt

forfeit ['fɔ:fɪt] n Einbuße f ♦ vt verwirken

forgave [fə'geɪv] pt of **forgive**

forge [fɔ:dʒ] n Schmiede f ♦ vt fälschen; (iron) schmieden; **~ ahead** vi Fortschritte machen; **~d** adj gefälscht; **~d banknotes** Blüten (inf) pl; **~r** n Fälscher m; **~ry** n Fälschung f

forget [fə'get] (pt **forgot**, pp **forgotten**) vt, vi vergessen; **~ful** adj vergesslich; **~-me-not** n Vergissmeinnicht nt

forgive [fə'gɪv] (pt **forgave**, pp **forgiven**) vt verzeihen; **to ~ sb (for sth)** jdm (etw) verzeihen; **~ness** n Verzeihung f

forgot [fə'gɒt] pt of **forget**; **~ten** pp of **forget**

fork [fɔ:k] n Gabel f; (in road) Gabelung f ♦ vi (road) sich gabeln; **~ out** (inf) vt (pay) blechen; **~-lift truck** n Gabelstapler m

forlorn [fə'lɔ:n] adj (person) verlassen; (hope) vergeblich

form [fɔ:m] n Form f; (type) Art f; (figure) Gestalt f; (SCH) Klasse f; (bench) (Schul)bank f; (document) Formular n ♦ vt formen; (be part of) bilden

formal ['fɔ:məl] adj formell; (occasion) offiziell; **~ly** adv (ceremoniously) formell; (officially) offiziell

format ['fɔ:mæt] n Format nt ♦ vt (COMPUT) formatieren

formation [fɔ:'meɪʃən] n Bildung f; (AVIAT) Formation f

formative ['fɔ:mətɪv] adj (years) formend

former ['fɔ:mə*] adj früher; (opposite of latter) erstere(r, s); **~ly** adv früher

formidable ['fɔ:mɪdəbl] adj furchtbar

formula ['fɔ:mjulə] (pl **~e** or **~s**) n Formel f; **~e** ['fɔ:mjuli:] npl of **formula**; **~te**

['fɔ:mjuleɪt] vt formulieren

fort [fɔ:t] n Feste f, Fort nt

forte ['fɔ:tɪ] n Stärke f, starke Seite f

forth [fɔ:θ] adv: **and so ~** und so weiter; **~coming** adj kommend; (character) entgegenkommend; **~right** adj offen; **~with** adv umgehend

fortify ['fɔ:tɪfaɪ] vt (ver)stärken; (protect) befestigen

fortitude ['fɔ:tɪtju:d] n Seelenstärke f

fortnight ['fɔ:tnaɪt] (BRIT) n vierzehn Tage pl; **~ly** (BRIT) adj zweiwöchentlich ♦ adv alle vierzehn Tage

fortress ['fɔ:trɪs] n Festung f

fortunate ['fɔ:tʃənɪt] adj glücklich; **~ly** adv glücklicherweise, zum Glück

fortune ['fɔ:tʃən] n Glück nt; (money) Vermögen nt; **~-teller** n Wahrsager(in) m(f)

forty ['fɔ:tɪ] num vierzig

forum ['fɔ:rəm] n Forum nt

forward ['fɔ:wəd] adj vordere(r, s); (movement) Vorwärts-; (person) vorlaut; (planning) Voraus- ♦ adv vorwärts ♦ n (SPORT) Stürmer m ♦ vt (send) schicken; (help) fördern; **~s** adv vorwärts

fossil ['fɒsl] n Fossil nt, Versteinerung f

foster ['fɒstə*] vt (talent) fördern; **~ child** n Pflegekind nt; **~ mother** n Pflegemutter f

fought [fɔ:t] pt, pp of **fight**

foul [faul] adj schmutzig; (language) gemein; (weather) schlecht ♦ n (SPORT) Foul nt ♦ vt (mechanism) blockieren; (SPORT) foulen; **~ play** n (SPORT) Foulspiel nt; (LAW) Verbrechen nt

found [faund] pt, pp of **find** ♦ vt gründen; **~ation** [faun'deɪʃən] n (act) Gründung f; (fig) Fundament nt; (also: **~ation cream**) Grundierungscreme f; **~ations** npl (of house) Fundament nt; **~er** n Gründer(in) m(f) ♦ vi sinken

foundry ['faundrɪ] n Gießerei f

fountain ['fauntɪn] n (Spring)brunnen m; **~ pen** n Füllfederhalter m

four [fɔ:*] num vier; **on all ~s** auf allen vieren; **~-poster** n Himmelbett nt; **~some** n Quartett nt; **~teen** num vierzehn;

~teenth *adj* vierzehnte(r, s); **~th** *adj* vierte(r, s)

wl [faul] *n* Huhn *nt*; (*food*) Geflügel *nt*

x [fɔks] *n* Fuchs *m* ♦ *vt* täuschen

yer ['fɔɪeɪ] *n* Foyer *nt*, Vorhalle *f*

action ['frækʃən] *n* (*MATH*) Bruch *m*; (*part*) Bruchteil *m*

acture ['fræktʃəʳ] *n* (*MED*) Bruch *m* ♦ *vt* brechen

agile ['frædʒaɪl] *adj* zerbrechlich

agment ['frægmənt] *n* Bruchstück *nt*; (*small part*) Splitter *m*

agrance ['freɪgrəns] *n* Duft *m*; **fragrant** ['freɪgrənt] *adj* duftend

ail [freɪl] *adj* schwach, gebrechlich

ame [freɪm] *n* Rahmen *m*; (*of spectacles: also:* **~s**) Gestell *nt*; (*body*) Gestalt *f* ♦ *vt* einrahmen; **to ~ sb** (*inf: incriminate*) jdm etwas anhängen; **~ of mind** Verfassung *f*; **~work** *n* Rahmen *m*; (*of society*) Gefüge *nt*

ance [frɑːns] *n* Frankreich *nt*

anchise ['fræntʃaɪz] *n* (*POL*) (aktives) Wahlrecht *nt*; (*COMM*) Lizenz *f*

ank [fræŋk] *adj* offen ♦ *vt* (*letter*) frankieren; **~ly** *adv* offen gesagt

antic ['fræntɪk] *adj* verzweifelt

aternal [frə'tɜːnl] *adj* brüderlich

aternity [frə'tɜːnɪtɪ] *n* (*club*) Vereinigung *f*; (*spirit*) Brüderlichkeit *f*; (*US: SCH*) Studentenverbindung *f*

aternize ['frætənaɪz] *vi* fraternisieren

aud [frɔːd] *n* (*trickery*) Betrug *m*; (*person*) Schwindler(in) *m(f)*; **~ulent** ['frɔːdjulənt] *adj* betrügerisch

aught [frɔːt] *adj*: **~ with** voller +*gen*

ay [freɪ] *vt, vi* ausfransen; **tempers were ~ed** die Gemüter waren erhitzt

eak [friːk] *n* Monstrosität *f* ♦ *cpd* (*storm etc*) anormal

eckle ['frekl] *n* Sommersprosse *f*

ee [friː] *adj* frei; (*loose*) lose; (*liberal*) freigebig ♦ *vt* (*set ~*) befreien; (*unblock*) freimachen; **~ (of charge)** gratis, umsonst; **for ~** gratis, umsonst; **~dom** ['friːdəm] *n* Freiheit *f*; **F~fone** ® *n*: **call F~fone 0800 ...** rufen Sie gebührenfrei 0800 ... an; **~-for-all** *n* (*fight*) allgemeine(s)

Handgemenge *nt*; **~ gift** *n* Geschenk *nt*; **~ kick** *n* Freistoß *m*; **~lance** *adj* frei; (*artist*) freischaffend; **~ly** *adv* frei; (*admit*) offen; **F~post** ® *n* ≃ Gebühr zahlt Empfänger; **~-range** *adj* (*hen*) Farmhof-; (*eggs*) Land-; **~ trade** *n* Freihandel *m*; **~way** (*US*) *n* Autobahn *f*; **~wheel** *vi* im Freilauf fahren; **~ will** *n*: **of one's own ~ will** aus freien Stücken

freeze [friːz] (*pt* **froze**, *pp* **frozen**) *vi* gefrieren; (*feel cold*) frieren ♦ *vt* (*also fig*) einfrieren ♦ *n* (*fig, FIN*) Stopp *m*; **~r** *n* Tiefkühltruhe *f*; (*in fridge*) Gefrierfach *nt*; **freezing** *adj* eisig; (*freezing cold*) eiskalt; **freezing point** *n* Gefrierpunkt *m*

freight [freɪt] *n* Fracht *f*; **~ train** *n* Güterzug *m*

French [frentʃ] *adj* französisch ♦ *n* (*LING*) Französisch *nt*; **the ~** *npl* (*people*) die Franzosen *pl*; **~ bean** *n* grüne Bohne *f*; **~ fried potatoes** (*BRIT*) *npl* Pommes frites *pl*; **~ fries** (*US*) *npl* Pommes frites *pl*; **~ horn** *n* (*MUS*) (Wald)horn *nt*; **~ kiss** *n* Zungenkuss *m*; **~ loaf** *n* Baguette *f*; **~man/woman** (*irreg*) *n* Franzose *m*/Französin *f*; **~ window** *n* Verandatür *f*

frenzy ['frenzɪ] *n* Raserei *f*

frequency ['friːkwənsɪ] *n* Häufigkeit *f*; (*PHYS*) Frequenz *f*

frequent [*adj* 'friːkwənt, *vb* frɪ'kwent] *adj* häufig ♦ *vt* (regelmäßig) besuchen; **~ly** *adv* (*often*) häufig, oft

fresh [freʃ] *adj* frisch; **~en** *vi* (*also:* **~en up**) (sich) auffrischen; (*person*) sich frisch machen; **~er** (*inf: BRIT*) *n* (*UNIV*) Erstsemester *nt*; **~ly** *adv* gerade; **~man** (*irreg*) (*US*) *n* = **fresher**; **~ness** *n* Frische *f*; **~water** *adj* (*fish*) Süßwasser-

fret [fret] *vi* sich *dat* Sorgen machen

friar ['fraɪəʳ] *n* Klosterbruder *m*

friction ['frɪkʃən] *n* (*also fig*) Reibung *f*

Friday ['fraɪdɪ] *n* Freitag *m*

fridge [frɪdʒ] (*BRIT*) *n* Kühlschrank *m*

fried [fraɪd] *adj* gebraten

friend [frend] *n* Freund(in) *m(f)*; **~ly** *adj* freundlich; (*relations*) freundschaftlich; **~ly fire** *n* Beschuss *m* durch die eigene Seite;

~ship n Freundschaft f

frieze [friːz] n Fries m

frigate ['frɪgɪt] n Fregatte f

fright [fraɪt] n Schrecken m; to take ~ es mit der Angst zu tun bekommen; ~en vt erschrecken; to be ~ened Angst haben; ~ening adj schrecklich; ~ful (inf) adj furchtbar

frigid ['frɪdʒɪd] adj frigide

frill [frɪl] n Rüsche f

fringe [frɪndʒ] n Besatz m; (BRIT: of hair) Pony m; (fig) Peripherie f; ~ benefits npl zusätzliche Leistungen pl

Frisbee ['frɪzbɪ] ® n Frisbee ® nt

frisk [frɪsk] vt durchsuchen

frisky ['frɪskɪ] adj lebendig, ausgelassen

fritter ['frɪtə*] vt: to ~ away vergeuden

frivolous ['frɪvələs] adj frivol

frizzy ['frɪzɪ] adj kraus

fro [frəu] adv see to

frock [frɔk] n Kleid nt

frog [frɔg] n Frosch m; ~man (irreg) n Froschmann m

frolic ['frɔlɪk] vi ausgelassen sein

KEYWORD

from [frɔm] prep 1 (indicating starting place) of; (indicating origin etc) aus +dat; a letter/ telephone call from my sister ein Brief/ Anruf von meiner Schwester; where do you come from? woher kommen Sie?; to drink from the bottle aus der Flasche trinken

2 (indicating time) von ... an; (: past) seit; from one o'clock to or until or till two von ein Uhr bis zwei; from January (on) ab Januar

3 (indicating distance) von ... (entfernt)

4 (indicating price, number etc) ab +dat; from £10 ab £10; there were from 20 to 30 people there es waren zwischen 20 und 30 Leute da

5 (indicating difference): he can't tell red from green er kann nicht zwischen Rot und Grün unterscheiden; to be different from sb/sth anders sein als jd/etw

6 (because of, based on): from what he says aus dem, was er sagt; weak from hunger schwach vor Hunger

front [frʌnt] n Vorderseite f; (of house) Fassade f; (promenade: also: sea ~) Strandpromenade f; (MIL, POL, MET) Front f; (fig: appearances) Fassade f ♦ adj (forward) vordere(r, s), Vorder-; (first) vorderste(r, s); in ~ vorne; in ~ of vor; ~age ['frʌntɪdʒ] n Vorderfront f; ~ door n Haustür f; ~ier ['frʌntɪə*] n Grenze f; ~ page n Titelseite f; ~ room (BRIT) n Wohnzimmer nt; ~-wheel drive n Vorderradantrieb m

frost [frɔst] n Frost m; ~bite n Erfrierung f; ~ed adj (glass) Milch-; ~y adj frostig

froth [frɔθ] n Schaum m

frown [fraun] n Stirnrunzeln nt ♦ vi die Stirn runzeln

froze [frəuz] pt of freeze

frozen ['frəuzn] pp of freeze

frugal ['fruːgl] adj sparsam, bescheiden

fruit [fruːt] n inv (as collective) Obst nt; (particular) Frucht f; ~ful adj fruchtbar; ~ion [fruːˈɪʃən] n: to come to ~ion in Erfüllung gehen; ~ juice n Fruchtsaft m; ~ machine (BRIT) n Spielautomat m; ~ salad n Obstsalat m

frustrate [frʌsˈtreɪt] vt vereiteln; ~d adj gehemmt; (PSYCH) frustriert

fry [fraɪ] (pt, pp fried) vt braten ♦ npl: small ~ kleine Fische pl; ~ing pan n Bratpfanne f

ft. abbr = foot; feet

fuddy-duddy ['fʌdɪdʌdɪ] n altmodische(r) Kauz m

fudge [fʌdʒ] n Fondant m

fuel ['fjuəl] n Treibstoff m; (for heating) Brennstoff m; (for lighter) Benzin nt; ~ oil n (diesel fuel) Heizöl nt; ~ tank n Tank m

fugitive ['fjuːdʒɪtɪv] n Flüchtling m

fulfil [fulˈfɪl] vt (duty) erfüllen; (promise) einhalten; ~ment n Erfüllung f

full [ful] adj (box, bottle, price) voll; (person: satisfied) satt; (member, power, employment) Voll-; (complete) vollständig, Voll-; (speed) höchste(r, s); (skirt) weit ♦ adv: ~ well sehr wohl; in ~ vollständig; a ~ two hours volle zwei Stunden; **~-length** adj (lifesize) lebensgroß; **a ~-length photograph** eine Ganzaufnahme; **~ moon** n Vollmond m; **~-scale** adj (attack) General-; (drawing) in Originalgröße; **~ stop** n Punkt m; **~-time** adj (job) Ganztags- ♦ adv (work) ganztags ♦ n (SPORT) Spielschluss nt; **~ly** adv völlig; **~y fledged** adj (also fig) flügge; **~y licensed** adj (hotel, restaurant) mit voller Schankkonzession or -erlaubnis

fumble ['fʌmbl] vi: **to ~ (with)** herumfummeln (an +dat)

fume [fjuːm] vi qualmen, (fig) kochen (inf); **~s** npl (of fuel, car) Abgase pl

fumigate ['fjuːmɪɡeɪt] vt ausräuchern

fun [fʌn] n Spaß m; **to make ~ of** sich lustig machen über +acc

function ['fʌŋkʃən] n Funktion f; (occasion) Veranstaltung f ♦ vi funktionieren; **~al** adj funktionell

fund [fʌnd] n (money) Geldmittel pl, Fonds m; (store) Vorrat m; **~s** npl (resources) Mittel pl

fundamental [fʌndə'mentl] adj fundamental, grundlegend

funeral ['fjuːnərəl] n Beerdigung f; **~ parlour** n Leichenhalle f; **~ service** n Trauergottesdienst m

unfair [ˈfɛəˀ] (BRIT) n Jahrmarkt m

fungi ['fʌŋɡaɪ] npl of **fungus**

fungus ['fʌŋɡəs] n Pilz m

unnel ['fʌnl] n Trichter m; (NAUT) Schornstein m

unny ['fʌnɪ] adj komisch

ur [fɜː] n Pelz m; **~ coat** n Pelzmantel m

urious ['fjuərɪəs] adj wütend; (attempt) heftig

urlong ['fɜːlɒŋ] n = 201.17 m

urnace ['fɜːnɪs] n (Brenn)ofen m

urnish ['fɜːnɪʃ] vt einrichten; (supply) versehen; **~ings** npl Einrichtung f

urniture ['fɜːnɪtʃəˀ] n Möbel pl; **piece of ~** Möbelstück nt

urrow ['fʌrəʊ] n Furche f

urry ['fɜːrɪ] adj (tongue) pelzig; (animal) Pelz-

urther ['fɜːðəˀ] adj weitere(r, s) ♦ adv weiter ♦ vt fördern; **~ education** n Weiterbildung f; Erwachsenenbildung f; **~more** adv ferner

furthest ['fɜːðɪst] superl of **far**

furtive ['fɜːtɪv] adj verstohlen

fury ['fjuərɪ] n Wut f, Zorn m

fuse [fjuːz] (US **fuze**) n (ELEC) Sicherung f; (of bomb) Zünder m ♦ vt verschmelzen ♦ vi (BRIT: ELEC) durchbrennen; **~ box** n Sicherungskasten m

fuselage ['fjuːzəlɑːʒ] n Flugzeugrumpf m

fusion ['fjuːʒən] n Verschmelzung f

fuss [fʌs] n Theater nt; **~y** adj kleinlich

futile ['fjuːtaɪl] adj zwecklos, sinnlos; **futility** [fjuː'tɪlɪtɪ] n Zwecklosigkeit f

future ['fjuːtʃəˀ] adj zukünftig ♦ n Zukunft f; **in (the) ~** in Zukunft

fuze [fjuːz] (US) = **fuse**

fuzzy ['fʌzɪ] adj (indistinct) verschwommen; (hair) kraus

G, g

G [dʒiː] n (MUS) G nt

G7 n abbr (= Group of Seven) G7 f

gabble ['ɡæbl] vi plappern

gable ['ɡeɪbl] n Giebel m

gadget ['ɡædʒɪt] n Vorrichtung f

Gaelic ['ɡeɪlɪk] adj gälisch ♦ n (LING) Gälisch nt

gaffe [ɡæf] n Fauxpas m

gag [ɡæɡ] n Knebel m; (THEAT) Gag m ♦ vt knebeln

gaiety ['ɡeɪtɪ] n Fröhlichkeit f

gain [ɡeɪn] vt (obtain) erhalten; (win) gewinnen ♦ vi (clock) vorgehen ♦ n Gewinn m; **to ~ in sth** an etw dat gewinnen; **~ on** vt fus einholen

gait [ɡeɪt] n Gang m

gal. abbr = **gallon**

gala ['ɡɑːlə] n Fest nt

galaxy ['ɡæləksɪ] n Sternsystem nt

gale [ɡeɪl] n Sturm m

gallant ['ɡælənt] adj tapfer; (polite) galant

gallbladder [ɡɔːl-] n Gallenblase f

gallery ['ɡælərɪ] n (also: **art ~**) Galerie f

galley ['ɡælɪ] n (ship's kitchen) Kombüse f; (ship) Galeere f

gallon ['gælən] n Gallone f

gallop ['gæləp] n Galopp m ♦ vi galoppieren

gallows ['gæləuz] n Galgen m

gallstone ['gɔːlstəun] n Gallenstein m

galore [gə'lɔːɾ] adv in Hülle und Fülle

galvanize ['gælvənaɪz] vt (metal) galvanisieren; (fig) elektrisieren

gambit ['gæmbɪt] n (fig): **opening ~** (einleitende(r)) Schachzug m

gamble ['gæmbl] vi (um Geld) spielen ♦ vt (risk) aufs Spiel setzen ♦ n Risiko nt; **~r** n Spieler(in) m(f); **gambling** n Glücksspiel nt

game [geɪm] n Spiel nt; (hunting) Wild nt ♦ adj: **~ (for)** bereit (zu); **~keeper** n Wildhüter m; **~s console** n (COMPUT) Gameboy m ®, Konsole f

gammon ['gæmən] n geräucherte(r) Schinken m

gamut ['gæmət] n Tonskala f

gang [gæŋ] n (of criminals, youths) Bande f; (of workmen) Kolonne f ♦ vi: **to ~ up on sb** sich gegen jdn verschwören

gangrene ['gæŋgriːn] n Brand m

gangster ['gæŋstəɾ] n Gangster m

gangway ['gæŋweɪ] n (NAUT) Laufplanke f; (aisle) Gang m

gaol [dʒeɪl] (BRIT) n, vt = **jail**

gap [gæp] n Lücke f

gape [geɪp] vi glotzen; **gaping** ['geɪpɪŋ] adj (wound) klaffend; (hole) gähnend

garage ['gærɑːʒ] n Garage f; (for repair) (Auto)reparaturwerkstatt f; (for petrol) Tankstelle f

garbage ['gɑːbɪdʒ] n Abfall m; **~ can** (US) n Mülltonne f

garbled ['gɑːbld] adj (story) verdreht

garden ['gɑːdn] n Garten m; **~s** npl (public park) Park m; (private) Gartenanlagen pl; **~er** n Gärtner(in) m(f); **~ing** n Gärtnern nt

gargle ['gɑːgl] vi gurgeln

gargoyle ['gɑːgɔɪl] n Wasserspeier m

garish ['gɛərɪʃ] adj grell

garland ['gɑːlənd] n Girlande f

garlic ['gɑːlɪk] n Knoblauch m

garment ['gɑːmənt] n Kleidungsstück nt

garnish ['gɑːnɪʃ] vt (food) garnieren

garrison ['gærɪsn] n Garnison f

garter ['gɑːtəɾ] n Strumpfband nt; (US) Strumpfhalter m

gas [gæs] n Gas nt; (esp US: petrol) Benzin nt ♦ vt vergasen; **~ cooker** (BRIT) n Gasherd m; **~ cylinder** n Gasflasche f; **~ fire** n Gasofen m

gash [gæʃ] n klaffende Wunde f ♦ vt tief verwunden

gasket ['gæskɪt] n Dichtungsring m

gas mask n Gasmaske f

gas meter n Gaszähler m

gasoline ['gæsəliːn] (US) n Benzin nt

gasp [gɑːsp] n keuchen; (in surprise) tief Luft holen ♦ n Keuchen nt

gas: ~ ring n Gasring m; **~ station** (US) n Tankstelle f; **~ tap** n Gashahn m

gastric ['gæstrɪk] adj Magen-

gate [geɪt] n Tor nt; (barrier) Schranke f

gateau ['gætəu] (pl **~x**) n Torte f

gatecrash ['geɪtkræʃ] (BRIT) vt (party) platzen in +acc

gateway ['geɪtweɪ] n Toreingang m

gather ['gæðəɾ] vt (people) versammeln; (things) sammeln; (understand) annehmen ♦ vi (assemble) sich versammeln; **to ~ speed** schneller werden; **to ~ (from)** schließen (aus); **~ing** n Versammlung f

gauche [gəuʃ] adj linkisch

gaudy ['gɔːdɪ] adj schreiend

gauge [geɪdʒ] n (instrument) Messgerät nt; (RAIL) Spurweite f; (dial) Anzeiger m; (measure) Maß nt ♦ vt (ab)messen; (fig) abschätzen

gaunt [gɔːnt] adj hager

gauze [gɔːz] n Gaze f

gave [geɪv] pt of **give**

gay [geɪ] adj (homosexual) schwul; (lively) lustig

gaze [geɪz] n Blick m ♦ vi starren; **to ~ at sth** etw dat anstarren

gazelle [gə'zɛl] n Gazelle f

gazumping [gə'zʌmpɪŋ] (BRIT) n Hausverkauf an Höherbietenden trotz Zusage an anderen

GB n abbr = **Great Britain**

GCE (BRIT) n abbr = **General Certificate of Education**

CSE (BRIT) n abbr = **General Certificate of Secondary Education**

ear [gɪəʳ] n Getriebe nt; (equipment) Ausrüstung f; (AUT) Gang m ♦ vt (fig: adapt): **to be ~ed to** ausgerichtet sein auf +acc; **top ~** höchste(r) Gang m; **high ~** (US) höchste(r) Gang m; **low ~** niedrige(r) Gang m; **in ~** eingekuppelt; **~ box** n Getriebe(gehäuse) nt; **~ lever** n Schalthebel m; **~ shift** (US) n Schalthebel m

eese [giːs] npl of **goose**

el [dʒel] n Gel nt

elatin(e) ['dʒelətiːn] n Gelatine f

em [dʒem] n Edelstein m; (fig) Juwel nt

iemini ['dʒemɪnaɪ] n Zwillinge pl

ender ['dʒendəʳ] n (GRAM) Geschlecht nt

ene [dʒiːn] n Gen nt

eneral ['dʒenərl] n General m ♦ adj allgemein; **~ delivery** (US) n Ausgabe(schalter m) f postlagernder Sendungen; **~ election** n allgemeine Wahlen pl; **~ize** vi verallgemeinern; **~ knowledge** n Allgemeinwissen nt; **~ly** adv allgemein, im Allgemeinen; **~ practitioner** n praktische(r) Arzt m, praktische Ärztin f

enerate ['dʒenəreɪt] vt erzeugen

eneration [dʒenə'reɪʃən] n Generation f; (act) Erzeugung f

enerator ['dʒenəreɪtəʳ] n Generator m

enerosity [dʒenə'rɒsɪti] n Großzügigkeit f

enerous ['dʒenərəs] adj großzügig

enetic [dʒɪ'netɪk] adj genetisch; **~ally** adv genetisch; **~ally modified** genmanipuliert; **~ engineering** n Gentechnik f; **~ fingerprinting** [-'fɪŋɡəprɪntɪŋ] n genetische Fingerabdrücke pl

enetics [dʒɪ'netɪks] n Genetik f

ieneva [dʒɪ'niːvə] n Genf nt

enial ['dʒiːnɪəl] adj freundlich, jovial

enitals ['dʒenɪtlz] npl Genitalien pl

enius ['dʒiːnɪəs] n Genie nt

enocide ['dʒenəusaɪd] n Völkermord m

ent [dʒent] n abbr = **gentleman**

enteel [dʒen'tiːl] adj (polite) wohlanständig; (affected) affektiert

entle ['dʒentl] adj sanft, zart

entleman ['dʒentlmən] (irreg) n Herr m;

(polite) Gentleman m

gentleness ['dʒentlnɪs] n Zartheit f, Milde f

gently ['dʒentli] adv zart, sanft

gentry ['dʒentri] n Landadel m

gents [dʒents] n: **G~** (lavatory) Herren pl

genuine ['dʒenjuɪn] adj echt

geographic(al) [dʒɪə'ɡræfɪk(l)] adj geografisch

geography [dʒɪ'ɒɡrəfɪ] n Geografie f

geological [dʒɪə'lɒdʒɪkl] adj geologisch

geology [dʒɪ'ɒlədʒɪ] n Geologie f

geometric(al) [dʒɪə'metrɪk(l)] adj geometrisch

geometry [dʒɪ'ɒmətri] n Geometrie f

geranium [dʒɪ'reɪnɪəm] n Geranie f

geriatric [dʒeri'ætrɪk] adj Alten- ♦ n Greis(in) m(f)

germ [dʒəːm] n Keim m; (MED) Bazillus m

German ['dʒəːmən] adj deutsch ♦ n Deutsche(r) f(m); (LING) Deutsch nt; **~ measles** n Röteln pl; **~y** n Deutschland nt

germination [dʒəːmɪ'neɪʃən] n Keimen nt

gesticulate [dʒes'tɪkjulert] vi gestikulieren

gesture ['dʒestjəʳ] n Geste f

KEYWORD

---

get [ɡet] (pt, pp **got**, pp **gotten** (US)) vi 1 (become, be) werden; **to get old/tired** alt/ müde werden; **to get married** heiraten
2 (go) (an)kommen, gehen
3 (begin): **to get to know sb** jdn kennen lernen; **let's get going** or **started!** fangen wir an!
4 (modal aux vb): **you've got to do it** du musst es tun

♦ vt 1: **to get sth done** (do) etw machen; (have done) etw machen lassen; **to get sth going** or **to go** etw in Gang bringen or bekommen; **to get sb to do sth** jdn dazu bringen, etw zu tun
2 (obtain: money, permission, results) erhalten; (find: job, flat) finden; (fetch: person, object) holen; **to get sth for sb** jdm etw besorgen; **get me Mr Jones, please** (TEL) verbinden Sie mich bitte mit Mr Jones
3 (receive: present, letter) bekommen, kriegen; (acquire: reputation etc) erwerben

4 (*catch*) bekommen, kriegen; (*hit: target etc*) treffen, erwischen; **get him!** (*to dog*) fass!
5 (*take, move*) bringen; **to get sth to sb** jdm etw bringen
6 (*understand*) verstehen; (*hear*) mitbekommen; **I've got it!** ich habs!
7 (*have, possess*): **to have got sth** etw haben
get about *vi* herumkommen; (*news*) sich verbreiten
get along *vi* (*people*) (gut) zurechtkommen; (*depart*) sich *acc* auf den Weg machen
get at *vt* (*facts*) herausbekommen; **to get at sb** (*nag*) an jdm herumnörgeln
get away *vi* (*leave*) sich *acc* davonmachen; (*escape*): **to get away from sth** von etw *dat* entkommen; **to get away with sth** mit etw davonkommen
get back *vi* (*return*) zurückkommen ♦ *vt* zurückbekommen
get by *vi* (*pass*) vorbeikommen; (*manage*) zurechtkommen
get down *vi* (her)untergehen ♦ *vt* (*depress*) fertig machen; **to get down to** in Angriff nehmen; (*find time to do*) kommen zu
get in *vi* (*train*) ankommen; (*arrive home*) heimkommen
get into *vt* (*enter*) hinein-/hereinkommen in +*acc*; (: *car, train etc*) einsteigen in +*acc*; (*clothes*) anziehen
get off *vi* (*from train etc*) aussteigen; (*from horse*) absteigen ♦ *vt* aussteigen aus; absteigen von
get on *vi* (*progress*) vorankommen; (*be friends*) auskommen; (*age*) alt werden; (*onto train etc*) einsteigen; (*onto horse*) aufsteigen ♦ *vt* einsteigen in +*acc*; auf etw *acc* aufsteigen
get out *vi* (*of house*) herauskommen; (*of vehicle*) aussteigen ♦ *vt* (*take out*) herausholen
get out of *vt* (*duty etc*) herumkommen um
get over *vt* (*illness*) sich *acc* erholen von;

(*surprise*) verkraften; (*news*) fassen; (*loss*) sich abfinden mit
get round *vt* herumkommen; (*fig: person*) herumkriegen
get through to *vt* (*TEL*) durchkommen zu
get together *vi* zusammenkommen
get up *vi* aufstehen ♦ *vt* hinaufbringen; (*go up*) hinaufgehen; (*organize*) auf die Beine stellen
get up to *vt* (*reach*) erreichen; (*prank etc*) anstellen

---

getaway ['gɛtəweɪ] *n* Flucht *f*
get-up ['gɛtʌp] (*inf*) *n* Aufzug *m*
geyser ['giːzə'] *n* Geiser *m*; (*heater*) Durchlauferhitzer *m*
ghastly ['gɑːstlɪ] *adj* grässlich
gherkin ['gəːkɪn] *n* Gewürzgurke *f*
ghetto ['gɛtəu] *n* G(h)etto *nt*; ~ **blaster** *n* (große(r)) Radiorekorder *m*
ghost [gəust] *n* Gespenst *nt*
giant ['dʒaɪənt] *n* Riese *m* ♦ *adj* riesig, Riesen-
gibberish ['dʒɪbərɪʃ] *n* dumme(s) Geschwätz *nt*
gibe [dʒaɪb] *n* spöttische Bemerkung *f*
giblets ['dʒɪblɪts] *npl* Geflügelinnereien *pl*
giddiness ['gɪdɪnɪs] *n* Schwindelgefühl *nt*
giddy ['gɪdɪ] *adj* schwindlig
gift [gɪft] *n* Geschenk *nt*; (*ability*) Begabung *f*; ~**ed** *adj* begabt; ~ **shop** *n* Geschenkladen *m*; ~ **token**, ~ **voucher** *n* Geschenkgutschein *m*
gigantic [dʒaɪ'gæntɪk] *adj* riesenhaft
giggle ['gɪgl] *vi* kichern ♦ *n* Gekicher *nt*
gild [gɪld] *vt* vergolden
gill [dʒɪl] *n* (*1/4 pint*) Viertelpinte *f*
gills [gɪlz] *npl* (*of fish*) Kiemen *pl*
gilt [gɪlt] *n* Vergoldung *f* ♦ *adj* vergoldet; ~~-**edged** *adj* mündelsicher
gimmick ['gɪmɪk] *n* Gag *m*
gin [dʒɪn] *n* Gin *m*
ginger ['dʒɪndʒə'] *n* Ingwer *m*; ~ **ale** *n* Ingwerbier *nt*; ~ **beer** *n* Ingwerbier *nt*; ~**bread** *n* Pfefferkuchen *m*; ~~-**haired** *adj* rothaarig
gingerly ['dʒɪndʒəlɪ] *adv* behutsam

gipsy ['dʒɪpsɪ] n Zigeuner(in) m(f)

giraffe [dʒɪ'rɑːf] n Giraffe f

girder ['gɜːdəʳ] n Eisenträger m

girdle ['gɜːdl] n Hüftgürtel m

girl [gɜːl] n Mädchen nt; **an English ~** eine (junge) Engländerin; **~friend** n Freundin f; **~ish** adj mädchenhaft

giro ['dʒaɪrəʊ] n (bank ~) Giro nt; (post office ~) Postscheckverkehr m

girth [gɜːθ] n (measure) Umfang m; (strap) Sattelgurt m

gist [dʒɪst] n Wesentliche(s) nt

give [gɪv] (pt **gave**, pp **given**) vt geben ♦ vi (break) nachgeben; **~ away** vt verschenken; (betray) verraten; **~ back** vt zurückgeben; **~ in** vi nachgeben ♦ vt (hand in) abgeben; **~ off** vt abgeben; **~ out** vt verteilen; (announce) bekannt geben; **~ up** vt, vi aufgeben; **to ~ o.s. up** sich stellen; (after siege) sich ergeben; **~ way** vi (BRIT: traffic) Vorfahrt lassen; (to feelings): **to ~ way to** nachgeben +dat

glacier ['glæsɪəʳ] n Gletscher m

glad [glæd] adj froh; **~ly** ['glædlɪ] adv gern(e)

glamorous ['glæmərəs] adj reizvoll

glamour ['glæməʳ] n Glanz m

glance [glɑːns] n Blick m ♦ vi: **to ~ (at)** (hin)blicken (auf +acc); **~ off** vt fus (fly off) abprallen von; **glancing** ['glɑːnsɪŋ] adj (blow) Streif-

gland [glænd] n Drüse f

glare [glɛəʳ] n (light) grelle(s) Licht nt; (stare) wilde(r) Blick m ♦ vi grell scheinen; (angrily): **to ~ at** böse ansehen; **glaring** ['glɛərɪŋ] adj (injustice) schreiend; (mistake) krass

glass [glɑːs] n Glas nt; (mirror: also: **looking ~**) Spiegel m; **~es** npl (spectacles) Brille f; **~house** n Gewächshaus nt; **~ware** n Glaswaren pl; **~y** adj glasig

glaze [gleɪz] vt verglasen; (finish with a ~) glasieren ♦ n Glasur f; **~d** adj (eye) glasig; (pot) glasiert; **glazier** ['gleɪzɪəʳ] n Glaser m

gleam [gliːm] n Schimmer m ♦ vi schimmern

glean [gliːn] vt (fig) ausfindig machen

glen [glɛn] n Bergtal nt

glib [glɪb] adj oberflächlich

glide [glaɪd] vi gleiten; **~r** n (AVIAT) Segelflugzeug nt; **gliding** ['glaɪdɪŋ] n Segelfliegen nt

glimmer ['glɪməʳ] n Schimmer m

glimpse [glɪmps] n flüchtige(r) Blick m ♦ vt flüchtig erblicken

glint [glɪnt] n Glitzern nt ♦ vi glitzern

glisten ['glɪsn] vi glänzen

glitter ['glɪtəʳ] vi funkeln ♦ n Funkeln nt

gloat [gləʊt] vi: **to ~ over** sich weiden an +dat

global ['gləʊbl] adj: **~ warming** globale(r) Temperaturanstieg m

globe [gləʊb] n Erdball m; (sphere) Globus m

gloom [gluːm] n (darkness) Dunkel nt; (depression) düstere Stimmung f; **~y** adj düster

glorify ['glɔːrɪfaɪ] vt verherrlichen

glorious ['glɔːrɪəs] adj glorreich

glory ['glɔːrɪ] n Ruhm m

gloss [glɒs] n (shine) Glanz m; **~ over** vt fus übertünchen

glossary ['glɒsərɪ] n Glossar nt

glossy ['glɒsɪ] adj (surface) glänzend

glove [glʌv] n Handschuh m; **~ compartment** n (AUT) Handschuhfach nt

glow [gləʊ] vi glühen ♦ n Glühen nt

glower ['glaʊəʳ] vi: **to ~ at** finster anblicken

glucose ['gluːkəʊs] n Traubenzucker m

glue [gluː] n Klebstoff m ♦ vt kleben

glum [glʌm] adj bedrückt

glut [glʌt] n Überfluss m

glutton ['glʌtn] n Vielfraß m; **a ~ for work** ein Arbeitstier m

glycerin(e) ['glɪsəriːn] n Glyzerin nt

GM abbr = **genetically modified**

gnarled [nɑːld] adj knorrig

gnat [næt] n Stechmücke f

gnaw [nɔː] vt nagen an +dat

gnome [nəʊm] n Gnom m

go [gəʊ] (pt **went**, pp **gone**, pl **~es**) vi gehen; (travel) reisen, fahren; (depart: train) (ab)fahren; (be sold) verkauft werden; (work) gehen, funktionieren; (fit, suit) passen; (become) werden; (break etc) nachgeben ♦ n (energy) Schwung m;

(*attempt*) Versuch m; **he's ~ing to do it** er wird es tun; **to ~ for a walk** spazieren gehen; **to ~ dancing** tanzen gehen; **how did it ~?** wie war's?; **to ~ with** (*be suitable*) passen zu; **to have a ~ at sth** etw versuchen; **to be on the ~** auf Trab sein; **whose ~ is it?** wer ist dran?; **~ about** vi (*rumour*) umgehen ♦ vt fus: **how do I ~ about this?** wie packe ich das an?; **~ after** vt fus (*pursue: person*) nachgehen +dat; **~ ahead** vi (*proceed*) weitergehen; **~ along** vi dahingehen, dahinfahren ♦ vt entlanggehen, entlangfahren; **to ~ along with** (*support*) zustimmen +dat; **~ away** vi (*depart*) weggehen; **~ back** vi (*return*) zurückgehen; **~ back on** vt fus (*promise*) nicht halten; **~ by** vi (*years, time*) vergehen ♦ vt fus sich richten nach; **~ down** vi (*sun*) untergehen ♦ vt fus hinuntergehen, hinunterfahren; **~ for** vt fus (*fetch*) holen (gehen); (*like*) mögen; (*attack*) sich stürzen auf +acc; **~ in** vi hineingehen; **~ in for** vt fus (*competition*) teilnehmen an; **~ into** vt fus (*enter*) hineingehen in +acc; (*study*) sich befassen mit; **~ off** vi (*depart*) weggehen; (*lights*) ausgehen; (*milk etc*) sauer werden; (*explode*) losgehen ♦ vt fus (*dislike*) nicht mehr mögen; **~ on** vi (*continue*) weitergehen; (*inf: complain*) meckern; (*lights*) angehen; **to ~ on with sth** mit etw weitermachen; **~ out** vi (*fire, light*) ausgehen; (*of house*) hinausgehen; **~ over** vi (*ship*) kentern ♦ vt fus (*examine, check*) durchgehen; **~ past** vi: **to ~ past sth** an etw dat vorbeigehen; **~ round** vi (*visit*): **to ~ round (to sb's)** (bei jdm) vorbeigehen; **~ through** vt fus (*town etc*) durchgehen, durchfahren; **~ up** vi (*price*) steigen; **~ with** vt fus (*suit*) zu etw passen; **~ without** vt fus sich behelfen ohne; (*food*) entbehren

goad [gəʊd] vt anstacheln

go-ahead ['gəʊəhɛd] adj zielstrebig; (*progressive*) fortschrittlich ♦ n grüne(s) Licht nt

goal [gəʊl] n Ziel nt; (SPORT) Tor nt; **~keeper** n Torwart m; **~ post** n

Torpfosten m

goat [gəʊt] n Ziege f

gobble ['gɒbl] vt (*also:* **~ down, ~ up**) hinunterschlingen

go-between ['gəʊbɪtwiːn] n Mittelsmann m

god [gɒd] n Gott m; **G~** n Gott m; **~child** n Patenkind nt; **~daughter** n Patentochter f; **~dess** n Göttin f; **~father** n Pate m; **~forsaken** adj gottverlassen; **~mother** n Patin f; **~send** n Geschenk nt des Himmels; **~son** n Patensohn m

goggles ['gɒglz] npl Schutzbrille f

going ['gəʊɪŋ] n (HORSE-RACING) Bahn f ♦ adj (*rate*) gängig; (*concern*) gut gehend; **it's hard ~** es ist schwierig

gold [gəʊld] n Gold nt ♦ adj golden; **~en** adj golden, Gold-; **~fish** n Goldfisch m; **~ mine** n Goldgrube f; **~-plated** adj vergoldet; **~smith** n Goldschmied(in) m(f)

golf [gɒlf] n Golf nt; **~ ball** n Golfball m; (*on typewriter*) Kugelkopf m; **~ club** n (*society*) Golfklub m; (*stick*) Golfschläger m; **~ course** n Golfplatz m; **~er** n Golfspieler(in) m(f)

gondola ['gɒndələ] n Gondel f

gone [gɒn] pp of **go**

gong [gɒŋ] n Gong m

good [gʊd] n (*benefit*) Wohl nt; (*moral excellence*) Güte f ♦ adj gut; **~s** npl (*merchandise etc*) Waren pl, Güter pl; **a ~ deal (of)** ziemlich viel; **a ~ many** ziemlich viele; **~ morning!** guten Morgen!; **~ afternoon!** guten Tag!; **~ evening!** guten Abend!; **~ night!** gute Nacht!; **would you be ~ enough to ...?** könnten Sie bitte ...?

goodbye [gʊd'baɪ] excl auf Wiedersehen!

good: G~ Friday n Karfreitag m; **~-looking** adj gut aussehend; **~-natured** adj gutmütig; (*joke*) harmlos; **~ness** n Güte f; (*virtue*) Tugend f; **~s train** n (BRIT) n Güterzug m; **~will** n (*favour*) Wohlwollen nt; (COMM) Firmenansehen nt

goose [guːs] n (pl **geese**) n Gans f

gooseberry ['guzbərɪ] n Stachelbeere f

gooseflesh ['guːsflɛʃ] n Gänsehaut f

goose pimples npl Gänsehaut f

gore [gɔːʳ] vt aufspießen ♦ n Blut nt

gorge [gɔːdʒ] n Schlucht f ♦ vt: **to ~ o.s.** (sich voll) fressen

gorgeous ['gɔːdʒəs] adj prächtig

gorilla [gə'rɪlə] n Gorilla m

gorse [gɔːs] n Stechginster m

gory ['gɔːrɪ] adj blutig

go-slow ['gəu'sləu] (BRIT) n Bummelstreik m

gospel ['gɔspl] n Evangelium nt

gossip ['gɔsɪp] n Klatsch m; (person) Klatschbase f ♦ vi klatschen

got [gɔt] pt, pp of **get**

gotten ['gɔtn] (US) pp of **get**

gout [gaut] n Gicht f

govern ['gʌvən] vt regieren; verwalten

governess ['gʌvənɪs] n Gouvernante f

government ['gʌvnmənt] n Regierung f

governor ['gʌvənər] n Gouverneur m

gown [gaun] n Gewand nt; (UNIV) Robe f

G.P. n abbr = **general practitioner**

grab [græb] vt packen

grace [greɪs] n Anmut f; (blessing) Gnade f; (prayer) Tischgebet nt ♦ vt (adorn) zieren; (honour) beehren; **5 days' ~** 5 Tage Aufschub; **~ful** adj anmutig

gracious ['greɪʃəs] adj gnädig; (kind) freundlich

grade [greɪd] n Grad m; (slope) Gefälle nt ♦ vt (classify) einstufen; **~ crossing** (US) n Bahnübergang m; **~ school** (US) n Grundschule f

gradient ['greɪdɪənt] n Steigung f; Gefälle nt

gradual ['grædjuəl] adj allmählich; **~ly** adv allmählich

graduate [n 'grædjuɪt, vb 'grædjueɪt] n: **to be a ~** das Staatsexamen haben ♦ vi das Staatsexamen machen; **graduation** [grædju'eɪʃən] n Abschlussfeier f

graffiti [grə'fiːtɪ] npl Graffiti pl

graft [grɑːft] n (hard work) Schufterei f; (MED) Verpflanzung f ♦ vt pfropfen; (fig) aufpfropfen; (MED) verpflanzen

grain [greɪn] n Korn nt; (in wood) Maserung f

gram [græm] n Gramm nt

grammar ['græmər] n Grammatik f; **~ school** (BRIT) n Gymnasium nt; **grammatical** [grə'mætɪkl] adj grammat(ikal)isch

gramme [græm] n = **gram**

granary ['grænərɪ] n Kornspeicher m

grand [grænd] adj großartig; **~child** (pl **~children**) n Enkelkind nt, Enkel(in) m(f); **~dad** n Opa m; **~daughter** n Enkelin f; **~eur** ['grændjər] n Erhabenheit f; **~father** n Großvater m; **~iose** ['grændɪəus] adj (imposing) großartig; (pompous) schwülstig; **~ma** n Oma f; **~mother** n Großmutter f; **~pa** n = **granddad**; **~parents** npl Großeltern pl; **~ piano** n Flügel m; **~son** n Enkel m; **~stand** n Haupttribüne f

granite ['grænɪt] n Granit m

granny ['grænɪ] n Oma f

grant [grɑːnt] vt gewähren ♦ n Unterstützung f; (UNIV) Stipendium nt; **to take sth for ~ed** etw als selbstverständlich (an)nehmen

granulated sugar ['grænjuleɪtɪd-] n Zuckerraffinade f

granule ['grænjuːl] n Körnchen nt

grape [greɪp] n (Wein)traube f

grapefruit ['greɪpfruːt] n Pampelmuse f, Grapefruit f

graph [grɑːf] n Schaubild nt; **~ic** ['græfɪk] adj (descriptive) anschaulich; (drawing) grafisch; **~ics** npl Grafik f

grapple ['græpl] vi: **to ~ with** kämpfen mit

grasp [grɑːsp] vt ergreifen; (understand) begreifen ♦ n Griff m; (of subject) Beherrschung f; **~ing** adj habgierig

grass [grɑːs] n Gras nt; **~hopper** n Heuschrecke f; **~land** n Weideland nt; **~-roots** adj an der Basis; **~ snake** n Ringelnatter f

grate [greɪt] n Kamin m ♦ vi (sound) knirschen ♦ vt (cheese etc) reiben; **to ~ on the nerves** auf die Nerven gehen

grateful ['greɪtful] adj dankbar

grater ['greɪtər] n Reibe f

gratify ['grætɪfaɪ] vt befriedigen; **~ing** adj erfreulich

grating ['greɪtɪŋ] n (iron bars) Gitter nt ♦ adj (noise) knirschend

gratitude ['grætɪtjuːd] n Dankbarkeit f

gratuity [grə'tjuːɪtɪ] n Gratifikation f

grave [greɪv] n Grab nt ♦ adj (serious) ernst

gravel ['grævl] n Kies m

gravestone ['greɪvstəun] n Grabstein m

graveyard ['greɪvjɑːd] n Friedhof m

gravity ['grævɪtɪ] n Schwerkraft f; (seriousness) Schwere f

gravy ['greɪvɪ] n (Braten)soße f

gray [greɪ] adj = **grey**

graze [greɪz] vi grasen ♦ vt (touch) streifen; (MED) abschürfen ♦ n Abschürfung f

grease [griːs] n (fat) Fett nt; (lubricant) Schmiere f ♦ vt (ab)schmieren; ~proof (BRIT) adj (paper) Butterbrot-; **greasy** ['griːsɪ] adj fettig

great [greɪt] adj groß; (inf: good) prima; G~ Britain n Großbritannien nt; ~-grandfather n Urgroßvater m; ~-grandmother n Urgroßmutter f; ~ly adv sehr

Greece [griːs] n Griechenland nt

greed [griːd] n (also: ~iness) Gier f; (meanness) Geiz m; ~(iness) for Gier nach; ~y adj gierig

Greek [griːk] adj griechisch ♦ n Grieche m, Griechin f; (LING) Griechisch nt

green [griːn] adj grün ♦ n (village ~) Dorfwiese f; ~ belt n Grüngürtel m; ~ card n (AUT) grüne Versicherungskarte f; ~ery n Grün nt; grüne(s) Laub nt; ~gage n Reneklode f, Reineclaude f; ~grocer (BRIT) n Obst- und Gemüsehändler m; ~house n Gewächshaus nt; ~house effect n Treibhauseffekt m; ~house gas n Treibhausgas nt

Greenland ['griːnlənd] n Grönland nt

greet [griːt] vt grüßen; ~ing n Gruß m; ~ing(s) card n Glückwunschkarte f

gregarious [grə'gɛərɪəs] adj gesellig

grenade [grə'neɪd] n Granate f

grew [gruː] pt of **grow**

grey [greɪ] adj grau; ~-haired adj grauhaarig; ~hound n Windhund m

grid [grɪd] n Gitter nt; (ELEC) Leitungsnetz nt; (on map) Gitternetz nt

gridlock ['grɪdlɒk] n (AUT: traffic jam) totale(r) Stau m; ~ed adj: **to be ~ed** (roads) total verstopft sein; (talks etc) festgefahren sein

grief [griːf] n Gram m, Kummer m

grievance ['griːvəns] n Beschwerde f

grieve [griːv] vi sich grämen ♦ vt betrüben

grievous ['griːvəs] adj: ~ **bodily harm** (JUR) schwere Körperverletzung f

grill [grɪl] n Grill m ♦ vt (BRIT) grillen; (question) in die Mangel nehmen

grille [grɪl] n (AUT) (Kühler)gitter nt

grim [grɪm] adj grimmig; (situation) düster

grimace [grɪ'meɪs] n Grimasse f ♦ vi Grimassen schneiden

grime [graɪm] n Schmutz m; **grimy** ['graɪmɪ] adj schmutzig

grin [grɪn] n Grinsen nt ♦ vi grinsen

grind [graɪnd] (pt, pp **ground**) vt mahlen; (US: meat) durch den Fleischwolf drehen; (sharpen) schleifen; (teeth) knirschen mit ♦ n (bore) Plackerei f

grip [grɪp] n Griff m; (suitcase) Handkoffer m ♦ vt packen; ~ping adj (exciting) spannend

grisly ['grɪzlɪ] adj grässlich

gristle ['grɪsl] n Knorpel m

grit [grɪt] n Splitt m; (courage) Mut m ♦ vt (teeth) zusammenbeißen; (road) (mit Splitt be)streuen

groan [grəun] n Stöhnen nt ♦ vi stöhnen

grocer ['grəusə'] n Lebensmittelhändler m; ~ies npl Lebensmittel pl; ~'s (shop) n Lebensmittelgeschäft nt

groggy ['grɒgɪ] adj benommen

groin [grɔɪn] n Leistengegend f

groom [gruːm] n (also: **bridegroom**) Bräutigam m; (for horses) Pferdeknecht m ♦ vt (horse) striegeln; **(well-)~ed** gepflegt

groove [gruːv] n Rille f, Furche f

grope [grəup] vi tasten; ~ **for** vt fus suchen nach

gross [grəus] adj (coarse) dick, plump; (bad) grob, schwer; (COMM) brutto; ~ly adv höchst

grotesque [grə'tɛsk] adj grotesk

grotto ['grɒtəu] n Grotte f

ground [graund] pt, pp of **grind** ♦ n Boden m; (land) Grundbesitz m; (reason) Grund m; (US: also: ~ **wire**) Endleitung f ♦ vi (run ashore) stranden, auflaufen; ~s npl (dregs) Bodensatz m; (around house)

(Garten)anlagen *pl*; **on the ~** am Boden; **to the ~** zu Boden; **to gain/lose ~** gewinnen/verlieren; **~ cloth** (*US*) *n* = **groundsheet;** **~ing** *n* (*instruction*) Anfangsunterricht *m*; **~less** *adj* grundlos; **~sheet** (*BRIT*) *n* Zeltboden *m*; **~ staff** *n* Bodenpersonal *nt*; **~work** *n* Grundlage *f*

oup [gru:p] *n* Gruppe *f* ♦ *vt* (*also:* **~ together**) gruppieren ♦ *vi* sich gruppieren

ouse [graus] *n inv* (*bird*) schottische(s) Moorhuhn *nt*

ove [grəuv] *n* Gehölz *nt*, Hain *m*

ovel ['grɒvl] *vi* (*fig*) kriechen

ow [grəu] (*pt* **grew**, *pp* **grown**) *vi* wachsen; (*become*) werden ♦ *vt* (*raise*) anbauen; **~ up** *vi* aufwachsen; **~er** *n* Züchter *m*; **~ing** *adj* zunehmend

owl [graul] *vi* knurren

own [grəun] *pp of* **grow**; **~-up** *n* Erwachsene(r) *mf*

owth [grəuθ] *n* Wachstum *nt*; (*increase*) Zunahme *f*; (*of beard etc*) Wuchs *m*

ub [grʌb] *n* Made *f*, Larve *f*; (*inf*: *food*) Futter *nt*; **~by** ['grʌbɪ] *adj* schmutzig

udge [grʌdʒ] *n* Groll *m* ♦ *vt*: **to ~ sb sth** jdm etw missgönnen; **to bear sb a ~** einen Groll gegen jdn hegen

uelling ['gruəlɪŋ] *adj* (*climb, race*) mörderisch

uesome ['gru:səm] *adj* grauenhaft

uff [grʌf] *adj* barsch

umble ['grʌmbl] *vi* murren

umpy ['grʌmpɪ] *adj* verdrießlich

unt [grʌnt] *vi* grunzen ♦ *n* Grunzen *nt*

-string ['dʒi:strɪŋ] *n* Minislip *m*

uarantee [gærən'ti:] *n* Garantie *f* ♦ *vt* garantieren

uard [ga:d] *n* (*sentry*) Wache *f*; (*BRIT*: *RAIL*) Zugbegleiter *m* ♦ *vt* bewachen; **~ed** ['ga:dɪd] *adj* vorsichtig; **~ian** ['ga:dɪən] *n* Vormund *m*; (*keeper*) Hüter *m*; **~'s van** ['ga:dz-] (*BRIT*) *n* (*RAIL*) Dienstwagen *m*

uerrilla [gə'rɪlə] *n* Guerilla(kämpfer) *m*; **~ warfare** *n* Guerillakrieg *m*

guess [ges] *vt*, *vi* (er)raten, schätzen ♦ *n* Vermutung *f*; **~work** *n* Raterei *f*

guest [gest] *n* Gast *m*; **~ house** *n* Pension *f*; **~ room** *n* Gastzimmer *nt*

guffaw [gʌ'fɔ:] *vi* schallend lachen

guidance ['gaɪdəns] *n* (*control*) Leitung *f*; (*advice*) Beratung *f*

guide [gaɪd] *n* Führer *m*; (*also:* **girl ~**) Pfadfinderin *f* ♦ *vt* führen; **~book** *n* Reiseführer *m*; **~ dog** *n* Blindenhund *m*; **~lines** *npl* Richtlinien *pl*

guild [gɪld] *n* (*HIST*) Gilde *f*

guillotine ['gɪlətiːn] *n* Guillotine *f*

guilt [gɪlt] *n* Schuld *f*; **~y** *adj* schuldig

guinea pig ['gɪnɪ-] *n* Meerschweinchen *nt*; (*fig*) Versuchskaninchen *nt*

guise [gaɪz] *n*: **in the ~ of** in der Form +*gen*

guitar [gɪ'tɑ:r] *n* Gitarre *f*

gulf [gʌlf] *n* Golf *m*; (*fig*) Abgrund *m*

gull [gʌl] *n* Möwe *f*

gullet ['gʌlɪt] *n* Schlund *m*

gullible ['gʌlɪbl] *adj* leichtgläubig

gully ['gʌlɪ] *n* (*Wasser*)rinne *f*

gulp [gʌlp] *vt* (*also:* **~ down**) hinunterschlucken ♦ *vi* (*gasp*) schlucken

gum [gʌm] *n* (*around teeth*) Zahnfleisch *nt*; (*glue*) Klebstoff *m*; (*also:* **chewing ~**) Kaugummi *m* ♦ *vt* gummieren; **~boots** (*BRIT*) *npl* Gummistiefel *pl*

gun [gʌn] *n* Schusswaffe *f*; **~boat** *n* Kanonenboot *nt*; **~fire** *n* Geschützfeuer *nt*; **~man** (*irreg*) *n* bewaffnete(r) Verbrecher *m*; **~point** *n*: **at ~point** mit Waffengewalt; **~powder** *n* Schießpulver *nt*; **~shot** *n* Schuss *m*

gurgle ['gə:gl] *vi* gluckern

gush [gʌʃ] *vi* (*rush out*) hervorströmen; (*fig*) schwärmen

gust [gʌst] *n* Windstoß *m*, Bö *f*

gusto ['gʌstəu] *n* Genuss *m*, Lust *f*

gut [gʌt] *n* (*ANAT*) Gedärme *pl*; (*string*) Darm *m*; **~s** *npl* (*fig*) Schneid *m*

gutter ['gʌtər] *n* Dachrinne *f*; (*in street*) Gosse *f*

guttural ['gʌtərl] *adj* guttural, Kehl-

guy [gaɪ] *n* (*also:* **~rope**) Halteseil *nt*; (*man*) Typ *m*, Kerl *m*

Guy Fawkes' Night

i Guy Fawkes' Night, *auch bonfire night genannt, erinnert an den Gunpowder Plot, einen Attentatsversuch auf James I. und sein Parlament am 5. November 1605. Einer der Verschwörer, Guy Fawkes, wurde auf frischer Tat ertappt, als er das Parlamentsgebäude in die Luft sprengen wollte. Vor der Guy Fawkes' Night basteln Kinder in Großbritannien eine Puppe des Guy Fawkes, mit der sie Geld für Feuerwerkskörper von Passanten erbetteln, und die dann am 5. November auf einem Lagerfeuer mit Feuerwerk verbrannt wird.*

---

guzzle ['gʌzl] vt, vi (drink) saufen; (eat) fressen

gym [dʒɪm] n (also: **~nasium**) Turnhalle f; (also: **~nastics**) Turnen nt

gymnast ['dʒɪmnæst] n Turner(in) m(f)

gymnastics [dʒɪm'næstɪks] n Turnen nt, Gymnastik f

gym shoes npl Turnschuhe pl

gynaecologist [gaɪnɪ'kɒlədʒɪst] (US **gynecologist**) n Frauenarzt(-ärztin) m(f)

gypsy ['dʒɪpsɪ] n = **gipsy**

gyrate [dʒaɪ'reɪt] vi kreisen

H, h

haberdashery [hæbə'dæʃərɪ] (BRIT) n Kurzwaren pl

habit ['hæbɪt] n (An)gewohnheit f; (monk's) Habit nt or m

habitable ['hæbɪtəbl] adj bewohnbar

habitat ['hæbɪtæt] n Lebensraum m

habitual [hə'bɪtjuəl] adj gewohnheitsmäßig; **~ly** adv gewöhnlich

hack [hæk] vt hacken ♦ n Hieb m; (writer) Schreiberling m

hacker ['hækə'] n (COMPUT) Hacker m

hackneyed ['hæknɪd] adj abgedroschen

had [hæd] pt, pp of **have**

haddock ['hædək] (pl **~** or **~s**) n Schellfisch m

hadn't ['hædnt] = **had not**

haemorrhage ['hemərɪdʒ] (US **hemorrhage**) n Blutung f

haemorrhoids ['hemərɔɪdz] (US **hemorrhoids**) npl Hämorr(ho)iden pl

haggard ['hægəd] adj abgekämpft

haggle ['hægl] vi feilschen

Hague [heɪg] n (GEOG) **The ~** Den Haag nt

hail [heɪl] n Hagel m ♦ vt umjubeln ♦ vi hageln; **~stone** n Hagelkorn nt

hair [heə'] n Haar nt, Haare pl; (one ~) Haar nt; **~brush** n Haarbürste f; **~cut** n Haarschnitt m; **to get a ~cut** sich dat die Haare schneiden lassen; **~do** n Frisur f; **~dresser** n Friseur m, Friseuse f; **~dresser's** n Friseursalon m; **~ dryer** n Trockenhaube f; (hand-held) Föhn m, Fön m ®; **~ gel** n Haargel nt; **~grip** n Klemme f; **~net** n Haarnetz nt; **~pin** n Haarnadel f; **~pin bend** (US **~pin curve**) n Haarnadelkurve f; **~-raising** adj haarsträubend; **~ removing cream** n Enthaarungscreme nt; **~ spray** n Haarspray nt; **~style** n Frisur f

hairy ['heərɪ] adj haarig

hake [heɪk] n Seehecht m

half [hɑːf] (pl **halves**) n Hälfte f ♦ adj halb ♦ adv halb, zur Hälfte; **~ an hour** eine halbe Stunde; **two and a ~** zweieinhalb; **to cut sth in ~** etw halbieren; **~ a dozen** ein halbes Dutzend, sechs; **~ board** n Halbpension f; **~-caste** n Mischling m; **~ fare** n halbe(r) Fahrpreis m; **~-hearted** adj lustlos; **~-hour** n halbe Stunde f; **~-price** n: **(at) ~-price** zum halben Preis; **~ term** (BRIT) n (SCH) Ferien pl in der Mitte des Trimesters; **~-time** n Halbzeit f; **~way** adv halbwegs, auf halbem Wege

halibut ['hælɪbət] n inv Heilbutt m

hall [hɔːl] n Saal m; (entrance ~) Hausflur m; (building) Halle f; **~ of residence** (BRIT) n Studentenwohnheim nt

hallmark ['hɔːlmɑːk] n Stempel m

hallo [hə'ləu] excl = **hello**

Hallowe'en ['hæləu'iːn] n Tag m vor Allerheiligen

---

allucination [həluːsɪˈneɪʃən] n Halluzination f

allway [ˈhɔːlweɪ] n Korridor m

alo [ˈheɪləʊ] n Heiligenschein m

alt [hɔːlt] n Halt m ♦ vt, vi anhalten

alve [hɑːv] vt halbieren

alves [hɑːvz] pl of **half**

am [hæm] n Schinken m

amburger [ˈhæmbɜːgəʳ] n Hamburger m

amlet [ˈhæmlɪt] n Weiler m

ammer [ˈhæməʳ] n Hammer m ♦ vt, vi hämmern

ammock [ˈhæmək] n Hängematte f

amper [ˈhæmpəʳ] vt (be)hindern ♦ n Picknickkorb m

amster [ˈhæmstəʳ] n Hamster m

and [hænd] n Hand f; (of clock) (Uhr)zeiger m; (worker) Arbeiter m ♦ vt (pass) geben; **to give sb a ~** jdm helfen; **at ~** nahe; **to ~ to** zur Hand; **in ~** (under control) unter Kontrolle; (being done) im Gange; (extra) übrig; **on ~** zur Verfügung; **on the one ~ ..., on the other ~ ...** einerseits ..., andererseits ...; ~ **in** vt abgeben; (forms) einreichen; ~ **out** vt austeilen; ~ **over** vt (deliver) übergeben; (surrender) abgeben; (: prisoner) ausliefern; ~**bag** n Handtasche f; ~**book** n Handbuch nt; ~**brake** n Handbremse f; ~**cuffs** npl Handschellen pl; ~**ful** n Hand f voll; (inf: person) Plage f

andicap [ˈhændɪkæp] n Handikap nt ♦ vt benachteiligen; **mentally/physically ~ped** geistig/körperlich behindert

andicraft [ˈhændɪkrɑːft] n Kunsthandwerk nt

handiwork [ˈhændɪwɜːk] n Arbeit f; (fig) Werk nt

handkerchief [ˈhæŋkətʃɪf] n Taschentuch nt

handle [ˈhændl] n (of door etc) Klinke f; (of cup etc) Henkel m; (for winding) Kurbel f ♦ vt (touch) anfassen; (deal with: things) sich befassen mit; (: people) umgehen mit; ~**bar(s)** n(pl) Lenkstange f

hand: ~ **luggage** n Handgepäck nt; ~**made** adj handgefertigt; ~**out** n (distribution) Verteilung f; (charity) Geldzuwendung f; (leaflet) Flugblatt nt; ~**rail** n Geländer nt; (on ship) Reling f; ~**set** n (TEL) Hörer m; **please replace the ~set** bitte legen Sie auf; ~**shake** n Händedruck f

handsome [ˈhænsəm] adj gut aussehend

handwriting [ˈhændraɪtɪŋ] n Handschrift f

handy [ˈhændɪ] adj praktisch; (shops) leicht erreichbar; ~**man** [ˈhændɪmæn] (irreg) n Bastler m

hang [hæŋ] (pt, pp hung) vt aufhängen; (pt, pp hanged: criminal) hängen ♦ vi hängen ♦ n: **to get the ~ of sth** (inf) den richtigen Dreh bei etw herauskriegen; ~ **about**, ~ **around** vi sich herumtreiben; ~ **on** vi (wait) warten; ~ **up** vi (TEL) auflegen

hangar [ˈhæŋəʳ] n Hangar m

hanger [ˈhæŋəʳ] n Kleiderbügel m

hanger-on [hæŋərˈɒn] n Anhänger(in) m(f)

hang [ˈhæŋ-]: ~**-gliding** n Drachenfliegen nt; ~**over** n Kater m; ~**-up** n Komplex m

hanker [ˈhæŋkəʳ] vi: **to ~ for** or **after** sich sehnen nach

hankie [ˈhæŋkɪ] n abbr = **handkerchief**

hanky [ˈhæŋkɪ] n abbr = **handkerchief**

haphazard [hæpˈhæzəd] adj zufällig

happen [ˈhæpən] vi sich ereignen, passieren; **as it ~s I'm going there today** zufällig(erweise) gehe ich heute (dort)hin; ~**ing** n Ereignis nt

happily [ˈhæpɪlɪ] adv glücklich; (fortunately) glücklicherweise

happiness [ˈhæpɪnɪs] n Glück nt

happy [ˈhæpɪ] adj glücklich; ~ **birthday!** alles Gute zum Geburtstag!; ~**-go-lucky** adj sorglos; ~ **hour** n Happy Hour f

harass [ˈhærəs] *vt* plagen; ~**ment** *n* Belästigung *f*

harbour [ˈhɑːbər] (*US* **harbor**) *n* Hafen *m* ♦ *vt* (*hope etc*) hegen; (*criminal etc*) Unterschlupf gewähren

hard [hɑːd] *adj* (*firm*) hart; (*difficult*) schwer; (*harsh*) hart(herzig) ♦ *adv* (*work*) hart; (*try*) sehr; (*push, hit*) fest; **no ~ feelings!** ich nehme es dir nicht übel; **~ of hearing** schwerhörig; **to be ~ done by** übel dran sein; ~**back** *n* kartonierte Ausgabe *f*; ~ **cash** *n* Bargeld *nt*; ~ **disk** *n* (*COMPUT*) Festplatte *f*; ~**en** *vt* erhärten; (*fig*) verhärten ♦ *vi* hart werden; (*fig*) sich verhärten; ~- **headed** *adj* nüchtern; ~ **labour** *n* Zwangsarbeit *f*

hardly [ˈhɑːdlɪ] *adv* kaum

hard: ~**ship** *n* Not *f*; ~ **shoulder** (*BRIT*) *n* (*AUT*) Seitenstreifen *m*; ~ **up** *adj* knapp bei Kasse; ~**ware** *n* Eisenwaren *pl*; (*COMPUT*) Hardware *f*; ~**ware shop** *n* Eisenwarenhandlung *f*; ~~**wearing** *adj* strapazierfähig; ~~**working** *adj* fleißig

hardy [ˈhɑːdɪ] *adj* widerstandsfähig

hare [hɛər] *n* Hase *m*; ~~**brained** *adj* schwachsinnig

harm [hɑːm] *n* Schaden *m* ♦ *vt* schaden +*dat*; **out of ~'s way** in Sicherheit; ~**ful** *adj* schädlich; ~**less** *adj* harmlos

harmonica [hɑːˈmɒnɪkə] *n* Mundharmonika *f*

harmonious [hɑːˈməʊnɪəs] *adj* harmonisch

harmonize [ˈhɑːmənaɪz] *vt* abstimmen ♦ *vi* harmonieren

harmony [ˈhɑːmənɪ] *n* Harmonie *f*

harness [ˈhɑːnɪs] *n* Geschirr *nt* ♦ *vt* (*horse*) anschirren; (*fig*) nutzbar machen

harp [hɑːp] *n* Harfe *f* ♦ *vi*: **to ~ on about sth** auf etw *dat* herumreiten

harpoon [hɑːˈpuːn] *n* Harpune *f*

harrowing [ˈhærəʊɪŋ] *adj* nervenaufreibend

harsh [hɑːʃ] *adj* (*rough*) rau; (*severe*) streng; ~**ness** *n* Härte *f*

harvest [ˈhɑːvɪst] *n* Ernte *f* ♦ *vt, vi* ernten

has [hæz] *vb see* **have**

hash [hæʃ] *vt* klein hacken ♦ *n* (*mess*) Kuddelmuddel *m*

hashish [ˈhæʃɪʃ] *n* Haschisch *nt*

hasn't [ˈhæznt] = **has not**

hassle [ˈhæsl] (*inf*) *n* Theater *nt*

haste [heɪst] *n* Eile *f*; ~**n** [ˈheɪsn] *vt* beschleunigen ♦ *vi* eilen; **hasty** *adj* hastig; (*rash*) vorschnell

hat [hæt] *n* Hut *m*

hatch [hætʃ] *n* (*NAUT: also:* ~**way**) Luke *f*; (*in house*) Durchreiche *f* ♦ *vi* (*young*) ausschlüpfen ♦ *vt* (*brood*) ausbrüten; (*plot*) aushecken; ~**back** [ˈhætʃbæk] *n* (*AUT*) (Auto *nt* mit) Heckklappe *f*

hatchet [ˈhætʃɪt] *n* Beil *nt*

hate [heɪt] *vt* hassen ♦ *n* Hass *m*; ~**ful** *adj* verhasst

hatred [ˈheɪtrɪd] *n* Hass *m*

haughty [ˈhɔːtɪ] *adj* hochnäsig, überheblich

haul [hɔːl] *vt* ziehen ♦ *n* (*catch*) Fang *m*; ~**age** *n* Spedition *f*; ~**ier** (*US* **hauler**) *n* Spediteur *m*

haunch [hɔːntʃ] *n* Lende *f*

haunt [hɔːnt] *vt* (*ghost*) spuken in +*dat*; (*memory*) verfolgen; (*pub*) häufig besuchen ♦ *n* Lieblingsplatz *m*; **the castle is ~ed** in dem Schloss spukt es

---
KEYWORD
---

have [hæv] (*pt, pp* **had**) *aux vb* 1 haben; (*esp with vbs of motion*) sein; **to have arrived/ slept** angekommen sein/geschlafen haben; **to have been** gewesen sein; **having eaten** *or* **when he had eaten, he left** nachdem er gegessen hatte, ging er

2 (*in tag questions*): **you've done it, haven't you?** du hast es doch gemacht, oder nicht?

3 (*in short answers and questions*): **you've made a mistake - so I have/no I haven't** du hast einen Fehler gemacht – ja, stimmt/nein; **we haven't paid - yes we have!** wir haben nicht bezahlt – doch; **I've been there before, have you?** ich war schon einmal da, du auch?

♦ *modal aux vb* (*be obliged*): **to have (got) to do sth** etw tun müssen; **you haven't to tell her** du darfst es ihr nicht erzählen

♦ *vt* 1 (*possess*) haben; **he has (got) blue**

eyes er hat blaue Augen; **I have (got) an idea** ich habe eine Idee
2 (*referring to meals etc*): **to have breakfast/a cigarette** frühstücken/eine Zigarette rauchen
3 (*receive, obtain etc*) haben; **may I have your address?** kann ich Ihre Adresse haben?; **to have a baby** ein Kind bekommen
4 (*maintain, allow*): **he will have it that he is right** er besteht darauf, dass er Recht hat; **I won't have it** das lasse ich mir nicht bieten
5: to have sth done etw machen lassen; **to have sb do sth** jdn etw machen lassen; **he soon had them all laughing** er brachte sie alle zum Lachen
6 (*experience, suffer*): **she had her bag stolen** man hat ihr die Tasche gestohlen; **he had his arm broken** er hat sich den Arm gebrochen
7 (*+noun: take, hold etc*): **to have a walk/rest** spazieren gehen/sich ausruhen; **to have a meeting/party** eine Besprechung/Party haben
have out *vt*: **to have it out with sb** (*settle problem*) etw mit jdm bereden

aven [ˈheɪvn] *n* Zufluchtsort *m*
aven't [ˈhævnt] = **have not**
avoc [ˈhævək] *n* Verwüstung *f*
awk [hɔːk] *n* Habicht *m*
ay [heɪ] *n* Heu *nt*; **~ fever** *n* Heuschnupfen *m*; **~stack** *n* Heuschober *m*
aywire [ˈheɪwaɪər] (*inf*) *adj* durcheinander
azard [ˈhæzəd] *n* Risiko *nt* ♦ *vt* aufs Spiel setzen; **~ous** *adj* gefährlich; **~ (warning) lights** *npl* (*AUT*) Warnblinklicht *nt*
aze [heɪz] *n* Dunst *m*
azelnut [ˈheɪzlnʌt] *n* Haselnuss *f*
azy [ˈheɪzɪ] *adj* (*misty*) dunstig; (*vague*) verschwommen
e [hiː] *pron* er
ead [hed] *n* Kopf *m*; (*leader*) Leiter *m* ♦ *vt* (an)führen, leiten; (*ball*) köpfen; **~s (or tails)** Kopf (oder Zahl); **~ first** mit dem Kopf nach unten; **~ over heels** kopfüber;

~ for *vt fus* zugehen auf +*acc*; **~ache** *n* Kopfschmerzen *pl*; **~dress** *n* Kopfschmuck *m*; **~ing** *n* Überschrift *f*; **~lamp** (*BRIT*) *n* Scheinwerfer *m*; **~land** *n* Landspitze *f*; **~light** *n* Scheinwerfer *m*; **~line** *n* Schlagzeile *f*; **~long** *adv* kopfüber; **~master** *n* (*of primary school*) Rektor *m*; (*of secondary school*) Direktor *m*; **~mistress** *n* Rektorin *f*; Direktorin *f*; **~ office** *n* Zentrale *f*; **~-on** *adj* Frontal-; **~phones** *npl* Kopfhörer *pl*; **~quarters** *npl* Zentrale *f*; (*MIL*) Hauptquartier *nt*; **~rest** *n* Kopfstütze *f*; **~room** *n* (*of bridges etc*) lichte Höhe *f*; **~scarf** *n* Kopftuch *nt*; **~strong** *adj* eigenwillig; **~teacher** (*BRIT*) *n* Schulleiter(in) *m(f)*; (*of secondary school also*) Direktor(in) *m*; **~ waiter** *n* Oberkellner *m*; **~way** *n* Fortschritte *pl*; **~wind** *n* Gegenwind *m*; **~y** *adj* berauschend
heal [hiːl] *vt* heilen ♦ *vi* verheilen
health [helθ] *n* Gesundheit *f*; **~ food** *n* Reformkost *f*; **H~ Service** (*BRIT*) *n*: **the H~ Service** das Gesundheitswesen; **~y** *adj* gesund
heap [hiːp] *n* Haufen *m* ♦ *vt* häufen
hear [hɪər] (*pt, pp* **heard**) *vt* hören; (*listen to*) anhören ♦ *vi* hören; **~d** [hɜːd] *pt, pp of* **hear**; **~ing** *n* Gehör *nt*; (*JUR*) Verhandlung *f*; **~ing aid** *n* Hörapparat *m*; **~say** *n* Hörensagen *nt*
hearse [hɜːs] *n* Leichenwagen *m*
heart [hɑːt] *n* Herz *nt*; **~s** *npl* (*CARDS*) Herz *nt*; **by ~** auswendig; **~ attack** *n* Herzanfall *m*; **~beat** *n* Herzschlag *m*; **~breaking** *adj* herzzerbrechend; **~broken** *adj* untröstlich; **~burn** *n* Sodbrennen *nt*; **~ failure** *n* Herzschlag *m*; **~felt** *adj* aufrichtig
hearth [hɑːθ] *n* Herd *m*
heartily [ˈhɑːtɪlɪ] *adv* herzlich; (*eat*) herzhaft
heartless [ˈhɑːtlɪs] *adj* herzlos
hearty [ˈhɑːtɪ] *adj* kräftig; (*friendly*) freundlich
heat [hiːt] *n* Hitze *f*; (*of food, water etc*) Wärme *f*; (*SPORT: also: qualifying ~*) Ausscheidungsrunde *f* ♦ *vt* (*house*) heizen; (*substance*) heiß machen, erhitzen; **~ up** *vi* warm werden ♦ *vt* aufwärmen; **~ed** *adj* erhitzt; (*fig*) hitzig; **~er** *n* (Heiz)ofen *m*

heath [hi:θ] (BRIT) n Heide f
heathen ['hi:ðən] n Heide m/Heidin f ♦ adj heidnisch, Heiden-
heather ['hɛðər] n Heidekraut nt
heat: ~ing n Heizung f; ~-seeking adj Wärme suchend; ~stroke n Hitzschlag m; ~ wave n Hitzewelle f
heave [hi:v] vt hochheben; (sigh) ausstoßen ♦ vi wogen; (breast) sich heben ♦ n Heben nt
heaven ['hɛvn] n Himmel m; ~ly adj himmlisch
heavily ['hɛvɪlɪ] adv schwer
heavy ['hɛvɪ] adj schwer; ~ goods vehicle n Lastkraftwagen m; ~weight n (SPORT) Schwergewicht nt
Hebrew ['hi:bru:] adj hebräisch ♦ n (LING) Hebräisch nt
Hebrides ['hɛbrɪdi:z] npl Hebriden pl
heckle ['hɛkl] vt unterbrechen
hectic ['hɛktɪk] adj hektisch
he'd [hi:d] = he had; he would
hedge [hɛdʒ] n Hecke f ♦ vt einzäunen ♦ vi (fig) ausweichen; to ~ one's bets sich absichern
hedgehog ['hɛdʒhɒg] n Igel m
heed [hi:d] vt (also: take ~ of) beachten ♦ n Beachtung f; ~less adj achtlos
heel [hi:l] n Ferse f; (of shoe) Absatz m ♦ vt mit Absätzen versehen
hefty ['hɛftɪ] adj (person) stämmig; (portion) reichlich
heifer ['hɛfər] n Färse f
height [haɪt] n (of person) Größe f; (of object) Höhe f; ~en vt erhöhen
heir [ɛər] n Erbe m; ~ess n ['ɛərɛs] n Erbin f; ~loom n Erbstück nt
held [hɛld] pt, pp of hold
helicopter ['hɛlɪkɒptər] n Hubschrauber m
heliport ['hɛlɪpɔ:t] n Hubschrauber-landeplatz m
hell [hɛl] n Hölle f ♦ excl verdammt!
he'll [hi:l] = he will; he shall
hellish ['hɛlɪʃ] adj höllisch, verteufelt
hello [hə'ləu] excl hallo
helm [hɛlm] n Ruder nt, Steuer nt
helmet ['hɛlmɪt] n Helm m

help [hɛlp] n Hilfe f ♦ vt helfen +dat; **I can't ~ it** ich kann nichts dafür; **~ yourself** bedienen Sie sich; ~er n Helfer m; ~ful adj hilfreich; ~ing n Portion f; ~less adj hilflos
hem [hɛm] n Saum m ♦ vt säumen; ~ **in** vt einengen
hemorrhage ['hɛmərɪdʒ] (US) n = **haemorrhage**
hemorrhoids ['hɛmərɔɪdz] (US) npl = **haemorrhoids**
hen [hɛn] n Henne f
hence [hɛns] adv von jetzt an; (therefore) daher; ~forth adv von nun an; (from then on) von da an
henchman ['hɛntʃmən] (irreg) n Gefolgsmann m
her [hə:r] pron (acc) sie; (dat) ihr ♦ adj ihr; see also **me; my**
herald ['hɛrəld] n (Vor)bote m ♦ vt verkünden
heraldry ['hɛrəldrɪ] n Wappenkunde f
herb [hə:b] n Kraut nt
herd [hə:d] n Herde f
here [hɪər] adv hier; (to this place) hierher; ~after [hɪər'ɑ:ftər] adv hernach, künftig ♦ n Jenseits nt; ~by [hɪə'baɪ] adv hiermit
hereditary [hɪ'rɛdɪtrɪ] adj erblich
heredity [hɪ'rɛdɪtɪ] n Vererbung f
heritage ['hɛrɪtɪdʒ] n Erbe nt
hermit ['hə:mɪt] n Einsiedler m
hernia ['hə:nɪə] n Bruch m
hero ['hɪərəu] (pl ~es) n Held m; ~ic [hɪ'rəuɪk] adj heroisch
heroin ['hɛrəuɪn] n Heroin nt
heroine ['hɛrəuɪn] n Heldin f
heroism ['hɛrəuɪzəm] n Heldentum nt
heron ['hɛrən] n Reiher m
herring ['hɛrɪŋ] n Hering m
hers [hə:z] pron ihre(r, s); see also **mine**[2]
herself [hə:'sɛlf] pron sich (selbst); (emphatic) selbst; see also **oneself**
he's [hi:z] = he is; he has
hesitant ['hɛzɪtənt] adj zögernd
hesitate ['hɛzɪteɪt] vi zögern; **hesitation** [hɛzɪ'teɪʃən] n Zögern nt
heterosexual ['hɛtərəu'sɛksjuəl] adj heterosexuell ♦ n Heterosexuelle(r) mf

W [hju:] (pt **hewed**, pp **hewn**) vt hauen,
acken

xagonal [hɛk'sægənl] adj sechseckig

yday ['heɪdeɪ] n Blüte f, Höhepunkt m

GV n abbr = **heavy goods vehicle**

[haɪ] excl he, hallo

ernate ['haɪbəneɪt] vi Winterschlaf m
alten; **hibernation** [haɪbə'neɪʃən] n
Vinterschlaf m

cough ['hɪkʌp] vi den Schluckauf haben;
-s npl Schluckauf m

cup ['hɪkʌp] = **hiccough**

I [hɪd] pt of **hide**; ~**den** [hɪdn] pp of **hide**
le [haɪd] (pt **hid**, pp **hidden**) n (skin) Haut
, Fell n ♦ vt verstecken ♦ vi sich
erstecken; ~**-and-seek** n Versteckspiel nt;
away n Versteck nt

eous ['hɪdɪəs] adj abscheulich

ling ['haɪdɪŋ] n (beating) Tracht f Prügel;
o be in ~ (concealed) sich versteckt halten;
place n Versteck nt

fi ['haɪfaɪ] n Hi-Fi nt ♦ adj Hi-Fi-

gh [haɪ] adj hoch; (wind) stark ♦ adv hoch;
t is 20m ~ es ist 20 Meter hoch; ~**brow**
dj (betont) intellektuell; ~**chair** n
lochstuhl m; ~**er education** n
lochschulbildung f; ~**-handed** adj
igenmächtig; ~**-heeled** adj hochhackig; ~
ump n (SPORT) Hochsprung m; H~**lands**
pl: **the H~lands** das schottische
lochland; ~**light** n (fig) Höhepunkt m ♦ vt
ervorheben; ~**ly** adv höchst; ~**ly strung**
dj überempfindlich; ~**ness** n Höhe f; **Her**
I~ness Ihre Hoheit f; ~**-pitched** adj hoch;
--**rise block** n Hochhaus nt; ~**school**
US) n Oberschule f; ~**season** (BRIT) n
lochsaison f; ~**street** (BRIT) n Hauptstraße

ghway ['haɪweɪ] n Landstraße f; H~ **Code**
BRIT) n Straßenverkehrsordnung f

ack ['haɪdʒæk] vt entführen; ~**er** n
ntführer(in) m(f)

ke [haɪk] vi wandern ♦ n Wanderung f; ~r
Wanderer m; **hiking** n Wandern nt

arious [hɪ'lɛərɪəs] adj lustig

I [hɪl] n Berg m; ~**side** n (Berg)hang m; ~
walking n Bergwandern nt; ~**y** adj hügelig

hilt [hɪlt] n Heft nt; **(up) to the** ~ ganz und
gar

him [hɪm] pron (acc) ihn; (dat) ihm; see also
me; ~**self** pron sich (selbst); (emphatic)
selbst; see also **oneself**

hind [haɪnd] adj hinter, Hinter-

hinder ['hɪndə'] vt (stop) hindern; (delay)
behindern; **hindrance** n (delay)
Behinderung f; (obstacle) Hindernis nt

hindsight ['haɪndsaɪt] n: **with ~** im
nachhinein

Hindu ['hɪndu:] n Hindu m

hinge [hɪndʒ] n Scharnier nt; (on door)
Türangel f ♦ vi (fig): **to ~ on** abhängen von

hint [hɪnt] n Tipp m; (trace) Anflug m ♦ vt: **to**
~ that andeuten, dass ♦ vi: **to ~ at**
andeuten

hip [hɪp] n Hüfte f

hippie ['hɪpɪ] n Hippie m

hippo ['hɪpəʊ] (inf) n Nilpferd nt

hippopotami [hɪpə'pɒtəmaɪ] npl of
hippopotamus

hippopotamus [hɪpə'pɒtəməs] (pl ~**es** or
hippopotami) n Nilpferd nt

hire ['haɪə'] vt (worker) anstellen; (BRIT: car)
mieten ♦ n Miete f; **for ~** (taxi) frei; ~**(d)**
car (BRIT) n Mietwagen m, Leihwagen m; ~
purchase (BRIT) n Teilzahlungskauf m

his [hɪz] adj sein ♦ pron seine(r, s); see also
my; mine²

hiss [hɪs] vi zischen ♦ n Zischen nt

historian [hɪ'stɔːrɪən] n Historiker m

historic [hɪ'stɒrɪk] adj historisch; ~**al** adj
historisch, geschichtlich

history ['hɪstərɪ] n Geschichte f

hit [hɪt] (pt, pp **hit**) vt schlagen; (injure)
treffen ♦ n (blow) Schlag m; (success) Erfolg
m; (MUS) Hit m; **to ~ it off with sb** prima
mit jdm auskommen; ~**-and-run driver** n
jemand, der Fahrerflucht begeht

hitch [hɪtʃ] vt festbinden; (also: ~ **up**)
hochziehen ♦ n (difficulty) Haken m; **to ~ a**
lift trampen; ~**hike** vi trampen; ~**hiker** n
Tramper m; ~**hiking** n Trampen nt

hi-tech ['haɪ'tɛk] adj Hightech- ♦ n
Spitzentechnologie f

hitherto [hɪðə'tu:] adv bislang

hit man (inf) (irreg) n Killer m
HIV n abbr: **HIV-negative/-positive** HIV-negativ/-positiv
hive [haɪv] n Bienenkorb m
HMS abbr = **His/Her Majesty's Ship**
hoard [hɔːd] n Schatz m ♦ vt horten, hamstern
hoarding ['hɔːdɪŋ] n Bretterzaun m; (BRIT: for posters) Reklamewand f
hoarse [hɔːs] adj heiser, rau
hoax [həʊks] n Streich m
hob [hɔb] n Kochmulde f
hobble ['hɔbl] vi humpeln
hobby ['hɔbɪ] n Hobby nt
hobby-horse ['hɔbɪhɔːs] n (fig) Steckenpferd nt
hobo ['həʊbəʊ] (US) n Tippelbruder m
hockey ['hɔkɪ] n Hockey nt
hoe [həʊ] n Hacke f ♦ vt hacken
hog [hɔg] n Schlachtschwein m ♦ vt mit Beschlag belegen; **to go the whole ~** aufs Ganze gehen
hoist [hɔɪst] n Winde f ♦ vt hochziehen
hold [həʊld] (pt, pp **held**) vt halten; (contain) enthalten; (be able to contain) fassen; (breath) anhalten; (meeting) abhalten ♦ vi (withstand pressure) aushalten ♦ n (grasp) Halt m; (NAUT) Schiffsraum m; **~ the line!** (TEL) bleiben Sie am Apparat!; **to ~ one's own** sich behaupten; **~ back** vt zurückhalten; **~ down** vt niederhalten; (job) behalten; **~ off** vt (enemy) abwehren; **~ on** vi sich festhalten; (resist) durchhalten; (wait) warten; **~ on to** vt fus festhalten an +dat; (keep) behalten; **~ out** vt hinhalten ♦ vi aushalten; **~ up** vt (delay) aufhalten; (rob) überfallen; **~all** (BRIT) n Reisetasche f; **~er** n Behälter m; **~ing** n (share) (Aktien)anteil m; **~up** n (BRIT: in traffic) Stockung f; (robbery) Überfall m; (delay) Verzögerung f
hole [həʊl] n Loch nt; **~ in the wall** (inf) n (cash dispenser) Geldautomat m
holiday ['hɔlɪdeɪ] n (day) Feiertag m; freie(r) Tag m; (vacation) Urlaub m; (SCH) Ferien pl; **~-maker** (BRIT) n Urlauber(in) m(f); **~ resort** n Ferienort m

Holland ['hɔlənd] n Holland nt
hollow ['hɔləʊ] adj hohl; (fig) leer ♦ n Vertiefung f; **~ out** vt aushöhlen
holly ['hɔlɪ] n Stechpalme f
holocaust ['hɔləkɔːst] n Inferno nt
holster ['həʊlstər] n Pistolenhalfter m
holy ['həʊlɪ] adj heilig; **H~ Ghost** or **Spirit** n: **the H~ Ghost** or **Spirit** der Heilige Geist
homage ['hɔmɪdʒ] n Huldigung f; **to pay ~ to** huldigen +dat
home [həʊm] n Zuhause nt; (institution) Heim nt, Anstalt f ♦ adj einheimisch; (POL) inner ♦ adv heim, nach Hause; **at ~** zu Hause; **~ address** n Heimatadresse f; **~coming** n Heimkehr f; **~land** n Heimat(land nt) f; **~less** adj obdachlos; **~ly** adj häuslich; (US: ugly) unscheinbar; **~made** adj selbst gemacht; **~ match** adj Heimspiel nt; **H~ Office** (BRIT) n Innenministerium nt; **~ page** n (COMPUT) Homepage f; **~ rule** n Selbstverwaltung f; **H~ Secretary** (BRIT) n Innenminister(in) m(f); **~sick** adj: **to be ~sick** Heimweh haben; **~ town** n Heimatstadt f; **~ward** adj (journey) Heim-; **~work** n Hausaufgaben pl
homicide ['hɔmɪsaɪd] (US) n Totschlag m
homoeopathic [həʊmɪə'pæθɪk] (US **homeopathic**) adj homöopathisch; **homoeopathy** [həʊmɪ'ɔpəθɪ] (US **homeopathy**) n Homöopathie f
homogeneous [hɔməʊ'dʒiːnɪəs] adj homogen
homosexual [hɔməʊ'seksjuəl] adj homosexuell ♦ n Homosexuelle(r) mf
honest ['ɔnɪst] adj ehrlich; **~ly** adv ehrlich; **~y** n Ehrlichkeit f
honey ['hʌnɪ] n Honig m; **~comb** n Honigwabe f; **~moon** n Flitterwochen pl, Hochzeitsreise f; **~suckle** ['hʌnɪsʌkl] n Geißblatt nt
honk [hɔŋk] vi hupen
honor etc ['ɔnər] (US) vt, n = **honour** etc
honorary ['ɔnərərɪ] adj Ehren-
honour ['ɔnər] (US **honor**) vt ehren; (cheque) einlösen ♦ n Ehre f; **~able** adj ehrenwert; (intention) ehrenhaft; **~s degree** n (UNIV) akademischer Grad mit Prüfung im

Spezialfach

ood [hud] *n* Kapuze *f*; (*BRIT: AUT*) Verdeck *nt*; (*US: AUT*) Kühlerhaube *f*

oof [huːf] (*pl* **hooves**) *n* Huf *m*

ook [huk] *n* Haken *m* ♦ *vt* einhaken

ooligan ['huːlɪgən] *n* Rowdy *m*

oop [huːp] *n* Reifen *m*

ooray [huː'reɪ] *excl* = **hurrah**

oot [huːt] *vi* (*AUT*) hupen; ~**er** *n* (*NAUT*) Dampfpfeife *f*; (*BRIT: AUT*) (Auto)hupe *f*

Hoover ['huːvə] (®; *BRIT*) *n* Staubsauger *m* ♦ *vt*: **to h~** staubsaugen, Staub saugen

ooves [huːvz] *pl of* **hoof**

op [hɔp] *vi* hüpfen, hopsen ♦ *n* (*jump*) Hopser *m*

ope [həup] *vt*, *vi* hoffen ♦ *n* Hoffnung *f*; **I ~ so/not** hoffentlich/hoffentlich nicht; ~**ful** *adj* hoffnungsvoll; (*promising*) viel versprechend; ~**fully** *adv* hoffentlich; ~**less** *adj* hoffnungslos

ops [hɔps] *npl* Hopfen *pl*

orizon [hə'raɪzn] *n* Horizont *m*; ~**tal** [hɔrɪ'zɔntl] *adj* horizontal

ormone ['hɔːməun] *n* Hormon *nt*

orn [hɔːn] *n* Horn *nt*; (*AUT*) Hupe *f*

ornet ['hɔːnɪt] *n* Hornisse *f*

orny ['hɔːnɪ] *adj* schwielig; (*US: inf*) scharf

oroscope ['hɔrəskəup] *n* Horoskop *nt*

orrendous [hə'rendəs] *adj* (*crime*) abscheulich; (*error*) schrecklich

orrible ['hɔrɪbl] *adj* fürchterlich

orrid ['hɔrɪd] *adj* scheußlich

orrify ['hɔrɪfaɪ] *vt* entsetzen

orror ['hɔrə] *n* Schrecken *m*; ~ **film** *n* Horrorfilm *m*

hors d'oeuvre [ɔː'dəːvrə] *n* Vorspeise *f*

horse [hɔːs] *n* Pferd *nt*; ~**back** *n*: **on ~back** beritten; ~ **chestnut** *n* Rosskastanie *f*; ~**man/woman** (*irreg*) *n* Reiter(in) *m(f)*; ~**power** *n* Pferdestärke *f*; ~**racing** *n* Pferderennen *nt*; ~**radish** *n* Meerrettich *m*; ~**shoe** *n* Hufeisen *nt*

horticulture ['hɔːtɪkʌltʃə] *n* Gartenbau *m*

hose [həuz] *n* (*also*: ~**pipe**) Schlauch *m*

hosiery ['həuzɪərɪ] *n* Strumpfwaren *pl*

hospitable ['hɔspɪtəbl] *adj* gastfreundlich

hospital ['hɔspɪtl] *n* Krankenhaus *nt*

hospitality [hɔspɪ'tælɪtɪ] *n* Gastfreundschaft *f*

host [həust] *n* Gastgeber *m*; (*innkeeper*) (Gast)wirt *m*; (*large number*) Heerschar *f*; (*ECCL*) Hostie *f*

hostage ['hɔstɪdʒ] *n* Geisel *f*

hostel ['hɔstl] *n* Herberge *f*; (*also*: **youth ~**) Jugendherberge *f*

hostess ['həustɪs] *n* Gastgeberin *f*

hostile ['hɔstaɪl] *adj* feindlich; **hostility** [hɔ'stɪlɪtɪ] *n* Feindschaft *f*; **hostilities** *npl* (*fighting*) Feindseligkeiten *pl*

hot [hɔt] *adj* heiß; (*food, water*) warm; (*spiced*) scharf; **I'm ~** mir ist heiß; ~**bed** *n* (*fig*) Nährboden *m*; ~ **dog** *n* heiße(s) Würstchen *nt*

hotel [həu'tel] *n* Hotel *nt*; ~**ier** [həu'telɪə] *n* Hotelier *m*

hot: ~**house** *n* Treibhaus *nt*; ~ **line** *n* (*POL*) heiße(r) Draht *m*; ~**ly** *adv* (*argue*) hitzig; ~**plate** *n* Kochplatte *f*; ~**pot** ['hɔtpɔt] (*BRIT*) *n* Fleischeintopf *m*; ~-**water bottle** *n* Wärmflasche *f*

hound [haund] *n* Jagdhund *m* ♦ *vt* hetzen

hour ['auə] *n* Stunde *f*; (*time of day*) (Tages)zeit *f*; ~**ly** *adj*, *adv* stündlich

house [*n* haus, *vb* hauz] *n* Haus *nt* ♦ *vt* unterbringen; **on the ~** auf Kosten des Hauses; ~ **arrest** *n* (*POL, MIL*) Hausarrest *m*; ~**boat** *n* Hausboot *nt*; ~**breaking** *n* Einbruch *m*; ~**coat** *n* Morgenmantel *m*; ~**hold** *n* Haushalt *m*; ~**keeper** *n* Haushälterin *f*; ~**keeping** *n* Haushaltung *f*; ~-**warming party** *n* Einweihungsparty *f*; ~**wife** (*irreg*) *n* Hausfrau *f*; ~**work** *n* Hausarbeit *f*

housing ['hauzɪŋ] *n* (*act*) Unterbringung *f*; (*houses*) Wohnungen *pl*; (*POL*) Wohnungsbau *m*; (*covering*) Gehäuse *nt*; ~ **estate** (*US* ~ **development**) *n* (Wohn)siedlung *f*

hovel ['hɔvl] *n* elende Hütte *f*

hover ['hɔvə] *vi* (*bird*) schweben; (*person*) herumstehen; ~**craft** *n* Luftkissenfahrzeug *nt*

how [hau] *adv* wie; ~ **are you?** wie geht es Ihnen?; ~ **much milk?** wie viel Milch?; ~

many people? wie viele Leute?

however [hau'evə'] *adv* (*but*) (je)doch, aber;
~ **you phrase it** wie Sie es auch
ausdrücken

howl [haul] *n* Heulen *nt* ♦ *vi* heulen

H.P. *abbr* = **hire purchase**

h.p. *abbr* = **horsepower**

H.Q. *abbr* = **headquarters**

HTML *abbr* (= *hypertext markup language*)
HTML

hub [hʌb] *n* Radnabe *f*

hubbub ['hʌbʌb] *n* Tumult *m*

hubcap ['hʌbkæp] *n* Radkappe *f*

huddle ['hʌdl] *vi*: **to ~ together** sich
zusammendrängen

hue [hju:] *n* Färbung *f*; ~ **and cry** *n*
Zetergeschrei *nt*

huff [hʌf] *n*: **to go into a ~** einschnappen

hug [hʌg] *vt* umarmen ♦ *n* Umarmung *f*

huge [hju:dʒ] *adj* groß, riesig

hulk [hʌlk] *n* (*ship*) abgetakelte(s) Schiff *nt*;
(*person*) Koloss *m*

hull [hʌl] *n* Schiffsrumpf *m*

hullo [hə'ləu] *excl* = **hello**

hum [hʌm] *vt*, *vi* summen

human ['hju:mən] *adj* menschlich ♦ *n* (*also*:
~ **being**) Mensch *m*

humane [hju:'mein] *adj* human

humanitarian [hju:mænɪ'teərɪən] *adj*
humanitär

humanity [hju:'mænɪtɪ] *n* Menschheit *f*;
(*kindliness*) Menschlichkeit *f*

humble ['hʌmbl] *adj* demütig; (*modest*)
bescheiden ♦ *vt* demütigen

humbug ['hʌmbʌg] *n* Humbug *m*; (*BRIT*:
sweet) Pfefferminzbonbon *nt*

humdrum ['hʌmdrʌm] *adj* stumpfsinnig

humid ['hju:mɪd] *adj* feucht; ~**ity** [hju:'mɪdɪtɪ]
n Feuchtigkeit *f*

humiliate [hju:'mɪlɪeɪt] *vt* demütigen; **hu-**
miliation [hju:mɪlɪ'eɪʃən] *n* Demütigung *f*

humility [hju:'mɪlɪtɪ] *n* Demut *f*

humor ['hju:mə'] (*US*) *n*, *vt* = **humour**

humorous ['hju:mərəs] *adj* humorvoll

humour ['hju:mə'] (*US* **humor**) *n* (*fun*)
Humor *m*; (*mood*) Stimmung *f* ♦ *vt* bei
Stimmung halten

hump [hʌmp] *n* Buckel *m*

hunch [hʌntʃ] *n*; (*premonition*)
(Vor)ahnung *f*; ~**back** *n* Bucklige(r) *mf*;
~**ed** *adj* gekrümmt

hundred ['hʌndrəd] *num* hundert; ~**weight**
n Zentner *m* (*BRIT* = 50.8 kg; *US* = 45.3 kg)

hung [hʌŋ] *pt*, *pp* of **hang**

Hungarian [hʌŋ'geərɪən] *adj* ungarisch ♦ *n*
Ungar(in) *m(f)*; (*LING*) Ungarisch *nt*

Hungary ['hʌŋgərɪ] *n* Ungarn *nt*

hunger ['hʌŋgə'] *n* Hunger *m* ♦ *vi* hungern

hungry ['hʌŋgrɪ] *adj* hungrig; **to be ~**
Hunger haben

hunk [hʌŋk] *n* (*of bread*) Stück *nt*

hunt [hʌnt] *vt*, *vi* jagen ♦ *n* Jagd *f*; **to ~ for**
suchen; ~**er** *n* Jäger *m*; ~**ing** *n* Jagd *f*

hurdle ['hə:dl] *n* (*also fig*) Hürde *f*

hurl [hə:l] *vt* schleudern

hurrah [hu'rɑ:] *n* Hurra *nt*

hurray [hu'reɪ] *n* Hurra *nt*

hurricane ['hʌrɪkən] *n* Orkan *m*

hurried ['hʌrɪd] *adj* eilig; (*hasty*) übereilt; ~**ly**
adv übereilt, hastig

hurry ['hʌrɪ] *n* Eile *f* ♦ *vi* sich beeilen ♦ *vt*
(an)treiben; (*job*) übereilen; **to be in a ~** es
eilig haben; ~ **up** *vi* sich beeilen ♦ *vt*
(*person*) zur Eile antreiben; (*work*)
vorantreiben

hurt [hə:t] (*pt*, *pp* **hurt**) *vt* wehtun +*dat*;
(*injure*, *fig*) verletzen ♦ *vi* wehtun; ~**ful** *adj*
schädlich; (*remark*) verletzend

hurtle ['hə:tl] *vi* sausen

husband ['hʌzbənd] *n* (Ehe)mann *m*

hush [hʌʃ] *n* Stille *f* ♦ *vt* zur Ruhe bringen
♦ *excl* pst, still

husky ['hʌskɪ] *adj* (*voice*) rau ♦ *n* Eskimohund *m*

hustle ['hʌsl] *vt* (*push*) stoßen; (*hurry*) antreiben ♦ *n*: ~ **and bustle** Geschäftigkeit *f*

hut [hʌt] *n* Hütte *f*

hutch [hʌtʃ] *n* (Kaninchen)stall *m*

hyacinth ['haɪəsɪnθ] *n* Hyazinthe *f*

hydrant ['haɪdrənt] *n* (*also*: **fire ~**) Hydrant *m*

hydraulic [haɪ'drɔ:lɪk] *adj* hydraulisch

hydroelectric ['haɪdrəuɪ'lektrɪk] *adj* (*energy*)
durch Wasserkraft erzeugt; ~ **power**
station *n* Wasserkraftwerk *nt*

hydrofoil ['haɪdrəfɔɪl] *n* Tragflügelboot *nt*

ydrogen ['haɪdrədʒən] n Wasserstoff m

yena [haɪ'iːnə] n Hyäne f

ygiene ['haɪdʒiːn] n Hygiene f; **hygienic** [haɪ'dʒiːnɪk] adj hygienisch

ymn [hɪm] n Kirchenlied nt

ype [haɪp] (inf) n Publicity f

ypermarket ['haɪpəmɑːkɪt] (BRIT) n Hypermarket m

ypertext ['haɪpətɛkst] n (COMPUT) Hypertext m

yphen ['haɪfn] n Bindestrich m

ypnosis [hɪp'nəusɪs] n Hypnose f

ypnotize ['hɪpnətaɪz] vt hypnotisieren

ypocrisy [hɪ'pɔkrɪsɪ] n Heuchelei f

ypocrite ['hɪpəkrɪt] n Heuchler m; **hypocritical** [hɪpə'krɪtɪkl] adj scheinheilig, heuchlerisch

ypothermia [haɪpə'θəːmɪə] n Unterkühlung f

ypotheses [haɪ'pɔθɪsiːz] npl of **hypothesis**

ypothesis [haɪ'pɔθɪsɪs] (pl **hypotheses**) n Hypothese f

ypothetic(al) [haɪpəυ'θetɪk(l)] adj hypothetisch

ysterical [hɪ'sterɪkl] adj hysterisch

ysterics [hɪ'sterɪks] npl hysterische(r) Anfall m

I, i

[aɪ] pron ich

ce [aɪs] n Eis nt ♦ vt (COOK) mit Zuckerguss überziehen ♦ vi (also: ~ up) vereisen; ~ axe n Eispickel m; ~berg n Eisberg m; ~box (US) n Kühlschrank m; ~ cream n Eis nt; ~ cube n Eiswürfel m; ~d [aɪst] adj (cake) mit Zuckerguss überzogen, glasiert; (tea, coffee) Eis-; ~ hockey n Eishockey nt

celand ['aɪslənd] n Island nt

ce: ~ lolly (BRIT) n Eis nt am Stiel; ~ rink n (Kunst)eisbahn f; ~ skating n Schlittschuhlaufen nt

cicle ['aɪsɪkl] n Eiszapfen m

cing ['aɪsɪŋ] n (on cake) Zuckerguss m; (on window) Vereisung f; ~ sugar (BRIT) n Puderzucker m

icon ['aɪkɔn] n Ikone f; (COMPUT) Icon nt

icy ['aɪsɪ] adj (slippery) vereist; (cold) eisig

I'd [aɪd] = **I would**; **I had**

idea [aɪ'dɪə] n Idee f

ideal [aɪ'dɪəl] n Ideal nt ♦ adj ideal

identical [aɪ'dentɪkl] adj identisch; (twins) eineiig

identification [aɪdentɪfɪ'keɪʃən] n Identifizierung f; **means of ~** Ausweispapiere pl

identify [aɪ'dentɪfaɪ] vt identifizieren; (regard as the same) gleichsetzen

Identikit [aɪ'dentɪkɪt] ® n: ~ **picture** Phantombild nt

identity [aɪ'dentɪtɪ] n Identität f; ~ **card** n Personalausweis m

ideology [aɪdɪ'ɔlədʒɪ] n Ideologie f

idiom ['ɪdɪəm] n (expression) Redewendung f; (dialect) Idiom nt; ~atic [ɪdɪə'mætɪk] adj idiomatisch

idiosyncrasy [ɪdɪəυ'sɪŋkrəsɪ] n Eigenart f

idiot ['ɪdɪət] n Idiot(in) m(f); ~ic [ɪdɪ'ɔtɪk] adj idiotisch

idle ['aɪdl] adj (doing nothing) untätig; (lazy) faul; (useless) nutzlos; (machine) still(stehend); (threat, talk) leer ♦ vi (machine) leer laufen ♦ vt: **to ~ away the time** die Zeit vertrödeln; ~**ness** n Müßiggang m; Faulheit f

idol ['aɪdl] n Idol nt; ~**ize** vt vergöttern

i.e. abbr (= id est) d. h.

KEYWORD

if [ɪf] conj 1 wenn; (in case also) falls; **if I were you** wenn ich Sie wäre

2 (although): **(even) if** (selbst or auch) wenn

3 (whether) ob

4: **if so/not** wenn ja/nicht; **if only ...** wenn ... doch nur ...; **if only I could** wenn ich doch nur könnte; see also **as**

ignite [ɪg'naɪt] vt (an)zünden ♦ vi sich entzünden; **ignition** [ɪg'nɪʃən] n Zündung f; **to switch on/off the ignition** den Motor anlassen/abstellen; **ignition key** n (AUT) Zündschlüssel m

ignorance ['ɪgnərəns] n Unwissenheit f

ignorant ['ɪgnərənt] adj unwissend; **to be ~ of** nicht wissen

ignore [ɪg'nɔː] vt ignorieren

I'll [aɪl] = **I will; I shall**

ill [ɪl] adj krank ♦ n Übel nt ♦ adv schlecht; **~-advised** adj unklug; **~-at-ease** adj unbehaglich

illegal [ɪ'liːgl] adj illegal

illegible [ɪ'ledʒɪbl] adj unleserlich

illegitimate [ɪlɪ'dʒɪtɪmət] adj unehelich

ill-fated [ɪl'feɪtɪd] adj unselig

ill feeling n Verstimmung f

illicit [ɪ'lɪsɪt] adj verboten

illiterate [ɪ'lɪtərət] adj ungebildet

ill-mannered [ɪl'mænəd] adj ungehobelt

illness ['ɪlnɪs] n Krankheit f

illogical [ɪ'lɒdʒɪkl] adj unlogisch

ill-treat [ɪl'triːt] vt misshandeln

illuminate [ɪ'luːmɪneɪt] vt beleuchten; **illumination** [ɪluːmɪ'neɪʃən] n Beleuchtung f; **illuminations** pl (decorative lights) festliche Beleuchtung f

illusion [ɪ'luːʒən] n Illusion f; **to be under the ~ that ...** sich dat einbilden, dass ...

illustrate ['ɪləstreɪt] vt (book) illustrieren; (explain) veranschaulichen; **illustration** [ɪlə'streɪʃən] n Illustration f; (explanation) Veranschaulichung f

illustrious [ɪ'lʌstrɪəs] adj berühmt

I'm [aɪm] = **I am**

image ['ɪmɪdʒ] n Bild nt; (public ~) Image nt; **~ry** n Symbolik f

imaginary [ɪ'mædʒɪnərɪ] adj eingebildet; (world) Fantasie-

imagination [ɪmædʒɪ'neɪʃən] n Einbildung f; (creative) Fantasie f

imaginative [ɪ'mædʒɪnətɪv] adj fantasiereich, einfallsreich

imagine [ɪ'mædʒɪn] vt sich vorstellen; (wrongly) sich einbilden

imbalance [ɪm'bæləns] n Unausgeglichenheit f

imbecile ['ɪmbəsiːl] n Schwachsinnige(r) mf

imitate ['ɪmɪteɪt] vt imitieren; **imitation** [ɪmɪ'teɪʃən] n Imitation f

immaculate [ɪ'mækjulət] adj makellos;

(dress) tadellos; (ECCL) unbefleckt

immaterial [ɪmə'tɪərɪəl] adj unwesentlich; **it is ~ whether ...** es ist unwichtig, ob ...

immature [ɪmə'tjuə] adj unreif

immediate [ɪ'miːdɪət] adj (instant) sofortig; (near) unmittelbar; (relatives) nächste(r, s); (needs) dringlich; **~ly** adv sofort; **~ly next to** direkt neben

immense [ɪ'mens] adj unermesslich

immerse [ɪ'məːs] vt eintauchen; **to be ~d in** (fig) vertieft sein in +acc

immersion heater [ɪ'məːʃən-] (BRIT) n Boiler m

immigrant ['ɪmɪgrənt] n Einwanderer m

immigrate ['ɪmɪgreɪt] vi einwandern; **immigration** [ɪmɪ'greɪʃən] n Einwanderung f

imminent ['ɪmɪnənt] adj bevorstehend

immobile [ɪ'məubaɪl] adj unbeweglich; **immobilize** [ɪ'məubɪlaɪz] vt lähmen

immoral [ɪ'mɔrl] adj unmoralisch; **~ity** [ɪmə'rælɪtɪ] n Unsittlichkeit f

immortal [ɪ'mɔːtl] adj unsterblich

immune [ɪ'mjuːn] adj (secure) sicher; (MED) immun; **~ from** sicher vor +dat; **immunity** n (MED, JUR) Immunität f; (fig) Freiheit f; **immunize** ['ɪmjunaɪz] vt immunisieren

impact ['ɪmpækt] n Aufprall m; (fig) Wirkung f

impair [ɪm'peə] vt beeinträchtigen

impart [ɪm'pɑːt] vt mitteilen; (knowledge) vermitteln; (exude) abgeben

impartial [ɪm'pɑːʃl] adj unparteiisch

impassable [ɪm'pɑːsəbl] adj unpassierbar

impassive [ɪm'pæsɪv] adj gelassen

impatience [ɪm'peɪʃəns] n Ungeduld f; **impatient** adj ungeduldig; **impatiently** adv ungeduldig

impeccable [ɪm'pekəbl] adj tadellos

impede [ɪm'piːd] vt (be)hindern; **impediment** [ɪm'pedɪmənt] n Hindernis nt; **speech impediment** Sprachfehler m

impending [ɪm'pendɪŋ] adj bevorstehend

impenetrable [ɪm'penɪtrəbl] adj (also fig) undurchdringlich

imperative [ɪm'perətɪv] adj (necessary) unbedingt erforderlich

nperceptible [ɪmpəˈsɛptɪbl] *adj* nicht wahrnehmbar

nperfect [ɪmˈpəːfɪkt] *adj* (*faulty*) fehlerhaft; **~ion** [ɪmpəˈfɛkʃən] *n* Unvollkommenheit *f*; (*fault*) Fehler *m*

nperial [ɪmˈpɪərɪəl] *adj* kaiserlich

npersonal [ɪmˈpəːsənl] *adj* unpersönlich

npersonate [ɪmˈpəːsəneɪt] *vt* sich ausgeben als; (*for fun*) imitieren

npertinent [ɪmˈpəːtɪnənt] *adj* unverschämt, frech

npervious [ɪmˈpəːvɪəs] *adj* (*fig*): **~ (to)** unempfänglich (für)

npetuous [ɪmˈpɛtjuəs] *adj* ungestüm

npetus [ˈɪmpətəs] *n* Triebkraft *f*; (*fig*) Auftrieb *m*

npinge [ɪmˈpɪndʒ]: **~ on** *vt* beeinträchtigen

nplacable [ɪmˈplækəbl] *adj* unerbittlich

nplement [*n* ˈɪmplɪmənt, *vb* ˈɪmplɪment] *n* Werkzeug *nt* ♦ *vt* ausführen

nplicate [ˈɪmplɪkeɪt] *vt* verwickeln; **implication** [ɪmplɪˈkeɪʃən] *n* (*effect*) Auswirkung *f*; (*in crime*) Verwicklung *f*

nplicit [ɪmˈplɪsɪt] *adj* (*suggested*) unausgesprochen; (*utter*) vorbehaltlos

nplore [ɪmˈplɔːʳ] *vt* anflehen

nply [ɪmˈplaɪ] *vt* (*hint*) andeuten; (*be evidence for*) schließen lassen auf *+acc*

npolite [ɪmpəˈlaɪt] *adj* unhöflich

nport [*vb* ɪmˈpɔːt, *n* ˈɪmpɔːt] *vt* einführen ♦ *n* Einfuhr *f*; (*meaning*) Bedeutung *f*

nportance [ɪmˈpɔːtns] *n* Bedeutung *f*

nportant [ɪmˈpɔːtənt] *adj* wichtig; **it's not ~** es ist unwichtig

nporter [ɪmˈpɔːtəʳ] *n* Importeur *m*

npose [ɪmˈpəʊz] *vt, vi*: **to ~ (on)** auferlegen (*+dat*); (*penalty, sanctions*) verhängen (*gegen*); **to ~ (o.s.) on sb** sich jdm aufdrängen

nposing [ɪmˈpəʊzɪŋ] *adj* eindrucksvoll

nposition [ɪmpəˈzɪʃən] *n* (*of burden, fine*) Auferlegung *f*; **to be an ~** (*on person*) eine Zumutung sein

npossible [ɪmˈpɒsɪbl] *adj* unmöglich

npostor [ɪmˈpɒstəʳ] *n* Hochstapler *m*

npotent [ˈɪmpətnt] *adj* machtlos; (*sexually*) impotent

impound [ɪmˈpaʊnd] *vt* beschlagnahmen

impoverished [ɪmˈpɒvərɪʃt] *adj* verarmt

impracticable [ɪmˈpræktɪkəbl] *adj* undurchführbar

impractical [ɪmˈpræktɪkl] *adj* unpraktisch

imprecise [ɪmprɪˈsaɪs] *adj* ungenau

impregnable [ɪmˈprɛgnəbl] *adj* (*castle*) uneinnehmbar

impregnate [ˈɪmprɛgneɪt] *vt* (*saturate*) sättigen; (*fertilize*) befruchten

impress [ɪmˈprɛs] *vt* (*influence*) beeindrucken; (*imprint*) (auf)drücken; **to ~ sth on sb** jdm etw einschärfen; **~ed** *adj* beeindruckt; **~ion** [ɪmˈprɛʃən] *n* Eindruck *m*; (*on wax, footprint*) Abdruck *m*; (*of book*) Auflage *f*; (*take-off*) Nachahmung *f*; **I was under the ~ion** ich hatte den Eindruck; **~ionable** *adj* leicht zu beeindrucken; **~ive** *adj* eindrucksvoll

imprint [ˈɪmprɪnt] *n* Abdruck *m*

imprison [ɪmˈprɪzn] *vt* ins Gefängnis schicken; **~ment** *n* Inhaftierung *f*

improbable [ɪmˈprɒbəbl] *adj* unwahrscheinlich

impromptu [ɪmˈprɒmptjuː] *adj, adv* aus dem Stegreif, improvisiert

improper [ɪmˈprɒpəʳ] *adj* (*indecent*) unanständig; (*unsuitable*) unpassend

improve [ɪmˈpruːv] *vt* verbessern ♦ *vi* besser werden; **~ment** *n* (Ver)besserung *f*

improvise [ˈɪmprəvaɪz] *vt, vi* improvisieren

imprudent [ɪmˈpruːdnt] *adj* unklug

impudent [ˈɪmpjudnt] *adj* unverschämt

impulse [ˈɪmpʌls] *n* Impuls *m*; **to act on ~** spontan handeln; **impulsive** [ɪmˈpʌlsɪv] *adj* impulsiv

impure [ɪmˈpjʊəʳ] *adj* (*dirty*) verunreinigt; (*bad*) unsauber; **impurity** [ɪmˈpjʊərɪtɪ] *n* Unreinheit *f*; (*TECH*) Verunreinigung *f*

KEYWORD

---

in [ɪn] *prep* **1** (*indicating place, position*) in *+dat*; (*with motion*) in *+acc*; **in here/there** hier/dort; **in London** in London; **in the United States** in den Vereinigten Staaten **2** (*indicating time: during*) in *+dat*; **in summer** im Sommer; **in 1988** (im Jahre)

1988; **in the afternoon** nachmittags, am Nachmittag
3 (*indicating time: in the space of*) innerhalb von; **I'll see you in 2 weeks** *or* **in 2 weeks' time** ich sehe Sie in zwei Wochen
4 (*indicating manner, circumstances, state etc*) in +*dat*; **in the sun/rain** in der Sonne/im Regen; **in English/French** auf Englisch/ Französisch; **in a loud/soft voice** mit lauter/leiser Stimme
5 (*with ratios, numbers*): **1 in 10** jeder Zehnte; **20 pence in the pound** 20 Pence pro Pfund; **they lined up in twos** sie stellten sich in Zweierreihe auf
6 (*referring to people, works*): **the disease is common in children** die Krankheit ist bei Kindern häufig; **in Dickens** bei Dickens; **we have a loyal friend in him** er ist uns ein treuer Freund
7 (*indicating profession etc*): **to be in teaching/the army** Lehrer(in)/beim Militär sein; **to be in publishing** im Verlagswesen arbeiten
8 (*with present participle*): **in saying this, I ...** wenn ich das sage, ... ich; **in accepting this view, he ...** weil er diese Meinung akzeptierte, ... er
♦ *adv*: **to be in** (*person: at home, work*) da sein; (*train, ship, plane*) angekommen sein; (*in fashion*) in sein; **to ask sb in** jdn hereinbitten; **to run/limp** *etc* **in** hereingerannt/gehumpelt *etc* kommen
♦ *n*: **the ins and outs** (*of proposal, situation etc*) die Feinheiten

---

in. *abbr* = **inch**
inability [ɪnəˈbɪlɪtɪ] *n* Unfähigkeit *f*
inaccessible [ɪnəkˈsesɪbl] *adj* unzugänglich
inaccurate [ɪnˈækjurət] *adj* ungenau; (*wrong*) unrichtig
inactivity [ɪnækˈtɪvɪtɪ] *n* Untätigkeit *f*
inadequate [ɪnˈædɪkwət] *adj* unzulänglich
inadvertently [ɪnədˈvəːtntlɪ] *adv* unabsichtlich
inadvisable [ɪnədˈvaɪzəbl] *adj* nicht ratsam
inane [ɪˈneɪn] *adj* dumm, albern
inanimate [ɪnˈænɪmət] *adj* leblos

inappropriate [ɪnəˈprəuprɪət] *adj* (*clothing*) ungeeignet; (*remark*) unangebracht
inarticulate [ɪnɑːˈtɪkjulət] *adj* unklar
inasmuch as [ɪnəzˈmʌtʃ-] *adv* da; (*in so far as*) so weit
inaudible [ɪnˈɔːdɪbl] *adj* unhörbar
inauguration [ɪnɔːgjuˈreɪʃən] *n* Eröffnung *f*; (*feierliche*) Amtseinführung *f*
inborn [ɪnˈbɔːn] *adj* angeboren
inbred [ɪnˈbred] *adj* angeboren
Inc. *abbr* = **incorporated**
incalculable [ɪnˈkælkjuləbl] *adj* (*consequences*) unabsehbar
incapable [ɪnˈkeɪpəbl] *adj*: ~ **(of doing sth)** unfähig(, etw zu tun)
incapacitate [ɪnkəˈpæsɪteɪt] *vt* untauglich machen
incapacity [ɪnkəˈpæsɪtɪ] *n* Unfähigkeit *f*
incarcerate [ɪnˈkɑːsəreɪt] *vt* einkerkern
incarnation [ɪnkɑːˈneɪʃən] *n* (*ECCL*) Menschwerdung *f*; (*fig*) Inbegriff *m*
incendiary [ɪnˈsendɪərɪ] *adj* Brand-
incense [*n* ˈɪnsens, *vb* ɪnˈsens] *n* Weihrauch *m* ♦ *vt* erzürnen
incentive [ɪnˈsentɪv] *n* Anreiz *m*
incessant [ɪnˈsesnt] *adj* unaufhörlich
incest [ˈɪnsest] *n* Inzest *m*
inch [ɪntʃ] *n* Zoll *m* ♦ *vi*: **to ~ forward** sich Stückchen für Stückchen vorwärts bewegen; **to be within an ~ of** kurz davor sein; **he didn't give an ~** er gab keinen Zentimeter nach
incidence [ˈɪnsɪdns] *n* Auftreten *nt*; (*of crime*) Quote *f*
incident [ˈɪnsɪdnt] *n* Vorfall *m*; (*disturbance*) Zwischenfall *m*
incidental [ɪnsɪˈdentl] *adj* (*music*) Begleit-; (*unimportant*) nebensächlich; (*remark*) beiläufig; ~**ly** *adv* übrigens
incinerator [ɪnˈsɪnəreɪtə*r*] *n* Verbrennungsofen *m*
incision [ɪnˈsɪʒən] *n* Einschnitt *m*
incisive [ɪnˈsaɪsɪv] *adj* (*style*) treffend; (*person*) scharfsinnig
incite [ɪnˈsaɪt] *vt* anstacheln
inclination [ɪnklɪˈneɪʃən] *n* Neigung *f*
incline [*n* ˈɪnklaɪn, *vb* ɪnˈklaɪn] *n* Abhang *m*

nclude [ɪnˈkluːd] vt einschließen; (on list, in group) aufnehmen; **including** prep: **including X** X inbegriffen; **inclusion** [ɪnˈkluːʒən] n Aufnahme f; **inclusive** [ɪnˈkluːsɪv] adj einschließlich; (COMM) inklusive; **inclusive of** einschließlich +gen

ncoherent [ɪnkəʊˈhɪərənt] adj zusammenhanglos

ncome [ˈɪnkʌm] n Einkommen nt; (from business) Einkünfte pl; ~ **tax** n Lohnsteuer f; (of self-employed) Einkommenssteuer f

ncoming [ˈɪnkʌmɪŋ] adj: ~ **flight** eintreffende Maschine f

ncomparable [ɪnˈkɒmpərəbl] adj unvergleichlich

ncompatible [ɪnkəmˈpætɪbl] adj unvereinbar; (people) unverträglich

ncompetence [ɪnˈkɒmpɪtns] n Unfähigkeit f; **incompetent** adj unfähig

ncomplete [ɪnkəmˈpliːt] adj unvollständig

ncomprehensible [ɪnkɒmprɪˈhensɪbl] adj unverständlich

nconceivable [ɪnkənˈsiːvəbl] adj unvorstellbar

ncongruous [ɪnˈkɒŋgruəs] adj seltsam; (remark) unangebracht

nconsiderate [ɪnkənˈsɪdərət] adj rücksichtslos

nconsistency [ɪnkənˈsɪstənsɪ] n Widersprüchlichkeit f; (state) Unbeständigkeit f

nconsistent [ɪnkənˈsɪstnt] adj (action, speech) widersprüchlich; (person, work) unbeständig; ~ **with** nicht übereinstimmend mit

nconspicuous [ɪnkənˈspɪkjuəs] adj unauffällig

ncontinent [ɪnˈkɒntɪnənt] adj (MED) nicht fähig, Stuhl und Harn zurückzuhalten

nconvenience [ɪnkənˈviːnjəns] n Unbequemlichkeit f; (trouble to others) Unannehmlichkeiten pl

nconvenient [ɪnkənˈviːnjənt] adj ungelegen; (journey) unbequem

incorporate [ɪnˈkɔːpəreɪt] vt (include) aufnehmen; (contain) enthalten; ~**d** adj: ~**d company** (US) eingetragene Aktiengesellschaft f

incorrect [ɪnkəˈrekt] adj unrichtig

incorrigible [ɪnˈkɒrɪdʒɪbl] adj unverbesserlich

incorruptible [ɪnkəˈrʌptɪbl] adj unzerstörbar; (person) unbestechlich

increase [n ˈɪnkriːs, vb ɪnˈkriːs] n Zunahme f; (pay ~) Gehaltserhöhung f; (in size) Vergrößerung f ♦ vt erhöhen; (wealth, rage) vermehren; (business) erweitern ♦ vi zunehmen; (prices) steigen; (in size) größer werden; (in number) sich vermehren; **increasing** adj (number) steigend; **increasingly** [ɪnˈkriːsɪŋlɪ] adv zunehmend

incredible [ɪnˈkredɪbl] adj unglaublich

incredulous [ɪnˈkredjuləs] adj ungläubig

increment [ˈɪnkrɪmənt] n Zulage f

incriminate [ɪnˈkrɪmɪneɪt] vt belasten

incubation [ɪnkjuˈbeɪʃən] n Ausbrüten nt

incubator [ˈɪnkjubeɪtər] n Brutkasten m

incumbent [ɪnˈkʌmbənt] n ♦ adj: **it is ~ on him to ...** es obliegt ihm, ...

incur [ɪnˈkəːr] vt sich zuziehen; (debts) machen

incurable [ɪnˈkjuərəbl] adj unheilbar

indebted [ɪnˈdetɪd] adj (obliged): ~ **(to sb)** (jdm) verpflichtet

indecent [ɪnˈdiːsnt] adj unanständig; ~ **assault** (BRIT) n Notzucht f; ~ **exposure** n Exhibitionismus m

indecisive [ɪndɪˈsaɪsɪv] adj (battle) nicht entscheidend; (person) unentschlossen

indeed [ɪnˈdiːd] adv tatsächlich, in der Tat; **yes ~!** allerdings!

indefinite [ɪnˈdefɪnɪt] adj unbestimmt; ~**ly** adv auf unbestimmte Zeit; (wait) unbegrenzt lange

indelible [ɪnˈdelɪbl] adj unauslöschlich

indemnity [ɪnˈdemnɪtɪ] n (insurance) Versicherung f; (compensation) Entschädigung f

independence [ɪndɪˈpendns] n Unabhängigkeit f; **independent** adj unabhängig

---

Independence Day

i **Independence Day** *(der 4. Juli)* ist in den USA ein gesetzlicher Feiertag zum Gedenken an die Unabhängigkeitserklärung am 4. Juli 1776, mit der die 13 amerikanischen Kolonien ihre Freiheit und Unabhängigkeit von Großbritannien erklärten.

---

indestructible [ɪndɪsˈtrʌktəbl] *adj* unzerstörbar

indeterminate [ɪndɪˈtəːmɪnɪt] *adj* unbestimmt

index [ˈɪndeks] *(pl* ~**es** *or* **indices)** *n* Index *m*; ~ **card** *n* Karteikarte *f*; ~ **finger** *n* Zeigefinger *m*; ~-**linked** *(US* ~**ed)** *adj* *(salaries)* der Inflationsrate *dat* angeglichen; *(pensions)* dynamisch

India [ˈɪndɪə] *n* Indien *nt*; ~**n** *adj* indisch ♦ *n* Inder(in) *m(f)*; **American** ~**n** Indianer(in) *m(f)*; ~**n Ocean** *n*: **the** ~**n Ocean** der Indische Ozean

indicate [ˈɪndɪkeɪt] *vt* anzeigen; *(hint)* andeuten; **indication** [ɪndɪˈkeɪʃən] *n* Anzeichen *nt*; *(information)* Angabe *f*; **indicative** [ɪnˈdɪkətɪv] *adj*: **indicative of** bezeichnend für; **indicator** *n* (An)zeichen *nt*; *(AUT)* Richtungsanzeiger *m*

indict [ɪnˈdaɪt] *vt* anklagen; ~**ment** *n* Anklage *f*

indifference [ɪnˈdɪfrəns] *n* Gleichgültigkeit *f*; Unwichtigkeit *f*; **indifferent** *adj* gleichgültig; *(mediocre)* mäßig

indigenous [ɪnˈdɪdʒɪnəs] *adj* einheimisch

indigestion [ɪndɪˈdʒestʃən] *n* Verdauungsstörung *f*

indignant [ɪnˈdɪgnənt] *adj*: **to be** ~ **about sth** über etw *acc* empört sein

indignation [ɪndɪgˈneɪʃən] *n* Entrüstung *f*

indignity [ɪnˈdɪgnɪtɪ] *n* Demütigung *f*

indirect [ɪndɪˈrekt] *adj* indirekt

indiscreet [ɪndɪsˈkriːt] *adj* *(insensitive)* taktlos; *(telling secrets)* indiskret; **indiscretion** [ɪndɪsˈkreʃən] *n* Taktlosigkeit *f*; Indiskretion *f*

indiscriminate [ɪndɪsˈkrɪmɪnət] *adj* wahllos; kritiklos

indispensable [ɪndɪsˈpensəbl] *adj* unentbehrlich

indisposed [ɪndɪsˈpəuzd] *adj* unpässlich

indisputable [ɪndɪsˈpjuːtəbl] *adj* unbestreitbar; *(evidence)* unanfechtbar

indistinct [ɪndɪsˈtɪŋkt] *adj* undeutlich

individual [ɪndɪˈvɪdjuəl] *n* Individuum *nt* ♦ *adj* individuell; *(case)* Einzel-; *(of, for one person)* eigen, individuell; *(characteristic)* eigentümlich; ~**ly** *adv* einzeln, individuell

indivisible [ɪndɪˈvɪzɪbl] *adj* unteilbar

indoctrinate [ɪnˈdɔktrɪneɪt] *vt* indoktrinieren

Indonesia [ɪndəˈniːzɪə] *n* Indonesien *nt*

indoor [ˈɪndɔːʳ] *adj* Haus-; Zimmer-; Innen-; *(SPORT)* Hallen-; ~**s** [ɪnˈdɔːz] *adv* drinnen, im Haus

induce [ɪnˈdjuːs] *vt* dazu bewegen; *(reaction)* herbeiführen

induction course [ɪnˈdʌkʃən-] *(BRIT)* *n* Einführungskurs *m*

indulge [ɪnˈdʌldʒ] *vt* *(give way)* nachgeben +*dat*; *(gratify)* frönen +*dat* ♦ *vi*: **to** ~ **(in)** frönen (+*dat*); ~**nce** *n* Nachsicht *f*; *(enjoyment)* Genuss *m*; ~**nt** *adj* nachsichtig; *(pej)* nachgiebig

industrial [ɪnˈdʌstrɪəl] *adj* Industrie-, industriell; *(dispute, injury)* Arbeits-; ~ **action** *n* Arbeitskampfmaßnahmen *pl*; ~ **estate** *(BRIT)* *n* Industriegebiet *nt*; ~**ist** *n* Industrielle(r) *mf*; ~**ize** *vt* industrialisieren; ~ **park** *(US)* *n* Industriegebiet *nt*

industrious [ɪnˈdʌstrɪəs] *adj* fleißig

industry [ˈɪndəstrɪ] *n* Industrie *f*; *(diligence)* Fleiß *m*

inebriated [ɪˈniːbrɪeɪtɪd] *adj* betrunken

inedible [ɪnˈedɪbl] *adj* ungenießbar

ineffective [ɪnɪˈfektɪv] *adj* unwirksam; *(person)* untauglich

ineffectual [ɪnɪˈfektʃuəl] *adj* = **ineffective**

inefficiency [ɪnɪˈfɪʃənsɪ] *n* Ineffizienz *f*

inefficient [ɪnɪˈfɪʃənt] *adj* ineffizient; *(ineffective)* unwirksam

inept [ɪˈnept] *adj* *(remark)* unpassend; *(person)* ungeeignet

inequality [ɪnɪˈkwɔlɪtɪ] *n* Ungleichheit *f*

inert [ɪˈnəːt] *adj* träge; *(CHEM)* inaktiv;

(*motionless*) unbeweglich

inescapable [ɪnɪˈskeɪpəbl] *adj* unvermeidbar

inevitable [ɪnˈevɪtəbl] *adj* unvermeidlich;
inevitably *adv* zwangsläufig

inexcusable [ɪnɪksˈkjuːzəbl] *adj*
unverzeihlich

inexhaustible [ɪnɪgˈzɔːstɪbl] *adj*
unerschöpflich

inexpensive [ɪnɪkˈspensɪv] *adj* preiswert

inexperience [ɪnɪkˈspɪərɪəns] *n*
Unerfahrenheit *f*; **~d** *adj* unerfahren

inexplicable [ɪnɪkˈsplɪkəbl] *adj* unerklärlich

inextricably [ɪnɪkˈstrɪkəblɪ] *adv* untrennbar

infallible [ɪnˈfælɪbl] *adj* unfehlbar

infamous [ˈɪnfəməs] *adj* (*deed*) schändlich;
(*person*) niederträchtig

infancy [ˈɪnfənsɪ] *n* frühe Kindheit *f*; (*fig*)
Anfangsstadium *nt*

infant [ˈɪnfənt] *n* kleine(s) Kind *nt*, Säugling
m; **~ile** [-aɪl] *adj* kindisch, infantil; **~
school** (*BRIT*) *n* Vorschule *f*

infatuated [ɪnˈfætjueɪtɪd] *adj* vernarrt; **to
become ~ with** sich vernarren in +*acc*;
infatuation [ɪnfætjuˈeɪʃən] *n*: **infatuation
(with)** Vernarrtheit *f* (in +*acc*)

infect [ɪnˈfekt] *vt* anstecken (*also fig*); **~ed
with** (*illness*) infiziert mit; **~ion** [ɪnˈfekʃən] *n*
Infektion *f*; **~ious** [ɪnˈfekʃəs] *adj* ansteckend

infer [ɪnˈfɜː] *vt* schließen

inferior [ɪnˈfɪərɪə] *adj* (*rank*) untergeordnet;
(*quality*) minderwertig ♦ *n* Untergebene(r)
m; **~ity** [ɪnfɪərɪˈɔrɪtɪ] *n* Minderwertigkeit *f*;
(*in rank*) untergeordnete Stellung *f*; **~ity
complex** *n* Minderwertigkeitskomplex *m*

infernal [ɪnˈfɜːnl] *adj* höllisch

infertile [ɪnˈfɜːtaɪl] *adj* unfruchtbar;
infertility [ɪnfəˈtɪlɪtɪ] *n* Unfruchtbarkeit *f*

infested [ɪnˈfestɪd] *adj*: **to be ~ with**
wimmeln von

infidelity [ɪnfɪˈdelɪtɪ] *n* Untreue *f*

infighting [ˈɪnfaɪtɪŋ] *n* Nahkampf *m*

infiltrate [ˈɪnfɪltreɪt] *vt* infiltrieren; (*spies*)
einschleusen ♦ *vi* (*MIL, liquid*) einsickern;
(*POL*): **to ~ (into)** unterwandern (+*acc*)

infinite [ˈɪnfɪnɪt] *adj* unendlich

infinitive [ɪnˈfɪnɪtɪv] *n* Infinitiv *m*

infinity [ɪnˈfɪnɪtɪ] *n* Unendlichkeit *f*

infirm [ɪnˈfɜːm] *adj* gebrechlich; **~ary** *n*
Krankenhaus *nt*

inflamed [ɪnˈfleɪmd] *adj* entzündet

inflammable [ɪnˈflæməbl] (*BRIT*) *adj*
feuergefährlich

inflammation [ɪnfləˈmeɪʃən] *n* Entzündung *f*

inflatable [ɪnˈfleɪtəbl] *adj* aufblasbar

inflate [ɪnˈfleɪt] *vt* aufblasen; (*tyre*)
aufpumpen; (*prices*) hoch treiben; **inflation**
[ɪnˈfleɪʃən] *n* Inflation *f*; **inflationary**
[ɪnˈfleɪʃənərɪ] *adj* (*increase*) inflationistisch;
(*situation*) inflationär

inflexible [ɪnˈfleksɪbl] *adj* (*person*) nicht
flexibel; (*opinion*) starr; (*thing*) unbiegsam

inflict [ɪnˈflɪkt] *vt*: **to ~ sth on sb** jdm etw
zufügen; (*wound*) jdm etw beibringen

influence [ˈɪnfluəns] *n* Einfluss *m* ♦ *vt*
beeinflussen

influential [ɪnfluˈenʃl] *adj* einflussreich

influenza [ɪnfluˈenzə] *n* Grippe *f*

influx [ˈɪnflʌks] *n* (*of people*) Zustrom *m*; (*of
ideas*) Eindringen *nt*

infomercial [ˈɪnfəumɜːʃl] *n*
Werbeinformationssendung *f*

inform [ɪnˈfɔːm] *vt* informieren ♦ *vi*: **to ~ on
sb** jdn denunzieren; **to keep sb ~ed** jdn
auf dem Laufenden halten

informal [ɪnˈfɔːml] *adj* zwanglos; **~ity**
[ɪnfɔːˈmælɪtɪ] *n* Ungezwungenheit *f*

informant [ɪnˈfɔːmənt] *n* Informant(in) *m(f)*

information [ɪnfəˈmeɪʃən] *n* Auskunft *f*,
Information *f*; **a piece of ~** eine Auskunft,
eine Information; **~ desk** *n*
Auskunftsschalter *m*; **~ office** *n*
Informationsbüro *nt*

informative [ɪnˈfɔːmətɪv] *adj* informativ;
(*person*) mitteilsam

informer [ɪnˈfɔːmə] *n* Denunziant(in) *m(f)*

infra-red [ɪnfrəˈred] *adj* infrarot

infrequent [ɪnˈfriːkwənt] *adj* selten

infringe [ɪnˈfrɪndʒ] *vt* (*law*) verstoßen gegen;
~ upon *vt* verletzen; **~ment** *n* Verstoß *m*,
Verletzung *f*

infuriating [ɪnˈfjuərɪeɪtɪŋ] *adj* ärgerlich

ingenuity [ɪndʒɪˈnjuːɪtɪ] *n* Genialität *f*

ingenuous [ɪnˈdʒenjuəs] *adj* aufrichtig;
(*naive*) naiv

ingot ['ɪŋgət] n Barren m

ingrained [ɪn'greɪnd] adj tief sitzend

ingratiate [ɪn'greɪʃɪeɪt] vt: **to ~ o.s. with sb** sich bei jdm einschmeicheln

ingratitude [ɪn'grætɪtjuːd] n Undankbarkeit f

ingredient [ɪn'griːdɪənt] n Bestandteil m; (COOK) Zutat f

inhabit [ɪn'hæbɪt] vt bewohnen; **~ant** n Bewohner(in) m(f); (of island, town) Einwohner(in) m(f)

inhale [ɪn'heɪl] vt einatmen; (MED, cigarettes) inhalieren

inherent [ɪn'hɪərənt] adj: **~ (in)** innewohnend (+dat)

inherit [ɪn'herɪt] vt erben; **~ance** n Erbe nt, Erbschaft f

inhibit [ɪn'hɪbɪt] vt hemmen; **to ~ sb from doing sth** jdn daran hindern, etw zu tun; **~ion** [ɪnhɪ'bɪʃən] n Hemmung f

inhospitable [ɪnhɔs'pɪtəbl] adj (person) ungastlich; (country) unwirtlich

inhuman [ɪn'hjuːmən] adj unmenschlich

initial [ɪ'nɪʃl] adj anfänglich, Anfangs- ♦ n Initiale f ♦ vt abzeichnen; (POL) paraphieren; **~ly** adv anfangs

initiate [ɪ'nɪʃɪeɪt] vt einführen; (negotiations) einleiten; **to ~ proceedings against sb** (JUR) gerichtliche Schritte gegen jdn einleiten; **initiation** [ɪnɪʃɪ'eɪʃən] n Einführung f; Einleitung f

initiative [ɪ'nɪʃətɪv] n Initiative f

inject [ɪn'dʒekt] vt einspritzen; (fig) einflößen; **~ion** [ɪn'dʒekʃən] n Spritze f

injunction [ɪn'dʒʌŋkʃən] n Verfügung f

injure ['ɪndʒər] vt verletzen; **~d** adj (person, arm) verletzt; **injury** ['ɪndʒərɪ] n Verletzung f; **to play injury time** (SPORT) nachspielen

injustice [ɪn'dʒʌstɪs] n Ungerechtigkeit f

ink [ɪŋk] n Tinte f

inkling ['ɪŋklɪŋ] n (dunkle) Ahnung f

inlaid ['ɪnleɪd] adj eingelegt, Einlege-

inland [adj 'ɪnlənd, adv ɪn'lænd] adj Binnen-; (domestic) Inlands- ♦ adv landeinwärts; **~ revenue** (BRIT) n Fiskus m

in-laws ['ɪnlɔːz] npl (parents-in-law) Schwiegereltern pl; (others) angeheiratete Verwandte pl

inlet ['ɪnlet] n Einlass m; (bay) kleine Bucht f

inmate ['ɪnmeɪt] n Insasse m

inn [ɪn] n Gasthaus nt, Wirtshaus nt

innate [ɪ'neɪt] adj angeboren

inner ['ɪnər] adj inner, Innen-; (fig) verborgen; **~ city** n Innenstadt f; **~ tube** n (of tyre) Schlauch m

innings ['ɪnɪŋz] n (CRICKET) Innenrunde f

innocence ['ɪnəsns] n Unschuld f; (ignorance) Unkenntnis f

innocent ['ɪnəsnt] adj unschuldig

innocuous [ɪ'nɔkjuəs] adj harmlos

innovation [ɪnəʊ'veɪʃən] n Neuerung f

innuendo [ɪnjuː'endəʊ] n (versteckte) Anspielung f

innumerable [ɪ'njuːmrəbl] adj unzählig

inoculation [ɪnɔkju'leɪʃən] n Impfung f

inopportune [ɪn'ɔpətjuːn] adj (remark) unangebracht; (visit) ungelegen

inordinately [ɪ'nɔːdɪnətlɪ] adv unmäßig

inpatient ['ɪnpeɪʃənt] n stationäre(r) Patient m/stationäre Patientin f

input ['ɪnput] n (COMPUT) Eingabe f; (power ~) Energiezufuhr f; (of energy, work) Aufwand m

inquest ['ɪnkwest] n gerichtliche Untersuchung f

inquire [ɪn'kwaɪər] vi sich erkundigen ♦ vt (price) sich erkundigen nach; **~ into** vt untersuchen; **inquiry** [ɪn'kwaɪərɪ] n (question) Erkundigung f; (investigation) Untersuchung f; **inquiries** Auskunft f; **inquiry office** (BRIT) n Auskunft(sbüro nt) f

inquisitive [ɪn'kwɪzɪtɪv] adj neugierig

ins. abbr = **inches**

insane [ɪn'seɪn] adj wahnsinnig; (MED) geisteskrank; **insanity** [ɪn'sænɪtɪ] n Wahnsinn m

insatiable [ɪn'seɪʃəbl] adj unersättlich

inscribe [ɪn'skraɪb] vt eingravieren; **inscription** [ɪn'skrɪpʃən] n (on stone) Inschrift f; (in book) Widmung f

insect ['ɪnsekt] n Insekt nt; **~icide** [ɪn'sektɪsaɪd] n Insektenvertilgungsmittel nt; **~ repellent** n Insektenbekämpfungsmittel nt

insecure [ɪnsɪ'kjuər] adj (person) unsicher;

(*thing*) nicht fest *or* sicher; **insecurity**
[ɪnsɪ'kjuərɪtɪ] *n* Unsicherheit *f*

semination [ɪnsemɪ'neɪʃən] *n*: **artificial ~**
künstliche Befruchtung *f*

sensible [ɪn'sensɪbl] *adj* (*unconscious*)
bewusstlos

sensitive [ɪn'sensɪtɪv] *adj* (*to pain*)
unempfindlich; (*unfeeling*) gefühllos

separable [ɪn'sepərəbl] *adj* (*people*)
unzertrennlich; (*word*) untrennbar

sert [*vb* ɪn'sə:t, *n* 'ɪnsə:t] *vt* einfügen; (*coin*)
einwerfen; (*stick into*) hineinstecken;
(*advertisement*) aufgeben ♦ *n* (*in book*)
Einlage *f*; (*in magazine*) Beilage *f*; **~ion**
[ɪn'sə:ʃən] *n* Einfügung *f*; (*PRESS*) Inserat *nt*

-service [ɪn'sə:vɪs] *adj* (*training*)
berufsbegleitend

shore ['ɪn'ʃɔ:r] *adj* Küsten- ♦ *adv* an der
Küste

side ['ɪn'saɪd] *n* Innenseite *f*, Innere(s) *nt*
♦ *adj* innere(r, s), Innen- ♦ *adv* (*place*)
innen; (*direction*) nach innen, hinein ♦ *prep*
(*place*) in +*dat*; (*direction*) in +*acc* ... hinein;
(*time*) innerhalb +*gen*; **~s** *npl* (*inf*)
Eingeweide *nt*; **~ 10 minutes** unter 10
Minuten; **~ information** *n* interne
Informationen *pl*; **~ lane** *n* (*AUT: in Britain*)
linke Spur; **~ out** *adv* linksherum; (*know*)
in- und auswendig

sider dealing, insider trading
[ɪn'saɪdər-] *n* (*STOCK EXCHANGE*) Insiderhandel
m

sidious [ɪn'sɪdɪəs] *adj* heimtückisch

sight ['ɪnsaɪt] *n* Einsicht *f*; **~ into** Einblick
m in +*acc*

significant [sɪg'nɪfɪkənt] *adj*
unbedeutend

sincere [ɪnsɪn'sɪər] *adj* unaufrichtig

sinuate [ɪn'sɪnjueɪt] *vt* (*hint*) andeuten

sipid [ɪn'sɪpɪd] *adj* fad(e)

sist [ɪn'sɪst] *vi*: **to ~ (on)** bestehen (auf
+*acc*); **~ence** *n* Bestehen *nt*; **~ent** *adj*
hartnäckig; (*urgent*) dringend

sole ['ɪnsəul] *n* Einlegesohle *f*

solence ['ɪnsələns] *n* Frechheit *f*

solent ['ɪnsələnt] *adj* frech

soluble [ɪn'sɔljubl] *adj* unlösbar; (*CHEM*)

unlöslich

insolvent [ɪn'sɔlvənt] *adj* zahlungsunfähig

insomnia [ɪn'sɔmnɪə] *n* Schlaflosigkeit *f*

inspect [ɪn'spekt] *vt* prüfen; (*officially*)
inspizieren; **~ion** [ɪn'spekʃən] *n* Inspektion *f*;
~or *n* (*official*) Inspektor *m*; (*police*)
Polizeikommissar *m*; (*BRIT: on buses, trains*)
Kontrolleur *m*

inspiration [ɪnspə'reɪʃən] *n* Inspiration *f*

inspire [ɪn'spaɪər] *vt* (*person*) inspirieren; **to ~**
sth in sb (*respect*) jdm etw einflößen;
(*hope*) etw in jdm wecken

instability [ɪnstə'bɪlɪtɪ] *n* Unbeständigkeit *f*,
Labilität *f*

install [ɪn'stɔ:l] *vt* (*put in*) installieren;
(*telephone*) anschließen; (*establish*)
einsetzen; **~ation** [ɪnstə'leɪʃən] *n* (*of person*)
(Amts)einsetzung *f*; (*of machinery*)
Installierung *f*; (*machines etc*) Anlage *f*

instalment [ɪn'stɔ:lmənt] (*US* **installment**) *n*
Rate *f*; (*of story*) Fortsetzung *f*; **to pay in ~s**
in Raten zahlen

instance ['ɪnstəns] *n* Fall *m*; (*example*)
Beispiel *nt*; **for ~** zum Beispiel; **in the first**
~ zunächst

instant ['ɪnstənt] *n* Augenblick *m* ♦ *adj*
augenblicklich, sofortig; **~aneous**
[ɪnstən'teɪnɪəs] *adj* unmittelbar; **~ coffee** *n*
Pulverkaffee *m*; **~ly** *adv* sofort

instead [ɪn'sted] *adv* stattdessen; **~ of** *prep*
anstatt +*gen*

instep ['ɪnstep] *n* Spann *m*; (*of shoe*) Blatt *nt*

instil [ɪn'stɪl] *vt* (*fig*): **to ~ sth in sb** jdm etw
beibringen

instinct ['ɪnstɪŋkt] *n* Instinkt *m*; **~ive**
[ɪn'stɪŋktɪv] *adj* instinktiv

institute ['ɪnstɪtju:t] *n* Institut *nt* ♦ *vt*
einführen; (*search*) einleiten

institution [ɪnstɪ'tju:ʃən] *n* Institution *f*;
(*home*) Anstalt *f*

instruct [ɪn'strʌkt] *vt* anweisen; (*officially*)
instruieren; **~ion** [ɪn'strʌkʃən] *n* Unterricht
m; **~ions** *npl* (*orders*) Anweisungen *pl*; (*for
use*) Gebrauchsanweisung *f*; **~or** *n* Lehrer
m

instrument ['ɪnstrumənt] *n* Instrument *nt*;
~al [ɪnstru'mentl] *adj* (*MUS*) Instrumental-;

(*helpful*): **~al (in)** behilflich (bei); **~ panel** n Armaturenbrett nt

insubordinate [ɪnsə'bɔːdənɪt] adj aufsässig, widersetzlich

insufferable [ɪn'sʌfrəbl] adj unerträglich

insufficient [ɪnsə'fɪʃənt] adj ungenügend

insular ['ɪnsjulə'] adj (*fig*) engstirnig

insulate ['ɪnsjuleɪt] vt (*ELEC*) isolieren; (*fig*): **to ~ (from)** abschirmen (vor +dat); **insulating tape** n Isolierband nt; **insulation** [ɪnsju'leɪʃən] n Isolierung f

insulin ['ɪnsjulɪn] n Insulin nt

insult [n 'ɪnsʌlt, vb ɪn'sʌlt] n Beleidigung f ♦ vt beleidigen

insurance [ɪn'ʃuərəns] n Versicherung f; **fire/life ~** Feuer-/Lebensversicherung; **~ agent** n Versicherungsvertreter m; **~ policy** n Versicherungspolice f

insure [ɪn'ʃuə'] vt versichern

intact [ɪn'tækt] adj unversehrt

intake ['ɪnteɪk] n (*place*) Einlaßöffnung f; (*act*) Aufnahme f; (*BRIT: SCH*): **an ~ of 200 a year** ein Neuzugang von 200 im Jahr

intangible [ɪn'tændʒɪbl] adj nicht greifbar

integral ['ɪntɪgrəl] adj (*essential*) wesentlich; (*complete*) vollständig; (*MATH*) Integral-

integrate ['ɪntɪgreɪt] vt integrieren ♦ vi sich integrieren

integrity [ɪn'tegrɪtɪ] n (*honesty*) Redlichkeit f, Integrität f

intellect ['ɪntəlekt] n Intellekt m; **~ual** [ɪntə'lektjuəl] adj geistig, intellektuell ♦ n Intellektuelle(r) mf

intelligence [ɪn'telɪdʒəns] n (*understanding*) Intelligenz f; (*news*) Information f; (*MIL*) Geheimdienst m; **~ service** n Nachrichtendienst m, Geheimdienst m

intelligent [ɪn'telɪdʒənt] adj intelligent; **~ly** adv klug; (*write, speak*) verständlich

intelligentsia [ɪntelɪ'dʒentsɪə] n Intelligenz f

intelligible [ɪn'telɪdʒɪbl] adj verständlich

intend [ɪn'tend] vt beabsichtigen; **that was ~ed for you** das war für dich gedacht

intense [ɪn'tens] adj stark, intensiv; (*person*) ernsthaft; **~ly** adv äußerst; (*study*) intensiv

intensify [ɪn'tensɪfaɪ] vt verstärken, intensivieren

intensity [ɪn'tensɪtɪ] n Intensität f

intensive [ɪn'tensɪv] adj intensiv; **~ care unit** n Intensivstation f

intent [ɪn'tent] n Absicht f ♦ adj: **to be ~ on doing sth** fest entschlossen sein, etw zu tun; **to all ~s and purposes** praktisch

intention [ɪn'tenʃən] n Absicht f; **~al** adj absichtlich

intently [ɪn'tentlɪ] adv konzentriert

interact [ɪntər'ækt] vi aufeinander einwirken; **~ion** [ɪntər'ækʃən] n Wechselwirkung f; **~ive** adj (*COMPUT*) interaktiv

intercept [ɪntə'sept] vt abfangen

interchange [n 'ɪntətʃeɪndʒ, vb ɪntə'tʃeɪndʒ] n (*exchange*) Austausch m; (*on roads*) Verkehrskreuz nt ♦ vt austauschen; **~able** [ɪntə'tʃeɪndʒəbl] adj austauschbar

intercom ['ɪntəkɔm] n (Gegen)sprechanlage f

intercourse ['ɪntəkɔːs] n (*exchange*) Beziehungen pl; (*sexual*) Geschlechtsverkehr m

interest ['ɪntrɪst] n Interesse nt; (*FIN*) Zinsen pl; (*COMM: share*) Anteil m; (*group*) Interessengruppe f ♦ vt interessieren; **~ed** adj (*having claims*) beteiligt; (*attentive*) interessiert; **to be ~ed in** sich interessieren für; **~ing** adj interessant; **~ rate** n Zinssatz m

interface ['ɪntəfeɪs] n (*COMPUT*) Schnittstelle f, Interface nt

interfere [ɪntə'fɪə'] vi: **to ~ (with)** (*meddle*) sich einmischen (in +acc); (*disrupt*) stören +acc; **~nce** [ɪntə'fɪərəns] n Einmischung f; (*TV*) Störung f

interim ['ɪntərɪm] n: **in the ~** inzwischen

interior [ɪn'tɪərɪə'] n Innere(s) nt ♦ adj innere(r, s), Innen-; **~ designer** n Innenarchitekt(in) m(f)

interjection [ɪntə'dʒekʃən] n Ausruf m

interlock [ɪntə'lɔk] vi ineinander greifen

interlude ['ɪntəluːd] n Pause f

intermediary [ɪntə'miːdɪərɪ] n Vermittler m

intermediate [ɪntə'miːdɪət] adj Zwischen-, Mittel-

interminable [ɪn'tə:mɪnəbl] adj endlos

intermission [ɪntə'mɪʃən] n Pause f

termittent [ɪntə'mɪtnt] *adj* periodisch, stoßweise

tern [*vb* ɪn'tɜːn, *n* 'ɪntɜːn] *vt* internieren ♦ *n* (*US*) Assistenzarzt *m*/-ärztin *f*

ternal [ɪn'tɜːnl] *adj* (*inside*) innere(r, s); (*domestic*) Inlands-; **~ly** *adv* innen; (*MED*) innerlich; **"not to be taken ~ly"** „nur zur äußerlichen Anwendung"; **Internal Revenue Service** (*US*) *n* Finanzamt *nt*

ternational [ɪntə'næʃənl] *adj* international ♦ *n* (*SPORT*) Nationalspieler(in) *m(f)*; (: *match*) internationale(s) Spiel *nt*

ternet ['ɪntənet] *n*: **the ~** das Internet; **~ café** *n* Internet-Café *nt*

terplay ['ɪntəpleɪ] *n* Wechselspiel *nt*

terpret [ɪn'tɜːprɪt] *vt* (*explain*) auslegen, interpretieren; (*translate*) dolmetschen; **~er** *n* Dolmetscher(in) *m(f)*

terrelated [ɪntərɪ'leɪtɪd] *adj* untereinander zusammenhängend

terrogate [ɪn'terəugeɪt] *vt* verhören; **interrogation** [ɪntərəu'geɪʃən] *n* Verhör *nt*

terrupt [ɪntə'rʌpt] *vt* unterbrechen; **~ion** [ɪntə'rʌpʃən] *n* Unterbrechung *f*

tersect [ɪntə'sekt] *vt* (durch)schneiden ♦ *vi* sich schneiden; **~ion** [ɪntə'sekʃən] *n* (*of roads*) Kreuzung *f*; (*of lines*) Schnittpunkt *m*

tersperse [ɪntə'spɜːs] *vt*: **to ~ sth with sth** etw mit etw durchsetzen

tertwine [ɪntə'twaɪn] *vt* verflechten ♦ *vi* sich verflechten

terval ['ɪntəvl] *n* Abstand *m*; (*BRIT: THEAT, SPORT*) Pause *f*; **at ~s** in Abständen

tervene [ɪntə'viːn] *vi* dazwischenliegen; (*act*): **to ~ (in)** einschreiten (gegen); **intervention** [ɪntə'venʃən] *n* Eingreifen *nt*, Intervention *f*

terview ['ɪntəvjuː] *n* (*PRESS etc*) Interview *nt*; (*for job*) Vorstellungsgespräch *nt* ♦ *vt* interviewen; **~er** *n* Interviewer *m*

testine [ɪn'testɪn] *n*: **large/small ~** Dick-/Dünndarm *m*

timacy ['ɪntɪməsɪ] *n* Intimität *f*

timate [*adj* 'ɪntɪmət, *vb* 'ɪntɪmeɪt] *adj* (*inmost*) innerste(r, s); (*knowledge*) eingehend; (*familiar*) vertraut; (*friends*) eng ♦ *vt* andeuten

intimidate [ɪn'tɪmɪdeɪt] *vt* einschüchtern

into ['ɪntu] *prep* (*motion*) in +*acc* ... hinein; **5 ~ 25** 25 durch 5

intolerable [ɪn'tɒlərəbl] *adj* unerträglich

intolerant [ɪn'tɒlərnt] *adj*: **~ of** unduldsam gegen(über)

intoxicate [ɪn'tɒksɪkeɪt] *vt* berauschen; **~d** *adj* betrunken; **intoxication** [ɪntɒksɪ'keɪʃən] *n* Rausch *m*

intractable [ɪn'træktəbl] *adj* schwer zu handhaben; (*problem*) schwer lösbar

intranet ['ɪntrænɪt] *n* Intranet *nt*

intransitive [ɪn'trænsɪtɪv] *adj* intransitiv

intravenous [ɪntrə'viːnəs] *adj* intravenös

in-tray ['ɪntreɪ] *n* Eingangskorb *m*

intrepid [ɪn'trepɪd] *adj* unerschrocken

intricate ['ɪntrɪkət] *adj* kompliziert

intrigue [ɪn'triːg] *n* Intrige *f* ♦ *vt* faszinieren ♦ *vi* intrigieren

intrinsic [ɪn'trɪnsɪk] *adj* innere(r, s); (*difference*) wesentlich

introduce [ɪntrə'djuːs] *vt* (*person*) vorstellen; (*sth new*) einführen; (*subject*) anschneiden; **to ~ sb to sb** jdm jdn vorstellen; **to ~ sb to sth** jdn in etw *acc* einführen; **introduction** [ɪntrə'dʌkʃən] *n* Einführung *f*; (*to book*) Einleitung *f*; **introductory** [ɪntrə'dʌktərɪ] *adj* Einführungs-, Vor-

introspective [ɪntrəu'spektɪv] *adj* nach innen gekehrt

introvert ['ɪntrəuvɜːt] *n* Introvertierte(r) *mf* ♦ *adj* introvertiert

intrude [ɪn'truːd] *vi*: **to ~ (on sb/sth)** (jdn/etw) stören; **~r** *n* Eindringling *m*

intrusion [ɪn'truːʒən] *n* Störung *f*

intrusive [ɪn'truːsɪv] *adj* aufdringlich

intuition [ɪntjuː'ɪʃən] *n* Intuition *f*

inundate ['ɪnʌndeɪt] *vt* überschwemmen

invade [ɪn'veɪd] *vt* einfallen in +*acc*; **~r** *n* Eindringling *m*

invalid¹ ['ɪnvəlɪd] *n* (*disabled*) Invalide *m* ♦ *adj* (*ill*) krank; (*disabled*) invalide

invalid² [ɪn'vælɪd] *adj* (*not valid*) ungültig

invaluable [ɪn'væljuəbl] *adj* unschätzbar

invariable [ɪn'veərɪəbl] *adj* unveränderlich; **invariably** *adv* ausnahmslos

invent [ɪn'vent] *vt* erfinden; **~ion** [ɪn'venʃən]

n Erfindung *f*; **~ive** *adj* erfinderisch; **~or** *n* Erfinder *m*

inventory ['ɪnvəntrɪ] *n* Inventar *nt*

inverse [ɪn'vɜːs] *n* Umkehrung *f* ♦ *adj* umgekehrt

invert [ɪn'vɜːt] *vt* umdrehen; **~ed commas** (BRIT) *npl* Anführungsstriche *pl*

invest [ɪn'vest] *vt* investieren

investigate [ɪn'vestɪgeɪt] *vt* untersuchen; **investigation** [ɪnvestɪ'geɪʃən] *n* Untersuchung *f*; **investigator** [ɪn'vestɪgeɪtəʳ] *n* Untersuchungsbeamte(r) *m*

investiture [ɪn'vestɪtʃəʳ] *n* Amtseinsetzung *f*

investment [ɪn'vestmənt] *n* Investition *f*

investor [ɪn'vestəʳ] *n* (Geld)anleger *m*

invigilate [ɪn'vɪdʒɪleɪt] *vi* (*in exam*) Aufsicht führen ♦ *vt* Aufsicht führen bei

invigorating [ɪn'vɪgəreɪtɪŋ] *adj* stärkend

invincible [ɪn'vɪnsɪbl] *adj* unbesiegbar

invisible [ɪn'vɪzɪbl] *adj* unsichtbar

invitation [ɪnvɪ'teɪʃən] *n* Einladung *f*

invite [ɪn'vaɪt] *vt* einladen

invoice ['ɪnvɔɪs] *n* Rechnung *f* ♦ *vt* (*goods*): **to ~ sb for sth** jdm etw *acc* in Rechnung stellen

invoke [ɪn'vəuk] *vt* anrufen

involuntary [ɪn'vɔləntrɪ] *adj* unabsichtlich

involve [ɪn'vɔlv] *vt* (*entangle*) verwickeln; (*entail*) mit sich bringen; **~d** *adj* verwickelt; **~ment** *n* Verwicklung *f*

inward ['ɪnwəd] *adj* innere(r, s); (*curve*) Innen- ♦ *adv* nach innen; **~ly** *adv* im Innern; **~s** *adv* nach innen

I/O *abbr* (COMPUT) (= input/output) I/O

iodine ['aɪəudiːn] *n* Jod *nt*

ioniser ['aɪənaɪzəʳ] *n* Ionisator *m*

iota [aɪ'əutə] *n* (*fig*) bisschen *nt*

IOU *n abbr* (= I owe you) Schuldschein *m*

IQ *n abbr* (= intelligence quotient) IQ *m*

IRA *n abbr* (= Irish Republican Army) IRA *f*

Iran [ɪ'rɑːn] *n* Iran *m*; **~ian** [ɪ'reɪnɪən] *adj* iranisch ♦ *n* Iraner(in) *m(f)*; (LING) Iranisch *nt*

Iraq [ɪ'rɑːk] *n* Irak *m*; **~i** *adj* irakisch ♦ *n* Iraker(in) *m(f)*

irate [aɪ'reɪt] *adj* zornig

Ireland ['aɪələnd] *n* Irland *nt*

iris ['aɪrɪs] (*pl* **~es**) *n* Iris *f*

Irish ['aɪrɪʃ] *adj* irisch ♦ *npl*: **the ~** die Iren *pl*, die Irländer *pl*; **~man** (*irreg*) *n* Ire *m*, Irländer *m*; **~ Sea** *n*: **the ~ Sea** die Irische See *f*; **~woman** (*irreg*) *n* Irin *f*, Irländerin *f*

irksome ['ɜːksəm] *adj* lästig

iron ['aɪən] *n* Eisen *nt*; (*for ~ing*) Bügeleisen *nt* ♦ *adj* eisern ♦ *vt* bügeln; **~ out** *vt* (*also fig*) ausbügeln; **Iron Curtain** *n* (HIST) Eiserne(r) Vorhang *m*

ironic(al) [aɪ'rɔnɪk(l)] *adj* ironisch; (*coincidence etc*) witzig

iron: **~ing** *n* Bügeln *nt*; (*laundry*) Bügelwäsche *f*; **~ing board** *n* Bügelbrett *nt*; **~monger's (shop)** *n* Eisen- und Haushaltswarenhandlung *f*

irony ['aɪrənɪ] *n* Ironie *f*

irrational [ɪ'ræʃənl] *adj* irrational

irreconcilable [ɪrekən'saɪləbl] *adj* unvereinbar

irrefutable [ɪrɪ'fjuːtəbl] *adj* unwiderlegbar

irregular [ɪ'regjuləʳ] *adj* unregelmäßig; (*shape*) ungleich(mäßig); (*fig*) unüblich; (: *behaviour*) ungehörig

irrelevant [ɪ'reləvənt] *adj* belanglos, irrelevant

irreparable [ɪ'reprəbl] *adj* nicht wieder gutzumachen

irreplaceable [ɪrɪ'pleɪsəbl] *adj* unersetzlich

irresistible [ɪrɪ'zɪstɪbl] *adj* unwiderstehlich

irrespective [ɪrɪ'spektɪv]: **~ of** *prep* ungeachtet *+gen*

irresponsible [ɪrɪ'spɔnsɪbl] *adj* verantwortungslos

irreverent [ɪ'revərnt] *adj* respektlos

irrevocable [ɪ'revəkəbl] *adj* unwiderrufbar

irrigate ['ɪrɪgeɪt] *vt* bewässern

irritable ['ɪrɪtəbl] *adj* reizbar

irritate ['ɪrɪteɪt] *vt* irritieren, reizen (*also* MED); **irritating** *adj* ärgerlich, irritierend; **he is irritating** er kann einem auf die Nerven gehen; **irritation** [ɪrɪ'teɪʃən] *n* (*anger*) Ärger *m*; (MED) Reizung *f*

IRS *n abbr* = **Internal Revenue Service**

is [ɪz] *vb see* **be**

Islam ['ɪzlɑːm] *n* Islam *m*; **~ic** [ɪz'læmɪk] *adj* islamisch

nd ['aɪlənd] *n* Insel *f*; **~er** *n*
    selbewohner(in) *m(f)*
    [aɪl] *n* (kleine) Insel *f*
t ['ɪznt] = **is not**
ate ['aɪsəleɪt] *vt* isolieren; **~d** *adj* isoliert;
    ɔse) Einzel-; **isolation** [aɪsə'leɪʃən] *n*
    lierung *f*
    n abbr (= *Internet Service Provider*)
    ternet-Anbieter *m*
el ['ɪzreɪl] *n* Israel *nt*; **~i** [ɪz'reɪlɪ] *adj*
    aelisch ♦ n Israeli *mf*
ue ['ɪʃjuː] *n* (*matter*) Frage *f*; (*outcome*)
    sgang *m*; (*of newspaper, shares*) Ausgabe
    (offspring) Nachkommenschaft *f* ♦ *vt*
    sgeben; (*warrant*) erlassen; (*documents*)
    sstellen; (*orders*) erteilen; (*books*)
    erausgeben; (*verdict*) aussprechen; **to be**
    ~ zur Debatte stehen; **to take ~ with sb**
    er sth jdm in etw *dat* widersprechen

    ] *pron* **1** (*specific: subject*) er/sie/es;
    direct object) ihn/sie/es; (: *indirect object*)
    m/ihr/ihm; **about/from/in/of it**
    arüber/davon/darin/davon
    (*impers*) es; **it's raining** es regnet; **it's**
    iday tomorrow morgen ist Freitag; **who**
    it? – it's me wer ist da? – ich (bins)

ian [ɪ'tæljən] *adj* italienisch ♦ *n*
    aliener(in) *m(f)*; (*LING*) Italienisch *nt*
ic [ɪ'tælɪk] *adj* kursiv; **~s** *npl* Kursivschrift *f*
y ['ɪtəlɪ] *n* Italien *nt*
    [ɪtʃ] *n* Juckreiz *m*; (*fig*) Lust *f* ♦ *vi* jucken;
    be ~ing to do sth darauf brennen, etw
    tun; ~y *adj* juckend
    ['ɪtd] = **it would; it had**
    n ['aɪtəm] *n* Gegenstand *m*; (*on list*)
    osten *m*; (*in programme*) Nummer *f*; (*in*
    genda) (Programm)punkt *m*; (*in newspaper*)
    eitungs)notiz *f*; **~ize** *vt* verzeichnen
erant [ɪ'tɪnərənt] *adj* umherreisend
erary [aɪ'tɪnərərɪ] *n* Reiseroute *f*
    ['ɪtl] = **it will; it shall**
    [ɪts] *adj* (*masculine, neuter*) sein; (*feminine*)
    r
    [ɪts] = **it is; it has**

itself [ɪt'sɛlf] *pron* sich (selbst); (*emphatic*)
    selbst
ITV (*BRIT*) *n abbr* = **Independent Television**
I.U.D. *n abbr* (= *intra-uterine device*) Pessar *nt*
I've [aɪv] = **I have**
ivory ['aɪvərɪ] *n* Elfenbein *nt*
ivy ['aɪvɪ] *n* Efeu *nt*

J, j

jab [dʒæb] *vt* (hinein)stechen ♦ *n* Stich *m*,
    Stoß *m*; (*inf*) Spritze *f*
jack [dʒæk] *n* (*AUT*) (Wagen)heber *m*; (*CARDS*)
    Bube *m*; **~ up** *vt* aufbocken
jackal ['dʒækl] *n* (*ZOOL*) Schakal *m*
jackdaw ['dʒækdɔː] *n* Dohle *f*
jacket ['dʒækɪt] *n* Jacke *f*; (*of book*)
    Schutzumschlag *m*; (*TECH*) Ummantelung *f*;
    ~ potatoes *npl* in der Schale gebackene
    Kartoffeln *pl*
jackknife ['dʒæknaɪf] *vi* (*truck*) sich
    zusammenschieben
jack plug *n* (*ELEC*) Buchsenstecker *m*
jackpot ['dʒækpɔt] *n* Haupttreffer *m*
jaded ['dʒeɪdɪd] *adj* ermattet
jagged ['dʒægɪd] *adj* zackig
jail [dʒeɪl] *n* Gefängnis *nt* ♦ *vt* einsperren;
    ~er *n* Gefängniswärter *m*
jam [dʒæm] *n* Marmelade *f*; (*also: traffic ~*)
    (Verkehrs)stau *m*; (*inf: trouble*) Klemme *f*
    ♦ *vt* (*wedge*) einklemmen; (*cram*)
    hineinzwängen; (*obstruct*) blockieren ♦ *vi*
    sich verklemmen; **to ~ sth into sth** etw in
    etw *acc* hineinstopfen
Jamaica [dʒə'meɪkə] *n* Jamaika *nt*
jam jar *n* Marmeladenglas *nt*
jammed [dʒæmd] *adj*: **it's ~** es klemmt
jam-packed [dʒæm'pækt] *adj* übenüllt,
    proppenvoll
jangle ['dʒæŋgl] *vt*, *vi* klimpern
janitor ['dʒænɪtə'] *n* Hausmeister *m*
January ['dʒænjʊərɪ] *n* Januar *m*
Japan [dʒə'pæn] *n* Japan *nt*; **~ese**
    [dʒæpə'niːz] *adj* japanisch ♦ *n inv* Japaner(in)
    m(f); (*LING*) Japanisch *nt*
jar [dʒɑː'] *n* Glas *nt* ♦ *vi* kreischen; (*colours*

etc) nicht harmonieren

jargon ['dʒɑːɡən] *n* Fachsprache *f*, Jargon *m*

jaundice ['dʒɔːndɪs] *n* Gelbsucht *f*; **~d** *adj* (*fig*) missgünstig

jaunt [dʒɔːnt] *n* Spritztour *f*

javelin ['dʒævlɪn] *n* Speer *m*

jaw [dʒɔː] *n* Kiefer *m*

jay [dʒeɪ] *n* (*ZOOL*) Eichelhäher *m*

jaywalker ['dʒeɪwɔːkə⁻] *n* unvorsichtige(r) Fußgänger *m*

jazz [dʒæz] *n* Jazz *m*; **~ up** *vt* (*MUS*) verjazzen; (*enliven*) aufpolieren

jealous ['dʒeləs] *adj* (*envious*) missgünstig; (*husband*) eifersüchtig; **~y** *n* Missgunst *f*; Eifersucht *f*

jeans [dʒiːnz] *npl* Jeans *pl*

Jeep [dʒiːp] ® *n* Jeep *m* ®

jeer [dʒɪə⁻] *vi*: **to ~ (at sb)** (über jdn) höhnisch lachen, (jdn) verspotten

Jehovah's Witness [dʒɪ'həʊvəz-] *n* Zeuge *m*/Zeugin *f* Jehovas

jelly ['dʒelɪ] *n* Gelee *nt*; (*dessert*) Grütze *f*; **~fish** *n* Qualle *f*

jeopardize ['dʒepədaɪz] *vt* gefährden

jeopardy ['dʒepədɪ] *n*: **to be in jeopardy** in Gefahr sein

jerk [dʒɜːk] *n* Ruck *m*; (*inf: idiot*) Trottel *m* ♦ *vt* ruckartig bewegen ♦ *vi* sich ruckartig bewegen

jerky ['dʒɜːkɪ] *adj* (*movement*) ruckartig; (*ride*) rüttelnd

jersey ['dʒɜːzɪ] *n* Pullover *m*

jest [dʒest] *n* Scherz *m* ♦ *vi* spaßen; **in ~** im Spaß

Jesus ['dʒiːzəs] *n* Jesus *m*

jet [dʒet] *n* (*stream: of water etc*) Strahl *m*; (*spout*) Düse *f*; (*AVIAT*) Düsenflugzeug *nt*; **~-black** *adj* rabenschwarz; **~ engine** *n* Düsenmotor *m*; **~ lag** *n* Jetlag *m*

jettison ['dʒetɪsn] *vt* über Bord werfen

jetty ['dʒetɪ] *n* Landesteg *m*, Mole *f*

Jew [dʒuː] *n* Jude *m*

jewel ['dʒuːəl] *n* (*also fig*) Juwel *nt*; **~ler** (*US* **jeweler**) *n* Juwelier *m*; **~ler's (shop)** *n* Juwelier *m*; **~lery** (*US* **jewelry**) *n* Schmuck *m*

Jewess ['dʒuːɪs] *n* Jüdin *f*

Jewish ['dʒuːɪʃ] *adj* jüdisch

jibe [dʒaɪb] *n* spöttische Bemerkung *f*

jiffy ['dʒɪfɪ] (*inf*) *n*: **in a ~** sofort

jigsaw ['dʒɪɡsɔː] *n* (*also: ~ puzzle*) Puzzle(spiel) *nt*

jilt [dʒɪlt] *vt* den Laufpass geben +*dat*

jingle ['dʒɪŋɡl] *n* (*advertisement*) Werbesong *m* ♦ *vi* klimpern; (*bells*) bimmeln ♦ *vt* klimpern mit; bimmeln lassen

jinx [dʒɪŋks] *n*: **there's a ~ on it** es ist verhext

jitters ['dʒɪtəz] (*inf*) *npl*: **to get the ~** einen Bammel kriegen

job [dʒɔb] *n* (*piece of work*) Arbeit *f*; (*position*) Stellung *f*; (*duty*) Aufgabe *f*; (*difficulty*) Mühe *f*; **it's a good ~ he …** es ist ein Glück, dass er …; **just the ~** genau das Richtige; **J~centre** (*BRIT*) *n* Arbeitsamt *nt*; **~less** *adj* arbeitslos

jockey ['dʒɔkɪ] *n* Jockei *m*, Jockey *m* ♦ *vi*: **to ~ for position** sich in eine gute Position drängeln

jocular ['dʒɔkjulə⁻] *adj* scherzhaft

jog [dʒɔɡ] *vt* (an)stoßen ♦ *vi* (*run*) joggen; **to ~ along** vor sich *acc* hinwursteln; (*work*) seinen Gang gehen; **~ging** *n* Jogging *nt*

join [dʒɔɪn] *vt* (*club*) beitreten +*dat*; (*person*) sich anschließen +*dat*; (*fasten*) **to ~ (sth to sth)** (etw mit etw) verbinden ♦ *vi* (*unite*) sich vereinigen ♦ *n* Verbindungsstelle *f*, Naht *f*; **~ in** *vt*, *vi*: **to ~ in (sth)** (bei etw) mitmachen; **~ up** *vi* (*MIL*) zur Armee gehen

joiner ['dʒɔɪnə⁻] *n* Schreiner *m*; **~y** *n* Schreinerei *f*

joint [dʒɔɪnt] *n* (*TECH*) Fuge *f*; (*of bones*) Gelenk *nt*; (*of meat*) Braten *m*; (*inf: place*) Lokal *nt* ♦ *adj* gemeinsam; **~ account** *n* (*with bank etc*) gemeinsame(s) Konto *nt*; **~ly** *adv* gemeinsam

joke [dʒəʊk] *n* Witz *m* ♦ *vi* Witze machen; **to play a ~ on sb** jdm einen Streich spielen

joker [dʒəʊkə⁻] *n* Witzbold *m*; (*CARDS*) Joker *m*

jolly ['dʒɔlɪ] *adj* lustig ♦ *adv* (*inf*) ganz schön

jolt [dʒəʊlt] *n* (*shock*) Schock *m*; (*jerk*) Stoß *m*

♦ vt (push) stoßen; (shake) durchschütteln; (fig) aufrütteln ♦ vi holpern

ordan ['dʒɔːdən] n Jordanien nt

ostle ['dʒɒsl] vt anrempeln

ot [dʒɒt] n: **not one ~** kein Jota nt; **~ down** vt notieren; **~ter** (BRIT) n Notizblock m

ournal ['dʒəːnl] n (diary) Tagebuch nt; (magazine) Zeitschrift f; **~ism** n Journalismus m; **~ist** n Journalist(in) m(f)

ourney ['dʒəːnɪ] n Reise f

ovial ['dʒəuvɪəl] adj jovial

oy [dʒɔɪ] n Freude f; **~ful** adj freudig; **~ous** adj freudig; **~ ride** n Schwarzfahrt f; **~rider** n Autodieb, der den Wagen nur für eine Spritztour stiehlt; **~stick** n Steuerknüppel m; (COMPUT) Joystick m

P. n abbr = **Justice of the Peace**

r abbr = **junior**

bilant ['dʒuːbɪlnt] adj triumphierend

bilee ['dʒuːbɪliː] n Jubiläum nt

dge [dʒʌdʒ] n Richter m; (fig) Kenner m ♦ vt (JUR: person) die Verhandlung führen über +acc; (case) verhandeln; (assess) beurteilen; (estimate) einschätzen; **~ment** n (JUR) Urteil nt; (ECCL) Gericht nt; (ability) Urteilsvermögen nt

dicial [dʒuːˈdɪʃl] adj gerichtlich, Justiz-

diciary [dʒuːˈdɪʃɪən] n Gerichtsbehörden pl; (judges) Richterstand m

dicious [dʒuːˈdɪʃəs] adj weise

do ['dʒuːdəu] n Judo nt

g [dʒʌɡ] n Krug m

ggernaut ['dʒʌɡənɔːt] (BRIT) n (huge truck) Schwertransporter m

ggle ['dʒʌɡl] vt, vi jonglieren; **~r** n Jongleur m

goslav etc ['juːɡəuˈslɑːv] = **Yugoslav** etc

ice [dʒuːs] n Saft m; **juicy** ['dʒuːsɪ] adj (also fig) saftig

kebox ['dʒuːkbɒks] n Musikautomat m

ly [dʒuːˈlaɪ] n Juli m

mble ['dʒʌmbl] n Durcheinander nt ♦ vt (also: **~ up**) durcheinander werfen; (facts) durcheinander bringen

mble sale (BRIT) n Basar m, Flohmarkt m

Jumble sale

🛈 **Jumble sale** ist ein Wohltätig-
keitsbasar, meist in einer Aula oder
einem Gemeindehaus abgehalten, bei
dem alle möglichen Gebrauchtwaren (vor
allem Kleidung, Spielzeug, Bücher, Geschirr
und Möbel) verkauft werden. Der Erlös
fließt entweder einer Wohltätigkeits-
organisation zu oder wird für örtliche
Zwecke verwendet, z.B. die Pfadfinder, die
Grundschule, Reparatur der Kirche
usw.

---

jumbo (jet) ['dʒʌmbəu-] n Jumbo(jet) m

jump [dʒʌmp] vi springen; (nervously) zusammenzucken ♦ vt überspringen ♦ n Sprung m; **to ~ the queue** (BRIT) sich vordrängeln

jumper ['dʒʌmpər] n (BRIT: pullover) Pullover m; (US: dress) Trägerkleid nt

jump leads BRIT, **jumper cables** US npl Überbrückungskabel nt

jumpy ['dʒʌmpɪ] adj nervös

Jun. abbr = **junior**

junction ['dʒʌŋkʃən] n (BRIT: of roads) (Straßen)kreuzung f; (RAIL) Knotenpunkt m

juncture ['dʒʌŋktʃər] n: **at this ~** in diesem Augenblick

June [dʒuːn] n Juni m

jungle ['dʒʌŋɡl] n Dschungel m

junior ['dʒuːnɪər] adj (younger) jünger; (after name) junior; (SPORT) Junioren-; (lower position) untergeordnet; (for young people) Junioren- ♦ n Jüngere(r) mf; **~ school** (BRIT) n Grundschule f

junk [dʒʌŋk] n (rubbish) Plunder m; (ship) Dschunke f; **~ bond** n (COMM) niedrig eingestuftes Wertpapier mit hohen Ertragschancen bei erhöhtem Risiko; **~ food** n Junk food nt; **~ mail** n Reklame, die unangefordert in den Briefkasten gesteckt wird; **~ shop** n Ramschladen m

Junr abbr = **junior**

jurisdiction [dʒuərɪsˈdɪkʃən] n Gerichtsbarkeit f; (range of authority) Zuständigkeit(sbereich m) f

juror ['dʒʊərə'] n Geschworene(r) mf; (in competition) Preisrichter m

jury ['dʒʊəri] n (court) Geschworene pl; (panel) Jury f

just [dʒʌst] adj gerecht ♦ adv (recently, now) gerade, eben; (barely) gerade noch; (exactly) genau, gerade; (only) nur, bloß; (a small distance) gleich; (absolutely) einfach; ~ **as I arrived** gerade als ich ankam; ~ **as nice** genauso nett; ~ **as well** umso besser; ~ **now** soeben, gerade; ~ **try** versuch es mal; **she's** ~ **left** sie ist gerade or (so)eben gegangen; **he's** ~ **done it** er hat es gerade or (so)eben getan; ~ **before** gerade or kurz bevor; ~ **enough** gerade genug; **he** ~ **missed** er hat fast or beinahe getroffen

justice ['dʒʌstɪs] n (fairness) Gerechtigkeit f; **J~ of the Peace** n Friedensrichter m

justifiable [dʒʌstɪ'faɪəbl] adj berechtigt

justification [dʒʌstɪfɪ'keɪʃən] n Rechtfertigung f

justify ['dʒʌstɪfaɪ] vt rechtfertigen; (text) justieren

justly ['dʒʌstlɪ] adv (say) mit Recht; (condemn) gerecht

jut [dʒʌt] vi (also: ~ **out**) herausragen, vorstehen

juvenile ['dʒuːvənaɪl] adj (young) jugendlich; (for the young) Jugend- ♦ n Jugendliche(r) mf

juxtapose ['dʒʌkstəpəuz] vt nebeneinander stellen

K, k

K [keɪ] abbr (= one thousand) Tsd.; (= kilobyte) K

kangaroo [kæŋgə'ruː] n Känguru nt

karate [kə'rɑːtɪ] n Karate nt

kebab [kə'bæb] n Kebab m

keel [kiːl] n Kiel m; **on an even** ~ (fig) im Lot

keen [kiːn] adj begeistert; (wind, blade, intelligence) scharf; (sight, hearing) gut; **to be** ~ **to do** or **on doing sth** etw unbedingt tun wollen; **to be** ~ **on sth/sb** scharf auf etw/jdn sein

keep [kiːp] (pt, pp **kept**) vt (retain) behalten; (have) haben; (animals, one's word) halten; (support) versorgen; (maintain in state) halten; (preserve) aufbewahren; (restrain) abhalten ♦ vi (continue in direction) sich halten; (food) sich halten; (remain: quiet etc) bleiben ♦ n Unterhalt m; (tower) Burgfried m; (inf): **for** ~s für immer; **to** ~ **sth to o.s.** etw für sich behalten; **it** ~s **happening** es passiert immer wieder; ~ **back** vt fern halten; (information) verschweigen; ~ **on** vi: ~ **on doing sth** etw immer weiter tun; ~ **out** vt nicht hereinlassen; **"~ out"** „Eintritt verboten!"; ~ **up** vi Schritt halten ♦ vt aufrechterhalten; (continue) weitermachen; **to** ~ **up with** Schritt halten mit; ~**er** n Wärter(in) m(f); (goalkeeper) Torhüter(in) m(f); ~**-fit** n Keep-fit nt; ~**ing** n (care) Obhut f; **in** ~**ing with** in Übereinstimmung mit; ~**sake** n Andenken nt

keg [keg] n Fass nt

kennel ['kenl] n Hundehütte f; ~s npl: **to put a dog in** ~s (for boarding) einen Hund in Pflege geben

Kenya ['kenjə] n Kenia nt; ~n adj kenianisch ♦ n Kenianer(in) m(f)

kept [kept] pt, pp of **keep**

kerb [kɜːb] (BRIT) n Bordstein m

kernel ['kɜːnl] n Kern m

kerosene ['kerəsiːn] n Kerosin nt

kettle ['ketl] n Kessel m; ~**drum** n Pauke f

key [kiː] n Schlüssel m; (of piano, typewriter) Taste f; (MUS) Tonart f ♦ vt (also: ~ **in**) eingeben; ~**board** n Tastatur f; ~**ed up** adj (person) überdreht; ~**hole** n Schlüsselloch nt; ~**hole surgery** n minimal invasive Chirurgie f, Schlüssellochchirurgie f; ~**note** n Grundton m; ~ **ring** n Schlüsselring m

khaki ['kɑːkɪ] n K(h)aki nt ♦ adj k(h)aki(farben)

kick [kɪk] vt einen Fußtritt geben +dat, treten ♦ vi treten; (baby) strampeln; (horse) ausschlagen ♦ n (Fuß)tritt m; (thrill) Spaß m; **he does it for** ~s er macht das aus Jux;

~ **off** vi (SPORT) anstoßen; ~-**off** n (SPORT)
Anstoß m

d [kɪd] n (inf: child) Kind nt; (goat) Zicklein
nt; (leather) Glacéleder nt, Glaceeleder nt
♦ vi (inf) Witze machen

dnap ['kɪdnæp] vt entführen; ~**per** n
Entführer m; ~**ping** n Entführung f

dney ['kɪdnɪ] n Niere f

ll [kɪl] vt töten, umbringen ♦ vi töten ♦ n
(hunting) (Jagd)beute f; ~**er** n Mörder(in)
m(f); ~**ing** n Mord m; ~**joy** n
Spaßverderber(in) m(f)

ln [kɪln] n Brennofen m

lo ['kiːləʊ] n Kilo nt; ~**byte** n (COMPUT)
Kilobyte nt; ~**gram(me)** n Kilogramm nt;
~**metre** ['kɪləmiːtə*] (US **kilometer**) n
Kilometer m; ~**watt** n Kilowatt nt

lt [kɪlt] n Schottenrock m

nd [kaɪnd] adj freundlich ♦ n Art f; **a ~ of**
eine Art von; **(two) of a ~** (zwei) von der
gleichen Art; **in ~** auf dieselbe Art; (in
goods) in Naturalien

ndergarten ['kɪndəgɑːtn] n Kindergarten
m

nd-hearted [kaɪnd'hɑːtɪd] adj gutherzig

ndle ['kɪndl] vt (set on fire) anzünden;
(rouse) reizen, (er)wecken

ndly ['kaɪndlɪ] adj freundlich ♦ adv
liebenswürdig(erweise); **would you ~ ...?**
wären Sie so freundlich und ...?

ndness ['kaɪndnɪs] n Freundlichkeit f

ndred ['kɪndrɪd] adj: ~ **spirit**
Gleichgesinnte(r) mf

ng [kɪŋ] n König m; ~**dom** n Königreich nt

ngfisher ['kɪŋfɪʃə*] n Eisvogel m

ng-size(d) ['kɪŋsaɪz(d)] adj (cigarette)
Kingsize

nky ['kɪŋkɪ] (inf) adj (person, ideas) verrückt;
(sexual) abartig

osk ['kiːɔsk] (BRIT) n (TEL) Telefonhäuschen
nt

pper ['kɪpə*] n Räucherhering m

ss [kɪs] n Kuss m ♦ vt küssen ♦ vi: **they ~ed**
sie küssten sich; ~ **of life** (BRIT) n: **the ~ of
life** Mund-zu-Mund-Beatmung f

t [kɪt] n Ausrüstung f; (tools) Werkzeug nt

tchen ['kɪtʃɪn] n Küche f; ~ **sink** n

Spülbecken nt

kite [kaɪt] n Drachen m

kitten ['kɪtn] n Kätzchen nt

kitty ['kɪtɪ] n (money) Kasse f

km abbr (= kilometre) km

knack [næk] n Dreh m, Trick m

knapsack ['næpsæk] n Rucksack m; (MIL)
Tornister m

knead [niːd] vt kneten

knee [niː] n Knie nt; ~**cap** n Kniescheibe f

kneel [niːl] (pt, pp **knelt**) vi (also: ~ **down**)
knien

knelt [nɛlt] pt, pp of **kneel**

knew [njuː] pt of **know**

knickers ['nɪkəz] (BRIT) npl Schlüpfer m

knife [naɪf] (pl **knives**) n Messer nt ♦ vt
erstechen

knight [naɪt] n Ritter m; (chess) Springer m;
~**hood** n (title): **to get a ~hood** zum Ritter
geschlagen werden

knit [nɪt] vt stricken ♦ vi stricken; (bones)
zusammenwachsen; ~**ting** n (occupation)
Stricken nt; (work) Strickzeug nt; ~**ting
needle** n Stricknadel f; ~**wear** n
Strickwaren pl

knives [naɪvz] pl of **knife**

knob [nɔb] n Knauf m; (on instrument) Knopf
m; (BRIT: of butter etc) kleine(s) Stück nt

knock [nɔk] vt schlagen; (criticize)
heruntermachen ♦ vi: **to ~ at** or **on the
door** an die Tür klopfen ♦ n Schlag m; (on
door) Klopfen nt; ~ **down** vt umwerfen;
(with car) anfahren; ~ **off** vt (do quickly)
hinhauen; (inf: steal) klauen ♦ vi (finish)
Feierabend machen; ~ **out** vt ausschlagen;
(BOXING) k. o. schlagen; ~ **over** vt (person,
object) umwerfen; (with car) anfahren; ~**er**
n (on door) Türklopfer m; ~**out** n
K.-o.-Schlag m; (fig) Sensation f

knot [nɔt] n Knoten m ♦ vt (ver)knoten

knotty ['nɔtɪ] adj (fig) kompliziert

know [nəʊ] (pt **knew**, pp **known**) vt, vi
wissen; (be able to) können; (be acquainted
with) kennen; (recognize) erkennen; **to ~
how to do sth** wissen, wie man etw
macht, etw tun können; **to ~ about** or **of
sth/sb** etw/jdn kennen; ~**-all** n Alleswisser

m; **~-how** *n* Kenntnis *f,* Know-how *nt;*
~ing *adj (look, smile)* wissend; **~ingly** *adv*
wissend; *(intentionally)* wissentlich
knowledge [ˈnɔlɪdʒ] *n* Wissen *nt,* Kenntnis
f; **~able** *adj* informiert
known [nəʊn] *pp of* **know**
knuckle [ˈnʌkl] *n* Fingerknöchel *m*
K.O. *n abbr* = **knockout**
Koran [kɔˈrɑːn] *n* Koran *m*
Korea [kəˈrɪə] *n* Korea *nt*
kosher [ˈkəʊʃəʳ] *adj* koscher

L, l

L [ɛl] *abbr (BRIT: AUT)* (= *learner*) am Auto
angebrachtes Kennzeichen für Fahrschüler; =
lake; (= *large*) gr.; (= *left*) l.
l. *abbr* = **litre**
lab [læb] *(inf) n* Labor *nt*
label [ˈleɪbl] *n* Etikett *nt* ♦ *vt* etikettieren
labor *etc* [ˈleɪbəʳ] *(US)* = **labour** *etc*
laboratory [ləˈbɔrətəri] *n* Laboratorium *nt*
laborious [ləˈbɔːrɪəs] *adj* mühsam
labour [ˈleɪbəʳ] *(US* **labor**) *n* Arbeit *f;*
(workmen) Arbeitskräfte *pl;* (*MED*) Wehen *pl*
♦ *vi:* **to ~ (at)** sich abmühen (mit) ♦ *vt*
breittreten *(inf);* **in ~** (*MED*) in den Wehen;
L~ *(BRIT: also:* **the L~ party**) die Labour
Party; **~ed** *adj (movement)* gequält; *(style)*
schwerfällig; **~er** *n* Arbeiter *m;* **farm ~er**
(Land)arbeiter *m*
lace [leɪs] *n (fabric)* Spitze *f;* *(of shoe)*
Schnürsenkel *m;* *(braid)* Litze *f* ♦ *vt (also: ~*
up) (zu)schnüren
lack [læk] *n* Mangel *m* ♦ *vt* nicht haben; **sb**
~s sth jdm fehlt etw *nom;* **to be ~ing**
fehlen; **sb is ~ing in sth** es fehlt jdm an
etw *dat;* **for** *or* **through ~** aus Mangel an
+dat
lacquer [ˈlækəʳ] *n* Lack *m*
lad [læd] *n* Junge *m*
ladder [ˈlædəʳ] *n* Leiter *f;* *(BRIT: in tights)*
Laufmasche *f* ♦ *vt (BRIT: tights)* Laufmaschen
bekommen in *+dat*
laden [ˈleɪdn] *adj* beladen, voll
ladle [ˈleɪdl] *n* Schöpfkelle *f*

lady [ˈleɪdɪ] *n* Dame *f;* *(title)* Lady *f;* **young ~**
junge Dame; **the ladies' (room)** die
Damentoilette; **~bird** *(US* **~bug**) *n*
Marienkäfer *m;* **~like** *adj* damenhaft,
vornehm; **~ship** *n:* **your L~ship** Ihre
Ladyschaft
lag [læg] *vi (also:* **~ behind**) zurückbleiben
♦ *vt (pipes)* verkleiden
lager [ˈlɑːgəʳ] *n* helle(s) Bier *nt*
lagging [ˈlægɪŋ] *n* Isolierung *f*
lagoon [ləˈguːn] *n* Lagune *f*
laid [leɪd] *pt, pp of* **lay;** **~ back** *(inf) adj* cool
lain [leɪn] *pp of* **lie**
lair [lɛəʳ] *n* Lager *nt*
lake [leɪk] *n* See *m*
lamb [læm] *n* Lamm *nt;* *(meat)* Lammfleisch
nt; **~ chop** *n* Lammkotelett *nt;* **~swool** *n*
Lammwolle *f*
lame [leɪm] *adj* lahm; *(excuse)* faul
lament [ləˈment] *n* Klage *f* ♦ *vt* beklagen
laminated [ˈlæmɪneɪtɪd] *adj* beschichtet
lamp [læmp] *n* Lampe *f;* *(in street)*
Straßenlaterne *f;* **~post** *n* Laternenpfahl *m;*
~shade *n* Lampenschirm *m*
lance [lɑːns] *n* Lanze *f;* **~ corporal** *(BRIT)*
Obergefreite(r) *m*
land [lænd] *n* Land *nt* ♦ *vi (from ship)* an
Land gehen; *(AVIAT, end up)* landen ♦ *vt*
(obtain) kriegen; *(passengers)* absetzen;
(goods) abladen; *(troops, space probe)*
landen; **~fill site** [ˈlændfɪl-] *n* Mülldeponie
f; **~ing** *n* Landung *f;* *(on stairs)*
(Treppen)absatz *m;* **~ing gear** *n*
Fahrgestell *nt;* **~ing stage** *(BRIT)* *n*
Landesteg *m;* **~ing strip** *n* Landebahn *f;*
~lady *n* (Haus)wirtin *f;* **~locked** *adj*
landumschlossen, Binnen-; **~lord** *n (of*
house) Hauswirt *m,* Besitzer *m;* *(of pub)*
Gastwirt *m;* *(of area)* Grundbesitzer *m;*
~mark *n* Wahrzeichen *nt;* *(fig)* Meilenstein
m; **~owner** *n* Grundbesitzer *m;* **~scape** *n*
Landschaft *f;* **~ gardener** *n*
Landschaftsgärtner(in) *m(f);* **~slide** *n*
(GEOG) Erdrutsch *m;* *(POL)*
überwältigende(r) Sieg *m*
lane [leɪn] *n (in town)* Gasse *f;* *(in country)*
Weg *m;* *(of motorway)* Fahrbahn *f,* Spur *f;*

(SPORT) Bahn f; **"get in ~"** „bitte einordnen"

language ['læŋgwɪdʒ] n Sprache f; **bad ~** unanständige Ausdrücke pl; **~ laboratory** n Sprachlabor nt

languish ['læŋgwɪʃ] vi schmachten

lank [læŋk] adj dürr

lanky ['læŋkɪ] adj schlaksig

lantern ['læntən] n Laterne f

lap [læp] n Schoß m; (SPORT) Runde f ♦ vt (also: **~ up**) auflecken ♦ vi (water) plätschern

lapel [lə'pel] n Revers nt or m

Lapland ['læplænd] n Lappland nt

lapse [læps] n (moral) Fehltritt m ♦ vi (decline) nachlassen; (expire) ablaufen; (claims) erlöschen; **to ~ into bad habits** sich schlechte Gewohnheiten angewöhnen

laptop (computer) ['læptɒp-] n Laptop(-Computer) m

lard [lɑːd] n Schweineschmalz nt

larder ['lɑːdə*] n Speisekammer f

large [lɑːdʒ] adj groß; **at ~** auf freiem Fuß; **~ly** adv zum größten Teil; **~-scale** adj groß angelegt, Groß-

lark [lɑːk] n (bird) Lerche f; (joke) Jux m; **~ about** (inf) vi herumalbern

laryngitis [lærɪn'dʒaɪtɪs] n Kehlkopfentzündung f

laser ['leɪzə*] n Laser m; **~ printer** n Laserdrucker m

lash [læʃ] n Peitschenhieb m; (eyelash) Wimper f ♦ vt (rain) schlagen gegen; (whip) peitschen; (bind) festbinden; **~ out** vi (with fists) um sich schlagen

lass [læs] n Mädchen nt

lasso [læ'suː] n Lasso nt

last [lɑːst] adj letzte(r, s) ♦ adv zuletzt; (~ time) das letzte Mal ♦ vi (continue) dauern; (remain good) sich halten; (money) ausreichen; **at ~** endlich; **~ night** gestern Abend; **~ week** letzte Woche; **~ but one** vorletzte(r, s); **~-ditch** adj (attempt) in letzter Minute; **~ing** adj dauerhaft; (shame etc) andauernd; **~ly** adv schließlich; **~-minute** adj in letzter Minute

latch [lætʃ] n Riegel m

late [leɪt] adj spät; (dead) verstorben ♦ adv spät; (after proper time) zu spät; **to be ~** zu spät kommen; **of ~** in letzter Zeit; **in ~ May** Ende Mai; **~comer** n Nachzügler(in) m(f); **~ly** adv in letzter Zeit; **later** ['leɪtə*] adj (date) später; (version) neuer ♦ adv später

lateral ['lætərəl] adj seitlich

latest ['leɪtɪst] adj (fashion) neueste(r, s) ♦ n (news) Neu(e)ste(s) nt; **at the ~** spätestens

lathe [leɪð] n Drehbank f

lather ['lɑːðə*] n (Seifen)schaum m ♦ vt einschäumen ♦ vi schäumen

Latin ['lætɪn] n Latein nt ♦ adj lateinisch; (Roman) römisch; **~ America** n Lateinamerika nt; **~ American** adj lateinamerikanisch

latitude ['lætɪtjuːd] n (GEOG) Breite f; (freedom) Spielraum m

latter ['lætə*] adj (second of two) letztere; (coming at end) letzte(r, s), später ♦ n: **the ~** der/die/das letztere, die letzteren; **~ly** adv in letzter Zeit

lattice ['lætɪs] n Gitter nt

laudable ['lɔːdəbl] adj löblich

laugh [lɑːf] n Lachen nt ♦ vi lachen; **~ at** vt lachen über +acc; **~ off** vt lachend abtun; **~able** adj lachhaft; **~ing stock** n Zielscheibe f des Spottes; **~ter** n Gelächter nt

launch [lɔːntʃ] n (of ship) Stapellauf m; (of rocket) Abschuss m; (boat) Barkasse f; (of product) Einführung f ♦ vt (set afloat) vom Stapel lassen; (rocket) (ab)schießen; (product) auf den Markt bringen; **~(ing) pad** n Abschussrampe f

launder ['lɔːndə*] vt waschen

Launderette [lɔːn'dret] (® BRIT) n Waschsalon m

Laundromat ['lɔːndrəmæt] (® US) n Waschsalon m

laundry ['lɔːndrɪ] n (place) Wäscherei f; (clothes) Wäsche f; **to do the ~** waschen

laureate ['lɔːrɪət] adj see **poet**

laurel ['lɒrl] n Lorbeer m

lava ['lɑːvə] n Lava f

lavatory ['lævətərɪ] n Toilette f

lavender ['lævəndə] n Lavendel m

lavish ['lævɪʃ] adj (extravagant) verschwenderisch; (generous) großzügig
♦ vt (money): **to ~ sth on sth** etw auf etw acc verschwenden; (attention, gifts): **to ~ sth on sb** jdn mit etw überschütten

law [lɔː] n Gesetz nt; (system) Recht nt; (as studies) Jura no art; **~abiding** adj gesetzestreu; **~ and order** n Recht nt und Ordnung f; **~ court** n Gerichtshof m; **~ful** adj gesetzlich; **~less** adj gesetzlos

lawn [lɔːn] n Rasen m; **~mower** n Rasenmäher m; **~ tennis** n Rasentennis m

law: **~ school** n Rechtsakademie f; **~suit** n Prozess m; **~yer** n Rechtsanwalt m, Rechtsanwältin f

lax [læks] adj (behaviour) nachlässig; (standards) lax

laxative ['læksətɪv] n Abführmittel nt

lay [leɪ] (pt, pp **laid**) pt of **lie** ♦ adj Laien- ♦ vt (place) legen; (table) decken; (egg) legen; (trap) stellen; (money) wetten; **~ aside** vt zurücklegen; **~ by** vt (set aside) beiseite legen; **~ down** vt hinlegen; (rules) vorschreiben; (arms) strecken; **to ~ down the law** Vorschriften machen; **~ off** vt (workers) (vorübergehend) entlassen; **~ on** vt (water, gas) anschließen; (concert etc) veranstalten; **~ out** vt (her)auslegen; (money) ausgeben; (corpse) aufbahren; **~ up** vt (subj: illness) ans Bett fesseln; **~about** n Faulenzer m; **~by** (BRIT) n Parkbucht f; (bigger) Rastplatz m

layer ['leɪə] n Schicht f

layman ['leɪmən] (irreg) n Laie m

layout ['leɪaʊt] n Anlage f; (ART) Lay-out nt, Layout nt

laze [leɪz] vi faulenzen

laziness ['leɪzɪnɪs] n Faulheit f

lazy ['leɪzɪ] adj faul; (slow-moving) träge

lb. abbr = **pound** (weight)

lead[1] [led] n (chemical) Blei nt; (of pencil) (Bleistift)mine f ♦ adj bleiern, Blei-

lead[2] [liːd] (pt, pp **led**) n (front position) Führung f; (distance, time ahead) Vorsprung f; (example) Vorbild nt; (clue) Tipp m; (of police) Spur f; (THEAT) Hauptrolle f; (dog's)

Leine f ♦ vt (guide) führen; (group etc) leiten ♦ vi (be first) führen; **in the ~** (SPORT, fig) in Führung; **~ astray** vt irreführen; **~ away** vt wegführen; (prisoner) abführen; **~ back** vi zurückführen; **~ on** vt anführen; **~ on to** vt (induce) dazu bringen; **~ to** vt (street) (hin)führen nach; (result in) führen zu; **~ up to** vt (drive) führen zu; (speaker etc) hinführen auf +acc

leaded petrol ['ledɪd-] n verbleites Benzin nt

leaden ['ledn] adj (sky, sea) bleiern; (heavy: footsteps) bleischwer

leader ['liːdə] n Führer m, Leiter m; (of party) Vorsitzende(r) m; (PRESS) Leitartikel m; **~ship** n (office) Leitung f; (quality) Führerschaft f

lead-free ['ledfriː] adj (petrol) bleifrei

leading ['liːdɪŋ] adj führend; **~ lady** n (THEAT) Hauptdarstellerin f; **~ light** n (person) führende(r) Geist m

lead singer [liːd-] n Leadsänger(in) m(f)

leaf [liːf] (pl **leaves**) n Blatt nt ♦ vi: **to ~ through** durchblättern; **to turn over a new ~** einen neuen Anfang machen

leaflet ['liːflɪt] n (advertisement) Prospekt m; (pamphlet) Flugblatt nt; (for information) Merkblatt nt

league [liːg] n (union) Bund m; (SPORT) Liga f; **to be in ~ with** unter einer Decke stecken mit

leak [liːk] n undichte Stelle f; (in ship) Leck nt ♦ vt (liquid etc) durchlassen ♦ vi (pipe etc) undicht sein; (liquid etc) auslaufen; **the information was ~ed to the enemy** die Information wurde dem Feind zugespielt; **~ out** vi (liquid etc) auslaufen; (information) durchsickern; **~y** ['liːkɪ] adj undicht

lean [liːn] (pt, pp **leaned** or **leant**) adj mager ♦ vi sich neigen ♦ vt (an)lehnen; **to ~ against sth** an etw dat angelehnt sein; sich an etw acc anlehnen; **~ back** vi sich zurücklehnen; **~ forward** vi sich vorbeugen; **~ on** vt fus sich stützen auf +acc; **~ out** vi sich hinauslehnen; **~ over** vi sich hinüberbeugen; **~ing** n Neigung f ♦ adj schief; **~t** [lent] pt, pp of **lean**; **~-to** n

Anbau m

eap [li:p] (pt, pp **leaped** or **leapt**) n Sprung m ♦ vi springen; **~frog** n Bockspringen nt; **~t** [lept] pt, pp of **leap**; **~ year** n Schaltjahr nt

earn [lə:n] (pt, pp **learned** or **learnt**) vt, vi lernen; (find out) erfahren; **to ~ how to do sth** etw (er)lernen; **~ed** ['lə:nɪd] adj gelehrt; **~er** n Anfänger(in) m(f); (AUT: BRIT: also: **~er driver**) Fahrschüler(in) m(f); **~ing** n Gelehrsamkeit f; **~t** [lə:nt] pt, pp of **learn**

ease [li:s] n (of property) Mietvertrag m ♦ vt pachten

eash [li:ʃ] n Leine f

east [li:st] adj geringste(r, s) ♦ adv am wenigsten ♦ n Mindeste(s) nt; **the ~ possible effort** möglichst geringer Aufwand; **at ~** zumindest; **not in the ~!** durchaus nicht!

eather ['leðər] n Leder nt

eave [li:v] (pt, pp **left**) vt verlassen; (~ behind) zurücklassen; (forget) vergessen; (allow to remain) lassen; (after death) hinterlassen; (entrust) **to ~ sth to sb** jdm etw überlassen ♦ vi weggehen, wegfahren; (for journey) abreisen; (bus, train) abfahren ♦ n Erlaubnis f; (MIL) Urlaub m; **to be left** (remain) übrig bleiben; **there's some milk left over** es ist noch etwas Milch übrig; **on ~** auf Urlaub; **~ behind** vt (person, object) dalassen; (forget) liegen lassen, stehen lassen; **~ out** vt auslassen; **~ of absence** n Urlaub m

eaves [li:vz] pl of **leaf**

Lebanon ['lebənən] n Libanon m

echerous ['letʃərəs] adj lüstern

ecture ['lektʃər] n Vortrag m; (UNIV) Vorlesung f ♦ vi einen Vortrag halten; (UNIV) lesen ♦ vt (scold) abkanzeln; **to give a ~ on sth** einen Vortrag über etw halten; **~r** ['lektʃərər] n Vortragende(r) mf; (BRIT: UNIV) Dozent(in) m(f)

~ed [led] pt, pp of **lead**²

edge [ledʒ] n Leiste f; (window ~) Sims m or nt; (of mountain) (Fels)vorsprung m

edger ['ledʒər] n Hauptbuch nt

eech [li:tʃ] n Blutegel m

leek [li:k] n Lauch m

leer [lɪər] vi: **to ~ (at sb)** (nach jdm) schielen

leeway ['li:weɪ] n (fig): **to have some ~** etwas Spielraum haben

left [left] pt, pp of **leave** ♦ adj linke(r, s) ♦ n (side) linke Seite f ♦ adv links; **on the ~** links; **to the ~** nach links; **the L~** (POL) die Linke f; **~-hand** adj: **~-hand drive** mit Linkssteuerung; **~-handed** adj linkshändig; **~-hand side** n linke Seite f; **~-luggage locker** n Gepäckschließfach nt; **~-luggage (office)** (BRIT) n Gepäckaufbewahrung f; **~-overs** npl Reste pl; **~-wing** adj linke(r, s)

leg [leg] n Bein nt; (of meat) Keule f; (stage) Etappe f; **1st/2nd ~** (SPORT) 1./2. Etappe

legacy ['legəsɪ] n Erbe nt, Erbschaft f

legal ['li:gl] adj gesetzlich; (allowed) legal; **~ holiday** (US) n gesetzliche(r) Feiertag m; **~ize** vt legalisieren; **~ly** adv gesetzlich; legal; **~ tender** n gesetzliche(s) Zahlungsmittel nt

legend ['ledʒənd] n Legende f; **~ary** adj legendär

leggings ['legɪŋz] npl Leggings pl

legible ['ledʒəbl] adj leserlich

legislation [ledʒɪs'leɪʃən] n Gesetzgebung f; **legislative** ['ledʒɪslətɪv] adj gesetzgebend; **legislature** ['ledʒɪslətʃər] n Legislative f

legitimate [lɪ'dʒɪtɪmət] adj rechtmäßig, legitim; (child) ehelich

legroom ['legru:m] n Platz m für die Beine

leisure ['leʒər] n Freizeit f; **to be at ~** Zeit haben; **~ centre** n Freizeitzentrum nt; **~ly** adj gemächlich

lemon ['lemən] n Zitrone f; (colour) Zitronengelb nt; **~ade** [lemə'neɪd] n Limonade f; **~ tea** n Zitronentee m

lend [lend] (pt, pp **lent**) vt leihen; **to ~ sb sth** jdm etw leihen; **~ing library** n Leihbibliothek f

length [leŋθ] n Länge f; (of road, pipe etc) Strecke f; (of material) Stück nt; **at ~** (lengthily) ausführlich; (at last) endlich; **~en** vt verlängern ♦ vi länger werden; **~ways** adv längs; **~y** adj sehr lang, langatmig

lenient ['li:nɪənt] adj nachsichtig

lens [lɛnz] n Linse f; (PHOT) Objektiv nt

Lent [lɛnt] n Fastenzeit f

lent [lɛnt] pt, pp of **lend**

lentil ['lɛntɪl] n Linse f

Leo ['li:əu] n Löwe m

leotard ['li:əta:d] n Trikot nt, Gymnastikanzug m

leper ['lɛpə*] n Leprakranke(r) f(m)

leprosy ['lɛprəsɪ] n Lepra f

lesbian ['lɛzbɪən] adj lesbisch ♦ n Lesbierin f

less [lɛs] adj, adv weniger ♦ n weniger ♦ pron weniger; **~ than half** weniger als die Hälfte; **~ than ever** weniger denn je; **~ and ~** immer weniger; **the ~ he works** je weniger er arbeitet; **~en** ['lɛsn] vi abnehmen ♦ vt verringern, verkleinern; **~er** ['lɛsə*] adj kleiner, geringer; **to a ~er extent** in geringerem Maße

lesson ['lɛsn] n (SCH) Stunde f; (unit of study) Lektion f; (fig) Lehre f; (ECCL) Lesung f; **a maths ~** eine Mathestunde

lest [lɛst] conj: **~ it happen** damit es nicht passiert

let [lɛt] (pt, pp **let**) vt lassen; (BRIT: lease) vermieten; **to ~ sb do sth** jdn etw tun lassen; **to ~ sb know sth** jdn etw wissen lassen; **~'s go!** gehen wir!; **~ him come** soll er doch kommen; **~ down** vt hinunterlassen; (disappoint) enttäuschen; **~ go** vi loslassen ♦ vt (things) loslassen; (person) gehen lassen; **~ in** vt hereinlassen; (water) durchlassen; **~ off** vt (gun) abfeuern; (steam) ablassen; (forgive) laufen lassen; **~ on** vi durchblicken lassen; (pretend) vorgeben; **~ out** vt herauslassen; (scream) fahren lassen; **~ up** vi nachlassen; (stop) aufhören

lethal ['li:θl] adj tödlich

lethargic [lɛ'θɑ:dʒɪk] adj lethargisch

letter ['lɛtə*] n Brief m; (of alphabet) Buchstabe m; **~ bomb** n Briefbombe f; **~box** (BRIT) n Briefkasten m; **~ing** n Beschriftung f; **~ of credit** n Akkreditiv m

lettuce ['lɛtɪs] n (Kopf)salat m

let-up ['lɛtʌp] (inf) n Nachlassen nt

leukaemia [lu:'ki:mɪə] (US **leukemia**) n Leukämie f

level ['lɛvl] adj (ground) eben; (at same height) auf gleicher Höhe; (equal) gleich gut; (head) kühl ♦ adv auf gleicher Höhe ♦ n (instrument) Wasserwaage f; (altitude) Höhe f; (flat place) ebene Fläche f; (position on scale) Niveau nt; (amount, degree) Grad m ♦ vt (ground) einebnen; **to draw ~ with** gleichziehen mit; **to be ~ with** auf einer Höhe sein mit; **A ~s** (BRIT) ≈ Abitur nt; **O ~s** (BRIT) ≈ mittlere Reife f; **on the ~** (fig: honest) ehrlich; **to ~ sth at sb** (blow) jdm etw versetzen; (remark) etw gegen jdn richten; **~ off** or **out** vi flach or eben werden; (fig) sich ausgleichen; (plane) horizontal fliegen ♦ vt (ground) planieren; (differences) ausgleichen; **~ crossing** (BRIT) n Bahnübergang m; **~-headed** adj vernünftig

lever ['li:və*] n Hebel m; (fig) Druckmittel nt ♦ vt (hoch)stemmen; **~age** n Hebelkraft f; (fig) Einfluss m

levy ['lɛvɪ] n (of taxes) Erhebung f; (tax) Abgaben pl; (MIL) Aushebung f ♦ vt erheben; (MIL) ausheben

lewd [lu:d] adj unzüchtig, unanständig

liability [laɪə'bɪlɪtɪ] n (burden) Belastung f; (duty) Pflicht f; (debt) Verpflichtung f; (responsibility) Haftung f; (proneness) Anfälligkeit f

liable ['laɪəbl] adj (responsible) haftbar; (prone) anfällig; **to be ~ for sth** etw dat unterliegen; **it's ~ to happen** es kann leicht vorkommen

liaise [li:'eɪz] vi: **to ~ (with sb)** (mit jdm) zusammenarbeiten; **liaison** n Verbindung f

liar ['laɪə*] n Lügner m

libel ['laɪbl] n Verleumdung f ♦ vt verleumden

liberal ['lɪbərl] adj (generous) großzügig; (open-minded) aufgeschlossen; (POL) liberal

liberate ['lɪbəreɪt] vt befreien; **liberation** [lɪbə'reɪʃən] n Befreiung f

liberty ['lɪbətɪ] n Freiheit f; (permission) Erlaubnis f; **to be at ~ to do sth** etw tun dürfen; **to take the ~ of doing sth** sich dat erlauben, etw zu tun

Libra ['li:brə] n Waage f

brarian [laɪˈbrɛərɪən] n Bibliothekar(in) m(f)

brary [ˈlaɪbrərɪ] n Bibliothek f; (lending ~) Bücherei f

ibya [ˈlɪbɪə] n Libyen nt; **~n** adj libysch ♦ n Libyer(in) m(f)

ce [laɪs] npl of **louse**

cence [ˈlaɪsns] (US **license**) n (permit) Erlaubnis f; (also: **driving ~**, (US) **driver's ~**) Führerschein m

cense [ˈlaɪsns] n (US) = **licence** ♦ vt genehmigen, konzessionieren; **~d** adj (for alcohol) konzessioniert (für den Alkoholausschank); **~ plate** (US) n (AUT) Nummernschild nt

chen [ˈlaɪkən] n Flechte f

ck [lɪk] vt lecken ♦ n Lecken nt; **a ~ of paint** ein bisschen Farbe

corice [ˈlɪkərɪs] (US) n = **liquorice**

d [lɪd] n Deckel m; (eyelid) Lid nt

e [laɪ] vi (rest, be situated) liegen; (put o.s. in position) sich legen; (pt, pp lied: tell lies) lügen ♦ n Lüge f; **to ~ low** (fig) untertauchen; **~ about** vi (things) herumliegen; (people) faulenzen; **~-down** (BRIT) n: **to have a ~-down** ein Nickerchen machen; **~-in** (BRIT) n: **to have a ~-in** sich ausschlafen

eu [luː] n: **in ~ of** anstatt +gen

eutenant [lefˈtenənt, (US) luːˈtenənt] n Leutnant m

fe [laɪf] (pl lives) n Leben nt; **~ assurance** (BRIT) n = **life insurance**; **~belt** (BRIT) n Rettungsring m; **~boat** n Rettungsboot nt; **~guard** n Rettungsschwimmer m; **~ insurance** n Lebensversicherung f; **~ jacket** n Schwimmweste f; **~less** adj (dead) leblos; (dull) langweilig; **~like** adj lebenswahr, naturgetreu; **~line** n Rettungsleine f; (fig) Rettungsanker m; **~long** adj lebenslang; **~ preserver** (US) n = **lifebelt**; **~-saver** n Lebensretter(in) m(f); **~-saving** adj lebensrettend, Rettungs-; **~ sentence** n lebenslängliche Freiheitsstrafe f; **~ span** n Lebensspanne f; **~style** n Lebensstil m; **~ support system** n (MED) Lebenserhaltungssystem nt; **~time** n: **in his ~time** während er lebte; **once in a**

~time einmal im Leben

lift [lɪft] vt hochheben ♦ vi sich heben ♦ n (BRIT: elevator) Aufzug m, Lift m; **to give sb a ~** jdn mitnehmen; **~-off** n Abheben nt (vom Boden)

ligament [ˈlɪgəmənt] n Band nt

light [laɪt] (pt, pp **lighted** or **lit**) n Licht nt; (for cigarette etc): **have you got a ~?** haben Sie Feuer? ♦ vt beleuchten; (lamp) anmachen; (fire, cigarette) anzünden ♦ adj (bright) hell; (pale) hell-; (not heavy, easy) leicht; (punishment) milde; (touch) leicht; **~s** npl (AUT) Beleuchtung f; **~ up** vi (lamp) angehen; (face) aufleuchten ♦ vt (illuminate) beleuchten; (~s) anmachen; **~ bulb** n Glühbirne f; (~ning) blitzen ♦ vt (give ~ to) erhellen; (hair) aufhellen; (gloom) aufheitern; (make less heavy) leichter machen; (fig) erleichtern; **~er** n Feuerzeug nt; **~-headed** adj (thoughtless) leichtsinnig; (giddy) schwindlig; **~-hearted** adj leichtherzig, fröhlich; **~house** n Leuchtturm m; **~ing** n (in road) Beleuchtung f; **~ly** adv leicht; (irresponsibly) leichtfertig; **to get off ~ly** mit einem blauen Auge davonkommen; **~ness** n (of weight) Leichtigkeit f; (of colour) Helle f

lightning [ˈlaɪtnɪŋ] n Blitz m; **~ conductor** (US **~ rod**) n Blitzableiter m

light: ~ pen n Lichtstift m; **~weight** adj (suit) leicht; (BOXING) Leichtgewichtler m; **~ year** n Lichtjahr nt

like [laɪk] vt mögen, gern haben ♦ prep wie ♦ adj (similar) ähnlich; (equal) gleich ♦ n: **the ~** dergleichen; **I would** or **I'd ~** ich möchte gern; **would you ~ a coffee?** möchten Sie einen Kaffee?; **to be** or **look ~ sb/sth** jdm/etw ähneln; **that's just ~ him** das ist typisch für ihn; **do it ~ this** mach es so; **it is nothing ~ ...** es ist nicht zu vergleichen mit ...; **what does it look ~?** wie sieht es aus?; **what does it sound ~?** wie hört es sich an?; **what does it taste ~?** wie schmeckt es?; **his ~s and dislikes** was er mag und was er nicht mag; **~able** adj sympathisch

likelihood [ˈlaɪklɪhud] n Wahrscheinlichkeit f

likely ['laɪklɪ] *adj* wahrscheinlich; **he's ~ to leave** er geht möglicherweise; **not ~!** wohl kaum!

likeness ['laɪknɪs] *n* Ähnlichkeit *f*; (*portrait*) Bild *nt*

likewise ['laɪkwaɪz] *adv* ebenso

liking ['laɪkɪŋ] *n* Zuneigung *f*; (*taste*) Vorliebe *f*

lilac ['laɪlək] *n* Flieder *m* ♦ *adj* (*colour*) fliederfarben

lily ['lɪlɪ] *n* Lilie *f*; **~ of the valley** *n* Maiglöckchen *nt*

limb [lɪm] *n* Glied *nt*

limber up ['lɪmbər-] *vi* sich auflockern; (*fig*) sich vorbereiten

limbo ['lɪmbəʊ] *n*: **to be in ~** (*fig*) in der Schwebe sein

lime [laɪm] *n* (*tree*) Linde *f*; (*fruit*) Limone *f*; (*substance*) Kalk *m*

limelight ['laɪmlaɪt] *n*: **to be in the ~** (*fig*) im Rampenlicht stehen

limestone ['laɪmstəʊn] *n* Kalkstein *m*

limit ['lɪmɪt] *n* Grenze *f*; (*inf*) Höhe *f* ♦ *vt* begrenzen, einschränken; **~ation** [lɪmɪ'teɪʃən] *n* Einschränkung *f*; **~ed** *adj* beschränkt; **to be ~ed to** sich beschränken auf **+acc**; **~ed (liability) company** (*BRIT*) *n* Gesellschaft *f* mit beschränkter Haftung

limousine ['lɪməziːn] *n* Limousine *f*

limp [lɪmp] *n* Hinken *nt* ♦ *vi* hinken ♦ *adj* schlaff

limpet ['lɪmpɪt] *n* (*fig*) Klette *f*

line [laɪn] *n* Linie *f*; (*rope*) Leine *f*; (*on face*) Falte *f*; (*row*) Reihe *f*; (*of hills*) Kette *f*; (*US: queue*) Schlange *f*; (*company*) Linie *f*, Gesellschaft *f*; (*RAIL*) Strecke *f*; (*TEL*) Leitung *f*; (*written*) Zeile *f*; (*direction*) Richtung *f*; (*fig: business*) Branche *f*; (*range of items*) Kollektion *f* ♦ *vt* (*coat*) füttern; (*border*) säumen; **~s** *npl* (*RAIL*) Gleise *pl*; **in ~ with** in Übereinstimmung mit; **~ up** *vi* sich aufstellen ♦ *vt* aufstellen; (*prepare*) sorgen für; (*support*) mobilisieren; (*surprise*) planen; **~ar** ['lɪnɪər] *adj* gerade; (*measure*) Längen-; **~d** *adj* (*face*) faltig; (*paper*) liniert

linen ['lɪnɪn] *n* Leinen *nt*; (*sheets etc*) Wäsche *f*

liner ['laɪnər] *n* Überseedampfer *m*

linesman ['laɪnzmən] (*irreg*) *n* (*SPORT*) Linienrichter *m*

line-up ['laɪnʌp] *n* Aufstellung *f*

linger ['lɪŋgər] *vi* (*remain long*) verweilen; (*taste*) (zurück)bleiben; (*delay*) zögern, verharren

lingerie ['lænʒəriː] *n* Damenunterwäsche *f*

lingering ['lɪŋgərɪŋ] *adj* (*doubt*) zurückbleibend; (*disease*) langwierig; (*taste*) nachhaltend; (*look*) lang

lingo ['lɪŋgəʊ] (*pl* **~es**) (*inf*) *n* Sprache *f*

linguist ['lɪŋgwɪst] *n* Sprachkundige(r) *m/f*; (*UNIV*) Sprachwissenschaftler(in) *m(f)*; **~ic** [lɪŋ'gwɪstɪk] *adj* sprachlich; sprachwissenschaftlich; **~ics** *n* Sprachwissenschaft *f*, Linguistik *f*

lining ['laɪnɪŋ] *n* Futter *nt*

link [lɪŋk] *n* Glied *nt*; (*connection*) Verbindung *f* ♦ *vt* verbinden; **~s** *npl* (*GOLF*) Golfplatz *m*; **~ up** *vt* verbinden ♦ *vi* zusammenkommen; (*companies*) sich zusammenschließen; **~-up** *n* (*TEL*) Verbindung *f*; (*of spaceships*) Kopplung *f*

lino ['laɪnəʊ] *n* = **linoleum**

linoleum [lɪ'nəʊlɪəm] *n* Linoleum *nt*

linseed oil ['lɪnsiːd-] *n* Leinöl *nt*

lion ['laɪən] *n* Löwe *m*; **~ess** *n* Löwin *f*

lip [lɪp] *n* Lippe *f*; (*of jug*) Schnabel *m*; **to pay ~ service (to)** ein Lippenbekenntnis ablegen (zu)

liposuction ['lɪpəʊsʌkʃən] *n* Fettabsaugen *nt*

lip: **~read** (*irreg*) *vi* von den Lippen ablesen; **~ salve** *n* Lippenbalsam *m*; **~stick** *n* Lippenstift *m*

liqueur [lɪ'kjuər] *n* Likör *m*

liquid ['lɪkwɪd] *n* Flüssigkeit *f* ♦ *adj* flüssig

liquidate ['lɪkwɪdeɪt] *vt* liquidieren

liquidize ['lɪkwɪdaɪz] *vt* (*COOK*) (im Mixer) pürieren; **~r** ['lɪkwɪdaɪzər] *n* Mixgerät *nt*

liquor ['lɪkər] *n* Alkohol *m*

liquorice ['lɪkərɪs] (*BRIT*) *n* Lakritze *f*

liquor store (*US*) *n* Spirituosengeschäft *nt*

Lisbon ['lɪzbən] *n* Lissabon *nt*

lisp [lɪsp] *n* Lispeln *nt* ♦ *vt, vi* lispeln

list [lɪst] *n* Liste *f*, Verzeichnis *nt*; (*of ship*) Schlagseite *f* ♦ *vt* (*write down*) eine Liste

machen von; (verbally) aufzählen ♦ vi (ship)
Schlagseite haben

listen ['lɪsn] vi hören; ~ **to** vt zuhören +dat;
~**er** n (Zu)hörer(in) m(f)

listless ['lɪstlɪs] adj lustlos

lit [lɪt] pt, pp of **light**

liter ['liːtər] (US) n = **litre**

literacy ['lɪtərəsɪ] n Fähigkeit f zu lesen und
zu schreiben

literal ['lɪtərəl] adj buchstäblich; (translation)
wortwörtlich; ~**ly** adv wörtlich;
buchstäblich

literary ['lɪtərərɪ] adj literarisch

literate ['lɪtərət] adj des Lesens und
Schreibens kundig

literature ['lɪtərɪtʃər] n Literatur f

litigation [lɪtɪ'geɪʃən] n Prozess m

litre ['liːtər] (US **liter**) n Liter m

litter ['lɪtər] n (rubbish) Abfall m; (of animals)
Wurf m ♦ vt in Unordnung bringen; **to be
~ed with** übersät sein mit; ~ **bin** (BRIT) n
Abfalleimer m

little ['lɪtl] adj klein ♦ adv, n wenig; **a** ~ ein
bisschen; ~ **by** ~ nach und nach

live[1] [laɪv] adj lebendig; (MIL) scharf; (ELEC)
geladen; (broadcast) live

live[2] [lɪv] vi leben; (dwell) wohnen ♦ vt (life)
führen; ~ **down** vt: **I'll never ~ it down**
das wird man mir nie vergessen; ~ **on** vi
weiterleben ♦ vt fus: **to ~ on sth** von etw
leben; ~ **together** vi zusammenleben;
(share a flat) zusammenwohnen; ~ **up to**
vt (standards) gerecht werden +dat;
(principles) anstreben; (hopes) entsprechen
+dat

livelihood ['laɪvlɪhʊd] n Lebensunterhalt m

lively ['laɪvlɪ] adj lebhaft, lebendig

liven up ['laɪvn-] vt beleben

liver ['lɪvər] n (ANAT) Leber f

lives [laɪvz] pl of **life**

livestock ['laɪvstɒk] n Vieh nt

livid ['lɪvɪd] adj bläulich; (furious)
fuchsteufelswild

living ['lɪvɪŋ] n (Lebens)unterhalt m ♦ adj
lebendig; (language etc) lebend; **to earn** or
make a ~ sich dat seinen Lebensunterhalt
verdienen; ~ **conditions** npl

Wohnverhältnisse pl; ~ **room** n
Wohnzimmer nt; ~ **standards** npl
Lebensstandard m; ~ **wage** n
ausreichender Lohn m

lizard ['lɪzəd] n Eidechse f

load [ləʊd] n (burden) Last f; (amount)
Ladung f ♦ vt (also: ~ **up**) (be)laden;
(COMPUT) laden; (camera) Film einlegen in
+acc; (gun) laden; **a ~ of**, ~**s of** (fig) jede
Menge; ~**ed** adj beladen; (dice) präpariert;
(question) Fang-; (inf: rich) steinreich; ~**ing
bay** n Ladeplatz m

loaf [ləʊf] (pl **loaves**) n Brot nt ♦ vi (also: ~
about, ~ **around**) herumlungern, faulenzen

loan [ləʊn] n Leihgabe f; (FIN) Darlehen nt
♦ vt leihen; **on** ~ geliehen

loath [ləʊθ] adj: **to be ~ to do sth** etw
ungern tun

loathe [ləʊð] vt verabscheuen

loaves [ləʊvz] pl of **loaf**

lobby ['lɒbɪ] n Vorhalle f; (POL) Lobby f ♦ vt
politisch beeinflussen (wollen)

lobster ['lɒbstər] n Hummer m

local ['ləʊkl] adj ortsansässig, Orts- ♦ n (pub)
Stammwirtschaft f; **the ~s** npl (people) die
Ortsansässigen pl; ~ **anaesthetic** n (MED)
örtliche Betäubung f; ~ **authority** n
städtische Behörden pl; ~ **call** n (TEL)
Ortsgespräch nt; ~ **government** n
Gemeinde-/Kreisverwaltung f; ~**ity**
[ləʊ'kælɪtɪ] n Ort m; ~**ly** adv örtlich, am Ort

locate [ləʊ'keɪt] vt ausfindig machen;
(establish) errichten; **location** [ləʊ'keɪʃən] n
Platz m, Lage f; **on location** (CINE) auf
Außenaufnahme

loch [lɒx] (SCOTTISH) n See m

lock [lɒk] n Schloss nt; (NAUT) Schleuse f; (of
hair) Locke f ♦ vt (fasten) (ver)schließen ♦ vi
(door etc) sich schließen (lassen); (wheels)
blockieren; ~ **up** vt (criminal, mental patient)
einsperren; (house) abschließen

locker ['lɒkər] n Spind m

locket ['lɒkɪt] n Medaillon nt

lock ['lɒk-]: ~**out** n Aussperrung f; ~**smith** n
Schlosser(in) m(f); ~**up** n (jail) Gefängnis nt;
(garage) Garage f

locum ['ləʊkəm] n (MED) Vertreter(in) m(f)

lodge [lɔdʒ] n (*gatehouse*) Pförtnerhaus nt; (*freemasons'*) Loge f ♦ vi (*get stuck*) stecken (bleiben); (*in Untermiete*): **to ~ (with)** wohnen (bei) ♦ vt (*protest*) einreichen; ~r n (Unter)mieter m; **lodgings** n (Miet)wohnung f

loft [lɔft] n (Dach)boden m

lofty ['lɔftɪ] adj hoch(ragend); (*proud*) hochmütig

log [lɔg] n Klotz m; (*book*) = **logbook**

logbook ['lɔgbʊk] n Bordbuch nt; (*for lorry*) Fahrtenschreiber m; (*AUT*) Kraftfahrzeugbrief m

loggerheads ['lɔgəhɛdz] npl: **to be at ~** sich in den Haaren liegen

logic ['lɔdʒɪk] n Logik f; ~al adj logisch

log in *or* **on** vi (*COMPUT*) einloggen

log off *or* **out** vi (*COMPUT*) ausloggen

logistics [lɔ'dʒɪstɪks] npl Logistik f

logo ['ləʊgəʊ] n Firmenzeichen nt

loin [lɔɪn] n Lende f

loiter ['lɔɪtəʳ] vi herumstehen

loll [lɔl] vi (*also:* **~ about**) sich rekeln *or* räkeln

lollipop ['lɔlɪpɔp] n (Dauer)lutscher m; **~ man/lady** (*irreg, BRIT*) n ≃ Schülerlotse m

---
Lollipop man/lady

ⓘ **Lollipop man/lady** *heißen in Großbritannien die Männer bzw. Frauen, die mit Hilfe eines runden Stopp-schildes den Verkehr anhalten, damit Schulkinder die Straße überqueren können. Der Name bezieht sich auf die Form des Schildes, die an einen Lutscher erinnert.*

---

lolly ['lɔlɪ] (*inf*) n (*sweet*) Lutscher m

London ['lʌndən] n London nt; ~er n Londoner(in) m(f)

lone [ləʊn] adj einsam

loneliness ['ləʊnlɪnɪs] n Einsamkeit f

lonely ['ləʊnlɪ] adj einsam

loner ['ləʊnəʳ] n Einzelgänger(in) m(f)

long [lɔŋ] adj lang; (*distance*) weit ♦ adv lange ♦ vi: **to ~ for** sich sehnen nach; **before ~** bald; **as ~ as** solange; **in the ~ run** auf die Dauer; **don't be ~!** beeil dich!;

how ~ is the street? wie lang ist die Straße?; **how ~ is the lesson?** wie lange dauert die Stunde?; **6 metres ~** 6 Meter lang; **6 months ~** 6 Monate lang; **all night ~** die ganze Nacht; **he no ~er comes** er kommt nicht mehr; **~ ago** vor langer Zeit; **~ before** lange vorher; **at ~ last** endlich; **~-distance** adj Fern-

longevity [lɔn'dʒevɪtɪ] n Langlebigkeit f

long: ~-haired adj langhaarig; **~hand** n Langschrift f; **~ing** n Sehnsucht f ♦ adj sehnsüchtig

longitude ['lɔŋgɪtjuːd] n Längengrad m

long: ~ jump n Weitsprung m; **~-life** adj (*batteries etc*) mit langer Lebensdauer; **~-lost** adj längst verloren geglaubt; **~-playing record** n Langspielplatte f; **~-range** adj Langstrecken-, Fern-; **~-sighted** adj weitsichtig; **~-standing** adj alt, seit langer Zeit bestehend; **~-suffering** adj schwer geprüft; **~-term** adj langfristig; **~wave** n Langwelle f; **~-winded** adj langatmig

loo [luː] (*BRIT: inf*) n Klo nt

look [lʊk] vi schauen; (*seem*) aussehen; (*building etc*): **to ~ on to the sea** aufs Meer gehen ♦ n Blick m; **~s** npl (*appearance*) Aussehen nt; **~ after** vt (*care for*) sorgen für; (*watch*) aufpassen auf +acc; **~ at** vt ansehen; (*consider*) sich überlegen; **~ back** vi sich umsehen; (*fig*) zurückblicken; **~ down on** vt (*fig*) herabsehen auf +acc; **~ for** vt (*seek*) suchen; **~ forward to** vt sich freuen auf +acc; (*in letters*): **we ~ forward to hearing from you** wir hoffen, bald von Ihnen zu hören; **~ into** vt untersuchen; **~ on** vi zusehen; **~ out** vi hinaussehen; (*take care*) aufpassen; **~ out for** vt Ausschau halten nach; (*be careful*) Acht geben auf +acc; **~ round** vi sich umsehen; **~ to** vt (*take care of*) Acht geben auf +acc; (*rely on*) sich verlassen auf +acc; **~ up** vi aufblicken; (*improve*) sich bessern ♦ vt (*word*) nachschlagen; (*person*) besuchen; **~ up to** vt aufsehen zu; **~out** n (*watch*) Ausschau f; (*person*) Wachposten m; (*place*) Ausguck m; (*prospect*) Aussichten pl; **to be on the ~ out**

for sth nach etw Ausschau halten
oom [lu:m] n Webstuhl m ♦ vi sich
abzeichnen
oony ['lu:nɪ] (inf) n Verrückte(r) mf
oop [lu:p] n Schlaufe f; ~**hole** n (fig)
Hintertürchen nt
oose [lu:s] adj lose, locker; (free) frei;
(inexact) unpräzise ♦ vt lösen, losbinden; ~
change n Kleingeld nt; ~ **chippings** npl
(on road) Rollsplit m; ~ **end** n: **to be at a ~
end** (BRIT) or **at ~ ends** (US) nicht wissen,
was man tun soll; ~**ly** adv locker, lose; ~**n**
vt lockern, losmachen
oot [lu:t] n Beute f ♦ vt plündern
op off [lɔp-] vt abhacken
opsided ['lɔp'saɪdɪd] adj schief
ord [lɔ:d] n (ruler) Herr m; (BRIT: title) Lord
m; **the L~** (God) der Herr; **the (House of)
L~s** das Oberhaus; ~**ship** n: **Your L~ship**
Eure Lordschaft
orry ['lɔrɪ] (BRIT) n Lastwagen m; ~ **driver**
(BRIT) n Lastwagenfahrer(in) m(f)
ose [lu:z] (pt, pp **lost**) vt verlieren; (chance)
verpassen ♦ vi verlieren; **to ~ (time)** (clock)
nachgehen; ~**r** n Verlierer m
oss [lɔs] n Verlust m; **at a ~** (COMM) mit
Verlust; (unable) außerstande, außer Stande
ost [lɔst] pt, pp of **lose** ♦ adj verloren; ~
property (US ~ **and found**) n Fundsachen
pl
ot [lɔt] n (quantity) Menge f; (fate, at auction)
Los nt; (inf: people, things) Haufen m; **the ~**
alles; (people) alle; **a ~ of** (with sg) viel; (with
pl) viele; ~**s of** massenhaft, viel(e); **I read a
~** ich lese viel; **to draw ~s for sth** etw verlosen
otion ['ləʊʃən] n Lotion f
ottery ['lɔtərɪ] n Lotterie f
oud [laud] adj laut; (showy) schreiend ♦ adv
laut; ~**ly** adv laut; ~**speaker** n
Lautsprecher m
ounge [laundʒ] n (in hotel)
Gesellschaftsraum m; (in house)
Wohnzimmer nt ♦ vi sich herumlümmeln
ouse [laus] (pl **lice**) n Laus f
ousy ['lauzɪ] adj (fig) miserabel
out [laut] n Lümmel m

louvre ['lu:vər] (US **louver**) adj (door, window)
Jalousie-
lovable ['lʌvəbl] adj liebenswert
love [lʌv] n Liebe f; (person) Liebling m;
(SPORT) null ♦ vt (person) lieben; (activity)
gerne mögen; **to be in ~ with sb** in jdn
verliebt sein; **to make ~** sich lieben; **for the
~ of** aus Liebe zu; **"15 ~"** (TENNIS) „15
null"; **to ~ to do sth** etw (sehr) gerne tun;
~ **affair** n (Liebes)verhältnis nt; ~ **letter** n
Liebesbrief m; ~ **life** n Liebesleben nt
lovely ['lʌvlɪ] adj schön
lover ['lʌvər] n Liebhaber(in) m(f)
loving ['lʌvɪŋ] adj liebend, liebevoll
low [ləu] adj niedrig; (rank) niedere(r, s);
(level, note, neckline) tief; (intelligence, density)
gering; (vulgar) ordinär; (not loud) leise;
(depressed) gedrückt ♦ adv (not high)
niedrig; (not loudly) leise ♦ n (~ point)
Tiefstand m; (MET) Tief nt; **to feel ~** sich
mies fühlen; **to turn (down)** ~ leiser stellen;
~ **alcohol** adj alkoholarm; ~~**calorie** adj
kalorienarm; ~~**cut** adj (dress) tief
ausgeschnitten; ~**er** vt herunterlassen;
(eyes, gun) senken; (reduce) herabsetzen,
senken ♦ vr: **to ~er o.s. to** (fig) sich
herablassen zu; ~**er sixth** (BRIT) n (SCOL) ≈
zwölfte Klasse; ~~**fat** adj fettarm, Mager-;
~**lands** npl (GEOG) Flachland nt; ~**ly** adj
bescheiden; ~~**lying** adj tief gelegen
loyal ['lɔɪəl] adj treu; ~**ty** n Treue f; ~**ty
card** n Kundenkarte f
lozenge ['lɔzɪndʒ] n Pastille f
L-plates ['ɛlpleɪts] (BRIT) npl L-Schild nt

L-Plates

ℹ Als **L-Plates** werden in Großbritannien
die weißen Schilder mit einem roten „L"
bezeichnet, die an jedem von einem
Fahrschüler geführten Fahrzeug befestigt
werden müssen. Fahrschüler bekommen einen
vorläufigen Führerschein und dürfen damit
unter Aufsicht eines erfahrenen Autofahrers
auf allen Straßen außer Autobahnen fahren.

Ltd abbr (= limited company) GmbH
lubricant ['lu:brɪkənt] n Schmiermittel nt

lubricate ['lu:brɪkeɪt] vt schmieren
lucid ['lu:sɪd] adj klar; (sane) bei klarem
Verstand; (moment) licht
luck [lʌk] n Glück nt; **bad** or **hard** or **tough**
~! (so ein) Pech!; **good ~!** viel Glück!; **~ily**
adv glücklicherweise, zum Glück; **~y** adj
Glücks-; **to be ~y** Glück haben
lucrative ['lu:krətɪv] adj einträglich
ludicrous ['lu:dɪkrəs] adj grotesk
lug [lʌg] vt schleppen
luggage ['lʌgɪdʒ] n Gepäck nt; **~ rack** n
Gepäcknetz nt
lukewarm ['lu:kwɔ:m] adj lauwarm;
(indifferent) lau
lull [lʌl] n Flaute f ♦ vt einlullen; (calm)
beruhigen
lullaby ['lʌləbaɪ] n Schlaflied nt
lumbago [lʌm'beɪgəu] n Hexenschuss m
lumber ['lʌmbəʳ] n Plunder m; (wood) Holz
nt; **~jack** n Holzfäller m
luminous ['lu:mɪnəs] adj Leucht-
lump [lʌmp] n Klumpen m; (MED)
Schwellung f; (in breast) Knoten m; (of
sugar) Stück nt ♦ vt (also: **~ together**)
zusammentun; (judge together) in einen
Topf werfen; **~ sum** n Pauschalsumme f;
~y adj klumpig
lunacy ['lu:nəsɪ] n Irrsinn m
lunar ['lu:nəʳ] adj Mond-
lunatic ['lu:nətɪk] n Wahnsinnige(r) mf ♦ adj
wahnsinnig, irr
lunch [lʌntʃ] n Mittagessen nt; **~eon**
['lʌntʃən] n Mittagessen nt; **~eon meat** n
Frühstücksfleisch nt; **~eon voucher** (BRIT)
n Essenmarke f; **~time** n Mittagszeit f
lung [lʌŋ] n Lunge f
lunge [lʌndʒ] vi (also: **~ forward**)
(los)stürzen; **to ~ at** sich stürzen auf +acc
lurch [lɜ:tʃ] vi taumeln; (NAUT) schlingern ♦ n
Ruck m; (NAUT) Schlingern nt; **to leave sb
in the ~** jdn im Stich lassen
lure [luəʳ] n Köder m; (fig) Lockung f ♦ vt
(ver)locken
lurid ['luərɪd] adj (shocking) grausig,
widerlich; (colour) grell
lurk [lɜ:k] vi lauern
luscious ['lʌʃəs] adj köstlich

lush [lʌʃ] adj satt; (vegetation) üppig
lust [lʌst] n Wollust f; (greed) Gier f ♦ vi: **to ~
after** gieren nach
lustre ['lʌstəʳ] (US **luster**) n Glanz m
Luxembourg ['lʌksəmbə:g] n Luxemburg nt
luxuriant [lʌg'zjuərɪənt] adj üppig
luxurious [lʌg'zjuərɪəs] adj luxuriös, Luxus-
luxury ['lʌkʃərɪ] n Luxus m ♦ cpd Luxus-
lying ['laɪɪŋ] n Lügen nt ♦ adj verlogen
lynx [lɪŋks] n Luchs m
lyric ['lɪrɪk] n Lyrik f ♦ adj lyrisch; **~s** pl (words
for song) (Lied)text m; **~al** adj lyrisch,
gefühlvoll

M, m

m abbr = **metre**; **mile**; **million**
M.A. n abbr = **Master of Arts**
mac [mæk] (BRIT: inf) n Regenmantel m
macaroni [mækə'rəunɪ] n Makkaroni pl
machine [mə'ʃi:n] n Maschine f ♦ vt (dress
etc) mit der Maschine nähen; **~ gun** n
Maschinengewehr nt; **~ language** n
(COMPUT) Maschinensprache f; **~ry** n
Maschinerie f
macho ['mætʃəu] adj macho
mackerel ['mækrɪl] n Makrele f
mackintosh ['mækɪntɒʃ] (BRIT) n
Regenmantel m
mad [mæd] adj verrückt; (dog) tollwütig;
(angry) wütend; **~ about** (fond of) verrückt
nach, versessen auf +acc
madam ['mædəm] n gnädige Frau f
madden ['mædn] vt verrückt machen; (make
angry) ärgern
made [meɪd] pt, pp of **make**
made-to-measure ['meɪdtə'meʒəʳ] (BRIT)
adj Maß-
mad [mæd-]: **~ly** adv wahnsinnig; **~man**
(irreg) n Verrückte(r) m, Irre(r) m; **~ness** n
Wahnsinn m
magazine [mægə'zi:n] n Zeitschrift f; (in
gun) Magazin nt
maggot ['mægət] n Made f
magic ['mædʒɪk] n Zauberei f, Magie f; (fig)
Zauber m ♦ adj magisch, Zauber-; **~al** adj

magisch; **~ian** [məˈdʒɪʃən] n Zauberer m

magistrate [ˈmædʒɪstreɪt] n (Friedens)richter m

magnanimous [mægˈnænɪməs] adj großmütig

magnet [ˈmægnɪt] n Magnet m; **~ic** [mægˈnetɪk] adj magnetisch; **~ic tape** n Magnetband nt; **~ism** n Magnetismus m; (fig) Ausstrahlungskraft f

magnificent [mægˈnɪfɪsnt] adj großartig

magnify [ˈmægnɪfaɪ] vt vergrößern; **~ing glass** n Lupe f

magnitude [ˈmægnɪtjuːd] n (size) Größe f; (importance) Ausmaß nt

magpie [ˈmægpaɪ] n Elster f

mahogany [məˈhɒgənɪ] n Mahagoni nt ♦ cpd Mahagoni-

maid [meɪd] n Dienstmädchen nt; **old ~** alte Jungfer f

maiden [ˈmeɪdn] n Maid f ♦ adj (flight, speech) Jungfern-; **~ name** n Mädchenname m

mail [meɪl] n Post f ♦ vt aufgeben; **~ box** (US) n Briefkasten m; **~ing list** n Anschreibeliste f; **~ order** n Bestellung f durch die Post; **~ order firm** n Versandhaus nt

maim [meɪm] vt verstümmeln

main [meɪn] adj hauptsächlich, Haupt- ♦ n (pipe) Hauptleitung f; **the ~s** npl (ELEC) das Stromnetz; **in the ~** im Großen und Ganzen; **~frame** n (COMPUT) Großrechner m; **~land** n Festland nt; **~ly** adv hauptsächlich; **~ road** n Hauptstraße f; **~stay** n (fig) Hauptstütze f; **~stream** n Hauptrichtung f

maintain [meɪnˈteɪn] vt (machine, roads) instand or in Stand halten; (support) unterhalten; (keep up) aufrechterhalten; (claim) behaupten; (innocence) beteuern

maintenance [ˈmeɪntənəns] n (TECH) Wartung f; (of family) Unterhalt m

maize [meɪz] n Mais m

majestic [məˈdʒestɪk] adj majestätisch

majesty [ˈmædʒɪstɪ] n Majestät f

major [ˈmeɪdʒəʳ] n Major m ♦ adj (MUS) Dur; (more important) Haupt-; (bigger) größer

Majorca [məˈjɔːkə] n Mallorca nt

majority [məˈdʒɒrɪtɪ] n Mehrheit f; (JUR) Volljährigkeit f

make [meɪk] (pt, pp made) vt machen; (appoint) ernennen (zu); (cause to do sth) veranlassen; (reach) erreichen; (in time) schaffen; (earn) verdienen ♦ n Marke f; **to ~ sth happen** etw geschehen lassen; **to ~ it** es schaffen; **what time do you ~ it?** wie spät hast du es?; **to ~ do with** auskommen mit; **~ for** vi gehen/fahren nach; **~ out** vt (write out) ausstellen; (understand) verstehen; **~ up** vt machen; (face) schminken; (quarrel) beilegen; (story etc) erfinden ♦ vi sich versöhnen; **~ up for** vt wieder gutmachen; (COMM) vergüten; **~-believe** n Fantasie f; **~r** n (COMM) Hersteller m; **~shift** adj behelfsmäßig, Not-; **~-up** n Schminke f, Make-up nt; **~-up remover** n Make-up-Entferner m; **making** n: **in the making** im Entstehen; **to have the makings of** das Zeug haben zu

malaria [məˈlɛərɪə] n Malaria f

Malaysia [məˈleɪzɪə] n Malaysia nt

male [meɪl] n Mann m; (animal) Männchen nt ♦ adj männlich

malevolent [məˈlevələnt] adj übel wollend

malfunction [mælˈfʌŋkʃən] n (MED) Funktionsstörung f; (of machine) Defekt m

malice [ˈmælɪs] n Bosheit f; **malicious** [məˈlɪʃəs] adj böswillig, gehässig

malign [məˈlaɪn] vt verleumden ♦ adj böse

malignant [məˈlɪgnənt] adj bösartig

mall [mɔːl] n (also: **shopping ~**) Einkaufszentrum nt

malleable [ˈmælɪəbl] adj formbar

mallet [ˈmælɪt] n Holzhammer m

malnutrition [mælnjuːˈtrɪʃən] n Unterernährung f

malpractice [mælˈpræktɪs] n Amtsvergehen nt

malt [mɔːlt] n Malz nt

Malta [ˈmɔːltə] n Malta nt; **Maltese** [mɔːlˈtiːz] adj inv maltesisch ♦ n inv Malteser(in) m(f)

maltreat [mælˈtriːt] vt misshandeln

mammal [ˈmæml] n Säugetier nt

mammoth ['mæməθ] n Mammut nt ♦ adj Mammut-

man [mæn] (pl **men**) n Mann m; (human race) der Mensch, die Menschen pl ♦ vt bemannen; **an old ~** ein alter Mann, ein Greis m; **~ and wife** Mann und Frau

manage ['mænɪdʒ] vi zurechtkommen ♦ vt (control) führen, leiten; (cope with) fertig werden mit; **~able** adj (person, animal) fügsam; (object) handlich; **~ment** n (control) Führung f, Leitung f; (directors) Management nt; **~r** n Geschäftsführer m; **~ress** [mænɪdʒə'rɛs] n Geschäftsführerin f; **~rial** [mænɪ'dʒɪərɪəl] adj (post) leitend; (problem etc) Management-; **managing** ['mænɪdʒɪŋ] adj: **managing director** Betriebsleiter m

mandarin ['mændərɪn] n (fruit) Mandarine f

mandatory ['mændətərɪ] adj obligatorisch

mane [meɪn] n Mähne f

maneuver [mə'nuːvər] (US) = **manoeuvre**

manfully ['mænfəlɪ] adv mannhaft

mangle ['mæŋgl] vt verstümmeln ♦ n Mangel f

mango ['mæŋgəʊ] (pl **~es**) n Mango(pflaume) f

mangy ['meɪndʒɪ] adj (dog) räudig

man [mæn-]: **~handle** vt grob behandeln; **~hole** n (Straßen)schacht m; **~hood** n Mannesalter nt; (~liness) Männlichkeit f; **~-hour** n Arbeitsstunde f; **~hunt** n Fahndung f

mania ['meɪnɪə] n Manie f; **~c** ['meɪnɪæk] n Wahnsinnige(r) mf

manic ['mænɪk] adj (behaviour, activity) hektisch

manicure ['mænɪkjʊər] n Maniküre f; **~ set** n Necessaire nt, Nessessär nt

manifest ['mænɪfɛst] vt offenbaren ♦ adj offenkundig; **~ation** [mænɪfɛs'teɪʃən] n (sign) Anzeichen nt

manifesto [mænɪ'fɛstəʊ] n Manifest nt

manipulate [mə'nɪpjʊleɪt] vt handhaben; (fig) manipulieren

man [mæn-]: **~kind** n Menschheit f; **~ly** ['mænlɪ] adj männlich; mannhaft; **~-made** adj (fibre) künstlich

manner ['mænər] n Art f, Weise f; **~s** npl (behaviour) Manieren pl; **in a ~ of speaking** sozusagen; **~ism** n (of person) Angewohnheit f; (of style) Manieriertheit f

manoeuvre [mə'nuːvər] (US **maneuver**) vt, vi manövrieren ♦ n (MIL) Feldzug m; (general) Manöver nt, Schachzug m

manor ['mænər] n Landgut nt

manpower ['mænpaʊər] n Arbeitskräfte pl

mansion ['mænʃən] n Villa f

manslaughter ['mænslɔːtər] n Totschlag m

mantelpiece ['mæntlpiːs] n Kaminsims m

manual ['mænjʊəl] adj manuell, Hand- ♦ n Handbuch nt

manufacture [mænjʊ'fæktʃər] vt herstellen ♦ n Herstellung f; **~r** n Hersteller m

manure [mə'njʊər] n Dünger m

manuscript ['mænjʊskrɪpt] n Manuskript nt

Manx [mæŋks] adj der Insel Man

many ['mɛnɪ] adj, pron viele; **a great ~** sehr viele; **~ a time** oft

map [mæp] n (Land)karte f; (of town) Stadtplan m ♦ vt eine Karte machen von; **~ out** vt (fig) ausarbeiten

maple ['meɪpl] n Ahorn m

mar [mɑːr] vt verderben

marathon ['mærəθən] n (SPORT) Marathonlauf m; (fig) Marathon m

marble ['mɑːbl] n Marmor m; (for game) Murmel f

March [mɑːtʃ] n März m

march [mɑːtʃ] vi marschieren ♦ n Marsch m

mare [mɛər] n Stute f

margarine [mɑːdʒə'riːn] n Margarine f

margin ['mɑːdʒɪn] n Rand m; (extra amount) Spielraum m; (COMM) Spanne f; **~al** adj (note) Rand-; (difference etc) geringfügig; **~al (seat)** n (POL) Wahlkreis, der nur mit knapper Mehrheit gehalten wird

marigold ['mærɪɡəʊld] n Ringelblume f

marijuana [mærɪ'wɑːnə] n Marihuana nt

marina [mə'riːnə] n Jachthafen m

marinate ['mærɪneɪt] vt marinieren

marine [mə'riːn] adj Meeres-, See- ♦ n (MIL) Marineinfanterist m

marital ['mærɪtl] adj ehelich, Ehe-; **~ status** n Familienstand m

maritime ['mærɪtaɪm] adj See-

mark [mɑːk] n (HIST: coin) Mark f; (spot) Fleck m; (scar) Kratzer m; (sign) Zeichen nt; (target) Ziel nt; (SCH) Note f ♦ vt (make ~ on) Flecken/Kratzer machen auf +acc; (indicate) markieren; (exam) korrigieren; to ~ time (also fig) auf der Stelle treten; ~ out vt bestimmen; (area) abstecken; ~ed adj deutlich; ~er n (in book) (Lese)zeichen nt; (on road) Schild nt

market ['mɑːkɪt] n Markt m; (stock ~) Börse f ♦ vt (COMM: new product) auf den Markt bringen; (sell) vertreiben; ~ garden (BRIT) n Handelsgärtnerei f; ~ing n Marketing nt; ~ research n Marktforschung f; ~ value n Marktwert m

marksman ['mɑːksmən] (irreg) n Scharfschütze m

marmalade ['mɑːməleɪd] n Orangenmarmelade f

maroon [mə'ruːn] vt aussetzen ♦ adj (colour) kastanienbraun

marquee [mɑː'kiː] n große(s) Zelt nt

marriage ['mærɪdʒ] n Ehe f; (wedding) Heirat f; ~ bureau n Heiratsinstitut nt; ~ certificate n Heiratsurkunde f

married ['mærɪd] adj (person) verheiratet; (couple, life) Ehe-

marrow ['mærəʊ] n (Knochen)mark nt; (BOT) Kürbis m

marry ['mærɪ] vt (join) trauen; (take as husband, wife) heiraten ♦ vi (also: get married) heiraten

marsh [mɑːʃ] n Sumpf m

marshal ['mɑːʃl] n (US) Bezirkspolizeichef m ♦ vt (an)ordnen, arrangieren

marshy ['mɑːʃɪ] adj sumpfig

martial law ['mɑːʃl] n Kriegsrecht nt

martyr ['mɑːtə*] n (also fig) Märtyrer(in) m(f) ♦ vt zum Märtyrer machen; ~dom n Martyrium nt

marvel ['mɑːvl] n Wunder nt ♦ vi: to ~ (at) sich wundern (über +acc); ~lous (US marvelous) adj wunderbar

Marxist ['mɑːksɪst] n Marxist(in) m(f)

marzipan ['mɑːzɪpæn] n Marzipan nt

mascara [mæs'kɑːrə] n Wimperntusche f

mascot ['mæskət] n Maskottchen nt

masculine ['mæskjʊlɪn] adj männlich

mash [mæʃ] n Brei m; ~ed potatoes npl Kartoffelbrei m or -püree nt

mask [mɑːsk] n (also fig) Maske f ♦ vt maskieren, verdecken

mason ['meɪsn] n (stonemason) Steinmetz m; (freemason) Freimaurer m; ~ry n Mauerwerk nt

masquerade [mæskə'reɪd] n Maskerade f ♦ vi: to ~ as sich ausgeben als

mass [mæs] n Masse f; (greater part) Mehrheit f; (REL) Messe f ♦ vi sich sammeln; the ~es npl (people) die Masse(n) f(pl)

massacre ['mæsəkə*] n Blutbad nt ♦ vt niedermetzeln, massakrieren

massage ['mæsɑːʒ] n Massage f ♦ vt massieren

massive ['mæsɪv] adj gewaltig, massiv

mass media npl Massenmedien pl

mass production n Massenproduktion f

mast [mɑːst] n Mast m

master ['mɑːstə*] n Herr m; (NAUT) Kapitän m; (teacher) Lehrer m; (artist) Meister m ♦ vt meistern; (language etc) beherrschen; ~ly adj meisterhaft; ~mind n Kapazität f ♦ vt geschickt lenken; M~ of Arts n Magister m der philosophischen Fakultät; M~ of Science n Magister m der naturwissenschaftlichen Fakultät; ~piece n Meisterwerk nt; ~ plan n kluge(r) Plan m; ~y n Können nt

masturbate ['mæstəbeɪt] vi masturbieren, onanieren

mat [mæt] n Matte f; (for table) Untersetzer m ♦ adj = matt

match [mætʃ] n Streichholz nt; (sth corresponding) Pendant nt; (SPORT) Wettkampf m; (ball games) Spiel nt ♦ vt (be like, suit) passen zu; (equal) gleichkommen +dat ♦ vi zusammenpassen; it's a good ~ (for) es passt gut (zu); ~box n Streichholzschachtel f; ~ing adj passend

mate [meɪt] n (companion) Kamerad m; (spouse) Lebensgefährte m; (of animal) Weibchen nt/Männchen nt; (NAUT) Schiffsoffizier m ♦ vi (animals) sich paaren

♦ *vt (animals)* paaren
material [mə'tɪərɪəl] *n* Material *nt*; *(for book, cloth)* Stoff *m* ♦ *adj (important)* wesentlich; *(damage)* Sach-; *(comforts etc)* materiell; **~s** *npl (for building etc)* Materialien *pl*; **~istic** [mətɪərɪə'lɪstɪk] *adj* materialistisch; **~ize** *vi* sich verwirklichen, zustande *or* zu Stande kommen
maternal [mə'tə:nl] *adj* mütterlich, Mutter-
maternity [mə'tə:nɪtɪ] *adj (dress)* Umstands-; *(benefit)* Wochen-; **~ hospital** *n* Entbindungsheim *nt*
math [mæθ] *(US) n* = **maths**
mathematical [mæθə'mætɪkl] *adj* mathematisch; **mathematics** *n* Mathematik *f*; **maths** *(US* math) *n* Mathe *f*
matinée ['mætɪneɪ] *n* Matinee *f*
matrices ['meɪtrɪsi:z] *npl of* matrix
matriculation [mətrɪkju'leɪʃən] *n* Immatrikulation *f*
matrimonial [mætrɪ'məʊnɪəl] *adj* ehelich, Ehe-
matrimony ['mætrɪmənɪ] *n* Ehestand *m*
matrix ['meɪtrɪks] *(pl* matrices*) n* Matrize *f*; *(GEOL etc)* Matrix *f*
matron ['meɪtrən] *n (MED)* Oberin *f*; *(SCH)* Hausmutter *f*
matt [mæt] *adj (paint)* matt
matted ['mætɪd] *adj* verfilzt
matter ['mætə*r*] *n (substance)* Materie *f*; *(affair)* Angelegenheit *f* ♦ *vi* darauf ankommen; **no ~ how/what** egal wie/was; **what is the ~?** was ist los?; **as a ~ of course** selbstverständlich; **as a ~ of fact** eigentlich; **it doesn't ~** es macht nichts; **~-of-fact** *adj* sachlich, nüchtern
mattress ['mætrɪs] *n* Matratze *f*
mature [mə'tjʊə*r*] *adj* reif ♦ *vi* reif werden; **maturity** [mə'tjʊərɪtɪ] *n* Reife *f*
maul [mɔ:l] *vt* übel zurichten
maxima ['mæksɪmə] *npl of* maximum
maximum ['mæksɪməm] *(pl* maxima*) adj* Höchst-, Maximal- ♦ *n* Maximum *nt*
May [meɪ] *n* Mai *m*
may [meɪ] *(conditional* might*) vi (be possible)* können; *(have permission)* dürfen; **he ~ come** er kommt vielleicht; **~be** ['meɪbi:]

adv vielleicht
May Day *n* der 1. Mai
mayhem ['meɪhɛm] *n* Chaos *nt*; *(US)* Körperverletzung *f*
mayonnaise [meɪə'neɪz] *n* Majonäse *f*, Mayonnaise *f*
mayor [mɛə*r*] *n* Bürgermeister *m*; **~ess** *n* Bürgermeisterin *f*; *(wife)* (die) Frau *f* Bürgermeister
maypole ['meɪpəʊl] *n* Maibaum *m*
maze [meɪz] *n* Irrgarten *m*; *(fig)* Wirrwarr *nt*
M.D. *abbr* = **Doctor of Medicine**

KEYWORD
---

me [mi:] *pron* **1** *(direct)* mich; **it's me** ich bins
2 *(indirect)* mir; **give them to me** gib sie mir
3 *(after prep: +acc)* mich; *(: +dat)* mir; **with/without me** mit mir/ohne mich
---

meadow ['mɛdəʊ] *n* Wiese *f*
meagre ['mi:gə*r*] *(US* meager*) adj* dürftig, spärlich
meal [mi:l] *n* Essen *nt*, Mahlzeit *f*; *(grain)* Schrotmehl *nt*; **to have a ~** essen (gehen); **~time** *n* Essenszeit *f*
mean [mi:n] *(pt, pp* meant*) adj (stingy)* geizig; *(spiteful)* gemein; *(average)* durchschnittlich, Durchschnitts- ♦ *vt (signify)* bedeuten; *(intend)* vorhaben, beabsichtigen ♦ *n (average)* Durchschnitt *m*; **~s** *npl (wherewithal)* Mittel *pl*; *(wealth)* Vermögen *nt*; **do you ~ me?** meinst du mich?; **do you ~ it?** meinst du das ernst?; **what do you ~?** was willst du damit sagen?; **to be ~t for sb/sth** für jdn/etw bestimmt sein; **by ~s of** durch; **by all ~s** selbstverständlich; **by no ~s** keineswegs
meander [mɪ'ændə*r*] *vi* sich schlängeln
meaning ['mi:nɪŋ] *n* Bedeutung *f*; *(of life)* Sinn *m*; **~ful** *adj* bedeutungsvoll; *(life)* sinnvoll; **~less** *adj* sinnlos
meanness ['mi:nnɪs] *n (stinginess)* Geiz *m*; *(spitefulness)* Gemeinheit *f*
meant [mɛnt] *pt, pp of* mean
meantime ['mi:ntaɪm] *adv* inzwischen

eanwhile ['miːnwaɪl] *adv* inzwischen
easles ['miːzlz] *n* Masern *pl*
easly ['miːzlɪ] (*inf*) *adj* poplig
easure ['meʒəʳ] *vt, vi* messen ♦ *Maß nt;*
(*step*) Maßnahme *f;* ~**ments** *npl* Maße *pl*
eat [miːt] *n* Fleisch *nt;* **cold** ~ Aufschnitt
m; ~ **ball** *n* Fleischkloß *m;* ~ **pie** *n*
Fleischpastete *f;* ~**y** *adj* fleischig; (*fig*)
gehaltvoll
ecca ['mekə] *n* Mekka *nt* (*also fig*)
echanic [mɪ'kænɪk] *n* Mechaniker *m;* ~**al**
adj mechanisch; ~**s** *n* Mechanik *f* ♦ *npl*
Technik *f*
echanism ['mekənɪzəm] *n* Mechanismus
m
echanize ['mekənaɪz] *vt* mechanisieren
edal ['medl] *n* Medaille *f;* (*decoration*)
Orden *m;* ~**list** (*US* **medalist**) *n*
Medaillengewinner(in) *m(f)*
eddle ['medl] *vi:* **to** ~ (**in**) sich einmischen
(**in** +*acc*); **to** ~ **with sth** sich an etw *dat* zu
schaffen machen
edia ['miːdɪə] *npl* Medien *pl*
ediaeval [medɪ'iːvl] *adj* = **medieval**
edian ['miːdɪən] (*US*) *n* (*also:* ~ **strip**)
Mittelstreifen *m*
ediate ['miːdɪeɪt] *vi* vermitteln; **mediator**
n Vermittler *m*
edicaid ['medɪkeɪd] (®) (*US*) *n*
medizinisches Versorgungsprogramm für
sozial Schwache
edical ['medɪkl] *adj* medizinisch; Medizin-;
ärztlich ♦ *n* (ärztliche) Untersuchung *f*
edicare ['medɪkeəʳ] (*US*) *n staatliche*
Krankenversicherung besonders für Ältere
edicated ['medɪkeɪtɪd] *adj* medizinisch
edication [medɪ'keɪʃən] *n* (*drugs etc*)
Medikamente *pl*
edicinal [me'dɪsɪnl] *adj* medizinisch, Heil-
edicine ['medsɪn] *n* Medizin *f;* (*drugs*)
Arznei *f*
edieval [medɪ'iːvl] *adj* mittelalterlich
ediocre [miːdɪ'əʊkəʳ] *adj* mittelmäßig
editate ['medɪteɪt] *vi* meditieren; **to** ~ (**on**
sth) (über etw *acc*) nachdenken; **meditation**
[medɪ'teɪʃən] *n* Nachsinnen *nt;* Meditation *f*
editerranean [medɪtə'reɪnɪən] *adj*

Mittelmeer-; (*person*) südländisch; **the** ~
(Sea) das Mittelmeer
medium ['miːdɪəm] *adj* mittlere(r, s), Mittel-,
mittel- ♦ *n* Mitte *f;* (*means*) Mittel *nt;*
(*person*) Medium *nt;* **happy** ~ goldener
Mittelweg; ~**-sized** *adj* mittelgroß; ~
wave *n* Mittelwelle *f*
medley ['medlɪ] *n* Gemisch *nt*
meek [miːk] *adj* sanft(mütig)
meet [miːt] (*pt, pp* **met**) *vt* (*encounter*)
treffen, begegnen +*dat;* (*by arrangement*)
sich treffen mit; (*difficulties*) stoßen auf +*acc;*
(*get to know*) kennen lernen; (*fetch*)
abholen; (*join*) zusammentreffen mit;
(*satisfy*) entsprechen +*dat* ♦ *vi* sich treffen;
(*become acquainted*) sich kennen lernen; ~
with *vt* (*problems*) stoßen auf +*acc;* (*US:*
people) zusammentreffen mit; ~**ing** *n*
Treffen *nt;* (*business ~ing*) Besprechung *f;* (*of*
committee) Sitzung *f;* (*assembly*)
Versammlung *f*
mega- ['megə-] (*inf*) *prefix* Mega-; ~**byte** *n*
(*COMPUT*) Megabyte *nt;* ~**phone** *n*
Megafon *nt,* Megaphon *nt*
melancholy ['melənkəlɪ] *adj* (*person*)
melancholisch; (*sight, event*) traurig
mellow ['meləʊ] *adj* mild, weich; (*fruit*) reif;
(*fig*) gesetzt ♦ *vi* reif werden
melodious [mɪ'ləʊdɪəs] *adj* wohlklingend
melody ['melədɪ] *n* Melodie *f*
melon ['melən] *n* Melone *f*
melt [melt] *vi* schmelzen; (*anger*) verfliegen
♦ *vt* schmelzen; ~ **away** *vi*
dahinschmelzen; ~ **down** *vt* einschmelzen;
~**down** *n* (*in nuclear reactor*) Kernschmelze
f; ~**ing point** *n* Schmelzpunkt *m;* ~**ing pot**
n (*fig*) Schmelztiegel *m*
member ['membəʳ] *n* Mitglied *nt;* (*of tribe,*
species) Angehörige(r) *f(m);* (*ANAT*) Glied *nt;*
M~ of Parliament (*BRIT*) *n*
Parlamentsmitglied *nt;* **M~ of the**
European Parliament (*BRIT*) *n* Mitglied *nt*
des Europäischen Parlaments; **M~ of the**
Scottish Parliament *n* Mitglied *nt* des
schottischen Parlaments; ~**ship** *n*
Mitgliedschaft *f;* **to seek ~ship of** einen
Antrag auf Mitgliedschaft stellen; ~**ship**

card n Mitgliedskarte f

memento [mə'mɛntəu] n Andenken nt

memo ['mɛməu] n Mitteilung f

memoirs ['mɛmwɑːz] npl Memoiren pl

memorable ['mɛmərəbl] adj denkwürdig

memoranda [mɛmə'rændə] npl of **memorandum**

memorandum [mɛmə'rændəm] (pl **memoranda**) n Mitteilung f

memorial [mɪ'mɔːrɪəl] n Denkmal nt ♦ adj Gedenk-

memorize ['mɛməraɪz] vt sich einprägen

memory ['mɛmərɪ] n Gedächtnis nt; (of computer) Speicher m; (sth recalled) Erinnerung f

men [mɛn] pl of **man** ♦ n (human race) die Menschen pl

menace ['mɛnɪs] n Drohung f; Gefahr f ♦ vt bedrohen; **menacing** adj drohend

menagerie [mɪ'nædʒərɪ] n Tierschau f

mend [mɛnd] vt reparieren, flicken ♦ vi (ver)heilen ♦ n ausgebesserte Stelle f; **on the ~** auf dem Wege der Besserung; **~ing** n (articles) Flickarbeit f

menial ['miːnɪəl] adj niedrig

meningitis [mɛnɪn'dʒaɪtɪs] n Hirnhautentzündung f, Meningitis f

menopause ['mɛnəupɔːz] n Wechseljahre pl, Menopause f

menstruation [mɛnstru'eɪʃən] n Menstruation f

mental ['mɛntl] adj geistig, Geistes-; (arithmetic) Kopf-; (hospital) Nerven-; (cruelty) seelisch; (inf: abnormal) verrückt; **~ity** [mɛn'tælɪtɪ] n Mentalität f

menthol ['mɛnθɒl] n Menthol nt

mention ['mɛnʃən] n Erwähnung f ♦ vt erwähnen; **don't ~ it!** bitte (sehr), gern geschehen

mentor ['mɛntɔː'] n Mentor m

menu ['mɛnjuː] n Speisekarte f

MEP n abbr = **Member of the European Parliament**

mercenary ['mɜːsɪnərɪ] adj (person) geldgierig ♦ n Söldner m

merchandise ['mɜːtʃəndaɪz] n (Handels)ware f

merchant ['mɜːtʃənt] n Kaufmann m; **~ bank** (BRIT) n Handelsbank f; **~ navy** (US **~ marine**) n Handelsmarine f

merciful ['mɜːsɪful] adj gnädig

merciless ['mɜːsɪlɪs] adj erbarmungslos

mercury ['mɜːkjurɪ] n Quecksilber nt

mercy ['mɜːsɪ] n Erbarmen nt; Gnade f; **at the ~ of** ausgeliefert +dat

mere [mɪə'] adj bloß; **~ly** adv bloß

merge [mɜːdʒ] vt verbinden; (COMM) fusionieren ♦ vi verschmelzen; (roads) zusammenlaufen; (COMM) fusionieren; **~r** (COMM) Fusion f

meringue [mə'ræŋ] n Baiser nt

merit ['mɛrɪt] n Verdienst nt; (advantage) Vorzug m ♦ vt verdienen

mermaid ['mɜːmeɪd] n Wassernixe f

merry ['mɛrɪ] adj fröhlich; **~-go-round** n Karussell nt

mesh [mɛʃ] n Masche f

mesmerize ['mɛzməraɪz] vt hypnotisieren; (fig) faszinieren

mess [mɛs] n Unordnung f; (dirt) Schmutz m; (trouble) Schwierigkeiten pl; (MIL) Messe f; **~ about** or **around** vi (play the fool) herumalbern; (do nothing in particular) herumgammeln; **~ about** or **around with** vt fus (tinker with) herummurksen an +dat; **~ up** vt verpfuschen; (make untidy) in Unordnung bringen

message ['mɛsɪdʒ] n Mitteilung f; **to get the ~** kapieren

messenger ['mɛsɪndʒə'] n Bote m

Messrs ['mɛsəz] abbr (on letters) die Herren

messy ['mɛsɪ] adj schmutzig; (untidy) unordentlich

met [mɛt] pt, pp of **meet**

metabolism [mɛ'tæbəlɪzəm] n Stoffwechsel m

metal ['mɛtl] n Metall nt; **~lic** adj metallisch; (made of ~) aus Metall

metaphor ['mɛtəfə'] n Metapher f

meteorology [miːtɪə'rɒlədʒɪ] n Meteorologie f

meter ['miːtə'] n Zähler m; (US) = **metre**

method ['mɛθəd] n Methode f; **~ical** [mɪ'θɒdɪkl] adj methodisch; **M~ist** n

['meθədɪst] *adj* methodistisch ♦ *n*
Methodist(in) *m(f)*; **~ology** [meθə'dɔlədʒɪ] *n*
Methodik *f*

eths [meθs] (*BRIT*) *n(pl)* = **methylated spirit(s)**

ethylated spirit(s) ['meθɪleɪtɪd-] (*BRIT*) *n*
(Brenn)spiritus *m*

eticulous [mɪ'tɪkjuləs] *adj* (über)genau

etre ['mi:tə'] (*US* **meter**) *n* Meter *m* or *nt*

etric ['metrɪk] *adj* (*also*: **~al**) metrisch

etropolitan [metrə'pɔlɪtn] *adj* der
Großstadt; **M~ Police** (*BRIT*) *n*: **the M~
Police** die Londoner Polizei

ettle ['metl] *n* Mut *m*

ew [mju:] *vi* (*cat*) miauen

ews [mju:z] *n*: **~ cottage** ehemaliges
Kutscherhäuschen

exican ['meksɪkən] *adj* mexikanisch ♦ *n*
Mexikaner(in) *m(f)*

exico ['meksɪkəu] *n* Mexiko *nt*

iaow [mi:'au] *vi* miauen

ice [maɪs] *pl of* **mouse**

icro ['maɪkrəu] *n* (*also*: **~computer**)
Mikrocomputer *m*; **~chip** *n* Mikrochip *m*;
~cosm ['maɪkrəukɔzəm] *n* Mikrokosmos *m*;
~phone *n* Mikrofon *m*, Mikrophon *nt*;
~scope *n* Mikroskop *nt*; **~wave** *n* (*also*:
~wave oven) Mikrowelle(nherd *m*) *f*

id [mɪd] *adj*: **in ~ afternoon** am
Nachmittag; **in ~ air** in der Luft; **in ~ May**
Mitte Mai

idday [mɪd'deɪ] *n* Mittag *m*

iddle ['mɪdl] *n* Mitte *f*; (*waist*) Taille *f* ♦ *adj*
mittlere(r, s), Mittel-; **in the ~ of** mitten in
+*dat*; **~-aged** *adj* mittleren Alters; **M~
Ages** *npl*: **the M~ Ages** das Mittelalter;
~-class *adj* Mittelstands-; **M~ East** *n*: **the
M~ East** der Nahe Osten; **~man** (*irreg*) *n*
(*COMM*) Zwischenhändler *m*; **~ name** *n*
zweiter Vorname *m*; **~ weight** *n* (*BOXING*)
Mittelgewicht *nt*

iddling ['mɪdlɪŋ] *adj* mittelmäßig

idge [mɪdʒ] *n* Mücke *f*

idget ['mɪdʒɪt] *n* Liliputaner(in) *m(f)*

idnight ['mɪdnaɪt] *n* Mitternacht *f*

idriff ['mɪdrɪf] *n* Taille *f*

idst [mɪdst] *n*: **in the ~ of** (*persons*) mitten

unter +*dat*; (*things*) mitten in +*dat*

mid [mɪd'-]: **~summer** *n* Hochsommer *m*;
~way *adv* auf halbem Wege ♦ *adj* Mittel-;
~week *adv* in der Mitte der Woche

midwife ['mɪdwaɪf] (*irreg*) *n* Hebamme *f*; **~ry**
['mɪdwɪfərɪ] *n* Geburtshilfe *f*

midwinter [mɪd'wɪntə'] *n* tiefste(r) Winter *m*

might [maɪt] *vi see* **may** ♦ *n* Macht *f*, Kraft *f*;
I ~ come ich komme vielleicht; **~y** *adj, adv*
mächtig

migraine ['mi:greɪn] *n* Migräne *f*

migrant ['maɪgrənt] *adj* Wander-; (*bird*) Zug-

migrate [maɪ'greɪt] *vi* (ab)wandern; (*birds*)
(fort)ziehen; **migration** [maɪ'greɪʃən] *n*
Wanderung *f*, Zug *m*

mike [maɪk] *n* = **microphone**

Milan [mɪ'læn] *n* Mailand *nt*

mild [maɪld] *adj* mild; (*medicine, interest*)
leicht; (*person*) sanft ♦ *n* (*beer*) leichtes
dunkles Bier

mildew ['mɪldju:] *n* (*on plants*) Mehltau *m*;
(*on food*) Schimmel *m*

mildly ['maɪldlɪ] *adv* leicht; **to put it ~**
gelinde gesagt

mile [maɪl] *n* Meile *f*; **~age** *n* Meilenzahl *f*;
~ometer *n* = **milometer**; **~stone** *n* (*also
fig*) Meilenstein *m*

militant ['mɪlɪtnt] *adj* militant ♦ *n*
Militante(r) *mf*

military ['mɪlɪtərɪ] *adj* militärisch, Militär-,
Wehr-

militate ['mɪlɪteɪt] *vi*: **to ~ against**
entgegenwirken +*dat*

militia [mɪ'lɪʃə] *n* Miliz *f*

milk [mɪlk] *n* Milch *f* ♦ *vt* (*also fig*) melken; **~
chocolate** *n* Milchschokolade *f*; **~man**
(*irreg*) *n* Milchmann *m*; **~ shake** *n*
Milchmixgetränk *nt*; **~y** *adj* milchig; **M~y
Way** *n* Milchstraße *f*

mill [mɪl] *n* Mühle *f*; (*factory*) Fabrik *f* ♦ *vt*
mahlen ♦ *vi* umherlaufen

millennia [mɪ'lenɪə] *npl of* **millennium**

millennium [mɪ'lenɪəm] (*pl* **~s** *or* **millennia**)
n Jahrtausend *nt*; **~ bug** *n* (*COMPUT*)
Jahrtausendfehler *m*

miller ['mɪlə'] *n* Müller *m*

milligram(me) ['mɪlɪgræm] *n* Milligramm *nt*

millimetre ['mɪlɪmiːtə'] (*US* **millimeter**) *n* Millimeter *m*

million ['mɪljən] *n* Million *f*; **a ~ times** tausendmal; **~aire** [mɪljə'neə'] *n* Millionär(in) *m(f)*

millstone ['mɪlstəun] *n* Mühlstein *m*

milometer [maɪ'lɒmɪtə'] *n* ≃ Kilometerzähler *m*

mime [maɪm] *n* Pantomime *f* ♦ *vt, vi* mimen

mimic ['mɪmɪk] *n* Mimiker *m* ♦ *vt, vi* nachahmen; **~ry** *n* Nachahmung *f*; (*BIOL*) Mimikry *f*

min. *abbr* = **minutes**; **minimum**

mince [mɪns] *vt* (zer)hacken ♦ *n* (*meat*) Hackfleisch *nt*; **~meat** *n* süße Pastetenfüllung *f*; **~ pie** *n* gefüllte (süße) Pastete *f*; **~r** *n* Fleischwolf *m*

mind [maɪnd] *n* Verstand *m*, Geist *m*; (*opinion*) Meinung *f* ♦ *vt* aufpassen auf +*acc*; (*object to*) etwas haben gegen; **on my ~** auf dem Herzen; **to my ~** meiner Meinung nach; **to be out of one's ~** wahnsinnig sein; **to bear** *or* **have in ~** bedenken; **to change one's ~** es sich *dat* anders überlegen; **to make up one's ~** sich entschließen; **I don't ~** das macht mir nichts aus; **~ you, ...** allerdings ...; **never ~!** macht nichts!; **"~ the step"** „Vorsicht Stufe"; **~ your own business** kümmern Sie sich um Ihre eigenen Angelegenheiten; **~er** *n* Aufpasser(in) *m(f)*; **~ful** *adj*: **~ful of** achtsam auf +*acc*; **~less** *adj* sinnlos

mine¹ [maɪn] *n* (*coalmine*) Bergwerk *nt*; (*MIL*) Mine *f* ♦ *vt* abbauen; (*MIL*) verminen

mine² [maɪn] *pron* meine(r, s); **that book is ~** das Buch gehört mir; **a friend of ~** ein Freund von mir

minefield ['maɪnfiːld] *n* Minenfeld *nt*

miner ['maɪnə'] *n* Bergarbeiter *m*

mineral ['mɪnərəl] *adj* mineralisch, Mineral- ♦ *n* Mineral *nt*; **~s** *npl* (*BRIT*: *soft drinks*) alkoholfreie Getränke *pl*; **~ water** *n* Mineralwasser *nt*

minesweeper ['maɪnswiːpə'] *n* Minensuchboot *nt*

mingle ['mɪŋgl] *vi*: **to ~ (with)** sich mischen (unter +*acc*)

miniature ['mɪnətʃə'] *adj* Miniatur- ♦ *n* Miniatur *f*

minibus ['mɪnɪbʌs] *n* Kleinbus *m*

Minidisc ['mɪnɪdɪsk] *n* Minidisc ® *f*

minimal ['mɪnɪml] *adj* minimal

minimize ['mɪnɪmaɪz] *vt* auf das Mindestmaß beschränken

minimum ['mɪnɪməm] (*pl* **minima**) *n* Minimum *nt* ♦ *adj* Mindest-

mining ['maɪnɪŋ] *n* Bergbau *m* ♦ *adj* Bergbau-, Berg-

miniskirt ['mɪnɪskəːt] *n* Minirock *m*

minister ['mɪnɪstə'] *n* (*BRIT*: *POL*) Minister *m*; (*ECCL*) Pfarrer *m* ♦ *vi*: **to ~ to sb/sb's needs** sich um jdn kümmern; **~ial** [mɪnɪs'tɪərɪəl] *adj* ministeriell, Minister-

ministry ['mɪnɪstrɪ] *n* (*BRIT*: *POL*) Ministerium *nt*; (*ECCL*: *office*) geistliche(s) Amt *nt*

mink [mɪŋk] *n* Nerz *m*

minnow ['mɪnəu] *n* Elritze *f*

minor ['maɪnə'] *adj* kleiner; (*operation*) leicht; (*problem, poet*) unbedeutend; (*MUS*) Moll ♦ *n* (*BRIT*: *under 18*) Minderjährige(r) *mf*

minority [maɪ'nɒrɪtɪ] *n* Minderheit *f*

mint [mɪnt] *n* Minze *f*; (*sweet*) Pfefferminzbonbon *nt* ♦ *vt* (*coins*) prägen; **the (Royal** (*BRIT*) *or* **US** (*US*)) **M~** die Münzanstalt; **in ~ condition** in tadellosem Zustand

minus ['maɪnəs] *n* Minuszeichen *nt*; (*amount*) Minusbetrag *m* ♦ *prep* minus, weniger

minuscule ['mɪnəskjuːl] *adj* winzig

minute¹ [maɪ'njuːt] *adj* winzig; (*detailed*) minutiös, minuziös

minute² ['mɪnɪt] *n* Minute *f*; (*moment*) Augenblick *m*; **~s** *npl* (*of meeting etc*) Protokoll *nt*

miracle ['mɪrəkl] *n* Wunder *nt*

miraculous [mɪ'rækjuləs] *adj* wunderbar

mirage ['mɪrɑːʒ] *n* Fata Morgana *f*

mire ['maɪə'] *n* Morast *m*

mirror ['mɪrə'] *n* Spiegel *m* ♦ *vt* (wider)spiegeln

mirth [məːθ] *n* Heiterkeit *f*

misadventure [mɪsəd'ventʃə'] *n* Missgeschick *nt*, Unfall *m*

misanthropist [mɪ'zænθrəpɪst] *n*

Menschenfeind *m*

isapprehension ['mɪsæprɪ'henʃən] *n*
Missverständnis *nt*

isbehave [mɪsbɪ'heɪv] *vi* sich schlecht
benehmen

iscalculate [mɪs'kælkjuleɪt] *vt* falsch
berechnen

iscarriage ['mɪskærɪdʒ] *n* (*MED*)
Fehlgeburt *f*; **~ of justice** Fehlurteil *nt*

iscellaneous [mɪsɪ'leɪnɪəs] *adj*
verschieden

ischief ['mɪstʃɪf] *n* Unfug *m*;

mischievous ['mɪstʃɪvəs] *adj* (*person*)
durchtrieben; (*glance*) verschmitzt; (*rumour*)
bösartig

isconception ['mɪskən'sepʃən] *n*
fälschliche Annahme *f*

isconduct [mɪs'kɒndʌkt] *n* Vergehen *nt*;
professional ~ Berufsvergehen *nt*

isconstrue [mɪskən'struː] *vt*
missverstehen

isdemeanour [mɪsdɪ'miːnəʳ] (*US*
misdemeanor) *n* Vergehen *nt*

iser ['maɪzəʳ] *n* Geizhals *m*

iserable ['mɪzərəbl] *adj* (*unhappy*)
unglücklich; (*headache, weather*)
fürchterlich; (*poor*) elend; (*contemptible*)
erbärmlich

iserly ['maɪzəlɪ] *adj* geizig

isery ['mɪzərɪ] *n* Elend *nt*, Qual *f*

isfire [mɪs'faɪəʳ] *vi* (*gun*) versagen; (*engine*)
fehlzünden; (*plan*) fehlgehen

isfit ['mɪsfɪt] *n* Außenseiter *m*

isfortune [mɪs'fɔːtʃən] *n* Unglück *nt*

isgiving(s) [mɪs'gɪvɪŋ(z)] *n(pl)* Bedenken
pl

isguided [mɪs'gaɪdɪd] *adj* fehlgeleitet;
(*opinions*) irrig

ishandle [mɪs'hændl] *vt* falsch handhaben

ishap ['mɪshæp] *n* Missgeschick *nt*

isinform [mɪsɪn'fɔːm] *vt* falsch
unterrichten

isinterpret [mɪsɪn'tɜːprɪt] *vt* falsch
auffassen

isjudge [mɪs'dʒʌdʒ] *vt* falsch beurteilen

islay [mɪs'leɪ] (*irreg: like* **lay**) *vt* verlegen

islead [mɪs'liːd] (*irreg: like* **lead**[2]) *vt*

(*deceive*) irreführen; **~ing** *adj* irreführend

mismanage [mɪs'mænɪdʒ] *vt* schlecht
verwalten

misnomer [mɪs'nəuməʳ] *n* falsche
Bezeichnung *f*

misplace [mɪs'pleɪs] *vt* verlegen

misprint ['mɪsprɪnt] *n* Druckfehler *m*

Miss [mɪs] *n* Fräulein *nt*

miss [mɪs] *vt* (*fail to hit, catch*) verfehlen; (*not
notice*) verpassen; (*be too late*) versäumen,
verpassen; (*omit*) auslassen; (*regret the
absence of*) vermissen ♦ *vi* fehlen ♦ *n* (*shot*)
Fehlschuss *m*; (*failure*) Fehlschlag *m*; **I ~ you**
du fehlst mir; **~ out** *vt* auslassen

misshapen [mɪs'ʃeɪpən] *adj* missgestaltet

missile ['mɪsaɪl] *n* Rakete *f*

missing ['mɪsɪŋ] *adj* (*person*) vermisst;
(*thing*) fehlend; **to be ~** fehlen

mission ['mɪʃən] *n* (*work*) Auftrag *m*;
(*people*) Delegation *f*; (*REL*) Mission *f*; **~ary**
n Missionar(in) *m(f)*; **~ statement** *n*
Kurzdarstellung *f* der Firmenphilosophie

misspell ['mɪs'spel] (*irreg: like* **spell**) *vt*
falsch schreiben

misspent ['mɪs'spent] *adj* (*youth*) vergeudet

mist [mɪst] *n* Dunst *m*, Nebel *m* ♦ *vi* (*also: ~
over, ~ up*) sich trüben; (*BRIT: windows*) sich
beschlagen

mistake [mɪs'teɪk] (*irreg: like* **take**) *n* Fehler
m ♦ *vt* (*misunderstand*) missverstehen; (*mix
up*): **to ~ (sth for sth)** (etw mit etw)
verwechseln; **to make a ~** einen Fehler
machen; **by ~** aus Versehen; **to ~ A for B** A
mit B verwechseln; **~n** *pp of* **mistake** ♦ *adj*
(*idea*) falsch; **to be ~n** sich irren

mister ['mɪstəʳ] *n* (*inf*) Herr *m*; *see* **Mr**

mistletoe ['mɪsltəu] *n* Mistel *f*

mistook [mɪs'tuk] *pt of* **mistake**

mistress ['mɪstrɪs] *n* (*teacher*) Lehrerin *f*; (*in
house*) Herrin *f*; (*lover*) Geliebte *f*; *see* **Mrs**

mistrust [mɪs'trʌst] *vt* misstrauen +*dat*

misty ['mɪstɪ] *adj* neblig

misunderstand [mɪsʌndə'stænd] (*irreg: like*
understand) *vt, vi* missverstehen, falsch
verstehen; **~ing** *n* Missverständnis *nt*;
(*disagreement*) Meinungsverschiedenheit *f*

misuse [*n* mɪs'juːs, *vb* mɪs'juːz] *n* falsche(r)

Gebrauch m ♦ vt falsch gebrauchen

mitigate ['mɪtɪɡeɪt] vt mildern

mitt(en) ['mɪt(n)] n Fausthandschuh m

mix [mɪks] vt (blend) (ver)mischen ♦ vi (liquids) sich (ver)mischen lassen; (people: get on) sich vertragen; (: associate) Kontakt haben ♦ n (~ture) Mischung f; ~ **up** vt zusammenmischen; (confuse) verwechseln; **~ed** adj gemischt; **~ed-up** adj durcheinander; **~er** n (for food) Mixer m; **~ture** n Mischung f; **~-up** n Durcheinander nt

mm abbr (= millimetre(s)) mm

moan [məʊn] n Stöhnen nt; (complaint) Klage f ♦ vi stöhnen; (complain) maulen

moat [məʊt] n (Burg)graben m

mob [mɔb] n Mob m; (the masses) Pöbel m ♦ vt herfallen über +acc

mobile ['məʊbaɪl] adj beweglich; (library etc) fahrbar ♦ n (decoration) Mobile nt; ~ **home** n Wohnwagen m; ~ **phone** n (TEL) Mobiltelefon nt; **mobility** [məʊ'bɪlɪtɪ] n Beweglichkeit f; **mobilize** ['məʊbɪlaɪz] vt mobilisieren

mock [mɔk] vt verspotten; (defy) trotzen +dat ♦ adj Schein-; **~ery** n Spott m; (person) Gespött nt

mod [mɔd] adj see **convenience**

mode [məʊd] n (Art f und) Weise f

model ['mɔdl] n Modell nt; (example) Vorbild nt; (in fashion) Mannequin nt ♦ adj (railway) Modell-; (perfect) Muster-; vorbildlich ♦ vt (make) bilden; (clothes) vorführen ♦ vi als Mannequin arbeiten

modem ['məʊdem] n (COMPUT) Modem nt

moderate [adj, n 'mɔdərət, vb 'mɔdəreɪt] adj gemäßigt ♦ n (POL) Gemäßigte(r) mf ♦ vi sich mäßigen ♦ vt mäßigen; **moderation** [mɔdə'reɪʃən] n Mäßigung f; **in moderation** mit Maßen

modern ['mɔdən] adj modern; (history, languages) neuere(r, s); **~ize** vt modernisieren

modest ['mɔdɪst] adj bescheiden; **~y** n Bescheidenheit f

modicum ['mɔdɪkəm] n bisschen nt

modification [mɔdɪfɪ'keɪʃən] n

(Ab)änderung f

modify ['mɔdɪfaɪ] vt abändern

module ['mɔdjuːl] n (component) (Bau)element nt; (SPACE) (Raum)kapsel f

mogul ['məʊɡl] n (fig) Mogul m

mohair ['məʊheə'] n Mohär m, Mohair m

moist [mɔɪst] adj feucht; **~en** ['mɔɪsn] vt befeuchten; **~ure** ['mɔɪstʃə'] n Feuchtigkeit f; **~urizer** ['mɔɪstʃəraɪzə'] n Feuchtigkeitscreme f

molar ['məʊlə'] n Backenzahn m

molasses [mə'læsɪz] n Melasse f

mold [məʊld] (US) = **mould**

mole [məʊl] n (spot) Leberfleck m; (animal) Maulwurf m; (pier) Mole f

molest [mə'lest] vt belästigen

mollycoddle ['mɔlɪkɔdl] vt verhätscheln

molt [məʊlt] (US) vi = **moult**

molten ['məʊltən] adj geschmolzen

mom [mɔm] (US) n = **mum**

moment ['məʊmənt] n Moment m, Augenblick m; (importance) Tragweite f; **at the ~** im Augenblick; **~ary** adj kurz; **~ous** [məʊ'mentəs] adj folgenschwer

momentum [məʊ'mentəm] n Schwung m; **to gather ~** in Fahrt kommen

mommy ['mɔmɪ] (US) n = **mummy**

Monaco ['mɔnəkəʊ] n Monaco nt

monarch ['mɔnək] n Herrscher(in) m(f); **~y** n Monarchie f

monastery ['mɔnəstərɪ] n Kloster nt

monastic [mə'næstɪk] adj klösterlich, Kloster-

Monday ['mʌndɪ] n Montag m

monetary ['mʌnɪtərɪ] adj Geld-; (of currency) Währungs-

money ['mʌnɪ] n Geld nt; **to make ~** Geld verdienen; ~ **belt** n Geldgürtel nt; **~lender** n Geldverleiher m; ~ **order** n Postanweisung f; **~-spinner** (inf) n Verkaufsschlager m

mongol ['mɔnɡəl] n (MED) mongoloide(s) Kind nt ♦ adj mongolisch; (MED) mongoloid

mongrel ['mʌnɡrəl] n Promenadenmischung f

monitor ['mɔnɪtə'] n (SCH) Klassenordner m; (television ~) Monitor m ♦ vt (broadcasts) abhören; (control) überwachen

monk [mʌŋk] n Mönch m

monkey ['mʌŋkɪ] n Affe m; ~ **nut** (BRIT) n
Erdnuss f; ~ **wrench** n (TECH) Engländer m,
Franzose m

monochrome ['mɒnəkrəum] adj schwarzweiß, schwarzweiß

monopolize [mə'nɒpəlaɪz] vt beherrschen

monopoly [mə'nɒpəlɪ] n Monopol nt

monosyllable ['mɒnəsɪləbl] n einsilbige(s)
Wort nt

monotone ['mɒnətəun] n gleich
bleibende(r) Ton(fall) m; **to speak in a ~**
monoton sprechen; **monotonous**
[mə'nɒtənəs] adj eintönig; **monotony**
[mə'nɒtənɪ] n Eintönigkeit f, Monotonie f

monsoon [mɒn'su:n] n Monsun m

monster ['mɒnstər] n Ungeheuer nt; (person)
Scheusal nt

monstrosity [mɒn'strɒsɪtɪ] n
Ungeheuerlichkeit f; (thing) Monstrosität f

monstrous ['mɒnstrəs] adj (shocking)
grässlich, ungeheuerlich; (huge) riesig

month [mʌnθ] n Monat m; ~**ly** adj
monatlich, Monats- ♦ adv einmal im Monat
♦ n (magazine) Monatsschrift f

monument ['mɒnjumənt] n Denkmal nt;
~**al** [mɒnju'mentl] adj (huge) gewaltig;
(ignorance) ungeheuer

moo [mu:] vi muhen

mood [mu:d] n Stimmung f, Laune f; **to be
in a good/bad ~** gute/schlechte Laune
haben; ~**y** adj launisch

moon [mu:n] n Mond m; ~**light** n
Mondlicht nt; ~**lighting** n Schwarzarbeit f;
~**lit** adj mondhell

moor [muər] n Heide f, Hochmoor m ♦ vt
(ship) festmachen, verankern ♦ vi anlegen;
~**ings** npl Liegeplatz m; ~**land** ['muələnd] n
Heidemoor nt

moose [mu:s] n Elch m

mop [mɒp] n Mopp m ♦ vt (auf)wischen; ~
up vt aufwischen

mope [məup] vi Trübsal blasen

moped ['məuped] n Moped nt

moral ['mɒrl] adj moralisch; (values) sittlich;
(virtuous) tugendhaft ♦ n Moral f; ~**s** npl

(ethics) Moral f

morale [mɒ'rɑ:l] n Moral f

morality [mə'rælɪtɪ] n Sittlichkeit f

morass [mə'ræs] n Sumpf m

morbid ['mɔ:bɪd] adj krankhaft; (jokes)
makaber

KEYWORD

more [mɔ:r] adj (greater in number etc) mehr;
(additional) noch mehr; **do you want
(some) more tea?** möchten Sie noch
etwas Tee?; **I have no** or **I don't have any
more money** ich habe kein Geld mehr
♦ pron (greater amount) mehr; (further or
additional amount) noch mehr; **is there any
more?** gibt es noch mehr?; (left over) ist
noch etwas da?; **there's no more** es ist
nichts mehr da
♦ adv mehr; **more dangerous/easily** etc
(than) gefährlicher/einfacher etc (als); **more
and more** immer mehr; **more and more
excited** immer aufgeregter; **more or less**
mehr oder weniger; **more than ever** mehr
denn je; **more beautiful than ever** schöner
denn je

---

moreover [mɔ:'rəuvər] adv überdies

morgue [mɔ:g] n Leichenschauhaus nt

Mormon ['mɔ:mən] n Mormone m,
Mormonin f

morning ['mɔ:nɪŋ] n Morgen m; **in the ~**
am Morgen; **7 o'clock in the ~** 7 Uhr
morgens; ~ **sickness** n
(Schwangerschafts)übelkeit f

Morocco [mə'rɒkəu] n Marokko nt

moron ['mɔ:rɒn] n Schwachsinnige(r) mf

morose [mə'rəus] adj mürrisch

morphine ['mɔ:fi:n] n Morphium nt

Morse [mɔ:s] n (also: ~ **code**)
Morsealphabet nt

morsel ['mɔ:sl] n Bissen m

mortal ['mɔ:tl] adj sterblich; (deadly) tödlich;
(very great) Todes- ♦ n (human being)
Sterbliche(r) mf; ~**ity** [mɔ:'tælɪtɪ] n
Sterblichkeit f; (death rate)
Sterblichkeitsziffer f

mortar ['mɔ:tər] n (for building) Mörtel m;

(*MIL*) Granatwerfer m

mortgage ['mɔːgɪdʒ] n Hypothek f ♦ vt hypothekarisch belasten; ~ **company** (*US*) n ≃ Bausparkasse f

mortify ['mɔːtɪfaɪ] vt beschämen

mortuary ['mɔːtjuərɪ] n Leichenhalle f

mosaic [məʊˈzeɪɪk] n Mosaik nt

Moscow ['mɔskəʊ] n Moskau nt

Moslem ['mɔzləm] = **Muslim**

mosque [mɔsk] n Moschee f

mosquito [mɔsˈkiːtəʊ] (pl ~**es**) n Moskito m

moss [mɔs] n Moos nt

most [məʊst] adj meiste(r, s) ♦ adv am meisten; (*very*) höchst ♦ n das meiste, der größte Teil; (*people*) die meisten; ~ **men** die meisten Männer; **at the (very)** ~ allerhöchstens; **to make the** ~ **of** das Beste machen aus; **a** ~ **interesting book** ein höchstinteressantes Buch; ~**ly** adv größtenteils

MOT (*BRIT*) n abbr (= Ministry of Transport): **the MOT (test)** ≃ der TÜV

motel [məʊˈtel] n Motel nt

moth [mɔθ] n Nachtfalter m; (*wool-eating*) Motte f; ~**ball** n Mottenkugel f

mother ['mʌðər] n Mutter f ♦ vt bemuttern; ~**hood** n Mutterschaft f; ~-**in-law** n Schwiegermutter f; ~**ly** adj mütterlich; ~-**of-pearl** n Perlmut nt; **M~'s Day** (*BRIT*) n Muttertag m; ~-**to-be** n werdende Mutter f; ~ **tongue** n Muttersprache f

motion ['məʊʃən] n Bewegung f; (*in meeting*) Antrag m ♦ vt, vi: **to** ~ **(to) sb** jdm winken, jdm zu verstehen geben; ~**less** adj regungslos; ~ **picture** n Film m

motivated ['məʊtɪveɪtɪd] adj motiviert

motivation [məʊtɪˈveɪʃən] n Motivierung f

motive ['məʊtɪv] n Motiv nt, Beweggrund m ♦ adj treibend

motley ['mɔtlɪ] adj bunt

motor ['məʊtər] n Motor m; (*BRIT: inf: vehicle*) Auto nt ♦ adj Motor-; ~**bike** n Motorrad nt; ~**boat** n Motorboot nt; ~**car** (*BRIT*) n Auto nt; ~**cycle** n Motorrad nt; ~**cyclist** n Motorradfahrer(in) m(f); ~**ing** (*BRIT*) n Autofahren nt ♦ adj Auto-; ~**ist** n Autofahrer(in) m(f); ~ **mechanic** n

Kraftfahrzeugmechaniker(in) m(f), Kfz-Mechaniker(in) m(f); ~ **racing** (*BRIT*) n Autorennen nt; ~ **vehicle** n Kraftfahrzeug nt; ~**way** (*BRIT*) n Autobahn f

mottled ['mɔtld] adj gesprenkelt

mould [məʊld] (*US* **mold**) n Form f; (*mildew*) Schimmel m ♦ vt (*also fig*) formen; ~**y** adj schimmelig

moult [məʊlt] (*US* **molt**) vi sich mausern

mound [maʊnd] n (Erd)hügel m

mount [maʊnt] n (*liter: hill*) Berg m; (*horse*) Pferd nt; (*for jewel etc*) Fassung f ♦ vt (*horse*) steigen auf +acc; (*put in setting*) fassen; (*exhibition*) veranstalten; (*attack*) unternehmen ♦ vi (*also:* ~ **up**) sich häufen; (*on horse*) aufsitzen

mountain ['maʊntɪn] n Berg m ♦ cpd Berg-; ~ **bike** n Mountainbike nt; ~**eer** n Bergsteiger(in) m(f); ~**eering** [maʊntɪˈnɪərɪŋ] n Bergsteigen nt; ~**ous** adj bergig; ~ **rescue team** n Bergwacht f; ~**side** n Berg(ab)hang m

mourn [mɔːn] vt betrauern, beklagen ♦ vi: **to** ~ **(for sb)** (um jdn) trauern; ~**er** n Trauernde(r) mf; ~**ful** adj traurig; ~**ing** n (*grief*) Trauer f ♦ cpd (*dress*) Trauer-; **in** ~**ing** (*period etc*) in Trauer; (*dress*) in Trauerkleidung f

mouse [maʊs] (pl **mice**) n Maus f; ~**trap** n Mausefalle f; ~ **mat**, ~ **pad** n (*COMPUT*) Mousepad m

mousse [muːs] n (*COOK*) Creme f; (*cosmetic*) Schaumfestiger m

moustache [məsˈtɑːʃ] n Schnurrbart m

mousy ['maʊsɪ] adj (*colour*) mausgrau; (*person*) schüchtern

mouth [maʊθ] n Mund m; (*opening*) Öffnung f; (*of river*) Mündung f; ~**ful** n Mund m voll; ~ **organ** n Mundharmonika f; ~**piece** n Mundstück nt; (*fig*) Sprachrohr nt; ~**wash** n Mundwasser nt; ~**watering** adj lecker, appetitlich

movable ['muːvəbl] adj beweglich

move [muːv] n (~*ment*) Bewegung f; (*in game*) Zug m; (*step*) Schritt m; (*of house*) Umzug m ♦ vt bewegen; (*people*) transportieren; (*in job*) versetzen;

(*emotionally*) bewegen ♦ *vi* sich bewegen; (*vehicle, ship*) fahren; (~ *house*) umziehen; **to get a ~ on** sich beeilen; **to ~ sb** to do sth jdn veranlassen, etw zu tun; ~ **about** *or* **around** *vi* sich hin und her bewegen; (*travel*) unterwegs sein; ~ **along** *vi* weitergehen; (*cars*) weiterfahren; ~ **away** *vi* weggehen; ~ **back** *vi* zurückgehen; (*to the rear*) zurückweichen; ~ **forward** *vi* vorwärts gehen, sich vorwärts bewegen ♦ *vt* vorschieben; (*time*) vorverlegen; ~ **s** *in vi* (*to house*) einziehen; (*troops*) einrücken; ~ **on** *vi* weitergehen ♦ *vt* weitergehen lassen; ~ **out** *vi* (*of house*) ausziehen; (*troops*) abziehen; ~ **over** *vi* zur Seite rücken; ~ **up** *vi* aufsteigen; (*in job*) befördert werden ♦ *vt* nach oben bewegen; (*in job*) befördern; ~**ment** ['mu:vmənt] *n* Bewegung *f*

movie ['mu:vɪ] *n* Film *m*; **to go to the ~s** ins Kino gehen; ~ **camera** *n* Filmkamera *f*

moving ['mu:vɪŋ] *adj* beweglich; (*touching*) ergreifend

mow [məu] (*pt* **mowed**, *pp* **mowed** *or* **mown**) *vt* mähen; ~ **down** *vt* (*fig*) niedermähen; ~**er** *n* (*lawnmower*) Rasenmäher *m*; ~**n** *pp of* **mow**

MP *n abbr* = **Member of Parliament**

MP3 player *n* MP3-Spieler *m*

m.p.h. *abbr* = **miles per hour**

Mr ['mɪstər] (*US* **Mr.**) *n* Herr *m*

Mrs ['mɪsɪz] (*US* **Mrs.**) *n* Frau *f*

Ms [mɪz] (*US* **Ms.**) *n* (= *Miss or Mrs*) Frau *f*

M.Sc. *n abbr* = **Master of Science**

MSP *n abbr* (= *Member of the Scottish Parliament*) Mitglied *nt* des schottischen Parlaments

much [mʌtʃ] *adj* viel ♦ *adv* sehr; viel ♦ *n* viel, eine Menge; **how ~ is it?** wie viel kostet das?; **too ~** zu viel; **it's not ~** es ist nicht viel; **as ~ as** so sehr, so viel; **however ~ he tries** sosehr er es auch versucht

muck [mʌk] *n* Mist *m*; (*fig*) Schmutz *m*; ~ **about** *or* **around** (*inf*) *vi*: **to ~ about** *or* **around (with sth)** (an etw *dat*) herumalbern; ~ **up** *vt* (*inf: ruin*) vermasseln; (*dirty*) dreckig machen; ~**y** *adj* (*dirty*) dreckig

mud [mʌd] *n* Schlamm *m*

muddle ['mʌdl] *n* Durcheinander *nt* ♦ *vt* (*also:* ~ **up**) durcheinander bringen; ~ **through** *vi* sich durchwursteln

mud ['mʌd-]: ~**dy** *adj* schlammig; ~**guard** *n* Schutzblech *nt*; ~**slinging** (*inf*) *n* Verleumdung *f*

muesli ['mju:zlɪ] *n* Müsli *nt*

muffin ['mʌfɪn] *n* süße(s) Teilchen *nt*

muffle ['mʌfl] *vt* (*sound*) dämpfen; (*wrap up*) einhüllen; ~**d** *adj* gedämpft; ~**r** (*US*) *n* (*AUT*) Schalldämpfer *m*

mug [mʌg] *n* (*cup*) Becher *m*; (*inf: face*) Visage *f*; (: *fool*) Trottel *m* ♦ *vt* überfallen und ausrauben; ~**ger** *n* Straßenräuber *m*; ~**ging** *n* Überfall *m*

muggy ['mʌgɪ] *adj* (*weather*) schwül

mule [mju:l] *n* Maulesel *m*

mull [mʌl]: ~ **over** *vt* nachdenken über +*acc*

multicoloured ['mʌltɪkʌləd] (*US* **multicolored**) *adj* mehrfarbig

multi-level ['mʌltɪlevl] (*US*) *adj* = **multistorey**

multiple ['mʌltɪpl] *n* Vielfache(s) *nt* ♦ *adj* mehrfach; (*many*) mehrere; ~ **sclerosis** *n* multiple Sklerose *f*

multiplex cinema ['mʌltɪpleks-] *n* Kinocenter *nt*

multiplication [mʌltɪplɪ'keɪʃən] *n* Multiplikation *f*; (*increase*) Vervielfachung *f*

multiply ['mʌltɪplaɪ] *vt*: **to ~ (by)** multiplizieren (mit) ♦ *vi* (*BIOL*) sich vermehren

multistorey ['mʌltɪ'stɔ:rɪ] (*BRIT*) *adj* (*building, car park*) mehrstöckig

multitude ['mʌltɪtju:d] *n* Menge *f*

mum [mʌm] *n* (*BRIT: inf*) Mutti *f* ♦ *adj*: **to keep ~ (about)** den Mund halten (über +*acc*)

mumble ['mʌmbl] *vt, vi* murmeln ♦ *n* Gemurmel *nt*

mummy ['mʌmɪ] *n* (*dead body*) Mumie *f*; (*BRIT: inf*) Mami *f*

mumps [mʌmps] *n* Mumps *m*

munch [mʌntʃ] *vt, vi* mampfen

mundane [mʌn'deɪn] *adj* banal

municipal [mju:'nɪsɪpl] *adj* städtisch, Stadt-

mural ['mjuərl] *n* Wandgemälde *nt*

murder ['mə:dər] *n* Mord *m* ♦ *vt* ermorden; ~**er** *n* Mörder *m*; ~**ous** *adj* Mord-; (*fig*) mörderisch

murky ['mɜːkɪ] *adj* finster

murmur ['mɜːmə*r*] *n* Murmeln *nt*; (*of water, wind*) Rauschen *nt* ♦ *vt*, *vi* murmeln

muscle ['mʌsl] *n* Muskel *m*; ~ **in** *vi* mitmischen; **muscular** ['mʌskjʊlə*r*] *adj* Muskel-; (*strong*) muskulös

museum [mjuːˈzɪəm] *n* Museum *nt*

mushroom ['mʌʃrʊm] *n* Champignon *m*; Pilz *m* ♦ *vi* (*fig*) emporschießen

music ['mjuːzɪk] *n* Musik *f*; (*printed*) Noten *pl*; ~**al** *adj* (*sound*) melodisch; (*person*) musikalisch ♦ *n* (*show*) Musical *nt*; ~**al instrument** *n* Musikinstrument *nt*; ~ **centre** *n* Stereoanlage *f*; ~ **hall** (*BRIT*) *n* Varietee *nt*, Varieté *nt*; ~**ian** [mjuːˈzɪʃən] *n* Musiker(in) *m(f)*

Muslim ['mʌzlɪm] *adj* moslemisch ♦ *n* Moslem *m*

muslin ['mʌzlɪn] *n* Musselin *m*

mussel ['mʌsl] *n* Miesmuschel *f*

must [mʌst] *vb aux* müssen; (*in negation*) dürfen ♦ *n* Muss *nt*; **the film is a ~** den Film muss man einfach gesehen haben

mustard ['mʌstəd] *n* Senf *m*

muster ['mʌstə*r*] *vt* (*MIL*) antreten lassen; (*courage*) zusammennehmen

mustn't ['mʌsnt] = **must not**

musty ['mʌstɪ] *adj* muffig

mute [mjuːt] *adj* stumm ♦ *n* (*person*) Stumme(r) *mf*; (*MUS*) Dämpfer *m*; ~**d** *adj* gedämpft

mutilate ['mjuːtɪleɪt] *vt* verstümmeln

mutiny ['mjuːtɪnɪ] *n* Meuterei *f* ♦ *vi* meutern

mutter ['mʌtə*r*] *vt*, *vi* murmeln

mutton ['mʌtn] *n* Hammelfleisch *nt*

mutual ['mjuːtʃʊəl] *adj* gegenseitig; beiderseitig; ~**ly** *adv* gegenseitig; für beide Seiten

muzzle ['mʌzl] *n* (*of animal*) Schnauze *f*; (*for animal*) Maulkorb *m*; (*of gun*) Mündung *f* ♦ *vt* einen Maulkorb anlegen +*dat*

my [maɪ] *adj* mein; **this is ~ car** das ist mein Auto; **I've washed ~ hair** ich habe mir die Haare gewaschen

myself [maɪˈself] *pron* mich *acc*; mir *dat*; (*emphatic*) selbst; *see also* **oneself**

mysterious [mɪsˈtɪərɪəs] *adj* geheimnisvoll

mystery ['mɪstərɪ] *n* (*secret*) Geheimnis *nt*; (*sth difficult*) Rätsel *nt*

mystify ['mɪstɪfaɪ] *vt* ein Rätsel *nt* sein +*dat*; verblüffen

mystique [mɪsˈtiːk] *n* geheimnisvolle Natur *f*

myth [mɪθ] *n* Mythos *m*; (*fig*) Erfindung *f*; ~**ology** [mɪˈθɒlədʒɪ] *n* Mythologie *f*

N, n

n/a *abbr* (= *not applicable*) nicht zutreffend

nab [næb] (*inf*) *vt* schnappen

naff [næf] (*BRIT*: *inf*) *adj* blöd

nag [næg] *n* (*horse*) Gaul *m*; (*person*) Nörgler(in) *m(f)* ♦ *vt*, *vi*: **to ~ (at) sb** an jdm herumnörgeln; ~**ging** *adj* (*doubt*) nagend ♦ *n* Nörgelei *f*

nail [neɪl] *n* Nagel *m* ♦ *vt* nageln; **to ~ sb down to doing sth** jdn darauf festnageln, etw zu tun; ~**brush** *n* Nagelbürste *f*; ~**file** *n* Nagelfeile *f*; ~ **polish** *n* Nagellack *m*; ~ **polish remover** *n* Nagellackentferner *m*; ~ **scissors** *npl* Nagelschere *f*; ~ **varnish** (*BRIT*) *n* = **nail polish**

naïve [naɪˈiːv] *adj* naiv

naked ['neɪkɪd] *adj* nackt

name [neɪm] *n* Name *m*; (*reputation*) Ruf *m* ♦ *vt* nennen; (*sth new*) benennen; (*appoint*) ernennen; **by ~** mit Namen; **I know him only by ~** ich kenne ihn nur dem Namen nach; **what's your ~?** wie heißen Sie?; **in the ~ of** im Namen +*gen*; (*for the sake of*) um +*gen* ... willen; ~**less** *adj* namenlos; ~**ly** *adv* nämlich; ~**sake** *n* Namensvetter *m*

nanny ['nænɪ] *n* Kindermädchen *nt*

nap [næp] *n* (*sleep*) Nickerchen *nt*; (*on cloth*) Strich *m* ♦ *vi*: **to be caught ~ping** (*fig*) überrumpelt werden

nape [neɪp] *n* Nacken *m*

napkin ['næpkɪn] *n* (*at table*) Serviette *f*; (*BRIT*: *for baby*) Windel *f*

nappy ['næpɪ] (*BRIT*) *n* (*for baby*) Windel *f*; ~ **rash** *n* wunde Stellen *pl*

narcotic [nɑːˈkɒtɪk] *adj* betäubend ♦ *n* Betäubungsmittel *nt*

narrative ['nærətɪv] n Erzählung f ♦ adj erzählend

narrator [nə'reɪtər] n Erzähler(in) m(f)

narrow ['nærəʊ] adj eng, schmal; (limited) beschränkt ♦ vi sich verengen; **to have a ~ escape** mit knapper Not davonkommen; **to ~ sth down to sth** etw auf etw acc einschränken; **~ly** adv (miss) knapp; (escape) mit knapper Not; **~-minded** adj engstirnig

nasty ['nɑːstɪ] adj ekelhaft, fies; (business, wound) schlimm

nation ['neɪʃən] n Nation f, Volk nt; **~al** ['næʃənl] adj national, National-, Landes- ♦ n Staatsangehörige(r) mf; **~al anthem** (BRIT) n Nationalhymne f; **~al dress** n Tracht f; **N~al Health Service** (BRIT) n staatliche(r) Gesundheitsdienst m; **N~al Insurance** (BRIT) n Sozialversicherung f; **~alism** ['næʃnəlɪzəm] n Nationalismus m; **~alist** ['næʃnəlɪst] n Nationalist(in) m(f) ♦ adj nationalistisch; **~ality** [næʃə'nælɪtɪ] n Staatsangehörigkeit f; **~alize** ['næʃnəlaɪz] vt verstaatlichen; **~ally** ['næʃnəlɪ] adv national, auf Staatsebene; **~al park** (BRIT) n Nationalpark m; **~wide** ['neɪʃənwaɪd] adj, adv allgemein, landesweit

---

National Trust

i Der **National Trust** ist ein 1895 gegründeter Natur- und Denkmalschutzverband in Großbritannien, der Gebäude und Gelände von besonderem historischen oder ästhetischen Interesse erhält und der Öffentlichkeit zugänglich macht. Viele Gebäude im Besitz des National Trust sind (z.T. gegen ein Eintrittsgeld) zu besichtigen.

---

native ['neɪtɪv] n (born in) Einheimische(r) mf; (original inhabitant) Eingeborene(r) mf ♦ adj einheimisch; Eingeborenen-; (belonging by birth) heimatlich, Heimat-; (inborn) angeboren, natürlich; **a ~ of Germany** ein gebürtiger Deutscher; **a ~ speaker of French** ein französischer Muttersprachler; **N~ American** n

Indianer(in) m(f), Ureinwohner(in) m(f) Amerikas; **~ language** n Muttersprache f

Nativity [nə'tɪvɪtɪ] n: **the ~** Christi Geburt no art

NATO ['neɪtəʊ] n abbr (= North Atlantic Treaty Organization) NATO f

natural ['nætʃrəl] adj natürlich; Natur-; (inborn) (an)geboren; **~ gas** n Erdgas nt; **~ist** n Naturkundler(in) m(f); **~ly** adv natürlich

nature ['neɪtʃər] n Natur f; **by ~** von Natur (aus)

naught [nɔːt] n = **nought**

naughty ['nɔːtɪ] adj (child) unartig, ungezogen; (action) ungehörig

nausea ['nɔːsɪə] n (sickness) Übelkeit f; (disgust) Ekel m; **~te** ['nɔːsɪeɪt] vt anekeln

nautical ['nɔːtɪkl] adj nautisch; See-; (expression) seemännisch

naval ['neɪvl] adj Marine-, Flotten-; **~ officer** n Marineoffizier m

nave [neɪv] n Kirchen(haupt)schiff nt

navel ['neɪvl] n Nabel m

navigate ['nævɪgeɪt] vi navigieren; **navigation** [nævɪ'geɪʃən] n Navigation f; **navigator** ['nævɪgeɪtər] n Steuermann m; (AVIAT) Navigator m; (AUT) Beifahrer(in) m(f)

navvy ['nævɪ] (BRIT) n Straßenarbeiter m

navy ['neɪvɪ] n (Kriegs)marine f ♦ adj (also: ~ **blue**) marineblau

Nazi ['nɑːtsɪ] n Nazi m

NB abbr (= nota bene) NB

near [nɪər] adj nah ♦ adv in der Nähe ♦ prep (also: ~ **to**: space) in der Nähe +gen; (: time) um +acc ... herum ♦ vt sich nähern +dat; **a ~ miss** knapp daneben; **~by** adj nahe (gelegen) ♦ adv in der Nähe; **~ly** adv fast; **I ~ly fell** ich wäre fast gefallen; **~side** n (AUT) Beifahrerseite f ♦ adj auf der Beifahrerseite; **~-sighted** adj kurzsichtig

neat [niːt] adj (tidy) ordentlich; (solution) sauber; (pure) pur; **~ly** adv (tidily) ordentlich

necessarily ['nesɪsrɪlɪ] adv unbedingt

necessary ['nesɪsrɪ] adj notwendig, nötig; **he did all that was ~** er erledigte alles, was nötig war; **it is ~ to/that ...** man muss ...

necessitate [nɪˈsesɪteɪt] *vt* erforderlich machen

necessity [nɪˈsesɪtɪ] *n* (*need*) Not *f*; (*compulsion*) Notwendigkeit *f*; **necessities** *npl* (*things needed*) das Notwendigste

neck [nek] *n* Hals *m* ♦ *vi* (*inf*) knutschen; **~ and ~** Kopf an Kopf; **~lace** [ˈneklɪs] *n* Halskette *f*; **~line** [ˈneklaɪn] *n* Ausschnitt *m*; **~tie** [ˈnektaɪ] (*US*) *n* Krawatte *f*

née [neɪ] *adj* geborene

need [niːd] *n* Bedürfnis *nt*; (*lack*) Mangel *m*; (*necessity*) Notwendigkeit *f*; (*poverty*) Not *f* ♦ *vt* brauchen; **I ~ to do it** ich muss es tun; **you don't ~ to go** du brauchst nicht zu gehen

needle [ˈniːdl] *n* Nadel *f* ♦ *vt* (*fig: inf*) ärgern

needless [ˈniːdlɪs] *adj* unnötig; **~ to say** natürlich

needlework [ˈniːdlwəːk] *n* Handarbeit *f*

needn't [ˈniːdnt] = **need not**

needy [ˈniːdɪ] *adj* bedürftig

negative [ˈnegətɪv] *n* (*PHOT*) Negativ *nt* ♦ *adj* negativ; (*answer*) abschlägig; **~ equity** *n* Differenz zwischen gefallenem Wert und hypothekarischer Belastung eines Wohneigentums

neglect [nɪˈglekt] *vt* vernachlässigen ♦ *n* Vernachlässigung *f*; **~ed** *adj* vernachlässigt

negligee [ˈneglɪʒeɪ] *n* Negligee *nt*, Negligé *nt*

negligence [ˈneglɪdʒəns] *n* Nachlässigkeit *f*

negligible [ˈneglɪdʒɪbl] *adj* unbedeutend, geringfügig

negotiable [nɪˈgəʊʃɪəbl] *adj* (*cheque*) übertragbar, einlösbar

negotiate [nɪˈgəʊʃɪeɪt] *vi* verhandeln ♦ *vt* (*treaty*) abschließen; (*difficulty*) überwinden; (*corner*) nehmen; **negotiation** [nɪgəʊʃɪˈeɪʃən] *n* Verhandlung *f*; **negotiator** *n* Unterhändler *m*

neigh [neɪ] *vi* wiehern

neighbour [ˈneɪbəʳ] (*US* **neighbor**) *n* Nachbar(in) *m(f)*; **~hood** *n* Nachbarschaft *f*; Umgebung *f*; **~ing** *adj* benachbart, angrenzend; **~ly** *adj* (*person, attitude*) nachbarlich

neither [ˈnaɪðəʳ] *adj, pron* keine(r, s) (von beiden) ♦ *conj*: **he can't do it, and ~ can I** er kann es nicht und ich auch nicht ♦ *adv*: **~ good nor bad** weder gut noch schlecht; **~ story is true** keine der beiden Geschichten stimmt

neon [ˈniːɒn] *n* Neon *nt*; **~ light** *n* Neonlampe *f*

nephew [ˈnevjuː] *n* Neffe *m*

nerve [nəːv] *n* Nerv *m*; (*courage*) Mut *m*; (*impudence*) Frechheit *f*; **to have a fit of ~s** in Panik geraten; **~-racking** *adj* nervenaufreibend

nervous [ˈnəːvəs] *adj* (*of the nerves*) Nerven-; (*timid*) nervös, ängstlich; **~ breakdown** *n* Nervenzusammenbruch *m*; **~ness** *n* Nervosität *f*

nest [nest] *n* Nest *nt* ♦ *vi* nisten; **~ egg** *n* (*fig*) Notgroschen *m*

nestle [ˈnesl] *vi* sich kuscheln

Net [net] *n*: **the ~** das Internet

net [net] *n* Netz *nt* ♦ *adj* netto, Netto- ♦ *vt* netto einnehmen; **~ball** *n* Netzball *m*

Netherlands [ˈneðələndz] *npl*: **the ~** die Niederlande *pl*

nett [net] *adj* = **net**

netting [ˈnetɪŋ] *n* Netz(werk) *nt*

nettle [ˈnetl] *n* Nessel *f*

network [ˈnetwəːk] *n* Netz *nt*

neurotic [njʊəˈrɒtɪk] *adj* neurotisch

neuter [ˈnjuːtəʳ] *adj* (*BIOL*) geschlechtslos; (*GRAM*) sächlich ♦ *vt* kastrieren

neutral [ˈnjuːtrəl] *adj* neutral ♦ *n* (*AUT*) Leerlauf *m*; **~ity** [njuːˈtrælɪtɪ] *n* Neutralität *f*; **~ize** *vt* (*fig*) ausgleichen

never [ˈnevəʳ] *adv* nie(mals); **I ~ went** ich bin gar nicht gegangen; **~ in my life** nie im Leben; **~-ending** *adj* endlos; **~theless** [nevəðəˈles] *adv* trotzdem, dennoch

new [njuː] *adj* neu; **N~ Age** *adj* Newage-, New-Age-; **~born** *adj* neugeboren; **~comer** [ˈnjuːkʌməʳ] *n* Neuankömmling *m*; **~fangled** (*pej*) *adj* neumodisch; **~found** *adj* neu entdeckt; **~ly** *adv* frisch, neu; **~lyweds** *npl* Frischvermählte *pl*; **~ moon** *n* Neumond *m*

news [njuːz] *n* Nachricht *f*; (*RAD, TV*) Nachrichten *pl*; **a piece of ~** eine

Nachricht; ~ **agency** n
Nachrichtenagentur f; ~**agent** (BRIT) n
Zeitungshändler m; ~**caster** n
Nachrichtensprecher(in) m(f); ~ **flash** n
Kurzmeldung f; ~**letter** n Rundschreiben
nt; ~**paper** n Zeitung f; ~**print** n
Zeitungspapier nt; ~**reader** n =
newscaster; ~**reel** n Wochenschau f; ~
stand n Zeitungsstand m

newt [njuːt] n Wassermolch m

New Year n Neujahr nt; ~'**s Day** n
Neujahrstag m; ~'**s Eve** n Silvester(abend
m) nt

New Zealand [-'ziːlənd] n Neuseeland nt;
~**er** n Neuseeländer(in) m(f)

next [nekst] adj nächste(r, s) ♦ adv (after)
dann, darauf; (~ time) das nächste Mal; **the
~ day** am nächsten or folgenden Tag; ~
time das nächste Mal; ~ **year** nächstes
Jahr; ~ **door** adv nebenan ♦ adj (neighbour,
flat) von nebenan; ~ **of kin** n nächste(r)
Verwandte(r) mf; ~ **to** prep neben; ~ **to
nothing** so gut wie nichts

NHS n abbr = **National Health Service**

nib [nɪb] n Spitze f

nibble ['nɪbl] vt knabbern an +dat

nice [naɪs] adj (person) nett; (thing) schön;
(subtle) fein; ~-**looking** adj gut aussehend;
~**ly** adv gut, nett; ~**ties** ['naɪsɪtɪz] npl
Feinheiten pl

nick [nɪk] n Einkerbung f ♦ vt (inf: steal)
klauen; **in the ~ of time** gerade rechtzeitig

nickel ['nɪkl] n Nickel nt; (US) Nickel m (5
cents)

nickname ['nɪkneɪm] n Spitzname m ♦ vt
taufen

nicotine patch ['nɪkəti:n-] n Nikotinpflaster
nt

niece [niːs] n Nichte f

Nigeria [naɪ'dʒɪərɪə] n Nigeria nt

niggling ['nɪglɪŋ] adj pedantisch; (doubt,
worry) quälend

night [naɪt] n Nacht f; (evening) Abend m;
the ~ before last vorletzte Nacht; **at** or **by
~** (before midnight) abends; (after midnight)
nachts; ~**cap** n (drink) Schlummertrunk m;
~**club** n Nachtlokal nt; ~**dress** n

Nachthemd nt; ~**fall** n Einbruch m der
Nacht; ~ **gown** n = **nightdress**; ~**ie** (inf) n
Nachthemd nt

nightingale ['naɪtɪŋgeɪl] n Nachtigall f

night: ~**life** ['naɪtlaɪf] n Nachtleben nt; ~**ly**
['naɪtlɪ] adj, adv jeden Abend; jede Nacht;
~**mare** ['naɪtmeəʳ] n Albtraum m; ~ **porter**
n Nachtportier m; ~ **school** n Abendschule
f; ~ **shift** n Nachtschicht f; ~**time** n Nacht
f

nil [nɪl] n Null f

Nile [naɪl] n: **the ~** der Nil

nimble ['nɪmbl] adj beweglich

nine [naɪn] num neun; ~**teen** num
neunzehn; ~**ty** num neunzig

ninth [naɪnθ] adj neunte(r, s)

nip [nɪp] vt kneifen ♦ n Kneifen nt

nipple ['nɪpl] n Brustwarze f

nippy ['nɪpɪ] (inf) adj (person) flink; (BRIT: car)
flott; (: cold) frisch

nitrogen ['naɪtrədʒən] n Stickstoff m

---KEYWORD---

no [nəʊ] (pl **noes**) adv (opposite of yes) nein;
to answer no (to question) mit Nein
antworten; (to request) Nein or nein sagen;
no thank you nein, danke
♦ adj (not any) kein(e); **I have no money/
time** ich habe kein Geld/keine Zeit; **"no
smoking"** „Rauchen verboten"
♦ n Nein nt; (no vote) Neinstimme f

nobility [nəʊ'bɪlɪtɪ] n Adel m

noble ['nəʊbl] adj (rank) adlig; (splendid)
nobel, edel

nobody ['nəʊbədɪ] pron niemand, keiner

nocturnal [nɔk'tɜːnl] adj (tour, visit)
nächtlich; (animal) Nacht-

nod [nɔd] vi nicken ♦ vt nicken mit ♦ n
Nicken nt; ~ **off** vi einnicken

noise [nɔɪz] n (sound) Geräusch nt;
(unpleasant, loud) Lärm m; **noisy** ['nɔɪzɪ] adj
laut; (crowd) lärmend

nominal ['nɔmɪnl] adj nominell

nominate ['nɔmɪneɪt] vt (suggest)
vorschlagen; (in election) aufstellen;
(appoint) ernennen; **nomination**

[nɔmɪ'neɪʃən] n (election) Nominierung f; (appointment) Ernennung f; **nominee** [nɔmɪ'niː] n Kandidat(in) m(f)

non... [nɔn] prefix Nicht-, un-; **~-alcoholic** adj alkoholfrei

nonchalant ['nɔnʃələnt] adj lässig

non-committal [nɔnkə'mɪtl] adj (reserved) zurückhaltend; (uncommitted) unverbindlich

nondescript ['nɔndɪskrɪpt] adj mittelmäßig

none [nʌn] adj, pron kein(e, er, es) ♦ adv: **he's ~ the worse for it** es hat ihm nicht geschadet; **~ of you** keiner von euch; **I've ~ left** ich habe keinen mehr

nonentity [nɔ'nentɪtɪ] n Null f (inf)

nonetheless ['nʌnðə'lɛs] adv nichtsdestoweniger

non-existent [nɔnɪg'zɪstənt] adj nicht vorhanden

non-fiction [nɔn'fɪkʃən] n Sachbücher pl

nonplussed [nɔn'plʌst] adj verdutzt

nonsense ['nɔnsəns] n Unsinn m

non: **~-smoker** n Nichtraucher(in) m(f); **~-smoking** adj Nichtraucher-; **~-stick** adj (pan, surface) Teflon- ®; **~-stop** adj Nonstop-, Non-Stop-

noodles ['nuːdlz] npl Nudeln pl

nook [nuk] n Winkel m; **~s and crannies** Ecken und Winkel

noon [nuːn] n (12 Uhr) Mittag m

no one ['nəuwʌn] pron = **nobody**

noose [nuːs] n Schlinge f

nor [nɔːr] conj = **neither** ♦ adv see **neither**

norm [nɔːm] n (convention) Norm f; (rule, requirement) Vorschrift f

normal ['nɔːməl] adj normal; **~ly** adv normal; (usually) normalerweise

Normandy ['nɔːməndɪ] n Normandie f

north [nɔːθ] n Norden m ♦ adj nördlich, Nord- ♦ adv nördlich, nach or im Norden; **N~ Africa** n Nordafrika nt; **N~ America** n Nordamerika nt; **~-east** n Nordosten m; **~erly** ['nɔːðəlɪ] adj nördlich; **~ern** ['nɔːðən] adj nördlich, Nord-; **N~ern Ireland** n Nordirland nt; **N~ Pole** n Nordpol m; **N~ Sea** n Nordsee f; **~ward(s)** ['nɔːθwəd(z)] adv nach Norden; **~-west** n Nordwesten m

Norway ['nɔːweɪ] n Norwegen nt

Norwegian [nɔː'wiːdʒən] adj norwegisch ♦ n Norweger(in) m(f); (LING) Norwegisch nt

nose [nəuz] n Nase f ♦ vi: **to ~ about** herumschnüffeln; **~bleed** n Nasenbluten nt; **~ dive** n Sturzflug m; **~y** adj = **nosy**

nostalgia [nɔs'tældʒɪə] n Nostalgie f; **nostalgic** adj nostalgisch

nostril ['nɔstrɪl] n Nasenloch nt

nosy ['nəuzɪ] (inf) adj neugierig

not [nɔt] adv nicht; **he is ~** or **isn't here** er ist nicht hier; **it's too late, isn't it?** es ist zu spät, oder or nicht wahr?; **~ yet/now** noch nicht/nicht jetzt; see also **all; only**

notably ['nəutəblɪ] adv (especially) besonders; (noticeably) bemerkenswert

notary ['nəutərɪ] n Notar(in) m(f)

notch [nɔtʃ] n Kerbe f, Einschnitt m

note [nəut] n (MUS) Note f, Ton m; (short letter) Nachricht f; (POL) Note f; (comment, attention) Notiz f; (of lecture etc) Aufzeichnung f; (banknote) Schein m; (fame) Ruf m ♦ vt (observe) bemerken; (also: **~ down**) notieren; **~book** n Notizbuch nt; **~d** adj bekannt; **~pad** n Notizblock m; **~paper** n Briefpapier nt

nothing ['nʌθɪŋ] n nichts; **~ new/much** nichts Neues/nicht viel; **for ~** umsonst

notice ['nəutɪs] n (announcement) Bekanntmachung f; (warning) Ankündigung f; (dismissal) Kündigung f ♦ vt bemerken; **to take ~ of** beachten; **at short ~** kurzfristig; **until further ~** bis auf weiteres; **to hand in one's ~** kündigen; **~able** adj merklich; **~ board** n Anschlagtafel f

notify ['nəutɪfaɪ] vt benachrichtigen

notion ['nəuʃən] n Idee f

notorious [nəu'tɔːrɪəs] adj berüchtigt

notwithstanding [nɔtwɪθ'stændɪŋ] adv trotzdem; **~ this** ungeachtet dessen

nought [nɔːt] n Null f

noun [naun] n Substantiv nt

nourish ['nʌrɪʃ] vt nähren; **~ing** adj nahrhaft; **~ment** n Nahrung f

novel ['nɔvl] n Roman m ♦ adj neu(artig); **~ist** n Schriftsteller(in) m(f); **~ty** n Neuheit f

November [nəu'vɛmbər] n November m

novice ['nɔvis] n Neuling m

now [nau] adv jetzt; **right ~** jetzt, gerade; **by ~** inzwischen; **just ~** gerade; **~ and then, ~ and again** ab und zu, manchmal; **from ~ on** von jetzt an; **~adays** adv heutzutage

nowhere ['nəuwɛər] adv nirgends

nozzle ['nɔzl] n Düse f

nuclear ['nju:kliər] adj (energy etc) Atom-, Kern-

nuclei ['nju:kliai] npl of **nucleus**

nucleus ['nju:kliəs] n Kern m

nude [nju:d] adj nackt ♦ n (ART) Akt m; **in the ~** nackt

nudge [nʌdʒ] vt leicht anstoßen

nudist ['nju:dist] n Nudist(in) m(f)

nudity ['nju:diti] n Nacktheit f

nuisance ['nju:sns] n Ärgernis nt; **what a ~!** wie ärgerlich!

nuke [nju:k] (inf) n Kernkraftwerk nt ♦ vt atomar vernichten

null [nʌl] adj: **~ and void** null und nichtig

numb [nʌm] adj taub, gefühllos ♦ vt betäuben

number ['nʌmbər] n Nummer f; (numeral also) Zahl f; (quantity) (An)zahl f ♦ vt nummerieren; (amount to) sein; **to be ~ed among** gezählt werden zu; **a ~ of** (several) einige; **they were ten in ~** sie waren zehn an der Zahl; **~ plate** (BRIT) n (AUT) Nummernschild nt

numeral ['nju:mərəl] n Ziffer f

numerate ['nju:mərit] adj rechenkundig

numerical [nju:'mɛrikl] adj (order) zahlenmäßig

numerous ['nju:mərəs] adj zahlreich

nun [nʌn] n Nonne f

nurse [nə:s] n Krankenschwester f; (for children) Kindermädchen nt ♦ vt (patient) pflegen; (doubt etc) hegen

nursery ['nə:səri] n (for children) Kinderzimmer nt; (for plants) Gärtnerei f; (for trees) Baumschule f; **~ rhyme** n Kinderreim m; **~ school** n Kindergarten m; **~ slope** (BRIT) n (SKI) Idiotenhügel m (inf), Anfängerhügel m

nursing ['nə:sɪŋ] n (profession) Krankenpflege f; **~ home** n Privatklinik f

nurture ['nə:tʃər] vt aufziehen

nut [nʌt] n Nuss f; (TECH) Schraubenmutter f; (inf) Verrückte(r) mf; **he's ~s** er ist verrückt; **~crackers** ['nʌtkrækəz] npl Nussknacker m

nutmeg ['nʌtmɛg] n Muskat(nuss f) m

nutrient ['nju:trɪənt] n Nährstoff m

nutrition [nju:'trɪʃən] n Nahrung f; **nutritious** [nju:'trɪʃəs] adj nahrhaft

nutshell ['nʌtʃɛl] n Nussschale f; **in a ~** (fig) kurz gesagt

nutter ['nʌtər] (BRIT: inf) n Spinner(in) m(f)

nylon ['nailɔn] n Nylon nt ♦ adj Nylon-

O, o

oak [əuk] n Eiche f ♦ adj Eichen(holz)-

O.A.P. abbr = **old-age pensioner**

oar [ɔ:r] n Ruder nt

oases [əu'eisi:z] npl of **oasis**

oasis [əu'eisis] n Oase f

oath [əuθ] n (statement) Eid m, Schwur m; (swearword) Fluch m

oatmeal ['əutmi:l] n Haferschrot m

oats [əuts] npl Hafer m

obedience [ə'bi:diəns] n Gehorsam m

obedient [ə'bi:diənt] adj gehorsam

obesity [əu'bi:siti] n Fettleibigkeit f

obey [ə'bei] vt, vi: **to ~ (sb)** (jdm) gehorchen

obituary [ə'bitjuəri] n Nachruf m

object [n 'ɔbdʒikt, vb əb'dʒɛkt] n (thing) Gegenstand m, Objekt nt; (purpose) Ziel nt ♦ vi dagegen sein; **expense is no ~** Ausgaben spielen keine Rolle; **I ~!** ich protestiere!; **to ~ to sth** Einwände gegen etw haben; (morally) Anstoß an etw acc nehmen; **to ~ that** einwenden, dass; **~ion** [əb'dʒɛkʃən] n (reason against) Einwand m, Einspruch m; (dislike) Abneigung f; **I have no ~ion to ...** ich habe nichts gegen ...; **~ionable** [əb'dʒɛkʃənəbl] adj nicht einwandfrei; (language) anstößig

objective [əb'dʒɛktiv] n Ziel nt ♦ adj objektiv

obligation [ɔbli'geiʃən] n Verpflichtung f; **without ~** unverbindlich; **obligatory**

[əˈblɪɡətərɪ] *adj* obligatorisch

oblige [əˈblaɪdʒ] *vt* (*compel*) zwingen; (*do a favour*) einen Gefallen tun +*dat*; **to be ~d to sb for sth** jdm für etw verbunden sein

obliging [əˈblaɪdʒɪŋ] *adj* entgegenkommend

oblique [əˈbliːk] *adj* schräg, schief ♦ *n* Schrägstrich *m*

obliterate [əˈblɪtəreɪt] *vt* auslöschen

oblivion [əˈblɪvɪən] *n* Vergessenheit *f*

oblivious [əˈblɪvɪəs] *adj* nicht bewusst

oblong [ˈɔblɔŋ] *n* Rechteck *nt* ♦ *adj* länglich

obnoxious [əbˈnɔkʃəs] *adj* widerlich

oboe [ˈəubəu] *n* Oboe *f*

obscene [əbˈsiːn] *adj* obszön; **obscenity** [əbˈsenɪtɪ] *n* Obszönität *f*; **obscenities** *npl* (*oaths*) Zoten *pl*

obscure [əbˈskjuə^r] *adj* unklar; (*indistinct*) undeutlich; (*unknown*) unbekannt, obskur; (*dark*) düster ♦ *vt* verdunkeln; (*view*) verbergen; (*confuse*) verwirren; **obscurity** [əbˈskjuərɪtɪ] *n* Unklarheit *f*; (*darkness*) Dunkelheit *f*

observance [əbˈzəːvəns] *n* Befolgung *f*

observant [əbˈzəːvənt] *adj* aufmerksam

observation [ɔbzəˈveɪʃən] *n* (*noticing*) Beobachtung *f*; (*surveillance*) Überwachung *f*; (*remark*) Bemerkung *f*

observatory [əbˈzəːvətrɪ] *n* Sternwarte *f*, Observatorium *nt*

observe [əbˈzəːv] *vt* (*notice*) bemerken; (*watch*) beobachten; (*customs*) einhalten; **~r** *n* Beobachter(in) *m(f)*

obsess [əbˈses] *vt* verfolgen, quälen; **~ion** [əbˈseʃən] *n* Besessenheit *f*, Wahn *m*; **~ive** *adj* krankhaft

obsolete [ˈɔbsəliːt] *adj* überholt, veraltet

obstacle [ˈɔbstəkl] *n* Hindernis *nt*; **~ race** *n* Hindernisrennen *nt*

obstetrics [ɔbˈstetrɪks] *n* Geburtshilfe *f*

obstinate [ˈɔbstɪnɪt] *adj* hartnäckig, stur

obstruct [əbˈstrʌkt] *vt* versperren; (*pipe*) verstopfen; (*hinder*) hemmen; **~ion** [əbˈstrʌkʃən] *n* Versperrung *f*; Verstopfung *f*; (*obstacle*) Hindernis *nt*

obtain [əbˈteɪn] *vt* erhalten, bekommen; (*result*) erzielen

obtrusive [əbˈtruːsɪv] *adj* aufdringlich

obvious [ˈɔbvɪəs] *adj* offenbar, offensichtlich; **~ly** *adv* offensichtlich

occasion [əˈkeɪʒən] *n* Gelegenheit *f*; (*special event*) Ereignis *nt*; (*reason*) Anlass *m* ♦ *vt* veranlassen; **~al** *adj* gelegentlich; **~ally** *adv* gelegentlich

occupant [ˈɔkjupənt] *n* Inhaber(in) *m(f)*; (*of house*) Bewohner(in) *m(f)*

occupation [ɔkjuˈpeɪʃən] *n* (*employment*) Tätigkeit *f*, Beruf *m*; (*pastime*) Beschäftigung *f*; (*of country*) Besetzung *f*, Okkupation *f*; **~al hazard** *n* Berufsrisiko *nt*

occupier [ˈɔkjupaɪə^r] *n* Bewohner(in) *m(f)*

occupy [ˈɔkjupaɪ] *vt* (*take possession of*) besetzen; (*seat*) belegen; (*live in*) bewohnen; (*position, office*) bekleiden; (*position in sb's life*) beanspruchen; **to ~ o.s. with sth** sich mit etw beschäftigen; **to ~ o.s. by doing sth** sich damit beschäftigen, etw zu tun

occur [əˈkəː^r] *vi* vorkommen; **to ~ to sb** jdm einfallen; **~rence** *n* (*event*) Ereignis *nt*; (*appearing*) Auftreten *nt*

ocean [ˈəuʃən] *n* Ozean *m*, Meer *nt*; **~-going** *adj* Hochsee-

o'clock [əˈklɔk] *adv*: **it is 5 ~** es ist 5 Uhr

OCR *n abbr* = **optical character reader**

octagonal [ɔkˈtæɡənl] *adj* achteckig

October [ɔkˈtəubə^r] *n* Oktober *m*

octopus [ˈɔktəpəs] *n* Krake *f*; (*small*) Tintenfisch *m*

odd [ɔd] *adj* (*strange*) sonderbar; (*not even*) ungerade; (*sock etc*) einzeln; (*surplus*) übrig; **60-~** so um die 60; **at ~ times** ab und zu; **to be the ~ one out** (*person*) das fünfte Rad am Wagen sein; (*thing*) nicht dazugehören; **~ity** *n* (*strangeness*) Merkwürdigkeit *f*; (*queer person*) seltsame(r) Kauz *m*; (*thing*) Kuriosität *f*; **~-job man** (*irreg*) *n* Mädchen *nt* für alles; **~ jobs** *npl* gelegentlich anfallende Arbeiten; **~ly** *adv* seltsam; **~ments** *npl* Reste *pl*; **~s** *npl* Chancen *pl*; (*betting*) Gewinnchancen *pl*; **it makes no ~s** es spielt keine Rolle; **~s and ends** *npl* Krimskrams *m*

odometer [ɔˈdɔmɪtə^r] (*esp US*) *n* Tacho(meter) *m*

dour ['əudər] (*US* **odor**) *n* Geruch *m*

f [ɒv, əv] *prep* 1 von +*dat*; *use of gen*; **the history of Germany** die Geschichte Deutschlands; **a friend of ours** ein Freund von uns; **a boy of 10** ein 10-jähriger Junge; **that was kind of you** das war sehr freundlich von Ihnen

2 (*expressing quantity, amount, dates etc*): **a kilo of flour** ein Kilo Mehl; **how much of this do you need?** wie viel brauchen Sie (davon)?; **there were 3 of them** (*people*) sie waren zu dritt; (*objects*) es gab 3 (davon); **a cup of tea/vase of flowers** eine Tasse Tee/Vase mit Blumen; **the 5th of July** der 5. Juli

3 (*from, out of*) aus; **a bridge made of wood** eine Holzbrücke, eine Brücke aus Holz

ff [ɒf] *adj, adv* (*absent*) weg, fort; (*switch*) aus(geschaltet), ab(geschaltet); (*BRIT: food: bad*) schlecht; (*cancelled*) abgesagt ♦ *prep* von +*dat*; **to be ~** (*to leave*) gehen; **to be ~ sick** krank sein; **a day ~** ein freier Tag; **to have an ~ day** einen schlechten Tag haben; **he had his coat ~** er hatte seinen Mantel aus; **10% ~** (*COMM*) 10% Rabatt; **5 km ~ (the road)** 5 km (von der Straße) entfernt; **~ the coast** vor der Küste; **I'm ~ meat** (*no longer eat it*) ich esse kein Fleisch mehr; (*no longer like it*) ich mag kein Fleisch mehr; **on the ~ chance** auf gut Glück

ffal ['ɒfl] *n* Innereien *pl*

ff-colour ['ɒf'kʌlər] *adj* nicht wohl

ffence [ə'fens] (*US* **offense**) *n* (*crime*) Vergehen *nt*, Straftat *f*; (*insult*) Beleidigung *f*; **to take ~ at** gekränkt sein wegen

ffend [ə'fend] *vt* beleidigen; **~er** *n* Gesetzesübertreter *m*

ffense [ə'fens] (*US*) *n* = **offence**

ffensive [ə'fensɪv] *adj* (*unpleasant*) übel, abstoßend; (*weapon*) Kampf-; (*remark*) verletzend ♦ *n* Angriff *m*

ffer ['ɒfər] *n* Angebot *f* ♦ *vt* anbieten; (*opinion*) äußern; (*resistance*) leisten; **on ~**

zum Verkauf angeboten; **~ing** *n* Gabe *f*

offhand [ɒf'hænd] *adj* lässig ♦ *adv* ohne weiteres

office ['ɒfɪs] *n* Büro *nt*; (*position*) Amt *nt*; **doctor's ~** (*US*) Praxis *f*; **to take ~** sein Amt antreten; (*POL*) die Regierung übernehmen; **~ automation** *n* Büroautomatisierung *f*; **~ block** (*US* **~ building**) *n* Büro(hoch)haus *nt*; **~ hours** *npl* Dienstzeit *f*; (*US: MED*) Sprechstunde *f*

officer ['ɒfɪsər] *n* (*MIL*) Offizier *m*; (*public ~*) Beamte(r) *m*

official [ə'fɪʃl] *adj* offiziell, amtlich ♦ *n* Beamte(r) *m*; **~dom** *n* Beamtentum *nt*

officiate [ə'fɪʃɪeɪt] *vi* amtieren

officious [ə'fɪʃəs] *adj* aufdringlich

offing ['ɒfɪŋ] *n*: **in the ~** in (Aus)sicht

Off-licence ist ein Geschäft (oder eine Theke in einer Gaststätte), wo man alkoholische Getränke kaufen kann, die aber anderswo konsumiert werden müssen. In solchen Geschäften, die oft von landesweiten Ketten betrieben werden, kann man auch andere Getränke, Süßigkeiten, Zigaretten und Knabbereien kaufen.

off: **~-licence** (*BRIT*) *n* (*shop*) Wein- und Spirituosenhandlung *f*; **~-line** *adj* (*COMPUT*) Offline- ♦ *adv* (*COMPUT*) offline; **~-peak** *adj* (*charges*) verbilligt; **~-putting** (*BRIT*) *adj* (*person, remark etc*) abstoßend; **~-road vehicle** *n* Geländefahrzeug *nt*; **~-season** *adj* außer Saison; **~set** (*irreg: like* **set**) *vt* ausgleichen ♦ *n* (*also:* **~set printing**) Offset(druck) *m*; **~shoot** *n* (*fig: of organization*) Zweig *m*; (: *of discussion etc*) Randergebnis *nt*; **~shore** *adv* in einiger Entfernung von der Küste ♦ *adj* küstennah, Küsten-; **~side** *adj* (*SPORT*) im Abseits ♦ *adv* abseits ♦ *n* (*AUT*) Fahrerseite *f*; **~spring** *n* Nachkommenschaft *f*; (*one*) Sprössling *m*; **~stage** *adv* hinter den Kulissen; **~-the-cuff** *adj* unvorbereitet, aus dem Stegreif; **~-the-peg** (*US* **~-the-rack**) *adv* von der Stange; **~-white** *adj* naturweiß

Oftel [ˈɔftel] n Überwachungsgremium zum Verbraucherschutz nach Privatisierung der Telekommunikationsindustrie

often [ˈɔfn] adv oft

Ofwat [ˈɔfwɔt] n Überwachungsgremium zum Verbraucherschutz nach Privatisierung der Wasserindustrie

ogle [ˈəʊgl] vt liebäugeln mit

oil [ɔɪl] n Öl nt ♦ vt ölen; **~can** n Ölkännchen nt; **~field** n Ölfeld nt; **~ filter** n (AUT) Ölfilter m; **~-fired** adj Öl-; **~ painting** n Ölgemälde nt; **~ rig** n Ölplattform f; **~skins** npl Ölzeug nt; **~ slick** n Ölteppich m; **~ tanker** n (Öl)tanker m; **~ well** n Ölquelle f; **~y** adj ölig; (dirty) ölbeschmiert

ointment [ˈɔɪntmənt] n Salbe f

O.K. [ˈəʊˈkeɪ] excl in Ordnung, O. K., o. k. ♦ adj in Ordnung ♦ vt genehmigen

okay [ˈəʊˈkeɪ] = **O.K.**

old [əʊld] adj alt; **how ~ are you?** wie alt bist du?; **he's 10 years ~** er ist 10 Jahre alt; **~er brother** ältere(r) Bruder m; **~ age** n Alter nt; **~-age pensioner** (BRIT) n Rentner(in) m(f); **~-fashioned** adj altmodisch

olive [ˈɔlɪv] n (fruit) Olive f; (colour) Olive nt ♦ adj Oliven-; (coloured) olivenfarbig; **~ oil** n Olivenöl nt

Olympic [əʊˈlɪmpɪk] adj olympisch; **the ~ Games, the ~s** die Olympischen Spiele

omelet(te) [ˈɔmlɪt] n Omelett nt

omen [ˈəʊmən] n Omen nt

ominous [ˈɔmɪnəs] adj bedrohlich

omission [əʊˈmɪʃən] n Auslassung f; (neglect) Versäumnis nt

omit [əʊˈmɪt] vt auslassen; (fail to do) versäumen

KEYWORD
---

on [ɔn] prep 1 (indicating position) auf +dat; (with vb of motion) auf +acc; (on vertical surface, part of body) an +dat/acc; **it's on the table** es ist auf dem Tisch; **she put the book on the table** sie legte das Buch auf den Tisch; **on the left** links
2 (indicating means, method, condition etc): **on foot** (go, be) zu Fuß; **on the train/**

plane (go) mit dem Zug/Flugzeug; (be) im Zug/Flugzeug; **on the telephone/ television** am Telefon/im Fernsehen; **to be on drugs** Drogen nehmen; **to be on holiday/business** im Urlaub/auf Geschäftsreise sein
3 (referring to time): **on Friday** (am) Freitag; **on Fridays** freitags; **on June 20th** am 20. Juni; **a week on Friday** Freitag in einer Woche; **on arrival he ...** als er ankam, ... er ...
4 (about, concerning) über +acc
♦ adv 1 (referring to dress) an; **she put her boots/hat on** sie zog ihre Stiefel an/setzte ihren Hut auf
2 (further, continuously) weiter; **to walk on** weitergehen
♦ adj 1 (functioning, in operation: machine, TV, light) an; (: tap) aufgedreht; (: brakes) angezogen; **is the meeting still on?** findet die Versammlung noch statt?; **there's a good film on** es läuft ein guter Film
2: **that's not on!** (inf: of behaviour) das liegt nicht drin!

---

once [wʌns] adv einmal ♦ conj wenn ... einmal; **~ he had left/it was done** nachdem er gegangen war/es fertig war; **at ~** sofort; (at the same time) gleichzeitig; **~ a week** einmal in der Woche; **~ more** noch einmal; **~ and for all** ein für alle Mal; **~ upon a time** es war einmal

oncoming [ˈɔnkʌmɪŋ] adj (traffic) Gegen-, entgegenkommend

KEYWORD
---

one [wʌn] num eins; (with noun, referring back to noun) ein/eine/ein; **it is one (o'clock)** es ist eins, es ist ein Uhr; **one hundred and fifty** einhundertfünfzig
♦ adj 1 (sole) einzige(r, s); **the one book which** das einzige Buch, welches
2 (same) derselbe/dieselbe/dasselbe; **they came in the one car** sie kamen alle in dem einen Auto
3 (indef): **one day I discovered ...** eines Tages bemerkte ich ...

♦ *pron* **1** eine(r, s); **do you have a red one?** haben Sie einen roten/eine rote/ein rotes?; **this one** diese(r, s); **that one** der/die/das; **which one?** welche(r, s)?; **one by one** einzeln

2: one another einander; **do you two ever see one another?** seht ihr beide euch manchmal?

3 (*impers*) man; **one never knows** man kann nie wissen; **to cut one's finger** sich in den Finger schneiden

one: **~-armed bandit** *n* einarmiger Bandit *m*; **~-day excursion** (*US*) *n* (*day return*) Tagesrückfahrkarte *f*; **~-man** *adj* Einmann-; **~-man band** *n* Einmannkapelle *f*; (*fig*) Einmannbetrieb *m*; **~-off** (*BRIT: inf*) *n* Einzelfall *m*

oneself [wʌn'sɛlf] *pron* (*reflexive: after prep*) sich; (*~ personally*) sich selbst *or* selber; (*emphatic*) (sich) selbst; **to hurt ~** sich verletzen

one: **~-sided** *adj* (*argument*) einseitig; **~-to-~** *adj* (*relationship*) eins-zu-eins; **~-upmanship** *n* die Kunst, anderen um eine Nasenlänge voraus zu sein; **~-way** *adj* (*street*) Einbahn-

ongoing ['ɔngəʊɪŋ] *adj* momentan; (*progressing*) sich entwickelnd

onion ['ʌnjən] *n* Zwiebel *f*

on-line ['ɔnlaɪn] *adj* (*COMPUT*) Online-

onlooker ['ɔnlʊkəʳ] *n* Zuschauer(in) *m(f)*

only ['əʊnlɪ] *adv* nur, bloß ♦ *adj* einzige(r, s) ♦ *conj* nur, bloß; **not ~ ... but also ...** nicht nur ..., sondern auch ...

onset ['ɔnsɛt] *n* (*start*) Beginn *m*

onshore ['ɔnʃɔːʳ] *adj* (*wind*) See-

onslaught ['ɔnslɔːt] *n* Angriff *m*

onto ['ɔntu] *prep* = **on to**

onus ['əʊnəs] *n* Last *f*, Pflicht *f*

onward(s) ['ɔnwəd(z)] *adv* (*place*) voran, vorwärts; **from that day ~** von dem Tag an; **from today ~** ab heute

ooze [uːz] *vi* sickern

opaque [əʊ'peɪk] *adj* undurchsichtig

OPEC ['əʊpɛk] *n abbr* (= *Organization of Petroleum-Exporting Countries*) OPEC *f*

open ['əʊpn] *adj* offen; (*public*) öffentlich; (*mind*) aufgeschlossen ♦ *vt* öffnen, aufmachen; (*trial, motorway, account*) eröffnen ♦ *vi* (*begin*) anfangen; (*shop*) aufmachen; (*door, flower*) aufgehen; (*play*) Premiere haben; **in the ~ (air)** im Freien; **~ on to** *vt fus* sich öffnen auf +*acc*; **~ up** *vt* (*route*) erschließen; (*shop, prospects*) eröffnen ♦ *vi* öffnen; **~ing** *n* (*hole*) Öffnung *f*; (*beginning*) Anfang *m*; (*good chance*) Gelegenheit *f*; **~ing hours** *npl* Öffnungszeiten *pl*; **~ learning centre** *n* Weiterbildungseinrichtung auf Teilzeitbasis; **~ly** *adv* offen; (*publicly*) öffentlich; **~-minded** *adj* aufgeschlossen; **~-necked** *adj* offen; **~-plan** *adj* (*office*) Großraum-; (*flat etc*) offen angelegt

---
Open University

🛈 **Open University** ist eine 1969 in Großbritannien gegründete Fernuniversität für Spätstudierende. Der Unterricht findet durch Fernseh- und Radiosendungen statt, schriftliche Arbeiten werden mit der Post verschickt, und der Besuch von Sommerkursen ist Pflicht. Die Studenten müssen eine bestimmte Anzahl von Unterrichtseinheiten in einem bestimmten Zeitraum absolvieren und für die Verleihung eines akademischen Grades eine Mindestzahl von Scheinen machen.

---

opera ['ɔpərə] *n* Oper *f*; **~ house** *n* Opernhaus *nt*

operate ['ɔpəreɪt] *vt* (*machine*) bedienen; (*brakes, light*) betätigen ♦ *vi* (*machine*) laufen, in Betrieb sein; (*person*) arbeiten; (*MED*): **to ~ on** operieren

operatic [ɔpə'rætɪk] *adj* Opern-

operating ['ɔpəreɪtɪŋ] *adj*: **~ table/theatre** Operationstisch *m*/-saal *m*

operation [ɔpə'reɪʃən] *n* (*working*) Betrieb *m*; (*MED*) Operation *f*; (*undertaking*) Unternehmen *nt*; (*MIL*) Einsatz *m*; **to be in ~** (*JUR*) in Kraft sein; (*machine*) in Betrieb sein; **to have an ~** (*MED*) operiert werden;

~al adj einsatzbereit

operative ['ɔpərətɪv] adj wirksam

operator ['ɔpəreɪtə'] n (of machine) Arbeiter m; (TEL) Telefonist(in) m(f)

opinion [ə'pɪnjən] n Meinung f; in my ~ meiner Meinung nach; ~ated adj starrsinnig; ~ poll n Meinungsumfrage f

opponent [ə'pəunənt] n Gegner m

opportunity [ɔpə'tjuːnɪtɪ] n Gelegenheit f, Möglichkeit f; to take the ~ of doing sth die Gelegenheit ergreifen, etw zu tun

oppose [ə'pəuz] vt entgegentreten +dat; (argument, idea) ablehnen; (plan) bekämpfen; to be ~d to sth gegen etw sein; as ~d to im Gegensatz zu; opposing adj gegnerisch; (points of view) entgegengesetzt

opposite ['ɔpəzɪt] adj (house) gegenüberliegend; (direction) entgegengesetzt ♦ adv gegenüber ♦ prep gegenüber ♦ n Gegenteil nt

opposition [ɔpə'zɪʃən] n (resistance) Widerstand m; (POL) Opposition f; (contrast) Gegensatz m

oppress [ə'pres] vt unterdrücken; (heat etc) bedrücken; ~ion [ə'preʃən] n Unterdrückung f; ~ive adj (authority, law) repressiv; (burden, thought) bedrückend; (heat) drückend

opt [ɔpt] vi: to ~ for sich entscheiden für; to ~ to do sth sich entscheiden, etw zu tun; to ~ out of sich drücken vor +dat

optical ['ɔptɪkl] adj optisch; ~ character reader n optische(s) Lesegerät nt

optician [ɔp'tɪʃən] n Optiker m

optimist ['ɔptɪmɪst] n Optimist m; ~ic [ɔptɪ'mɪstɪk] adj optimistisch

optimum ['ɔptɪməm] adj optimal

option ['ɔpʃən] n Wahl f; (COMM) Option f; to keep one's ~s open sich alle Möglichkeiten offen halten; ~al adj freiwillig; (subject) wahlfrei; ~al extras npl Extras auf Wunsch

or [ɔː'] conj oder; he could not read ~ write er konnte weder lesen noch schreiben; ~ else sonst

oral ['ɔːrəl] adj mündlich ♦ n (exam)

mündliche Prüfung f

orange ['ɔrɪndʒ] n (fruit) Apfelsine f, Orange f; (colour) Orange nt ♦ adj orange

orator ['ɔrətə'] n Redner(in) m(f)

orbit ['ɔːbɪt] n Umlaufbahn f

orbital (motorway) ['ɔːbɪtəl-] n Ringautobahn f

orchard ['ɔːtʃəd] n Obstgarten m

orchestra ['ɔːkɪstrə] n Orchester nt; (US: seating) Parkett nt; ~l [ɔː'kestrəl] adj Orchester-, orchestral

orchid ['ɔːkɪd] n Orchidee f

ordain [ɔː'deɪn] vt (ECCL) weihen

ordeal [ɔː'diːl] n Qual f

order ['ɔːdə'] n (sequence) Reihenfolge f; (good arrangement) Ordnung f; (command) Befehl m; (JUR) Anordnung f; (peace) Ordnung f; (condition) Zustand m; (rank) Klasse f; (COMM) Bestellung f; (ECCL, honour) Orden m ♦ vt (also: put in ~) ordnen; (command) befehlen; (COMM) bestellen; in ~ in der Reihenfolge; in (working) ~ in gutem Zustand; in ~ to do etw um etw zu tun; on ~ (COMM) auf Bestellung; to ~ sb to do sth jdm befehlen, etw zu tun; to ~ sth (command) etw acc befehlen; ~ form n Bestellschein m; ~ly n (MIL) Sanitäter m; (MED) Pfleger m ♦ adj (tidy) ordentlich; (well-behaved) ruhig

ordinary ['ɔːdnrɪ] adj gewöhnlich ♦ n: out of the ~ außergewöhnlich

Ordnance Survey ['ɔːdnəns-] (BRIT) n amtliche(r) Kartografiedienst m

ore [ɔː'] n Erz nt

organ ['ɔːgən] n (MUS) Orgel f; (BIOL, fig) Organ nt

organic [ɔː'gænɪk] adj (food, farming etc) biodynamisch

organization [ɔːgənaɪ'zeɪʃən] n Organisation f; (make-up) Struktur f

organize ['ɔːgənaɪz] vt organisieren; ~r n Organisator m, Veranstalter m

orgasm ['ɔːgæzəm] n Orgasmus m

orgy ['ɔːdʒɪ] n Orgie f

Orient ['ɔːrɪənt] n Orient m; o~al [ɔːrɪ'entl] adj orientalisch

origin ['ɔrɪdʒɪn] n Ursprung m; (of the world)

Anfang m, Entstehung f; ~al [ə'rɪdʒɪnl] adj
(first) ursprünglich; (painting) original; (idea)
originell ♦ n Original nt; ~ally adv
ursprünglich; originell; ~ate [ə'rɪdʒɪneɪt] vi
entstehen ♦ vt ins Leben rufen; to ~ate
from stammen aus

Orkney ['ɔːknɪ] npl (also: **the ~ Islands**) die
Orkneyinseln pl

ornament ['ɔːnəmənt] n Schmuck m; (on
mantelpiece) Nippesfigur f; ~al [ɔːnə'mɛntl]
adj Zier-

ornate [ɔː'neɪt] adj reich verziert

orphan ['ɔːfn] n Waise f, Waisenkind nt ♦ vt:
to be ~ed Waise werden; ~age n
Waisenhaus nt

orthodox ['ɔːθədɒks] adj orthodox; ~y n
Orthodoxie f; (fig) Konventionalität f

orthopaedic [ɔːθə'piːdɪk] (US **orthopedic**)
adj orthopädisch

ostentatious [ɒstɛn'teɪʃəs] adj großtuerisch,
protzig

ostracize ['ɒstrəsaɪz] vt ausstoßen

ostrich ['ɒstrɪtʃ] n Strauß m

other ['ʌðə*] adj andere(r, s) ♦ pron andere(r,
s) ♦ adv: **~ than** anders als; **the ~ (one)**
der/die/das andere; **the ~ day** neulich; **~s**
(~ people) andere; **~wise** adv (in a different
way) anders; (or else) sonst

otter ['ɒtə*] n Otter m

ouch [autʃ] excl aua

ought [ɔːt] vb aux sollen; **I ~ to do it** ich
sollte es tun; **this ~ to have been
corrected** das hätte korrigiert werden
sollen

ounce [auns] n Unze f

our ['auə*] adj unser; see also **my**; **~s** pron
unsere(r, s); see also **mine**[2]; **~selves** pron
uns (selbst); (emphatic) (wir) selbst; see also
oneself

oust [aust] vt verdrängen

out [aut] adv hinaus/heraus; (not indoors)
draußen; (not alight) aus; (unconscious)
bewusstlos; (results) bekannt gegeben; **to
eat/go ~** auswärts essen/ausgehen; **~
there** da draußen; **he is ~** (absent) er ist
nicht da; **he was ~ in his calculations**
seine Berechnungen waren nicht richtig; **~**

loud laut; **~ of** aus; (away from) außerhalb
+gen; **to be ~ of milk** etc keine Milch etc
mehr haben; **~ of order** außer Betrieb; **~-
and-~** adj (liar, thief etc) ausgemacht;
~back n Hinterland nt; **~board (motor)** n
Außenbordmotor m; **~break** n Ausbruch
m; **~burst** n Ausbruch m; **~cast** n
Ausgestoßene(r) mf; **~come** n Ergebnis nt;
~crop n (of rock) Felsnase f; **~cry** n Protest
m; **~dated** adj überholt; **~do** (irreg: like
do) vt übertrumpfen; **~door** adj Außen-;
(SPORT) im Freien; **~doors** adv im Freien

outer ['autə*] adj äußere(r, s); **~ space** n
Weltraum m

outfit ['autfɪt] n Kleidung f

out: ~going adj (character) aufgeschlossen;
~goings (BRIT) npl Ausgaben pl; **~grow**
(irreg: like **grow**) vt (clothes) herauswachsen
aus; (habit) ablegen; **~house** n
Nebengebäude nt

outing ['autɪŋ] n Ausflug m

outlandish [aut'lændɪʃ] adj eigenartig

out: ~law n Geächtete(r) f(m) ♦ vt ächten;
(thing) verbieten; **~lay** n Auslage f; **~let** n
Auslass m, Abfluss m; (also: **retail ~let**)
Absatzmarkt m; (US: ELEC) Steckdose f; (for
emotions) Ventil nt

outline ['autlaɪn] n Umriss m

out: ~live vt überleben; **~look** n (also fig)
Aussicht f; (attitude) Einstellung f; **~lying**
adj entlegen; (district) Außen-; **~moded** adj
veraltet; **~number** vt zahlenmäßig
überlegen sein +dat; **~-of-date** adj
(passport) abgelaufen; (clothes etc)
altmodisch; (ideas etc) überholt; **~-of-the-
way** adj abgelegen; **~patient** n
ambulante(r) Patient m/ambulante
Patientin f; **~post** n (MIL, fig) Vorposten m;
~put n Leistung f, Produktion f; (COMPUT)
Ausgabe f

outrage ['autreɪdʒ] n (cruel deed)
Ausschreitung f; (indecency) Skandal m ♦ vt
(morals) verstoßen gegen; (person)
empören; **~ous** [aut'reɪdʒəs] adj unerhört

outreach worker [aut'riːtʃ-] n
Streetworker(in) m(f)

outright [adv aut'raɪt, adj 'autraɪt] adv (at

once) sofort; (*openly*) ohne Umschweife
♦ *adj* (*denial*) völlig; (*sale*) Total-; (*winner*) unbestritten

outset ['autset] *n* Beginn *m*

outside [aut'said] *n* Außenseite *f* ♦ *adj* äußere(r, s), Außen-; (*chance*) gering ♦ *adv* außen ♦ *prep* außerhalb +*gen*; **at the ~** (*fig*) maximal; (*time*) spätestens; **to go ~** nach draußen gehen; **~ lane** *n* (*AUT*) äußere Spur *f*; **~ line** *n* (*TEL*) Amtsanschluss *m*; **~r** *n* Außenseiter(in) *m(f)*

out: **~size** *adj* übergroß; **~skirts** *npl* Stadtrand *m*; **~spoken** *adj* freimütig; **~standing** *adj* hervorragend; (*debts etc*) ausstehend; **~stay** *vt*: **to ~stay one's welcome** länger bleiben als erwünscht; **~stretched** *adj* ausgestreckt; **~strip** *vt* übertreffen; **~ tray** *n* Ausgangskorb *m*

outward ['autwəd] *adj* äußere(r, s); (*journey*) Hin-; (*freight*) ausgehend ♦ *adv* nach außen; **~ly** *adv* äußerlich

outweigh [aut'wei] *vt* (*fig*) überwiegen

outwit [aut'wit] *vt* überlisten

oval ['əuvl] *adj* oval ♦ *n* Oval *nt*

Oval Office

ⓘ **Oval Office**, *ein großer ovaler Raum im Weißen Haus, ist das private Büro des amerikanischen Präsidenten. Im weiteren Sinne bezieht sich dieser Begriff oft auf die Präsidentschaft selbst.*

---

ovary ['əuvəri] *n* Eierstock *m*

ovation [əu'veiʃən] *n* Beifallssturm *m*

oven ['ʌvn] *n* Backofen *m*; **~proof** *adj* feuerfest

over ['əuvə'] *adv* (*across*) hinüber/herüber; (*finished*) vorbei; (*left*) übrig; (*again*) wieder, noch einmal ♦ *prep* über ♦ *prefix* (*excessively*) übermäßig; **~ here** hier(hin); **~ there** dort(hin); **all ~** (*everywhere*) überall; (*finished*) vorbei; **~ and ~** immer wieder; **~ and above** darüber hinaus; **to ask sb ~** jdn einladen; **to bend ~** sich bücken

overall [*adj*, *n* 'əuvərɔːl, *adv* əuvər'ɔːl] *adj* (*situation*) allgemein; (*length*) Gesamt- ♦ *n* (*BRIT*) Kittel *m* ♦ *adv* insgesamt; **~s** *npl* (*for*

man) Overall *m*

over: **~awe** *vt* (*frighten*) einschüchtern; (*make impression*) überwältigen; **~balance** *vi* Übergewicht bekommen; **~bearing** *adj* aufdringlich; **~board** *adv* über Bord; **~book** *vi* überbuchen

overcast ['əuvəkɑːst] *adj* bedeckt

overcharge [əuvə'tʃɑːdʒ] *vt*: **to ~ sb** von jdm zu viel verlangen

overcoat ['əuvəkəut] *n* Mantel *m*

overcome [əuvə'kʌm] (*irreg: like* come) *vt* überwinden

over: **~crowded** *adj* überfüllt; **~crowding** *n* Überfüllung *f*; **~do** (*irreg: like* do) *vt* (*cook too much*) verkochen; (*exaggerate*) übertreiben; **~done** *adj* übertrieben; (*COOK*) verbraten, verkocht; **~dose** *n* Überdosis *f*; **~draft** *n* (Konto)überziehung *f*; **~drawn** *adj* (*account*) überzogen; **~due** *adj* überfällig; (*remark*) verspätet; **~estimate** *vt* überschätzen; **~excited** *adj* überreizt; (*children*) aufgeregt

overflow [əuvə'fləu] *vi* überfließen ♦ *n* (*excess*) Überschuss *m*; (*also*: **~ pipe**) Überlaufrohr *nt*

overgrown [əuvə'grəun] *adj* (*garden*) verwildert

overhaul [*vb* əuvə'hɔːl, *n* 'əuvəhɔːl] *vt* (*car*) überholen; (*plans*) überprüfen ♦ *n* Überholung *f*

overhead [*adv* əuvə'hed, *adj*, *n* 'əuvəhed] *adv* oben ♦ *adj* Hoch-; (*wire*) oberirdisch; (*lighting*) Decken- ♦ *n* (*US*) = **overheads**; **~s** *npl* (*costs*) allgemeine Unkosten *pl*; **~ projector** *n* Overheadprojektor *m*

over: **~hear** (*irreg: like* hear) *vt* (mit an)hören; **~heat** *vi* (*engine*) heiß laufen; **~joyed** *adj* überglücklich; **~kill** *n* (*fig*) Rundumschlag *m*

overland ['əuvəlænd] *adj* Überland- ♦ *adv* (*travel*) über Land

overlap [*vb* əuvə'læp, *n* 'əuvəlæp] *vi* sich überschneiden; (*objects*) sich teilweise decken ♦ *n* Überschneidung *f*

over: **~leaf** *adv* umseitig; **~load** *vt* überladen; **~look** *vt* (*view from above*) überblicken; (*not notice*) übersehen; (*pardon*) hinwegsehen über +*acc*

ernight [*adv* əuvə'naɪt, *adj* 'əuvənaɪt] *adv*
ıber Nacht ♦ *adj* (*journey*) Nacht-; **~ stay**
Übernachtung *f*; **to stay ~** übernachten
erpass ['əuvəpɑːs] *n* Überführung *f*
erpower [əuvə'pauər] *vt* überwältigen
er: **~rate** *vt* überschätzen; **~ ride** (*irreg:
ike* **ride**) *vt* (*order, decision*) aufheben;
objection) übergehen; **~riding** *adj*
vorherrschend; **~rule** *vt* verwerfen; **~run**
irreg: like **run**) *vt* (*country*) einfallen in; (*time
imit*) überziehen
erseas [əuvə'siːz] *adv* nach/in Übersee
♦ *adj* überseeisch, Übersee-
erseer ['əuvəsɪər] *n* Aufseher *m*
ershadow [əuvə'ʃædəu] *vt* überschatten
ershoot [əuvə'ʃuːt] (*irreg: like* **shoot**) *vt*
runway) hinausschießen über +*acc*
ersight ['əuvəsaɪt] *n* (*mistake*) Versehen *nt*
er: **~sleep** (*irreg: like* **sleep**) *vi*
verschlafen; **~spill** *n*
(Bevölkerungs)überschuss *m*; **~state** *vt*
übertreiben; **~step** *vt*: **to ~step the mark**
zu weit gehen
ert [əu'vəːt] *adj* offen(kundig)
ertake [əuvə'teɪk] (*irreg: like* **take**) *vt, vi*
überholen
er: **~throw** (*irreg: like* **throw**) *vt* (*POL*)
stürzen; **~time** *n* Überstunden *pl*; **~tone** *n*
(*fig*) Note *f*
erture ['əuvətʃuər] *n* Ouvertüre *f*
er: **~turn** *vt, vi* umkippen; **~weight** *adj*
zu dick; **~whelm** *vt* überwältigen; **~work**
n Überarbeitung *f* ♦ *vt* überlasten ♦ *vi* sich
überarbeiten; **~wrought** *adj* überreizt
we [əu] *vt* schulden; **to ~ sth to sb** (*money*)
jdm etw schulden; (*favour etc*) jdm etw
verdanken; **owing to** *prep* wegen +*gen*
wl [aul] *n* Eule *f*
wn [əun] *vt* besitzen ♦ *adj* eigen; **a room of
my ~** mein eigenes Zimmer; **to get one's
~ back** sich rächen; **on one's ~** allein; **~
up** *vi*: **to ~ up (to sth)** (etw) zugeben; **~er**
n Besitzer(in) *m(f)*; **~ership** *n* Besitz *m*
x [ɔks] (*pl* **~en**) *n* Ochse *m*
xtail ['ɔksteɪl] *n*: **~ soup** Ochsen-
schwanzsuppe *f*
xygen ['ɔksɪdʒən] *n* Sauerstoff *m*; **~ mask**

n Sauerstoffmaske *f*; **~ tent** *n* Sauerstoffzelt
nt
oyster ['ɔɪstər] *n* Auster *f*
oz. *abbr* = **ounce(s)**
ozone ['əuzəun] *n* Ozon *nt*; **~-friendly** *adj*
(*aerosol*) ohne Treibgas; (*fridge*) FCKW-frei;
~ hole *n* Ozonloch *nt*; **~ layer** *n*
Ozonschicht *f*

P, p

p *abbr* = **penny; pence**
pa [pɑː] (*inf*) *n* Papa *m*
P.A. *n abbr* = **personal assistant; public
address system**
p.a. *abbr* = **per annum**
pace [peɪs] *n* Schritt *m*; (*speed*) Tempo *nt*
♦ *vi* schreiten; **to keep ~ with** Schritt halten
mit; **~maker** *n* Schrittmacher *m*
pacific [pə'sɪfɪk] *adj* pazifisch ♦ *n*: **the P~
(Ocean)** der Pazifik
pacifist ['pæsɪfɪst] *n* Pazifist *m*
pacify ['pæsɪfaɪ] *vt* befrieden; (*calm*)
beruhigen
pack [pæk] *n* (*of goods*) Packung *f*; (*of
hounds*) Meute *f*; (*of cards*) Spiel *nt*; (*gang*)
Bande *f* ♦ *vt* (*case*) packen; (*clothes*)
einpacken ♦ *vi* packen; **to ~ sb off to ...**
jdn nach ... schicken; **~ it in!** lass es gut
sein!
package ['pækɪdʒ] *n* Paket *nt*; **~ tour** *n*
Pauschalreise *f*
packed [pækt] *adj* abgepackt; **~ lunch** *n*
Lunchpaket *nt*
packet ['pækɪt] *n* Päckchen *nt*
packing ['pækɪŋ] *n* (*action*) Packen *nt*;
(*material*) Verpackung *f*; **~ case** *n*
(Pack)kiste *f*
pact [pækt] *n* Pakt *m*, Vertrag *m*
pad [pæd] *n* (*of paper*) (Schreib)block *m*;
(*stuffing*) Polster *nt* ♦ *vt* polstern; **~ding** *n*
Polsterung *f*
paddle ['pædl] *n* Paddel *nt*; (*US: SPORT*)
Schläger *m* ♦ *vt* (*boat*) paddeln ♦ *vi* (*in sea*)
plan(t)schen; **~ steamer** *n* Raddampfer *m*
paddling pool ['pædlɪŋ-] (*BRIT*) *n*

Plan(t)schbecken nt

paddock ['pædək] n Koppel f

paddy field ['pædɪ-] n Reisfeld nt

padlock ['pædlɔk] n Vorhängeschloss nt ♦ vt verschließen

paediatrics [piːdɪˈætrɪks] (US **pediatrics**) n Kinderheilkunde f

pagan ['peɪgən] adj heidnisch ♦ n Heide m, Heidin f

page [peɪdʒ] n Seite f; (person) Page m ♦ vt (in hotel) ausrufen lassen

pageant ['pædʒənt] n Festzug m; ~ry n Gepränge nt

pager ['peɪdʒər] n (TEL) Funkrufempfänger m, Piepser m (inf)

paging device ['peɪdʒɪŋ-] n (TEL) = **pager**

paid [peɪd] pt, pp of **pay** ♦ adj bezahlt; **to put ~ to** (BRIT) zunichte machen

pail [peɪl] n Eimer m

pain [peɪn] n Schmerz m; **to be in ~** Schmerzen haben; **on ~ of death** bei Todesstrafe; **to take ~s to do sth** sich dat Mühe geben, etw zu tun; ~**ed** adj (expression) gequält; ~**ful** adj (physically) schmerzhaft; (embarrassing) peinlich; (difficult) mühsam; ~**fully** adv (fig: very) schrecklich; ~**killer** n Schmerzmittel nt; ~**less** adj schmerzlos; ~**staking** ['zteɪkɪŋ] adj gewissenhaft

paint [peɪnt] n Farbe f ♦ vt anstreichen; (picture) malen; **to ~ the door blue** die Tür blau streichen; ~**brush** n Pinsel m; ~**er** n Maler m; ~**ing** n Malerei f; (picture) Gemälde nt; ~**work** n Anstrich m; (of car) Lack m

pair [peər] n Paar nt; **~ of scissors** Schere f; **~ of trousers** Hose f

pajamas [pəˈdʒɑːməz] (US) npl Schlafanzug m

Pakistan [pɑːkɪˈstɑːn] n Pakistan nt; ~**i** adj pakistanisch ♦ n Pakistani mf

pal [pæl] (inf) n Kumpel m

palace ['pæləs] n Palast m, Schloss nt

palatable ['pælɪtəbl] adj schmackhaft

palate ['pælɪt] n Gaumen m

palatial [pəˈleɪʃəl] adj palastartig

pale [peɪl] adj blass, bleich ♦ n: **to be**

beyond the ~ die Grenzen überschreiten

Palestine ['pælɪstaɪn] n Palästina nt; **Palestinian** [pælɪsˈtɪnɪən] adj palästinensisch ♦ n Palästinenser(in) m(f)

palette ['pælɪt] n Palette f

paling ['peɪlɪŋ] n (stake) Zaunpfahl m; (fence) Lattenzaun m

pall [pɔːl] vi jeden Reiz verlieren, verblassen

pallet ['pælɪt] n (for goods) Palette f

pallid ['pælɪd] adj blass, bleich

pallor ['pælər] n Blässe f

palm [pɑːm] n (of hand) Handfläche f; (also: **~ tree**) Palme f ♦ vt: **to ~ sth off on sb** jdm etw andrehen; **P~ Sunday** n Palmsonntag m

palpable ['pælpəbl] adj (also fig) greifbar

palpitation [pælpɪˈteɪʃən] n Herzklopfen nt

paltry ['pɔːltrɪ] adj armselig

pamper ['pæmpər] vt verhätscheln

pamphlet ['pæmflət] n Broschüre f

pan [pæn] n Pfanne f ♦ vi (CINE) schwenken

panache [pəˈnæʃ] n Schwung m

pancake ['pænkeɪk] n Pfannkuchen m

pancreas ['pæŋkrɪəs] n Bauchspeicheldrüse f

panda ['pændə] n Panda m; **~ car** (BRIT) n (Funk)streifenwagen m

pandemonium [pændɪˈməʊnɪəm] n Hölle f; (noise) Höllenlärm m

pander ['pændər] vi: **to ~ to** sich richten nach

pane [peɪn] n (Fenster)scheibe f

panel ['pænl] n (of wood) Tafel f; (TV) Diskussionsrunde f; ~**ling** (US **paneling**) n Täfelung f

pang [pæŋ] n: **~s of hunger** quälende(r) Hunger m; **~s of conscience** Gewissensbisse pl

panic ['pænɪk] n Panik f ♦ vi in Panik geraten; **don't ~** (nur) keine Panik; ~**ky** adj (person) überängstlich; ~**-stricken** adj von panischem Schrecken erfasst; (look) panisch

pansy ['pænzɪ] n Stiefmütterchen nt; (inf) Schwule(r) m

pant [pænt] vi keuchen; (dog) hecheln

panther ['pænθər] n Pant(h)er m

anties ['pæntɪz] *npl* (Damen)slip *m*

antihose ['pæntɪhəuz] (*US*) *n* Strumpfhose *f*

antomime ['pæntəmaɪm] (*BRIT*) *n* Märchenkomödie *f* um Weihnachten

---

Pantomime

i **Pantomime** *oder umgangssprachlich* **panto** *ist in Großbritannien ein zur Weihnachtszeit aufgeführtes Märchenspiel mit possenhaften Elementen, Musik, Standardrollen (ein als Frau verkleideter Mann, ein Junge, ein Bösewicht) und aktuellen Witzen. Publikumsbeteiligung wird gern gesehen (z.B. warnen die Kinder den Helden mit dem Ruf „He's behind you" vor einer drohenden Gefahr), und viele der Witze sprechen vor allem Erwachsene an, so dass pantomimes Unterhaltung für die ganze Familie bieten.*

---

antry ['pæntrɪ] *n* Vorratskammer *f*

ants [pænts] *npl* (*BRIT: woman's*) Schlüpfer *m*; (*: man's*) Unterhose *f*; (*US: trousers*) Hose *f*

apal ['peɪpəl] *adj* päpstlich

aper ['peɪpəʳ] *n* Papier *nt*; (*newspaper*) Zeitung *f*; (*essay*) Referat *nt* ♦ *adj* Papier-, aus Papier ♦ *vt* (*wall*) tapezieren; **~s** *npl* (*identity ~s*) Ausweis(papiere *pl*) *m*; **~back** *n* Taschenbuch *nt*; **~ bag** *n* Tüte *f*; **~ clip** *n* Büroklammer *f*; **~ hankie** *n* Tempotaschentuch *nt* ®; **~weight** *n* Briefbeschwerer *m*; **~work** *n* Schreibarbeit *f*

ar [pɑːʳ] *n* (*COMM*) Nennwert *m*; (*GOLF*) Par *nt*; **on a ~ with** ebenbürtig +*dat*

arable ['pærəbl] *n* (*REL*) Gleichnis *nt*

arachute ['pærəʃuːt] *n* Fallschirm *m* ♦ *vi* (mit dem Fallschirm) abspringen

arade [pə'reɪd] *n* Parade *f* ♦ *vt* aufmarschieren lassen; (*fig*) zur Schau stellen ♦ *vi* paradieren, vorbeimarschieren

aradise ['pærədaɪs] *n* Paradies *nt*

aradox ['pærədɔks] *n* Paradox *nt*; **~ically** [pærə'dɔksɪklɪ] *adv* paradoxerweise

araffin ['pærəfɪn] (*BRIT*) *n* Paraffin *nt*

paragraph ['pærəgrɑːf] *n* Absatz *m*

parallel ['pærəlel] *adj* parallel ♦ *n* Parallele *f*

paralyse ['pærəlaɪz] (*US* **paralyze**) *vt* (*MED*) lähmen, paralysieren; (*fig: organization, production etc*) lahm legen; **~d** *adj* gelähmt; **paralysis** [pə'rælɪsɪs] *n* Lähmung *f*

paralyze ['pærəlaɪz] (*US*) = **paralyse** *vt*

parameter [pə'ræmɪtəʳ] *n* Parameter *m*; **~s** *npl* (*framework, limits*) Rahmen *m*

paramount ['pærəmaunt] *adj* höchste(r, s), oberste(r, s)

paranoid ['pærənɔɪd] *adj* (*person*) an Verfolgungswahn leidend, paranoid; (*feeling*) krankhaft

parapet ['pærəpɪt] *n* Brüstung *f*

paraphernalia [pærəfə'neɪlɪə] *n* Zubehör *nt*, Utensilien *pl*

paraphrase ['pærəfreɪz] *vt* umschreiben

paraplegic [pærə'pliːdʒɪk] *n* Querschnittsgelähmte(r) *f(m)*

parasite ['pærəsaɪt] *n* (*also fig*) Schmarotzer *m*, Parasit *m*

parasol ['pærəsɔl] *n* Sonnenschirm *m*

paratrooper ['pærətruːpəʳ] *n* Fallschirmjäger *m*

parcel ['pɑːsl] *n* Paket *nt* ♦ *vt* (*also: ~ up*) einpacken

parch [pɑːtʃ] *vt* (aus)dörren; **~ed** *adj* ausgetrocknet; (*person*) am Verdursten

parchment ['pɑːtʃmənt] *n* Pergament *nt*

pardon ['pɑːdn] *n* Verzeihung *f* ♦ *vt* (*JUR*) begnadigen; **~ me!, I beg your ~!** verzeihen Sie bitte!; **~ me?** (*US*) wie bitte?; **(I beg your) ~?** wie bitte?

parent ['pεərənt] *n* Elternteil *m*; **~s** *npl* (*mother and father*) Eltern *pl*; **~al** [pə'rentl] *adj* elterlich, Eltern-

parentheses [pə'renθɪsiːz] *npl* of **parenthesis**

parenthesis [pə'renθɪsɪs] *n* Klammer *f*; (*sentence*) Parenthese *f*

Paris ['pærɪs] *n* Paris *nt*

parish ['pærɪʃ] *n* Gemeinde *f*

park [pɑːk] *n* Park *m* ♦ *vt, vi* parken

parking ['pɑːkɪŋ] *n* Parken *nt*; **"no ~"** „Parken verboten"; **~ lot** (*US*) *n* Parkplatz *m*; **~ meter** *n* Parkuhr *f*; **~ ticket** *n*

Strafzettel m

parlance [ˈpɑːləns] n Sprachgebrauch m

parliament [ˈpɑːləmənt] n Parlament nt; **~ary** [pɑːləˈmentərɪ] adj parlamentarisch, Parlaments-

parlour [ˈpɑːlə*] (US **parlor**) n Salon m

parochial [pəˈrəukɪəl] adj (narrow-minded) eng(stirnig)

parole [pəˈrəul] n: **on ~** (prisoner) auf Bewährung

parrot [ˈpærət] n Papagei m

parry [ˈpærɪ] vt parieren, abwehren

parsley [ˈpɑːslɪ] n Petersilie m

parsnip [ˈpɑːsnɪp] n Pastinake f

parson [ˈpɑːsn] n Pfarrer m

part [pɑːt] n (piece) Teil m; (THEAT) Rolle f; (of machine) Teil nt ♦ adv = **partly**; ♦ vt trennen; (hair) scheiteln ♦ vi (people) sich trennen; **to take ~ in** teilnehmen an +dat; **to take sth in good ~** etw nicht übel nehmen; **to take sb's ~** sich auf jds Seite acc stellen; **for my ~** ich für meinen Teil; **for the most ~** meistens, größtenteils; **in ~ exchange** (BRIT) in Zahlung; **~ with** vt fus hergeben; (renounce) aufgeben; **~ial** [ˈpɑːʃl] adj (incomplete) teilweise; (biased) parteiisch; **to be ~ial to** eine (besondere) Vorliebe haben für

participant [pɑːˈtɪsɪpənt] n Teilnehmer(in) m(f)

participate [pɑːˈtɪsɪpeɪt] vi: **to ~ (in)** teilnehmen (an +dat); **participation** [pɑːtɪsɪˈpeɪʃən] n Teilnahme f; (sharing) Beteiligung f

participle [ˈpɑːtɪsɪpl] n Partizip nt

particle [ˈpɑːtɪkl] n Teilchen nt

particular [pəˈtɪkjulə*] adj bestimmt; (exact) genau; (fussy) eigen; **in ~** besonders; **~ly** adv besonders

particulars npl (details) Einzelheiten pl; (of person) Personalien pl

parting [ˈpɑːtɪŋ] n (separation) Abschied m; (BRIT: of hair) Scheitel m ♦ adj Abschieds-

partition [pɑːˈtɪʃən] n (wall) Trennwand f; (division) Teilung f ♦ vt aufteilen

partly [ˈpɑːtlɪ] adv zum Teil, teilweise

partner [ˈpɑːtnə*] n Partner m ♦ vt der

Partner sein von; **~ship** n Partnerschaft f; (COMM) Teilhaberschaft f

partridge [ˈpɑːtrɪdʒ] n Rebhuhn nt

part-time [ˈpɑːtˈtaɪm] adj Teilzeit- ♦ adv stundenweise

party [ˈpɑːtɪ] n (POL, JUR) Partei f; (group) Gesellschaft f; (celebration) Party f ♦ adj (dress) Party-; (politics) Partei-; **~ line** n (TEL) Gemeinschaftsanschluss m

pass [pɑːs] vt (on foot) vorbeigehen an +dat; (driving) vorbeifahren an +dat; (surpass) übersteigen; (hand on) weitergeben; (approve) genehmigen; (time) verbringen; (exam) bestehen ♦ vi (go by) vorbeigehen, vorbeifahren; (years) vergehen; (be successful) bestehen ♦ n (in mountains, SPORT) Pass m; (permission) Passierschein m; (in exam): **to get a ~** bestehen; **to ~ sth through sth** etw durch etw führen; **to make a ~ at sb** (inf) bei jdm Annäherungsversuche machen; **~ away** vi (euph) verscheiden; **~ by** vi vorbeigehen; vorbeifahren; (years) vergehen; **~ on** vt weitergeben; **~ out** vi (faint) ohnmächtig werden; **~ up** vt vorbeigehen lassen; **~able** adj (road) passierbar; (fairly good) passabel

passage [ˈpæsɪdʒ] n (corridor) Gang m; (in book) (Text)stelle f; (voyage) Überfahrt f; **~way** n Durchgang m

passbook [ˈpɑːsbuk] n Sparbuch nt

passenger [ˈpæsɪndʒə*] n Passagier m; (on bus) Fahrgast m

passer-by [pɑːsəˈbaɪ] n Passant(in) m(f)

passing [ˈpɑːsɪŋ] adj (car) vorbeifahrend; (thought, affair) momentan ♦ n: **in ~** beiläufig; **~ place** n (AUT) Ausweichstelle f

passion [ˈpæʃən] n Leidenschaft f; **~ate** adj leidenschaftlich

passive [ˈpæsɪv] adj passiv; (LING) passivisch; **~ smoking** n Passivrauchen nt

Passover [ˈpɑːsəuvə*] n Passahfest nt

passport [ˈpɑːspɔːt] n (Reise)pass m; **~ control** n Passkontrolle f; **~ office** n Passamt nt

password [ˈpɑːswɜːd] n Parole f, Kennwort nt, Losung f

ast [pɑːst] *prep (motion)* an +*dat* ... vorbei; *(position)* hinter +*dat*; *(later than)* nach ♦ *adj (years)* vergangen; *(president etc)* ehemalig ♦ *n* Vergangenheit *f*; **he's ~ forty** er ist über vierzig; **for the ~ few/3 days** in den letzten paar/3 Tagen; **to run ~** vorbeilaufen; **ten/quarter ~ eight** zehn/ Viertel nach acht

asta ['pæstə] *n* Teigwaren *pl*

aste [peɪst] *n (fish ~ etc)* Paste *f*; *(glue)* Kleister *m* ♦ *vt* kleben

asteurized ['pæstʃəraɪzd] *adj* pasteurisiert

astime ['pɑːstaɪm] *n* Zeitvertreib *m*

astor ['pɑːstər] *n* Pfarrer *m*

astry ['peɪstrɪ] *n* Blätterteig *m*; **pastries** *npl (tarts etc)* Stückchen *pl*

asture ['pɑːstʃər] *n* Weide *f*

asty [*n* 'pæstɪ, *adj* 'peɪstɪ] *n* (Fleisch)pastete *f* ♦ *adj* blässlich, käsig

at [pæt] *n* leichte(r) Schlag *m*, Klaps *m* ♦ *vt* tätscheln

atch [pætʃ] *n* Fleck *m* ♦ *vt* flicken; **(to go through) a bad ~** eine Pechsträhne (haben); **~ up** *vt* flicken; *(quarrel)* beilegen; **~ed** *adj* geflickt; **~y** *adj (irregular)* ungleichmäßig

âté ['pæteɪ] *n* Pastete *f*

atent ['peɪtnt] *n* Patent *nt* ♦ *vt* patentieren lassen; *(by authorities)* patentieren ♦ *adj* offenkundig; **~ leather** *n* Lackleder *nt*

aternal [pə'tɜːnl] *adj* väterlich

aternity [pə'tɜːnɪtɪ] *n* Vaterschaft *f*

ath [pɑːθ] *n* Pfad *m*; Weg *m*

athetic [pə'θetɪk] *adj (very bad)* kläglich

athological [pæθə'lɒdʒɪkl] *adj* pathologisch

athology [pə'θɒlədʒɪ] *n* Pathologie *f*

athos ['peɪθɒs] *n* Rührseligkeit *f*

athway ['pɑːθweɪ] *n* Weg *m*

atience ['peɪʃns] *n* Geduld *f*; *(BRIT: CARDS)* Patience *f*

atient ['peɪʃnt] *n* Patient(in) *m(f)*, Kranke(r) *mf* ♦ *adj* geduldig

atio ['pætɪəʊ] *n* Terrasse *f*

atriotic [pætrɪ'ɒtɪk] *adj* patriotisch

atrol [pə'trəʊl] *n* Patrouille *f*; *(police)* Streife *f* ♦ *vt* patrouillieren in +*dat* ♦ *vi (police)* die Runde machen; *(MIL)* patrouillieren; **~ car** *n* Streifenwagen *m*; **~man** *(US) (irreg) n* (Streifen)polizist *m*

patron ['peɪtrən] *n (in shop)* (Stamm)kunde *m*; *(in hotel)* (Stamm)gast *m*; *(supporter)* Förderer *m*; **~ of the arts** Mäzen *m*; **~age** ['pætrənɪdʒ] *n* Schirmherrschaft *f*; **~ize** ['pætrənaɪz] *vt (support)* unterstützen; *(shop)* besuchen; *(treat condescendingly)* von oben herab behandeln; **~ saint** *n* Schutzpatron(in) *m(f)*

patter ['pætər] *n (sound: of feet)* Trappeln *nt*; *(: of rain)* Prasseln *nt*; *(sales talk)* Gerede *nt* ♦ *vi (feet)* trappeln; *(rain)* prasseln

pattern ['pætən] *n* Muster *nt*; *(SEWING)* Schnittmuster *nt*; *(KNITTING)* Strickanleitung *f*

pauper ['pɔːpər] *n* Arme(r) *mf*

pause [pɔːz] *n* Pause *f* ♦ *vi* innehalten

pave [peɪv] *vt* pflastern; **to ~ the way for** den Weg bahnen für

pavement ['peɪvmənt] *(BRIT) n* Bürgersteig *m*

pavilion [pə'vɪlɪən] *n* Pavillon *m*; *(SPORT)* Klubhaus *nt*

paving ['peɪvɪŋ] *n* Straßenpflaster *nt*; **~ stone** *n* Pflasterstein *m*

paw [pɔː] *n* Pfote *f*; *(of big cats)* Tatze *f*, Pranke *f* ♦ *vt (scrape)* scharren; *(handle)* betatschen

pawn [pɔːn] *n* Pfand *nt*; *(chess)* Bauer *m* ♦ *vt* verpfänden; **~broker** *n* Pfandleiher *m*; **~shop** *n* Pfandhaus *nt*

pay [peɪ] *(pt, pp paid) n* Bezahlung *f*, Lohn *m* ♦ *vt* bezahlen ♦ *vi* zahlen; *(be profitable)* sich bezahlt machen; **to ~ attention (to)** Acht geben (auf +*acc*); **to ~ sb a visit** jdn besuchen; **~ back** *vt* zurückzahlen; **~ for** *vt fus* bezahlen; **~ in** *vt* einzahlen; **~ off** *vt* abzahlen ♦ *vi (scheme, decision)* sich bezahlt machen; **~ up** *vt* bezahlen; **~able** *adj* zahlbar, fällig; **~ee** *n* Zahlungsempfänger *m*; **~ envelope** *(US) n* Lohntüte *f*; **~ment** *n* Bezahlung *f*; **advance ~ment** Vorauszahlung *f*; **monthly ~ment** monatliche Rate *f*; **~ packet** *(BRIT) n* Lohntüte *f*; **~phone** *n* Münzfernsprecher

m; ~roll *n* Lohnliste *f*; ~ slip *n* Lohn-/
Gehaltsstreifen *m*; ~ television *n*
Abonnenten-Fernsehen *nt*
PC *n abbr* = **personal computer**
p.c. *abbr* = **per cent**
pea [pi:] *n* Erbse *f*
peace [pi:s] *n* Friede(n) *m*; ~able *adj*
friedlich; ~ful *adj* friedlich, ruhig;
~keeping *adj* Friedens-
peach [pi:tʃ] *n* Pfirsich *m*
peacock ['pi:kɔk] *n* Pfau *m*
peak [pi:k] *n* Spitze *f*; (*of mountain*) Gipfel *m*;
(*fig*) Höhepunkt *m*; ~ hours *npl* (*traffic*)
Hauptverkehrszeit *f*; (*telephone, electricity*)
Hauptbelastungszeit *f*; ~ period *n* Stoßzeit
f, Hauptzeit *f*
peal [pi:l] *n* (Glocken)läuten *nt*; ~s of
laughter schallende(s) Gelächter *nt*
peanut ['pi:nʌt] *n* Erdnuss *f*; ~ butter *n*
Erdnussbutter *f*
pear [pɛər] *n* Birne *f*
pearl [pə:l] *n* Perle *f*
peasant ['peznt] *n* Bauer *m*
peat [pi:t] *n* Torf *m*
pebble ['pebl] *n* Kiesel *m*
peck [pek] *vt, vi* picken ♦ *n* (*with beak*)
Schnabelhieb *m*; (*kiss*) flüchtige(r) Kuss *m*;
~ing order *n* Hackordnung *f*; ~ish (*BRIT:*
inf) *adj* ein bisschen hungrig
peculiar [pɪ'kju:lɪər] *adj* (*odd*) seltsam; ~ to
charakteristisch für; ~ity [pɪkju:lɪ'ærɪtɪ] *n*
(*singular quality*) Besonderheit *f*;
(*strangeness*) Eigenartigkeit *f*
pedal ['pedl] *n* Pedal *nt* ♦ *vt, vi* (*cycle*) fahren,
Rad fahren
pedantic [pɪ'dæntɪk] *adj* pedantisch
peddler ['pedlər] *n* Hausierer(in) *m(f)*; (*of*
drugs) Drogenhändler(in) *m(f)*
pedestal ['pedəstl] *n* Sockel *m*
pedestrian [pɪ'destrɪən] *n* Fußgänger *m*
♦ *adj* Fußgänger-; (*humdrum*) langweilig; ~
crossing (*BRIT*) *n* Fußgängerüberweg *m*;
~ized *n* in eine Fußgängerzone
umgewandelt; ~ precinct (*BRIT*), ~ zone
(*US*) *n* Fußgängerzone *f*
pediatrics [pi:dɪ'ætrɪks] (*US*) *n* = **paediatrics**
pedigree ['pedɪgri:] *n* Stammbaum *m* ♦ *cpd*

(*animal*) reinrassig, Zucht-
pee [pi:] (*inf*) *vi* pissen, pinkeln
peek [pi:k] *vi* gucken
peel [pi:l] *n* Schale *f* ♦ *vt* schälen ♦ *vi* (*paint*
etc) abblättern; (*skin*) sich schälen
peep [pi:p] *n* (*BRIT: look*) kurze(r) Blick *m*;
(*sound*) Piepsen *nt* ♦ *vi* (*BRIT: look*) gucken;
~ out *vi* herausgucken; ~hole *n* Guckloch
nt
peer [pɪər] *vi* starren; (*peep*) gucken ♦ *n*
(*nobleman*) Peer *m*; (*equal*) Ebenbürtige(r)
m; ~age *n* Peerswürde *f*
peeved [pi:vd] *adj* (*person*) sauer
peg [peg] *n* (*stake*) Pflock *m*; (*BRIT: also:*
clothes ~) Wäscheklammer *f*
Pekinese [pi:kɪ'ni:z] *n* (*dog*) Pekinese *m*
pelican ['pelɪkən] *n* Pelikan *m*; ~ crossing
(*BRIT*) *n* (*AUT*) Ampelüberweg *m*
pellet ['pelɪt] *n* Kügelchen *nt*
pelmet ['pelmɪt] *n* Blende *f*
pelt [pelt] *vt* bewerfen ♦ *vi* (*rain*) schütten
♦ *n* Pelz *m*, Fell *nt*
pelvis ['pelvɪs] *n* Becken *nt*
pen [pen] *n* (*fountain* ~) Federhalter *m*; (*ball-*
point ~) Kuli *m*; (*for sheep*) Pferch *m*
penal ['pi:nl] *adj* Straf-; ~ize *vt* (*punish*)
bestrafen; (*disadvantage*) benachteiligen
penalty ['penltɪ] *n* Strafe *f*; (*FOOTBALL*)
Elfmeter *m*; ~ (kick) *n* Elfmeter *m*
penance ['penəns] *n* Buße *f*
pence [pens] (*BRIT*) *npl of* **penny**
pencil ['pensl] *n* Bleistift *m*; ~ case *n*
Federmäppchen *nt*; ~ sharpener *n*
Bleistiftspitzer *m*
pendant ['pendnt] *n* Anhänger *m*
pending ['pendɪŋ] *prep* bis (zu) ♦ *adj*
unentschieden, noch offen
pendulum ['pendjuləm] *n* Pendel *nt*
penetrate ['penɪtreɪt] *vt* durchdringen;
(*enter into*) eindringen in +*acc*;
penetration [penɪ'treɪʃən] *n* Durchdringen
nt; Eindringen *nt*
penfriend ['penfrend] (*BRIT*) *n* Brieffreund(in)
m(f)
penguin ['peŋgwɪn] *n* Pinguin *m*
penicillin [penɪ'sɪlɪn] *n* Penizillin *nt*
peninsula [pə'nɪnsjulə] *n* Halbinsel *f*

enis ['pi:nɪs] n Penis m

enitentiary [penɪ'tenʃərɪ] (US) n Zuchthaus nt

enknife ['pennaɪf] n Federmesser nt

en name n Pseudonym nt

enniless ['penɪlɪs] adj mittellos

enny ['penɪ] (pl pennies or (BRIT) pence) n Penny m; (US) Centstück nt

enpal ['penpæl] n Brieffreund(in) m(f)

ension ['penʃən] n Rente f; ~er (BRIT) n Rentner(in) m(f); ~ fund n Rentenfonds m; ~ plan n Rentenversicherung f

ensive ['pensɪv] adj nachdenklich

Pentagon

i Pentagon *heißt das fünfeckige Gebäude in Arlington, Virginia, in dem das amerikanische Verteidigungsministerium untergebracht ist. Im weiteren Sinne bezieht sich dieses Wort auf die amerikanische Militärführung.*

entathlon [pen'tæθlən] n Fünfkampf m

entecost ['pentɪkɔst] n Pfingsten pl or nt

enthouse ['penthaus] n Dach-terrassenwohnung f

ent-up ['pentʌp] adj (feelings) angestaut

enultimate [pe'nʌltɪmət] adj vorletzte(r, s)

eople ['pi:pl] n (nation) Volk nt ♦ npl (persons) Leute pl; (inhabitants) Bevölkerung f ♦ vt besiedeln; **several ~ came** mehrere Leute kamen; **~ say that ...** man sagt, dass ...

epper ['pepər] n Pfeffer m; (vegetable) Paprika m ♦ vt (pelt) bombardieren; ~ mill n Pfeffermühle f; ~mint n (plant) Pfefferminze f; (sweet) Pfefferminz nt

ep talk [pep-] (inf) n Anstachelung f

er [pə:r] prep pro; ~ day/person pro Tag/Person; ~ annum adv pro Jahr; ~ capita adj (income) Pro-Kopf- ♦ adv pro Kopf

erceive [pə'si:v] vt (realize) wahrnehmen; (understand) verstehen

er cent n Prozent nt; percentage [pə'sentɪdʒ] n Prozentsatz m

erception [pə'sepʃən] n Wahrnehmung f; (insight) Einsicht f

perceptive [pə'septɪv] adj (person) aufmerksam; (analysis) tief gehend

perch [pə:tʃ] n Stange f; (fish) Flussbarsch m ♦ vi sitzen, hocken

percolator ['pə:kəleɪtər] n Kaffeemaschine f

percussion [pə'kʌʃən] n (MUS) Schlagzeug nt

perennial [pə'renɪəl] adj wiederkehrend; (everlasting) unvergänglich

perfect [adj, n 'pə:fɪkt, vb pə'fekt] adj vollkommen; (crime, solution) perfekt ♦ n (GRAM) Perfekt nt ♦ vt vervollkommnen; ~ion n Vollkommenheit f; ~ly adv vollkommen, perfekt; (quite) ganz, einfach

perforate ['pə:fəreɪt] vt durchlöchern; perforation [pə:fə'reɪʃən] n Perforieren nt; (line of holes) Perforation f

perform [pə'fɔ:m] vt (carry out) durch- or ausführen; (task) verrichten; (THEAT) spielen, geben ♦ vi (THEAT) auftreten; ~ance n Durchführung f; (efficiency) Leistung f; (show) Vorstellung f; ~er n Künstler(in) m(f)

perfume ['pə:fju:m] n Duft m; (lady's) Parfüm nt

perhaps [pə'hæps] adv vielleicht

peril ['perɪl] n Gefahr f

perimeter [pə'rɪmɪtər] n Peripherie f; (of circle etc) Umfang m

period ['pɪərɪəd] n Periode f; (GRAM) Punkt m; (MED) Periode f ♦ adj (costume) historisch; ~ic [pɪərɪ'ɔdɪk] adj periodisch; ~ical [pɪərɪ'ɔdɪkl] n Zeitschrift f; ~ically [pɪərɪ'ɔdɪklɪ] adv periodisch

peripheral [pə'rɪfərəl] adj Rand-, peripher ♦ n (COMPUT) Peripheriegerät nt

perish ['perɪʃ] vi umkommen; (fruit) verderben; ~able adj leicht verderblich

perjury ['pə:dʒərɪ] n Meineid m

perk [pə:k] (inf) n (fringe benefit) Vergünstigung f; ~ up vi munter werden; ~y adj keck

perm [pə:m] n Dauerwelle f

permanent ['pə:mənənt] adj dauernd, ständig

permeate ['pə:mɪeɪt] vt, vi durchdringen

permissible [pə'mɪsɪbl] adj zulässig

permission [pə'mɪʃən] n Erlaubnis f

permissive [pə'mɪsɪv] *adj* nachgiebig; **the ~ society** die permissive Gesellschaft

permit [*n* 'pɜːmɪt, *vb* pə'mɪt] *n* Zulassung *f* ♦ *vt* erlauben, zulassen

perpendicular [pɜːpən'dɪkjuləʳ] *adj* senkrecht

perpetrate ['pɜːpɪtreɪt] *vt* begehen

perpetual [pə'petjuəl] *adj* dauernd, ständig

perpetuate [pə'petjueɪt] *vt* verewigen, bewahren

perplex [pə'pleks] *vt* verblüffen

persecute ['pɜːsɪkjuːt] *vt* verfolgen; **persecution** [pɜːsɪ'kjuːʃən] *n* Verfolgung *f*

perseverance [pɜːsɪ'vɪərns] *n* Ausdauer *f*

persevere [pɜːsɪ'vɪəʳ] *vi* durchhalten

Persian ['pɜːʃən] *adj* persisch ♦ *n* Perser(in) *m(f)*; **the (Persian) Gulf** der Persische Golf

persist [pə'sɪst] *vi* (*in belief etc*) bleiben; (*rain, smell*) andauern; (*continue*) nicht aufhören; **to ~ in** bleiben bei; **~ence** *n* Beharrlichkeit *f*; **~ent** *adj* beharrlich; (*unending*) ständig

person ['pɜːsn] *n* Person *f*; **in ~** persönlich; **~able** *adj* gut aussehend; **~al** *adj* persönlich; (*private*) privat; (*of body*) körperlich, Körper-; **~al assistant** *n* Assistent(in) *m(f)*; **~al column** *n* private Kleinanzeigen *pl*; **~al computer** *n* Personalcomputer *m*; **~ality** [pɜːsə'nælɪtɪ] *n* Persönlichkeit *f*; **~ally** *adv* persönlich; **~al organizer** *n* Terminplaner *m*, Zeitplaner *m*; (*electronic*) elektronisches Notizbuch *nt*; **~al stereo** *n* Walkman *m* ℝ; **~ify** [pɜː'sɒnɪfaɪ] *vt* verkörpern

personnel [pɜːsə'nel] *n* Personal *nt*

perspective [pə'spektɪv] *n* Perspektive *f*

Perspex ['pɜːspeks] ℝ *n* Acrylglas *nt*, Akrylglas *nt*

perspiration [pɜːspɪ'reɪʃən] *n* Transpiration *f*

perspire [pə'spaɪəʳ] *vi* transpirieren

persuade [pə'sweɪd] *vt* überreden; (*convince*) überzeugen

persuasion [pə'sweɪʒən] *n* Überredung *f*; Überzeugung *f*

persuasive [pə'sweɪsɪv] *adj* überzeugend

pert [pɜːt] *adj* keck

pertaining [pɜː'teɪnɪŋ]: **~ to** *prep* betreffend +*acc*

pertinent ['pɜːtɪnənt] *adj* relevant

perturb [pə'tɜːb] *vt* beunruhigen

pervade [pə'veɪd] *vt* erfüllen

perverse [pə'vɜːs] *adj* pervers; (*obstinate*) eigensinnig

pervert [*n* 'pɜːvɜːt, *vb* pə'vɜːt] *n* perverse(r) Mensch *m* ♦ *vt* verdrehen; (*morally*) verderben

pessimist ['pesɪmɪst] *n* Pessimist *m*; **~ic** *adj* pessimistisch

pest [pest] *n* (*insect*) Schädling *m*; (*fig: person*) Nervensäge *f*; (: *thing*) Plage *f*; **~er** ['pestəʳ] *vt* plagen; **~icide** ['pestɪsaɪd] *n* Insektenvertilgungsmittel *nt*

pet [pet] *n* (*animal*) Haustier *nt* ♦ *vt* liebkosen, streicheln

petal ['petl] *n* Blütenblatt *nt*

peter out ['piːtə-] *vi* allmählich zu Ende gehen

petite [pə'tiːt] *adj* zierlich

petition [pə'tɪʃən] *n* Bittschrift *f*

petrified ['petrɪfaɪd] *adj* versteinert; (*person*) starr (vor Schreck)

petrify ['petrɪfaɪ] *vt* versteinern; (*person*) erstarren lassen

petrol ['petrəl] (*BRIT*) *n* Benzin *nt*, Kraftstoff *m*; **two-/four-star ~** ≈ Normal-/Superbenzin *nt*; **~ can** *n* Benzinkanister *m*

petroleum [pə'trəuliəm] *n* Petroleum *nt*

petrol: ~ pump (*BRIT*) *n* (*in car*) Benzinpumpe *f*; (*at garage*) Zapfsäule *f*; **~ station** (*BRIT*) *n* Tankstelle *f*; **~ tank** (*BRIT*) *n* Benzintank *m*

petticoat ['petɪkəut] *n* Unterrock *m*

petty ['petɪ] *adj* (*unimportant*) unbedeutend; (*mean*) kleinlich; **~ cash** *n* Portokasse *f*; **~ officer** *n* Maat *m*

pew [pjuː] *n* Kirchenbank *f*

pewter ['pjuːtəʳ] *n* Zinn *nt*

phantom ['fæntəm] *n* Phantom *nt*

pharmacist ['fɑːməsɪst] *n* Pharmazeut *m*; (*druggist*) Apotheker *m*

pharmacy ['fɑːməsɪ] *n* Pharmazie *f*; (*shop*) Apotheke *f*

phase [feɪz] *n* Phase *f* ♦ *vt*: **to ~ sth in** etw allmählich einführen; **to ~ sth out** etw auslaufen lassen

Ph.D. n abbr = **Doctor of Philosophy**

pheasant ['feznt] n Fasan m

phenomena [fə'nɔmɪnə] npl of **phenomenon**

phenomenon [fə'nɔmɪnən] n Phänomen nt

philanthropist [fɪ'lænθrəpɪst] n Philanthrop m, Menschenfreund m

Philippines ['fɪlɪpiːnz] npl: **the ~** die Philippinen pl

philosopher [fɪ'lɔsəfə'] n Philosoph m; **philosophical** [fɪlə'sɔfɪkl] adj philosophisch; **philosophy** [fɪ'lɔsəfɪ] n Philosophie f

phlegm [flem] n (MED) Schleim m

phobia ['fəubjə] n (irrational fear: of insects, flying, water etc) Phobie f

phone [fəun] n Telefon nt ♦ vt, vi telefonieren, anrufen; **to be on the ~** telefonieren; **~ back** vt, vi zurückrufen; **~ up** vt, vi anrufen; **~ bill** n Telefonrechnung f; **~ book** n Telefonbuch nt; **~ booth** n Telefonzelle f; **~ box** n Telefonzelle f; **~ call** n Telefonanruf m; **~ card** n (TEL) Telefonkarte f; **~-in** n (RAD, TV) Phone-in nt; **~ number** n Telefonnummer f

phonetics [fə'netɪks] n Phonetik f

phoney ['fəunɪ] (inf) adj unecht ♦ n (person) Schwindler m; (thing) Fälschung f; (banknote) Blüte f

phony ['fəunɪ] adj, n = **phoney**

photo ['fəutəu] n Foto nt; **~copier** ['fəutəukɔpɪə'] n Kopiergerät nt; **~copy** ['fəutəukɔpɪ] n Fotokopie f ♦ vt fotokopieren; **~genic** [fəutəu'dʒenɪk] adj fotogen; **~graph** n Fotografie f, Aufnahme f ♦ vt fotografieren; **~grapher** ['fəutəgræf] n Fotograf m; **~graphic** [fəutə'græfɪk] adj fotografisch; **~graphy** [fə'tɔgrəfɪ] n Fotografie f

phrase [freɪz] n Satz m; (expression) Ausdruck m ♦ vt ausdrücken, formulieren; **~ book** n Sprachführer m

physical ['fɪzɪkl] adj physikalisch; (bodily) körperlich, physisch; **~ education** n Turnen nt; **~ly** adv physikalisch

physician [fɪ'zɪʃən] n Arzt m

physicist ['fɪzɪsɪst] n Physiker(in) m(f)

physics ['fɪzɪks] n Physik f

physiotherapist [fɪzɪəu'θerəpɪst] n Physiotherapeut(in) m(f)

physiotherapy [fɪzɪəu'θerəpɪ] n Heilgymnastik f, Physiotherapie f

physique [fɪ'ziːk] n Körperbau m

pianist ['piːənɪst] n Pianist(in) m(f)

piano [pɪ'ænəu] n Klavier nt

pick [pɪk] n (tool) Pickel m; (choice) Auswahl f ♦ vt (fruit) pflücken; (choose) aussuchen; **take your ~** such dir etwas aus; **to ~ sb's pocket** jdn bestehlen; **~ on** vt fus (person) herumhacken auf +dat; **~ out** vt auswählen; **~ up** vi (improve) sich erholen ♦ vt (lift up) aufheben; (learn) (schnell) mitbekommen; (collect) abholen; (girl) (sich dat) anlachen; (AUT: passenger) mitnehmen; (speed) gewinnen an +dat; **to ~ o.s. up** aufstehen

picket ['pɪkɪt] n (striker) Streikposten m ♦ vt (factory) (Streik)posten aufstellen vor +dat ♦ vi (Streik)posten stehen

pickle ['pɪkl] n (salty mixture) Pökel m; (inf) Klemme f ♦ vt (in Essig) einlegen; einpökeln

pickpocket ['pɪkpɔkɪt] n Taschendieb m

pick-up ['pɪkʌp] n (BRIT: on record player) Tonabnehmer m; (small truck) Lieferwagen m

picnic ['pɪknɪk] n Picknick nt ♦ vi picknicken; **~ area** n Rastplatz m

pictorial [pɪk'tɔ:rɪəl] adj in Bildern

picture ['pɪktʃə'] n Bild n ♦ vt (visualize) sich dat vorstellen; **the ~s** npl (BRIT) das Kino; **~ book** n Bilderbuch nt; **~ message** n Bildnachricht f

picturesque [pɪktʃə'resk] adj malerisch

pie [paɪ] n (meat) Pastete f; (fruit) Torte f

piece [piːs] n Stück nt ♦ vt: **to ~ together** zusammenstückeln; (fig) sich dat zusammenreimen; **to take to ~s** in Einzelteile zerlegen; **~meal** adv stückweise, Stück für Stück; **~work** n Akkordarbeit f

pie chart n Kreisdiagramm nt

pier [pɪə'] n Pier m, Mole f

pierce [pɪəs] vt durchstechen, durchbohren (also look); **~d** adj durchgestochen; **piercing** ['pɪəsɪŋ] adj (cry) durchdringend

pig [pɪg] n Schwein nt

pigeon ['pɪdʒən] n Taube f; **~hole** n (compartment) Ablegefach nt

piggy bank ['pɪgɪ-] n Sparschwein nt

pig: **~headed** ['pɪg'hedɪd] adj dickköpfig; **~let** ['pɪglɪt] n Ferkel nt; **~skin** ['pɪgskɪn] n Schweinsleder nt; **~sty** ['pɪgstaɪ] n Schweinestall m; **~tail** ['pɪgteɪl] n Zopf m

pike [paɪk] n Pike f; (fish) Hecht m

pilchard ['pɪltʃəd] n Sardine f

pile [paɪl] n Haufen m; (of books, wood) Stapel m; (in ground) Pfahl m; (on carpet) Flausch m ♦ vt (also: ~ **up**) anhäufen ♦ vi (also: ~ **up**) sich anhäufen

piles [paɪlz] npl Hämorr(ho)iden pl

pile-up ['paɪlʌp] n (AUT) Massenzusammenstoß m

pilfering ['pɪlfərɪŋ] n Diebstahl m

pilgrim ['pɪlgrɪm] n Pilger(in) m(f); **~age** n Wallfahrt f

pill [pɪl] n Tablette f, Pille f; **the ~** die (Antibaby)pille

pillage ['pɪlɪdʒ] vt plündern

pillar ['pɪlə*] n Pfeiler m, Säule f (also fig); ~ **box** (BRIT) n Briefkasten m

pillion ['pɪljən] n Soziussitz m

pillow ['pɪləu] n Kissen nt; **~case** n Kissenbezug m

pilot ['paɪlət] n Pilot m; (NAUT) Lotse m ♦ adj (scheme etc) Versuchs- ♦ vt führen; (ship) lotsen; ~ **light** n Zündflamme f

pimp [pɪmp] n Zuhälter m

pimple ['pɪmpl] n Pickel m

PIN n abbr (= personal identification number) PIN f

pin [pɪn] n Nadel f; (for sewing) Stecknadel f; (TECH) Stift m, Bolzen m ♦ vt stecken; (keep in one position) pressen, drücken; **to ~ sth to sth** etw an etw acc heften; **to ~ sth on sb** (fig) jdm etw anhängen; **~s and needles** Kribbeln nt; ~ **down** vt (fig: person): **to ~ sb down (to sth)** jdn (auf etw acc) festnageln

pinafore ['pɪnəfɔː*] n Schürze f; ~ **dress** n Kleiderrock m

pinball ['pɪnbɔːl] n Flipper m

pincers ['pɪnsəz] npl Kneif- or Beißzange f; (MED) Pinzette f

pinch [pɪntʃ] n Zwicken nt, Kneifen nt; (of salt) Prise f ♦ vt zwicken, kneifen; (inf: steal) klauen ♦ vi (shoe) drücken; **at a ~** notfalls, zur Not

pincushion ['pɪnkuʃən] n Nadelkissen nt

pine [paɪn] n (also: ~ **tree**) Kiefer f ♦ vi: **to ~ for** sich sehnen nach; ~ **away** vi sich zu Tode sehnen

pineapple ['paɪnæpl] n Ananas f

ping [pɪŋ] n Klingeln nt; **~-pong** ® n Pingpong nt

pink [pɪŋk] adj rosa inv ♦ n Rosa nt; (BOT) Nelke f

pinnacle ['pɪnəkl] n Spitze f

PIN (number) n Geheimnummer f

pinpoint ['pɪnpɔɪnt] vt festlegen

pinstripe ['pɪnstraɪp] n Nadelstreifen m

pint [paɪnt] n Pint nt; (BRIT: inf: of beer) große(s) Bier nt

pioneer [paɪə'nɪə*] n Pionier m; (fig also) Bahnbrecher m

pious ['paɪəs] adj fromm

pip [pɪp] n Kern m; **the ~s** npl (BRIT: RAD) das Zeitzeichen

pipe [paɪp] n (smoking) Pfeife f; (tube) Rohr nt; (in house) (Rohr)leitung f ♦ vt (durch Rohre) leiten; (MUS) blasen; **~s** npl (also: **bagpipes**) Dudelsack m; ~ **down** vi (be quiet) die Luft anhalten; ~ **cleaner** n Pfeifenreiniger m; ~ **dream** n Luftschloss nt; **~line** n (for oil) Pipeline f; **~r** n Pfeifer m; (bagpipes) Dudelsackbläser m

piping ['paɪpɪŋ] adv: ~ **hot** siedend heiß

pique ['piːk] n gekränkte(r) Stolz m

pirate ['paɪərət] n Pirat m, Seeräuber m; **~d** adj: **~d version** Raubkopie f; ~ **radio** (BRIT) n Piratensender m

Pisces ['paɪsiːz] n Fische pl

piss [pɪs] (inf) vi pissen; **~ed** (inf) adj (drunk) voll

pistol ['pɪstl] n Pistole f

piston ['pɪstən] n Kolben m

pit [pɪt] n Grube f; (THEAT) Parterre nt; (orchestra ~) Orchestergraben m ♦ vt (mark with scars) zerfressen; (compare): **to ~ sb against sb** jdn an jdm messen; **the ~s** npl (MOTOR RACING) die Boxen pl

pitch [pɪtʃ] n Wurf m; (of trader) Stand m; (SPORT) (Spiel)feld nt; (MUS) Tonlage f; (substance) Pech m ♦ vt werfen; (set up) aufschlagen ♦ vi (NAUT) rollen; **to ~ a tent** ein Zelt aufbauen; **~-black** adj pechschwarz; **~ed battle** n offene Schlacht f

piteous ['pɪtɪəs] adj kläglich, erbärmlich

pitfall ['pɪtfɔ:l] n (fig) Falle f

pith [pɪθ] n Mark nt

pithy ['pɪθɪ] adj prägnant

pitiful ['pɪtɪful] adj (deserving pity) bedauernswert; (contemptible) jämmerlich

pitiless ['pɪtɪlɪs] adj erbarmungslos

pittance ['pɪtns] n Hungerlohn m

pity ['pɪtɪ] n (sympathy) Mitleid nt ♦ vt Mitleid haben mit; **what a ~!** wie schade!

pivot ['pɪvət] n Drehpunkt m ♦ vi: **to ~ (on)** sich drehen (um)

pizza ['pi:tsə] n Pizza f

placard ['plækɑ:d] n Plakat nt, Anschlag m

placate [plə'keɪt] vt beschwichtigen

place [pleɪs] n Platz m; (spot) Stelle f; (town etc) Ort m ♦ vt setzen, stellen, legen; (order) aufgeben; (SPORT) platzieren; (identify) unterbringen; **to take ~** stattfinden; **out of ~** nicht am rechten Platz; (fig: remark) unangebracht; **in the first ~** erstens; **to change ~s with sb** mit jdm den Platz tauschen; **to be ~d third** (in race, exam) auf dem dritten Platz liegen

placid ['plæsɪd] adj gelassen, ruhig

plagiarism ['pleɪdʒərɪzəm] n Plagiat nt

plague [pleɪg] n Pest f; (fig) Plage f ♦ vt plagen

plaice [pleɪs] n Scholle f

plaid [plæd] n Plaid nt

plain [pleɪn] adj (clear) klar, deutlich; (simple) einfach, schlicht; (not beautiful) alltäglich ♦ n Ebene f; **in ~ clothes** (police) in Zivil(kleidung); **~ chocolate** n Bitterschokolade f

plaintiff ['pleɪntɪf] n Kläger m

plaintive ['pleɪntɪv] adj wehleidig

plait [plæt] n Zopf m ♦ vt flechten

plan [plæn] n Plan m ♦ vt, vi planen; **according to ~** planmäßig; **to ~ to do sth**

vorhaben, etw zu tun

plane [pleɪn] n Ebene f; (AVIAT) Flugzeug nt; (tool) Hobel m; (tree) Platane f

planet ['plænɪt] n Planet m

plank [plæŋk] n Brett nt

planning ['plænɪŋ] n Planung f; **family ~** Familienplanung f; **~ permission** n Baugenehmigung f

plant [plɑ:nt] n Pflanze f; (TECH) (Maschinen)anlage f; (factory) Fabrik f, Werk nt ♦ vt pflanzen; (set firmly) stellen; **~ation** [plæn'teɪʃən] n Plantage f

plaque [plæk] n Gedenktafel f; (on teeth) (Zahn)belag m

plaster ['plɑ:stər] n Gips m; (in house) Verputz m; (BRIT: also: **sticking ~**) Pflaster nt; (for fracture: **~ of Paris**) Gipsverband m ♦ vt gipsen; (hole) zugipsen; (ceiling) verputzen; (fig: with pictures etc) bekleben, verkleben; **~ed** (inf) adj besoffen; **~er** n Gipser m

plastic ['plæstɪk] n Plastik nt or f ♦ adj (made of ~) Plastik-; (ART) plastisch, bildend; **~ bag** n Plastiktüte f

plasticine ['plæstɪsi:n] ® n Plastilin nt

plastic surgery n plastische Chirurgie f

plate [pleɪt] n Teller m; (gold/silver ~) vergoldete(s)/versilberte(s) Tafelgeschirr nt; (in book) (Bild)tafel f

plateau ['plætəʊ] (pl **~s** or **~x**) n (GEOG) Plateau nt, Hochebene f

plateaux ['plætəʊz] npl of **plateau**

plate glass n Tafelglas nt

platform ['plætfɔ:m] n (at meeting) Plattform f, Podium nt; (RAIL) Bahnsteig m; (POL) Parteiprogramm nt; **~ ticket** n Bahnsteigkarte f

platinum ['plætɪnəm] n Platin nt

platoon [plə'tu:n] n (MIL) Zug m

platter ['plætər] n Platte f

plausible ['plɔ:zɪbl] adj (theory, excuse, statement) plausibel; (person) überzeugend

play [pleɪ] n (also TECH) Spiel nt; (THEAT) (Theater)stück nt ♦ vt spielen; (another team) spielen gegen ♦ vi spielen; **to ~ safe** auf Nummer sicher or Sicher gehen; **~ down** vt herunterspielen; **~ up** vi (cause

trouble) frech werden; (*bad leg etc*) wehtun
♦ *vt* (*person*) plagen; **to ~ up to sb** jdm
flattieren; **~acting** *n* Schauspielerei *f*; **~er**
n Spieler(in) *m(f)*; **~ful** *adj* spielerisch;
~ground *n* Spielplatz *m*; **~group** *n*
Kindergarten *m*; **~ing card** *n* Spielkarte *f*;
~ing field *n* Sportplatz *m*; **~mate** *n*
Spielkamerad *m*; **~off** *n* (SPORT)
Entscheidungsspiel *nt*; **~pen** *n* Laufstall *m*;
~school *n* = **playgroup**; **~thing** *n*
Spielzeug *nt*; **~time** *n* (kleine) Pause *f*;
~wright ['pleɪraɪt] *n* Theaterschriftsteller *m*

plc *abbr* (= *public limited company*) AG

plea [pli:] *n* Bitte *f*; (*general appeal*) Appell *m*;
(JUR) Plädoyer *nt*; **~ bargaining** *n* (LAW)
Aushandeln der Strafe zwischen
Staatsanwaltschaft und Verteidigung

plead [pli:d] *vt* (*poverty*) zur Entschuldigung
anführen; (JUR: *sb's case*) vertreten ♦ *vi* (*beg*)
dringend bitten; (JUR) plädieren; **to ~ with
sb** jdn dringend bitten

pleasant ['plɛznt] *adj* angenehm; **~ries** *npl*
(*polite remarks*) Nettigkeiten *pl*

please [pli:z] *vt, vi* (*be agreeable to*) gefallen
+*dat*; **~!** bitte!; **~ yourself!** wie du willst!;
~d *adj* zufrieden; (*glad*): **~d (about sth)**
erfreut (über etw *acc*); **~d to meet you**
angenehm; **pleasing** ['pli:zɪŋ] *adj* erfreulich

pleasure ['plɛʒə*] *n* Freude *f* ♦ *cpd*
Vergnügungs-; **"it's a ~"** „gern
geschehen"

pleat [pli:t] *n* Falte *f*

plectrum ['plɛktrəm] *n* Plektron *nt*

pledge [plɛdʒ] *n* Pfand *nt*; (*promise*)
Versprechen *nt* ♦ *vt* verpfänden; (*promise*)
geloben, versprechen

plentiful ['plɛntɪful] *adj* reichlich

plenty ['plɛntɪ] *n* Fülle *f*, Überfluss *m*; **~ of**
eine Menge, viel

pleurisy ['pluərɪsɪ] *n* Rippenfellentzündung *f*

pliable ['plaɪəbl] *adj* biegsam; (*person*)
beeinflussbar

pliers ['plaɪəz] *npl* (Kneif)zange *f*

plight [plaɪt] *n* (Not)lage *f*

plimsolls ['plɪmsəlz] (BRIT) *npl* Turnschuhe *pl*

plinth [plɪnθ] *n* Sockel *m*

P.L.O. *n* abbr (= *Palestine Liberation*

Organization) PLO *f*

plod [plɒd] *vi* (*work*) sich abplagen; (*walk*)
trotten

plonk [plɒŋk] *n* (BRIT: *inf*: *wine*) billige(r)
Wein *m* ♦ *vt*: **to ~ sth down** etw hinknallen

plot [plɒt] *n* Komplott *nt*; (*story*) Handlung *f*;
(*of land*) Grundstück *nt* ♦ *vt* markieren;
(*curve*) zeichnen; (*movements*) nachzeichnen
♦ *vi* (*plan secretly*) sich verschwören

plough [plau] (US **plow**) *n* Pflug *m* ♦ *vt*
pflügen; **~ back** *vt* (COMM) wieder in das
Geschäft stecken; **~ through** *vt fus* (*water*)
durchpflügen; (*book*) sich kämpfen durch

plow [plau] (US) = **plough**

ploy [plɔɪ] *n* Masche *f*

pluck [plʌk] *vt* (*fruit*) pflücken; (*guitar*)
zupfen; (*goose etc*) rupfen ♦ *n* Mut *m*; **to ~
up courage** all seinen Mut
zusammennehmen

plug [plʌg] *n* Stöpsel *m*; (ELEC) Stecker *m*;
(*inf*: *publicity*) Schleichwerbung *f*; (AUT)
Zündkerze *f* ♦ *vt* (zu)stopfen; (*inf*: *advertise*)
Reklame machen für; **~ in** *vt* (ELEC)
anschließen

plum [plʌm] *n* Pflaume *f*, Zwetsch(g)e *f*

plumage ['plu:mɪdʒ] *n* Gefieder *nt*

plumber ['plʌmə*] *n* Klempner *m*,
Installateur *m*; **plumbing** ['plʌmɪŋ] *n* (*craft*)
Installieren *nt*; (*fittings*) Leitungen *pl*

plummet ['plʌmɪt] *vi* (ab)stürzen

plump [plʌmp] *adj* rundlich, füllig ♦ *vt*
plumpsen lassen; **to ~ for** (*inf*: *choose*) sich
entscheiden für

plunder ['plʌndə*] *n* Plünderung *f*; (*loot*)
Beute *f* ♦ *vt* plündern

plunge [plʌndʒ] *n* Sturz *m* ♦ *vt* stoßen ♦ *vi*
(sich) stürzen; **to take the ~** den Sprung
wagen; **plunging** ['plʌndʒɪŋ] *adj* (*neckline*)
offenherzig

plural ['pluərl] *n* Plural *m*, Mehrzahl *f*

plus [plʌs] *n* (*also*: **~ sign**) Plus(zeichen) *nt*
♦ *prep* plus, und; **ten/twenty ~** mehr als
zehn/zwanzig

plush [plʌʃ] *adj* (*also*: **~y**: *inf*) feudal

ply [plaɪ] *vt* (*trade*) (be)treiben; (*with
questions*) zusetzen +*dat*; (*ship, taxi*)
befahren ♦ *vi* (*ship, taxi*) verkehren ♦ *n*:

three-~ (*wool*) Dreifach-; **to ~ sb with drink** jdn zum Trinken animieren; **~wood** *n* Sperrholz *nt*

P.M. *n abbr* = **prime minister**

p.m. *adv abbr* (= *post meridiem*) nachmittags

pneumatic drill *n* Presslufthammer *m*

pneumonia [nju:'məʊnɪə] *n* Lungenentzündung *f*

poach [pəʊtʃ] *vt* (*COOK*) pochieren; (*game*) stehlen ♦ *vi* (*steal*) wildern; **~ed** *adj* (*egg*) verloren; **~er** *n* Wilddieb *m*

P.O. Box *n abbr* = **Post Office Box**

pocket ['pɒkɪt] *n* Tasche *f*; (*of resistance*) (Widerstands)nest *nt* ♦ *vt* einstecken; **to be out of ~** (*BRIT*) draufzahlen; **~book** *n* Taschenbuch *nt*; **~ calculator** *n* Taschenrechner *m*; **~ knife** *n* Taschenmesser *nt*; **~ money** *n* Taschengeld *nt*

pod [pɒd] *n* Hülse *f*; (*of peas also*) Schote *f*

podgy ['pɒdʒɪ] *adj* pummelig

podiatrist [pɒ'di:ətrɪst] (*US*) *n* Fußpfleger(in) *m(f)*

poem ['pəʊɪm] *n* Gedicht *nt*

poet ['pəʊɪt] *n* Dichter *m*, Poet *m*; **~ic** [pəʊ'etɪk] *adj* poetisch, dichterisch; **~ laureate** *n* Hofdichter *m*; **~ry** *n* Poesie *f*; (*poems*) Gedichte *pl*

poignant ['pɔɪnjənt] *adj* (*touching*) ergreifend

point [pɔɪnt] *n* (*also in discussion, scoring*) Punkt *m*; (*spot*) Punkt *m*, Stelle *f*; (*sharpened tip*) Spitze *f*; (*moment*) (Zeit)punkt *m*; (*purpose*) Zweck *m*; (*idea*) Argument *nt*; (*decimal*) Dezimalstelle *f*; (*personal characteristic*) Seite *f* ♦ *vt* zeigen mit; (*gun*) richten ♦ *vi* zeigen; **~s** *npl* (*RAIL*) Weichen *pl*; **to be on the ~ of doing sth** drauf und dran sein, etw zu tun; **to make a ~ of** Wert darauf legen; **to get the ~** verstehen, worum es geht; **to come to the ~** zur Sache kommen; **there's no ~ (in doing sth)** es hat keinen Sinn(, etw zu tun); **~ out** *vt* hinweisen auf +*acc*; **~ to** *vt fus* zeigen auf +*acc*; **~-blank** *adv* (*at close range*) aus nächster Entfernung; (*bluntly*) unverblümt; **~ed** *adj* (*also fig*) spitz, scharf;

~edly *adv* (*fig*) spitz; **~er** *n* Zeigestock *m*; (*on dial*) Zeiger *m*; **~less** *adj* sinnlos; **~ of view** *n* Stand- *or* Gesichtspunkt *m*

poise [pɔɪz] *n* Haltung *f*; (*fig*) Gelassenheit *f*

poison ['pɔɪzn] *n* (*also fig*) Gift *nt* ♦ *vt* vergiften; **~ing** *n* Vergiftung *f*; **~ous** *adj* giftig, Gift-

poke [pəʊk] *vt* stoßen; (*put*) stecken; (*fire*) schüren; (*hole*) bohren; **~ about** *vi* herumstochern; (*nose around*) herumwühlen

poker ['pəʊkə*r*] *n* Schürhaken *m*; (*CARDS*) Poker *nt*

poky ['pəʊkɪ] *adj* eng

Poland ['pəʊlənd] *n* Polen *nt*

polar ['pəʊlə*r*] *adj* Polar-, polar; **~ bear** *n* Eisbär *m*

Pole [pəʊl] *n* Pole *m*, Polin *f*

pole [pəʊl] *n* Stange *f*, Pfosten *m*; (*flagpole, telegraph ~*) Stange *f*, Mast *m*; (*ELEC, GEOG*) Pol *m*; (*SPORT: vaulting ~*) Stab *m*; (*ski ~*) Stock *m*; **~ bean** (*US*) *n* (*runner bean*) Stangenbohne *f*; **~ vault** *n* Stabhochsprung *m*

police [pə'li:s] *n* Polizei *f* ♦ *vt* kontrollieren; **~ car** *n* Polizeiwagen *m*; **~man** (*irreg*) *n* Polizist *m*; **~ state** *n* Polizeistaat *m*; **~ station** *n* (Polizei)revier *nt*, Wache *f*; **~woman** (*irreg*) *n* Polizistin *f*

policy ['pɒlɪsɪ] *n* Politik *f*; (*insurance*) (Versicherungs)police *f*

polio ['pəʊlɪəʊ] *n* (spinale) Kinderlähmung *f*, Polio *f*

Polish ['pəʊlɪʃ] *adj* polnisch ♦ *n* (*LING*) Polnisch *nt*

polish ['pɒlɪʃ] *n* Politur *f*; (*for floor*) Wachs *nt*; (*for shoes*) Creme *f*; (*for nails*) Lack *m*; (*shine*) Glanz *m*; (*of furniture*) Politur *f*; (*fig*) Schliff *m* ♦ *vt* polieren; (*shoes*) putzen; (*fig*) den letzten Schliff geben +*dat*; **~ off** *vt* (*inf: food*) wegputzen; (: *drink*) hinunterschütten; **~ed** *adj* glänzend; (*manners*) verfeinert

polite [pə'laɪt] *adj* höflich; **~ly** *adv* höflich; **~ness** *n* Höflichkeit *f*

politic-: **~al** [pə'lɪtɪkl] *adj* politisch; **~ally** [pə'lɪtɪklɪ] *adv* politisch; **~ally correct**

politisch korrekt; **~ian** [pɒlɪ'tɪʃən] *n* Politiker *m*; **~s** *npl* Politik *f*

polka dot ['pɒlkə-] *n* Tupfen *m*

poll [pəul] *n* Abstimmung *f*; (*in election*) Wahl *f*; (*votes cast*) Wahlbeteiligung *f*; (*opinion ~*) Umfrage *f* ♦ *vt* (*votes*) erhalten

pollen ['pɒlən] *n* (BOT) Blütenstaub *m*, Pollen *m*

polling ['pəulɪŋ-]: **~ booth** (BRIT) *n* Wahlkabine *f*; **~ day** (BRIT) *n* Wahltag *m*; **~ station** (BRIT) *n* Wahllokal *nt*

pollute [pə'lu:t] *vt* verschmutzen, verunreinigen; **~d** *adj* verschmutzt; **pollution** [pə'lu:ʃən] *n* Verschmutzung *f*

polo ['pəuləu] *n* Polo *nt*; **~ neck** *n* (*also:* **~-necked sweater**) Rollkragen *m*; Rollkragenpullover *m*; **~ shirt** *n* Polohemd *nt*

polystyrene [pɒlɪ'staɪri:n] *n* Styropor *nt*

polytechnic [pɒlɪ'tɛknɪk] *n* technische Hochschule *f*

polythene ['pɒlɪθi:n] *n* Plastik *nt*; **~ bag** *n* Plastiktüte *f*

pomegranate ['pɒmɪɡrænɪt] *n* Granatapfel *m*

pompom ['pɒmpɒm] *n* Troddel *f*, Pompon *m*

pompous ['pɒmpəs] *adj* aufgeblasen; (*language*) geschwollen

pond [pɒnd] *n* Teich *m*, Weiher *m*

ponder ['pɒndər] *vt* nachdenken über +*acc*; **~ous** *adj* schwerfällig

pong [pɒŋ] (BRIT: *inf*) *n* Mief *m*

pontiff ['pɒntɪf] *n* Pontifex *m*

pontoon [pɒn'tu:n] *n* Ponton *m*; (CARDS) 17-und-4 *nt*

pony ['pəunɪ] *n* Pony *nt*; **~tail** *n* Pferdeschwanz *m*; **~ trekking** (BRIT) *n* Ponyreiten *nt*

poodle ['pu:dl] *n* Pudel *m*

pool [pu:l] *n* (*swimming ~*) Schwimmbad *nt*; (: *private*) Swimmingpool *m*; (*of liquid, blood*) Lache *f*; (*fund*) (gemeinsame) Kasse *f*; (*billiards*) Poolspiel *nt* ♦ *vt* (*money etc*) zusammenlegen; **(football) ~s** Toto *nt*

poor [puər] *adj* arm; (*not good*) schlecht ♦ *npl*: **the ~** die Armen *pl*; **~ in** (*resources*)

arm an +*dat*; **~ly** *adv* schlecht; (*dressed*) ärmlich ♦ *adj* schlecht

pop [pɒp] *n* Knall *m*; (*music*) Popmusik *f*; (*drink*) Limo(nade) *f*; (US: *inf*) Pa *m* ♦ *vt* (*put*) stecken; (*balloon*) platzen lassen ♦ *vi* knallen; **~ in** *vi* kurz vorbeigehen *or* vorbeikommen; **~ out** *vi* (*person*) kurz rausgehen; (*thing*) herausspringen; **~ up** *vi* auftauchen; **~corn** *n* Puffmais *m*

pope [pəup] *n* Papst *m*

poplar ['pɒplər] *n* Pappel *f*

poppy ['pɒpɪ] *n* Mohn *m*

Popsicle ['pɒpsɪkl] (®US) *n* (*ice lolly*) Eis *nt* am Stiel

populace ['pɒpjuləs] *n* Volk *nt*

popular ['pɒpjulər] *adj* beliebt, populär; (*of the people*) volkstümlich; (*widespread*) allgemein; **~ity** [pɒpju'lærɪtɪ] *n* Beliebtheit *f*, Popularität *f*; **~ly** *adv* allgemein, überall

population [pɒpju'leɪʃən] *n* Bevölkerung *f*; (*of town*) Einwohner *pl*

populous ['pɒpjuləs] *adj* dicht besiedelt

porcelain ['pɔ:slɪn] *n* Porzellan *nt*

porch [pɔ:tʃ] *n* Vorbau *m*, Veranda *f*

porcupine ['pɔ:kjupaɪn] *n* Stachelschwein *nt*

pore [pɔ:r] *n* Pore *f* ♦ *vi*: **to ~ over** brüten über +*dat*

pork [pɔ:k] *n* Schweinefleisch *nt*

porn [pɔ:n] *n* Porno *m*; **~ographic** [pɔ:nə'ɡræfɪk] *adj* pornografisch; **~ography** [pɔ:'nɒɡrəfɪ] *n* Pornografie *f*

porous ['pɔ:rəs] *adj* porös; (*skin*) porig

porpoise ['pɔ:pəs] *n* Tümmler *m*

porridge ['pɒrɪdʒ] *n* Haferbrei *m*

port [pɔ:t] *n* Hafen *m*; (*town*) Hafenstadt *f*; (NAUT: *left side*) Backbord *nt*; (*wine*) Portwein *m*; **~ of call** Anlaufhafen *m*

portable ['pɔ:təbl] *adj* tragbar

porter ['pɔ:tər] *n* Pförtner(in) *m(f)*; (*for luggage*) (Gepäck)träger *m*

portfolio [pɔ:t'fəulɪəu] *n* (*case*) Mappe *f*; (POL) Geschäftsbereich *m*; (FIN) Portefeuille *nt*; (*of artist*) Kollektion *f*

porthole ['pɔ:thəul] *n* Bullauge *nt*

portion ['pɔ:ʃən] *n* Teil *m*, Stück *nt*; (*of food*) Portion *f*

portrait ['pɔ:treɪt] *n* Porträt *nt*

portray [pɔː'treɪ] vt darstellen; ~al n Darstellung f

Portugal ['pɔːtjʊgl] n Portugal nt

Portuguese [pɔːtjʊ'giːz] adj portugiesisch ♦ n inv Portugiese m, Portugiesin f; (LING) Portugiesisch nt

pose [pəʊz] n Stellung f, Pose f; (affectation) Pose f ♦ vi posieren ♦ vt stellen

posh [pɔʃ] (inf) adj (piek)fein

position [pə'zɪʃən] n Stellung f; (place) Lage f; (job) Stelle f; (attitude) Standpunkt m ♦ vt aufstellen

positive ['pɔzɪtɪv] adj positiv; (convinced) sicher; (definite) eindeutig

posse ['pɔsɪ] (US) n Aufgebot nt

possess [pə'zɛs] vt besitzen; ~ion [pə'zɛʃən] n Besitz m; ~ive adj besitzergreifend, eigensüchtig

possibility [pɔsɪ'bɪlɪtɪ] n Möglichkeit f

possible ['pɔsɪbl] adj möglich; **as big as ~** so groß wie möglich, möglichst groß; **possibly** adv möglicherweise, vielleicht; **I cannot possibly come** ich kann unmöglich kommen

post [pəʊst] n (BRIT: letters, delivery) Post f; (pole) Pfosten m, Pfahl m; (place of duty) Posten m; (job) Stelle f ♦ vt (notice) anschlagen; (BRIT: letters) aufgeben; (: appoint) versetzen; (soldiers) aufstellen; ~age n Postgebühr f, Porto nt; ~al adj Post-; ~al order n Postanweisung f; ~box (BRIT) n Briefkasten m; ~card n Postkarte f; ~code (BRIT) n Postleitzahl f

postdate ['pəʊst'deɪt] vt (cheque) nachdatieren

poster ['pəʊstər] n Plakat nt, Poster nt

poste restante [pəʊst'restɑːnt] n Aufbewahrungsstelle f für postlagernde Sendungen

posterior [pɔs'tɪərɪər] (inf) n Hintern m

posterity [pɔs'tɛrɪtɪ] n Nachwelt f

postgraduate ['pəʊst'grædjʊət] n Weiterstudierende(r) mf

posthumous ['pɔstjʊməs] adj post(h)um

postman ['pəʊstmən] (irreg) n Briefträger m

postmark ['pəʊstmɑːk] n Poststempel m

post-mortem [pəʊst'mɔːtəm] n Autopsie f

post office n Postamt nt, Post f; (organization) Post f; **Post Office Box** n Postfach nt

postpone [pəʊs'pəʊn] vt verschieben

postscript ['pəʊstskrɪpt] n Postskript nt; (to affair) Nachspiel nt

posture ['pɔstʃər] n Haltung f ♦ vi posieren

postwar [pəʊst'wɔːr] adj Nachkriegs-

postwoman ['pəʊstwʊmən] (irreg) n Briefträgerin f

posy ['pəʊzɪ] n Blumenstrauß m

pot [pɔt] n Topf m; (teapot) Kanne f; (inf: marijuana) Hasch m ♦ vt (plant) eintopfen; **to go to ~** (inf: work) auf den Hund kommen

potato [pə'teɪtəʊ] (pl ~es) n Kartoffel f; ~ **peeler** n Kartoffelschäler m

potent ['pəʊtnt] adj stark; (argument) zwingend

potential [pə'tɛnʃl] adj potenziell, potentiell ♦ n Potenzial nt, Potential nt; ~ly adv potenziell, potentiell

pothole ['pɔthəʊl] n (in road) Schlagloch nt; (BRIT: underground) Höhle f; **potholing** (BRIT) n: **to go potholing** Höhlen erforschen

potion ['pəʊʃən] n Trank m

potluck [pɔt'lʌk] n: **to take ~ with sth** etw auf gut Glück nehmen

pot plant n Topfpflanze f

potter ['pɔtər] n Töpfer m ♦ vi herumhantieren; ~y n Töpferwaren pl; (place) Töpferei f

potty ['pɔtɪ] adj (inf: mad) verrückt ♦ n Töpfchen nt

pouch [paʊtʃ] n Beutel m

pouf(fe) [puːf] n Sitzkissen nt

poultry ['pəʊltrɪ] n Geflügel nt

pounce [paʊns] vi sich stürzen ♦ n Sprung m, Satz m; **to ~ on** sich stürzen auf +acc

pound [paʊnd] n (FIN, weight) Pfund nt; (for cars, animals) Auslösestelle f ♦ vt (zer)stampfen ♦ vi klopfen, hämmern; ~ **sterling** n Pfund Sterling nt

pour [pɔːr] vt gießen, schütten ♦ vi gießen; (crowds etc) strömen; ~ **away** vt abgießen; ~ **in** vi (people) hereinströmen; ~ **off** vt abgießen; ~ **out** vi (people) herausströmen

♦ vt (*drink*) einschenken; ~ing adj: **~ing rain** strömende(r) Regen m

pout [paut] vi schmollen

poverty ['pɒvətɪ] n Armut f; **~-stricken** adj verarmt, sehr arm

powder ['paudəʳ] n Pulver nt; (*cosmetic*) Puder m ♦ vt pulverisieren; **to ~ one's nose** sich dat die Nase pudern; ~ **compact** n Puderdose f; ~**ed milk** n Milchpulver nt; ~ **room** n Damentoilette f; ~**y** adj pulverig

power ['pauəʳ] n (*also POL*) Macht f; (*ability*) Fähigkeit f; (*strength*) Stärke f; (*MATH*) Potenz f; (*ELEC*) Strom m ♦ vt betreiben, antreiben; **to be in ~** (*POL etc*) an der Macht sein; ~ **cut** n Stromausfall m; ~**ed** adj: **~ed by** betrieben mit; ~ **failure** (*US*) n Stromausfall m; ~**ful** adj (*person*) mächtig; (*engine, government*) stark; ~**less** adj machtlos; ~ **point** (*BRIT*) n elektrische(r) Anschluss m; ~ **station** n Elektrizitätswerk nt; ~ **struggle** n Machtkampf m

p.p. abbr (= per procurationem): **p.p. J. Smith** i. A. J. Smith

PR n abbr = **public relations**

practicable ['præktɪkəbl] adj durchführbar

practical ['præktɪkl] adj praktisch; ~**ity** [præktɪ'kælɪtɪ] n (*of person*) praktische Veranlagung f; (*of situation etc*) Durchführbarkeit f; ~ **joke** n Streich m; ~**ly** adv praktisch

practice ['præktɪs] n Übung f; (*reality, also of doctor, lawyer*) Praxis f; (*custom*) Brauch m; (*in business*) Usus m ♦ vt, vi (*US*) = **practise**; **in ~** (*in reality*) in der Praxis; **out of ~** außer Übung; **practicing** (*US*) adj = **practising**

practise ['præktɪs] (*US* **practice**) vt üben; (*profession*) ausüben ♦ vi (sich) üben; (*doctor, lawyer*) praktizieren; **practising** (*US* **practicing**) adj praktizierend; (*Christian etc*) aktiv

practitioner [præk'tɪʃənəʳ] n praktische(r) Arzt m, praktische Ärztin f

pragmatic [præg'mætɪk] adj pragmatisch

prairie ['prɛərɪ] n Prärie f, Steppe f

praise [preɪz] n Lob nt ♦ vt loben; ~**worthy** adj lobenswert

pram [præm] (*BRIT*) n Kinderwagen m

prance [prɑːns] vi (*horse*) tänzeln; (*person*) stolzieren

prank [præŋk] n Streich m

prawn [prɔːn] n Garnele f; Krabbe f; ~ **cocktail** n Krabbencocktail m

pray [preɪ] vi beten; ~**er** [prɛəʳ] n Gebet nt

preach [priːtʃ] vi predigen; ~**er** n Prediger m

preamble [prɪ'æmbl] n Einleitung f

precarious [prɪ'kɛərɪəs] adj prekär, unsicher

precaution [prɪ'kɔːʃən] n (*Vorsichts*)maßnahme f

precede [prɪ'siːd] vi vorausgehen ♦ vt vorausgehen +dat; ~**nce** ['presɪdəns] n Vorrang m; ~**nt** ['presɪdənt] n Präzedenzfall m; **preceding** [prɪ'siːdɪŋ] adj vorhergehend

precinct ['priːsɪŋkt] n (*US: district*) Bezirk m; ~**s** npl (*round building*) Gelände nt; (*area, environs*) Umgebung f; **pedestrian ~** Fußgängerzone f; **shopping ~** Geschäftsviertel nt

precious ['preʃəs] adj kostbar, wertvoll; (*affected*) pretiös, preziös, geziert

precipice ['presɪpɪs] n Abgrund m

precipitate [adj prɪ'sɪpɪtɪt, vb prɪ'sɪpɪteɪt] adj überstürzt, übereilt ♦ vt hinunterstürzen; (*events*) heraufbeschwören

precise [prɪ'saɪs] adj genau, präzis; ~**ly** adv genau, präzis

precision [prɪ'sɪʒən] n Präzision f

preclude [prɪ'kluːd] vt ausschließen

precocious [prɪ'kəʊʃəs] adj frühreif

preconceived [priːkən'siːvd] adj (*idea*) vorgefasst

precondition ['priːkən'dɪʃən] n Vorbedingung f, Voraussetzung f

precursor [priː'kɜːsəʳ] n Vorläufer m

predator ['predətəʳ] n Raubtier nt

predecessor ['priːdɪsesəʳ] n Vorgänger m

predicament [prɪ'dɪkəmənt] n missliche Lage f

predict [prɪ'dɪkt] vt voraussagen; ~**able** adj vorhersagbar; ~**ion** [prɪ'dɪkʃən] n Voraussage f

predominantly [prɪ'dɒmɪnəntlɪ] adv

überwiegend, hauptsächlich

redominate [prɪ'dɔmɪneɪt] vi vorherrschen; (fig) vorherrschen, überwiegen

re-eminent [priː'emɪnənt] adj hervorragend, herausragend

re-empt [priː'emt] vt (action, decision) vorwegnehmen

reen [priːn] vt putzen; **to ~ o.s.** (person) sich brüsten

refab [priːfæb] n Fertighaus nt

reface [priːfəs] n Vorwort nt

refect [priːfekt] n Präfekt m; (SCH) Aufsichtsschüler(in) m(f)

refer [prɪ'fɜːʳ] vt vorziehen, lieber mögen; **to ~ to do sth** etw lieber tun; **~ably** [prefrəblɪ] adv vorzugsweise, am liebsten; **~ence** [prefrəns] n Präferenz f, Vorzug m; **~ential** [prefə'renʃəl] adj bevorzugt, Vorzugs-

refix [priːfɪks] n Vorsilbe f, Präfix nt

regnancy [pregnənsɪ] n Schwangerschaft f

regnant [pregnənt] adj schwanger

rehistoric [priːhɪs'tɔrɪk] adj prähistorisch, vorgeschichtlich

rejudice [predʒudɪs] n (bias) Voreingenommenheit f; (opinion) Vorurteil nt; (harm) Schaden m ♦ vt beeinträchtigen; **~d** adj (person) voreingenommen

reliminary [prɪ'lɪmɪnərɪ] adj einleitend, Vor-

relude [preljuːd] n Vorspiel nt; (fig) Auftakt m

remarital [priː'mærɪtl] adj vorehelich

remature [premətʃuəʳ] adj vorzeitig, verfrüht; (birth) Früh-

remeditated [priː'medɪteɪtɪd] adj geplant; (murder) vorsätzlich

remenstrual syndrome [priː'menstruəl-] n prämenstruelles Syndrom nt

remier [premɪəʳ] adj erste(r, s) ♦ n Premier m

remière [premɪɛəʳ] n Premiere f; Uraufführung f

remier League [-liːg] n ≈ 1. Bundesliga (höchste Spielklasse im Fußball)

remise [premɪs] n Voraussetzung f,

Prämisse f; **~s** npl (shop) Räumlichkeiten pl; (grounds) Gelände nt; **on the ~s** im Hause

premium [priːmɪəm] n Prämie f; **to be at a ~** über pari stehen; **~ bond** (BRIT) n Prämienanleihe f

premonition [premə'nɪʃən] n Vorahnung f

preoccupation [priːɔkju'peɪʃən] n Sorge f

preoccupied [priː'ɔkjupaɪd] adj (look) geistesabwesend

prep [prep] n (SCH) Hausaufgabe f

prepaid [priː'peɪd] adj vorausbezahlt; (letter) frankiert

preparation [prepə'reɪʃən] n Vorbereitung f

preparatory [prɪ'pærətərɪ] adj Vor(bereitungs)-; **~ school** n (BRIT) private Vorbereitungsschule für die Public School; (US) private Vorbereitungsschule für die Hochschule

prepare [prɪ'peəʳ] vt vorbereiten ♦ vi sich vorbereiten; **to ~ for/prepare sth for** sich/etw vorbereiten auf +acc; **to be ~d to ...** bereit sein zu ...

preponderance [prɪ'pɔndərns] n Übergewicht nt

preposition [prepə'zɪʃən] n Präposition f, Verhältniswort nt

preposterous [prɪ'pɔstərəs] adj absurd

prep school n = **preparatory school**

prerequisite [priː'rekwɪzɪt] n (unerlässliche) Voraussetzung f

prerogative [prɪ'rɔgətɪv] n Vorrecht nt

Presbyterian [prezbɪ'tɪərɪən] adj presbyterianisch ♦ n Presbyterier(in) m(f)

preschool [priː'skuːl] adj Vorschul-

prescribe [prɪ'skraɪb] vt vorschreiben; (MED) verschreiben

prescription [prɪ'skrɪpʃən] n (MED) Rezept nt

presence [prezns] n Gegenwart f; **~ of mind** Geistesgegenwart f

present [adj, n 'preznt, vb prɪ'zent] adj (here) anwesend; (current) gegenwärtig ♦ n Gegenwart f; (gift) Geschenk nt ♦ vt vorlegen; (introduce) vorstellen; (show) zeigen; (give) **to ~ sb with sth** jdm etw überreichen; **at ~** im Augenblick; **to give sb a ~** jdm ein Geschenk machen; **~able** [prɪ'zentəbl] adj präsentabel; **~ation**

[prezn'teɪʃən] n Überreichung f; ~-day adj
heutig; ~er [prɪ'zentər] n (RAD, TV)
Moderator(in) m(f); ~ly adv bald; (at ~) im
Augenblick

preservation [prezə'veɪʃən] n Erhaltung f
preservative [prɪ'zɜ:vətɪv] n
Konservierungsmittel nt

preserve [prɪ'zɜ:v] vt erhalten; (food)
einmachen ♦ n (jam) Eingemachte(s) nt;
(reserve) Schutzgebiet nt

preside [prɪ'zaɪd] vi den Vorsitz haben

president ['prezɪdənt] n Präsident m; ~ial
[prezɪ'denʃl] adj Präsidenten-; (election)
Präsidentschafts-; (system) Präsidial-

press [pres] n Presse f; (printing house)
Druckerei f ♦ vt drücken; (iron) bügeln;
(urge) (be)drängen ♦ vi (push) drücken; **to
be ~ed for time** unter Zeitdruck stehen; **~
for sth** drängen auf etw acc; **~ on** vi
vorwärts drängen; **~ agency** n
Presseagentur f; **~ conference** n
Pressekonferenz f; **~ed** adj (clothes)
gebügelt; **~ing** adj dringend; **~ stud** (BRIT)
n Druckknopf m; **~-up** (BRIT) n Liegestütz m

pressure ['preʃər] n Druck m; **~ cooker** n
Schnellkochtopf m; **~ gauge** n
Druckmesser m

pressurized ['preʃəraɪzd] adj Druck-

prestige [pres'ti:ʒ] n Prestige nt

prestigious [pres'tɪdʒəs] adj Prestige-

presumably [prɪ'zju:məblɪ] adv vermutlich

presume [prɪ'zju:m] vt, vi annehmen; **to ~
to do sth** sich erlauben, etw zu tun;
presumption [prɪ'zʌmpʃən] n Annahme f;
presumptuous [prɪ'zʌmpʃəs] adj
anmaßend

pretence [prɪ'tens] (US **pretense**) n Vorgabe
f, Vortäuschung f; (false claim) Vorwand m

pretend [prɪ'tend] vt vorgeben, so tun als
ob ... ♦ vi so tun; **to ~ to sth** Anspruch
erheben auf etw acc

pretense [prɪ'tens] (US) n = **pretence**

pretension [prɪ'tenʃən] n Anspruch m;
(impudent claim) Anmaßung f

pretentious [prɪ'tenʃəs] adj angeberisch

pretext ['pri:tekst] n Vorwand m

pretty ['prɪtɪ] adj hübsch ♦ adv (inf) ganz

schön

prevail [prɪ'veɪl] vi siegen; (custom)
vorherrschen; **to ~ against** or **over** siegen
über +acc; **to ~ (up)on sb to do sth** jdn
dazu bewegen, etw zu tun; **~ing** adj
vorherrschend

prevalent ['prevələnt] adj vorherrschend

prevent [prɪ'vent] vt (stop) verhindern,
verhüten; **to ~ sb from doing sth** jdn
(daran) hindern, etw zu tun; **~ative** n
Vorbeugungsmittel nt; **~ion** [prɪ'venʃən] n
Verhütung f; **~ive** adj vorbeugend, Schutz-

preview ['pri:vju:] n private Voraufführung
f; (trailer) Vorschau f

previous ['pri:vɪəs] adj früher, vorherig; **~ly**
adv früher

prewar [pri:'wɔ:r] adj Vorkriegs-

prey [preɪ] n Beute f; **~ on** vt fus Jagd
machen auf +acc; **it was ~ing on his mind**
es quälte sein Gewissen

price [praɪs] n Preis m; (value) Wert m ♦ vt
(label) auszeichnen; **~less** adj (also fig)
unbezahlbar; **~ list** n Preisliste f

prick [prɪk] n Stich m ♦ vt, vi stechen; **to ~
up one's ears** die Ohren spitzen

prickle ['prɪkl] n Stachel m, Dorn m

prickly ['prɪklɪ] adj stachelig; (fig: person)
reizbar; **~ heat** n Hitzebläschen pl

pride [praɪd] n Stolz m; (arrogance) Hochmut
m ♦ vt: **to ~ o.s. on sth** auf etw acc stolz
sein

priest [pri:st] n Priester m; **~hood** n
Priesteramt nt

prim [prɪm] adj prüde

primarily ['praɪmərɪlɪ] adv vorwiegend

primary ['praɪmərɪ] adj (main) Haupt-; (SCH)
Grund-; **~ school** (BRIT) n Grundschule f

prime [praɪm] adj erste(r, s); (excellent)
erstklassig ♦ vt vorbereiten; (gun) laden; **in
the ~ of life** in der Blüte der Jahre; **~
minister** n Premierminister m,
Ministerpräsident m; **~r** ['praɪmər] n Fibel f

primeval [praɪ'mi:vl] adj vorzeitlich; (forests)
Ur-

primitive ['prɪmɪtɪv] adj primitiv

primrose ['prɪmrəʊz] n (gelbe) Primel f

primus (stove) ['praɪməs-] (® BRIT) n

Primuskocher m

prince [prɪns] n Prinz m; (ruler) Fürst m; **princess** [prɪnˈses] n Prinzessin f; Fürstin f

principal [ˈprɪnsɪpl] adj Haupt- ♦ n (SCH) (Schul)direktor m, Rektor m; (money) (Grund)kapital nt

principle [ˈprɪnsɪpl] n Grundsatz m, Prinzip nt; **in ~** im Prinzip; **on ~** aus Prinzip, prinzipiell

print [prɪnt] n Druck m; (made by feet, fingers) Abdruck m; (PHOT) Abzug m ♦ vt drucken; (name) in Druckbuchstaben schreiben; (PHOT) abziehen; **out of ~** vergriffen; ~ed **matter** n Drucksache f; ~er n Drucker m; ~ing n Drucken nt; (of photos) Abziehen nt; ~out n (COMPUT) Ausdruck m

prior [ˈpraɪər] adj früher ♦ n Prior m; **~ to sth** vor etw dat; **~ to going abroad, she had ...** bevor sie ins Ausland ging, hatte sie ...

priority [praɪˈɔrɪtɪ] n Vorrang m; Priorität f

prise [praɪz] vt: **to ~ open** aufbrechen

prison [ˈprɪzn] n Gefängnis nt ♦ adj Gefängnis-; (system etc) Strafvollzugs-; ~er n Gefangene(r) mf

pristine [ˈprɪstiːn] adj makellos

privacy [ˈprɪvəsɪ] n Ungestörtheit f, Ruhe f; Privatleben nt

private [ˈpraɪvɪt] adj privat, Privat-; (secret) vertraulich, geheim ♦ n einfache(r) Soldat m; "**~**" (on envelope) „persönlich"; (on door) „Privat"; **in ~** privat, unter vier Augen; ~ **enterprise** n Privatunternehmen nt; ~ **eye** n Privatdetektiv m; ~ **property** n Privatbesitz m; ~ **school** n Privatschule f; **privatize** vt privatisieren

privet [ˈprɪvɪt] n Liguster m

privilege [ˈprɪvɪlɪdʒ] n Privileg nt; ~d adj bevorzugt, privilegiert

privy [ˈprɪvɪ] adj geheim, privat; **P~ Council** n Geheime(r) Staatsrat m

prize [praɪz] n Preis m ♦ adj (example) erstklassig; (idiot) Voll- ♦ vt (hoch) schätzen; ~-**giving** n Preisverteilung f; ~**winner** n Preisträger(in) m(f)

pro [prəu] n (professional) Profi m; **the ~s and cons** das Für und Wider

probability [prɔbəˈbɪlɪtɪ] n

Wahrscheinlichkeit f

probable [ˈprɔbəbl] adj wahrscheinlich; **probably** adv wahrscheinlich

probation [prəˈbeɪʃən] n Probe(zeit) f; (JUR) Bewährung f; **on ~** auf Probe; auf Bewährung

probe [prəub] n Sonde f; (enquiry) Untersuchung f ♦ vt, vi erforschen

problem [ˈprɔbləm] n Problem nt; ~**atic** [prɔbləˈmætɪk] adj problematisch

procedure [prəˈsiːdʒər] n Verfahren nt

proceed [prəˈsiːd] vi (advance) vorrücken; (start) anfangen; (carry on) fortfahren; (set about) vorgehen; ~**ings** npl Verfahren nt (PHOT) Entwickeln nt

proceeds [ˈprəusiːdz] npl Erlös m

process [ˈprəuses] n Prozess m; (method) Verfahren nt ♦ vt bearbeiten; (food) verarbeiten; (film) entwickeln; ~**ing** n (PHOT) Entwickeln nt

procession [prəˈseʃən] n Prozession f, Umzug m; **funeral ~** Trauerprozession f

pro-choice [prəuˈtʃɔɪs] adj (movement) Pro-Abtreibungs-; ~ **campaigner** Abtreibungsbefürworter(in) m(f)

proclaim [prəˈkleɪm] vt verkünden

procrastinate [prəuˈkræstɪneɪt] vi zaudern

procure [prəˈkjuər] vt beschaffen

prod [prɔd] vt stoßen ♦ n Stoß m

prodigal [ˈprɔdɪgl] adj: **~ (with or of)** verschwenderisch (mit)

prodigy [ˈprɔdɪdʒɪ] n Wunder nt

produce [n ˈprɔdjuːs, vb prəˈdjuːs] n (AGR) (Boden)produkte pl, (Natur)erzeugnis nt ♦ vt herstellen, produzieren; (cause) hervorrufen; (farmer) erzeugen; (yield) liefern, bringen; (play) inszenieren; ~r n Hersteller m, Produzent m (also CINE); Erzeuger m

product [ˈprɔdʌkt] n Produkt nt, Erzeugnis nt; ~**ion** [prəˈdʌkʃən] n Produktion f, Herstellung f; (thing) Erzeugnis nt, Produkt nt; (THEAT) Inszenierung f; ~**ion line** n Fließband nt; ~**ive** [prəˈdʌktɪv] adj produktiv; (fertile) ertragreich, fruchtbar

productivity [prɔdʌkˈtɪvɪtɪ] n Produktivität f

profane [prəˈfeɪn] adj weltlich, profan; (language etc) gotteslästerlich

profess [prəˈfes] *vt* bekennen; (*show*) zeigen; (*claim to be*) vorgeben

profession [prəˈfeʃən] *n* Beruf *m*; (*declaration*) Bekenntnis *nt*; ~al *n* Fachmann *m*; (*SPORT*) Berufsspieler(in) *m(f)* ♦ *adj* Berufs-; (*expert*) fachlich; (*player*) professionell; ~ally *adv* beruflich; fachmännisch

professor [prəˈfesər] *n* Professor *m*

proficiency [prəˈfiʃənsɪ] *n* Können *nt*

proficient [prəˈfiʃənt] *adj* fähig

profile [ˈprəufaɪl] *n* Profil *nt*; (*fig: report*) Kurzbiografie *f*

profit [ˈprɒfɪt] *n* Gewinn *m* ♦ *vi*: **to ~ (by** or **from)** profitieren (von); ~**ability** [prɒfɪtəˈbɪlɪtɪ] *n* Rentabilität *f*; ~**able** *adj* einträglich, rentabel; ~**eering** [prɒfɪˈtɪərɪŋ] *n* Profitmacherei *f*

profound [prəˈfaund] *adj* tief

profuse [prəˈfjuːs] *adj* überreich; ~**ly** [prəˈfjuːslɪ] *adv* überschwänglich; (*sweat*) reichlich; **profusion** [prəˈfjuːʒən] *n*: **profusion (of)** Überfülle *f* (von), Überfluss *m* (an +*dat*)

program [ˈprəugræm] *n* (*COMPUT*) Programm *nt* ♦ *vt* (*machine*) programmieren; ~**me** (*US* **program**) *n* Programm *nt* ♦ *vt* planen; (*computer*) programmieren; ~**mer** (*US* **programer**) *n* Programmierer(in) *m(f)*

progress [*n* ˈprəugres, *vb* prəˈgres] *n* Fortschritt *m* ♦ *vi* fortschreiten, weitergehen; **in ~** im Gang; ~**ion** [prəˈgreʃən] *n* Folge *f*; ~**ive** [prəˈgresɪv] *adj* fortschrittlich, progressiv

prohibit [prəˈhɪbɪt] *vt* verbieten; **to ~ sb from doing sth** jdm untersagen, etw zu tun; ~**ion** [prəuɪˈbɪʃən] *n* Verbot *nt*; (*US*) Alkoholverbot *nt*, Prohibition *f*; ~**ive** *adj* unerschwinglich

project [*n* ˈprɒdʒekt, *vb* prəˈdʒekt] *n* Projekt *nt* ♦ *vt* vorausplanen; (*film etc*) projizieren; (*personality, voice*) zum Tragen bringen ♦ *vi* (*stick out*) hervorragen, (her)vorstehen

projectile [prəˈdʒektaɪl] *n* Geschoss *nt*

projection [prəˈdʒekʃən] *n* Projektion *f*; (*sth prominent*) Vorsprung *m*

projector [prəˈdʒektər] *n* Projektor *m*

proletariat [prəulɪˈtɛərɪət] *n* Proletariat *nt*

pro-life [prəuˈlaɪf] *adj* (*movement*) Anti-Abtreibungs-; ~ **campaigner** Abtreibungsgegner(in) *m(f)*

prolific [prəˈlɪfɪk] *adj* fruchtbar; (*author etc*) produktiv

prologue [ˈprəulɒg] *n* Prolog *m*; (*event*) Vorspiel *nt*

prolong [prəˈlɒŋ] *vt* verlängern

prom [prɒm] *n abbr* = **promenade**; **promenade concert**

Prom

ⓘ **Prom** (*promenade concert*) ist in *Großbritannien ein Konzert, bei dem ein Teil der Zuhörer steht (ursprünglich spazieren ging). Die seit 1895 alljährlich stattfindenden Proms (seit 1941 immer in der Londoner Royal Albert Hall) zählen zu den bedeutendsten Musikereignissen in England. Der letzte Abend der Proms steht ganz im Zeichen des Patriotismus und gipfelt im Singen des Lieds „Land of Hope and Glory". In den USA und Kanada steht das Wort für* **promenade**, *ein Ball an einer* **High School** *oder einem* **College**.

---

promenade [prɒməˈnɑːd] *n* Promenade *f*; ~ **concert** *n* Promenadenkonzert *nt*

prominence [ˈprɒmɪnəns] *n* (große) Bedeutung *f*

prominent [ˈprɒmɪnənt] *adj* bedeutend; (*politician*) prominent; (*easily seen*) herausragend, auffallend

promiscuous [prəˈmɪskjuəs] *adj* lose

promise [ˈprɒmɪs] *n* Versprechen *nt*; (*hope*: ~ *of sth*) Aussicht *f* auf etw *acc* ♦ *vt, vi* versprechen; **promising** *adj* viel versprechend

promontory [ˈprɒməntrɪ] *n* Vorsprung *m*

promote [prəˈməut] *vt* befördern; (*help on*) fördern, unterstützen; ~**r** *n* (*in entertainment, sport*) Veranstalter *m*; (*for charity etc*) Organisator *m*; **promotion** [prəˈməuʃən] *n* (*in rank*) Beförderung *f*; (*furtherance*) Förderung *f*; (*COMM*): **promotion (of)** Werbung *f* (für)

prompt [prɒmpt] *adj* prompt, schnell ♦ *adv* (*punctually*) genau ♦ *n* (COMPUT) Meldung *f* ♦ *vt* veranlassen; (THEAT) soufflieren +*dat*; **to ~ sb to do sth** jdn dazu veranlassen, etw zu tun; **~ly** *adv* sofort

prone [prəʊn] *adj* hingestreckt; **to be ~ to sth** zu etw neigen

prong [prɒŋ] *n* Zinke *f*

pronoun ['prəʊnaʊn] *n* Fürwort *nt*

pronounce [prə'naʊns] *vt* aussprechen; (JUR) verkünden ♦ *vi*: **to ~ (on)** sich äußern (zu)

pronunciation [prənʌnsɪ'eɪʃən] *n* Aussprache *f*

proof [pruːf] *n* Beweis *m*; (PRINT) Korrekturfahne *f*; (*of alcohol*) Alkoholgehalt *m* ♦ *adj* sicher

prop [prɒp] *n* (*also fig*) Stütze *f*; (THEAT) Requisit *nt* ♦ *vt* (*also*: **~ up**) (ab)stützen

propaganda [prɒpə'gændə] *n* Propaganda *f*

propel [prə'pel] *vt* (an)treiben; **~ler** *n* Propeller *m*; **~ling pencil** (BRIT) *n* Drehbleistift *m*

propensity [prə'pensɪtɪ] *n* Tendenz *f*

proper ['prɒpə*] *adj* richtig; (*seemly*) schicklich; **~ly** *adv* richtig; **~ noun** *n* Eigenname *m*

property ['prɒpətɪ] *n* Eigentum *nt*; (*quality*) Eigenschaft *f*; (*land*) Grundbesitz *m*; **~ owner** *n* Grundbesitzer *m*

prophecy ['prɒfɪsɪ] *n* Prophezeiung *f*

prophesy ['prɒfɪsaɪ] *vt* prophezeien

prophet ['prɒfɪt] *n* Prophet *m*

proportion [prə'pɔːʃən] *n* Verhältnis *nt*; (*share*) Teil *m* ♦ *vt*: **to ~ (to)** abstimmen (auf +*acc*); **~al** *adj* proportional; **~ate** *adj* verhältnismäßig

proposal [prə'pəʊzl] *n* Vorschlag *m*; (*of marriage*) Heiratsantrag *m*

propose [prə'pəʊz] *vt* vorschlagen; (*toast*) ausbringen ♦ *vi* (*offer marriage*) einen Heiratsantrag machen; **to ~ to do sth** beabsichtigen, etw zu tun

proposition [prɒpə'zɪʃən] *n* Angebot *nt*; (*statement*) Satz *m*

proprietor [prə'praɪətə*] *n* Besitzer *m*, Eigentümer *m*

propriety [prə'praɪətɪ] *n* Anstand *m*

pro rata [prəʊ'rɑːtə] *adv* anteilmäßig

prose [prəʊz] *n* Prosa *f*

prosecute ['prɒsɪkjuːt] *vt* (strafrechtlich) verfolgen; **prosecution** [prɒsɪ'kjuːʃən] *n* (JUR) strafrechtliche Verfolgung *f*; (*party*) Anklage *f*; **prosecutor** *n* Vertreter *m* der Anklage; **Public Prosecutor** Staatsanwalt *m*

prospect [*n* 'prɒspekt, *vb* prə'spekt] *n* Aussicht *f* ♦ *vt* auf Bodenschätze hin untersuchen ♦ *vi*: **to ~ (for)** suchen (nach); **~ing** ['prɒspektɪŋ] *n* (*for minerals*) Suche *f*; **~ive** [prə'spektɪv] *adj* (*son-in-law etc*) zukünftig; (*customer, candidate*) voraussichtlich

prospectus [prə'spektəs] *n* (Werbe)prospekt *m*

prosper ['prɒspə*] *vi* blühen, gedeihen; (*person*) erfolgreich sein; **~ity** [prɒ'sperɪtɪ] *n* Wohlstand *m*; **~ous** *adj* wohlhabend, reich

prostitute ['prɒstɪtjuːt] *n* Prostituierte *f*

prostrate ['prɒstreɪt] *adj* ausgestreckt (liegend)

protagonist [prə'tægənɪst] *n* Hauptperson *f*, Held *m*

protect [prə'tekt] *vt* (be)schützen; **~ed species** *n* geschützte Art; **~ion** [prə'tekʃən] *n* Schutz *m*; **~ive** *adj* Schutz-, (be)schützend

protégé ['prəʊteʒeɪ] *n* Schützling *m*

protein ['prəʊtiːn] *n* Protein *nt*, Eiweiß *nt*

protest [*n* 'prəʊtest, *vb* prə'test] *n* Protest *m* ♦ *vi* protestieren ♦ *vt* (*affirm*) beteuern

Protestant ['prɒtɪstənt] *adj* protestantisch ♦ *n* Protestant(in) *m(f)*

protester [prə'testə*] *n* (*demonstrator*) Demonstrant(in) *m(f)*

protracted [prə'træktɪd] *adj* sich hinziehend

protrude [prə'truːd] *vi* (her)vorstehen

proud [praʊd] *adj*: **~ (of)** stolz (auf +*acc*)

prove [pruːv] *vt* beweisen ♦ *vi*: **to ~ (to be) correct** sich als richtig erweisen; **to ~ o.s.** sich bewähren

proverb ['prɒvɜːb] *n* Sprichwort *nt*; **~ial** [prə'vɜːbɪəl] *adj* sprichwörtlich

provide [prə'vaɪd] *vt* versehen; (*supply*) besorgen; **to ~ sb with sth** jdn mit etw versorgen; ~ **for** vt fus sorgen für; (*emergency*) Vorkehrungen treffen für; ~**d** (*that*) conj vorausgesetzt(, dass)

providing [prə'vaɪdɪŋ] conj vorausgesetzt(, dass)

province ['prɒvɪns] n Provinz f; (*division of work*) Bereich m; **provincial** [prə'vɪnʃəl] adj provinziell, Provinz-

provision [prə'vɪʒən] n Vorkehrung f; (*condition*) Bestimmung f; ~**s** npl (*food*) Vorräte pl, Proviant m; ~**al** adj provisorisch

proviso [prə'vaɪzəu] n Bedingung f

provocative [prə'vɒkətɪv] adj provozierend

provoke [prə'vəuk] vt provozieren; (*cause*) hervorrufen

prowess ['prauɪs] n überragende(s) Können nt

prowl [praul] vi herumstreichen; (*animal*) schleichen ♦ n: **on the** ~ umherstreifend; ~**er** n Herumtreiber(in) m(f)

proximity [prɒk'sɪmɪtɪ] n Nähe f

proxy ['prɒksɪ] n (*Stell*)vertreter m; (*authority, document*) Vollmacht f; **by** ~ durch einen Stellvertreter

prudent ['pru:dnt] adj klug, umsichtig

prudish ['pru:dɪʃ] adj prüde

prune [pru:n] n Backpflaume f ♦ vt ausputzen; (*fig*) zurechtstutzen

pry [praɪ] vi: **to** ~ (**into**) seine Nase stecken (in +*acc*)

PS n abbr (= postscript) PS

pseudonym ['sju:dənɪm] n Pseudonym nt, Deckname m

psychiatric [saɪkɪ'ætrɪk] adj psychiatrisch

psychiatrist [saɪ'kaɪətrɪst] n Psychiater m

psychic ['saɪkɪk] adj (*also:* ~**al**) übersinnlich; (*person*) paranormal begabt

psychoanalyse [saɪkəu'ænəlaɪz] (*US* **psychoanalyze**) vt psychoanalytisch behandeln; **psychoanalyst** [saɪkəu'ænəlɪst] n Psychoanalytiker(in) m(f)

psychological [saɪkə'lɒdʒɪkl] adj psychologisch; **psychologist** [saɪ'kɒlədʒɪst] n Psychologe m, Psychologin f; **psychology** [saɪ'kɒlədʒɪ] n Psychologie f

PTO abbr = **please turn over**

pub [pʌb] n abbr (= public house) Kneipe f

Pub

i **Pub** *ist ein Gasthaus mit einer Lizenz zum Ausschank von alkoholischen Getränken. Ein Pub besteht meist aus verschiedenen gemütlichen (***lounge, snug***) oder einfacheren Räumen (***public bar***), in der oft auch Spiele wie Darts, Domino und Poolbillard zur Verfügung stehen. In Pubs werden vor allem mittags oft auch Mahlzeiten angeboten. Pubs sind normalerweise von 11 bis 23 Uhr geöffnet, aber manchmal nachmittags geschlossen.*

---

pubic ['pju:bɪk] adj Scham-

public ['pʌblɪk] adj öffentlich ♦ n (*also:* **general** ~) Öffentlichkeit f; **in** ~ in der Öffentlichkeit; ~ **address system** n Lautsprecheranlage f

publican ['pʌblɪkən] n Wirt m

publication [pʌblɪ'keɪʃən] n Veröffentlichung f

public: ~ **company** n Aktiengesellschaft f; ~ **convenience** (*BRIT*) n öffentliche Toiletten pl; ~ **holiday** n gesetzliche(r) Feiertag m; ~ **house** (*BRIT*) n Lokal nt, Kneipe f

publicity [pʌb'lɪsɪtɪ] n Publicity f, Werbung f

publicize ['pʌblɪsaɪz] vt bekannt machen; (*advertise*) Publicity machen für

publicly ['pʌblɪklɪ] adv öffentlich

public: ~ **opinion** n öffentliche Meinung f; ~ **relations** npl Publicrelations pl, Public Relations pl; ~ **school** n (*BRIT*) Privatschule f; (*US*) staatliche Schule f; ~-**spirited** adj mit Gemeinschaftssinn; ~ **transport** n öffentliche Verkehrsmittel pl

publish ['pʌblɪʃ] vt veröffentlichen; (*event*) bekannt geben; ~**er** n Verleger m; ~**ing** n (*business*) Verlagswesen n

pub lunch n in Pubs servierter Imbiss

pucker ['pʌkə*] vt (*face*) verziehen; (*lips*) kräuseln

pudding ['pudɪŋ] n (*BRIT: course*) Nachtisch m; Pudding m; **black** ~ ≈ Blutwurst f

puddle ['pʌdl] n Pfütze f

puff [pʌf] n (*of wind etc*) Stoß m; (*cosmetic*)

Puderquaste f ♦ vt blasen, pusten; (*pipe*)
paffen ♦ vi keuchen, schnaufen; (*smoke*)
paffen; **to ~ out smoke** Rauch ausstoßen;
~ pastry (*US* **= paste**) n Blätterteig m; **~y**
adj aufgedunsen

pull [pul] n Ruck m; (*influence*) Beziehung f
♦ vt ziehen; (*trigger*) abdrücken ♦ vi ziehen;
to ~ sb's leg jdn auf den Arm nehmen; **to
~ to pieces** in Stücke reißen; (*fig*)
verreißen; **to ~ one's punches** sich
zurückziehen; **to ~ one's weight** sich in die
Riemen legen; **to ~ o.s. together** sich
zusammenreißen; **~ apart** vt (*break*)
zerreißen; (*dismantle*) auseinander nehmen;
(*separate*) trennen; **~ down** vt (*house*)
abreißen; **~ in** vi hineinfahren; (*stop*)
anhalten; (*RAIL*) einfahren; **~ off** vt (*deal
etc*) abschließen; **~ out** vi (*car*)
herausfahren; (*fig: partner*) aussteigen ♦ vt
herausziehen; **~ over** vi (*AUT*) an die Seite
fahren; **~ through** vi durchkommen; **~
up** vi anhalten ♦ vt (*uproot*) herausreißen;
(*stop*) anhalten

pulley ['puli] n Rolle f, Flaschenzug m

pullover ['puləuvər] n Pullover m

pulp [pʌlp] n Brei m; (*of fruit*) Fruchtfleisch nt

pulpit ['pulpit] n Kanzel f

pulsate [pʌl'seit] vi pulsieren

pulse [pʌls] n Puls m; **~s** npl (*BOT*)
Hülsenfrüchte pl

pummel ['pʌml] vt mit den Fäusten
bearbeiten

pump [pʌmp] n Pumpe f; (*shoe*) leichter
(Tanz)schuh m ♦ vt pumpen; **~ up** vt (*tyre*)
aufpumpen

pumpkin ['pʌmpkin] n Kürbis m

pun [pʌn] n Wortspiel nt

punch [pʌntʃ] n (*tool*) Locher m; (*blow*)
(Faust)schlag m; (*drink*) Punsch m, Bowle f
♦ vt lochen; (*strike*) schlagen, boxen; **~ line**
n Pointe f; **~-up** n (*BRIT: inf*) n Keilerei f

punctual ['pʌŋktjuəl] adj pünktlich

punctuate ['pʌŋktjueit] vt mit Satzzeichen
versehen; (*fig*) unterbrechen; **punctuation**
[pʌŋktju'eiʃən] n Zeichensetzung f,
Interpunktion f

puncture ['pʌŋktʃər] n Loch nt; (*AUT*)

Reifenpanne f ♦ vt durchbohren

pundit ['pʌndit] n Gelehrte(r) m

pungent ['pʌndʒənt] adj scharf

punish ['pʌniʃ] vt bestrafen; (*in boxing etc*)
übel zurichten; **~ment** n Strafe f; (*action*)
Bestrafung f

punk [pʌŋk] n (*also: ~ rocker*) Punker(in)
m(f); (*also: ~ rock*) Punk m; (*US: inf:
hoodlum*) Ganove m

punt [pʌnt] n Stechkahn m

punter ['pʌntər] (*BRIT*) n (*better*) Wetter m

puny ['pju:ni] adj kümmerlich

pup [pʌp] n = **puppy**

pupil ['pju:pl] n Schüler(in) m(f); (*in eye*)
Pupille f

puppet ['pʌpit] n Puppe f; Marionette f

puppy ['pʌpi] n junge(r) Hund m

purchase ['pə:tʃis] n Kauf m; (*grip*) Halt m
♦ vt kaufen, erwerben; **~r** n Käufer(in) m(f)

pure [pjuər] adj (*also fig*) rein; **~ly** ['pjuəli]
adv rein

purgatory ['pə:gətəri] n Fegefeuer nt

purge [pə:dʒ] n (*also POL*) Säuberung f ♦ vt
reinigen; (*body*) entschlacken

purify ['pjuərifai] vt reinigen

purity ['pjuəriti] n Reinheit f

purple ['pə:pl] adj violett; (*face*) dunkelrot

purport [pə:'pɔ:t] vi vorgeben

purpose ['pə:pəs] n Zweck m, Ziel nt; (*of
person*) Absicht f; **on ~** absichtlich; **~ful** adj
zielbewusst, entschlossen

purr [pə:r] n Schnurren nt ♦ vi schnurren

purse [pə:s] n Portemonnaie nt, Portmonee
nt, Geldbeutel m ♦ vt (*lips*)
zusammenpressen, schürzen

purser ['pə:sər] n Zahlmeister m

pursue [pə'sju:] vt verfolgen; (*study*)
nachgehen +dat; **~r** n Verfolger m; **pursuit**
[pə'sju:t] n Verfolgung f; (*occupation*)
Beschäftigung f

pus [pʌs] n Eiter m

push [puʃ] n Stoß m, Schub m; (*MIL*) Vorstoß
m ♦ vt stoßen, schieben; (*button*) drücken;
(*idea*) durchsetzen ♦ vi stoßen, schieben; **~
aside** vt beiseite schieben; **~ off** (*inf*) vi
abschieben; **~ on** vi weitermachen; **~
through** vt durchdrücken; (*policy*)

durchsetzen; ~ **up** vt (total) erhöhen; (prices) hoch treiben; ~**chair** (BRIT) n (Kinder)sportwagen m; ~**er** n (drug dealer) Pusher m; ~**over** (inf) n Kinderspiel nt; ~**up** (US) n (press-up) Liegestütz m; ~**y** (inf) adj aufdringlich

puss [pus] n Mieze(katze) f; ~**y**(cat) n Mieze(katze) f

put [put] (pt, pp **put**) vt setzen, stellen, legen; (express) ausdrücken, sagen; (write) schreiben; ~ **about** vi (turn back) wenden ♦ vt (spread) verbreiten; ~ **across** vt (explain) erklären; ~ **away** vt weglegen; (store) beiseite legen; ~ **back** vt zurückstellen or -legen; ~ **by** vt zurücklegen, sparen; ~ **down** vt hinstellen or -legen; (rebellion) niederschlagen; (animal) einschläfern; (in writing) niederschreiben; ~ **forward** vt (idea) vorbringen; (clock) vorstellen; ~ **in** vt (application, complaint) einreichen; ~ **off** vt verschieben; (discourage): **to ~ sb off sth** jdn von etw abbringen; ~ **on** vt (clothes etc) anziehen; (light etc) anschalten, anmachen; (play etc) aufführen; (brake) anziehen; ~ **out** vt (hand etc) (her)ausstrecken; (news, rumour) verbreiten; (light etc) ausschalten, ausmachen; ~ **through** vt (TEL: person) verbinden; (: call) durchstellen; ~ **up** vt (tent) aufstellen; (building) errichten; (price) erhöhen; (person) unterbringen; ~ **up with** vt fus sich abfinden mit

putrid ['pju:trɪd] adj faul

putt [pʌt] vt (golf) putten ♦ n (golf) Putten nt; ~**ing green** n kleine(r) Golfplatz m nur zum Putten

putty ['pʌtɪ] n Kitt m; (fig) Wachs nt

put-up ['putʌp] adj: ~ **job** abgekartete(s) Spiel nt

puzzle ['pʌzl] n Rätsel nt; (toy) Geduldspiel nt ♦ vt verwirren ♦ vi sich den Kopf zerbrechen; ~**d** adj verdutzt, verblüfft; **puzzling** adj rätselhaft, verwirrend

pyjamas [pə'dʒɑ:məz] (BRIT) npl Schlafanzug m, Pyjama m

pylon ['paɪlən] n Mast m

pyramid ['pɪrəmɪd] n Pyramide f

Q, q

quack [kwæk] n Quaken nt; (doctor) Quacksalber m ♦ vi quaken

quad [kwɔd] n abbr = **quadrangle**; **quadruplet**

quadrangle ['kwɔdræŋgl] n (court) Hof m; (MATH) Viereck nt

quadruple [kwɔ'dru:pl] adj ♦ vi sich vervierfachen ♦ vt vervierfachen

quadruplets [kwɔ'dru:plɪts] npl Vierlinge pl

quagmire ['kwæɡmaɪə*] n Morast m

quail [kweɪl] n (bird) Wachtel f ♦ vi (vor Angst) zittern

quaint [kweɪnt] adj kurios; malerisch

quake [kweɪk] vi beben, zittern ♦ n abbr = **earthquake**

qualification [kwɔlɪfɪ'keɪʃən] n Qualifikation f; (sth which limits) Einschränkung f

qualified ['kwɔlɪfaɪd] adj (competent) qualifiziert; (limited) bedingt

qualify ['kwɔlɪfaɪ] vt (prepare) befähigen; (limit) einschränken ♦ vi sich qualifizieren; **to ~ as a doctor/lawyer** sein medizinisches/juristisches Staatsexamen machen

quality ['kwɔlɪtɪ] n Qualität f; (characteristic) Eigenschaft f

---
Quality press

ⓘ **Quality press** bezeichnet die seriösen Tages- und Wochenzeitungen, im Gegensatz zu den Massenblättern. Diese Zeitungen sind fast alle großformatig und wenden sich an den anspruchsvolleren Leser, der voll informiert sein möchte und bereit ist, für die Zeitungslektüre viel Zeit aufzuwenden. Siehe auch **tabloid press**.

---

quality time n intensiv genutzte Zeit

qualm [kwɑ:m] n Bedenken nt

quandary ['kwɔndrɪ] n: **to be in a ~** in Verlegenheit sein

quantity ['kwɔntɪtɪ] n Menge f; ~ **surveyor**

n Baukostenkalkulator m

uarantine ['kwɔrntiːn] n Quarantäne f

uarrel ['kwɔrl] n Streit m ♦ vi sich streiten;
~**some** adj streitsüchtig

uarry ['kwɔrɪ] n Steinbruch m; (animal)
Wild nt; (fig) Opfer nt

uarter ['kwɔːtəʳ] n Viertel nt; (of year)
Quartal nt ♦ vt (divide) vierteln; (MIL)
einquartieren; ~**s** npl (esp MIL) Quartier nt;
~ **of an hour** Viertelstunde f; ~ **final** n
Viertelfinale nt; ~**ly** adj vierteljährlich

uartet(te) [kwɔːˈtɛt] n Quartett nt

uartz [kwɔːts] n Quarz m

uash [kwɔʃ] vt (verdict) aufheben

uaver ['kweɪvəʳ] vi (tremble) zittern

uay [kiː] n Kai m

ueasy ['kwiːzɪ] adj übel

ueen [kwiːn] n Königin f; ~ **mother** n
Königinmutter f

ueer [kwɪəʳ] adj seltsam ♦ n (inf:
homosexual) Schwule(r) m

uell [kwɛl] vt unterdrücken

uench [kwɛntʃ] vt (thirst) löschen

uerulous ['kwɛruləs] adj nörglerisch

uery ['kwɪərɪ] n (question) (An)frage f;
(question mark) Fragezeichen nt ♦ vt in
Zweifel ziehen, infrage or in Frage stellen

uest [kwɛst] n Suche f

uestion ['kwɛstʃən] n Frage f ♦ vt (ask)
(be)fragen; (suspect) verhören; (doubt)
infrage or in Frage stellen, bezweifeln;
beyond ~ ohne Frage; **out of the ~**
ausgeschlossen; ~**able** adj zweifelhaft; ~
mark n Fragezeichen nt

uestionnaire [kwɛstʃəˈnɛəʳ] n Fragebogen
m

ueue [kjuː] n (BRIT) Schlange f ♦ vi (also: ~
up) Schlange stehen

uibble ['kwɪbl] vi kleinlich sein

uick [kwɪk] adj schnell ♦ n (of nail)
Nagelhaut f; **be ~!** mach schnell!; **cut to
the ~** (fig) tief getroffen; ~**en** vt (hasten)
beschleunigen ♦ vi sich beschleunigen; ~**ly**
adv schnell; ~**sand** n Treibsand m; ~-
witted adj schlagfertig

uid [kwɪd] (BRIT: inf) n Pfund nt

uiet ['kwaɪət] adj (without noise) leise;

(peaceful, calm) still, ruhig ♦ n Stille f, Ruhe f
♦ vt, vi (US) = **quieten**; **keep ~!** sei still!;
~**en** vi (also: ~**en down**) ruhig werden ♦ vt
beruhigen; ~**ly** adv leise, ruhig; ~**ness** n
Ruhe f, Stille f

quilt [kwɪlt] n (continental ~) Steppdecke f

quin [kwɪn] n abbr = **quintuplet**

quintuplets [kwɪnˈtjuːplɪts] npl Fünflinge pl

quip [kwɪp] n witzige Bemerkung f

quirk [kwɜːk] n (oddity) Eigenart f

quit [kwɪt] (pt, pp quit or quitted) vt
verlassen ♦ vi aufhören

quite [kwaɪt] adv (completely) ganz, völlig;
(fairly) ziemlich; ~ **a few of them** ziemlich
viele von ihnen; ~ **(so)!** richtig!

quits [kwɪts] adj quitt; **let's call it ~** lassen
wirs gut sein

quiver ['kwɪvəʳ] vi zittern ♦ n (for arrows)
Köcher m

quiz [kwɪz] n (competition) Quiz nt ♦ vt
prüfen; ~**zical** adj fragend

quota ['kwəʊtə] n Anteil m; (COMM) Quote f

quotation [kwəʊˈteɪʃən] n Zitat nt; (price)
Kostenvoranschlag m; ~ **marks** npl
Anführungszeichen pl

quote [kwəʊt] n = **quotation** ♦ vi (from book)
zitieren ♦ vt zitieren; (price) angeben

R, r

rabbi ['ræbaɪ] n Rabbiner m; (title) Rabbi m

rabbit ['ræbɪt] n Kaninchen nt; ~ **hole** n
Kaninchenbau m; ~ **hutch** n Kaninchenstall
m

rabble ['ræbl] n Pöbel m

rabies ['reɪbiːz] n Tollwut f

RAC (BRIT) n abbr = **Royal Automobile Club**

raccoon [rəˈkuːn] n Waschbär m

race [reɪs] n (species) Rasse f; (competition)
Rennen nt; (on foot) Rennen nt, Wettlauf m;
(rush) Hetze f ♦ vt um die Wette laufen mit;
(horses) laufen lassen ♦ vi (run) rennen; (in
contest) am Rennen teilnehmen; ~ **car** (US)
n = **racing car**; ~ **car driver** (US) n =
racing driver; ~**course** n (for horses)
Rennbahn f; ~**horse** n Rennpferd nt; ~**r** n

(person) Rennfahrer(in) m(f); (car)
Rennwagen m; ~**track** n (for cars etc)
Rennstrecke f

racial ['reɪʃl] adj Rassen-

racing ['reɪsɪŋ] n Rennen nt; ~ **car** (BRIT) n
Rennwagen m; ~ **driver** (BRIT) n
Rennfahrer m

racism ['reɪsɪzəm] n Rassismus m; **racist**
['reɪsɪst] n Rassist m ♦ adj rassistisch

rack [ræk] n Ständer m, Gestell nt ♦ vt
plagen; **to go to ~ and ruin** verfallen; **to ~
one's brains** sich dat den Kopf zerbrechen

racket ['rækɪt] n (din) Krach m; (scheme)
(Schwindel)geschäft nt; (TENNIS)
(Tennis)schläger m

racquet ['rækɪt] n (Tennis)schläger m

racy ['reɪsɪ] adj gewagt; (style) spritzig

radar ['reɪdɑːʳ] n Radar nt or m

radial ['reɪdɪəl] adj (also: US: ~**ply**) radial

radiant ['reɪdɪənt] adj strahlend; (giving out
rays) Strahlungs-

radiate ['reɪdɪeɪt] vi ausstrahlen; (roads, lines)
strahlenförmig wegführen ♦ vt ausstrahlen;
radiation [reɪdɪ'eɪʃən] n (Aus)strahlung f

radiator ['reɪdɪeɪtəʳ] n (for heating)
Heizkörper m; (AUT) Kühler m

radical ['rædɪkl] adj radikal

radii ['reɪdɪaɪ] npl of **radius**

radio ['reɪdɪəʊ] n Rundfunk m, Radio nt; (set)
Radio nt, Radioapparat m; **on the ~** im
Radio; ~**active** ['reɪdɪəʊ'æktɪv] adj
radioaktiv; ~ **cassette** n Radiorekorder m;
~**controlled** adj ferngesteuert; ~**logy**
[reɪdɪ'ɒlədʒɪ] n Strahlenkunde f; ~ **station** n
Rundfunkstation f; ~**therapy**
['reɪdɪəʊ'θerəpɪ] n Röntgentherapie f

radish ['rædɪʃ] n (big) Rettich m; (small)
Radieschen nt

radius ['reɪdɪəs] (pl **radii**) n Radius m; (area)
Umkreis m

RAF n abbr = **Royal Air Force**

raffle ['ræfl] n Verlosung f, Tombola f ♦ vt
verlosen

raft [rɑːft] n Floß nt

rafter ['rɑːftəʳ] n Dachsparren m

rag [ræg] n (cloth) Lumpen nt, Lappen m;
(inf: newspaper) Käseblatt nt; (UNIV: for

charity) studentische Sammelaktion f ♦ vt
(BRIT) auf den Arm nehmen; ~**s** npl (cloth)
Lumpen pl; ~ **doll** n Flickenpuppe f

rage [reɪdʒ] n Wut f; (fashion) große Mode f
♦ vi wüten, toben

ragged ['rægɪd] adj (edge) gezackt; (clothes)
zerlumpt

raid [reɪd] n Überfall m; (MIL) Angriff m; (by
police) Razzia f ♦ vt überfallen

rail [reɪl] n (also RAIL) Schiene f; (on stair)
Geländer nt; (of ship) Reling f; ~**s** npl (RAIL)
Geleise pl; **by** ~ per Bahn; ~**ing(s)** n(pl)
Geländer nt; ~**road** (US) n Eisenbahn f;
~**way** (BRIT) n Eisenbahn f; ~**way line**
(BRIT) n (Eisen)bahnlinie f; (track) Gleis nt;
~**wayman** (irreg; BRIT) n Eisenbahner m;
~**way station** (BRIT) n Bahnhof m

rain [reɪn] n Regen m ♦ vt, vi regnen; **in the
~** im Regen; **it's ~ing** es regnet; ~**bow** n
Regenbogen m; ~**coat** n Regenmantel m;
~**drop** n Regentropfen m; ~**fall** n
Niederschlag m; ~**forest** n Regenwald m;
~**y** adj (region, season) Regen-; (day)
regnerisch, verregnet

raise [reɪz] n (esp US: increase)
(Gehalts)erhöhung f ♦ vt (lift) (hoch)heben;
(increase) erhöhen; (question) aufwerfen;
(doubts) äußern; (funds) beschaffen; (family)
großziehen; (livestock) züchten; **to ~ one's
voice** die Stimme erheben

raisin ['reɪzn] n Rosine f

rake [reɪk] n Rechen m, Harke f; Wüstling m
♦ vt rechen, harken; (search) (durch)suchen

rally ['rælɪ] n (POL etc) Kundgebung f; (AUT)
Rallye f ♦ vt (MIL) sammeln ♦ vi Kräfte
sammeln; ~ **round** vt fus (sich) scharen
um; (help) zu Hilfe kommen +dat ♦ vi zu
Hilfe kommen

RAM [ræm] n abbr (= random access memory)
RAM m

Ramadan ['ræmədɑːn] n Ramadan m

ram [ræm] n Widder m ♦ vt (hit) rammen;
(stuff) (hinein)stopfen

ramble ['ræmbl] n Wanderung f ♦ vi (talk)
schwafeln; ~**r** n Wanderer m; **rambling** adj
(speech) weitschweifig; (town) ausgedehnt

ramp [ræmp] n Rampe f; **on/off** ~ (US: AUT)

Ein-/Ausfahrt f

rampage [ræm'peɪdʒ] n: **to be on the ~** randalieren ♦ vi randalieren

rampant ['ræmpənt] adj wild wuchernd

rampart ['ræmpɑːt] n (Schutz)wall m

ram raid n Raubüberfall, bei dem eine Geschäftsfront mit einem Fahrzeug gerammt wird

ramshackle ['ræmʃækl] adj baufällig

ran [ræn] pt of **run**

ranch [rɑːntʃ] n Ranch f

rancid ['rænsɪd] adj ranzig

rancour ['ræŋkə*] (US **rancor**) n Verbitterung f, Groll m

random ['rændəm] adj ziellos, wahllos ♦ n: **at ~** aufs Geratewohl; **~ access** n (COMPUT) wahlfreie(r) Zugriff m

randy ['rændɪ] (BRIT: inf) adj geil, scharf

rang [ræŋ] pt of **ring**

range [reɪndʒ] n Reihe f; (of mountains) Kette f; (COMM) Sortiment nt; (reach) (Reich)weite f; (of gun) Schussweite f; (for shooting practice) Schießplatz m; (stove) (großer) Herd m ♦ vt (set in row) anordnen, aufstellen; (roam) durchstreifen ♦ vi: **to ~ over** (wander) umherstreifen in +dat; (extend) sich erstrecken auf +acc; **a ~ of** (selection) eine (große) Auswahl an +dat; **prices ranging from £5 to £10** Preise, die sich zwischen £5 und £10 bewegen; **~r** ['reɪndʒə*] n Förster m

rank [ræŋk] n (row) Reihe f; (BRIT: also: **taxi ~**) (Taxi)stand m; (MIL) Rang m; (social position) Stand m ♦ vi (have ~): **to ~ among** gehören zu ♦ adj (strong-smelling) stinkend; (extreme) kraß; **the ~ and file** (fig) die breite Masse

rankle ['ræŋkl] vi nagen

ransack ['rænsæk] vt (plunder) plündern; (search) durchwühlen

ransom ['rænsəm] n Lösegeld nt; **to hold sb to ~** jdn gegen Lösegeld festhalten

rant [rænt] vi hochtrabend reden

rap [ræp] n Schlag m; (music) Rap m ♦ vt klopfen

rape [reɪp] n Vergewaltigung f; (BOT) Raps m ♦ vt vergewaltigen; **~(seed) oil** n Rapsöl nt

rapid ['ræpɪd] adj rasch, schnell; **~ity** [rə'pɪdɪtɪ] n Schnelligkeit f; **~s** npl Stromschnellen pl

rapist ['reɪpɪst] n Vergewaltiger m

rapport [ræ'pɔːr] n gute(s) Verhältnis nt

rapture ['ræptʃə*] n Entzücken nt; **rapturous** ['ræptʃərəs] adj (applause) stürmisch; (expression) verzückt

rare [reə*] adj selten, rar; (underdone) nicht durchgebraten; **~ly** ['reəlɪ] adv selten

raring ['reərɪŋ] adj: **to be ~ to go** (inf) es kaum erwarten können, dass es losgeht

rarity ['reərɪtɪ] n Seltenheit f

rascal ['rɑːskl] n Schuft m

rash [ræʃ] adj übereilt; (reckless) unbesonnen ♦ n (Haut)ausschlag m

rasher ['ræʃə*] n Speckscheibe f

raspberry ['rɑːzbərɪ] n Himbeere f

rasping ['rɑːspɪŋ] adj (noise) kratzend; (voice) krächzend

rat [ræt] n (animal) Ratte f; (person) Halunke m

rate [reɪt] n (proportion) Rate f; (price) Tarif m; (speed) Tempo nt ♦ vt (ein)schätzen; **~s** npl (BRIT: tax) Grundsteuer f; **to ~ as** für etw halten; **~able value** (BRIT) n Einheitswert m (als Bemessungsgrundlage); **~payer** (BRIT) n Steuerzahler(in) m(f)

rather ['rɑːðə*] adv (in preference) lieber, eher; (to some extent) ziemlich; **I would** or **I'd ~ go** ich würde lieber gehen; **it's ~ expensive** (quite) es ist ziemlich teuer; (too) es ist etwas zu teuer; **there's ~ a lot** es ist ziemlich viel

ratify ['rætɪfaɪ] vt (POL) ratifizieren

rating ['reɪtɪŋ] n Klasse f

ratio ['reɪʃɪəʊ] n Verhältnis nt; **in the ~ of 100 to 1** im Verhältnis 100 zu 1

ration ['ræʃən] n (usu pl) Ration f ♦ vt rationieren

rational ['ræʃənl] adj rational

rationale [ræʃə'nɑːl] n Grundprinzip nt

rationalize ['ræʃnəlaɪz] vt rationalisieren

rat race n Konkurrenzkampf m

rattle ['rætl] n (sound) Rasseln nt; (toy) Rassel f ♦ vi ratteln, klappern ♦ vt rasseln mit; **~snake** n Klapperschlange f

raucous ['rɔːkəs] adj heiser, rau

rave [reɪv] vi (talk wildly) fantasieren; (rage) toben ♦ n (BRIT: inf: party) Rave m, Fete f

raven ['reɪvən] n Rabe m

ravenous ['rævənəs] adj heißhungrig

ravine [rə'viːn] n Schlucht f

raving ['reɪvɪŋ] adj: ~ **lunatic** völlig Wahnsinnige(r) mf

ravishing ['rævɪʃɪŋ] adj atemberaubend

raw [rɔː] adj roh; (tender) wund (gerieben); (inexperienced) unerfahren; **to get a ~ deal** (inf) schlecht wegkommen; ~ **material** n Rohmaterial nt

ray [reɪ] n (of light) Strahl m; ~ **of hope** Hoffnungsschimmer m

raze [reɪz] vt (also: ~ **to the ground**) dem Erdboden gleichmachen

razor ['reɪzər] n Rasierapparat m; ~ **blade** n Rasierklinge f

Rd abbr = **road**

RE (BRIT: SCH) abbr (= religious education) Religionsunterricht m

re [riː] prep (COMM) betreffs +gen

reach [riːtʃ] n Reichweite f; (of river) Strecke f ♦ vt (arrive at) erreichen; (give) reichen ♦ vi (stretch) sich erstrecken; **within ~** (shops etc) in erreichbarer Weite or Entfernung; **out of ~** außer Reichweite; **to ~ for** (try to get) langen nach; ~ **out** vi die Hand ausstrecken; **to ~ out for sth** nach etw greifen

react [riː'ækt] vi reagieren; ~**ion** [riː'ækʃən] n Reaktion f; ~**or** [riː'æktər] n Reaktor m

read¹ [rɛd] pt, pp of **read²**

read² [riːd] (pt, pp **read**) vt, vi lesen; (aloud) vorlesen; ~ **out** vt vorlesen; ~**able** adj leserlich; (worth ~ing) lesenswert; ~**er** n (person) Leser(in) m(f); ~**ership** n Leserschaft f

readily ['rɛdɪlɪ] adv (willingly) bereitwillig; (easily) prompt

readiness ['rɛdɪnɪs] n (willingness) Bereitwilligkeit f; (being ready) Bereitschaft f; **in ~** (prepared) bereit

reading ['riːdɪŋ] n Lesen nt

readjust [riːə'dʒʌst] vt neu einstellen ♦ vi (person): **to ~ to** sich wieder anpassen an

+acc

ready ['rɛdɪ] adj (prepared, willing) bereit ♦ adv: ~-**cooked** vorgekocht ♦ n: **at the ~** bereit; ~-**made** adj gebrauchsfertig, Fertig-; (clothes) Konfektions-; ~ **money** n Bargeld nt; ~ **reckoner** n Rechentabelle f; ~-**to-wear** adj Konfektions-

real [rɪəl] adj wirklich; (actual) eigentlich; (not fake) echt; **in ~ terms** effektiv; ~ **estate** n Grundbesitz m; ~**istic** [rɪə'lɪstɪk] adj realistisch

reality [riː'ælɪtɪ] n Wirklichkeit f, Realität f; **in ~** in Wirklichkeit

realization [rɪəlaɪ'zeɪʃən] n (understanding) Erkenntnis f; (fulfilment) Verwirklichung f

realize ['rɪəlaɪz] vt (understand) begreifen; (make real) verwirklichen; **I didn't ~ ...** ich wusste nicht, ...

really ['rɪəlɪ] adv wirklich; ~? (indicating interest) tatsächlich?; (expressing surprise) wirklich?

realm [rɛlm] n Reich nt

realtor ['rɪəltɔːr] (US) n Grundstücksmakler(in) m(f)

reap [riːp] vt ernten

reappear [riːə'pɪər] vi wieder erscheinen

rear [rɪər] adj hintere(r, s), Rück- ♦ n Rückseite f; (last part) Schluss m ♦ vt (bring up) aufziehen ♦ vi (horse) sich aufbäumen; ~**guard** n Nachhut f

rearmament [riː'ɑːməmənt] n Wiederaufrüstung f

rearrange [riːə'reɪndʒ] vt umordnen

rear-view mirror ['rɪəvjuː-] n Rückspiegel m

reason ['riːzn] n (cause) Grund m; (ability to think) Verstand m; (sensible thoughts) Vernunft f ♦ vi (think) denken; (use arguments) argumentieren; **it stands to ~ that** es ist logisch, dass; **to ~ with sb** mit jdm diskutieren; ~**able** adj vernünftig; ~**ably** adv vernünftig; (fairly) ziemlich; ~**ed** adj (argument) durchdacht; ~**ing** n Urteilen nt; (argumentation) Beweisführung f

reassurance [riːə'ʃuərəns] n Beruhigung f; (confirmation) Bestätigung f; **reassure** [riːə'ʃuər] vt beruhigen; **to reassure sb of**

sth jdm etw versichern

rebate ['ri:beit] n Rückzahlung f

rebel [n 'rebl, vb rɪ'bel] n Rebell m ♦ vi rebellieren; **~lion** [rɪ'beljən] n Rebellion f, Aufstand m; **~lious** [rɪ'beljəs] adj rebellisch

rebirth [ri:'bə:θ] n Wiedergeburt f

rebound [vb rɪ'baund, n 'ri:baund] vi zurückprallen ♦ n Rückprall m

rebuff [rɪ'bʌf] n Abfuhr f ♦ vt abblitzen lassen

rebuild [ri:'bɪld] (irreg) vt wieder aufbauen; (fig) wieder herstellen

rebuke [rɪ'bju:k] n Tadel m ♦ vt tadeln, rügen

rebut [rɪ'bʌt] vt widerlegen

recall [vb rɪ'kɔ:l, n 'ri:kɔ:l] vt (call back) zurückrufen; (remember) sich erinnern an +acc ♦ n Rückruf m

recap ['ri:kæp] vt, vi wiederholen

rec'd abbr (= received) Eing.

recede [rɪ'si:d] vi zurückweichen; **receding** adj: **receding hairline** Stirnglatze f

receipt [rɪ'si:t] n (document) Quittung f; (receiving) Empfang m; **~s** npl (ECON) Einnahmen pl

receive [rɪ'si:v] vt erhalten; (visitors etc) empfangen; **~r** n (TEL) Hörer m

recent ['ri:snt] adj vor kurzem (geschehen), neulich; (modern) neu; **~ly** adv kürzlich, neulich

receptacle [rɪ'septɪkl] n Behälter m

reception [rɪ'sepʃən] n Empfang m; **~ desk** n Empfang m; (in hotel) Rezeption f; **~ist** n (in hotel) Empfangschef m, Empfangsdame f; (MED) Sprechstundenhilfe f

receptive [rɪ'septɪv] adj aufnahmebereit

recess [rɪ'ses] n (break) Ferien pl; (hollow) Nische f

recession [rɪ'seʃən] n Rezession f

recharge [ri:'tʃɑːdʒ] vt (battery) aufladen

recipe ['resɪpɪ] n Rezept nt

recipient [rɪ'sɪpɪənt] n Empfänger m

reciprocal [rɪ'sɪprəkl] adj gegenseitig; (mutual) wechselseitig

recital [rɪ'saɪtl] n Vortrag m

recite [rɪ'saɪt] vt vortragen, aufsagen

reckless ['rekləs] adj leichtsinnig; (driving)

fahrlässig

reckon ['rekən] vt (count) rechnen, berechnen, errechnen; (estimate) schätzen; (think): **I ~ that ...** ich nehme an, dass ...; **~ on** vt fus rechnen mit; **~ing** n (calculation) Rechnen nt

reclaim [rɪ'kleɪm] vt (expenses) zurückverlangen; (land): **to ~ (from sth)** (etw dat) gewinnen; (Reclamation) [reklə'meɪʃən] n (of land) Gewinnung f

recline [rɪ'klaɪn] vi sich zurücklehnen; **reclining** adj Liege-

recluse [rɪ'klu:s] n Einsiedler m

recognition [rekəg'nɪʃən] n (recognizing) Erkennen nt; (acknowledgement) Anerkennung f; **transformed beyond ~** völlig verändert

recognizable ['rekəgnaɪzəbl] adj erkennbar

recognize ['rekəgnaɪz] vt erkennen; (POL, approve) anerkennen; **to ~ as** anerkennen als; **to ~ by** erkennen an +dat

recoil [rɪ'kɔɪl] vi (in horror) zurückschrecken; (rebound) zurückprallen; (person): **to ~ from doing sth** davor zurückschrecken, etw zu tun

recollect [rekə'lekt] vt sich erinnern an +acc; **~ion** [rekə'lekʃən] n Erinnerung f

recommend [rekə'mend] vt empfehlen; **~ation** [rekəmen'deɪʃən] n Empfehlung f

recompense ['rekəmpens] n (compensation) Entschädigung f; (reward) Belohnung f ♦ vt entschädigen; belohnen

reconcile ['rekənsaɪl] vt (facts) vereinbaren; (people) versöhnen; **to ~ o.s. to sth** sich mit etw abfinden; **reconciliation** [rekənsɪlɪ'eɪʃən] n Versöhnung f

recondition [ri:kən'dɪʃən] vt (machine) generalüberholen

reconnoitre [rekə'nɔɪtər] (US **reconnoiter**) vt erkunden ♦ vi aufklären

reconsider [ri:kən'sɪdər] vt von neuem erwägen, noch einmal überdenken ♦ vi es noch einmal überdenken

reconstruct [ri:kən'strʌkt] vt wieder aufbauen; (crime) rekonstruieren

record [n 'rekɔːd, vb rɪ'kɔːd] n Aufzeichnung f; (MUS) Schallplatte f; (best performance)

Rekord *m* ♦ *vt* aufzeichnen; (*music etc*)
aufnehmen; **off the ~** vertraulich, im
Vertrauen; **in ~ time** in Rekordzeit; **~ card**
n (*in file*) Karteikarte *f*; **~ed delivery** (*BRIT*)
n (*POST*) Einschreiben *nt*; **~er** *n* (*TECH*)
Registriergerät *nt*; (*MUS*) Blockflöte *f*; **~
holder** *n* (*SPORT*) Rekordinhaber *m*; **~ing** *n*
(*MUS*) Aufnahme *f*; **~ player** *n*
Plattenspieler *m*
recount [rɪ'kaunt] *vt* (*tell*) berichten
re-count ['ri:kaunt] *n* Nachzählung *f*
recoup [rɪ'ku:p] *vt*: **to ~ one's losses**
seinen Verlust wieder gutmachen
recourse [rɪ'kɔ:s] *n*: **to have ~ to** Zuflucht
nehmen zu *or* bei
recover [rɪ'kʌvər] *vt* (*get back*)
zurückerhalten ♦ *vi* sich erholen
re-cover [ri:'kʌvər] *vt* (*quilt etc*) neu
überziehen
recovery [rɪ'kʌvərɪ] *n* Wiedererlangung *f*; (*of
health*) Erholung *f*
recreate [ri:krɪ'eɪt] *vt* wieder herstellen
recreation [rekrɪ'eɪʃən] *n* Erholung *f*; **~al** *adj*
Erholungs-; **~al drug** *n* Freizeitdroge *f*
recrimination [rɪkrɪmɪ'neɪʃən] *n*
Gegenbeschuldigung *f*
recruit [rɪ'kru:t] *n* Rekrut *m* ♦ *vt* rekrutieren;
~ment *n* Rekrutierung *f*
rectangle ['rektæŋgl] *n* Rechteck *nt*;
rectangular [rek'tæŋgjulər] *adj* rechteckig,
rechtwinklig
rectify ['rektɪfaɪ] *vt* berichtigen
rector ['rektər] *n* (*REL*) Pfarrer *m*; (*SCH*)
Direktor(in) *m(f)*; **~y** ['rektərɪ] *n* Pfarrhaus *nt*
recuperate [rɪ'kju:pəreɪt] *vi* sich erholen
recur [rɪ'kə:r] *vi* sich wiederholen; **~rence** *n*
Wiederholung *f*; **~rent** *adj* wiederkehrend
recycle [ri:'saɪkl] *vt* wieder verwerten,
wieder aufbereiten; **recycling** *n* Recycling
nt
red [red] *n* Rot *nt*; (*POL*) Rote(r) *m* ♦ *adj* rot;
in the ~ in den roten Zahlen; **~ carpet
treatment** *n* Sonderbehandlung *f*,
große(r) Bahnhof *m*; **R~ Cross** *n* Rote(s)
Kreuz *nt*; **~currant** *n* rote Johannisbeere *f*;
~den *vi* sich röten; (*blush*) erröten ♦ *vt*
röten; **~dish** *adj* rötlich

redecorate [ri:'dekəreɪt] *vt* neu tapezie
neu streichen
redeem [rɪ'di:m] *vt* (*COMM*) einlösen; (.
retten; **~ing** *adj*: **~ing feature**
versöhnende(s) Moment *nt*
redeploy [ri:dɪ'plɔɪ] *vt* (*resources*)
umverteilen
red: **~-haired** [red'heəd] *adj* rothaarig;
handed [red'hændɪd] *adv*: **to be caug**
handed auf frischer Tat ertappt werde
~head ['redhed] *n* Rothaarige(r) *mf*; **~**
herring *n* Ablenkungsmanöver *nt*; **~**
[red'hɔt] *adj* rot glühend
redirect [ri:daɪ'rekt] *vt* umleiten
red light *n*: **to go through a ~** (*AUT*) b
über die Ampel fahren; **red-light dis**
n Strichviertel *nt*
redo [ri:'du:] (*irreg: like* **do**) *vt* nochmals
machen
redolent ['redələnt] *adj*: **~ of** (*fig*) erinr
an **+acc**
redouble [ri:'dʌbl] *vt*: **to ~ one's effor**
seine Anstrengungen verdoppeln
redress [rɪ'dres] *vt* wieder gutmachen
red: **R~ Sea** *n*: **the R~ Sea** das Rote N
~skin ['redskɪn] *n* Rothaut *f*; **~ tape** *n*
Bürokratismus *m*
reduce [rɪ'dju:s] *vt* (*speed, temperature*)
vermindern; (*photo*) verkleinern; **"~ sp**
now" (*AUT*) ≃ „langsam"; **to ~ the p**
(to) den Preis herabsetzen (auf **+acc**);
~d price zum ermäßigten Preis
reduction [rɪ'dʌkʃən] *n* Verminderung
Verkleinerung *f*; Herabsetzung *f*; (*amo*
money) Nachlass *m*
redundancy [rɪ'dʌndənsɪ] *n* Überflüssi
f; (*of workers*) Entlassung *f*
redundant [rɪ'dʌndnt] *adj* überflüssig;
(*workers*) ohne Arbeitsplatz; **to be ma**
arbeitslos werden
reed [ri:d] *n* Schilf *nt*; (*MUS*) Rohrblatt *n*
reef [ri:f] *n* Riff *nt*
reek [ri:k] *vi*: **to ~ (of)** stinken (nach)
reel [ri:l] *n* Spule *f*, Rolle *f* ♦ *vt* (*also: ~*
wickeln, spulen ♦ *vi* (*stagger*) taumeln
ref [ref] (*inf*) *n abbr* (= *referee*) Schiri *m*
refectory [rɪ'fektərɪ] *n* (*UNIV*) Mensa *f*;

Speisesaal *m*; (*ECCL*) Refektorium *nt*

efer [rɪ'fɜːʳ] *vt*: **to ~ sb to sb/sth** jdn an jdn/etw verweisen ♦ *vi*: **to ~ to** (*to book*) nachschlagen in +*dat*; (*mention*) sich beziehen auf +*acc*

eferee [refə'riː] *n* Schiedsrichter *m*; (*BRIT: for job*) Referenz *f* ♦ *vt* schiedsrichtern

eference ['refrəns] *n* (*for job*) Referenz *f*; (*in book*) Verweis *m*; (*number, code*) Aktenzeichen *nt*; (*allusion*): **~ (to)** Anspielung (auf +*acc*); **with ~ to** in Bezug auf +*acc*; **~ book** *n* Nachschlagewerk *nt*; **~ number** *n* Aktenzeichen *nt*

eferenda [refə'rendə] *npl* of **referendum**

eferendum [refə'rendəm] (*pl* **-da**) *n* Volksabstimmung *f*

efill [*vb* riː'fɪl, *n* 'riːfɪl] *vt* nachfüllen ♦ *n* (*for pen*) Ersatzmine *f*

efine [rɪ'faɪn] *vt* (*purify*) raffinieren; **~d** *adj* kultiviert; **~ment** *n* Kultiviertheit *f*; **~ry** *n* Raffinerie *f*

eflect [rɪ'flekt] *vt* (*light*) reflektieren; (*fig*) (wider)spiegeln ♦ *vi* (*meditate*): **to ~ (on)** nachdenken (über +*acc*); **it ~s badly/well on him** das stellt ihn in ein schlechtes/ gutes Licht; **~ion** [rɪ'flekʃən] *n* Reflexion *f*; (*image*) Spiegelbild *nt*; (*thought*) Überlegung *f*; **on ~ion** wenn man sich *dat* das recht überlegt

eflex ['riːfleks] *adj* Reflex- ♦ *n* Reflex *m*; **~ive** [rɪ'fleksɪv] *adj* reflexiv

eform [rɪ'fɔːm] *n* Reform *f* ♦ *vt* (*person*) bessern; **~atory** (*US*) *n* Besserungsanstalt *f*

efrain [rɪ'freɪn] *vi*: **to ~ from** unterlassen ♦ *n* Refrain *m*

efresh [rɪ'freʃ] *vt* erfrischen; **~er course** (*BRIT*) *n* Wiederholungskurs *m*; **~ing** *adj* erfrischend; **~ments** *npl* Erfrischungen *pl*

efrigeration [rɪfrɪdʒə'reɪʃən] *n* Kühlung *f*

efrigerator [rɪ'frɪdʒəreɪtə'] *n* Kühlschrank *m*

efuel [riː'fjuːəl] *vt, vi* auftanken

efuge ['refjuːdʒ] *n* Zuflucht *f*; **to take ~ in** sich flüchten in +*acc*; **~e** [refjuː'dʒiː] *n* Flüchtling *m*

efund [*n* 'riːfʌnd, *vb* rɪ'fʌnd] *n* Rückvergütung *f* ♦ *vt* zurückerstatten

efurbish [riː'fɜːbɪʃ] *vt* aufpolieren

refusal [rɪ'fjuːzəl] *n* (Ver)weigerung *f*; **first ~** Vorkaufsrecht *nt*

refuse[1] [rɪ'fjuːz] *vt* abschlagen ♦ *vi* sich weigern

refuse[2] ['refjuːs] *n* Abfall *m*, Müll *m*; **~ collection** *n* Müllabfuhr *f*

refute [rɪ'fjuːt] *vt* widerlegen

regain [rɪ'geɪn] *vt* wiedergewinnen; (*consciousness*) wiedererlangen

regal ['riːgl] *adj* königlich

regalia [rɪ'geɪlɪə] *npl* Insignien *pl*

regard [rɪ'gɑːd] *n* Achtung *f* ♦ *vt* ansehen; **to send one's ~s to sb** jdn grüßen lassen; **"with kindest ~s"** "mit freundlichen Grüßen"; **~ing** *or* **as ~s** *or* **with ~ to** bezüglich +*gen*, in Bezug auf +*acc*; **~less** *adj*: **~less of** ohne Rücksicht auf +*acc* ♦ *adv* trotzdem

regenerate [rɪ'dʒenəreɪt] *vt* erneuern

régime [reɪ'ʒiːm] *n* Regime *nt*

regiment [*n* 'redʒɪmənt, *vb* 'redʒɪmənt] *n* Regiment *nt* ♦ *vt* (*fig*) reglementieren; **~al** [redʒɪ'mentl] *adj* Regiments-

region ['riːdʒən] *n* Region *f*; **in the ~ of** (*fig*) so um; **~al** *adj* örtlich, regional

register ['redʒɪstə'] *n* Register *nt* ♦ *vt* (*list*) registrieren; (*emotion*) zeigen; (*write down*) eintragen ♦ *vi* (*at hotel*) sich eintragen; (*with police*) sich melden; (*make impression*) wirken, ankommen; **~ed** (*BRIT*) *adj* (*letter*) Einschreibe-, eingeschrieben; **~ed trademark** *n* eingetragene(s) Warenzeichen *nt*

registrar ['redʒɪstrɑː'] *n* Standesbeamte(r) *m*

registration [redʒɪs'treɪʃən] *n* (*act*) Registrierung *f*; (*AUT: also:* **~ number**) polizeiliche(s) Kennzeichen *nt*

registry ['redʒɪstrɪ] *n* Sekretariat *nt*; **~ office** (*BRIT*) *n* Standesamt *nt*; **to get married in a ~ office** standesamtlich heiraten

regret [rɪ'gret] *n* Bedauern *nt* ♦ *vt* bedauern; **~fully** *adv* mit Bedauern, ungern; **~table** *adj* bedauerlich

regroup [riː'gruːp] *vt* umgruppieren ♦ *vi* sich umgruppieren

regular ['regjulə'] *adj* regelmäßig; (*usual*) üblich; (*inf*) regelrecht ♦ *n* (*client etc*)

Stammkunde m; ~ity [regju'læriti] n
Regelmäßigkeit f; ~ly adv regelmäßig
regulate ['regjuleit] vt regeln, regulieren;
regulation [regju'leiʃən] n (rule) Vorschrift f;
(control) Regulierung f
rehabilitation ['ri:əbili'teiʃən] n (of criminal)
Resozialisierung f
rehearsal [rɪ'hɜːsəl] n Probe f
rehearse [rɪ'hɜːs] vt proben
reign [reɪn] n Herrschaft f ♦ vi herrschen
reimburse [ri:ɪm'bɜːs] vt: to ~ sb for sth
jdn für etw entschädigen, jdm etw
zurückzahlen
rein [reɪn] n Zügel m
reincarnation [ri:ɪnkɑː'neiʃən] n
Wiedergeburt f
reindeer ['reɪndɪə'] n Ren nt
reinforce [ri:ɪn'fɔːs] vt verstärken; ~d
concrete n Stahlbeton m; ~ment n
Verstärkung f; ~ments npl (MIL)
Verstärkungstruppen pl
reinstate [ri:ɪn'steɪt] vt wieder einsetzen
reissue [ri:'ɪʃju:] vt neu herausgeben
reiterate [ri:'ɪtəreɪt] vt wiederholen
reject [n 'ri:dʒekt, vb rɪ'dʒekt] n (COMM)
Ausschuss(artikel) m ♦ vt ablehnen; ~ion
[rɪ'dʒekʃən] n Zurückweisung f
rejoice [rɪ'dʒɔɪs] vi: to ~ at or over sich
freuen über +acc
rejuvenate [rɪ'dʒu:vəneɪt] vt verjüngen
rekindle [ri:'kɪndl] vt wieder anfachen
relapse [rɪ'læps] n Rückfall m
relate [rɪ'leɪt] vt (tell) erzählen; (connect)
verbinden ♦ vi: to ~ to zusammenhängen
mit; (form relationship) eine Beziehung
aufbauen zu; ~d adj: ~d (to) verwandt
(mit); relating prep: relating to bezüglich
+gen; relation [rɪ'leɪʃən] n Verwandte(r) mf;
(connection) Beziehung f; relationship n
Verhältnis nt, Beziehung f
relative ['relətɪv] n Verwandte(r) mf ♦ adj
relativ; ~ly adv verhältnismäßig
relax [rɪ'læks] vi (slacken) sich lockern;
(muscles, person) sich entspannen ♦ vt (ease)
lockern, entspannen; ~ation [ri:læk'seɪʃən] n
Entspannung f; ~ed adj entspannt, locker;
~ing adj entspannend

relay [n 'ri:leɪ, vb rɪ'leɪ] n (SPORT) Staffel f ♦ vt
(message) weiterleiten; (RAD, TV) übertragen
release [rɪ'li:s] n (freedom) Entlassung f;
(TECH) Auslöser m ♦ vt befreien; (prisoner)
entlassen; (report, news) verlautbaren,
bekannt geben
relegate ['relɪgeɪt] vt (SPORT): to be ~d
absteigen
relent [rɪ'lent] vi nachgeben; ~less adj
unnachgiebig
relevant ['relɪvənt] adj wichtig, relevant; ~
to relevant für
reliability [rɪlaɪə'bɪlɪtɪ] n Zuverlässigkeit f
reliable [rɪ'laɪəbl] adj zuverlässig; reliably
adv zuverlässig; to be reliably informed
that ... aus zuverlässiger Quelle wissen,
dass ...
reliance [rɪ'laɪəns] n: ~ (on) Abhängigkeit f
(von)
relic ['relɪk] n (from past) Überbleibsel nt;
(REL) Reliquie f
relief [rɪ'li:f] n Erleichterung f; (help) Hilfe f;
(person) Ablösung f
relieve [rɪ'li:v] vt (ease) erleichtern; (help)
entlasten; (person) ablösen; to ~ sb of sth
jdm etw abnehmen; to ~ o.s. (euph) sich
erleichtern (euph); ~d adj erleichtert
religion [rɪ'lɪdʒən] n Religion f; religious
[rɪ'lɪdʒəs] adj religiös
relinquish [rɪ'lɪŋkwɪʃ] vt aufgeben
relish ['relɪʃ] n Würze f ♦ vt genießen; to ~
doing gern tun
relocate [ri:ləu'keɪt] vt verlegen ♦ vi
umziehen
reluctance [rɪ'lʌktəns] n Widerstreben nt,
Abneigung f
reluctant [rɪ'lʌktənt] adj widerwillig; ~ly adv
ungern
rely [rɪ'laɪ] vt fus: to ~ on sich verlassen auf
+acc
remain [rɪ'meɪn] vi (be left) übrig bleiben;
(stay) bleiben; ~der n Rest m; ~ing adj
übrig (geblieben); ~s npl Überreste pl
remake ['ri:meɪk] n (CINE) Neuverfilmung f
remand [rɪ'mɑːnd] n: on ~ in
Untersuchungshaft ♦ vt: to ~ in custody in
Untersuchungshaft schicken; ~ home

(BRIT) n Untersuchungsgefängnis nt für Jugendliche

emark [rɪˈmɑːk] n Bemerkung f ♦ vt bemerken; **~able** adj bemerkenswert; **remarkably** adv außergewöhnlich

emarry [riːˈmærɪ] vi sich wieder verheiraten

emedial [rɪˈmiːdɪəl] adj Heil-; (teaching) Hilfsschul-

emedy [ˈremədɪ] n Mittel nt ♦ vt (pain) abhelfen +dat; (trouble) in Ordnung bringen

emember [rɪˈmembəʳ] vt sich erinnern an +acc; **remembrance** [rɪˈmembrəns] n Erinnerung f; (official) Gedenken nt; **R~ Day** ≈ Volkstrauertag m

---
Remembrance Day

🛈 **Remembrance Day** oder **Remembrance Sunday** ist der britische Gedenktag für die Gefallenen der beiden Weltkriege und anderer Konflikte. Er fällt auf einen Sonntag vor oder nach dem 11. November (am 11. November 1918 endete der erste Weltkrieg) und wird mit einer Schweigeminute, Kranzniederlegungen an Kriegerdenkmälern und dem Tragen von Anstecknadeln in Form einer Mohnblume begangen.

---

emind [rɪˈmaɪnd] vt: **to ~ sb to do sth** jdn daran erinnern, etw zu tun; **to ~ sb of sth** jdn an etw acc erinnern; **she ~s me of her mother** sie erinnert mich an ihre Mutter; **~er** n Mahnung f

eminisce [remɪˈnɪs] vi in Erinnerungen schwelgen; **~nt** [remɪˈnɪsnt] adj: **to be ~nt of sth** an etw acc erinnern

emiss [rɪˈmɪs] adj nachlässig

emission [rɪˈmɪʃən] n Nachlass m; (of debt, sentence) Erlass m

emit [rɪˈmɪt] vt (money): **to ~ (to)** überweisen (an +acc); **~tance** n Geldanweisung f

emnant [ˈremnənt] n Rest m; **~s** npl (COMM) Einzelstücke pl

emorse [rɪˈmɔːs] n Gewissensbisse pl; **~ful** adj reumütig; **~less** adj unbarmherzig

emote [rɪˈməut] adj abgelegen; (slight)

gering; **~ control** n Fernsteuerung f; **~ly** adv entfernt

remould [ˈriːməuld] (BRIT) n runderneuerte(r) Reifen m

removable [rɪˈmuːvəbl] adj entfernbar

removal [rɪˈmuːvəl] n Beseitigung f; (of furniture) Umzug m; (from office) Entlassung f; **~ van** (BRIT) n Möbelwagen m

remove [rɪˈmuːv] vt beseitigen, entfernen; **~rs** npl Möbelspedition f

remuneration [rɪmjuːnəˈreɪʃən] n Vergütung f, Honorar nt

render [ˈrendəʳ] vt machen; (translate) übersetzen; **~ing** n (MUS) Wiedergabe f

rendezvous [ˈrɒndɪvuː] n (meeting) Rendezvous nt; (place) Treffpunkt m ♦ vi sich treffen

renew [rɪˈnjuː] vt erneuern; (contract, licence) verlängern; (replace) ersetzen; **~able** adj regenerierbar; **~al** n Erneuerung f; Verlängerung f

renounce [rɪˈnauns] vt (give up) verzichten auf +acc; (disown) verstoßen

renovate [ˈrenəveɪt] vt renovieren; (building) restaurieren

renown [rɪˈnaun] n Ruf m; **~ed** adj namhaft

rent [rent] n Miete f; (for land) Pacht f ♦ vt (hold as tenant) mieten; pachten; (let) vermieten; verpachten; (car etc) mieten; (firm) vermieten; **~al** n Miete f

renunciation [rɪnʌnsɪˈeɪʃən] n: **~ (of)** Verzicht m (auf +acc)

reorganize [riːˈɔːɡənaɪz] vt umgestalten, reorganisieren

rep [rep] n abbr (COMM) = **representative**; (THEAT) = **repertory**

repair [rɪˈpeəʳ] n Reparatur f ♦ vt reparieren; (damage) wieder gutmachen; **in good / bad ~** in gutem/schlechtem Zustand; **~ kit** n Werkzeugkasten m

repartee [repɑːˈtiː] n Witzeleien pl

repatriate [riːˈpætrɪeɪt] vt in die Heimat zurückschicken

repay [riːˈpeɪ] (irreg) vt zurückzahlen; (reward) vergelten; **~ment** n Rückzahlung f; (fig) Vergeltung f

repeal [rɪˈpiːl] vt aufheben

repeat [rɪ'piːt] n (RAD, TV) Wiederholung(ssendung) f ♦ vt wiederholen; **~edly** adv wiederholt

repel [rɪ'pel] vt (drive back) zurückschlagen; (disgust) abstoßen; **~lent** adj abstoßend ♦ n: **insect ~lent** Insektenmittel nt

repent [rɪ'pent] vt, vi: **to ~ (of)** bereuen; **~ance** n Reue f

repercussion [riːpə'kʌʃən] n Auswirkung f; **to have ~s** ein Nachspiel haben

repertory ['repətəri] n Repertoire nt

repetition [repɪ'tɪʃən] n Wiederholung f

repetitive [rɪ'petɪtɪv] adj sich wiederholend

replace [rɪ'pleɪs] vt ersetzen; (put back) zurückstellen; **~ment** n Ersatz m

replay ['riːpleɪ] n (of match) Wiederholungsspiel nt; (of tape, film) Wiederholung f

replenish [rɪ'plenɪʃ] vt ergänzen

replica ['replɪkə] n Kopie f

reply [rɪ'plaɪ] n Antwort f ♦ vi antworten; **~ coupon** n Antwortschein m

report [rɪ'pɔːt] n Bericht m; (BRIT: SCH) Zeugnis nt ♦ vt (tell) berichten; (give information against) melden; (to police) anzeigen ♦ vi (make ~) Bericht erstatten; (present o.s.): **to ~ (to sb)** sich (bei jdm) melden; **~ card** n (US, SCOTTISH) Zeugnis nt; **~edly** adv wie verlautet; **~er** n Reporter m

reprehensible [reprɪ'hensɪbl] adj tadelnswert

represent [reprɪ'zent] vt darstellen; (speak for) vertreten; **~ation** [reprɪzen'teɪʃən] n Darstellung f; (being ~ed) Vertretung f; **~ations** npl (protest) Vorhaltungen pl; **~ative** n (person) Vertreter m; (US: POL) Abgeordnete(r) mf ♦ adj repräsentativ

repress [rɪ'pres] vt unterdrücken; **~ion** [rɪ'preʃən] n Unterdrückung f

reprieve [rɪ'priːv] n (JUR) Begnadigung f; (fig) Gnadenfrist f ♦ vt (JUR) begnadigen

reprimand ['reprɪmɑːnd] n Verweis m ♦ vt einen Verweis erteilen +dat

reprint [n 'riːprɪnt, vb riː'prɪnt] n Neudruck m ♦ vt wieder abdrucken

reprisal [rɪ'praɪzl] n Vergeltung f

reproach [rɪ'prəutʃ] n Vorwurf m ♦ vt Vorwürfe machen +dat; **to ~ sb with sth** jdm etw vorwerfen; **~ful** adj vorwurfsvoll

reproduce [riːprə'djuːs] vt reproduzieren ♦ vi (have offspring) sich vermehren; **reproduction** [riːprə'dʌkʃən] n (ART, PHOT) Reproduktion f; (breeding) Fortpflanzung f; **reproductive** [riːprə'dʌktɪv] adj reproduktiv; (breeding) Fortpflanzungs-

reprove [rɪ'pruːv] vt tadeln

reptile ['reptaɪl] n Reptil nt

republic [rɪ'pʌblɪk] n Republik f

repudiate [rɪ'pjuːdɪeɪt] vt zurückweisen

repugnant [rɪ'pʌgnənt] adj widerlich

repulse [rɪ'pʌls] vt (drive back) zurückschlagen; (reject) abweisen

repulsive [rɪ'pʌlsɪv] adj abstoßend

reputable ['repjutəbl] adj angesehen

reputation [repju'teɪʃən] n Ruf m

reputed [rɪ'pjuːtɪd] adj angeblich; **~ly** [rɪ'pjuːtɪdlɪ] adv angeblich

request [rɪ'kwest] n Bitte f ♦ vt (thing) erbitten; **to ~ sth of** or **from sb** jdn um etw bitten; (formally) jdn um etw ersuchen; **~ stop** (BRIT) n Bedarfshaltestelle f

require [rɪ'kwaɪə*] vt (need) brauchen; (demand) erfordern; **~ment** n (condition) Anforderung f; (need) Bedarf m

requisite ['rekwɪzɪt] adj erforderlich

requisition [rekwɪ'zɪʃən] n Anforderung f ♦ vt beschlagnahmen

rescue ['reskjuː] n Rettung f ♦ vt retten; **~ party** n Rettungsmannschaft f; **~r** n Retter m

research [rɪ'səːtʃ] n Forschung f ♦ vi forschen ♦ vt erforschen; **~er** n Forscher m

resemblance [rɪ'zembləns] n Ähnlichkeit f

resemble [rɪ'zembl] vt ähneln +dat

resent [rɪ'zent] vt übel nehmen; **~ful** adj nachtragend, empfindlich; **~ment** n Verstimmung f, Unwille m

reservation [rezə'veɪʃən] n (booking) Reservierung f; (THEAT) Vorbestellung f; (doubt) Vorbehalt m; (land) Reservat nt

reserve [rɪ'zəːv] n (store) Vorrat m, Reserve f; (manner) Zurückhaltung f; (game ~) Naturschutzgebiet nt; (SPORT)

Ersatzspieler(in) m(f) ♦ vt reservieren; (judgement) sich dat vorbehalten; **~s** npl (MIL) Reserve f; **in ~** in Reserve; **~d** adj reserviert

eshuffle [riːˈʃʌfl] n (POL): **cabinet ~** Kabinettsumbildung f ♦ vt (POL) umbilden

eside [rɪˈzaɪd] vi wohnen, ansässig sein

esidence [ˈrezɪdəns] n (house) Wohnsitz m; (living) Aufenthalt m; **~ permit** (BRIT) n Aufenthaltserlaubnis f

esident [ˈrezɪdənt] n (in house) Bewohner m; (in area) Einwohner m ♦ adj wohnhaft, ansässig; **~ial** [rezɪˈdenʃəl] adj Wohn-

esidue [ˈrezɪdjuː] n Rest m; (CHEM) Rückstand m; (fig) Bodensatz m

esign [rɪˈzaɪn] vt (office) aufgeben, zurücktreten von ♦ vi (from office) zurücktreten; (employee) kündigen; **to be ~ed to sth, to ~ o.s. to sth** sich mit etw abfinden; **~ation** [rezɪgˈneɪʃən] n (from job) Kündigung f; (POL) Rücktritt m; (submission) Resignation f; **~ed** adj resigniert

esilience [rɪˈzɪlɪəns] n Spannkraft f; (of person) Unverwüstlichkeit f; **resilient** [rɪˈzɪlɪənt] adj unverwüstlich

esin [ˈrezɪn] n Harz nt

esist [rɪˈzɪst] vt widerstehen +dat; **~ance** n Widerstand m

esit [vb riːˈsɪt, n ˈriːsɪt] vt (exam) wiederholen ♦ n Wiederholung(sprüfung) f

esolute [ˈrezəluːt] adj entschlossen, resolut; **resolution** [rezəˈluːʃən] n (firmness) Entschlossenheit f; (intention) Vorsatz m; (decision) Beschluss m

esolve [rɪˈzɒlv] n Entschlossenheit f ♦ vt (decide) beschließen ♦ vi sich lösen; **~d** adj (fest) entschlossen

esonant [ˈrezənənt] adj voll

esort [rɪˈzɔːt] n (holiday place) Erholungsort m; (help) Zuflucht f ♦ vi: **to ~ to** Zuflucht nehmen zu; **as a last ~** als letzter Ausweg

esound [rɪˈzaund] vi: **to ~ (with)** widerhallen (von); **~ing** adj nachhallend; (success) groß

source [rɪˈsɔːs] n Findigkeit f; **~s** npl (financial) Geldmittel pl; (natural) Bodenschätze pl; **~ful** adj findig

respect [rɪsˈpekt] n Respekt m ♦ vt achten, respektieren; **~s** npl (regards) Grüße pl; **with ~ to** in Bezug auf +acc, hinsichtlich +gen; **in this ~** in dieser Hinsicht; **~able** adj anständig; (not bad) leidlich; **~ful** adj höflich

respective [rɪsˈpektɪv] adj jeweilig; **~ly** adv beziehungsweise

respiration [respɪˈreɪʃən] n Atmung f

respite [ˈrespaɪt] n Ruhepause f

resplendent [rɪsˈplendənt] adj strahlend

respond [rɪsˈpɒnd] vi antworten; (react): **to ~ (to)** reagieren (auf +acc); **response** [rɪsˈpɒns] n Antwort f; Reaktion f; (to advert) Resonanz f

responsibility [rɪspɒnsɪˈbɪlɪtɪ] n Verantwortung f

responsible [rɪsˈpɒnsɪbl] adj verantwortlich; (reliable) verantwortungsvoll

responsive [rɪsˈpɒnsɪv] adj empfänglich

rest [rest] n Ruhe f; (break) Pause f; (remainder) Rest m ♦ vi sich ausruhen; (be supported) (auf)liegen ♦ vt (lean): **to ~ sth on/against sth** etw gegen etw acc lehnen; **the ~ of them** die Übrigen; **it ~s with him to ...** es liegt bei ihm, zu ...

restaurant [ˈrestərɒŋ] n Restaurant nt; **~ car** (BRIT) n Speisewagen m

restful [ˈrestful] adj erholsam, ruhig

rest home n Erholungsheim nt

restive [ˈrestɪv] adj unruhig

restless [ˈrestlɪs] adj unruhig

restoration [restəˈreɪʃən] n Rückgabe f; (of building etc) Rückerstattung f

restore [rɪsˈtɔː] vt (order) wieder herstellen; (customs) wieder einführen; (person to position) wieder einsetzen; (give back) zurückgeben; (renovate) restaurieren

restrain [rɪsˈtreɪn] vt zurückhalten; (curiosity etc) beherrschen; (person): **to ~ sb from doing sth** jdn davon abhalten, etw zu tun; **~ed** adj (style etc) gedämpft, verhalten; **~t** n (self-control) Zurückhaltung f

restrict [rɪsˈtrɪkt] vt einschränken; **~ion** [rɪsˈtrɪkʃən] n Einschränkung f; **~ive** adj einschränkend

rest room (US) n Toilette f

restructure [riː'strʌktʃər] vt umstrukturieren

result [rɪ'zʌlt] n Resultat nt, Folge f; (of exam, game) Ergebnis nt ♦ vi: **to ~ in sth** etw zur Folge haben; **as a ~ of** als Folge +gen

resume [rɪ'zjuːm] vt fortsetzen; (occupy again) wieder einnehmen ♦ vi (work etc) wieder beginnen

résumé ['reɪzjuːmeɪ] n Zusammenfassung f

resumption [rɪ'zʌmpʃən] n Wiederaufnahme f

resurgence [rɪ'sɜːdʒəns] n Wiedererwachen nt

resurrection [rezə'rekʃən] n Auferstehung f

resuscitate [rɪ'sʌsɪteɪt] vt wieder beleben; **resuscitation** [rɪsʌsɪ'teɪʃən] n Wiederbelebung f

retail [n, adj 'riːteɪl, vb 'riːteɪl] n Einzelhandel m ♦ adj Einzelhandels- ♦ vt im Kleinen verkaufen ♦ vi im Einzelhandel kosten; **~er** ['riːteɪlər] n Einzelhändler m, Kleinhändler m; **~ price** n Ladenpreis m

retain [rɪ'teɪn] vt (keep) (zurück)behalten; **~er** n (fee) (Honorar)vorschuss m

retaliate [rɪ'tælieɪt] vi zum Vergeltungsschlag ausholen; **retaliation** [rɪtælɪ'eɪʃən] n Vergeltung f

retarded [rɪ'tɑːdɪd] adj zurückgeblieben

retch [retʃ] vi würgen

retentive [rɪ'tentɪv] adj (memory) gut

reticent ['retɪsnt] adj schweigsam

retina ['retɪnə] n Netzhaut f

retire [rɪ'taɪər] vi (from work) in den Ruhestand treten; (withdraw) sich zurückziehen; (go to bed) schlafen gehen; **~d** adj (person) pensioniert, im Ruhestand; **~ment** n Ruhestand m

retiring [rɪ'taɪərɪŋ] adj zurückhaltend

retort [rɪ'tɔːt] n (reply) Erwiderung f ♦ vi (sharp) erwidern

retrace [riː'treɪs] vt zurückverfolgen; **to ~ one's steps** denselben Weg zurückgehen

retract [rɪ'trækt] vt (statement) zurücknehmen; (claws) einziehen ♦ vi einen Rückzieher machen; **~able** adj (aerial) ausziehbar

retrain [riː'treɪn] vt umschulen

retread ['riːtred] n (tyre) Reifen m mit erneuerter Lauffläche

retreat [rɪ'triːt] n Rückzug m; (place) Zufluchtsort m ♦ vi sich zurückziehen

retribution [retrɪ'bjuːʃən] n Strafe f

retrieval [rɪ'triːvəl] n Wiedergewinnung f

retrieve [rɪ'triːv] vt wiederbekommen; (rescue) retten; **~r** n Apportierhund m

retrograde ['retrəgreɪd] adj (step) Rück-; (policy) rückschrittlich

retrospect ['retrəspekt] n: **in ~** im Rückblick, rückblickend; **~ive** [retrə'spektɪv] adj (action) rückwirkend; (look) rückblickend

return [rɪ'tɜːn] n Rückkehr f; (profits) Ertrag m; (BRIT: rail ticket etc) Rückfahrkarte f; (: plane ticket) Rückflugkarte f ♦ adj (journey, match) Rück- ♦ vi zurückkehren, zurückkommen ♦ vt zurückgeben, zurücksenden; (pay back) zurückzahlen; (elect) wählen; (verdict) aussprechen; **~s** npl (COMM) Gewinn m; (receipts) Einkünfte pl; **in ~** dafür; **by ~ of post** postwendend; **many happy ~s!** herzlichen Glückwunsch zum Geburtstag!

reunion [riː'juːnɪən] n Wiedervereinigung f; (SCH etc) Treffen nt

reunite [riːjuː'naɪt] vt wieder vereinigen

reuse [riː'juːz] vt wieder verwenden, wieder verwerten

rev [rev] n abbr (AUT: = revolution) Drehzahl f

revamp [riː'væmp] vt aufpolieren

reveal [rɪ'viːl] vt enthüllen; **~ing** adj aufschlussreich

revel ['revl] vi: **to ~ in sth/in doing sth** seine Freude an etw dat haben/daran haben, etw zu tun

revelation [revə'leɪʃən] n Offenbarung f

revelry ['revlrɪ] n Rummel m

revenge [rɪ'vendʒ] n Rache f; **to take ~ on** sich rächen an +dat

revenue ['revənjuː] n Einnahmen pl

reverberate [rɪ'vɜːbəreɪt] vi widerhallen

revere [rɪ'vɪər] vt (ver)ehren; **~nce** ['revərəns] n Ehrfurcht f

Reverend ['revərənd] adj: **the ~ Robert Martin** ≃ Pfarrer Robert Martin

reversal [rɪ'vɜːsl] n Umkehrung f

reverse [rɪ'vɜːs] n Rückseite f; (AUT: gear)

Rückwärtsgang m ♦ adj (order, direction) entgegengesetzt ♦ vt umkehren ♦ vi (BRIT: AUT) rückwärts fahren; ~-**charge call** (BRIT) n R-Gespräch nt; **reversing lights** npl (AUT) Rückfahrscheinwerfer pl

evert [rɪ'vəːt] vi: **to ~ to** zurückkehren zu; (to bad state) zurückfallen in +acc

eview [rɪ'vjuː] n (of book) Rezension f; (magazine) Zeitschrift f ♦ vt Rückschau halten auf +acc; (MIL) mustern; (book) rezensieren; (reexamine) von neuem untersuchen; ~**er** n (critic) Rezensent m

evise [rɪ'vaɪz] vt (book) überarbeiten; (reconsider) ändern, revidieren; **revision** [rɪ'vɪʒən] n Prüfung f; (COMM) Revision f; (SCH) Wiederholung f

evitalize [riː'vaɪtəlaɪz] vt neu beleben

evival [rɪ'vaɪvl] n Wiederbelebung f; (REL) Erweckung f; (THEAT) Wiederaufnahme f

evive [rɪ'vaɪv] vt wieder beleben; (fig) wieder auffrischen ♦ vi wieder erwachen; (fig) wieder aufleben

evoke [rɪ'vəuk] vt aufheben

evolt [rɪ'vəult] n Aufstand m, Revolte f ♦ vi sich auflehnen ♦ vt entsetzen; ~**ing** adj widerlich

evolution [rɛvə'luːʃən] n (turn) Umdrehung f; (POL) Revolution f; ~**ary** adj revolutionär ♦ n Revolutionär m; ~**ize** vt revolutionieren

evolve [rɪ'vɔlv] vi kreisen; (on own axis) sich drehen

evolver [rɪ'vɔlvər] n Revolver m

evolving door [rɪ'vɔlvɪŋ-] n Drehtür f

evulsion [rɪ'vʌlʃən] n Ekel m

eward [rɪ'wɔːd] n Belohnung f ♦ vt belohnen; ~**ing** adj lohnend

ewind [riː'waɪnd] (irreg: like **wind**) vt (tape etc) zurückspulen

ewire [riː'waɪər] vt (house) neu verkabeln

eword [riː'wəːd] vt anders formulieren

ewrite [riː'raɪt] (irreg: like **write**) vt umarbeiten, neu schreiben

eumatism ['ruːmətɪzəm] n Rheumatismus m, Rheuma nt

hine [raɪn] n: **the ~** der Rhein

inoceros [raɪ'nɔsərəs] n Nashorn nt

hone [rəun] n: **the ~** die Rhone

rhubarb ['ruːbɑːb] n Rhabarber m

rhyme [raɪm] n Reim m

rhythm ['rɪðm] n Rhythmus m

rib [rɪb] n Rippe f ♦ vt (mock) hänseln, aufziehen

ribbon ['rɪbən] n Band nt; **in ~s** (torn) in Fetzen

rice [raɪs] n Reis m; ~ **pudding** n Milchreis m

rich [rɪtʃ] adj reich; (food) reichhaltig ♦ npl: **the ~** die Reichen pl; ~**es** npl Reichtum m; ~**ly** adv reich; (deserve) völlig

rickets ['rɪkɪts] n Rachitis f

rickety ['rɪkɪtɪ] adj wack(e)lig

rickshaw ['rɪkʃɔː] n Rikscha f

ricochet ['rɪkəʃeɪ] n Abprallen nt; (shot) Querschläger m ♦ vi abprallen

rid [rɪd] (pt, pp rid) vt befreien; **to get ~ of** loswerden

riddle ['rɪdl] n Rätsel nt ♦ vt: **to be ~d with** völlig durchlöchert sein von

ride [raɪd] (pt rode, pp ridden) n (in vehicle) Fahrt f; (on horse) Ritt m ♦ vt (horse) reiten; (bicycle) fahren ♦ vi fahren, reiten; **to take sb for a ~** mit jdm eine Fahrt etc machen; (fig) jdn aufs Glatteis führen; ~**r** n Reiter m

ridge [rɪdʒ] n Kamm m; (of roof) First m

ridicule ['rɪdɪkjuːl] n Spott m ♦ vt lächerlich machen

ridiculous [rɪ'dɪkjuləs] adj lächerlich

riding ['raɪdɪŋ] n Reiten nt; ~ **school** n Reitschule f

rife [raɪf] adj weit verbreitet; **to be ~** grassieren; **to be ~ with** voll sein von

riffraff ['rɪfræf] n Pöbel m

rifle ['raɪfl] n Gewehr nt ♦ vt berauben; ~ **range** n Schießstand m

rift [rɪft] n Spalte f; (fig) Bruch m

rig [rɪg] n (oil ~) Bohrinsel f ♦ vt (election etc) manipulieren; ~ **out** (BRIT) vt ausstatten; ~ **up** vt zusammenbasteln; ~**ging** n Takelage f

right [raɪt] adj (correct, just) richtig, recht; (~ side) rechte(r, s) ♦ n Recht nt; (not left, POL) Rechte f ♦ adv (on the ~) rechts; (to the ~) nach rechts; (look, work) richtig, recht; (directly) gerade; (exactly) genau ♦ vt in

Ordnung bringen, korrigieren ♦ *excl* gut;
on the ~ rechts; **to be in the ~** im Recht
sein; **by ~s** von Rechts wegen; **to be ~**
Recht haben; **~ away** sofort; **~ now** in
diesem Augenblick, eben; **~ in the middle**
genau in der Mitte; **~ angle** *n* rechte(r)
Winkel *m*; **~eous** ['raɪtʃəs] *adj*
rechtschaffen; **~ful** *adj* rechtmäßig; **~-**
hand *adj*: **~-hand drive** mit
Rechtssteuerung; **~-handed** *adj*
rechtshändig; **~-hand man** (*irreg*) *n* rechte
Hand *f*; **~-hand side** *n* rechte Seite *f*; **~ly**
adv mit Recht; **~ of way** *n* Vorfahrt *f*; **~-**
wing *adj* rechtsorientiert
rigid ['rɪdʒɪd] *adj* (*stiff*) starr, steif; (*strict*)
streng; **~ity** [rɪ'dʒɪdɪtɪ] *n* Starrheit *f*; Strenge *f*
rigmarole ['rɪgmərəʊl] *n* Gewäsch *nt*
rigor ['rɪgə*] (*US*) *n* = **rigour**
rigorous ['rɪgərəs] *adj* streng
rigour ['rɪgə*] (*US* **rigor**) *n* Strenge *f*, Härte *f*
rile [raɪl] *vt* ärgern
rim [rɪm] *n* (*edge*) Rand *m*; (*of wheel*) Felge *f*
rind [raɪnd] *n* Rinde *f*
ring [rɪŋ] (*pt* **rang**, *pp* **rung**) *n* Ring *m*; (*of
people*) Kreis *m*; (*arena*) Manege *f*; (*of
telephone*) Klingeln *nt* ♦ *vt*, *vi* (*bell*) läuten;
(*BRIT*) anrufen; **~ back** (*BRIT*) *vt*, *vi*
zurückrufen; **~ off** (*BRIT*) *vi* aufhängen; **~**
up (*BRIT*) *vt* anrufen; **~ binder** *n* Ringbuch
nt; **~ing** *n* Klingeln *nt*; (*of large bell*) Läuten
nt; (*in ears*) Klingen *nt*; **~ing tone** *n* (*TEL*)
Rufzeichen *nt*
ringleader ['rɪŋliːdə*] *n* Anführer *m*,
Rädelsführer *m*
ringlets ['rɪŋlɪts] *npl* Ringellocken *pl*
ring road (*BRIT*) *n* Umgehungsstraße *f*
ringtone ['rɪŋtəʊn] *n* Klingelton *m*
rink [rɪŋk] *n* (*ice ~*) Eisbahn *f*
rinse [rɪns] *n* Spülen *nt* ♦ *vt* spülen
riot ['raɪət] *n* Aufruhr *m* ♦ *vi* randalieren; **to**
run ~ (*people*) randalieren; (*vegetation*)
wuchern; **~er** *n* Aufrührer *m*; **~ous** *adj*
aufrührerisch; (*noisy*) lärmend
rip [rɪp] *n* Schlitz *m*, Riss *m* ♦ *vt*, *vi*
(zer)reißen; **~cord** *n* Reißleine *f*
ripe [raɪp] *adj* reif; **~n** *vi* reifen ♦ *vt* reifen
lassen

rip-off ['rɪpɒf] (*inf*) *n*: **it's a ~~~!** das ist
Wucher!
ripple ['rɪpl] *n* kleine Welle *f* ♦ *vt* kräuseln
♦ *vi* sich kräuseln
rise [raɪz] (*pt* **rose**, *pp* **risen**) *n* (*slope*)
Steigung *f*; (*esp in wages*: *BRIT*) Erhöhung *f*;
(*growth*) Aufstieg *m* ♦ *vi* (*sun*) aufgehen;
(*smoke*) aufsteigen; (*mountain*) sich
erheben; (*ground*) ansteigen; (*prices*)
steigen; (*in revolt*) sich erheben; **to give ~**
to Anlass geben zu; **to ~ to the occasion**
sich der Lage gewachsen zeigen; **~n** [rɪzn]
pp of **rise**; **~r** ['raɪzə*] *n*: **to be an early ~r**
ein(e) Frühaufsteher(in) *m(f)* sein; **rising**
['raɪzɪŋ] *adj* (*tide, prices*) steigend; (*sun,
moon*) aufgehend ♦ *n* (*uprising*) Aufstand *m*
risk [rɪsk] *n* Gefahr *f*, Risiko *nt* ♦ *vt* (*venture*)
wagen; (*chance loss of*) riskieren, aufs Spiel
setzen; **to take** *or* **run the ~ of doing sth**
das Risiko eingehen, etw zu tun; **at ~** in
Gefahr; **at one's own ~** auf eigene Gefahr;
~y *adj* riskant
risqué ['riːskeɪ] *adj* gewagt
rissole ['rɪsəʊl] *n* Fleischklößchen *nt*
rite [raɪt] *n* Ritus *m*; **last ~s** Letzte Ölung *f*
ritual ['rɪtjʊəl] *n* Ritual *nt* ♦ *adj* ritual, Ritual-;
(*fig*) rituell
rival ['raɪvl] *n* Rivale *m*, Konkurrent *m* ♦ *adj*
rivalisierend ♦ *vt* rivalisieren mit; (*COMM*)
konkurrieren mit; **~ry** *n* Rivalität *f*;
Konkurrenz *f*
river ['rɪvə*] *n* Fluss *m*, Strom *m* ♦ *cpd* (*port,
traffic*) Fluss-; **up/down ~** flussaufwärts/
-abwärts; **~bank** *n* Flussufer *nt*; **~bed** *n*
Flussbett *nt*
rivet ['rɪvɪt] *n* Niete *f* ♦ *vt* (*fasten*) (ver)nieten
Riviera [rɪvɪ'eərə] *n*: **the ~** die Riviera
road [rəʊd] *n* Straße *f* ♦ *cpd* (*port*) Straßen-;
major/minor ~ Haupt-/Nebenstraße *f*; **~**
accident *n* Verkehrsunfall *m*; **~block** *n*
Straßensperre *f*; **~hog** *n* Verkehrsrowdy *m*;
~ map *n* Straßenkarte *f*; **~ rage** *n*
Aggressivität *f* im Straßenverkehr; **~ safety**
n Verkehrssicherheit *f*; **~side** *n* Straßenrand
m ♦ *adj* an der Landstraße (gelegen); **~**
sign *n* Straßenschild *nt*; **~ user** *n*
Verkehrsteilnehmer *m*; **~way** *n* Fahrbahn *f*;

~ **works** npl Straßenbauarbeiten pl; ~**worthy** adj verkehrssicher

roam [rəum] vi (umher)streifen ♦ vt durchstreifen

roar [rɔːʳ] n Brüllen nt, Gebrüll nt ♦ vi brüllen; **to ~ with laughter** vor Lachen brüllen; **to do a ~ing trade** ein Riesengeschäft machen

roast [rəust] n Braten m ♦ vt braten, schmoren; ~ **beef** n Roastbeef nt

rob [rɔb] vt bestehlen, berauben; (bank) ausrauben; **to ~ sb of sth** jdm etw rauben; ~**ber** n Räuber m; ~**bery** n Raub m

robe [rəub] n (dress) Gewand nt; (US) Hauskleid nt; (judge's) Robe f

robin ['rɔbin] n Rotkehlchen nt

robot ['rəubɔt] n Roboter m

robust [rəu'bʌst] adj (person) robust; (appetite, economy) gesund

rock [rɔk] n Felsen m; (BRIT: sweet) Zuckerstange f ♦ vt, vi wiegen, schaukeln; **on the ~s** (drink) mit Eis(würfeln); (marriage) gescheitert; (ship) aufgelaufen; ~ **and roll** n Rock and Roll m; ~**-bottom** n (fig) Tiefpunkt m; ~**ery** n Steingarten m

rocket ['rɔkit] n Rakete f

rocking chair ['rɔkiŋ-] n Schaukelstuhl m

rocking horse n Schaukelpferd nt

rocky ['rɔki] adj felsig

rod [rɔd] n (bar) Stange f; (stick) Rute f

rode [rəud] pt of **ride**

rodent ['rəudnt] n Nagetier nt

roe [rəu] n (also: ~ **deer**) Reh nt; (of fish: also: **hard ~**) Rogen m; **soft ~** Milch f

rogue [rəug] n Schurke m

role [rəul] n Rolle f; ~ **play** n Rollenspiel nt

roll [rəul] n Rolle f; (bread) Brötchen nt; (list) (Namens)liste f; (of drum) Wirbel m ♦ vt (turn) rollen, (herum)wälzen; (grass etc) walzen ♦ vi (swing) schlingern; (sound) rollen, grollen; ~ **about** or **around** vi herumkugeln; (ship) schlingern; (dog etc) sich wälzen; ~ **by** vi (time) verfließen; ~ **over** vi sich (herum)drehen; ~ **up** vi (arrive) kommen, auftauchen ♦ vt (carpet) aufrollen; ~ **call** n Namensaufruf m; ~**er** n Rolle f, Walze f; (road ~er) Straßenwalze f;

R~**erblade** ® n Rollerblade m; ~**er coaster** n Achterbahn f; ~**er skates** npl Rollschuhe pl; ~**-skating** n Rollschuhlaufen nt

rolling ['rəuliŋ] adj (landscape) wellig; ~ **pin** n Nudel- or Wellholz nt; ~ **stock** n Wagenmaterial nt

ROM [rɔm] n abbr (= read only memory) ROM m

Roman ['rəumən] adj römisch ♦ n Römer(in) m(f); ~ **Catholic** adj römisch-katholisch ♦ n Katholik(in) m(f)

romance [rə'mæns] n Romanze f; (story) (Liebes)roman m

Romania [rəu'meiniə] n = **Rumania**; ~**n** n = **Rumanian**

Roman numeral n römische Ziffer

romantic [rə'mæntik] adj romantisch; ~**ism** [rə'mæntisizəm] n Romantik f

Rome [rəum] n Rom nt f

romp [rɔmp] n Tollen nt ♦ vi (also: ~ **about**) herumtollen

rompers ['rɔmpəz] npl Spielanzug m

roof [ruːf] (pl ~**s**) n Dach nt; (of mouth) Gaumen m ♦ vt überdachen, überdecken; ~**ing** n Deckmaterial nt; ~ **rack** n (AUT) Dachgepäckträger m

rook [ruk] n (bird) Saatkrähe f; (chess) Turm m

room [ruːm] n Zimmer nt, Raum m; (space) Platz m; (fig) Spielraum m; ~**s** npl (accommodation) Wohnung f; "~**s to let** (BRIT) or **for rent** (US)" „Zimmer zu vermieten"; **single/double** ~ Einzel-/ Doppelzimmer nt; ~**ing house** n (US) Mietshaus nt (mit möblierten Wohnungen); ~**mate** n Mitbewohner(in) m(f); ~ **service** n Zimmerbedienung f; ~**y** adj geräumig

roost [ruːst] n Hühnerstange f ♦ vi auf der Stange hocken

rooster ['ruːstəʳ] n Hahn m

root [ruːt] n (also fig) Wurzel f ♦ vi wurzeln; ~ **about** vi (fig) herumwühlen; ~ **for** vt fus Stimmung machen für; ~ **out** vt ausjäten; (fig) ausrotten

rope [rəup] n Seil nt ♦ vt (tie) festschnüren; **to know the ~s** sich auskennen; **to ~ sb in** jdn gewinnen; ~ **off** vt absperren;

~ ladder n Strickleiter f

rosary ['rəʊzərɪ] n Rosenkranz m

rose [rəʊz] pt of **rise ♦** n Rose f **♦** adj Rosen-, rosenrot

rosé ['rəʊzeɪ] n Rosé m

rosebud ['rəʊzbʌd] n Rosenknospe f

rosebush ['rəʊzbʊʃ] n Rosenstock m

rosemary ['rəʊzmərɪ] n Rosmarin m

rosette [rəʊ'zɛt] n Rosette f

roster ['rɒstə] n Dienstplan m

rostrum ['rɒstrəm] n Rednerbühne f

rosy ['rəʊzɪ] adj rosig

rot [rɒt] n Fäulnis f; (nonsense) Quatsch m **♦** vi verfaulen **♦** vt verfaulen lassen

rota ['rəʊtə] n Dienstliste f

rotary ['rəʊtərɪ] adj rotierend

rotate [rəʊ'teɪt] vt rotieren lassen; (take turns) turnusmäßig wechseln **♦** vi rotieren; **rotating** adj rotierend; **rotation** [rəʊ'teɪʃən] n Umdrehung f

rote [rəʊt] n: **by ~** auswendig

rotten ['rɒtn] adj faul; (fig) schlecht, gemein; **to feel ~** (ill) sich elend fühlen

rotund [rəʊ'tʌnd] adj rundlich

rouble ['ruːbl] (US **ruble**) n Rubel m

rough [rʌf] adj (not smooth) rau; (path) uneben; (violent) roh, grob; (crossing) stürmisch; (without comforts) hart, unbequem; (unfinished, makeshift) grob; (approximate) ungefähr **♦** n (BRIT: person) Rowdy m, Rohling m; (GOLF): **in the ~** im Rau **♦** vt: **to ~ it** primitiv leben; **to sleep ~** im Freien schlafen; **~age** n Ballaststoffe pl; **~-and-ready** adj provisorisch; (work) zusammengehauen; **~ copy** n Entwurf m; **~ draft** n Entwurf m; **~ly** adv grob; (about) ungefähr; **~ness** n Rauheit f; (of manner) Ungeschliffenheit f

roulette [ruː'lɛt] n Roulett(e) nt

Roumania [ruː'meɪnɪə] n = **Rumania**

round [raʊnd] adj rund; (figures) aufgerundet **♦** adv (in a circle) rundherum **♦** prep um ... herum **♦** n Runde f; (of ammunition) Magazin nt **♦** vt (corner) biegen um; **all ~** überall; **the long way ~** der Umweg; **all the year ~** das ganze Jahr über; **it's just ~ the corner** (fig) es ist gerade um die Ecke;

~ the clock rund um die Uhr; **to go ~ to sb's (house)** jdn besuchen; **to go ~ the back** hintenherum gehen; **enough to go ~** genug für alle; **to go the ~s** (story) die Runde machen; **a ~ of applause** ein Beifall m; **a ~ of drinks** eine Runde Drinks; **a ~ of sandwiches** ein Sandwich nt or m, ein belegtes Brot; **~ off** vt (end) abschließen; (figures) aufrunden; (criminals) hochnehmen; **~about** n (BRIT: traffic) Kreisverkehr m; (: merry-go-~) Karussell nt **♦** adj auf Umwegen; **~ers** npl (game) ≈ Schlagball m; **~ly** adv (fig) gründlich; **~-shouldered** adj mit abfallenden Schultern; **~ trip** n Rundreise f; **~up** n Zusammentreiben nt, Sammeln nt

rouse [raʊz] vt (waken) (auf)wecken; (stir up) erregen; **rousing** adj (welcome) stürmisch; (speech) zündend

route [ruːt] n Weg m, Route f; **~ map** (BRIT) n (for journey) Streckenkarte f

routine [ruː'tiːn] n Routine f **♦** adj Routine-

row¹ [rəʊ] n (noise) Lärm m; (dispute) Streit m **♦** vi sich streiten

row² [rəʊ] n (line) Reihe f **♦** vt, vi (boat) rudern; **in a ~** (fig) hintereinander; **~boat** ['rəʊbəʊt] (US) n Ruderboot nt

rowdy ['raʊdɪ] adj rüpelhaft **♦** n (person) Rowdy m

rowing ['rəʊɪŋ] n Rudern nt; (SPORT) Rudersport m; **~ boat** (BRIT) n Ruderboot nt

royal ['rɔɪəl] adj königlich, Königs-; **R~ Air Force** n Königliche Luftwaffe f; **~ty** ['rɔɪəltɪ] n (family) königliche Familie f; (for novel etc) Tantieme f

rpm abbr (= revs per minute) U/min

R.S.V.P. abbr (= répondez s'il vous plaît) u. A. w. g.

Rt. Hon. (BRIT) abbr (= Right Honourable) Abgeordnete(r) mf

rub [rʌb] n (with cloth) Polieren nt; (on person) Reiben nt **♦** vt reiben; **to ~ sb up** (BRIT) or **to ~ sb** (US) **the wrong way** jdn aufreizen; **~ off** vi (also fig): **to ~ off (on)** abfärben (auf +acc); **~ out** vt herausreiben; (with eraser) ausradieren

rubber ['rʌbə] n Gummi m; (BRIT)

Radiergummi *m*; ~ **band** *n* Gummiband
nt; ~ **plant** *n* Gummibaum *m*

ubbish ['rʌbɪʃ] *n* (*waste*) Abfall *m*;
(*nonsense*) Blödsinn *m*, Quatsch *m*; ~ **bin**
(*BRIT*) *n* Mülleimer *m*; ~ **dump** *n*
Müllabladeplatz *m*

ubble ['rʌbl] *n* (*Stein*)schutt *m*

uby ['ru:bɪ] *n* Rubin *m* ♦ *adj* rubinrot

ucksack ['rʌksæk] *n* Rucksack *m*

udder ['rʌdər] *n* Steuerruder *nt*

uddy ['rʌdɪ] *adj* (*colour*) rötlich; (*inf: bloody*)
verdammt

ude [ru:d] *adj* unverschämt; (*shock*) hart;
(*awakening*) unsanft; (*unrefined, rough*) grob;
~**ness** *n* Unverschämtheit *f*; Grobheit *f*

udiment ['ru:dɪmənt] *n* Grundlage *f*

ueful ['ru:ful] *adj* reuevoll

uffian ['rʌfɪən] *n* Rohling *m*

uffle ['rʌfl] *vt* kräuseln

ug [rʌg] *n* Brücke *f*; (*in bedroom*)
Bettvorleger *m*; (*BRIT: for knees*) (Reise)decke
f

ugby ['rʌgbɪ] *n* (*also:* ~ **football**) Rugby *nt*

ugged ['rʌgɪd] *adj* (*coastline*) zerklüftet;
(*features*) markig

ugger ['rʌgər] (*BRIT: inf*) *n* = **rugby**

uin ['ru:ɪn] *n* Ruine *f*; (*downfall*) Ruin *m* ♦ *vt*
ruinieren; ~**s** *npl* (*fig*) Trümmer *pl*; ~**ous**
adj ruinierend

ule [ru:l] *n* Regel *f*; (*government*) Regierung
f; (*for measuring*) Lineal *nt* ♦ *vt* (*govern*)
herrschen über +*acc*, regieren; (*decide*)
anordnen, entscheiden; (*make lines on*)
linieren ♦ *vi* herrschen, regieren;
entscheiden; **as a** ~ in der Regel; ~ **out** *vt*
ausschließen; ~**d** *adj* (*paper*) liniert; ~**r** *n*
Lineal *nt*; Herrscher *m*; **ruling** ['ru:lɪŋ] *adj*
(*party*) Regierungs-; (*class*) herrschend ♦ *n*
(*JUR*) Entscheid *m*

um [rʌm] *n* Rum *m*

Rumania [ru:'meɪnɪə] *n* Rumänien *nt*; ~**n** *adj*
rumänisch ♦ *n* Rumäne *m*, Rumänin *f*;
(*LING*) Rumänisch *nt*

rumble ['rʌmbl] *n* Rumpeln *nt*; (*of thunder*)
Grollen *nt* ♦ *vi* rumpeln; grollen

rummage ['rʌmɪdʒ] *vi* durchstöbern

rumour ['ru:mər] (*US* **rumor**) *n* Gerücht *nt*

♦ *vt*: **it is** ~ed that man sagt *or* man
munkelt, dass

rump [rʌmp] *n* Hinterteil *nt*; ~ **steak** *n*
Rumpsteak *nt*

rumpus ['rʌmpəs] *n* Spektakel *m*

run [rʌn] (*pt* **ran**, *pp* **run**) *n* Lauf *m*; (*in car*)
(Spazier)fahrt *f*; (*series*) Serie *f*, Reihe *f*; (*ski*
~) (Ski)abfahrt *f*; (*in stocking*) Laufmasche *f*
♦ *vt* (*cause to* ~) laufen lassen; (*car, train,
bus*) fahren; (*race, distance*) laufen, rennen;
(*manage*) leiten; (*COMPUT*) laufen lassen;
(*pass: hand, eye*) gleiten lassen ♦ *vi* laufen;
(*move quickly*) laufen, rennen; (*bus, train*)
fahren; (*flow*) fließen, laufen; (*colours*)
(ab)färben; **there was a** ~ **on** (*meat, tickets*)
es gab einen Ansturm auf +*acc*; **on the** ~
auf der Flucht; **in the long** ~ auf die Dauer;
I'll ~ **you to the station** ich fahre dich zum
Bahnhof; **to** ~ **a risk** ein Risiko eingehen; ~
about *or* **around** (*children*)
umherspringen; ~ **across** *vt fus* (*find*)
stoßen auf +*acc*; ~ **away** *vi* weglaufen; ~
down *vi* (*clock*) ablaufen ♦ *vt* (*production,
factory*) allmählich auflösen; (*with car*)
überfahren; (*talk against*) heruntermachen;
to be ~ **down** erschöpft *or* abgespannt
sein; ~ **in** (*BRIT*) *vt* (*car*) einfahren; ~ **into**
vt fus (*meet: person*) zufällig treffen; (*trouble*)
bekommen; (*collide with*) rennen gegen;
fahren gegen; ~ **off** *vi* fortlaufen; ~ **out** *vi*
(*person*) hinausrennen; (*liquid*) auslaufen;
(*lease*) ablaufen; (*money*) ausgeben; **he ran
out of money/petrol** ihm ging das Geld/
Benzin aus; ~ **over** *vt* (*in accident*)
überfahren; ~ **through** *vt* (*instructions*)
durchgehen; ~ **up** *vt* (*debt, bill*) machen; ~
up against *vt fus* (*difficulties*) stoßen auf
+*acc*; ~**away** *adj* (*horse*) ausgebrochen;
(*person*) flüchtig

rung [rʌŋ] *pp of* **ring** ♦ *n* Sprosse *f*

runner ['rʌnər] *n* Läufer(in) *m(f)*; (*for sleigh*)
Kufe *f*; ~ **bean** (*BRIT*) *n* Stangenbohne *f*;
~**-up** *n* Zweite(r) *mf*

running ['rʌnɪŋ] *n* (*of business*) Leitung *f*; (*of
machine*) Betrieb *m* ♦ *adj* (*water*) fließend;
(*commentary*) laufend; **to be in/out of the**
~ **for sth** im/aus dem Rennen für etw sein;

3 days ~ 3 Tage lang *or* hintereinander; **~ costs** *npl* (*of car, machine*) Unterhaltungskosten *pl*

runny ['rʌnɪ] *adj* dünn; (*nose*) laufend

run-of-the-mill ['rʌnəvðə'mɪl] *adj* gewöhnlich, alltäglich

runt [rʌnt] *n* (*animal*) Kümmerer *m*

run-up ['rʌnʌp] *n*: **the ~~ to** (*election etc*) die Endphase *vor +dat*

runway ['rʌnweɪ] *n* Startbahn *f*

rupture ['rʌptʃər] *n* (*MED*) Bruch *m*

rural ['ruərl] *adj* ländlich, Land-

ruse [ru:z] *n* Kniff *m*, List *f*

rush [rʌʃ] *n* Eile *f*, Hetze *f*; (*FIN*) starke Nachfrage *f* ♦ *vt* (*carry along*) auf dem schnellsten Wege schaffen *or* transportieren; (*attack*) losstürmen auf *+acc* ♦ *vi* (*hurry*) eilen, stürzen; **don't ~ me** dräng mich nicht; **~ hour** *n* Hauptverkehrszeit *f*

rusk [rʌsk] *n* Zwieback *m*

Russia ['rʌʃə] *n* Russland *nt*; **~n** *adj* russisch ♦ *n* Russe *m*, Russin *f*; (*LING*) Russisch *nt*

rust [rʌst] *n* Rost *m* ♦ *vi* rosten

rustic ['rʌstɪk] *adj* bäuerlich, ländlich

rustle ['rʌsl] *vi* rauschen, rascheln ♦ *vt* rascheln lassen

rustproof ['rʌstpru:f] *adj* rostfrei

rusty ['rʌstɪ] *adj* rostig

rut [rʌt] *n* (*in track*) Radspur *f*; **to be in a ~** im Trott stecken

ruthless ['ru:θlɪs] *adj* rücksichtslos

rye [raɪ] *n* Roggen *m*; **~ bread** *n* Roggenbrot *nt*

S, s

sabbath ['sæbəθ] *n* Sabbat *m*

sabotage ['sæbətɑ:ʒ] *n* Sabotage *f* ♦ *vt* sabotieren

saccharin ['sækərɪn] *n* Sa(c)charin *nt*

sachet ['sæʃeɪ] *n* (*of shampoo etc*) Briefchen *nt*, Kissen *nt*

sack [sæk] *n* Sack *m* ♦ *vt* (*inf*) hinauswerfen; (*pillage*) plündern; **to get the ~** rausfliegen; **~ing** *n* (*material*) Sackleinen *nt*; (*inf*)

Rausschmiss *m*

sacrament ['sækrəmənt] *n* Sakrament *nt*

sacred ['seɪkrɪd] *adj* heilig

sacrifice ['sækrɪfaɪs] *n* Opfer *nt* ♦ *vt* (*also fig*) opfern

sacrilege ['sækrɪlɪdʒ] *n* Schändung *f*

sad [sæd] *adj* traurig; **~den** *vt* traurig machen, betrüben

saddle ['sædl] *n* Sattel *m* ♦ *vt* (*burden*): **to ~ sb with sth** jdm etw aufhalsen; **~bag** *n* Satteltasche *f*

sadistic [sə'dɪstɪk] *adj* sadistisch

sadly ['sædlɪ] *adv* traurig; (*unfortunately*) leider

sadness ['sædnɪs] *n* Traurigkeit *f*

s.a.e. *abbr* (= *stamped addressed envelope*) adressierte(r) Rückumschlag *m*

safe [seɪf] *adj* (*careful*) vorsichtig ♦ *n* Safe *m*; **~ and sound** gesund und wohl; **(just) to be on the ~ side** um ganz sicherzugehen; **~ from** (*attack*) sicher vor *+dat*; **~-conduct** *n* freie(s) Geleit *nt*; **~-deposit** *n* (*vault*) Tresorraum *m*; (*box*) Banksafe *m*; **~guard** *n* Sicherung *f* ♦ *vt* sichern, schützen; **~keeping** *n* sichere Verwahrung *f*; **~ly** *adv* sicher; (*arrive*) wohlbehalten; **~ sex** *n* geschützter Sex *m*

safety ['seɪftɪ] *n* Sicherheit *f*; **~ belt** *n* Sicherheitsgurt *m*; **~ pin** *n* Sicherheitsnadel *f*; **~ valve** *n* Sicherheitsventil *nt*

sag [sæg] *vi* (durch)sacken

sage [seɪdʒ] *n* (*herb*) Salbei *m*; (*person*) Weise(r) *mf*

Sagittarius [sædʒɪ'teərɪəs] *n* Schütze *m*

Sahara [sə'hɑ:rə] *n*: **the ~ (Desert)** die (Wüste) Sahara

said [sed] *pt, pp of* **say**

sail [seɪl] *n* Segel *nt*; (*trip*) Fahrt *f* ♦ *vt* segeln ♦ *vi* segeln; (*begin voyage: person*) abfahren; (*: ship*) auslaufen; (*fig: cloud etc*) dahinsegeln; **to go for a ~** segeln gehen; **they ~ed into Copenhagen** sie liefen in Kopenhagen ein; **~ through** *vt fus, vi* (*fig*) (es) spielend schaffen; **~boat** (*US*) *n* Segelboot *nt*; **~ing** *n* Segeln *nt*; **~ing ship** *n* Segelschiff *nt*; **~or** *n* Matrose *m*, Seemann *m*

saint [seɪnt] n Heilige(r) mf; **~ly** adj heilig, fromm

sake [seɪk] n: **for the ~ of** um +gen willen

salad ['sæləd] n Salat m; **~ bowl** n Salatschüssel f; **~ cream** (BRIT) n Salatmayonnaise f, Salatmajonäse f; **~ dressing** n Salatsoße f

salary ['sælərɪ] n Gehalt nt

sale [seɪl] n Verkauf m; (reduced prices) Schlussverkauf m; **"for ~"** „zu verkaufen"; **on ~** zu verkaufen; **~room** n Verkaufsraum m; **~s assistant** n Verkäufer(in) m(f); **~s clerk** (US) n Verkäufer(in) m(f); **~sman** (irreg) n Verkäufer m; (representative) Vertreter m; **~s rep** n (COMM) Vertreter(in) m(f); **~swoman** (irreg) n Verkäuferin f

salient ['seɪlɪənt] adj bemerkenswert

saliva [sə'laɪvə] n Speichel m

sallow ['sæləʊ] adj fahl; (face) bleich

salmon ['sæmən] n Lachs m

salon ['sælɒn] n Salon m

saloon [sə'luːn] n (BRIT: AUT) Limousine f; (ship's lounge) Salon m; **~ car** (BRIT) n Limousine f

salt [sɔːlt] n Salz nt ♦ vt (cure) einsalzen; (flavour) salzen; **~cellar** n Salzfass nt; **~water** adj Salzwasser-; **~y** adj salzig

salute [sə'luːt] n (MIL) Gruß m; (with guns) Salutschüsse pl ♦ vt (MIL) salutieren

salvage ['sælvɪdʒ] n (from ship) Bergung f; (property) Rettung f ♦ vt bergen; retten

salvation [sæl'veɪʃən] n Rettung f; **S~ Army** n Heilsarmee f

same [seɪm] adj, pron (similar) gleiche(r, s); (identical) derselbe/dieselbe/dasselbe; **the ~ book as** das gleiche Buch wie; **at the ~ time** zur gleichen Zeit, gleichzeitig; (however) zugleich, andererseits; **all** or **just the ~** trotzdem; **the ~ to you!** gleichfalls!; **to do the ~ (as sb)** das Gleiche tun (wie jd)

sample ['sɑːmpl] n Probe f ♦ vt probieren

sanctify ['sæŋktɪfaɪ] vt weihen

sanctimonious [sæŋktɪ'məʊnɪəs] adj scheinheilig

sanction ['sæŋkʃən] n Sanktion f

sanctity ['sæŋktɪtɪ] n Heiligkeit f; (fig) Unverletzlichkeit f

sanctuary ['sæŋktjʊərɪ] n (for fugitive) Asyl nt; (refuge) Zufluchtsort m; (for animals) Schutzgebiet nt

sand [sænd] n Sand m ♦ vt (furniture) schmirgeln

sandal ['sændl] n Sandale f

sand: **~box** (US) n = **sandpit**; **~castle** n Sandburg f; **~ dune** n (Sand)düne f; **~paper** n Sandpapier nt; **~pit** n Sandkasten m; **~stone** n Sandstein m

sandwich ['sændwɪtʃ] n Sandwich m or nt ♦ vt (also: **~ in**) einklemmen; **cheese/ham ~** Käse-/Schinkenbrot; **~ed between** eingeklemmt zwischen; **~ board** n Reklametafel f; **~ course** (BRIT) n Theorie und Praxis abwechselnde(r) Ausbildungsgang m

sandy ['sændɪ] adj sandig; (hair) rotblond

sane [seɪn] adj geistig gesund or normal; (sensible) vernünftig, gescheit

sang [sæŋ] pt of **sing**

sanitary ['sænɪtərɪ] adj hygienisch; **~ towel** n (Monats)binde f

sanitation [sænɪ'teɪʃən] n sanitäre Einrichtungen pl; **~ department** (US) n Stadtreinigung f

sanity ['sænɪtɪ] n geistige Gesundheit f; (sense) Vernunft f

sank [sæŋk] pt of **sink**

Santa Claus [sæntə'klɔːz] n Nikolaus m, Weihnachtsmann m

sap [sæp] n (of plants) Saft m ♦ vt (strength) schwächen

sapling ['sæplɪŋ] n junge(r) Baum m

sapphire ['sæfaɪə*] n Saphir m

sarcasm ['sɑːkæzm] n Sarkasmus m

sarcastic [sɑː'kæstɪk] adj sarkastisch

sardine [sɑː'diːn] n Sardine f

Sardinia [sɑː'dɪnɪə] n Sardinien nt

sardonic [sɑː'dɒnɪk] adj zynisch

sash [sæʃ] n Schärpe f

sat [sæt] pt, pp of **sit**

Satan ['seɪtn] n Satan m

satchel ['sætʃl] n (for school) Schulmappe f

satellite ['sætəlaɪt] n Satellit m; **~ dish** n (TECH) Parabolantenne f, Satellitenantenne *f;* **~ television** *n* Satellitenfernsehen *nt*

satisfaction [sætɪsˈfækʃən] *n* Befriedigung *f*, Genugtuung *f;* **satisfactory** [sætɪsˈfæktərɪ] *adj* zufrieden stellend, befriedigend; **satisfied** *adj* befriedigt

satisfy [ˈsætɪsfaɪ] *vt* befriedigen, zufrieden stellen; (*convince*) überzeugen; (*conditions*) erfüllen; **~ing** *adj* befriedigend; (*meal*) sättigend

saturate [ˈsætʃəreɪt] *vt* (durch)tränken

Saturday [ˈsætədɪ] *n* Samstag *m*, Sonnabend *m*

sauce [sɔːs] *n* Soße *f*, Sauce *f;* **~pan** *n* Kasserolle *f*

saucer [ˈsɔːsər] *n* Untertasse *f*

saucy [ˈsɔːsɪ] *adj* frech, keck

Saudi [ˈsaʊdɪ]: **~ Arabia** *n* Saudi-Arabien *nt;* **~ (Arabian)** *adj* saudi-arabisch ♦ *n* Saudi-Araber(in) *m(f)*

sauna [ˈsɔːnə] *n* Sauna *f*

saunter [ˈsɔːntər] *vi* schlendern

sausage [ˈsɒsɪdʒ] *n* Wurst *f;* **~ roll** *n* Wurst *f* im Schlafrock, Wurstpastete *f*

sauté [ˈsəʊteɪ] *adj* Röst-

savage [ˈsævɪdʒ] *adj* wild ♦ *n* Wilde(r) *mf* ♦ *vt* (*animals*) zerfleischen

save [seɪv] *vt* retten; (*money, electricity etc*) sparen; (*strength etc*) aufsparen; (*COMPUT*) speichern ♦ *vi* (*also:* **~ up**) sparen ♦ *n* (*SPORT*) (Ball)abwehr *f* ♦ *prep, conj* außer, ausgenommen

saving [ˈseɪvɪŋ] *adj:* **the ~ grace of** das Versöhnende an +*dat* ♦ *n* Sparen *nt*, Ersparnis *f;* **~s** *npl* (*money*) Ersparnisse *pl;* **~s account** *n* Sparkonto *nt;* **~s bank** *n* Sparkasse *f*

saviour [ˈseɪvjər] (*US* **savior**) *n* (*REL*) Erlöser *m*

savour [ˈseɪvər] (*US* **savor**) *vt* (*taste*) schmecken; (*fig*) genießen; **~y** *adj* pikant, würzig

saw [sɔː] (*pt* **sawed**, *pp* **sawed** *or* **sawn**) *pt* *of* **see** ♦ *n* (*tool*) Säge *f* ♦ *vt, vi* sägen; **~dust** *n* Sägemehl *nt;* **~mill** *n* Sägewerk *nt;* **~n** *pp* *of* **saw;** **~n-off shotgun** *n* Gewehr *nt* mit abgesägtem Lauf

sax [sæks] (*inf*) *n* Saxofon *nt*, Saxophon *nt*

saxophone [ˈsæksəfəʊn] *n* Saxofon *nt*,

Saxophon *nt*

say [seɪ] (*pt, pp* **said**) *n:* **to have a/no ~ in sth** Mitspracherecht/kein Mitspracherecht bei etw haben ♦ *vt, vi* sagen; **let him have his ~** lass ihn doch reden; **to ~ yes/no** Ja/Nein *or* ja/nein sagen; **that goes without ~ing** das versteht sich von selbst; **that is to ~** das heißt; **~ing** *n* Sprichwort *nt*

scab [skæb] *n* Schorf *m;* (*pej*) Streikbrecher *m*

scaffold [ˈskæfəld] *n* (*for execution*) Schafott *nt;* **~ing** *n* (Bau)gerüst *nt*

scald [skɔːld] *n* Verbrühung *f* ♦ *vt* (*burn*) verbrühen

scale [skeɪl] *n* (*of fish*) Schuppe *f;* (*MUS*) Tonleiter *f;* (*on map, size*) Maßstab *m;* (*gradation*) Skala *f* ♦ *vt* (*climb*) erklimmen; **~s** *npl* (*balance*) Waage *f;* **on a large ~** (*fig*) im Großen, in großem Umfang; **~ of charges** Gebührenordnung *f;* **~ down** *vt* verkleinern; **~ model** *n* maßstabgetreue(s) Modell *nt*

scallop [ˈskɒləp] *n* Kammmuschel *f*

scalp [skælp] *n* Kopfhaut *f*

scamper [ˈskæmpər] *vi:* **to ~ away** *or* **off** sich davonmachen

scampi [ˈskæmpɪ] *npl* Scampi *pl*

scan [skæn] *vt* (*examine*) genau prüfen; (*quickly*) überfliegen; (*horizon*) absuchen

scandal [ˈskændl] *n* Skandal *m;* (*piece of gossip*) Skandalgeschichte *f*

Scandinavia [skændɪˈneɪvɪə] *n* Skandinavien *nt;* **~n** *adj* skandinavisch ♦ *n* Skandinavier(in) *m(f)*

scant [skænt] *adj* knapp; **~ily** *adv* knapp, dürftig; **~y** *adj* knapp, unzureichend

scapegoat [ˈskeɪpgəʊt] *n* Sündenbock *m*

scar [skɑː] *n* Narbe *f* ♦ *vt* durch Narben entstellen

scarce [skɛəs] *adj* selten, rar; (*goods*) knapp; **~ly** *adv* kaum; **scarcity** *n* Mangel *m*

scare [skɛər] *n* Schrecken *m* ♦ *vt* erschrecken; **bomb ~** Bombendrohung *f;* **to ~ sb stiff** jdn zu Tode erschrecken; **to be ~d** Angst haben; **~ away** *vt* (*animal*) verscheuchen; **~ off** *vt* = **scare away;**

~**crow** n Vogelscheuche f

scarf [skɑːf] (pl **scarves**) n Schal m; (headscarf) Kopftuch nt

scarlet ['skɑːlɪt] adj scharlachrot ♦ n Scharlachrot nt; ~ **fever** n Scharlach m

scarves [skɑːvz] npl of **scarf**

scary ['skɛərɪ] (inf) adj schaurig

scathing ['skeɪðɪŋ] adj scharf, vernichtend

scatter ['skætəʳ] vt (sprinkle) (ver)streuen; (disperse) zerstreuen ♦ vi sich zerstreuen; ~**brained** adj flatterhaft, schusselig

scavenger ['skævəndʒəʳ] n (animal) Aasfresser m

scenario [sɪ'nɑːrɪəu] n (THEAT, CINE) Szenarium nt; (fig) Szenario nt

scene [siːn] n (of happening) Ort m; (of play, incident) Szene f; (view) Anblick m; (argument) Szene f, Auftritt m; ~**ry** n (THEAT) Bühnenbild nt; (landscape) Landschaft f

scenic ['siːnɪk] adj landschaftlich

scent [sɛnt] n Parfüm nt; (smell) Duft m ♦ vt parfümieren

sceptical ['skɛptɪkl] (US **skeptical**) adj skeptisch

schedule ['ʃɛdjuːl, (US) 'skɛdjuːl] n (list) Liste f; (plan) Programm nt; (of work) Zeitplan m ♦ vt planen; **on** ~ pünktlich; **to be ahead of/behind** ~ dem Zeitplan voraus/im Rückstand sein; ~**d flight** n (not charter) Linienflug m

scheme [skiːm] n Schema nt; (dishonest) Intrige f; (plan of action) Plan m ♦ vi intrigieren ♦ vt planen; **scheming** ['skiːmɪŋ] adj intrigierend

scholar ['skɒləʳ] n Gelehrte(r) m; (holding ~ship) Stipendiat m; ~**ly** adj gelehrt; ~**ship** n Gelehrsamkeit f; (grant) Stipendium nt

school [skuːl] n Schule f; (UNIV) Fakultät f ♦ vt schulen; ~ **age** n schulpflichtige(s) Alter nt; ~**book** n Schulbuch nt; ~**boy** n Schüler m; ~**children** npl Schüler pl, Schulkinder pl; ~**days** npl (alte) Schulzeit f; ~**girl** n Schülerin f; ~**ing** n Schulung f, Ausbildung f; ~**master** n Lehrer m; ~**mistress** n Lehrerin f; ~**teacher** n Lehrer(in) m(f)

sciatica [saɪ'ætɪkə] n Ischias m or nt

science ['saɪəns] n Wissenschaft f; (natural ~) Naturwissenschaft f; ~ **fiction** n Sciencefiction f; **scientific** [saɪən'tɪfɪk] adj wissenschaftlich; (natural ~s) naturwissenschaftlich; **scientist** ['saɪəntɪst] n Wissenschaftler(in) m(f)

scintillating ['sɪntɪleɪtɪŋ] adj sprühend

scissors ['sɪzəz] npl Schere f; **a pair of** ~ eine Schere

scoff [skɔf] vt (BRIT: inf: eat) fressen ♦ vi (mock): **to** ~ (**at**) spotten (über +acc)

scold [skəuld] vt schimpfen

scone [skɒn] n weiche(s) Teegebäck nt

scoop [skuːp] n Schaufel f; (news) sensationelle Erstmeldung f; ~ **out** vt herausschaufeln; ~ **up** vt aufschaufeln; (liquid) aufschöpfen

scooter ['skuːtəʳ] n Motorroller m; (child's) Roller m

scope [skəup] n Ausmaß nt; (opportunity) (Spiel)raum m

scorch [skɔːtʃ] n Brandstelle f ♦ vt versengen; ~**ing** adj brennend

score [skɔːʳ] n (in game) Punktzahl f; (final ~) (Spiel)ergebnis nt; (MUS) Partitur f; (line) Kratzer m; (twenty) zwanzig, zwanzig Stück ♦ vt (goal) schießen; (points) machen; (mark) einritzen ♦ vi (keep record) Punkte zählen; **on that** ~ in dieser Hinsicht; **what's the** ~? wie stehts?; **to** ~ **6 out of 10** 6 von 10 Punkten erzielen; ~ **out** vt ausstreichen; ~**board** n Anschreibetafel f; ~**r** n Torschütze m; (recorder) (Auf)schreiber m

scorn [skɔːn] n Verachtung f ♦ vt verhöhnen; ~**ful** adj verächtlich

Scorpio ['skɔːpɪəu] n Skorpion m

scorpion ['skɔːpɪən] n Skorpion m

Scot [skɒt] n Schotte m, Schottin f

Scotch [skɒtʃ] n Scotch m

scotch [skɒtʃ] vt (end) unterbinden

scot-free ['skɒt'friː] adv: **to get off** ~~ (unpunished) ungeschoren davonkommen

Scotland ['skɒtlənd] n Schottland nt

Scots [skɒts] adj schottisch; ~**man/woman** (irreg) n Schotte m/Schottin f

Scottish ['skɒtɪʃ] adj schottisch

scoundrel ['skaundrl] n Schuft m

scour ['skauəʳ] vt (search) absuchen; (clean) schrubben

scourge [skə:dʒ] n (whip) Geißel f; (plague) Qual f

scout [skaut] n (MIL) Späher m; (also: **boy ~**) Pfadfinder m; **~ around** vi: **to ~ around (for)** sich umsehen (nach)

scowl [skaul] n finstere(r) Blick m ♦ vi finster blicken

scrabble ['skræbl] vi (also: **~ around**: search) (herum)tasten; (claw): **to ~ (at)** kratzen (an +dat) ♦ n: **S~** ® Scrabble nt ®

scraggy ['skrægɪ] adj dürr, hager

scram [skræm] (inf) vi abhauen

scramble ['skræmbl] n (climb) Kletterei f; (struggle) Kampf m ♦ vi klettern; (fight) sich schlagen; **to ~ out/through** krabbeln aus/ durch; **to ~ for sth** sich um etw raufen; **~d eggs** npl Rührei nt

scrap [skræp] n (bit) Stückchen nt; (fight) Keilerei f; (also: **~ iron**) Schrott m ♦ vt verwerfen ♦ vi (fight) streiten, sich prügeln; **~s** npl (leftovers) Reste pl; (waste) Abfall m; **~book** n Einklebealbum nt; **~ dealer** n Schrotthändler(in) m(f)

scrape [skreɪp] n Kratzen nt; (trouble) Klemme f ♦ vt kratzen; (car) zerkratzen; (clean) abkratzen ♦ vi (make harsh noise) kratzen; **to ~ through** gerade noch durchkommen; **~r** n Kratzer m

scrap: **~ heap** n Schrotthaufen m; **on the ~ heap** (fig) beim alten Eisen; **~ iron** n Schrott m; **~ merchant** (BRIT) n Altwarenhändler(in) m(f); **~ paper** n Schmierpapier nt

scrappy ['skræpɪ] adj zusammengestoppelt

scratch [skrætʃ] n (wound) Kratzer m, Schramme f ♦ adj: **~ team** zusammengewürfelte Mannschaft ♦ vt kratzen; (car) zerkratzen ♦ vi (sich) kratzen; **to start from ~** ganz von vorne anfangen; **to be up to ~** den Anforderungen entsprechen

scrawl [skrɔ:l] n Gekritzel nt ♦ vt, vi kritzeln

scrawny ['skrɔ:nɪ] adj (person, neck) dürr

scream [skri:m] n Schrei m ♦ vi schreien

scree [skri:] n Geröll(halde f) nt

screech [skri:tʃ] n Schrei m ♦ vi kreischen

screen [skri:n] n (protective) Schutzschirm m; (CINE) Leinwand f; (TV) Bildschirm m ♦ vt (shelter) (be)schirmen; (film) zeigen, vorführen; **~ing** n (MED) Untersuchung f; **~play** n Drehbuch nt; **~ saver** n (COMPUT) Bildschirmschoner m

screw [skru:] n Schraube f ♦ vt (fasten) schrauben; (vulgar) bumsen; **~ up** vt (paper etc) zerknüllen; (inf: ruin) vermasseln (inf); **~driver** n Schraubenzieher m

scribble ['skrɪbl] n Gekritzel nt ♦ vt kritzeln

script [skrɪpt] n (handwriting) Handschrift f; (for film) Drehbuch nt; (THEAT) Manuskript nt, Text m

Scripture ['skrɪptʃəʳ] n Heilige Schrift f

scroll [skrəul] n Schriftrolle f

scrounge [skraundʒ] (inf) vt: **to ~ sth off or from sb** etw bei jdm abstauben ♦ n: **on the ~** beim Schnorren

scrub [skrʌb] n (clean) Schrubben nt; (in countryside) Gestrüpp nt ♦ vt (clean) schrubben

scruff [skrʌf] n: **by the ~ of the neck** am Genick

scruffy ['skrʌfɪ] adj unordentlich, vergammelt

scrum(mage) ['skrʌm(ɪdʒ)] n Getümmel nt

scruple ['skru:pl] n Skrupel m, Bedenken nt

scrupulous ['skru:pjuləs] adj peinlich genau, gewissenhaft

scrutinize ['skru:tɪnaɪz] vt genau prüfen;

scrutiny ['skru:tɪnɪ] n genaue Untersuchung f

scuff [skʌf] vt (shoes) abstoßen

scuffle ['skʌfl] n Handgemenge nt

sculptor ['skʌlptəʳ] n Bildhauer(in) m(f)

sculpture ['skʌlptʃəʳ] n (ART) Bildhauerei f; (statue) Skulptur f

scum [skʌm] n (also fig) Abschaum m

scurry ['skʌrɪ] vi huschen

scuttle ['skʌtl] n (also: **coal ~**) Kohleneimer m ♦ vt (ship) versenken ♦ vi (scamper): **to ~ away** or **off** sich davonmachen

scythe [saɪð] n Sense f

SDP (BRIT) n abbr = **Social Democratic**

Party

sea [siː] *n* Meer *nt*, See *f*; (*fig*) Meer *nt* ♦ *adj* Meeres-, See-; **by ~** (*travel*) auf dem Seeweg; **on the ~** (*boat*) auf dem Meer; (*town*) am Meer; **out to ~** aufs Meer hinaus; **out at ~** aufs Meer; **~board** *n* Küste *f*; **~food** *n* Meeresfrüchte *pl*; **~ front** *n* Strandpromenade *f*; **~going** *adj* seetüchtig, Hochsee-; **~gull** *n* Möwe *f*

seal [siːl] *n* (*animal*) Robbe *f*, Seehund *m*; (*stamp, impression*) Siegel *nt* ♦ *vt* versiegeln; **~ off** *vt* (*place*) abriegeln

sea level *n* Meeresspiegel *m*

sea lion *n* Seelöwe *m*

seam [siːm] *n* Saum *m*; (*edges joining*) Naht *f*; (*of coal*) Flöz *nt*

seaman [ˈsiːmən] (*irreg*) *n* Seemann *m*

seaplane [ˈsiːpleɪn] *n* Wasserflugzeug *nt*

seaport [ˈsiːpɔːt] *n* Seehafen *m*

search [sɜːtʃ] *n* (*for person, thing*) Suche *f*; (*of drawer, pockets, house*) Durchsuchung *f* ♦ *vi* suchen ♦ *vt* durchsuchen; **in ~ of** auf der Suche nach; **to ~ for** suchen nach; **~ through** *vt* durchsuchen; **~ engine** *n* (*COMPUT*) Suchmaschine *f*; **~ing** *adj* (*look*) forschend; **~light** *n* Scheinwerfer *m*; **~ party** *n* Suchmannschaft *f*; **~ warrant** *n* Durchsuchungsbefehl *m*

sea: **~shore** [ˈsiːʃɔːr] *n* Meeresküste *f*; **~sick** [ˈsiːsɪk] *adj* seekrank; **~side** [ˈsiːsaɪd] *n* Küste *f*; **~side resort** *n* Badeort *m*

season [ˈsiːzn] *n* Jahreszeit *f*; (*Christmas etc*) Zeit *f*, Saison *f* ♦ *vt* (*flavour*) würzen; **~al** *adj* Saison-; **~ed** *adj* (*fig*) erfahren; **~ing** *n* Gewürz *nt*, Würze *f*; **~ ticket** *n* (*RAIL*) Zeitkarte *f*; (*THEAT*) Abonnement *nt*

seat [siːt] *n* Sitz *m*, Platz *m*; (*in Parliament*) Sitz *m*; (*part of body*) Gesäß *nt*; (*of trousers*) Hosenboden *m* ♦ *vt* (*place*) setzen; (*have space for*) Sitzplätze bieten für; **to be ~ed** sitzen; **~ belt** *n* Sicherheitsgurt *m*

sea: **~ water** *n* Meerwasser *nt*; **~weed** [ˈsiːwiːd] *n* (*See*)tang *m*; **~worthy** [ˈsiːwəːðɪ] *adj* seetüchtig

sec. *abbr* (= *second(s)*) Sek.

secluded [sɪˈkluːdɪd] *adj* abgelegen

seclusion [sɪˈkluːʒən] *n* Zurückgezogenheit *f*

second [ˈsekənd] *adj* zweite(r,s) ♦ *adv* (*in ~ position*) an zweiter Stelle ♦ *n* Sekunde *f*; (*person*) Zweite(r) *mf*; (*COMM: imperfect*) zweite Wahl *f*; (*SPORT*) Sekundant *m*; (*AUT: also:* **~ gear**) zweite(r) Gang *m*; (*BRIT: UNIV: degree*) mittlere Note bei Abschlussprüfungen ♦ *vt* (*support*) unterstützen; **~ary** *adj* zweitrangig; **~ary school** *n* höhere Schule *f*, Mittelschule *f*; **~-class** *adj* zweiter Klasse; **~hand** *adj* aus zweiter Hand; (*car etc*) gebraucht; **~ hand** *n* (*on clock*) Sekundenzeiger *m*; **~ly** *adv* zweitens

secondment [sɪˈkɒndmənt] (*BRIT*) *n* Abordnung *f*

second-rate [ˈsekəndreɪt] *adj* mittelmäßig

second thoughts *npl*: **to have ~** es sich *dat* anders überlegen; **on ~** (*BRIT*) *or* **thought** (*US*) oder lieber (nicht)

secrecy [ˈsiːkrəsɪ] *n* Geheimhaltung *f*

secret [ˈsiːkrɪt] *n* Geheimnis *nt* ♦ *adj* geheim, Geheim-; **in ~** geheim

secretarial [sekrɪˈtɛərɪəl] *adj* Sekretärinnen-

secretary [ˈsekrətərɪ] *n* Sekretär(in) *m(f)*; **S~ of State** (*BRIT*) *n* (*POL*): **S~ of State (for)** Minister(in) *m(f)* (für)

secretion [sɪˈkriːʃən] *n* Absonderung *f*

secretive [ˈsiːkrətɪv] *adj* geheimtuerisch

secretly [ˈsiːkrɪtlɪ] *adv* geheim

sectarian [sekˈtɛərɪən] *adj* (*riots etc*) Konfessions-, zwischen den Konfessionen

section [ˈsekʃən] *n* Teil *m*; (*department*) Abteilung *f*; (*of document*) Abschnitt *m*

sector [ˈsektər] *n* Sektor *m*

secular [ˈsekjulər] *adj* weltlich, profan

secure [sɪˈkjuər] *adj* (*safe*) sicher; (*firmly fixed*) fest ♦ *vt* (*make firm*) befestigen, sichern; (*obtain*) sichern; **security** [sɪˈkjuərɪtɪ] *n* Sicherheit *f*; (*pledge*) Pfand *nt*; (*document*) Wertpapier *nt*; (*national security*) Staatssicherheit *f*; **security guard** *n* Sicherheitsbeamte(r) *m*, Wächter *m*, Wache *f*

sedan [səˈdæn] (*US*) *n* (*AUT*) Limousine *f*

sedate [sɪˈdeɪt] *adj* gesetzt ♦ *vt* (*MED*) ein Beruhigungsmittel geben +*dat*; **sedation** [sɪˈdeɪʃən] *n* (*MED*) Einfluss *m* von Beruhigungsmitteln; **sedative** [ˈsedɪtɪv] *n*

Beruhigungsmittel nt ♦ adj beruhigend, einschläfernd

sediment ['sedɪmənt] n (Boden)satz m

seduce [sɪ'dju:s] vt verführen; **seductive** [sɪ'dʌktɪv] adj verführerisch

see [si:] (pt saw, pp seen) vt sehen; (understand) (ein)sehen, erkennen; (visit) besuchen ♦ vi (be aware) sehen; (find out) nachsehen ♦ n (ECCL: R.C.) Bistum nt; (: Protestant) Kirchenkreis m; **to ~ sb to the door** jdn hinausbegleiten; **to ~ that** (ensure) dafür sorgen, dass; **~ you soon!** bis bald!; **~ about** vt fus sich kümmern um; **~ off** vt: **to ~ sb off** jdn zum Zug etc begleiten; **~ through** vt: **to ~ sth through** etw durchfechten; **to ~ through sb/sth** jdn/ etw durchschauen; **~ to** vt fus: **to ~ to it** dafür sorgen

seed [si:d] n Samen m ♦ vt (TENNIS) platzieren; **to go to ~** (plant) schießen; (fig) herunterkommen; **~ling** n Setzling m; **~y** adj (café) übel; (person) zweifelhaft

seeing ['si:ɪŋ] conj: **~ (that)** da

seek [si:k] (pt, pp sought) vt suchen

seem [si:m] vi scheinen; **it ~s that ... es** scheint, dass ...; **~ingly** adv anscheinend

seen [si:n] pp of **see**

seep [si:p] vi sickern

seesaw ['si:sɔ:] n Wippe f

seethe [si:ð] vi: **to ~ with anger** vor Wut kochen

see-through ['si:θru:] adj (dress etc) durchsichtig

segment ['segmənt] n Teil m; (of circle) Ausschnitt m

segregate ['segrɪgeɪt] vt trennen

seize [si:z] vt (grasp) (er)greifen, packen; (power) ergreifen; (take legally) beschlagnahmen; **~ (up)on** vt fus sich stürzen auf +acc; **~ up** vi (TECH) sich festfressen; **seizure** ['si:ʒə] n (illness) Anfall m

seldom ['seldəm] adv selten

select [sɪ'lekt] adj ausgewählt ♦ vt auswählen; **~ion** [sɪ'lekʃən] n Auswahl f; **~ive** adj (person) wählerisch

self [self] (pl **selves**) pron selbst ♦ n Selbst

nt, Ich nt; **the ~** das Ich; **~-assured** adj selbstbewusst; **~-catering** (BRIT) adj für Selbstversorger; **~-centred** (US **self-centered**) adj egozentrisch; **~-coloured** (US **self-colored**) adj (of one colour) einfarbig, uni; **~-confidence** n Selbstvertrauen nt, Selbstbewusstsein nt; **~-conscious** adj gehemmt, befangen; **~-contained** adj (complete) (in sich) geschlossen; (person) verschlossen; (BRIT: flat) separat; **~-control** n Selbstbeherrschung f; **~-defence** (US **self-defense**) n Selbstverteidigung f; (JUR) Notwehr f; **~-discipline** n Selbstdisziplin f; **~-employed** adj frei(schaffend); **~-evident** adj offensichtlich; **~-governing** adj selbst verwaltet; **~-indulgent** adj zügellos; **~-interest** n Eigennutz m

selfish ['selfɪʃ] adj egoistisch, selbstsüchtig; **~ness** n Egoismus m, Selbstsucht f

self: **~lessly** adv selbstlos; **~-made** adj: **~-made man** Selfmademan m; **~-pity** n Selbstmitleid nt; **~-portrait** n Selbstbildnis nt; **~-possessed** adj selbstbeherrscht; **~-preservation** n Selbsterhaltung f; **~-reliant** adj unabhängig; **~-respect** n Selbstachtung f; **~-righteous** adj selbstgerecht; **~-sacrifice** n Selbstaufopferung f; **~-satisfied** adj selbstzufrieden; **~-service** adj Selbstbedienungs-; **~-sufficient** adj selbstgenügsam; **~-taught** adj selbst erlernt; **~-taught person** Autodidakt m

sell [sel] (pt, pp **sold**) vt verkaufen ♦ vi verkaufen; (goods) sich verkaufen; **to ~ at** or **for £10** für £10 verkaufen; **~ off** vt verkaufen; **~ out** vi alles verkaufen; **~-by date** n Verfalldatum nt; **~er** n Verkäufer m; **~ing price** n Verkaufspreis m

Sellotape ['seləuteɪp] (® BRIT) n Tesafilm m ®

sellout ['selaut] n (of tickets): **it was a ~** es war ausverkauft

selves [selvz] npl of **self**

semaphore ['seməfɔ:] n Winkzeichen pl

semblance ['semblns] n Anschein m

semen ['si:mən] n Sperma nt

emester [sɪˈmɛstər] (*US*) *n* Semester *nt*

emi [ˈsɛmɪ] *n* = **semidetached house**;
~**circle** *n* Halbkreis *m*; ~**colon** *n*
Semikolon *nt*; ~**conductor** *n* Halbleiter *m*;
~**detached house** (*BRIT*) *n* halbe(s)
Doppelhaus *nt*; ~**final** *n* Halbfinale *nt*

eminary [ˈsɛmɪnərɪ] *n* (*REL*) Priesterseminar
nt

emiskilled [sɛmɪˈskɪld] *adj* angelernt

emi-skimmed [sɛmɪˈskɪmd] *adj* (*milk*)
teilentrahmt, Halbfett-

enate [ˈsɛnɪt] *n* Senat *m*; **senator** *n*
Senator *m*

end [sɛnd] (*pt, pp* **sent**) *vt* senden,
schicken; (*inf: inspire*) hinreißen; ~ **away**
vt wegschicken; ~ **away for** *vt fus*
anfordern; ~ **back** *vt* zurückschicken; ~
for *vt fus* holen lassen; ~ **off** *vt* (*goods*)
abschicken; (*BRIT: SPORT: player*) vom Feld
schicken; ~ **out** *vt* (*invitation*) aussenden; ~
up *vt* hinaufsenden; (*BRIT: parody*) verulken;
~**er** *n* Absender *m*; ~**-off** *n*: **to give sb a**
good ~-off jdn (ganz) groß verabschieden

enior [ˈsiːnɪər] *adj* (*older*) älter; (*higher rank*)
Ober- ♦ *n* (*older person*) Ältere(r) *mf*; (*higher*
ranking) Rangälteste(r) *mf*; ~ **citizen** *n*
ältere(r) Mitbürger(in) *m(f)*; ~**ity** [siːnɪˈɔrɪtɪ]
n (*of age*) höhere(s) Alter *nt*; (*in rank*)
höhere(r) Dienstgrad *m*

ensation [sɛnˈseɪʃən] *n* Gefühl *nt*;
(*excitement*) Sensation *f*, Aufsehen *nt*; ~**al**
adj (*wonderful*) wunderbar; (*result*)
sensationell; (*headlines etc*) reißerisch

ense [sɛns] *n* Sinn *m*; (*understanding*)
Verstand *m*, Vernunft *f*; (*feeling*) Gefühl *nt*
♦ *vt* fühlen, spüren; ~ **of humour** Humor
m; **to make** ~ Sinn ergeben; ~**less** *adj*
sinnlos; (*unconscious*) besinnungslos

ensibility [sɛnsɪˈbɪlɪtɪ] *n* Empfindsamkeit *f*;
(*feeling hurt*) Empfindlichkeit *f*; **sensibilities**
npl (*feelings*) Zartgefühl *nt*

ensible [ˈsɛnsɪbl] *adj* vernünftig

ensitive [ˈsɛnsɪtɪv] *adj*: ~ **(to)** empfindlich
(gegen); **sensitivity** [sɛnsɪˈtɪvɪtɪ] *n*
Empfindlichkeit *f*; (*artistic*) Feingefühl *nt*;
(*tact*) Feinfühligkeit *f*

ensual [ˈsɛnsjuəl] *adj* sinnlich

sensuous [ˈsɛnsjuəs] *adj* sinnlich

sent [sɛnt] *pt, pp of* **send**

sentence [ˈsɛntns] *n* Satz *m*; (*JUR*) Strafe *f*;
Urteil *nt* ♦ *vt*: **to ~ sb to death/to 5 years**
jdn zum Tode/zu 5 Jahren verurteilen

sentiment [ˈsɛntɪmənt] *n* Gefühl *nt*;
(*thought*) Gedanke *m*; ~**al** [sɛntɪˈmɛntl] *adj*
sentimental; (*of feelings rather than reason*)
gefühlsmäßig

sentry [ˈsɛntrɪ] *n* (Schild)wache *f*

separate [*adj* ˈsɛprɪt, *vb* ˈsɛpəreɪt] *adj*
getrennt, separat ♦ *vt* trennen ♦ *vi* sich
trennen; ~**ly** *adv* getrennt; ~**s** *npl* (*clothes*)
Röcke, Pullover *etc*; **separation** [sɛpəˈreɪʃən]
n Trennung *f*

September [sɛpˈtɛmbər] *n* September *m*

septic [ˈsɛptɪk] *adj* vereitert, septisch; ~ **tank**
n Klärbehälter *m*

sequel [ˈsiːkwl] *n* Folge *f*

sequence [ˈsiːkwəns] *n* (Reihen)folge *f*

sequin [ˈsiːkwɪn] *n* Paillette *f*

Serbia [ˈsɜːbɪə] *n* Serbien *nt*

serene [sɪˈriːn] *adj* heiter

sergeant [ˈsɑːdʒənt] *n* Feldwebel *m*; (*POLICE*)
(Polizei)wachtmeister *m*

serial [ˈsɪərɪəl] *n* Fortsetzungsroman *m*; (*TV*)
Fernsehserie *f* ♦ *adj* (*number*) (fort)laufend;
~**ize** *vt* in Fortsetzungen veröffentlichen; in
Fortsetzungen senden

series [ˈsɪərɪz] *n inv* Serie *f*, Reihe *f*

serious [ˈsɪərɪəs] *adj* ernst; (*injury*) schwer;
~**ly** *adv* ernst(haft); (*hurt*) schwer; ~**ness** *n*
Ernst *m*, Ernsthaftigkeit *f*

sermon [ˈsɜːmən] *n* Predigt *f*

serrated [sɪˈreɪtɪd] *adj* gezackt

servant [ˈsɜːvənt] *n* Diener(in) *m(f)*

serve [sɜːv] *vt* dienen +*dat*; (*guest, customer*)
bedienen; (*food*) servieren ♦ *vi* dienen,
nützen; (*at table*) servieren; (*TENNIS*) geben,
aufschlagen; **it ~s him right** das geschieht
ihm recht; **that'll ~ as a table** das geht als
Tisch; **to ~ a summons (on sb)** (jdn) vor
Gericht laden; ~ **out** *or* **up** *vt* (*food*)
auftragen, servieren

service [ˈsɜːvɪs] *n* (*help*) Dienst *m*; (*trains etc*)
Verbindung *f*; (*hotel*) Service *m*, Bedienung
f; (*set of dishes*) Service *nt*; (*REL*)

Gottesdienst *m*; (*car*) Inspektion *f*; (*for TVs etc*) Kundendienst *m*; (*TENNIS*) Aufschlag *m* ♦ *vt* (*AUT, TECH*) warten, überholen; **the S~s** *npl* (*armed forces*) die Streitkräfte *pl*; **to be of ~ to sb** jdm einen großen Dienst erweisen; **~ included/not included** Bedienung inbegriffen/nicht inbegriffen; **~able** *adj* brauchbar; **~ area** *n* (*on motorway*) Raststätte *f*; **~ charge** (*BRIT*) *n* Bedienung *f*; **~man** (*irreg*) *n* (*soldier etc*) Soldat *m*; **~ station** *n* (Groß)tankstelle *f*

serviette [sə:vɪˈɛt] *n* Serviette *f*

servile [ˈsəːvaɪl] *adj* unterwürfig

session [ˈsɛʃən] *n* Sitzung *f*; (*POL*) Sitzungsperiode *f*; **to be in ~** tagen

set [sɛt] (*pt, pp* **set**) *n* (*collection of things*) Satz *m*, Set *nt*; (*RAD, TV*) Apparat *m*; (*TENNIS*) Satz *m*; (*group of people*) Kreis *m*; (*CINE*) Szene *f*; (*THEAT*) Bühnenbild *nt* ♦ *adj* festgelegt; (*ready*) bereit ♦ *vt* (*place*) setzen, stellen, legen; (*arrange*) (an)ordnen; (*table*) decken; (*time, price*) festsetzen; (*alarm, watch, task*) stellen; (*jewels*) (ein)fassen; (*exam*) ausarbeiten ♦ *vi* (*sun*) untergehen; (*become hard*) fest werden; (*bone*) zusammenwachsen; **to be ~ on doing sth** etw unbedingt tun wollen; **to ~ to music** vertonen; **to ~ on fire** anstecken; **to ~ free** freilassen; **to ~ sth going** etw in Gang bringen; **to ~ sail** losfahren; **~ about** *vt fus* (*task*) anpacken; **~ aside** *vt* beiseite legen; **~ back** *vt*: **to ~ back (by)** zurückwerfen (um); **~ off** *vi* aufbrechen ♦ *vt* (*explode*) sprengen; (*alarm*) losgehen lassen; (*show up well*) hervorheben; **~ out** *vi*: **to ~ out to do sth** vorhaben, etw zu tun ♦ *vt* (*arrange*) anlegen, arrangieren; (*state*) darlegen; **~ up** *vt* (*organization*) aufziehen; (*record*) aufstellen; (*monument*) erstellen; **~back** *n* Rückschlag *m*; **~ meal** *n* Menü *nt*; **~ menu** *n* Tageskarte *f*

settee [sɛˈtiː] *n* Sofa *nt*

setting [ˈsɛtɪŋ] *n* Hintergrund *m*

settle [ˈsɛtl] *vt* beruhigen; (*pay*) begleichen, bezahlen; (*agree*) regeln ♦ *vi* sich einleben; (*come to rest*) sich niederlassen; (*sink*) sich setzen; (*calm down*) sich beruhigen; **to ~ for**

sth sich mit etw zufrieden geben; **to ~ on sth** sich für etw entscheiden; **to ~ up with sb** mit jdm abrechnen; **~ down** *vi* (*feel at home*) sich einleben; (*calm down*) sich beruhigen; **~ in** *vi* sich eingewöhnen; **~ment** *n* Regelung *f*; (*payment*) Begleichung *f*; (*colony*) Siedlung *f*; **~r** *n* Siedler *m*

setup [ˈsɛtʌp] *n* (*situation*) Lage *f*

seven [ˈsɛvn] *num* sieben; **~teen** *num* siebzehn; **~th** *adj* siebte(r, s) ♦ *n* Siebtel *nt*; **~ty** *num* siebzig

sever [ˈsɛvəʳ] *vt* abtrennen

several [ˈsɛvrəl] *adj* mehrere, verschiedene ♦ *pron* mehrere; **~ of us** einige von uns

severance [ˈsɛvərəns] *n*: **~ pay** Abfindung *f*

severe [sɪˈvɪəʳ] *adj* (*strict*) streng; (*serious*) schwer; (*climate*) rau; **severity** [sɪˈvɛrɪtɪ] *n* Strenge *f*; Schwere *f*; Rauheit *f*

sew [səu] (*pt* sewed, *pp* sewn) *vt, vi* nähen; **~ up** *vt* zunähen

sewage [ˈsuːɪdʒ] *n* Abwässer *pl*

sewer [ˈsuːəʳ] *n* (Abwasser)kanal *m*

sewing [ˈsəuɪŋ] *n* Näharbeit *f*; **~ machine** *n* Nähmaschine *f*

sewn [səun] *pp of* sew

sex [sɛks] *n* Sex *m*; (*gender*) Geschlecht *nt*; **to have ~ with sb** mit jdm Geschlechtsverkehr haben; **~ism** *n* Sexismus *m*; **~ist** *adj* sexistisch ♦ *n* Sexist(in) *m(f)*; **~ual** [ˈsɛksjuəl] *adj* sexuell, geschlechtlich, Geschlechts-; **~uality** [sɛksjuˈælɪtɪ] *n* Sexualität *f*; **~y** *adj* sexy

shabby [ˈʃæbɪ] *adj* (*also fig*) schäbig

shack [ʃæk] *n* Hütte *f*

shackles [ˈʃæklz] *npl* (*also fig*) Fesseln *pl*, Ketten *pl*

shade [ʃeɪd] *n* Schatten *m*; (*for lamp*) Lampenschirm *m*; (*colour*) Farbton *m* ♦ *vt* abschirmen; **in the ~** im Schatten; **a ~ smaller** ein bisschen kleiner

shadow [ˈʃædəu] *n* Schatten *m* ♦ *vt* (*follow*) beschatten ♦ *adj*: **~ cabinet** (*BRIT: POL*) Schattenkabinett *nt*; **~y** *adj* schattig

shady [ˈʃeɪdɪ] *adj* schattig; (*fig*) zwielichtig

shaft [ʃɑːft] *n* (*of spear etc*) Schaft *m*; (*in mine*) Schacht *m*; (*TECH*) Welle *f*; (*of light*)

Strahl m

raggy ['ʃægɪ] adj struppig

hake [ʃeɪk] (pt **shook**, pp **shaken**) vt schütteln, rütteln; (shock) erschüttern ♦ vi (move) schwanken; (tremble) zittern, beben ♦ n (jerk) Schütteln nt, Rütteln nt; **to ~ hands with** die Hand geben +dat; **to ~ one's head** den Kopf schütteln; **~ off** vt abschütteln; **~ up** vt aufschütteln; (fig) aufrütteln; **~n** ['ʃeɪkn] pp of **shake**; **shaky** ['ʃeɪkɪ] adj zittrig; (weak) unsicher

hall [ʃæl] vb aux: **I ~ go** ich werde gehen; **~ I open the door?** soll ich die Tür öffnen?; **I'll buy some cake, ~ I?** soll ich Kuchen kaufen?, ich kaufe Kuchen, oder?

hallow ['ʃæləʊ] adj seicht

ham [ʃæm] n Schein m ♦ adj unecht, falsch

rambles ['ʃæmblz] n Durcheinander nt

hame [ʃeɪm] n Scham f; (disgrace, pity) Schande f ♦ vt beschämen; **it is a ~ that** ist schade, dass; **it is a ~ to do ...** es ist eine Schande, ... zu tun; **what a ~!** wie schade!; **~faced** adj beschämt; **~ful** adj schändlich; **~less** adj schamlos

hampoo [ʃæm'pu:] n Shampoo(n) nt ♦ vt (hair) waschen; **~ and set** n Waschen nt und Legen

hamrock ['ʃæmrɔk] n Kleeblatt nt

handy ['ʃændɪ] n Bier nt mit Limonade

han't [ʃɑ:nt] = **shall not**

hape [ʃeɪp] n Form f ♦ vt formen, gestalten ♦ vi (also: **~ up**) sich entwickeln; **to take ~** Gestalt annehmen; **~d** suffix: **heart-~d** herzförmig; **~less** adj formlos; **~ly** adj wohlproportioniert

hare [ʃeə] n (An)teil m; (FIN) Aktie f ♦ vt teilen; **to ~ out (among/between)** verteilen (unter/zwischen); **~holder** n Aktionär(in) m(f)

hark [ʃɑ:k] n Hai(fisch) m; (swindler) Gauner m

harp [ʃɑ:p] adj scharf; (pin) spitz; (person) clever; (MUS) erhöht ♦ n Kreuz nt ♦ adv zu hoch; **nine o'clock ~** Punkt neun; **~en** vt schärfen; (pencil) spitzen; **~ener** n (also: **pencil ~ener**) Anspitzer m; **~-eyed** adj

scharfsichtig; **~ly** adv (turn, stop) plötzlich; (stand out, contrast) deutlich; (criticize, retort) scharf

shatter ['ʃætə] vt zerschmettern; (fig) zerstören ♦ vi zerspringen

shave [ʃeɪv] n Rasur f ♦ vt rasieren ♦ vi sich rasieren; **to have a ~** sich rasieren (lassen); **~r** n (also: **electric ~r**) Rasierapparat m

shaving ['ʃeɪvɪŋ] n (action) Rasieren nt; **~s** npl (of wood etc) Späne pl; **~ brush** n Rasierpinsel m; **~ cream** n Rasiercreme f; **~ foam** n Rasierschaum m

shawl [ʃɔ:l] n Schal m, Umhang m

she [ʃi:] pron sie ♦ adj weiblich

sheaf [ʃi:f] (pl **sheaves**) n Garbe f

shear [ʃɪə] (pt **sheared**, pp **sheared** or **shorn**) vt scheren; **~ off** vi abbrechen; **~s** npl Heckenschere f

sheath [ʃi:θ] n Scheide f; (condom) Kondom m or nt

sheaves [ʃi:vz] npl of **sheaf**

shed [ʃed] (pt, pp **shed**) n Schuppen m; (for animals) Stall m ♦ vt (leaves etc) verlieren; (tears) vergießen

she'd [ʃi:d] = **she had**; **she would**

sheen [ʃi:n] n Glanz m

sheep [ʃi:p] n inv Schaf nt; **~dog** n Schäferhund m; **~ish** adj verlegen; **~skin** n Schaffell nt

sheer [ʃɪə] adj bloß, rein; (steep) steil; (transparent) (hauch)dünn ♦ adv (directly) direkt

sheet [ʃi:t] n Betttuch nt, Bettlaken nt; (of paper) Blatt nt; (of metal etc) Platte f; (of ice) Fläche f

sheik(h) [ʃeɪk] n Scheich m

shelf [ʃelf] (pl **shelves**) n Bord nt, Regal nt

shell [ʃel] n Schale f; (seashell) Muschel f; (explosive) Granate f ♦ vt (peas) schälen; (fire on) beschießen

she'll [ʃi:l] = **she will**; **she shall**

shellfish ['ʃelfɪʃ] n Schalentier nt; (as food) Meeresfrüchte pl

shell suit n Ballonseidenanzug m

shelter ['ʃeltə] n Schutz m; (air-raid ~) Bunker m ♦ vt schützen, bedecken; (refugees) aufnehmen ♦ vi sich unterstellen;

~ed adj (life) behütet; (spot) geschützt; ~ housing n (for old people) Altenwohnungen pl; (for handicapped people) Behindertenwohnungen pl

shelve [ʃɛlv] vt aufschieben ♦ vi abfallen

shelves [ʃɛlvz] npl of **shelf**

shepherd [ˈʃɛpəd] n Schäfer m ♦ vt treiben, führen; ~'s pie n Auflauf aus Hackfleisch und Kartoffelbrei

sheriff [ˈʃɛrɪf] n Sheriff m; (SCOTTISH) Friedensrichter m

she's [ʃiːz] = **she is; she has**

Shetland [ˈʃɛtlənd] n (also: **the ~s, the ~ Isles**) die Shetlandinseln pl

shield [ʃiːld] n Schild m; (fig) Schirm m ♦ vt (be)schirmen; (TECH) abschirmen

shift [ʃɪft] n Verschiebung f; (work) Schicht f ♦ vt (ver)rücken, verschieben; (arm) wegnehmen ♦ vi sich verschieben; ~less adj (person) träge; ~ work n Schichtarbeit f; ~y adj verschlagen

shilly-shally [ˈʃɪlɪʃælɪ] vi zögern

shin [ʃɪn] n Schienbein nt

shine [ʃaɪn] (pt, pp **shone**) n Glanz m, Schein m ♦ vt polieren ♦ vi scheinen; (fig) glänzen; **to ~ a torch on sb** jdn (mit einer Lampe) anleuchten

shingle [ˈʃɪŋgl] n Strandkies m; ~s npl (MED) Gürtelrose f

shiny [ˈʃaɪnɪ] adj glänzend

ship [ʃɪp] n Schiff nt ♦ vt verschiffen; ~building n Schiffbau m; ~ment n Schiffsladung f; ~per n Verschiffer m; ~ping n (act) Verschiffung f; (~s) Schiffahrt f; ~wreck n Schiffbruch m; (destroyed ~) Wrack nt ♦ vt: **to be ~wrecked** Schiffbruch erleiden; ~yard n Werft f

shire [ʃaɪə] (BRIT) n Grafschaft f

shirk [ʃəːk] vt ausweichen +dat

shirt [ʃəːt] n (Ober)hemd nt; **in ~ sleeves** in Hemdsärmeln

shit [ʃɪt] (inf!) excl Scheiße (!)

shiver [ˈʃɪvə] n Schauer m ♦ vi frösteln, zittern

shoal [ʃəʊl] n (Fisch)schwarm m

shock [ʃɔk] n Erschütterung f; (mental)

Schock m; (ELEC) Schlag m ♦ vt erschüttern; (offend) schockieren; ~ **absorber** n Stoßdämpfer m; ~ed adj geschockt, schockiert, erschüttert; ~ing adj unerhört

shod [ʃɔd] pt, pp of **shoe**

shoddy [ˈʃɔdɪ] adj schäbig

shoe [ʃuː] (pt, pp **shod**) n Schuh m; (of horse) Hufeisen nt ♦ vt (horse) beschlagen; ~brush n Schuhbürste f; ~horn n Schuhlöffel m; ~lace n Schnürsenkel m; ~ **polish** n Schuhcreme f; ~ **shop** n Schuhgeschäft nt; ~string n (fig): **on a ~string** mit sehr wenig Geld

shone [ʃɔn] pt, pp of **shine**

shoo [ʃuː] excl sch; (to dog etc) pfui

shook [ʃuk] pt of **shake**

shoot [ʃuːt] (pt, pp **shot**) n (branch) Schössling m ♦ vt (gun) abfeuern; (goal, arrow) schießen; (person) anschießen; (kill) erschießen; (film) drehen ♦ vi (move quickly) schießen; **to ~ (at)** schießen (auf +acc); ~ **down** vt abschießen; ~ **in** vi hineinschießen; ~ **out** vi hinausschießen; ~ **up** vi (fig) aus dem Boden schießen; ~ing n Schießerei f; ~ing star n Sternschnuppe f

shop [ʃɔp] n (esp BRIT) Geschäft nt, Laden m; (workshop) Werkstatt f ♦ vi (also: **go ~ping**) einkaufen gehen; ~ **assistant** (BRIT) n Verkäufer(in) m(f); ~ **floor** (BRIT) n Werkstatt f; ~ **keeper** n Geschäftsinhaber m; ~ **lifting** n Ladendiebstahl m; ~ **per** n Käufer(in) m(f); ~ **ping** n Einkaufen nt, Einkauf m; ~ **ping bag** n Einkaufstasche f; ~ **ping centre** (US **shopping center**) n Einkaufszentrum nt; ~ **-soiled** adj angeschmutzt; ~ **steward** (BRIT) n (INDUSTRY) Betriebsrat m; ~ **window** n Schaufenster nt

shore [ʃɔː] n Ufer nt; (of sea) Strand m ♦ vt: **to ~ up** abstützen

shorn [ʃɔːn] pp of **shear**

short [ʃɔːt] adj kurz; (person) klein; (curt) kurz angebunden; (measure) zu knapp ♦ n (also: ~ **film**) Kurzfilm m ♦ adv (suddenly) plötzlich ♦ vi (ELEC) einen Kurzschluss haben; ~s npl (clothes) Shorts pl; **to be ~ of sth** nicht genug von etw haben; **in ~** kurz gesagt; **~ of doing sth** ohne so weit zu gehen, etw zu tun; **everything ~ of ...** alles außer ...; **it is ~ for** das ist die Kurzform von; **to cut ~** abkürzen; **to fall ~ of sth** etw nicht erreichen; **to stop ~** plötzlich anhalten; **to stop ~ of** Halt machen vor; **~age** n Knappheit f, Mangel m; **~bread** n Mürbegebäck nt; **~-change** vt: **to ~-change sb** jdm zu wenig herausgeben; **~-circuit** n Kurzschluss m ♦ vi einen Kurzschluss haben ♦ vt kurzschließen; **~coming** n Mangel m; **~(crust) pastry** (BRIT) n Mürbeteig m; **~ cut** n Abkürzung f; **~en** vt (ab)kürzen; (clothes) kürzer machen; **~fall** n Defizit nt; **~hand** (BRIT) n Stenografie f; **~hand typist** (BRIT) n Stenotypistin f; **~ list** (BRIT) n (for job) engere Wahl f; **~-lived** adj kurzlebig; **~ly** adv bald; **~ notice** n: **at ~ notice** kurzfristig; **~-sighted** (BRIT) adj (also fig) kurzsichtig; **~-staffed** adj: **to be ~-staffed** zu wenig Personal haben; **~-stay** n (car park) Kurzparken nt; **~ story** n Kurzgeschichte f; **~-tempered** adj leicht aufbrausend; **~-term** adj (effect) kurzfristig; **~ wave** n (RAD) Kurzwelle f

hot [ʃɔt] pt, pp of **shoot** ♦ n (from gun) Schuss m; (person) Schütze m; (try) Versuch m; (injection) Spritze f; (PHOT) Aufnahme f; **like a ~** wie der Blitz; **~gun** n Schrotflinte f

hould [ʃud] vb aux: **I ~ go now** ich sollte jetzt gehen; **he ~ be there now** er sollte eigentlich schon da sein; **I ~ go if I were you** ich würde gehen, wenn ich du wäre; **I ~ like to** ich möchte gerne

houlder [ˈʃəuldəʳ] n Schulter f; (BRIT: of road): **hard ~** Seitenstreifen m ♦ vt (rifle) schultern; (fig) auf sich nehmen; **~ bag** n Umhängetasche f; **~ blade** n Schulterblatt nt; **~ strap** n (of dress etc) Träger m

houldn't [ˈʃudnt] = **should not**

hout [ʃaut] n Schrei m; (call) Ruf m ♦ vt rufen ♦ vi schreien; **~ down** vt niederbrüllen; **~ing** n Geschrei nt

hove [ʃʌv] n Schubs m, Stoß m ♦ vt

schieben, stoßen, schubsen; (inf: put): **to ~ sth in(to) sth** etw in etw acc hineinschieben; **~ off** vi (NAUT) abstoßen; (fig: inf) abhauen

shovel [ˈʃʌvl] n Schaufel f ♦ vt schaufeln

show [ʃəu] (pt **showed**, pp **shown**) n (display) Schau f; (exhibition) Ausstellung f; (CINE, THEAT) Vorstellung f, Show f ♦ vt zeigen; (kindness) erweisen ♦ vi te sehen sein; **to be on ~** (exhibits etc) ausgestellt sein; **to ~ sb in** jdn hereinführen; **to ~ sb out** jdn hinausbegleiten; **~ off** vi (pej) angeben ♦ vt (display) ausstellen; **~ up** vi (stand out) sich abheben; (arrive) erscheinen ♦ vt aufzeigen; (unmask) bloßstellen; **~ business** n Showbusiness nt; **~down** n Kraftprobe f

shower [ˈʃauəʳ] n Schauer m; (of stones) (Stein)hagel m; (~ bath) Dusche f ♦ vi duschen ♦ vt: **to ~ sb with sth** jdn mit etw überschütten; **~proof** adj Wasser abstoßend

showing [ˈʃəuɪŋ] n Vorführung f

show jumping n Turnierreiten nt

shown [ʃəun] pp of **show**

show: ~-off [ˈʃəuɔf] n Angeber(in) m(f); **~piece** [ˈʃəupiːs] n Paradestück nt; **~room** [ˈʃəurum] n Ausstellungsraum m

shrank [ʃræŋk] pt of **shrink**

shred [ʃred] n Fetzen m ♦ vt zerfetzen; (COOK) raspeln; **~der** n (COOK) Gemüseschneider m; (for documents) Reißwolf m

shrewd [ʃruːd] adj clever

shriek [ʃriːk] n Schrei m ♦ vt, vi kreischen, schreien

shrill [ʃrɪl] adj schrill

shrimp [ʃrɪmp] n Krabbe f, Garnele f

shrine [ʃraɪn] n Schrein m; (fig) Gedenkstätte f

shrink [ʃrɪŋk] (pt **shrank**, pp **shrunk**) vi schrumpfen, eingehen ♦ vt einschrumpfen lassen; **to ~ from doing sth** davor zurückschrecken, etw zu tun; **~age** n Schrumpfung f; **~-wrap** vt einschweißen

shrivel [ˈʃrɪvl] vt, vi (also: **~ up**) schrumpfen, schrumpeln

shroud [ʃraud] *n* Leichentuch *nt* ♦ *vt*: **~ed in mystery** mit einem Geheimnis umgeben

Shrove Tuesday ['ʃrəuv-] *n* Fastnachtsdienstag *m*

shrub [ʃrʌb] *n* Busch *m*, Strauch *m*; **~bery** *n* Gebüsch *nt*

shrug [ʃrʌg] *n* Achselzucken *nt* ♦ *vt*, *vi*: **to ~ (one's shoulders)** die Achseln zucken; **~ off** *vt* auf die leichte Schulter nehmen

shrunk [ʃrʌŋk] *pp* of **shrink**

shudder ['ʃʌdə^r] *n* Schauder *m* ♦ *vi* schaudern

shuffle ['ʃʌfl] *vt* (*cards*) mischen; **to ~ (one's feet)** schlurfen

shun [ʃʌn] *vt* scheuen, (ver)meiden

shunt [ʃʌnt] *vt* rangieren

shut [ʃʌt] (*pt, pp* **shut**) *vt* schließen, zumachen ♦ *vi* sich schließen (lassen); **~ down** *vt, vi* schließen; **~ off** *vt* (*supply*) abdrehen; **~ up** *vi* (*keep quiet*) den Mund halten ♦ *vt* (*close*) zuschließen; **~ter** *n* Fensterladen *m*; (*PHOT*) Verschluss *m*

shuttle ['ʃʌtl] *n* (*plane, train etc*) Pendelflugzeug *nt*/-zug *m etc*; (*space ~*) Raumtransporter *m*; (*also:* **~ service**) Pendelverkehr *m*; **~cock** ['ʃʌtlkɔk] *n* Federball *m*; **~ diplomacy** *n* Pendeldiplomatie *f*

shy [ʃaɪ] *adj* schüchtern; **~ness** *n* Schüchternheit *f*

Siamese [saɪə'miːz] *adj*: **~ cat** Siamkatze *f*

Siberia [saɪ'bɪərɪə] *n* Sibirien *nt*

sibling ['sɪblɪŋ] *n* Geschwister *nt*

Sicily ['sɪsɪlɪ] *n* Sizilien *nt*

sick [sɪk] *adj* krank; (*joke*) makaber; **I feel ~** mir ist schlecht; **I was ~** ich habe gebrochen; **to be ~ of sb/sth** jdn/etw satt haben; **~ bay** *n* (Schiffs)lazarett *nt*; **~en** *vt* (*disgust*) krank machen ♦ *vi* krank werden; **~ening** *adj* (*annoying*) zum Weinen

sickle ['sɪkl] *n* Sichel *f*

sick: ~ leave *n*: **to be on ~ leave** krankgeschrieben sein; **~ly** *adj* kränklich, blass; (*causing nausea*) widerlich; **~ness** *n* Krankheit *f*; (*vomiting*) Übelkeit *f*, Erbrechen *nt*; **~ note** *n* Arbeitsunfähigkeitsbescheinigung *f*; **~ pay** *n* Krankengeld

nt

side [saɪd] *n* Seite *f* ♦ *adj* (*door, entrance*) Seiten-, Neben- ♦ *vi*: **to ~ with sb** jds Partei ergreifen; **by the ~ of** neben; **~ by ~** nebeneinander; **on all ~s** von allen Seiten; **to take ~s (with)** Partei nehmen (für); **from all ~s** von allen Seiten; **~board** *n* Sideboard *nt*; **~boards** (*BRIT*) *npl* Koteletten *pl*; **~burns** *npl* Koteletten *pl*; **~car** *n* Beiwagen *m*; **~ drum** *n* (*MUS*) kleine Trommel; **~ effect** *n* Nebenwirkung *f*; **~light** *n* (*AUT*) Parkleuchte *f*; **~line** *n* (*SPORT*) Seitenlinie *f*; (*fig: hobby*) Nebenbeschäftigung *f*; **~long** *adj* Seiten-; **~ order** *n* Beilage *f*; **~saddle** *adv* im Damensattel; **~ show** *n* Nebenausstellung *f*; **~step** *vt* (*fig*) ausweichen; **~ street** *n* Seitenstraße *f*; **~track** *vt* (*fig*) ablenken; **~walk** (*US*) *n* Bürgersteig *m*; **~ways** *adv* seitwärts

siding ['saɪdɪŋ] *n* Nebengleis *nt*

sidle ['saɪdl] *vi*: **to ~ up (to)** sich heranmachen (an +*acc*)

siege [siːdʒ] *n* Belagerung *f*

sieve [sɪv] *n* Sieb *nt* ♦ *vt* sieben

sift [sɪft] *vt* sieben; (*fig*) sichten

sigh [saɪ] *n* Seufzer *m* ♦ *vi* seufzen

sight [saɪt] *n* (*power of seeing*) Sehvermögen *nt*; (*look*) Blick *m*; (*fact of seeing*) Anblick *m*; (*of gun*) Visier *nt* ♦ *vt* sichten; **in ~** in Sicht; **out of ~** außer Sicht; **~seeing** *n* Besuch *m* von Sehenswürdigkeiten; **to go ~seeing** Sehenswürdigkeiten besichtigen

sign [saɪn] *n* Zeichen *nt*; (*notice, road ~ etc*) Schild *nt* ♦ *vt* unterschreiben; **to ~ sth over to sb** jdm etw überschreiben; **~ on** *vi* (*as unemployed*) sich (arbeitslos) melden ♦ *vt* (*employee*) anstellen; **~ up** *vi* (*MIL*) sich verpflichten ♦ *vt* verpflichten

signal ['sɪgnl] *n* Signal *nt* ♦ *vt* ein Zeichen geben +*dat*; **~man** (*irreg*) *n* (*RAIL*) Stellwerkswärter *m*

signature ['sɪgnətʃə^r] *n* Unterschrift *f*; **~ tune** *n* Erkennungsmelodie *f*

signet ring ['sɪgnət-] *n* Siegelring *m*

significance [sɪg'nɪfɪkəns] *n* Bedeutung *f*

significant [sɪg'nɪfɪkənt] *adj* (*meaning sth*)

bedeutsam; (*important*) bedeutend

gnify ['sɪgnɪfaɪ] *vt* bedeuten; (*show*) andeuten, zu verstehen geben

gn language *n* Zeichensprache *f*, Fingersprache *f*

gnpost ['saɪnpəʊst] *n* Wegweiser *m*

ilence ['saɪləns] *n* Stille *f*; (*of person*) Schweigen *nt* ♦ *vt* zum Schweigen bringen; **~r** *n* (*on gun*) Schalldämpfer *m*; (*BRIT: AUT*) Auspufftopf *m*

ilent ['saɪlənt] *adj* still; (*person*) schweigsam; **to remain ~** schweigen; **~ partner** *n* (*COMM*) stille(r) Teilhaber *m*

ilicon chip ['sɪlɪkən-] *n* Siliciumchip *m*, Siliziumchip *m*

ilk [sɪlk] *n* Seide *f* ♦ *adj* seiden, Seiden-; **~y** *adj* seidig

illy ['sɪlɪ] *adj* dumm, albern

ilt [sɪlt] *n* Schlamm *m*, Schlick *m*

ilver ['sɪlvər] *n* Silber *nt* ♦ *adj* silbern, Silber-; **~ paper** (*BRIT*) *n* Silberpapier *nt*; **~-plated** *adj* versilbert; **~smith** *n* Silberschmied *m*; **~ware** *n* Silber *nt*; **~y** *adj* silbern

imilar ['sɪmɪlər] *adj*: **~ (to)** ähnlich (+*dat*); **~ity** [sɪmɪ'lærɪtɪ] *n* Ähnlichkeit *f*; **~ly** *adv* in ähnlicher Weise

immer ['sɪmər] *vi* sieden ♦ *vt* sieden lassen

imple ['sɪmpl] *adj* einfach; **~(-minded)** *adj* einfältig

implicity [sɪm'plɪsɪtɪ] *n* Einfachheit *f*; (*of person*) Einfältigkeit *f*

implify ['sɪmplɪfaɪ] *vt* vereinfachen

imply ['sɪmplɪ] *adv* einfach

imulate ['sɪmjuleɪt] *vt* simulieren

imultaneous [sɪməl'teɪnɪəs] *adj* gleichzeitig

in [sɪn] *n* Sünde *f* ♦ *vi* sündigen

ince [sɪns] *adv* seither ♦ *prep* seit, seitdem ♦ *conj* (*time*) seit; (*because*) da, weil; **~ then** seitdem

incere [sɪn'sɪər] *adj* aufrichtig; **~ly** *adv*: **yours ~ly** mit freundlichen Grüßen; **sincerity** [sɪn'serɪtɪ] *n* Aufrichtigkeit *f*

inew ['sɪnjuː] *n* Sehne *f*

inful ['sɪnful] *adj* sündig, sündhaft

ing [sɪŋ] (*pt* sang, *pp* sung) *vt*, *vi* singen

ingapore [sɪŋgə'pɔːr] *n* Singapur *nt*

singe [sɪndʒ] *vt* versengen

singer ['sɪŋər] *n* Sänger(in) *m(f)*

singing ['sɪŋɪŋ] *n* Singen *nt*, Gesang *m*

single ['sɪŋgl] *adj* (*one only*) einzig; (*bed, room*) Einzel-, einzeln; (*unmarried*) ledig; (*BRIT: ticket*) einfach; (*having one part only*) einzeln ♦ *n* (*BRIT: also:* **~ ticket**) einfache Fahrkarte *f*; **in ~ file** hintereinander; **~ out** *vt* aussuchen, auswählen; **~ bed** *n* Einzelbett *nt*; **~-breasted** *adj* einreihig; **~-handed** *adj* allein; **~-minded** *adj* zielstrebig; **~ parent** *n* Alleinerziehende(r) *f(m)*; **~ room** *n* Einzelzimmer *nt*; **~s** *n* (*TENNIS*) Einzel *nt*; **~-track road** *n* einspurige Straße (mit Ausweichstellen); **singly** *adv* einzeln, allein

singular ['sɪŋgjulər] *adj* (*odd*) merkwürdig, seltsam ♦ *n* (*GRAM*) Einzahl *f*, Singular *m*

sinister ['sɪnɪstər] *adj* (*evil*) böse; (*ghostly*) unheimlich

sink [sɪŋk] (*pt* sank, *pp* sunk) *n* Spülbecken *nt* ♦ *vt* (*ship*) versenken ♦ *vi* sinken; **to ~ sth into** (*teeth, claws*) etw schlagen in +*acc*; **~ in** *vi* (*news etc*) eingehen

sinner ['sɪnər] *n* Sünder(in) *m(f)*

sinus ['saɪnəs] *n* (*ANAT*) Sinus *m*

sip [sɪp] *n* Schlückchen *nt* ♦ *vt* nippen an +*dat*

siphon ['saɪfən] *n* Siphon(flasche *f*) *m*; **~ off** *vt* absaugen; (*fig*) abschöpfen

sir [sər] *n* (*respect*) Herr *m*; (*knight*) Sir *m*; **S~ John Smith** Sir John Smith; **yes ~** ja(wohl, mein Herr)

siren ['saɪərn] *n* Sirene *f*

sirloin ['səːlɔɪn] *n* Lendenstück *nt*

sissy ['sɪsɪ] (*inf*) *n* Waschlappen *m*

sister ['sɪstər] *n* Schwester *f*; (*BRIT: nurse*) Oberschwester *f*; (*nun*) Ordensschwester *f*; **~-in-law** *n* Schwägerin *f*

sit [sɪt] (*pt*, *pp* sat) *vi* sitzen; (*hold session*) tagen ♦ *vt* (*exam*) machen; **~ down** *vi* sich hinsetzen; **~ in on** *vt fus* dabei sein bei; **~ up** *vi* (*after lying*) sich aufsetzen; (*straight*) sich gerade setzen; (*at night*) aufbleiben

sitcom ['sɪtkɔm] *n abbr* (= situation comedy) Situationskomödie *f*

site [saɪt] *n* Platz *m*; (*also:* **building ~**)

Baustelle f ♦ vt legen

sitting ['sɪtɪŋ] n (meeting) Sitzung f; ~ **room** n Wohnzimmer nt

situated ['sɪtjueɪtɪd] adj: **to be** ~ liegen

situation [sɪtju'eɪʃən] n Situation f, Lage f; (place) Lage f; (employment) Stelle f; **"~s vacant"** (BRIT) „Stellenangebote" pl

six [sɪks] num sechs; ~**teen** num sechzehn; ~**th** adj sechste(r, s) ♦ n Sechstel f; ~**ty** num sechzig

size [saɪz] n Größe f; (of project) Umfang m; ~ **up** vt (assess) abschätzen, einschätzen; ~**able** adj ziemlich groß, ansehnlich

sizzle ['sɪzl] vi zischen; (COOK) brutzeln

skate [skeɪt] n Schlittschuh m; (fish: pl inv) Rochen m ♦ vi Schlittschuh laufen; ~**board** n Skateboard nt; ~**boarding** n Skateboardfahren nt; ~**r** n Schlittschuhläufer(in) m(f); **skating** ['skeɪtɪŋ] n Eislauf m; **to go skating** Eis laufen gehen; **skating rink** n Eisbahn f

skeleton ['skelɪtn] n Skelett nt; (fig) Gerüst nt; ~ **key** n Dietrich m; ~ **staff** n Notbesetzung f

skeptical ['skeptɪkl] (US) adj = **sceptical**

sketch [sketʃ] n Skizze f; (THEAT) Sketch m ♦ vt skizzieren; ~**book** n Skizzenbuch nt; ~**y** adj skizzenhaft

skewer ['skjuːə'] n Fleischspieß m

ski [skiː] n Ski m, Schi m ♦ vi Ski or Schi laufen; ~ **boot** n Skistiefel m

skid [skɪd] n (AUT) Schleudern nt ♦ vi rutschen; (AUT) schleudern

ski: ~**er** ['skiːə'] n Skiläufer(in) m(f); ~**ing** ['skiːɪŋ] n: **to go ~ing** Ski laufen gehen; ~~**jump** n Sprungschanze f ♦ vi Ski springen

skilful ['skɪlful] adj geschickt

ski-lift n Skilift m

skill [skɪl] n Können nt; (worker) Fach-, gelernt

skim [skɪm] vt (liquid) abschöpfen; (glide over) gleiten über +acc ♦ vi: ~ **through** (book) überfliegen; ~**med milk** n Magermilch f

skimp [skɪmp] vt (do carelessly) oberflächlich tun; ~**y** adj (dress) knapp

skin [skɪn] n Haut f; (peel) Schale f ♦ vt

abhäuten; schälen; ~ **cancer** n Hautkrebs m; ~~**deep** adj oberflächlich; ~ **diving** n Schwimmtauchen nt; ~**head** n Skinhead m; ~**ny** adj dünn; ~**tight** adj (dress etc) hauteng

skip [skɪp] n Sprung m ♦ vi hüpfen; (with rope) Seil springen ♦ vt (pass over) übergehen

ski: ~ **pants** npl Skihosen pl; ~ **pass** n Skipass nt; ~ **pole** n Skistock m

skipper ['skɪpə'] n Kapitän m ♦ vt führen

skipping rope ['skɪpɪŋ-] (BRIT) n Hüpfseil nt

skirmish ['skɜːmɪʃ] n Scharmützel nt

skirt [skɜːt] n Rock m ♦ vt herumgehen um; (fig) umgehen; ~**ing board** (BRIT) n Fußleiste f

ski suit n Skianzug m

skit [skɪt] n Parodie f

ski tow n Schlepplift m

skittle ['skɪtl] n Kegel m; ~**s** n (game) Kegeln nt

skive [skaɪv] (BRIT: inf) vi schwänzen

skulk [skʌlk] vi sich herumdrücken

skull [skʌl] n Schädel m

skunk [skʌŋk] n Stinktier nt

sky [skaɪ] n Himmel m; ~**light** n Oberlicht nt; ~**scraper** n Wolkenkratzer m

slab [slæb] n (of stone) Platte f

slack [slæk] adj (loose) locker; (business) flau; (careless) nachlässig, lasch ♦ vi nachlässig sein ♦ n: **to take up the** ~ straff ziehen; ~**s** npl (trousers) Hose(n pl) f; ~**en** vi (also: ~**en off**) locker werden; (: slow down) stocken, nachlassen ♦ vt (: loosen) lockern

slag [slæg] (BRIT) vt: ~ **off** (criticize) (he)runtermachen

slag heap [slæg-] n Halde f

slain [sleɪn] pp of **slay**

slam [slæm] n Knall m ♦ vt (door) zuschlagen; (throw down) knallen ♦ vi zuschlagen

slander ['slɑːndə'] n Verleumdung f ♦ vt verleumden

slang [slæŋ] n Slang m; (jargon) Jargon m

slant [slɑːnt] n Schräge f; (fig) Tendenz f ♦ vt schräg legen ♦ vi schräg liegen; ~**ed** adj schräg; ~**ing** adj schräg

slap [slæp] n Klaps m ♦ vt einen Klaps geben +dat ♦ adv (directly) geradewegs; ~dash adj salopp; ~stick n (comedy) Klamauk m; ~-up (BRIT) (meal) erstklassig, prima

slash [slæʃ] n Schnittwunde f ♦ vt (auf)schlitzen

slat [slæt] n Leiste f

slate [sleɪt] n (stone) Schiefer m; (roofing) Dachziegel m ♦ vt (criticize) verreißen

slaughter ['slɔːtə^r] n (of animals) Schlachten nt; (of people) Gemetzel nt ♦ vt schlachten; (people) niedermetzeln; ~house n Schlachthof m

Slav [slɑːv] adj slawisch

slave [sleɪv] n Sklave m, Sklavin f ♦ vi schuften, sich schinden; ~ry n Sklaverei f

slay [sleɪ] (pt slew, pp slain) vt ermorden

sleazy ['sliːzɪ] adj (place) schmierig

sledge [sledʒ] n Schlitten m

sledgehammer ['sledʒhæmə^r] n Schmiedehammer m

sledging n Schlittenfahren nt

sleek [sliːk] adj glatt; (shape) rassig

sleep [sliːp] (pt, pp slept) n Schlaf m ♦ vi schlafen; **to go to ~** einschlafen; **~ in** vi ausschlafen; (oversleep) verschlafen; ~er n (person) Schläfer m; (BRIT: RAIL) Schlafwagen m; (: beam) Schwelle f; ~ing bag n Schlafsack m; ~ing car n Schlafwagen m; ~ing partner n = silent partner; ~ing pill n Schlaftablette f; ~less adj (night) schlaflos; ~walker n Schlafwandler(in) m(f); ~y adj schläfrig

sleet [sliːt] n Schneeregen m

sleeve [sliːv] n Ärmel m; (of record) Umschlag m; ~less adj ärmellos

sleigh [sleɪ] n Pferdeschlitten m

sleight [slaɪt] n: ~ **of hand** Fingerfertigkeit f

slender ['slendə^r] adj schlank; (fig) gering

slept [slept] pt, pp of **sleep**

slew [sluː] vi (veer) (herum)schwenken ♦ pt of **slay**

slice [slaɪs] n Scheibe f ♦ vt in Scheiben schneiden

slick [slɪk] adj (clever) raffiniert, aalglatt ♦ n Ölteppich m

slid [slɪd] pt, pp of **slide**

slide [slaɪd] n (pt, pp slid) n Rutschbahn f; (PHOT) Dia(positiv) nt; (BRIT: for hair) (Haar)spange f ♦ vt schieben ♦ vi (slip) gleiten, rutschen; **sliding** ['slaɪdɪŋ] adj (door) Schiebe-; **sliding scale** n gleitende Skala f

slight [slaɪt] adj zierlich; (trivial) geringfügig; (small) gering ♦ n Kränkung f ♦ vt (offend) kränken; **not in the ~est** nicht im Geringsten; ~ly adv etwas, ein bisschen

slim [slɪm] adj schlank; (book) dünn; (chance) gering ♦ vi eine Schlankheitskur machen

slime [slaɪm] n Schleim m

slimming ['slɪmɪŋ] n Schlankheitskur f

slimy ['slaɪmɪ] adj glitschig; (dirty) schlammig; (person) schmierig

sling [slɪŋ] (pt, pp slung) n Schlinge f; (weapon) Schleuder f ♦ vt schleudern

slip [slɪp] n (mistake) Flüchtigkeitsfehler m; (petticoat) Unterrock m; (of paper) Zettel m ♦ vt (put) stecken, schieben ♦ vi (lose balance) ausrutschen; (move) gleiten, rutschen; (decline) nachlassen; (move smoothly): **to ~ in/out** (person) hinein-/ hinausschlüpfen; **to give sb the ~** jdm entwischen; **~ of the tongue** Versprecher m; **it ~ped my mind** das ist mir entfallen; **to ~ sth on/off** etw über-/abstreifen; ~ **away** vi sich wegstehlen; ~ **in** vt hineingleiten lassen ♦ vi (errors) sich einschleichen; ~ped disc n Bandscheibenschaden m

slipper ['slɪpə^r] n Hausschuh m

slippery ['slɪpərɪ] adj glatt

slip: ~ **road** (BRIT) n Auffahrt f/Ausfahrt f; ~**shod** adj schlampig; ~-up n Panne f; ~**way** n Auslaufbahn f

slit [slɪt] (pt, pp slit) n Schlitz m ♦ vt aufschlitzen

slither ['slɪðə^r] vi schlittern; (snake) sich schlängeln

sliver ['slɪvə^r] n (of glass, wood) Splitter m; (of cheese) Scheibchen nt

slob [slɒb] (inf) n Klotz m

slog [slɒg] vi (work hard) schuften ♦ n: **it was a ~** es war eine Plackerei

slogan ['sləʊgən] n Schlagwort nt; (COMM)

Werbespruch m

slop [slɔp] vi (also: ~ **over**) überschwappen
♦ vt verschütten

slope [sləup] n Neigung f; (of mountains)
(Ab)hang m ♦ vi: **to ~ down** sich senken; **to
~ up** ansteigen; **sloping** ['sləupɪŋ] adj
schräg

sloppy ['slɔpɪ] adj schlampig

slot [slɔt] n Schlitz m ♦ vt: **to ~ sth in** etw
einlegen

sloth [sləuθ] n (laziness) Faulheit f

slot machine n (BRIT) Automat m; (for
gambling) Spielautomat m

slouch [slautʃ] vi: **to ~ about** (laze)
herumhängen (inf)

slovenly ['slʌvənlɪ] adj schlampig; (speech)
salopp

slow [sləu] adj langsam ♦ adv langsam; **to
be ~** (clock) nachgehen; (stupid)
begriffsstutzig sein; "**~**" (road sign)
„Langsam"; **in ~ motion** in Zeitlupe; **~
down** vi langsamer werden ♦ vt
verlangsamen; **~ up** vi sich verlangsamen,
sich verzögern ♦ vt aufhalten, langsamer
machen; **~ly** adv langsam

sludge [slʌdʒ] n Schlamm m

slug [slʌg] n Nacktschnecke f; (inf: bullet)
Kugel f

sluggish ['slʌgɪʃ] adj träge; (COMM)
schleppend

sluice [slu:s] n Schleuse f

slum [slʌm] n (house) Elendsquartier nt

slump [slʌmp] n Rückgang m ♦ vi fallen,
stürzen

slung [slʌŋ] pt, pp of **sling**

slur [slɜ:r] n Undeutlichkeit f; (insult)
Verleumdung f; **~red** [slɜ:d] adj
(pronunciation) undeutlich

slush [slʌʃ] n (snow) Schneematsch m; ~
fund n Schmiergeldfonds m

slut [slʌt] n Schlampe f

sly [slaɪ] adj schlau

smack [smæk] n Klaps m ♦ vt einen Klaps
geben +dat ♦ vi: **to ~ of** riechen nach; **to ~
one's lips** schmatzen, sich dat die Lippen
lecken

small [smɔ:l] adj klein; **in the ~ hours** in den
frühen Morgenstunden; ~ **ads** (BRIT) npl
Kleinanzeigen pl; ~ **change** n Kleingeld nt;
~holder (BRIT) n Kleinbauer m; **~pox** n
Pocken pl; ~ **talk** n Geplauder nt

smart [smɑ:t] adj (fashionable) elegant,
schick; (neat) adrett; (clever) clever; (quick)
scharf ♦ vi brennen, schmerzen; ~ **card** n
Chipkarte f; **~en up** vi sich in Schale
werfen ♦ vt herausputzen

smash [smæʃ] n Zusammenstoß m; (TENNIS)
Schmetterball m ♦ vt (break) zerschmettern;
(destroy) vernichten ♦ vi (break) zersplittern,
zerspringen; **~ing** (inf) adj toll

smattering ['smætərɪŋ] n oberflächliche
Kenntnis f

smear [smɪər] n Fleck m ♦ vt beschmieren

smell [smel] (pt, pp **smelt** or **smelled**) n
Geruch m; (sense) Geruchssinn m ♦ vt
riechen ♦ vi: **to ~ (of)** riechen (nach);
(fragrantly) duften (nach); **~y** adj übel
riechend

smile [smaɪl] n Lächeln nt ♦ vi lächeln

smiling ['smaɪlɪŋ] adj lächelnd

smirk [smɜ:k] n blöde(s) Grinsen nt

smock [smɔk] n Kittel m

smoke [sməuk] n Rauch m ♦ vt rauchen;
(food) räuchern ♦ vi rauchen; **~d** adj
(bacon) geräuchert; (glass) Rauch-; **~r** n
Raucher(in) m(f); (RAIL) Raucherabteil nt; ~
screen n Rauchwand f

smoking ['sməukɪŋ] n: "**no ~**" „Rauchen
verboten"; ~ **compartment** (BRIT), ~ **car**
(US) n Raucherabteil nt

smoky ['sməukɪ] adj rauchig; (room)
verraucht; (taste) geräuchert

smolder ['sməuldər] (US) vi = **smoulder**

smooth [smu:ð] adj glatt ♦ vt (also: ~ **out**)
glätten, glatt streichen

smother ['smʌðər] vt ersticken

smoulder ['sməuldər] (US **smolder**) vi
schwelen

smudge [smʌdʒ] n Schmutzfleck m ♦ vt
beschmieren

smug [smʌg] adj selbstgefällig

smuggle ['smʌgl] vt schmuggeln; **~r** n
Schmuggler m

smuggling ['smʌglɪŋ] n Schmuggel m

smutty ['smʌtɪ] *adj* schmutzig

snack [snæk] *n* Imbiss *m*; **~ bar** *n* Imbissstube *f*

snag [snæg] *n* Haken *m*

snail [sneɪl] *n* Schnecke *f*

snake [sneɪk] *n* Schlange *f*

snap [snæp] *n* Schnappen *nt*; *(photograph)* Schnappschuss *m* ♦ *adj (decision)* schnell ♦ *vt (break)* zerbrechen; *(PHOT)* knipsen ♦ *vi (break)* brechen; *(speak)* anfauchen; **to ~ shut** zuschnappen; **~ at** *vt fus* schnappen nach; **~ off** *vt (break)* abbrechen; **~ up** *vt* aufschnappen; **~shot** *n* Schnappschuss *m*

snare [snɛəˈ] *n* Schlinge *f* ♦ *vt* mit einer Schlinge fangen

snarl [snɑːl] *n* Zähnefletschen *nt* ♦ *vi (dog)* knurren

snatch [snætʃ] *n (small amount)* Bruchteil *m* ♦ *vt* schnappen, packen

sneak [sniːk] *vi* schleichen ♦ *n (inf)* Petze(r) *mf*; **~ers** ['sniːkəz] *(US)* npl Freizeitschuhe *pl*; **~y** ['sniːkɪ] *adj* raffiniert

sneer [snɪəˈ] *n* Hohnlächeln *nt* ♦ *vi* spötteln

sneeze [sniːz] *n* Niesen *nt* ♦ *vi* niesen

sniff [snɪf] *n* Schnüffeln *nt* ♦ *vi* schnieben; *(smell)* schnüffeln ♦ *vt* schnuppern

snigger ['snɪgəˈ] *n* Kichern *nt* ♦ *vi* hämisch kichern

snip [snɪp] *n* Schnippel *m*, Schnipsel *m* ♦ *vt* schnippeln

sniper ['snaɪpəˈ] *n* Heckenschütze *m*

snippet ['snɪpɪt] *n* Schnipsel *m*; *(of conversation)* Fetzen *m*

snivelling ['snɪvlɪŋ] *adj* weinerlich

snob [snɒb] *n* Snob *m*

snooker ['snuːkəˈ] *n* Snooker *nt*

snoop [snuːp] *vi*: **to ~ about** herumschnüffeln

snooze [snuːz] *n* Nickerchen *nt* ♦ *vi* ein Nickerchen machen, dösen

snore [snɔːˈ] *vi* schnarchen ♦ *n* Schnarchen *nt*

snorkel ['snɔːkl] *n* Schnorchel *m*

snort [snɔːt] *n* Schnauben *nt* ♦ *vi* schnauben

snout [snaut] *n* Schnauze *f*

snow [snəu] *n* Schnee *m* ♦ *vi* schneien; **~ball** *n* Schneeball *m* ♦ *vi* eskalieren; **~bound** *adj* eingeschneit; **~drift** *n* Schneewehe *f*; **~drop** *n* Schneeglöckchen *nt*; **~fall** *n* Schneefall *m*; **~flake** *n* Schneeflocke *f*; **~man** *(irreg)* *n* Schneemann *m*; **~plough** *(US* **snowplow)** *n* Schneepflug *m*; **~ shoe** *n* Schneeschuh *m*; **~storm** *n* Schneesturm *m*

snub [snʌb] *vt* schroff abfertigen ♦ *n* Verweis *m*; **~-nosed** *adj* stupsnasig

snuff [snʌf] *n* Schnupftabak *m*

snug [snʌg] *adj* gemütlich, behaglich

snuggle ['snʌgl] *vi*: **to ~ up to sb** sich an jdn kuscheln

---

KEYWORD

so [səu] *adv* **1** *(thus)* so; *(likewise)* auch; **so saying he walked away** indem er das sagte, ging er; **if so** wenn ja; **I didn't do it – you did so!** ich hab das nicht gemacht – hast du wohl!; **so do I, so am I** *etc* ich auch; **so it is!** tatsächlich!; **I hope/think so** hoffentlich/ich glaube schon; **so far** bis jetzt

2 *(in comparisons etc: to such a degree)* so; **so quickly/big (that)** so schnell/groß, dass; **I'm so glad to see you** ich freue mich so, dich zu sehen

3: **so many** so viele; **so much work** so viel Arbeit; **I love you so much** ich liebe dich so sehr

4 *(phrases)*: **10 or so** etwa 10; **so long!** *(inf: goodbye)* tschüss!

♦ *conj* **1** *(expressing purpose)*: **so as to** um ... zu; **so (that)** damit

2 *(expressing result)* also; **so I was right after all** ich hatte also doch Recht; **so you see ...** wie du siehst ...

---

soak [səuk] *vt* durchnässen; *(leave in liquid)* einweichen ♦ *vi* (ein)weichen; **~ in** *vi* einsickern; **~ up** *vt* aufsaugen; **~ed** *adj* völlig durchnässt; **~ing** *adj* klitschnass, patschnass

so-and-so ['səuənsəu] *n (somebody)* Soundso *m*

soap [səup] *n* Seife *f*; **~flakes** *npl* Seifenflocken *pl*; **~ opera** *n* Familienserie *f*

(*im Fernsehen, Radio*); **~ powder** *n*
Waschpulver *nt*; **~y** *adj* seifig, Seifen-
soar [sɔːr] *vi* aufsteigen; (*prices*) in die Höhe
schnellen
sob [sɔb] *n* Schluchzen *nt* ♦ *vi* schluchzen
sober ['səubər] *adj* (*also fig*) nüchtern; **~ up**
vi nüchtern werden
so-called ['səu'kɔːld] *adj* so genannt
soccer ['sɔkər] *n* Fußball *m*
sociable ['səuʃəbl] *adj* gesellig
social ['səuʃl] *adj* sozial; (*friendly, living with
others*) gesellig ♦ *n* gesellige(r) Abend *m*; **~
club** *n* Verein *m* (*für Freizeitgestaltung*);
~ism *n* Sozialismus *m*; **~ist** *n* Sozialist(in)
m(f) ♦ *adj* sozialistisch; **~ize** *vi*: **to ~ize
(with)** gesellschaftlich verkehren (mit); **~ly**
adv gesellschaftlich, privat; **~ security** *n*
Sozialversicherung *f*; **~ work** *n* Sozialarbeit
f; **~ worker** *n* Sozialarbeiter(in) *m(f)*
society [sə'saɪətɪ] *n* Gesellschaft *f*;
(*fashionable world*) die große Welt
sociology [səusɪ'ɔlədʒɪ] *n* Soziologie *f*
sock [sɔk] *n* Socke *f*
socket ['sɔkɪt] *n* (*ELEC*) Steckdose *f*; (*of eye*)
Augenhöhle *f*
sod [sɔd] *n* Rasenstück *nt*; (*inf!*) Saukerl *m* (!)
soda ['səudə] *n* Soda *f*; (*also:* **~ water**)
Soda(wasser) *nt*; (*US: also:* **~ pop**)
Limonade *f*
sodden ['sɔdn] *adj* durchweicht
sodium ['səudɪəm] *n* Natrium *nt*
sofa ['səufə] *n* Sofa *nt*
soft [sɔft] *adj* weich; (*not loud*) leise; (*weak*)
nachgiebig; **~ drink** *n* alkoholfreie(s)
Getränk *nt*; **~en** ['sɔfn] *vt* weich machen;
(*blow*) abschwächen, mildern ♦ *vi* weich
werden; **~ly** *adv* sanft; leise; **~ness** *n*
Weichheit *f*; (*fig*) Sanftheit *f*
software ['sɔftweər] *n* (*COMPUT*) Software *f*
soggy ['sɔgɪ] *adj* (*ground*) sumpfig; (*bread*)
aufgeweicht
soil [sɔɪl] *n* Erde *f* ♦ *vt* beschmutzen
solace ['sɔlɪs] *n* Trost *m*
solar ['səulər] *adj* Sonnen-; **~ cell** *n*
Solarzelle *f*; **~ energy** *n* Sonnenenergie *f*;
~ panel *n* Sonnenkollektor *m*; **~ power** *n*
Sonnenenergie *f*

sold [səuld] *pt, pp of* **sell**; **~ out** (*COMM*)
ausverkauft
solder ['səuldər] *vt* löten
soldier ['səuldʒər] *n* Soldat *m*
sole [səul] *n* Sohle *f*; (*fish*) Seezunge *f* ♦ *adj*
alleinig, Allein-; **~ly** *adv* ausschließlich
solemn ['sɔləm] *adj* feierlich
sole trader *n* (*COMM*) Einzelunternehmen
nt
solicit [sə'lɪsɪt] *vt* (*request*) bitten um ♦ *vi*
(*prostitute*) Kunden anwerben
solicitor [sə'lɪsɪtər] *n* Rechtsanwalt *m*/-
anwältin *f*
solid ['sɔlɪd] *adj* (*hard*) fest; (*of same material,
not hollow*) massiv; (*without break*) voll,
ganz; (*reliable, sensible*) solide ♦ *n* Festkörper
m; **~arity** [sɔlɪ'dærɪtɪ] *n* Solidarität *f*; **~ify**
[sə'lɪdɪfaɪ] *vi* fest werden
solitary ['sɔlɪtərɪ] *adj* einsam, einzeln; **~
confinement** *n* Einzelhaft *f*
solitude ['sɔlɪtjuːd] *n* Einsamkeit *f*
solo ['səuləu] *n* Solo *nt*; **~ist** ['səuləuɪst] *n*
Solist(in) *m(f)*
soluble ['sɔljubl] *adj* (*substance*) löslich;
(*problem*) (auf)lösbar
solution [sə'luːʃən] *n* (*also fig*) Lösung *f*; (*of
mystery*) Erklärung *f*
solve [sɔlv] *vt* (auf)lösen
solvent ['sɔlvənt] *adj* (*FIN*) zahlungsfähig ♦ *n*
(*CHEM*) Lösungsmittel *nt*
sombre ['sɔmbər] (*US* **somber**) *adj* düster

---KEYWORD---

some [sʌm] *adj* **1** (*a certain amount or
number of*) einige; (*a few*) ein paar; (*with
singular nouns*) etwas; **some tea/biscuits**
etwas Tee/ein paar Plätzchen; **I've got
some money, but not much** ich habe ein
bisschen Geld, aber nicht viel
2 (*certain: in contrasts*) manche(r, s); **some
people say that ...** manche Leute sagen,
dass ...
3 (*unspecified*) irgendein(e); **some woman
was asking for you** da hat eine Frau nach
Ihnen gefragt; **some day** eines Tages;
some day next week irgendwann nächste
Woche

♦ *pron* 1 (*a certain number*) einige; **have you got some?** haben Sie welche?
2 (*a certain amount*) etwas; **I've read some of the book** ich habe das Buch teilweise gelesen
♦ *adv*: **some 10 people** etwa 10 Leute

somebody ['sʌmbədɪ] *pron* = **someone**
somehow ['sʌmhaʊ] *adv* (*in some way, for some reason*) irgendwie
someone ['sʌmwʌn] *pron* jemand; (*direct obj*) jemand(en); (*indirect obj*) jemandem
someplace ['sʌmpleɪs] (*US*) *adv* = **somewhere**
somersault ['sʌməsɔːlt] *n* Salto *m* ♦ *vi* einen Salto machen
something ['sʌmθɪŋ] *pron* etwas
sometime ['sʌmtaɪm] *adv* (*irgend*)einmal
sometimes ['sʌmtaɪmz] *adv* manchmal
somewhat ['sʌmwɒt] *adv* etwas
somewhere ['sʌmweəʳ] *adv* irgendwo; (*to a place*) irgendwohin; **~ else** irgendwo anders
son [sʌn] *n* Sohn *m*
sonar ['səʊnɑːʳ] *n* Echolot *nt*
song [sɒŋ] *n* Lied *nt*
sonic boom ['sɒnɪk-] *n* Überschallknall *m*
son-in-law ['sʌnɪnlɔː] *n* Schwiegersohn *m*
soon [suːn] *adv* bald; **~ afterwards** kurz danach; **~er** *adv* (*time*) früher; (*for preference*) lieber; **~er or later** früher oder später
soot [sʊt] *n* Ruß *m*
soothe [suːð] *vt* (*person*) beruhigen; (*pain*) lindern
sophisticated [sə'fɪstɪkeɪtɪd] *adj* (*person*) kultiviert; (*machinery*) hoch entwickelt
sophomore ['sɒfəmɔːʳ] (*US*) *n* College-student *m* im 2. Jahr
soporific [sɒpə'rɪfɪk] *adj* einschläfernd
sopping ['sɒpɪŋ] *adj* patschnass
soppy ['sɒpɪ] (*inf*) *adj* schmalzig
soprano [sə'prɑːnəʊ] *n* Sopran *m*
sorcerer ['sɔːsərəʳ] *n* Hexenmeister *m*
sordid ['sɔːdɪd] *adj* erbärmlich
sore [sɔːʳ] *adj* schmerzend; (*point*) wund ♦ *n* Wunde *f*; **~ly** *adv* (*tempted*) stark, sehr

sorrow ['sɒrəʊ] *n* Kummer *m*, Leid *nt*; **~ful** *adj* sorgenvoll
sorry ['sɒrɪ] *adj* traurig, erbärmlich; **~!** Entschuldigung!; **to feel ~ for sb** jdn bemitleiden; **I feel ~ for him** er tut mir Leid; **~?** (*pardon*) wie bitte?
sort [sɔːt] *n* Art *f*, Sorte *f* ♦ *vt* (*also*: **~ out**: *papers*) sortieren; (: *problems*) sichten, in Ordnung bringen; **~ing office** *n* Sortierstelle *f*
SOS *n* SOS *nt*
so-so ['səʊsəʊ] *adv* so(so) lala
sought [sɔːt] *pt, pp of* **seek**
soul [səʊl] *n* Seele *f*; (*music*) Soul *m*; **~-destroying** *adj* trostlos; **~ful** *adj* seelenvoll
sound [saʊnd] *adj* (*healthy*) gesund; (*safe*) sicher; (*sensible*) vernünftig; (*theory*) stichhaltig; (*thorough*) tüchtig, gehörig ♦ *adv*: **to be ~ asleep** fest schlafen ♦ *n* (*noise*) Geräusch *nt*, Laut *m*; (*GEOG*) Sund *m* ♦ *vt* erschallen lassen; (*alarm*) (Alarm) schlagen ♦ *vi* (*make a ~*) schallen, tönen; (*seem*) klingen; **to ~ like** sich anhören wie; **~ out** *vt* erforschen; (*person*) auf den Zahn fühlen *+dat*; **~ barrier** *n* Schallmauer *f*; **~ bite** *n* (*RAD, TV*) prägnante(s) Zitat *nt*; **~ effects** *npl* Toneffekte *pl*; **~ly** *adv* (*sleep*) fest; (*beat*) tüchtig; **~proof** *adj* (*room*) schalldicht; **~ track** *n* Tonstreifen *m*; (*music*) Filmmusik *f*
soup [suːp] *n* Suppe *f*; **~ plate** *n* Suppenteller *m*; **~spoon** *n* Suppenlöffel *m*
sour ['saʊəʳ] *adj* (*also fig*) sauer; **it's ~ grapes** (*fig*) die Trauben hängen zu hoch
source [sɔːs] *n* (*also fig*) Quelle *f*
south [saʊθ] *n* Süden *m* ♦ *adj* Süd-, südlich ♦ *adv* nach Süden, südwärts; **S~ Africa** *n* Südafrika *nt*; **S~ African** *adj* südafrikanisch ♦ *n* Südafrikaner(in) *m(f)*; **S~ America** *n* Südamerika *nt*; **S~ American** *adj* südamerikanisch ♦ *n* Südamerikaner(in) *m(f)*; **~-east** *n* Südosten *m*; **~erly** ['sʌðəlɪ] *adj* südlich; **~ern** ['sʌðən] *adj* südlich, Süd-; **S~ Pole** *n* Südpol *m*; **S~ Wales** *n* Südwales *nt*; **~ward(s)** *adv* südwärts, nach Süden; **~-west** *n* Südwesten *m*
souvenir [suːvə'nɪəʳ] *n* Souvenir *nt*

sovereign ['sɒvrɪn] n (ruler) Herrscher(in) m(f) ♦ adj (independent) souverän

soviet ['səuvɪət] adj sowjetisch; **the S~ Union** die Sowjetunion

sow[1] [sau] n Sau f

sow[2] [səu] (pt **sowed**, pp **sown**) vt (also fig) säen

soya ['sɔɪə] (US **soy**) n: **~ bean** Sojabohne f; **~ sauce** Sojasauce f

spa [spɑː] n (place) Kurort m

space [speɪs] n Platz m, Raum m; (universe) Weltraum m, All nt; (length of time) Abstand m ♦ vt (also: **~ out**) verteilen; **~craft** n Raumschiff nt; **~man** (irreg) n Raumfahrer m; **~ ship** n Raumschiff nt

spacing ['speɪsɪŋ] n Abstand m; (also: **~ out**) Verteilung f

spacious ['speɪʃəs] adj geräumig, weit

spade [speɪd] n Spaten m; **~s** npl (CARDS) Pik nt

Spain [speɪn] n Spanien nt

span [spæn] n Spanne f; (of bridge etc) Spannweite f ♦ vt überspannen

Spaniard ['spænjəd] n Spanier(in) m(f)

spaniel ['spænjəl] n Spaniel m

Spanish ['spænɪʃ] adj spanisch ♦ n (LING) Spanisch nt; **the ~** npl (people) die Spanier pl

spank [spæŋk] vt verhauen, versohlen

spanner ['spænər] (BRIT) n Schraubenschlüssel m

spar [spɑːr] n (NAUT) Sparren m ♦ vi (BOXING) einen Sparring machen

spare [spɛər] adj Ersatz- ♦ n = **spare part** ♦ vt (lives, feelings) verschonen; (trouble) ersparen; **to ~** (surplus) übrig; **~ part** n Ersatzteil nt; **~ time** n Freizeit f; **~ wheel** n (AUT) Reservereifen m

sparing ['spɛərɪŋ] adj: **to be ~ with** geizen mit; **~ly** adv sparsam; (eat, spend etc) in Maßen

spark [spɑːk] n Funken m; **~(ing) plug** n Zündkerze f

sparkle ['spɑːkl] n Funkeln nt; (gaiety) Schwung m ♦ vi funkeln; **sparkling** adj funkelnd; (wine) Schaum-; (mineral water) mit Kohlensäure; (conversation) spritzig,

geistreich

sparrow ['spærəu] n Spatz m

sparse [spɑːs] adj spärlich

spasm ['spæzəm] n (MED) Krampf m; (fig) Anfall m; **~odic** [spæz'mɔdɪk] adj (fig) sprunghaft

spastic ['spæstɪk] (old) n Spastiker(in) m(f) ♦ adj spastisch

spat [spæt] pt, pp of **spit**

spate [speɪt] n (fig) Flut f, Schwall m; **in ~** (river) angeschwollen

spatter ['spætər] vt bespritzen, verspritzen

spatula ['spætjulə] n Spatel m

spawn [spɔːn] vi laichen ♦ n Laich m

speak [spiːk] (pt **spoke**, pp **spoken**) vt sprechen, reden; (truth) sagen; (language) sprechen ♦ vi: **to ~ (to)** sprechen (mit or zu); **to ~ to sb** of or **about sth** mit jdm über etw acc sprechen; **~ up!** sprich lauter!; **~er** n Sprecher(in) m(f), Redner(in) m(f); (loudspeaker) Lautsprecher m; (POL): **the S~er** der Vorsitzende des Parlaments (BRIT) or des Kongresses (US)

spear [spɪər] n Speer m ♦ vt aufspießen; **~head** vt (attack etc) anführen

spec [spɛk] (inf) n: **on ~** auf gut Glück

special ['spɛʃl] adj besondere(r, s); **~ist** n (TECH) Fachmann m; (MED) Facharzt m/Fachärztin f; **~ity** [spɛʃɪ'ælɪtɪ] n Spezialität f; (study) Spezialgebiet nt; **~ize** vi: **to ~ize (in)** sich spezialisieren (auf +acc); **~ly** adv besonders; (explicitly) extra; **~ty** (esp US) n = **speciality**

species ['spiːʃiːz] n Art f

specific [spə'sɪfɪk] adj spezifisch; **~ally** adv spezifisch

specification [spɛsɪfɪ'keɪʃən] n Angabe f; (stipulation) Bedingung f; **~s** npl (TECH) technische Daten pl

specify ['spɛsɪfaɪ] vt genau angeben

specimen ['spɛsɪmən] n Probe f

speck [spɛk] n Fleckchen nt

speckled ['spɛkld] adj gesprenkelt

specs [spɛks] (inf) npl Brille f

spectacle ['spɛktəkl] n Schauspiel nt; **~s** npl (glasses) Brille f

spectacular [spek'tækjulər] *adj* sensationell; (*success etc*) spektakulär

spectator [spek'teɪtər] *n* Zuschauer(in) *m(f)*

spectre ['spektər] (*US* **specter**) *n* Geist *m*, Gespenst *nt*

speculate ['spekjuleɪt] *vi* spekulieren

speech [spi:tʃ] *n* Sprache *f*; (*address*) Rede *f*; (*way one speaks*) Sprechweise *f*; ~**less** *adj* sprachlos

speed [spi:d] *n* Geschwindigkeit *f*; (*gear*) Gang *m* ♦ *vi* (*JUR*) (zu) schnell fahren; **at full** *or* **top** ~ mit Höchstgeschwindigkeit; ~ **up** *vt* beschleunigen ♦ *vi* schneller werden; schneller fahren; ~**boat** *n* Schnellboot *nt*; ~**ily** *adv* schleunigst; ~**ing** *n* Geschwindigkeitsüberschreitung *f*; ~ **limit** *n* Geschwindigkeitsbegrenzung *f*; ~**ometer** [spɪ'dɔmɪtər] *n* Tachometer *m*; ~**way** *n* (*bike racing*) Motorradrennstrecke *f*; ~**y** *adj* schnell

spell [spel] (*pt, pp* **spelt** (*BRIT*) *or* **spelled**) *n* (*magic*) Bann *m*; (*period of time*) (eine) Zeit lang ♦ *vt* buchstabieren; (*imply*) bedeuten; **to cast a ~ on sb** jdn verzaubern; ~**bound** *adj* (wie) gebannt; ~**ing** *n* Rechtschreibung *f*

spelt [spelt] (*BRIT*) *pt, pp of* **spell**

spend [spend] (*pt, pp* **spent**) *vt* (*money*) ausgeben; (*time*) verbringen; ~**thrift** *n* Verschwender(in) *m(f)*

spent [spent] *pt, pp of* **spend**

sperm [spə:m] *n* (*BIOL*) Samenflüssigkeit *f*

spew [spju:] *vt* (er)brechen

sphere [sfɪər] *n* (*globe*) Kugel *f*; (*fig*) Sphäre *f*, Gebiet *nt*; **spherical** ['sferɪkl] *adj* kugelförmig

spice [spaɪs] *n* Gewürz *nt* ♦ *vt* würzen

spick-and-span ['spɪkən'spæn] *adj* blitzblank

spicy ['spaɪsɪ] *adj* (*food*) stark gewürzt; (*fig*) pikant

spider ['spaɪdər] *n* Spinne *f*

spike [spaɪk] *n* Dorn *m*, Spitze *f*

spill [spɪl] (*pt, pp* **spilt** *or* **spilled**) *vt* verschütten ♦ *vi* sich ergießen; ~ **over** *vi* überlaufen; (*fig*) sich ausbreiten

spilt [spɪlt] *pt, pp of* **spill**

spin [spɪn] (*pt, pp* **spun**) *n* (*trip in car*) Spazierfahrt *f*; (*AVIAT*) (Ab)trudeln *nt*; (*on ball*) Drall *m* ♦ *vt* (*thread*) spinnen; (*like top*) (herum)wirbeln ♦ *vi* sich drehen; ~ **out** *vt* in die Länge ziehen

spinach ['spɪnɪtʃ] *n* Spinat *m*

spinal ['spaɪnl] *adj* Rückgrat-; ~ **cord** *n* Rückenmark *nt*

spindly ['spɪndlɪ] *adj* spindeldürr

spin doctor *n* PR-Fachmann *m*, PR-Fachfrau *f*

spin-dryer [spɪn'draɪər] (*BRIT*) *n* Wäscheschleuder *f*

spine [spaɪn] *n* Rückgrat *nt*; (*thorn*) Stachel *m*; ~**less** *adj* (*also fig*) rückgratlos

spinning ['spɪnɪŋ] *n* Spinnen *nt*; ~ **top** *n* Kreisel *m*; ~ **wheel** *n* Spinnrad *nt*

spin-off ['spɪnɔf] *n* Nebenprodukt *nt*

spinster ['spɪnstər] *n* unverheiratete Frau *f*; (*pej*) alte Jungfer *f*

spiral ['spaɪərl] *n* Spirale *f* ♦ *adj* spiralförmig; (*movement etc*) in Spiralen ♦ *vi* sich (hoch)winden; ~ **staircase** *n* Wendeltreppe *f*

spire ['spaɪər] *n* Turm *m*

spirit ['spɪrɪt] *n* Geist *m*; (*humour, mood*) Stimmung *f*; (*courage*) Mut *m*; (*verve*) Elan *m*; (*alcohol*) Alkohol *m*; ~**s** *npl* (*drink*) Spirituosen *pl*; **in good** ~**s** gut aufgelegt; ~**ed** *adj* beherzt; ~ **level** *n* Wasserwaage *f*

spiritual ['spɪrɪtjuəl] *adj* geistig, seelisch; (*REL*) geistlich ♦ *n* Spiritual *nt*

spit [spɪt] (*pt, pp* **spat**) *n* (*for roasting*) (Brat)spieß *m*; (*saliva*) Spucke *f* ♦ *vi* spucken; (*rain*) sprühen; (*make a sound*) zischen; (*cat*) fauchen

spite [spaɪt] *n* Gehässigkeit *f* ♦ *vt* kränken; **in** ~ **of** trotz; ~**ful** *adj* gehässig

spittle ['spɪtl] *n* Speichel *m*, Spucke *f*

splash [splæʃ] *n* Spritzer *m*; (*of colour*) (Farb)fleck *m* ♦ *vt* bespritzen ♦ *vi* spritzen

spleen [spli:n] *n* (*ANAT*) Milz *f*

splendid ['splendɪd] *adj* glänzend

splendour ['splendər] (*US* **splendor**) *n* Pracht *f*

splint [splɪnt] *n* Schiene *f*

splinter ['splɪntər] *n* Splitter *m* ♦ *vi* (zer)splittern

split [splɪt] (*pt, pp* **split**) *n* Spalte *f*; (*fig*) Spaltung *f*; (*division*) Trennung *f* ♦ *vt* spalten *vi* ♦ *vi* (*divide*) reißen; ~ **up** *vi* sich trennen

splutter ['splʌtər] *vi* stottern

spoil [spɔɪl] (*pt, pp* **spoilt** *or* **spoiled**) *vt* (*ruin*) verderben; (*child*) verwöhnen; ~s *npl* Beute *f*; ~**sport** *n* Spielverderber *m*; ~**t** *pt, pp of* **spoil**

spoke [spəuk] *pt of* **speak** ♦ *n* Speiche *f*; ~**n** *pp of* **speak**

spokesman ['spəuksmən] (*irreg*) *n* Sprecher *m*; **spokeswoman** ['spəukswumən] (*irreg*) *n* Sprecherin *f*

sponge [spʌndʒ] *n* Schwamm *m* ♦ *vt* abwaschen ♦ *vi*: **to ~ on** auf Kosten +*gen* leben; ~ **bag** (*BRIT*) *n* Kulturbeutel *m*; ~ **cake** *n* Rührkuchen *m*

sponsor ['spɔnsər] *n* Sponsor *m* ♦ *vt* fördern; ~**ship** *n* Finanzierung *f*; (*public*) Schirmherrschaft *f*

spontaneous [spɔn'teɪnɪəs] *adj* spontan

spooky ['spuːkɪ] (*inf*) *adj* gespenstisch

spool [spuːl] *n* Spule *f*, Rolle *f*

spoon [spuːn] *n* Löffel *m*; ~**-feed** (*irreg*) *vt* mit dem Löffel füttern; (*fig*) hochpäppeln; ~**ful** *n* Löffel *m* (voll)

sport [spɔːt] *n* Sport *m*; (*person*) feine(r) Kerl *m*; ~**ing** *adj* (*fair*) sportlich, fair; **to give sb a ~ing chance** jdm eine faire Chance geben; ~ **jacket** (*US*) *n* = **sports jacket**; ~**s car** *n* Sportwagen *m*; ~**s jacket** *n* Sportjackett *nt*; ~**sman** (*irreg*) *n* Sportler *m*; ~**smanship** *n* Sportlichkeit *f*; ~**swear** *n* Sportkleidung *f*; ~**swoman** (*irreg*) *n* Sportlerin *f*; ~**y** *adj* sportlich

spot [spɔt] *n* Punkt *m*; (*dirty*) Fleck(en) *m*; (*place*) Stelle *f*; (*MED*) Pickel *m* ♦ *vt* erspähen; (*mistake*) bemerken; **on the ~** an Ort und Stelle; (*at once*) auf der Stelle; ~ **check** *n* Stichprobe *f*; ~**less** *adj* fleckenlos; ~**light** *n* Scheinwerferlicht *nt*; (*lamp*) Scheinwerfer *m*; ~**ted** *adj* gefleckt; ~**ty** *adj* (*face*) pickelig

spouse [spaus] *n* Gatte *m*/Gattin *f*

spout [spaut] *n* (*of pot*) Tülle *f*; (*jet*) Wasserstrahl *m* ♦ *vi* speien

sprain [spreɪn] *n* Verrenkung *f* ♦ *vt* verrenken

sprang [spræŋ] *pt of* **spring**

sprawl [sprɔːl] *vi* sich strecken

spray [spreɪ] *n* Spray *nt*; (*off sea*) Gischt *f*; (*of flowers*) Zweig *m* ♦ *vt* besprühen, sprayen

spread [spred] (*pt, pp* **spread**) *n* (*extent*) Verbreitung *f*; (*inf: meal*) Schmaus *m*; (*for bread*) Aufstrich *m* ♦ *vt* ausbreiten; (*scatter*) verbreiten; (*butter*) streichen ♦ *vi* sich ausbreiten; ~ **out** *vi* (*move apart*) sich verteilen; ~~-**eagled** ['spredɪːgld] *adj*: **to be** ~~-**eagled** alle viere von sich strecken; ~**sheet** *n* Tabellenkalkulation *f*

spree [spriː] *n* (*shopping*) Einkaufsbummel *m*; **to go on a** ~ einen draufmachen

sprightly ['spraɪtlɪ] *adj* munter, lebhaft

spring [sprɪŋ] (*pt* **sprang**, *pp* **sprung**) *n* (*leap*) Sprung *m*; (*TECH*) Feder *f*; (*season*) Frühling *m*; (*water*) Quelle *f* ♦ *vi* (*leap*) springen; ~ **up** *vi* (*problem*) auftauchen; ~**board** *n* Sprungbrett *nt*; ~~-**clean** *n* (*also:* ~~-**cleaning**) Frühjahrsputz *m*; ~**time** *n* Frühling *m*; ~**y** *adj* federnd, elastisch

sprinkle ['sprɪŋkl] *vt* (*salt*) streuen; (*liquid*) sprenkeln; **to ~ water on, to ~ with water** mit Wasser besprengen; ~**r** ['sprɪŋklər] *n* (*for lawn*) Sprenger *m*; (*for fire fighting*) Sprinkler *m*

sprint [sprɪnt] *n* (*race*) Sprint *m* ♦ *vi* (*run fast*) rennen; (*SPORT*) sprinten; ~**er** *n* Sprinter(in) *m(f)*

sprout [spraut] *vi* sprießen

sprouts [sprauts] *npl* (*also:* **Brussels ~**) Rosenkohl *m*

spruce [spruːs] *n* Fichte *f* ♦ *adj* schmuck, adrett

sprung [sprʌŋ] *pp of* **spring**

spry [spraɪ] *adj* flink, rege

spun [spʌn] *pt, pp of* **spin**

spur [spəːr] *n* Sporn *m*; (*fig*) Ansporn *m* ♦ *vt* (*also:* ~ **on**: *fig*) anspornen; **on the ~ of the moment** spontan

spurious ['spjuərɪəs] *adj* falsch

spurn [spəːn] *vt* verschmähen

spurt [spəːt] *n* (*jet*) Strahl *m*; (*acceleration*) Spurt *m* ♦ *vi* (*liquid*) schießen

spy [spaɪ] n Spion(in) m(f) ♦ vi spionieren
♦ vt erspähen; ~**ing** n Spionage f

sq. abbr = **square**

squabble ['skwɒbl] n Zank m ♦ vi sich
zanken

squad [skwɒd] n (MIL) Abteilung f; (POLICE)
Kommando nt

squadron ['skwɒdrən] n (cavalry) Schwadron
f; (NAUT) Geschwader nt; (air force) Staffel f

squalid ['skwɒlɪd] adj verkommen

squall [skwɔːl] n Bö(e) f, Windstoß m

squalor ['skwɒlər] n Verwahrlosung f

squander ['skwɒndər] vt verschwenden

square [skwɛər] n Quadrat nt; (open space)
Platz m; (instrument) Winkel m; (inf: person)
Spießer m ♦ adj viereckig; (inf: ideas, tastes)
spießig ♦ vt (arrange) ausmachen; (MATH)
ins Quadrat erheben ♦ vi (agree)
übereinstimmen; **all ~** quitt; **a ~ meal** eine
ordentliche Mahlzeit; **2 metres ~** 2 Meter
im Quadrat; **1 ~ metre** 1 Quadratmeter;
~**ly** adv fest, gerade

squash [skwɒʃ] n (BRIT: drink) Saft m; (game)
Squash nt ♦ vt zerquetschen

squat [skwɒt] adj untersetzt ♦ vi hocken;
~**ter** n Hausbesetzer m

squawk [skwɔːk] vi kreischen

squeak [skwiːk] vi quiek(s)en; (spring, door
etc) quietschen

squeal [skwiːl] vi schrill schreien

squeamish ['skwiːmɪʃ] adj empfindlich

squeeze [skwiːz] vt pressen, drücken;
(orange) auspressen; ~ **out** vt
ausquetschen

squelch [skwɛltʃ] vi platschen

squib [skwɪb] n Knallfrosch m

squid [skwɪd] n Tintenfisch m

squiggle ['skwɪgl] n Schnörkel m

squint [skwɪnt] vi schielen ♦ n: **to have a ~**
schielen; **to ~ at sb/sth** nach jdm/etw
schielen

squirm [skwəːm] vi sich winden

squirrel ['skwɪrəl] n Eichhörnchen nt

squirt [skwəːt] vt, vi spritzen

Sr abbr (= senior) sen.

St abbr (= saint) hl., St.; (= street) Str.

stab [stæb] n (blow) Stich m; (inf: try) Versuch

m ♦ vt erstechen

stabilize ['steɪbəlaɪz] vt stabilisieren ♦ vi sich
stabilisieren

stable ['steɪbl] adj stabil ♦ n Stall m

stack [stæk] n Stapel m ♦ vt stapeln

stadium ['steɪdɪəm] n Stadion nt

staff [stɑːf] n (stick, MIL) Stab m; (personnel)
Personal nt; (BRIT: SCH) Lehrkräfte pl ♦ vt
besetzen

stag [stæg] n Hirsch m

stage [steɪdʒ] n Bühne f; (of journey) Etappe
f; (degree) Stufe f; (point) Stadium nt ♦ vt
(put on) aufführen; (simulate) inszenieren;
(demonstration) veranstalten; **in ~s**
etappenweise; ~**coach** n Postkutsche f; ~
door n Bühneneingang m; ~ **manager** n
Intendant m

stagger ['stægər] vi wanken, taumeln ♦ vt
(amaze) verblüffen; (hours) staffeln; ~**ing**
adj unglaublich

stagnant ['stægnənt] adj stagnierend;
(water) stehend; **stagnate** [stæg'neɪt] vi
stagnieren

stag party n Männerabend m (vom
Bräutigam vor der Hochzeit gegeben)

staid [steɪd] adj gesetzt

stain [steɪn] n Fleck m ♦ vt beflecken; ~**ed
glass window** buntes Glasfenster nt; ~**less**
adj (steel) rostfrei; ~ **remover** n
Fleckentferner m

stair [stɛər] n (Treppen)stufe f; ~**s** npl (flight
of steps) Treppe f; ~**case** n Treppenhaus
nt, Treppe f; ~**way** n Treppenaufgang m

stake [steɪk] n (post) Pfahl m; (money) Einsatz
m ♦ vt (bet: money) setzen; **to be at ~** auf
dem Spiel stehen

stale [steɪl] adj alt; (bread) altbacken

stalemate ['steɪlmeɪt] n (CHESS) Patt nt; (fig)
Stillstand m

stalk [stɔːk] n Stängel m, Stiel m ♦ vt (game)
jagen; ~ **off** vi abstolzieren

stall [stɔːl] n (in stable) Stand m, Box f; (in
market) (Verkaufs)stand m ♦ vt (AUT)
abwürgen ♦ vi (AUT) stehen bleiben; (fig)
Ausflüchte machen; ~**s** npl (BRIT: THEAT)
Parkett nt

stallion ['stæljən] n Zuchthengst m

stalwart ['stɔːlwət] n treue(r) Anhänger m

stamina ['stæmɪnə] n Durchhaltevermögen nt, Zähigkeit f

stammer ['stæmər] n Stottern nt ♦ vt, vi stottern, stammeln

stamp [stæmp] n Briefmarke f; (for document) Stempel m ♦ vi stampfen ♦ vt (mark) stempeln; (mail) frankieren; (foot) stampfen mit; ~ **album** n Briefmarkenalbum nt; ~ **collecting** n Briefmarkensammeln nt

stampede [stæm'piːd] n panische Flucht f

stance [stæns] n Haltung f

stand [stænd] (pt, pp **stood**) n (for objects) Gestell nt; (seats) Tribüne f ♦ vi stehen; (rise) aufstehen; (decision) feststehen ♦ vt setzen, stellen; (endure) aushalten; (person) ausstehen; (nonsense) dulden; **to make a ~** Widerstand leisten; **to ~ for parliament** (BRIT) für das Parlament kandidieren; ~ **by** vi (be ready) bereitstehen ♦ vt fus (opinion) treu bleiben +dat; ~ **down** vi (withdraw) zurücktreten; ~ **for** vt fus (signify) stehen für; (permit, tolerate) hinnehmen; ~ **in for** vt fus einspringen für; ~ **out** vi (be prominent) hervorstechen; ~ **up** vi (rise) aufstehen; ~ **up for** vt fus sich einsetzen für; ~ **up to** vt fus: **to ~ up to sth** einer Sache dat gewachsen sein; **to ~ up to sb** sich jdm gegenüber behaupten

standard ['stændəd] n (measure) Norm f; (flag) Fahne f ♦ adj (size etc) Normal-; ~**s** npl (morals) Maßstäbe pl; ~**ize** vt vereinheitlichen; ~ **lamp** (BRIT) n Stehlampe f; ~ **of living** n Lebensstandard m

stand-by n Reserve f; **to be on ~-by** in Bereitschaft sein; ~-**by ticket** n (AVIAT) Standbyticket nt; ~-**in** ['stændɪn] n Ersatz m

standing ['stændɪŋ] adj (erect) stehend; (permanent) ständig; (invitation) offen ♦ n (duration) Dauer f; (reputation) Ansehen nt; **of many years'** ~ langjährig; ~ **order** (BRIT) n (at bank) Dauerauftrag m; ~ **room** n Stehplatz m

stand: ~-**offish** [stænd'ɔfɪʃ] adj zurückhaltend, sehr reserviert; ~**point** ['stændpɔɪnt] n Standpunkt m; ~**still**

['stændstɪl] n: **to be at a ~still** stillstehen; **to come to a ~still** zum Stillstand kommen

stank [stæŋk] pt of **stink**

staple ['steɪpl] n (in paper) Heftklammer f; (article) Haupterzeugnis nt ♦ adj Grund-, Haupt- ♦ vt (fest)klammern; ~**r** n Heftmaschine f

star [stɑːr] n Stern m; (person) Star m ♦ vi die Hauptrolle spielen ♦ vt: ~**ring** ... in der Hauptrolle/den Hauptrollen ...

starboard ['stɑːbɔːd] n Steuerbord nt

starch [stɑːtʃ] n Stärke f

stardom ['stɑːdəm] n Berühmtheit f

stare [steər] n starre(r) Blick m ♦ vi: **to ~ at** starren auf +acc, anstarren

starfish ['stɑːfɪʃ] n Seestern m

stark [stɑːk] adj öde ♦ adv: ~ **naked** splitternackt

starling ['stɑːlɪŋ] n Star m

starry ['stɑːrɪ] adj Sternen-; ~-**eyed** adj (innocent) blauäugig

start [stɑːt] n Anfang m; (SPORT) Start m; (lead) Vorsprung m ♦ vt in Gang setzen; (car) anlassen ♦ vi anfangen; (car) anspringen; (on journey) aufbrechen; (SPORT) starten; (with fright) zusammenfahren; **to ~ doing** or **to do sth** anfangen, etw zu tun; ~ **off** vi anfangen; (begin moving) losgehen; losfahren; ~ **up** vi anfangen ♦ vt beginnen; (car) anlassen; (engine) starten; ~**er** n (AUT) Anlasser m; (for race) Starter m; (BRIT: COOK) Vorspeise f; ~**ing point** n Ausgangspunkt m

startle ['stɑːtl] vt erschrecken; **startling** adj erschreckend

starvation [stɑː'veɪʃən] n Verhungern nt

starve [stɑːv] vi verhungern ♦ vt verhungern lassen; **I'm starving** ich sterbe vor Hunger

state [steɪt] n (condition) Zustand m; (POL) Staat m ♦ vt erklären; (facts) angeben; **the S~s** (USA) die Staaten; **to be in a ~** durchdrehen; ~**ly** adj würdevoll; ~**ly home** n herrschaftliches Anwesen nt, Schloss nt; ~**ment** n Aussage f; (POL) Erklärung f; ~**sman** (irreg) n Staatsmann m

static ['stætɪk] n (also: ~ **electricity**) Reibungselektrizität f

station ['steɪʃən] n (RAIL etc) Bahnhof m; (police etc) Wache f; (in society) Stand m ♦ vt stationieren

stationary ['steɪʃnərɪ] adj stillstehend; (car) parkend

stationer's n (shop) Schreibwarengeschäft nt; ~y n Schreibwaren pl

station master n Bahnhofsvorsteher m

station wagon n Kombiwagen m

statistics [stə'tɪstɪks] n Statistik f

statue ['stætjuː] n Statue f

stature ['stætʃəʳ] n Größe f

status ['steɪtəs] n Status m

statute ['stætjuːt] n Gesetz nt; **statutory** ['stætjutrɪ] adj gesetzlich

staunch [stɔːntʃ] adj standhaft

stay [steɪ] n Aufenthalt m ♦ vi bleiben; (reside) wohnen; **to ~ put** an Ort und Stelle bleiben; **to ~ the night** übernachten; **~ behind** vi zurückbleiben; **~ in** vi (at home) zu Hause bleiben; **~ on** vi (continue) länger bleiben; **~ out** vi (of house) wegbleiben; **~ up** vi (at night) aufbleiben; **~ing power** n Durchhaltevermögen nt

stead [sted] n: **in sb's ~** an jds Stelle dat; **to stand sb in good ~** jdm zugute kommen

steadfast ['stedfɑːst] adj standhaft, treu

steadily ['stedɪlɪ] adv stetig, regelmäßig

steady ['stedɪ] adj (firm) fest, stabil; (regular) gleichmäßig; (reliable) beständig; (hand) ruhig; (job, boyfriend) fest ♦ vt festigen; **to ~ o.s. on/against sth** sich stützen auf/ gegen etw acc

steak [steɪk] n Steak nt; (fish) Filet nt

steal [stiːl] (pt stole, pp stolen) vt stehlen ♦ vi stehlen; (go quietly) sich stehlen

stealth [stelθ] n Heimlichkeit f; **~y** adj verstohlen, heimlich

steam [stiːm] n Dampf m ♦ vt (COOK) im Dampfbad erhitzen ♦ vi dampfen; **~ engine** n Dampfmaschine f; **~er** n Dampfer m; **~roller** n Dampfwalze f; **~ship** n = **steamer**; **~y** adj dampfig

steel [stiːl] n Stahl m ♦ adj Stahl-; (fig) stählern; **~works** n Stahlwerke pl

steep [stiːp] adj steil; (price) gepfeffert ♦ vt einweichen

steeple ['stiːpl] n Kirchturm m; **~chase** n Hindernisrennen nt

steer [stɪəʳ] vt, vi steuern; (car etc) lenken; **~ing** n (AUT) Steuerung f; **~ing wheel** n Steuer- or Lenkrad nt

stem [stem] n Stiel m ♦ vt aufhalten; **~ from** vt fus abstammen von

stench [stentʃ] n Gestank m

stencil ['stensl] n Schablone f ♦ vt (auf)drucken

stenographer [ste'nɔgrəfəʳ] (US) n Stenograf(in) m(f)

step [step] n Schritt m; (stair) Stufe f ♦ vi treten, schreiten; **~s** npl (BRIT) = **stepladder; to take ~s** Schritte unternehmen; **in/out of ~ (with)** im/nicht im Gleichklang (mit); **~ down** vi (fig) abtreten; **~ off** vt fus aussteigen aus; **~ up** vt steigern

stepbrother ['stepbrʌðəʳ] n Stiefbruder m

stepdaughter ['stepdɔːtəʳ] n Stieftochter f

stepfather ['stepfɑːðəʳ] n Stiefvater m

stepladder ['steplædəʳ] n Trittleiter f

stepmother ['stepmʌðəʳ] n Stiefmutter f

stepping stone ['stepɪŋ-] n Stein m; (fig) Sprungbrett nt

stepsister ['stepsɪstəʳ] n Stiefschwester f

stepson ['stepsʌn] n Stiefsohn m

stereo ['stɛrɪəu] n Stereoanlage f ♦ adj (also: **~phonic**) stereofonisch, stereophonisch

stereotype ['stɪərɪətaɪp] n (fig) Klischee nt ♦ vt stereotypieren; (fig) stereotyp machen

sterile ['stɛraɪl] adj steril; (person) unfruchtbar; **sterilize** vt sterilisieren

sterling ['stɜːlɪŋ] adj (FIN) Sterling-; (character) gediegen ♦ n (ECON) das Pfund Sterling; **a pound ~** ein Pfund Sterling

stern [stɜːn] adj streng ♦ n Heck nt, Achterschiff nt

stew [stjuː] n Eintopf m ♦ vt, vi schmoren

steward ['stjuːəd] n Steward m; **~ess** n Stewardess f

stick [stɪk] (pt, pp stuck) n Stock m; (of chalk etc) Stück nt ♦ vt (stab) stechen; (put) stellen; (gum) (an)kleben; (inf: tolerate) vertragen ♦ vi (stop) stecken bleiben; (get stuck) klemmen; (hold fast) kleben, haften; **~ out** vi (*project*) hervorstehen; **~ up** vi (*project*) in die Höhe stehen; **~ up for** vt fus (*defend*) eintreten für; **~er** n Aufkleber m; **~ing plaster** n Heftpflaster nt

stickler ['stıklə'] n: **~ (for)** Pedant m (in +acc)

stick-up ['stıkʌp] (inf) n (Raub)überfall m

sticky ['stıkı] adj klebrig; (*atmosphere*) stickig

stiff [stıf] adj steif; (*difficult*) hart; (*paste*) dick; (*drink*) stark; **to have a ~ neck** einen steifen Hals haben; **~en** vt versteifen, (ver)stärken ♦ vi sich versteifen

stifle ['staıfl] vt unterdrücken; **stifling** adj drückend

stigma ['stıgmə] (pl BOT, MED, REL **~ta**; fig **~s**) n Stigma nt

stigmata [stıg'mɑ:tə] npl of **stigma**

stile [staıl] n Steige f

stiletto [stı'letəu] (BRIT) n (also: **~ heel**) Pfennigabsatz m

still [stıl] adj still ♦ adv (*immer*) noch; (*anyhow*) immerhin; **~born** adj tot geboren; **~ life** n Stillleben nt

stilt [stılt] n Stelze f

stilted ['stıltıd] adj gestelzt

stimulate ['stımjuleıt] vt anregen, stimulieren

stimuli ['stımjulaı] npl of **stimulus**

stimulus ['stımjuləs] (pl **-li**) n Anregung f, Reiz m

sting [stıŋ] (pt, pp **stung**) n Stich m; (*organ*) Stachel m ♦ vi stechen; (*on skin*) brennen ♦ vt stechen

stingy ['stındʒı] adj geizig, knauserig

stink [stıŋk] (pt **stank**, pp **stunk**) n Gestank m ♦ vi stinken; **~ing** adj (fig) widerlich

stint [stınt] n (*period*) Betätigung f; **to do one's ~** seine Arbeit tun; (*share*) seinen Teil beitragen

stipulate ['stıpjuleıt] vt festsetzen

stir [stə:'] n Bewegung f; (COOK) Rühren nt; (*sensation*) Aufsehen nt ♦ vt (um)rühren ♦ vi sich rühren; **~ up** vt (mob) aufhetzen; (*mixture*) umrühren; (*dust*) aufwirbeln

stirrup ['stırəp] n Steigbügel m

stitch [stıtʃ] n (*with needle*) Stich m; (MED)

Faden m; (*of knitting*) Masche f; (*pain*) Stich m ♦ vt nähen

stoat [stəut] n Wiesel nt

stock [stɔk] n Vorrat m; (COMM) (Waren)lager nt; (*livestock*) Vieh nt; (COOK) Brühe f; (FIN) Grundkapital nt ♦ adj stets vorrätig; (*standard*) Normal- ♦ vt (*in shop*) führen; **~s** npl (FIN) Aktien pl; **in/out of ~** vorrätig/nicht vorrätig; **to take ~ of** Inventur machen von; (fig) Bilanz ziehen aus; **~s and shares** Effekten pl; **~ up** vi: **to ~ up (with)** Reserven anlegen (von); **~broker** ['stɔkbrəukə'] n Börsenmakler m; **~ cube** n Brühwürfel m; **~ exchange** n Börse f

stocking ['stɔkıŋ] n Strumpf m

stock: **~ market** n Börse f; **~ phrase** n Standardsatz m; **~pile** n Vorrat m ♦ vt aufstapeln; **~taking** (BRIT) n (COMM) Inventur f, Bestandsaufnahme f

stocky ['stɔkı] adj untersetzt

stodgy ['stɔdʒı] adj pampig

stoke [stəuk] vt schüren

stole [stəul] pt of **steal** ♦ n Stola f

stolen ['stəuln] pp of **steal**

stomach ['stʌmək] n Bauch m, Magen m ♦ vt vertragen; **~-ache** n Magen- or Bauchschmerzen pl

stone [stəun] n Stein m; (BRIT: *weight*) *Gewichtseinheit = 6.35 kg* ♦ vt (*olive*) entkernen; (*kill*) steinigen; **~-cold** adj eiskalt; **~-deaf** adj stocktaub; **~work** n Mauerwerk nt; **stony** ['stəunı] adj steinig

stood [stud] pt, pp of **stand**

stool [stu:l] n Hocker m

stoop [stu:p] vi sich bücken

stop [stɔp] n Halt m; (*bus* ~) Haltestelle f; (*punctuation*) Punkt m ♦ vt anhalten; (*bring to an end*) aufhören (mit), ein lassen ♦ vi aufhören; (*clock*) stehen bleiben; (*remain*) bleiben; **to ~ doing sth** aufhören, etw zu tun; **to ~ dead** innehalten; **~ off** vi kurz Halt machen; **~ up** vt (*hole*) zustopfen, verstopfen; **~gap** n Notlösung f; **~lights** npl (AUT) Bremslichter pl; **~over** n (*on journey*) Zwischenaufenthalt m; **~page** ['stɔpıdʒ] n (An)halten nt; (*traffic*)

Verkehrsstockung f; (strike)
Arbeitseinstellung f; ~**per** ['stɔpər] n
Propfen m, Stöpsel m; ~ **press** n letzte
Meldung f; ~**watch** ['stɒpwɒtʃ] n Stoppuhr f

storage ['stɔːrɪdʒ] n Lagerung f; ~ **heater** n
(Nachtstrom)speicherofen m

store [stɔːr] n Vorrat m; (place) Lager nt,
Warenhaus nt; (BRIT: large shop) Kaufhaus
nt; (US) Laden m ♦ vt lagern; ~**s** npl
(supplies) Vorräte pl; ~ **up** vt sich
eindecken mit; ~**room** n Lagerraum m,
Vorratsraum m

storey ['stɔːrɪ] (US **story**) n Stock m

stork [stɔːk] n Storch m

storm [stɔːm] n (also fig) Sturm m ♦ vt, vi
stürmen; ~**y** adj stürmisch

story ['stɔːrɪ] n Geschichte f; (lie) Märchen
nt; (US) = **storey**; ~**book** n
Geschichtenbuch nt; ~**teller** n
Geschichtenerzähler m

stout [staut] adj (bold) tapfer; (fat) beleibt
♦ n Starkbier nt; (also: **sweet** ~) ≈ Malzbier
nt

stove [stəuv] n (Koch)herd m; (for heating)
Ofen m

stow [stəu] vt verstauen; ~**away** n blinde(r)
Passagier m

straddle ['strædl] vt (horse, fence) rittlings
sitzen auf +dat; (fig) überbrücken

straggle ['strægl] vi (people) nachhinken; ~**r**
n Nachzügler m; **straggly** adj (hair) zottig

straight [streɪt] adj (honest) offen,
ehrlich; (drink) pur ♦ adv (direct) direkt,
geradewegs; **to put** or **get sth** ~ etw in
Ordnung bringen; ~ **away** sofort; ~ **off**
sofort; ~**en** vt (also: ~**en out**) gerade
machen; (fig) klarstellen; ~**-faced** adv ohne
die Miene zu verziehen ♦ adj: **to be** ~-
faced keine Miene verziehen; ~**forward**
adj einfach, unkompliziert

strain [streɪn] n Belastung f; (streak, trace)
Zug m; (of music) Fetzen m ♦ vt
überanstrengen; (stretch) anspannen;
(muscle) zerren; (filter) (durch)seihen ♦ vi
sich anstrengen; ~**ed** adj (laugh)
gezwungen; (relations) gespannt; ~**er** n
Sieb nt

strait [streɪt] n Straße f, Meerenge f;
~**jacket** n Zwangsjacke f; ~**-laced** adj
engherzig, streng

strand [strænd] n (of hair) Strähne f; (also fig)
Faden m

stranded ['strændɪd] adj (also fig) gestrandet

strange [streɪndʒ] adj fremd; (unusual)
seltsam; ~**r** n Fremde(r) mf

strangle ['stræŋgl] vt erwürgen; ~**hold** n
(fig) Umklammerung f

strap [stræp] n Riemen m; (on clothes) Träger
m ♦ vt (fasten) festschnallen

strapping ['stræpɪŋ] adj stramm

strata ['strɑːtə] npl of **stratum**

strategic [strəˈtiːdʒɪk] adj strategisch

strategy ['strætɪdʒɪ] n (fig) Strategie f

stratum ['strɑːtəm] (pl **-ta**) n Schicht f

straw [strɔː] n Stroh nt; (single stalk, drinking
~) Strohhalm m; **that's the last** ~! das ist
der Gipfel!

strawberry ['strɔːbərɪ] n Erdbeere f

stray [streɪ] adj (animal) verirrt ♦ vi
herumstreunen

streak [striːk] n Streifen m; (in character)
Einschlag m; (in hair) Strähne f ♦ vt streifen
♦ vi zucken; (move quickly) flitzen; ~ **of bad
luck** Pechsträhne f; ~**y** adj gestreift; (bacon)
durchwachsen

stream [striːm] n (brook) Bach m; (fig) Strom
m ♦ vt (SCH) in (Leistungs)gruppen einteilen
♦ vi strömen; **to** ~ **in/out** (people) hinein-/
hinausströmen

streamer ['striːmər] n (flag) Wimpel m; (of
paper) Luftschlange f

streamlined ['striːmlaɪnd] adj
stromlinienförmig; (effective) rationell

street [striːt] n Straße f ♦ adj Straßen-; ~**car**
(US) n Straßenbahn f; ~ **lamp** n
Straßenlaterne f; ~ **plan** n Stadtplan m;
~**wise** (inf) adj: **to be** ~**wise** wissen, wo es
langgeht

strength [streŋθ] n (also fig) Stärke f; Kraft f;
~**en** vt (ver)stärken

strenuous ['strenjʊəs] adj anstrengend

stress [stres] n Druck m; (mental) Stress m;
(GRAM) Betonung f ♦ vt betonen

stretch [stretʃ] n Strecke f ♦ vt ausdehnen,

strecken ♦ *vi* sich erstrecken; *(person)* sich strecken; ~ **out** *vi* sich ausstrecken ♦ *vt* ausstrecken

stretcher ['strɛtʃər] *n* Tragbahre *f*

stretchy ['strɛtʃɪ] *adj*: ~ **with** übersät mit

strewn [struːn] *adj*: ~ **with** übersät mit

stricken ['strɪkən] *adj (person)* ergriffen; *(city, country)* heimgesucht; ~ **with** *(disease)* leidend unter +*dat*

strict [strɪkt] *adj (exact)* genau; *(severe)* streng; ~**ly** *adv* streng, genau

stridden ['strɪdn] *pp of* **stride**

stride [straɪd] *(pt* **strode***, pp* **stridden***) n* lange(r) Schritt *m* ♦ *vi* schreiten

strident ['straɪdnt] *adj* schneidend, durchdringend

strife [straɪf] *n* Streit *m*

strike [straɪk] *(pt, pp* **struck***) n* Streik *m*; *(attack)* Schlag *m* ♦ *vt (hit)* schlagen; *(collide)* stoßen gegen; *(come to mind)* einfallen +*dat*; *(stand out)* auffallen +*dat*; *(find)* finden ♦ *vi (stop work)* streiken; *(attack)* zuschlagen; *(clock)* schlagen; **on ~** *(workers)* im Streik; **to ~ a match** ein Streichholz anzünden; ~ **down** *vt (lay low)* niederschlagen; ~ **out** *vt (cross out)* ausstreichen; ~ **up** *vt (music)* anstimmen; *(friendship)* schließen; ~**r** *n* Streikende(r) *mf*; **striking** ['straɪkɪŋ] *adj* auffallend

string [strɪŋ] *(pt, pp* **strung***) n* Schnur *f*; *(row)* Reihe *f*; *(MUS)* Saite *f* ♦ *vt*: **to ~ together** aneinander reihen ♦ *vi*: **to ~ out** *(sich)* verteilen; **the ~s** *npl (MUS)* die Streichinstrumente *pl*; **to pull ~s** *(fig)* Fäden ziehen; ~ **bean** *n* grüne Bohne *f*; ~**(ed) instrument** *n (MUS)* Saiteninstrument *nt*

stringent ['strɪndʒənt] *adj* streng

strip [strɪp] *n* Streifen *m* ♦ *vt (uncover)* abstreifen, abziehen; *(clothes)* ausziehen; *(TECH)* auseinander nehmen ♦ *vi (undress)* sich ausziehen; ~ **cartoon** *n* Bildserie *f*

stripe [straɪp] *n* Streifen *m*; ~**d** *adj* gestreift

strip lighting *n* Neonlicht *nt*

stripper ['strɪpər] *n* Stripteasetänzerin *f*

strip-search ['strɪpsɜːtʃ] *n* Leibesvisitation *f (bei der man sich ausziehen muss)* ♦ *vt*: **to be ~~ed** sich ausziehen müssen und

durchsucht werden

stripy ['straɪpɪ] *adj* gestreift

strive [straɪv] *(pt* **strove***, pp* **striven***) vi*: **to ~ (for)** streben (nach)

strode [strəʊd] *pt of* **stride**

stroke [strəʊk] *n* Schlag *m*; *(SWIMMING, ROWING)* Stoß *m*; *(MED)* Schlaganfall *m*; *(caress)* Streicheln *nt* ♦ *vt* streicheln; **at a ~** mit einem Schlag

stroll [strəʊl] *n* Spaziergang *m* ♦ *vi* schlendern; ~**er** *(US) n (pushchair)* Sportwagen *m*

strong [strɒŋ] *adj* stark; *(firm)* fest; **they are 50 ~** sie sind 50 Mann stark; ~**box** *n* Kassette *f*; ~**hold** *n* Hochburg *f*; ~**ly** *adv* stark; ~**room** *n* Tresor *m*

strove [strəʊv] *pt of* **strive**

struck [strʌk] *pt, pp of* **strike**

structure ['strʌktʃər] *n* Struktur *f*, Aufbau *m*; *(building)* Bau *m*

struggle ['strʌgl] *n* Kampf *m* ♦ *vi (fight)* kämpfen

strum [strʌm] *vt (guitar)* klimpern auf +*dat*

strung [strʌŋ] *pt, pp of* **string**

strut [strʌt] *n* Strebe *f*, Stütze *f* ♦ *vi* stolzieren

stub [stʌb] *n* Stummel *m*; *(of cigarette)* Kippe *f* ♦ *vt*: **to ~ one's toe** sich *dat* den Zeh anstoßen; ~ **out** *vt* ausdrücken

stubble ['stʌbl] *n* Stoppel *f*

stubborn ['stʌbən] *adj* hartnäckig

stuck [stʌk] *pt, pp of* **stick** ♦ *adj (jammed)* klemmend; ~**-up** *adj* hochnäsig

stud [stʌd] *n (button)* Kragenknopf *m*; *(place)* Gestüt *nt* ♦ *vt (fig)*: ~**ded with** übersät mit

student ['stjuːdənt] *n* Student(in) *m(f)*; *(US)* Student(in) *m(f)*, Schüler(in) *m(f)* ♦ *adj* Studenten-; ~ **driver** *(US) n* Fahrschüler(in) *m(f)*

studio ['stjuːdɪəʊ] *n* Studio *nt*; *(for artist)* Atelier *nt*; ~ **apartment** *(US) n* Appartement *nt*; ~ **flat** *n* Appartement *nt*

studious ['stjuːdɪəs] *adj* lernbegierig

study ['stʌdɪ] *n (investigation)* Studium *nt*, Untersuchung *f*; *(room)* Arbeitszimmer *nt*; *(essay etc)* Studie *f* ♦ *vt* studieren; *(face)* erforschen; *(evidence)* prüfen ♦ *vi* studieren

stuff [stʌf] n Stoff m; (inf) Zeug nt ♦ vt stopfen, füllen; (animal) ausstopfen; **~ing** n Füllung f; **~y** adj (room) schwül; (person) spießig

stumble ['stʌmbl] vi stolpern; **to ~ across** (fig) zufällig stoßen auf +acc

stumbling block ['stʌmblɪŋ-] n Hindernis nt

stump [stʌmp] n Stumpf m

stun [stʌn] vt betäuben; (shock) niederschmettern

stung [stʌŋ] pt, pp of **sting**

stunk [stʌŋk] pp of **stink**

stunned adj benommen, fassungslos

stunning ['stʌnɪŋ] adj betäubend; (news) überwältigend, umwerfend

stunt [stʌnt] n Kunststück nt, Trick m

stunted ['stʌntɪd] adj verkümmert

stuntman ['stʌntmæn] (irreg) n Stuntman m

stupefy ['stjuːpɪfaɪ] vt betäuben; (by news) bestürzen

stupendous [stjuːˈpɛndəs] adj erstaunlich, enorm

stupid ['stjuːpɪd] adj dumm; **~ity** [stjuːˈpɪdɪtɪ] n Dummheit f

stupor ['stjuːpəʳ] n Betäubung f

sturdy ['stɜːdɪ] adj kräftig, robust

stutter ['stʌtəʳ] n Stottern nt ♦ vi stottern

sty [staɪ] n Schweinestall m

stye [staɪ] n Gerstenkorn nt

style [staɪl] n Stil m; (fashion) Mode f; **stylish** ['staɪlɪʃ] adj modisch; **stylist** ['staɪlɪst] n (hair stylist) Friseur m, Friseuse f

stylus ['staɪləs] n (Grammofon)nadel f

suave [swɑːv] adj zuvorkommend

sub... [sʌb] prefix Unter...; **~conscious** adj unterbewusst ♦ n: **the ~conscious** das Unterbewusste; **~contract** vt (vertraglich) untervermitteln; **~divide** vt unterteilen; **~dued** adj (lighting) gedämpft; (person) still

subject [n, adj 'sʌbdʒɪkt, vb səbˈdʒɛkt] n (of kingdom) Untertan m; (citizen) Staatsangehörige(r) mf; (topic) Thema nt; (SCH) Fach nt; (GRAM) Subjekt nt ♦ adj: **to be ~ to** unterworfen sein +dat; (exposed) ausgesetzt sein +dat ♦ vt (subdue) unterwerfen; (expose) aussetzen; **~ive** [səbˈdʒɛktɪv] adj subjektiv; **~ matter** n Thema nt

sublet [sʌbˈlɛt] (irreg: like **let**) vt untervermieten

sublime [səˈblaɪm] adj erhaben

submachine gun ['sʌbməˈʃiːn-] n Maschinenpistole f

submarine [sʌbməˈriːn] n Unterseeboot nt, U-Boot nt

submerge [səbˈmɜːdʒ] vt untertauchen; (flood) überschwemmen ♦ vi untertauchen

submission [səbˈmɪʃən] n (obedience) Gehorsam m; (claim) Behauptung f; (of plan) Unterbreitung f; **submissive** [səbˈmɪsɪv] adj demütig, unterwürfig (pej)

submit [səbˈmɪt] vt behaupten; (plan) unterbreiten ♦ vi sich ergeben

subnormal [sʌbˈnɔːml] adj minderbegabt

subordinate [səˈbɔːdɪnət] adj untergeordnet ♦ n Untergebene(r) mf

subpoena [səˈpiːnə] n Vorladung f ♦ vt vorladen

subscribe [səbˈskraɪb] vi: **to ~ to** (view etc) unterstützen; (newspaper) abonnieren; **~r** n (to periodical) Abonnent m; (TEL) Telefonteilnehmer m

subscription [səbˈskrɪpʃən] n Abonnement nt; (money subscribed) (Mitglieds)beitrag m

subsequent ['sʌbsɪkwənt] adj folgend, später; **~ly** adv später

subside [səbˈsaɪd] vi sich senken; **~nce** [səbˈsaɪdns] n Senkung f

subsidiarity [səbsɪdɪˈærɪtɪ] n (POL) Subsidiarität f

subsidiary [səbˈsɪdɪərɪ] adj Neben- ♦ n Tochtergesellschaft f

subsidize ['sʌbsɪdaɪz] vt subventionieren

subsidy ['sʌbsɪdɪ] n Subvention f

subsistence [səbˈsɪstəns] n Unterhalt m

substance ['sʌbstəns] n Substanz f

substantial [səbˈstænʃl] adj (strong) fest, kräftig; (important) wesentlich; **~ly** adv erheblich

substantiate [səbˈstænʃɪeɪt] vt begründen, belegen

substitute ['sʌbstɪtjuːt] n Ersatz m ♦ vt ersetzen; **substitution** [sʌbstɪˈtjuːʃən] n

Ersetzung f

subterfuge ['sʌbtəfjuːdʒ] n Vorwand m; (trick) Trick m

subterranean [sʌbtə'reɪnɪən] adj unterirdisch

subtitle ['sʌbtaɪtl] n Untertitel m; ~d adj untertitelt, mit Untertiteln versehen

subtle ['sʌtl] adj fein; ~ty n Feinheit f

subtotal [sʌb'təʊtl] n Zwischensumme f

subtract [səb'trækt] vt abziehen; ~ion [səb'trækʃən] n Abziehen nt, Subtraktion f

suburb ['sʌbəːb] n Vorort m; **the ~s** die Außenbezirke pl; ~an [sə'bəːbən] adj Vorort(s)-; ~ia [sə'bəːbɪə] n Vorstadt f

subversive [səb'vəːsɪv] adj subversiv

subway ['sʌbweɪ] n (US) U-Bahn f; (BRIT) Unterführung f

succeed [sək'siːd] vi (person) erfolgreich sein, Erfolg haben; (plan etc also) gelingen ♦ vt (nach)folgen +dat; **he ~ed in doing it** es gelang ihm, es zu tun; ~ing adj (nach)folgend

success [sək'ses] n Erfolg m; ~ful adj erfolgreich; **to be ~ful (in doing sth)** Erfolg haben (bei etw); ~fully adv erfolgreich

succession [sək'seʃən] n (Aufeinander)folge f; (to throne) Nachfolge f

successive [sək'sesɪv] adj aufeinander folgend

successor [sək'sesəʳ] n Nachfolger(in) m(f)

succinct [sək'sɪŋkt] adj knapp

succulent ['sʌkjulənt] adj saftig

succumb [sə'kʌm] vi: **to ~ (to)** erliegen (+dat); (yield) nachgeben (+dat)

such [sʌtʃ] adj solche(r, s); ~ **a book** so ein Buch; ~ **books** solche Bücher; ~ **courage** so ein Mut; ~ **a long trip** so eine lange Reise; ~ **a lot of** so viel(e); ~ **as** wie; **a noise** ~ **as** to in derartiger Lärm, dass; **as** ~ an sich; ~~**and**-~ **a time** die und die Zeit

suck [sʌk] vt saugen; (lollipop etc) lutschen

sucker ['sʌkəʳ] (inf) n Idiot m

suction ['sʌkʃən] n Saugkraft f

sudden ['sʌdn] adj plötzlich; **all of a** ~ auf einmal; ~ly adv plötzlich

suds [sʌdz] npl Seifenlauge f; (lather) Seifenschaum m

sue [suː] vt verklagen

suede [sweɪd] n Wildleder nt

Suez ['suːɪz] n: **the ~ Canal** der Suezkanal

suffer ['sʌfəʳ] vt (er)leiden ♦ vi leiden; ~er n Leidende(r) mf; ~ing n Leiden nt

suffice [sə'faɪs] vi genügen

sufficient [sə'fɪʃənt] adj ausreichend; ~ly adv ausreichend

suffix ['sʌfɪks] n Nachsilbe f

suffocate ['sʌfəkeɪt] vt, vi ersticken

suffrage ['sʌfrɪdʒ] n Wahlrecht nt

sugar ['ʃʊgəʳ] n Zucker m ♦ vt zuckern; ~ **beet** n Zuckerrübe f; ~ **cane** n Zuckerrohr nt; ~y adj süß

suggest [sə'dʒest] vt vorschlagen; (show) schließen lassen auf +acc; ~ion [sə'dʒestʃən] n Vorschlag m; ~ive adj anregend; (indecent) zweideutig

suicide ['suɪsaɪd] n Selbstmord m; **to commit ~** Selbstmord begehen ~ **bomber** n Selbstmordattentäter(in) m(f)

suit [suːt] n Anzug m; (CARDS) Farbe f ♦ vt passen +dat; (clothes) stehen +dat; **well ~ed** (well matched) gut zusammenpassend; ~**able** adj geeignet, passend; ~**ably** adv passend, angemessen

suitcase ['suːtkeɪs] n (Hand)koffer m

suite [swiːt] n (of rooms) Zimmerflucht f; (of furniture) Einrichtung f; (MUS) Suite f

suitor ['suːtəʳ] n (JUR) Kläger(in) m(f)

sulfur ['sʌlfəʳ] (US) n = **sulphur**

sulk [sʌlk] vi schmollen; ~y adj schmollend

sullen ['sʌlən] adj mürrisch

sulphur ['sʌlfəʳ] (US **sulfur**) n Schwefel m

sultana [sʌl'tɑːnə] n (fruit) Sultanine f

sultry ['sʌltrɪ] adj schwül

sum [sʌm] n Summe f; (money) Betrag m, Summe f; (arithmetic) Rechenaufgabe f; ~ **up** vt, vi zusammenfassen

summarize ['sʌməraɪz] vt kurz zusammenfassen

summary ['sʌmərɪ] n Zusammenfassung f ♦ adj (justice) kurzerhand erteilt

summer ['sʌməʳ] n Sommer m ♦ adj Sommer-; ~**house** n (in garden) Gartenhaus nt; ~**time** n Sommerzeit f

summit ['sʌmɪt] n Gipfel m; ~

(conference) n Gipfelkonferenz f

summon ['sʌmən] vt herbeirufen; (JUR) vorladen; (gather up) aufbringen; **~s** (JUR) n Vorladung f ♦ vt vorladen

sump [sʌmp] (BRIT) n (AUT) Ölwanne f

sumptuous ['sʌmptjuəs] adj prächtig

sun [sʌn] n Sonne f; **~bathe** vi sich sonnen; **~block** n Sonnenschutzcreme f; **~burn** n Sonnenbrand m; **~burnt** adj sonnenverbrannt, sonnengebräunt; **to be ~burnt** (painfully) einen Sonnenbrand haben

Sunday ['sʌndɪ] n Sonntag m; **~ school** n Sonntagsschule f

sundial ['sʌndaɪəl] n Sonnenuhr f

sundown ['sʌndaun] n Sonnenuntergang m

sundries ['sʌndrɪz] npl (miscellaneous items) Verschiedene(s) nt

sundry ['sʌndrɪ] adj verschieden; **all and ~** alle

sunflower ['sʌnflauəʳ] n Sonnenblume f

sung [sʌŋ] pp of **sing**

sunglasses ['sʌnglɑːsɪz] npl Sonnenbrille f

sunk [sʌŋk] pp of **sink**

sun: ~light ['sʌnlaɪt] n Sonnenlicht nt; **~lit** ['sʌnlɪt] adj sonnenbeschienen; **~ny** ['sʌnɪ] adj sonnig; **~rise** n Sonnenaufgang m; **~ roof** n (AUT) Schiebedach nt; **~screen** ['sʌnskriːn] n Sonnenschutzcreme f; **~set** ['sʌnsɛt] n Sonnenuntergang m; **~shade** ['sʌnʃeɪd] n Sonnenschirm m; **~shine** ['sʌnʃaɪn] n Sonnenschein m; **~stroke** ['sʌnstrəuk] n Hitzschlag m; **~tan** ['sʌntæn] n (Sonnen)bräune f; **~tan oil** n Sonnenöl nt

super ['suːpəʳ] (inf) adj prima, klasse

superannuation [suːpərænjuˈeɪʃən] n Pension f

superb [suːˈpəːb] adj ausgezeichnet, hervorragend

supercilious [suːpəˈsɪlɪəs] adj herablassend

superficial [suːpəˈfɪʃəl] adj oberflächlich

superfluous [suˈpəːfluəs] adj überflüssig

superhuman [suːpəˈhjuːmən] adj (effort) übermenschlich

superimpose ['suːpərɪmˈpəuz] vt übereinander legen

superintendent [suːpərɪnˈtɛndənt] n Polizeichef m

superior [suˈpɪərɪəʳ] adj überlegen; (better) besser ♦ n Vorgesetzte(r) mf; **~ity** [supɪərɪˈɒrɪtɪ] n Überlegenheit f

superlative [suˈpəːlatɪv] adj überragend

super: ~man ['suːpəmæn] (irreg) n Übermensch m; **~market** ['suːpəmɑːkɪt] n Supermarkt m; **~natural** [suːpəˈnætʃərəl] adj übernatürlich; **~power** ['suːpəpauəʳ] n Weltmacht f

supersede [suːpəˈsiːd] vt ersetzen

supersonic ['suːpəˈsɔnɪk] adj Überschall-

superstition [suːpəˈstɪʃən] n Aberglaube m; **superstitious** [suːpəˈstɪʃəs] adj abergläubisch

supervise ['suːpəvaɪz] vt beaufsichtigen, kontrollieren; **supervision** [suːpəˈvɪʒən] n Aufsicht f; **supervisor** ['suːpəvaɪzəʳ] n Aufsichtsperson f; **supervisory** ['suːpəvaɪzəɪ] adj Aufsichts-

supper ['sʌpəʳ] n Abendessen nt

supplant [səˈplɑːnt] vt (person, thing) ersetzen

supple ['sʌpl] adj geschmeidig

supplement [n 'sʌplɪmənt, vb sʌplɪˈmɛnt] n Ergänzung f; (in book) Nachtrag m ♦ vt ergänzen; **~ary** [sʌplɪˈmɛntərɪ] adj ergänzend; **~ary benefit** (BRIT: old) n ≈ Sozialhilfe f

supplier [səˈplaɪəʳ] n Lieferant m

supplies [səˈplaɪz] npl (food) Vorräte pl; (MIL) Nachschub m

supply [səˈplaɪ] vt liefern ♦ n Vorrat m; (~ing) Lieferung f; see also **supplies**; **~ teacher** (BRIT) n Vertretung f

support [səˈpɔːt] n Unterstützung f; (TECH) Stütze f ♦ vt (hold up) stützen, tragen; (provide for) ernähren; (be in favour of) unterstützen; **~er** n Anhänger(in) m(f)

suppose [səˈpəuz] vt, vi annehmen; **to be ~d to do sth** etw tun sollen; **~dly** [səˈpəuzɪdlɪ] adv angeblich; **supposing** conj angenommen; **supposition** [sʌpəˈzɪʃən] n Voraussetzung f

suppress [səˈprɛs] vt unterdrücken

supremacy [suˈprɛməsɪ] n Vorherrschaft f, Oberhoheit f

supreme [su'pri:m] *adj* oberste(r, s), höchste(r, s)

surcharge ['sə:tʃɑ:dʒ] *n* Zuschlag *m*

sure [ʃuər] *adj* sicher, gewiss; **~!** (*of course*) klar!; **to make ~ of sth/that** sich einer Sache *gen* vergewissern/vergewissern, dass; **~ enough** (*with past*) tatsächlich; (*with future*) ganz bestimmt; **~-footed** *adj* sicher (auf den Füßen); **~ly** *adv* (*certainly*) sicherlich, gewiss; **~ly it's wrong** das ist doch wohl falsch

surety ['ʃuərəti] *n* Sicherheit *f*

surf [sə:f] *n* Brandung *f*

surface ['sə:fɪs] *n* Oberfläche *f* ♦ *vt* (*roadway*) teeren ♦ *vi* auftauchen; **~ mail** *n* gewöhnliche Post *f*

surfboard ['sə:fbɔ:d] *n* Surfbrett *nt*

surfeit ['sə:fɪt] *n* Übermaß *nt*

surfing ['sə:fɪŋ] *n* Surfen *nt*

surge [sə:dʒ] *n* Woge *f* ♦ *vi* wogen

surgeon ['sə:dʒən] *n* Chirurg(in) *m(f)*

surgery ['sə:dʒəri] *n* (*BRIT: place*) Praxis *f*; (: *time*) Sprechstunde *f*; (*treatment*) Operation *f*; **to undergo ~** operiert werden; **~ hours** (*BRIT*) *npl* Sprechstunden *pl*

surgical ['sə:dʒɪkl] *adj* chirurgisch; **~ spirit** (*BRIT*) *n* Wundbenzin *nt*

surly ['sə:lɪ] *adj* verdrießlich, grob

surmount [sə:'maunt] *vt* überwinden

surname ['sə:neɪm] *n* Zuname *m*

surpass [sə:'pɑ:s] *vt* übertreffen

surplus ['sə:pləs] *n* Überschuss *m* ♦ *adj* überschüssig, Über(schuss)-

surprise [sə'praɪz] *n* Überraschung *f* ♦ *vt* überraschen; **~d** *adj* überrascht; **surprising** *adj* überraschend; **surprisingly** *adv* überraschend(erweise)

surrender [sə'rendər] *n* Kapitulation *f* ♦ *vi* sich ergeben

surreptitious [sʌrəp'tɪʃəs] *adj* heimlich; (*look also*) verstohlen

surrogate ['sʌrəgɪt] *n* Ersatz *m*; **~ mother** *n* Leihmutter *f*

surround [sə'raund] *vt* umgeben; **~ing** *adj* (*countryside*) umliegend; **~ings** *npl* Umgebung *f*; (*environment*) Umwelt *f*

surveillance [sə:'veɪləns] *n* Überwachung *f*

survey [*n* 'sə:veɪ, *vb* sə:'veɪ] *n* Übersicht *f* ♦ *vt* überblicken; (*land*) vermessen; **~or** [sə'veɪər] *n* Land(ver)messer(in) *m(f)*

survival [sə'vaɪvl] *n* Überleben *nt*

survive [sə'vaɪv] *vt, vi* überleben; **survivor** [sə'vaɪvər] *n* Überlebende(r) *mf*

susceptible [sə'septəbl] *adj*: **~ (to)** empfindlich (gegen); (*charms etc*) empfänglich (für)

suspect [*n* 'sʌspekt, *vb* səs'pekt] *n* Verdächtige(r) *mf* ♦ *adj* verdächtig ♦ *vt* verdächtigen; (*think*) vermuten

suspend [səs'pend] *vt* verschieben; (*from work*) suspendieren; (*hang up*) aufhängen; (*SPORT*) sperren; **~ed sentence** *n* (*JUR*) zur Bewährung ausgesetzte Strafe; **~er belt** *n* Strumpf(halter)gürtel *m*; **~ers** *npl* (*BRIT*) Strumpfhalter *m*; (*US*) Hosenträger *m*

suspense [səs'pens] *n* Spannung *f*

suspension [səs'penʃən] *n* (*from work*) Suspendierung *f*; (*SPORT*) Sperrung *f*; (*AUT*) Federung *f*; **~ bridge** *n* Hängebrücke *f*

suspicion [səs'pɪʃən] *n* Misstrauen *nt*; Verdacht *m*; **suspicious** [səs'pɪʃəs] *adj* misstrauisch; (*causing ~*) verdächtig

sustain [səs'teɪn] *vt* (*maintain*) aufrechterhalten; (*confirm*) bestätigen; (*injury*) davontragen; **~able** *adj* (*development, growth etc*) aufrechtzuerhalten; **~ed** *adj* (*effort*) anhaltend

sustenance ['sʌstɪnəns] *n* Nahrung *f*

swab [swɔb] *n* (*MED*) Tupfer *m*

swagger ['swægər] *vi* stolzieren

swallow ['swɔləu] *n* (*bird*) Schwalbe *f*; (*of food etc*) Schluck *m* ♦ *vt* (ver)schlucken; **~ up** *vt* verschlingen

swam [swæm] *pt of* **swim**

swamp [swɔmp] *n* Sumpf *m* ♦ *vt* überschwemmen

swan [swɔn] *n* Schwan *m*

swap [swɔp] *n* Tausch *m* ♦ *vt*: **to ~ sth (for sth)** etw (gegen etw) tauschen *or* eintauschen

swarm [swɔ:m] *n* Schwarm *m* ♦ *vi*: **to ~** *or* **be ~ing with** wimmeln von

swarthy ['swɔːðɪ] *adj* dunkel, braun

swastika ['swɒstɪkə] *n* Hakenkreuz *nt*

swat [swɒt] *vt* totschlagen

sway [sweɪ] *vi* schaukeln, sich wiegen; (*branches*) schaukeln, sich wiegen ♦ *vt* schwenken; (*influence*) beeinflussen

swear [sweəʳ] (*pt* **swore**, *pp* **sworn**) *vi* (*promise*) schwören; (*curse*) fluchen; **to ~ to sth** schwören auf etw *acc*; ~**word** *n* Fluch *m*

sweat [swet] *n* Schweiß *m* ♦ *vi* schwitzen

sweater ['swetəʳ] *n* Pullover *m*

sweatshirt ['swetʃəːt] *n* Sweatshirt *nt*

sweaty ['swetɪ] *adj* verschwitzt

Swede [swiːd] *n* Schwede *m*, Schwedin *f*

swede [swiːd] (*BRIT*) *n* Steckrübe *f*

Sweden ['swiːdn] *n* Schweden *nt*

Swedish ['swiːdɪʃ] *adj* schwedisch ♦ *n* (*LING*) Schwedisch *nt*

sweep [swiːp] (*pt, pp* **swept**) *n* (*chimney ~*) Schornsteinfeger *m* ♦ *vt* fegen, kehren; ~ **away** *vt* wegfegen; ~ **past** *vi* vorbeisausen; ~ **up** *vt* zusammenkehren; ~**ing** *adj* (*gesture*) schwungvoll; (*statement*) verallgemeinernd

sweet [swiːt] *n* (*course*) Nachtisch *m*; (*candy*) Bonbon *nt* ♦ *adj* süß; ~**corn** *n* Zuckermais *m*; ~**en** *vt* süßen; (*fig*) versüßen; ~**heart** *n* Liebste(r) *mf*; ~**ness** *n* Süße *f*; ~ **pea** *n* Gartenwicke *f*

swell [swel] (*pt* **swelled**, *pp* **swollen** *or* **swelled**) *n* Seegang *m* ♦ *adj* (*inf*) todschick ♦ *vt* (*numbers*) vermehren ♦ *vi* (*also*: ~ **up**) (an)schwellen; ~**ing** *n* Schwellung *f*

sweltering ['sweltərɪŋ] *adj* drückend

swept [swept] *pt, pp of* **sweep**

swerve [swəːv] *vt, vi* ausscheren

swift [swɪft] *n* Mauersegler *m* ♦ *adj* geschwind, schnell, rasch; ~**ly** *adv* geschwind, schnell, rasch

swig [swɪg] *n* Zug *m*

swill [swɪl] *n* (*for pigs*) Schweinefutter *nt* ♦ *vt* spülen

swim [swɪm] (*pt* **swam**, *pp* **swum**) *n*: **to go for a ~** schwimmen gehen ♦ *vi* schwimmen ♦ *vt* (*cross*) (durch)schwimmen; ~**mer** *n* Schwimmer(in) *m(f)*; ~**ming** *n* Schwimmen *nt*; ~**ming cap** *n* Badehaube *f*, Badekappe *f*; ~**ming costume** (*BRIT*) *n* Badeanzug *m*; ~**ming pool** *n* Schwimmbecken *nt*; (*private*) Swimmingpool *m*; ~**ming trunks** *npl* Badehose *f*; ~**suit** *n* Badeanzug *m*

swindle ['swɪndl] *n* Schwindel *m*, Betrug *m* ♦ *vt* betrügen

swine [swaɪn] *n* (*also fig*) Schwein *nt*

swing [swɪŋ] (*pt, pp* **swung**) *n* (*child's*) Schaukel *f*; (*movement*) Schwung *m* ♦ *vt* schwingen ♦ *vi* schwingen, schaukeln; (*turn quickly*) schwenken; **in full ~** in vollem Gange; ~ **bridge** *n* Drehbrücke *f*; ~ **door** (*BRIT*) *n* Schwingtür *f*

swingeing ['swɪndʒɪŋ] (*BRIT*) *adj* hart; (*taxation, cuts*) extrem

swinging door ['swɪŋɪŋ-] (*US*) *n* Schwingtür *f*

swipe [swaɪp] *n* Hieb *m* ♦ *vt* (*inf: hit*) hart schlagen; (: *steal*) klauen

swirl [swəːl] *vi* wirbeln

swish [swɪʃ] *adj* (*inf: smart*) schick ♦ *vi* zischen; (*grass, skirts*) rascheln

Swiss [swɪs] *adj* Schweizer, schweizerisch ♦ *n* Schweizer(in) *m(f)*; **the ~** *npl* (*people*) die Schweizer *pl*

switch [swɪtʃ] *n* (*ELEC*) Schalter *m*; (*change*) Wechsel *m* ♦ *vt* (*ELEC*) schalten; (*change*) wechseln ♦ *vi* wechseln; ~ **off** *vt* ab- *or* ausschalten; ~ **on** *vt* an- *or* einschalten; ~**board** *n* Zentrale *f*; (*board*) Schaltbrett *nt*

Switzerland ['swɪtsələnd] *n* die Schweiz

swivel ['swɪvl] *vt* (*also*: ~ **round**) drehen ♦ *vi* (*also*: ~ **round**) sich drehen

swollen ['swəʊlən] *pp of* **swell**

swoon [swuːn] *vi* (*old*) in Ohnmacht fallen

swoop [swuːp] *n* Sturzflug *m*; (*esp by police*) Razzia *f* ♦ *vi* (*also*: ~ **down**) stürzen

swop [swɒp] = **swap**

sword [sɔːd] *n* Schwert *nt*; ~**fish** *n* Schwertfisch *m*

swore [swɔːʳ] *pt of* **swear**

sworn [swɔːn] *pp of* **swear**

swot [swɒt] *vt, vi* pauken

swum [swʌm] *pp of* **swim**

swung [swʌŋ] *pt, pp of* **swing**

sycamore ['sɪkəmɔ:ʳ] n (US) Platane f; (BRIT) Bergahorn m

syllable ['sɪləbl] n Silbe f

syllabus ['sɪləbəs] n Lehrplan m

symbol ['sɪmbl] n Symbol nt; ~ic(al) [sɪm'bɒlɪk(l)] adj symbolisch

symmetry ['sɪmɪtrɪ] n Symmetrie f

sympathetic [sɪmpə'θetɪk] adj mitfühlend

sympathize ['sɪmpəθaɪz] vi mitfühlen; ~r n (POL) Sympathisant(in) m(f)

sympathy ['sɪmpəθɪ] n Mitleid nt, Mitgefühl nt; (condolence) Beileid nt; **with our deepest ~** mit tief empfundenem Beileid

symphony ['sɪmfənɪ] n Sinfonie f

symptom ['sɪmptəm] n Symptom nt; ~atic [sɪmptə'mætɪk] adj (fig): **~atic of** bezeichnend für

synagogue ['sɪnəgɒg] n Synagoge f

synchronize ['sɪŋkrənaɪz] vt synchronisieren

syndicate ['sɪndɪkɪt] n Konsortium nt

synonym ['sɪnənɪm] n Synonym nt; ~ous [sɪ'nɒnɪməs] adj gleichbedeutend

synopsis [sɪ'nɒpsɪs] n Zusammenfassung f

synthetic [sɪn'θetɪk] adj synthetisch; ~**s** npl (man-made fabrics) Synthetik f

syphon ['saɪfən] = **siphon**

Syria ['sɪrɪə] n Syrien nt

syringe [sɪ'rɪndʒ] n Spritze f

syrup ['sɪrəp] n Sirup m; (of sugar) Melasse f

system ['sɪstəm] n System nt; ~atic [sɪstə'mætɪk] adj systematisch; ~ **disk** n (COMPUT) Systemdiskette f; ~ **analyst** n Systemanalytiker(in) m(f)

T, t

ta [tɑ:] (BRIT: inf) excl danke!

tab [tæb] n Aufhänger m; (name ~) Schild nt; **to keep ~s on** (fig) genau im Auge behalten

tabby ['tæbɪ] n (also: ~ **cat**) getigerte Katze f

table ['teɪbl] n Tisch m; (list) Tabelle f ♦ vt (PARL: propose) vorlegen, einbringen; **to lay** or **set the ~** den Tisch decken; ~**cloth** n Tischtuch nt; ~ **d'hôte** [tɑ:bl'dəʊt] n Tagesmenü nt; ~ **lamp** n Tischlampe f;

~**mat** n Untersatz m; ~ **of contents** n Inhaltsverzeichnis nt; ~**spoon** n Esslöffel m; ~**spoonful** n Esslöffel m (voll)

tablet ['tæblɪt] n (MED) Tablette f

table tennis n Tischtennis nt

table wine n Tafelwein m

tabloid ['tæblɔɪd] n Zeitung f in kleinem Format; (pej) Boulevardzeitung f

---
tabloid press

ⓘ *Der Ausdruck* **tabloid press** *bezieht sich auf kleinformatige Zeitungen (ca 30 x 40cm); sie sind in Großbritannien fast ausschließlich Massenblätter. Im Gegensatz zur* **quality press** *verwenden diese Massenblätter viele Fotos und einen knappen, oft reißerischen Stil. Sie kommen den Lesern entgegen, die mehr Wert auf Unterhaltung legen.*

---

tabulate ['tæbjuleɪt] vt tabellarisch ordnen

tacit ['tæsɪt] adj stillschweigend

taciturn ['tæsɪtɜːn] adj wortkarg

tack [tæk] n (small nail) Stift m; (US: thumbtack) Reißzwecke f; (stitch) Heftstich m; (NAUT) Lavieren nt; (course) Kurs m ♦ vt (nail) nageln; (stitch) heften ♦ vi aufkreuzen

tackle ['tækl] n (for lifting) Flaschenzug m; (NAUT) Takelage f; (SPORT) Tackling nt ♦ vt (deal with) anpacken, in Angriff nehmen; (person) festhalten; (player) angehen

tacky ['tækɪ] adj klebrig

tact [tækt] n Takt m; ~**ful** adj taktvoll

tactical ['tæktɪkl] adj taktisch

tactics ['tæktɪks] npl Taktik f

tactless ['tæktlɪs] adj taktlos

tadpole ['tædpəʊl] n Kaulquappe f

taffy ['tæfɪ] (US) n Sahnebonbon nt

tag [tæg] n (label) Schild nt, Anhänger m; (maker's name) Etikett nt; ~ **along** vi mitkommen

tail [teɪl] n Schwanz m; (of list) Schluss m ♦ vt folgen +dat; ~ **away** or **off** vi abfallen, schwinden; ~**back** (BRIT) n (AUT) (Rück)stau m; ~ **coat** n Frack m; ~ **end** n Schluss m, Ende nt; ~**gate** n (AUT) Heckklappe f

tailor ['teɪləʳ] n Schneider m; ~**ing** n

Schneidern nt; **~-made** adj
maßgeschneidert; (fig): **~-made for sb** jdm
wie auf den Leib geschnitten

tailwind ['teɪlwɪnd] n Rückenwind m

tainted ['teɪntɪd] adj verdorben

take [teɪk] (pt **took**, pp **taken**) vt nehmen;
(trip, exam, PHOT) machen; (capture: person)
fassen; (: town; also COMM, FIN) einnehmen;
(carry to a place) bringen; (get for o.s.) sich
dat nehmen; (gain, obtain) bekommen; (put
up with) hinnehmen; (respond to)
aufnehmen; (interpret) auffassen; (assume)
annehmen; (contain) Platz haben für;
(GRAM) stehen mit; **to ~ sth from sb** jdm
etw wegnehmen; **to ~ sth from sth** (MATH:
subtract) etw von etw abziehen; (extract,
quotation) etw einer Sache dat entnehmen;
~ after vt fus ähnlich sein +dat; **~ apart**
vt auseinander nehmen; **~ away** vt
(remove) wegnehmen; (carry off)
wegbringen; **~ back** vt (return)
zurückbringen; (retract) zurücknehmen; **~
down** vt (pull down) abreißen; (write down)
aufschreiben; **~ in** vt (deceive) hereinlegen;
(understand) begreifen; (include)
einschließen; **~ off** vi (plane) starten ♦ vt
(remove) wegnehmen; (clothing) ausziehen;
(imitate) nachmachen; **~ on** vt (undertake)
übernehmen; (engage) einstellen;
(opponent) antreten gegen; **~ out** vt (girl,
dog) ausführen; (extract) herausnehmen;
(insurance) abschließen; (licence) sich dat
geben lassen; (book) ausleihen; (remove)
entfernen; **to ~ sth out of sth** (drawer,
pocket etc) etw aus etw herausnehmen; **~
over** vt übernehmen ♦ vi: **to ~ over from
sb** jdn ablösen; **~ to** vt fus (like) mögen;
(adopt as practice) sich dat angewöhnen; **~
up** vt (raise) aufnehmen; (dress etc) kürzer
machen; (occupy) in Anspruch nehmen;
(engage in) sich befassen mit; **~away** adj
zum Mitnehmen; **~-home pay** n
Nettolohn m; **~n** pp of **take**; **~off** n (AVIAT)
Start m; (imitation) Nachahmung f; **~out**
(US) adj = **takeaway**; **~over** n (COMM)
Übernahme f; **takings** ['teɪkɪŋz] npl (COMM)
Einnahmen pl

talc [tælk] n (also: **~um powder**)
Talkumpuder m

tale [teɪl] n Geschichte f, Erzählung f; **to tell
~s** (fig: lie) Geschichten erfinden

talent ['tælnt] n Talent nt; **~ed** adj begabt

talk [tɔːk] n (conversation) Gespräch nt;
(rumour) Gerede nt; (speech) Vortrag m ♦ vi
sprechen, reden; **~s** npl (POL etc) Gespräche
pl; **to ~ about** sprechen von +dat or über
+acc; **to ~ sb into doing sth** jdn
überreden, etw zu tun; **to ~ sb out of
doing sth** jdm ausreden, etw zu tun; **to ~
shop** fachsimpeln; **~ over** vt besprechen;
~ative adj gesprächig

tall [tɔːl] adj groß; (building) hoch; **to be 1 m
80 ~** 1,80 m groß sein; **~boy** (BRIT) n
Kommode f; **~ story** n übertriebene
Geschichte f

tally ['tælɪ] n Abrechnung f ♦ vi
übereinstimmen

talon ['tælən] n Kralle f

tame [teɪm] adj zahm; (fig) fade

tamper ['tæmpə*] vi: **to ~ with**
herumpfuschen an +dat

tampon ['tæmpɔn] n Tampon m

tan [tæn] n (Sonnen)bräune f; (colour)
Gelbbraun nt ♦ adj (colour) (gelb)braun ♦ vt
bräunen ♦ vi braun werden

tang [tæŋ] n Schärfe f

tangent ['tændʒənt] n Tangente f; **to go off
at a ~** (fig) vom Thema abkommen

tangerine [tændʒəˈriːn] n Mandarine f

tangible ['tændʒəbl] adj greifbar

tangle ['tæŋgl] n Durcheinander nt; (trouble)
Schwierigkeiten pl; **to get in(to) a ~** sich
verheddern

tank [tæŋk] n (container) Tank m, Behälter m;
(MIL) Panzer m; **~er** ['tæŋkə*] n (ship) Tanker
m; (vehicle) Tankwagen m

tanned [tænd] adj gebräunt

tantalizing ['tæntəlaɪzɪŋ] adj verlockend;
(annoying) quälend

tantamount ['tæntəmaunt] adj: **~ to**
gleichbedeutend mit

tantrum ['tæntrəm] n Wutanfall m

tap [tæp] n Hahn m; (gentle blow) Klopfen nt
♦ vt (strike) klopfen; (supply) anzapfen;

(*telephone*) abhören; **on ~** (*fig: resources*) zur Hand; **~-dancing** *n* Steppen *nt*

tape [teɪp] *n* Band *nt*; (*magnetic*) (Ton)band *nt*; (*adhesive*) Klebstreifen *m* ♦ *vt* (*record*) aufnehmen; **~ deck** *n* Tapedeck *nt*; **~ measure** *n* Maßband *nt*

taper ['teɪpə'] *vi* spitz zulaufen

tape recorder *n* Tonbandgerät *nt*

tapestry ['tæpɪstrɪ] *n* Wandteppich *m*

tar [tɑː] *n* Teer *m*

target ['tɑːgɪt] *n* Ziel *nt*; (*board*) Zielscheibe *f*

tariff ['tærɪf] *n* (*duty paid*) Zoll *m*; (*list*) Tarif *m*

tarmac ['tɑːmæk] *n* (*AVIAT*) Rollfeld *nt*

tarnish ['tɑːnɪʃ] *vt* matt machen; (*fig*) beflecken

tarpaulin [tɑː'pɔːlɪn] *n* Plane *f*

tarragon ['tærəgən] *n* Estragon *m*

tart [tɑːt] *n* (Obst)torte *f*; (*inf*) Nutte *f* ♦ *adj* scharf; **~ up** (*inf*) *vt* aufmachen; (*person*) auftakeln

tartan ['tɑːtn] *n* Schottenkaro *nt* ♦ *adj* mit Schottenkaro

tartar ['tɑːtə'] *n* Zahnstein *m*

tartar(e) sauce ['tɑːtə-] *n* Remoulade *f*

task [tɑːsk] *n* Aufgabe *f*; **to take sb to ~** sich *dat* jdn vornehmen; **~ force** *n* Sondertrupp *m*

tassel ['tæsl] *n* Quaste *f*

taste [teɪst] *n* Geschmack *m*; (*sense*) Geschmackssinn *m*; (*small quantity*) Kostprobe *f*; (*liking*) Vorliebe *f* ♦ *vt* schmecken; (*try*) probieren ♦ *vi* schmecken; **can I have a ~ of this wine?** kann ich diesen Wein probieren?; **to have a ~ for sth** etw mögen; **in good/bad ~** geschmackvoll/geschmacklos; **you can ~ the garlic (in it)** man kann den Knoblauch herausschmecken; **to ~ of sth** nach einer Sache schmecken; **~ful** *adj* geschmackvoll; **~less** *adj* (*insipid*) fade; (*in bad ~*) geschmacklos; **tasty** ['teɪstɪ] *adj* schmackhaft

tattered ['tætəd] *adj* = **in tatters**

tatters ['tætəz] *npl*: **in ~** in Fetzen

tattoo [tə'tuː] *n* (*MIL*) Zapfenstreich *m*; (*on skin*) Tätowierung *f* ♦ *vt* tätowieren

tatty ['tætɪ] (*BRIT: inf*) *adj* schäbig

taught [tɔːt] *pt, pp* of **teach**

taunt [tɔːnt] *n* höhnische Bemerkung *f* ♦ *vt* verhöhnen

Taurus ['tɔːrəs] *n* Stier *m*

taut [tɔːt] *adj* straff

tawdry ['tɔːdrɪ] *adj* (bunt und) billig

tax [tæks] *n* Steuer *f* ♦ *vt* besteuern; (*strain*) strapazieren; (*strength*) angreifen; **~able** *adj* (*income*) steuerpflichtig; **~ation** [tæk'seɪʃən] *n* Besteuerung *f*; **~ avoidance** *n* Steuerumgehung *f*; **~ disc** (*BRIT*) *n* (*AUT*) Kraftfahrzeugsteuerplakette *f*; **~ evasion** *n* Steuerhinterziehung *f*; **~-free** *adj* steuerfrei

taxi ['tæksɪ] *n* Taxi *nt* ♦ *vi* (*plane*) rollen; **~ driver** *n* Taxifahrer *m*; **~ rank** (*BRIT*) *n* Taxistand *m*; **~ stand** *n* Taxistand *m*

tax: **~payer** *n* Steuerzahler *m*; **~ relief** *n* Steuerermäßigung *f*; **~ return** *n* Steuererklärung *f*

TB *n abbr* (= *tuberculosis*) Tb *f*, Tbc *f*

tea [tiː] *n* Tee *m*; (*meal*) (frühes) Abendessen *nt*; **high ~** (*BRIT*) Abendessen *nt*; **~ bag** *n* Teebeutel *m*; **~ break** (*BRIT*) *n* Teepause *f*

teach [tiːtʃ] (*pt, pp* **taught**) *vt* lehren; (*SCH*) lehren, unterrichten; (*show*): **to ~ sb sth** jdm etw beibringen ♦ *vi* lehren, unterrichten; **~er** *n* Lehrer(in) *m(f)*; **~er's pet** *n* Lehrers Liebling *m*; **~ing** *n* (*~er's work*) Unterricht *m*; (*doctrine*) Lehre *f*

tea: **~ cloth** *n* Geschirrtuch *nt*; **~ cosy** *n* Teewärmer *m*; **~cup** *n* Teetasse *f*; **~ leaves** *npl* Teeblätter *pl*

team [tiːm] *n* (*workers*) Team *nt*; (*SPORT*) Mannschaft *f*; (*animals*) Gespann *nt*; **~work** *n* Gemeinschaftsarbeit *f*, Teamarbeit *f*

teapot ['tiːpɔt] *n* Teekanne *f*

tear¹ [tɛə'] (*pt* **tore**, *pp* **torn**) *n* Riss *m* ♦ *vt* zerreißen; (*muscle*) zerren ♦ *vi* (zer)reißen; (*rush*) rasen; **~ along** *vi* (*rush*) entlangrasen; **~ up** *vt* (*sheet of paper etc*) zerreißen

tear² [tɪə'] *n* Träne *f*; **~ful** ['tɪəful] *adj* weinend; (*voice*) weinerlich; **~ gas** ['tɪəgæs] *n* Tränengas *nt*

tearoom ['tiːruːm] *n* Teestube *f*

tease [tiːz] *n* Hänsler *m* ♦ *vt* necken

tea set *n* Teeservice *nt*

teaspoon ['tiːspuːn] n Teelöffel m

teat [tiːt] n Brustwarze f; (of animal) Zitze f; (of bottle) Sauger m

tea time n (in the afternoon) Teestunde f; (mealtime) Abendessen nt

tea towel n Geschirrtuch nt

technical ['tɛknɪkl] adj technisch; (knowledge, terms) Fach-; ~ity [tɛknɪ'kælɪtɪ] n technische Einzelheit f; (JUR) Formsache f; ~ly adv technisch; (speak) spezialisiert; (fig) genau genommen

technician [tɛk'nɪʃən] n Techniker m

technique [tɛk'niːk] n Technik f

techno ['tɛknəu] n Techno m

technological [tɛknə'lɔdʒɪkl] adj technologisch

technology [tɛk'nɔlədʒɪ] n Technologie f

teddy (bear) ['tɛdɪ-] n Teddybär m

tedious ['tiːdɪəs] adj langweilig, ermüdend

tee [tiː] n (GOLF: object) Tee nt

teem [tiːm] vi (swarm): **to ~ (with)** wimmeln (von); **it is ~ing (with rain)** es gießt in Strömen

teenage ['tiːneɪdʒ] adj (fashions etc) Teenager-, jugendlich; ~r n Teenager m, Jugendliche(r) mf

teens [tiːnz] npl Teenageralter nt

tee-shirt ['tiːʃəːt] n T-Shirt nt

teeter ['tiːtər] vi schwanken

teeth [tiːθ] npl of **tooth**

teethe [tiːð] vi zahnen; **teething ring** n Beißring m; **teething troubles** npl (fig) Kinderkrankheiten pl

teetotal ['tiː'təutl] adj abstinent

tele: ~communications npl Fernmeldewesen nt; ~**conferencing** n Telefon- or Videokonferenz f; ~**gram** n Telegramm nt; ~**graph** n Telegraf m; ~**graph pole** n Telegrafenmast m

telephone ['tɛlɪfəun] n Telefon nt, Fernsprecher m ♦ vt anrufen; (message) telefonisch mitteilen; **to be on the ~** (talking) telefonieren; (possessing phone) Telefon haben; ~ **booth** n Telefonzelle f; ~ **box** (BRIT) n Telefonzelle f; ~ **call** n Telefongespräch nt, Anruf m; ~ **directory** n Telefonbuch nt; ~ **number** n

Telefonnummer f; **telephonist** [tə'lɛfənɪst] (BRIT) n Telefonist(in) m(f)

telephoto lens ['tɛlɪ'fəutəu-] n Teleobjektiv nt

telesales ['tɛlɪseɪlz] n Telefonverkauf m

telescope ['tɛlɪskəup] n Teleskop nt, Fernrohr nt ♦ vt ineinander schieben

televise ['tɛlɪvaɪz] vt durch das Fernsehen übertragen

television ['tɛlɪvɪʒən] n Fernsehen nt; **on ~** im Fernsehen; ~ **(set)** n Fernsehapparat m, Fernseher m

teleworking ['tɛlɪwəːkɪŋ] n Telearbeit f

telex ['tɛlɛks] n Telex nt ♦ vt per Telex schicken

tell [tɛl] (pt, pp **told**) vt (story) erzählen; (secret) ausplaudern; (say, make known) sagen; (distinguish) erkennen; (be sure) wissen ♦ vi (talk) sprechen; (be sure) wissen; (divulge) es verraten; (have effect) sich auswirken; **to ~ sb to do sth** jdm sagen, dass er etw tun soll; **to ~ sb sth** or **sth to sb** jdm etw sagen; **to ~ sb by sth** jdn an etw dat erkennen; **to ~ sth from** etw unterscheiden von; **to ~ of sth** von etw sprechen; ~ **off** vt: **to ~ sb off** jdn ausschimpfen

teller ['tɛlər] n Kassenbeamte(r) mf

telling ['tɛlɪŋ] adj verräterisch; (blow) hart

telltale ['tɛlteɪl] adj verräterisch

telly ['tɛlɪ] (BRIT: inf) n abbr (= television) TV nt

temp [tɛmp] n abbr (= temporary) Aushilfssekretärin f

temper ['tɛmpər] n (disposition) Temperament nt; (anger) Zorn m ♦ vt (tone down) mildern; (metal) härten; **to be in a (bad) ~** wütend sein; **to lose one's ~** die Beherrschung verlieren

temperament ['tɛmprəmənt] n Temperament nt; ~**al** [tɛmprə'mɛntl] adj (moody) launisch

temperate ['tɛmprət] adj gemäßigt

temperature ['tɛmprətʃər] n Temperatur f; (MED: high ~) Fieber nt; **to have** or **run a ~** Fieber haben

template ['tɛmplɪt] n Schablone f

temple ['tɛmpl] n Tempel m; (ANAT) Schläfe f

temporal ['tempərl] *adj (of time)* zeitlich; *(worldly)* irdisch, weltlich

temporarily ['tempərərılı] *adv* zeitweilig, vorübergehend

temporary ['tempərərı] *adj* vorläufig; *(road, building)* provisorisch

tempt [tempt] *vt (persuade)* verleiten; *(attract)* reizen, (ver)locken; **to ~ sb into doing sth** jdn dazu verleiten, etw zu tun; **~ation** [temp'teıʃən] *n* Versuchung *f*; **~ing** *adj (person)* verführerisch; *(object, situation)* verlockend

ten [ten] *num* zehn

tenable ['tenəbl] *adj* haltbar

tenacious [tə'neıʃəs] *adj* zäh, hartnäckig

tenacity [tə'næsıtı] *n* Zähigkeit *f*, Hartnäckigkeit *f*

tenancy ['tenənsı] *n* Mietverhältnis *nt*

tenant ['tenənt] *n* Mieter *m*; *(of larger property)* Pächter *m*

tend [tend] *vt (look after)* sich kümmern um ♦ *vi:* **to ~ to do sth** etw gewöhnlich tun

tendency ['tendənsı] *n* Tendenz *f*; *(of person)* Tendenz *f*, Neigung *f*

tender ['tendə*] *adj* zart; *(loving)* zärtlich ♦ *n (COMM: offer)* Kostenanschlag *m* ♦ *vt* (an)bieten; *(resignation)* einreichen; **~ness** *n* Zartheit *f*; *(being loving)* Zärtlichkeit *f*

tendon ['tendən] *n* Sehne *f*

tenement ['tenəmənt] *n* Mietshaus *nt*

tennis ['tenıs] *n* Tennis *nt*; **~ ball** *n* Tennisball *m*; **~ court** *n* Tennisplatz *m*; **~ player** *n* Tennisspieler(in) *m(f)*; **~ racket** *n* Tennisschläger *m*; **~ shoes** *npl* Tennisschuhe *pl*

tenor ['tenə*] *n* Tenor *m*

tenpin bowling ['tenpın-] *n* Bowling *nt*

tense [tens] *adj* angespannt ♦ *n* Zeitform *f*

tension ['tenʃən] *n* Spannung *f*

tent [tent] *n* Zelt *nt*

tentacle ['tentəkl] *n* Fühler *m*; *(of sea animals)* Fangarm *m*

tentative ['tentətıv] *adj (movement)* unsicher; *(offer)* Probe-; *(arrangement)* vorläufig; *(suggestion)* unverbindlich; **~ly** *adv* versuchsweise; *(try, move)* vorsichtig

tenterhooks ['tentəhuks] *npl:* **to be on ~** auf die Folter gespannt sein

tenth [tenθ] *adj* zehnte(r, s)

tent peg *n* Hering *m*

tent pole *n* Zeltstange *f*

tenuous ['tenjuəs] *adj* schwach

tenure ['tenjuə*] *n (of land)* Besitz *m*; *(of office)* Amtszeit *f*

tepid ['tepıd] *adj* lauwarm

term [tə:m] *n (period of time)* Zeit(raum *m*) *f*; *(limit)* Frist *f*; *(SCH)* Quartal *nt*; *(UNIV)* Trimester *nt*; *(expression)* Ausdruck *m* ♦ *vt* (be)nennen; **~s** *npl (conditions)* Bedingungen *pl*; **in the short/long ~** auf kurze/lange Sicht; **to be on good ~s with sb** gut mit jdm auskommen; **to come to ~s with** *(person)* sich einigen mit; *(problem)* sich abfinden mit

terminal ['tə:mınl] *n (BRIT: also:* **coach ~**) Endstation *f*; *(AVIAT)* Terminal *m*; *(COMPUT)* Terminal *nt* or *m* ♦ *adj* Schluss-; *(MED)* unheilbar; **~ly** *adj (MED):* **~ly ill** unheilbar krank

terminate ['tə:mıneıt] *vt* beenden ♦ *vi* enden, aufhören

termini ['tə:mınaı] *npl of* **terminus**

terminus ['tə:mınəs] *(pl* **termini**) *n* Endstation *f*

terrace ['terəs] *n (BRIT: row of houses)* Häuserreihe *f*; *(in garden etc)* Terrasse *f*; **the ~s** *npl (BRIT: SPORT)* die Ränge; **~d** *adj (garden)* terrassenförmig angelegt; *(house)* Reihen-

terrain [te'reın] *n* Gelände *nt*

terrible ['terıbl] *adj* schrecklich, entsetzlich, fürchterlich; **terribly** *adv* fürchterlich

terrier ['terıə*] *n* Terrier *m*

terrific [tə'rıfık] *adj* unwahrscheinlich; **~!** klasse!

terrified *adj:* **to be ~ of sth** vor etw schreckliche Angst haben

terrify ['terıfaı] *vt* erschrecken

territorial [terı'tɔ:rıəl] *adj* Gebiets-, territorial

territory ['terıtərı] *n* Gebiet *nt*

terror ['terə*] *n* Schrecken *m*

terrorism ['terərızəm] *n* Terrorismus *m*; **~ist** *n* Terrorist(in) *m(f)*; **~ize** *vt* terrorisieren

terse [tɜːs] adj knapp, kurz, bündig
test [test] n Probe f; (examination) Prüfung f; (PSYCH, TECH) Test m ♦ vt prüfen; (PSYCH) testen
testicle ['testɪkl] n (ANAT) Hoden m
testify ['testɪfaɪ] vi aussagen; **to ~ to sth** etw bezeugen
testimony ['testɪmənɪ] n (JUR) Zeugenaussage f; (fig) Zeugnis nt
test match n (SPORT) Länderkampf m
test tube n Reagenzglas nt
tether ['teðər] vt anbinden ♦ n: **at the end of one's ~** völlig am Ende
text [tekst] n Text m; (of document) Wortlaut m; (text message) SMS-Nachricht f; ♦ vti eine SMS schicken; **ich schicke dir eine SMS** I'll send you a text; **~book** n Lehrbuch nt
textiles ['tekstaɪlz] npl Textilien pl
texture ['tekstʃər] n Beschaffenheit f
Thai [taɪ] adj thailändisch ♦ n Thailänder(in) m(f); **~land** n Thailand nt
Thames [temz] n: **the ~** die Themse
than [ðæn, ðən] prep (in comparisons) als
thank [θæŋk] vt danken +dat; **you've him to ~ for your success** Sie haben Ihren Erfolg ihm zu verdanken; **~ you (very much)** danke (vielmals), danke schön; **~ful** adj dankbar; **~less** adj undankbar; **~s** npl Dank m ♦ excl danke!; **~s to** dank +gen; **T~sgiving (Day)** (US) n Thanksgiving Day m

Thanksgiving (Day)

ⓘ **Thanksgiving (Day)** *ist ein Feiertag in den USA, der auf den vierten Donnerstag im November fällt. Er soll daran erinnern, wie die Pilgerväter die gute Ernte im Jahre 1621 feierten. In Kanada gibt es einen ähnlichen Erntedanktag (der aber nichts mit dem Pilgervätern zu tun hat) am zweiten Montag im Oktober.*

KEYWORD

that [ðæt, ðət] adj (demonstrative: pl those) der/die/das; jene(r, s); **that one** das da

♦ pron 1 (demonstrative: pl those) das; **who's/what's that?** wer ist da/was ist das?; **is that you?** bist du das?; **that's what he said** genau das hat er gesagt; **what happened after that?** was passierte danach?; **that is** das heißt
2 (relative: subj) der/die/das, die; (: direct obj) den/die/das, die; (: indirect obj) dem/der/dem, denen; **all (that) I have** alles, was ich habe
3 (relative: of time): **the day (that)** an dem Tag, als; **the winter (that) he came** in dem Winter, in dem er kam
♦ conj dass; **he thought that I was ill** er dachte, dass ich krank sei, er dachte, ich sei krank
♦ adv (demonstrative) so; **I can't work that much** ich kann nicht so viel arbeiten

thatched [θætʃt] adj strohgedeckt; (cottage) mit Strohdach
thaw [θɔː] n Tauwetter nt ♦ vi tauen; (frozen foods, fig: people) auftauen ♦ vt (auf)tauen lassen

KEYWORD

the [ðiː, ðə] def art 1 der/die/das; **to play the piano/violin** Klavier/Geige spielen; **I'm going to the butcher's/the cinema** ich gehe zum Fleischer/ins Kino; **Elizabeth the First** Elisabeth die Erste
2 (+adj to form noun) das, die; **the rich and the poor** die Reichen und die Armen
3 (in comparisons): **the more he works the more he earns** je mehr er arbeitet, desto mehr verdient er

theatre ['θɪətər] (US **theater**) n Theater nt; (for lectures etc) Saal m; (MED) Operationssaal m; **~goer** n Theaterbesucher(in) m(f); **theatrical** [θɪˈætrɪkl] adj Theater-; (career) Schauspieler-; (showy) theatralisch
theft [θeft] n Diebstahl m
their [ðeər] adj ihr; see also **my**; **~s** pron ihre(r, s); see also **mine**[2]
them [ðem, ðəm] pron (acc) sie; (dat) ihnen; see also **me**

theme [θiːm] *n* Thema *nt*; (*MUS*) Motiv *nt*; ~ **park** *n* (thematisch gestalteter) Freizeitpark *m*; ~ **song** *n* Titelmusik *f*

themselves [ðəmˈselvz] *pl pron* (*reflexive*) sich (selbst); (*emphatic*) selbst; *see also* **oneself**

then [ðen] *adv* (*at that time*) damals; (*next*) dann ♦ *conj* also, folglich; (*furthermore*) ferner ♦ *adj* damalig; **from ~ on** von da an; **by ~** bis dahin; **the ~ president** der damalige Präsident

theology [θɪˈɔlədʒɪ] *n* Theologie *f*

theoretical [θɪəˈretɪkl] *adj* theoretisch; ~**ly** *adv* theoretisch

theory [ˈθɪərɪ] *n* Theorie *f*

therapist [ˈθerəpɪst] *n* Therapeut(in) *m(f)*

therapy [ˈθerəpɪ] *n* Therapie *f*

KEYWORD
---

there [ðeəʳ] *adv* **1**: **there is, there are** es *or* da ist/sind; (*there exists/exist also*) es gibt; **there are 3 of them** (*people, things*) es gibt 3 davon; **there has been an accident** da war ein Unfall

2 (*place*) da, dort; (*direction*) dahin, dorthin; **put it in/on there** leg es dahinein/ dorthinauf

3: **there, there** (*esp to child*) na, na

there: ~**abouts** [ˈðeərəˈbauts] *adv* (*place*) dort in der Nähe, dort irgendwo; (*amount*): **20 or ~abouts** ungefähr 20; ~**after** [ðeərˈɑːftəʳ] *adv* danach; ~**by** [ˈðeəbaɪ] *adv* dadurch, damit

therefore [ˈðeəfɔːʳ] *adv* deshalb, daher

there's [ˈðeəz] = **there is**; **there has**

thermometer [θəˈmɔmɪtəʳ] *n* Thermometer *nt*

Thermos [ˈθəːməs] ® *n* Thermosflasche *f*

thesaurus [θɪˈsɔːrəs] *n* Synonymwörterbuch *nt*

these [ðiːz] *pron, adj* (*pl*) diese

theses [ˈθiːsiːz] *npl of* **thesis**

thesis [ˈθiːsɪs] (*pl* **theses**) *n* (*for discussion*) These *f*; (*UNIV*) Dissertation *f*, Doktorarbeit *f*

they [ðeɪ] *pl pron* sie; (*people in general*) man; ~ **say that ...** (*it is said that*) es wird gesagt,

dass ; ~**'d** = **they had**; **they would**; ~= **they shall**; **they will**; ~= **they are**; ~= **they have**

thick [θɪk] *adj* dick; (*forest*) dicht; (*liquid*) dickflüssig; (*slow, stupid*) dumm, schwer von Begriff ♦ *n*: **in the ~ of** mitten in +*dat*; **it's 20 cm ~** es ist 20 cm dick *or* stark; ~**en** *vi* (*fog*) dichter werden ♦ *vt* (*sauce etc*) verdicken; ~**ness** *n* Dicke *f*; Dichte *f*; Dickflüssigkeit *f*; ~**set** *adj* untersetzt; ~**skinned** *adj* dickhäutig

thief [θiːf] (*pl* **thieves**) *n* Dieb(in) *m(f)*

thieves [θiːvz] *npl of* **thief**

thieving [ˈθiːvɪŋ] *n* Stehlen *nt* ♦ *adj* diebisch

thigh [θaɪ] *n* Oberschenkel *m*

thimble [ˈθɪmbl] *n* Fingerhut *m*

thin [θɪn] *adj* dünn, mager; (*excuse*) schwach ♦ *vt*: **to ~ (down)** (*sauce, paint*) verdünnen

thing [θɪŋ] *n* Ding *nt*; (*affair*) Sache *f*; **my ~s** meine Sachen *pl*; **the best ~ would be to ...** das Beste wäre, ...; **how are ~s?** wie gehts?

think [θɪŋk] (*pt, pp* **thought**) *vt, vi* denken; **what did you ~ of them?** was halten Sie von ihnen?; **to ~ about sth/sb** nachdenken über etw/jdn; **I'll ~ about it** ich überlege es mir; **to ~ of doing sth** vorhaben *or* beabsichtigen, etw zu tun; **I ~ so/not** ich glaube (schon)/glaube ich nicht; **to ~ well of sb** viel von jdm halten; ~ **over** *vt* überdenken; ~ **up** *vt* sich *dat* ausdenken

think tank *n* Expertengruppe *f*

thinly [ˈθɪnlɪ] *adv* dünn; (*disguised*) kaum

third [θəːd] *adj* dritte(r, s) ♦ *n* (*person*) Dritte(r) *mf*; (*part*) Drittel *nt*; ~**ly** *adv* drittens; ~ **party insurance** (*BRIT*) *n* Haftpflichtversicherung *f*; ~**-rate** *adj* minderwertig; **T~ World** *n*: **the T~ World** die Dritte Welt *f*

thirst [θəːst] *n* (*also fig*) Durst *m*; ~**y** *adj* (*person*) durstig; (*work*) durstig machend; **to be ~y** Durst haben

thirteen [θəːˈtiːn] *num* dreizehn

thirty [ˈθəːtɪ] *num* dreißig

this [ðɪs] adj (demonstrative: pl these) diese(r, s); **this evening** heute Abend; **this one** diese(r, s) (da)
♦ pron (demonstrative: pl these) dies, das; **who/what is this?** wer/was ist das?; **this is where I live** hier wohne ich; **this is what he said** das hat er gesagt; **this is Mr Brown** dies ist Mr Brown; (on telephone) hier ist Mr Brown
♦ adv (demonstrative): **this high/long** etc so groß/lang etc

thistle ['θɪsl] n Distel f

thorn [θɔ:n] n Dorn m; ~**y** adj dornig; (problem) schwierig

thorough ['θʌrə] adj gründlich; ~**bred** n Vollblut nt ♦ adj reinrassig, Vollblut-; ~**fare** n Straße f; **"no ~fare"** „Durchfahrt verboten"; ~**ly** adv gründlich; (extremely) äußerst

those [ðəuz] pl pron die (da), jene ♦ adj die, jene

though [ðəu] conj obwohl ♦ adv trotzdem

thought [θɔ:t] pt, pp of **think** ♦ n (idea) Gedanke m; (thinking) Denken nt, Denkvermögen nt; ~**ful** adj (thinking) gedankenvoll, nachdenklich; (kind) rücksichtsvoll, aufmerksam; ~**less** adj gedankenlos, unbesonnen; (unkind) rücksichtslos

thousand ['θauzənd] num tausend; **two** ~ zweitausend; ~**s of** tausende or Tausende (von); ~**th** adj tausendste(r, s)

thrash [θræʃ] vt verdreschen; (fig) (vernichtend) schlagen; ~ **about** vi um sich schlagen; ~ **out** vt ausdiskutieren

thread [θred] n Faden m, Garn nt; (TECH) Gewinde nt; (in story) Faden m ♦ vt (needle) einfädeln; ~**bare** adj fadenscheinig

threat [θret] n Drohung f; (danger) Gefahr f; ~**en** vt bedrohen ♦ vi drohen; **to ~en sb with sth** jdm etw androhen

three [θri:] num drei; ~~**dimensional** adj dreidimensional; ~~**piece suite** n dreiteilige Polstergarnitur f; ~~**wheeler** n Dreiradwagen m

thresh [θreʃ] vt, vi dreschen

threshold ['θreʃhəuld] n Schwelle f

threw [θru:] pt of **throw**

thrift [θrɪft] n Sparsamkeit f; ~**y** adj sparsam

thrill [θrɪl] n Reiz m, Erregung f ♦ vt begeistern, packen; **to be ~ed with** (gift etc) sich unheimlich freuen über +acc; ~**er** n Krimi m; ~**ing** adj spannend; (news) aufregend

thrive [θraɪv] (pt thrived, pp thrived) vi: **to ~ (on)** gedeihen (bei); **thriving** ['θraɪvɪŋ] adj blühend

throat [θrəut] n Hals m, Kehle f; **to have a sore ~** Halsschmerzen haben

throb [θrɔb] vi klopfen, pochen

throes [θrəuz] npl: **in the ~ of** mitten in +dat

throne [θrəun] n Thron m; **on the ~** auf dem Thron

throng ['θrɔŋ] n (Menschen)schar f ♦ vt sich drängen in +dat

throttle ['θrɔtl] n Gashebel m ♦ vt erdrosseln

through [θru:] prep durch; (time) während +gen; (because of) aus, durch ♦ adv durch ♦ adj (ticket, train) durchgehend; (finished) fertig; **to put sb ~ (to)** jdn verbinden (mit); **to be ~** (TEL) eine Verbindung haben; (have finished) fertig sein; **no ~ way** (BRIT) Sackgasse f; ~**out** [θru:'aut] prep (place) überall in +dat; (time) während +gen ♦ adv überall; die ganze Zeit

throw [θrəu] (pt threw, pp thrown) n Wurf m ♦ vt werfen; **to ~ a party** eine Party geben; ~ **away** vt wegwerfen; (waste) verschenken; (money) verschwenden; ~ **off** vt abwerfen; (pursuer) abschütteln; ~ **out** vt hinauswerfen; (rubbish) wegwerfen; (plan) verwerfen; ~ **up** vt, vi (vomit) speien; ~**away** adj Wegwerf-; ~~**in** n Einwurf m; ~**n** pp of **throw**

thru [θru:] (US) = **through**

thrush [θrʌʃ] n Drossel f

thrust [θrʌst] (pt, pp thrust) vt, vi (push) stoßen

thud [θʌd] n dumpfe(r) (Auf)schlag m

thug [θʌg] n Schlägertyp m

thumb [θʌm] *n* Daumen *m* ♦ *vt* (*book*) durchblättern; **to ~ a lift** per Anhalter fahren (wollen); **~tack** (*US*) *n* Reißzwecke *f*

thump [θʌmp] *n* (*blow*) Schlag *m*; (*noise*) Bums *m* ♦ *vi* hämmern, pochen ♦ *vt* schlagen auf +*acc*

thunder ['θʌndər] *n* Donner *m* ♦ *vi* donnern; (*train etc*): **to ~ past** vorbeidonnern ♦ *vt* brüllen; **~bolt** *n* Blitz *nt*; **~clap** *n* Donnerschlag *m*; **~storm** *n* Gewitter *nt*, Unwetter *nt*; **~y** *adj* gewitterschwül

Thursday ['θɜːzdɪ] *n* Donnerstag *m*

thus [ðʌs] *adv* (*in this way*) so; (*therefore*) somit, also, folglich

thwart [θwɔːt] *vt* vereiteln, durchkreuzen; (*person*) hindern

thyme [taɪm] *n* Thymian *m*

thyroid ['θaɪrɔɪd] *n* Schilddrüse *f*

tiara [tɪ'ɑːrə] *n* Diadem *nt*

tic [tɪk] *n* Tick *m*

tick [tɪk] *n* (*sound*) Ticken *nt*; (*mark*) Häkchen *nt* ♦ *vi* ticken ♦ *vt* abhaken; **in a ~** (*BRIT*: *inf*) sofort; **~ off** *vt* abhaken; (*person*) ausschimpfen; **~ over** *vi* (*engine*) im Leerlauf laufen; (*fig*) auf Sparflamme laufen

ticket ['tɪkɪt] *n* (*for travel*) Fahrkarte *f*; (*for entrance*) (Eintritts)karte *f*; (*price ~*) Preisschild *nt*; (*luggage ~*) (Gepäck)schein *m*; (*raffle ~*) Los *nt*; (*parking ~*) Strafzettel *m*; (*in car park*) Parkschein *m*; **~ collector** *n* Fahrkartenkontrolleur *m*; **~ inspector** *n* Fahrkartenkontrolleur *m*; **~ office** *n* (*THEAT etc*) Kasse *f*; (*RAIL etc*) Fahrkartenschalter *m*

tickle ['tɪkl] *n* Kitzeln *nt* ♦ *vt* kitzeln; (*amuse*) amüsieren; **ticklish** ['tɪklɪʃ] *adj* (*also fig*) kitzlig

tidal ['taɪdl] *adj* Flut-, Tide-; **~ wave** *n* Flutwelle *f*

tidbit ['tɪdbɪt] (*US*) *n* Leckerbissen *m*

tiddlywinks ['tɪdlɪwɪŋks] *n* Floh(hüpf)spiel *nt*

tide [taɪd] *n* Gezeiten *pl*; **high/low ~** Flut *f*/ Ebbe *f*

tidy ['taɪdɪ] *adj* ordentlich ♦ *vt* aufräumen, in Ordnung bringen

tie [taɪ] *n* (*BRIT*: *neck*) Krawatte *f*, Schlips *m*; (*sth connecting*) Band *nt*; (*SPORT*)

Unentschieden *nt* ♦ *vt* (*fasten, restrict*) binden; *vi* (*SPORT*) unentschieden spielen; (*in competition*) punktgleich sein; **to ~ in a bow** zur Schleife binden; **to ~ a knot in sth** einen Knoten in etw *acc* machen; **~ down** *vt* festbinden; **to ~ sb down to** jdn binden an +*acc*; **~ up** *vt* (*dog*) anbinden; (*parcel*) verschnüren; (*boat*) festmachen; (*person*) fesseln; **to be ~d up** (*busy*) beschäftigt sein

tier [tɪər] *n* Rang *m*; (*of cake*) Etage *f*

tiff [tɪf] *n* Krach *m*

tiger ['taɪgər] *n* Tiger *m*

tight [taɪt] *adj* (*close*) eng, knapp; (*schedule*) gedrängt; (*firm*) fest; (*control*) streng; (*stretched*) stramm, (an)gespannt; (*inf: drunk*) blau, stramm ♦ *adv* (*squeeze*) fest; **~en** *vt* anziehen, anspannen; (*restrictions*) verschärfen ♦ *vi* sich spannen; **~-fisted** *adj* knauserig; **~ly** *adv* eng; fest; (*stretched*) straff; **~-rope** *n* Seil *nt*; **~s** *npl* (*esp BRIT*) Strumpfhose *f*

tile [taɪl] *n* (*on roof*) Dachziegel *m*; (*on wall or floor*) Fliese *f*; **~d** *adj* (*roof*) gedeckt, Ziegel-; (*floor, wall*) mit Fliesen belegt

till [tɪl] *n* Kasse *f* ♦ *vt* bestellen ♦ *prep, conj* = **until**

tiller ['tɪlər] *n* Ruderpinne *f*

tilt [tɪlt] *vt* kippen, neigen ♦ *vi* sich neigen

timber ['tɪmbər] *n* (*wood*) Holz *nt*

time [taɪm] *n* Zeit *f*; (*occasion*) Mal *nt*; (*rhythm*) Takt *m* ♦ *vt* zur rechten Zeit tun, zeitlich einrichten; (*SPORT*) stoppen; **in 2 weeks'** ~ in 2 Wochen; **a long ~** lange; **for the ~ being** vorläufig; **4 at a ~** zu jeweils 4; **from ~ to ~** gelegentlich; **to have a good ~** sich amüsieren; **in ~** (*soon enough*) rechtzeitig; (*after some ~*) mit der Zeit; (*MUS*) im Takt; **in no ~** im Handumdrehen; **any ~** jederzeit; **on ~** pünktlich, rechtzeitig; **five ~s 5** fünfmal 5; **what ~ is it?** wie viel Uhr ist es?, wie spät ist es?; **at ~s** manchmal; **~ bomb** *n* Zeitbombe *f*; **~less** *adj* (*beauty*) zeitlos; **~ limit** *n* Frist *f*; **~ly** *adj* rechtzeitig; günstig; **~ off** *n* freie Zeit *f*; **~r** *n* (*timer switch*: *in kitchen*) Schaltuhr *f*; **~ scale** *n* Zeitspanne *f*; **~-share** *adj* Timesharing-; **~ switch**

(BRIT) n Zeitschalter m; **~table** n Fahrplan m; (SCH) Stundenplan m; **~ zone** n Zeitzone f

imid ['tɪmɪd] adj ängstlich, schüchtern

iming ['taɪmɪŋ] n Wahl f des richtigen Zeitpunkts, Timing nt

impani ['tɪmpənɪ] npl Kesselpauken pl

in [tɪn] n (metal) Blech nt; (BRIT: can) Büchse f, Dose f; **~foil** n Stanniolpapier nt

inge [tɪndʒ] n (colour) Färbung f; (fig) Anflug m ♦ vt färben; **~d with** mit einer Spur von

ingle ['tɪŋgl] n Prickeln nt ♦ vi prickeln

inker ['tɪŋkər] n Kesselflicker m; **~ with** vt fus herumpfuschen an +dat

inkle ['tɪŋkl] vi klingeln

inned [tɪnd] (BRIT) adj (food) Dosen-, Büchsen-

in opener [-əupnər] (BRIT) n Dosen- or Büchsenöffner m

insel ['tɪnsl] n Rauschgold nt

int [tɪnt] n Farbton m; (slight colour) Anflug m; (hair) Tönung f; **~ed** adj getönt

iny ['taɪnɪ] adj winzig

ip [tɪp] n (pointed end) Spitze f; (money) Trinkgeld nt; (hint) Wink m, Tipp m ♦ vt (slant) kippen; (hat) antippen; (~ over) umkippen; (waiter) ein Trinkgeld geben +dat; **~-off** n Hinweis m, Tipp m; **~ped** (BRIT) adj (cigarette) Filter-

ipsy ['tɪpsɪ] adj beschwipst

iptoe ['tɪptəu] n: **on ~** auf Zehenspitzen

iptop [tɪp'tɔp] adj: **in ~ condition** tipptopp, erstklassig

ire ['taɪər] n (US) = tyre ♦ vt, vi ermüden, müde machen/werden; **~d** adj müde; **to be ~d of sth** etw satt haben; **~less** adj unermüdlich; **~some** adj lästig

iring ['taɪərɪŋ] adj ermüdend

issue ['tɪʃu:] n Gewebe nt; (paper handkerchief) Papiertaschentuch nt; **~ paper** n Seidenpapier nt

it [tɪt] n (bird) Meise f; **~ for tat** wie du mir, so ich dir

itbit ['tɪtbɪt] (US tidbit) n Leckerbissen m

itillate ['tɪtɪleɪt] vt kitzeln

itle ['taɪtl] n Titel m; **~ deed** n Eigentumsurkunde f; **~ role** n Hauptrolle f

titter ['tɪtər] vi kichern

titular ['tɪtjulər] adj (in name only) nominell

TM abbr (= trademark) Wz

KEYWORD

to [tu:, tə] prep 1 (direction) zu, nach; **I go to France/school** ich gehe nach Frankreich/zur Schule; **to the left** nach links

2 (as far as) bis

3 (with expressions of time) vor; **a quarter to 5** Viertel vor 5

4 (for, of) für; **secretary to the director** Sekretärin des Direktors

5 (expressing indirect object): **to give sth to sb** jdm etw geben; **to talk to sb** mit jdm sprechen; **I sold it to a friend** ich habe es einem Freund verkauft

6 (in relation to) zu; **30 miles to the gallon** 30 Meilen pro Gallone

7 (purpose, result) zu; **to my surprise** zu meiner Überraschung

♦ with vb 1 (infin): **to go/eat** gehen/essen; **to want to do sth** etw tun wollen; **to try/start to do sth** versuchen/anfangen, etw zu tun; **he has a lot to lose** er hat viel zu verlieren

2 (with vb omitted): **I don't want to** ich will (es) nicht

3 (purpose, result) um; **I did it to help you** ich tat es, um dir zu helfen

4 (after adj etc): **ready to use** gebrauchsfertig; **too old/young to ...** zu alt/jung, um ... zu ...

♦ adv: **push/pull the door to** die Tür zuschieben/zuziehen

toad [təud] n Kröte f; **~stool** n Giftpilz m

toast [təust] n (bread) Toast m; (drinking) Trinkspruch m ♦ vt trinken auf +acc; (bread) toasten; (warm) wärmen; **~er** n Toaster m

tobacco [tə'bækəu] n Tabak m; **~nist** [tə'bækənɪst] n Tabakhändler m; **~nist's (shop)** n Tabakladen m

toboggan [tə'bɔgən] n (Rodel)schlitten m; **~ing** n Rodeln nt

today [tə'deɪ] adv heute; (at the present time) heutzutage

toddler ['tɒdlə'] n Kleinkind nt

toddy ['tɒdɪ] n (Whisky)grog m

to-do [tə'duː] n Theater nt

toe [təʊ] n Zehe f; (of sock, shoe) Spitze f
♦ vt: **to ~ the line** (fig) sich einfügen; ~**nail** n Zehennagel m

toffee ['tɒfɪ] n Sahnebonbon nt; ~ **apple** (BRIT) n kandierte(r) Apfel

together [tə'ɡɛðə'] adv zusammen; (at the same time) gleichzeitig; ~ **with** zusammen mit; gleichzeitig mit

toil [tɔɪl] n harte Arbeit f, Plackerei f ♦ vi sich abmühen, sich plagen

toilet ['tɔɪlət] n Toilette f ♦ cpd Toiletten-; ~ **bag** n Waschbeutel m; ~ **paper** n Toilettenpapier nt; ~**ries** ['tɔɪlətrɪz] npl Toilettenartikel pl; ~ **roll** n Rolle f Toilettenpapier; ~ **water** n Toilettenwasser nt

token ['təʊkən] n Zeichen nt; (gift ~) Gutschein m; **book/record ~** (BRIT) Bücher-/Plattengutschein m

Tokyo ['təʊkjəʊ] n Tokio nt

told [təʊld] pt, pp of **tell**

tolerable ['tɒlərəbl] adj (bearable) erträglich; (fairly good) leidlich

tolerant ['tɒlərnt] adj: **be ~ (of)** vertragen +acc

tolerate ['tɒləreɪt] vt dulden; (noise) ertragen

toll [təʊl] n Gebühr f ♦ vi (bell) läuten

tomato [tə'mɑːtəʊ] (pl **-es**) n Tomate f

tomb [tuːm] n Grab(mal) nt

tomboy ['tɒmbɔɪ] n Wildfang m

tombstone ['tuːmstəʊn] n Grabstein m

tomcat ['tɒmkæt] n Kater m

tomorrow [tə'mɒrəʊ] n Morgen nt ♦ adv morgen; **the day after ~** übermorgen; ~ **morning** morgen früh; **a week ~** morgen in einer Woche

ton [tʌn] n Ton m (BRIT = 1016kg; US = 907kg); ~**s of** (inf) eine Unmenge von

tone [təʊn] n Ton m; ~ **down** vt (criticism, demands) mäßigen; (colours) abtönen; ~ **up** vt in Form bringen; ~**-deaf** adj ohne musikalisches Gehör

tongs [tɒŋz] npl Zange f; (curling ~) Lockenstab m

tongue [tʌŋ] n Zunge f; (language) Sprache f; **with ~ in cheek** scherzhaft; ~**-tied** adj stumm, sprachlos; ~ **twister** n Zungenbrecher m

tonic ['tɒnɪk] n (drink) Tonic nt; (MED) Stärkungsmittel nt

tonight [tə'naɪt] adv heute Abend

tonsil ['tɒnsl] n Mandel f; ~**litis** [tɒnsɪ'laɪtɪs] n Mandelentzündung f

too [tuː] adv zu; (also) auch; ~ **bad!** Pech!; ~ **many** zu viele

took [tʊk] pt of **take**

tool [tuːl] n (also fig) Werkzeug nt; ~**box** n Werkzeugkasten m

toot [tuːt] n Hupen nt ♦ vi tuten; (AUT) hupen

tooth [tuːθ] (pl **teeth**) n Zahn m; ~**ache** n Zahnschmerzen pl, Zahnweh nt; ~**brush** n Zahnbürste f; ~**paste** n Zahnpasta f; ~**pick** n Zahnstocher m

top [tɒp] n Spitze f; (of mountain) Gipfel m; (of tree) Wipfel m; (toy) Kreisel m; (~ gear) vierte(r)/fünfte(r) Gang m ♦ adj oberste(r, s) ♦ vt (list) an erster Stelle stehen auf +dat; **on ~ of** oben auf +dat; **from ~ to bottom** von oben bis unten; ~ **off** (US) vt auffüllen; ~ **up** vt auffüllen; ~ **floor** n oberste(s) Stockwerk nt; ~ **hat** n Zylinder m; ~**-heavy** adj kopflastig

topic ['tɒpɪk] n Thema nt, Gesprächsgegenstand m; ~**al** adj aktuell

top: ~**less** ['tɒplɪs] adj (bather etc) oben ohne; ~**-level** ['tɒplɛvl] adj auf höchster Ebene; ~**most** ['tɒpməʊst] adj oberste(r, s)

topple ['tɒpl] vt, vi stürzen, kippen

top-secret ['tɒp'siːkrɪt] adj streng geheim

topsy-turvy ['tɒpsɪ'tɜːvɪ] adv durcheinander ♦ adj auf den Kopf gestellt

torch [tɔːtʃ] n (BRIT: ELEC) Taschenlampe f; (with flame) Fackel f

tore [tɔː'] pt of **tear1**

torment [n 'tɔːmɛnt, vb tɔː'mɛnt] n Qual f ♦ vt (distress) quälen

torn [tɔːn] pp of **tear1** ♦ adj hin- und hergerissen

torrent ['tɒrnt] n Sturzbach m; ~**ial** [tɔ'rɛnʃl] adj wolkenbruchartig

torrid ['tɒrɪd] adj heiß
tortoise ['tɔːtəs] n Schildkröte f; **~shell**
['tɔːtəʃel] n Schildpatt m
torture ['tɔːtʃəʳ] n Folter f ♦ vt foltern
Tory ['tɔːrɪ] (BRIT) n (POL) Tory m ♦ adj Tory-,
konservativ
toss [tɒs] vt schleudern; **to ~ a coin** or **to ~
up for sth** etw mit einer Münze
entscheiden; **to ~ and turn** (in bed) sich hin
und her werfen
tot [tɒt] n (small quantity) bisschen nt; (small
child) Knirps m
total ['təʊtl] n Gesamtheit f; (money)
Endsumme f ♦ adj Gesamt-, total ♦ vt (add
up) zusammenzählen; (amount to) sich
belaufen auf
totalitarian [təʊtælɪ'tɛərɪən] adj totalitär
totally ['təʊtəlɪ] adv total
totter ['tɒtəʳ] vi wanken, schwanken
touch [tʌtʃ] n Berührung f; (sense of feeling)
Tastsinn m ♦ vt (feel) berühren; (come
against) leicht anstoßen; (emotionally)
rühren; **a ~ of** (fig) eine Spur von; **to get in
~ with sb** sich mit jdm in Verbindung
setzen; **to lose ~** (friends) Kontakt verlieren;
~ on vt fus (topic) berühren, erwähnen; **~
up** vt (paint) auffrischen; **~-and-go** adj
riskant, knapp; **~down** n Landen nt,
Niedergehen nt; **~ed** adj (moved) gerührt;
~ing adj rührend; **~line** n Seitenlinie f; **~-
sensitive screen** n (COMPUT)
berührungsempfindlicher Bildschirm m; **~y**
adj empfindlich, reizbar
tough [tʌf] adj zäh; (difficult) schwierig ♦ n
Schläger(typ) m; **~en** vt zäh machen;
(make strong) abhärten
toupee ['tuːpeɪ] n Toupet nt
tour ['tuəʳ] n Tour f ♦ vi umherreisen; (THEAT)
auf Tour sein; auf Tour gehen; **~ guide** n
Reiseleiter(in) m(f)
tourism ['tuərɪzm] n Fremdenverkehr m,
Tourismus m
tourist ['tuərɪst] n Tourist(in) m(f) ♦ cpd
(class) Touristen-; **~ office** n Verkehrsamt
nt
tournament ['tuənəmənt] n Turnier nt
tousled ['tauzld] adj zerzaust

tout [taut] vi: **to ~ for** auf Kundenfang gehen
für ♦ n: **ticket ~** Kundenschlepper(in) m(f)
tow [təu] vt (ab)schleppen; **on** (BRIT) or **in**
(US) **~** (AUT) im Schlepp
toward(s) [tə'wɔːd(z)] prep (with time)
gegen; (in direction of) nach
towel ['tauəl] n Handtuch nt; **~ling** n (fabric)
Frottee nt or m; **~ rack** (US) n
Handtuchstange f; **~ rail** n
Handtuchstange f
tower ['tauəʳ] n Turm m; **~ block** (BRIT) n
Hochhaus nt
town [taun] n Stadt f; **to go to ~** (fig) sich
ins Zeug legen; **~ centre** n Stadtzentrum
nt; **~ clerk** n Stadtdirektor m; **~ council** n
Stadtrat m; **~ hall** n Rathaus nt; **~ plan** n
Stadtplan m; **~ planning** n Stadtplanung f
towrope ['təurəup] n Abschlepptau nt
tow truck (US) n Abschleppwagen m
toxic ['tɒksɪk] adj giftig, Gift-
toy [tɔɪ] n Spielzeug nt; **~ with** vt fus spielen
mit; **~shop** n Spielwarengeschäft nt
trace [treɪs] n Spur f ♦ vt (follow a course)
nachspüren +dat; (find out) aufspüren;
(copy) durchpausen; **tracing paper** n
Pauspapier n
track [træk] n (mark) Spur f; (path) Weg m;
(racetrack) Rennbahn f; (RAIL) Gleis nt ♦ vt
verfolgen; **to keep ~ of sb** jdn im Auge
behalten; **~ down** vt aufspüren; **~suit** n
Trainingsanzug m
tract [trækt] n (of land) Gebiet nt
traction ['trækʃən] n (power) Zugkraft f; (AUT:
grip) Bodenhaftung f; (MED): **in ~** im
Streckverband
tractor ['træktəʳ] n Traktor m
trade [treɪd] n (commerce) Handel m;
(business) Geschäft nt, Gewerbe nt; (people)
Geschäftsleute pl; (skilled manual work)
Handwerk nt ♦ vi: **to ~ (in)** handeln (mit)
♦ vt tauschen; **~ in** vt in Zahlung geben; **~
fair** n Messe nt; **~-in price** n Preis, zu dem
etw in Zahlung genommen wird; **~mark** n
Warenzeichen nt; **~ name** n
Handelsbezeichnung f; **~r** n Händler m;
~sman (irreg) n (shopkeeper)
Geschäftsmann m; (workman) Handwerker

m; (*delivery man*) Lieferant *m*; ~ **union** *n*
Gewerkschaft *f*; ~ **unionist** *n*
Gewerkschaftler(in) *m(f)*

trading ['treɪdɪŋ] *n* Handel *m*; ~ **estate**
(*BRIT*) *n* Industriegelände *nt*

tradition [trə'dɪʃən] *n* Tradition *f*; ~**al** *adj*
traditionell, herkömmlich

traffic ['træfɪk] *n* Verkehr *m*; (*esp in drugs*): ~
(in) Handel *m* (mit) ♦ *vi*: **to ~ in** (*esp drugs*)
handeln mit; ~ **calming** *n*
Verkehrsberuhigung *f*; ~ **circle** (*US*) *n*
Kreisverkehr *m*; ~ **jam** *n* Verkehrsstauung *f*;
~ **lights** *npl* Verkehrsampel *f*; ~ **warden** *n*
≈ Verkehrspolizist *m* (*ohne amtliche
Befugnisse*), Politesse *f* (*ohne amtliche
Befugnisse*)

tragedy ['trædʒədɪ] *n* Tragödie *f*

tragic ['trædʒɪk] *adj* tragisch

trail [treɪl] *n* (*track*) Spur *f*; (*of smoke*)
Rauchfahne *f*; (*of dust*) Staubwolke *f*; (*road*)
Pfad *m*, Weg *m* ♦ *vt* (*animal*) verfolgen;
(*person*) folgen +*dat*; (*drag*) schleppen ♦ *vi*
(*hang loosely*) schleifen; (*plants*) sich ranken;
(*be behind*) hinterherhinken; (*SPORT*) weit
zurückliegen; (*walk*) zuckeln; ~ **behind** *vi*
zurückbleiben; ~**er** *n* Anhänger *m*; (*US*:
caravan) Wohnwagen *m*; (*for film*) Vorschau
f; ~**er truck** (*US*) *n* Sattelschlepper *m*

train [treɪn] *n* Zug *m*; (*of dress*) Schleppe *f*;
(*series*) Folge *f* ♦ *vt* (*teach: person*) ausbilden;
(: *animal*) abrichten; (: *mind*) schulen;
(*SPORT*) trainieren; (*aim*) richten ♦ *vi*
(*exercise*) trainieren; (*study*) ausgebildet
werden; ~ **of thought** Gedankengang *m*; **to
~ sth on** (*aim*) etw richten auf +*acc*; ~**ed**
adj (*eye*) geschult; (*person, voice*)
ausgebildet; ~**ee** *n* Lehrling *m*;
Praktikant(in) *m(f)*; ~**er** *n* (*SPORT*) Trainer *m*;
Ausbilder *m*; ~**ers** *npl* Turnschuhe *pl*; ~**ing**
n (*for occupation*) Ausbildung *f*; (*SPORT*)
Training *nt*; **in ~ing** im Training; ~**ing
college** *n* pädagogische Hochschule *f*,
Lehrerseminar *nt*; ~**ing shoes** *npl*
Turnschuhe *pl*

traipse [treɪps] *vi* latschen

trait [treɪt] *n* Zug *m*, Merkmal *nt*

traitor ['treɪtər] *n* Verräter *m*

trajectory [trə'dʒɛktərɪ] *n* Flugbahn *f*

tram [træm] (*BRIT*) *n* (*also:* ~**car**)
Straßenbahn *f*

tramp [træmp] *n* Landstreicher *m* ♦ *vi*
(*trudge*) stampfen, stapfen

trample ['træmpl] *vt* (*nieder*)trampeln ♦ *vi*
(*herum*)trampeln; **to ~ (underfoot)**
herumtrampeln auf +*dat*

trampoline ['træmpəliːn] *n* Trampolin *m*

tranquil ['træŋkwɪl] *adj* ruhig, friedlich; ~**lity**
[træŋ'kwɪlɪtɪ] (*US* **tranquility**) *n* Ruhe *f*;
~**lizer** (*US* **tranquilizer**) *n*
Beruhigungsmittel *nt*

transact [træn'zækt] *vt* abwickeln; ~**ion**
[træn'zækʃən] *n* Abwicklung *f*; (*piece of
business*) Geschäft *nt*, Transaktion *f*

transcend [træn'send] *vt* übersteigen

transcription [træn'skrɪpʃən] *n* Transkription
f; (*product*) Abschrift *f*

transfer [*n* 'trænsfər, *vb* træns'fɜːr] *n* (~*ring*)
Übertragung *f*; (*of business*) Umzug *m*;
(*being ~red*) Versetzung *f*; (*design*)
Abziehbild *nt*; (*SPORT*) Transfer *m* ♦ *vt*
(*business*) verlegen; (*person*) versetzen;
(*prisoner*) überführen; (*drawing*) übertragen;
(*money*) überweisen; **to ~ the charges**
(*BRIT: TEL*) ein R-Gespräch führen; ~ **desk** *n*
(*AVIAT*) Transitschalter *m*

transform [træns'fɔːm] *vt* umwandeln;
~**ation** [trænsfə'meɪʃən] *n* Umwandlung *f*,
Verwandlung *f*

transfusion [træns'fjuːʒən] *n*
Blutübertragung *f*, Transfusion *f*

transient ['trænzɪənt] *adj* kurz(lebig)

transistor [træn'zɪstər] *n* (*ELEC*) Transistor *m*;
(*RAD*) Transistorradio *nt*

transit ['trænzɪt] *n*: **in ~** unterwegs

transition [træn'zɪʃən] *n* Übergang *m*; ~**al**
adj Übergangs-

transit lounge *n* Warteraum *m*

translate [trænz'leɪt] *vt, vi* übersetzen;
translation [trænz'leɪʃən] *n* Übersetzung *f*;
translator [trænz'leɪtər] *n* Übersetzer(in)
m(f)

transmission [trænz'mɪʃən] *n* (*of
information*) Übermittlung *f*; (*ELEC, MED, TV*)
Übertragung *f*; (*AUT*) Getriebe *nt*

transmit [trænz'mɪt] vt (message) übermitteln; (ELEC, MED, TV) übertragen; ~ter n Sender m

transparency [træns'pɛərnsɪ] n Durchsichtigkeit f; (BRIT: PHOT) Dia(positiv) nt

transparent [træns'pærnt] adj durchsichtig; (fig) offenkundig

transpire [træns'paɪər] vi (turn out) sich herausstellen; (happen) passieren

transplant [vb træns'plɑːnt, n 'trænsplɑːnt] vt umpflanzen; (MED, also fig: person) verpflanzen ♦ n (MED) Transplantation f; (organ) Transplantat nt

transport [n 'trænspɔːt, vb træns'pɔːt] n Transport m, Beförderung f ♦ vt befördern; transportieren; **means of ~** Transportmittel nt; **~ation** [trænspɔː'teɪʃən] n Transport m, Beförderung f; (means) Beförderungsmittel nt; (cost) Transportkosten pl; **~ café** (BRIT) n Fernfahrerlokal nt

trap [træp] n Falle f; (carriage) zweirädrige(r) Einspänner m; (inf: mouth) Klappe f ♦ vt fangen; (person) in eine Falle locken; **~door** n Falltür f

trappings ['træpɪŋz] npl Aufmachung f

trash [træʃ] n (rubbish) Plunder m; (nonsense) Mist m; **~ can** (US) n Mülleimer m; **~y** (inf) adj minderwertig, wertlos; (novel) Schund-

traumatic [trɔː'mætɪk] adj traumatisch

travel ['trævl] n Reisen nt ♦ vi reisen ♦ vt (distance) zurücklegen; (country) bereisen; **~s** npl (journeys) Reisen pl; **~ agency** n Reisebüro nt; **~ agent** n Reisebürokaufmann(-frau) m(f); **~ler** (US **traveler**) n Reisende(r) mf; (salesman) Handlungsreisende(r) m; **~ler's cheque** (US **traveler's check**) n Reisescheck m; **~ling** (US **traveling**) n Reisen nt; **~sick** adj reisekrank; **~ sickness** n Reisekrankheit f

trawler ['trɔːlər] n (NAUT, FISHING) Fischdampfer m, Trawler m

tray [treɪ] n (tea ~) Tablett nt; (for mail) Ablage f

treacherous ['tretʃərəs] adj verräterisch; (road) tückisch

treachery ['tretʃərɪ] n Verrat m

treacle ['triːkl] n Sirup m, Melasse f

tread [tred] (pt **trod**, pp **trodden**) n Schritt m, Tritt m; (of stair) Stufe f; (on tyre) Profil nt ♦ vi treten; **~ on** vt fus treten auf +acc

treason ['triːzn] n Verrat m

treasure ['treʒər] n Schatz m ♦ vt schätzen

treasurer ['treʒərər] n Kassenverwalter m, Schatzmeister m

treasury ['treʒərɪ] n (POL) Finanzministerium nt

treat [triːt] n besondere Freude f ♦ vt (deal with) behandeln; **to ~ sb to sth** jdm etw spendieren

treatise ['triːtɪz] n Abhandlung f

treatment ['triːtmənt] n Behandlung f

treaty ['triːtɪ] n Vertrag m

treble ['trebl] adj dreifach ♦ vt verdreifachen; **~ clef** n Violinschlüssel m

tree [triː] n Baum m; **~ trunk** n Baumstamm m

trek [trek] n Treck m, Zug m; (inf) anstrengende(r) Weg m ♦ vi trecken

trellis ['trelɪs] n Gitter nt; (for gardening) Spalier nt

tremble ['trembl] vi zittern; (ground) beben

tremendous [trɪ'mendəs] adj gewaltig, kolossal; (inf: good) prima

tremor ['tremər] n Zittern nt; (of earth) Beben nt

trench [trentʃ] n Graben m; (MIL) Schützengraben m

trend [trend] n Tendenz f; **~y** (inf) adj modisch

trepidation [trepɪ'deɪʃən] n Beklommenheit f

trespass ['trespəs] vi: **to ~ on** widerrechtlich betreten; **"no ~ing"** „Betreten verboten"

trestle ['tresl] n Bock m; **~ table** n Klapptisch m

trial ['traɪəl] n (JUR) Prozess m; (test) Versuch m, Probe f; (hardship) Prüfung f; **by ~ and error** durch Ausprobieren; **~ period** n Probezeit f

triangle ['traɪæŋgl] n Dreieck nt; (MUS) Triangel f; **triangular** [traɪ'æŋgjulər] adj dreieckig

tribal ['traɪbl] adj Stammes-

tribe [traɪb] n Stamm m; **~sman** (irreg) n

Stammesangehörige(r) *m*

tribulation [trɪbjuˈleɪʃən] *n* Not *f*, Mühsal *f*

tribunal [traɪˈbjuːnl] *n* Gericht *nt*; (*inquiry*) Untersuchungsausschuss *m*

tributary [ˈtrɪbjutərɪ] *n* Nebenfluss *m*

tribute [ˈtrɪbjuːt] *n* (*admiration*) Zeichen *nt* der Hochachtung; **to pay ~ to sb/sth** jdm/einer Sache Tribut zollen

trick [trɪk] *n* Trick *m*; (*CARDS*) Stich *m* ♦ *vt* überlisten, beschwindeln; **to play a ~ on sb** jdm einen Streich spielen; **that should do the ~** daß müsste eigentlich klappen; **~ery** *n* Tricks *pl*

trickle [ˈtrɪkl] *n* Tröpfeln *nt*; (*small river*) Rinnsal *n* ♦ *vi* tröpfeln; (*seep*) sickern

tricky [ˈtrɪkɪ] *adj* (*problem*) schwierig; (*situation*) kitzlig

tricycle [ˈtraɪsɪkl] *n* Dreirad *nt*

trifle [ˈtraɪfl] *n* Kleinigkeit *f*; (*COOK*) Trifle *m* ♦ *adv*: **a ~ ...** ein bisschen ...; **trifling** *adj* geringfügig

trigger [ˈtrɪɡər] *n* Drücker *m*; **~ off** *vt* auslösen

trim [trɪm] *adj* gepflegt; (*figure*) schlank ♦ *n* (*gute*) Verfassung *f*; (*embellishment, on car*) Verzierung *f* ♦ *vt* (*clip*) schneiden; (*trees*) stutzen; (*decorate*) besetzen; (*sails*) trimmen; **~mings** *npl* (*decorations*) Verzierung *f*, Verzierungen *pl*; (*extras*) Zubehör *nt*

Trinity [ˈtrɪnɪtɪ] *n*: **the ~** die Dreieinigkeit *f*

trinket [ˈtrɪŋkɪt] *n* kleine(s) Schmuckstück *nt*

trip [trɪp] *n* (*kurze*) Reise *f*; (*outing*) Ausflug *m*; (*stumble*) Stolpern *nt* ♦ *vi* (*stumble*) stolpern; **on a ~** auf Reisen; **~ up** *vi* stolpern; (*fig*) stolpern, einen Fehler machen ♦ *vt* zu Fall bringen; (*fig*) hereinlegen

tripe [traɪp] *n* (*food*) Kutteln *pl*; (*rubbish*) Mist *m*

triple [ˈtrɪpl] *adj* dreifach

triplets [ˈtrɪplɪts] *npl* Drillinge *pl*

triplicate [ˈtrɪplɪkət] *n*: **in ~** in dreifacher Ausfertigung

tripod [ˈtraɪpɒd] *n* (*PHOT*) Stativ *nt*

trite [traɪt] *adj* banal

triumph [ˈtraɪʌmf] *n* Triumph *m* ♦ *vi*: **to ~ (over)** triumphieren (über +*acc*); **~ant** [traɪˈæmfənt] *adj* triumphierend

trivia [ˈtrɪvɪə] *npl* Trivialitäten *pl*

trivial [ˈtrɪvɪəl] *adj* gering(fügig), trivial

trod [trɒd] *pt* of **tread**; **~den** *pp* of **tread**

trolley [ˈtrɒlɪ] *n* Handwagen *m*; (*in shop*) Einkaufswagen *m*; (*for luggage*) Kofferkuli *m*; (*table*) Teewagen *m*; **~ bus** *n* Oberleitungsbus *m*, Obus *m*

trombone [trɒmˈbəun] *n* Posaune *f*

troop [truːp] *n* Schar *f*; (*MIL*) Trupp *m*; **~s** *npl* (*MIL*) Truppen *pl*; **~ in/out** *vi* hinein-/hinausströmen; **~ing the colour** *n* (*ceremony*) Fahnenparade *f*

trophy [ˈtrəufɪ] *n* Trophäe *f*

tropic [ˈtrɒpɪk] *n* Wendekreis *m*; **~al** *adj* tropisch

trot [trɒt] *n* Trott *m* ♦ *vi* trotten; **on the ~** (*BRIT: fig: inf*) in einer Tour

trouble [ˈtrʌbl] *n* (*problems*) Ärger *m*; (*worry*) Sorge *f*; (*in country, industry*) Unruhen *pl*; (*effort*) Mühe *f*; (*MED*): **stomach ~** Magenbeschwerden *pl* ♦ *vt* (*disturb*) stören; **~s** *npl* (*POL etc*) Unruhen *pl*; **to ~ to do sth** sich bemühen, etw zu tun; **to be in ~** Probleme *or* Ärger haben; **to go to the ~ of doing sth** sich die Mühe machen, etw zu tun; **what's the ~?** was ist los?; (*to sick person*) wo fehlts?; **~d** *adj* (*person*) beunruhigt; (*country*) geplagt; **~free** *adj* sorglos; **~maker** *n* Unruhestifter *m*; **~shooter** *n* Vermittler *m*; **~some** *adj* lästig, unangenehm; (*child*) schwierig

trough [trɒf] *n* Trog *m*; (*channel*) Rinne *f*, Kanal *m*; (*MET*) Tief *nt*

trousers [ˈtrauzəz] *npl* Hose *f*

trout [traut] *n* Forelle *f*

trowel [ˈtrauəl] *n* Kelle *f*

truant [ˈtruənt] *n*: **to play ~** (*BRIT*) (die Schule) schwänzen

truce [truːs] *n* Waffenstillstand *m*

truck [trʌk] *n* Lastwagen *m*; (*RAIL*) offene(r) Güterwagen *m*; **~ driver** *n* Lastwagenfahrer *m*; **~ farm** (*US*) *n* Gemüsegärtnerei *f*

trudge [trʌdʒ] *vi* sich (mühselig) dahinschleppen

true [truː] *adj* (*exact*) wahr; (*genuine*) echt; (*friend*) treu

truffle ['trʌfl] *n* Trüffel *f or m*

truly ['truːlɪ] *adv* wirklich; **yours ~** Ihr sehr ergebener

trump [trʌmp] *n* (*CARDS*) Trumpf *m*

trumpet ['trʌmpɪt] *n* Trompete *f*

truncheon ['trʌntʃən] *n* Gummiknüppel *m*

trundle ['trʌndl] *vt* schieben ♦ *vi*: **to ~ along** entlangrollen

trunk [trʌŋk] *n* (*of tree*) (Baum)stamm *m*; (*ANAT*) Rumpf *m*; (*box*) Truhe *f*, Überseekoffer *m*; (*of elephant*) Rüssel *m*; (*US: AUT*) Kofferraum *m*; **~s** *npl* (*also:* **swimming ~s**) Badehose *f*

truss *vt* (*also:* **~ up**) fesseln

trust [trʌst] *n* (*confidence*) Vertrauen *nt*; (*for land etc*) Treuhandvermögen *nt* ♦ *vt* (*rely on*) vertrauen +*dat*, sich verlassen auf +*acc*; (*hope*) hoffen; (*entrust*): **to ~ sth to sb** jdm etw anvertrauen; **~ed** *adj* treu; **~ee** [trʌsˈtiː] *n* Vermögensverwalter *m*; **~ful** *adj* vertrauensvoll; **~ing** *adj* vertrauensvoll; **~worthy** *adj* vertrauenswürdig; (*account*) glaubwürdig

truth [truːθ] *n* Wahrheit *f*; **~ful** *adj* ehrlich

try [traɪ] *n* Versuch *m* ♦ *vt* (*attempt*) versuchen; (*test*) (aus)probieren; (*JUR: person*) unter Anklage stellen; (: *case*) verhandeln; (*courage, patience*) auf die Probe stellen ♦ *vi* (*make effort*) versuchen, sich bemühen; **to have a ~** es versuchen; **to ~ to do sth** versuchen, etw zu tun; **~ on** *vt* (*dress*) anprobieren; (*hat*) aufprobieren; **~ out** *vt* ausprobieren; **~ing** *adj* schwierig

T-shirt ['tiːʃəːt] *n* T-Shirt *nt*

T-square ['tiːskwɛəʳ] *n* Reißschiene *f*

tub [tʌb] *n* Wanne *f*, Kübel *m*; (*for margarine etc*) Becher *m*

tubby ['tʌbɪ] *adj* rundlich

tube [tjuːb] *n* Röhre *f*, Rohr *nt*; (*for toothpaste etc*) Tube *f*; (*underground*) U-Bahn *f*; (*AUT*) Schlauch *m*

tuberculosis [tjubəːkjuˈləusɪs] *n* Tuberkulose *f*

tube station *n* (*in London*) U-Bahnstation *f*;

tubing ['tjuːbɪŋ] *n* Schlauch *m*; **tubular** ['tjuːbjuləʳ] *adj* röhrenförmig

TUC (*BRIT*) *n abbr* = **Trades Union Congress**

tuck [tʌk] *n* (*fold*) Falte *f*, Einschlag *m* ♦ *vt* (*put*) stecken; (*gather*) fälteln, einschlagen; **~ away** *vt* wegstecken; **~ in** *vt* hineinstecken; (*blanket etc*) feststecken; (*person*) zudecken ♦ *vi* (*eat*) hineinhauen, zulangen; **~ up** *vt* (*child*) warm zudecken; **~ shop** *n* Süßwarenladen *m*

Tuesday ['tjuːzdɪ] *n* Dienstag *m*

tuft [tʌft] *n* Büschel *nt*

tug [tʌg] *n* (*jerk*) Zerren *nt*, Ruck *m*; (*NAUT*) Schleppdampfer *m* ♦ *vt*, *vi* zerren, ziehen; (*boat*) schleppen; **~ of war** *n* Tauziehen *nt*

tuition [tjuːˈɪʃən] *n* (*BRIT*) Unterricht *m*; (: *private ~*) Privatunterricht *m*; (*US: school fees*) Schulgeld *nt*

tulip ['tjuːlɪp] *n* Tulpe *f*

tumble ['tʌmbl] *n* (*fall*) Sturz *m* ♦ *vi* fallen, stürzen; **~ to** *vt fus* kapieren; **~down** *adj* baufällig; **~ dryer** (*BRIT*) *n* Trockner *m*; **~r** ['tʌmbləʳ] *n* (*glass*) Trinkglas *nt*

tummy ['tʌmɪ] *n* (*inf*) Bauch *m*; **~ upset** *n* Magenverstimmung *f*

tumour ['tjuːməʳ] (*US* **tumor**) *n* Geschwulst *f*, Tumor *m*

tumultuous [tjuːˈmʌltjuəs] *adj* (*welcome, applause etc*) stürmisch

tuna ['tjuːnə] *n* T(h)unfisch *m*

tune [tjuːn] *n* Melodie *f* ♦ *vt* (*MUS*) stimmen; (*AUT*) richtig einstellen; **to sing in ~/out of ~** richtig/falsch singen; **to be out of ~ with** nicht harmonieren mit; **~ in** *vi* einschalten; **~ up** *vi* (*MUS*) stimmen; **~ful** *adj* melodisch; **~r** *n* (*RAD*) Tuner *m*; (*person*) (Instrumenten)stimmer *m*; **piano ~r** Klavierstimmer(in) *m(f)*

tunic ['tjuːnɪk] *n* Waffenrock *m*; (*loose garment*) lange Bluse *f*

tuning ['tjuːnɪŋ] *n* (*RAD, AUT*) Einstellen *nt*; (*MUS*) Stimmen *nt*; **~ fork** *n* Stimmgabel *f*

Tunisia [tjuːˈnɪzɪə] *n* Tunesien *nt*

tunnel ['tʌnl] *n* Tunnel *m*, Unterführung *f* ♦ *vi* einen Tunnel anlegen

turbulent ['təːbjulənt] *adj* stürmisch

tureen [təˈriːn] *n* Terrine *f*

turf [tɜːf] *n* Rasen *m*; (*piece*) Sode *f* ♦ *vt* mit Grassoden belegen; **~ out** (*inf*) *vt* rauswerfen

turgid [ˈtɜːdʒɪd] *adj* geschwollen

Turk [tɜːk] *n* Türke *m*, Türkin *f*

Turkey [ˈtɜːkɪ] *n* Türkei *f*

turkey [ˈtɜːkɪ] *n* Puter *m*, Truthahn *m*

Turkish [ˈtɜːkɪʃ] *adj* türkisch ♦ *n* (*LING*) Türkisch *nt*

turmoil [ˈtɜːmɔɪl] *n* Aufruhr *m*, Tumult *m*

turn [tɜːn] *n* (*rotation*) (Um)drehung *f*; (*performance*) (Programm)nummer *f*; (*MED*) Schock *m* ♦ *vt* (*rotate*) drehen; (*change position of*) umdrehen, wenden; (*page*) umblättern; (*transform*): **to ~ sth into sth** etw in etw *acc* verwandeln; (*direct*) zuwenden ♦ *vi* (*rotate*) sich drehen; (*change direction: in car*) abbiegen; (*: wind*) drehen; (*~ round*) umdrehen, wenden; (*become*) werden; (*leaves*) sich verfärben; (*milk*) sauer werden; (*weather*) umschlagen; **to do sb a good ~** jdm etwas Gutes tun; **it's your ~** du bist dran *or* an der Reihe; **in ~, by ~s** abwechselnd; **to take ~s** sich abwechseln; **it gave me quite a ~** das hat mich schön erschreckt; **"no left ~"** (*AUT*) „Linksabbiegen verboten"; **~ away** *vi* sich abwenden; **~ back** *vt* umdrehen; (*person*) zurückschicken; (*clock*) zurückstellen ♦ *vi* umkehren; **~ down** *vt* (*refuse*) ablehnen; (*fold down*) umschlagen; **~ in** *vi* (*go to bed*) ins Bett gehen ♦ *vt* (*fold inwards*) einwärts biegen; **~ off** *vi* abbiegen ♦ *vt* ausschalten; (*tap*) zudrehen; (*machine, electricity*) abstellen; **~ on** *vt* (*light*) anschalten, einschalten; (*tap*) aufdrehen; (*machine*) anstellen; **~ out** *vt* (*prove to be*) sich erweisen; (*people*) sich entwickeln ♦ *vt* (*light*) ausschalten; (*gas*) abstellen; (*produce*) produzieren; **how did the cake ~ out?** wie ist der Kuchen geworden?; **~ over** *vi* (*person*) sich umdrehen ♦ *vt* (*object*) umdrehen, wenden; (*page*) umblättern; **~ round** *vi* (*person, vehicle*) sich herumdrehen; (*rotate*) sich drehen; **~ up** *vi* auftauchen ♦ *vt* (*collar*) hochklappen,

hochstellen; (*nose*) rümpfen; (*increase: radio*) lauter stellen; (*: heat*) höher drehen; **~ing** *n* (*in road*) Abzweigung *f*; **~ing point** *n* Wendepunkt *m*

turnip [ˈtɜːnɪp] *n* Steckrübe *f*

turnout [ˈtɜːnaʊt] *n* (Besucher)zahl *f*

turnover [ˈtɜːnəʊvə*] *n* Umsatz *m*; (*of staff*) Wechsel *m*

turnpike [ˈtɜːnpaɪk] (*US*) *n* gebührenpflichtige Straße *f*

turn: **~stile** [ˈtɜːnstaɪl] *n* Drehkreuz *nt*; **~table** [ˈtɜːnteɪbl] *n* (*of record player*) Plattenteller *m*; (*RAIL*) Drehscheibe *f*; **~-up** [ˈtɜːnʌp] (*BRIT*) *n* (*on trousers*) Aufschlag *m*

turpentine [ˈtɜːpəntaɪn] *n* Terpentin *nt*

turquoise [ˈtɜːkwɔɪz] *n* (*gem*) Türkis *m*; (*colour*) Türkis *m* ♦ *adj* türkisfarben

turret [ˈtʌrɪt] *n* Turm *m*

turtle [ˈtɜːtl] *n* Schildkröte *f*; **~ neck (sweater)** *n* Pullover *m* mit Schildkrötkragen

tusk [tʌsk] *n* Stoßzahn *m*

tussle [ˈtʌsl] *n* Balgerei *f*

tutor [ˈtjuːtə*] *n* (*teacher*) Privatlehrer *m*; (*college instructor*) Tutor *m*; **~ial** [tjuːˈtɔːrɪəl] *n* (*UNIV*) Kolloquium *nt*, Seminarübung *f*

tuxedo [tʌkˈsiːdəʊ] (*US*) *n* Smoking *m*

TV [tiːˈviː] *n abbr* (= *television*) TV *nt*

twang [twæŋ] *n* scharfe(r) Ton *m*; (*of voice*) Näseln *nt*

tweezers [ˈtwiːzəz] *npl* Pinzette *f*

twelfth [twelfθ] *adj* zwölfte(r, s)

twelve [twelv] *num* zwölf; **at ~ o'clock** (*midday*) um 12 Uhr; (*midnight*) um null Uhr

twentieth [ˈtwentɪɪθ] *adj* zwanzigste(r, s)

twenty [ˈtwentɪ] *num* zwanzig

twice [twaɪs] *adv* zweimal; **~ as much** doppelt so viel

twiddle [ˈtwɪdl] *vt, vi*: **to ~ (with) sth** an etw *dat* herumdrehen; **to ~ one's thumbs** (*fig*) Däumchen drehen

twig [twɪg] *n* dünne(r) Zweig *m* ♦ *vt* (*inf*) kapieren, merken

twilight [ˈtwaɪlaɪt] *n* Zwielicht *nt*

twin [twɪn] *n* Zwilling *m* ♦ *adj* Zwillings-; (*very similar*) Doppel- ♦ *vt* (*towns*) zu

Partnerstädten machen; **~-bedded room**
n Zimmer nt mit zwei Einzelbetten; **~ beds**
npl zwei (gleiche) Einzelbetten pl
twine [twaɪn] n Bindfaden m ♦ vi (plants)
sich ranken
twinge [twɪndʒ] n stechende(r) Schmerz m,
Stechen nt
twinkle ['twɪŋkl] n Funkeln nt, Blitzen nt ♦ vi
funkeln
twinned adj: **to be ~ with** die Partnerstadt
von ... sein
twirl [twɜːl] n Wirbel m ♦ vt, vi
(herum)wirbeln
twist [twɪst] n (~ing) Drehung f; (bend) Kurve
f ♦ vt (turn) drehen; (make crooked)
verbiegen; (distort) verdrehen ♦ vi (wind)
sich drehen; (curve) sich winden
twit [twɪt] (inf) n Idiot m
twitch [twɪtʃ] n Zucken nt ♦ vi zucken
two [tuː] num zwei; **to put ~ and ~ together**
seine Schlüsse ziehen; **~-door** adj
zweitürig; **~-faced** adj falsch; **~-fold** adj,
adv zweifach, doppelt; **to increase ~fold**
verdoppeln; **~-piece** adj zweiteilig; **~-
piece (suit)** n Zweiteiler m; **~-piece
(swimsuit)** n zweiteilige(r) Badeanzug m;
~-seater n (plane, car) Zweisitzer m;
~some n Paar nt; **~-way** adj (traffic)
Gegen-
tycoon [taɪ'kuːn] n: **(business) ~**
(Industrie)magnat m
type [taɪp] n Typ m, Art f; (PRINT) Type f ♦ vt,
vi Maschine schreiben, tippen; **~-cast** adj
(THEAT, TV) auf eine Rolle festgelegt; **~face**
n Schrift f; **~script** n
maschinegeschriebene(r) Text m; **~writer**
n Schreibmaschine f; **~written** adj
maschinegeschrieben
typhoid ['taɪfɔɪd] n Typhus m
typical ['tɪpɪkl] adj: **~ (of)** typisch (für)
typify ['tɪpɪfaɪ] vt typisch sein für
typing ['taɪpɪŋ] n Maschineschreiben nt
typist ['taɪpɪst] n Maschinenschreiber(in)
m(f), Tippse f (inf)
tyrant ['taɪərnt] n Tyrann m
tyre ['taɪər] (US **tire**) n Reifen m; **~ pressure**
n Reifendruck m

U, u

U-bend ['juːbɛnd] n (in pipe) U-Bogen m
udder ['ʌdər] n Euter nt
UFO ['juːfəʊ] n abbr (= unidentified flying
object) UFO nt
ugh [əːh] excl hu
ugliness ['ʌɡlɪnɪs] n Hässlichkeit f
ugly ['ʌɡlɪ] adj hässlich; (bad) böse, schlimm
UHT abbr (= ultra heat treated): **UHT milk**
H-Milch f
UK n abbr = **United Kingdom**
ulcer ['ʌlsər] n Geschwür nt
Ulster ['ʌlstər] n Ulster nt
ulterior [ʌl'tɪərɪər] adj: **~ motive**
Hintergedanke m
ultimate ['ʌltɪmət] adj äußerste(r, s),
allerletzte(r, s); **~ly** adv schließlich, letzten
Endes
ultrasound ['ʌltrəsaʊnd] n (MED) Ultraschall
m
umbilical cord [ʌm'bɪlɪkl-] n Nabelschnur f
umbrella [ʌm'brɛlə] n Schirm m
umpire ['ʌmpaɪər] n Schiedsrichter m ♦ vt, vi
schiedsrichtern
umpteenth [ʌmp'tiːnθ] (inf) adj zig; **for the
~ time** zum x-ten Mal
UN n abbr = **United Nations**
unable [ʌn'eɪbl] adj: **to be ~ to do sth** etw
nicht tun können
unacceptable [ʌnək'sɛptəbl] adj
unannehmbar, nicht akzeptabel
unaccompanied [ʌnə'kʌmpənɪd] adj ohne
Begleitung
unaccountably [ʌnə'kaʊntəblɪ] adv
unerklärlich
unaccustomed [ʌnə'kʌstəmd] adj nicht
gewöhnt; (unusual) ungewohnt; **~ to** nicht
gewöhnt an +acc
unanimous [juː'nænɪməs] adj einmütig;
(vote) einstimmig; **~ly** adv einmütig;
einstimmig
unarmed [ʌn'ɑːmd] adj unbewaffnet
unashamed [ʌnə'ʃeɪmd] adj schamlos
unassuming [ʌnə'sjuːmɪŋ] adj bescheiden

unattached [ʌnə'tætʃt] *adj* ungebunden
unattended [ʌnə'tendɪd] *adj* (*person*) unbeaufsichtigt; (*thing*) unbewacht
unauthorized [ʌn'ɔːθəraɪzd] *adj* unbefugt
unavoidable [ʌnə'vɔɪdəbl] *adj* unvermeidlich
unaware [ʌnə'weəʳ] *adj*: **to be ~ of sth** sich *dat* einer Sache *gen* nicht bewusst sein; **~s** *adv* unversehens
unbalanced [ʌn'bælənst] *adj* unausgeglichen; (*mentally*) gestört
unbearable [ʌn'beərəbl] *adj* unerträglich
unbeatable [ʌn'biːtəbl] *adj* unschlagbar
unbeknown(st) [ʌnbɪ'nəun(st)] *adv*: **~ to me** ohne mein Wissen
unbelievable [ʌnbɪ'liːvəbl] *adj* unglaublich
unbend [ʌn'bend] (*irreg: like* **bend**) *vt* gerade biegen ♦ *vi* aus sich herausgehen
unbias(s)ed [ʌn'baɪəst] *adj* unparteiisch
unborn [ʌn'bɔːn] *adj* ungeboren
unbreakable [ʌn'breɪkəbl] *adj* unzerbrechlich
unbridled [ʌn'braɪdld] *adj* ungezügelt
unbroken [ʌn'brəukən] *adj* (*period*) ununterbrochen; (*spirit*) ungebrochen; (*record*) unübertroffen
unburden [ʌn'bɜːdn] *vt*: **to ~ o.s.** (jdm) sein Herz ausschütten
unbutton [ʌn'bʌtn] *vt* aufknöpfen
uncalled-for [ʌn'kɔːldfɔːʳ] *adj* unnötig
uncanny [ʌn'kænɪ] *adj* unheimlich
unceasing [ʌn'siːsɪŋ] *adj* unaufhörlich
unceremonious [ʌnserɪ'məunɪəs] *adj* (*abrupt, rude*) brüsk; (*exit, departure*) überstürzt
uncertain [ʌn'sɜːtn] *adj* unsicher; (*doubtful*) ungewiss; (*unreliable*) unbeständig; (*vague*) undeutlich, vag(e); **~ty** *n* Ungewissheit *f*
unchanged [ʌn'tʃeɪndʒd] *adj* unverändert
unchecked [ʌn'tʃekt] *adj* ungeprüft; (*not stopped: advance*) ungehindert
uncivilized [ʌn'sɪvɪlaɪzd] *adj* unzivilisiert
uncle ['ʌŋkl] *n* Onkel *m*
uncomfortable [ʌn'kʌmfətəbl] *adj* unbequem, ungemütlich
uncommon [ʌn'kɔmən] *adj* ungewöhnlich; (*outstanding*) außergewöhnlich

uncompromising [ʌn'kɔmprəmaɪzɪŋ] *adj* kompromisslos, unnachgiebig
unconcerned [ʌnkən'sɜːnd] *adj* unbekümmert; (*indifferent*) gleichgültig
unconditional [ʌnkən'dɪʃənl] *adj* bedingungslos
unconscious [ʌn'kɔnʃəs] *adj* (*MED*) bewusstlos; (*not meant*) unbeabsichtigt ♦ *n*: **the ~** das Unbewusste; **~ly** *adv* unbewusst
uncontrollable [ʌnkən'trəuləbl] *adj* unkontrollierbar, unbändig
unconventional [ʌnkən'venʃənl] *adj* unkonventionell
uncouth [ʌn'kuːθ] *adj* grob
uncover [ʌn'kʌvəʳ] *vt* aufdecken
undecided [ʌndɪ'saɪdɪd] *adj* unschlüssig
undeniable [ʌndɪ'naɪəbl] *adj* unleugbar
under ['ʌndəʳ] *prep* unter ♦ *adv* darunter; **~ there** da drunter; **~ repair** in Reparatur
underage [ʌndər'eɪdʒ] *adj* minderjährig
undercarriage ['ʌndəkærɪdʒ] (*BRIT*) *n* (*AVIAT*) Fahrgestell *nt*
undercharge [ʌndə'tʃɑːdʒ] *vt*: **to ~ sb** jdm zu wenig berechnen
undercoat ['ʌndəkəut] *n* (*paint*) Grundierung *f*
undercover [ʌndə'kʌvəʳ] *adj* Geheim-
undercurrent ['ʌndəkʌrnt] *n* Unterströmung *f*
undercut [ʌndə'kʌt] (*irreg: like* **cut**) *vt* unterbieten
underdeveloped ['ʌndədɪ'veləpt] *adj* Entwicklungs-, unterentwickelt
underdog ['ʌndədɔg] *n* Unterlegene(r) *mf*
underdone [ʌndə'dʌn] *adj* (*COOK*) nicht gar, nicht durchgebraten
underestimate ['ʌndər'estɪmeɪt] *vt* unterschätzen
underexposed ['ʌndərɪks'pəuzd] *adj* unterbelichtet
underfoot [ʌndə'fut] *adv* am Boden
undergo [ʌndə'gəu] (*irreg: like* **go**) *vt* (*experience*) durchmachen; (*test, operation*) sich unterziehen +*dat*
undergraduate [ʌndə'grædjuɪt] *n* Student(in) *m(f)*
underground ['ʌndəgraund] *n* U-Bahn *f*

♦ adj Untergrund-

undergrowth ['ʌndəgrəυθ] n Gestrüpp nt, Unterholz nt

underhand(ed) [ʌndə'hænd(ɪd)] adj hinterhältig

underlie [ʌndə'laɪ] (irreg: like **lie**) vt zugrunde or zu Grunde liegen +dat

underline [ʌndə'laɪn] vt unterstreichen; (emphasize) betonen

underling ['ʌndəlɪŋ] n Handlanger m

undermine [ʌndə'maɪn] vt untergraben

underneath [ʌndə'niːθ] adv darunter ♦ prep unter

underpaid [ʌndə'peɪd] adj unterbezahlt

underpants ['ʌndəpænts] npl Unterhose f

underpass ['ʌndəpɑːs] (BRIT) n Unterführung f

underprivileged [ʌndə'prɪvɪlɪdʒd] adj benachteiligt, unterprivilegiert

underrate [ʌndə'reɪt] vt unterschätzen

undershirt ['ʌndəʃəːt] (US) n Unterhemd nt

undershorts ['ʌndəʃɔːts] (US) npl Unterhose f

underside ['ʌndəsaɪd] n Unterseite f

underskirt ['ʌndəskəːt] (BRIT) n Unterrock m

understand [ʌndə'stænd] (irreg: like **stand**) vt, vi verstehen; **I ~ that ...** ich habe gehört, dass ...; **am I to ~ that ...?** soll das (etwa) heißen, dass ...?; **what do you ~ by that?** was verstehen Sie darunter?; **it is understood that ...** es wurde vereinbart, dass ...; **to make o.s. understood** sich verständlich machen; **is that understood?** ist das klar?; **~able** adj verständlich; **~ing** n Verständnis nt ♦ adj verständnisvoll

understatement ['ʌndəsteɪtmənt] n (quality) Untertreibung f; **that's an ~!** das ist untertrieben!

understood [ʌndə'stud] pt, pp of **understand** ♦ adj klar; (implied) angenommen

understudy ['ʌndəstʌdɪ] n Ersatz(schau)spieler(in) m(f)

undertake [ʌndə'teɪk] (irreg: like **take**) vt unternehmen ♦ vi: **to ~ to do sth** sich verpflichten, etw zu tun

undertaker ['ʌndəteɪkər] n Leichenbestat-

ter m

undertaking ['ʌndəteɪkɪŋ] n (enterprise) Unternehmen nt; (promise) Verpflichtung f

undertone ['ʌndətəun] n: **in an ~** mit gedämpfter Stimme

underwater ['ʌndə'wɔːtər] adv unter Wasser ♦ adj Unterwasser-

underwear ['ʌndəwɛər] n Unterwäsche f

underworld ['ʌndəwəːld] n (of crime) Unterwelt f

underwriter ['ʌndəraɪtər] n Assekurant m

undesirable [ʌndɪ'zaɪərəbl] adj unerwünscht

undies ['ʌndɪz] (inf) npl (Damen)unterwäsche f

undisputed ['ʌndɪs'pjuːtɪd] adj unbestritten

undo [ʌn'duː] (irreg: like **do**) vt (unfasten) öffnen, aufmachen; (work) zunichte machen; **~ing** n Verderben nt

undoubted [ʌn'dautɪd] adj unbezweifelt; **~ly** adv zweifellos, ohne Zweifel

undress [ʌn'drɛs] vt ausziehen ♦ vi sich ausziehen

undue [ʌn'djuː] adj übermäßig

undulating ['ʌndjuleɪtɪŋ] adj wellenförmig; (country) wellig

unduly [ʌn'djuːlɪ] adv übermäßig

unearth [ʌn'əːθ] vt (dig up) ausgraben; (discover) ans Licht bringen

unearthly [ʌn'əːθlɪ] adj (hour) nachtschlafen

uneasy [ʌn'iːzɪ] adj (worried) unruhig; (feeling) ungut

uneconomic(al) [ʌni:kə'nɔmɪk(l)] adj unwirtschaftlich

uneducated [ʌn'edjukeɪtɪd] adj ungebildet

unemployed [ʌnɪm'plɔɪd] adj arbeitslos ♦ npl: **the ~** die Arbeitslosen pl

unemployment [ʌnɪm'plɔɪmənt] n Arbeitslosigkeit f

unending [ʌn'endɪŋ] adj endlos

unerring [ʌn'əːrɪŋ] adj unfehlbar

uneven [ʌn'iːvn] adj (surface) uneben; (quality) ungleichmäßig

unexpected [ʌnɪks'pektɪd] adj unerwartet; **~ly** adv unerwartet

unfailing [ʌn'feɪlɪŋ] adj nie versagend

unfair [ʌn'fɛər] adj ungerecht, unfair

unfaithful [ʌn'feɪθful] adj untreu

unfamiliar [ʌnfəˈmɪlɪəʳ] *adj* ungewohnt; (*person, subject*) unbekannt; **to be ~ with** nicht kennen +*acc*, nicht vertraut sein mit

unfashionable [ʌnˈfæʃnəbl] *adj* unmodern; (*area etc*) nicht in Mode

unfasten [ʌnˈfɑːsn] *vt* öffnen, aufmachen

unfavourable [ʌnˈfeɪvrəbl] (*US* **unfavorable**) *adj* ungünstig

unfeeling [ʌnˈfiːlɪŋ] *adj* gefühllos, kalt

unfinished [ʌnˈfɪnɪʃt] *adj* unvollendet

unfit [ʌnˈfɪt] *adj* ungeeignet; (*in bad health*) nicht fit; **~ for sth** zu *or* für etw ungeeignet

unfold [ʌnˈfəʊld] *vt* entfalten; (*paper*) auseinander falten ♦ *vi* (*develop*) sich entfalten

unforeseen [ˈʌnfɔːˈsiːn] *adj* unvorhergesehen

unforgettable [ʌnfəˈgetəbl] *adj* unvergesslich

unforgivable [ʌnfəˈgɪvəbl] *adj* unverzeihlich

unfortunate [ʌnˈfɔːtʃənət] *adj* unglücklich, bedauerlich; **~ly** *adv* leider

unfounded [ʌnˈfaʊndɪd] *adj* unbegründet

unfriendly [ʌnˈfrendlɪ] *adj* unfreundlich

ungainly [ʌnˈgeɪnlɪ] *adj* linkisch

ungodly [ʌnˈgɒdlɪ] *adj* (*hour*) nachtschlafend; (*row*) heillos

ungrateful [ʌnˈgreɪtfʊl] *adj* undankbar

unhappiness [ʌnˈhæpɪnɪs] *n* Unglück *nt*, Unglückseligkeit *f*

unhappy [ʌnˈhæpɪ] *adj* unglücklich; **~ with** (*arrangements etc*) unzufrieden mit

unharmed [ʌnˈhɑːmd] *adj* wohlbehalten, unversehrt

UNHCR *n abbr* (= *United Nations High Commission for Refugees*) Flüchtlingshochkommissariat der Vereinten Nationen

unhealthy [ʌnˈhelθɪ] *adj* ungesund

unheard-of [ʌnˈhɜːdɒv] *adj* unerhört

unhurt [ʌnˈhɜːt] *adj* unverletzt

unidentified [ʌnaɪˈdentɪfaɪd] *adj* unbekannt, nicht identifiziert

uniform [ˈjuːnɪfɔːm] *n* Uniform *f* ♦ *adj* einheitlich; **~ity** [juːnɪˈfɔːmɪtɪ] *n* Einheitlichkeit *f*

unify [ˈjuːnɪfaɪ] *vt* vereinigen

unilateral [juːnɪˈlætərəl] *adj* einseitig

uninhabited [ʌnɪnˈhæbɪtɪd] *adj* unbewohnt

unintentional [ʌnɪnˈtenʃənəl] *adj* unabsichtlich

union [ˈjuːnjən] *n* (*uniting*) Vereinigung *f*; (*alliance*) Bund *m*, Union *f*; (*trade ~*) Gewerkschaft *f*; **U~ Jack** *n* Union Jack *m*

unique [juːˈniːk] *adj* einzig(artig)

UNISON [ˈjuːnɪsn] *n* Gewerkschaft der Angestellten im öffentlichen Dienst

unison [ˈjuːnɪsn] *n* Einstimmigkeit *f*; **in ~** einstimmig

unit [ˈjuːnɪt] *n* Einheit *f*; **kitchen ~** Küchenelement *nt*

unite [juːˈnaɪt] *vt* vereinigen ♦ *vi* sich vereinigen; **~d** *adj* vereinigt; (*together*) vereint; **U~d Kingdom** *n* Vereinigte(s) Königreich *nt*; **U~d Nations (Organization)** *n* Vereinte Nationen *pl*; **U~d States (of America)** *n* Vereinigte Staaten *pl* (von Amerika)

unit trust (*BRIT*) *n* Treuhandgesellschaft *f*

unity [ˈjuːnɪtɪ] *n* Einheit *f*; (*agreement*) Einigkeit *f*

universal [juːnɪˈvɜːsl] *adj* allgemein

universe [ˈjuːnɪvɜːs] *n* (*Welt*)all *nt*

university [juːnɪˈvɜːsɪtɪ] *n* Universität *f*

unjust [ʌnˈdʒʌst] *adj* ungerecht

unkempt [ʌnˈkempt] *adj* ungepflegt

unkind [ʌnˈkaɪnd] *adj* unfreundlich

unknown [ʌnˈnəʊn] *adj*: **~ (to sb)** (jdm) unbekannt

unlawful [ʌnˈlɔːfʊl] *adj* illegal

unleaded [ˈʌnˈledɪd] *adj* bleifrei, unverbleit; **I use ~** ich fahre bleifrei

unleash [ʌnˈliːʃ] *vt* entfesseln

unless [ʌnˈles] *conj* wenn nicht, es sei denn; **~ he comes** es sei denn, er kommt; **~ otherwise stated** sofern nicht anders angegeben

unlike [ʌnˈlaɪk] *adj* unähnlich ♦ *prep* im Gegensatz zu

unlikely [ʌnˈlaɪklɪ] *adj* (*not likely*) unwahrscheinlich; (*unexpected: combination etc*) merkwürdig

unlimited [ʌnˈlɪmɪtɪd] *adj* unbegrenzt

unlisted [ˈʌnˈlɪstɪd] (*US*) *adj* nicht im

Telefonbuch stehend

unload [ʌn'ləʊd] *vt* entladen

unlock [ʌn'lɒk] *vt* aufschließen

unlucky [ʌn'lʌkɪ] *adj* unglücklich; *(person)* unglückselig; **to be ~** Pech haben

unmarried [ʌn'mærɪd] *adj* unverheiratet, ledig

unmask [ʌn'mɑːsk] *vt* entlarven

unmistakable [ʌnmɪs'teɪkəbl] *adj* unverkennbar

unmitigated [ʌn'mɪtɪgeɪtɪd] *adj* ungemildert, ganz

unnatural [ʌn'nætʃrəl] *adj* unnatürlich

unnecessary [ʌn'nesəsərɪ] *adj* unnötig

unnoticed [ʌn'nəʊtɪst] *adj*: **to go ~** unbemerkt bleiben

UNO ['juːnəʊ] *n abbr* = **United Nations Organization**

unobtainable [ʌnəb'teɪnəbl] *adj*: **this number is ~** kein Anschluss unter dieser Nummer

unobtrusive [ʌnəb'truːsɪv] *adj* unauffällig

unofficial [ʌnə'fɪʃl] *adj* inoffiziell

unpack [ʌn'pæk] *vt, vi* auspacken

unparalleled [ʌn'pærəleld] *adj* beispiellos

unpleasant [ʌn'pleznt] *adj* unangenehm

unplug [ʌn'plʌg] *vt* den Stecker herausziehen von

unpopular [ʌn'pɒpjʊlər] *adj* *(person)* unbeliebt; *(decision etc)* unpopulär

unprecedented [ʌn'presɪdentɪd] *adj* beispiellos

unpredictable [ʌnprɪ'dɪktəbl] *adj* unvorhersehbar; *(weather, person)* unberechenbar

unprofessional [ʌnprə'feʃənl] *adj* unprofessionell

UNPROFOR *n abbr* (= *United Nations Protection Force*) UNPROFOR *f*

unqualified [ʌn'kwɒlɪfaɪd] *adj* *(success)* uneingeschränkt, voll; *(person)* unqualifiziert

unquestionably [ʌn'kwestʃənəblɪ] *adv* fraglos

unravel [ʌn'rævl] *vt* *(disentangle)* ausfasern, entwirren; *(solve)* lösen

unreal [ʌn'rɪəl] *adj* unwirklich

unrealistic ['ʌnrɪə'lɪstɪk] *adj* unrealistisch

unreasonable [ʌn'riːznəbl] *adj* unvernünftig; *(demand)* übertrieben

unrelated [ʌnrɪ'leɪtɪd] *adj* ohne Beziehung; *(family)* nicht verwandt

unrelenting [ʌnrɪ'lentɪŋ] *adj* unerbittlich

unreliable [ʌnrɪ'laɪəbl] *adj* unzuverlässig

unremitting [ʌnrɪ'mɪtɪŋ] *adj* *(efforts, attempts)* unermüdlich

unreservedly [ʌnrɪ'zɜːvɪdlɪ] *adv* offen; *(believe, trust)* uneingeschränkt; *(cry)* rückhaltlos

unrest [ʌn'rest] *n (discontent)* Unruhe *f*; *(fighting)* Unruhen *pl*

unroll [ʌn'rəʊl] *vt* aufrollen

unruly [ʌn'ruːlɪ] *adj* *(child)* undiszipliniert; schwer lenkbar

unsafe [ʌn'seɪf] *adj* nicht sicher

unsaid [ʌn'sed] *adj*: **to leave sth ~** etw ungesagt lassen

unsatisfactory ['ʌnsætɪs'fæktərɪ] *adj* unbefriedigend; unzulänglich

unsavoury [ʌn'seɪvərɪ] *(US* **unsavory**) *adj* *(fig)* widerwärtig

unscathed [ʌn'skeɪðd] *adj* unversehrt

unscrew [ʌn'skruː] *vt* aufschrauben

unscrupulous [ʌn'skruːpjʊləs] *adj* skrupellos

unsettled [ʌn'setld] *adj* *(person)* rastlos; *(weather)* wechselhaft

unshaven [ʌn'ʃeɪvn] *adj* unrasiert

unsightly [ʌn'saɪtlɪ] *adj* unansehnlich

unskilled [ʌn'skɪld] *adj* ungelernt

unspeakable [ʌn'spiːkəbl] *adj* *(joy)* unsagbar; *(crime)* scheußlich

unstable [ʌn'steɪbl] *adj* instabil; *(mentally)* labil

unsteady [ʌn'stedɪ] *adj* unsicher

unstuck [ʌn'stʌk] *adj*: **to come ~** sich lösen; *(fig)* ins Wasser fallen

unsuccessful [ʌnsək'sesful] *adj* erfolglos

unsuitable [ʌn'suːtəbl] *adj* unpassend

unsure [ʌn'ʃʊər] *adj* unsicher; **to be ~ of o.s.** unsicher sein

unsuspecting [ʌnsəs'pektɪŋ] *adj* nichts ahnend

unsympathetic ['ʌnsɪmpə'θetɪk] *adj* gefühllos; *(response)* abweisend; *(unlikeable)* unsympathisch

untapped [ʌn'tæpt] *adj* (*resources*) ungenützt

unthinkable [ʌn'θɪŋkəbl] *adj* unvorstellbar

untidy [ʌn'taɪdɪ] *adj* unordentlich

untie [ʌn'taɪ] *vt* aufschnüren

until [ən'tɪl] *prep, conj* bis; **~ he comes** bis er kommt; **~ then** bis dann; **~ now** bis jetzt

untimely [ʌn'taɪmlɪ] *adj* (*death*) vorzeitig

untold [ʌn'təʊld] *adj* unermesslich

untoward [ʌntə'wɔːd] *adj* widrig

untranslatable [ʌntrænz'leɪtəbl] *adj* unübersetzbar

unused [ʌn'juːzd] *adj* unbenutzt

unusual [ʌn'juːʒʊəl] *adj* ungewöhnlich

unveil [ʌn'veɪl] *vt* enthüllen

unwanted [ʌn'wɒntɪd] *adj* unerwünscht

unwavering [ʌn'weɪvərɪŋ] *adj* standhaft, unerschütterlich

unwelcome [ʌn'welkəm] *adj* (*at a bad time*) unwillkommen; (*unpleasant*) unerfreulich

unwell [ʌn'wel] *adj*: **to feel** *or* **be ~** sich nicht wohl fühlen

unwieldy [ʌn'wiːldɪ] *adj* sperrig

unwilling [ʌn'wɪlɪŋ] *adj*: **to be ~ to do sth** nicht bereit sein, etw zu tun; **~ly** *adv* widerwillig

unwind [ʌn'waɪnd] (*irreg: like* **wind**[2]) *vt* abwickeln ♦ *vi* (*relax*) sich entspannen

unwise [ʌn'waɪz] *adj* unklug

unwitting [ʌn'wɪtɪŋ] *adj* unwissentlich

unworkable [ʌn'wɔːkəbl] *adj* (*plan*) undurchführbar

unworthy [ʌn'wɜːðɪ] *adj* (*person*): **~ (of sth)** (einer Sache *gen*) nicht wert

unwrap [ʌn'ræp] *vt* auspacken

unwritten [ʌn'rɪtn] *adj* ungeschrieben

KEYWORD

up [ʌp] *prep*: **to be up sth** oben auf etw *dat* sein; **to go up sth** (auf) etw *acc* hinaufgehen; **go up that road** gehen Sie die Straße hinauf

♦ *adv* **1** (*upwards, higher*) oben; **put it up a bit higher** stell es etwas weiter nach oben; **up there** da oben, dort oben; **up above** hoch oben

2: **to be up** (*out of bed*) auf sein; (*prices, level*) gestiegen sein; (*building, tent*) stehen

3: **up to** (*as far as*) bis; **up to now** bis jetzt

4: **to be up to** (*depending on*): **it's up to you** das hängt von dir ab; (*equal to*): **he's not up to it** (*job, task etc*) er ist dem nicht gewachsen; (*inf: be doing*): **what is he up to?** was führt er im Schilde?; **it's not up to me to decide** die Entscheidung liegt nicht bei mir; **his work is not up to the required standard** seine Arbeit entspricht nicht dem geforderten Niveau

♦ *n*: **ups and downs** (*in life, career*) Höhen und Tiefen *pl*

up-and-coming [ʌpənd'kʌmɪŋ] *adj* aufstrebend

upbringing ['ʌpbrɪŋɪŋ] *n* Erziehung *f*

update [ʌp'deɪt] *vt* auf den neuesten Stand bringen

upgrade [ʌp'greɪd] *vt* höher einstufen

upheaval [ʌp'hiːvl] *n* Umbruch *m*

uphill ['ʌp'hɪl] *adj* ansteigend; (*fig*) mühsam ♦ *adv*: **to go ~** bergauf gehen/fahren

uphold [ʌp'həʊld] (*irreg: like* **hold**) *vt* unterstützen

upholstery [ʌp'həʊlstərɪ] *n* Polster *nt*; Polsterung *f*

upkeep ['ʌpkiːp] *n* Instandhaltung *f*

upon [ə'pɒn] *prep* auf

upper ['ʌpər] *n* (*on shoe*) Oberleder *nt* ♦ *adj* obere(r, s); höhere(r, s); **to have the ~ hand** die Oberhand haben; **~-class** *adj* vornehm; **~most** *adj* oberste(r, s), höchste(r, s); **what was ~most in my mind** was mich in erster Linie beschäftigte; **~ sixth** (*BRIT: SCOL*) *n* Abschlussklasse *f*

upright ['ʌpraɪt] *adj* aufrecht

uprising ['ʌpraɪzɪŋ] *n* Aufstand *m*

uproar ['ʌprɔːr] *n* Aufruhr *m*

uproot [ʌp'ruːt] *vt* ausreißen

upset [*n* 'ʌpset, *vb, adj* ʌp'set] (*irreg: like* **set**) *n* Aufregung *f* ♦ *vt* (*overturn*) umwerfen; (*disturb*) aufregen, bestürzen; (*plans*) durcheinander bringen ♦ *adj* (*person*) aufgeregt; (*stomach*) verdorben

pshot ['ʌpʃɔt] n (End)ergebnis nt

pside-down ['ʌpsaɪd-] adv verkehrt herum

pstairs [ʌp'steəz] adv oben; (go) nach oben
♦ adj (room) obere(r, s), Ober- ♦ n obere(s)
Stockwerk nt

pstart ['ʌpstɑːt] n Emporkömmling m

pstream [ʌp'striːm] adv stromaufwärts

ptake ['ʌpteɪk] n: **to be quick on the ~**
schnell begreifen; **to be slow on the ~**
schwer von Begriff sein

ptight [ʌp'taɪt] (inf) adj (nervous) nervös;
(inhibited) verklemmt

p-to-date ['ʌptə'deɪt] adj (clothes) modisch,
modern; (information) neueste(r, s)

pturn ['ʌptɜːn] n Aufschwung m

pward ['ʌpwəd] adj nach oben gerichtet;
~(s) adv aufwärts

ranium [juə'reɪnɪəm] n Uran nt

rban ['ɜːbən] adj städtisch, Stadt-; **~
clearway** n Stadtautobahn f

rchin ['ɜːtʃɪn] n (boy) Schlingel m; (sea ~)
Seeigel m

rge [ɜːdʒ] n Drang m ♦ vt: **to ~ sb to do
sth** jdn (dazu) drängen, etw zu tun

rgency ['ɜːdʒənsɪ] n Dringlichkeit f

rgent ['ɜːdʒənt] adj dringend

rinal ['juərɪnl] n (public) Pissoir nt

rinate ['juərɪneɪt] vi urinieren

rine ['juərɪn] n Urin m, Harn m

rn [ɜːn] n Urne f; (tea ~) Teemaschine f

S n abbr = **United States**

s [ʌs] pron uns; see also **me**

SA n abbr = **United States of America**

sage ['juːzɪdʒ] n Gebrauch m; (esp LING)
Sprachgebrauch m

se [n juːs, vb juːz] n (employment) Gebrauch
m; (point) Zweck m ♦ vt gebrauchen; **in ~**
in Gebrauch; **out of ~** außer Gebrauch; **to
be of ~** nützlich sein; **it's no ~** es hat
keinen Zweck; **what's the ~?** was solls?;
~d to (accustomed to) gewöhnt an +acc;
she ~d to live here (formerly) sie hat früher
mal hier gewohnt; **~ up** vt aufbrauchen,
verbrauchen; **~d** adj (car) Gebraucht-; **~ful**
adj nützlich; **~fulness** n Nützlichkeit f;
~less adj nutzlos, unnütz; **~r** n Benutzer
m; **~r-friendly** adj (computer)

benutzerfreundlich

usher ['ʌʃə'] n Platzanweiser m; **~ette**
[ʌʃə'rɛt] n Platzanweiserin f

usual ['juːʒʊəl] adj gewöhnlich, üblich; **as ~**
wie üblich; **~ly** adv gewöhnlich

usurp [juː'zɜːp] vt an sich reißen

utensil [juː'tɛnsl] n Gerät nt; **kitchen ~s**
Küchengeräte pl

uterus ['juːtərəs] n Gebärmutter f

utilitarian [juːtɪlɪ'tɛərɪən] adj Nützlichkeits-

utility [juː'tɪlɪtɪ] n (usefulness) Nützlichkeit f;
(also: **public ~**) öffentliche(r)
Versorgungsbetrieb m; **~ room** n
Hauswirtschaftsraum m

utilize ['juːtɪlaɪz] vt benützen

utmost ['ʌtməʊst] adj äußerste(r, s) ♦ n: **to
do one's ~** sein Möglichstes tun

utter ['ʌtə'] adj äußerste(r, s), höchste(r, s),
völlig ♦ vt äußern, aussprechen; **~ance** n
Äußerung f; **~ly** adv äußerst, absolut, völlig

U-turn ['juː'tɜːn] n (AUT) Kehrtwendung f

V, v

v. abbr = **verse**; **versus**; **volt**; (= vide) see

vacancy ['veɪkənsɪ] n (BRIT: job) offene Stelle
f; (room) freie(s) Zimmer nt; **"no
vacancies"** „belegt"

vacant ['veɪkənt] adj leer; (unoccupied) frei;
(house) leer stehend, unbewohnt; (stupid)
(gedanken)leer; **~ lot** (US) n unbebaute(s)
Grundstück nt

vacate [və'keɪt] vt (seat) frei machen; (room)
räumen

vacation [və'keɪʃən] n Ferien pl, Urlaub m;
~ist (US) n Ferienreisende(r) f(m)

vaccinate ['væksɪneɪt] vt impfen

vaccine ['væksiːn] n Impfstoff m

vacuum ['vækjʊm] n Vakuum nt; **~ bottle**
(US) n Thermosflasche f; **~ cleaner** n
Staubsauger m; **~ flask** (BRIT) n
Thermosflasche f; **~-packed** adj
vakuumversiegelt

vagina [və'dʒaɪnə] n Scheide f

vague [veɪg] adj vag(e); (absent-minded)
geistesabwesend; **~ly** adv unbestimmt,

vag(e)

vain [veɪn] *adj* eitel; (*attempt*) vergeblich; **in ~** vergebens, umsonst

valentine ['væləntaɪn] *n* (*also*: **~ card**) Valentinsgruß *m*; **V~'s Day** *n* Valentinstag *m*

valet ['vælɪt] *n* Kammerdiener *m*

valiant ['vælɪənt] *adj* tapfer

valid ['vælɪd] *adj* gültig; (*argument*) stichhaltig; (*objection*) berechtigt; **~ity** [və'lɪdɪtɪ] *n* Gültigkeit *f*

valley ['vælɪ] *n* Tal *nt*

valour ['vælər] (*US* **valor**) *n* Tapferkeit *f*

valuable ['væljʊəbl] *adj* wertvoll; (*time*) kostbar; **~s** *npl* Wertsachen *pl*

valuation [væljʊ'eɪʃən] *n* (*FIN*) Schätzung *f*; Beurteilung *f*

value ['vælju:] *n* Wert *m*; (*usefulness*) Nutzen *m* ♦ *vt* (*prize*) (hoch) schätzen, werthalten; (*estimate*) schätzen; **~ added tax** (*BRIT*) *n* Mehrwertsteuer *f*; **~d** *adj* (hoch) geschätzt

valve [vælv] *n* Ventil *nt*; (*BIOL*) Klappe *f*; (*RAD*) Röhre *f*

van [væn] *n* Lieferwagen *m*; (*BRIT*: *RAIL*) Waggon *m*

vandal ['vændl] *n* Rowdy *m*; **~ism** *n* mutwillige Beschädigung *f*; **~ize** *vt* mutwillig beschädigen

vanguard ['vænɡɑːd] *n* (*fig*) Spitze *f*

vanilla [və'nɪlə] *n* Vanille *f*; **~ ice cream** *n* Vanilleeis *nt*

vanish ['vænɪʃ] *vi* verschwinden

vanity ['vænɪtɪ] *n* Eitelkeit *f*; **~ case** *n* Schminkkoffer *m*

vantage ['vɑːntɪdʒ] *n*: **~ point** gute(r) Aussichtspunkt *m*

vapour ['veɪpər] (*US* **vapor**) *n* (*mist*) Dunst *m*; (*gas*) Dampf *m*

variable ['vɛərɪəbl] *adj* wechselhaft, veränderlich; (*speed, height*) regulierbar

variance ['vɛərɪəns] *n*: **to be at ~ (with)** nicht übereinstimmen (mit)

variation [vɛərɪ'eɪʃən] *n* Variation *f*; (*in prices etc*) Schwankung *f*

varicose ['værɪkəʊs] *adj*: **~ veins** Krampfadern *pl*

varied ['vɛərɪd] *adj* unterschiedlich; (*life*) abwechslungsreich

variety [və'raɪətɪ] *n* (*difference*) Abwechslung *f*; (*varied collection*) Vielfalt *f*; (*COMM*) Auswahl *f*; (*sort*) Sorte *f*, Art *f*; **~ show** *n* Varietee *nt*, Varieté *nt*

various ['vɛərɪəs] *adj* verschieden; (*several*) mehrere

varnish ['vɑːnɪʃ] *n* Lack *m*; (*on pottery*) Glasur *f* ♦ *vt* lackieren

vary ['vɛərɪ] *vt* (*alter*) verändern; (*give variety to*) abwechslungsreicher gestalten ♦ *vi* sich (ver)ändern; (*prices*) schwanken; (*weather*) unterschiedlich sein

vase [vɑːz] *n* Vase *f*

Vaseline ['væsɪliːn] ® *n* Vaseline *f*

vast [vɑːst] *adj* weit, groß, riesig

VAT [væt] *n abbr* (= *value added tax*) MwSt *f*

vat [væt] *n* große(s) Fass *nt*

vault [vɔːlt] *n* (*of roof*) Gewölbe *nt*; (*tomb*) Gruft *f*; (*in bank*) Tresorraum *m*; (*leap*) Sprung *m* ♦ *vt* (*also*: **~ over**) überspringen

vaunted ['vɔːntɪd] *adj*: **much-~** viel gerühmt

VCR *n abbr* = **video cassette recorder**

VD *n abbr* = **venereal disease**

VDU *n abbr* = **visual display unit**

veal [viːl] *n* Kalbfleisch *nt*

veer [vɪər] *vi* sich drehen; (*of car*) ausscheren

vegan ['viːɡən] *n* Vegan *m*, radikale(r) Vegetarier(in) *m(f)*

vegeburger ['vedʒɪbɜːɡər] *n* vegetarische Frikadelle *f*

vegetable ['vedʒtəbl] *n* Gemüse *nt* ♦ *adj* Gemüse-; **~s** *npl* (*CULIN*) Gemüse *nt*

vegetarian [vedʒɪ'tɛərɪən] *n* Vegetarier(in) *m(f)* ♦ *adj* vegetarisch

vegetate ['vedʒɪteɪt] *vi* (dahin)vegetieren

veggieburger ['vedʒɪbɜːɡər] *n* = **vegeburger**

vehement ['viːɪmənt] *adj* heftig

vehicle ['viːɪkl] *n* Fahrzeug *nt*; (*fig*) Mittel *nt*

veil [veɪl] *n* (*also fig*) Schleier *m* ♦ *vt* verschleiern

vein [veɪn] *n* Ader *f*; (*mood*) Stimmung *f*

velocity [vɪ'lɒsɪtɪ] *n* Geschwindigkeit *f*

velvet ['velvɪt] *n* Samt *m* ♦ *adj* Samt-

vendetta [ven'detə] *n* Fehde *f*; (*in family*)

Blutrache f

vending machine ['vendɪŋ-] n Automat m

vendor ['vendər] n Verkäufer m

veneer [və'nɪər] n Furnier(holz) nt; (fig) äußere(r) Anstrich m

venereal disease [vɪ'nɪərɪəl-] n Geschlechtskrankheit f

Venetian blind [vɪ'ni:ʃən-] n Jalousie f

vengeance ['vendʒəns] n Rache f; **with a ~** gewaltig

venison ['venɪsn] n Reh(fleisch) nt

venom ['venəm] n Gift nt

vent [vent] n Öffnung f; (in coat) Schlitz m; (fig) Ventil nt ♦ vt (emotion) abreagieren

ventilate ['ventɪleɪt] vt belüften; **ventilator** ['ventɪleɪtər] n Ventilator m

ventriloquist [ven'trɪləkwɪst] n Bauchredner m

venture ['ventʃər] n Unternehmung f, Projekt nt ♦ vt wagen; (life) aufs Spiel setzen ♦ vi sich wagen

venue ['venju:] n Schauplatz m

verb [və:b] n Zeitwort nt, Verb nt; **~al** adj (spoken) mündlich; (translation) wörtlich; **~ally** adv mündlich

verbatim [və:'beɪtɪm] adv Wort für Wort ♦ adj wortwörtlich

verbose [və:'bəus] adj wortreich

verdict ['və:dɪkt] n Urteil nt

verge [və:dʒ] n (BRIT) Rand m ♦ vi: **to ~ on** grenzen an +acc; **"soft ~s"** (BRIT: AUT) „Seitenstreifen nicht befahrbar"; **on the ~ of doing sth** im Begriff, etw zu tun

verify ['verɪfaɪ] vt (über)prüfen; (confirm) bestätigen; (theory) beweisen

veritable ['verɪtəbl] adj wirklich, echt

vermin ['və:mɪn] npl Ungeziefer nt

vermouth ['və:məθ] n Wermut m

versatile ['və:sətaɪl] adj vielseitig

verse [və:s] n (poetry) Poesie f; (stanza) Strophe f; (of Bible) Vers m; **in ~** in Versform

version ['və:ʃən] n Version f; (of car) Modell nt

versus ['və:səs] prep gegen

vertebrate ['və:tɪbrɪt] adj Wirbel-

vertical ['və:tɪkl] adj senkrecht

vertigo ['və:tɪgəu] n Schwindel m

very ['verɪ] adv sehr ♦ adj (extreme) äußerste(r, s); **the ~ book which** genau das Buch, welches; **the ~ last ...** der/die/das allerletzte ...; **at the ~ least** allerwenigstens; **~ much** sehr

vessel ['vesl] n (ship) Schiff nt; (container) Gefäß nt

vest [vest] n (BRIT) Unterhemd nt; (US: waistcoat) Weste f

vested interests ['vestɪd-] npl finanzielle Beteiligung f; (people) finanziell Beteiligte pl; (fig) persönliche(s) Interesse nt

vestige ['vestɪdʒ] n Spur f

vestry ['vestrɪ] n Sakristei f

vet [vet] n abbr (= veterinary surgeon) Tierarzt m/-ärztin f

veteran ['vetərn] n Veteran(in) m(f)

veterinarian [vetrɪ'nɛərɪən] n (US) Tierarzt m/-ärztin f

veterinary ['vetrɪnərɪ] adj Veterinär-; **~ surgeon** (BRIT) n Tierarzt m/-ärztin f

veto ['vi:təu] n (pl **~es**) Veto nt ♦ vt sein Veto einlegen gegen

vex [veks] vt ärgern; **~ed** adj verärgert; **~ed question** umstrittene Frage f

VHF abbr (= very high frequency) UKW f

via ['vaɪə] prep über +acc

viable ['vaɪəbl] adj (plan) durchführbar; (company) rentabel

vibrant ['vaɪbrnt] adj (lively) lebhaft; (bright) leuchtend; (full of emotion: voice) bebend

vibrate [vaɪ'breɪt] vi zittern, beben; (machine, string) vibrieren; **vibration** [vaɪ'breɪʃən] n Schwingung f; (of machine) Vibrieren nt

vicar ['vɪkər] n Pfarrer m; **~age** n Pfarrhaus nt

vice [vaɪs] n (evil) Laster nt; (TECH) Schraubstock m

vice-chairman [vaɪs'tʃɛəmən] n stellvertretende(r) Vorsitzende(r) m

vice-president [vaɪs'prezɪdənt] n Vizepräsident m

vice squad n ≈ Sittenpolizei f

vice versa ['vaɪsɪ'və:sə] adv umgekehrt

vicinity [vɪ'sɪnɪtɪ] n Umgebung f; (closeness) Nähe f

vicious ['vɪʃəs] *adj* gemein, böse; ~ **circle** *n* Teufelskreis *m*

victim ['vɪktɪm] *n* Opfer *nt*

victor ['vɪktə'] *n* Sieger *m*

Victorian [vɪk'tɔːrɪən] *adj* viktorianisch; *(fig)* (sitten)streng

victorious [vɪk'tɔːrɪəs] *adj* siegreich

victory ['vɪktərɪ] *n* Sieg *m*

video ['vɪdɪəʊ] *adj* Fernseh-, Bild- ♦ *n* (~ *film*) Video *nt*; *(also: ~ cassette)* Videokassette *f*; *(also: ~ cassette recorder)* Videorekorder *m*; ~ **tape** *n* Videoband *nt*; ~ **wall** *n* Videowand *m*

vie [vaɪ] *vi* wetteifern

Vienna [vɪ'ɛnə] *n* Wien *nt*

Vietnam ['vjɛt'næm] *n* Vietnam *nt*; ~**ese** *adj* vietnamesisch ♦ *n inv (person)* Vietnamese *m*, Vietnamesin *f*

view [vju:] *n (sight)* Sicht *f*, Blick *m*; *(scene)* Aussicht *f*; *(opinion)* Ansicht *f*; *(intention)* Absicht *f* ♦ *vt (situation)* betrachten; *(house)* besichtigen; **to have sth in ~** etw beabsichtigen; **on ~** ausgestellt; **in ~ of** wegen +*gen*, angesichts +*gen*; ~**er** *n (PHOT: small projector)* Gucki *m*; *(TV)* Fernsehzuschauer(in) *m(f)*; ~**finder** *n* Sucher *m*; ~**point** *n* Standpunkt *m*

vigil ['vɪdʒɪl] *n* (Nacht)wache *f*; ~**ant** *adj* wachsam

vigorous ['vɪgərəs] *adj* kräftig; *(protest)* energisch, heftig

vile [vaɪl] *adj (mean)* gemein; *(foul)* abscheulich

villa ['vɪlə] *n* Villa *f*

village ['vɪlɪdʒ] *n* Dorf *nt*; ~**r** *n* Dorfbewohner(in) *m(f)*

villain ['vɪlən] *n* Schurke *m*

vindicate ['vɪndɪkeɪt] *vt* rechtfertigen

vindictive [vɪn'dɪktɪv] *adj* nachtragend, rachsüchtig

vine [vaɪn] *n* Rebstock *m*, Rebe *f*

vinegar ['vɪnɪgə'] *n* Essig *m*

vineyard ['vɪnjɑːd] *n* Weinberg *m*

vintage ['vɪntɪdʒ] *n (of wine)* Jahrgang *m*; ~ **car** *n* Oldtimer *m (zwischen 1919 und 1930 gebaut)*; ~ **wine** *n* edle(r) Wein *m*

viola [vɪ'əʊlə] *n* Bratsche *f*

violate ['vaɪəleɪt] *vt (law)* übertreten; *(rights, rule, neutrality)* verletzen; *(sanctity, woman)* schänden; **violation** [vaɪə'leɪʃən] *n* Übertretung *f*; Verletzung *f*

violence ['vaɪələns] *n (force)* Heftigkeit *f*; *(brutality)* Gewalttätigkeit *f*

violent ['vaɪələnt] *adj (strong)* heftig; *(brutal)* gewalttätig, brutal; *(contrast)* krass; *(death)* gewaltsam

violet ['vaɪələt] *n* Veilchen *nt* ♦ *adj* veilchenblau, violett

violin [vaɪə'lɪn] *n* Geige *f*, Violine *f*; ~**ist** *n* Geiger(in) *m(f)*

VIP *n abbr (= very important person)* VIP *m*

virgin ['vɜːdʒɪn] *n* Jungfrau *f* ♦ *adj* jungfräulich, unberührt; ~**ity** [vɜː'dʒɪnɪtɪ] *n* Unschuld *f*

Virgo ['vɜːgəʊ] *n* Jungfrau *f*

virile ['vɪraɪl] *adj* männlich; **virility** [vɪ'rɪlɪtɪ] *n* Männlichkeit *f*

virtually ['vɜːtjʊəlɪ] *adv* praktisch, fast

virtual reality ['vɜːtjʊəl-] *n (COMPUT)* virtuelle Realität *f*

virtue ['vɜːtjuː] *n (moral goodness)* Tugend *f*; *(good quality)* Vorteil *m*, Vorzug *m*; **by ~ of** aufgrund *or* auf Grund +*gen*

virtuous ['vɜːtjʊəs] *adj* tugendhaft

virulent ['vɪrʊlənt] *adj (poisonous)* bösartig; *(bitter)* scharf, geharnischt

virus ['vaɪərəs] *n (also COMPUT)* Virus *m*

visa ['viːzə] *n* Visum *nt*

vis-à-vis [viːzə'viː] *prep* gegenüber

viscous ['vɪskəs] *adj* zähflüssig

visibility [vɪzɪ'bɪlɪtɪ] *n (MET)* Sicht(weite) *f*

visible ['vɪzəbl] *adj* sichtbar; **visibly** *adv* sichtlich

vision ['vɪʒən] *n (ability)* Sehvermögen *nt*; *(foresight)* Weitblick *m*; *(in dream, image)* Vision *f*

visit ['vɪzɪt] *n* Besuch *m* ♦ *vt* besuchen; *(town, country)* fahren nach; ~**ing hours** *npl (in hospital etc)* Besuchszeiten *pl*; ~**or** *n (in house)* Besucher(in) *m(f)*; *(in hotel)* Gast *m*; ~**or centre** *n* Touristeninformation *f*

visor ['vaɪzə'] *n* Visier *nt*; *(on cap)* Schirm *m*; *(AUT)* Blende *f*

vista ['vɪstə] *n* Aussicht *f*

visual ['vɪzjuəl] *adj* Seh-, visuell; ~ **aid** *n* Anschauungsmaterial *nt*; ~ **display unit** *n* Bildschirm(gerät *nt*) *m*; ~**ize** *vt* sich +*dat* vorstellen; ~**ly-impaired** *adj* sehbehindert

vital ['vaɪtl] *adj* (*important*) unerlässlich; (*necessary for life*) Lebens-, lebenswichtig; (*lively*) vital; ~**ity** [vaɪ'tælɪtɪ] *n* Vitalität *f*; ~**ly** *adv*: ~**ly important** äußerst wichtig; ~ **statistics** *npl* (*fig*) Maße *pl*

vitamin ['vɪtəmɪn] *n* Vitamin *nt*

vivacious [vɪ'veɪʃəs] *adj* lebhaft

vivid ['vɪvɪd] *adj* (*graphic*) lebendig; (*memory*) lebhaft; (*bright*) leuchtend; ~**ly** *adv* lebendig; lebhaft; leuchtend

V-neck ['viːnɛk] *n* V-Ausschnitt *m*

vocabulary [vəu'kæbjulərɪ] *n* Wortschatz *m*, Vokabular *nt*

vocal ['vəukl] *adj* Vokal-, Gesang-; (*fig*) lautstark; ~ **cords** *npl* Stimmbänder *pl*

vocation [vəu'keɪʃən] *n* (*calling*) Berufung *f*; ~**al** *adj* Berufs-

vociferous [və'sɪfərəs] *adj* lautstark

vodka ['vɒdkə] *n* Wodka *m*

vogue [vəug] *n* Mode *f*

voice [vɔɪs] *n* Stimme *f*; (*fig*) Mitspracherecht *n* ♦ *vt* äußern; ~ **mail** *n* (*TEL*) Voicemail *f*

void [vɔɪd] *n* Leere *f* ♦ *adj* (*invalid*) nichtig, ungültig; (*empty*): ~ **of** ohne, bar +*gen*; *see* **null**

volatile ['vɒlətaɪl] *adj* (*gas*) flüchtig; (*person*) impulsiv; (*situation*) brisant

volcano [vɒl'keɪnəu] *n* Vulkan *m*

volition [və'lɪʃən] *n* Wille *m*; **of one's own** ~ aus freiem Willen

volley ['vɒlɪ] *n* (*of guns*) Salve *f*; (*of stones*) Hagel *m*; (*tennis*) Flugball *m*; ~**ball** *n* Volleyball *m*

volt [vəult] *n* Volt *nt*; ~**age** *n* Spannung *f*

volume ['vɒljuːm] *n* (*book*) Band *m*; (*size*) Umfang *m*; (*space*) Rauminhalt *m*; (*of sound*) Lautstärke *f*

voluntarily ['vɒləntrɪlɪ] *adv* freiwillig

voluntary ['vɒləntərɪ] *adj* freiwillig

volunteer [vɒlən'tɪəʳ] *n* Freiwillige(r) *mf* ♦ *vi* sich freiwillig melden; **to ~ to do sth** sich anbieten, etw zu tun

vomit ['vɒmɪt] *n* Erbrochene(s) *nt* ♦ *vt* spucken ♦ *vi* sich übergeben

vote [vəut] *n* Stimme *f*; (*ballot*) Abstimmung *f*; (*result*) Abstimmungsergebnis *nt*; (*franchise*) Wahlrecht *nt* ♦ *vt, vi* wählen; ~ **of thanks** *n* Dankesworte *pl*; ~**r** *n* Wähler(in) *m(f)*; **voting** ['vəutɪŋ] *n* Wahl *f*

voucher ['vautʃəʳ] *n* Gutschein *m*

vouch for [vautʃ-] *vt* bürgen für

vow [vau] *n* Versprechen *nt*; (*REL*) Gelübde *nt* ♦ *vt* geloben

vowel ['vauəl] *n* Vokal *m*

voyage ['vɔɪdʒ] *n* Reise *f*

vulgar ['vʌlgəʳ] *adj* (*rude*) vulgär; ~**ity** [vʌl'gærɪtɪ] *n* Vulgarität *f*

vulnerable ['vʌlnərəbl] *adj* (*easily injured*) verwundbar; (*sensitive*) verletzlich

vulture ['vʌltʃəʳ] *n* Geier *m*

W, w

wad [wɒd] *n* (*bundle*) Bündel *nt*; (*of paper*) Stoß *m*; (*of money*) Packen *m*

waddle ['wɒdl] *vi* watscheln

wade [weɪd] *vi*: **to ~ through** waten durch

wafer ['weɪfəʳ] *n* Waffel *f*; (*REL*) Hostie *f*; (*COMPUT*) Wafer *f*

waffle ['wɒfl] *n* Waffel *f*; (*inf: empty talk*) Geschwafel *nt* ♦ *vi* schwafeln

waft [wɒft] *vt, vi* wehen

wag [wæg] *vt* (*tail*) wedeln mit ♦ *vi* wedeln

wage [weɪdʒ] *n* (*also:* ~**s**) (Arbeits)lohn *m* ♦ *vt*: **to ~ war** Krieg führen; ~ **earner** *n* Lohnempfänger(in) *m(f)*; ~ **packet** *n* Lohntüte *f*

wager ['weɪdʒəʳ] *n* Wette *f* ♦ *vt, vi* wetten

waggle ['wægl] *vi* wackeln

wag(g)on ['wægən] *n* (*horse-drawn*) Fuhrwerk *nt*; (*US: AUT*) Wagen *m*; (*BRIT: RAIL*) Wag(g)on *m*

wail [weɪl] *n* Wehgeschrei *nt* ♦ *vi* wehklagen, jammern

waist [weɪst] *n* Taille *f*; ~**coat** (*BRIT*) *n* Weste *f*; ~**line** *n* Taille *f*

wait [weɪt] *n* Wartezeit *f* ♦ *vi* warten; **to lie in** ~ **for sb** jdm auflauern; **I can't** ~ **to see**

him ich kanns kaum erwarten ihn zu sehen; **"no ~ing"** (*BRIT: AUT*) „Halteverbot"; **~ behind** *vi* zurückbleiben; **~ for** *vt fus* warten auf +*acc*; **~ on** *vt fus* bedienen; **~er** *n* Kellner *m*; **~ing list** *n* Warteliste *f*; **~ing room** *n* (*MED*) Wartezimmer *nt*; (*RAIL*) Wartesaal *m*; **~ress** *n* Kellnerin *f*

waive [weɪv] *vt* verzichten auf +*acc*

wake [weɪk] (*pt* **woke, waked**, *pp* **woken**) *vt* wecken ♦ *vi* (*also*: **~ up**) aufwachen ♦ *n* (*NAUT*) Kielwasser *nt*; (*for dead*) Totenwache *f*; **to ~ up to** (*fig*) sich bewusst werden +*gen*

waken [ˈweɪkn] *vt* aufwecken

Wales [weɪlz] *n* Wales *nt*

walk [wɔːk] *n* Spaziergang *m*; (*gait*) Gang *m*; (*route*) Weg *m* ♦ *vi* gehen; (*stroll*) spazieren gehen; (*longer*) wandern; **~s of life** Sphären *pl*; **a 10-minute ~** 10 Minuten zu Fuß; **to ~ out on sb** (*inf*) jdn sitzen lassen; **~er** *n* Spaziergänger *m*; (*hiker*) Wanderer *m*; **~ie-talkie** [ˈwɔːkɪˈtɔːkɪ] *n* tragbare(s) Sprechfunkgerät *nt*; **~ing** *n* Gehen *nt*; (*hiking*) Wandern *nt* ♦ *adj* Wander-; **~ing shoes** *npl* Wanderschuhe *pl*; **~ing stick** *n* Spazierstock *m*; **W~man** [ˈwɔːkmən] ® *n* Walkman *m* ®; **~out** *n* Streik *m*; **~over** (*inf*) *n* leichte(r) Sieg *m*; **~way** *n* Fußweg *m*

wall [wɔːl] *n* (*inside*) Wand *f*; (*outside*) Mauer *f*; **~ed** *adj* von Mauern umgeben

wallet [ˈwɔlɪt] *n* Brieftasche *f*

wallflower [ˈwɔːlflauə*] *n* Goldlack *m*; **to be a ~** (*fig*) ein Mauerblümchen sein

wallop [ˈwɔləp] (*inf*) *vt* schlagen, verprügeln

wallow [ˈwɔləu] *vi* sich wälzen

wallpaper [ˈwɔːlpeɪpə*] *n* Tapete *f*

walnut [ˈwɔːlnʌt] *n* Walnuss *f*

walrus [ˈwɔːlrəs] *n* Walross *nt*

waltz [wɔːlts] *n* Walzer *m* ♦ *vi* Walzer tanzen

wan [wɔn] *adj* bleich

wand [wɔnd] *n* (*also*: **magic ~**) Zauberstab *m*

wander [ˈwɔndə*] *vi* (*roam*) (herum)wandern; (*fig*) abschweifen

wane [weɪn] *vi* abnehmen; (*fig*) schwinden

wangle [ˈwæŋgl] (*BRIT: inf*) *vt*: **to ~ sth** etw richtig hindrehen

want [wɔnt] *n* (*lack*) Mangel *m* ♦ *vt* (*need*) brauchen; (*desire*) wollen; (*lack*) nicht haben; **~s** *npl* (*needs*) Bedürfnisse *pl*; **for ~ of** aus Mangel an +*dat*; mangels +*gen*; **to ~ to do sth** etw tun wollen; **to ~ sb to do sth** wollen, dass jd etw tut; **~ed** *adj* (*criminal etc*) gesucht; **"cook ~ed"** (*in adverts*) „Koch/Köchin gesucht"; **~ing** *adj*: **to be found ~ing** sich als unzulänglich erweisen

wanton [ˈwɔntn] *adj* mutwillig, zügellos

war [wɔː] *n* Krieg *m*; **to make ~** Krieg führen

ward [wɔːd] *n* (*in hospital*) Station *f*; (*of city*) Bezirk *m*; (*child*) Mündel *nt*; **~ off** *vt* abwenden, abwehren

warden [ˈwɔːdn] *n* (*guard*) Wächter *m*, Aufseher *m*; (*BRIT: in youth hostel*) Herbergsvater *m*; (*UNIV*) Heimleiter *m*; (*BRIT: also*: **traffic ~**) ≃ Verkehrspolizist *m*, ≃ Politesse *f*

warder [ˈwɔːdə*] (*BRIT*) *n* Gefängniswärter *m*

wardrobe [ˈwɔːdrəub] *n* Kleiderschrank *m*; (*clothes*) Garderobe *f*

warehouse [ˈwɛəhaus] *n* Lagerhaus *nt*

wares [wɛəz] *npl* Ware *f*

warfare [ˈwɔːfɛə*] *n* Krieg *m*; Kriegsführung *f*

warhead [ˈwɔːhed] *n* Sprengkopf *m*

warily [ˈwɛərɪlɪ] *adv* vorsichtig

warlike [ˈwɔːlaɪk] *adj* kriegerisch

warm [wɔːm] *adj* warm; (*welcome*) herzlich ♦ *vt, vi* wärmen; **I'm ~** mir ist warm; **it's ~** es ist warm; **~ up** *vt* aufwärmen ♦ *vi* warm werden; **~-hearted** *adj* warmherzig; **~ly** *adv* warm; herzlich; **~th** *n* Wärme *f*; Herzlichkeit *f*

warn [wɔːn] *vt*: **to ~** (*of or against*) warnen (vor +*dat*); **~ing** *n* Warnung *f*; **without ~ing** unerwartet; **~ing light** *n* Warnlicht *nt*; **~ing triangle** *n* (*AUT*) Warndreieck *nt*

warp [wɔːp] *vt* verziehen; **~ed** *adj* wellig; (*fig*) pervers

warrant [ˈwɔrnt] *n* (*for arrest*) Haftbefehl *m*

warranty [ˈwɔrəntɪ] *n* Garantie *f*

warren [ˈwɔrən] *n* Labyrinth *nt*

Warsaw [ˈwɔːsɔː] *n* Warschau *nt*

warship [ˈwɔːʃɪp] *n* Kriegsschiff *nt*

wart [wɔːt] *n* Warze *f*

wartime ['wɔːtaɪm] n Krieg m
wary ['weərɪ] adj misstrauisch
was [wɔz] pt of **be**
wash [wɔʃ] n Wäsche f ♦ vt waschen; (dishes) abwaschen ♦ vi sich waschen; (do ~ing) waschen; **to have a ~** sich waschen; **~ away** vt abwaschen, wegspülen; **~ off** vt abwaschen; **~ up** vt (BRIT) spülen; (US) sich waschen; **~able** adj waschbar; **~basin** n Waschbecken nt; **~ bowl** (US) n Waschbecken nt; **~ cloth** (US) n (face cloth) Waschlappen m; **~er** n (TECH) Dichtungsring m; (machine) Waschmaschine f; **~ing** n Wäsche f; **~ing machine** n Waschmaschine f; **~ing powder** (BRIT) n Waschpulver nt; **~ing-up** n Abwasch m; **~ing-up liquid** n Spülmittel nt; **~-out** (inf) n (event) Reinfall m; (person) Niete f; **~room** n Waschraum m
wasn't ['wɔznt] = **was not**
wasp [wɔsp] n Wespe f
wastage ['weɪstɪdʒ] n Verlust m; **natural ~** Verschleiß m
waste [weɪst] n (wasting) Verschwendung f; (what is ~d) Abfall m ♦ adj (useless) überschüssig, Abfall- ♦ vt (object) verschwenden; (time, life) vergeuden ♦ vi: **to ~ away** verfallen, verkümmern; **~s** npl (land) Einöde f; **~ disposal unit** (BRIT) n Müllschlucker m; **~ful** adj verschwenderisch; (process) aufwändig, aufwendig; **~ ground** (BRIT) n unbebaute(s) Grundstück nt; **~land** n Ödland nt; **~paper basket** n Papierkorb m; **~ pipe** n Abflussrohr nt
watch [wɔtʃ] n Wache f; (for time) Uhr f ♦ vt ansehen; (observe) beobachten; (be careful of) aufpassen auf +acc; (guard) bewachen ♦ vi zusehen; **to be on the ~ (for sth)** (auf etw acc) aufpassen; **to ~ TV** fernsehen; **to ~ sb doing sth** jdm bei etw zuschauen; **~ out** vi Ausschau halten; (be careful) aufpassen; **~ out!** pass auf!; **~dog** n Wachhund m; (fig) Wächter m; **~ful** adj wachsam; **~maker** n Uhrmacher m; **~man** (irreg) n (also: **night ~man**) (Nacht)wächter m; **~ strap** n Uhrarmband nt

water ['wɔːtər] n Wasser nt ♦ vt (be)gießen; (river) bewässern; (horses) tränken ♦ vi (eye) tränen; **~s** npl (of sea, river etc) Gewässer nt; **~ down** vt verwässern; **~ closet** (BRIT) n (Wasser)klosett nt; **~colour** (US **watercolor**) n (painting) Aquarell nt; (paint) Wasserfarbe f; **~cress** n (Brunnen)kresse f; **~fall** n Wasserfall m; **~ heater** n Heißwassergerät nt; **~ing can** n Gießkanne f; **~ level** n Wasserstand m; **~lily** n Seerose f; **~line** n Wasserlinie f; **~logged** adj (ground) voll Wasser; **~ main** n Haupt(wasser)leitung f; **~mark** n Wasserzeichen nt; (on wall) Wasserstandsmarke f; **~melon** n Wassermelone f; **~ polo** n Wasserball(spiel) nt; **~proof** adj wasserdicht; **~shed** n Wasserscheide f; **~-skiing** n Wasserskilaufen nt; **~ tank** n Wassertank m; **~tight** adj wasserdicht; **~way** n Wasserweg m; **~works** npl Wasserwerk nt; **~y** adj wäss(e)rig
watt [wɔt] n Watt nt
wave [weɪv] n Welle f; (with hand) Winken nt ♦ vt (move to and fro) schwenken; (hand, flag) winken mit ♦ vi (person) winken; (flag) wehen; **~length** n (also fig) Wellenlänge f
waver ['weɪvər] vi schwanken
wavy ['weɪvɪ] adj wellig
wax [wæks] n Wachs nt; (sealing ~) Siegellack m; (in ear) Ohrenschmalz nt ♦ vt (floor) (ein)wachsen ♦ vi (moon) zunehmen; **~works** npl Wachsfigurenkabinett nt
way [weɪ] n Weg m; (method) Art und Weise f; (direction) Richtung f; (habit) Gewohnheit f; (distance) Entfernung f; (condition) Zustand m; **which ~? - this ~** welche Richtung? - hier entlang; **on the ~** (en route) unterwegs; **to be in the ~** im Weg sein; **to go out of one's ~ to do sth** sich besonders anstrengen, um etw zu tun; **to lose one's ~** sich verirren; **"give ~"** (BRIT: AUT) „Vorfahrt achten!"; **in a ~** in gewisser Weise; **by the ~** übrigens; **in some ~s** in gewisser Hinsicht; **"~ in"** (BRIT) „Eingang"; **"~ out"** (BRIT) „Ausgang"
waylay [weɪ'leɪ] (irreg: like **lay**) vt auflauern

+*dat*

wayward [ˈweɪwəd] *adj* eigensinnig

W.C. (*BRIT*) *n* WC *nt*

we [wiː] *pl pron* wir

weak [wiːk] *adj* schwach; **~en** *vt* schwächen ♦ *vi* schwächer werden; **~ling** *n* Schwächling *m*; **~ness** *n* Schwäche *f*

wealth [wɛlθ] *n* Reichtum *m*; (*abundance*) Fülle *f*; **~y** *adj* reich

wean [wiːn] *vt* entwöhnen

weapon [ˈwɛpən] *n* Waffe *f*

wear [wɛəʳ] (*pt* **wore**, *pp* **worn**) *n* (*clothing*): **sports/baby ~** Sport-/Babykleidung *f*; (*use*) Verschleiß *m* ♦ *vt* (*have on*) tragen; (*smile etc*) haben; (*use*) abnutzen ♦ *vi* (*last*) halten; (*become old*) (sich) verschleißen; **evening ~** Abendkleidung *f*; **~ and tear** Verschleiß *m*; **~ away** *vt* verbrauchen ♦ *vi* schwinden; **~ down** *vt* (*people*) zermürben; **~ off** *vi* sich verlieren; **~ out** *vt* verschleißen; (*person*) erschöpfen

weary [ˈwɪərɪ] *adj* müde ♦ *vt* ermüden ♦ *vi* überdrüssig werden

weasel [ˈwiːzl] *n* Wiesel *nt*

weather [ˈwɛðəʳ] *n* Wetter *nt* ♦ *vt* verwittern lassen; (*resist*) überstehen; **under the ~** (*fig: ill*) angeschlagen (*inf*); **~-beaten** *adj* verwittert; **~cock** *n* Wetterhahn *m*; **~ forecast** *n* Wettervorhersage *f*; **~ vane** *n* Wetterfahne *f*

weave [wiːv] (*pt* **wove**, *pp* **woven**) *vt* weben; **~r** *n* Weber(in) *m(f)*; **weaving** *n* (*craft*) Webkunst *f*

Web [wɛb] *n*: **the ~** das Web

web [wɛb] *n* Netz *nt*; (*membrane*) Schwimmhaut *f*; **~ site** *n* (*COMPUT*) Website *f*, Webseite *f*

wed [wɛd] (*pt*, *pp* **wedded**) *vt* heiraten ♦ *n*: **the newly-~s** *npl* die Frischvermählten *pl*

we'd [wiːd] = **we had; we would**

wedding [ˈwɛdɪŋ] *n* Hochzeit *f*; **silver/ golden ~ anniversary** Silberhochzeit *f/* goldene Hochzeit *f*; **~ day** *n* Hochzeitstag *m*; **~ dress** *n* Hochzeitskleid *nt*; **~ ring** *n* Trauring *m*, Ehering *m*

wedge [wɛdʒ] *n* Keil *m*; (*of cheese etc*) Stück *nt* ♦ *vt* (*fasten*) festklemmen; (*pack tightly*) einkeilen

Wednesday [ˈwɛnzdɪ] *n* Mittwoch *m*

wee [wiː] (*SCOTTISH*) *adj* klein, winzig

weed [wiːd] *n* Unkraut *nt* ♦ *vt* jäten; **~-killer** *n* Unkrautvertilgungsmittel *nt*

weedy [ˈwiːdɪ] *adj* (*person*) schmächtig

week [wiːk] *n* Woche *f*; **a ~ today/on Friday** heute/Freitag in einer Woche; **~day** *n* Wochentag *m*; **~end** *n* Wochenende *nt*; **~ly** *adj* wöchentlich; (*wages, magazine*) Wochen- ♦ *adv* wöchentlich

weep [wiːp] (*pt*, *pp* **wept**) *vi* weinen; **~ing willow** *n* Trauerweide *f*

weigh [weɪ] *vt*, *vi* wiegen; **to ~ anchor** den Anker lichten; **~ down** *vt* niederdrücken; **~ up** *vt* abschätzen

weight [weɪt] *n* Gewicht *nt*; **to lose/put on ~** abnehmen/zunehmen; **~ing** *n* (*allowance*) Zulage *f*; **~lifter** *n* Gewichtheber *m*; **~lifting** *n* Gewichtheben *nt*; **~y** *adj* (*heavy*) gewichtig; (*important*) schwerwiegend, schwer wiegend

weir [wɪəʳ] *n* (Stau)wehr *nt*

weird [wɪəd] *adj* seltsam

welcome [ˈwɛlkəm] *n* Willkommen *nt*, Empfang *m* ♦ *vt* begrüßen; **thank you - you're ~!** danke - nichts zu danken

welder [ˈwɛldəʳ] *n* (*person*) Schweißer(in) *m(f)*

welding [ˈwɛldɪŋ] *n* Schweißen *nt*

welfare [ˈwɛlfɛəʳ] *n* Wohl *nt*; (*social*) Fürsorge *f*; **~ state** *n* Wohlfahrtsstaat *m*; **~ work** *n* Fürsorge *f*

well [wɛl] *n* Brunnen *m*; (*oil ~*) Quelle *f* ♦ *adj* (*in good health*) gesund ♦ *adv* gut ♦ *excl* nun!, na schön!; **I'm ~** es geht mir gut; **get ~ soon!** gute Besserung!; **as ~** auch; **as ~ as** sowohl als auch; **~ done!** gut gemacht!; **to do ~** (*person*) gut zurechtkommen; (*business*) gut gehen; **~ up** *vi* emporsteigen; (*fig*) aufsteigen

we'll [wiːl] = **we will; we shall**

well: **~-behaved** [ˈwɛlbɪˈheɪvd] *adj* wohlerzogen; **~-being** [ˈwɛlˈbiːɪŋ] *n* Wohl *nt*; **~-built** [ˈwɛlˈbɪlt] *adj* kräftig gebaut; **~-deserved** [ˈwɛldɪˈzɜːvd] *adj* wohlverdient; **~-dressed** [ˈwɛlˈdrɛst] *adj* gut gekleidet; **~-heeled** [ˈwɛlˈhiːld] (*inf*) *adj* (*wealthy*) gut gepolstert

wellingtons ['wɛlɪŋtənz] *npl* (*also:* **wellington boots**) Gummistiefel *pl*

well: ~**-known** ['wɛl'nəʊn] *adj* bekannt; ~**-mannered** ['wɛl'mænəd] *adj* wohlerzogen; ~**-meaning** ['wɛl'miːnɪŋ] *adj* (*person*) wohlmeinend; (*action*) gut gemeint; ~**-off** ['wɛl'ɔf] *adj* gut situiert; ~**-read** ['wɛl'rɛd] *adj* (sehr) belesen; ~**-to-do** ['wɛltə'duː] *adj* wohlhabend; ~**-wisher** ['wɛlwɪʃər] *n* Gönner *m*

Welsh [wɛlʃ] *adj* walisisch ♦ *n* (*LING*) Walisisch *nt*; **the** ~ *npl* (*people*) die Waliser *pl*; ~ **Assembly** *n* walisische Versammlung *f*; ~**man/woman** (*irreg*) *n* Waliser(in) *m(f)*

went [wɛnt] *pt of* **go**

wept [wɛpt] *pt, pp of* **weep**

were [wəːr] *pt pl of* **be**

we're [wɪər] = **we are**

weren't [wəːnt] = **were not**

west [wɛst] *n* Westen *m* ♦ *adj* West-, westlich ♦ *adv* westwärts, nach Westen; **the W~** der Westen; **W~ Country** (*BRIT*) *n*: **the W~ Country** der Südwesten Englands; ~**erly** *adj* westlich; ~**ern** *adj* westlich, West- ♦ *n* (*CINE*) Western *m*; **W~ Indian** *adj* westindisch ♦ *n* Westindier(in) *m(f)*; **W~ Indies** *npl* Westindische Inseln *pl*; ~**ward(s)** *adv* westwärts

wet [wɛt] *adj* nass; **to get** ~ nass werden; "~ **paint**" "frisch gestrichen"; ~ **blanket** *n* (*fig*) Triefel *m*; ~ **suit** *n* Taucheranzug *m*

we've [wiːv] = **we have**

whack [wæk] *n* Schlag *m* ♦ *vt* schlagen

whale [weɪl] *n* Wal *m*

wharf [wɔːf] *n* Kai *m*

wharves [wɔːvz] *npl of* **wharf**

KEYWORD

what [wɔt] *adj* **1** (*in questions*) welche(r, s), was für ein(e); **what size is it?** welche Größe ist das?

2 (*in exclamations*) was für ein(e); **what a mess!** was für ein Durcheinander!

♦ *pron* (*interrogative/relative*) was; **what are you doing?** was machst du gerade?; **what are you talking about?** wovon reden Sie?;

what is it called? wie heißt das?; **what about ...?** wie wärs mit ...?; **I saw what you did** ich habe gesehen, was du gemacht hast

♦ *excl* (*disbelieving*) wie, was; **what, no coffee!** wie, kein Kaffee?; **I've crashed the car - what!** ich hatte einen Autounfall - was!

whatever [wɔt'ɛvər] *adj*: ~ **book** welches Buch auch immer ♦ *pron*: **do** ~ **is necessary** tu, was (immer auch) nötig ist; ~ **happens** egal, was passiert; **nothing** ~ überhaupt *or* absolut gar nichts; **do** ~ **you want** tu, was (immer) du (auch) möchtest; **no reason** ~ **or whatsoever** überhaupt *or* absolut kein Grund

whatsoever [wɔtsəʊ'ɛvər] *adj see* **whatever**

wheat [wiːt] *n* Weizen *m*

wheedle ['wiːdl] *vt*: **to** ~ **sb into doing sth** jdn dazu überreden, etw zu tun; **to** ~ **sth out of sb** jdm etw abluchsen

wheel [wiːl] *n* Rad *nt*; (*steering* ~) Lenkrad *nt*; (*disc*) Scheibe *f* ♦ *vt* schieben; ~**barrow** *n* Schubkarren *m*; ~**chair** *n* Rollstuhl *m*; ~ **clamp** *n* (*AUT*) Parkkralle *f*

wheeze [wiːz] *vi* keuchen

KEYWORD

when [wɛn] *adv* wann

♦ *conj* **1** (*at, during, after the time that*) wenn; (*in past*) als; **she was reading when I came in** sie las, als ich hereinkam; **be careful when you cross the road** seien Sie vorsichtig, wenn Sie über die Straße gehen **2** (*on, at which*) als; **on the day when I met him** an dem Tag, an dem ich ihn traf **3** (*whereas*) wo ... doch

whenever [wɛn'ɛvər] *adv* wann (auch) immer; (*every time that*) jedes Mal wenn ♦ *conj* (*any time*) wenn

where [weər] *adv* (*place*) wo; (*direction*) wohin; ~ **from** woher; **this is** ~ ... hier ...; ~**abouts** ['weərəbaʊts] *adv* wo ♦ *n* Aufenthaltsort *m*; **nobody knows his** ~**abouts** niemand weiß, wo er ist; ~**as**

[weər'æz] *conj* während, wo ... doch; **~by** *pron* woran, wodurch, womit, wovon; **~upon** *conj* worauf, wonach; (*at beginning of sentence*) daraufhin; **~ver** [weər'evər] *adv* wo (immer)

wherewithal ['weəwıðɔːl] *n* nötige (Geld)mittel *pl*

whet [wet] *vt* (*appetite*) anregen

whether ['weðər] *conj* ob; **I don't know ~ to accept or not** ich weiß nicht, ob ich es annehmen soll oder nicht; **~ you go or not** ob du gehst oder nicht; **it's doubtful/ unclear ~ ...** es ist zweifelhaft/nicht klar, ob ...

KEYWORD

which [wıtʃ] *adj* **1** (*interrogative: direct, indirect*) welche(r, s); **which one?** welche(r, s)?

2: in which case in diesem Fall; **by which time** zu dieser Zeit

♦ *pron* **1** (*interrogative*) welche(r, s); (*of people also*) wer

2 (*relative*) der/die/das; (*referring to people*) was; **the apple which you ate/which is on the table** der Apfel, den du gegessen hast/der auf dem Tisch liegt; **he said he saw her, which is true** er sagte, er habe sie gesehen, was auch stimmt

---

whichever [wıtʃ'evər] *adj* welche(r, s) auch immer; (*no matter which*) ganz gleich welche(r, s); **~ book you take** welches Buch du auch nimmst; **~ car you prefer** egal welches Auto du vorziehst

whiff [wıf] *n* Hauch *m*

while [waıl] *n* Weile *f* ♦ *conj* während; **for a ~** eine Zeit lang; **~ away** *vt* (*time*) sich *dat* vertreiben

whim [wım] *n* Laune *f*

whimper ['wımpər] *n* Wimmern *nt* ♦ *vi* wimmern

whimsical ['wımzıkəl] *adj* launisch

whine [waın] *n* Gewinsel *nt*, Gejammer *nt* ♦ *vi* heulen, winseln

whip [wıp] *n* Peitsche *f*; (*POL*) Fraktionsführer *m* ♦ *vt* (*beat*) peitschen; (*snatch*) reißen;

~ped cream *n* Schlagsahne *f*

whip-round ['wıpraund] (*BRIT: inf*) *n* Geldsammlung *f*

whirl [wəːl] *n* Wirbel *m* ♦ *vt, vi* (herum)wirbeln; **~pool** *n* Wirbel *m*; **~wind** *n* Wirbelwind *m*

whirr [wəːr] *vi* schwirren, surren

whisk [wısk] *n* Schneebesen *m* ♦ *vt* (*cream etc*) schlagen; **to ~ sb away** *or* **off** mit jdm davon sausen

whisker ['wıskər] *n*: **~s** (*of animal*) Barthaare *pl*; (*of man*) Backenbart *m*

whisky ['wıskı] (*US, IRISH* **whiskey**) *n* Whisky *m*

whisper ['wıspər] *n* Flüstern *nt* ♦ *vt, vi* flüstern

whistle ['wısl] *n* Pfiff *m*; (*instrument*) Pfeife *f* ♦ *vt, vi* pfeifen

white [waıt] *n* Weiß *nt*; (*of egg*) Eiweiß *nt* ♦ *adj* weiß; **~ coffee** (*BRIT*) *n* Kaffee *m* mit Milch; **~-collar worker** *n* Angestellte(r) *m*; **~ elephant** *n* (*fig*) Fehlinvestition *f*; **~ lie** *n* Notlüge *f*; **~ paper** *n* (*POL*) Weißbuch *nt*; **~wash** *n* (*paint*) Tünche *f*; (*fig*) Ehrenrettung *f* ♦ *vt* weißen, tünchen; (*fig*) rein waschen

whiting ['waıtıŋ] *n* Weißfisch *m*

Whitsun ['wıtsn] *n* Pfingsten *nt*

whittle ['wıtl] *vt*: **to ~ away** *or* **down** stutzen, verringern

whizz [wız] *vi*: **to ~ past** *or* **by** vorbeizischen, vorbeischwirren; **~ kid** (*inf*) *n* Kanone *f*

KEYWORD

who [huː] *pron* **1** (*interrogative*) wer; (*acc*) wen; (*dat*) wem; **who is it?, who's there?** wer ist da?

2 (*relative*) der/die/das; **the woman/man who spoke to me** die Frau/der Mann, die/ der mit mir sprach

---

whodu(n)nit [huː'dʌnıt] (*inf*) *n* Krimi *m*

whoever [huː'evər] *pron* wer/wen/wem auch immer; (*no matter who*) ganz gleich wer/ wen/wem

whole [həul] *adj* ganz ♦ *n* Ganze(s) *nt*; **the ~ of the town** die ganze Stadt; **on the ~** im

Großen und Ganzen; **as a ~** im Großen
und Ganzen; **~food(s)** ['həʊlfuːd(z)] *n(pl)*
Vollwertkost *f*; **~hearted** [həʊl'hɑːtɪd] *adj*
rückhaltlos; **~heartedly** *adv* von ganzem
Herzen; **~meal** *adj (bread, flour)* Vollkorn-;
~sale *n* Großhandel *m* ♦ *adj (trade)*
Großhandels-; *(destruction)* Massen-; **~saler**
n Großhändler *m*; **~some** *adj* bekömmlich,
gesund; **~wheat** *adj* = **wholemeal**

wholly ['həʊlɪ] *adv* ganz, völlig

KEYWORD

whom [huːm] *pron* 1 *(interrogative: acc)* wen;
(: *dat)* wem; **whom did you see?** wen
haben Sie gesehen?; **to whom did you
give it?** wem haben Sie es gegeben?
2 *(relative: acc)* den/die/das; (: *dat)* dem/
der/dem; **the man whom I saw/to whom
I spoke** der Mann, den ich sah/mit dem
ich sprach

whooping cough ['huːpɪŋ-] *n* Keuchhusten
m

whore [hɔːʳ] *n* Hure *f*

whose [huːz] *adj (possessive: interrogative)*
wessen; (: *relative)* dessen; *(after f and pl)*
deren ♦ *pron* wessen; **~ book is this?**, **~ is
this book?** wessen Buch ist dies?; **~ is
this?** wem gehört das?

KEYWORD

why [waɪ] *adv* warum, weshalb
♦ *conj* warum, weshalb; **that's not why I'm
here** ich bin nicht deswegen hier; **that's
the reason why** deshalb
♦ *excl (expressing surprise, shock)* na so was;
(explaining) also dann; **why, it's you!** na so
was, du bist es!

wick [wɪk] *n* Docht *m*

wicked ['wɪkɪd] *adj* böse

wicker ['wɪkəʳ] *n (also: ~work)* Korbgeflecht
nt

wicket ['wɪkɪt] *n* Tor *nt*, Dreistab *m*

wide [waɪd] *adj* breit; *(plain)* weit; *(in firing)*
daneben ♦ *adv:* **to open ~** weit öffnen; **to
shoot ~** danebenschießen; **~-angle lens** *n*
Weitwinkelobjektiv *nt*; **~-awake** *adj*
hellwach; **~ly** *adv* weit; *(known)* allgemein;
~n *vt* erweitern; **~ open** *adj* weit geöffnet;
~spread *adj* weitverbreitet, weit verbreitet

widow ['wɪdəʊ] *n* Witwe *f*; **~ed** *adj*
verwitwet; **~er** *n* Witwer *m*

width [wɪdθ] *n* Breite *f*, Weite *f*

wield [wiːld] *vt* schwingen, handhaben

wife [waɪf] *(pl* **wives)** *n* (Ehe)frau *f*, Gattin *f*

wig [wɪg] *n* Perücke *f*

wiggle ['wɪgl] *n* Wackeln *nt* ♦ *vt* wackeln mit
♦ *vi* wackeln

wild [waɪld] *adj* wild; *(violent)* heftig; *(plan,
idea)* verrückt; **~erness** ['wɪldənɪs] *n*
Wildnis *f*, Wüste *f*; **~-goose chase** *n (fig)*
fruchtlose(s) Unternehmen *nt*; **~life** *n*
Tierwelt *f*; **~ly** *adv* wild, ungestüm;
(exaggerated) irrsinnig; **~s** *npl:* **the ~s** die
Wildnis *f*

wilful ['wɪlfʊl] *(US* **willful)** *adj (intended)*
vorsätzlich; *(obstinate)* eigensinnig

KEYWORD

will [wɪl] *aux vb* 1 *(forms future tense)* werden;
I will finish it tomorrow ich mache es
morgen zu Ende
2 *(in conjectures, predictions):* **he will** *or* **he'll
be there by now** er dürfte jetzt da sein;
that will be the postman das wird der
Postbote sein
3 *(in commands, requests, offers):* **will you be
quiet!** sei endlich still!; **will you help me?**
hilfst du mir?; **will you have a cup of tea?**
trinken Sie eine Tasse Tee?; **I won't put up
with it!** das lasse ich mir nicht gefallen!
♦ *vt* wollen
♦ *n* Wille *m*; *(JUR)* Testament *nt*

willing ['wɪlɪŋ] *adj* gewillt, bereit; **~ly** *adv*
bereitwillig, gern; **~ness** *n* (Bereit)willigkeit
f

willow ['wɪləʊ] *n* Weide *f*

willpower ['wɪl'paʊəʳ] *n* Willenskraft *f*

willy-nilly ['wɪlɪ'nɪlɪ] *adv* einfach so

wilt [wɪlt] *vi* (ver)welken

wily ['waɪlɪ] *adj* gerissen

win [wɪn] *(pt, pp* **won)** *n* Sieg *m* ♦ *vt, vi*

gewinnen; **to ~ sb over** or **round** jdn gewinnen; **to ~ sb over** or **round** jdn gewinnen

wince [wɪns] vi zusammenzucken

winch [wɪntʃ] n Winde f

wind[1] [wɪnd] n Wind m; (MED) Blähungen pl

wind[2] [waɪnd] (pt, pp **wound**) vt (rope) winden; (bandage) wickeln ♦ vi (turn) sich winden; **~ up** vt (clock) aufziehen; (debate) (ab)schließen

windfall ['wɪndfɔːl] n unverhoffte(r) Glücksfall m

winding ['waɪndɪŋ] adj (road) gewunden

wind instrument ['wɪnd-] n Blasinstrument nt

windmill ['wɪndmɪl] n Windmühle f

window ['wɪndəu] n Fenster nt; **~ box** n Blumenkasten m; **~ cleaner** n Fensterputzer m; **~ envelope** n Fensterbriefumschlag m; **~ ledge** n Fenstersims m; **~ pane** n Fensterscheibe f; **~-shopping** n Schaufensterbummel m; **to go ~-shopping** einen Schaufensterbummel machen; **~sill** n Fensterbank f

wind: **~pipe** n Luftröhre f; **~ power** n Windenergie f; **~screen** (BRIT) n Windschutzscheibe f; **~screen washer** n Scheibenwaschanlage f; **~screen wiper** n Scheibenwischer m; **~shield** (US) n = **windscreen**; **~swept** adj vom Wind gepeitscht; (person) zerzaust; **~y** adj windig

wine [waɪn] n Wein m; **~ bar** n Weinlokal nt; **~ cellar** n Weinkeller m; **~glass** n Weinglas nt; **~ list** n Weinkarte f; **~ merchant** n Weinhändler m; **~ tasting** n Weinprobe f; **~ waiter** n Weinkellner m

wing [wɪŋ] n Flügel m; (MIL) Gruppe f; **~s** npl (THEAT) Seitenkulisse f; **~er** n (SPORT) Flügelstürmer m

wink [wɪŋk] n Zwinkern nt ♦ vi zwinkern, blinzeln

winner ['wɪnə*] n Gewinner m; (SPORT) Sieger m

winning ['wɪnɪŋ] adj (team) siegreich, Sieger-; (goal) entscheidend; **~ post** n Ziel nt; **~s** npl Gewinn m

winter ['wɪntə*] n Winter m ♦ adj (clothes) Winter- ♦ vi überwintern; **~ sports** npl

Wintersport m; **wintry** ['wɪntrɪ] adj Winter-, winterlich

wipe [waɪp] n: **to give sth a ~** etw (ab)wischen ♦ vt wischen; **~ off** vt abwischen; **~ out** vt (debt) löschen; (destroy) auslöschen; **~ up** vt aufwischen

wire ['waɪə*] n Draht m; (telegram) Telegramm nt ♦ vt telegrafieren; **to ~ sb** jdm telegrafieren; **~less** ['waɪəlɪs] (BRIT) n Radio(apparat m) nt

wiring ['waɪərɪŋ] n elektrische Leitungen pl

wiry ['waɪərɪ] adj drahtig

wisdom ['wɪzdəm] n Weisheit f; (of decision) Klugheit f; **~ tooth** n Weisheitszahn m

wise [waɪz] adj klug, weise ♦ suffix: **timewise** zeitlich gesehen

wisecrack ['waɪzkræk] n Witzelei f

wish [wɪʃ] n Wunsch m ♦ vt wünschen; **best ~es** (on birthday etc) alles Gute; **with best ~es** herzliche Grüße; **to ~ sb goodbye** jdn verabschieden; **he ~ed me well** er wünschte mir Glück; **to ~ to do sth** etw tun wollen; **~ for** vt fus sich dat wünschen; **~ful thinking** n Wunschdenken nt

wishy-washy ['wɪʃɪ'wɒʃɪ] (inf) adj (ideas, argument) verschwommen

wisp [wɪsp] n (Haar)strähne f; (of smoke) Wölkchen nt

wistful ['wɪstful] adj sehnsüchtig

wit [wɪt] n (also: **~s**) Verstand m no pl; (amusing ideas) Witz m; (person) Witzbold m

witch [wɪtʃ] n Hexe f; **~craft** n Hexerei f

KEYWORD

with [wɪð, wɪθ] prep 1 (accompanying, in the company of) mit; **we stayed with friends** wir übernachteten bei Freunden; **I'll be with you in a minute** einen Augenblick, ich bin sofort da; **I'm not with you** (I don't understand) das verstehe ich nicht; **to be with it** (inf: up-to-date) auf dem Laufenden sein; (: alert) (voll) da sein (inf)

2 (descriptive, indicating manner etc) mit; **the man with the grey hat** der Mann mit dem grauen Hut; **red with anger** rot vor Wut

withdraw [wɪθ'drɔː] (irreg: like **draw**) vt

zurückziehen; (*money*) abheben; (*remark*) zurücknehmen ♦ *vi* sich zurückziehen; **~al** *n* Zurückziehung *f*; Abheben *nt*; Zurücknahme *f*; **~n** *adj* (*person*) verschlossen

wither ['wɪðə'] *vi* (ver)welken

withhold [wɪθ'həʊld] (*irreg: like* **hold**) *vt*: **to ~ sth (from sb)** (jdm) etw vorenthalten

within [wɪð'ɪn] *prep* innerhalb +*gen* ♦ *adv* innen; **~ sight of** in Sichtweite von; **the week** innerhalb dieser Woche; **~ a mile of** weniger als eine Meile von

without [wɪð'aʊt] *prep* ohne; **~ sleeping** *etc* ohne zu schlafen *etc*

withstand [wɪθ'stænd] (*irreg: like* **stand**) *vt* widerstehen +*dat*

witness ['wɪtnɪs] *n* Zeuge *m*, Zeugin *f* ♦ *vt* (*see*) sehen, miterleben; (*document*) beglaubigen; **~ box** *n* Zeugenstand *m*; **~ stand** (*US*) *n* Zeugenstand *m*

witticism ['wɪtɪsɪzəm] *n* witzige Bemerkung *f*

witty ['wɪtɪ] *adj* witzig, geistreich

wives [waɪvz] *pl of* **wife**

wk *abbr* = **week**

wobble ['wɒbl] *vi* wackeln

woe [wəʊ] *n* Kummer *m*

woke [wəʊk] *pt of* **wake**

woken ['wəʊkn] *pp of* **wake**

wolf [wʊlf] (*pl* **wolves**) *n* Wolf *m*

woman ['wʊmən] (*pl* **women**) *n* Frau *f*; **~ doctor** *n* Ärztin *f*; **~ly** *adj* weiblich

womb [wuːm] *n* Gebärmutter *f*

women ['wɪmɪn] *npl of* **woman**; **~'s lib** (*inf*) *n* Frauenrechtsbewegung *f*

won [wʌn] *pt, pp of* **win**

wonder ['wʌndə'] *n* (*marvel*) Wunder *nt*; (*surprise*) Staunen *nt*, Verwunderung *f* ♦ *vi* sich wundern ♦ *vt*: **I ~ whether ...** ich frage mich, ob ...; **it's no ~ that** es ist kein Wunder, dass; **to ~ at** sich wundern über +*acc*; **to ~ about** sich Gedanken machen über +*acc*; **~ful** *adj* wunderbar, herrlich

won't [wəʊnt] = **will not**

woo [wuː] *vt* (*audience etc*) umwerben

wood [wʊd] *n* Holz *nt*; (*forest*) Wald *m*; **~ carving** *n* Holzschnitzerei *f*; **~ed** *adj* bewaldet; **~en** *adj* (*also fig*) hölzern;

~pecker *n* Specht *m*; **~wind** *n* Blasinstrumente *pl*; **~work** *n* Holzwerk *nt*; (*craft*) Holzarbeiten *pl*; **~worm** *n* Holzwurm *m*

wool [wʊl] *n* Wolle *f*; **to pull the ~ over sb's eyes** (*fig*) jdm Sand in die Augen streuen; **~len** (*US* **woolen**) *adj* Woll-; **~lens** *npl* Wollsachen *pl*; **~ly** (*US* **wooly**) *adj* wollig; (*fig*) schwammig

word [wəːd] *n* Wort *nt*; (*news*) Bescheid *m* ♦ *vt* formulieren; **in other ~s** anders gesagt; **to break/keep one's ~** sein Wort brechen/halten; **~ing** *n* Wortlaut *m*; **~ processing** *n* Textverarbeitung *f*; **~ processor** *n* Textverarbeitung *f*

wore [wɔː'] *pt of* **wear**

work [wəːk] *n* Arbeit *f*; (*ART, LITER*) Werk *nt* ♦ *vi* arbeiten; (*machine*) funktionieren; (*medicine*) wirken; (*succeed*) klappen; **~s** *n sg* (*BRIT: factory*) Fabrik *f*, Werk *nt* ♦ *npl* (*of watch*) Werk *nt*; **to be out of ~** arbeitslos sein; **in ~ing order** in betriebsfähigem Zustand; **~ loose** *vi* sich lockern; **~ on** *vi* weiterarbeiten ♦ *vt fus* arbeiten an +*dat*; (*influence*) bearbeiten; **~ out** *vi* (*sum*) aufgehen; (*plan*) klappen ♦ *vt* (*problem*) lösen; (*plan*) ausarbeiten; **it ~s out at £100** das gibt *or* macht £100; **~ up** *vt*: **to get ~ed up** sich aufregen; **~able** *adj* (*soil*) bearbeitbar; (*plan*) ausführbar; **~aholic** [wəːkə'hɒlɪk] *n* Arbeitssüchtige(r) *f(m)*; **~er** *n* Arbeiter(in) *m(f)*; **~ experience** *n* Praktikum *nt*; **~force** *n* Arbeiterschaft *f*; **~ing class** *n* Arbeiterklasse *f*; **~ing-class** *adj* Arbeiter-; **~man** (*irreg*) *n* Arbeiter *m*; **~manship** *n* Arbeit *f*, Ausführung *f*; **~sheet** *n* Arbeitsblatt *nt*; **~shop** *n* Werkstatt *f*; **~ station** *n* Arbeitsplatz *m*; **~to-rule** (*BRIT*) *n* Dienst *m* nach Vorschrift

world [wəːld] *n* Welt *f*; **to think the ~ of sb** große Stücke auf jdn halten; **~ly** *adj* weltlich, irdisch; **~-wide** *adj* weltweit

World-Wide Web ['wəːld'waɪd-] *n* World Wide Web *nt*

worm [wəːm] *n* Wurm *m*

worn [wɔːn] *pp of* **wear** ♦ *adj* (*clothes*) abgetragen; **~-out** *adj* (*object*) abgenutzt;

(*person*) völlig erschöpft

worried ['wʌrɪd] *adj* besorgt, beunruhigt

worry ['wʌrɪ] *n* Sorge *f* ♦ *vt* beunruhigen ♦ *vi* (*feel uneasy*) sich sorgen, sich *dat* Gedanken machen; **~ing** *adj* beunruhigend

worse [wɜːs] *adj* schlechter, schlimmer ♦ *adv* schlimmer, ärger ♦ *n* Schlimmere(s) *nt*, Schlechtere(s) *nt*; **a change for the ~** eine Verschlechterung; **~n** *vt* verschlimmern ♦ *vi* sich verschlechtern; **~ off** *adj* (*fig*) schlechter dran

worship ['wɜːʃɪp] *n* Verehrung *f* ♦ *vt* anbeten; **Your W~** (*BRIT: to mayor*) Herr/ Frau Bürgermeister; (*: to judge*) Euer Ehren

worst [wɜːst] *adj* schlimmste(r, s), schlechteste(r, s) ♦ *adv* am schlimmsten, am ärgsten ♦ *n* Schlimmste(s) *nt*, Ärgste(s) *nt*; **at ~** schlimmstenfalls

worth [wɜːθ] *n* Wert *m* ♦ *adj* wert; **it's ~ it** es lohnt sich; **to be ~ one's while (to do sth)** die Mühe wert sein(, etw zu tun); **~less** *adj* wertlos; (*person*) nichtsnutzig; **~while** *adj* lohnend, der Mühe wert; **~y** *adj* wert, würdig

───────────────
| *KEYWORD* |
───────────────

would [wud] *aux vb* **1** (*conditional tense*): **if you asked him he would do it** wenn du ihn fragtest, würde er es tun; **if you had asked him he would have done it** wenn du ihn gefragt hättest, hätte er es getan

2 (*in offers, invitations, requests*): **would you like a biscuit?** möchten Sie ein Plätzchen?; **would you ask him to come in?** würden Sie ihn bitte hineinbitten?

3 (*in indirect speech*): **I said I would do it** ich sagte, ich würde es tun

4 (*emphatic*): **it WOULD have to snow today!** es musste ja ausgerechnet heute schneien!

5 (*insistence*): **she wouldn't behave** sie wollte sich partout nicht anständig benehmen

6 (*conjecture*): **it would have been midnight** es mag ungefähr Mitternacht gewesen sein; **it would seem so** es sieht wohl so aus

7 (*indicating habit*): **he would go there on Mondays** er ging jeden Montag dorthin

───────────────

would-be ['wudbiː] (*pej*) *adj* Möchtegern-

wouldn't ['wudnt] = **would not**

wound¹ [wuːnd] *n* (*also fig*) Wunde *f* ♦ *vt* verwunden, verletzen (*also fig*)

wound² [waund] *pt, pp of* **wind²**

wove [wəuv] *pt of* **weave**; **~n** *pp of* **weave**

wrangle ['ræŋgl] *n* Streit *m* ♦ *vi* sich zanken

wrap [ræp] *vt* einwickeln; **~ up** *vt* einwickeln; (*deal*) abschließen; **~per** *n* Umschlag *m*, Schutzhülle *f*; **~ping paper** *n* Einwickelpapier *nt*

wrath [rɔθ] *n* Zorn *m*

wreak [riːk] *vt* (*havoc*) anrichten; (*vengeance*) üben

wreath [riːθ] *n* Kranz *m*

wreck [rek] *n* (*ship*) Wrack *nt*; (*sth ruined*) Ruine *f* ♦ *vt* zerstören; **~age** *n* Trümmer *pl*

wren [ren] *n* Zaunkönig *m*

wrench [rentʃ] *n* (*spanner*) Schraubenschlüssel *m*; (*twist*) Ruck *m* ♦ *vt* reißen, zerren; **to ~ sth from sb** jdm etw entreißen *or* entwinden

wrestle ['resl] *vi*: **to ~ (with sb)** (mit jdm) ringen; **~r** *n* Ringer(in) *m(f)*; **wrestling** *n* Ringen *nt*

wretched ['retʃɪd] *adj* (*inf*) verflixt

wriggle ['rɪgl] *n* Schlängeln *nt* ♦ *vi* sich winden

wring [rɪŋ] (*pt, pp* **wrung**) *vt* wringen

wrinkle ['rɪŋkl] *n* Falte *f*, Runzel *f* ♦ *vt* runzeln ♦ *vi* sich runzeln; (*material*) knittern; **~d** *adj* faltig, schrumpelig

wrist [rɪst] *n* Handgelenk *nt*; **~watch** *n* Armbanduhr *f*

writ [rɪt] *n* gerichtliche(r) Befehl *m*

write [raɪt] (*pt* **wrote**, *pp* **written**) *vt, vi* schreiben; **~ down** *vt* aufschreiben; **~ off** *vt* (*dismiss*) abschreiben; **~ out** *vt* (*essay*) abschreiben; (*cheque*) ausstellen; **~ up** *vt* schreiben; **~-off** *n*: **it is a ~-off** das kann man abschreiben; **~r** *n* Schriftsteller *m*

writhe [raɪð] *vi* sich winden

writing ['raɪtɪŋ] *n* (*act*) Schreiben *nt*; (*handwriting*) (Hand)schrift *f*; **in ~** schriftlich;

~ **paper** n Schreibpapier nt
written ['rɪtn] pp of **write**
wrong [rɒŋ] adj (incorrect) falsch; (morally) unrecht ♦ n Unrecht nt ♦ vt Unrecht tun +dat; **he was ~ in doing that** es war nicht recht von ihm, das zu tun; **you are ~ about that, you've got it ~** da hast du Unrecht; **to be in the ~** im Unrecht sein; **what's ~ with your leg?** was ist mit deinem Bein los?; **to go ~** (plan) schief gehen; (person) einen Fehler machen; ~**ful** adj unrechtmäßig; ~**ly** adv falsch; (accuse) zu Unrecht
wrong number n (TEL): **you've got the ~** Sie sind falsch verbunden
wrote [rəut] pt of **write**
wrought [rɔːt] adj: ~ **iron** Schmiedeeisen nt
wrung [rʌŋ] pt, pp of **wring**
wry [raɪ] adj ironisch
wt. abbr = **weight**
WWW n abbr (= World Wide Web): **the ~** das WWW.

X, x

Xmas ['eksməs] n abbr = **Christmas**
X-ray ['eksreɪ] n Röntgenaufnahme f ♦ vt röntgen; ~~~**s** npl Röntgenstrahlen pl
xylophone ['zaɪləfəun] n Xylofon nt, Xylophon nt

Y, y

yacht [jɒt] n Jacht f; ~**ing** n (Sport)segeln nt; ~**sman** (irreg) n Sportsegler m
Yank [jæŋk] (inf) n Ami m
yap [jæp] vi (dog) kläffen
yard [jɑːd] n Hof m; (measure) (englische) Elle f, Yard nt (0,91 m); ~**stick** n (fig) Maßstab m
yarn [jɑːn] n (thread) Garn nt; (story) (Seemanns)garn nt
yawn [jɔːn] n Gähnen nt ♦ vi gähnen; ~**ing** adj (gap) gähnend
yd. abbr = **yard(s)**

yeah [jɛə] (inf) adv ja
year [jɪəʳ] n Jahr nt; **to be 8 ~s old** acht Jahre alt sein; **an eight-year-old child** ein achtjähriges Kind; ~**ly** adj, adv jährlich
yearn [jɜːn] vi: **to ~ (for)** sich sehnen (nach); ~**ing** n Verlangen nt, Sehnsucht f
yeast [jiːst] n Hefe f
yell [jɛl] n gellende(r) Schrei m ♦ vi laut schreien
yellow ['jɛləu] adj gelb ♦ n Gelb nt
yelp [jɛlp] n Gekläff nt ♦ vi kläffen
yes [jɛs] adv ja ♦ n Ja nt, Jawort nt; **to say ~** Ja or ja sagen; **to answer ~** mit Ja antworten
yesterday ['jestədɪ] adv gestern ♦ n Gestern nt; ~ **morning/evening** gestern Morgen/Abend; **all day ~** gestern den ganzen Tag; **the day before ~** vorgestern
yet [jet] adv noch; (in question) schon; (up to now) bis jetzt ♦ conj doch, dennoch; **it is not finished ~** es ist noch nicht fertig; **the best ~** das bisher Beste; **as ~** bis jetzt; (in past) bis dahin
yew [juː] n Eibe f
yield [jiːld] n Ertrag m ♦ vt (result, crop) hervorbringen; (interest, profit) abwerfen; (concede) abtreten ♦ vi nachgeben; (MIL) sich ergeben; "~" (US: AUT) „Vorfahrt gewähren"
YMCA n abbr (= Young Men's Christian Association) CVJM m
yob [jɒb] (BRIT: inf) n Halbstarke(r) f(m)
yoga ['jəugə] n Joga m
yog(h)urt ['jəugət] n Jog(h)urt m
yoke [jəuk] n (also fig) Joch nt
yolk [jəuk] n Eidotter m, Eigelb nt

─────────────────
KEYWORD
─────────────────

you [juː] pron 1 (subj, in comparisons: familiar form: sg) du; (: pl) ihr; (in letters also) du, ihr; (: polite form) Sie; **you Germans** ihr Deutschen; **she's younger than you** sie ist jünger als du/Sie
2 (direct object, after prep +acc: familiar form: sg) dich; (: pl) euch; (in letters also) dich, euch; (: polite form) Sie; **I know you** ich kenne dich/euch/Sie

3 (*indirect object, after prep +dat: familiar form: sg*) dir; (: *pl*) euch; (*in letters also*) dir, euch; (: *polite form*) Ihnen; **I gave it to you** ich gab es dir/euch/Ihnen

4 (*impers: one: subj*) man; (: *direct object*) einen; (: *indirect object*) einem; **fresh air does you good** frische Luft tut gut

you'd [juːd] = **you had; you would**

you'll [juːl] = **you will; you shall**

young [jʌŋ] *adj* jung ♦ *npl*: **the ~** die Jungen *pl*; **~ster** *n* Junge *m*, junge(r) Bursche *m*, junge(s) Mädchen *nt*

your [jɔːʳ] *adj* (*familiar: sg*) dein; (: *pl*) euer, eure *pl*; (*polite*) Ihr; *see also* **my**

you're [juəʳ] = **you are**

yours [jɔːz] *pron* (*familiar: sg*) deine(r, s); (: *pl*) eure(r, s); (*polite*) Ihre(r, s); *see also* **mine²**

yourself [jɔːˈsɛlf] *pron* (*emphatic*) selbst; (*familiar: sg: acc*) dich (selbst); (: *dat*) dir (selbst); (: *pl*) euch (selbst); (*polite*) sich (selbst); *see also* **oneself**; **yourselves** *pl pron* (*reflexive: familiar*) euch; (: *polite*) sich; (*emphatic*) selbst; *see also* **oneself**

youth [juːθ] *n* Jugend *f*; (*young man*) junge(r) Mann *m*; **~s** *npl* (*young people*) Jugendliche *pl*; **~ club** *n* Jugendzentrum *nt*; **~ful** *adj* jugendlich; **~ hostel** *n* Jugendherberge *f*

you've [juːv] = **you have**

YTS (*BRIT*) *n abbr* (= *Youth Training Scheme*) staatliches Förderprogramm für arbeitslose Jugendliche

Yugoslav [ˈjuːɡəuslɑːv] *adj* jugoslawisch ♦ *n* Jugoslawe *m*, Jugoslawin *f*; **~ia**

[juːɡəuˈslɑːvɪə] *n* Jugoslawien *nt*

yuppie [ˈjʌpɪ] (*inf*) *n* Yuppie *m* ♦ *adj* yuppiehaft, Yuppie-

YWCA *n abbr* (= *Young Women's Christian Association*) CVJF *m*

Z, z

zany [ˈzeɪnɪ] *adj* (*ideas, sense of humour*) verrückt

zap [zæp] *vt* (*COMPUT*) löschen

zeal [ziːl] *n* Eifer *m*; **~ous** [ˈzɛləs] *adj* eifrig

zebra [ˈziːbrə] *n* Zebra *nt*; **~ crossing** (*BRIT*) *n* Zebrastreifen *m*

zero [ˈzɪərəu] *n* Null *f*; (*on scale*) Nullpunkt *m*

zest [zɛst] *n* Begeisterung *f*

zigzag [ˈzɪɡzæɡ] *n* Zickzack *m*

Zimbabwe [zɪmˈbɑːbwɪ] *n* Zimbabwe *nt*

Zimmer frame [ˈzɪmə-] *n* Laufgestell *nt*

zip [zɪp] *n* Reißverschluss *m* ♦ *vt* (*also:* **~ up**) den Reißverschluss zumachen +*gen*

zip code (*US*) *n* Postleitzahl *f*

zipper [ˈzɪpəʳ] (*US*) *n* Reißverschluss *m*

zit [zɪt] (*inf*) *n* Pickel *m*

zodiac [ˈzəudɪæk] *n* Tierkreis *m*

zombie [ˈzɒmbɪ] *n*: **like a ~** (*fig*) wie im Tran

zone [zəun] *n* (*also MIL*) Zone *f*, Gebiet *nt*; (*in town*) Bezirk *m*

zoo [zuː] *n* Zoo *m*

zoology [zuːˈɒlədʒɪ] *n* Zoologie *f*

zoom [zuːm] *vi*: **to ~ past** vorbeisausen; **~ lens** *n* Zoomobjektiv *nt*

zucchini [zuːˈkiːnɪ] (*US*) *npl* Zucchini *pl*

GERMAN IRREGULAR VERBS
*with 'sein'

infinitive	present indicative (2nd, 3rd sg)	imperfect	past participle
aufschrecken*	schrickst auf, schrickt auf	schrak or schreckte auf	aufgeschreckt
ausbedingen	bedingst aus, bedingt aus	bedang or bedingte aus	ausbedungen
backen	bäckst, bäckt	backte or buk	gebacken
befehlen	befiehlst, befiehlt	befahl	befohlen
beginnen	beginnst, beginnt	begann	begonnen
beißen	beißt, beißt	biss	gebissen
bergen	birgst, birgt	barg	geborgen
bersten*	birst, birst	barst	geborsten
bescheißen*	bescheißt, bescheißt	beschiss	beschissen
bewegen	bewegst, bewegt	bewog	bewogen
biegen	biegst, biegt	bog	gebogen
bieten	bietest, bietet	bot	geboten
binden	bindest, bindet	band	gebunden
bitten	bittest, bittet	bat	gebeten
blasen	bläst, bläst	blies	geblasen
bleiben*	bleibst, bleibt	blieb	geblieben
braten	brätst, brät	briet	gebraten
brechen*	brichst, bricht	brach	gebrochen
brennen	brennst, brennt	brannte	gebrannt
bringen	bringst, bringt	brachte	gebracht
denken	denkst, denkt	dachte	gedacht
dreschen	drisch(e)st, drischt	drosch	gedroschen
dringen*	dringst, dringt	drang	gedrungen
dürfen	darfst, darf	durfte	gedurft
empfehlen	empfiehlst, empfiehlt	empfahl	empfohlen
erbleichen*	erbleichst, erbleicht	erbleichte	erblichen
erlöschen*	erlischst, erlischt	erlosch	erloschen
erschrecken*	erschrickst, erschrickt	erschrak	erschrocken
essen	isst, isst	aß	gegessen
fahren*	fährst, fährt	fuhr	gefahren
fallen*	fällst, fällt	fiel	gefallen

infinitive	present indicative (2nd, 3rd sg)	imperfect	past participle
fangen	fängst, fängt	fing	gefangen
fechten	fichtst, ficht	focht	gefochten
finden	findest, findet	fand	gefunden
flechten	flichtst, flicht	flocht	geflochten
fliegen*	fliegst, fliegt	flog	geflogen
fliehen*	fliehst, flieht	floh	geflohen
fließen*	fließt, fließt	floss	geflossen
fressen	frisst, frisst	fraß	gefressen
frieren	frierst, friert	fror	gefroren
gären*	gärst, gärt	gor	gegoren
gebären	gebierst, gebiert	gebar	geboren
geben	gibst, gibt	gab	gegeben
gedeihen*	gedeihst, gedeiht	gedieh	gediehen
gehen*	gehst, geht	ging	gegangen
gelingen*	——, gelingt	gelang	gelungen
gelten	giltst, gilt	galt	gegolten
genesen*	gene(se)st, genest	genas	genesen
genießen	genießt, genießt	genoss	genossen
geraten*	gerätst, gerät	geriet	geraten
geschehen*	——, geschieht	geschah	geschehen
gewinnen	gewinnst, gewinnt	gewann	gewonnen
gießen	gießt, gießt	goss	gegossen
gleichen	gleichst, gleicht	glich	geglichen
gleiten*	gleitest, gleitet	glitt	geglitten
glimmen	glimmst, glimmt	glomm	geglommen
graben	gräbst, gräbt	grub	gegraben
greifen	greifst, greift	griff	gegriffen
haben	hast, hat	hatte	gehabt
halten	hältst, hält	hielt	gehalten
hängen	hängst, hängt	hing	gehangen
hauen	haust, haut	haute	gehauen
heben	hebst, hebt	hob	gehoben
heißen	heißt, heißt	hieß	geheißen
helfen	hilfst, hilft	half	geholfen
kennen	kennst, kennt	kannte	gekannt
klimmen*	klimmst, klimmt	klomm	geklommen
klingen	klingst, klingt	klang	geklungen
kneifen	kneifst, kneift	kniff	gekniffen
kommen*	kommst, kommt	kam	gekommen
können	kannst, kann	konnte	gekonnt
kriechen*	kriechst, kriecht	kroch	gekrochen
laden	lädst, lädt	lud	geladen
lassen	lässt, lässt	ließ	gelassen
laufen*	läufst, läuft	lief	gelaufen
leiden	leidest, leidet	litt	gelitten

infinitive	present indicative (2nd, 3rd sg)	imperfect	past participle
leihen	leihst, leiht	lieh	geliehen
lesen	liest, liest	las	gelesen
liegen*	liegst, liegt	lag	gelegen
lügen	lügst, lügt	log	gelogen
mahlen	mahlst, mahlt	mahlte	gemahlen
meiden	meidest, meidet	mied	gemieden
melken	melkst, melkt	melkte	gemolken
messen	misst, misst	maß	gemessen
misslingen*	——, misslingt	misslang	misslungen
mögen	magst, mag	mochte	gemocht
müssen	musst, muss	musste	gemusst
nehmen	nimmst, nimmt	nahm	genommen
nennen	nennst, nennt	nannte	genannt
pfeifen	pfeifst, pfeift	pfiff	gepfiffen
preisen	preist, preist	pries	gepriesen
quellen*	quillst, quillt	quoll	gequollen
raten	rätst, rät	riet	geraten
reiben	reibst, reibt	rieb	gerieben
reißen*	reißt, reißt	riss	gerissen
reiten*	reitest, reitet	ritt	geritten
rennen*	rennst, rennt	rannte	gerannt
riechen	riechst, riecht	roch	gerochen
ringen	ringst, ringt	rang	gerungen
rinnen*	rinnst, rinnt	rann	geronnen
rufen	rufst, ruft	rief	gerufen
salzen	salzt, salzt	salzte	gesalzen
saufen	säufst, säuft	soff	gesoffen
saugen	saugst, saugt	sog	gesogen
schaffen	schaffst, schafft	schuf	geschaffen
scheiden	scheidest, scheidet	schied	geschieden
scheinen	scheinst, scheint	schien	geschienen
schelten	schiltst, schilt	schalt	gescholten
scheren	scherst, schert	schor	geschoren
schieben	schiebst, schiebt	schob	geschoben
schießen	schießt, schießt	schoss	geschossen
schinden	schindest, schindet	schindete	geschunden
schlafen	schläfst, schläft	schlief	geschlafen
schlagen	schlägst, schlägt	schlug	geschlagen
schleichen*	schleichst, schleicht	schlich	geschlichen
schleifen	schleifst, schleift	schliff	geschliffen
schließen	schließt, schließt	schloss	geschlossen
schlingen	schlingst, schlingt	schlang	geschlungen

infinitive	present indicative (2nd, 3rd sg)	imperfect	past participle
schmeißen	schmeißt, schmeißt	schmiss	geschmissen
schmelzen*	schmilzt, schmilzt	schmolz	geschmolzen
schneiden	schneidest, schneidet	schnitt	geschnitten
schreiben	schreibst, schreibt	schrieb	geschrieben
schreien	schreist, schreit	schrie	geschrie(e)n
schreiten	schreitest, schreitet	schritt	geschritten
schweigen	schweigst, schweigt	schwieg	geschwiegen
schwellen*	schwillst, schwillt	schwoll	geschwollen
schwimmen*	schwimmst, schwimmt	schwamm	geschwommen
schwinden*	schwindest, schwindet	schwand	geschwunden
schwingen	schwingst, schwingt	schwang	geschwungen
schwören	schwörst, schwört	schwor	geschworen
sehen	siehst, sieht	sah	gesehen
sein*	bist, ist	war	gewesen
senden	sendest, sendet	sandte	gesandt
singen	singst, singt	sang	gesungen
sinken*	sinkst, sinkt	sank	gesunken
sinnen	sinnst, sinnt	sann	gesonnen
sitzen*	sitzt, sitzt	saß	gesessen
sollen	sollst, soll	sollte	gesollt
speien	speist, speit	spie	gespie(e)n
spinnen	spinnst, spinnt	spann	gesponnen
sprechen	sprichst, spricht	sprach	gesprochen
sprießen*	sprießt, sprießt	spross	gesprossen
springen*	springst, springt	sprang	gesprungen
stechen	stichst, sticht	stach	gestochen
stecken	steckst, steckt	steckte or stak	gesteckt
stehen	stehst, steht	stand	gestanden
stehlen	stiehlst, stiehlt	stahl	gestohlen
steigen*	steigst, steigt	stieg	gestiegen
sterben*	stirbst, stirbt	starb	gestorben
stinken	stinkst, stinkt	stank	gestunken
stoßen	stößt, stößt	stieß	gestoßen
streichen	streichst, streicht	strich	gestrichen
streiten*	streitest, streitet	stritt	gestritten
tragen	trägst, trägt	trug	getragen
treffen	triffst, trifft	traf	getroffen
treiben*	treibst, treibt	trieb	getrieben

infinitive	present indicative (2nd, 3rd sg)	imperfect	past participle
treten*	trittst, tritt	trat	getreten
trinken	trinkst, trinkt	trank	getrunken
trügen	trügst, trügt	trog	getrogen
tun	tust, tut	tat	getan
verderben	verdirbst, verdirbt	verdarb	verdorben
verdrießen	verdrießt, verdrießt	verdross	verdrossen
vergessen	vergisst, vergisst	vergaß	vergessen
verlieren	verlierst, verliert	verlor	verloren
verschleißen	verschleißt, verschleißt	verschliss	verschlissen
wachsen*	wächst, wächst	wuchs	gewachsen
weben	webst, webt	webte or wob	gewoben
wägen	wägst, wägt	wog	gewogen
waschen	wäschst, wäscht	wusch	gewaschen
weichen*	weichst, weicht	wich	gewichen
weisen	weist, weist	wies	gewiesen
wenden	wendest, wendet	wandte	gewandt
werben	wirbst, wirbt	warb	geworben
werden*	wirst, wird	wurde	geworden
werfen	wirfst, wirft	warf	geworfen
wiegen	wiegst, wiegt	wog	gewogen
winden	windest, windet	wand	gewunden
wissen	weißt, weiß	wusste	gewusst
wollen	willst, will	wollte	gewollt
wringen	wringst, wringt	wrang	gewrungen
zeihen	zeihst, zeiht	zieh	geziehen
ziehen*	ziehst, zieht	zog	gezogen
zwingen	zwingst, zwingt	zwang	gezwungen

GERMAN SPELLING CHANGES

In July 1996, all German-speaking countries signed a declaration concerning the reform of German spelling, with the result that the new spelling rules are now taught in all schools. To ensure that you have the most up-to-date information at your fingertips, the following list contains the old and new spellings of all German headwords and translations in this dictionary which are affected by the reform.

ALT/OLD	NEU/NEW	ALT/OLD	NEU/NEW
abend	Abend	aufsein	auf sein
Abfluß	Abfluss	aufwendig	aufwendig
Abflußrohr	Abflussrohr		or aufwändig
Abschluß	Abschluss	auseinanderbrechen	auseinander brechen
Abschlußexamen	Abschlussexamen	auseinanderbringen	auseinander bringen
Abschlußfeier	Abschlussfeier	auseinanderfallen	auseinander fallen
Abschlußklasse	Abschlussklasse	auseinanderfalten	auseinander falten
Abschlußprüfung	Abschlussprüfung	auseinandergehen	auseinander gehen
Abschuß	Abschuss	auseinanderhalten	auseinander halten
Abschußrampe	Abschussrampe	auseinandernehmen	auseinander nehmen
Abszeß	Abszess	auseinandersetzen	auseinander setzen
achtgeben	Acht geben	Ausfluß	Ausfluss
Adreßbuch	Adressbuch	Ausguß	Ausguss
Alleinerziehende(r)	Alleinerziehende(r)	Auslaß	Auslass
	or allein Erziehende(r)	Ausschluß	Ausschluss
alleinstehend	allein stehend	Ausschuß	Ausschuss
allgemeingültig	allgemein gültig	Ausschuß(artikel)	Ausschuss(artikel)
allzuoft	allzu oft	aussein	aus sein
allzuviel	allzu viel	außerstande	außer Stande
Alptraum	Alptraum	Autobiographie	Autobiographie
	or Albtraum		or Autobiografie
Amboß	Amboss	Baß	Bass
Amtsanschluß	Amtsanschluss	Baßstimme	Bassstimme
(Amts)mißbrauch	(Amts)missbrauch		or Bass-Stimme
andersdenkend	anders denkend	Ballettänzer(in)	Balletttänzer(in)
aneinandergeraten	aneinander geraten		or Ballett-Tänzer(in)
aneinanderreihen	aneinander reihen	beeinflußbar	beeinflussbar
Anlaß	Anlass	beiseitelegen	beiseite legen
anläßlich	anlässlich	bekanntgeben	bekannt geben
Anschluß	Anschluss	bekanntmachen	bekannt machen
Anschlußflug	Anschlussflug	Beschluß	Beschluss
As	Ass	Beschuß	Beschuss
aufeinanderfolgen	aufeinander folgen	bessergehen	besser gehen
aufeinanderfolgend	aufeinander folgend	Bettuch	Betttuch
aufeinanderlegen	aufeinander legen		or Bett-Tuch
aufeinanderprallen	aufeinander prallen	(Bevölkerungs)überschuß	
Aufschluß	Aufschluss		(Bevölkerungs)überschuss
aufschlußreich	aufschlussreich	bewußt	bewusst
aufsehenerregend	Aufsehen erregend	bewußtlos	bewusstlos

ALT/OLD	NEU/NEW	ALT/OLD	NEU/NEW
Bewußtlosigkeit	Bewusstlosigkeit	durchnumerieren	durchnummerieren
Bewußtsein	Bewusstsein	ehrfurchtgebietend	Ehrfurcht gebietend
bezug	Bezug	Einfluß	Einfluss
Bibliographie	Bibliographie	Einflußbereich	Einflussbereich
	or Bibliografie	einflußreich	einflussreich
Biographie	Biographie	einigemal	einige Mal
	or Biografie	einiggehen	einig gehen
Biß	Biss	Einlaß	Einlass
biß	biss	ekelerregend	Ekel erregend
bißchen	bisschen	Elsaß	Elsass
blaß	blass	Engpaß	Engpass
bläßlich	blässlich	Entschluß	Entschluss
bleibenlassen	bleiben lassen	entschlußfreudig	entschlussfreudig
Bluterguß	Bluterguss	Entschlußkraft	Entschlusskraft
Boß	Boss	epochemachend	Epoche machend
braungebrannt	braun gebrannt	Erdgeschoß	Erdgeschoss
breitmachen	breit machen	Erdnuß	Erdnuss
Brennessel	Brennnessel	Erdnußbutter	Erdnussbutter
	or Brenn-Nessel	erfolgversprechend	Erfolg versprechend
Büroschluß	Büroschluss	Erguß	Erguss
Butterfaß	Butterfass	Erlaß	Erlass
Cashewnuß	Cashewnuss	ernstgemeint	ernst gemeint
Chicorée	Chicorée	erstemal	erste Mal
	or Schikoree	Eß–	Ess–
Choreograph(in)	Choreograph(in)	erstenmal	ersten Mal
	or Choreograf(in)	eßbar	essbar
Computertomographie	Computertomographie	Eßbesteck	Essbesteck
	or Computertomografie	Eßecke	Essecke
dabeisein	dabei sein	Eßgeschirr	Essgeschirr
dafürkönnen	dafür können	Eßkastanie	Esskastanie
dahinterkommen	dahinter kommen	Eßlöffel	Esslöffel
daraffolgend	darauf folgend	Eßlöffel(voll)	Esslöffel (voll)
dasein	da sein	(Eß)stäbchen	(Ess)stäbchen
daß	dass		or (Ess-)Stäbchen
Dekolleté	Dekolleté	Eßtisch	Esstisch
	or Dekolletee	Eßwaren	Esswaren
Delphin	Delphin	Eßzimmer	Esszimmer
	or Delfin	Expreß	Express
dessenungeachtet	dessen ungeachtet	Expreß–	Express–
dichtbevölkert	dicht bevölkert	Expreßgut	Expressgut
diensthabend	Dienst habend	Expreßzug	Expresszug
differential	differential	Exzeß	Exzess
	or differenzial	Facette	Facette
Differentialrechnung	Differentialrechnung		or Fassette
	or Differenzialrechnung	Fährenanschluß	Fährenanschluss
Diktaphon	Diktaphon	Fairneß	Fairness
	or Diktafon	fallenlassen	fallen lassen
dreiviertel	drei Viertel	Faß	Fass
durcheinanderbringen	durcheinander bringen	faßbar	fassbar
durcheinanderreden	durcheinander reden	Fehlschuß	Fehlschuss
durcheinanderwerfen	durcheinander werfen	fernhalten	fern halten

ALT/OLD	NEU/NEW	ALT/OLD	NEU/NEW
fertigbringen	fertig bringen	gewiß	gewiss
fertigmachen	fertig machen	Gewißheit	Gewissheit
fertigstellen	fertig stellen	gewußt	gewusst
fertigwerden	fertig werden	glattrasiert	glatt rasiert
festangestellt	fest angestellt	glattstreichen	glatt streichen
Fitneß	Fitness	gleichbleibend	gleich bleibend
fleischfressend	Fleisch fressend	gleichgesinnt	gleich gesinnt
floß	floss	Glimmstengel	Glimmstängel
Fluß	Fluss	Grammophon	Grammophon
Fluß–	Fluss–		or Grammofon
flußabwärts	flussabwärts	(Grammophon)nadel	(Grammophon)nadel
Flußbarsch	Flussbarsch		or (Grammofon)nadel
Flußbett	Flussbett	Graphiker(in)	Graphiker(in)
Flußdiagramm	Flussdiagramm		or Grafiker(in)
flüssigmachen	flüssig machen	graphisch	graphisch
Flußufer	Flussufer		or grafisch
Fön ®	Fön	gräßlich	grässlich
	or Föhn ®	Greuel	Gräuel
fönen	föhnen	Greueltat	Gräueltat
Fönfrisur	Föhnfrisur	greulich	gräulich
Friedensschluß	Friedensschluss	Grundriß	Grundriss
Frischvermählte	frisch Vermählte	Guß	Guss
Frischvermählten	frisch Vermählten	Gußeisen	Gusseisen
frißt	frisst	gutaussehend	gut aussehend
fritieren	frittieren	gutgehen	gut gehen
Gebiß	Gebiss	gutgehend	gut gehend
Gebührenerlaß	Gebührenerlass	gutgemeint	gut gemeint
gefangen(gehalten)	gefangen (gehalten)	guttun	gut tun
gefangenhalten	gefangen halten	haftenbleiben	haften bleiben
gefangennehmen	gefangen nehmen	halboffen	halb offen
gefaßt	gefasst	haltmachen	Halt machen
geheimhalten	geheim halten	Hämorrhoiden	Hämorrhoiden
gehenlassen	gehen lassen		or Hämorriden
Gemeinschaftsanschluß		Handvoll	Hand voll
	Gemeinschaftsanschluss	hängenbleiben	hängen bleiben
Gemse	Gämse	hängenlassen	hängen lassen
gemußt	gemusst	hartgekocht	hart gekocht
genaugenommen	genau genommen	Haselnuß	Haselnuss
Genuß	Genuss	Haß	Hass
genüßlich	genüsslich	häßlich	hässlich
Genußmittel	Genussmittel	Häßlichkeit	Hässlichkeit
Geograph	Geograph	haushalten	haushalten
	or Geograf		or Haus halten
Geographie	Geographie	heiligsprechen	heilig sprechen
	or Geografie	Hexenschuß	Hexenschuss
geographisch	geographisch	hierbehalten	hier behalten
	or geografisch	hierbleiben	hier bleiben
geringachten	gering achten	hierlassen	hier lassen
Geschäftsschluß	Geschäftsschluss	hierzulande	hierzulande
Geschoß	Geschoss		or hier zu Lande
gewinnbringend	Gewinn bringend	hochachten	hoch achten

ALT/OLD	NEU/NEW	ALT/OLD	NEU/NEW
hochbegabt	hoch begabt	kompromißlos	kompromisslos
hochdotiert	hoch dotiert	Kompromißlösung	Kompromisslösung
hochentwickelt	hoch entwickelt	Kongreß	Kongress
(hoch)geschätzt	(hoch) geschätzt	Kongreßzentrum	Kongresszentrum
(hoch)schätzen	(hoch) schätzen	Kontrabaß	Kontrabass
(Honorar)vorschuß	(Honorar)vorschuss	kraß	krass
Imbiß	Imbiss	Kreppapier	Krepppapier
Imbißhalle	Imbisshalle		or Krepp-Papier
Imbißraum	Imbissraum	kriegführend	Krieg führend
Imbißstube	Imbissstube	krummnehmen	krumm nehmen
	or Imbiss-Stube	Kurzbiographie	Kurzbiographie
immerwährend	immer während		or Kurzbiografie
imstande	imstande	kurzhalten	kurz halten
	or im Stande	Kurzschluß	Kurzschluss
ineinandergreifen	ineinander greifen	Kuß	Kuss
ineinanderschieben	ineinander schieben	Ladenschluß	Ladenschluss
Intercity-Expreßzug	Intercity-Expresszug	Laufpaß	Laufpass
ißt	isst	leerlaufen	leer laufen
Jahresabschluß	Jahresabschluss	leerstehend	leer stehend
jedesmal	jedes Mal	leichtfallen	leicht fallen
Joghurt	Joghurt	leichtmachen	leicht machen
	or Jogurt	Lenkradschloß	Lenkradschloss
kahlgeschoren	kahl geschoren	letztemal	letzte Mal
kaltbleiben	kalt bleiben	liebgewinnen	lieb gewinnen
Kammuschel	Kammmuschel	liebhaben	lieb haben
	or Kamm-Muschel	liegenbleiben	liegen bleiben
Känguruh	Känguru	liegenlassen	liegen lassen
Karamel	Karamell	Litfaßsäule	Litfasssäule
Karamelbonbon	Karamellbonbon		or Litfass-Säule
Katarrh	Katarrh	Lithographie	Lithographie
	or Katarr		or Lithografie
Kellergeschoß	Kellergeschoss	Luftschloß	Luftschloss
kennenlernen	kennen lernen	maschineschreiben	Maschine schreiben
keß	kess	maßhalten	Maß halten
klarsehen	klar sehen	Megaphon	Megaphon
klarwerden	klar werden		or Megafon
klassenbewußt	klassenbewusst	Meldeschluß	Meldeschluss
Klassenbewußtsein	Klassenbewusstsein	meßbar	messbar
klatschnaß	klatschnass	Meßbecher	Messbecher
kleinhacken	klein hacken	Meßgerät	Messgerät
kleinschneiden	klein schneiden	Mikrophon	Mikrophon
klitschnaß	klitschnass		or Mikrofon
knapphalten	knapp halten	Miß-	Miss-
Kokosnuß	Kokosnuss	mißachten	missachten
Koloß	Koloss	Mißachtung	Missachtung
Kombinationsschloß	Kombinationsschloss	Mißbehagen	Missbehagen
Kommuniqué	Kommuniqué	Mißbildung	Missbildung
	or Kommunikee	mißbilligen	missbilligen
Kompaß	Kompass	Mißbilligung	Missbilligung
Kompromiß	Kompromiss	Mißbrauch	Missbrauch
kompromißbereit	kompromissbereit	mißbrauchen	missbrauchen

ALT/OLD	NEU/NEW	ALT/OLD	NEU/NEW
Mißerfolg	Misserfolg	Nebenanschluß	Nebenanschluss
Mißfallen	Missfallen	nebeneinanderlegen	nebeneinander legen
mißfallen	missfallen	nebeneinanderstellen	nebeneinander stellen
Mißgeburt	Missgeburt	Nebenfluß	Nebenfluss
Mißgeschick	Missgeschick	Necessaire	Necessaire
mißgestaltet	missgestaltet		or Nessessär
mißglücken	missglücken	Negligé	Negligé
mißgönnen	missgönnen		or Negligee
Mißgriff	Missgriff	Netzanschluß	Netzanschluss
Mißgunst	Missgunst	neuentdeckt	neu entdeckt
mißgünstig	missgünstig	nichtsahnend	nichts ahnend
mißhandeln	misshandeln	nichtssagend	nichts sagend
Mißhandlung	Misshandlung	Nonstop-	Nonstop-
Mißklang	Missklang		or Non-Stop-
Mißkredit	Misskredit	notleidend	Not leidend
mißlich	misslich	numerieren	nummerieren
mißlingen	misslingen	Nuß	Nuss
mißlungen	misslungen	Nußbaum	Nussbaum
Mißmut	Missmut	Nußknacker	Nussknacker
mißmutig	missmutig	Nußschale	Nussschale
mißraten	missraten		or Nuss-Schale
Mißstand	Missstand	obenerwähnt	oben erwähnt
	or Miss-Stand	obengenannt	oben genannt
Mißtrauen	Misstrauen	Obergeschoß	Obergeschoss
mißtrauen	misstrauen	offenbleiben	offen bleiben
Mißtrauensantrag	Misstrauensantrag	offenhalten	offen halten
Mißtrauensvotum	Misstrauensvotum	offenlassen	offen lassen
mißtrauisch	misstrauisch	offenstehen	offen stehen
Mißverhältnis	Missverhältnis	Ölmeßstab	Ölmessstab
Mißverständnis	Missverständnis		or Ölmess-Stab
mißverstehen	missverstehen	Orthographie	Orthographie
Mißwirtschaft	Misswirtschaft		or Orthografie
mittag	Mittag	orthographisch	orthographisch
Mop	Mopp		or orthografisch
Muß	Muss	paarmal	paar Mal
mußte	musste	Panther	Panther
nachhinein	Nachhinein		or Panter
Nachlaß	Nachlass	Paragraph	Paragraph
nahegehen	nahe gehen		or Paragraf
nahekommen	nahe kommen	Paranuß	Paranuss
nahelegen	nahe legen	Parlamentsbeschluß	Parlamentsbeschluss
naheliegen	nahe liegen	Paß	Pass
naheliegend	nahe liegend	Paß-	Pass-
näherkommen	näher kommen	Paßamt	Passamt
näherrücken	näher rücken	Paßbild	Passbild
nahestehen	nahe stehen	Paßkontrolle	Passkontrolle
nahestehend	nahe stehend	Paßstelle	Passstelle
nahetreten	nahe treten		or Pass-Stelle
naß	nass	Paßstraße	Passstraße
naßkalt	nasskalt		or Pass-Straße
Naßrasur	Nassrasur	patschnaß	patschnass

ALT/OLD	NEU/NEW	ALT/OLD	NEU/NEW
pflichtbewußt	pflichtbewusst	rotglühend	rot glühend
Phantasie	Phantasie	Rückschluß	Rückschluss
	or Fantasie	Rußland	Russland
Phantasie–	Phantasie–	Safe(r) Sex	Safe(r) Sex
	or Fantasie–		or Safe(r)-sex
phantasielos	phantasielos	Salzfaß	Salzfass
	or fantasielos	sauberhalten	sauber halten
phantasiereich	phantasiereich	Saxophon	Saxophon
	or fantasiereich		or Saxofon
phantasieren	phantasieren	Schattenriß	Schattenriss
	or fantasieren	schiefgehen	schief gehen
phantasievoll	phantasievoll	Schiffahrt	Schifffahrt
	or fantasievoll		or Schiff–Fahrt
phantastisch	phantastisch	Schiffahrtslinie	Schifffahrtslinie
	or fantastisch	Schlangenbiß	Schlangenbiss
platschnaß	platschnass	schlechtgehen	schlecht gehen
plazieren	platzieren	schlechtmachen	schlecht machen
Pornographie	Pornographie	Schlegel	Schlägel
	or Pornografie	Schloß	Schloss
pornographisch	pornographisch	schloß	schloss
	or pornografisch	Schluß	Schluss
Portemonnaie	Portemonnaie	Schluß–	Schluss–
	or Portmonee	(Schluß)folgerung	(Schluss)folgerung
Potential	Potential	Schlußlicht	Schlusslicht
	or Potenzial	Schlußrunde	Schlussrunde
potentiell	potentiell	Schlußrundenteilnehmer	
	or potenziell		Schlussrundenteilnehmer
preisbewußt	preisbewusst	Schlußstrich	Schlussstrich
Preßluft	Pressluft		or Schluss–Strich
Preßluftbohrer	Pressluftbohrer	Schlußverkauf	Schlussverkauf
Preßlufthammer	Presslufthammer	Schmiß	Schmiss
Prozeß	Prozess	Schnappschloß	Schnappschloss
Prüfungsausschuß	Prüfungsausschuss	Schnappschuß	Schnappschuss
radfahren	Rad fahren	Schnellimbiß	Schnellimbiss
(Raketen)abschuß	(Raketen)abschuss	schneuzen	schnäuzen
Rassenhaß	Rassenhass	schoß	schoss
rauh	rau	Schößling	Schössling
Rauhreif	Raureif	Schrittempo	Schritttempo
Raumschiffahrt	Raumschifffahrt		or Schritt–Tempo
	or Raumschiff–Fahrt	Schuß	Schuss
Rausschmiß	Rausschmiss	Schußbereich	Schussbereich
Rechnungsabschluß	Rechnungsabschluss	Schußlinie	Schusslinie
reinwaschen	rein waschen	Schußverletzung	Schussverletzung
Reisepaß	Reisepass	Schußwaffe	Schusswaffe
Reißverschluß	Reißverschluss	Schußweite	Schussweite
richtigstellen	richtig stellen	schwererziehbar	schwer erziehbar
Riß	Riss	schwerfallen	schwer fallen
Rolladen	Rollladen	schwermachen	schwer machen
	or Roll–Laden	schwernehmen	schwer nehmen
Roß	Ross	schwertun	schwer tun
Roßkastanie	Rosskastanie	schwerverdaulich	schwer verdaulich

ALT/OLD	NEU/NEW	ALT/OLD	NEU/NEW
			or telegrafieren
schwerverletzt	schwer verletzt		
Seismograph	Seismograph	Thunfisch	Thunfisch
	or Seismograf		or Tunfisch
selbständig	selbständig	tiefausgeschnitten	tief ausgeschnitten
	or selbstständig	tiefgehend	tief gehend
Selbständigkeit	Selbständigkeit	tiefgekühlt	tief gekühlt
	or Selbstständigkeit	tiefgreifend	tief greifend
selbstbewußt	selbstbewusst	tiefschürfend	tief schürfend
Selbstbewußtsein	Selbstbewusstsein	Tip	Tipp
selbstgemacht	selbst gemacht	topographisch	topographisch
selbstverständlich	selbst verständlich		or topografisch
selbstverwaltet	selbst verwaltet	totenblaß	totenblass
seßhaft	sesshaft	totgeboren	tot geboren
Showbusineß	Showbusiness	Trugschluß	Trugschluss
Sicherheitsschloß	Sicherheitsschloss	tschüs	tschüs
sitzenbleiben	sitzen bleiben		or tschüss
sitzenlassen	sitzen lassen	übelgelaunt	übel gelaunt
Skipaß	Skipass	übelnehmen	übel nehmen
sogenannt	so genannt	übelriechend	übel riechend
Sommerschlußverkauf		übelwollend	übel wollend
	Sommerschlussverkauf	Überdruß	Überdruss
sonstjemand	sonst jemand	übereinanderlegen	übereinander legen
sonstwo	sonst wo	Überfluß	Überfluss
sonstwoher	sonst woher	Überschuß	Überschuss
sonstwohin	sonst wohin	überschwenglich	überschwänglich
Spannbettuch	Spannbetttuch	übrigbleiben	übrig bleiben
	or Spannbett-Tuch	übriggeblieben	übrig geblieben
spazierenfahren	spazieren fahren	übriglassen	übrig lassen
spazierengehen	spazieren gehen	Umriß	Umriss
Sprößling	Sprössling	unbewußt	unbewusst
steckenbleiben	stecken bleiben	Unbewußte	Unbewusste
steckenlassen	stecken lassen	unerläßlich	unerlässlich
stehenbleiben	stehen bleiben	unermeßlich	unermesslich
stehenlassen	stehen lassen	unfaßbar	unfassbar
Stengel	Stängel	ungewiß	ungewiss
Stenographie	Stenographie	Ungewißheit	Ungewissheit
	or Stenografie	unmißverständlich	unmissverständlich
stenographieren	stenographieren	unpäßlich	unpässlich
	or stenografieren	unselbständig	unselbständig
Stenograph(in)	Stenograph(in)		or unselbstständig
	or Stenograf(in)		
stereophonisch	stereophonisch	unterbewußt	unterbewusst
	or stereofonisch	Unterbewußte	Unterbewusste
Stewardeß	Stewardess	Unterbewußtsein	Unterbewusstsein
Stilleben	Stillleben	Untergeschoß	Untergeschoss
	or Still-Leben	Untersuchungsausschuß	
stillegen	stilllegen		Untersuchungsausschuss
Streifschuß	Streifschuss	unvergeßlich	unvergesslich
strenggenommen	streng genommen	Varieté	Varieté
Streß	Stress		or Varietee
telegrahieren	telegraphieren	verantwortungsbewußt	
			verantwortungsbewusst

ALT/OLD	NEU/NEW	ALT/OLD	NEU/NEW
Verdruß	Verdruss	wiedergutzumachen	wieder gutzumachen
vergeßlich	vergesslich	wiederherstellen	wieder herstellen
Vergeßlichkeit	Vergesslichkeit	wiedersehen	wieder sehen
Vergißmeinnicht	Vergissmeinnicht	wiedervereinigen	wieder vereinigen
vergißt	vergisst	wiederverwenden	wieder verwenden
verhaßt	verhasst	wiederverwerten	wieder verwerten
Verlaß	Verlass	wieviel	wie viel
verläßlich	verlässlich	Wißbegier(de)	Wissbegier(de)
verlorengehen	verloren gehen	wißbegierig	wissbegierig
vermißt	vermisst	wohltun	wohl tun
Verschluß	Verschluss	wußte	wusste
vertrauenerweckend	Vertrauen erweckend	Xylophon	Xylophon
vielsagend	viel sagend		or Xylofon
vielversprechend	viel versprechend	Zahlenschloß	Zahlenschloss
(voll)fressen	(voll) fressen	zeitlang	Zeit lang
vollgepfropft	voll gepfropft	zielbewußt	zielbewusst
vollpfropfen	voll pfropfen	Zuckerguß	Zuckerguss
vollstopfen	voll stopfen	zufriedengeben	zufrieden geben
volltanken	voll tanken	zufriedenstellen	zufrieden stellen
vorgefaßt	vorgefasst	zufriedenstellend	zufrieden stellend
Vorhängeschloß	Vorhängeschloss	zugrunde	zugrunde
vorhinein	Vorhinein		or zu Grunde
vorliebnehmen	vorlieb nehmen	zugunsten	zugunsten
Vorschuß	Vorschuss		or zu Gunsten
vorwärtsbewegen	vorwärts bewegen	zuleide	zuleide
vorwärtsdrängen	vorwärts drängen		or zu Leide
vorwärtsgehen	vorwärts gehen	zumute	zumute
vorwärtskommen	vorwärts kommen		or zu Mute
Waggon	Waggon	Zündschloß	Zündschloss
	or Wagon	Zungenkuß	Zungenkuss
Walnuß	Walnuss	zunutze	zunutze
Walroß	Walross		or zu Nutze
wasserabstoßend	Wasser abstoßend	Zusammenschluß	Zusammenschluss
wäßrig	wässrig	zuschulden	zuschulden
Weißrußland	Weißrussland		or zu Schulden
weitblickend	weitblickend	Zuschuß	Zuschuss
	or weit blickend	zustande	zustande
weitreichend	weitreichend		or zu Stande
	or weit reichend	zustande bringen	zustande bringen
weitverbreitet	weitverbreitet		or zu Stande bringen
	or weit verbreitet	zustande kommen	zustande kommen
wiederaufbauen	wieder aufbauen		or zu Stande kommen
wiederaufbereiten	wieder aufbereiten	zutage	zutage
wiederaufnehmen	wieder aufnehmen		or zu Tage
wiederbeleben	wieder beleben	zuviel	zu viel
wiedereinsetzen	wieder einsetzen	zuwege	zuwege
wiedererkennen	wieder erkennen		or zu Wege
wiedererwachen	wieder erwachen	zuwenig	zu wenig
wiedergutmachen	wieder gutmachen		